L.A. WILDING'S
GREEK FOR BEGINNERS

L.A. WILDING'S
GREEK FOR BEGINNERS

REVISED AND EXPANDED BY

C.W. SHELMERDINE
UNIVERSITY OF TEXAS

Focus Publishing / R. Pullins Co.
Newburyport MA 01950

TABLE OF CONTENTS

PREFACE TO THE CURRENT EDITION .... *xiii*

Map of Greece and the Aegean .... *xv*

Map of the Ancient World .... *xvi*

CHAPTER 1 1

1. The Greek alphabet, with pronunciation 1
2. Consonant groups 2
3. Vowel groups (diphthongs) 2
4. Accents 2
5. Breathings 3
6. Elision 4
7. Punctuation and capital letters 4

CHAPTER 2 6

1. Verb forms: terminology 6
2. The present active indicative of thematic verbs 6
3. Verb accents 7
4. The negative 8
5. Common conjunctions 8
   Chapter 2 Vocabulary 8

CHAPTER 3 9

1. Noun forms: terminology 9
2. The definite article 9
3. Feminine nouns of the 1st declension 9
4. Noun and adjective accents 10
5. Accents of 1st declension nouns 10
6. Prepositions 11
7. Future active indicative 12
   Chapter 3 Vocabulary 13

CHAPTER 4 14

1. The definite article 14
2. Masculine nouns of the 1st declension 14
3. Imperfect active indicative 14
4. Some uses of the article 15
5. Word order 16
6. Word order with dependent genitive 16
7. Uses of the dative 16
8. Verbs taking genitive or dative 17
   Chapter 4 Vocabulary 18

CHAPTER 5 19

1. Masculine and feminine nouns of the 2nd declension 19
2. The aorist active indicative 19

	Review Exercises	20
	Chapter 5 Vocabulary	21
CHAPTER 6		22
1.	Neuter nouns of the 2nd declension	22
2.	Neuter plural with singular verb	22
3.	The noun γῆ, 'earth, land'	22
4.	The perfect active indicative	23
	Chapter 6 Vocabulary	24
CHAPTER 7		25
1.	1st and 2nd declension adjectives	25
2.	Attributive and predicate position	25
3.	Enclitics	26
4.	The present indicative of εἰμί, 'be'	27
5.	Dative of possession	27
6.	The pluperfect active indicative	28
	Chapter 7 Vocabulary	29
CHAPTER 8		30
1.	Third declension nouns	30
2.	3rd declension nouns: stems in -κ, -τ	30
3.	The present active imperative, second person	31
4.	The present active infinitive	31
5.	Connections	32
6.	μέν and δέ	33
7.	αὐτός	34
8.	αὐτός, intensive use	34
9.	αὐτός as personal pronoun, 3rd person	34
10.	οἷός τέ εἰμι	36
	Chapter 8 Vocabulary	37
CHAPTER 9		38
1.	3rd declension nouns: stems in -τ, -δ, -θ	38
2.	The future indicative of εἰμί, 'be'	39
3.	3rd declension nouns: stems in -ντ, -κτ	39
4.	The imperfect (active) indicative of εἰμί, 'be'	40
5.	The relative pronoun	40
	Chapter 9 Vocabulary	42
CHAPTER 10		43
1.	3rd declension nouns: stems in -ρ	43
2.	Syllabic and temporal augments	43
3.	Augments of compound verbs	44
4.	3rd declension nouns: stems in -ν	45
5.	Principal parts of palatal stem verbs	45
6.	Augmented and reduplicated perfects	46
7.	Strong perfect	46
8.	Strong aorist	46
	Chapter 10 Vocabulary	49

CHAPTER 11 50
  1. Review of word order 50
  2. More uses of the article 50
  3. Compounds of εἰμί, 'be' 51
  4. Conditions 51
  5. Simple conditions 52
  6. Contrary-to-fact conditions 52
     Chapter 11 Vocabulary 54

CHAPTER 12 55
  1. Numbers 55
  2. Declension of numbers 56
  3. Ways of expressing time 56
  4. 3rd declension nouns: stems in -σ 57
  5. Principal parts of dental stem verbs 58
  6. Directional suffixes 58
     Chapter 12 Vocabulary 60

CHAPTER 13 61
  1. 3rd declension nouns: stems in -ι, -υ 61
  2. Principal parts of labial stem verbs 61
  3. Elision of δέ, τε, etc. 62
     Review Exercises 63
     Chapter 13 Vocabulary 64

CHAPTER 14 65
  1. 3rd declension nouns: stems in diphthongs 65
  2. The present and imperfect passive indicative of thematic verbs ... 65
  3. Genitive of agent 66
  4. Irregular 3rd declension nouns 66
  5. The aorist and future passive indicative 67
     Chapter 14 Vocabulary 68

CHAPTER 15 69
  1. Regular comparison of adjectives 69
  2. The use of ἤ and the genitive of comparison 69
  3. Genitive with the superlative 70
  4. The perfect and pluperfect passive indicative 70
     Chapter 15 Vocabulary 72

CHAPTER 16 73
  1. The middle voice: meaning 73
  2. The middle voice: formation 73
  3. Infinitives of thematic verbs (present and aorist) 75
  4. Infinitives of εἰμί, 'be' 75
  5. Aspect 75
  6. Use of the imperfect and aorist indicative 76
  7. More principal parts 76
  8. Contract adjectives 77
     Chapter 16 Vocabulary 78

CHAPTER 17 79
  1. Imperatives of thematic verbs 79
  2. Imperatives of εἰμί, 'be' 79
  3. Infinitives of thematic verbs (future and perfect) 80
  4. Personal pronouns, 1st and 2nd persons 81
  5. Possessive adjectives, 1st and 2nd persons 82
     Chapter 17 Vocabulary 83
CHAPTER 18 84
  1. Contract verbs 84
  2. Contract verbs in -εω 85
  3. Contract verbs in -αω 86
  4. Contract verbs in -οω 88
     Chapter 18 Vocabulary 90
CHAPTER 19 91
  1. Adjectives of the ἡδύς type 91
  2. Adjectives of the εὔφρων and εὐγενής types 92
  3. μέγας, πολύς and adjectives of the τάλας type 92
     Chapter 19 Vocabulary 95
CHAPTER 20 96
  1. Participles 96
  2. The present active participle in -ων 96
  3. The future active participle 99
  4. The aorist active participle 99
  5. The perfect active participle 100
  6. The adjective πᾶς 100
  7. Present middle/passive participles 101
  8. Future, aorist and perfect middle and passive participles ... 102
     Chapter 20 Vocabulary 104
CHAPTER 21 105
  1. The perfect middle/passive of consonant stem verbs 105
  2. The aorist and future passive of consonant stem verbs .. 106
  3. Principal Parts 106
  4. The liquid future 108
  5. The liquid aorist 108
  6. The strong aorist of βαίνω 109
  7. Supplementary participles with τυγχάνω, λανθάνω and φθάνω ... 109
     Chapter 21 Vocabulary 112
CHAPTER 22 113
  1. Further comparison of adjectives in -τερος, -τατος 113
  2. Further comparison of adjectives in -ιων, -ιστος 113
  3. Adverbs 114
  4. ἔχω + adverb 115
     Chapter 22 Vocabulary 116

CHAPTER 23 117
  1. αὐτός   117
  2. Reflexive pronouns   117
  3. Reflexive possessive pronouns   118
  4. The reciprocal pronoun   118
  5. Questions   119
  6. Demonstrative pronouns   119
  7. τοιοῦτος, τοσοῦτος   120
    Chapter 23 Vocabulary   122
CHAPTER 24 123
  1. The subjunctive mood   123
  2. Exhortations   124
  3. Prohibitions with 2nd person   125
  4. Prohibitions with 3rd person   125
  5. The interrogative pronoun   126
  6. The indefinite pronoun   126
  7. Interrogative and indefinite adverbs   126
    Chapter 24 Vocabulary   128
CHAPTER 25 129
  1. The optative mood   129
  2. The optative in wishes for the future   131
  3. ἀφικνέομαι, γίγνομαι and ἔρχομαι   131
  4. The genitive absolute   132
  5. εἶμι, 'go'   132
    Chapter 25 Vocabulary   135
CHAPTER 26 136
  1. Purpose (final) clauses   136
  2. δεῖ   137
  3. Future participle to express purpose   137
    Chapter 26 Vocabulary   139
CHAPTER 27 140
  1. Result (consecutive) clauses   140
  2. Clauses of fearing   140
    Chapter 27 Vocabulary   142
CHAPTER 28 143
  1. οἶδα and φημί   143
  2. Indirect statement   144
  3. The infinitive in indirect statement   144
  4. The participle in indirect statement   146
  5. Indirect statement with ὅτι or ὡς   147
    Chapter 28 Vocabulary   148
CHAPTER 29 149
  1. Indirect questions   149
  2. Accusative of respect   150
  3. Irregular strong aorists   150
    Chapter 29 Vocabulary   152

CHAPTER 30 153
  1. Conditions with subjunctive and optative 153
  2. Conditions with the subjunctive 153
  3. Conditions with the optative 154
    Chapter 30 Vocabulary 156
CHAPTER 31 157
  1. The indefinite relative pronoun/adjective ὅστις 157
  2. Correlative pronouns/adjectives 157
  3. Correlative adverbs 158
  4. Indefinite relative clauses 158
  5. Temporal clauses with ἕως and μέχρι 159
  6. Temporal clauses with πρίν 159
    Chapter 31 Vocabulary 160
CHAPTER 32 161
  1. Athematic (-μι) verbs, first principal part 161
  2. Athematic (-μι) verbs, first principal part (δείκνυμι, τίθημι, ἵστημι, δίδωμι) 161
  3. Athematic verbs, 3rd principal part 164
  4. ἵημι 166
    Chapter 32 Vocabulary 168
SUMMARY OF FORMS 169
  Definite Article 169
  Nouns 169
  Adjectives 171
  Participles 173
  Pronouns 176
  Numbers 178
  Regular Thematic Verbs 179
  Contract Thematic Verbs 182
  Regular Athematic Verbs 184
  Verb Ending Charts 191
GREEK-ENGLISH VOCABULARY 194
ENGLISH-GREEK VOCABULARY 208

to my Greek students,
who made this book necessary
made it happen
and made it fun

ὁ ἡ τό, y'all

Preface to Current Edition

This book was born of my experience over the last two decades teaching Greek to American university students. These students bear little resemblance to the audience (British schoolboys with some knowledge of Latin) for which most older textbooks were intended. They appreciate having their maturity and intelligence acknowledged, and most find a new paradigm, for example, easier to remember if they understand the linguistic pattern behind it. At the same time their grasp of English grammar may be imperfect, and many have never taken Latin. Thus they need more help with forms and usage than older textbooks supply. Finally, they want results: they want to absorb the grammar and to start reading Greek, real Greek, as soon as possible. Newer textbooks which are based on invented reading passages may take a year or more to get through. Retention rates suggest that many students are not willing to invest two or three semesters in a language if at the end of that time they will still be learning basic syntax, and not reading the authors who inspired them to learn the language in the first place.

This textbook is designed to give today's Greek students what they want and need. Classes which meet four or five hours a week can finish it by the middle of the second semester, allowing time thereafter for simply reading Greek. It starts from one of the best of the older books, L.A. Wilding's *Greek for Beginners*. That work had several appealing features:

1) Points of Greek morphology and syntax were introduced in logical order.

2) The Greek vocabulary emphasized common words, especially from prose authors like Xenophon and Herodotus.

3) The readings were thoughtfully chosen for interest and relevance to Greek history.

4) There were plenty of practice sentences, both Greek-to-English and English-to-Greek.

However, it was essentially a collection of exercises. For presentation of forms and explanations of grammar, a student was expected to refer to a primer of Greek grammar. Wilding also assumed a knowledge of Latin on the part of all Greek students.

What I have done is essentially to create a full textbook based on Wilding's sentences and readings. I have rearranged the order of presentation somewhat, and modified the readings so that they are closer to the original. I have also added material Wilding did not cover, like athematic verbs, relative clauses and conditions. Paradigms are given whenever new forms are introduced. All points of grammar and syntax are fully explained in terms of English usage, without reference to Latin. I have tried to strike a balance between simply presenting forms to be learned, and explaining the linguistic reasons for their appearance. Some points in the development of the Greek language, such as the great vowel shift and the function of the thematic vowel, are addressed in the text. However, only those things are included which have proven empirically to be helpful and interesting to a first-year Greek student. The goal has been to make the book complete but compact, so that students can do as soon as possible what they came to do: read Greek. The epigraphs which appear at the beginning of some chapters illustrate a point of grammar covered in that chapter. They are there for teacher and student to enjoy together if they wish; the words are not included in the book's vocabulary list.

I want to thank the generous colleagues who have taught from this book over the past eight years, catching mistakes and suggesting helpful changes. Many thanks also to Susan Shelmerdine, whose careful scrutiny of the final draft made further improvements possible. My greatest debt is to the students who have learned Greek with this textbook. They have shown me which explanations worked and which did not; they have encouraged its evolution; and they have given me the pleasure of shared discoveries which is one of the best things about teaching.

Cynthia W. Shelmerdine

January 2001

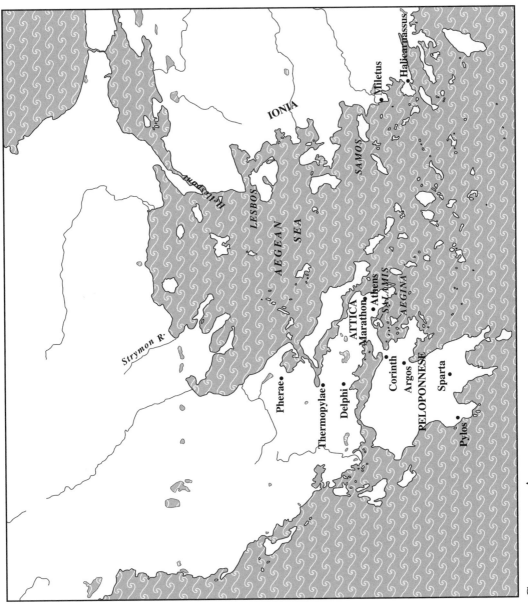

GREECE AND THE AEGEAN

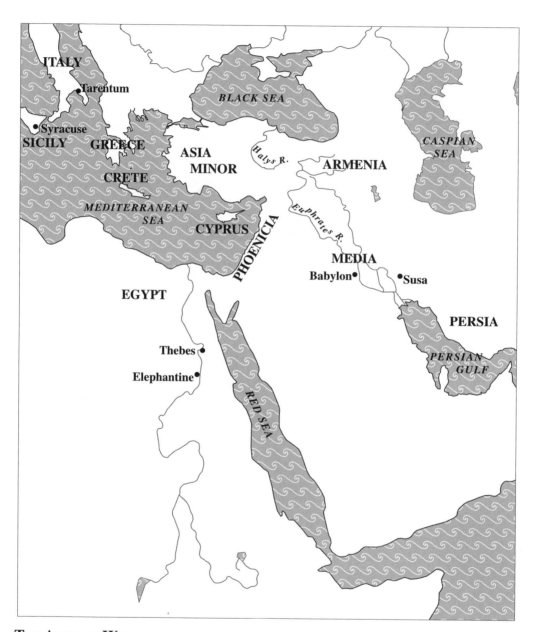

THE ANCIENT WORLD

1. The Greek alphabet, with pronunciation

Form		Name	Pronounced like
A	α	Alpha	short: second **a** in *drama*; long: first **a** in *drama*
B	β	Beta	**b**
Γ	γ	Gamma	**g** in *good*
Δ	δ	Delta	**d**
E	ε	Epsilon (short **e**)	**e** in *bet*
Z	ζ	Zeta	**sd** in *wisdom*
H	η	Eta (long **a, e**)	**a** in *hate* or (more correctly) in *man*
Θ	θ	Theta	**th** in *thick* or (more correctly) in *hothead*
I	ι	Iota	short: **i** in *hit*; long: **i** in *machine*
K	κ	Kappa	**k**
Λ	λ	Lambda	**l**
M	μ	Mu	**m**
N	ν	Nu	**n**
Ξ	ξ	Xi	**x** in *hex* (**ks**)
O	o	Omicron (short **o**)	**ou** in *thought*
Π	π	Pi	**p**
P	ρ	Rho	**r**
Σ	σ, ς	Sigma	**s**
T	τ	Tau	**t**
Y	υ	Upsilon	short: **u** in *put*; long: **u** in *cute*
Φ	φ	Phi	**ph** (**f**) in *photo* or (more correctly) in *hiphop*
X	χ	Chi	**kh** (**ch**) in *chorus* or (more correctly) in *backhand*
Ψ	ψ	Psi	**ps**
Ω	ω	Omega (long **o**)	**o** in *bone* or (more correctly) in *long*

Gamma: when γ is followed by γ, κ, χ or ξ it is pronounced **ng** as in *angle, ankle*.

Omicron and Omega: the words describe the long and short vowels: μικρόν means 'small', and μέγα means 'big'.

Sigma: written ς at the end of a word, σ elsewhere in most books you will see. Another ancient option was the *lunate* sigma, ϲ, used in place of both σ and ς. In the 1980s, Greek texts began to appear using the lunate sigma.

Latin spelling: Romans adjusted the spelling of Greek words, particularly proper names, to conform to the Latin alphabet. English frequently uses the Latinized forms:

c for κ: Περικλῆς becomes 'Pericles'.
y for υ: κύκλος ('circle') gives us the word 'cycle'.
ae for αι: Αἴσχυλος becomes 'Aeschylus'.
oe for οι: Οἰδίπους becomes 'Oedipus'.

A more recent practice has been to keep the Greek spelling as much as possible: Aiskhylos, Oidipous.

2. Consonant groups

The following table shows how consonants can be grouped according to how and where in the mouth they are produced. *Labial* consonants are produced with the lips, *dental* or *lingual* consonants with the tongue against the teeth (or the hard palate just behind the teeth), and *palatal* or *velar* consonants with the soft palate or velum.

	Labial	Dental	Palatal	
stops:	π	τ	κ	unvoiced
	β	δ	γ	voiced
	φ	θ	χ	aspirated
	ψ	σ	ξ	+ σ
nasals:	μ	ν	γκ, γγ, γχ, γξ	

The table also shows another way of distinguishing nouns, as *unvoiced* (produced with no vibration from the voice box), *voiced* (produced with vibration) and *aspirated* (adding the sound **h**). The aspirated stops in ancient Greek were actually pronounced like the unvoiced stop accompanied by a puff of air, and the unvoiced stops were pronounced with no puff of air. Native English speakers do this inadvertently: 'spot' contains an unaspirated **p**, while in 'pot' the **p** is aspirated (put your hand in front of your mouth and try saying the words!). However, it is difficult for an English speaker to make the distinction voluntarily. This is why many English speakers settle for mispronouncing θ as **th**, φ as **f**, and χ as **kh** = **k**.

3. Vowel groups (diphthongs)

Diphthongs (δίφθογγοι) are two vowels combined into a single syllable. The second vowel is always ι or υ. They are pronounced as they look, with the sound of the first vowel followed by the sound of the second vowel:

αι, ᾱι as in *aisle* (θεαί, θεᾷ / θεᾶι)   αυ as in *plow* (ταῦτα)
ει, ηι as in *lei* (Δαρεῖος, τιμῇ / τιμῆι)   ευ, ηυ as in *Europe* (Ζεύς, ηὕρηκα)
οι, ωι as in *boil* (οἶνος, οἴνῳ / οἴνωι)   ου as in boot or (more correctly) as ο + υ
υι as in *sweet* (λελυκυῖα)   (Μοῦσα)

When ι follows a long vowel—ᾱ, η or ω—the ι is often written *subscript* underneath the long vowel, where it is not usually pronounced. (If the long vowel is upper case, the ι appears *adscript*, written on the line and pronounced normally.) In the 1980s, Greek texts began to appear using the iota adscript even after lower case vowels.

4. Accents

Greek has three accents: acute, ´, grave, `, and circumflex, ˆ. They are part of the spelling of most Greek words. In ancient Greek the accents indicated pitch, but for convenience most modern students pronounce them as stress accents, indicating which syllable of a word to emphasize.

An accent is written over a vowel; it appears on one of the last three syllables of a word. For each position, there is a rule for what form the accent must take. The following table shows all possible accents and their positions, using the following symbols:

○ = short or long syllable (length determined by length of vowel)

Ⓢ = short syllable: ε, ο; sometimes α, ι, υ; αι, οι when they end a word

Ⓛ = long syllable: η, ω; sometimes α, ι, υ; diphthongs (exception above)

3 antepenult	2 penult	1 ultima
Ó ○ Ⓢ	○ Ⓛ̂ Ⓢ	○ ○ Ⓛ̂
	○ Ⓛ́ Ⓛ	○ ○ Ⓢ́
	○ Ⓢ́ Ⓛ	○ ○ Ó Nom./Acc.
	○ Ⓢ́ Ⓢ	

Position 3: accent on antepenult. Only acute, and only if **last** syllable is short.

Position 2: accent on penult. If penult is long **and** followed by a short syllable, accent is circumflex; otherwise, acute.

Position 1: accent on ultima. If ultima is long, accent is circumflex; if ultima is short, accent is acute.

EXCEPTION: nominative/accusative/vocative accents always acute. "Nominative/accusative acute" is a good memorizing device.

Note: An acute accent on ultima becomes grave when another word follows (unless that word is *enclitic*; see Ch. 7.3).

Accents appear directly over a lower case vowel (καλόν). They appear over the second vowel of a diphthong (Ζεύς). For accents on vowels that begin a word, see section 5 below on breathings.

5. Breathings

A breathing mark always appears on an *initial* vowel, diphthong or ρ —i.e., one that begins a word. Like accents, the breathing is part of the spelling:

A *smooth breathing*, written like an apostrophe, is silent: ἐγώ ('eh-GO').
A *rough breathing*, written like a backward apostrophe, adds an **h** sound:
ὕδρα ('HUdra').

Note: initial ρ and υ always have a rough breathing.

A breathing mark appears directly over a lower case letter, and to the left of an upper case letter: ἐγώ, Ἥρα. The breathing is written over the second vowel of a diphthong: εἰρήνη, Αἰσχυλος. If a syllable has both a breathing and an acute (or grave) accent, the breathing comes first; it stands underneath a circumflex accent: ἄγω, ἥ, ἦγον (for accents see section 4 above).

6. Elision

Short vowels at the end of a word may be *elided* or cut off when the next word begins with a vowel. Greek spelling shows this: the vowel is omitted and an apostrophe marks its omission: μετὰ ἐμοῦ becomes μετ' ἐμοῦ, 'with me'. When the vowel that begins the next word has a rough breathing, the aspiration or **h**-sound affects the preceding consonant. π becomes φ, and τ becomes θ: μετὰ ἡμῶν becomes μεθ' ἡμῶν, 'with us'.

7. Punctuation and capital letters

Period, comma: as English.

Colon, semicolon: a period written above the line: ἀγαθός·

Question mark: as English semicolon: ἀγαθός;

Capital letters: Not used at the start of every sentence in Greek. They are used to begin a paragraph, and in proper nouns, and to introduce quotations.

Quotation marks: Not used in Greek, although some textbooks occasionally add quotation marks for extra clarity.

EXERCISE 1. The following English words are Greek in origin. Write them out in the Greek alphabet; don't worry about accents, but do include correct breathings. Follow *spelling* rules, not sound: what English letter corresponds to what Greek letter? Remember to convert Latinized spellings to proper Greek spellings! Long vowels ē (η) and ō (ω) are marked; plain **e** and **o** are short (ε, ο).

EXAMPLES: isoscelēs = ἰσοσκελης; hydrophobia = ὑδροφοβια

1. drama	9. genesis	17. calyx
2. rhinocerōs	10. mētropolis	18. rhododendron
3. nectar	11. thōrax	19. iris
4. sarcophagus	12. analysis	20. parenthesis
5. crisis	13. critērion	21. climax
6. canōn	14. basis	22. horizōn
7. paralysis	15. acrophobia	23. catastrophē
8. comma	16. cōlon	24. acropolis

EXERCISE 2. The following are all figures in Greek myths. Write in English, using Latinized spelling.

1. Ποσειδῶν	9. Ἀφροδίτη	17. Ἄρης
2. Ἄρτεμις	10. Προμηθεύς	18. Ψυχή
3. Ἑρμῆς	11. Ἥρα	19. Ἀθήνη
4. Κίρκη	12. Περσεφόνη	20. Ὀδυσσεύς
5. Κύκλωψ	13. Ἡρακλῆς	21. Ὑπερίων
6. Θησεύς	14. Ἀγαμέμνων	22. Ἕκτωρ
7. Μίδας	15. Ἀνδρομάχη	23. Χάρων
8. Δημήτηρ	16. Ἠλέκτρα	24. Ἄλκηστις

EXERCISE 3. The following are names of Greek people and places. Write them out in Greek letters (don't worry about accents). Long vowels are marked.

(a) 1. Dēmosthenēs
     2. Solōn
     3. Leōnidas
     4. Euripidēs

     5. Nicias
     6. Cleisthenēs
     7. Pythagoras
     8. Xerxēs

     9. Themistoclēs
    10. Alcibiadēs
    11. Hippias
    12. Philocratēs

(b) 1. Argos
     2. Dēlos
     3. Mytilēnē
     4. Samos

     5. Olympia
     6. Naxos
     7. Chios
     8. Thasos

     9. Eretria
    10. Pylos
    11. Phōcis
    12. Mycēnae

CHAPTER 2

1. Verb forms: terminology

Like English verbs, Greek verbs express *person* (1st: I/we; 2nd: you/you; 3rd: he, she, it/they), and *number* (singular/dual/plural). However, they do so differently than English. Greek is an *inflected* language; person and number are indicated not by pronouns, but by endings attached to the verb stem. This book covers only the singular and plural forms; the dual, used of two persons or things, is much less common.

Of course Greek verbs also come in various *tenses* (present, future, etc.), *voices* (active, middle, passive) and *moods* (indicative or main verb, subjunctive, etc.). The Greek verb has six *principal parts*; each is the basis for forming one or more tenses. A particular identifying marker distinguishes each principal part from the others. The complete list of principal parts is as follows:

P.P.	REGULAR MARKER	EXAMPLE	FORMS THE FOLLOWING TENSES
First:		λύω	present, imperfect active, middle, passive
Second:	σ	λύσω	future active, middle
Third:	augment/σα	ἔλυσα	aorist active, middle
Fourth:	reduplication/κα	λέλυκα	perfect, pluperfect active
Fifth:	reduplication	λέλυμαι	perfect, pluperfect middle, passive
Sixth:	augment/θη	ἐλύθην	aorist, future passive

This lesson covers only the present active indicative; the rest will come later.

2. The present active indicative of thematic verbs

The present tense has several forms in English, for example 'I go', 'I do go', 'I am going'; 'I walk', 'I do walk', 'I am walking'. The present tense in Greek covers all of these meanings. You'll notice that all the present active verb forms contain some form of an **o** or **e** vowel:

	SINGULAR				PLURAL		
1st	(I)	-ω	o		(we)	-ο-μεν	o
2nd	(you)	-εις	e		(you)	-ε-τε	e
3rd	(he)	-ει	e		(they)	-ουσι	o

This is the *thematic vowel*, which regularly appears in certain forms as an **e**, in others as an **o**. We can describe a *thematic verb* like λύω as consisting of three parts: stem, thematic vowel, and personal ending. Here is the present indicative active of λύω, 'I loose', 'I am loosing'. The hyphens are not part of the spelling, but are inserted here to show the different components (in the singular and the third person plural, the thematic vowel and the ending are combined).

	SINGULAR		PLURAL	
1st	λύ-ω .	I loose	λύ-ο-μεν	we loose
2nd	λύ-εις	you loose	λύ-ε-τε	you loose
3rd	λύ-ει	he/she/it looses	λύ-ουσῖ(ν)	they loose

The -ι of the 3rd person plural is short. The -ν in parenthesis on this form is not used when the next word begins with a consonant. It is added when the next word begins with a vowel, or when a punctuation mark follows. Because it moves on and off the form as needed, it is called *nu movable* (more formally *paragogic nu*).

3. Verb accents

The accent on a verb is *recessive*; that is, it always goes back toward the start of the word as far as accent rules (Ch. 1.4) permit, thus:

last syllable short: accent recedes to antepenult (must be acute—why?)
last syllable long: accent recedes to penult (must be acute—why?)

Note: The verb accent always recedes, and the same rules always apply, so you should be able to reason out the correct accent for any verb form.

PRACTICE A. Add accent and breathing, and translate (see lesson vocabulary):

1. φερει
2. πεμπουσι
3. κωλυετε
4. γραφομεν
5. αγεις
6. φυλασσω

EXERCISE 4.

Verbs used: ἄγω   κωλύω   (see vocabulary list at
          γράφω   πέμπω   end of chapter)
          θύω   φέρω

Translate into English:

1. κωλύεις
2. θύομεν
3. ἄγει
4. πέμπετε
5. φέρουσι
6. ἄγομεν
7. γράφεις
8. πέμπουσιν
9. κωλύει
10. θύετε
11. γράφουσι
12. ἄγετε
13. πέμπομεν
14. φέρεις
15. θύει

EXERCISE 5. Translate into Greek:

1. We hinder
2. You (s.) sacrifice
3. You (pl.) hinder
4. He is writing
5. They lead
6. We carry
7. They sacrifice
8. You (s.) send
9. You (pl.) write
10. She carries
11. You (pl.) are carrying
12. He sends
13. They hinder
14. We write
15. You (s.) lead

EXERCISE 6.

New verbs:	διώκω	τοξεύω
	ἔχω	φεύγω
	πείθω	φυλάσσω

Translate into English:

1. φυλάσσομεν
2. διώκουσι
3. φεύγει
4. φυλάσσεις

5. διώκετε
6. φεύγουσιν
7. ἔχεις
8. πείθετε

9. τοξεύομεν
10. ἔχει
11. πείθουσι
12. τοξεύετε

EXERCISE 7. Translate into Greek:

1. They guard
2. We are fleeing
3. He persuades
4. You (s.) pursue

5. She shoots
6. You (pl.) have
7. We persuade
8. They are shooting

9. You (pl.) guard
10. It is pursuing
11. We have
12. You (s.) flee

4. The negative

The negative used with main verbs appears as οὐ (before consonants), οὐκ (before vowels with smooth breathing, to ease pronunciation), and οὐχ (before vowels with rough breathing—why? see Ch. 1.2). It commonly stands just before the word it negates.

Note: οὐ is a *proclitic* word; this means it has no accent of its own, and this lack of accent does not affect neighboring words.

5. Common conjunctions

καί, 'and, also, even', and ἀλλά, 'but' are used and placed just as in English.

EXERCISE 8. Translate:

1. οὐ γράφει
2. διώκομεν καὶ τοξεύομεν
3. οὐ διώκει, ἀλλὰ φεύγει
4. οὐκ ἔχομεν
5. γράφουσι καὶ πείθουσιν

6. We write and persuade
7. You do not persuade
8. He does not shoot
9. They do not guard, but they flee
10. You are not leading

Chapter 2 Vocabulary

Verbs:

ἄγω	lead, bring	πείθω	persuade
γράφω	write	πέμπω	send
διώκω	pursue, seek after	τοξεύω	shoot (with arrows)
ἔχω	have	φέρω	carry, bear
θύω	sacrifice	φεύγω	flee
κωλύω	hinder, prevent	φυλάσσω	guard
λύω	loose, set free		

Adverbs:

καί	also, even	οὐ, οὐκ, οὐχ	not

Conjunctions:

ἀλλά	but	καί	and

CHAPTER 3

1. Noun forms: terminology

Like verbs, Greek nouns consist of a stem and an ending. These endings indicate *number* (singular, dual, plural). They also show grammatical *gender* (masculine, feminine, neuter—whether or not the noun has a natural gender). Finally, the endings show the *case* of the noun, and thereby its grammatical function. There are five cases in Greek, with the following names and functions:

CASE	FUNCTION	EXAMPLE
Nominative:	subject	*The goddess* writes.
	predicate	She is *a goddess*.
Genitive:	possessive ("s" is the sign)	The honor *of the goddess*; *the goddess'* honor
Dative:	indirect object ('to' or 'for')	I sacrifice *to the goddess*.
Accusative:	direct object	I worship *the goddess*.
Vocative:	used in direct address	*Goddess*, I write.

2. The definite article

The definite article in Greek corresponds to English 'the'. The indefinite article, 'a', 'an' in English, does not exist in Greek; it is indicated by omitting the definite article.

The definite article is an adjective, and *agrees with* a noun. Agreement means it has the same gender, number and case. This chapter includes the feminine forms of the article, which agree with the 1st declension nouns introduced in the next section. (For other forms, see Ch. 4.1.)

3. Feminine nouns of the 1st declension

The set of case endings belonging to each noun defines its *declension*. In Greek there are three declensions. The first comprises nouns whose stem ends in -α or -η. (To find the stem of a noun, remove the genitive ending; whatever is left is the stem.) There are three types of 1st declension feminine nouns. They are all identical in the plural, but different in the singular:

(a) τιμή type. Singular forms have the vowel -η. Originally this type ended in long -ᾱ. However, in the Dark Ages a change in pronunciation took place in some dialects, including Attic, which you are learning. This raised the ᾱ sound to η. This change, which did not affect short α, is called the *great vowel shift*.

(b) χώρᾱ type. Singular forms have the vowel -ᾱ. In this type of noun, the -ᾱ is preceded by ε, ι or ρ. This protected it from the great vowel shift in Attic Greek. The noun thus preserves its original form, with so-called 'pure' ᾱ.

(c) Μοῦσα / γέφυρα type. The nominative, accusative and vocative singular end in short -α. The genitive and dative endings are long, and were therefore affected by the great vowel shift. Thus the vowel in those cases appears as η (unless preceded by ε, ι or ρ as in γέφυρα, when it appears as ᾱ).

		(article)	honor	country	**Muse**	**bridge**
SING.	Nom.	ἡ	τιμή	χώρᾱ	Μοῦσᾰ	γέφυρᾰ
	Gen.	τῆς	τιμῆς	χώρᾱς	Μούσης	γεφύρᾱς
	Dat.	τῇ	τιμῇ	χώρᾳ	Μούσῃ	γεφύρᾳ
	Acc.	τὴν	τιμήν	χώρᾱν	Μοῦσᾰν	γέφυρᾰν
	Voc.	(ὦ)	τιμή	χώρᾱ	Μοῦσᾰ	γέφυρᾰ
PLUR.	Nom.	αἱ	τιμαί	χῶραι	Μοῦσαι	γέφυραι
	Gen.	τῶν	τιμῶν	χωρῶν	Μουσῶν	γεφυρῶν
	Dat.	ταῖς	τιμαῖς	χώραις	Μούσαις	γεφύραις
	Acc.	τὰς	τιμάς	χώρας	Μούσας	γεφύρας
	Voc.	(ὦ)	τιμαί	χῶραι	Μοῦσαι	γέφυραι

Recitation Only — (Voc. rows, handwritten annotations)

Note: In the vocative, ὦ is not a form of the definite article. It is an interjection that always precedes a vocative form in Greek. Its literal translation would be 'O' but since we do not use this in English (we say 'Fred!', not 'O Fred!' in direct address), ὦ should not be translated.

If confronted by a noun in an *oblique* case (genitive, dative or accusative), you can find the nominative by the following rules:

STEM ENDS IN	NOM. SING.	EXAMPLE
ε, ι or ρ	long or short -α (χώρα / γέφυρα types)	ἀγορῶν from ἀγορά
σ, double consonant (ζ, ξ, ψ) or two consonants (λλ, σσ, ττ)	short -α (Μοῦσα type)	θαλάσσῃ from θάλασσα
any other letter	-η (τιμή type)	ἐπιστολαῖς from ἐπιστολή

4. Noun and adjective accents

Noun and adjective accents are *persistent*; that is, wherever the accent appears in the nominative singular, there it remains as long as accent rules permit, and follows the rule for that position (Ch. 1.4).

Note: When the accent is on the ultima (Position 1), it is always acute/grave in the nominative, vocative and accusative—even when normal accent rules would suggest a circumflex.

5. Accents of 1st declension nouns

Some words ending in short -α have their accent on the antepenult (Position 3). In the genitive and dative singular, and in the dative and accusative plural, the ultima is long, and the accent moves forward to the penult (Position 2) to comply with accent rules (for the genitive plural, see below).

There are several accent rules that affect individual cases:

Nom. sing.: the accent rules can help you determine whether an α is long or short:
θάλασσα has its accent in Position 3; therefore the ultima is short.
χώρα has an acute accent (not circumflex); therefore the ultima is long.

Nom./Voc. pl.: αι at the end of a word is always counted short for accent purposes.

Gen. pl.: the genitive plural of 1st declension nouns always has a circumflex accent
on the last syllable (Position 1). This is because, like the other cases, this one originally had
an α at the end of the stem. By normal accent rules, this α originally carried the accent.
However, the α contracts with the ω of the ending: α + ω = ω. The accent remains on the
contracted syllable, and follows the rule for Position 1.

Acc. pl.: the ᾱ in this declension is always long.

6. Prepositions

Prepositions each take a particular case, sometimes a choice of cases depending on their
meaning. Here are three common prepositions which take only one case. This is because the
genitive case typically describes motion *out of* or *away from*, the dative typically describes a
stationary position, and the accusative typically describes motion *into* or *toward*.

Note: The following prepositions are *proclitic*, and have no accent (like the negative οὐ,
Ch. 2.4).

Gen.	ἐκ τῆς χώρας	out of the country	(where from)
Gen.	ἐξ οἰκίας	out of a house	(where from)
Dat.	ἐν τῇ χώρᾳ	in the country	(where)
Acc.	εἰς τὴν χώραν	into the country	(where to)

Note: When ἐκ is followed by a vowel, it is written ἐξ.

EXERCISE 9.

1. ἡ θεὰ ἔχει τιμήν.
2. γράφει ἐπιστολάς.
3. φεύγομεν εἰς τὴν χώραν.
4. θύουσιν ἐν τῇ ἀγορᾷ.
5. θεραπεύετε τὴν θεάν.
6. τράπεζαν οὐκ ἔχομεν.
7. ἡ θεὰ φυλάσσει τὴν ἀγοράν.
8. διώκομεν τὴν στρατιὰν εἰς τὴν θάλασσαν.
9. αἱ Μοῦσαι δόξαν ἔχουσιν.
10. θεραπεύεις τὴν θεάν; (; is a question mark; see Ch. 1.7)

EXERCISE 10.

1. They send a letter.
2. The sea hinders the army.
3. We honor the Muses.
4. The army has glory.
5. You (pl.) are pursuing the army into the country.
6. Do they flee from the sea?
7. I am not carrying letters.
8. They sacrifice to the goddesses.

9. In the marketplace they are honoring the goddess.
10. We do not pursue the army, but flee.

EXERCISE 11.

1. Give the acc. sing. of: φωνή, ἑσπέρα, ἅμιλλα, θεά, σοφία.
2. Give the acc. and gen. sing. of: μάχη, θύρα, πύλη, ἅμαξα, στρατιά.
3. Give the nom. and dat. sing. of: οἰκιῶν, φωνῆς, δίψαν, γεφύραις.

7. Future active indicative

The future active ('I will go', 'I will sacrifice', etc.) is formed from the second principal part (Ch. 2.1). The present and the future are *primary* tenses (the other primary tenses are the perfect and the future perfect, a rare combination of the future and the perfect). The regular marker for the future is σ, inserted between the verb stem and the thematic vowel. When the verb stem ends in a vowel, this is no problem. (Verbs whose stem ends in a consonant will be discussed starting in Ch. 10.) The personal endings of the future are identical to those of the present:

	SINGULAR		PLURAL	
1st	λύσω	I shall loose	λύσομεν	we shall loose
2nd	λύσεις	you will loose	λύσετε	you will loose
3rd	λύσει	he/she/it will loose	λύσουσῖ(ν)	they will loose

EXERCISE 12.

1. ἡ θεὰ παύσει τὴν μάχην.
2. θεραπεύσουσι τὴν θεάν.
3. ἕλκομεν τὴν ἅμαξαν εἰς τὴν κώμην.
4. ἡ θάλασσα οὐ κωλύσει τὴν στρατιάν.
5. οὐκ ἄγομεν τὴν στρατιὰν εἰς τὴν γέφυραν.
6. ἄγετε τὴν στρατιὰν ἐκ τῆς χώρας.
7. αἱ ἅμαξαι κωλύσουσι τὴν μάχην.
8. θύσομεν τῇ θεᾷ ἐν τῇ κώμῃ.
9. στρατεύσετε εἰς τὴν θάλασσαν;
10. οὐ λύσομεν τὴν στρατιάν.

EXERCISE 13.

1. We will set free the village.
2. I shall stop the battle.
3. Will you sacrifice to the goddess?
4. They will not march out of the country.
5. We will honor the Muses.
6. He is not writing the letter.
7. They are dragging the wagons from the marketplace.
8. You will hunt in the country.
9. We shall not prevent the contest.
10. Will they stop the army?

Chapter 3 Vocabulary

Verbs:

ἕλκω	drag	παύω	stop
θεραπεύω	honor, worship	στρατεύω	march
θηρεύω	hunt		

Nouns: (noun entries include nominative, genitive ending and article)

ἀγορά, -ᾶς, ἡ	marketplace	θύρα, -ας, ἡ	door
ἅμαξα, -ης, ἡ	wagon	κώμη, -ης, ἡ	village
ἅμιλλα, -ης, ἡ	contest	μάχη, -ης, ἡ	battle
γέφυρα, -ας, ἡ	bridge	Μοῦσα, -ης, ἡ	Muse
γλῶσσα, -ης, ἡ	tongue	οἰκία, -ας, ἡ	house
δίψα, -ης, ἡ	thirst	πύλη, -ης, ἡ	gate
δόξα, -ης, ἡ	glory	σοφία, -ας, ἡ	wisdom
ἐπιστολή, -ῆς, ἡ	letter	στρατιά, -ᾶς, ἡ	army
ἑσπέρα, -ας, ἡ	evening	τιμή, -ῆς, ἡ	honor
ἡμέρα, -ας, ἡ	day	τράπεζα, -ης, ἡ	table
θάλασσα, -ης, ἡ	sea	φωνή, -ῆς, ἡ	voice
θεά, -ᾶς, ἡ	goddess	χώρα, -ας, ἡ	country

Article:

ἡ	the (feminine form)

Prepositions: (in parentheses, the case of the noun governed by the preposition)

εἰς (+ *acc.*)	into, onto, to	ἐν (+ *dat.*)	in, on, at
ἐκ (+ *gen.*)	out of, from		
ἐξ when followed by word starting with a vowel			

Other:

ὦ	(used with voc.)

1. The definite article

Here is the complete declension of the definite article (see also Ch. 3.2). The masculine forms agree with the 1st declension nouns introduced in the next section.

Test

		SINGULAR			PLURAL	
	M	**F**	**N**	**M**	**F**	**N**
Nom.	ὁ	ἡ	τό	οἱ	αἱ	τά
Gen.	τοῦ	τῆς	τοῦ	τῶν	τῶν	τῶν
Dat.	τῷ	τῇ	τῷ	τοῖς	ταῖς	τοῖς
Acc.	τόν	τήν	τό	τούς	τάς	τά

2. Masculine nouns of the 1st declension

There are two types of 1st declension masculine nouns. The plurals are identical to those learned in Chapter 3. In the singular, the κριτής type corresponds to the τιμή type (Ch. 3.3), and the νεανίας type corresponds to the χώρα type.

		(article)	judge	young man
SING.	Nom.	ὁ	κριτής	νεανίας
	Gen.	τοῦ	κριτοῦ	νεανίου
	Dat.	τῷ	κριτῇ	νεανίᾳ
	Acc.	τὸν	κριτήν	νεανίαν
	Voc.	ὦ	κριτά	νεανία
PLUR.	Nom.	οἱ	κριταί	νεανίαι
	Gen.	τῶν	κριτῶν	νεανιῶν
	Dat.	τοῖς	κριταῖς	νεανίαις
	Acc.	τοὺς	κριτάς	νεανίας
	Voc.	ὦ	κριταί	νεανίαι

3. Imperfect active indicative

The imperfect is a past tense, also known as a *historic* or *secondary* tense. It is formed from the first principal part of the verb (Ch. 2.1)—that is, it uses the present stem. It has its own set of endings, and it also has an *augment*, like all secondary tenses. For verbs beginning with a consonant, the augment is the letter ε preceding the verb stem. (Verbs that begin with a vowel are augmented by lengthening the vowel; see Ch. 10.2.)

Note: The thematic vowel follows the same pattern in the imperfect as in the present tense: **o** for 1st singular, 1st and 3rd plural; **e** for 2nd and 3rd singular, 2nd plural.

	SINGULAR			PLURAL
1st	ἔ-λυ-ο-ν	I was loosing	ἐ-λύ-ο-μεν	we were loosing
2nd	ἔ-λυ-ε-ς	you were loosing	ἐ-λύ-ε-τε	you were loosing
3rd	ἔ-λυ-ε(ν)	he/she/it was loosing	ἔ-λυ-ο-ν	they were loosing

The imperfect in English describes an ongoing or repeated past action: 'I was going', 'I used to go'. These are its two most common meanings in Greek also. It can also mean 'I tried to go' (the *conative* imperfect) and 'I began to go' (the *inchoative* imperfect).

> οἱ πολῖται ἐθεράπευον τὴν θεάν.
> The citizens used to worship the goddess.

> ὁ νεανίας ἐδίωκε τὴν ἅμαξαν.
> The young man was pursuing the wagon.

> οἱ πολῖται ἔπειθον τὸν κριτήν.
> The citizens tried to persuade the judge.

> ὁ νεανίας ἐδίωκε τὴν ἅμαξαν.
> The young man began to pursue the wagon.

PRACTICE A. Translate:

1. ἔθυεν
2. ἐπαύομεν
3. ἐκώλυον
4. ἔφερες
5. ἐπέμπετε

6. He was writing
7. You (pl.) were sacrificing
8. I used to hunt
9. We began to loose
10. You (s.) tried to stop

4. Some uses of the article

In Greek the article has several uses which go beyond its function in English. Among its common uses:

1) In place of a possessive adjective, when the context makes the meaning clear:
> ἄγει τὴν στρατιάν. He leads his army.

2) With nouns denoting a class or type in general:
> οἱ ποιηταὶ παρέχουσι τὴν τιμήν. Poets provide honor.

3) With abstract nouns, especially when the noun is the subject of the sentence, or the topic of discussion:
> ἡ δικαιοσύνη παρέχει τὴν εἰρήνην. Justice causes peace.

4) With proper nouns, especially after the first time the person or place is mentioned:
> ἡ Ἀθήνη, 'Athena'; αἱ Ἀθῆναι, 'Athens'.

EXERCISE 14.

1. οἱ στρατιῶται ἔλυον τὸν πολίτην.
2. οἱ ποιηταὶ θεραπεύουσι τὴν Μοῦσαν.
3. ὁ κριτὴς τὴν ἅμιλλαν ἔπαυεν.
4. οἱ κριταὶ διώκουσι τὴν δικαιοσύνην.
5. οἱ στρατιῶται ἔφευγον εἰς τὰς Ἀθήνας.

6. ἐθύετε ἐν τῇ κώμῃ;
7. ὁ Βορέας τὴν μάχην ἐκώλυεν.
8. στρατεύσετε, ὦ νεανίαι, εἰς τὴν χώραν.
9. οἱ πολῖται ἔθυον ταῖς Μούσαις.
10. οἱ στρατιῶται ἐκώλυον τοὺς ναύτας ἀπὸ τῆς κώμης.

EXERCISE 15.

1. We were not hindering the soldiers.
2. The sailor was sacrificing to the goddess.
3. Will Athena stop the battle?
4. The sailor flees to his house.
5. The soldiers were not hindering the steward.
6. We used to train the young men in the village.
7. Poets will always honor Sparta.
8. Will you set free the soldiers, citizens?
9. The citizens tried to keep the soldiers from the houses.
10. We were honoring the Muses.

5. Word order

Since the ending of a word, rather than its position in the sentence, shows its grammatical function, word order in Greek is generally flexible. There is no rule that puts, for example, the verb at the end of the sentence. It is often good Greek to follow English word order. The most important point is that the order should be logical and the meaning clear. This flexibility has certain advantages. To emphasize a word, a Greek author may just move it from its natural place toward the beginning of the sentence; this gives it prominence, as underlining does in English. Sometimes, too, a certain word order will be chosen for its harmonious sound.

There are, however, some situations which require a particular word order; one of these is given in the next section.

6. Word order with dependent genitive

A possessive or *dependent* genitive must follow the article of the noun it depends on. Usually this is done by sandwiching the genitive phrase between that article and its noun:

ὁ τῆς οἰκίας ταμίας, the steward of the house

ἡ τοῦ κριτοῦ οἰκία, the judge's house

It is equally good Greek to write ἡ οἰκία ἡ τοῦ κριτοῦ. In this construction the genitive phrase still comes right after the article of the noun it depends on, because this article is repeated after its noun. Greek authors used this construction both for emphasis and simply for variation.

7. Uses of the dative

1) indirect object:

θύομεν τῇ θεᾷ. We sacrifice *to the goddess*.

Note: In expressions of motion *to* or *toward* a place, the dative is not used: to say 'to the house' Greek uses a preposition with the accusative (Ch. 3.6).

2) with the preposition ἐν:

    a) literally, place where:

        θύομεν ἐν τῇ ἀγορᾷ.   We sacrifice *in the marketplace*.

    b) metaphorically:

        παιδεύομεν τοὺς νεανίας ἐν τῇ σοφίᾳ. We educate the young men *in wisdom*.

3) means/instrument:

        τὸν κριτὴν ἐκώλυες τῇ φωνῇ. You were hindering the judge *with your voice*.

        ἁμάξῃ διώκει τὴν στρατιάν. He pursues the army *by means of a wagon*.

8. Verbs taking genitive or dative

Some verbs take an object in the genitive or dative, instead of a normal direct object in the accusative. Often one can see the logic behind the usage, as in the two such verbs introduced in this lesson. Verbs of ruling take the genitive, like βασιλέυω 'reign, be king' (be king *of*):

        βασιλεύει τῆς χώρας. He is king of the country.

πιστεύω 'trust, believe' takes the dative (put one's trust *in*, give credence *to*):

        πιστεύουσι τῇ θεᾷ. They trust the goddess.

Note: If a verb takes the genitive or the dative, it always says so in the vocabulary.

EXERCISE 16.

1. οἱ νεανίαι πιστεύουσι τοῖς ναύταις.
2. τὴν σοφίαν διώκομεν.
3. οἱ στρατιῶται ἐφύλασσον τὰς τῶν πολιτῶν οἰκίας.
4. οἱ νεανίαι εἰς τὴν Σπάρτην στρατεύσουσιν.
5. ἡ Ἀθήνη κωλύει τὸν νεανίαν.
6. ἐθεραπεύομεν τὴν τῆς χώρας θεάν.
7. ἡ στρατιὰ ἡ τοῦ Ξέρξου φεύγει.
8. τῷ ταμίᾳ οὐκ ἐπιστεύομεν.
9. ὁ Ξέρξης παύσει τὴν μάχην τῇ φωνῇ.
10. ὁ Ξέρξης ἐβασίλευε τῶν Περσῶν.

EXERCISE 17.

1. The sailor was not trusting the north wind.
2. The citizens used to believe the judge.
3. We were marching into the country of the Persians.
4. Young men do not always seek after wisdom.
5. Xerxes does not trust his soldiers.
6. The judge will educate the young man in justice and wisdom.
7. We will not hinder the citizen's wagon.
8. The young men began to flee toward the door of the house.
9. Do you rule the country?
10. We will keep the Persians from Athens.

Chapter 4 Vocabulary

Verbs:

βασιλεύω (+ *gen.*)	be king, reign	πιστεύω (+ *dat.*)	trust, believe
κωλύω	keep (someone) away	παρέχω	produce, cause, provide
παιδεύω	educate, teach, train		

Nouns:

Ἀθῆναι, -ῶν, αἱ	Athens	Ξέρξης, -ου, ὁ	Xerxes
Ἀθήνη, -ης, ἡ	Athena	Πέρσης, -ου, ὁ	a Persian
Βορέας, -ου, ὁ	North Wind	ποιητής, -οῦ, ὁ	poet
δικαιοσύνη, -ης, ἡ	justice	πολίτης, -ου, ὁ	citizen (long ι)
εἰρήνη, -ης, ἡ	peace	Σπάρτη, -ης, ἡ	Sparta
κριτής, -οῦ, ὁ	judge	στρατιώτης, -ου, ὁ	soldier
ναύτης, -ου, ὁ	sailor	ταμίας, -ου, ὁ	steward
νεανίας, -ου, ὁ	young man		

Article:

ὁ, ἡ, τό	the

Adverb:

ἀεί	always

Prepositions:

ἀπό (+ *gen.*)	from	πρός (+ *acc.*)	to, toward

Ἐν ἀρχῇ ἦν ὁ λόγος, καὶ ὁ λόγος ἦν πρὸς τὸν θεόν, καὶ θεὸς ἦν
ὁ λόγος. οὗτος ἦν ἐν ἀρχῇ πρὸς τὸν θεόν.

— Gospel according to St. John, 1.1

1. Masculine and feminine nouns of the 2nd declension

Both masculine and (less common) feminine nouns of the second declension have stems
that end in -o. The pattern of long and short endings is the same as for the Μοῦσα / γέφυρα
type of 1st declension nouns (Ch. 3.3): short in Nom., Acc. sing., Voc.; long in Gen., Dat.,
Acc. plur.

			word		island
Sing.	Nom.	ὁ	λόγος	ἡ	νῆσος
	Gen.	τοῦ	λόγου	τῆς	νήσου
	Dat.	τῷ	λόγῳ	τῇ	νήσῳ
	Acc.	τὸν	λόγον	τὴν	νῆσον
	Voc.	ὦ	λόγε	ὦ	νῆσε
Plur.	Nom.	οἱ	λόγοι	αἱ	νῆσοι
	Gen.	τῶν	λόγων	τῶν	νήσων
	Dat.	τοῖς	λόγοις	ταῖς	νήσοις
	Acc.	τοὺς	λόγους	τὰς	νήσους
	Voc.	ὦ	λόγοι	ὦ	νῆσοι

2. The aorist active indicative

The *aorist* is the simple past tense, which corresponds to English 'I went', 'I watched',
'I did not watch', etc. Unlike the imperfect it does not say that the action was ongoing or
repeated, simply that it happened. Contrast the following imperfects and simple pasts in
English:

Imperfect	Simple past
I was going	I went
it was happening	it happened
they were running	they ran

The aorist active is the third principal part of a Greek verb, after the present and the
future (see Ch. 2.1). It is formed in one of two ways. In English, some verbs form the past
tense by adding the ending **-ed** to the present stem ('I watch' / 'I watched'); these are called

weak verbs. Other verbs change their stem instead ('I go' / 'I went'); these are called *strong verbs*. The same distinction applies in Greek: a verb has either a weak or a strong aorist (also referred to as first and second aorist). The strong aorist will be presented in Ch. 10. 8. In the weak or first aorist -**σα**- is the regular marker; it replaces the thematic vowel (except -**σε** shows in the 3rd singular). The personal endings are the same as those of the imperfect, and like all past tense indicatives the aorist begins with an augment (Ch. 4.3):

		IMPERFECT		**AORIST**	
Sing.	1st	ἔ-λυ-ο-ν	I was loosing	ἔ-λυ-σα	I loosed
	2nd	ἔ-λυ-ε-ς	you were loosing	ἔ-λυ-σα-ς	you loosed
	3rd	ἔ-λυ-ε͡(ν)	he was loosing	ἔ-λυ-σε(ν)	he loosed
Plur.	1st	ἐ-λύ-ο-μεν	we were loosing	ἐ-λύ-σα-μεν	we loosed
	2nd	ἐ-λύ-ε-τε	you were loosing	ἐ-λύ-σα-τε	you loosed
	3rd	ἔ-λυ-ο-ν	they were loosing	ἔ-λυ-σα-ν	they loosed

EXERCISE 18.

1. ὁ δοῦλος ἔλυσε τὸν ἵππον.
2. ἐπιστεύσαμεν τοῖς τοῦ νεανίου λόγοις.
3. ὁ δοῦλος γράφει ἐν τῇ βίβλῳ.
4. ὁ τῆς οἰκίας ταμίας ἐπαίδευσε τοὺς δούλους.
5. ὁ ἰατρὸς ἐθεράπευσε τὴν νόσον.
6. ὁ ποταμὸς οὐκ ἐκώλυε τοὺς ἵππους.
7. ἡ νόσος τὸν πόλεμον οὐκ ἔπαυσεν.
8. οἱ Ἀθηναῖοι ἔθυσαν ἐν τῇ νήσῳ.
9. ἐτοξεύσαμεν τοὺς τῶν Ἀθηναίων ἵππους.
10. ὁ Ξέρξης ἄγει τὴν στρατιὰν ἐν τῇ ὁδῷ.

EXERCISE 19.

1. We set free [use aorist] the slaves.
2. The Athenians trained their horses.
3. We seek after wisdom in books.
4. You ran risks on the road.
5. You healed the slave, doctor.
6. The soldiers believed the general's words.
7. We were fleeing to the island.
8. The young man trusted the words of the book.
9. The doctors did not keep the plague from Athens.
10. We are leading the horses to the river.

Review Exercises

EXERCISE 20.

1. οἱ ἰατροὶ τὰς νόσους θεραπεύουσιν.
2. ὁ δοῦλος ἐκώλυσε τοὺς ἵππους ἀπὸ τοῦ ποταμοῦ.
3. οἱ Ἀθηναῖοι ἐπαίδευον τοὺς νεανίας ἐν τῇ σοφίᾳ.
4. οἱ τῆς βίβλου λόγοι οὐ πείθουσι τοὺς Ἀθηναίους.
5. οἱ στρατιῶται ἐφύλασσον τὴν ὁδόν;
6. πέμπομεν ἐπιστολὴν εἰς τὴν νῆσον.

7. οἱ Ἀθηναῖοι ἔθυσαν τῇ θεᾷ.
8. πιστεύσομεν τῇ φωνῇ τῇ τῆς θεᾶς.
9. ἡ τοῦ Ξέρξου στρατιὰ ἐκινδύνευσεν ἐν τῷ πολέμῳ.
10. ἡ τοῦ ποιητοῦ γλῶσσα πείθει τοὺς πολίτας.

EXERCISE 21.

1. The citizens were fleeing into Athens.
2. The Persians will keep the Athenians from the island.
3. We trusted the doctor's words.
4. Thirst and illness hinder the Athenians.
5. The soldiers were guarding the gates of the village.
6. You did not set free the slaves.
7. The voice of the citizen began to persuade the judges.
8. The sailors are guarding the island.
9. The river will not hinder the army of the Athenians.
10. The doctor cured the young man's illness.

Chapter 5 Vocabulary

Verbs:

| θεραπεύω | heal, cure, tend | κινδυνεύω | run risks |

Nouns:

Ἀθηναῖος, -ου, ὁ	Athenian	νῆσος, -ου, ἡ	island
βίβλος, -ου, ἡ	book	νόσος, -ου, ἡ	illness, plague
δοῦλος, -ου, ὁ	slave	ὁδός, -οῦ, ἡ	road, way, journey
ἰατρός, -οῦ, ὁ	doctor	πόλεμος, -ου, ὁ	war
ἵππος, -ου, ὁ	horse	ποταμός, -οῦ, ὁ	river
λόγος, -ου, ὁ	word	στρατηγός, -οῦ, ὁ	general

CHAPTER 6

τὰ δ᾽ ἄλλα σιγῶ· βοῦς ἐπὶ γλώσσῃ μέγας
βέβηκεν·

— Aeschylus, *Agamemnon* 36-37

ἤ που ἔτι ζώει καὶ ὁρᾷ φάος ἠελίοιο,
ἦ ἤδη τέθνηκε καὶ εἰν Ἀΐδαο δόμοισιν.

— Homer, *Odyssey* 4.833-834

1. Neuter nouns of the 2nd declension

Neuter nouns of the 2nd declension have the same endings as neuter forms of the article, except that the nom., acc. and voc. singular end in **-ov**. In neuter nouns and adjectives, the accusative and the nominative are always the same. There is only one type of 2nd declension neuter noun.

yoke

	SINGULAR		PLURAL	
Nom.	τὸ	ζυγόν	τὰ	ζυγά
Gen.	τοῦ	ζυγοῦ	τῶν	ζυγῶν
Dat.	τῷ	ζυγῷ	τοῖς	ζυγοῖς
Acc.	τὸ	ζυγόν	τὰ	ζυγά
Voc.	ὦ	ζυγόν	ὦ	ζυγά

2. Neuter plural with singular verb

If the subject is neuter, the verb is singular—even if the subject is plural:

τὸ δένδρον παρέχει καρπόν. The tree produces fruit.
τὰ δένδρα παρέχει καρπόν. The trees produce fruit.

3. The noun γῆ, 'earth, land'

The 1st-declension noun γῆ appears to violate normal accent rules. The underlying form is actually γέα: η results from a *contraction* of a stem vowel ε with α. An accent on a contracted syllable is always circumflex. Thus γῆ has a circumflex accent on the nominative and accusative singular (there is no plural):

Nom.	ἡ	γῆ
Gen.	τῆς	γῆς
Dat.	τῇ	γῇ
Acc.	τὴν	γῆν
Voc.	ὦ	γῆ

4. The perfect active indicative

Like the present and future, the perfect is a *primary* tense in Greek. It refers to the present result of a past action, rather than to the action itself: 'I have climbed', 'he has arrived'. Compare the following English examples:

- Aorist: I climbed the tree (yesterday).
  Perfect: I have climbed the tree (and here I am at the top).

The perfect tense, and its past (historic or secondary) equivalent the pluperfect (Ch. 7.6), are formed from the fourth principal part of the Greek verb (Ch. 2.1).

(κ) Tense Marker

	SINGULAR		PLURAL	
1st	λέ-λυ-κα	I have loosed	λε-λύ-κα-μεν	we have loosed
2nd	λέ-λυ-κας	you have loosed	λε-λύ-κα-τε	you have loosed
3rd	λέ-λυ-κε(ν)	he has loosed	λε-λύ-κα-σῐ(ν)	they have loosed

The regular marker for weak perfect forms is -κα-; it replaces the thematic vowel. The personal endings are very similar to the weak aorist endings (Ch. 5.2). The exception is the 3rd plural, which has the primary tense ending -σι(ν). A further marker of the perfect is the *reduplicated* first letter, for verbs beginning with a consonant.

Note: If the first letter is an aspirated stop (φ, θ or χ), the unvoiced equivalent (π, τ or κ) is used for the reduplication: τέθυκα from θύω. (For other perfect active formations see Ch. 10.6-7.)

EXERCISE 22.

1. οἱ δοῦλοι λελύκασι τὰ τῶν ἵππων ζυγά.
2. ὁ νεανίας κόπτει τὸ δένδρον.
3. ὁ ποιητὴς πεπαίδευκε τὰ τέκνα.
4. τὰ τῶν πολεμίων ἔργα βλάπτει τοὺς πολίτας.
5. κεκωλύκατε τοὺς πολεμίους ἀπὸ τοῦ στρατοπέδου.
6. ἐπέμπομεν δῶρα πρὸς τὸν στρατηγόν.
7. τὰ τοῦ ταμίου τέκνα τεθεράπευκε τοὺς ἵππους.
8. τὰ ὅπλα βλάπτει τοὺς στρατιώτας.
9. ὁ ταμίας λέλυκε τοὺς δούλους.
10. βασιλεύεις τῆς γῆς;

EXERCISE 23.

1. The trees of the island provide food.
2. We have kept the horses from the river.
3. The slave has loosed the yoke.
4. Gifts do not always persuade.
5. They were marching into the land.
6. The sailor's children are carrying fruit.
7. We are cutting the trees of the enemy.
8. You have hindered the Persians with your weapons.
9. They have sacrificed to the goddess of the country.
10. The gifts have loosed the sailor's tongue.

EXERCISE 24.

1. οἱ πολέμιοι κινδυνεύουσιν ἐν τῷ στρατοπέδῳ.
2. λελύκαμεν τὸν καρπὸν ἀπὸ τῶν δένδρων.
3. οἱ στρατιῶται ἔκοπτον τὰ τῶν Ἀθηναίων δένδρα.
4. τὸ ζυγὸν βλάπτει τὸν τοῦ ταμίου ἵππον.
5. τὰ τῶν πολιτῶν ἔργα κεκώλυκε τοὺς πολεμίους.
6. οἱ ποιηταὶ τὴν δόξαν παρέχουσι τοῖς Ἀθηναίοις.
7. τὰ ὅπλα οὐ βλάπτει τὸν ναύτην.
8. οἱ στρατιῶται φέρουσι δένδρα πρὸς τὸν ποταμόν.
9. ὁ ταμίας πεπαίδευκε τὸν ἵππον ζυγῷ.
10. οἱ νεανίαι τεθηρεύκασι ζῷα ἐν τῇ νήσῳ.

EXERCISE 25.

1. The children are carrying gifts from the market place.
2. We have prevented a battle in the island.
3. The poet was writing among the trees.
4. We were marching to the villages of the enemy.
5. The glory of the contest has loosed the poet's tongue.
6. The soldiers' deeds have honor among the citizens.
7. We are sending a letter to the general.
8. The Athenians are seeking not after war, but after friendship.
9. I have trained the general's horse.
10. Weapons do not produce peace.

Chapter 6 Vocabulary

Verbs:

| βλάπτω | harm, injure, damage | κόπτω | cut, cut down |

Nouns:

γῆ, γῆς, ἡ	earth, land	ζῷον, -ου, τό	animal
δένδρον, -ου, τό	tree	πολέμιοι, -ων, οἱ	enemy (group)
δῶρον, -ου, τό	gift	σῖτος, -ου, ὁ	food
ἔργον, -ου, τό	work, deed	στρατόπεδον, -ου, τό	army camp
ζυγόν, -οῦ, τό	yoke	τέκνον, -ου, τό	child
καρπός, -οῦ, ὁ	fruit	φιλία, -ας, ἡ	friendship
ὅπλα, - ων, τά	arms, weapons		

Preposition:

| ἐν (+ *dat. plural*) | among |

CHAPTER 7

σκηνὴ πᾶς ὁ βίος.　　　　　　　　　— Palatine Anthology X.72.1

ἄνδρες γὰρ πόλις, καὶ οὐ τείχη οὐδὲ νῆες ἀνδρῶν κεναί.
　　　　　　　　　　　　　　　　　— Thucydides, *Histories* 7.77.7

1. 1st and 2nd declension adjectives

Adjectives exist in all three genders, so that they can agree with any noun. The masculine and neuter forms of most adjectives have second declension endings (Ch. 5.1, 6.1). The feminine forms have 1st declension endings of the τιμή or χώρα / γέφυρα type (Ch. 3.3). Thus most feminine singulars will have **-η**, but after **ε, ι** and **ρ** the long **-ᾱ** will appear.

Note: The genitive plural of the feminine is accented like the masculine and neuter, not as in 1st declension nouns.

		wise			**friendly**		
		M	**F**	**N**	**M**	**F**	**N**
Sing.	Nom.	σοφός	σοφή	σοφόν	φίλιος	φιλία	φίλιον
	Gen.	σοφοῦ	σοφῆς	σοφοῦ	φιλίου	φιλίας	φιλίου
	Dat.	σοφῷ	σοφῇ	σοφῷ	φιλίῳ	φιλίᾳ	φιλίῳ
	Acc.	σοφόν	σοφήν	σοφόν	φίλιον	φιλίαν	φίλιον
	Voc.	σοφέ	σοφή	σοφόν	φίλιε	φιλία	φίλιον
Plur.	Nom.	σοφοί	σοφαί	σοφά	φίλιοι	φίλιαι	φίλια
	Gen.	σοφῶν	σοφῶν	σοφῶν	φιλίων	φιλίων	φιλίων
	Dat.	σοφοῖς	σοφαῖς	σοφοῖς	φιλίοις	φιλίαις	φιλίοις
	Acc.	σοφούς	σοφάς	σοφά	φιλίους	φιλίας	φίλια
	Voc.	σοφοί	σοφαί	σοφά	φίλιοι	φίλιαι	φίλια

2. Attributive and predicate position

An *attributive* adjective simply defines a noun within a noun phrase: 'the good soldier', 'the wise king'. In Greek, as in English, it is normally placed between the article and the noun. Alternatively the article may be repeated, with the adjective following it. These same two options exist for any attributive word or phrase (cf. the dependent genitive, Ch. 4.6). If there is no article, the word order is flexible.

οἱ σοφοὶ λόγοι	the wise words
οἱ λόγοι οἱ σοφοί	the wise words
λόγοι σοφοὶ	wise words

An adjective may also be *predicate*. A predicate adjective appears with a noun phrase and the verb 'be'; the present 3rd person (singular and plural) of this verb is often omitted, however. The position of the adjective distinguishes the predicate from the attributive: an attributive adjective always follows the article, a predicate never does. The predicate adjective agrees with the subject noun it modifies.

ὁ λόγος (ἐστὶ) σοφός.	The word is wise.
σοφός ὁ λόγος.	The word is wise.

Nouns can also be predicate. Because the verb 'be' states an equality or equivalency, the predicate noun, like a predicate adjective, is in the same case as the subject.

ὁ στρατιώτης ποιητής.	The soldier is a poet.
ποιητής ὁ στρατιώτης.	The soldier is a poet.

Since the subject and the predicate in the sentence above are both nominative nouns, how do you know which is the subject? Here is the rule: if only **one** of the nouns has an article, that is the subject; if both do, the subject comes first. An article always accompanies one noun or both.

ὁ στρατιώτης ποιητής.	The soldier is a poet.
ποιητὴς ὁ στρατιώτης.	The soldier is a poet.
ὁ ποιητὴς ὁ στρατιώτης.	The poet is the soldier.

3. Enclitics

An *enclitic* (from ἐν + κλίνω, 'lean on') is a word which has no accent of its own, but leans on the previous word for its accent. The effect is like adding a syllable to the previous word. An enclitic can never be the first word of a clause or sentence; if it were, there would be nothing for it to lean on. The verb 'be' is enclitic in the present indicative, except in the 2nd singular.

Enclitics can be one or two syllables long. The following diagram shows how accents work for a one-syllable enclitic (**e**) and for a two-syllable enclitic (**ee**). Generally you take care of the enclitic by adding an acute accent to the last syllable of the previous word, or in Position 1-acute by leaving the accent acute. The one exception is Position 2-acute.

Position 3	(ó o o):	ó o ó e	ó o ó ee	πόλεμός τις	πόλεμός ἐστι
Position 2	(o ô o):	o ô ó e	o ô ó ee	δῶρόν τι	δῶρόν ἐστι
	(o ó o):	o ó o e	o ó o eé or eê	λόγος τις	λόγος ἐστί, λόγων τινῶν
Position 1	(o o ó):	o o ó e	o o ó ee	σοφός τις	σοφός ἐστι
	(o o ô):	o o ô e	o o ô ee	σοφοῦ μου	σοφοῦ τινος

The reason Position 2-acute has an accent on the enclitic is that the effect of the acute only reaches the first syllable. The second syllable of the enclitic must have an accent to cover it. Why not just put another acute on the last syllable of the previous word, as in Position 2-circumflex? Because of the way pitch accents affected pronunciation (Ch. 1.4), the Greeks avoided two acute accents in a row. Instead they put the accent on the second syllable of the enclitic —acute or circumflex as appropriate (by normal accent rules).

Note: Suppose a sentence contains several enclitics in a row. Each has its accent on the previous word, thus: ποταμός τίς ἐστί σοι.

> You take care of σοι by adding an accent to the last syllable of ἐστι.
> You take care of ἐστι by adding an accent to the last (only) syllable of τις.
> You take care of τις by leaving the accent on ποταμός acute.

4. The present indicative of εἰμί, 'be'

The 2nd singular of this irregular verb has its own accent. The other forms are enclitic. By convention, acute accents are shown on the ultima; they would only be used if the previous word had a Position 2-acute accent.

	SINGULAR		PLURAL	
1st	εἰμί	I am	ἐσμέν	we are
2nd	εἶ	you are	ἐστέ	you are
3rd	ἐστί(ν)	he/she/it is	εἰσί(ν)	they are

ἐστί and εἰσί often mean 'there is/there exists' and 'there are/there exist'. If the sense is not emphatic, these forms may be omitted altogether; when they appear, they are enclitic. If the sense is emphatic, these forms appear with an accent on the penultimate. Since the emphatic forms have their own accents, they can stand first in a clause or sentence.

> not emphatic: τέκνον (ἐστὶν) ἐν τῇ οἰκίᾳ.   There is a child in the house.
> A child is in the house.

> emphatic: οὐκ ἔστι δικαιοσύνη.   There is no justice.
> Justice does not exist.

5. Dative of possession

ἐστί and εἰσί can be used with a dative of the possessor (only in simple sentences of the following type). Though the construction literally means 'X is to/for Y', it is better to translate into good English: 'Y has X'.

> κίνδυνοί εἰσι τοῖς στρατιώταις.   The soldiers have dangers.
> τῷ τέκνῳ ὁ ἵππος ἐστίν.   The child has the horse.

EXERCISE 26.

1. ὁ σοφὸς κριτὴς πείθει τὸν νεανίαν.
2. οἱ τοῦ ποιητοῦ λόγοι εἰσὶ καλοί.
3. τῷ ποιητῇ εἰσι καλοὶ λόγοι.
4. οὐ πιστεύομεν τοῖς τῶν κακῶν λόγοις.
5. δεινὰ ὅπλα ἐστὶ τοῖς Πέρσαις.
6. ἡ σοφία ἐστὶν ἀγαθὸν δῶρον.
7. ἡ τῆς οἰκίας θύρα ἐστὶν ἰσχυρά.
8. τοῖς πολίταις ἐστὶ πόλεμος χαλεπὸς καὶ μακρός.
9. οἱ πολέμιοι ἔκοπτον τὰ καλὰ δένδρα.
10. οὐ πλούσιοί ἐσμεν, ὦ Ἀθηναῖοι.

EXERCISE 27.

1. The strong gate hindered the soldiers.
2. The slave is a bad steward.
3. Rich men are not always wise.
4. The goddess is friendly to the Athenians.
5. You are a wise doctor.
6. The judge's letter is long.
7. The poet has a beautiful voice.
8. There are beautiful trees on the earth.
9. Bad trees do not produce good fruit.
10. The Athenians have strong weapons.

6. The pluperfect active indicative

The pluperfect tense stands in the same relation to the perfect (Ch. 6.4) as the imperfect does to the present. It presents the result of a previous action, all within past time: 'He had arrived (by the time I came)'; 'I had climbed the tree (when the bull reached it)'.

Like the imperfect and the aorist it is a past (*historic* or *secondary*) tense. Thus it has an augment and secondary endings. It is reduplicated like the perfect from which it is formed; weak forms have the -**κ**- which also marks the weak perfect, with some form of **e**-vowel.

	SINGULAR		PLURAL	
1st	ἐ-λε-λύ-κην	I had loosed	ἐ-λε-λύ-κεμεν	we had loosed
2nd	ἐ-λε-λύ-κης	you had loosed	ἐ-λε-λύ-κετε	you had loosed
3rd	ἐ-λε-λύ-κει(ν)	he had loosed	ἐ-λε-λύ-κεσαν	they had loosed

EXERCISE 28.

1. οἱ δοῦλοι οἱ ἀγαθοὶ ἤδη ἐλελύκεσαν τοὺς ἵππους.
2. ἐθηρεύομεν δεινὰ ζῷα ἐν τῇ γῇ.
3. ὁ ταμίας ἐπεπαιδεύκει τοὺς δούλους.
4. οἱ τῆς κώμης πολῖται ἐχθροί εἰσι τοῖς Ἀθηναίοις.
5. οὐκ ἀεὶ πιστεύομεν τοῖς τῶν σοφῶν λόγοις.
6. ὁ νεανίας ἀγγέλλει νίκην καλήν.
7. οἱ βάρβαροι ἐκεκωλύκεσαν τοὺς Ἀθηναίους ἀπὸ τοῦ ποταμοῦ.
8. τὰ ζῷά ἐστιν ἐχθρὰ τοῖς νεανίαις.
9. ὁ τοῦ δένδρου καρπὸς ἀγαθὸς τοῖς ἀνθρώποις.
10. διὰ τὸν κίνδυνον οὐκ ἐλελύκεμεν τοὺς ἵππους ἀπὸ τῆς ἁμάξης.

EXERCISE 29.

1. The river is dangerous for horses.
2. The sea had loosed the bridge.
3. The foreigners are hostile to the Athenians.
4. Good trees do not always produce fruit.
5. Do the long weapons injure the soldiers?
6. You had already set free the good slaves.
7. The general has honor on account of a fine victory.
8. The island produces strange animals.
9. Bad masters do not have good slaves.
10. The goddess of the island is friendly to the sailors.

Chapter 7 Vocabulary

Verbs:

ἀγγέλλω	announce, report	εἰμί	be

Nouns:

ἄνθρωπος, -ου, ὁ	man, human	κίνδυνος, -ου, ὁ	danger
βάρβαρος, -ου, ὁ	foreigner	νίκη, -ης, ἡ	victory
δεσπότης, -ου, ὁ	master (of a household)		

Adjectives:

ἀγαθός, -ή, -όν	good	καλός, -ή, -όν	beautiful, fine
ἀνδρεῖος, -α, -ον	brave	μακρός, -ά, -όν	long
δεινός, -ή, -όν	strange, terrible, clever	πλούσιος, -α, -ον	rich
ἐχθρός, -ά, -όν	hostile	σοφός, -ή, -όν	wise
ἰσχυρός, -ά, -όν	strong	φίλιος, -α, -ον	friendly
κακός, -ή, -όν	bad	χαλεπός, -ή, -όν	difficult, danger-ous, harsh

Adverb:

ἤδη	already

Preposition:

διά (+ *acc.*)	on account of

CHAPTER 8

1. 3rd declension nouns

There is one set of endings for both masculine and feminine nouns of the 3rd declension, and one set for neuter nouns; genitive and dative are the same in both sets. The vowels are short except the genitive plural.

		M/F	**N**
Sing.	Nom.	-ς or none	——
	Gen.	-ος	-ος
	Dat.	-ῐ	ῐ
	Acc.	-ᾰ	as nom.
	Voc.	(often as nom.)	as nom.
Plur.	Nom.	-ες	-ᾰ
	Gen.	-ων	-ων
	Dat.	-σῐ(ν)	-σῐ(ν)
	Acc.	-ᾰς	as nom.
	Voc.	as nom.	as nom.

It is not clear from the nominative what the stem of a 3rd declension noun is; remove the ending from the genitive, what remains is the stem. The 3rd declension is also called the *consonant declension*, because the stem ends in a consonant. The α and ι in the endings are all short. The dative plural, and sometimes the nominative singular, has an ending which starts with a consonant; the following chart shows what happens when the consonant of the stem is followed by σ (see also Ch. 1.2):

labials: π
          β + σ = ψ
          φ

palatals: κ
          γ + σ = ξ
          χ

dentals: τ
          δ + σ = σ
          θ

nasals: μ
          ν + σ = σ
          γγ, γκ, γχ + σ = ξ

2. 3rd declension nouns: stems in -κ, -τ

The following types are typical of 3rd declension nouns. κῆρυξ is masculine, σῶμα is neuter.

			herald		**body**
SING.	Nom.	ὁ	κῆρυξ	τὸ	σῶμα
	Gen.		κήρυκος		σώματος
	Dat.		κήρυκι		σώματι
	Acc.		κήρυκα		σῶμα
	Voc.		κῆρυξ		σῶμα
PLUR.	Nom.		κήρυκες		σώματα
	Gen.		κηρύκων		σωμάτων
	Dat.		κήρυξι(ν)		σώμασι(ν)
	Acc.		κήρυκας		σώματα
	Voc.		κήρυκες		σώματα

3. The present active imperative, second person

There are four *moods* in Greek: indicative, imperative, subjunctive and optative. Thus far all the verb forms you have learned have been in the *indicative mood*, that is, they have been main verbs which make a statement or ask a simple question, and have a subject in the nominative case. *Imperative* verbs are also main verbs, but this mood expresses a direct command, in Greek as in English: 'Sit!', 'Stay!'. The 2nd person of the present imperative is formed by adding -ε (singular) or -ετε (plural) to the present stem: λῦε, 'loose!'; γράφετε, 'write!'. This means that the 2nd plural imperative and the 2nd plural indicative are identical in form. The context will make it clear which mood is intended.

The present imperative expresses a command when the action is ongoing or repeated. A person is addressed in the vocative, usually preceded by ὦ (Ch. 3.3).

Note: With few exceptions, the negative for moods other than the indicative is μή, not οὐ.

μένε ἐν τῇ κώμῃ, ὦ νεανία.
    Stay in the village, young man.

ἀεὶ πιστεύετε τοῖς ἀγαθοῖς ἀνθρώποις.
    Always trust good people.

μὴ λῦε τὸν ἵππον, ὦ στρατιῶτα.
    Don't loose the horse, soldier.

4. The present active infinitive

The *infinitive* is a verbal noun, corresponding to the English infinitive: 'to loose', 'to write'. The present active infinitive consists of the present active stem (from first principal part) + the thematic vowel ε + the ending εν. The two ε's contract to ει: λύειν, γράφειν. The accent is on the last syllable of the stem (Position 2, penult).

The infinitive can be a subject, as in the first example below. It can also complement a main verb, just as in English: ἐθέλω πέμπειν, 'I want to send'. The other examples below show this usage. It can take a regular direct object in the accusative. The negative is μή, not οὐ. In the first example below, notice that '*it* is dangerous' requires a *neuter* adjective. (For other infinitive forms, see Ch. 16.3, 17.3.)

χαλεπόν ἐστι διαβαίνειν τὸν ποταμόν.
    To cross the river is dangerous./It is dangerous to cross the river.

ἐθέλομεν εὑρίσκειν τὸν φύλακα.
    We wish to find the guard.

ἐκελεύσαμεν τοὺς φύλακας φεύγειν.
We ordered the guards to flee.

κελεύσομεν τοὺς φύλακας μὴ φεύγειν.
We will order the guards not to flee.

EXERCISE 30.

1. οἱ πολέμιοι ἐτόξευον τοὺς φύλακας.
2. οἱ στρατιῶται ὁπλίζουσι τὰ σώματα θώραξιν.
3. παίδευε τοὺς δούλους, ὦ ταμία.
4. διώκετε τοὺς πολεμίους, ὦ στρατιῶται.
5. ἐκέλευσα τοὺς στρατιώτας λαμβάνειν τὰς κώμας.
6. ῥᾴδιόν ἐστι λαμβάνειν τὴν νῆσον.
7. ὁ κῆρυξ ἀγγέλλει τὴν νίκην τῇ σάλπιγγι.
8. τῷ ταμίᾳ ἐστὶ τὰ χρήματα.
9. οἱ πολέμιοι οὐκ ἐθέλουσι πιστεύειν τῷ κήρυκι.
10. ὁ στρατηγὸς ἐκέλευσε τὸν φύλακα μὴ φεύγειν ἀπὸ τῆς πύλης.

EXERCISE 31.

1. The general will order the soldiers to flee.
2. The island has a beautiful name.
3. The voice of the herald announces a victory.
4. The general is leading his army to the sea.
5. The soldier is carrying his breastplate.
6. Flee from the village, citizens.
7. The general ordered the soldiers to save the children.
8. It is difficult to train horses.
9. We ordered the young men not to hunt the animals.
10. The soldier shot the general through the breastplate.

5. Connections

In English, a conjunction ('and', 'but') is used to connect two main clauses within a sentence. In Greek there are many conjunctions which perform this function. Also, in a Greek paragraph, every sentence is connected to the previous one by means of a conjunction, to show how the new matter is related to what went before.

The commonest conjunctions are:

1) coming first in the clause or sentence: καί, 'and', 'also'; ἀλλά, 'but'
2) coming second (*postpositive*) in the clause or sentence: δέ, 'and', 'but'; γάρ, 'for', 'because'; οὖν, 'therefore'

Another common connective particle is the enclitic τε. It is used in combination with καί to mean 'both...and'. Because it has no accent, it cannot be the first word in a phrase. Usually it stands second: οἵ τε στρατιῶται καὶ οἱ ναῦται, 'both the soldiers and the sailors'. It can also come at the end of a phrase, right before καί: οἱ στρατιῶταί τε καὶ ὁ στρατηγός, 'both the soldiers and the general'.

τε also appears written as one word with οὐ in the compound negative οὔτε...οὔτε, 'neither...nor'.

οἱ στρατιῶται (οὐ) διώκουσιν οὔτε τοὺς Πέρσας οὔτε τοὺς Ἀθηναίους.
The soldiers pursue neither the Persians nor the Athenians.

As a proclitic οὐ normally has no accent (see Ch. 2.4). οὔτε is accented thus to cover the enclitic τε. οὐ also carries an accent when it appears at the end of a sentence: οὔ. Examples appear below in section 6.

Note: If the proper negative is μή instead of οὐ, the compound is μήτε instead of οὔτε:

> ἐθέλω μήτε διώκειν μήτε φεύγειν.
> I want neither to pursue nor to flee.

6. μέν and δέ

μέν and δέ signal words or clauses which correspond to or contrast with each other. μέν signals the first part of the contrast, δέ the second part (and subsequent parts, if they exist). These two words are both *postpositive*; each comes second in the phrase or clause which is the point of the contrast. μέν shows that a correspondence or contrast is being set up; there is no need to translate it. As usual δέ can mean 'and' or 'but'.

> ῥᾴδιον μέν ἐστι λέγειν, χαλεπὸν δὲ πείθειν.
> It is easy to speak, but difficult to persuade.

> ὁ μὲν ποιητὴς γράφει, ὁ δὲ κριτὴς διδάσκει.
> The poet writes, and the judge teaches.

> ὁ ποιητὴς γράφει μέν, διδάσκει δὲ οὔ.
> The poet writes, but he does not teach.

> ὁ ποιητὴς γράφει καλὰ μέν, μακρὰ δέ.
> The poet writes beautiful things, but long ones.

Sometimes, rather than contrasting two nouns, a Greek sentence compares two sets of the same noun. In this case the noun is expressed in the μέν clause, but does not need to be repeated in the δέ clause. In fact, any term of the correspondence that remains the same in both clauses need not be repeated.

> οἱ μὲν στρατιῶται ἐδίωκον, οἱ δὲ ἔφευγον.
> Some soldiers were pursuing, and others were fleeing.

> οἱ μὲν τῶν ποιητῶν πείθουσιν, οἱ δὲ οὔ.
> Some of the poets persuade, but others do not.

When the contrast is between 'some (men)' and 'others', etc., no noun is necessary at all. The article will give the gender, and thus suggest the right pronoun.

> οἱ μὲν πιστεύουσι τοῖς λόγοις, οἱ δὲ τοῖς ὅπλοις.
> Some (men/people) trust in words, others in weapons.

> αἱ μὲν πλούσιαι, αἱ δὲ οὔ.
> Some (women) are rich, but others are not.

ὁ/ἡ/τὸ δέ and οἱ/αἱ/τὰ δέ may start a sentence 'and he/they/etc.', but only when they refer to a preceding noun or pronoun in an *oblique* case (gen., dat., acc.). μέν does not serve as a link with what has gone before.

EXERCISE 32. Reading passage. The vocabulary for reading exercises is not given in the chapter vocabulary list, but will be found at the end of the book.

UNDERGROUND DWELLINGS

The Armenia being referred to lay to the southeast of the Black Sea.

οἱ δὲ Ἀρμένιοι ἔχουσι τὰς οἰκίας κατὰ τῆς γῆς· ταῖς δὲ οἰκίαις τὸ μὲν στόμα μικρόν, κάτω δὲ μεγάλαι. αἱ δὲ εἴσοδοι τοῖς μὲν ὑποζυγίοις ὀρυκταί εἰσιν, οἱ δὲ ἄνθρωποι καταβαίνουσιν ἐπὶ κλίμακος. ἐν δὲ ταῖς οἰκίαις εἰσὶν αἶγές τε καὶ ἄλλα ζῷα· οἱ δὲ Ἀρμένιοι τρέφουσι τὰ ζῷα ἔνδον χιλῷ. ἐν δὲ ἀγγείοις ἐστὶν οἶνος· καὶ τὸν οἶνον εἰς τὸ στόμα μύζουσι καλάμοις.

Adapted from Xenophon, *Anabasis* IV.v.25-27

7. αὐτός

The pronoun αὐτός, -ή, -ό is declined like a regular 1st and 2nd declension adjective, except that the nom. and acc. neuter singular end in -ο, not -ον. There is no vocative case.

	SINGULAR			PLURAL		
	M	**F**	**N**	**M**	**F**	**N**
Nom.	αὐτός	αὐτή	αὐτό	αὐτοί	αὐταί	αὐτά
Gen.	αὐτοῦ	αὐτῆς	αὐτοῦ	αὐτῶν	αὐτῶν	αὐτῶν
Dat.	αὐτῷ	αὐτῇ	αὐτῷ	αὐτοῖς	αὐταῖς	αὐτοῖς
Acc.	αὐτόν	αὐτήν	αὐτό	αὐτούς	αὐτάς	αὐτά

8. αὐτός, intensive use

One use of this pronoun is to emphasize a noun or pronoun: 'himself / herself / itself'. αὐτός has this intensive meaning when it appears either by itself in the nominative, or in the predicate position agreeing with a noun (in all cases). The predicate may either precede or follow the noun/article phrase. You will see that in the third example, the English sentence is ambiguous (does 'himself' refer to 'He' or 'the child'?), but in Greek the ending of αὐτός makes the meaning clear:

ὁ στρατηγὸς αὐτὸς ἄγει τοὺς στρατιώτας.
The general himself leads the soldiers.

πέμπω τὸν ἄγγελον εἰς αὐτὴν τὴν κώμην.
I send the messenger into the village itself.

αὐτὸς ἐδίωκε τὸν τέκνον.
He was pursuing the child himself.

9. αὐτός as personal pronoun, 3rd person

αὐτός is also used as the personal pronoun 'him/her/it/them'. It has this meaning only when it appears alone in the oblique cases. The verb ending already indicates 'he/she/it/ they' in the nominative case, so if αὐτὸς appears in the nominative it is always emphatic (section 8 above).

πέμπομεν αὐτὸν εἰς τὴν κώμην.
We send him into the village.

ἔγραφον ἐπιστολὴν αὐτῇ.
I was writing a letter to her.

οἱ λόγοι αὐτῆς πείθουσι τοὺς πολίτας.
Her words [The words of her] persuade the citizens.

Oblique forms of αὐτός can refer to a noun mentioned earlier in the sentence, but not to the subject. The pronoun will have the same gender as the noun it refers to, but the case may be different. In the first example below, αὐτήν is feminine to agree with ἐπιστολήν, 'letter'. In the second example, 'her' is feminine to agree with 'goddess', but it is in the dative case after πιστεύσομεν:

γράφω ἐπιστολὴν καὶ πέμπω αὐτήν.
I write a letter and send it.

θεραπεύσομεν τὴν θεὰν καὶ πιστεύσομεν αὐτῇ.
We shall honor the goddess and trust her.

The possessive genitive forms of this pronoun always follow the noun they depend on; they are not sandwiched between article and noun like regular possessive adjectives.

EXERCISE 33.

1. οἱ μὲν Ἀθηναῖοι ἐστράτευον, οἱ δὲ Λακεδαιμόνιοι ἔθυον.
2. ὁ στρατηγὸς αὐτὸς ἀγγέλλει τὴν νίκην ἐν τῇ ἐκκλησίᾳ.
3. ἐδιώκομεν αὐτὸν ἀπὸ τῆς χώρας.
4. οἱ μὲν φεύγουσιν, οἱ δὲ μένουσιν.
5. οἵ τε Λακεδαιμόνιοι καὶ οἱ Ἀθηναῖοι ἐστράτευον ἐπὶ τοὺς Πέρσας.
6. ὁ κριτὴς αὐτὸς διδάσκει τὸν νεανίαν.
7. οἱ μὲν τῶν στρατιωτῶν ἐφύλασσον τὴν πύλην, οἱ δ' ἔφευγον ἀπ' αὐτῆς.[1]
8. κελεύσομεν τὰ τέκνα μὴ φεύγειν ἐκ τῆς κώμης αὐτῆς.
9. σοφοὶ μέν ἐστε, κακοὶ δέ.
10. ἡ μὲν εἰρήνη καλή, ὁ δὲ πόλεμος κακός.

EXERCISE 34.

1. Both the Persians and the allies were fleeing.
2. The island is small, but the guards are hostile.
3. Some of the trees are beautiful, others useful.
4. The herald is announcing the victory to the general himself.
5. We are pursuing the enemy and driving them to the gates.
6. They are clever, but cowardly.
7. Some trust money, others wisdom.
8. The goddess herself ordered the army to honor them.
9. The horse is easy to catch, but difficult to train.
10. The young man is neither brave nor wise.

---

[1] δ' = δέ; ἀπ' = ἀπό. Some final vowels can be dropped, like the ε of δέ and the ending vowel of a two-syllable preposition, if the next word begins with a vowel.

10. οἷός τέ εἰμι

In the following reading from Herodotus you will see an idiomatic way to say 'I can/am able'. It has three components:

οἷος, οἵα, οἷον :   adjective, fully declinable; literally 'of such a kind'.

τε :   enclitic conjunction, meaning 'and'; not translated here. Before a vowel, usually abbreviated τ'.

εἰμί :   enclitic verb 'be', fully conjugated.

Thus to say 'we are able', οἷοι must be plural, and ἐσμεν must be first person plural, present. Some more examples:

οἷοί τ' εἰσι	they are able
οἵα τ' ἐστί	she is able
οἷός τ' εἶ	you (sing.) are able

EXERCISE 35.

CYRUS IS HELPED BY CAMELS

Croesus, king of Lydia (in Asia Minor), after conquering most of the Greek cities east of the Aegean, invaded Persia in 546 BC in an attempt to crush the power of Cyrus the Great, king of the Medes and Persians.

ὁ δὲ Κροῖσος, ὅτε ἐβασίλευε τῶν Λυδῶν, ἐστράτευσεν ἐπὶ τοὺς Πέρσας. τὸ γὰρ μαντεῖον ἔπειθεν αὐτόν, ὡς ἐνόμιζε, καταλύειν τὴν τῶν Περσῶν ἀρχήν. πρῶτον μὲν οὖν ποταμὸν (τὸ ὄνομά ἐστιν "Αλυς) διαβαίνει καὶ φθείρει τὴν χώραν, ἔπειτα δὲ τάσσει τὸ στράτευμα εἰς μάχην. *(This battle was indecisive.)* μετὰ δὲ τὴν μάχην, ὁ Κροῖσος ἀπήλαυνε εἰς τὰς Σάρδις·[1] ἤθελε γὰρ κήρυκας πέμπειν πρὸς τοὺς συμμάχους. *(Before the allies can arrive, Cyrus appears before Sardis with a large army.)* ἀνάγκη δὲ τῷ Κύρῳ ἐστὶν ἐξάγειν τὴν στρατιὰν εἰς μάχην. ἀθροίζει δ' οὖν τὰς καμήλους καὶ κελεύει στρατιώτας ἀναβαίνειν καὶ ἐλαύνειν αὐτὰς πρὸς τὴν τοῦ Κροίσου ἵππον,[2] τοὺς δὲ πεζοὺς τάσσει ὄπισθε τῶν καμήλων, τὴν δὲ ἵππον ὄπισθε τῶν πεζῶν· οἱ γὰρ ἵπποι οὐχ οἷοί τέ εἰσι φέρειν οὔτε τὴν ἰδέαν οὔτε τὴν ὀδμὴν τῶν καμήλων. ἐν δὲ τῇ μάχῃ αἱ κάμηλοι δεινὸν φόβον παρέχουσι τοῖς ἵπποις. οὕτω δὲ ὁ Κῦρος ἀναγκάζει τοὺς τοῦ Κροίσου στρατιώτας φεύγειν.

Adapted from Herodotus I.76-80

---

[1] Sardis was the capital city of Lydia.

[2] ἵππος, -ου, ἡ, 'the cavalry'.

Chapter 8 Vocabulary

Verbs:

διαβαίνω	cross	λαμβάνω	take, capture, catch
διδάσκω	teach	λέγω	say, speak, tell
ἐθέλω	wish, be willing	μένω	stay, remain
ἐλαύνω	drive	οἷός τέ εἰμι	be able, can
εὑρίσκω	find, find out	ὁπλίζω	arm
θαυμάζω	wonder (at), admire	σῴζω	save
κελεύω	order		

Nouns:

ἐκκλησία, -ας, ἡ	assembly	στράτευμα, -ατος, τό	army
θώραξ, -ακος, ὁ	breastplate		
κῆρυξ, -υκος, ὁ	herald	σύμμαχος, -ου, ὁ	ally
Λακεδαιμόνιος, -ου, ὁ	a Spartan	σῶμα, -ατος, τό	body
		φύλαξ, -ακος, ὁ	guard
ὄνομα, -ατος, τό	name	χρῆμα, -ατος, τό	thing; pl., money
σάλπιγξ, -ιγγος, ἡ	trumpet		

Pronoun:

αὐτός, -ή, -ό	self (predicate with noun); him, her, it (in oblique cases)

Adjectives:

δειλός, -ή, -όν	cowardly	ῥᾴδιος, -α, -ον	easy
μικρός, -ά, -όν	small	χρήσιμος, -η -ον	useful

Adverb:

μή	not

Prepositions:

διά (+ gen.)	through	ἐπί (+ acc.)	against, onto

Conjunctions:

γάρ	for, because (postpos.)	οὖν	therefore (postpos.)
δέ	and, but (postpos.)	οὔτε...οὔτε	neither...nor
μέν	(sets up contrast with δέ; postpos.)	τε	and
οἱ μὲν...οἱ δέ	some...others	τε...καί	both...and (τε postpos.)

ὦ ξεῖν᾽, ἀγγέλλειν Λακεδαιμονίοις ὅτι τῆδε
κείμεθα τοῖς κείνων ῥήμασι πειθόμενοι.

— Epitaph of the Spartans at Thermopylae (Herodotus VII.228.2)

τῶν ἐν Θερμοπύλαις θανόντων
εὐκλεὴς μὲν ἁ τύχα, καλὸς δ᾽ ὁ πότμος,
βωμὸς δ᾽ ὁ τάφος, πρὸ γόων δὲ μνᾶστις, ὁ δ᾽ οἶκτος ἔπαινος·
ἐντάφιον δὲ τοιοῦτον οὔτ᾽ εὐρὼς
οὔθ᾽ ὁ πανδαμάτωρ ἀμαυρώσει χρόνος.
ἀνδρῶν ἀγαθῶν ὅδε σηκὸς οἰκέταν εὐδοξίαν
Ἑλλάδος εἵλετο· μαρτυρεῖ δὲ καὶ Λεωνίδας,
Σπάρτας βασιλεύς, ἀρετᾶς μέγαν λελοιπὼς
κόσμον ἀέναόν τε κλέος.

— Simonides 4 (Bergk)

1. 3rd declension nouns: stems in -τ, -δ, -θ

These nouns have generally the same endings as those in Ch. 8. When the stem is followed by σ, the dental disappears (see Ch. 8.1). Nouns with nominatives in -ις or -υς, unless accented on the last syllable, usually form the accusative singular by dropping the dental and adding -ν. However, in Homer, Herodotus and Attic poetry the accusative has the normal ending in -α.

Most one-syllable nominatives like ὁ/ἡ παῖς, παιδός accent their gen. and dat. singular and plural on the last syllable. παῖς itself actually violates this rule; the gen. plural is παίδων.

			love		torch		grace		child
Sing.	Nom.	ὁ	ἔρως	ἡ	λαμπάς	ἡ	χάρις	ὁ/ἡ	παῖς
	Gen.		ἔρωτος		λαμπάδος		χάριτος		παιδός
	Dat.		ἔρωτι		λαμπάδι		χάριτι		παιδί
	Acc.		ἔρωτα		λαμπάδα		χάριν		παῖδα
	Voc.		ἔρως		λαμπάς		χάρις		παῖ
Plur.	Nom.		ἔρωτες		λαμπάδες		χάριτες		παῖδες
	Gen.		ἐρώτων		λαμπάδων		χαρίτων		παίδων
	Dat.		ἔρωσι(ν)		λαμπάσι(ν)		χάρισι(ν)		παισί(ν)
	Acc.		ἔρωτας		λαμπάδας		χάριτας		παῖδας
	Voc.		ἔρωτες		λαμπάδες		χάριτες		παῖδες

2. The future indicative of εἰμί, 'be':

The future of εἰμί, unlike most of the present (Ch. 7.4), is not enclitic. The endings are those of the *middle* voice (Ch. 16).

	SINGULAR		PLURAL	
1st	ἔσομαι	I shall be	ἐσόμεθα	we shall be
2nd	ἔσῃ / ἔσει	you will be	ἔσεσθε	you will be
3rd	ἔσται	he will be	ἔσονται	they will be

EXERCISE 36.

1. ῥᾴδιον ἔσται λαμβάνειν τὴν ὄρνιν.
2. οἱ σύμμαχοι ἔσονται χρήσιμοι τοῖς Ἀθηναίοις.
3. χάριν ἔχομεν ὅτι σῴζετε τὴν πατρίδα.
4. οἱ παῖδες αὐτῶν χάριν ἔχουσι τῷ δούλῳ.
5. ἀνδρεῖοι ἔσεσθε, ὦ στρατιῶται, καὶ ἄξιοι τῆς τιμῆς.
6. αἱ Ἀθῆναι ἔσονται ἐλεύθεραι· οἱ γὰρ πολῖται ἐθέλουσιν ἀποθνῄσκειν ὑπὲρ τῆς πατρίδος.
7. τοῖς ὁπλίταις εἰσὶ κόρυθές τε καὶ ἀσπίδες.
8. αἱ τῶν Περσῶν ἐλπίδες εἰσὶ χαλεπαὶ τοῖς Ἀθηναίοις.
9. οἱ φυγάδες ἀπὸ τῆς Ἑλλάδος ἔφευγον.
10. τὰ τόξα ἐστὶν ἑτοῖμα τοῖς παισίν.

EXERCISE 37.

1. The Athenians will not be slaves.
2. It will be useful to have shields.
3. Some Persians die, and others flee from Greece.
4. Greece will be both strong and free.
5. The boys are carrying torches in the marketplace.
6. The enemy will be friendly to the exiles and honor them.
7. The exiles feel grateful to the Athenians.
8. We wish to drive the enemy from our country.
9. The girls were sacrificing to the goddess.
10. The soldiers trust neither shields nor helmets.

3. 3rd declension nouns: stems in -ντ, -κτ

The only form of these nouns that needs explanation is the dative plural of nouns in -ντ. The dental drops out before σ, and then so does the ν; because the series of consonants made for a long syllable, the vowel is lengthened to preserve the length of the syllable, and to compensate for losing two consonants. This is called *compensatory lengthening*. One-syllable nouns have gen. and dat. accents on the last syllable (section 1 above). The proper name Xenophon has a contracted syllable, so its accent pattern is different.

			giant		**tooth**		**night**		**lion**		**Xenophon**
SING.	Nom.	ὁ	γίγας	ὁ	ὀδούς	ἡ	νύξ	ὁ	λέων	ὁ	Ξενοφῶν
	Gen.		γίγαντος		ὀδόντος		νυκτός		λέοντος		Ξενοφῶντος
	Dat.		γίγαντι		ὀδόντι		νυκτί		λέοντι		Ξενοφῶντι
	Acc.		γίγαντα		ὀδόντα		νύκτα		λέοντα		Ξενοφῶντα
	Voc.		(γίγαν)		ὀδούς		νύξ		(λέον)		Ξενοφῶν
PLUR.	Nom.		γίγαντες		ὀδόντες		νύκτες		λέοντες		
	Gen.		γιγάντων		ὀδόντων		νυκτῶν		λεόντων		
	Dat.		γίγᾱσι(ν)		ὀδοῦσι(ν)		νυξί(ν)		λέουσι(ν)		
	Acc.		γίγαντας		ὀδόντας		νύκτας		λέοντας		
	Voc.		γίγαντες		ὀδόντες		νύκτες		λέοντες		

4. The imperfect indicative of εἰμί, 'be'

This is the only historic (past) tense of εἰμί. Its forms are not enclitic.

	SINGULAR		PLURAL	
1st	ἦ / ἦν	I was	ἦμεν	we were
2nd	ἦσθα	you were	ἦτε	you were
3rd	ἦν	he was	ἦσαν	they were

5. The relative pronoun

The relative pronoun introduces a *relative clause*. This is a subordinate clause which refers to a noun (or pronoun) in the main clause. All forms except the nom. sing. masculine look like the definite article, with a rough breathing replacing the initial τ-.

	SINGULAR			PLURAL		
	M	**F**	**N**	**M**	**F**	**N**
Nom.	ὅς	ἥ	ὅ	οἵ	αἵ	ἅ
Gen.	οὗ	ἧς	οὗ	ὧν	ὧν	ὧν
Dat.	ᾧ	ᾗ	ᾧ	οἷς	αἷς	οἷς
Acc.	ὅν	ἥν	ὅ	οὕς	ἅς	ἅ

A relative pronoun has the same *gender* and *number* as the noun to which it refers (its antecedent); this is how you identify its antecedent. However, its *case* depends on its function in the relative clause. The relative clause is underlined in the following examples:

> ὁ παῖς <u>ὃν διδάσκω</u> ἔχει ἵππον.
> The child <u>(whom) I teach</u> has a horse.

(rel. pronoun is masc. sing., agreeing with 'child'; it is accusative as direct object)

> ὁ παῖς <u>ὃς πέμπει δῶρον</u> ἀγαθός ἐστιν.
> The child <u>who sends a gift</u> is good.

(rel. pronoun is masc. sing., agreeing with 'child'; it is nominative as subject)

> πιστεύσομεν τῷ παιδὶ <u>ὃς ἀγαθὰ λέγει.</u>
> We will trust the child <u>who says good things</u>.

(rel. pronoun is masc. sing., agreeing with 'child'; it is nominative as subject)

ὁ παῖς ᾧ λέγω ἀγαθός ἐστιν.
The child <u>to whom I speak</u> is good.

(rel. pronoun is masc. sing., agreeing with 'child'; it is dative as indirect object)

ὁ παῖς οὗ ὁ δοῦλος λέγει ἀγαθός ἐστιν.
The child <u>whose slave is speaking</u> is good.

(rel. pronoun is masc. sing., agreeing with 'child'; it is genitive as possessive)

EXERCISE 38.

1. ἡ κώμη πολεμία ἦν τῷ βαρβάρῳ οὗ ἡ στρατιὰ ἐστράτευεν.
2. ἡ νῆσος ἐν ᾗ ἦν καλὰ δένδρα οὐ μικρὰ ἦν.
3. χαλεπόν ἐστι θηρεύειν τοὺς λέοντας καὶ λαμβάνειν αὐτούς.
4. οἱ φυγάδες οἳ ἔμενον ἐν τῷ στρατοπέδῳ ἦσαν ἐν κινδύνῳ.
5. ὁ Ξενοφῶν ἔπαυσε τὴν μάχην διὰ τὴν νύκτα.
6. οἱ ὀδόντες οἱ τῶν γιγάντων ἦσαν δεινοί.
7. οὐκ ἦσθα δίκαιος, ὦ κριτά.
8. οἱ μὲν νεανίαι εἰσὶν ἀνδρεῖοι, οἱ δὲ γέροντες σοφοί.
9. οἱ Ἀθηναῖοι ἐθέλουσι σῴζειν τούς τε γέροντας καὶ τοὺς παῖδας.
10. οἱ στρατηγοὶ οἷς πιστεύομεν δίκαιοί εἰσιν.

EXERCISE 39.

1. Always honor old men, children.
2. The lion is strong and his teeth are dangerous.
3. It was not easy to kill the giant who was damaging the houses.
4. We were once slaves, Athenians, but now we are free.
5. There were dangerous animals on the island.
6. The slaves will be faithful to the old man.
7. We loose the animals which we capture in battle.
8. Night stopped the battle which was keeping the Persians away.
9. The young men were pursuing the enemy, but the old men were fleeing from them.
10. The poet does not wish to die in a war.

EXERCISE 40. There are no quotation marks in Greek. The first word of a quotation is capitalized, and you must rely on context and common sense to see where the quotation ends.

THE BATTLE OF THERMOPYLAE

In 480 BC three hundred Spartans with their king, Leonidas, heroically tried to defend Greece against the invading army of Xerxes, king of Persia. The battle took place at Thermopylae, a narrow pass in the south of Thessaly.

ὅτε δὲ ὁ Ξέρξης ἐστράτευεν ἐπὶ τὴν Ἑλλάδα, οἱ Λακεδαιμόνιοι ἐφύλασσον τὴν ἐν ταῖς

Θερμοπύλαις εἰσβολήν· καὶ πρὸ τῆς μάχης λέγει τις τῶν συμμάχων, Τοσοῦτός ἐστιν ὁ

ἀριθμὸς τῶν βαρβάρων, ὥστε ἀποκρύπτουσι τὸν ἥλιον τοῖς τοξεύμασιν. Ἀγαθὰ ἀγγέλλεις,

λέγει Λακεδαιμόνιός τις, ᾧ ἦν ὄνομα Διηνέκης· ὑπὸ οὖν σκιᾷ ἔσται πρὸς αὐτοὺς ἡ μάχη, καὶ οὐκ ἐν ἡλίῳ. ὁ δὲ Λεωνίδας, ὃς ἦν ὁ τῶν Λακεδαιμονίων στρατηγός, ἐκέλευσε τοὺς στρατιώτας μένειν οὗ [where] ἦσαν.

ἐν δὲ τῇ μάχῃ αὐτῇ οἱ λοχαγοὶ ἐποτρύνουσι τοὺς Πέρσας μάστιξιν· οἱ γὰρ βάρβαροι οὐκ ἀνδρεῖοι ἦσαν. οἱ δὲ Λακεδαιμόνιοι ἀνδρείως μὲν ἐφύλασσον τὴν εἰσβολὴν ὑπὲρ τῆς πατρίδος, μάτην δέ· μόνον γὰρ τριακόσιοι ἦσαν. ὁ δὲ Λεωνίδας αὐτὸς ἐν τῇ μάχῃ πίπτει· καὶ σήμερόν ἐστιν ἐπὶ τῷ τάφῳ αὐτοῦ λίθινος λέων.

Adapted from Herodotus VII.225-226

Chapter 9 Vocabulary

Verbs:

ἀποθνήσκω	die	χάριν ἔχω	feel grateful
ἀποκτείνω	kill		

Nouns:

ἀσπίς, -ίδος, ἡ	shield	Ξενοφῶν, -ῶντος	Xenophon
γέρων, -οντος, ὁ	old man	ὀδούς, -όντος, ὁ	tooth
γίγας, -αντος, ὁ	giant	ὁπλίτης, -ου, ὁ	hoplite
Ἑλλάς, -άδος, ἡ	Greece	ὄρνις, -ιθος, ὁ/ἡ	bird
ἐλπίς, -ίδος, ἡ	hope, expectation	παῖς, -δός, ὁ/ἡ	child, boy, girl
ἔρως, -τος, ὁ	love, desire	πατρίς, -ίδος, ἡ	fatherland, own country
θεός, -οῦ, ὁ	god		
κόρυς, -υθος, ἡ	helmet	τόξον, -ου, τό	bow
λαμπάς, -άδος, ἡ	torch	ὕλη, -ης, ἡ	wood, forest
λέων, -οντος, ὁ	lion	φυγάς, -άδος, ὁ/ἡ	exile (a person)
νύξ, -κτός, ἡ	night	χάρις, -τος, ἡ	grace, thanks

Adjectives:

ἄξιος, -α, -ον	worthy (+ *gen.*)	ἑτοῖμος, -η, -ον	ready
δίκαιος, -α, -ον	just	πιστός, -ή, -όν	faithful
ἐλεύθερος, -α, -ον	free		

Pronoun:

ὅς, ἥ, ὅ	who, which

Adverbs:

νῦν	now	ποτέ	once, ever (enclitic)

Preposition:

ὑπέρ (+ *gen.*)	on behalf of, for

Conjunction:

ὅτι	because

CHAPTER 10

1. 3rd declension nouns: stems in -ρ

ῥήτωρ, 'orator' is an example of a regular 3rd declension noun whose stem ends in -ρ. The noun θήρ, 'wild beast' (compare θηρεύω) is declined like it, but follows the accent rule for one-syllable nouns (Ch. 9.1).

μήτηρ, 'mother' and πατήρ, 'father' have an ε vowel (long in the nominative and short elsewhere) which is missing in the gen. and dat. sing. and the dat. pl. This omission of a stem vowel is called *syncope*. The dat. pl. has another peculiarity. The ρα represents an original **r** which made for a whole syllable (*syllabic* **r**); this Indo-European consonant appears in Attic Greek as ρα (occasionally αρ). θυγάτηρ, 'daughter' is declined exactly the same way. Another word declined like μήτηρ is ἀνήρ, 'man', 'husband'. Here the ε vowel is missing except in the nom. sing. The δ appears just because the combination νρ was hard to pronounce without it.

			orator		**wild beast**		**mother**		**father**		**man**
Sing.	Nom.	ὁ	ῥήτωρ	ὁ	θήρ	ἡ	μήτηρ	ὁ	πατήρ	ὁ	ἀνήρ
	Gen.		ῥήτορος		θηρός		μητρός		πατρός		ἀνδρός
	Dat.		ῥήτορι		θηρί		μητρί		πατρί		ἀνδρί
	Acc.		ῥήτορα		θῆρα		μητέρα		πατέρα		ἄνδρα
	Voc.		ῥῆτορ		θήρ		μῆτερ		πάτερ		ἄνερ
Plur.	Nom.		ῥήτορες		θῆρες		μητέρες		πατέρες		ἄνδρες
	Gen.		ῥητόρων		θηρῶν		μητέρων		πατέρων		ἀνδρῶν
	Dat.		ῥήτορσι(ν)		θηρσί(ν)		μητράσι(ν)		πατράσι(ν)		ἀνδράσι(ν)
	Acc.		ῥήτορας		θῆρας		μητέρας		πατέρας		ἄνδρας
	Voc.		ῥήτορες		θῆρες		μητέρες		πατέρες		ἄνδρες

2. Syllabic and temporal augments

You have seen that when a verb stem begins with a consonant, it is augmented by adding the prefix ε- (Ch. 4.3). This form is called a *syllabic augment*, because it adds a syllable to the verb. When the verb stem begins with a vowel, it is augmented by lengthening the vowel (a *temporal augment*). Sometimes the lengthening is visible: α and ε to η, and ο to ω. The vowels η, ι, υ and ω, however, look no different when lengthened. If a verb begins with a diphthong, the first vowel is lengthened. Some examples:

ἄγω	ἦγον	ἱκετεύω	ἱκέτευον
ἐθέλω	ἤθελον	οἰκίζω	ᾤκιζον or ᾤκιζον
ἥκω	ἧκον	ὀνομάζω	ὠνόμαζον

Note: ἔχω has an unusual imperfect, εἶχον, which seems to violate this rule. This is because the verb stem was originally *σεχ-, with a normal syllabic augment: *ἔσεχ-. The σ between vowels was weak, though, and eventually dropped out; the contraction of the two vowels produced ει (ε + ε = ει).

3. Augments of compound verbs

Sometimes a verb has a preposition preceding the actual stem; for example, ἀποπέμπω, 'send away', εἰσάγω, 'lead into'. The preposition added to these *compound* verbs never affects the augment of the verb, or its accent. That is, the augment is never added in front of the preposition. Instead, it appears as usual in front of the verb stem. This is because the prefixes were originally adverbs, and not attached to the verb as a single word.

There are several rules governing the combination of prefix and verb stem.

1) Most two-syllable prepositions drop their final vowel before the augment: ἀπέπεμπον. The exception is περί, which neither drops a syllable nor contracts with the augment: περιέβαλλον.

2) A one-syllable preposition that ends in a vowel (πρό) contracts with the augment (ο + ε = ου): προύπεμπον.

3) The preposition ἐκ becomes ἐξ before a vowel: ἐξ ᾿Αθηνῶν. This includes augments, and verbs whose stem starts with a vowel: ἐξάγω, ἐξέπεμπον.

4) The preposition σύν becomes συμ- when the verb begins with a labial consonant (π, β, φ). Before an augment it appears as συν-: συνεβούλευον.

5) A verb accent can only recede as far as the augment. It does not appear on a prefix: ἐπῆγον. (An exception is the enclitic verb εἰμί; see Ch. 11.3.)

PRACTICE A. From what verb does each of the following forms come?
example: ἐξέπεμπον comes from ἐκπέμπω

1. ὥπλιζον
2. ἤλαυνον
3. ἐξῆγον
4. ἀπέβαλλον
5. προσέφερον

EXERCISE 41. Give the 1st person sing. Greek form of the imperfect indicative active of the following verbs.

1. ἀγγέλλω	8. ὀνομάζω	15. προπέμπω
2. ὁπλίζω	9. ἔχω	16. διαβαίνω
3. ἀναγκάζω	10. ἄγω	17. περιπέμπω
4. ἐλαύνω	11. εὑρίσκω	18. συμβουλεύω
5. ψεύδω	12. ἥκω	19. εἰσβάλλω
6. οἰκίζω	13. ἀκούω	20. ἐκπέμπω
7. ἄρχω	14. ἁρπάζω	21. ἀποφεύγω

EXERCISE 42.

1. ὁ τοῦ Ξέρξου πατὴρ ἦν Δαρεῖος, ὃς εἰσέβαλλεν εἰς τὴν Ἑλλάδα.
2. οἱ παῖδες χάριν ἔχουσι τῇ μητρὶ ἣ τρέφει αὐτούς.
3. οἱ ἄνδρες ἤλαυνον τοὺς θῆρας ἐκ τῆς ὕλης.
4. οἱ Ἀθηναῖοι ἐθαύμαζον τοὺς λόγους οὓς ὁ ῥήτωρ ἔλεξεν.
5. οἶνός ἐστιν ἐν τῇ οἰκίᾳ.
6. ὁ στρατηγὸς ὥπλιζε τοὺς ἄνδρας θώραξί τε καὶ κόρυσιν.
7. ἐν πολέμῳ οἱ μὲν παῖδες ἀποθνήσκουσιν, οἱ δὲ πατέρες θάπτουσιν αὐτούς.
8. ὁ γέρων ἤκουε τὴν τῆς πιστῆς θυγατρὸς φωνήν.
9. χαλεπὸν ἦν τοῖς ἀνδράσι φυλάσσειν τὴν εἰσβολήν.
10. ὁ θὴρ ἥρπαζε τὸ ζῷον τοῖς ὀδοῦσιν.

EXERCISE 43.

1. The general himself was crossing the river, but he was sending the old men around.
2. The mothers were sending forth their boys to the war.
3. The men were escaping from the wild beasts who were pursuing them.
4. The orator was advising the citizens.
5. In peace children bury their fathers.
6. We did not believe the words of the judge.
7. The mothers of the Spartans admire the brave.
8. It is not always easy for fathers to educate their children.
9. The exiles were founding a colony.
10. They used to call the earth their mother.

4. 3rd declension nouns: stems in -ν

Some of these keep long η or ω throughout; in others this vowel is short except in the nominative singular.

		Greek	**contest**	**shepherd**	**leader**	**dolphin**
SING.	Nom.	ὁ Ἕλλην	ὁ ἀγών	ὁ ποιμήν	ὁ ἡγεμών	ὁ δελφίς
	Gen.	Ἕλληνος	ἀγῶνος	ποιμένος	ἡγεμόνος	δελφῖνος
	Dat.	Ἕλληνι	ἀγῶνι	ποιμένι	ἡγεμόνι	δελφῖνι
	Acc.	Ἕλληνα	ἀγῶνα	ποιμένα	ἡγεμόνα	δελφῖνα
	Voc.	Ἕλλην	ἀγών	ποιμήν	ἡγεμών	δελφίς
PLUR.	Nom.	Ἕλληνες	ἀγῶνες	ποιμένες	ἡγεμόνες	δελφῖνες
	Gen.	Ἑλλήνων	ἀγώνων	ποιμένων	ἡγεμόνων	δελφίνων
	Dat.	Ἕλλησι(ν)	ἀγῶσι(ν)	ποιμέσι(ν)	ἡγεμόσι(ν)	δελφῖσι(ν)
	Acc.	Ἕλληνας	ἀγῶνας	ποιμένας	ἡγεμόνας	δελφῖνας
	Voc.	Ἕλληνες	ἀγῶνες	ποιμένες	ἡγεμόνες	δελφῖνες

5. Principal parts of palatal stem verbs

You have now covered all the tenses formed from the first four principal parts of the Greek verb. When a verb stem ends in a vowel, it is no problem to add the consonant that marks a principal part (σ for the future, for example). When the stem ends in a consonant, however, the resulting consonant cluster must be resolved. You have already seen how various consonants combine with σ (Ch. 1.2, 8.1). Palatal verb stems end in -κ, -γ, -χ. When a palatal consonant is followed by **σ**, the result is always **ξ**. Here are the first four principal parts for the regular palatal stem verbs you have already learned. Also included is the common irregular verb ἔχω:

PRESENT	FUTURE	AORIST ACT.	PERFECT ACT.
ἄγω	ἄξω	ἤγαγον	ἦχα
ἄρχω	ἄρξω	ἦρξα	ἦρχα
διδάσκω	διδάξω	ἐδίδαξα	δεδίδαχα
διώκω	διώξω	ἐδίωξα	δεδίωχα
ἕλκω	ἕλξω	εἷλξα	——
ἔχω	ἕξω / σχήσω[1]	ἔσχον	ἔσχηκα
λέγω	λέξω	ἔλεξα	εἴρηκα[2]
πράσσω	πράξω	ἔπραξα	πέπραχα / πέπραγα
ταράσσω	ταράξω	ἐτάραξα	——
τάσσω	τάξω	ἔταξα	τέταχα
φεύγω	φεύξομαι[3]	ἔφυγον	πέφευγα
φυλάσσω	φυλάξω	ἐφύλαξα	πεφύλαχα

6. Augmented and reduplicated perfects

You have learned that when a verb stem begins with a consonant, the perfect tense is reduplicated (Ch. 6.3). When the verb stem begins with a vowel, as in ἄρχω above, the vowel is lengthened in the perfect; that is, the perfect has an augment like the aorist.

Note: When a verb stem begins with a double consonant (**ζ, ξ, ψ**) or with two consonants where the second one is a stop (Ch. 1.2), the vowel **ε** is prefixed *without* the reduplicated consonant. This is the case with ἔσχηκα above.

7. Strong perfect

Perfects like λέλυκα are weak (first) forms, with the tense marker -**κα**- (Ch. 6.4). Many verbs, including a number on the list above, have a strong (second) perfect instead. Strong perfects have the same endings as the weak perfect, but instead of the consonant **κ** they show the consonant which ends the stem, or an aspirated version of it. Thus δεδίωχα from διώκω, etc.

Sometimes there are two forms with a distinction in meaning between them. On the list above, for example, πράσσω has two perfect forms. πέπραχα means 'I have done'; πέπραγα means 'I have fared'.

8. Strong aorist

Like the perfect, the aorist tense also has weak and strong forms. The aorist forms you have learned so far are all *weak* or *first aorists*. Some verbs, like ἄγω, ἔχω and φεύγω above, have a *strong* or *second aorist* instead (Ch. 5.2) This type uses the thematic vowel instead of the marker **σα**. It has the same *endings* as the imperfect, but its *stem* is different from the present stem, which is the basis for the imperfect tense. Compare the strong aorist of ἄγω with its imperfect:

---

[1]   ἕξω means 'I will (go on) having'; σχήσω means 'I will (acquire and) have'.
[2]   εἴρηκα comes from a stem unrelated to λέγω.
[3]   For future conjugation see Ch. 16.2.

	IMPERFECT		AORIST	
1st	ἦγ-ον	ἤγ-ομεν	ἤγαγ-ον	ἠγάγ-ομεν
2nd	ἦγ-ες	ἤγ-ετε	ἤγαγ-ες	ἠγάγ-ετε
3rd	ἦγ-ε	ἦγ-ον	ἤγαγ-ε	ἤγαγ-ον

Here are the first four principal parts of the other verbs learned so far which have strong aorists:

PRESENT	FUTURE	AORIST ACT.	PERFECT ACT.
ἀποθνῄσκω	ἀποθανοῦμαι[1]	ἀπέθανον	(τέθνηκα)[2]
εὑρίσκω	εὑρήσω	ηὗρον / εὗρον	ηὕρηκα / εὕρηκα
λαμβάνω	λήψομαι[3]	ἔλαβον	εἴληφα
φέρω	οἴσω	ἤνεγκον	ἐνήνοχα

EXERCISE 44.

1. ὁ Λεωνίδας ἔταξε τοὺς Ἕλληνας εἰς μάχην.
2. ὁ Ξέρξης οὐ σχήσει τὴν Ἑλλάδα.
3. οἱ ποιμένες ἤγαγον τοὺς αἶγας εἰς τὸν λειμῶνα.
4. εὖ ἔλεξας ὑπὲρ τῶν φυγάδων οὓς ἐλάβομεν.
5. ὁ στρατηγὸς τέταχε τοὺς συμμάχους.
6. οἱ Λακεδαιμόνιοι μάτην πεφυλάχασι τὴν εἰσβολὴν.
7. αἱ κάμηλοι ἐτάραξαν τοὺς ἵππους.
8. οἱ γίγαντες οἳ ἔμενον ἐν τῇ νήσῳ ἦσαν δεινοί τε καὶ ἰσχυροί.
9. διὰ τὸν χειμῶνα ὁ ἡγεμὼν οὐχ ηὗρε τὴν ὁδόν.
10. οἱ νεανίαι εὖ πεπράγασιν ἐν τοῖς ἀγῶσιν.

EXERCISE 45.

1. The Persians will not throw them into confusion.
2. The shepherd found the animals in the meadow.
3. The Athenians have pursued the Persians into the sea.
4. On account of the danger we will guard the harbor.
5. Cyrus has drawn up his soldiers behind the camels.
6. Xerxes, who was Darius' child, ruled the country after his death.
7. The tyrant had a beautiful daughter.
8. The guides led the enemy who were invading to the pass.
9. We did not fare well in the contest.
10. The Spartans died in the mountain pass, but they saved Greece from the enemy.

---

[1] For future conjugation see Ch. 21.4.
[2] This form does not exist in the compound version ἀπο-θνῄσκω.
[3] For future conjugation see Ch. 16.2.

EXERCISE 46.

XERXES WHIPS THE SEA

The bridges referred to were built across the Hellespont between Abydos and Sestos and were nearly a mile long. This was in preparation for Xerxes' invasion of Greece in 480 BC. King Darius had died in 485 BC.

μετὰ δὲ τὸν τοῦ πατρὸς θάνατον ὁ Ξέρξης ἦρχε τῶν Περσῶν. ὅτι δὲ ἤθελε κολάζειν τοὺς Ἕλληνας διὰ τὰς ἀδικίας αὐτῶν,[1] ἐβούλευσε διαβαίνειν τὸν Ἑλλήσποντον καὶ ἄγειν στράτευμα διὰ τῆς Εὐρώπης ἐπὶ τὴν Ἑλλάδα· ἐκέλευσεν οὖν Φοίνικας καὶ Αἰγυπτίους, οἳ σύμμαχοι ἦσαν τῶν Περσῶν, δύο γεφύρας κατασκευάζειν. ἐπεὶ δὲ ἔπραξαν τὸ ἔργον, χειμὼν μέγιστος διέλυσε τὰς γεφύρας. ὁ οὖν Ξέρξης, ὅτε μανθάνει, μάλιστα ἐχαλέπαινε καὶ ἐκέλευσε τοὺς ἄνδρας οὐ μόνον τόν τε Ἑλλήσποντον τριακοσίαις πληγαῖς τύπτειν καὶ δύο πέδας εἰς αὐτὸν βάλλειν, ἀλλὰ καὶ ἀποτέμνειν τὰς τῶν ἐπιστατῶν κεφαλάς. ἔπειτα δὲ ἄλλους ἐπιστάτας ἐκέλευσε κατασκευάζειν τὰς γεφύρας.

Adapted from Herodotus VII.34-36

---

[1] Darius had wanted to punish the Greek cities of Athens and Eretria for helping the Greeks of Ionia (in Asia Minor) to revolt against the Persians in 499 BC. His expedition had been defeated at Marathon in 490 BC; Xerxes thus had a further motive for his invasion in 480 BC.

Chapter 10 Vocabulary

Verbs:

ἀκούω	hear, listen to	καταλύω	destroy
(+ *acc.* thing,		οἰκίζω	found (a colony)
+ *gen.* person)			
ἀναγκάζω	compel/ force	ὀνομάζω	name, call
ἀποφεύγω	flee away, escape	περιπέμπω	send around
ἁρπάζω	snatch	πράσσω	do, manage; fare
ἄρχω (+ *gen.*)	rule, command	προπέμπω	send forth
εἰσβάλλω (+ εἰς)	throw into, invade, flow into	συμβουλεύω (+ *dat.*)	advise
εὖ πράσσω	fare well, manage well	ταράσσω	throw into confusion
ἥκω	have come	τάσσω	draw up
θάπτω	bury	ψεύδω	tell a lie
ἱκετεύω	entreat, supplicate		

Nouns:

ἀγών, -ῶνος, ὁ	contest, game	κάμηλος, -ου, ὁ/ἡ	camel
αἴξ, αἰγός, ὁ/ἡ	goat	Κῦρος, -ου, ὁ	Cyrus
ἀνήρ, ἀνδρός, ὁ	man, husband	λειμών, -ῶνος, ὁ	meadow
ἀποικία, -ας, ἡ	colony	Λεωνίδας, -ου, ὁ	Leonidas
Δαρεῖος, -ου, ὁ	Darius	λιμήν, -ένος, ὁ	harbor
δελφίς, -ῖνος, ὁ	dolphin	μήτηρ, μητρός, ἡ	mother
εἰσβολή, -ῆς, ἡ	(mountain) pass	οἶνος, -ου, ὁ	wine
Ἕλλην, -ηνος, ὁ	a Greek	πατήρ, πατρός, ὁ	father
ἡγεμών, -όνος, ὁ	leader, guide	ποιμήν -ένος, ὁ	shepherd
θάνατος, -ου, ὁ	death	ῥήτωρ, -ορος, ὁ	orator
θήρ, θηρός, ὁ	wild beast	τύραννος, -ου, ὁ	tyrant
θυγάτηρ, -τρός, ἡ	daughter	χειμών, -ῶνος, ὁ	storm, winter

Adjective:

μωρός, -ά, -όν	foolish

Adverbs:

εὖ	well	μάτην	in vain

Prepositions:

εἰς (+ *acc.*)	for (a purpose)	ὄπισθε(ν) (+ *gen.*)	behind
μετά (+ *gen.*)	with	σύν (+ *dat.*)	with
μετά (+ *acc.*)	after		

CHAPTER 11

1. Review of word order

You already know that an attributive adjective always follows an article, if the noun phrase contains one (Ch. 7.2). A dependent genitive adjective likewise appears either sandwiched between article and noun (Ch. 4.6), or following the repeated article. (The possessive form of the pronoun αὐτοῦ, αὐτῆς, αὐτοῦ is predicate instead; Ch. 8.9). Prepositional phrases that modify nouns behave in the same way.

ὁ σοφὸς ἀνήρ	or	ὁ ἀνὴρ ὁ σοφός
ὁ τοῦ στρατηγοῦ ἵππος	or	ὁ ἵππος ὁ τοῦ στρατηγοῦ
τὰ ἐν τῇ νήσῳ δένδρα	or	τὰ δένδρα τὰ ἐν τῇ νήσῳ

When a sentence contains a prepositional phrase it is important to check whether or not this is part of a noun phrase, that is, whether or not it follows an article. Contrast the following pairs of sentences:

1. a) εὑρίσκομεν τοὺς στρατιώτας ἐν τῷ λιμένι.
      We find the soldiers in the harbor. (answers the question *where?*)
   b) εὑρίσκομεν τοὺς στρατιώτας τοὺς ἐν τῷ λιμένι.
      We find the soldiers in the harbor. (answers the question *which soldiers?*)

2. a) ἡ μήτηρ ἀκούει τοῦ ῥήτορος ἐν τῇ οἰκίᾳ.
      The mother hears the orator in the house. (answers the question *where?*)
   b) ἡ μήτηρ ἀκούει τοῦ ἐν τῇ οἰκίᾳ ῥήτορος.
      The mother hears the orator in the house. (answers the question *which orator?*)

2. More uses of the article

The article can never stand all by itself, but it can be combined with other words to make a noun phrase. The noun itself can be omitted, since the context supplies it. You have already seen this happen with ὁ μέν and ὁ δέ (Ch. 8.6). Other examples:

1. with a genitive noun:
   τὰ τῆς πατρίδος, 'the [affairs] of the fatherland'
   οἱ τῆς Ἑλλάδος, 'the [people] of Greece'

2. with an adjective, prepositional phrase or adverb:

ὁ σοφός, 'the wise [man]'	αἱ πάλαι, 'the [women] of old'
οἱ ἐκεῖ, 'the [people] there'	τὰ ἐν τῇ οἰκίᾳ, 'the [things] in the house'

3. Compounds of εἰμί, 'be'

Normally a verb accent can only recede as far as the augment; it cannot stand on the prefix of a compound verb (Ch. 10.3). However, in the present tense of εἰμί most forms are enclitic, so they cannot carry their own accent. In compound verbs like ἄπειμι, 'be absent', therefore, the accent appears on the prefix:

	Singular	Plural
1st	ἄπειμι	ἄπεσμεν
2nd	ἄπει	ἄπεστε
3rd	ἄπεστι(ν)	ἄπεισι(ν)

Note: The future and imperfect tenses are not enclitic, so they are accented normally: ἀπέσται, ἀπῆσαν.

EXERCISE 47.

1. ἡ μάχη ἡ ἐν τῷ λιμένι ἦν μακρά.
2. οἱ Ἀθηναῖοι ἐτάραξαν τοὺς ἐν τῇ νήσῳ.
3. ἐθέλομεν εὑρίσκειν, ὦ ἡγεμών, τὴν διὰ τῆς ὕλης ὁδόν.
4. οἱ Λακεδαιμόνιοι χάριν ἔχουσι τοῖς μετὰ τοῦ Λεωνίδου.
5. εὖ ἐπράξατε τὰ τῆς πατρίδος ὑπὲρ τῶν πολιτῶν.
6. ὁ Λεωνίδας ἤγαγε τὴν στρατιὰν διὰ τῆς Ἀττικῆς.
7. οἱ στρατιῶται οἳ ἄπεισιν ἀπὸ τῆς μάχης οὐ σχήσουσι τιμήν.
8. οἱ Ἀθηναῖοι ἐθαύμαζον τοὺς πάλαι.
9. οὐ κακῶς ἔπραξαν οἱ δοῦλοι· ὁ γὰρ δεσπότης ἀπῆν.
10. χαλεπὸν ἦν αὐτοῖς ἀπελαύνειν τοὺς Πέρσας οἳ εἰσέβαλλον· οἱ γὰρ σύμμαχοι ἀπέθανον.

EXERCISE 48.

1. We led the men on the island into the sea.
2. Some were cutting down trees, others carried food.
3. The boys found a lion in the house.
4. The people there were pitying the prisoners, for they did not have hope.
5. The Athenians have trained their animals.
6. Night will not stop the contest.
7. The generals managed the affairs of Greece.
8. The trumpets threw the horses into confusion.
9. We ordered the women who were in the village to flee.
10. The general himself falls in the battle.

4. Conditions

A conditional sentence describes the condition under which an action occurs, or may occur. A subordinate clause, the *protasis* or if-clause, expresses the condition. The *apodosis* or main clause, states the outcome: "If John thinks that, he is wrong"; "If it rains, we will stay home." There are several types of conditional sentences in Greek, each constructed in a particular way. Conditions using only the indicative are presented here; other types will be discussed in Ch. 30.

Note: The negative used in the protasis of any condition is μή, while οὐ is used in the apodosis.

5. Simple conditions

A simple condition is the most basic type of conditional sentence. It may refer to the present, or to the past, but not to the future:

> εἰ ὁ παῖς μὴ ἀγαθός, οἰκτείρω τὸν πατέρα.
> If the child is not good, I pity the father.

> εἰ ὁ στρατηγὸς σοφὸς ἦν, οὐκ ἐπίστευσε τῷ ἡγεμόνι.
> If the general was wise, he did not trust the guide.

6. Contrary-to-fact conditions

A contrary-to-fact condition describes what might have happened, but did not, because the necessary condition was not fulfilled:

> If I were rich [but I'm not], I would be happy [but I'm not].
> If it had not rained [but it did], I would have gone out [but I didn't].

In each case, both clauses describe a situation contrary to the known facts: I'm not rich, and I'm not happy; it did rain, and I didn't go out.

Contrary-to-fact conditions are constructed as follows. The word εἰ, 'if' introduces the protasis as in simple conditions. The negative used in the protasis is μή. The apodosis always includes the untranslated signal word ἄν. It usually stands second in the verb phrase, so it comes after the verb itself, or between οὐ or an adverb and the verb. (It generally stands in front of the verb εἰμί, even in non-enclitic forms.) The verb itself is imperfect in either clause if it refers to the present ('if I were marching'; 'I would be marching'), and aorist if it refers to the past ('if I had stayed home'; 'I would have stayed home'). The two clauses do not have to be in the same tense. Here are examples of a present, a past, and a mixed contrary-to-fact condition.

> εἰ δοῦλος ἦν, οὐκ εὖ ἄν ἔπρασσεν.
> If he were a slave, he would not be faring well.

> εἰ ὁ στρατηγὸς ἐφύλαξε τὸ στρατόπεδον, οἱ αἰχμάλωτοι οὐκ ἄν ἔφυγον.
> If the general had guarded the camp, the prisoners of war would not have escaped.

> εἰ οἱ Ἀθηναῖοι μὴ ἐδίωξαν τοὺς Πέρσας ἐκ τῆς Ἑλλάδος, δοῦλοι νῦν ἄν ἦσαν.
> If the Athenians had not pursued the Persians out of Greece, they would now be slaves.

Construction Summary

TYPE OF CONDITION	PROTASIS (NEGATIVE μή)	APODOSIS (NEGATIVE οὐ)
simple:	εἰ + indicative	indicative
contrary to fact:	εἰ + indicative	indicative + ἄν
	imperfect for present	imperfect for present
	aorist for past	aorist for past

EXERCISE 49.

1. εἰ ὁ χειμὼν χαλεπός ἐστιν, μένετε ἐν τῷ λιμένι.
2. ἔτι ἐν κινδύνῳ ἄν ἦμεν, εἰ ἡ θεὰ μὴ ἔπαυσε τὴν μάχην.
3. εἰ ὁ στρατηγὸς μὴ ἐκέλευσε τοὺς στρατιώτας μένειν ἐκεῖ, οἱ πολέμιοι ηὗρον ἄν αὐτούς.

4. εἰ οἱ θῆρες ἐν τῇ κώμῃ εἰσίν, ἐθέλω ἀπελαύνειν αὐτούς.
5. οἱ πολῖται ἐπίστευον ἄν τῷ ῥήτορι, εἰ σοφοὶ ἦσαν.
6. εἰ ἡ νῆσος μικρὰ ἦν, οἱ παῖδες οὐκ ἄν ἔμενον ἐν αὐτῇ.
7. σοφοί ἐστε εἰ ἀκούετε τοῦ Ξενοφῶντος.
8. εἰ μὴ ἐφύλαξα τὸν δοῦλον ἔφυγεν ἄν.
9. εἰ ὁ ναύτης τοῖς θεοῖς ἔθυσε, δῶρα ἄν ἔπεμπον πρὸς αὐτόν.
10. εἰ τὰ χρήματα πείθει τοὺς παῖδας, μωροί εἰσιν.

EXERCISE 50.

1. If there is a camel in the house, do not stay!
2. I would have fled away from the village if I were rich.
3. If they stayed in the forest they were in danger.
4. If the storm were dangerous, we would not be marching out of Athens.
5. Xerxes would have destroyed Greece if the Athenians had not stopped him.
6. If we were not faithful, we would have fled away.
7. If the soldiers had not guarded the camp, the enemy would have captured it.
8. If he wants to hunt the lion, I admire him.
9. If he had not died, he would be a general now.
10. The orator would have advised them if they had listened to him.

EXERCISE 51.

ADMETUS AND ALCESTIS

The following is the outline of the plot of the Alcestis, *one of the best known plays of Euripides* (c. 485-406 BC). *Pherae was a town in Thessaly.*

ὁ Ἄδμητος, ὃς ἐβασίλευε τῶν Φερῶν, ἦν ὁ τῆς Ἀλκήστιδος ἀνήρ· ἐπεὶ δὲ ἡ ὥρα ἧκεν αὐτῷ ἀποθνῄσκειν, ὁ Ἀπόλλων ἔλεξεν ὅτι διὰ τὴν πρὶν εὔνοιαν ἐξῆν αὐτῷ ἔτι βίον διάγειν, εἴ τις τῶν οἰκείων ἤθελε ὑπὲρ αὐτοῦ ἀποθανεῖν. ἀλλ᾽ ὁ Ἄδμητος οὐχ οἷός τε ἦν πείθειν οὔτε τὸν πατέρα οὔτε τὴν μητέρα· καὶ δὴ ἡ Ἄλκηστις μόνη ἤθελε σῴζειν τὸν ἄνδρα· ἐκέλευσεν οὖν χαίρειν τόν τε υἱὸν καὶ τὴν θυγατέρα καὶ τὸν ἄνδρα αὐτόν. μετὰ δὲ τὸν τῆς Ἀλκήστιδος θάνατον ὁ Ἡρακλῆς παρῆν εἰς τὰ βασίλεια. ὁ δὲ Ἄδμητος ἐξένιζε μὲν αὐτόν, ἔκρυπτε δὲ τὴν συμφοράν· εἰ γὰρ ἔλεξε τὰ ἀληθῆ [the truth] τῷ φίλῳ, ὁ Ἡρακλῆς ἂν ἔφυγεν. τέλος δὲ ὁ Ἡρακλῆς, ὡς ηὗρε τὰ περὶ τῆς Ἀλκήστιδος παρὰ τῆς θεραπαίνης, εἰς τὸν τάφον ἔτρεξε καὶ ἔλαβε τὴν Ἀλκήστιδα πρὸς βίαν ἀπὸ τοῦ Θανάτου· εἶτα δὲ πρὸς τὸν ἄνδρα ἤγαγεν αὐτήν.

Chapter 11 Vocabulary

Verbs:

ἄπειμι	be absent	οἰκτείρω	pity
ἀπελαύνω	drive away	πίπτω	fall
κακῶς πράσσω	fare badly		

Nouns:

αἰχμάλωτος, -ου, ὁ	prisoner (of war)	Ἀττική, -ῆς, ἡ	Attica

Adverbs:

ἐκεῖ	there	κακῶς	badly
ἔτι	still, yet	πάλαι	of old, long ago

Conjunction:

εἰ	if

Particle:

ἄν	conditional particle

CHAPTER 12

τὸ μὲν γὰρ ἓν στιγμή, τὰ δὲ δύο γραμμή, τὰ δὲ τρία τρίγωνον, τὰ δὲ τέσσερα πυραμίς. ταῦτα δὲ πάντα ἐστὶ πρῶτα καὶ ἀρχαὶ τῶν καθ᾽ ἕκαστον ὁμογενῶν….τὰ αὐτὰ δὲ καὶ ἐν τῇ γενέσι· πρώτη μὲν γὰρ ἀρχὴ εἰς μέγεθος στιγμή, δευτέρα γραμμή, τρίτη ἐπιφάνεια, τέταρτον στερεόν.

— Pythagorean belief, recorded by Speusippos, *ap.*
Theologumena Arithemeticae p. 84.10 (de Falco)

1. Numbers

Here are the Greek cardinal (one, two, three...) and ordinal (first, second, third...) numbers from 1 to 100. All the ordinals are fully declinable (like σοφός, except that δεύτερος retains α throughout the singular, like φίλιος, Ch. 7.1). Of the cardinals, only 1-4 are declined (Ch. 12.2).

	Cardinal	**Ordinal**
1.	εἷς, μία, ἕν	πρῶτος, -η, -ον
2.	δύο	δεύτερος, -α, -ον
3.	τρεῖς, τρία	τρίτος, -η, -ον
4.	τέσσαρες, τέσσαρα	τέταρτος, -η, -ον
5.	πέντε	πέμπτος, -η, -ον
6.	ἕξ	ἕκτος, -η, -ον
7.	ἑπτά	ἕβδομος, -η, -ον
8.	ὀκτώ	ὄγδοος, -η, -ον
9.	ἐννέα	ἔνατος, -η, -ον
10.	δέκα	δέκατος, -η, -ον
11.	ἕνδεκα	ἑνδέκατος, -η, -ον
12.	δώδεκα	δωδέκατος, -η, -ον
13.	τρεῖς καὶ δέκα	τρίτος καὶ δέκατος
14.	τέσσαρες καὶ δέκα	τέταρτος καὶ δέκατος
15.	πεντεκαίδεκα	πέμπτος καὶ δέκατος
16.	ἑκκαίδεκα	ἕκτος καὶ δέκατος
17.	ἑπτακαίδεκα	ἕβδομος καὶ δέκατος
18.	ὀκτωκαίδεκα	ὄγδοος καὶ δέκατος
19.	ἐννεακαίδεκα	ἔνατος καὶ δέκατος
20.	εἴκοσι(ν)	εἰκοστός, -ή, -όν
21.	εἷς καὶ εἴκοσι, εἴκοσι καὶ εἷς, etc.	πρῶτος καὶ εἰκοστός etc.

	Cardinal	Ordinal
30.	τριάκοντα	τριακοστός, -ή, -όν
40.	τεσσαράκοντα	τεσσαρακοστός, -ή, -όν
50.	πεντήκοντα	πεντηκοστός, -ή, -όν
60.	ἑξήκοντα	ἑξηκοστός, -ή, -όν
70.	ἑβδομήκοντα	ἑβδομηκοστός, -ή, -όν
80.	ὀγδοήκοντα	ὀγδοηκοστός, -ή, -όν
90.	ἐνενήκοντα	ἐνενηκοστός, -ή, -όν
100.	ἑκατόν	ἑκατοστός, -ή, -όν

2. Declension of numbers

The numbers 1 to 4 are declined as follows:

	one			two	three		four	
	M	**F**	**N**	**M/F/N**	**M/F**	**N**	**M/F**	**N**
Nom.	εἷς	μία	ἕν	δύο	τρεῖς	τρία	τέσσαρες	τέσσαρα
Gen.	ἑνός	μιᾶς	ἑνός	δυοῖν	τριῶν	τριῶν	τεσσάρων	τεσσάρων
Dat.	ἑνί	μιᾷ	ἑνί	δυοῖν	τρισί(ν)	τρισί(ν)	τέσσαρσι(ν)	τέσσαρσι(ν)
Acc.	ἕνα	μίαν	ἕν	δύο	τρεῖς	τρία	τέσσαρας	τέσσαρα
Voc.	εἷς	μία	ἕν	δύο	τρεῖς	τρία	τέσσαρες	τέσσαρα

The Greek word for 'no one', 'nothing' joins the negative οὐδέ, 'not even', with the number one: οὐδείς. Wherever μή is used instead of οὐ, μηδείς replaces οὐδείς. They are declined the same way. There is no plural, of course.

	M	**F**	**N**
Nom.	οὐδείς	οὐδεμία	οὐδέν
Gen.	οὐδενός	οὐδεμίας	οὐδενός
Dat.	οὐδενί	οὐδεμίᾳ	οὐδενί
Acc.	οὐδένα	οὐδεμίαν	οὐδέν
Voc.	οὐδείς	οὐδεμία	οὐδέν

Note: οὐδείς can appear both alone as a pronoun, and as an adjective modifying a noun:

οὐδέν ἐστι ῥᾴδιον. οὐδεὶς στρατηγὸς δειλός.
Nothing is easy. No general is cowardly.

3. Ways of expressing time

The oblique cases in Greek (gen., dat., acc.) are used without preposition for different expressions of time. The accusative expresses *duration* or *length* of time, how long something lasts:

οἱ πολέμιοι ἔφευγον πέντε ἡμέρας.
The enemy were fleeing *for five days.*

The dative expresses a *point in time*, the time at which something happens:

ὁ στρατηγὸς ἔταξε τὸ στράτευμα τῇ τρίτῃ ἡμέρᾳ.
The general drew up his army *on the third day.*

The genitive expresses a range of time *within which* something happens:

> πέμψει τοὺς στρατιώτας πέντε ἡμερῶν.
> He will send the soldiers *within five days.*

So too, τῆς νυκτός, during the night; χειμῶνος, in winter.

Some people find it helpful to visualize the accusative expression as a *line* along which an event continues; the dative as a *point* pinpointing the moment of an event; and the genitive as a *circle* representing the time within which an event occurs.

EXERCISE 52.

1. ἐμένομεν τὸν Ξενοφῶντα ἐν τῇ νήσῳ ἓξ ἡμέρας.
2. μακρὸν χρόνον τεθηρεύκαμεν τὸν λέοντα ὃς ἐτάραξε τοὺς ἐν τῷ λειμῶνι αἶγας.
3. θύσομεν τῇ θεᾷ τῷ τετάρτῳ μηνί.
4. οἱ ἑκατὸν στρατιῶται παρασκευάζουσι τὰ ὅπλα τῆς νυκτός.
5. ὀκτὼ ἡμέρας τὸ στράτευμα αὐτῶν ἦν ἐν κινδύνῳ.
6. τὰ ὅπλα ἦν ἑτοῖμα τῇ δευτέρᾳ ἡμέρᾳ.
7. ὀλίγων ἡμερῶν ἡ Ἑλλὰς ἐλευθέρα ἔσται.
8. εἰ αὐτὸς ἐπαίδευσας τὸν ἵππον δέκα ἡμέρας, εὖ ἂν ἔπραξας ἐν τῷ ἀγῶνι.
9. τὸ στράτευμα οὐχ οἷόν τε ἔσται διαβαίνειν τὸν ποταμὸν μιᾶς ἡμέρας.
10. οἱ Λακεδαιμόνιοι, οἳ μόνον τριακόσιοι ἦσαν, μάτην ἐφύλαξαν τὴν εἰσβολήν.

EXERCISE 53.

1. For five nights we were waiting for the moon.
2. Within twenty days I shall bring back the soldiers who are staying on the island.
3. On the second day we pursued the enemy to the sea.
4. In the fourth month he stopped the war.
5. If he were a good doctor, he would have cured the boy in seven days.
6. For ten months the exiles were in danger.
7. The slave was absent for two days and one night.
8. No one crosses the river at night.
9. You yourself will be free within a few months.
10. Some rest by night, others by day.

4. 3rd declension nouns: stems in -σ

In these nouns the σ drops out between vowels, and the vowels contract, as follows:

ε + ε = ει	ε + ο = ου
ε + α = η , ει (acc. pl.)	ε + ω = ω

Masculine and feminine nouns of this type are declined like τριήρης, neuters like τεῖχος. Σωκράτης, 'Socrates' is a noun of this type (singular only).

			trireme		**wall**
SING.	Nom.	ἡ	τριήρης	τὸ	τεῖχος
	Gen.		τριήρους		τείχους
	Dat.		τριήρει		τείχει
	Acc.		τριήρη		τεῖχος
	Voc.		(τριῆρες)		τεῖχος

		trireme	**wall**
PLUR.	Nom.	τριήρεις	τείχη
	Gen.	τριηρῶν	τειχῶν
	Dat.	τριήρεσι(ν)	τείχεσι(ν)
	Acc.	τριήρεις	τείχη
	Voc.	τριήρεις	τείχη

5. Principal parts of dental stem verbs

The stems of these verbs end in -τ, -δ, -θ. Stems in -ζ also belong to this group, since ζ actually represents the consonant cluster **sd** (Ch. 1.1). When a dental consonant is followed by σ, the dental disappears (Ch. 1.2, 8.1). Here are the first four principal parts of the dental stem verbs you have learned:

PRESENT	FUTURE	AORIST ACT.	PERFECT ACT.
ἀναγκάζω	ἀναγκάσω	ἠνάγκασα	ἠνάγκακα
ἁρπάζω	ἁρπάσω	ἥρπασα	ἥρπακα
θαυμάζω	θαυμάσω	ἐθαύμασα	τεθαύμακα
οἰκίζω	οἰκίσω	ᾤκισα	——
ὀνομάζω	ὀνομάσω	ὠνόμασα	ὠνόμακα
ὁπλίζω	ὁπλίσω	ὥπλισα	——
πείθω	πείσω	ἔπεισα	πέπεικα or πέποιθα[1]
σῴζω	σώσω	ἔσωσα	σέσωκα

6. Directional suffixes

-δε, 'toward', and -θεν, 'from' can be attached to place names and a few other words. Thus οἴκαδε = 'homeward'; ὅθεν = 'from which'. More examples:

οἴκοθεν	from home
Ἀθήνηθεν	from Athens
Ἀθήναζε	to Athens (Ἀθήνας + δε: ζ = σδ)

EXERCISE 54.

1. ὁ Δημοσθένης ἔπεισε τοὺς Ἀθηναίους πέμπειν στράτευμα.
2. εἰ ἀγαθὰ ὅπλα ἦν τοῖς Ἕλλησιν, ἠνάγκασαν ἂν τοὺς Πέρσας ἀποφεύγειν.
3. πείσομεν τοὺς συμμάχους πέμπειν τρεῖς τριήρεις.
4. τῷ δεκάτῳ ἔτει οἱ στρατηγοὶ ἤγαγον τὸ στράτευμα οἴκαδε.
5. οἱ Ἀθηναῖοι ἐφύλασσον τὴν ὁδὸν μακροῖς τείχεσιν.
6. οἱ πολῖται πεφυλάχασι τὴν πατρίδα δέκα ἔτη.
7. σεσώκατε τὴν πατρίδα, ὦ πολῖται.
8. τοὺς μὲν ἐπείσαμεν φεύγειν, οἱ δὲ ἀπέθανον ἐν τῇ μάχῃ.
9. ἐπιστεύσαμεν τῷ Σωκράτει οὗ οἱ λόγοι σοφοὶ ἦσαν.
10. εἰ τὸ ὄρος ὑψηλόν, οὐκ ἐθέλω ἀναβαίνειν αὐτό.

EXERCISE 55.

1. He compelled the sailors to remain in the harbor.
2. We persuaded the exiles to escape to Athens by night.
3. The general has saved both the old men and the children.

---

[1] πέπεικα = 'I have persuaded'; πέποιθα = 'I trust' (present sense).

4. If the Athenians had persuaded their allies to send triremes and sailors, they would not be in danger now.
5. The enemy compelled the Athenians to destroy the long walls.
6. Is it easy to cross the mountain in summer?
7. Within three years the triremes which we are waiting for will be ready.
8. The Persians will not force the Spartans to flee.
9. The lion compels the soldiers to flee from home.
10. The young men were listening to the words of Socrates himself.

EXERCISE 56.

THE WOODEN WALL

Between the two Persian invasions of 490 and 480 BC a rich vein of silver was discovered in Attica. It was used to develop the Athenian navy, which fought first against the people of Aegina (an island southwest of Attica, and a strong naval power), and then against the Persians, especially in the decisive victory off Salamis in 480.

ἦν δέ ποτε ἀνὴρ Ἀθηναῖος ὀνόματι Θεμιστοκλῆς· ὅτε δὲ ἦν χρήματα οὐκ ὀλίγα ἐκ τῶν μετάλλων ἐν τῷ κοινῷ, οἱ μὲν ἤθελον παρέχειν δέκα δραχμὰς ἑκάστῳ τῶν Ἀθηναίων. ὁ δὲ Θεμιστοκλῆς ἔπεισεν αὐτοὺς κατασκευάζειν διακοσίας τριήρεις εἰς τὸν πρὸς τοὺς Αἰγινήτας πόλεμον· καὶ οὕτως ἠνάγκασε τοὺς Ἀθηναίους ἀριστεύειν κατὰ θάλασσαν.

ἐν δὲ τῷ πρὸς τοὺς Πέρσας πολέμῳ οἱ Ἀθηναῖοι ἔπεμψαν ἄνδρας εἰς Δελφούς, ὅτι ἐν μεγίστῳ κινδύνῳ ἦσαν. καὶ ἡ Πυθία, Εἰ ἐθέλετε σῶσαι τὴν πατρίδα, ἔφη, πιστεύετε τῷ ξυλίνῳ τείχει. ὁ δὲ Θεμιστοκλῆς ὧδε συνεβούλευσε τοῖς πολίταις· Ὁ θεὸς τῷ ξυλίνῳ τείχει οὐ τὴν ἀκρόπολιν σημαίνει, ἀλλὰ τὸ ναυτικόν, καὶ κελεύει τοὺς πολίτας ταῖς τριήρεσι πιστεύειν. οἱ δὲ πλεῖστοι ἐπίστευσαν αὐτῷ, καὶ οὕτω ἔπεισε τοὺς Ἀθηναίους καὶ ἄλλο ναυτικὸν κατασκευάζειν. καὶ δὴ εἰ μὴ ἔσχον ναυτικὸν καλόν, οὐκ ἂν κατέλυσαν τοὺς Πέρσας.

μετὰ δὲ τὴν ἐν ταῖς Θερμοπύλαις μάχην, οἱ μὲν Πελοποννήσιοι ἐφύλασσον τὸν Ἰσθμὸν τείχει, οἱ δὲ Ἀθηναῖοι ἐξεκόμισαν τά τε τέκνα καὶ τοὺς οἰκέτας ἐκ τῆς Ἀττικῆς, τοὺς μὲν εἰς Τροιζῆνα, τοὺς δὲ εἰς Αἴγιναν, τοὺς δὲ εἰς Σαλαμῖνα, καὶ οὕτως ἔσωσαν αὐτούς. οἱ δὲ Πέρσαι εἰσέβαλον εἰς τὴν Ἀττικὴν καὶ κατέλαβον τὰς Ἀθήνας καὶ ἔκαυσαν τὴν ἀκρόπολιν, ἐν ᾗ ἦσαν οἱ ὀλίγοι οἳ οὐκ ἐπίστευσαν τῷ Θεμιστοκλεῖ.

Adapted from Herodotus VII.141-144, VIII.41, 53

Chapter 12 Vocabulary

Verbs:

ἀναβαίνω	mount, climb (up)	μένω	wait for, stay,
ἀπάγω	lead away, bring back		remain
ἡσυχάζω	rest, remain quiet	παρασκευάζω	prepare

Nouns:

Ἄδμητος, -ου, ὁ	Admetus	σελήνη, -ης, ἡ	moon
Δημοσθένης, -ους, ὁ	Demosthenes	Σωκράτης, -ους, ὁ	Socrates
ἔτος, ἔτους, τό	year	τεῖχος, -ους, τό	wall
θέρος, -ους, τό	summer	τριήρης, -ους, ἡ	trireme
μήν, μηνός, ὁ	month	χρόνος, -ου, ὁ	time
ὄρος, ὄρους, τό	mountain		

Pronouns:

μηδείς, μηδεμία, μηδέν	no one, nothing	οὐδείς, οὐδεμία, οὐδέν	no one, nothing

Adjectives:

μηδείς, μηδεμία, μηδέν	not one, no	ὀλίγος, -η, -ον	little, few
οὐδείς, οὐδεμία, οὐδέν	not one, no	τριακόσιοι, -αι, -α	three hundred
		ὑψηλός, -ή, -όν	high

Other:

Ἀθήναζε	to Athens	οἴκαδε	homeward
Ἀθήνηθεν	from Athens	οἴκοθεν	from home

Numbers: see Ch. 12.1

CHAPTER 13

1. 3rd declension nouns: stems in -ι, -υ

These nouns look irregular in some forms, and must be learned carefully. Most -ι stems and some -υ stems show **ε** in many forms instead of their true vowel. πόλις, 'city', πρέσβυς, 'elder' and ἄστυ, 'town' are examples of this type. The true vowel appears in ἰχθύς, 'fish'.

			city		**elder**		**town**		**fish**
SING.	Nom.	ἡ	πόλις	ὁ	πρέσβυς	τὸ	ἄστυ	ὁ	ἰχθύς
	Gen.		πόλεως		πρέσβεως		ἄστεως		ἰχθύος
	Dat.		πόλει		πρέσβει		ἄστει		ἰχθύϊ
	Acc.		πόλιν		πρέσβυν		ἄστυ		ἰχθύν
	Voc.		πόλι		πρέσβυ		ἄστυ		ἰχθύ
PLUR.	Nom.		πόλεις		πρέσβεις		ἄστη		ἰχθύες
	Gen.		πόλεων		πρέσβεων		ἄστεων		ἰχθύων
	Dat.		πόλεσι(ν)		πρέσβεσι(ν)		ἄστεσι(ν)		ἰχθύσι(ν)
	Acc.		πόλεις		πρέσβεις		ἄστη		ἰχθύας, ἰχθῦς
	Voc.		πόλεις		πρέσβεις		ἄστη		ἰχθύες

The accent on the genitive sing. and plural of πόλις seems to violate normal rules. The gen. sing. form was originally πόληος, with the regular ending. However, the length of the last two vowels was switched, lengthening the **o** and shortening the **η** (a process called *quantitative metathesis*). The accent was not adjusted to the new form; the gen. plural copies the singular.

2. Principal parts of labial stem verbs

The stems of these verbs end in -**π**, -**β**, -**φ**. When a labial consonant is followed by **σ**, the result is **ψ** (Ch. 1.2, 8.1). Here are the first four principal parts of the labial stem verbs you have learned:

PRESENT	FUTURE	AORIST ACT.	PERFECT ACT.
βλάπτω	βλάψω	ἔβλαψα	βέβλαφα
γράφω	γράψω	ἔγραψα	γέγραφα
κόπτω	κόψω	ἔκοψα	κέκοφα
κρύπτω	κρύψω	ἔκρυψα	κέκρυφα
λείπω	λείψω	ἔλιπον[1]	λέλοιπα
πέμπω	πέμψω	ἔπεμψα	πέπομφα
πίπτω	πεσοῦμαι[2]	ἔπεσον	πέπτωκα
τύπτω	τύψω/τυπτήσω	ἔτυψα/ἔτυπον	—

3. Elision of δέ, τε, etc.

Conjunctions like δέ, τε and ἀλλά, and two-syllable prepositions like ἀπό and μετά, are among the words that can drop their last letter when the next word begins with a vowel. (You already know that prepositions behave this way in compound verbs; Ch. 10.3). The elision is marked by an apostrophe: ἡ δ᾽ οἰκία, οἱοί τ᾽ εἰσιν, μετ᾽ αὐτοῦ. When the following vowel has a rough breathing, an unvoiced consonant (π, τ, κ) will shift to its aspirated form (φ, θ, χ): ὁ θ᾽ ἡγεμών, μεθ᾽ ἕξ ἡμέρας.

EXERCISE 57.

1. εἰ ἐπέμψαμεν πρέσβεις εἰς τὴν πόλιν αὐτῶν, εἰρήνην νῦν ἂν εἴχομεν.
2. οἱ πολέμιοι οὐκ ἔβλαψαν οὔτε τοὺς παῖδας οὔτε τοὺς γέροντας.
3. οἱ γέροντες ἔτυψαν τοὺς Πέρσας λίθοις.
4. οἱ παῖδες κεκρύφασι τὰ χρήματα ἐν τῇ ὕλῃ.
5. οἱ δ᾽ Ἀθηναῖοι ἔγραψαν τὰ τῶν στρατιωτῶν ὀνόματα ἐν λίθῳ.
6. οἱ πολέμιοι κατέλιπον ἐν τῷ ἄστει τὰ ὅπλα ἃ ἔλαβον.
7. ὁ στρατηγὸς αὐτὸς ἐπιστολὴν γέγραφε περὶ τῆς νίκης.
8. πεπόμφαμεν δέκα ἵππους εἰς τὸ ἄστυ.
9. ἐλίπομεν τοὺς μικροὺς ἰχθῦς ἐν τῇ θαλάσσῃ.
10. οὐκ ἰσχυρὰ ἦν ἡ τοῦ ναυτικοῦ δύναμις· ὀλίγαι γὰρ ἦσαν αἱ τριήρεις.

EXERCISE 58.

1. The cavalry whom we were pursuing hid their horses in the wood.
2. The Persians will damage the city, but they will not destroy it.
3. The men whom the general drew up on the wall will hit the enemy with stones.
4. The ambassador has written five letters to the Athenians.
5. The Athenians sent their allies' children out of the city.
6. The enemy struck the gate with stones.
7. The young man found a fish and he will send it to her.
8. The power of the orator's words was small.
9. The Athenians have sent ambassadors to the Persians.
10. The Spartans had few towns.

---

[1]   Strong aorist; see Ch. 10.8 for conjugation.
[2]   See Ch. 21.4 for future conjugation.

Review Exercises

EXERCISE 59.

1. φυλάξομεν τὰς τῆς πόλεως πύλας.
2. εἰ οἱ τοῦ ῥήτορος λόγοι μὴ ἔπεισαν τοὺς πολίτας, μωροὶ ἦσαν.
3. οὐ ῥᾴδιον ἦν τῷ γίγαντι διώκειν τοὺς ναύτας.
4. ὁ Θεμιστοκλῆς ἔπεισε τοὺς Ἀθηναίους τῷ ναυτικῷ πιστεύειν.
5. ἠναγκάσατε τοὺς πολεμίους διαβαίνειν τὸν ποταμόν;
6. ὁ Λεωνίδας ἦρχε τῶν Λακεδαιμονίων ἐν τῇ μάχῃ.
7. τὰ τῶν πολεμίων ὅπλα ἀπέκρυψε τὸν ἥλιον.
8. οἱ πολέμιοι οὐκ ἔλαβον τὰς καμήλους αἳ ἐτάραξαν τοὺς ἵππους.
9. χαλεπὸν ἦν ἀναγκάζειν τοὺς ἵππους ἐν τῇ μάχῃ μένειν.
10. ὁ κῆρυξ ἧκεν εἰς τὴν Σπάρτην τῇ δευτέρᾳ ἡμέρᾳ.

EXERCISE 60.

1. It is not easy to invade Greece, for there are high mountains there.
2. The three hundred men on the wall were not in danger.
3. Pericles managed the affairs of the Athenians.
4. Ten triremes will be ready in three months.
5. The old man to whom I sent the letter is worthy of honor.
6. I ordered the boy not to hit the horse, and he escaped into the house.
7. If the enemy were already on the mountain, we would be fleeing.
8. The boy threw the small fish which he caught into the sea.
9. The Athenians admire wisdom, the Spartans courage.
10. Demosthenes persuaded the citizens themselves to march against the enemy.

EXERCISE 61.

THE TEN THOUSAND REACH THE SEA

In 401 BC Cyrus the Younger rebels against his brother Artaxerxes, king of Persia, with the aid of Greek mercenaries. Cyrus is killed at the battle of Cunaxa, not far from Babylon. Xenophon, who is chosen as one of the leaders of the Greeks, describes their return to the sea.

μετὰ δὲ τὸν πόλεμον ὁ Ξενοφῶν ἤγαγε τοὺς Ἕλληνας διὰ τῆς Ἀρμενίας. ἧκον δ' εἰς χώραν καλήν, ἧς ὁ ἄρχων τοῖς Ἕλλησιν ἡγεμόνα ἔπεμψεν. καὶ ὁ ἡγεμών, Πέντε ἡμερῶν, ἔφη, ἄξω τὸ στράτευμα εἰς χωρίον ὅθεν ἡ θάλασσα ἔσται φανερά. εἰ δὲ μή, ἐθέλω ἀποθανεῖν. οὐ μέντοι τῆς πρὸς τοὺς Ἕλληνας εὐνοίας ἕνεκα ἦγεν αὐτούς· ἡ γὰρ ὁδὸς ἡ τῆς στρατιᾶς ἦν διὰ χώρας ἣ πολεμία ἦν τῷ ἄρχοντι. ἔπεισεν οὖν τοὺς Ἕλληνας ἐν τῇ ὁδῷ αἴθειν καὶ φθείρειν τὴν χώραν. τῇ δὲ πέμπτῃ ἡμέρᾳ ἤγαγεν αὐτοὺς εἰς τὸ ὄρος, ᾧ τὸ ὄνομα ἦν Θήχης. τότε ἔθεον οἱ στρατιῶται, ἐπεὶ δὲ οἱ πρῶτοι ἦσαν ἐπὶ τοῦ ὄρους, ὁ Ξενοφῶν καὶ οἱ μετ' αὐτοῦ ἤκουσαν κραυγὴν μακράν. ὁ δ' οὖν Ξενοφῶν ἀναβαίνει ἐφ' ἵππον καὶ ἀκούει τὴν βοήν, Θάλασσα, θάλασσα. ἐπεὶ δὲ τὸ ὅλον στράτευμα ἧκεν ἐπὶ τὸ ἄκρον, περιέβαλλον ἀλλήλους καὶ στρατηγοὺς καὶ λοχαγοὺς καὶ ἐδάκρυον. καὶ οἱ στρατιῶται ἤνεγκον λίθους, ὡς ἤθελον κολωνὸν παρασκευάζειν. τῷ δὲ ἡγεμόνι παρέσχον δῶρα, ἵππον καὶ φιάλην καὶ σκευὴν Περσικὴν καὶ δαρεικοὺς δέκα, καὶ ἐπεὶ ἑσπέρα ἦν, οἴκαδε αὐτὸν ἀπέπεμψαν.   .

Adapted from Xenophon, *Anabasis*, IV.vii

Chapter 13 Vocabulary

Verbs:

ἀποκρύπτω	hide away	λείπω	leave
καταλείπω	leave behind	ἔλιπον (strong aorist)	
κρύπτω	hide	τύπτω	strike, hit

Nouns:

ἀνδρεία, -ας, ἡ	courage, bravery	λίθος, -ου, ὁ	stone
ἄστυ, ἄστεως, τό	town	ναυτικόν, -οῦ, τό	fleet, navy
δύναμις, -εως, ἡ	power	Περικλῆς, -έους, ὁ	Pericles
ἥλιος, -ου, ὁ	sun	πόλις, -εως, ἡ	city
Θεμιστοκλῆς, -έους, ὁ	Themistocles	πρέσβυς, -εως, ὁ	elder
		πρέσβεις, -εων, οἱ	ambassadors
ἰχθύς, -ύος, ὁ	fish		

Preposition:

περί (+ *gen.*)	about, concerning

Ἄριστον μὲν ὕδωρ, ὁ δὲ χρυσὸς αἰθόμενον πῦρ
ἅτε διαπρέπει νυκτὶ μεγάνορος ἔξοχα πλούτου·
—Pindar, *Olympian* 1.1-2

1. 3rd declension nouns: stems in diphthongs

The long nom. plural ending of the βασιλεύς type is the result of a contraction. That type underwent the same process of quantitative metathesis as the πόλις type (Ch. 13.1).

		king	**ox**	**old woman**
SING.	Nom.	ὁ βασιλεύς	ὁ βοῦς	ἡ γραῦς
	Gen.	βασιλέως	βοός	γρᾱός
	Dat.	βασιλεῖ	βοΐ	γρᾱΐ
	Acc.	βασιλέᾱ	βοῦν	γραῦν
	Voc.	βασιλεῦ	βοῦ	γραῦ
PLUR.	Nom.	βασιλεῖς/ -ῆς	βόες	γρᾶες
	Gen.	βασιλέων	βοῶν	γρᾱῶν
	Dat.	βασιλεῦσι(ν)	βουσί(ν)	γραυσί(ν)
	Acc.	βασιλέᾱς	βοῦς	γραῦς
	Voc.	βασιλεῖς/ -ῆς	βόες	γρᾶες

2. The present and imperfect passive indicative of thematic verbs

So far all the verb forms you have learned belong to the *active voice*, where the subject performs the action. In the *passive voice*, the subject of the verb is the object or receiver of the action: 'the boy is taught', 'the horse is being ridden'. There is a set of passive as well as active endings for each Greek verb tense.

PRESENT: the present passive ('I am loosed', 'I am being loosed') has the same endings as the future tense of εἰμί, 'be' (Ch. 9.2), and uses the thematic vowel.

	SINGULAR		PLURAL	
1st	λύ-ο-μαι	I am loosed	λυ-ό-μεθα	we are loosed
2nd	λύ-ῃ / -ει	you are loosed	λύ-ε-σθε	you are loosed
3rd	λύ-ε-ται	he is loosed	λύ-ο-νται	they are loosed

The 2nd singular ending is -σαι, but σ is weak between vowels and drops out. ε and α contract; thus the proper form should be -ῃ (Ch. 12.4). However, to avoid confusion with the subjunctive, which also ends in -ῃ, -ει is often used in the indicative.

IMPERFECT: The imperfect passive ('I was being loosed') also uses the thematic vowel, and the same consonants as the present passive endings. The 2nd singular ending is -σο, but the σ drops out. When ε contracts with ο the result is -ου.

	SINGULAR			PLURAL	
1st	ἐ-λυ-ό-μην	I was being loosed	ἐ-λυ-ό-μεθα	we were being loosed
2nd	ἐ-λύ-ου	you were being loosed	ἐ-λύ-ε-σθε	you were being loosed
3rd	ἐ-λύ-ε-το	he was being loosed	ἐ-λύ-ο-ντο	they were being loosed

3. Genitive of agent

The person or *agent* responsible for the action of a passive verb is expressed in Greek by the preposition ὑπό and a genitive noun or pronoun. The thing or *instrument* used is expressed by the dative without preposition; this is a version of the dative of means (Ch. 4.7).

διωκόμεθα ὑπὸ τῶν πολεμίων.
    We are being pursued *by the enemy.*

διωκόμεθα ὑπὸ θηρῶν.
    We are being pursued *by wild beasts.*

τὸ τεῖχος βάλλεται λίθοις.
    The wall is pelted *with stones.*

ὁ ναύτης τύπτεται τοῖς ὅπλοις.
    The sailor is struck *by the weapons.*

EXERCISE 62.

1. οἱ δὲ στρατιῶται τάσσονται ὑπὸ τοῦ βασιλέως.
2. ὁ Ξενοφῶν χάριν εἶχε τῷ ἡγεμόνι· ηὗρε γὰρ τὴν ὁδόν.
3. ἡ τῆς πόλεως πύλη φυλάσσεται ὑπὸ τῶν πολεμίων.
4. οἱ δ᾽ ἱππεῖς οὓς ἐδιώκομεν ἔφευγον πρὸς τὸ τεῖχος.
5. ταῖς γραυσὶν ἦν μόνον εἷς ὁδούς.
6. εἰ οἱ πολέμιοι λίθοις ἐτύπτοντο, οὐκ ἂν οἷοί τ᾽ ἦσαν μένειν.
7. πέμπεσθε εἰς τὰς νήσους, ὦ παῖδες;
8. οἱ παῖδες ἤλαυνον τοὺς βοῦς εἰς τὸν λειμῶνα.
9. τὰ τῆς πόλεως ἐπράσσετο ὑπὸ τῶν στρατηγῶν.
10. διωκόμεθα ὑπὸ τῶν βασιλέως[1] ἵππων.

EXERCISE 63.

1. The oxen are being set free by the boy.
2. Ambassadors are being sent by the Persians concerning peace.
3. The king whose army was being pursued by the Greeks destroyed the town.
4. The soldier's helmet is struck by a stone.
5. If their country is ruled by a giant, I do not want to invade it.
6. The cavalry were being led by a faithful guide.
7. The enemy did not harm the old women in the city.
8. The door of the house was being guarded by five soldiers.
9. Themistocles sent a letter to the king of Persia.
10. His daughter was leading the old man through the marketplace.

4. Irregular 3rd declension nouns

Some 3rd declension nouns are irregular, though they mainly have normal 3rd declension endings. 'Zeus' exists only in the singular.

---

1   βασιλεύς without the article means 'the king of Persia'.

			woman		ship		water		Zeus
SING.	Nom.	ἡ	γυνή	ἡ	ναῦς	τὸ	ὕδωρ	ὁ	Ζεύς
	Gen.		γυναικός		νεώς		ὕδατος		Διός
	Dat.		γυναικί		νηΐ		ὕδατι		Διΐ
	Acc.		γυναῖκα		ναῦν		ὕδωρ		Δία
	Voc.		γύναι		ναῦ		ὕδωρ		Ζεῦ
PLUR.	Nom.		γυναῖκες		νῆες		ὕδατα		
	Gen.		γυναικῶν		νεῶν		ὑδάτων		
	Dat.		γυναιξί(ν)		ναυσί(ν)		ὕδασι(ν)		
	Acc.		γυναῖκας		ναῦς		ὕδατα		
	Voc.		γυναῖκες		νῆες		ὕδατα		

5. The aorist and future passive indicative

AORIST: The aorist passive ('I was loosed') is a new principal part, the sixth (Ch. 2.1; the fifth principal part will be presented in Ch. 15.4). From it both the aorist and the future passive are formed. As with the aorist active, some verbs have weak forms and others have strong forms. The formation of strong forms will be presented in Ch. 21.2. The tense marker for the weak aorist passive indicative is -θη-. The endings resemble *active* past tense endings.

	SINGULAR		PLURAL	
1st	ἐ-λύ-θη-ν	I was loosed	ἐ-λύ-θη-μεν	we were loosed
2nd	ἐ-λύ-θη-ς	you were loosed	ἐ-λύ-θη-τε	you were loosed
3rd	ἐ-λύ-θη	he was loosed	ἐ-λύ-θη-σαν	they were loosed

FUTURE: The future passive ('I will be loosed') is formed off the aorist passive stem. It is marked by both the -θη- of this principal part and the -σ- of the future tense. The endings are the same as those of the present passive.

	SINGULAR		PLURAL	
1st	λυ-θή-σ-ο-μαι	I will be loosed	λυ-θη-σ-ό-μεθα	we will be loosed
2nd	λυ-θή-σ-ει / -ῃ	you will be loosed	λυ-θή-σ-ε-σθε	you will be loosed
3rd	λυ-θή-σ-ε-ται	he will be loosed	λυ-θή-σ-ο-νται	they will be loosed

EXERCISE 64.
1. τριῶν ἡμερῶν ἐλύθησαν ὑπὸ τῶν συμμάχων.
2. ἡ ναῦς ἐκωλύθη τῷ χειμῶνι.
3. οἱ Πέρσαι οἳ ἔφευγον οὐκ ἐκωλύθησαν ὑπὸ τῶν Λακεδαιμονίων.
4. πέμπετε τάς τε γυναῖκας καὶ τοὺς παῖδας ἐκ τῆς πόλεως.
5. οἱ νεανίαι παιδευθήσονται εἰς τὸν πόλεμον.
6. οἱ ἱερεῖς ἔθυον τὸν βοῦν τῷ Διΐ.
7. ἀγαθός μέν ἐστιν ὁ οἶνος, ἄριστον δὲ τὸ ὕδωρ.
8. ἡ ναυμαχία ἐπαύθη ὑπὸ βασιλέως.
9. εἰ ὁ Ἄδμητος μὴ ἔπεισε τὴν γυναῖκα ἀποθνήσκειν, αὐτὸς ἂν ἀπέθανεν.
10. τῇ ἑσπέρᾳ οἱ βόες ἀπὸ τῶν ζυγῶν λυθήσονται.

EXERCISE 65.
1. Was the faithful slave set free by his master?
2. The women were hindered by the children on the journey.
3. The horses which were trained by the cavalry are good in battle.
4. The war will be stopped by the king.

5. It is difficult for the soldiers to find water in the island.
6. The god whom the Greeks used to worship was Zeus.
7. Admetus was set free from death by his wife.
8. The ships will not be hindered by the storm.
9. Themistocles was trusted by the Athenians.
10. The cities sent earth and water[1] to the king of Persia.

EXERCISE 66.

THE CUNNING OF ARTEMISIA

The following episode took place at the battle of Salamis, where in 480 BC the Greeks defeated the Persian fleet.

παρῆν δὲ ἐν τῇ ναυμαχίᾳ ἡ τῶν Ἁλικαρνασσέων[2] βασίλεια, ὀνόματι Ἀρτεμισία. ἐπεὶ δ᾽ αἱ τῶν Περσῶν νῆες ἐπιέζοντο καὶ μάλιστα ἐβλάπτοντο ὑπὸ τῶν Ἑλλήνων, ἡ τῆς Ἀρτεμισίας ναῦς ἐδιώκετο ὑπὸ νεὼς Ἀττικῆς· ἐπεὶ δ᾽ ἡ Ἀρτεμισία οὐχ οἵα τ᾽ ἦν διαφυγεῖν (ἔμπροσθε γὰρ αὐτῆς ἦσαν ἄλλαι νῆες φίλιαι), ἐκέλευσεν τοὺς ναύτας ἐμβάλλειν νηὶ φιλίᾳ. ὡς δὲ ἐνέβαλέ τε καὶ κατέδυσεν αὐτὴν, εὐτυχίᾳ ἡ βασιλεία διπλᾶ ἑαυτὴν ἀγαθὰ ἔπραξεν. ὁ μὲν γὰρ τῆς Ἀττικῆς νεὼς τριήραρχος ἐνόμισε τὴν ναῦν τὴν τῆς Ἀρτεμισίας ἢ Ἑλληνικὴν εἶναι ἢ τοὺς ναύτας αὐτομόλους εἶναι ἐκ τῶν βαρβάρων. οὐκέτι οὖν ἐδίωκεν αὐτήν, ἀλλ᾽ ἐνέβαλλεν ἄλλαις ναυσίν· καὶ οὕτως ἡ Ἀρτεμισία ἐκ τῆς μάχης διέφυγεν.

τὸ δὲ τῆς βασιλείας ἔργον οὐκ ἐλάνθανε τὸν Ξέρξην· βασιλεὺς γὰρ αὐτὸς ἐν ὑψηλῷ θρόνῳ ἐπὶ τῆς ἀκτῆς ἐκάθιζεν. λέγει δέ τις τῶν μετ᾽ αὐτοῦ· Δέσποτα, ἡ Ἀρτεμισία ναῦν τῶν πολεμίων κατέδυσεν. ὁ δὲ Ξέρξης πρῶτον μὲν οὐκ ἐπίστευεν αὐτῷ, τέλος δ᾽ ἐπείθετο· μάλιστα δ᾽ ἐθαύμαζε τὴν τῆς βασιλείας ἀρετήν. Οἱ μὲν ἄνδρες, ἔφη, νῦν εἰσι γυναῖκες, αἱ δὲ γυναῖκες ἄνδρες.

Adapted from Herodotus VIII.87-88

Chapter 14 Vocabulary

Nouns:

βασιλεύς, -έως, ὁ	king	ἱερεύς, -έως, ὁ	priest
βοῦς, βοός, ὁ/ἡ	ox	ἱππεύς, -έως, ὁ	cavalryman
γραῦς, γραός, ἡ	old woman	ἱππεῖς, -έων, οἱ	cavalry
γυνή, γυναικός, ἡ	woman, wife	ναυμαχία, -ας, ἡ	sea battle
ἐρέτης, -ου, ὁ	rower	ναῦς, νεώς, ἡ	ship
Ζεύς, Διός, ὁ	Zeus	ὕδωρ, ὕδατος, τό	water

Adjectives:

ἄριστος, -η, -ον	best	διακόσιοι, -αι, α	two hundred

Adverb:

μόνον	only

Preposition:

ὑπό	by (+ *gen.* of agent)

---

[1] A traditional symbol of surrender.
[2] Herodotus was born in Halicarnassus, a city in Caria, in Asia Minor (modern Turkey).

CHAPTER 15

1. Regular comparison of adjectives

The *comparative* in Greek shares its English meaning: 'wiser', 'more wise'. It can also mean 'fairly wise'. The *superlative* shares the English meaning: 'wisest', 'most wise'. It can also mean 'very wise'. Some adjectives in English form the comparative by adding **-er** to the *positive* form, and the superlative by adding -est: wise, wiser, wisest. These are the regular forms. Other adjectives are irregular in form: bad, worse, worst. Greek also has both regular and irregular forms of comparison; this chapter deals with regular comparison.

The regular comparative and superlative in Greek are declined like 1st and 2nd declension adjectives. The comparative ending is -τερος, -τερα, -τερον; the superlative ends in -τατος, -τατη, -τατον. These endings are attached directly to the ο which ends the adjective stem. This ο may be long or short, depending on the length of the previous syllable:

previous syllable long / short **ο**	previous syllable short / long **ο**
μωρός, -ά, -όν / μωρότερος	σοφός, -ή, -όν / σοφώτερος

Usually the length of a syllable is clear; long vowels and diphthongs (including αι and οι) make long syllables, short vowels make short syllables (Ch. 1.4). A syllable is also long if the vowel is followed by two consonants (πιστός) or by a double consonant (ζ, ξ, ψ).

If the vowel in a syllable is α, ι or υ, you will not be able to tell its length just by looking at it. The following is a list of such adjectives you have had so far, which form their comparatives and superlatives in the regular way. The long (ῡ) and short (ῠ) vowels are marked in the positive form.

POSITIVE		COMPARATIVE	SUPERLATIVE
ἄξῐος, -α, -ον	worthy	ἀξιώτερος, -α, -ον	ἀξιώτατος, -η, -ον
ἰσχῡρός, -ά, -όν	strong	ἰσχυρότερος, -α, -ον	ἰσχυρότατος, -η, -ον
μᾱκρός, -ά, -όν	long	μακρότερος, -α, -ον	μακρότατος, -η, -ον
μῑκρός, -ά, -όν	small	μικρότερος, -α, -ον	μικρότατος, -η, -ον
πλούσῐος, -α, -ον	rich	πλουσιώτερος, -α, -ον	πλουσιώτατος, -η, -ον
φίλῐος, -α, -ον	friendly	φιλιώτερος, -α, -ον	φιλιώτατος, -η, -ον
χρήσῐμος, -η ον	useful	χρησιμώτερος, -α, -ον	χρησιμώτατος, -η, -ον

2. The use of ἤ and the genitive of comparison

There are two ways in Greek to form a comparison ('X is *bigger than* Y'). One is to use the word ἤ, 'than'.

οἱ Ἕλληνες ἔχουσι μικρότερον ναυτικὸν ἢ οἱ βάρβαροι.
The Greeks have a smaller fleet <u>than the foreigners</u>.

In this construction the two nouns compared must be in the same case. Compare the following sentences:

1. a)   αἱ κάμηλοι δεινότεραι ἦσαν τοῖς στρατιώταις <u>ἢ οἱ ναῦται</u>.
        The camels were more terrible to the soldiers <u>than the sailors (were)</u>.

  b)   αἱ κάμηλοι δεινότεραι ἦσαν τοῖς στρατιώταις <u>ἢ τοῖς ναύταις</u>.
        The camels were more terrible to the soldiers <u>than (to) the sailors</u>.

2. a)   ἡ τοῦ ποιητοῦ γυνὴ σοφωτέρα ἐστὶν <u>ἢ ἡ τοῦ δούλου</u>.
        The poet's wife is wiser <u>than the slave's (wife)</u>.

  b)   ἡ τοῦ ποιητοῦ γυνὴ σοφωτέρα ἐστὶν <u>ἢ ὁ δοῦλος</u>.
        The poet's wife is wiser <u>than the slave</u>.

The other way to express the comparison 'X is bigger than Y' is with the *genitive of comparison*. In this construction 'than Y' is expressed by the genitive (without a preposition).

ὁ Σωκράτης σοφώτερος ἦν <u>τῶν ἄλλων</u>.
Socrates was wiser <u>than the others</u>.

3. Genitive with the superlative

The genitive is also used with the superlative, just as in English:

ὁ Σωκράτης ἦν σοφώτατος <u>τῶν Ἀθηναίων</u>.
Socrates was wisest <u>of the Athenians</u>.

4. The perfect and pluperfect passive indicative

PERFECT: The perfect passive is the fifth principal part of the verb (Ch. 2.1). From it are formed the perfect passive ('I have been loosed') and the pluperfect passive ('I had been loosed'). Because the perfect is a primary tense, it has primary endings, just like the perfect active (Ch. 6.4). These are attached directly to the stem without the thematic vowel; the only marker is the reduplication or lengthening (Ch. 6.4, 10.6) which starts the word:

	SINGULAR		PLURAL	
1st	λέ-λυ-μαι	I have been loosed	λε-λύ-μεθα	we have been loosed
2nd	λέ-λυ-σαι	you have been loosed	λέ-λυ-σθε	you have been loosed
3rd	λέ-λυ-ται	he has been loosed	λέ-λυ-νται	they have been loosed

Note: For stems beginning with an aspirated stop (φ, θ, χ), the reduplication uses the unvoiced equivalent (π, τ, κ): τέθυμαι from θύω (Ch. 6.4).

PLUPERFECT: The pluperfect passive is formed off the perfect principal part. The secondary endings are attached directly to the stem.

	SINGULAR		PLURAL	
1st	ἐ-λε-λύ-μην	I had been loosed	ἐ-λε-λύ-μεθα	we had been loosed
2nd	ἐ-λέ-λυ-σο	you had been loosed	ἐ-λέ-λυ-σθε	you had been loosed
3rd	ἐ-λέ-λυ-το	he had been loosed	ἐ-λέ-λυ-ντο	they had been loosed

EXERCISE 67.

1. οἱ Λακεδαιμόνιοι ἀνδρειότεροί εἰσι τῶν Περσῶν.
2. ὁ πιστότατος δοῦλος λέλυται ὑπὸ τοῦ δεσπότου.
3. ὁ Ἡρακλῆς ἦν ἰσχυρότατος τῶν τότε.
4. οἱ νεανίαι οἳ πεπαίδευνται ἐν ταῖς Ἀθήναις σοφώτατοί εἰσιν.
5. αἱ τριακόσιαι κάμηλοι δεινότεραι ἦσαν τοῖς στρατιώταις ἢ τὰ ὅπλα.
6. αἱ τριήρεις τρεῖς ἡμέρας ἐκεκώλυντο τῷ χειμῶνι.
7. ὁ χειμὼν ἦν χαλεπώτερος τοῖς Πέρσαις ἢ τοῖς Ἀθηναίοις.
8. ἡ δὲ μάχη ἐπέπαυτο τῇ νυκτί.
9. ἡ Ἄλκηστίς ἐστιν ἡ ἀξιωτάτη γυναικῶν, ἢ τῶν νῦν ἢ τῶν τότε.
10. οὔπω λελύμεθα ὑπὸ τοῦ φύλακος.

EXERCISE 68.

1. We have been trained by the general who led the Athenians into battle.
2. Herakles was stronger than either the lion or the other animals.
3. The yokes of the oxen have been loosed.
4. We are not wiser than Socrates.
5. Those with Odysseus had been hindered by the giant.
6. We are hurrying by a more difficult road (*use dative*) than the enemy.
7. The prisoners had not yet been set free.
8. The navy was very useful in the war.
9. The war has been stopped by the winter.
10. The city itself was more ancient than the walls.

EXERCISE 69.

1. οἱ Ἀθηναῖοι ἐλευθερώτεροι ἦσαν τῶν Λακεδαιμονίων.
2. οἱ ἄλλοι νεανίαι ἐπεπαίδευντο εἰς χαλεπώτατον ἀγῶνα.
3. οὐδένα φίλον ἔχομεν δικαιότερον ἢ τὸν Σωκράτη.
4. οἱ δ᾽ ἐν τῇ νήσῳ οὐ λέλυνται ὑπὸ τῶν Λακεδαιμονίων.
5. αἱ νῆες βεβαιότεραι ἦσαν ἢ τὸ τεῖχος.
6. ἡ οἰκία χρησίμη ἐστὶν ἢ θέρει ἢ χειμῶνι.
7. νομίζομεν τοὺς Λακεδαιμονίους ἀνδρειοτέρους ἢ τοὺς Πέρσας.
8. αἱ Ἀθῆναι κατελέλυντο ὑπὸ τῶν Περσῶν.
9. ἐλευθερώτατοί ἐσμεν τῶν Ἑλλήνων.
10. εκωλύμεθα ὑψηλοτάτῳ ὄρει.

EXERCISE 70.

1. If Socrates was the wisest of the Greeks, the bravest was Leonidas.
2. The women have been hindered by the children.
3. Some men are wiser, others are stronger.
4. The river was more dangerous than the mountain.
5. An ox had been sacrificed to the goddess.
6. A stronger army has been trained by the Spartans than by the Athenians.
7. The judges think the old woman wiser than the others.
8. Was Alcestis more worthy of honor than her husband?
9. The horses have not yet been loosed.
10. The richest men are not always the wisest.

EXERCISE 71.

HOW THE EGYPTIANS AVOIDED GNATS

ἐν δὲ τῇ Αἰγύπτῳ εἰσὶ κώνωπες πλεῖστοι. οἱ μὲν οὖν Αἰγύπτιοι οἳ τὰς κώμας ἄνω τῶν λιμνῶν ἔχουσι τῆς νυκτὸς ἀναβαίνουσιν εἰς πύργους ὑψηλοὺς καὶ ἐκεῖ καθεύδουσιν· οἱ γὰρ κώνωπες ὑπὸ τῶν ἀνέμων οὐχ οἷοί τ' εἰσιν ἀναβαίνειν ἐκεῖσε· οἱ δὲ περὶ τὰς λίμνας Αἰγύπτιοι ἀντὶ τῶν πύργων τὰ σώματα ὧδε φυλάσσουσιν· πᾶς ἀνὴρ αὐτῶν ἀμφίβληστρον ἔχει, ᾧ τῆς μὲν ἡμέρας ἰχθῦς θηρεύει, τῆς δὲ νυκτὸς περὶ κοίτην βάλλει τὸ ἀμφίβληστρον καὶ ὑπ' αὐτῷ καθεύδει. οἱ δὲ κώνωπες, εἴ τις μόνον ἐν ἱματίῳ καθεύδει, δι' αὐτοῦ δάκνουσιν, διὰ δὲ τοῦ ἀμφιβλήστρου οὔ.

Adapted from Herodotus II.95

Chapter 15 Vocabulary

Verbs:

νομίζω	think	σπεύδω	hasten, hurry

Nouns:

Ἄλκηστις, -ιδος, ἡ	Alcestis	Ὀδυσσεύς, -έως, ὁ	Odysseus
Ἡρακλῆς, -έους, ὁ	Herakles		

Adjectives:

ἀρχαῖος, -α, -ον	ancient	βέβαιος, -α, -ον	sure, trusty
ἄλλος, -η, -ο	other, another (endings as rel. pronoun)		

Adverbs:

οὔπω	not yet	τότε	then

Conjunction:

ἤ	or, than	ἤ...ἤ	either...or

CHAPTER 16

1. The middle voice: meaning

In addition to the active and passive, Greek has a third voice, appropriately called the *middle*. It has several connotations that distinguish it from the active voice.

1) The most straightforward is its reflexive (or intransitive) sense. For example παύω, 'I stop (someone else)'; παύομαι, 'I cease/stop (myself)'. Many active verbs have middle forms for this reflexive use, which can also be extended as follows:

a) what you do to yourself (English reflexive):

παύομαι	I stop (myself)/cease from
παύομαι τοῦ πολέμου.	I cease from the war.
παύω τὸν πόλεμον.	I stop the war.

b) what you do for yourself (in your own interest):

λαμβάνομαι ἰχθύν.	I catch myself a fish.
λαμβάνω ἰχθύν.	I catch a fish.

c) what you get someone to do for you (in your own interest):

διδάσκομαι τὸν υἱόν.	I have my son taught.
διδάσκω τὸν υἱόν.	I teach my son.

2) Some verbs have *only* middle forms, in some or all tenses. For example: δέχομαι, 'receive', μάχομαι, 'fight' (+ *dat.* = 'fight against'). The meaning is still active, even though the forms are not. Such verbs are called *deponent* verbs.

3) Other verbs take on a special meaning in the middle which is different from their meaning in the active. For example: πείθω, 'I persuade'; πείθομαι, 'I obey' (+ *dat.*). For the Greeks, obedience was linked to persuasion, rather than to compulsion.

2. The middle voice: formation

Even though the translation of a middle form sounds active in meaning, the formation is different from the active.

PRESENT, IMPERFECT; PERFECT, PLUPERFECT. The indicative middle endings are identical to the passive in the present and imperfect (Ch. 14.2), and in the perfect and pluperfect (Ch. 15.4). Translation of these tenses will thus depend on context and common sense:

Middle	Passive
διδασκόμεθα τοὺς υἱούς.	διδασκόμεθα ἐν τῇ κώμῃ.
We have our sons taught.	We are taught in the village.
ἐπείθετο τοῖς νόμοις.	ἐπείθετο ὑπὸ τοῦ ῥήτορος.
He was obeying the laws.	He was being persuaded by the orator.
πέπαυνται τοῦ πολέμου.	πέπαυνται ὑπὸ τῶν πολεμίων.
They have ceased from the war.	They have been stopped by the enemy.

FUTURE. The future middle is formed by adding primary middle/passive endings to the future active stem (2nd principal part):

	Singular	Plural
1st	λύ-σ-ο-μαι	λυ-σ-ό-μεθα
2nd	λύ-σ-ει / -ῃ (-ε-σαι)	λύ-σ-ε-σθε
3rd	λύ-σ-ε-ται	λύ-σ-ο-νται

AORIST. The aorist middle is formed by adding secondary middle/passive endings to the aorist active stem (3rd principal part). Here are the paradigms for the first (weak) aorist of λύομαι, 'ransom', and the second (strong) aorist of πείθομαι, 'obey'.

	Singular	Plural
1st	ἐ-λυ-σά-μην	ἐ-λυ-σά-μεθα
2nd	ἐ-λύ-σω (-σα-σο)	ἐ-λύ-σα-σθε
3rd	ἐ-λύ-σα-το	ἐ-λύ-σα-ντο

	Singular	Plural
1st	ἐ-πιθ-ό-μην	ἐ-πιθ-ό-μεθα
2nd	ἐ-πίθ-ου (-ε-σο)	ἐ-πίθ-ε-σθε
3rd	ἐ-πίθ-ε-το	ἐ-πίθ-ο-ντο

EXERCISE 72.

1. λυσόμεθα τοὺς ἐν τῇ νήσῳ.
2. οἱ Πέρσαι ἐβουλεύοντο περὶ τῆς εἰρήνης.
3. εἰ τὸ τῶν Ἑλλήνων στράτευμα πρὸς τὴν θάλασσαν ἐπορεύετο, οἱ πολέμιοι οὐκ ἂν ἐστράτευον ἐπὶ τοὺς Ἀθηναίους.
4. ἡ μάχη οὐ παύσεται πρὸ τῆς ἑσπέρας.
5. ὁ νεανίας φέρεται καλὰ ἆθλα ἐν τοῖς ἀγῶσιν.
6. οἱ παῖδες ἐπαύσαντο τοῦ ἔργου.
7. οὐκ ἐπιθόμεθα τοῖς τοῦ ῥήτορος λόγοις.
8. οἱ Ἕλληνες ἐστρατοπεδεύσαντο παρὰ τῷ ποταμῷ.
9. οἱ Ἀθηναῖοι ἐμάχοντο τοῖς Πέρσαις ὑπὲρ τῆς πατρίδος.
10. οἱ στρατιῶται εἶχον τὸ στρατόπεδον ἐγγὺς τῆς κώμης.

EXERCISE 73.

1. We ransomed the general who was a prisoner of the Persians.
2. The soldiers were marching to the gates of the city.
3. Wise men obey the laws.
4. The old men deliberated about the war for five days.
5. We shall cease from the battle before night.

6. We get our children taught in Athens.
7. The Persians were fighting the Greeks.
8. We encamped outside the walls of the city.
9. The general ransomed the prisoners after the battle.
10. The Athenian poet is winning the prize.

3. Infinitives of thematic verbs (present and aorist)

The infinitive ('to loose', 'to persuade' etc.) is a *verbal noun*. That is, it has some features of a verb, but in other ways it is like a noun.

verb features:
  • tense (present, future, etc.)
  • voice (active, middle, passive)
  • it can have a subject and an object

noun features:
  • it can be the subject of a sentence, 'To fight is dangerous.'
  • accent is fixed, not recessive

Greek infinitives exist in the present, future, aorist and perfect tenses, and in all three voices; you already know the present active infinitive (Ch. 8.4). The following summary shows how to form and accent the present and aorist infinitive. The future and perfect tenses will be presented in Ch. 17.3. Note that unlike the indicative, the aorist infinitive has no augment.

PRESENT

Active:	present stem + ε + -εν	= -ειν	λύειν, πείθειν
Mid./Pass.:	present stem + ε + -σθαι	= -εσθαι	λύεσθαι, πείθεσθαι

accent: on the last syllable of the verb stem

WEAK AORIST

Active:	aorist stem + -αι	= -σαι	λῦσαι, πεῖσαι
Middle:	aorist stem + -σθαι	= -σασθαι	λύσασθαι
Passive:	aorist stem + -ναι	= -θηναι	λυθῆναι

accent: active/middle: on the last syllable of the verb stem; passive: on the -θη-

STRONG AORIST

Active:	aorist stem + ε + -εν	= -ειν	ἀγαγεῖν
Middle:	aorist stem + ε + -σθαι	= -εσθαι	πιθέσθαι

accent: on the -ε-

4. Infinitives of εἰμί, 'be'

The present infinitive of εἰμί is εἶναι; the future is ἔσεσθαι. There is no aorist or perfect tense of this verb.

5. Aspect

The *aspect* of a verb shows whether it describes a single, simple act or an ongoing or repeated action. In the indicative, the difference between the imperfect (ongoing action) and the aorist (single act) is one of aspect. In the other moods (imperative, subjunctive, optative), and in many uses of the infinitive and participle, this same distinction is made between the present (ongoing action) and the aorist (single act). Even word formation can reflect this difference. For example, you saw in Ch. 10.5 that ἔχω has two future forms:

> ἕξω (present stem) = ongoing aspect: 'have (and go on having)'
> σχήσω (aorist stem) = single aspect: '(acquire and) have'.

Aspect is always a factor in using complementary infinitives. You learned the present tense of these infinitives in Ch. 8.4. However, both present and aorist complementary infinitive can refer to present time: the aorist infinitive describes a single act and the present infinitive an ongoing action. It does not matter what tense the main verb is.

Note: The negative used with all complementary infinitives is μή, not οὐ.

> ἐκέλευσα τοὺς ἄνδρας μὴ διῶξαι τὸν ἵππον.
> I ordered the men not to pursue the horse. (single act)

> ἐκέλευσα τοὺς ἄνδρας ἀεὶ διώκειν τὴν τιμήν.
> I ordered the men always to keep pursuing honor. (ongoing action)

6. Use of the imperfect and aorist indicative

Some verbs naturally imply a single, simple act: παύω, 'stop'. These occur in the aorist much more often than the imperfect. Other verbs naturally imply an ongoing action: μέλλω, 'intend'; μένω, 'remain'; φαίνομαι, 'appear'. In the following exercises, use the imperfect, not the aorist, for the past tense of these verbs.

7. More principal parts

Some of the verbs in recent lessons have irregular principal parts. A full list will be presented in Ch. 21.3, but the following may be useful now.

PRESENT	FUTURE A/M	AORIST A/M	PERFECT A	PERFECT M/P	AORIST P
ἀποθνῄσκω	ἀποθανοῦμαι[1]	ἀπέθανον	ἀποτέθνηκα	——	——
λαμβάνω	λήψομαι	ἔλαβον	εἴληφα	εἴλημμαι	ἐλήφθην
μάχομαι	μαχοῦμαι[1]	ἐμαχεσάμην	——	μεμάχημαι	——
μέλλω	μελλήσω	ἐμέλλησα	——	——	——
πείθομαι	πείσομαι	ἐπιθόμην	——	πέπεισμαι	——
σῴζω	σώσω	ἔσωσα	σέσωκα	σέσω(σ)μαι	ἐσώθην
φαίνομαι	φανοῦμαι[1]	——	——	πέφασμαι	ἐφάνθην

EXERCISE 74.

1. ἀκούετε τοῦ πρέσβεως εἰ ἐθέλετε λύσασθαι τοὺς αἰχμαλώτους.
2. κακόν ἐστι μὴ πείθεσθαι τοῖς νόμοις.
3. ὁ Ξέρξης ἐκέλευσε τοὺς λοχαγοὺς παρασκευάζειν μὲν τὰς ναῦς, μαχέσασθαι δὲ τοῖς Ἕλλησιν.
4. ὁ ποιητὴς ἄξιός ἐστι δέξασθαι τὸ ἆθλον.
5. ἐπείσαμεν τοὺς Λακεδαιμονίους πέμψαι τὸ στράτευμα.
6. ἡ Ἄλκηστις ἀπέθανεν ὑπὲρ τοῦ ἀνδρός.
7. αἰσχρὸν ἦν τῷ Κροίσῳ κωλυθῆναι ὑπὸ τῶν καμήλων.
8. ὁ Σωκράτης ἐφαίνετο εἶναι σοφώτατος.
9. οὐχ οἷοί τ' ἐσόμεθα παύσασθαι τῆς ναυμαχίας πρὸ τῆς νυκτός.
10. οἱ Ἀθηναῖοι ἤθελον λαβεῖν τοὺς βοῦς οἳ ἀπέφυγον ἀπὸ τοῦ λειμῶνος.

---

[1] Liquid futures; for conjugation, see Ch. 21.4.

EXERCISE 75.

1. The general ordered the soldiers to save both the women and the children.
2. We are not able to send the army immediately.
3. It will be difficult to cease from work before night.
4. The Spartans wanted to pursue the enemy, but the other Greeks prevented them.
5. It was fine for them to be educated by Socrates.
6. The citizens appeared to be friendly.
7. We persuaded the Armenians to send a guide.
8. It was difficult to encamp on the mountain.
9. The enemy were not willing to ransom the prisoners.
10. It was shameful to leave the old man behind.

8. Contract adjectives

The stem of certain adjectives ends in the vowel ε, which contracts with the vowel of the ending. You have seen several instances of contraction already. ε contracts in adjectives with other vowels as follows:

$$\varepsilon + \alpha = \bar{\alpha}, \eta \qquad \varepsilon + o = ov$$
$$\varepsilon + \eta = \eta \qquad \varepsilon + \omega = \omega$$

The reading in this chapter uses the contract adjective ἀργυροῦς, 'silver'. You will see from its declension that when an accented syllable is involved in a contraction, the accent stays on the contracted syllable, and follows the accent rule for that position. In the nominative masculine singular, the accented syllable was originally the penult; after contraction it is the ultima, so the accent becomes circumflex. The usual exception for nominatives and accusatives does not apply to contracted syllables. The long α in the feminine singular remains α because of the preceding ρ; contrast χρυσοῦς, χρυσῆ, χρυσοῦν, 'gold'. No vocative forms occur.

		M	F	N
SING.	Nom.	ἀργυροῦς (-έος)	ἀργυρᾶ (-έα)	ἀργυροῦν (-έον)
	Gen.	ἀργυροῦ	ἀργυρᾶς	ἀργυροῦ
	Dat.	ἀργυρῷ	ἀργυρᾷ	ἀργυρῷ
	Acc.	ἀργυροῦν	ἀργυρᾶν	ἀργυροῦν
PLUR.	Nom.	ἀργυροῖ	ἀργυραῖ	ἀργυρᾶ
	Gen.	ἀργυρῶν	ἀργυρῶν	ἀργυρῶν
	Dat.	ἀργυροῖς	ἀργυραῖς	ἀργυροῖς
	Acc.	ἀργυροῦς	ἀργυρᾶς	ἀργυρᾶ

EXERCISE 76.

VICTORY IN BAD WEATHER

Here are further episodes in the march of the Ten Thousand.

ἕως δὲ οἱ Ἕλληνες στρατοπεδεύονται, τῆς νυκτὸς ἐπιπίπτει χιὼν πλείστη, ἣ ἀπέκρυψε καὶ τὰ ὅπλα καὶ τοὺς ἀνθρώπους· καὶ τὰ ὑποζύγια ἐκώλυσεν ἡ χιών· οἱ δὲ στρατιῶται ἐν ἀθυμίᾳ ἦσαν. ἐπεὶ δὲ Ξενοφῶν ἐτόλμησε γυμνὸς ἀναστῆναι [to get up] καὶ σχίζειν ξύλα, εὐθὺς καὶ ἄλλοι ἔσχιζον καὶ πῦρ ἔκαιον. ἔπειτα δὲ ὁ Ξενοφῶν ἐκέλευσε τοὺς στρατιώτας ἀπολιπεῖν τὸ χωρίον οὗ ἐστρατοπεδεύοντο, καὶ σπεύδειν εἰς τὰς κώμας εἰς στέγας.

ἀγγέλλει δ᾽ αὐτοῖς αἰχμάλωτός τις ὅτι πολέμιοι ἐγγύς εἰσι καὶ μέλλουσιν αὐτοῖς προσβαλεῖν ἐν τῇ τοῦ ὄρους εἰσβολῇ. οἱ οὖν στρατηγοὶ συνήγαγον τὸ στράτευμα ἀπὸ τῶν κωμῶν καὶ ἐκέλευσαν τοὺς μὲν φυλάσσειν τὸ στρατόπεδον, τοὺς δὲ πορεύεσθαι ἐπὶ τοὺς βαρβάρους· ὁ δὲ αἰχμάλωτος ἡγεμὼν ἦν αὐτοῖς. ἐπεὶ δὲ ὑπερέβαλλον τὸ ὄρος, οἱ πελτασταὶ οὐκ ἔμενον τοὺς ὁπλίτας, ἀλλὰ κραυγῇ ἔθεον ἐπὶ τὸ τῶν βαρβάρων στρατόπεδον. οἱ δὲ βάρβαροι, ὡς ἤκουσαν τὸν θόρυβον, οὐχ ὑπέμενον, ἀλλ᾽ ἔφευγον. οἱ δὲ Ἕλληνες ὀλίγους τῶν βαρβάρων ἀποκτείνουσι καὶ λαμβάνουσιν εἴκοσιν ἵππους καὶ τὴν τοῦ ἄρχοντος σκηνὴν καὶ ἐν αὐτῇ κλίνας ἀργυρᾶς καὶ ἐκπώματα. οἱ δὲ τῶν ὁπλιτῶν στρατηγοὶ τῇ σάλπιγγι ἐκέλευσαν τοὺς πελταστὰς παύσασθαι τῆς μάχης καὶ πορεύεσθαι πάλιν εἰς τὸ τῶν Ἑλλήνων στρατόπεδον.

Adapted from Xenophon, *Anabasis* IV.iv

Chapter 16 Vocabulary

Verbs:

βουλεύομαι	deliberate	πορεύομαι	march, journey
δέχομαι	receive	στρατοπεδεύομαι	encamp
λύομαι	ransom	φαίνομαι	seem, appear
μάχομαι (+ *dat.*)	fight	φέρομαι	win (a prize)
παύομαι (+ *gen.*)	cease from	(see Ch. 21.3	
πείθομαι (+ *dat.*)	obey	for principal	
aor. ἐπιθόμην		parts of φέρω)	

Nouns:

ἆθλον, -ου, τό	prize	λοχαγός, -οῦ, ὁ	captain
Ἀρμένιος, -ου, ὁ	an Armenian	νόμος, -ου, ὁ	law
δειλία, -ας, ἡ	cowardice	υἱός, -οῦ, ὁ	son
Κροῖσος, -ου, ὁ	Croesus		

Adjectives:

αἰσχρός, -ά, -όν	shameful	χρυσοῦς, -ῆ, -οῦν	of gold
ἀργυροῦς, -ᾶ, -οῦν	of silver		

Adverbs:

ἐγγύς	near	εὐθύς	immediately, at once

Prepositions:

ἐγγύς (+ *gen.*)	near	παρά (+ *dat.*)	beside
ἔξω (+ *gen.*)	outside	πρό (+ *gen.*)	before, in front of

CHAPTER 17

1. Imperatives of thematic verbs

You learned the present second person imperatives in Ch. 8.3. There are also third person imperatives, corresponding to English 'Let him come!', 'They are to stay!'. These imperatives all exist in the aorist tense as well. The difference between the present and aorist imperatives is one of aspect, not time (Ch. 16.5). When it refers to a continuing action, the imperative is present: μενόντων οἱ ναῦται, 'let the sailors remain'. When it refers to a single act, the imperative is aorist: λῦσον τὸν βοῦν, 'loose the ox'.

The present and aorist imperatives are formed as follows. (There is also a rare perfect imperative, which need not be learned now.)

		ACTIVE	MIDDLE	PASSIVE
PRESENT				
Sing.	2nd	λῦε	λύου (λυ-ε-σο)	λύου (λυ-ε-σο)
	3rd	λυέτω	λυέσθω	λυέσθω
Plur.	2nd	λύετε	λύεσθε	λύεσθε
	3rd	λυόντων	λυέσθων	λυέσθων
WEAK AORIST				
Sing.	2nd	λῦσον	λῦσαι	λύθητι
	3rd	λυσάτω	λυσάσθω	λυθήτω
Plur.	2nd	λύσατε	λύσασθε	λύθητε
	3rd	λυσάντων	λυσάσθων	λυθέντων

STRONG AORIST (λαμβάνω; for principal parts see Ch. 16.7)

Sing.	2nd	λάβε	λαβοῦ	λήφθητι
	3rd	λαβέτω	λαβέσθω	ληφθήτω
Plur.	2nd	λάβετε	λάβεσθε	λήφθητε
	3rd	λαβόντων	λαβέσθων	ληφθέντων

2. Imperatives of εἰμί, 'be'

The only tense of the imperative of εἰμί is the present:

Sing.	2nd	ἴσθι	Plur.	2nd	ἔστε
	3rd	ἔστω		3rd	ὄντων

3. Infinitives of thematic verbs (future and perfect)

The future and perfect infinitives are formed and accented as follows:

FUTURE

Active:	future stem + ε + -εν	= -σειν	λύσειν, πείσειν
Middle:	future stem + ε + -σθαι	= -σεσθαι	λύσεσθαι, πείσεσθαι
Passive:	future stem + ε + -σθαι	= -θησεσθαι	λυθήσεσθαι

accent: active/middle: on the last syllable of the verb stem; passive: on the -**θη**-

PERFECT

Active:	perfect stem + ε + -ναι	= -εναι	λελυκέναι, πεποιθέναι
Mid./Pass.:	perfect stem + -σθαι	= -σθαι	λελύσθαι, πεπεῖσθαι

accent: active: on the -ε-; middle/passive: on the last syllable of the verb stem

Both tenses have only rare and specific uses. A future infinitive is used after the verb μέλλω, 'intend' 'be about to', and also after ἐλπίζω, 'hope', 'expect' when it refers to the future: μέλλω θύσειν, "I am about to sacrifice." Otherwise complementary infinitives are in the present or aorist tense, depending on aspect (Ch. 16.5). The perfect infinitive is used for a completed action: ἀγαθόν ἐστι πεπαῦσθαι τοῦ ἔργου, "It is good to have ceased from work."

EXERCISE 77.

1. σώσατε τὴν πατρίδα, ὦ στρατιῶται.
2. πιστευόντων οἱ νεανίαι τοῖς τοῦ Σωκράτους λόγοις.
3. ὁ νεανίας μέλλει λύσειν τὸν βοῦν.
4. εὐθὺς λυθέντων οἱ αἰχμάλωτοι.
5. σῶσον τὸν γέροντα, ὦ νεανία.
6. μενέτω ἡ εἰρήνη, ὦ πολῖται.
7. βουλευέσθων οἱ σύμμαχοι περὶ τοῦ πολέμου.
8. ἐλπίζομεν λυθήσεσθαι ὑπὸ τῶν τριηρῶν.
9. οἱ μετὰ τοῦ Ξενοφῶντος ἔμελλον πορεύσεσθαι πρὸς τὴν θάλασσαν.
10. καλὸν ἦν τοῖς Ἀθηναίοις σεσωκέναι τὴν πατρίδα.

EXERCISE 78.

1. Persuade the three hundred allies to remain.
2. Trust the ships, citizens.
3. The enemy intended to ransom the general.
4. Let there be peace in the city.
5. The soldiers are about to destroy the enemy.
6. The faithful steward hopes to be rich.
7. Order him not to say foolish things.
8. The men in the city were about to be saved by the allies.
9. Send the allies homeward immediately.
10. Let the Persians ransom the prisoners.

4. Personal pronouns, 1st and 2nd persons

The personal pronouns 'I/we' and 'you' are formed in Greek as follows:

		I/we	you
SING.	Nom.	ἐγώ	σύ
	Gen.	ἐμοῦ, μου	σοῦ, σου
	Dat.	ἐμοί, μοι	σοί, σοι
	Acc.	ἐμέ, με	σέ, σε
PLUR.	Nom.	ἡμεῖς	ὑμεῖς
	Gen.	ἡμῶν	ὑμῶν
	Dat.	ἡμῖν	ὑμῖν
	Acc.	ἡμᾶς	ὑμᾶς

The forms without accents are enclitic; therefore they can never begin a clause. Nor are they used after a preposition. The accented forms are more emphatic. The nominative is *only* used for extra emphasis, since the verb ending already gives the same information:

πείθεταί μοι.	He obeys me.
πείθεται ἐμοί.	He obeys <u>me</u> (and not <u>you</u>).
πείθομαι τοῖς νόμοις.	I obey the laws.
ἐγὼ πείθομαι τοῖς νόμοις.	I obey the laws (but <u>you</u> don't).
ἔσωσας τὴν στρατιάν.	You saved the army.
σὺ ἔσωσας τὴν στρατιάν.	It was <u>you</u> who saved the army.

EXERCISE 79.

1. ὁ στρατηγὸς ἔλαβε μὲν δύο ναῦς, ἐκέλευσε δ' ὑμᾶς φέρειν αὐτὰς εἰς τὸν λιμένα.
2. ὑμεῖς μὲν ἀνδρεῖοί ἐστε, ἐγὼ δὲ δειλός.
3. οὐδείς ἐστι πιστότερος σοῦ.
4. ὁ δοῦλος οὐκ ἤθελε μένειν μετ' ἐμοῦ.
5. ὁ θεὸς κελεύει ἡμᾶς πιστεύειν ταῖς ναυσίν ἃς παρεσκευάσαμεν.
6. ἡμεῖς μὲν εἰς τὰς νήσους ἐκομιζόμεθα, οἱ δὲ γέροντες ἐν τῇ πόλει ἔμενον.
7. ἡ Ἄλκηστίς σε σώσει, ὦ Ἄδμητε.
8. ὁ βασιλεὺς ἐπιστολὴν πρὸς ἐμὲ ἔπεμψεν.
9. ὑμεῖς φέρεσθε τὸ ἆθλον, ὦ Λακεδαιμόνιοι.
10. ἀεὶ πεισόμεθά σοι, ὦ στρατηγέ.

EXERCISE 80.

1. The Persians compelled us to flee.
2. We shall never persuade you to fight.
3. If you are wise, Socrates is wiser.
4. It is difficult for me to trust you.
5. The allies are not willing to die on our behalf.
6. I am a soldier, but you are a sailor.
7. We will obey you, Socrates.
8. The general ordered you not to remain on the wall.
9. It was you who captured the city.
10. I ordered the slaves to escape with me.

5. Possessive adjectives, 1st and 2nd persons

These adjectives are formed from the personal pronouns and mean 'my', 'our', 'your'. They are declined like regular 1st and 2nd declension adjectives.

ἐμός, ἐμή, ἐμόν	my		σός, σή, σόν	your (sing.)
ἡμέτερος, ᾱ, -ον	our		ὑμέτερος, -ᾱ, -ον	your (plur.)

For the first and second person there are two ways to express possession in Greek: with a possessive adjective, or with the genitive of the personal pronoun. These phrases always include the article. The possessive adjective is always attributive (preceded by the article); the pronoun is always predicate.

> ἡ ἐμὴ βίβλος   my book
> ἡ βίβλος μου   my book

Note: For the third person there is no possessive adjective; possession is expressed with the genitive pronoun αὐτοῦ, αὐτῆς, αὐτοῦ (Ch. 8.9):

> ἔλυσα τὸν δοῦλον αὐτοῦ.   I set free his slave.

EXERCISE 81.

1. ὁ ἐμὸς υἱὸς οὐκ ἀεὶ πείθεται τῷ διδασκάλῳ.
2. οἱ πολέμιοι οὐ καταλύσουσι τὴν ἡμετέραν πόλιν.
3. βουλευσόμεθα περὶ τῆς ὑμετέρας σωτηρίας.
4. ὁ Ἡρακλῆς οἰκτείρει τὸν Ἄδμητον καὶ ἐθέλει σῶσαι τὴν γυναῖκα αὐτοῦ.
5. ἡ Ἀρτεμισία παρῆν ἐν τῇ ναυμαχίᾳ· ὁ δὲ Ξέρξης ἐθαύμαζε τὴν ἀνδρείαν αὐτῆς.
6. ἐπιστεύσαμεν τῷ Δημοσθένει καὶ ἐπιθόμεθα τοῖς λόγοις αὐτοῦ.
7. θαυμάζομεν τὴν σὴν θυγατέρα καὶ τὴν σοφίαν αὐτῆς.
8. οἱ ὑμέτεροι σύμμαχοι ἔφυγον ἐκ τοῦ στρατοπέδου.
9. ἡ ἐμὴ γυνὴ καὶ ἐγὼ ἐφεύγομεν μετὰ τῆς θυγατρὸς αὐτοῦ.
10. οὐδεμία πόλις οὐκ ἔστι τιμῆς ἀξιωτέρα τῆς ἡμετέρας.

EXERCISE 82.

1. Our city will always be free.
2. My son was running with him.
3. Is your fleet smaller than ours?
4. I ransomed my son from the enemy.
5. The Athenians sacrifice to the goddess and guard her temple.
6. We persuaded your father not to remain.
7. The Persians admired the Spartans' general and his army.
8. Our fleet was fighting in a narrow place.
9. My slave is wiser than yours.
10. We are fleeing with our children.

EXERCISE 83.

DOUBLE DEALINGS OF THEMISTOCLES

Although the Greeks had won a decisive naval victory at Salamis, the Persian army was not yet defeated, and this accounts for the attitude of the Spartans shown in this piece. When later in his life Themistocles lost his countrymen's trust and was exiled, he claimed credit from the Persians for having tried to help them.

μετὰ δὲ τὴν ἐν Σαλαμῖνι ναυμαχίαν ὁ Θεμιστοκλῆς πρῶτον συνεβούλευε τοῖς

Ἕλλησι διῶξαι τὸ τῶν Περσῶν ναυτικὸν καὶ λῦσαι τὰς ἐν τῷ Ἑλλησπόντῳ γεφύρας. ὁ δὲ

Εὐρυβιάδης, ὁ τῶν Λακεδαιμονίων στρατηγός, ἔπεισε τοὺς Ἕλληνας μὴ καταλῦσαι τὰς γεφύρας. Ἄλλως γάρ, ἔλεξεν, ἀναγκαῖον ἔσται τῷ Πέρσῃ ἐνθάδε μένειν· οὕτως δὲ οἷός τ' ἔσται καταστρέψασθαι τὴν ὅλην Εὐρώπην· οὐ γὰρ μέλλει ἡσυχάσειν. ταύτης[1] δὲ εἴχοντο τῆς γνώμης καὶ Πελοποννησίων τῶν ἄλλων οἱ στρατηγοί.

ὡς δὲ ἐμάνθανε ὅτι οὐ πείσει τοὺς στρατηγοὺς πλεῖν εἰς τὸν Ἑλλήσποντον, ὁ Θεμιστοκλῆς ἔλεγεν αὐτοῖς ὧδε· Οὐχ ἡμεῖς σεσώκαμεν ἡμᾶς αὐτούς τε καὶ τὴν Ἑλλάδα, ἀλλ' οἱ θεοὶ οἳ οὐκ ἤθελον ἄνδρα ἕνα τῆς τε Ἀσίας καὶ τῆς Εὐρώπης βασιλεῦσαι, ὄντα [being] ἀνόσιόν τε καὶ ἀτάσθαλον· ὃς τὰ ἱερὰ ἔκαυσέ τε καὶ κατέβαλε τὰ τῶν θεῶν ἀγάλματα· ὃς καὶ τὴν θάλασσαν μάστιξιν ἔτυψεν καὶ πέδας εἰς αὐτὴν ἔβαλεν. νῦν οὖν ἀγαθόν ἐστιν τῷ μὲν Πέρσῃ οἴκαδε ἀποφυγεῖν, ἡμῖν δ' ἐν τῇ Ἑλλάδι καταμένειν καὶ θεραπεύειν τοὺς ἡμετέρους. Θεμιστοκλῆς μὲν οὕτως ἔλεξεν, ὡς ἀποθήκην ἔμελλε σχήσειν χάριτος πρὸς βασιλεῖ, οἱ δὲ Ἀθηναῖοι ἐπείθοντο· ἐφαίνετο γὰρ αὐτοῖς εἶναι σοφώτατος ἀνήρ.

ἔπειτα δὲ ὁ Θεμιστοκλῆς ἔπεμψεν ἀγγέλους ὡς βασιλέα, ἐν οἷς καὶ Σίκιννος ὁ οἰκέτης ἦν· καὶ ὁ Σίκιννος ἔλεξεν τῷ Ξέρξῃ ὧδε· Ἔπεμψέ με ὁ Θεμιστοκλῆς, στρατηγὸς μὲν Ἀθηναίων, ἀνὴρ δὲ τῶν συμμάχων ἄριστος καὶ σοφώτατος· ὡς βούλεται εὐεργέτης σοι εἶναι, ἔπεισε τοὺς Ἕλληνας μήτε διώκειν τὰς σὰς ναῦς μήτε τὰς ἐν τῷ Ἑλλησπόντῳ γεφύρας καταλύειν. καὶ νῦν οἷός τ' ἔσει σῴζεσθαι εἰς τὴν σὴν χώραν.

Adapted from Herodotus VIII.108-110

Chapter 17 Vocabulary

Verbs:

ἐλπίζω (+ *fut. inf.*)	hope, expect	πάρειμι	be present
κομίζω	convey	τρέχω	run
μέλλω (+ *fut. inf.*)	be about to, intend	(ἔδραμον, strong aor.)	

Nouns:

Ἀρτεμισία, -ας, ἡ	Artemisia	σωτηρία, -ας, ἡ	safety
διδάσκαλος, -ου, ὁ	teacher	τόπος, -ου, ὁ	place
ἱερόν, -οῦ, τό	temple		

Pronouns:

ἐγώ, ἐμοῦ	I	σύ, σοῦ	you (sing.)
ἡμεῖς, ἡμῶν	we	ὑμεῖς, ὑμῶν	you (pl.)

Adjectives:

ἐμός, -ή, -όν	my	σός, σή, σόν	your (sing.)
ἡμέτερος, -α, -ον	our	ὑμέτερος, -α, -ον	your (pl.)
στενός, -ή, -όν	narrow		

Adverb:

οὔποτε	never

---

[1] from οὗτος, αὕτη, τοῦτο, 'this' (Ch. 23. 6)

CHAPTER 18

1. Contract verbs

Contract verbs are thematic verbs whose stems end in a vowel (α, ε or o), which must contract with the thematic vowel. The lexicon lists such verbs in their uncontracted form, but even the 1st singular is always contracted in Attic usage. Because the imperfect tense is formed from the present stem, it also has contract forms.

As you saw with contract adjectives (Ch. 16.8), the accent is in place before the contraction. If an accented syllable is contracted, the accent remains on the contracted syllable, and follows the accent rule for its new position.

You will see from the following chart that ε is the weakest vowel, and o/ω the strongest. Contractions always result in a long form of the stronger vowel involved:

ε + ε = ει	α + ε = ᾱ	o + ε = ου
ε + ει = ει	α + ει = ᾳ	o + ει = οι
ε + o = ου	α + o = ω	o + o = ου
ε + ου = ου	α + ου = ω	o + ου = ου
ε + ω = ω	α + ω = ω	o + ω = ω

The other principal parts do not involve contractions. They show a long version of the contract vowel. In the following list ἐθέλω is not a contract verb, but its principal parts resemble those of φιλέω and τιμάω.

	PRESENT	FUTURE A/M	AORIST A/M	PERFECT A	PERFECT M/P	AORIST P
love	φιλέω	φιλήσω	ἐφίλησα	πεφίληκα	πεφίλημαι	ἐφιλήθην
honor	τιμάω	τιμήσω	ἐτίμησα	τετίμηκα	τετίμημαι	ἐτιμήθην
show	δηλόω	δηλώσω	ἐδήλωσα	δεδήλωκα	δεδήλωμαι	ἐδηλώθην
wish	ἐθέλω	ἐθελήσω	ἠθέλησα	ἠθέληκα	——	

Note: βοηθέω has a shortened aorist passive form, ἐβοήθην. A few contract verbs have some irregular principal parts. The only ones you need to learn now are βοηθέω, 'help' and ὁράω, 'see':

help	βοηθέω	βοηθήσω	ἐβοήθησα	βεβοήθηκα	βεβοήθημαι	ἐβοήθην
see	ὁράω	ὄψομαι	εἶδον	ἑώρακα	ἑώραμαι	ὤφθην

2. Contract verbs in -εω

		ACTIVE		MIDDLE/PASSIVE	

INDICATIVE
Present

SING.	1st	φιλῶ	(φιλέ-ω)	φιλοῦμαι	(φιλέ-ομαι)
	2nd	φιλεῖς	(φιλέ-εις)	φιλῇ/φιλεῖ	(φιλέ-εσαι)
	3rd	φιλεῖ	(φιλέ-ει)	φιλεῖται	(φιλέ-εται)
PLUR.	1st	φιλοῦμεν	(φιλέ-ομεν)	φιλούμεθα	(φιλε-όμεθα)
	2nd	φιλεῖτε	(φιλέ-ετε)	φιλεῖσθε	(φιλέ-εσθε)
	3rd	φιλοῦσι	(φιλέ-ουσι)	φιλοῦνται	(φιλέ-ονται)

Imperfect

SING.	1st	ἐφίλουν	(ἐφίλε-ον)	ἐφιλούμην	(ἐφιλε-όμην)
	2nd	ἐφίλεις	(ἐφίλε-ες)	ἐφιλοῦ	(ἐφιλέ-εσο)
	3rd	ἐφίλει	(ἐφίλε-ε)	ἐφιλεῖτο	(ἐφιλέ-ετο)
PLUR.	1st	ἐφιλοῦμεν	(ἐφιλέ-ομεν)	ἐφιλούμεθα	(ἐφιλε-όμεθα)
	2nd	ἐφιλεῖτε	(ἐφιλέ-ετε)	ἐφιλεῖσθε	(ἐφιλέ-εσθε)
	3rd	ἐφίλουν	(ἐφίλε-ον)	ἐφιλοῦντο	(ἐφιλέ-οντο)

IMPERATIVE

SING.	2nd	φίλει	(φίλε-ε)	φιλοῦ	(φιλέ-εσο)
	3rd	φιλείτω	(φιλε-έτω)	φιλείσθω	(φιλε-έσθω)
PLUR.	2nd	φιλεῖτε	(φιλέ-ετε)	φιλεῖσθε	(φιλέ-εσθε)
	3rd	φιλούντων	(φιλε-όντων)	φιλείσθων	(φιλε-έσθων)

INFINITIVE	φιλεῖν	(φιλέ-ε-εν)	φιλεῖσθαι	(φιλέ-εσθαι)

EXERCISE 84. Identify and translate the following forms.

(a)
1. φιλοῦμεν
2. ζητεῖται
3. βοηθεῖτε
4. ἐποιεῖτο
5. ζητοῦσι
6. ἐβοηθοῦμεν
7. ἐφιλεῖσθε
8. ἐβοηθήσαμεν
9. βοηθεῖν
10. ποιήσουσι
11. ἐβοήθουν
12. ἐφίλησε
13. ζητεῖς
14. πεποίηκα
15. ἐζήτει

(b)
1. They made
2. You (pl.) make
3. We were seeking
4. He loves
5. You (s.) are helping
6. To be loved
7. They loved
8. He was helped
9. I will make
10. You (s.) were being helped
11. They have been loved
12. We helped
13. To keep seeking
14. Seek (s.)
15. He was helping

EXERCISE 85.

1. φιλοῦμεν τὴν πατρίδα, ὦ Λακεδαιμόνιοι.
2. εἰ οἱ φυγάδες φιλοῦσι τοὺς Πέρσας, μωροί εἰσιν.
3. οἱ πολέμιοι οἷς ἐμαχεσάμεθα εὖ πεποιήκασι τάς τε γυναῖκας καὶ τὰ τέκνα.

4. οἱ Ἀθηναῖοι ἐποίουν ναῦς εἰς τὸν πόλεμον.
5. πρότερον μὲν ὁ Θεμιστοκλῆς ἐφιλεῖτο, νῦν δὲ οὔ.
6. ἀεὶ φιληθήσεται ἡ ἡμετέρα πατρίς.
7. ῥᾴδιον μέν ἐστι ζητεῖν, χαλεπὸν δὲ εὑρίσκειν.
8. ἡ Ἄλκηστις ἀποθνῄσκει ὑπὲρ τοῦ ἀνδρός, ὡς αὐτὸν φιλεῖ.
9. ὁ λέων ἐζητεῖτο ἒξ ἡμέρας ὑπὸ τῶν παίδων.
10. ἐλπίζετε ὄψεσθαι τὴν θάλασσαν ἀπὸ τοῦ ὄρους, ὦ σύμμαχοι;

EXERCISE 86.

1. Xerxes never treated the captains well.
2. We were helping the king with our army.
3. We sought the river in vain.
4. The ship has at last been made.
5. Some masters treat slaves well, others badly.
6. You will always be loved, because you saved your city.
7. Always love your country, citizens.
8. The king ordered the man's son to be sought.
9. Peace was made in the tenth year.
10. If the cavalry had captured the general of the allies we would not be seeking him now.

3. Contract verbs in -αω

		ACTIVE		MIDDLE/PASSIVE	
INDICATIVE					
Present					
SING.	1st	τιμῶ	(τιμά-ω)	τιμῶμαι	(τιμά-ομαι)
	2nd	τιμᾷς	(τιμά-εις)	τιμᾷ	(τιμά-εσαι)
	3rd	τιμᾷ	(τιμά-ει)	τιμᾶται	(τιμά-εται)
PLUR.	1st	τιμῶμεν	(τιμά-ομεν)	τιμώμεθα	(τιμα-όμεθα)
	2nd	τιμᾶτε	(τιμά-ετε)	τιμᾶσθε	(τιμά-εσθε)
	3rd	τιμῶσι	(τιμά-ουσι)	τιμῶνται	(τιμά-ονται)
Imperfect					
SING.	1st	ἐτίμων	(ἐτίμα-ον)	ἐτιμώμην	(ἐτιμα-όμην)
	2nd	ἐτίμας	(ἐτίμα-ες)	ἐτιμῶ	(ἐτιμά-εσο)
	3rd	ἐτίμα	(ἐτίμα-ε)	ἐτιμᾶτο	(ἐτιμά-ετο)
PLUR.	1st	ἐτιμῶμεν	(ἐτιμά-ομεν)	ἐτιμώμεθα	(ἐτιμα-όμεθα)
	2nd	ἐτιμᾶτε	(ἐτιμάετε)	ἐτιμᾶσθε	(ἐτιμά-εσθε)
	3rd	ἐτίμων	(ἐτίμα-ον)	ἐτιμῶντο	(ἐτιμά-οντο)
IMPERATIVE					
SING.	2nd	τίμα	(τίμα-ε)	τιμῶ	(τιμά-εσο)
	3rd	τιμάτω	(τιμα-έτω)	τιμάσθω	(τιμα-έσθω)
PLUR.	2nd	τιμᾶτε	(τιμά-ετε)	τιμᾶσθε	(τιμά-εσθε)
	3rd	τιμώντων	(τιμα-όντων)	τιμάσθων	(τιμα-έσθων)
INFINITIVE		τιμᾶν	(τιμά-ε-εν)	τιμᾶσθαι	(τιμά-εσθαι)

EXERCISE 87. Identify and translate the following forms.

(a) 1. νικῶσι
     2. ἐτιμώμεθα
     3. ὁρᾷ
     4. ἐνίκων
     5. νικᾶτε

     6. βοᾶν
     7. ὁρῶμεν
     8. νικηθήσεται
     9. ἐτίμησας
    10. τίμα

    11. νενίκηνται
    12. ἐβόα
    13. ὁρᾷς
    14. νενικήκαμεν
    15. τιμᾶσθαι

(b) 1. We conquer
     2. They are seen
     3. You (s.) honor
     4. You (pl.) see
     5. They were shouting
     6. I will conquer
     7. He shouts
     8. He was honoring

     9. They will be honored
    10. To honor (aor.)
    11. He has been conquered
    12. You (pl.) have honored
    13. You (s.) were conquered
    14. Honor (pl.)
    15. Shout (s.)

EXERCISE 88.

1. χαλεπὸν ἦν τοῖς Ἕλλησι νικῆσαι τοὺς Πέρσας.
2. οἱ δειλοὶ οὔποτε ἐτιμῶντο ὑπὸ τοῦ δήμου.
3. οἱ Πέρσαι νικήσουσι τοὺς Λακεδαιμονίους.
4. ὁ Ξέρξης ὁρᾷ τὴν ναυμαχίαν ἐν ᾗ ἡ Ἀρτεμισία κατέδυσε ναῦν φιλίαν.
5. ἀγαθόν ἐστι τιμᾶσθαι ὑπὸ τοῦ δήμου.
6. νικᾶσθε, ὦ πολῖται, διὰ τὴν ὑμετέραν δειλίαν.
7. ἐνικήθημεν τοῦ θέρους τῇ νόσῳ.
8. τιμᾶσθε ὑπὸ τῶν παίδων, ὦ γέροντες.
9. ἐτίμας τὴν θεάν, ὦ θύγατερ;
10. τιμῶμεν ὑμᾶς, ὦ παῖδες, εἰ πείθεσθε τοῖς τε πατράσι καὶ ταῖς μητράσιν.

EXERCISE 89.

1. The Athenians were honoring the young men after the contest.
2. You do not honor the cowardly.
3. The poet is honored by the people.
4. Death did not conquer Alcestis.
5. Wise men were not always honored by the Athenians.
6. The Persians will be conquered in the sea battle within a few days.
7. Demosthenes wished to be honored by the citizens.
8. We have conquered the army of the enemy.
9. We hope to be honored.
10. The poet was honoring Athens by his words.

4. Contract verbs in -οω

		ACTIVE		MIDDLE/PASSIVE	
INDICATIVE					
Present					
SING.	1st	δηλῶ	(δηλό-ω)	δηλοῦμαι	(δηλό-ομαι)
	2nd	δηλοῖς	(δηλό-εις)	δηλοῖ	(δηλό-εσαι)
	3rd	δηλοῖ	(δηλό-ει)	δηλοῦται	(δηλό-εται)
PLUR.	1st	δηλοῦμεν	(δηλό-ομεν)	δηλούμεθα	(δηλο-όμεθα)
	2nd	δηλοῦτε	(δηλό-ετε)	δηλοῦσθε	(δηλό-εσθε)
	3rd	δηλοῦσι	(δηλό-ουσι)	δήλοῦνται	(δηλό-ονται)
Imperfect					
SING.	1st	ἐδήλουν	(ἐδήλο-ον)	ἐδηλούμην	(ἐδηλο-όμην)
	2nd	ἐδήλους	(ἐδήλο-ες)	ἐδηλοῦ	(ἐδηλό-εσο)
	3rd	ἐδήλου	(ἐδήλο-ε)	ἐδηλοῦτο	(ἐδηλό-ετο)
PLUR.	1st	ἐδηλοῦμεν	(ἐδηλό-ομεν)	ἐδηλούμεθα	(ἐδηλο-όμεθα)
	2nd	ἐδηλοῦτε	(ἐδηλό-ετε)	ἐδηλοῦσθε	(ἐδηλό-εσθε)
	3rd	ἐδήλουν	(ἐδήλο-ον)	ἐδηλοῦντο	(ἐδηλό-οντο)
IMPERATIVE					
SING.	2nd	δήλου	(δήλο-ε)	δηλοῦ	(δηλό-εσο)
	3rd	δηλούτω	(δηλο-έτω)	δηλούσθω	(δηλο-έσθω)
PLUR.	2nd	δηλοῦτε	(δηλό-ετε)	δηλοῦσθε	(δηλό-εσθε)
	3rd	δηλούντων	(δηλο-όντων)	δηλούσθων	(δηλο-έσθων)
INFINITIVE		δηλοῦν	(δηλό-ε-εν)	δηλοῦσθαι	(δηλό-εσθαι)

EXERCISE 90. Identify and translate the following forms.

(a) 1. δηλοῖ
2. ἐδήλους
3. ἐδουλώθη
4. ἐδουλοῦμεν
5. ἐδήλωσας

6. ἐλευθερούμεθα
7. δήλου
8. δουλοῦσθαι
9. ἐδήλου
10. δεδούλωται

11. δουλώσετε
12. δηλοῦν
13. ἠλευθεροῦντο
14. δεδηλώκασι
15. ἐλευθεροῖ

(b) 1. We show
2. They were enslaving
3. You (s.) are shown
4. You (pl.) are freeing
5. He enslaves
6. To enslave
7. To be shown
8. I was showing

9. He was freeing
10. We shall show
11. They enslaved
12. Show (pl.)
13. He has shown
14. They were freed
15. It has been shown

EXERCISE 91.

1. κακόν ἐστι δουλοῦν συμμάχους πιστούς.
2. ὁ ἡγεμὼν δηλοῖ τὴν ὁδὸν τοῖς Ἕλλησιν.
3. χαλεπὸν ἔσται ἐλευθεροῦσθαι ἀπὸ τῶν βαρβάρων.

4. οὐ μέλλομεν δουλώσειν ὑμᾶς, ὦ ἄνδρες.
5. ἐδηλοῦμεν τῷ στρατηγῷ τὸ τῶν πολεμίων στρατόπεδον.
6. ὁ νεανίας δηλοῖ τὰ ἆθλα τῷ πατρί.
7. ἡ Ἑλλὰς οὔποτε δουλωθήσεται ὑπὸ τῶν βαρβάρων.
8. ἡ πόλις ἐλευθεροῦται ὑπὸ τοῦ στρατηγοῦ.
9. αἱ νῆσοι δεδούλωνται ὑπὸ τῶν Ἀθηναίων.
10. ὁ στρατηγὸς δηλοῖ τὴν βουλὴν τοῖς συμμάχοις.

EXERCISE 92.

1. The general is enslaving the citizens.
2. We do not show the way to traitors.
3. The soldiers are freeing the country from the enemy.
4. The citizen was showing to me the house of Socrates.
5. We will see the road to the harbor.
6. We shall free the citizens within five days.
7. The city was enslaved by the foreigners.
8. It is not easy to free the island.
9. The general's plan has been shown to the soldiers.
10. Free your city from the Persians, citizens.

EXERCISE 93.

POLYCRATES AND THE RING

Polycrates was tyrant of Samos, an island off the coast of Ionia, from 532 to 523 BC. He grew so prosperous that Amasis, king of Egypt, warned him that his success would provoke the jealousy of the gods. Amasis suggested that he should appease them by throwing away his most valuable possession.

ὁ Πολυκράτης, ὃς ἦν ὁ τῆς Σάμου τύραννος, ἦν δυνατώτατος· φιλίαν δὲ ἐποιήσατο πρὸς Ἄμασιν τὸν Αἰγύπτου βασιλέα· ἔπεμψεν οὖν δῶρα καὶ ἄλλα ἐδέξατο παρ' αὐτοῦ. ἐν χρόνῳ δὲ ὀλίγῳ ὁ Πολυκράτης ἐστράτευε πανταχοῦ καὶ εὖ ἔπρασσε τῇ στρατιᾷ· ἦσαν γὰρ αὐτῷ πεντηκόντεροί θ' ἑκατὸν καὶ χίλιοι τοξόται. συχνῶν μὲν δὴ τῶν τε νήσων ἐκράτησε καὶ τῶν ἐν τῇ ἠπείρῳ πόλεων. ἐπεὶ δὲ τοὺς Λεσβίους[1] ναυμαχίᾳ ἐνίκησε, τοὺς αἰχμαλώτους καὶ ἠνάγκασε ὀρύσσειν τάφρον περὶ τὴν τῶν Σαμίων πόλιν.

ἡ δὲ τοῦ Πολυκράτους εὐτυχία οὐκ ἐλάνθανε τὸν Ἄμασιν, ἀλλὰ ἄλγος ἦν αὐτῷ. ἔγραψεν οὖν ἐπιστολὴν καὶ ἔπεμψεν εἰς Σάμον· Ἄμασις Πολυκράτει ὧδε λέγει. ἡδὺ μέν ἐστιν, ὦ φίλε, πυνθάνεσθαι ὅτι ἀνὴρ φίλος καὶ ξένος εὖ πράσσει, ἐμοὶ δὲ αἱ σαὶ εὐτυχίαι οὐκ ἀρέσκουσιν. εἰ γάρ τις ἀεὶ εὐτυχεῖ, οἱ θεοὶ φθονοῦσιν. πείθου οὖν ἐμοὶ καὶ ὧδε ποίει· τῶν σῶν κτημάτων τὸ πλείστου ἄξιον ἀπόβαλε οὕτω ὅπως μηκέτι ἥξει εἰς ἀνθρώπους.

ὁ δὲ Πολυκράτης δέχεται τὴν ἐπιστολὴν καὶ ἀναγιγνώσκει, καὶ νόῳ ἔλαβε ὡς εὖ συνεβούλευεν ὁ Ἄμασις· ἦν δ' αὐτῷ σφραγὶς σμαράγδου λίθου χρυσόδετος. ἐπεὶ οὖν

---

[1]   Lesbos was another Greek island off the Asia Minor coast, well to the north of Samos.

ἐδόκει αὐτῷ ἀποβαλεῖν, ἐποίει ὧδε· πεντηκόντερον πληροῖ ἀνδρῶν καὶ εἰσβαίνει εἰς αὐτόν, μετὰ δὲ ἀναγαγεῖν κελεύει εἰς τὸ πέλαγος· ὡς δὲ ἀπὸ τῆς νήσου ἑκὰς ἦσαν, βάλλει τὴν σφραγῖδα εἰς τὸ πέλαγος.

τῇ δὲ πέμπτῃ ἢ τῇ ἕκτῃ ἡμέρᾳ ἀνὴρ ἁλιεὺς ἰχθὺν μέγιστον καὶ καλὸν ἔλαβε καὶ ἠξίου αὐτὸν Πολυκράτει δῶρον φέρειν. βαίνει οὖν εἰς ὄψιν Πολυκράτει καὶ λέγει· Ὦ βασιλεῦ, ἐγὼ τὸν ἰχθὺν οὐκ ἐδικαίωσα φέρειν εἰς ἀγοράν, ἀλλά μοι ἐδόκει σοῦ τε εἶναι ἄξιος καὶ τῆς σῆς ἀρχῆς· αἰτῶ σε αὐτὸν δέξασθαι. ὁ δὲ ἥδεται τοῖς λόγοις καὶ λέγει· Εὖ τε ἐποίησας καὶ χάρις διπλῆ τῶν τε λόγων καὶ τοῦ δώρου· καί σε ἐπὶ δεῖπνον καλοῦμεν. ὁ μὲν οὖν ἁλιεὺς μάλιστα ἥδεται, ὅτι οὕτω τιμᾶται, καὶ οἴκαδε ἀποχωρεῖ· οἱ δὲ θεράποντες, ὡς τέμνουσι τὸν ἰχθύν, εὑρίσκουσιν ἐν τῇ γαστρὶ τὴν Πολυκράτους σφραγῖδα ἣν ἀπέβαλεν. ὡς δὲ εἶδόν τε καὶ ἔλαβον αὐτήν, εὐθὺς παρὰ τὸν Πολυκράτη φέρουσι καὶ τὸ πρᾶγμα ἐξηγοῦνται. ὁ δὲ Ἄμασις, ἐπεὶ ἤκουσε περὶ τοῦ θαύματος, ἐμάνθανε ὅτι ἐκκομίζειν τε ἀδύνατόν ἐστι ἀνθρώπῳ ἄνθρωπον ἐκ τοῦ μέλλοντος γίγνεσθαι πράγματος [the thing which is/was going to happen] καὶ ὅτι οὐκ εὖ ἀποθανεῖται Πολυκράτης εὐτυχὴς τὰ πάντα [in all things]. κήρυκα δὲ αὐτῷ ἔπεμψεν εἰς Σάμον καὶ διελύσατο τὴν φιλίαν· οὐ γὰρ ἤθελεν, ὅτε δεινή τις συμφορὰ τὸν Πολυκράτη καταλήψεται, αὐτὸς ἄλγος πάσχειν ὡς περὶ ξένου ἀνδρός.

Adapted from Herotodus III.39-43

Chapter 18 Vocabulary

Verbs:

βοάω	shout	καταδύω	sink
βοηθέω (+ *dat.*)	help	νικάω	win; conquer, defeat
δηλόω	show	ὁράω	see
δουλόω	enslave	(Attic impf. ἑώρων)	
ἐλευθερόω	free	πίνω	drink
εὖ ποιέω	treat well	ποιέω	make, do; treat
ζητέω	seek	τιμάω	honor
κακῶς ποιέω	treat badly	φιλέω	love

Nouns:

βίος, -ου, ὁ	life	Μιλτιάδης, -ου, ὁ	Miltiades
βουλή, -ῆς, ἡ	plan	προδότης, -ου, ὁ	traitor
δῆμος, -ου, ὁ	people	Σοφοκλῆς, -κλέους	Sophocles
ἑορτή, -ῆς, ἡ	feast	χιών, -όνος, ἡ	snow

Adverbs:

πρότερον	before, formerly	τέλος	at last

Conjunction:

ὡς	since, because; as

CHAPTER 19

ὁ βίος βραχύς, ἡ δὲ τέχνη μακρή.

— Hippocratic Aphorisms 1.1

1. Adjectives of the ἡδύς type

Adjectives like ἡδύς, 'sweet' 'pleasant' have 3rd declension masculine and neuter forms, and 1st declension feminine forms.

sweet

	SINGULAR			PLURAL		
	M	**F**	**N**	**M**	**F**	**N**
Nom.	ἡδύς	ἡδεῖα	ἡδύ	ἡδεῖς	ἡδεῖαι	ἡδέα
Gen.	ἡδέος	ἡδείας	ἡδέος	ἡδέων	ἡδειῶν	ἡδέων
Dat.	ἡδεῖ	ἡδείᾳ	ἡδεῖ	ἡδέσι(ν)	ἡδείαις	ἡδέσι(ν)
Acc.	ἡδύν	ἡδεῖαν	ἡδύ	ἡδεῖς	ἡδείας	ἡδέα
Voc.	ἡδύς	ἡδεῖα	ἡδύ	ἡδεῖς	ἡδεῖαι	ἡδέα

EXERCISE 94.

1. ἡδύ ἐστιν ἀκούειν τὴν τοῦ ποιητοῦ φωνήν.
2. διεβαίνομεν ποταμὸν εὐρύν τε καὶ βαθύν.
3. τὰ τῶν στρατιωτῶν ὅπλα ἦν βαρέα.
4. οἱ Ἀθηναῖοι ἔλαβον πέντε ταχείας τριήρεις.
5. ἡ διὰ τῆς ὕλης ὁδὸς ἦν βραδεῖα.
6. βραχεῖς μὲν ἦσαν οἱ τοῦ ῥήτορος λόγοι, ἡδεῖς δέ.
7. εἰ ἐδιώξαμεν τοὺς θῆρας ὅπλοις ὀξέσιν, ἐλάβομεν ἂν αὐτούς.
8. ἐνικήσαμεν ἂν τοὺς πολεμίους, εἰ αἱ νῆες αὐτῶν ἦσαν βραδεῖαι.
9. ἡδεῖα ἦν ἡ τοῦ ὄρνιθος φωνή ἣν ἤκουον τῆς νυκτός.
10. εἰ ἐν τοῖς βαρβάροις ἦμεν ἐπίνομεν ἂν οἶνον γλυκύν.

EXERCISE 95.

1. Short is the life of man.
2. We sent a swift ship to the island.
3. It was pleasant to be honored by the citizens whom we saved.
4. The snow on the mountain was deep.
5. The snow was deep on the mountain.
6. We were marching by a short and quick way to the sea.
7. The guide showed us the wide and deep river.

8. The shields of the foreigners were not heavy.
9. The cavalry of the enemy are slow.
10. The water on the island was not sweet.

2. Adjectives of the εὔφρων and εὐγενής types

These types have one set of endings for the masculine and feminine, and another for the neuter gender. For the M/F endings of εὔφρων, compare ἡγεμών, -όνος, ὁ (Ch. 10.4); for εὐγενής, compare τριήρης, -ους, ἡ (Ch. 12.4).

		kindly		well-born	
		M/F	N	M/F	N
SING.	Nom.	εὔφρων	εὔφρον	εὐγενής	εὐγενές
	Gen.	εὔφρονος	εὔφρονος	εὐγενοῦς	εὐγενοῦς
	Dat.	εὔφρονι	εὔφρονι	εὐγενεῖ	εὐγενεῖ
	Acc.	εὔφρονα	εὔφρον	εὐγενῆ	εὐγενές
	Voc.	εὔφρον	εὔφρον	εὐγενές	εὐγενές
PLUR.	Nom.	εὔφρονες	εὔφρονα	εὐγενεῖς	εὐγενῆ
	Gen.	εὐφρόνων	εὐφρόνων	εὐγενῶν	εὐγενῶν
	Dat.	εὔφροσι(ν)	εὔφροσι(ν)	εὐγενέσι(ν)	εὐγενέσι(ν)
	Acc.	εὔφρονας	εὔφρονα	εὐγενεῖς	εὐγενῆ
	Voc.	εὔφρονες	εὔφρονα	εὐγενεῖς	εὐγενῆ

EXERCISE 96.

1. οἱ πλούσιοι οὐκ ἀεὶ εὐδαίμονές εἰσιν.
2. ὁ Ἄδμητος ἐφαίνετο μὲν εἶναι εὐτυχής, ἦν δ᾽ οὔ.
3. ἐπιτρέπομεν τὴν ἀρχὴν τοῖς εὐγενέσιν.
4. ὁ Θεμιστοκλῆς οὐκ ἔγραψε τὰ ἀληθῆ.
5. ἡ πρὸς τὴν θάλασσαν ὁδὸς οὐκ ἦν σαφής.
6. οὐκ ἀσφαλές ἐστι πιστεύειν τοῖς τείχεσιν.
7. ὁ Ἄμασις οὐκ ἐνόμισε τὸν Πολυκράτη εἶναι σώφρονα.
8. πολλοὶ μέν εἰσιν οἱ τοῦ ῥήτορος λόγοι, ψευδεῖς δέ.
9. οἱ Ἀθηναῖοι ἔπεμψαν τοὺς ἀσθενεῖς εἰς τὰς νήσους.
10. σῶφρόν ἐστι τὰ ἀληθῆ λέγειν.

EXERCISE 97.

1. If the orator's words were not clear we would not have trusted them.
2. The Greeks were being led by a false guide.
3. The walls of the city were weak.
4. Few men are always fortunate.
5. The rule of the well-born was harsh.
6. Citizens, I am telling you the truth.
7. The Athenians will be safe on account of their fleet.
8. Socrates was both wise and prudent.
9. The words of the messenger were false.
10. The soldiers were being led by a prudent general.

3. μέγας, πολύς and adjectives of the τάλας type

Adjectives of the τάλας type have 3rd declension masculine and neuter forms and 1st declension feminine forms. μέγας and πολύς are variants of this type, with irregular forms.

Only the nom., acc. and voc. singular of the masculine and neuter are 3rd declension; otherwise these adjectives have 1st and 2nd declension endings.

wretched

	SINGULAR			PLURAL		
	M	**F**	**N**	**M**	**F**	**N**
Nom.	τάλας	τάλαινα	τάλαν	τάλανες	τάλαιναι	τάλανα
Gen.	τάλανος	ταλαίνης	τάλανος	ταλάνων	ταλαινῶν	ταλάνων
Dat.	τάλανι	ταλαίνῃ	τάλανι	τάλασι(ν)	ταλαίναις	τάλασι(ν)
Acc.	τάλανα	τάλαιναν	τάλαν	τάλανας	ταλαίνας	τάλανα
Voc.	τάλαν	τάλαινα	τάλαν	τάλανες	τάλαιναι	τάλανα

big   **much, many**

		M	**F**	**N**	**M**	**F**	**N**
SING.	Nom.	μέγας	μεγάλη	μέγα	πολύς	πολλή	πολύ
	Gen.	μεγάλου	μεγάλης	μεγάλου	πολλοῦ	πολλῆς	πολλοῦ
	Dat.	μεγάλῳ	μεγάλῃ	μεγάλῳ	πολλῷ	πολλῇ	πολλῷ
	Acc.	μέγαν	μεγάλην	μέγα	πολύν	πολλήν	πολύ
	Voc.	μεγάλε	μεγάλη	μέγα	πολύς	πολλή	πολύ
PLUR.	Nom.	μεγάλοι	μεγάλαι	μεγάλα	πολλοί	πολλαί	πολλά
	Gen.	μεγάλων	μεγάλων	μεγάλων	πολλῶν	πολλῶν	πολλῶν
	Dat.	μεγάλοις	μεγάλαις	μεγάλοις	πολλοῖς	πολλαῖς	πολλοῖς
	Acc.	μεγάλους	μεγάλας	μεγάλα	πολλούς	πολλάς	πολλά
	Voc.	μεγάλοι	μεγάλαι	μεγάλα	πολλοί	πολλαί	πολλά

EXERCISE 98.

1. ὁ Πολυκράτης ἔλαβε πολλὰς τῶν νησῶν.
2. ὁ Περικλῆς ἐβούλετο ποιεῖν τὴν πόλιν μεγάλην καὶ καλήν.
3. πολλαὶ νῆες κατεδύθησαν ἐν τῇ Σαλαμῖνι.
4. ὁ γίγας ὃς ἐν τῇ νήσῳ ἔμενε μεγάλῃ φωνῇ ἐβόα.
5. οἱ θεράποντες εὑρίσκουσι σφραγῖδα ἐν ἰχθύϊ μεγάλῳ.
6. πολὺν χρόνον οἱ Ἀθηναῖοι ἔμενον τοὺς Λακεδαιμονίους.
7. πολλὰ ἔλεγεν ὁ Δημοσθένης.
8. ὁ τάλας τύραννος ἐν πολλῇ ἀπορίᾳ ἦν.
9. οἱ Ἀθηναῖοι παρεσκεύαζον τεῖχος μέγα.
10. οἱ Κορίνθιοι ᾤκισαν πολλὰς ἀποικίας ἐν τῇ Σικελίᾳ.

EXERCISE 99.

1. Many of the ships were swift.
2. We have come to a river which is both wide and deep.
3. The Athenians sent many soldiers against the Persians.
4. There was a large ship outside the harbor.
5. Many trees were being cut down by the Spartans.
6. The fisherman was carrying the big fish to Polycrates.
7. The Spartans who remained in the island for many days were wretched.
8. Xerxes was leading a large army into Greece.
9. If we had had much money we would have ransomed the prisoners.
10. There was not much water in the river.

EXERCISE 100.

XERXES AND THE HELMSMAN

On his way back from Greece to Asia, says Herodotus, Xerxes actually returned by land to the Hellespont and was ferried across, as the bridges had been destroyed by a storm. He writes that the following alternative account "seems quite unworthy of belief."

ἐπεὶ δὲ ὁ Ξέρξης ἐκ τῶν Ἀθηνῶν ἧκεν ἐπὶ τὸν Στρυμόνα,[1] ἐντεῦθεν οὐκέτι κατὰ γῆν ἐπορεύετο, ἀλλὰ τὴν μὲν στρατιὰν τῷ στρατηγῷ ἐπέτρεψε ἀπάγειν εἰς τὸν Ἑλλήσποντον, αὐτὸς δ᾽ ἐπὶ νεὼς Φοινίσσης ἐκομίζετο εἰς τὴν Ἀσίαν. ἡ δὲ ναῦς μάλιστα ἐπιέζετο ἀνέμῳ τε καὶ χειμῶνι καὶ ἔμελλε καταδύσεσθαι· συχνοὶ γὰρ Πέρσαι μετὰ βασιλέως ἐκομίζοντο καὶ ἐπὶ τοῦ καταστρώματος ἐπῆσαν. ὁ οὖν Ξέρξης καὶ ὁ κυβερνήτης περὶ τοῦ κινδύνου ἐβουλεύοντο· καὶ ὁ κυβερνήτης λέγει· Δέσποτα, εἰ βούλει σῴζειν τὴν σὴν ψυχήν, ἀναγκαῖόν ἐστιν ἀπαλλάσσεσθαι τῶν ἐπιβατῶν. ὁ δὲ Ξέρξης λέγει τοῖς Πέρσαις, Ἄνδρες Πέρσαι, νῦν καιρός[2] ἐστιν ὑμῖν ἀποφαίνειν τὴν ὑμετέραν πρὸς ἐμὲ φιλίαν· ἐν ὑμῖν γὰρ δοκεῖ εἶναι ἐμοὶ ἡ σωτηρία. οἱ δὲ εὐθὺς ἐξάλλονται εἰς τὴν θάλασσαν· καὶ οὕτως ἔσωσαν βασιλέα, ἐπεὶ ἡ ναῦς νῦν ἦν κουφοτέρα. ὁ δὲ Ξέρξης, ὡς ἀποβαίνει εἰς γῆν, ὅτι μὲν ἔσωσε βασιλέως τὴν ψυχήν, παρέχει τῷ κυβερνήτῃ χρυσοῦν στέφανον, ὅτι δὲ ἠνάγκασε συχνοὺς Πέρσας ἀποθανεῖν, ἀποτέμνει τὴν κεφαλὴν αὐτοῦ.

Adapted from Herodotus VIII.118

---

[1]   The Strymon river in Macedonia.

[2]   καιρός, 'precise moment', 'opportunity' as opposed to χρόνος, 'time'.

Chapter 19 Vocabulary

Verbs:

βούλομαι	want, wish, be willing	ἐπιτρέπω	entrust
βουλήσομαι, etc.			

Nouns:

τὰ ἀληθῆ	the truth	Κορίνθιος, -ου, ὁ	a Corinthian
ἁλιεύς, -έως, ὁ	fisherman	Πολυκράτης,	Polycrates
Ἄμασις, -ιος, ὁ	Amasis	-ους, ὁ	
ἀπορία, -ας, ἡ	difficulty, want (of something)	Σαλαμίς, -ῖνος, ἡ	Salamis
		Σικελία, -ας, ἡ	Sicily
ἀρχή, -ῆς, ἡ	rule, empire, command	σφραγίς, -ῖδος, ἡ	ring
θεράπων, -οντος, ὁ	(male) servant		

Adjectives:

ἀληθής, -ές	true	εὐτυχής, -ές	fortunate
ἀσθενής, -ές	weak	εὔφρων, -ον	kindly
ἀσφαλής, -ές	safe	ἡδύς, -εῖα, -ύ	sweet, pleasant
βαθύς, -εῖα, -ύ	deep	μέγας, -άλη, -α	big, great, large
βαρύς, -εῖα, -ύ	heavy	ὀξύς, -εῖα, -ύ	sharp
βραδύς, -εῖα, -ύ	slow	πολύς, πολλή,	much, many
βραχύς, -εῖα, -ύ	short	πολύ	
γλυκύς, -εῖα, -ύ	sweet	σαφής, -ές	clear
εὐγενής, -ές	well-born	σώφρων, -ον	prudent
εὐδαίμων,	happy	τάλας, -αινα, -αν	wretched
εὔδαιμον		ταχύς, -εῖα, -ύ	swift, quick
εὐρύς, -εῖα, -ύ	wide	ψευδής, -ές	false

CHAPTER 20

πάντων χρημάτων μέτρον ἐστὶν ἄνθρωπος, τῶν μὲν
ὄντων ὡς ἔστιν, τῶν δὲ μὴ ὄντων ὡς οὔκ ἐστιν.

—Protagoras

1. Participles

A participle is the adjectival form of a verb (active: 'calling', 'having called'; passive: 'being called', 'having been called'). Because they are verb forms, participles come in all tenses (except the imperfect and pluperfect). Because they are adjectives, they also have case, gender and number, so they can agree with whatever noun they modify.

Endings: **Active** participles, and the **aorist passive**, have 3rd declension M/N endings and 1st declension F endings. Most **middle** and **passive** participles have 2nd declension M/N endings and 1st declension F endings.

2. The present active participle in -ων

A: Form. Here are the present participial forms of the verb εἰμί ('being'). They are also the *endings* for the present active participle of thematic verbs. The present participle has the thematic vowel o.

	SINGULAR			PLURAL		
	M	**F**	**N**	**M**	**F**	**N**
Nom.	ὤν	οὖσα	ὄν	ὄντες	οὖσαι	ὄντα
Gen.	ὄντος	οὔσης	ὄντος	ὄντων	οὐσῶν	ὄντων
Dat.	ὄντι	οὔσῃ	ὄντι	οὖσι(ν)	οὔσαις	οὖσι(ν)
Acc.	ὄντα	οὖσαν	ὄν	ὄντας	οὔσας	ὄντα
Voc.	ὤν	οὖσα	ὄν	ὄντες	οὖσαι	ὄντα

Note: The masc. and neuter dative plural have the same ending as the third person plural present active indicative verb. Here are the forms of **λύων**, 'loosing':

	SINGULAR			PLURAL		
	M	**F**	**N**	**M**	**F**	**N**
Nom.	λύων	λύουσα	λῦον	λύοντες	λύουσαι	λύοντα
Gen.	λύοντος	λυούσης	λύοντος	λυόντων	λυουσῶν	λυόντων
Dat.	λύοντι	λυούσῃ	λύοντι	λύουσι(ν)	λυούσαις	λύουσι(ν)
Acc.	λύοντα	λύουσαν	λῦον	λύοντας	λυούσας	λύοντα
Voc.	λύων	λύουσα	λῦον	λύοντες	λύουσαι	λύοντα

Note: The accent of these present active participles is on the last syllable of the stem, except that as usual the fem. genitive plural has a circumflex on the ultima (Ch. 3.5).

In the present tense of contract verbs, the vowel of the stem contracts as usual with the thematic vowel **o** (Ch. 18).

φιλῶν (φιλέ-ων)   φιλοῦσα (φιλέ-ουσα)   φιλοῦν (φιλέ-ον)
φιλοῦντος (φιλέ-οντος), etc., 'loving'

τιμῶν (τιμά-ων)   τιμῶσα (τιμά-ουσα)   τιμῶν (τιμά-ον)
τιμῶντος (τιμά-οντος), etc., 'honoring'

δηλῶν (δηλό-ων)   δηλοῦσα (δηλό-ουσα)   δηλοῦν (δηλό-ον)
δηλοῦντος (δηλό-οντος), etc., 'showing'

B.1: Meaning. The *attributive participle* modifies a noun, and behaves like any attributive adjective (Ch. 7.2).

αἱ σοφαί γυναῖκες   the wise women
οἱ φεύγοντες ἄνδρες   the fleeing men, the men who are fleeing

When an attributive participle appears with a noun, it must be in the attributive position:

οἱ διώκοντες στρατηγοί   the pursuing generals, the generals who are pursuing
οἱ στρατηγοὶ οἱ διώκοντες   the pursuing generals, the generals who are pursuing

Note: As you see above, one way to translate the attributive participle is to use a relative clause. Greek uses participial phrases much more frequently than English; a relative clause is often a better English translation.

Like any adjective, the participle can also be used with an article to create a noun phrase: οἱ διώκοντες, 'those (the men) who are pursuing', αἱ σοφαί, 'those (the women) who are wise'. In this case too a relative clause is usually a good translation, as in the following examples:

οὐ τιμῶμεν τοὺς ἐκ τῆς μάχης φεύγοντας.
    We do not honor <u>those who flee</u> from battle.

οἱ ἐν τῇ πόλει μένοντες ἀκούουσι τοῦ ῥήτορος.
    <u>Those who remain</u> in the city are listening to the orator.

B.2: Meaning. The *circumstantial participle*. Alone or in a phrase, the participle can also express a variety of circumstances. This is common in English:

I saw him *sitting by the fire.*
Running into the room, he tripped and fell.

It is even more common in Greek, which often uses a participle where English would use a subordinate clause. A clause beginning 'if', 'when', 'since' or 'although' is often a good translation of a Greek participial phrase. The least common of these is the 'although' clause; the word καίπερ, 'although', is sometimes included to make the meaning clear.

<u>φίλους ἔχοντες</u> εὐδαίμονες ἐσόμεθα.
    If we have friends we will be happy.

<u>φίλους ἔχοντες</u> εὐδαίμονες ἐσόμεθα.
    When we have friends we will be happy.

<u>φίλους ἔχοντες</u> εὐδαίμονές ἐσμεν.
    Since we have friends we are happy.

(καίπερ) <u>φίλους</u> <u>ἔχοντες</u> εὐδαίμονες οὔκ ἐσμεν.
Although we have friends, we are not happy.

In each of the sentences above the participle is nominative plural, because it refers to a plural subject. The ending makes a participle agree with a particular noun (there is no such thing in Greek as a dangling participle!). Compare the following sentences:

ὁρῶμεν τοὺς ἵππους <u>τρέχοντες</u> ἐν τῷ λειμῶνι.
While running in the meadow, we see the horses.

ὁρῶμεν τοὺς ἵππους <u>τρέχοντας</u> ἐν τῷ λειμῶνι.
We see the horses running in the meadow.

ὁρῶμεν τοὺς ἵππους τοὺς <u>τρέχοντας</u> ἐν τῷ λειμῶνι.
We see the horses which are running in the meadow.

B. 3: Meaning. Here is an easy way to distinguish the attributive from the circumstantial participle when you first look at a sentence: the attributive participle always has its own article; the circumstantial participle never does. Contrast the following:

a)   ὁρῶμεν τοὺς τρέχοντας ἵππους.
     We see the running horses. (attributive)

b)   ὁρῶμεν τοὺς ἵππους τρέχοντας.
     We see the horses running. (circumstantial)

a)   ὁρῶμεν τοὺς ἄνδρας τοὺς ζῷα διώκοντας.
     We see the men who are pursuing animals. (attributive)

b)   ὁρῶμεν τοὺς ἄνδρας ζῷα διώκοντας.
     We see the men pursuing animals. (circumstantial)

C: Tense of the participle. The tense of a participle expresses time relative to that of the main verb. The present participle refers to the *same* time as the main verb; in the following example, the seeing and the pursuing take place at the same time.

διώκων τὸν ἵππον παῖδα εἶδεν.
While pursuing the horse, he saw a child.

EXERCISE 101.

1.   οἱ ἐν τῇ πόλει μένοντες μωροί εἰσιν.
2.   οἱ πολέμιοι διώκοντες ἐκωλύθησαν τῷ χειμῶνι.
3.   ἀκούεις τὰς τῶν θυόντων φωνάς;
4.   τὸν ποταμὸν διαβαίνοντες ὁρῶνται ὑπὸ τῶν φίλων.
5.   ὁ Λεωνίδας πίπτει ἐν τῇ μάχῃ ἄγων τοὺς τριακοσίους Λακεδαιμονίους.
6.   τιμᾶτε τοὺς πολίτας τοὺς ὑπὲρ τῆς πατρίδος κινδυνεύοντας.
7.   πιστεύομεν τοῖς τὴν πύλην φυλάσσουσιν.
8.   ὁρῶμεν τὰς καμήλους διωκούσας τοὺς ἵππους.
9.   τιμῶμεν τοὺς ἐπὶ τοὺς Λακεδαιμονίους στρατεύοντας.
10. οἱ νεανίαι οἱ ἐν τοῖς ἀγῶσι νικῶντες τιμηθήσονται ὑπὸ τοῦ δήμου.

EXERCISE 102.

1.   We see the enemy cutting down the trees.
2.   Those who flee are not worthy of honor.
3.   The Athenians honor those who are willing to fight.
4.   While crossing the mountain we were hindered by the enemy.

5. Honor those who write beautiful poems.
6. We can see the Persians fleeing.
7. Those who were pursuing could not find the river.
8. While fleeing from the city, our friends were hindered by the snow.
9. Orators who speak well do not always persuade.
10. Since we do not have faithful allies, we shall not be able to conquer.

3. The future active participle

A: Form. The *future active* participle is formed from the second principal part. It has the same thematic vowel and endings as the present; they are attached to the future stem. The accent is always on the stem, except in the fem. genitive plural (section 2A above; Ch. 3.5).

λύσων   λύσουσα   λῦσον
λύσοντος, etc.

B: Meaning. The future participle is used for an action which will occur after that of the main verb. This relationship must be translated by a clause, since there is no future participle in English:

τιμῶ τοὺς σώσοντας τὴν πόλιν.
I honor those who will save the city.

4. The aorist active participle

A: Form. The *weak* or *first aorist active* participle is formed from the third principal part. Except in the nom. sing., the only difference from the present participle is that the tense marker σα substitutes for the thematic vowel o, just as it does in the indicative. The accent is on the stem, except in the fem. genitive plural (section 2A above; Ch. 3.5).

	SINGULAR			PLURAL		
	M	**F**	**N**	**M**	**F**	**N**
Nom.	λύσας	λύσασα	λῦσαν	λύσαντες	λύσασαι	λύσαντα
Gen.	λύσαντος	λυσάσης	λύσαντος	λυσάντων	λυσασῶν	λυσάντων
Dat.	λύσαντι	λυσάσῃ	λύσαντι	λύσασι(ν)	λυσάσαις	λύσασι(ν)
Acc.	λύσαντα	λύσασαν	λῦσαν	λύσαντας	λυσάσας	λύσαντα
Voc.	λύσας	λύσασα	λῦσαν	λύσαντες	λύσασαι	λύσαντα

The *strong* or *second aorist active* participle, like the indicative and infinitive, uses the thematic vowel o instead of the weak aorist marker σα. Thus this form has the same endings as the present. However, the accent is on the thematic vowel, except in the fem. genitive plural (section 2A above; Ch. 3.5).

	SINGULAR			PLURAL		
	M	**F**	**N**	**M**	**F**	**N**
Nom.	λιπών	λιποῦσα	λιπόν	λιπόντες	λιποῦσαι	λιπόντα
Gen.	λιπόντος	λιπούσης	λιπόντος	λιπόντων	λιπουσῶν	λιπόντων
Dat.	λιπόντι	λιπούσῃ	λιπόντι	λιποῦσι(ν)	λιπούσαις	λιποῦσι(ν)
Acc.	λιπόντα	λιποῦσαν	λιπόν	λιπόντας	λιπούσας	λιπόντα
Voc.	λιπών	λιποῦσα	λιπόν	λιπόντες	λιποῦσαι	λιπόντα

B: Meaning. The aorist participle is used for an action that occurs before that of the main verb. The participles in the following sentences could be translated in several equivalent ways, but the time relative to the main verb must always be clear.

οἱ διώξαντες τοὺς πολεμίους νικήσουσιν.

Those having pursued
Those who pursued
} the enemy will conquer.

διώξαντες τοὺς πολεμίους εἰς τὸν ποταμόν, ἐπαυσάμεθα τῆς μάχης.

Having pursued
After pursuing
After/when we had pursued
} the enemy to the river, we ceased from battle.

5. The perfect active participle

A: Form. The *perfect active* participle is formed from the fourth principal part, with a new set of endings.

	SINGULAR			PLURAL		
	M	**F**	**N**	**M**	**F**	**N**
Nom.	λελυκώς	λελυκυῖα	λελυκός	λελυκότες	λελυκυῖαι	λελυκότα
Gen.	λελυκότος	λελυκυίας	λελυκότος	λελυκότων	λελυκυιῶν	λελυκότων
Dat.	λελυκότι	λελυκυίᾳ	λελυκότι	λελυκόσι(ν)	λελυκυίαις	λελυκόσι(ν)
Acc.	λελυκότα	λελυκυῖαν	λελυκός	λελυκότας	λελυκυίας	λελυκότα
Voc.	λελυκός	λελυκυῖα	λελυκός	λελυκότες	λελυκυῖαι	λελυκότα

B: Meaning. Like the perfect indicative, the perfect participle is only used to express the result of a completed action; for example, οἱ τεθνηκότες, 'the dead', 'those who have died'.[1] The simple translation is 'having — ed'. An aorist participle may be translated the same way, for example 'having pursued'. But with the perfect, the verb itself may carry the idea of completion: 'having arrived2', 'having finished'. The difference is clearer when the participle is translated as a relative clause: οἱ ἀποθανόντες, 'those who died'; οἱ τεθνηκότες, 'those who have died'.

6. The adjective πᾶς

The adjective πᾶς, πᾶσα, πᾶν, 'all', has the same endings as the aorist active participle, though the accent is different.

	SINGULAR			PLURAL		
	M	**F**	**N**	**M**	**F**	**N**
Nom.	πᾶς	πᾶσα	πᾶν	πάντες	πᾶσαι	πάντα
Gen.	παντός	πάσης	παντός	πάντων	πασῶν	πάντων
Dat.	παντί	πάσῃ	παντί	πᾶσι(ν)	πάσαις	πᾶσι(ν)
Acc.	πάντα	πᾶσαν	πᾶν	πάντας	πάσας	πάντα
Voc.	πᾶς	πᾶσα	πᾶν	πάντες	πᾶσαι	πάντα

---

[1]   The form τέθνηκα, from the simple verb θνήσκω, 'die', is used in the perfect tense instead of the compound ἀποθνήσκω.

πᾶς has the following range of meanings:

•'whole', in attributive position	ἡ πᾶσα χώρα	the whole country
	οἱ πάντες πολῖται	the whole (body of) citizens
•'all', in predicate position	πάντες οἱ πολῖται	all the citizens
•'every' (sing.), 'all' (plur.),	πᾶσα χώρα	every country
without an article	πάντες πολῖται	all citizens

Note: The word order of the English translation is the same as the Greek word order.

EXERCISE 103.

1. πείσας τὴν γυναῖκα ἀποθνῄσκειν, ὁ Ἄδμητος ἔτι ἐβασίλευεν.
2. τιμήσομεν τοὺς τὴν πόλιν σώσαντας.
3. λύσας τοὺς βοῦς, ὁ γέρων οὐκ ἔμενεν ἐν τῷ λειμῶνι.
4. οἱ ἐν τῇ πόλει ἐφύλασσον τὰς πύλας τὴν πᾶσαν νύκτα.
5. κολάσομεν τοὺς παῖδας τοὺς τὰ δένδρα βλάψαντας.
6. ὁ στρατηγὸς ἔλυσε πάντας τοὺς αἰχμαλώτους τοὺς ἔτι μένοντας ἐν τῇ νήσῳ.
7. οὐ πιστεύομεν τοῖς τὸν ἄγγελον πέμψασιν.
8. χάριν ἔχομεν τοῖς φίλοις τοῖς τὴν πατρίδα σεσωκόσιν.
9. τιμῶμεν τοὺς ἡμᾶς εὖ πεποιηκότας.
10. ἦν ἡδὺ πᾶσι τοῖς μετὰ τοῦ Ξενοφῶντος ὁρᾶν τὴν θάλασσαν.

EXERCISE 104.

1. Having persuaded the allies to send help, the general began to march.
2. All the prisoners will be set free in three days.
3. After capturing the city, the allies are marching homeward.
4. After sending away all the women and children, the Athenians trusted their ships and their friends.
5. It is wise to trust those who trust us.
6. Those who conquered in the sea battle are worthy of honor.
7. Socrates was the wisest of all the Greeks.
8. We shall guard the ships that remain in the harbor.
9. Xerxes ordered all the cities to send earth and water.
10. Few are those who will send help.

7. Present middle/passive participles

A: Form. There is only one set of endings for middle and passive participles, except for the aorist passive (section 8 below). They are declined like normal first and second declension adjectives. In the present tense these endings are attached to the present stem with the thematic vowel **o**.

	SINGULAR			PLURAL		
	M	**F**	**N**	**M**	**F**	**N**
Nom.	λυόμενος	λυομένη	λυόμενον	λυόμενοι	λυόμεναι	λυόμενα
Gen.	λυομένου	λυομένης	λυομένου	λυομένων	λυομένων	λυομένων
Dat.	λυομένῳ	λυομένη	λυομένῳ	λυομένοις	λυομέναις	λυομένοις
Acc.	λυόμενον	λυομένην	λυόμενον	λυομένους	λυομένας	λυόμενα
Voc.	λυόμενε	λυομένη	λυόμενον	λυόμενοι	λυόμεναι	λυόμενα

In the present tense of contract verbs, the vowel of the stem contracts as usual with the thematic vowel:

φιλούμενος	φιλουμένη	φιλούμενον	(φιλε-όμενος, -η, ον)
φιλουμένου, etc.			
τιμώμενος	τιμωμένη	τιμώμενον	(τιμα-όμενος, -η, ον)
τιμωμένου, etc.			
δηλούμενος	δηλουμένη	δηλούμενον	(δηλο-όμενος, -η, ον)
δηλουμένου, etc.			

B: Meaning. The middle participle has the same range of active meanings as the middle indicative: λυόμενος, 'ransoming', μαχόμενος, 'fighting', etc.

8. Future, aorist and perfect middle and passive participles

A: Form. The *future middle* participle has the same endings as the present middle/passive, attached to the future stem (second principal part).

λυσόμενος	λυσομένη	λυσόμενον
λυσομένου, etc.		

B: Meaning. Like the active, the future middle participle must be translated by a clause.

μένομεν τοὺς λυσομένους ἡμᾶς.   We await those who will ransom us.

A: Form. The *weak* or *first aorist middle* participle has the same endings as the present middle/passive, attached to the weak aorist stem (third principal part).

λυσάμενος	λυσαμένη	λυσάμενον
λυσαμένου, etc.		

The *strong* or *second aorist middle* participle has the same endings as the present middle/passive, attached to the strong aorist stem (third principal part).

πιθόμενος	πιθομένη	πιθόμενον
πιθομένου, etc.		

B: Meaning. Like the active, the aorist middle participle has a range of meanings indicating time before the main verb.

τιμῶμεν τοὺς λυσαμένους τοὺς συμμάχους.
We honor those who ransomed the allies.

λυσάμενοι τοὺς συμμάχους, οἴκαδε ἐπορευσάμεθα.
Having ransomed
After ransoming   } our allies, we journeyed homeward.
After/when we had ransomed

A: Form. The *perfect middle/passive* participle is formed from the fifth principal part, with the same set of endings as above. The accent is on the **ε** of the ending throughout.

λελυμένος	λελυμένη	λελυμένον
λελυμένου, etc.		

B: Meaning. The perfect participle is only used to emphasize the present result of a past action. The middle can be translated 'having —ed', 'those who have —ed', etc. The passive is translated 'having been —ed', 'those who have been —ed', etc. As in the active, the difference between aorist and perfect is only clear when you translate the participle as a clause.

A: Form. The *aorist passive* participle is formed from the sixth principal part (for the strong aorist formation, see Ch. 21.2). Like the indicative, its endings resemble those of active participles. They are attached to the aorist passive stem, with a shortened tense marker -θε- (-θει- in the masc. nom. and the fem.). The accent is on this syllable.

> λυθείς   λυθεῖσα   λυθέν
> λυθέντος, etc.

B: Meaning. The aorist passive participle can be translated 'having been —ed', 'those who have were —ed', etc.: οἱ νικηθέντες, 'those who were conquered'.

A: Form. The *future passive* participle is also formed from the sixth principal part + σ. It has regular middle/passive endings.

> λυθησόμενος   λυθησομένη   λυθησόμενον
> λυθησομένου, etc.

B: Meaning. The future passive participle, like other future participles, must be translated by a clause.

> οἱ λυθησόμενοι ἵπποι εἰσὶν ἐν τῷ λειμῶνι.
> The horses which will be freed are in the meadow.

EXERCISE 105.

1. οἱ Ἀθηναῖοι λυσάμενοι τοὺς αἰχμαλώτους τὴν εἰρήνην ἐποιήσαντο.
2. διωκόμενοι ὑπὸ τῶν Ἀθηναίων, οἱ Πέρσαι φεύγουσιν εἰς τὴν θάλασσαν.
3. τῷ ποταμῷ κωλυθείς, ὁ στρατηγὸς ἐκέλευσεν ἡμᾶς στρατοπεδεύεσθαι.
4. οἱ ἡμᾶς λυσόμενοι οὐ σπεύδουσιν.
5. οἰκτείρομεν τοὺς τεθνηκότας.
6. οἱ λυθέντες οἴκαδε ἀπεχώρησαν.
7. ὁ Μιλτιάδης στρατηγὸς ποιηθεὶς ἐνίκησε τοὺς Πέρσας.
8. πολὺν χρόνον βουλευσάμενοι, οἱ στρατηγοὶ ἐκέλευσαν τὴν στρατιὰν προχωρεῖν.
9. σώσομεν τοὺς δεδουλωμένους.
10. ἡ ναῦς ἡ τῷ χειμῶνι κωλυθεῖσα ἔμενεν ἐγγὺς τῆς νήσου.

EXERCISE 106.

1. Having been hindered by the broad river, the enemy went away.
2. The general ordered those who had been set free to encamp.
3. Those who have been conquered are hurrying homeward.
4. We are willing to wait for those who will ransom us.
5. The women who have been set free are rejoicing.
6. Leonidas falls while fighting the Persians.
7. Those who have been made generals will manage the affairs of the city.
8. Obeying the god, the Athenians trusted not the wooden walls themselves, but their ships.
9. While marching through Armenia, the Greeks were in great danger.
10. Are those who are taught wiser than those who teach?

EXERCISE 107.

THE INGENUITY OF CYRUS

Cyrus the Great, who ruled Persia from 549 to 529 BC, after conquering Lydia and Ionia, turned East and captured Babylon in 538; his campaigns had extended as far as India.

οἱ δὲ Βαβυλώνιοι, νικηθέντες ὑπὸ τῶν Περσῶν μάχῃ ἔξω τῶν τειχῶν, εἰς τὴν πόλιν ἀπεχώρησαν. ἔπειτα δὲ ὁ Κῦρος μάλιστα ἠπόρει, ὅτι τοῖς Βαβυλωνίοις ἦν σῖτος ἐτῶν δὴ πολλῶν. εἴτε δὴ οὖν ἄλλος αὐτῷ ἀποροῦντι συνεβούλευσεν, εἴτε καὶ αὐτὸς ἐμάνθανε καλὴν βουλήν, ἐποίει ὧδε· τάξας τὴν στρατιὰν πᾶσαν ἐξ ἐμβολῆς τοῦ Εὐφράτου καλουμένου ποταμοῦ, ᾗ εἰς τὴν πόλιν εἰσβάλλει, καὶ ὄπισθεν αὖθις τῆς πόλεως τάξας ἑτέρους, ᾗ ἐκβαίνει ἐκ τῆς πόλεως ὁ ποταμός, ἐκέλευσεν τὸν στρατόν, ἐπεὶ ὄψονται τὸ ῥεῖθρον διαβατὸν ὄντα, εἰσβαίνειν αὐτῷ εἰς τὴν πόλιν.

ἔπειτα δὲ ὁ Κῦρος ἤγαγε τοὺς λοιποὺς τῶν ἀνδρῶν πρὸς τὴν λίμνην, ἣν ἡ τῶν Βαβυλωνίων βασίλεια ἔπραξεν ἐν τῷ πρὶν χρόνῳ ἐγγὺς τοῦ ποταμοῦ. ὁ δὲ Κῦρος τὸν ποταμὸν διώρυχι εἰσαγαγὼν εἰς τὴν λίμνην οὖσαν ἕλος, τὸ ἀρχαῖον ῥεῖθρον διαβατὸν εἶναι ἐποίησεν. καὶ οὕτως οἱ Πέρσαι οἱ ταχθέντες ἔξω τῆς πόλεως κατὰ τὸ ῥεῖθρον οἷοί τ᾽ ἦσαν εἰσβαίνειν εἰς τὴν Βαβυλῶνα. εἰ μὲν ἐπύθοντο οἱ Βαβυλώνιοι τὸ ἐκ τοῦ Κύρου ποιούμενον, ὁρῶντες τοὺς Πέρσας εἰσβαίνοντας εἰς τὴν πόλιν κατέλυσαν ἂν αὐτούς. νῦν δὲ οὐκ εἶδον· ὑπὸ γὰρ μεγέθους τῆς πόλεως, τὸν θάνατον τὸν τῶν περὶ τὰ ἔσχατα οἰκούντων οἱ ἐν τῷ μέσῳ οὐκ ἐμάνθανον, ἀλλὰ (τύχῃ γὰρ ἑορτή ἦν) ἐχόρευον πολὺν χρόνον καὶ ἐν εὐπαθείαις ἦσαν [were making merry], ἕως δὴ καὶ τὰ ἀληθῆ ἐμάνθανον. καὶ Βαβυλὼν οὕτω τότε πρῶτον ᾑρέθη.

Adapted from Herodotus I.190-191

Chapter 20 Vocabulary

Verbs:

ἀποπέμπω	send away	θνήσκω, θανοῦμαι,	die
ἀπορέω	be at a loss	ἔθανον, τέθνηκα	
ἀποχωρέω	go away	κολάζω	punish
βουλεύω	plan	προχωρέω	advance
		χαίρω	rejoice

Nouns:

ἄγγελος, -ου, ὁ	messenger	ποίημα, -ατος, τό	poem
Ἀρμενία, -ας, ἡ	Armenia	φίλος, -ου, ὁ	friend
βοήθεια, -ας, ἡ	help		

Adjectives:

ξύλινος, -η, -ον	of wood, wooden	πᾶς, πᾶσα, πᾶν	all, every, whole

Conjunction:

καίπερ	although

CHAPTER 21

1. The perfect middle/passive of consonant stem verbs

Since the perfect middle/passive endings are added directly to the stem of the fifth principal part, some consonant clusters will result. You have already seen how stops combine with **σ** (Ch. 8.1). The complete list follows. You will see that stops become voiced / unvoiced / aspirated when the following consonant is voiced / unvoiced / aspirated. Similar adjustments are made in English: we say 'practical' but 'pragmatic'.

π	π	π	π
β + μ = μμ	β + σ = ψ	β + τ = πτ	β + σθ = φθ
φ	φ	φ	φ
τ	τ	τ	τ
δ + μ = σμ	δ + σ = σ	δ + τ = στ	δ + σθ = σθ
θ	θ	θ	θ
κ	κ	κ	κ
γ + μ = γμ	γ + σ = ξ	γ + τ = κτ	γ + σθ = χθ
χ	χ	χ	χ

The following examples show the perfect and pluperfect of a labial stem (γράφω), a dental stem (πείθω) and a palatal stem (ἄγω).

Note: In the third person plural, the consonant cluster would be so complicated that it is avoided altogether. Instead, the nominative plural participle appears with a third plural form of the verb εἰμί, 'be':

perfect:	part. + present	γεγραμμένοι εἰσί	they have been written
pluperfect:	part. + imperfect	γεγραμμένοι ἦσαν	they had been written

		γράφω	**πείθω**	**ἄγω**
INDICATIVE				
Perfect				
SING.	1st	γέγραμμαι	πέπεισμαι	ἦγμαι
	2nd	γέγραψαι	πέπεισαι	ἦξαι
	3rd	γέγραπται	πέπεισται	ἦκται
PLUR.	1st	γεγράμμεθα	πεπείσμεθα	ἤγμεθα
	2nd	γέγραφθε	πέπεισθε	ἦχθε
	3rd	γεγραμμένοι εἰσί(ν)	πεπεισμένοι εἰσί(ν)	ἠγμένοι εἰσί(ν)

		γράφω	πείθω	ἄγω
INDICATIVE				
Pluperfect				
SING.	1st	ἐγεγράμμην	ἐπεπείσμην	ἤγμην
	2nd	ἐγέγραψο	ἐπέπεισο	ἦξο
	3rd	ἐγέγραπτο	ἐπέπειστο	ἦκτο
PLUR.	1st	ἐγεγράμμεθα	ἐπεπείσμεθα	ἤγμεθα
	2nd	ἐγέγραφθε	ἐπέπεισθε	ἦχθε
	3rd	γεγραμμένοι ἦσαν	πεπεισμένοι ἦσαν	ἠγμένοι ἦσαν
INFINITIVE		γέγραφθαι	πέπεισθαι	ἦχθαι
PARTICIPLE		γεγραμμένος, -η, -ον	πεπεισμένος, -η, -ον	ἠγμένος, -η, -ον
		γεγραμμένου, etc.	πεπεισμένου, etc.	ἠγμένου, etc.

2. The aorist and future passive of consonant stem verbs

Many consonant stem verbs have strong aorist passives. The endings are the same as those of the regular weak passive (Ch. 14.5). However, instead of the **θ** that marks the weak forms, these verbs either add or substitute another consonant. The form cannot always be predicted, but there are a few consistent patterns.

a) Verbs with dental stems, and some others, have -**σθ**-:

παύω   ἐπαύσθην
πείθω   ἐπείσθην

b) Verbs with labial or palatal stems may keep their own consonant, or aspirate it before the **θ**:

γράφω   ἐγράφην   βλάπτω   ἐβλάβην
λείπω   ἐλείφθην   διώκω   ἐδιώχθην

The future passive of these verbs has the same stem as the aorist passive + **σ**, and regular future passive endings: ἐγράφην, γραφήσομαι; ἐδιώχθην, διωχθήσομαι; etc.

3. Principal parts

You have now met all six principal parts of the Greek verb (Ch. 2.1). The following list reviews which principal part is the basis for which tense(s):

P.P.	FORMS THE FOLLOWING TENSES
First:	present and imperfect active, middle, passive
Second:	future active, middle
Third:	aorist active, middle
Fourth:	perfect and pluperfect active
Fifth:	perfect and pluperfect middle, passive
Sixth:	aorist and future passive

A number of common verbs show a stem change or other irregularity in one or more principal parts. Some of these are predictable; others are not. The following list gives the principal parts of the most important irregular verbs in Ch. 2-21.

PRESENT	FUTURE A/M	AORIST A/M	PERFECT A	PERFECT M/P	AORIST P
ἀγγέλλω	ἀγγελῶ	ἤγγειλα	ἤγγελκα	ἤγγελμαι	ἠγγέλθην
ἄγω	ἄξω	ἤγαγον	ἦχα	ἦγμαι	ἤχθην
αἱρέω	αἱρήσω	εἷλον	ᾕρηκα	ᾕρημαι	ᾑρέθην
ἀκούω	ἀκούσομαι	ἤκουσα	ἀκήκοα	—	ἠκούσθην
ἀποθνήσκω	ἀποθανοῦμαι	ἀπέθανον	(τέθνηκα)[1]	—	—
ἄρχω	ἄρξω	ἦρξα	ἦρχα	ἦργμαι	ἤρχθην
βαίνω	βήσομαι	ἔβην	βέβηκα	—	—
βάλλω	βαλῶ	ἔβαλον	βέβληκα	βέβλημαι	ἐβλήθην
βλάπτω	βλάψω	ἔβλαψα	βέβλαφα	βέβλαμμαι	ἐβλάβην
					ἐβλάφθην
βοηθέω	βοηθήσω	ἐβοήθησα	βεβοήθηκα	βεβοήθημαι	ἐβοήθην
βούλομαι	βουλήσομαι	ἐβουλησάμην	—	βεβούλημαι	ἐβουλήθην
γράφω	γράψω	ἔγραψα	γέγραφα	γέγραμμαι	ἐγράφην
διώκω	διώξω	ἐδίωξα	δεδίωχα	δεδίωγμαι	ἐδιώχθην
ἐθέλω	ἐθελήσω	ἠθέλησα	ἠθέληκα	—	—
εἰμί	ἔσομαι	—		—	—
ἕλκω	ἕλξω	εἵλκυσα	—	εἵλκυσμαι	εἱλκύσθην
		εἷλξα			
εὑρίσκω	εὑρήσω	ηὗρον	ηὕρηκα	ηὕρημαι	ηὑρέθην
		εὗρον	εὕρηκα	εὕρημαι	
ἔχω	ἕξω/σχήσω	ἔσχον	ἔσχηκα	—	—
ἥκω	ἥξω	—		—	—
κρύπτω	κρύψω	ἔκρυψα	κέκρυφα	κέκρυμμαι	ἐκρύφθην
λαμβάνω	λήψομαι	ἔλαβον	εἴληφα	εἴλημμαι	ἐλήφθην
λανθάνω	λήσω	ἔλαθον	λέληθα	—	—
λέγω	λέξω	ἔλεξα	εἴρηκα	λέλεγμαι	ἐλέχθην
		εἶπον			
λείπω	λείψω	ἔλιπον	λέλοιπα	λέλειμμαι	ἐλείφθην
μανθάνω	μαθήσομαι	ἔμαθον	μεμάθηκα	—	—
μάχομαι	μαχοῦμαι	ἐμαχεσάμην	—	μεμάχημαι	—
μέλλω	μελλήσω	ἐμέλλησα	—	—	—
μένω	μενῶ	ἔμεινα	μεμένηκα	—	—
οἰκτείρω	οἰκτερῶ	ᾤκτειρα	—	—	—
ὁράω	ὄψομαι	εἶδον	ἑώρακα	ἑώραμαι	ὤφθην
πάσχω	πείσομαι	ἔπαθον	πέπονθα	—	—
παύω	παύσω	ἔπαυσα	πέπαυκα	πέπαυμαι	ἐπαύσθην
πείθομαι	πείσομαι	ἐπιθόμην	—	πέπεισμαι	—
πείθω	πείσω	ἔπεισα	πέπεικα	πέπεισμαι	ἐπείσθην
			πέποιθα		
πέμπω	πέμψω	ἔπεμψα	πέπομφα	πέπεμμαι	ἐπέμφθην
πίπτω	πεσοῦμαι	ἔπεσον	πέπτωκα	—	—
πράσσω	πράξω	ἔπραξα	πέπραχα	πέπραγμαι	ἐπράχθην
σῴζω	σώσω	ἔσωσα	σέσωκα	σέσω(σ)μαι	ἐσώθην
τάσσω	τάξω	ἔταξα	τέταχα	τέταγμαι	ἐτάχθην
τρέφω	θρέψω	ἔθρεψα	τέτροφα	τέθραμμαι	ἐτράφην
τρέχω	δραμοῦμαι	ἔδραμον	δεδράμηκα	—	—

---

[1] The simple verb θνῄσκω is used instead of the compound in the perfect tense.

PRESENT	FUTURE A/M	AORIST A/M	PERFECT A	PERFECT M/P	AORIST P
τυγχάνω	τεύξομαι	ἔτυχον	τετύχηκα	——	——
τύπτω	τύψω	ἔτυψα	τέτυφα	τέτυμμαι	ἐτύπην
φαίνομαι	φανοῦμαι	——	——	πέφασμαι	ἐφάνθην
φέρω	οἴσω	ἤνεγκον	ἐνήνοχα	ἐνήνεγμαι	ἠνέχθην
φεύγω	φεύξομαι	ἔφυγον	πέφευγα	——	——
φθάνω	φθήσομαι	ἔφθασα ἔφθην	——	——	——
φυλάσσω	φυλάξω	ἐφύλαξα	πεφύλαχα	πεφύλαγμαι	ἐφυλάχθην

4. The liquid future

Verbs whose stems end in a liquid (λ, ρ) or a nasal (μ, ν) have an ε contract vowel in the future instead of the usual marker σ. They are conjugated just like the present tense of φιλέω. For this reason, the *liquid future* is also called the *contract future*, or the *Attic future*, because it is a feature of this dialect. The future of μένω, 'stay' and πίπτω, 'fall' show the active and middle forms respectively.

	μένω		**πίπτω**	
	SINGULAR	PLURAL	SINGULAR	PLURAL
1st	μενῶ	μενοῦμεν	πεσοῦμαι	πεσούμεθα
2nd	μενεῖς	μενεῖτε	πεσεῖ	πεσεῖσθε
3rd	μενεῖ	μενοῦσι(ν)	πεσεῖται	πεσοῦνται
	inf.	μενεῖν	inf.	πεσεῖσθαι
	part.	μενῶν, -οῦσα, -οῦν	part.	πεσούμενος, -μένη, -μενον

Note: Several of the verbs you have learned (section 3 above) have liquid futures:

ἀγγέλλω	οἰκτείρω
ἀποθνῄσκω	πίπτω
βάλλω	τρέχω
μάχομαι	φαίνομαι
μένω	

5. The liquid aorist

A few verbs whose stems end in a liquid (λ, ρ) or a nasal (μ, ν) have *liquid aorists* as well as liquid futures. These are weak aorist forms, but the liquid followed by the tense marker σα creates an unacceptable consonant cluster. The σ therefore drops out, and the stem vowel is lengthened to compensate for losing the σ, and to maintain the long syllable which liquid + σ had created. This is an example of *compensatory lengthening* in verbs; you have already met it in nouns (Ch. 9.3.) The aorist of μένω shows how the pattern works:

	SINGULAR	PLURAL
1st	ἔμεινα	ἐμείναμεν
2nd	ἔμεινας	ἐμείνατε
3rd	ἔμεινε	ἔμειναν
	inf. μεῖναι	
	part. μείνας, -ασα, -αν	

Note: Among the verbs you have learned, ἀγγέλλω and οἰκτείρω also have liquid aorists.

6. The strong aorist of βαίνω

ἄγω represents the normal type of strong aorist active (Ch. 10.8). The strong aorist of βαίνω is of a different type:

1st	ἔβην	ἔβημεν
2nd	ἔβης	ἔβητε
3rd	ἔβη	ἔβησαν

        inf. βῆναι
        part. βάς, βᾶσα, βάν (declined like πᾶς, πᾶσα, πᾶν, Ch. 20.6; but
             note that accent differs in nom. sing.)

EXERCISE 108.

1. εἰ τὸ στράτευμα ἡμῶν εὐθὺς ἐτάχθη εἰς τὴν μάχην, οἱ πολέμιοι οὐκ ἂν ἔμειναν.
2. οἱ πολέμιοι δεδιωγμένοι εἰσὶν εἰς τὴν θάλασσαν.
3. ἡ πόλις ἐν ᾗ ἐλίπομεν τὰς γυναῖκας οὐ βέβλαπται ὑπὸ τῶν πολεμίων.
4. οἱ Ἕλληνες ἐπείσθησαν μὴ καταλῦσαι τὴν γέφυραν.
5. αἱ Ἀθῆναι σωθήσονται τῷ ξυλίνῳ τείχει.
6. οἱ Πέρσαι ἠναγκάσθησαν ἀποφεύγειν ἐκ τῆς Ἀττικῆς.
7. πολλοὶ πεισθήσονται τοῖς τοῦ Δημοσθένους λόγοις.
8. λελείμμεθα, ὦ ἄνδρες, ὑπὸ τῶν συμμάχων.
9. τὸ ἔργον τριῶν ἡμερῶν ἐπέπρακτο.
10. ὁ στρατὸς ὃς ἐτάχθη ὑπὸ τοῦ Κύρου οὐ πεσεῖται τοῖς Ἀθηναίοις.

EXERCISE 109.

1. We have been persuaded to fight for our country.
2. Few men have been left in Athens.
3. The cavalry were pursued by the camels.
4. The work which your father ordered us to do has now been done.
5. If the Greeks had been led to the sea by a guide, they would already be in Greece.
6. The letter which has been written will be sent to the king.
7. The women and children will not be left in the city.
8. Not many allies had been sent.
9. Citizens, you have been harmed by the orator's words.
10. You have been drawn up near your allies, soldiers.

7. Supplementary participles with τυγχάνω, λανθάνω and φθάνω

Some verbs need a *supplementary* participle in Greek to complete their meaning. τυγχάνω, 'happen (to be)' is one of these. In English an infinitive completes the meaning of this verb: 'I happened <u>to meet</u> him', 'he happens <u>to be doing</u> this', etc. A smooth English translation of τυγχάνω + participle will change the participle to an infinitive. The participle itself agrees with the subject in gender and number.

The tense of the supplementary participle is usually the same as the main verb.

        ὁ στρατηγὸς τυγχάνει τάσσων τοὺς στρατιώτας.
        The general happens to be drawing up his soldiers.

        οἱ παῖδες ἔτυχον ἰδόντες τὸν Σωκράτη.
        The children happened to see Socrates.

Note: After a present or imperfect main verb, the aorist participle may express previous time.

οἱ παῖδες τυγχάνουσιν ἰδόντες τὸν Σωκράτη.
The children happen to have seen Socrates.

λανθάνω and φθάνω are likewise followed by a supplementary participle to complete their meanings. These verbs have no really good English equivalent, so translation need not be literal. In both cases, the participle describes the action taking place, so it is best expressed in English by a main verb. The main verb in the Greek sentence describes *how* the action took place, and can be translated with an adverbial phrase.

The literal meaning of λανθάνω is something like 'escape the notice (of)'. It signifies that the action of the participle is not noticed by someone: "I λανθάνω you, doing something." It can also be used without a direct object. There are several ways to express this construction in good English.

οἱ πολέμιοι λανθάνουσι τοὺς φύλακας φεύγοντες.
The enemy runs away without the guards seeing them.
The enemy runs away unbeknownst to the guards.

οἱ πολέμιοι ἔλαθον φυγόντες.
The enemy fled unnoticed.
The enemy fled without being seen.

φθάνω works in a very similar way. Its literal meaning is something like 'outstrip', 'anticipate'. It signifies that the action of the participle occurs before something else happens: "I φθάνω you, doing something."

ἡ γυνὴ φθάνει τοὺς παῖδας ὁρῶσα τὸν ἵππον.
The woman sees the horse before the children do.

ἡ γυνὴ ἔφθασε ἰδοῦσα τὸν ἵππον.
The woman saw the horse first.

EXERCISE 110.

1. ἀναγκασθησόμεθα ἀναλίσκειν πολλὰ χρήματα.
2. οὐ βέβλαψαι ὑπὸ τῶν Ἑλλήνων, ὦ βασιλεῦ.
3. πολλοὶ πολῖται τετυμμένοι εἰσὶ τοῖς λίθοις οὓς ἔβαλον οἱ παῖδες.
4. ὁ ῥήτωρ ἐτύγχανε λέγων τοῖς πολίταις.
5. οἱ ναῦται οὐκ ἔλαθον τοὺς πολεμίους πορευόμενοι εἰς τὸν λιμένα.
6. φυλαχθήσεσθε ταῖς ναυσίν, ὦ πολῖται.
7. ὁ ποιητὴς ἔφθασε τὸν φίλον βὰς εἰς τὴν πόλιν.
8. οὐ πολλοὶ ἐλείφθησαν ἐν τῇ πόλει.
9. πάντα τὰ ἀναγκαῖα πραχθήσεται ὑπὲρ τῆς πατρίδος.
10. οἱ Ἕλληνες πεπεισμένοι ἦσαν μὴ διώκειν τὰς τῶν Περσῶν ναῦς.

EXERCISE 111.

1. The allies had been persuaded to go away.
2. We were saved by the Spartans.
3. A large army was led by Xerxes.
4. The enemy will attack before our soldiers do.
5. We happened to find five trees on the island.

6. The island will be saved within a few days.
7. Many soldiers seem to have been hidden in the wood.
8. Not much money was left in the city from which we escaped.
9. The city's affairs will be managed by the generals.
10. Without Polycrates knowing it, the ring has been saved.

EXERCISE 112.

VAIN APPEAL TO SPARTA

The expedition sent by Darius in 490 BC *to punish Athens and Eretria for their roles in the Ionian revolt (Ch. 10 reading note, Ch. 24 Reading) sailed up the west coast of Euboea and sacked Eretria. The Persians then landed in Attica in the bay of Marathon.*

οἱ δὲ Ἀθηναῖοι ἦσαν ἐν μεγάλῳ κινδύνῳ· ὁ οὖν Φιλιππίδης ἐπέμφθη κῆρυξ εἰς
Σπάρτην ὑπὸ τῶν στρατηγῶν· καὶ δευτεραῖος ἐκ τοῦ Ἀθηναίων ἄστεως ἦν ἐν Σπάρτῃ,[1]
ἥκων δὲ ἐπὶ τοὺς ἄρχοντας ἔλεγε· Ὦ Λακεδαιμόνιοι, οἱ Ἀθηναῖοι αἰτοῦσιν ὑμᾶς αὑτοῖς
βοηθῆσαι μηδὲ ἐᾶν πόλιν ἀρχαιοτάτην ἐν τοῖς Ἕλλησι δουλοῦσθαι ὑπὸ βαρβάρων
ἀνδρῶν· καὶ γὰρ νῦν Ἐρετρία δεδούλωται καὶ πόλει τιμῆς ἀξίᾳ ἡ Ἑλλάς ἐστιν
ἀσθενεστέρα.[2] οἱ δὲ Λακεδαιμόνιοι ἤθελον μὲν βοηθεῖν τοῖς Ἀθηναίοις, ἀδύνατον δὲ ἦν
αὐτοῖς τὸ εὐθὺς ποιεῖν αὐτό οὐ βουλομένοις λύειν τὸν νόμον· ἔδει γὰρ αὐτοὺς τὴν
πανσέληνον μένειν.

Adapted from Herodotus VI.105-106

EXERCISE 113.

THE BATTLE OF MARATHON

ἐν δὲ τῷ μεταξὺ οἱ μὲν βάρβαροι ἤχθησαν εἰς τὸν Μαραθῶνα ὑπὸ τοῦ Ἱππίου τοῦ
Πεισιστράτου υἱοῦ,[3] καὶ ἐκβάντες εἰς γῆν ἐτάχθησαν· οἱ δὲ Ἀθηναῖοι ἐκεῖ τεταγμένοι
ἦσαν. τοῖς δὲ Ἀθηναίων στρατηγοῖς δύο ἦσαν αἱ γνῶμαι· οἱ μὲν οὐκ ἤθελον εὐθὺς
μάχεσθαι (οἱ μὲν γὰρ Ἀθηναῖοι ἦσαν ὀλίγοι, οἱ δὲ Πέρσαι πολλοί), οἱ δὲ ἐβούλοντο, ἐν οἷς
καὶ Μιλτιάδης ἦν. τέλος δὲ ἔβη ὁ Μιλτιάδης πρὸς τὸν πολέμαρχον,[4] ὀνόματι Καλλίμαχος,
καὶ ἔλεξεν ὧδε· Ἐν σοὶ νῦν ἐστιν, ὦ Καλλίμαχε, ἢ δουλῶσαι τὰς Ἀθήνας ἢ ἐλευθέρας
ποιήσαντα μνημόσυνον λιπέσθαι εἰς τὸν πάντα ἀνθρώπων βίον. ἡμῶν γὰρ τῶν στρατηγῶν
ὄντων δέκα δύο αἱ γνῶμαι, τῶν μὲν κελευόντων μάχεσθαι, τῶν δὲ οὔ. πάντα οὖν ἐκ σοῦ

---

[1] The distance was 140 miles.
[2] Comparative + dative: 'weaker by'
[3] Both Pisistratus and his son Hippias had been tyrants of Athens in the 6th century BC. Hippias, having fled to Persia after his expulsion from Athens in 510 BC, served as advisor to king Darius.
[4] The Polemarch, as commander-in-chief, had a vote.

ἄρτηται [depends on you]. ὁ δὲ Καλλίμαχος ἐπείσθη ὑπὸ τοῦ Μιλτιάδου μάχην ψηφίζεσθαι.

ἐν δὲ τῇ μάχῃ οἱ Ἀθηναῖοι δρόμῳ προυχώρησαν ἐπὶ τοὺς βαρβάρους καὶ ἀνδρείως ἐμάχοντο. καὶ τὸ μὲν μέσον⁵ ἐνικῶντο οἱ Ἀθηναῖοι καὶ ἐδιώχθησαν εἰς τὴν μεσόγειαν· τὸ δὲ κέρας ἑκάτερον⁵ οἱ Ἀθηναῖοι ἐνίκων. ἔπειτα δὲ οἱ Ἀθηναῖοι συναγαγόντες ἀμφότερα τὰ κέρατα προσέβαλον τοῖς τὸ μέσον τρέψασιν, καὶ ἐνίκων. καὶ οὕτως οἱ Πέρσαι ἐδιώχθησαν εἰς τὴν θάλασσαν.

Adapted from Herodotus VI.107-113

Chapter 21 Vocabulary

Verbs:

αἱρέω	take, capture	πάσχω	suffer
ἀναλίσκω	spend (money)	τρέφω	feed, nourish
βαίνω	go, walk	τυγχάνω (+ *part.*)	happen to
βάλλω	throw		(aor. ἔτυχον)
λανθάνω	(escape the	φθάνω	(outstrip, anticipate)
(aor. ἔλαθον)	notice of)		
μανθάνω	learn		
(aor. ἔμαθον)			

Nouns:

στρατός, -οῦ, ὁ	army	τάφος, -ου, ὁ	tomb

Adjective:

ἀναγκαῖος, -α, -ον	necessary

Preposition:

ὡς (+ *acc.*)	to (a person)

---

5 'in the center'; 'on each wing': accusatives of respect (see Ch. 29.2).

CHAPTER 22

1. Further comparison of adjectives in -τερος, -τατος

Most 3rd- (or 3rd- and 1st-) declension adjectives have the same comparative and superlative endings as the regular 1st- and 2nd-declension adjectives presented in Ch. 15.1. These endings are usually added directly to the nominative neuter singular form. εὔφρων and σώφρων, however, follow a different pattern.

	POSITIVE	COMPARATIVE	SUPERLATIVE
true	ἀληθής, -ές	ἀληθέστερος, -α, -ον	ἀληθέστατος, -α, -ον
safe	ἀσφαλής, -ές	ἀσφαλέστερος, -α, -ον	ἀσφαλέστατος, -η, -ον
deep	βαθύς, -εῖα, -ύ	βαθύτερος, -α, -ον	βαθύτατος, -η, -ον
heavy	βαρύς, -εῖα, -ύ	βαρύτερος, -α, -ον	βαρύτατος, -η, -ον
slow	βραδύς, -εῖα, -ύ	βραδύτερος, -α, -ον	βραδύτατος, -η, -ον
sweet	γλυκύς, -εῖα, -ύ	γλυκύτερος, -α, -ον	γλυκύτατος, -η, -ον
wide	εὐρύς, -εῖα, -ύ	εὐρύτερος, -α, -ον	εὐρύτατος, -η, -ον
kindly	εὔφρων, -ον	εὐφρονέστερος, -α, -ον	εὐφρονέστατος, -η, -ον
fortunate	εὐτυχής, -ές	εὐτυχέστερος, -α, -ον	εὐτυχέστατος, -η, -ον
sharp	ὀξύς, -εῖα, -ύ	ὀξύτερος, -α, -ον	ὀξύτατος, -η, -ον
clear	σαφής, -ές	σαφέστερος, -α, -ον	σαφέστατος, -η, -ον
prudent	σώφρων, -ον	σωφρονέστερος, -α, -ον	σωφρονέστατος, -η, -ον

2. Further comparison of adjectives in -ιων, -ιστος

Some other adjectives change to a different stem in the comparative and superlative. The comparative of these adjectives has 3rd-declension endings, one set for masculine and feminine forms and one for neuter. In the superlative, the 1st- and 2nd-declension endings -ιστος, -η, -ον are added to the new stem used for the comparative. A few adjectives have a second optional form; these are included on the following list:

	POSITIVE	COMPARATIVE	SUPERLATIVE
good	ἀγαθός, -ή, -όν	ἀμείνων, ἄμεινον	ἄριστος, -η, -ον
shameful	αἰσχρός, -ά, -όν	αἰσχίων, αἴσχιον	αἴσχιστος, -η, -ον
short	βραχύς, -εῖα, -ύ	βραχίων, βράχιον	βράχιστος, -η, -ον
		βραχύτερος, -α, -ον	βραχύτατος, -η, -ον
hostile	ἐχθρός, -ά, -όν	ἐχθίων, ἔχθιον	ἔχθιστος, -η, -ον
sweet	ἡδύς, -εῖα, -ύ	ἡδίων, ἥδιον	ἥδιστος, -η, -ον
bad	κακός, -ή, -όν	κακίων, κάκιον	κάκιστος, -η, -ον
beautiful, fine	καλός, -ή, -όν	καλλίων, κάλλιον	κάλλιστος, -η, -ον

	POSITIVE	COMPARATIVE	SUPERLATIVE
big, great	μέγας, -γάλη, -γα	μείζων, μεῖζον	μέγιστος, -η, -ον
small	μικρός, -ά, -όν	ἐλάσσων, ἔλασσον	ἐλάχιστος -η, -ον
		μικρότερος, -α, -ον	μικρότατος, -η, -ον
little, few	ὀλίγος, -η, -ον	μείων, μεῖον	ὀλίγιστος, -η, -ον
		ἐλάσσων, ἔλασσον	ἐλάχιστος -η, -ον
much	πολύς, πολλή, πολύ	πλείων, πλεῖον	πλεῖστος, -η, -ον
easy	ῥᾴδιος, -α, -ον	ῥᾴων, ῥᾷον	ῥᾷστος, -η, -ον
swift	ταχύς, -εῖα, -ύ	θάσσων, θᾶσσον	τάχιστος, -η, -ον

The 3rd-declension comparative forms all have short o in the stem, like εὔφρων, -ον, 'kindly' (Ch. 19.2). The comparative of ἡδίων, -ον, 'sweeter' is shown here; the short forms of the nom. and acc. plural are optional Attic forms.

	SINGULAR		PLURAL	
	M/F	N	M/F	N
Nom.	ἡδίων	ἥδιον	ἡδίονες, ἡδίους	ἡδίονα
Gen.	ἡδίονος	ἡδίονος	ἡδιόνων	ἡδιόνων
Dat.	ἡδίονι	ἡδίονι	ἡδίοσι(ν)	ἡδίοσι(ν)
Acc.	ἡδίονα	ἥδιον	ἡδίονας, ἡδίους	ἡδίονα
Voc.	ἥδιον	ἥδιον	ἡδίονες	ἡδίονα

EXERCISE 114.

1. εἰ αἱ τῶν πολεμίων νῆες θάσσονες ἦσαν τῶν ἡμετέρων, οὐκ ἂν ἐνικήσαμεν αὐτούς.
2. ὁ οἶνος ὃν ἔχομεν γλυκύτερός ἐστι τοῦ ὕδατος.
3. ὁ Πολυκράτης ἦν πάντων ἀνθρώπων ὁ εὐτυχέστατος.
4. οἱ λόγοι οὓς ὁ θεὸς ἔλεξεν ἦσαν ἀληθέστατοι.
5. ἦν μεγίστη ναυμαχία ἐν τῷ λιμένι.
6. οἱ ἀποφεύγοντες ἐχθίονες ἡμῖν εἰσι τῶν πολεμίων αὐτῶν.
7. τὸ τῶν Περσῶν ναυτικὸν ἦν μεῖζον ἢ τὸ τῶν Ἀθηναίων.
8. ἀσφαλέστερόν ἐστι μὴ πιστεύειν τῷ ῥήτορι.
9. ἀσθενέστεροί ἐσμεν ἢ οἱ πολέμιοι.
10. αἴσχιστον ἔσται καταλείπειν τοὺς γέροντας.

EXERCISE 115.

1. We shall be safer in the islands.
2. The plan of the enemy was now very clear.
3. Xerxes was leading a bigger army than Leonidas.
4. The swiftest ships are not always the safest.
5. We think Socrates greater than his enemies.
6. I never heard truer words.
7. The men whom we found in the village were very hostile to Xenophon's army.
8. Cyrus captured Babylon, which is a very big city.
9. The son was more fortunate than his father.
10. It is more shameful to flee than to be conquered.

3. Adverbs

To form an adverb ('happily', 'swiftly', etc.), take the genitive plural of any adjective and replace -ν with -ς:

ADJ.	GEN. PL.	ADV.
δίκαιος	δικαίων	δικαίως
καλός	καλῶν	καλῶς
εὐτυχής	εὐτυχῶν	εὐτυχῶς
σώφρων	σωφρόνων	σωφρόνως

A comparative adverb ('more —ly') is the nom./acc. neuter singular of the comparative adjective. A superlative adverb ('most —ly') is the nom./acc. neuter plural of the superlative adjective.

Note: ὡς + superlative (adjective or adverb) means 'as...as possible':

ὡς σοφώτατος ἦν ὁ Σωκράτης.   Socrates was as wise as possible.
ὡς τάχιστα ἔσπευδον.   They were hurrying as quickly as possible.

The following adverb is quite common, as are its comparative and superlative:

μάλα   much, very   μᾶλλον   more   μάλιστα   very much

4. ἔχω + adverb:

ἔχω can be used with an adverb to describe a state of being:

ἔχω καλῶς.   I am (doing) well.
κακῶς ἔχει.   It is going badly.
ἔμενε ὡς εἶχε.   He stayed as he was.

EXERCISE 116.

1. ἐλάσσονας ξίφη ἐστὶν ἡμῖν ἢ τοῖς πολεμίοις.
2. ἄμεινόν ἐστιν ἀποχωρεῖν ἢ ἐν τῇ πόλει μένειν.
3. οἱ Ἀθηναῖοι ἐποίησαν ἱερὰ κάλλιστα.
4. κατεδύσαμεν πλείους ναῦς ἢ οἱ πολέμιοι.
5. ῥᾷόν ἐστι λέγειν ἢ πείθειν.
6. κάκιστα πάσχομεν ἐν τῷ πολέμῳ.
7. ταχέως ἔτρεχον οἱ Πέρσαι πρὸς τὴν θάλασσαν.
8. οἱ ἀνδρείως μαχόμενοι τιμῶνται ὑπὸ τῶν Λακεδαιμονίων.
9. οἱ Ἀθηναῖοι μάλιστα ἀπελαύνουσι τοὺς τυράννους.
10. οὐ ῥᾳδίως νικηθησόμεθα ὑπὸ τῶν ἱππέων οἷς προσεβάλομεν καμήλοις.

EXERCISE 117.

1. The army of the Spartans was very small.
2. Do not hinder the soldiers who are guarding the town.
3. If most of the enemy had retreated at once, they would not have been conquered.
4. When doing well, even the worst men have friends.
5. Few cities are more beautiful than Athens.
6. We have more ships than the enemy.
7. The best of the ships were sunk.
8. The more hostile men took the swords which were in the house.
9. The giant was shouting terribly.
10. Pericles managed the affairs of the city more wisely than Cleon, who was younger and less prudent.

EXERCISE 118.

CROCODILES

Cambyses, son of Cyrus the Great, invades Egypt, and Herodotus with his typical thoroughness devotes a whole book to an account of the country—including the crocodiles of the Nile.

ὁ δὲ κροκόδειλος τοὺς τέσσαρας μῆνας τοῦ χειμῶνος ἐσθίει οὐδέν. ἡ δὲ θήλεια τίκτει μὲν ᾠὰ ἐν γῇ καὶ ἐκλέπει καὶ ἐκεῖ διατρίβει τὸ πολὺ [most] τῆς ἡμέρας, τὴν δὲ νύκτα πᾶσαν ἐν τῷ ποταμῷ· θερμότερον γὰρ δή ἐστι τὸ ὕδωρ τῆς δρόσου. πάντων δὲ ὧν ἡμεῖς γιγνώσκομεν ζῴων ὁ κροκόδειλος ἐξ ἐλαχίστου μέγιστον γίγνεται· τὰ μὲν γὰρ ᾠὰ χηνῶν οὐ πολλῷ μείζονα τίκτει, αὐξανόμενος δὲ γίγνεται [reaches] καὶ εἰς ἑπτακαίδεκα πήχεις καὶ μείζων ἔτι. ἔχει δὲ ὀφθαλμοὺς μὲν ὑός, ὀδόντας δὲ μεγάλους· γλῶσσαν δὲ μόνον θηρίων οὐκ ἔχει. οὐδὲ κινεῖ τὴν κάτω γνάθον, ἀλλὰ καὶ τοῦτο[1] μόνον θηρίων τὴν ἄνω γνάθον προσάγει τῇ κάτω.

τοῖς μὲν δὴ τῶν Αἰγυπτίων ἱεροί εἰσι οἱ κροκόδειλοι, τοῖς δὲ οὔ, ἀλλὰ ὡς πολεμίους περιέπουσι. οἱ δὲ περὶ Θήβας[1] οἰκοῦντες καὶ μάλιστα νομίζουσιν αὐτοὺς εἶναι ἱερούς. ἐκ πάντων δὲ ἕνα τρέφουσι κροκόδειλον, καὶ τὰ τ᾽ ὦτα καὶ τοὺς πόδας κοσμοῦσι χρυσῷ. οἱ δὲ περὶ Ἐλεφαντίνην[2] πόλιν οἰκοῦντες καὶ ἐσθίουσιν αὐτούς, οὐ νομίζοντες ἱεροὺς εἶναι. ὁ δὲ βουλόμενος κροκόδειλον αἱρεῖν δελεάζει νῶτον ὑὸς περὶ ἄγκιστρον καὶ εἰσβάλλει εἰς μέσον τὸν ποταμόν· αὐτὸς δὲ ἐν τῇ γῇ ἔχων ὗν ζωόν, αὐτὸν τύπτει. ἀκούσας δὲ τὴν φωνήν ὁ κροκόδειλος σπεύδει πρὸς τὴν φωνήν, εὑρὼν δὲ τὸ νῶτον καταπίνει· οἱ δὲ ἐν τῇ γῇ ἕλκουσιν. πρῶτον δὲ πάντων ὁ θηρευτὴς πηλῷ καλύπτει τοὺς ὀφθαλμοὺς αὐτοῦ· ἔπειτα αὐτὸν ῥᾷστα ἀποκτείνει.

Adapted from Herodotus II.68-70

Chapter 22 Vocabulary

Verbs:

ἀναχωρέω	retreat	προσβάλλω (+ *dat.*)	attack

Nouns:

Βαβυλών, -ῶνος, ἡ	Babylon	ξίφος, -ους, τό	sword
Κλέων, -ωνος, ὁ	Cleon		

Adverbs:

ἡδέως	gladly	μάλιστα	very much
μάλα	much, very	ὡς (+ *sup.*)	as...as possible
μᾶλλον	more		

---

[1] From οὗτος, αὕτη, τοῦτο, 'this' (Ch. 23.6)

[2] Egyptian Thebes (modern Luxor) with its hundred gates was destroyed by Cambyses. It lay some 550 miles upstream from the Nile delta; Elephantine was about 120 miles beyond it.

CHAPTER 23

ούκ έστ᾽ έτυμος λόγος οὗτος,
οὐδ᾽ ἔβας ἐν νηυσὶν εὐσέλμοις,
οὐδ᾽ ἵκεο πέργαμα Τροίας.

—Stesichorus 32 (Bergk)

1. αὐτός

You have already learned three uses of the pronoun αὐτός, αὐτή, αὐτό (Ch. 8.7-9).

1) in all cases, meaning 'himself', etc.

ὁ ἀνὴρ αὐτός	the man himself

2) in oblique cases (gen., dat., acc.), meaning 'him/her/it/them'

ἔπεμψα αὐτόν	I sent him

3) in the genitive, meaning (non-reflexive) 'his, her, its, their'

τὸν υἱὸν αὐτῶν	their son

Another use of αὐτός is as an adjective, preceded by the article, meaning 'the same'.

αἱ αὐταὶ γυναῖκες	the same women
τὸ αὐτό	the same thing

Note: The difference in word order between 'the same man' and 'the man himself' is the same as in English.

ὁ αὐτὸς ἀνήρ	the same man
ὁ ἀνὴρ αὐτός	the man himself

2. Reflexive pronouns

The reflexive pronoun in English is 'myself', 'ourselves', etc. The Greek reflexive is formed by combining a personal pronoun with the correct form of αὐτός, '-self' (the third person uses an old personal pronoun ἑ): σῴζω ἐμαυτόν, 'I save myself'. In the singular the pronoun and -αυτός are combined and written as one word. In the plural, the first and second person forms are written as two words.

		myself/ourselves		yourself/yourselves	
		M	**F**	**M**	**F**
Sing.	Gen.	ἐμαυτοῦ	ἐμαυτῆς	σεαυτοῦ	σεαυτῆς
	Dat.	ἐμαυτῷ	ἐμαυτῇ	σεαυτῷ	σεαυτῇ
	Acc.	ἐμαυτόν	ἐμαυτήν	σεαυτόν	σεαυτήν

		myself/ourselves		yourself/yourselves	
		M	F	M	F
PLUR.	Gen.	ἡμῶν αὐτῶν	ἡμῶν αὐτῶν	ὑμῶν αὐτῶν	ὑμῶν αὐτῶν
	Dat.	ἡμῖν αὐτοῖς	ἡμῖν αὐταῖς	ὑμῖν αὐτοῖς	ὑμῖν αὐταῖς
	Acc.	ἡμᾶς αὐτούς	ἡμᾶς αὐτάς	ὑμᾶς αὐτούς	ὑμᾶς αὐτάς

For the third person, one-word and two-word versions both exist, but the one-word version given here is far more common.

		himself/herself/itself/themselves		
		M	F	N
SING.	Gen.	ἑαυτοῦ	ἑαυτῆς	ἑαυτοῦ
	Dat.	ἑαυτῷ	ἑαυτῇ	ἑαυτῷ
	Acc.	ἑαυτόν	ἑαυτήν	ἑαυτό
PLUR.	Gen.	ἑαυτῶν	ἑαυτῶν	ἑαυτῶν
	Dat.	ἑαυτοῖς	ἑαυταῖς	ἑαυτοῖς
	Acc.	ἑαυτούς	ἑαυτάς	ἑαυτά

Note: Reflexive pronouns exist only in the oblique cases. In the nominative case αὐτός, αὐτή, αὐτό alone means 'himself', 'herself', etc. (Ch. 8.8).

3. Reflexive possessive pronouns

The genitive singular and plural of the reflexive pronouns are used to express the reflexive possessive 'his own', 'our own' etc. They stand in the attributive position, sandwiched between article and noun.

> ἡ Ἀθήνη φυλάσσει τοὺς ἑαυτῆς πολίτας.
> Athena protects her own citizens.

> οἱ Πέρσαι προυχώρησαν εἰς τὴν ἑαυτῶν χώραν.
> The Persians advanced into their own country.

In the first sentence above ἑαυτῆς is fem. sing. because it refers to Athena. In the second sentence ἑαυτῶν refers to the Persians, the subject of the sentence. In each case, the reflexive pronoun refers to the subject of its own clause (*direct reflexive*). Sometimes, though, a reflexive in a subordinate clause refers to the subject of the main clause (*indirect reflexive*):

> ὁ στρατηγὸς ἐκέλευσεν ἡμᾶς ἐλθεῖν εἰς τὴν ἑαυτοῦ χώραν.
> The general ordered us to come into his own country.

Note: Remember that when a third-person possessive is not reflexive, but refers to a different person or group, the genitive of αὐτός, -ή, -ό is used (Ch. 8.9).

> ἡ θεὰ φυλάσσει τοὺς πολίτας αὐτῶν.
> The goddess protects their citizens.

> οἱ Πέρσαι προυχώρησαν εἰς τὴν χώραν αὐτῶν.
> The Persians advanced into their (someone else's) country.

4. The reciprocal pronoun

The reciprocal pronoun 'each other' is formed by doubling the stem of ἄλλος, 'other': ἀλλήλων. There is no singular, since this pronoun must always refer to more than one person. Like reflexive pronouns, ἀλλήλων exists only in the oblique cases: φιλοῦμεν ἀλλήλους, "we love each other."

		M	**F**	**N**
PLUR.	Gen.	ἀλλήλων	ἀλλήλων	ἀλλήλων
	Dat.	ἀλλήλοις	ἀλλήλαις	ἀλλήλοις
	Acc.	ἀλλήλους	ἀλλήλας	ἄλληλα

each other

Note: The neuter accusative ends in a short vowel, allowing the accent to stand on the antepenult. In all other forms the long last syllable moves the accent to the penult.

5. Questions

Simple questions ('does he...?') may be introduced with ἆρα; it is just a marker, and is not translated. Two more specialized markers also exist:

ἆρα μή expects the answer 'no' ('he doesn't..., does he?', 'surely...not?')
ἆρα μὴ φιλεῖ τοὺς κακούς; Surely he doesn't love bad men?

ἆρα οὐ expects the answer 'yes' ('you do..., don't you?', 'don't you...?')
ἆρα οὐ λέγεις τὰ ἀληθή; You are telling the truth, aren't you?

EXERCISE 119.

1. ἔγραψα πολλὰς ἐπιστολὰς τῇ αὐτῇ ἡμέρᾳ.
2. ἡ Ἄλκηστις αὐτὴ ἐθέλει ἀποθνῄσκειν ὑπὲρ τοῦ ἀνδρός.
3. ἆρα ὁ Ἄδμητος ᾤκτειρεν ἑαυτὸν κακῶς ἔχοντα;
4. ἆρα οὐχ ὁ Ἀγαμέμνων ἔθυσε τὴν ἑαυτοῦ θυγατέρα;
5. ἡ αὐτὴ λίμνη ἦν χρησίμη τῷ Κύρῳ.
6. ἡ Ἀρτεμισία ἔσωσεν ἑαυτὴν ἐν τῇ ναυμαχίᾳ.
7. ὁ Θεμιστοκλῆς οὐ διώκει βασιλέα, ἀλλ' ἀγγέλους ὡς αὐτὸν πέμπει.
8. ἐπεὶ οἱ ναῦται ἀπέβαλον ἑαυτοὺς ἐκ τῆς νεώς, οἷός τ' εἶ σῶσαι σεαυτόν.
9. ἆρα μὴ οἱ σοφοὶ θαυμάζουσιν ἑαυτούς;
10. οἱ τύραννοι οὐκ ἐπίστευον τοῖς ἑαυτῶν.

EXERCISE 120.

1. Xerxes did not trust his own soldiers.
2. The fisherman finds the same ring in the fish.
3. Most men are willing to fight for their own country.
4. Good men love others more than themselves.
5. The Athenians feared Xerxes and his army.
6. The orator always says the same things.
7. It is difficult for me to save myself.
8. The same queen made Babylon more beautiful.
9. Many of the Athenians admired Socrates and his wisdom, didn't they?
10. In the same year the Greeks conquered both by land and by sea.

6. Demonstrative pronouns

The demonstratives ὅδε, οὗτος and ἐκεῖνος correspond to English 'this' and 'that'. ἐκεῖνος means 'that', while ὅδε and οὗτος both mean 'this'. ὅδε specifically refers to something actually present, that you can point at: ὅδε ὁ ἀνήρ, 'this man here'.

that

	SINGULAR			PLURAL		
	M	**F**	**N**	**M**	**F**	**N**
Nom.	ἐκεῖνος	ἐκείνη	ἐκεῖνο	ἐκεῖνοι	ἐκεῖναι	ἐκεῖνα
Gen.	ἐκείνου	ἐκείνης	ἐκείνου	ἐκείνων	ἐκείνων	ἐκείνων
Dat.	ἐκείνῳ	ἐκείνῃ	ἐκείνῳ	ἐκείνοις	ἐκείναις	ἐκείνοις
Acc.	ἐκεῖνον	ἐκείνην	ἐκεῖνο	ἐκείνους	ἐκείνας	ἐκεῖνα

this

	SINGULAR			PLURAL		
	M	**F**	**N**	**M**	**F**	**N**
Nom.	ὅδε	ἥδε	τόδε	οἵδε	αἵδε	τάδε
Gen.	τοῦδε	τῆσδε	τοῦδε	τῶνδε	τῶνδε	τῶνδε
Dat.	τῷδε	τῇδε	τῷδε	τοῖσδε	ταῖσδε	τοῖσδε
Acc.	τόνδε	τήνδε	τόδε	τούσδε	τάσδε	τάδε

Note: ὅδε is just the definite article with the suffix -δε added to it.

this

	SINGULAR			PLURAL		
	M	**F**	**N**	**M**	**F**	**N**
Nom.	οὗτος	αὕτη	τοῦτο	οὗτοι	αὗται	ταῦτα
Gen.	τούτου	ταύτης	τούτου	τούτων	τούτων	τούτων
Dat.	τούτῳ	ταύτῃ	τούτῳ	τούτοις	ταύταις	τούτοις
Acc.	τοῦτον	ταύτην	τοῦτο	τούτους	ταύτας	ταῦτα

Used by themselves, these demonstratives are pronouns: οὗτοι, 'these men'; ἐκείνη, 'that woman', etc.

They may also be used as adjectives. The definite article is always present, and the demonstrative is always in the predicate position: ἥδε ἡ γυνή, 'this woman'; τὰ δένδρα ταῦτα, 'these trees'; etc.

The adverbs from these demonstratives are οὕτω (before consonants)/οὕτως (before vowels), ἐκείνως and ὧδε.

7. τοιοῦτος, τοσοῦτος

These demonstratives are compounds of οὗτος, and are declined just like it. τοιοῦτος, τοιαύτη, τοιοῦτο refers to the *quality* of a person or thing: τοιοῦτος ἀνήρ, 'this kind of man', 'such a man as this'. τοσοῦτος, τοσαύτη, τοσοῦτο refers to *quantity*: τοσαύτη στρατιά, 'such a great army as this'; τοσαῦτα δένδρα, 'so many trees', 'this many trees'. (For related words see Ch. 31.2.)

Here is the paradigm of τοιοῦτος, -η, -ον; τοσοῦτος works in just the same way.

this kind

	SINGULAR			PLURAL		
	M	**F**	**N**	**M**	**F**	**N**
Nom.	τοιοῦτος	τοιαύτη	τοιοῦτο	τοιοῦτοι	τοιαῦται	τοιαῦτα
Gen.	τοιούτου	τοιαύτης	τοιούτου	τοιούτων	τοιούτων	τοιούτων
Dat.	τοιούτῳ	τοιαύτῃ	τοιούτῳ	τοιούτοις	τοιαύταις	τοιούτοις
Acc.	τοιοῦτον	τοιαύτην	τοιοῦτο	τοιούτους	τοιαύτας	τοιαῦτα

Note: When these words are used with the article, they are always in the attributive position: ὁ τοιοῦτος ἀνήρ.

EXERCISE 121.

1. οἵδε οἱ στρατιῶται ἀνδρειότατα ἐμάχοντο.
2. ἡ σφραγὶς ἦν ἐν τῷδε τῷ ἰχθύϊ.
3. μετὰ τοῦτο ὁ Ξέρξης ἐκ τῆς Ἀττικῆς ἀπεχώρησεν.
4. ἐκείνη ἡ ναῦς κατεδύθη ὑπὸ τῆς Ἀρτεμισίας.
5. οὗτοί εἰσιν ἀξιώτεροι τῆς τιμῆς ἢ ἐκεῖνοι.
6. ὁ Θεμιστοκλῆς πέμπει τὴν τοιαύτην ἐπιστολὴν ὡς βασιλέα.
7. τοιαύτη ἐστὶν ἡ τοῦ Ἀδμήτου γυνή.
8. μακραί εἰσιν αὗται αἱ ἐπιστολαὶ ἃς οἱ πρέσβεις ἔπεμψαν ἀλλήλοις.
9. ἐκείνῳ τῷ ἔτει οἱ Πέρσαι ἐνικήθησαν ὑπὸ τῶν Ἑλλήνων.
10. τοσαῦτα δένδρα βέβλαπται ὑπὸ τῶν Λακεδαιμονίων.

EXERCISE 122.

1. This city is very beautiful.
2. That tyrant is always fortunate and his city is doing well.
3. This many gifts were sent to Apollo by Croesus.
4. On account of this we shall march towards the river.
5. She has been saved by the friend of Admetus.
6. If this sword is better than that one, take it.
7. These men have been persuaded by Demosthenes to fight.
8. This is the son of Socrates.
9. We cannot conquer this kind of army.
10. The general ordered us to cross that mountain before night.

EXERCISE 123.

A STRANGE RESCUE

This interesting story is a mere digression of Herodotus. Periander was tyrant of Corinth about 600 BC; he promoted both commerce and the arts. Arion is said to have invented a new form of poetry.

ἦν δέ ποτε ἐν Κορίνθῳ κιθαρῳδός τις, ὀνόματι Ἀρίων, οὐδενὸς δεύτερος τῶν τότε ὄντων· καὶ οὗτος ὁ Ἀρίων, ὡς λέγουσι, τὸν πολὺν τοῦ χρόνου διατρίβων παρὰ Περιάνδρῳ, τῷ Κορίνθου τυράννῳ, ἐβούλετο πλεῦσαι εἰς Ἰταλίαν τε καὶ Σικελίαν, ἐργασάμενος δὲ ἐκεῖ χρήματα μεγάλα ἠθέλησεν εἰς Κόρινθον ἐπανέρχεσθαι. ὡρμήσατο μὲν νῦν ἐκ Τάραντος,[1] πιστεύων δὲ οὐδενὶ μᾶλλον ἢ τοῖς Κορινθίοις ἐμισθώσατο πλοῖον ἀνδρῶν Κορινθίων· οἱ δὲ ἐν τῷ πελάγει ἐπεβούλευσαν τὸν Ἀρίονα ἐκβαλόντες ἔχειν τὰ χρήματα· ὁ δέ, τοῦτο μαθών, ᾔτησεν αὐτοὺς χρήματα μὲν λαβεῖν, τὴν δ᾽ ἑαυτοῦ ψυχὴν σῶσαι. ἀλλ᾽ οὐ πεισθέντες οἱ ναῦται ἐκέλευσαν αὐτὸν ἢ ἑαυτὸν ἀποκτείνειν, εἰ ἐθέλει τάφον ἐν γῇ, ἢ ἐκπηδᾶν εἰς τὴν θάλασσαν τάχιστα. ὁ δὲ Ἀρίων εἶπεν αὐτοῖς· Ἐᾶτέ με πρῶτον ἐν τῇ σκευῇ

---

1   Taras or Tarentum, in Southern Italy, was the only colony founded by Sparta.

πάσῃ ἀείδειν. οἱ δὲ ἀνεχώρησαν ἐκ τῆς πρύμνης εἰς μέσην τὴν ναῦν. ἔπειτα δὲ ὁ μὲν
Ἀρίων, λαβὼν τὴν κιθάραν καὶ ἀείσας, ἔβαλεν ἑαυτὸν εἰς τὴν θάλασσαν, ὡς εἶχε τῇ
σκευῇ πάσῃ. οἱ δὲ ναῦται ἀπέπλευσαν εἰς Κόρινθον.

κ αὶ τότε δὴ μέγιστον θαῦμα ἐγένετο· δελφὶς γὰρ αὐτὸν ὑπολαβὼν ἐκόμισεν εἰς γῆν. ὁ
μὲν οὖν Ἀρίων πορεύεται εἰς Κόρινθον σὺν τῇ σκευῇ καὶ ἥκων πᾶν τὸ πρᾶγμα ἐξηγεῖται τῷ
Περιάνδρῳ· ὁ δὲ ὑπὸ ἀπιστίας ἔχει αὐτὸν ἐν φυλακῇ. ἐπεὶ δὲ τέλος οἱ ναῦται εἰς Κόρινθον
ἀφίκοντο, ἠρώτησεν αὐτοὺς περὶ τοῦ Ἀρίωνος· οἱ δὲ ἀπεκρίναντο ὅτι ἔλιπον αὐτὸν εὖ
πράσσοντα ἐν Τάραντι. ἕως δὲ ἔτι τοῦτο λέγουσιν, ἐπιφαίνεται αὐτοῖς ὁ Ἀρίων αὐτός
ὥσπερ ἔχων ἔβαλεν ἑαυτὸν εἰς τὴν θάλασσαν· οἱ δὲ ναῦται τῷδε τῷ τρόπῳ ἐλέγχονται.

Adapted from Herodotus I.23-24

Chapter 23 Vocabulary

Verb:

ἀποβάλλω	throw away	φοβέομαι	fear
		φοβήσομαι, ἐφοβησάμην, ——,	
		πεφόβημαι, ἐφοβήθην	

Nouns:

Ἀπόλλων, -ωνος, ὁ	Apollo	λίμνη, -ης, ἡ	lake, marsh

Pronouns:

ἀλλήλων, -ων, -ων	each other	ἡμῶν αὐτῶν	ourselves
ἑαυτοῦ, -ῆς, -οῦ	himself, herself, etc.	σεαυτοῦ, -ῆς, -οῦ	yourself
ἐμαυτοῦ, -ῆς, -οῦ	myself	ὑμῶν αὐτῶν	yourselves

Adjectives:

ἐκεῖνος, -η, -ο	that	τοιοῦτος, -αύτη, -οῦτο	this kind, such
ὅδε, ἥδε, τόδε	this		
οὗτος, αὕτη, τοῦτο	this	τοσοῦτος, -αύτη, -οῦτο	so much, so great, so many

Adverbs:

ἐκείνως	in that way	ὧδε	thus, in this way
οὕτω(ς)	thus, in this way		

Preposition:

κατά (+ *acc.*)	by way of	κατὰ γῆν	by land

Conjunction:

ἐπεί	when, since, as

Particle:

ἆρα	(introduces a question)

ἐπάμεροι· τί δέ τις; τί δ᾽ οὔ τις; σκιᾶς ὄναρ
ἄνθρωπος.

—Pindar, *Pythian* 8.95-96

1. The subjunctive mood

The subjunctive in Greek has various uses, as you will see. It is associated with primary tenses of the main verb, and has primary endings.

The subjunctive is marked by a long thematic vowel. The same primary endings are used for both the present and aorist. The difference is one of aspect only (Ch. 16.5): the present for a continuing action, the aorist for a single, simple act.

The perfect subjunctive consists of the perfect participle (active or middle/passive) plus the subjunctive forms of εἰμί. There is no future subjunctive.

Note: The negative used with subjunctives is always μή.

	SINGULAR	PLURAL	SINGULAR	PLURAL
PRESENT	**Active**		**Middle/Passive**	
1st	λύ-ω	λύ-ωμεν	λύ-ωμαι	λυ-ώμεθα
2nd	λύ-ῃς	λύ-ητε	λύ-ῃ	λύ-ησθε
3d	λύ-ῃ	λύ-ωσι(ν)	λύ-ηται	λύ-ωνται
WEAK AORIST	**Active**		**Middle**	
1st	λύσω	λύσωμεν	λύσωμαι	λυσώμεθα
2nd	λύσῃς	λύσητε	λύσῃ	λύσησθε
3rd	λύσῃ	λύσωσι(ν)	λύσηται	λύσωνται
STRONG AORIST	**Active**		**Middle**	
1st	λάβω	λάβωμεν	λάβωμαι	λαβώμεθα
2nd	λάβῃς	λάβητε	λάβῃ	λάβησθε
3rd	λάβῃ	λάβωσι(ν)	λάβηται	λάβωνται
PERFECT	**Active**		**Middle/Passive**	
1st	λελυκὼς ὦ	λελυκότες ὦμεν	λελυμένος ὦ	λελυμένοι ὦμεν
2nd	λελυκὼς ᾖς	λελυκότες ἦτε	λελυμένος ᾖς	λελυμένοι ἦτε
3rd	λελυκὼς ᾖ	λελυκότες ὦσι(ν)	λελυμένος ᾖ	λελυμένοι ὦσι(ν)

	SINGULAR	PLURAL
AORIST		**Passive**
1st	λυθῶ	λυθῶμεν
2nd	λυθῇς	λυθῆτε
3rd	λυθῇ	λυθῶσι(ν)

Contract Verbs

	SINGULAR	PLURAL	SINGULAR	PLURAL
PRESENT	**Active**		**Middle/Passive**	
1st	φιλῶ	φιλῶμεν	φιλῶμαι	φιλώμεθα
2nd	φιλῇς	φιλῆτε	φιλῇ	φιλῆσθε
3rd	φιλῇ	φιλῶσι(ν)	φιλῆται	φιλῶνται
1st	τιμῶ	τιμῶμεν	τιμῶμαι	τιμώμεθα
2nd	τιμᾷς	τιμᾶτε	τιμᾷ	τιμᾶσθε
3rd	τιμᾷ	τιμῶσι(ν)	τιμᾶται	τιμῶνται
1st	δηλῶ	δηλῶμεν	δηλῶμαι	δηλώμεθα
2nd	δηλοῖς	δηλῶτε	δηλῶ	δηλῶσθε
3rd	δηλοῖ	δηλῶσι(ν)	δηλῶται	δηλῶνται

PRACTICE A. Fill in the blanks:

	FORM	TENSE	VOICE	PERSON/NUMBER	(VERB)
1.	_____	aorist	active	3rd singular	(νομίζω)
2.	παυσθῶσι	_____	_____	_____	_____
3.	λέγητε	_____	_____	_____	_____
4.	_____	present	middle	3rd plural	(γράφω)
5.	_____	perfect	active	1st plural	(φεύγω)
6.	τιμήσω	_____	_____	_____	_____
7.	πεπεμμένος ᾖς	_____	_____	_____	_____
8.	_____	aorist	active	3rd singular	(λαμβάνω)
9.	φιλῇ	_____	_____	_____	_____

2. Exhortations

The 1st plural of the subjunctive is used to express an exhortation, such as English 'Let's do it!'. The negative is μή. The difference in meaning between the present and aorist subjunctive is one of aspect only. Thus in exhortations the aorist subjunctive is preferred for single acts, the present for ongoing actions.

> θαυμάζωμεν τοὺς ἀγαθούς.
>> Let us admire the good (people).
> λύσωμεν τὸν βοῦν.
>> Let's loose the ox.

μὴ παυσώμεθα τοῦδε τοῦ πολέμου.

Let us not cease from this war.

3. Prohibitions with 2nd person

μή is used with the 2nd singular and plural forms of the aorist subjunctive (never the imperative) to express a specific prohibition, that is, one that refers to a specific occasion. A general prohibition is expressed by μή with the 2nd singular and plural forms of the present imperative (Ch. 17.1).

μὴ ἀποπέμψῃς τοὺς συμμάχους.

Don't send away the allies (right now).

μὴ βλάπτε τοὺς φίλους.

Don't (ever) injure your friends.

4. Prohibitions with 3rd person

μή and μηδείς, μηδεμία, μηδέν are used with the 3rd singular and plural forms of the aorist subjunctive (occasionally the imperative) to express a specific prohibition directed at a third party. A general prohibition is expressed by μή, μηδείς etc. with the 3rd singular and plural forms of the present imperative.

μηδεὶς πιστεύσῃ τῷ ῥήτορι.

Let no one believe the orator (right now).

μὴ οἱ γέροντες βλαπτέσθων.

Let the old men not be injured (ever).

EXERCISE 124.

1. ἀεὶ τὰ ἀληθῆ λέγωμεν.
2. μὴ βλάπτετε ἀλλήλους, ὦ παῖδες.
3. φύγωμεν εἰς τὰ ὄρη, ἐπεὶ οἱ πολέμιοι προσβάλλουσι τῇ πόλει.
4. μὴ κωλύσῃς τοὺς τῇ πόλει βοηθοῦντας.
5. μὴ λυθῶσιν οἱ αἰχμάλωτοι.
6. ἀεὶ πράσσωμεν ἀξίως τὰ τῆς πόλεως.
7. μὴ παύσησθε τοῦ ἔργου, ὦ νεανίαι.
8. μηδεὶς βοηθείτω τοῖς πολεμίοις.
9. μήτε διώξητε τοὺς Πέρσας, ὦ ἄνδρες, μήτε αὐτοὺς κωλύσητε.
10. καίπερ κακῶς ἔχοντες μὴ πέμψωμεν ἀγγέλους ὡς βασιλέα.

EXERCISE 125.

1. Let us educate our children.
2. Do not cut down these trees.
3. Let no one be persuaded by money.
4. Let us not cease from the sea battle.
5. Do not draw up the cavalry beside the lake.
6. Let us neither hinder nor pursue each other.
7. Let us always fight in a manner worthy of our country.
8. Do not treat prisoners badly.
9. Let the soldiers not attack the city before night.
10. Do not be enslaved by the king, citizens.

5. The interrogative pronoun

The interrogative pronoun τίς, τί, 'who?' 'what?' always has an acute accent, never grave. It is used as in English, to introduce questions.

who? what?

	SINGULAR		PLURAL	
	M/F	**N**	**M/F**	**N**
Nom.	τίς	τί	τίνες	τίνα
Gen.	τίνος	τίνος	τίνων	τίνων
Dat.	τίνι	τίνι	τίσι	τίσι
Acc.	τίνα	τί	τίνας	τίνα

Besides standing alone as a pronoun, τίς, τί is also used as an adjective ('what', 'which'), with an accompanying noun. It usually precedes the noun.

τίς λέγει;	Who is speaking?
τί βούλεσθε;	What do you want?
τίς στρατηγὸς ἄξει αὐτούς;	What general will lead them?

Note: τί is also an adverb meaning 'why': τί φεύγεις; Why are you fleeing?

6. The indefinite pronoun

The indefinite pronoun τις, τι ('someone', 'something', 'anyone', 'anything') is identical in formation to the interrogative pronoun, except that it has no accent of its own, and is therefore enclitic.

Besides standing alone as a pronoun, τις, τι is also used as an adjective ('some', 'any', 'a certain'), to make an accompanying noun indefinite. It always follows the noun.

κόπτει τις τὰ δένδρα.
Someone is cutting down the trees.

πέμψω δῶρά τινα ὡς βασιλέα.
I will send some gifts to the king of Persia.

ζῷά τινα εἴδετε ἐν τῇ νήσῳ;
Did you see any animals on the island?

ἁλιεύς τις ἰχθὺν μέγιστον λαμβάνει.
A certain fisherman catches a very large fish.

7. Interrogative and indefinite adverbs

There are a number of interrogative adverbs in Greek. Those relating to place and manner are used in this lesson (for other types, see Ch. 31.3). Each of these is made indefinite by removing its accent and making it enclitic. These forms can carry an acute accent before punctuation, or for a following enclitic:

ποῦ, 'where?'	που, 'somewhere'
πόθεν, 'from where?'	ποθέν, 'from somewhere'
ποῖ, 'to where?'	ποι, 'to somewhere'
πῶς, 'how?'	πως, 'somehow'

EXERCISE 126.

1. τῶν Ἀθηναίων τινὲς οὐκ ἐφίλουν τὸν Δημοσθένη.
2. ἦν Ἀθηναῖός τις, ὀνόματι Θεμιστοκλῆς.

3. ἆρα πιστεύετε τῷ ὑμετέρῳ στρατηγῷ;
4. τίς βάρβαρος ἔβη ποθὲν εἰς τὴν πόλιν ἐκείνην;
5. ποῦ ᾤκισαν οἱ Λακεδαιμόνιοι τὴν ἀποικίαν;
6. ἆρ᾽ οὐ μάλιστα ἐφίλησε τὸν Ἄδμητον ἡ Ἄλκηστις;
7. ποῖ καὶ τί πορεύονται οἱ Πέρσαι;
8. ἆρα καταλείψετε τοὺς ὑμετέρους συμμάχους;
9. ὁ ἁλιεὺς εὗρέ που μέγαν ἰχθύν.
10. ἐκείνη ἡ παῖς ἐπαίδευσέ πως τὸν ἵππον.

EXERCISE 127.

1. Someone was announcing the victory of the Athenians.
2. Where did you hide the money?
3. A certain messenger, Sicinnus by name, was sent to the king.
4. From where were the enemy marching?
5. Some of the allies were not willing to help the Athenians.
6. Surely you do not admire this traitor?
7. Why are you marching through our country?
8. What do you intend to do in this danger, citizens?
9. How did the orator persuade you to do this?
10. The Greeks were journeying quickly to somewhere.

EXERCISE 128.

ARISTAGORAS AND HIS MAP

The Greeks in Ionia, as has already been said, had been subjected in turn to Lydia and Persia. In 499 BC Aristagoras resigned his position as tyrant in Miletus (a city in Ionia, southeast of Samos) and headed the revolt against Persia. He attempted to get help from Sparta, before going to Athens and Eretria.

ὁ δὲ Ἀρισταγόρας, ὁ τῆς Μιλήτου τύραννος, ἐβούλετο ἐλευθεροῦν τοὺς Ἴωνας ἀπὸ τῆς τῶν Περσῶν ἀρχῆς. ἔπλευσεν οὖν εἰς τὴν Σπάρτην καὶ διελέγετο τῷ Κλεομένει, τῷ τὴν ἀρχὴν ἔχοντι· καὶ ἔφερεν, ὡς οἱ Λακεδαιμόνιοι λέγουσι, χαλκοῦν πίνακα, ἐν ᾧ γῆς πάσης περίοδος ἐγέγραπτο καὶ θάλασσά τε πᾶσα καὶ ποταμοὶ πάντες. Κλεόμενες, ἔφη, μὴ θαυμάσῃς ὅτι δεῦρο ἥκω· ὅτι οἱ τῶν Ἰώνων παῖδές εἰσι δοῦλοι ἀντ᾽ ἐλευθέρων μέγιστον μὲν γὰρ ἄλγος ἐστὶν ἡμῖν αὐτοῖς, ἔτι δὲ τῶν λοιπῶν ὑμῖν, οἳ πρωτεύετε ἐν τῇ Ἑλλάδι. νῦν οὖν πρὸς θεῶν ['by the gods'] σώσατε Ἴωνας ἐκ δουλοσύνης, ἄνδρας ὁμαίμονας. ῥᾴδιον δὲ ὑμῖν ἐστι ταῦτα ποιεῖν· οὔτε γὰρ οἱ βάρβαροι ἀνδρεῖοί εἰσιν, ὑμεῖς τε ἐν πολέμῳ ἀριστεύετε. ἥ τε μάχη αὐτῶν ἐστιν ὧδε, τόξα καὶ αἰχμὴ βραχεῖα· ἀναξυρίδας δὲ ἔχοντες ἔρχονται εἰς τὰς μάχας καὶ κυρβασίας ἐπὶ ταῖς κεφαλαῖς. οὕτω ῥᾴδιοι νικηθῆναί εἰσιν. ἔστι δὲ καὶ ἀγαθὰ τοῖς τὴν ἤπειρον ἐκείνην οἰκοῦσιν ὅσα οὐδενὶ ἄλλῳ, χρυσός τε καὶ ἄργυρος, καὶ ὑποζύγιά τε καὶ ἀνδράποδα· ἃ βουλόμενοι αὐτοὶ οἷοί τ᾽ ἐστε ἔχειν.

δηλῶν δὲ ἔλεγε ταῦτα τὴν τῆς γῆς περίοδον, ἣν ἔφερε ἐν τῷ πίνακι γεγραμμένην· ἐξηγεῖτο δὲ τὰς χώρας πάντων τῶν βαρβάρων, ἐξηγούμενος τὸν πλοῦτον ἑκάστης, καὶ τὰ

Σοῦσα[1] αὐτά, ἐν οἷς οἱ βασιλέως μεγάλου θησαυροὶ ἐνῆσαν. Λαβόντες ταύτην τὴν πόλιν, ἔφη, πλουσιώτατοι γενήσεσθε. ἀλλὰ περὶ χώρας οὐ πολλῆς οὐδὲ οὕτω χρησίμης δεῖ ὑμᾶς μάχας παῦσαι, πρός τε Μεσσηνίους καὶ Ἀργείους,[2] οἷς οὔτε χρυσός ἐστιν οὔτε ἄργυρος. Ἀρισταγόρας μὲν ταῦτα ἔλεξε, Κλεομένης δὲ εἶπε τάδε· Ὦ ξένε Μιλήσιε, τριῶν ἡμερῶν ἀποκρινοῦμαι. ἐπεὶ δὲ ἡ κυρία ἡμέρα ἐγένετο, ὁ Κλεομένης ἠρώτησε, Πόσων ἡμερῶν ἐστιν ἡ ὁδὸς ἀπὸ τῆς τῶν Ἰώνων θαλάσσης παρὰ βασιλέα; ὁ δὲ Ἀρισταγόρας εἶπεν, Τριῶν μηνῶν. ὁ δὲ Κλεομένης εὐθὺς ἀπεκρίνατο· Ὦ ξένε Μιλήσιε, ἀποχώρησον ἐκ Σπάρτης πρὸ ἡλίου δυσμῶν· οὐ γὰρ εὖ συμβουλεύεις τοῖς Λακεδαιμονίοις, ἐθέλων αὐτοὺς ἀπὸ θαλάσσης τριῶν μηνῶν ὁδὸν ἀγαγεῖν.

Adapted from Herodotus V.49-50

Chapter 24 Vocabulary

Noun:

Σίκιννος, -ου, ὁ	Sicinnus

Pronouns:

τίς, τί	who?, what?
τις, τι	someone, something; anyone, anything

Interrogative adverbs:

πόθεν	from where?	πῶς	how?
ποῖ	to where?	τί	why?
ποῦ	where?		

Indefinite adverbs:

ποθέν	from somewhere	που	somewhere
ποι	to somewhere	πως	somehow

---

[1] Susa, the capital of the Persian empire, lay north of the Persian Gulf; the Royal Road ran all the way there from Ephesus in Ionia.

[2] Sparta's neighbors in the Peloponnese, Messenians to the west and Argives to the northeast.

CHAPTER 25

1. The optative mood

The optative mood, like the subjunctive, is used in a variety of constructions in Greek. It is associated with secondary tenses of the main verb; it has its own set of active and aorist passive endings, but uses the regular middle/passive secondary endings in other middle/passive tenses.

The marker for the present, future and strong aorist optatives is the addition of ι to the thematic vowel ο, making οι. As in the indicative, σα replaces the thematic vowel in the weak aorist active and middle, making σαι. The perfect optative consists of the perfect participle (active or middle/passive) plus the optative forms of εἰμί. Here are the active and middle optatives of λύω.

	Singular	Plural	Singular	Plural
	Active		**Middle**	
PRESENT				
1st	λύ-οιμι	λύ-οιμεν	λυ-οίμην	λυ-οίμεθα
2nd	λύ-οις	λύ-οιτε	λύ-οιο (οι-σο)	λύ-οισθε
3rd	λύ-οι	λύ-οιεν	λύ-οιτο	λύ-οιντο
FUTURE				
1st	λύσοιμι	λύσοιμεν	λυσοίμην	λυσοίμεθα
2nd	λύσοις	λύσοιτε	λύσοιο	λύσοισθε
3rd	λύσοι	λύσοιεν	λύσοιτο	λύσοιντο
WEAK AORIST				
1st	λύσαιμι	λύσαιμεν	λυσαίμην	λυσαίμεθα
2nd	λύσαις	λύσαιτε	λύσαιο	λύσαισθε
3rd	λύσαι	λύσαιεν	λύσαιτο	λύσαιντο
STRONG AORIST				
1st	λάβοιμι	λάβοιμεν	λαβοίμην	λαβοίμεθα
2nd	λάβοις	λάβοιτε	λάβοιο	λάβοισθε
3rd	λάβοι	λάβοιεν	λάβοιτο	λάβοιντο
PERFECT				
1st	λελυκὼς εἴην	λελυκότες εἶμεν	λελυμένος εἴην	λελυμένοι εἶμεν
2nd	λελυκὼς εἴης	λελυκότες εἶτε	λελυμένος εἴης	λελυμένοι εἶτε
3rd	λελυκὼς εἴη	λελυκότες εἶεν	λελυμένος εἴη	λελυμένοι εἶεν

Note: diphthongs in the 3rd singular active endings count as long for accent purposes. Thus the aorist active infinitive of λύω is λῦσαι, but the optative form is λύσαι.

As usual, the passive forms are the same as the middle forms in the present and perfect tenses. The aorist and future passive optative are formed from the sixth principal part, with ι added to the marker -(θ)ε-.

	SINGULAR	PLURAL	SINGULAR	PLURAL
	Weak Aorist Passive		**Future Passive**	
1st	λυθείην	λυθεῖμεν	λυθησοίμην	λυθησοίμεθα
2nd	λυθείης	λυθεῖτε	λυθήσοιο	λυθήσοισθε
3rd	λυθείη	λυθεῖεν	λυθήσοιτο	λυθήσοιντο
	Strong Aorist Passive (γράφω)		**Future Passive**	
1st	γραφείην	γραφεῖμεν	γραφησοίμην	γραφησοίμεθα
2nd	γραφείης	γραφεῖτε	γραφήσοιο	γραφήσοισθε
3rd	γραφείη	γραφεῖεν	γραφήσοιτο	γραφήσοιντο

Contract Verbs

In the present tense of contract verbs, the usual contractions take place between the stem and thematic vowels. In addition, contract verbs have a different set of endings in the present optative active singular (the active plural and the middle/passive have regular endings). The present optatives of contract verbs are formed as follows:

-εω: ε + οι = οι	φιλοίην, etc.
-αω: α + οι = ῳ	τιμῴην, etc.
-οω: ο + οι = οι	δηλοίην, etc.

	SINGULAR	PLURAL	SINGULAR	PLURAL
PRESENT	**Active**		**Middle/Passive**	
1st	φιλοίην	φιλοῖμεν/φιλοίημεν	φιλοίμην	φιλοίμεθα
2nd	φιλοίης	φιλοῖτε/φιλοίητε	φιλοῖο	φιλοῖσθε
3rd	φιλοίη	φιλοῖεν/φιλοίησαν	φιλοῖτο	φιλοῖντο
1st	τιμῴην	τιμῷμεν/τιμῴημεν	τιμῴμην	τιμῴμεθα
2nd	τιμῴης	τιμῷτε/τιμῴητε	τιμῷο	τιμῷσθε
3rd	τιμῴη	τιμῷεν/τιμῴησαν	τιμῷτο	τιμῷντο
1st	δηλοίην	δηλοῖμεν/δηλοίημεν	δηλοίμην	δηλοίμεθα
2nd	δηλοίης	δηλοῖτε/δηλοίητε	δηλοῖο	δηλοῖσθε
3rd	δηλοίη	δηλοῖεν/δηλοίησαν	δηλοῖτο	δηλοῖντο

The other tenses of contract verbs do not involve contractions, so they have regular conjugations like that of λύω: future φιλήσοιμι, aorist φιλήσαιμι, etc.

PRACTICE A. Fill in the blanks:

	FORM	TENSE	VOICE	PERSON/NUMBER	(VERB)
1.	_____	aorist	active	3rd singular	(νομίζω)
2.	δηλοῖο	_____	_____	_____	_____
3.	πέμψαιμι	_____	_____	_____	_____
4.	_____	present	middle	3rd plural	(τιμάω)
5.	_____	perfect	active	1st plural	(φεύγω)
6.	ἔξοιτε	_____	_____	_____	_____
7.	γραφείης	_____	_____	_____	_____
8.	_____	aorist	active	3rd singular	(λαμβάνω)
9.	λελοιπὼς εἴη	_____	_____	_____	_____

2. The optative in wishes for the future

Wishes referring to a future time are expressed by the optative. They are usually (but not always) introduced by εἴθε or εἰ γάρ; in English, phrases like 'if only', 'would that', 'may' are good phrases to signify a wish.

Verb tense conveys the aspect: present optative for a continuous action, aorist for a single act.

> εἰ γὰρ ἡ θεὰ ἀεὶ ἡμᾶς φυλάσσοι.
> If only the goddess might always protect us.

> ἡ θεὰ μὴ βλάψαι ἡμᾶς.
> Would that the goddess might not harm us.

> εἴθε οἱ πολέμιοι μὴ νικήσαιεν ἡμᾶς.
> May the enemy not conquer us.

Note: The negative is always μή.

3. ἀφικνέομαι, γίγνομαι and ἔρχομαι

ἀφικνέομαι (+ εἰς) means 'arrive', 'reach'; γίγνομαι means 'become', 'happen', and ἔρχομαι means both 'come' and 'go'. These are deponent verbs, with active meaning but middle forms in some or all tenses (cf. Ch. 16.1, part 2). Each of these verbs has a strong aorist, as well as some other irregularities in the principal parts.

PRESENT	FUTURE A/M	AORIST A/M	PERFECT A	PERFECT M/P	AORIST P
ἀφικνέομαι	ἀφίξομαι	ἀφικόμην	——	ἀφῖγμαι	——
γίγνομαι	γενήσομαι	ἐγενόμην	γέγονα	γεγένημαι	ἐγενήθην
ἔρχομαι	ἐλεύσομαι	ἦλθον	ἐλήλυθα	——	——

γίγνομαι takes a predicate nominative, like εἰμί, instead of a direct object:

> ὁ ποιητὴς ἐγένετο σοφός.   The poet became wise.
> ὁ νεανίας γενήσεται στρατιώτης.   The young man will become a soldier.

EXERCISE 129.

1. εἴθε ὁ στρατηγὸς λύσαι τοὺς αἰχμαλώτους.
2. ἄξιοι εἶμεν τῆς πόλεως.
3. εἰ γὰρ μὴ τοῦτο γένοιτο.
4. εἴθε ὁ Δημοσθένης πείσαι τοὺς πολίτας.
5. ἀνδρειότερον μαχώμεθα ὑπὲρ τῆς πατρίδος.
6. εἰ γὰρ ἀφικοίμεθα εἰς τὴν πόλιν πρὸ τῆς νυκτός.
7. εἴθε οἱ στρατιῶται εὖ φυλάσσοιεν τὰς πύλας.
8. μὴ νικηθείη τὸ στράτευμα.
9. εἴθε μὴ βλάπτοιτε τὰ ἱερά.
10. μὴ γράψῃς ἐπιστολὴν σήμερον.

EXERCISE 130.

1. Would that we might set free our friends.
2. May he be wiser than his father.
3. May the orator always speak the truth.
4. If only the enemy might not reach the river.
5. Polycrates, who was a tyrant, was most fortunate.
6. Would that some guide would show us the way.
7. Do not order the allies to go away.
8. May we be set free from this danger.
9. I wish I might become a sailor.
10. May the women and children not be harmed.

4. The genitive absolute

When a circumstantial participle refers to a noun in the main clause, it agrees with that noun. When the participle refers to a noun not present in the main clause, it is said to be *absolute*. What, then, should be the case of the participle and the noun it agrees with? In Greek, they both appear in the genitive case.

Like any other circumstantial participial phrase, the genitive absolute is often best translated with a clause beginning 'if', 'when'/'while', 'since' or 'although' (Ch. 20.2, part B).

> τάξας τοὺς ἄνδρας ὁ στρατηγὸς ἀπεχώρησεν.
> > After he had drawn up his men, the general went away.
> τοῦ στρατηγοῦ τάξαντος τοὺς ἄνδρας, ἀπεχωρήσαμεν.
> > After the general had drawn up his men, we went away.

> ὁ ῥήτωρ εὖ λέγων πείθει ἡμᾶς.
> > The orator, when he speaks well, persuades us.
> τοῦ ῥήτορος εὖ λέγοντος, πειθόμεθα.
> > Since the orator is speaking well, we are persuaded.
> τοῦ ῥήτορος εὖ λέγοντος, πεισθησόμεθα.
> > If the orator speaks well, we will be persuaded.

5. εἶμι, 'go'

Though it is present in form, the indicative of εἶμι, 'go' often has the future meaning 'I shall go'. The subjunctive always has this future meaning. The infinitive, participle and optative can have either a present or a future sense.

The forms of εἶμι are distinguished from those of εἰμί, 'be' both by the accent and by the presence of ι in all forms. Here are the two paradigms for comparison.

PRESENT SYSTEM

	εἶμι, 'go'		εἰμί, 'be'	
	SINGULAR	PLURAL	SINGULAR	PLURAL

INDICATIVE
Present

1st	εἶμι	ἴμεν	εἰμί	ἐσμέν
2nd	εἶ(ς)[1]	ἴτε	εἶ	ἐστέ
3rd	εἶσι(ν)	ἴᾱσι(ν)	ἐστί(ν)	εἰσί(ν)

Imperfect

1st	ᾖα/ᾔειν	ᾖμεν	ἦ / ἦν	ἦμεν
2nd	ᾔεισθα	ᾖτε	ἦσθα	ἦτε
3rd	ᾔειν/ᾔει	ᾖσαν/ᾔεσαν	ἦν	ἦσαν

SUBJUNCTIVE

1st	ἴω	ἴωμεν	ὦ	ὦμεν
2nd	ἴῃς	ἴητε	ᾖς	ἦτε
3rd	ἴῃ	ἴωσι(ν)	ᾖ	ὦσι(ν)

OPTATIVE

1st	ἴοιμι	ἴοιμεν	εἴην	εἶμεν
2nd	ἴοις	ἴοιτε	εἴης	εἶτε
3rd	ἴοι	ἴοιεν	εἴη	εἶεν

IMPERATIVE

2nd	ἴθι	ἴτε	ἴσθι	ἔστε
3rd	ἴτω	ἰόντων	ἔστω	ἔστων/ὄντων

INFINITIVE   ἰέναι   εἶναι

PARTICIPLE   ἰών, ἰοῦσα, ἰόν   ὤν, οὖσα, ὄν

EXERCISE 131.

1. τῶν πολεμίων ἀπελθόντων, ἐστρατοπεδευσάμεθα.
2. ἰδόντες τὴν θάλασσαν, πάντες ἐβοῶμεν.
3. τοῦ ναυτικοῦ νικηθέντος, ὁ Ξέρξης ἠπόρει.
4. οἱ πολέμιοι προσέβαλον ἡμῖν τὸν ποταμὸν διαβαίνουσιν.
5. ἡμῶν εἰς τὴν Βαβυλῶνα εἰσιόντων, οἱ πολῖται ἀπέβησαν.
6. κελεύσαντος τοῦ Κύρου, τῶν στρατιωτῶν τινες ἐτάχθησαν ὄπισθε τῆς πόλεως.
7. λαβόντες τοὺς ἐν τῇ νήσῳ, οἱ Ἀθηναῖοι ἔχαιρον.
8. ὁ Ἄδμητος ἐδάκρυε τῇ γυναικὶ ἀποθανούσῃ.
9. ἐπιφαινομένου τοῦ Ἀρίονος, οἱ ναῦται μάλιστα ἀποροῦσιν.
10. τοῦ Ξενοφῶντος ἄρχοντος, οἱ Ἕλληνες εἰς τὴν θάλασσαν ἀφίκοντο.

EXERCISE 132.

1. When the Greeks had reached the sea, the guide went away.
2. After conquering him in a sea battle, the Greeks did not pursue Xerxes.
3. While this general was in command, the Athenians fared well.
4. When Darius died, Xerxes became king.
5. When they had been defeated, the Persians went away from Attica.
6. As the Persians were very many, Leonidas was easily defeated.
7. When the enemy had ransomed the prisoners, we went away.

---

1   εἶ is the Attic form, while εἰς is more common elsewhere.

8. As our friends are not there, we will return to the city.
9. Since my father is wiser, I will obey him.
10. When the fleet had sailed away we went homeward.

EXERCISE 133.

BORN TO BE KING

Astyages, the last king of the Medes, dreamt that he would be overthrown by his grandson Cyrus, whose father Cambyses was a Persian. As soon as Cyrus was born, Astyages ordered him to be put to death, but a herdsman to whom the deed was entrusted substituted his own dead baby, and brought up Cyrus as his own son. Years later, Cyrus organized a rebellion and became king of the Medes and Persians in 549 BC. The empire of Media, founded in about 700 BC, had stretched from the Caspian Sea to the Persian Gulf and included Assyria and Persia.

ὁ δὲ Κῦρος, ὅτε ἦν δεκαετὴς καὶ ἔτι ἐνομίζετο εἶναι υἱὸς τοῦ βουκόλου, ἔπαιζεν ἐν τῇ κώμῃ μετ᾽ ἄλλων τινῶν παίδων. καὶ οἱ παῖδες παίζοντες εἵλοντο ἑαυτῶν βασιλέα εἶναι αὐτόν. τοῦ δὲ Κύρου κελεύσαντος, οἱ μὲν αὐτῶν οἰκίας παρεσκεύαζον, οἱ δὲ δορυφόροι ἦσαν, οἱ δὲ ἄλλα ἔργα ἐποίουν. εἷς δὴ τούτων τῶν παίδων, υἱὸς ὢν Ἀρτεμβάρους, ἀνδρὸς δοκίμου ἐν Μήδοις, οὐ γὰρ δὴ ἐποίησεν ἃ ὁ Κῦρος προσέταξεν, ἐκέλευε ὁ Κῦρος τοὺς ἄλλους παῖδας αὐτὸν λαβεῖν. πειθομένων δὲ τῶν παίδων, ὁ Κῦρος τὸν παῖδα μάστιγι ἐκόλασεν· ὁ δέ, ἐπεὶ ἀπέφυγεν, μάλιστα ὀργιζόμενος δι᾽ ἃ ἔπαθεν, ἤγγειλε τὸ γενόμενον τῷ πατρί. ὁ δ᾽ Ἀρτεμβάρης, ὀργῇ ὡς εἶχε ἐλθὼν παρὰ τὸν Ἀστυάγη καὶ ἅμα ἄγων τὸν παῖδα, εἶπεν, Ὦ βασιλεῦ, ὑπὸ τοῦ σοῦ δούλου, βουκόλου δὲ παιδὸς ὧδε ὑβρίσμεθα, δηλώσας τοὺς τοῦ παιδὸς ὤμους. ἀκούσας δὲ καὶ ἰδών, ὁ Ἀστυάγης ἐθέλων κολάσαι τὸν παῖδα τιμῆς τῆς Ἀρτεμβάρους ἕνεκα, μετεπέμπετο τόν τε βουκόλον καὶ τὸν παῖδα.

τούτων δὲ παρόντων, βλέψας πρὸς τὸν Κῦρον ὁ Ἀστυάγης ἔφη· Σὺ δὴ ὢν υἱὸς βουκόλου, ἐτόλμησας τὸν τοῦδε υἱὸν ὄντος πρώτου παρ᾽ ἐμοὶ ὧδε ὑβρίζειν; ὁ δὲ ἀπεκρίνατο ὧδε· Ὦ δέσποτα, ἐγὼ ταῦτα δικαίως ἐποίησα. οἱ γάρ με ἐκ τῆς κώμης παῖδες, ὧν καὶ ὅδε ἦν, παίζοντες ἑαυτῶν ἐποίησαν βασιλέα. ἐδόκουν γὰρ αὐτοῖς εἶναι εἰς τοῦτο ἐπιτηδειότατος. οἱ μὲν οὖν ἄλλοι παῖδες ἃ ἐκέλευσα ἔπραξαν, οὗτος δὲ οὐκ ἐπείθετο, ἕως ἐκολάσθη. εἰ οὖν δὴ τούτου ἕνεκα ἄξιος κακοῦ τινός εἰμι, ὅδε πάρειμι. ταῦτα λέγοντος τοῦ παιδός, ὁ Ἀστυάγης ἐδόκει ἀναγνωρίζειν τὸ πρόσωπον αὐτοῦ καὶ πολὺν χρόνον ἄφθογγος ἦν. τοῦ δὲ Ἀρτεμβάρους ἀποπεμφθέντος, ἐκέλευσε τοὺς θεράποντας ἔσω ἄγειν τὸν Κῦρον.

ἐπεὶ δὲ ὑπελέλειπτο ὁ βουκόλος μόνος, ὁ ᾽Αστυάγης αὐτὸν ἠρώτησεν πόθεν ἔλαβε τὸν παῖδα. ὁ δὲ ἀπεκρίνατο ὅτι ἐστὶν ὁ ἑαυτοῦ υἱός. ὁ δὲ ᾽Αστυάγης ἐσήμαινε τοῖς δορυφόροις συλλαμβάνειν καὶ τύπτειν αὐτόν. ὁ δὲ ἐν μεγίστῃ ἀπορίᾳ ὤν, ἀληθῶς πάντα ἐξηγεῖτο καὶ ᾔτησε τὸν βασιλέα ἑαυτῷ συγγιγνώσκειν.

Adapted from Herodotus I.114-116

Chapter 25 Vocabulary

Verbs:

ἀπέρχομαι	go away	εἴσειμι (εἶμι, 'go')	enter
ἀποβαίνω	go away	ἐπανέρχομαι	return
ἀποπλέω	sail away	ἐπιφαίνομαι	appear
ἀφικνέομαι (+ εἰς)	arrive, reach	ἔρχομαι	come, go
γίγνομαι	become, happen	πλέω, πλεύσομαι,	sail
δακρύω	weep	ἔπλευσα, πέπλευκα,	
εἶμι	go (future sense)	πέπλευσμαι, ἐπλεύσθην	

Adjective:
    ἱερός, -ά, -όν   sacred

Adverb:
    σήμερον   today

Particle:
    εἰ γάρ, εἴθε   if only, would that, may

CHAPTER 26

1. Purpose (final) clauses

The subjunctive and optative are used in similar ways in several kinds of subordinate clauses. The subjunctive has primary endings, as you learned, and it is associated with primary tenses. Thus when the main verb in a sentence is in a primary tense (present, future, perfect), the subordinate clause uses the subjunctive. When the main verb is in a secondary tense (imperfect, aorist, pluperfect), the subordinate clause uses the optative. This division of labor between subjunctive and optative has a good parallel in the thematic vowel, which appears in certain environments as **e**, and in certain others as **o**, always with similar functions.

One subordinate clause where the subjunctive and optative appear is the purpose clause, which expresses the reason something is done. In English, as in Greek, the form of the subordinate verb can vary depending on the tense of the main verb:

I <u>come</u> so that I <u>may</u> see you. / I come in order to see you.

I <u>came</u> so that you <u>might</u> see me.

A purpose clause is introduced in Greek by ἵνα, ὡς or ὅπως. The negative is μή. The tense of the subjunctive or optative shows aspect (Ch. 16.5): the present for an ongoing or repeated action, the aorist for a single, simple act.

> τρέχομεν ἵνα παύσωμεν τὴν μάχην.
> We are running in order to stop the battle.

> ἐδράμομεν ἵνα παύσαιμεν τὴν μάχην.
> We ran in order to stop the battle.

> νόμοις πειθόμεθα ὅπως εἰρήνην ἔχωμεν.
> We obey laws in order to have peace / so that we may have peace.

> ἐλευσόμεθα ἵνα οἱ παῖδες μὴ φοβῶνται.
> We will come so that the children may not be afraid.

> ἐμαχεσάμεθα ἵνα οἱ στρατιῶται μὴ νικηθεῖεν.
> We fought so that the soldiers might not be conquered.

Construction Summary

primary verb:	+ ἵνα + subjunctive (negative μή):	"He goes <u>in order to do x</u>."
secondary verb:	+ ἵνα + optative (negative μή):	"He went <u>in order to do x</u>."

Note: Some authors occasionally use the subjunctive in place of the optative after a secondary tense main verb; this makes the construction more vivid and immediate, since it effectively treats the past as present.

EXERCISE 134.

1. οἱ Λακεδαιμόνιοι ἐπέμφθησαν ἵνα τὰ δένδρα κόψαιεν.
2. πάρεσμεν ὅπως τῷ θεῷ θύωμεν.
3. ὁ Ξέρξης ἄξει στράτευμα, ἵνα οἱ Ἀθηναῖοι κολασθῶσιν.
4. οἱ πολέμιοι ἔμενον ἐπὶ τοῦ ὄρους, ὡς προσβάλοιεν τοῖς Ἕλλησιν.
5. ἵνα μὴ ληφθεῖεν, οἱ Πέρσαι πρὸς τὴν θάλασσαν ἔφυγον.
6. ὁ Πολυκράτης ἀποπλεῖ, ὅπως ἀποβάλῃ τὴν σφραγῖδα.
7. οἱ Ἀθηναῖοι ἀπέπεμψαν τὰς γυναῖκας, ὅπως αὐταὶ ἀσφαλεῖς εἶεν.
8. οὐκ ἀεὶ τρέχομεν ἵνα ἆθλα φερώμεθα.
9. ἡ Ἀρτεμισία κατέδυσε τὴν ναῦν ὅπως ἑαυτὴν σώσαι.
10. ὁ Ἀρίων ἐκπηδᾷ εἰς τὴν θάλασσαν, ἵνα μὴ ἀποθάνῃ.

EXERCISE 135.

1. The general is sending cavalry in order that he may hinder the enemy.
2. The Greeks and Persians fought each other bravely.
3. We shall flee out of the city so that the foreigners may not capture us.
4. We sent many soldiers to guard the bridge.
5. The Athenians sent for the general so that they might honor him.
6. A guide arrived to lead the Greeks to the sea.
7. The king waited for three days, so that the generals might deliberate with him.
8. So that they might not be defeated, the Athenians asked for help.
9. We are crossing the river to escape from danger.
10. Themistocles persuaded the citizens to prepare ships to save their country.

2. δεῖ:

The verb δέω is used impersonally in the third person singular to mean 'it is necessary'. It is followed by the accusative and an infinitive (negative μή), but English translation can be more flexible, as the following examples show.

> δεῖ ἡμᾶς μὴ διῶξαι τὸν ἵππον.
> > It is necessary for us not to pursue the horse.
> > We must not pursue the horse.

> ἔδει τὸν στρατηγὸν διώκειν τοὺς πολεμίους.
> > It was necessary for the general to pursue the enemy.
> > The general had to pursue the enemy.

> δεήσει τὸν παῖδα αἰτεῖν τὰ χρήματα.
> > It will be necessary for the child to ask for money.
> > The child will have to ask for money.

Note: The future is δεήσει, 'it will be necessary', and the imperfect is ἔδει, 'it was necessary'. The aorist is not used for this construction.

3. Future participle to express purpose:

Another way to express purpose (especially after verbs of motion, like 'go', 'send' etc.) is with the future participle (without ἵνα or ὅπως; with or without ὡς). The participle agrees with the subject of the action. The negative is οὐ, but it is rarely needed; most purposes are positive.

> ἔπεμψα τὸν παῖδα λύσοντα τοὺς βοῦς.
> > I sent the boy to loose the oxen.

> ἐλευσόμεθα τοῦ ῥήτορος ἀκουσόμενοι.
> > We will come in order to hear the orator.

EXERCISE 136.

1. ὁ Ἀρισταγόρας ἦλθεν εἰς Σπάρτην, ἵνα πείσαι τοὺς Λακεδαιμονίους βοηθεῖν τοῖς Ἴωσιν.
2. ἔδει τοὺς κροκοδείλους νυκτὸς ἀποβῆναι εἰς τὴν γῆν, ὅπως καθεύδσιεν.
3. βοηθεῖτε ἡμῖν, ὦ πολῖται, ἵνα μὴ δουλωθῶμεν ὑπὸ τῶν βαρβάρων.
4. ὁ Κῦρος εἰσήγαγε τὸν ποταμὸν εἰς τὴν λίμνην, ὡς οἱ στρατιῶται λάβοιεν τὴν Βαβυλῶνα.
5. ὁ ἁλιεὺς φέρει τὸν ἰχθὺν εἰς τὰ βασίλεια, ἵνα τὸν Πολυκράτη τιμήσῃ.
6. ἐπέμψαμεν κήρυκα τοὺς στρατιώτας λυσόμενον.
7. δεῖ ἡμᾶς ἰέναι Ἀθήναζε τοὺς στρατηγοὺς τιμήσοντες.
8. οἱ Πέρσαι εἰς τὴν θάλασσαν ἐξεπήδησαν, ἵνα ἡ ναῦς μὴ καταδυθείη.
9. δεῖ ἡμᾶς ἡγεμόνα ἔχειν ἵνα δηλῷ ἡμῖν τὴν ὁδόν.
10. οἱ Λακεδαιμόνιοι εἰσῆλθον εἰς τὴν Ἀττικήν, ἡμῖν προσβαλοῦντες.

EXERCISE 137.

1. The Egyptians have nets so that they may protect their bodies from gnats.
2. We will advance to the mountain to attack the enemy.
3. Cyrus sent for the boy in order to punish him.
4. We went to the temple to honor the goddess.
5. So that he might not die himself, Admetus persuaded his wife to die for him.
6. In order to save himself, Arion wanted the sailors to take his money.
7. Croesus sends these gifts to honor the god.
8. Tell the truth in order that you may be trusted.
9. We were compelled to retreat in order to save ourselves.
10. Flee to your ships that you may not be captured.

EXERCISE 138.

AN ARGUMENT ABOUT COMMAND

In the autumn of 481 BC a congress of Greeks was held at the Isthmus of Corinth to decide upon measures for resisting the threatened invasion by Xerxes. Ambassadors were sent to ask for help from various states, including Syracuse in Sicily. Syracuse had been founded by Corinth, and was ruled at this time by the tyrant Gelon.

Ὡς δὲ οἱ ἄγγελοι ἀφίκοντο εἰς τὰς Συρακούσας, τῷ Γέλωνι ἔλεγον τάδε· Ἔπεμψαν ἡμᾶς οἵ τε Λακεδαιμόνιοι καὶ οἱ Ἀθηναῖοι καὶ οἱ τούτων σύμμαχοι, παραληψομένους σε πρὸς τὸν βάρβαρον· Πέρσης γὰρ ἀνὴρ μέλλει, διαβαίνων τὸν Ἑλλήσποντον καὶ ἐπάγων πάντα τὸν στρατὸν ἐκ τῆς Ἀσίας, στρατεύσειν ἐπὶ τὴν Ἑλλάδα. ὡς δέ σοι, τῷ τῆς Σικελίας ἄρχοντι, μοῖρά ἐστιν οὐκ ἐλαχίστη τῆς Ἑλλάδος, βοήθει τοῖς τὴν Ἑλλάδα ἐλευθεροῦσι καὶ ἅμα ἐλευθέρου σεαυτόν· νικηθέντων γὰρ ἡμῶν, καὶ σὺ νικηθήσει.

ὁ δὲ Γέλων ἀπεκρίνατο· Ἄνδρες Ἕλληνες, ἐτολμήσατε μὲν δεῦρο ἐλθεῖν, ὅπως ἐμὲ σύμμαχον ἐπὶ τὸν βάρβαρον παρακαλέσαιτε· αὐτοὶ δέ, ὅτε ἐμοὶ πρὸς τοὺς Καρχηδονίους[1] πόλεμος ἦν, οὐκ ἤλθετε ὡς βοηθήσοντες. νῦν δέ, ἐπεὶ ὁ πόλεμος ἀφῖκται εἰς ὑμᾶς, Γέλωνος

---

[1] No details are known of this war, but in 480 the Carthaginians invaded Sicily and were decisively defeated at the battle of Himera, said to have been fought on the same day as the battle of Salamis.

μέμνησθε. ἀτιμηθεὶς δὲ ὑφ᾽ ὑμῶν, οὐχ ὑμᾶς ἀτιμήσω, ἀλλ᾽ ἑτοῖμός εἰμι βοηθεῖν καὶ παρέχειν διακοσίας τριήρεις καὶ δισμυρίους ὁπλίτας καὶ δισχιλίους ἱππέας, αὐτὸς ὢν στρατηγός τε καὶ ἡγεμὼν τῶν Ἑλλήνων πρὸς τὸν βάρβαρον· ἐπὶ λόγῳ τούτῳ [on this condition] τάδε ὑπισχνοῦμαι. ἐπ᾽ ἄλλῳ δὲ λόγῳ οὔτ᾽ αὐτὸς ἐλεύσομαι οὔτ᾽ ἄλλους πέμψω.

ἄγγελος δέ τις Λακεδαιμόνιος, ταῦτα ἀκούσας, εἶπε τάδε· Οὔ σοι ἐπιτρέψομεν τὴν ἡγεμονίαν· ἀλλ᾽ εἰ μὲν βούλει βοηθεῖν τῇ Ἑλλάδι, γίγνωσκε ὅτι ἀρχθήσει ὑπὸ Λακεδαιμονίων· εἰ δὲ μὴ δικαιοῖς ἄρχεσθαι, σὺ δὲ μηδὲ δικαίου βοηθεῖν. καὶ πρὸς τάδε ὁ Γέλων ἀπεκρίνατο· Ὦ ξένε Λακεδαιμόνιε, ὧδ᾽ ἐμὲ ὑβρίσας, οὔ με ἔπεισας ὑβρίζειν σε. εἰ δὲ καί μοί ἐστι πολλῷ μὲν μείζων ἡ στρατιά, πολλῷ δὲ πλείονες αἱ νῆες, ὑπείξομέν τι. εἰ τοῦ μὲν πεζοῦ ὑμεῖς ἡγεμονεύετε, τοῦ δὲ ναυτικοῦ ἐγώ· εἰ δὲ ὑμῖν ἡδύ ἐστι κατὰ θάλασσαν ἡγεμονεύειν, τοῦ πεζοῦ ἐγὼ ἐθέλω. καὶ δεῖ ὑμᾶς ἢ τόδε ἐᾶν ἢ ἀπιέναι ἄνευ συμμάχων.

ὁ δὲ τῶν Ἀθηναίων ἄγγελος εὐθὺς εἶπε τάδε· Ὦ βασιλεῦ Συρακοσίων, ἡ Ἑλλὰς ἀπέπεμψεν ἡμᾶς πρός σε οὐχ ἵνα ἡγεμόνα αἰτήσαιμεν, ἀλλὰ στρατιάν· εἰ δὲ καὶ ὁ Λακεδαιμόνιος βούλεταί σοι ἐπιτρέπειν τὴν τοῦ ναυτικοῦ ἀρχήν, ἡμεῖς οὐ βουλόμεθα· ἡμετέρα γάρ ἐστιν αὕτη, εἰ μὴ οἱ Λακεδαιμόνιοι αὐτοὶ βούλονται αὐτὴν ἔχειν. ἀπεκρίνατο δὲ Γέλων· Ξένε Ἀθηναῖε, ὑμεῖς δοκεῖτε τοὺς μὲν ἄρχοντας ἔχειν, τοὺς δὲ ἀρχομένους οὐχ ἕξειν. ἐπεὶ τοίνυν, οὐδὲν ὑπείκοντες, ἔχειν τὸ πᾶν ἐθέλετε, ἀποχωρήσατε ὡς τάχιστα εἰς τὴν Ἑλλάδα.

Adapted from Herodotus VII.157-162

Chapter 26 Vocabulary

Verbs:

αἰτέω	ask for, demand	ἐκπηδάω	leap out
δεῖ	it is necessary	καθεύδω	sleep
εἰσάγω	lead in, bring in	μεταπέμπομαι	send for
εἰσέρχομαι	come in	σῴζω	protect

Nouns:

Αἰγύπτιος, -ου, ὁ	an Egyptian	Ἀρίων, -ονος, ὁ	Arion
ἀμφίβληστρον, -ου, τό	net	βασίλεια, -ων, τά	palace
		Ἴωνες, -ων, οἱ	Ionians
Ἀρισταγόρας, -ου, ὁ	Aristagoras	κροκόδειλος, -ου, ὁ	crocodile
		κώνωψ, -ωπος, ὁ	gnat

Adverb:

ἐκεῖσε	to that place

Preposition:

ἐπί (+ *gen.*)	on, upon

Conjunction:

ἵνα	in order that	ὡς	in order that
ὅπως	in order that		

CHAPTER 27

1. Result (consecutive) clauses

A result clause expresses either an actual, specific result (in the indicative, negative οὐ), or a probable, general result (in the infinitive, negative μή). It is introduced in either case by ὥστε. In a probable result clause, the subject of the infinitive is in the accusative, if it is different from the subject of the main verb. The infinitive is usually either present or aorist, depending on aspect.

> ἀγαθὸς στρατηγὸς ἦν ὥστε ἔπαυσε τὴν μάχην.
>> He was a good general and so he stopped the battle.

> οὕτω σοφός ἐστιν ὥστε ἀεὶ λέγειν καλῶς.
>> He is so wise as to speak well always (that he speaks well always).

> οὕτω μωρός ἐστιν ὥστε οὐ πιστεύομεν αὐτῷ.
>> He is so foolish that we do not trust him (now).

> οὕτω μωρός ἐστιν ὥστε ἡμᾶς μὴ πιστεύειν αὐτῷ.
>> He is so foolish that we do not believe him (ever).

After a comparative, ἢ ὥστε is used.

> ὁ Σωκράτης σοφώτερός ἐστιν ἢ ὥστε τοῦτο λέξαι.
>> Socrates is too wise (lit., wiser than) to say this.

Construction Summary

ὥστε + indicative (negative οὐ):	actual result	"He is so wise <u>that x happened</u>."
ὥστε + infinitive (negative μή):	general result	"He is so wise <u>as to do y</u>."

2. Clauses of fearing

Clauses of fearing are always introduced by a verb of fearing + μή; if there is a negative in the following clause οὐ is added. Fear may be expressed about the past, present or future. When the fear refers to the present or past, the verb is in the indicative; the tense is the same as it would be in a main clause.

> φοβοῦμαι μὴ οὐ πιστεύει μοι.   φοβοῦμαι μὴ οὐκ ἦλθεν.
>> I am afraid he does not trust me.   I am afraid he did not come.

When the fear concerns the future, the same division of labor you learned for purpose clauses applies: the subjunctive is used after a main verb in a primary tense, the optative after a secondary tense. As usual, aspect determines whether the subjunctive or optative is present or aorist.

140

φοβοῦμαι μὴ ἔλθῃ.
   I am afraid he may come.

φοβοῦμαι μὴ οὐ μένῃ.
   I am afraid he may not stay.

ἐφοβούμην μὴ οἱ πολέμιοι ἔλθοιεν.
   I was afraid that the enemy would come.

ἐφοβούμην μὴ οὐ μένοι ὁ στρατηγός.
   I was afraid that the general might not stay.

Construction Summary

present fear:	φοβοῦμαι μὴ + present indicative	"I fear he does/ is doing x."
past fear:	φοβοῦμαι μὴ + past indicative	"I fear he did/ was doing x."
	ἐφοβούμην μὴ + past indicative	"I feared he had done x."
future fear:	φοβοῦμαι μὴ + subjunctive	"I fear he will do x."
	ἐφοβούμην μὴ + optative	"I feared he would do x."

EXERCISE 139.

1. οἱ Λακεδαιμόνιοι οὕτως ἀνδρεῖοί εἰσιν, ὥστε ἀεὶ εὖ μάχεσθαι.
2. ἐφοβεῖτο μὴ ὁ στρατηγὸς ὁ τῶν πολεμίων ῥαδίως νικήῃ τὴν στρατιὰν ἡμῶν.
3. τοσοῦτός ἐστιν ὁ κίνδυνος ὥστε φοβοῦμαι μὴ οὐκ ἀποφύγω.
4. ὁ ποταμός ἐστιν οὕτω χαλεπός, ὥστε μηδένα αὐτὸν διαβαίνειν.
5. ὁ Ξέρξης οὐκ ἦν οὕτω μωρὸς ὥστε μένειν ἐν τῇ Ἑλλάδι.
6. τοσοῦτοι ἦσαν οἱ Πέρσαι ὥστε οἱ Ἀθηναῖοι οὐκέτι ἔμειναν ἐν τῇ πόλει.
7. οἱ βάρβαροι δειλότεροι ἦσαν ἢ ὥστε μάχεσθαι.
8. φοβεῖ μὴ οὐκ ἔχῃς πολλὰ χρήματα;
9. οἱ τριακόσιοι οὕτως ἀνδρείως ἐμαχέσαντο, ὥστε ἀεὶ ἐτιμῶντο ὑπὸ τῶν Ἑλλήνων.
10. τὸ τεῖχός ἐστιν οὕτως ὑψηλὸν ὥστε μηδένα οἷόν τε εἶναι αὐτὸ ὑπερβῆναι.

EXERCISE 140.

1. Were you afraid that the orator would persuade us?
2. The enemy were so few that we quickly defeated them.
3. The Persians were so many that nobody hindered them.
4. We are afraid that they hit each other with stones.
5. The Athenians attacked the enemy so bravely that they pursued them into the sea.
6. The men were afraid that the storm was very great.
7. The general was too prudent to cross the mountain by night.
8. I fear we will not win the battle.
9. Few men are so foolish as not to honor their country.
10. The ship sailed away so quickly that we did not catch it.

EXERCISE 141.

PYLOS AND SPHACTERIA: (1) AN ILL WIND

In the year 425 BC, *during the Peloponnesian War, when Athens had to face both Sparta and Corinth, an Athenian fleet on its way to Sicily was overtaken by a storm off the coast of Messenia in the Peloponnese.*

Τοσοῦτος δὲ ἦν ὁ χειμών, ὥστε αἱ νῆες ἠναγκάσθησαν καταφυγεῖν εἰς τὴν Πύλον·

ἔδοξε δὲ τῷ Δημοσθένει, ὃς ἦν στρατηγός, τειχίζειν τὸ χωρίον· εὐπορία γὰρ ἦν ξύλων τε

καὶ λίθων. οἱ δὲ στρατιῶται οὕτω ταχέως εἰργάζοντο, ὥστε ἐξ ἡμερῶν τὸ χωρίον ἐτείχισαν· οἱ δὲ Ἀθηναῖοι τὸν μὲν Δημοσθένη ἐνταῦθα κατέλιπον φύλακα μετὰ νεῶν πέντε, ταῖς δὲ ἄλλαις ναυσὶ εἰς Σικελίαν ἀπέπλευσαν. οἱ δὲ Λακεδαιμόνιοι εὐθὺς ἐπορεύοντο ἐπὶ τὴν Πύλον, καὶ ἐκέλευσαν τοὺς συμμάχους πέμψαι ἐκεῖσε ἑξήκοντα ναῦς· ἐν δὲ τούτῳ ὁ Δημοσθένης μετεπέμψατο ἄλλας ναῦς. οἱ δὲ Λακεδαιμόνιοι παρεσκευάζοντο ὡς τῷ τειχίσματι προσβαλοῦντες κατά τε γῆν καὶ κατὰ θάλασσαν, ἐλπίζοντες ῥᾳδίως αἱρήσειν τὸ χωρίον, ἀνθρώπων ὀλίγων ἐνόντων· διεβίβασαν δὲ ὁπλίτας εἰς τὴν νῆσον Σφακτηρίαν, ἣ ἐπίκειται τῇ Πύλῳ, καὶ εἰς τὴν ἤπειρον. μετὰ δὲ τοῦτο προσέβαλον μὲν τῷ τειχίσματι τῷ τε κατὰ γῆν στρατῷ καὶ ναυσὶν ἅμα, μάτην δέ.

ἐπεὶ δὲ πεντήκοντα ἄλλαι νῆες ἀφίκοντο, οἱ Ἀθηναῖοι προσέπεσον τῷ τῶν Λακεδαιμονίων ναυτικῷ, ὥστε ἔκοψαν μὲν πολλὰς ναῦς, πέντε δὲ ἔλαβον καὶ μίαν τούτων αὐτοῖς ναύταις,[1] καὶ ἀπέλαβον πολλοὺς ἄνδρας ἐν τῇ νήσῳ. μετὰ δὲ τὴν ναυμαχίαν ἔδοξε τοῖς Ἀθηναίοις εὐθὺς τὴν νῆσον περιπλεῖν καὶ ἐν φυλακῇ ἔχειν. ὡς δὲ εἰς τὴν Σπάρτην ἠγγέλθη τὰ περὶ Πύλον γενόμενα, ἔδοξε τοῖς Λακεδαιμονίοις σπονδὰς ποιήσασθαι καὶ πέμψαι εἰς τὰς Ἀθήνας πρέσβεις, ὅπως τοὺς ἄνδρας ὡς τάχιστα κομίσαιντο.

Adapted from Thucydides IV.3-15

Chapter 27 Vocabulary

Verb:

ὑπερβαίνω	climb over

Adverbs:

οὐκέτι	no longer	οὕτω(ς) (before cons.)	so
		οὕτως (before vowel)	

Conjunction:

ὥστε	(so) that, (so) as to

---

1   'Sailors and all'; an idiom which often includes the article: αὐτοῖς τοῖς ναύταις.

CHAPTER 28

1. οἶδα and φημί

οἶδα ('know') is related to the aorist εἶδον, 'saw'; it is perfect in form, with the present meaning 'I know' (because I have seen). The pluperfect forms have the imperfect meaning 'I knew'. The future, εἴσομαι, is regular (like λύσομαι).

φημί, 'say' is enclitic in the present tense. The principal parts of both verbs are given here, and the paradigms of unpredictable tenses.

PRESENT	FUTURE A/M	AORIST A/M	PERFECT A	PERFECT M/P	AORIST P
——	εἴσομαι	——	οἶδα	——	——
φημί	φήσω	ἔφησα	——	πέφασμαι	——

	οἶδα		φημί	
	SINGULAR	PLURAL	SINGULAR	PLURAL
INDICATIVE				
Perfect			**Present**	
1st	οἶδα	ἴσμεν	φημί	φαμέν
2nd	οἶσθα	ἴστε	φής	φατέ
3rd	οἶδε(ν)	ἴσασι(ν)	φησί(ν)	φασί(ν)
Pluperfect			**Imperfect**	
1st	ᾔδη/ᾔδειν	ᾖσμεν/ᾔδεμεν	ἔφην	ἔφαμεν
2nd	ᾔδησθα/ᾔδεις	ᾖστε/ᾔδετε	ἔφησθα/ἔφης	ἔφατε
3rd	ᾔδει(ν)	ᾖσαν/ᾔδεσαν	ἔφη	ἔφασαν
SUBJUNCTIVE				
1st	εἰδῶ	εἰδῶμεν	φῶ	φῶμεν
2nd	εἰδῇς	εἰδῆτε	φῇς	φῆτε
3rd	εἰδῇ	εἰδῶσι(ν)	φῇ	φῶσι(ν)
OPTATIVE				
1st	εἰδείην	εἰδεῖμεν/εἰδείημεν	φαίην	φαῖμεν/φαίημεν
2nd	εἰδείης	εἰδεῖτε/εἰδείητε	φαίης	φαῖτε/φαίητε
3rd	εἰδείη	εἰδεῖεν/εἰδείησαν	φαίη	φαῖεν/φαίησαν

	οἶδα		φημί	
	SINGULAR	PLURAL	SINGULAR	PLURAL
IMPERATIVE				
2nd	ἴσθι	ἴστε	φάθι, φαθί	φάτε
3rd	ἴστω	ἴστων	φάτω	φάντων
INFINITIVE	εἰδέναι		φάναι	
PARTICIPLE	εἰδώς, εἰδυῖα, εἰδός εἰδότος, etc.		φάς, φᾶσα, φάν φάντος, etc.	

Note: The negative οὔ φημι means 'I deny', 'I say...not...'. For 'I do not say' you must use another verb, like οὐ λέγω.

2. Indirect statement

A *direct* statement is like a quotation: it gives a person's words or thoughts in their original form: "They are coming." An *indirect* statement reports the original words or thoughts at second hand: "I think that they are coming"; "He said they were coming." In Greek each main verb that introduces an indirect statement takes one of three particular constructions.

Note: The negative in indirect statement is always οὐ.

3. The infinitive in indirect statement

After most verbs of thinking and some verbs of saying, the verb of an indirect statement is in the infinitive. νομίζω, 'think' and φημί, 'say' are two common verbs of this type which you will be using. νομίζω has a liquid future, νομιῶ (Ch. 21.4).

If the subject of the main verb (the reporter) is also the subject of the infinitive, it does not have to be repeated before the infinitive. However, any noun or adjective modifying it must be nominative. In the following example, the general is the reporter.

> ὁ στρατηγὸς νομίζει σοφὸς εἶναι.
> The general thinks he is wise.

> ὁ στρατηγός φησι αὐτὸς σοφὸς εἶναι.
> The general says that he himself is wise.

If the subject of the infinitive is different from the reporter, it appears in the accusative, and any noun or adjective modifying it must also be accusative.

> ὁ στρατηγὸς νομίζει τὴν γυναῖκα σοφὴν εἶναι.
> The general thinks the woman is wise.

The infinitive expresses time relative to the main verb of thinking or saying. The tense of the main verb itself has no effect on this relative relationship.

> present infinitive: same time as the main verb
> future infinitive: later time than the main verb
> aorist infinitive: earlier time than the main verb

This is different from (and easier than) the English system, where changing the tense of the main verb also changes the tense of the verb in the indirect statement.

> νομίζω τὸν στρατηγὸν πέμπειν συμμάχους.   (same time; *present* inf.)
> I think (that) the general sends / is sending allies.

> ἐνόμιζον τὸν στρατηγὸν πέμπειν συμμάχους.   (same time; *present* inf.)
> I thought (that) the general was sending allies.

νομίζω τὸν στρατηγὸν οὐ πέμψειν συμμάχους.   (later time; *future* inf.)
    I think (that) the general will not send allies.

ἐνόμιζον τὸν στρατηγὸν οὐ πέμψειν συμμάχους.   (later time; *future* inf.)
    I thought (that) the general would not send allies.

νομίζω τὸν στρατηγὸν πέμψαι συμμάχους.   (earlier time; *aorist* inf.)
    I think (that) the general sent allies.

ἐνόμιζον τὸν στρατηγὸν πέμψαι συμμάχους.   (earlier time; *aorist* inf.)
    I thought (that) the general had sent allies.

Another way to look at the tense of the infinitive is to say that it corresponds to the verb tense of the original direct statement on which the report is based. In the first two examples on the previous page, the original statement was "The general is sending allies." The present infinitive is therefore used in the indirect statement. In the third and fourth examples above, the direct statement was "The general will send allies"; thus the infinitive is future. In the final two examples, the direct statement was "The general sent allies."

PRACTICE A. Before translating the following sentences, write out in English the direct statement on which each reports.

1. They say that the men will come.
2. He said that he would come.
3. We think that we ourselves speak well.
4. We think that the orator spoke well.
5. The man says that his wife wrote to the general.
6. The woman says that her child is not speaking the truth.
7. The sailor thought the slave had taken the money.

EXERCISE 142.

1. ὁ ἄγγελος ἔφη τοὺς πολεμίους ὀλίγους εἶναι.
2. ἐνομίζομεν τοὺς Πέρσας οὐκ εὐθὺς ἀποχωρήσειν.
3. ὁ Σωκράτης οὐκ ἐνόμιζεν σοφὸς εἶναι.
4. ἡ Ἄλκηστις ἔφη αὐτὴ ἀποθανεῖσθαι.
5. οἱ ναῦται ἔφασαν ἀπολιπεῖν τὸν Ἀρίονα εὖ πράσσοντα ἐν τῇ Ἰταλίᾳ.
6. ὁ τύραννος οὐκ ἔφη πέμψειν στρατιώτας εἰς τὴν Ἑλλάδα.
7. ἆρα νομίζετε τοῦτο εἶναι ἀληθές;
8. ὁ ἁλιεὺς ἔφη αὐτὸς λαβεῖν τὸν ἰχθύν.
9. ὁ Ξέρξης ἐνόμισε δουλώσειν τοὺς Ἕλληνας.
10. οὔ φαμεν σύμμαχοι εἶναι ἀλλήλων.

EXERCISE 143.

1. The soldiers said that the enemy were fleeing.
2. We think that the orator is not wise.
3. Polycrates said that he had thrown away his ring.
4. The tyrant said that he wanted to lead the Greeks himself.
5. Surely you do not think that you will capture the city?
6. The Athenians said that they would prepare more triremes.
7. The citizens said that they did not trust the general.
8. The messenger said that the fleet had sailed away.
9. Even the Persians thought that the Spartans were brave.
10. The citizen said that he himself would educate his children.

4. The participle in indirect statement

Verbs of knowing and perceiving take a construction very similar to the one you have just learned. The only difference is that it uses a participle instead of an infinitive. The participle agrees with its subject (whether nominative or accusative) in gender, number and case. As in the infinitive construction, the tense of the participle expresses time relative to the main verb: present for same time, future for later time, aorist for earlier time.

Verbs that take this construction include the following:

αἰσθάνομαι, 'perceive'
γιγνώσκω, 'know', 'perceive'
οἶδα, 'know'
ὁράω, 'see', ἀκούω, 'hear', and other verbs of sense perception

PRESENT	FUTURE A/M	AORIST A/M	PERFECT A	PERFECT M/P	AORIST P
αἰσθάνομαι	αἰσθήσομαι	ᾐσθόμην	——	ᾔσθημαι	——
γιγνώσκω	γνώσομαι	ἔγνων[1]	ἔγνωκα	ἔγνωσμαι	ἐγνώσθην

οἶδα οὐ σοφὸς ὤν.
I know that I am not wise.

εἶδον τὴν ἐμὴν θυγατέρα σοφὴν οὖσαν.
I saw that my daughter was wise.

οἶδεν αὐτὸς ποιήσας τοῦτο.
He knows that he himself did this.

ἀκούομεν τοὺς ἵππους ἐλευσομένους εὐθύς.
We hear that the horses will come immediately.

EXERCISE 144.

1. ὁ τύραννος οἶδεν ὢν εὐτυχέστατος.
2. ὁ ἁλιεὺς εἶδε τὸν ἰχθὺν ὄντα μέγαν.
3. ὁ Πολυκράτης ᾔσθετο τὴν σφραγῖδα σωθεῖσαν.
4. εἴδομεν τοὺς πολεμίους προχωροῦντας πρὸς τὸν ποταμόν.
5. ὁ Σωκράτης οὐκ ᾔδει αὐτὸς ὢν σοφώτατος.
6. ὁ Κροῖσος ᾔσθετο τοὺς ἵππους φοβουμένους τὰς καμήλους.
7. ἡ Ἀρτεμισία ὁρᾷ αὐτὴ οὖσα ἐν κινδύνῳ.
8. ἠκούσαμεν τοὺς Πέρσας εἰς τὴν πόλιν ἐλθόντας.
9. ᾐσθόμεθα οὐχ οἷοί τε ὄντες ἀποφυγεῖν.
10. οἱ Πέρσαι ᾔδεσαν οὐ πολλοὺς ἐνόντας ἐν τῇ ἀκροπόλει.

EXERCISE 145.

1. We know that we are not safe.
2. The Athenians perceived that the enemy had departed.
3. We saw that the enemy were fortifying the mountain.
4. Cyrus did not know that he himself was the son of a king.
5. The general saw that the island would be useful.
6. The Athenians heard that the Spartans would not come at once.
7. We perceived that we were being pursued by the enemy.
8. The sailors did not know that Arion had been saved.

---

[1]   For the aorist conjugation, see Ch. 29.3.

9. Xenophon perceived that many of the soldiers were weak.
10. Who does not know that the Greeks were saved by their fleet?

5. Indirect statement with ὅτι or ὡς

This construction is closest to English wording. It uses a regular nominative subject and indicative verb, introduced by ὅτι or ὡς, meaning 'that'. (ὅτι usually indicates an objective fact, ὡς a personal opinion.)

Several common verbs can introduce this construction, including the following:

λέγω, 'say'
εἶπον, 'said' (the second aorist, with inf. εἰπεῖν, part. εἰπών)
ἀγγέλλω, 'announce' (for principal parts see Ch. 21.3)
ἀποκρίνομαι, 'answer'

PRESENT	FUTURE A/M	AORIST A/M	PERFECT A	PERFECT M/P	AORIST P
ἀποκρίνομαι	ἀποκρινοῦμαι	ἀπεκρινάμην	——	ἀποκέκριμαι	ἀπεκρίθην

As in the infinitive and participle constructions, the tense of the verb in the indirect statement expresses time relative to the main verb: present for same time, future for later time, aorist for earlier time.

Note: In this construction, it is always correct for the verb in the indirect statement to be indicative. A second option also exists when the verb of saying is in a secondary tense. In that case, the verb in the ὅτι / ὡς clause is sometimes put in the optative mood (same tense as the indicative).

ἀγγέλλουσιν ὅτι ὁ Σωκράτης πάρεστιν.
They announce that Socrates is present.

εἶπον ὡς ὁ Σωκράτης σοφός ἐστιν.
They said that Socrates was wise.

εἶπον ὅτι ὁ Σωκράτης σοφὸς εἴη.
They said that Socrates was wise.

EXERCISE 146.

1. ὁ ἄγγελος λέγει ὅτι οἱ πολέμιοι πάρεισιν.
2. ὁ Ἄμασις εἶπεν ὡς ὁ Πολυκράτης ἐστὶν εὐτυχής.
3. ὁ Γέλων εἶπεν ὡς οὐ βοηθήσει τοῖς Ἕλλησιν.
4. ὁ Ἀρισταγόρας ἤγγειλεν ὡς οἱ βάρβαροι οὐκ ἀνδρεῖοι εἶεν.
5. οἱ Ἀθηναῖοι εἶπον ὅτι ἐν μεγάλῳ κινδύνῳ εἰσίν.
6. ὁ ἡγεμὼν ἀπεκρίνατο ὅτι τοὺς Ἕλληνας ἀπάξει πρὸς τὴν θάλασσαν.
7. ὁ Θεμιστοκλῆς εἶπεν ὡς δεῖ τοὺς Ἀθηναίους πιστεύειν τῷ ναυτικῷ.
8. ἠγγέλθη ὅτι ὁ Λεωνίδας ἀπέθανεν.
9. ὁ ἄγγελος εἶπεν ὅτι οἱ Ἀθηναῖοι τειχίσαιεν τὴν Πύλον.
10. οἱ Λακεδαιμόνιοι ἀπεκρίναντο ὡς πέμψοιεν πρέσβεις.

EXERCISE 147.

1. The prisoner announces that the Persians are fleeing.
2. The sailors said that the ship was ready.
3. Cyrus said that he had punished the boy justly.
4. Aristagoras said that it was easy to conquer the Persians.
5. Admetus' father replied that he would not save his son.
6. The messenger announced that ten ships had been captured.

7. His friends said that Socrates was not worthy of death.
8. The Athenians said that the enemy would easily capture the city.
9. I replied that I had not heard this.
10. Some say that this is true, others that it is false.

EXERCISE 148.

PYLOS AND SPHACTERIA: (2) STALEMATE

οἱ δὲ πρέσβεις ἀφικόμενοι εἰς τὰς Ἀθήνας ἔφασαν τοὺς Λακεδαιμονίους

προκαλεῖσθαι μὲν τοὺς Ἀθηναίους εἰς εἰρήνην καὶ συμμαχίαν, ἀνταιτεῖν δὲ τοὺς ἐκ τῆς

νήσου ἄνδρας. οἱ γὰρ Λακεδαιμόνιοι ἐνόμισαν τοὺς Ἀθηναίους, ἤδη πολλάκις

νικηθέντας, εἰρήνην ἀσμένως δέξεσθαι. οἱ δέ, ἔχοντες τοὺς ἄνδρας τοὺς ἐν τῇ νήσῳ, ἔτι

πλείονα ἕξειν ἤλπιζον. μάλιστα δὲ αὐτοὺς ἐνῆγε Κλέων, ἀνὴρ δεινότατος· οἱ δὲ πρέσβεις

ἀνεχώρησαν ἐκ τῶν Ἀθηνῶν ἄπρακτοι.

Ἀφικομένων δὲ αὐτῶν εἰς τὴν Πύλον, αἱ σπονδαὶ εὐθὺς διελύοντο. οἱ δὲ Ἀθηναῖοι ἔτι

ἐπολιόρκουν τοὺς ἐν τῇ νήσῳ Λακεδαιμονίους, καὶ ἡ τῶν Λακεδαιμονίων στρατιὰ ἔμενεν

οὗ ἦν ἐν τῇ ἠπείρῳ. χαλεπὴ δ᾽ ἦν τοῖς Ἀθηναίοις ἡ φυλακὴ δι᾽ ἀπορίαν σίτου τε καὶ

ὕδατος. πρὸς δὲ τούτῳ μάλιστα ἠθύμουν, ὡς ἐνόμιζον ἐκπολιορκήσειν τοὺς πολεμίους

ἡμερῶν ὀλίγων. οἱ δὲ Λακεδαιμόνιοι ὑπέσχοντο πολὺ ἀργύριον τοῖς βουλομένοις εἰς τὴν

νῆσον εἰσάγειν σῖτόν τε καὶ οἶνον· μάλιστα δὲ εἰσῆγον οἱ Εἵλωτες.[1]

Ἐν δὲ ταῖς Ἀθήναις, πυνθανόμενοι ὅτι ἡ στρατιὰ οὐκ εὖ πράσσει, καὶ σῖτος τοῖς ἐν τῇ

νήσῳ εἰσάγεται, οἱ πολῖται ἠπόρουν. Κλέων δὲ πρῶτον μὲν οὐκ ἔφη τοὺς ἀγγέλλοντας τὰ

ἀληθῆ λέγειν, ὕστερον δὲ εἶπε τῷ Νικίᾳ, στρατηγῷ ὄντι, ὡς ῥᾴδιόν ἐστι λαβεῖν τοὺς ἐν τῇ

νήσῳ καὶ αὐτὸς οἷός τε ἔσται τοῦτο ποιῆσαι. ὁ δὲ Νικίας ἐκέλευε τὸν Κλέωνα στρατιὰν

λαβόντα ἐπιχειρεῖν ἀντὶ τῶν στρατηγῶν. ὁ δὲ ἀνεχώρει καὶ οὐκ ἔφη αὐτὸς ἀλλ᾽ ἐκεῖνον

στρατηγὸν εἶναι. οἱ δὲ Ἀθηναῖοι ἐβόων ὡς δεῖ τὸν Κλέωνα πλεῖν· τέλος δὲ ἔφη τοῦτο

ποιήσειν καὶ ἡμερῶν εἴκοσιν ἢ ἄξειν τοὺς Λακεδαιμονίους ζῶντας ἢ ἐκεῖ ἀποκτενεῖν.

Adapted from Thucydides IV.16-28

Chapter 28 Vocabulary

Verbs:

αἰσθάνομαι	perceive	εἶπον (aorist)	said
ἀπέρχομαι	depart	ἔνειμι	be in, be among
ἀποκρίνομαι	answer, reply	οἶδα	know
ἀπολείπω	abandon	τειχίζω	fortify
γιγνώσκω	know, perceive	φημί	say

Nouns:

ἀκρόπολις, -εως, ἡ	acropolis	Ἰταλία, -ας, ἡ	Italy
Γέλων, -ωνος, ὁ	Gelon	Πύλος, -ου, ἡ	Pylos

---

[1]   The Helots were the original inhabitants of territory taken over by Sparta; they were reduced
to the position of serfs, and in wartime served as light-armed troops.

CHAPTER 29

τυφλὸς τά τ᾽ ὦτα τόν τε νοῦν τά τ᾽ ὄμματ᾽ εἶ.
—Sophocles, *Oedipus Tyrannus* 371

1. Indirect questions

Sometimes questions, like statements, are reported. These *indirect questions* are expressed just like indirect statements of the ὅτι or ὡς type (Ch. 28.5). That is, the indicative is normally used, though the optative may be substituted after a secondary tense main verb. As in indirect statement, the tense of the verb is relative to the main verb: present for same time, future for later time, aorist for earlier time.

Indirect questions can be introduced by any interrogative word. In addition to εἰ, 'if' and πότερον, 'whether', this includes the interrogative pronoun τίς, τί, 'who, what' (Ch. 24.5) and interrogative adverbs (Ch. 24.7, 31.3).

An *indefinite relative* pronoun or adverb can be used instead of its interrogative equivalent. Here are the indefinite relative adverbs relating to place, and the corresponding interrogative adverbs you learned in Ch. 24.7. The other indefinite relatives will be presented in Ch. 31.

Interrogative	Indefinite Relative
ποῦ, 'where?'	ὅπου, 'where', 'wherever'
πόθεν, 'from where?'	ὁπόθεν, 'from where', 'from wherever'
ποῖ, 'to where?'	ὅποι, 'to where', 'to wherever'

ἐρωτᾷ τὸν ἄγγελον τίνες οἱ πολέμιοί εἰσιν.
    He asks the messenger who the enemy are.

ἤρετο ὅπου οἱ πολέμιοί εἰσιν (or εἶεν).
    He asked where the enemy were.

εὕρομεν τί προσέβαλον (or προσβάλοιεν).
    We found out why they had attacked.

ἠρόμεθα αὐτοὺς τί ποιήσουσιν (or ποιήσοιεν).
    We asked them what they would do.

οὐκ ᾖσμεν εἰ ἐνίκησαν ἢ οὔ.
    We did not know if they had won or not.

Note: After εἰ, the negative can be either οὐ or μή. οὐ is usually used after interrogative pronouns, adjectives and adverbs.

You can see from these examples that the main verb which introduces an indirect question is often not a verb of asking at all. Verbs of saying, warning, seeing, hearing, finding out, knowing, etc. can also introduce an indirect question. Since these verbs can also introduce indirect statements, it is important to distinguish between the two. Compare the following:

οἶδα αὐτὸν παρόντα.	I know that he is here.
οἶδα τί πάρεστιν.	I know why he is here.

2. Accusative of respect

The accusative without preposition can indicate the respect in which something is true. The appropriate English translation can vary:

ἀγαθός ἐστι τὴν μάχην.	He is good at battle.
ἐβλάβη τὴν κεφαλήν.	He was hurt in the head.

The infinitive can be used in the same way:

δεινὸς λέγειν	clever at speaking
ἀγαθὸς τρέχειν	good at running

EXERCISE 149.

1. ἐρωτήσω τοὺς ἄνδρας εἰ ἐβλάβησαν τὴν κεφαλήν.
2. οὐκ ἴσμεν ὅποι οἱ πολέμιοι ἔφυγον.
3. ὁ τύραννος ἤρετο τὸν ἁλιέα ὅπου τὸν ἰχθὺν εὗρεν.
4. ἐβουλόμεθα εὑρίσκειν ποῖ οἱ Πέρσαι πορεύοιντο.
5. ἆρ᾽ οἶσθα πότερον ὁ στρατηγὸς νενίκηκε τοὺς Πέρσας;
6. ἠρωτήσαμεν εἰ οἱ πολέμιοι προσβαλοῦσιν ἡμῖν ἐκείνῃ τῇ ἡμέρᾳ.
7. ἐβουλόμεθα εὑρίσκειν ὁδὸν ᾗ ἀσφαλὴς εἴη θήρας.
8. οἱ Ἀθηναῖοι ἠρώτων εἰ ἡ γέφυρα καταλυθήσεται.
9. οὐκ ᾖσμεν εἰ οἱ σύμμαχοι ἀγαθοὶ εἶεν μάχεσθαι.
10. οἱ πολῖται ἤροντο τίνες ἐσμὲν καὶ πόθεν ἤλθομεν.

EXERCISE 150.

1. We are asking who he is.
2. The enemy wanted to know where the road was.
3. We wanted to discover where the allies had gone.
4. I asked that sailor whether the ship had arrived.
5. Have you heard where the ships are being sent?
6. The Greeks did not know whether the Persians had crossed the river or not.
7. We could not find out what the enemy would do.
8. The general asked the messenger where the enemy's camp was.
9. Demosthenes asked the Athenians whether they wanted to save their country.
10. The citizens were good at speaking but bad at fighting.

3. Irregular strong aorists

A few verbs have irregular strong aorists. Here are the full aorist active paradigms of βαίνω (cf. Ch. 21.6) and γιγνώσκω (for principal parts, cf. Ch. 28.4).

	βαίνω		γιγνώσκω	
	Singular	Plural	Singular	Plural

INDICATIVE

1st	ἔβην	ἔβημεν	ἔγνων	ἔγνωμεν
2nd	ἔβης	ἔβητε	ἔγνως	ἔγνωτε
3rd	ἔβη	ἔβησαν	ἔγνω	ἔγνωσαν

SUBJUNCTIVE

1st	βῶ	βῶμεν	γνῶ	γνῶμεν
2nd	βῇς	βῆτε	γνῷς	γνῶτε
3rd	βῇ	βῶσι(ν)	γνῷ	γνῶσι(ν)

OPTATIVE

1st	βαίην	βαῖμεν	γνοίην	γνοῖμεν
2nd	βαίης	βαῖτε	γνοίης	γνοῖτε
3rd	βαίη	βαῖεν	γνοίη	γνοῖεν

IMPERATIVE

2nd	βῆθι	βῆτε	γνῶθι	γνῶτε
3rd	βήτω	βάντων	γνώτω	γνόντων

INFINITIVE   βῆναι   γνῶναι

PARTICIPLE   βάς, βᾶσα, βάν   γνούς, γνοῦσα, γνόν
βάντος, etc.   γνόντος, etc.

EXERCISE 151.

PYLOS AND SPHACTERIA: (3) A BOAST FULFILLED

Ἐν δὲ τούτῳ, ἐπεὶ ἡ ἐν τῇ νήσῳ ὕλη ὑπὸ στρατιώτου τινὸς ὡς ἐπὶ τὸ πολὺ [for the most part] κατεκαύθη, ῥᾷον ἦν τῷ Δημοσθένει εὑρίσκειν ὁπόσοι εἰσὶν οἱ Λακεδαιμόνιοι καὶ ὅπου ἔξεστιν ἀποβαίνειν. Κλέων δέ, ὃς τὸν Δημοσθένη προσείλετο, ἔχων στρατιὰν ἀφικνεῖται εἰς Πύλον. οἱ δὲ στρατηγοί, πάντας τοὺς ὁπλίτας νυκτὸς ἐπιβιβάσαντες ἐπ᾽ ὀλίγας ναῦς, ἑκατέρωθεν τῆς νήσου ἀπέβαινον καὶ ἐχώρουν δρόμῳ ἐπὶ τὸ πρῶτον φυλακτήριον· τοὺς δὲ φύλακας εὐθὺς διαφθείρουσιν ἔτι ἀναλαμβάνοντας τὰ ὅπλα. ὕστερον δὲ πᾶς ὁ ἄλλος στρατὸς ἀπέβαινε πλὴν τῶν ἐν τῇ Πύλῳ φυλάκων. οἱ δὲ Λακεδαιμόνιοι, ὡς εἶδον τὸ φυλακτήριον διεφθαρμένον καὶ στρατὸν ἐπιόντα, τοῖς ὁπλίταις τῶν Ἀθηναίων ἐπῇσαν, βουλόμενοι εἰς χεῖρας ἐλθεῖν [come to grips]. οἱ δὲ Ἀθηναῖοι, αἰσθόμενοι αὐτοὶ πολλῷ πλείονες ὄντες τῶν πολεμίων, ἔβαλλον λίθοις τε καὶ τοξεύμασιν. τέλος δὲ οἱ Λακεδαιμόνιοι ἐχώρησαν εἰς τὸ ἔσχατον ἔρυμα τῆς νήσου.

χρόνον μὲν οὖν πολὺν ἀμφότεροι ἐμάχοντο, πιεζόμενοι τῇ μάχῃ καὶ δίψῃ καὶ ἡλίῳ· προσελθὼν δὲ ὁ τῶν Μεσσηνίων[1] στρατηγὸς Κλέωνι καὶ Δημοσθένει ἔφη ἐκείνους μὲν μάτην πονεῖν, αὐτὸς δέ, εἰ βούλονται ἑαυτῷ παρέχειν τοξότας καὶ ψιλούς, περιιέναι κατὰ νώτου. λαβὼν δὲ τούτους λάθρα περιῆλθεν, ὥστε τοὺς πολεμίους μὴ ἰδεῖν, καὶ αὐτοὺς ἐξέπληξεν. καὶ οἱ Λακεδαιμόνιοι βαλλόμενοι ἑκατέρωθεν οὐκέτι ἀντεῖχον. ὁ δὲ Κλέων καὶ ὁ Δημοσθένης, βουλόμενοι λαβεῖν αὐτοὺς ζῶντας, ἔπαυσαν τὴν μάχην. καὶ οὕτως ὁ Κλέων εἴκοσιν ἡμερῶν ἤγαγε τοὺς ἄνδρας Ἀθήναζε, ὥσπερ ὑπέσχετο.

Adapted from Thucydides IV.29-39

Chapter 29 Vocabulary

Verb:

ἐρωτάω	ask
aor. ἠρόμην or ἠρώτησα	

Noun:

κεφαλή, -ῆς, ἡ	head

Pronouns:

ὁπόσος, -η, -ον	as much/many as; how much/many
πότερος, -α, -ον	which of two

Adverbs:

ὅποι	to where, to wherever	ὅπου	where, wherever
ὁπόθεν	from where, from wherever	πότερον	whether

---

1   Helots in Messenia had revolted in 464 BC; when Sparta suppressed the rebellion, they were given a settlement by the Athenians at Naupactus on the Corinthian Gulf.

CHAPTER 30

ἐὰν ᾖς φιλομαθής, ἔσει πολυμαθής.
——Isocrates 1.18
ἀρετὴ δὲ κἂν θάνῃ τις οὐκ ἀπόλλυται.
——Euripides fr. 734.1 Nauck

1. Conditions with subjunctive and optative

Ch. 11.4-6 covered simple and contrary-to-fact conditions. Both those types use only indicative verbs. This chapter introduces other types of conditions, which require the subjunctive or optative.

Future conditions: There are two kinds of conditions referring to the future. Compare the following two sentences:

> If it rains we will stay home.
> If it should rain we would stay home.

In Greek, the first is called a *future more vivid* condition, and the second a *future less vivid* condition. A future more vivid condition sounds more likely to happen. It uses a more vivid or definite form of expression for both the condition (if-clause or protasis) and the outcome (then-clause or apodosis). The verb in the if-clause is subjunctive. A future less vivid condition sounds more doubtful, and the use of the optative in both clauses reflects this.

General conditions: Also presented below are *present general* and *past general* conditions. These state an outcome that is (was) always true every time the condition is (was) fulfilled.

> If Socrates speaks, we (always) listen.
> If the general gave an order, the soldiers (always) obeyed him.

Since the subjunctive is associated with primary tenses, it is used in present general conditions. Since the optative is associated with secondary tenses, it is used in past general conditions.

Note: The negative is μή in the protasis of all types of condition, οὐ in the apodosis.

2. Conditions with the subjunctive

Future More Vivid: Expresses a strong probability that the condition will be fulfilled. The protasis is introduced by the word ἐάν, a combination of εἰ, 'if' and the conditional particle ἄν, which you encountered in the apodosis of contrary-to-fact conditions (Ch. 11.6). In future more vivid conditions only the protasis is in doubt; ἄν appears there with εἰ.

example: If he comes, we will persuade him.

construction: protasis: ἐάν + subjunctive; apodosis: future indicative

Aspect is shown by using the present subjunctive for an ongoing action, or the aorist subjunctive for a single, simple act:

> ἐὰν χρήματα ἔχῃς, φίλους ἕξεις.
>> If you have money, you will have friends.

> ἐὰν ἔλθῃ, πείσομεν αὐτόν.
>> If he comes, we will persuade him.

Present General: Expresses an outcome that is always true, if the condition is fulfilled. As in future more vivid conditions, the apodosis is not in doubt; the particle ἄν appears in the protasis.

example: If you have money, you always have friends.

construction: protasis: ἐάν + subjunctive; apodosis: present indicative

Aspect is shown by using the present or aorist subjunctive:

> ἐὰν χρήματα ἔχῃς, φίλους ἔχεις.
>> If you have money, you have friends.

> ἐὰν πέμψωμεν δῶρον αὐτῷ, ἀεὶ χάριν ἔχει ἡμῖν.
>> If we send him a gift, he is always grateful to us.

PRACTICE A. Identify the type of condition; then translate:

1. ἐὰν διώκῃς τὴν ἀρετήν, εὐτυχὴς εἶ.
2. ἐὰν οἱ πολέμιοι ἔλθωσιν οὐ μενοῦμεν ἐν τῇ οἰκίᾳ.
3. οἱ πολῖται πείσονται τῷ ῥήτορι ἐὰν πιστεύωσι τοῖς λόγοις αὐτοῦ.
4. If the children obey their father, he treats them well.
5. You will arrive before night if you march quickly.

3. Conditions with the optative

Future Less Vivid: Expresses a more remote probability that the condition will be fulfilled. Both clauses are in doubt; εἰ alone introduces the protasis, and ἄν appears in the apodosis. The protasis can be translated in various ways.

example:
If he came,	
If he should come,	} we would persuade him.
If he were to come,	

construction: protasis: εἰ + optative; apodosis: optative + ἄν

Aspect is shown by using the present or aorist optative:

> εἰ χρήματα ἔχοις, ἔχοις ἂν φίλους.
>> If you should have money, you would have friends.

> εἰ ἔλθοι, πείθοιμεν ἂν αὐτόν.
>> If he should come, we would persuade him.

Past General: Expresses an outcome that was always true, if the condition was fulfilled. In this type the particle ἄν does not appear at all.

example: If you had money, you had friends.

construction: protasis: εἰ + optative; apodosis: imperfect indicative

Aspect is shown by using the present or aorist optative:

εἰ χρήματα ἔχοις, φίλους εἶχες.
If you had money, you had friends.

εἰ πέμψαιμεν δῶρον αὐτῷ, ἀεὶ χάριν εἶχε ἡμῖν.
If we sent him a gift, he was always grateful to us.

PRACTICE B. Identify the type of condition; then translate:

1. μαχοίμεθα ἂν ὑπὲρ τῆς πατρίδος, εἰ οἱ Πέρσαι προσβάλλοιεν ἡμῖν.
2. εἰ ἡ μήτηρ κελεύσαι, οἱ υἱοὶ ἀεὶ ἐπείθοντο αὐτῇ.
3. εἰ ναύτης εἴην, ἡδέως ἂν πορευοίμην ναυσίν.
4. If the king wanted a fish, he always had it.
5. The men would not leave the island if the enemy should come.

Construction Summary

TYPE OF CONDITION	PROTASIS (NEGATIVE μή)	APODOSIS (NEGATIVE οὐ)
future more vivid:	ἐάν + subjunctive	future indicative
present general:	ἐάν + subjunctive	present indicative
future less vivid:	εἰ + optative	optative + ἄν
past general:	εἰ + optative	imperfect indicative
simple:	εἰ + indicative	indicative
contrary to fact:	εἰ + indicative	indicative + ἄν
	imperfect for present	imperfect for present
	aorist for past	aorist for past

EXERCISE 152. Identify the type of condition and translate.

1. κακὸν ἂν εἴη εἰ ποιήσαιμεν τοῦτο.
2. ἐὰν ἀδικῆτε, ἀποθανεῖσθε.
3. ἐὰν ὁ τύραννος εὖ ἄρξῃ τῆς πόλεως, οἱ πολῖται εὐδαίμονές εἰσίν.
4. ἡ γυνὴ ἡδέως ἤκουε τοῦ ῥήτορος εἰ τὰ ἀληθὲς λέγοι.
5. ὁ Ἄδμητος εὐτυχής ἐστιν εἰ ἡ γυνὴ ἐθέλει ἀποθανεῖν ὑπὲρ ἑαυτοῦ.
6. τίς κωλύσει τοὺς πολεμίους ἐὰν ὁ στρατηγὸς ἀποθάνῃ;
7. εἰ οἱ παῖδες λάβοιεν τὰ χρήματα οἱ ἑαυτῶν πατέρες τύπτοιεν ἂν αὐτούς.
8. ἐάν τις πιστεύηται ὑπὸ τῶν πολιτῶν τιμὴν ἔχει.
9. εἰ ἔμαθες τὸ καλὸν οὐκ ἂν ἠδίκεις νῦν.
10. ἐὰν ὁ Ἄμασις ὁρᾷ τὸν Πολυκράτη εὐτυχῆ ὄντα, οὐ φιλίαν ποιήσεται πρὸς αὐτόν.

EXERCISE 153. Identify the type of condition and translate.

1. If the general had come more quickly, we would not have been conquered.
2. If you send me these things I will love you.
3. Nobody would honor him if he abandoned his country.
4. Everyone believes you if you speak the truth.
5. If we were able to do that, we would be doing it.
6. What would you do if the enemy came?
7. If the king were wiser, he would still be ruling the citizens.
8. If the child sent a gift, his father always wrote a letter to him.
9. If the sailors reach the harbor, they will stop the war.
10. If you know these foreigners, you know what they will do.

EXERCISE 154.

SOCRATES' DEFENSE SPEECH

In 399 BC Socrates went on trial in Athens. The charges were that he (1) introduced strange new gods; (2) corrupted the youth; (3) made the weaker argument appear the stronger. The first charge in particular is without apparent foundation; nevertheless Socrates was found guilty. After proposing an insufficient lesser penalty, he was sentenced to death. This section of his defense speech comes after his conviction is announced, and the penalty is under debate.

ἴσως οὖν ἄν τις εἴποι· Σιγῶν δὲ καὶ ἡσυχίαν ἄγων, ὦ Σώκρατες, οὐχ οἷός τ᾽ ἔσει ζῆν ἐν ἄλλῃ τινὶ χώρᾳ; τοῦτο δή ἐστι πάντων χαλεπώτατον πεῖσαί τινας ὑμῶν. ἐὰν μὲν γὰρ λέγω ὅτι τῷ θεῷ ἀπειθεῖν τοῦτ᾽ ἔστι καὶ διὰ τοῦτ᾽ ἀδύνατον ἡσυχίαν ἄγειν, οὐ πείσεσθέ μοι· ἐὰν δὲ λέγω ὅτι τοῦτο τυγχάνει μέγιστον ἀγαθὸν ὂν ἀνθρώπῳ, ἑκάστης ἡμέρας περὶ ἀρετῆς τοὺς λόγους ποιεῖσθαι καὶ τῶν ἄλλων περὶ ὧν ὑμεῖς ἐμοῦ ἀκούετε διαλεγομένου καὶ ἐμαυτὸν καὶ ἄλλους ἐξετάζοντος, ὁ δ᾽ ἀνεξέταστος βίος οὐ βιωτὸς ἀνθρώπῳ,—ταῦτα δ᾽ ἔτι ἧσσον πείσεσθέ μοι λέγοντι. εἰ μὲν γὰρ ἦν μοι χρήματα, ἐτιμησάμην ἂν χρημάτων ὅσα ἔμελλον ἐκτείσειν· οὐδὲν γὰρ ἂν ἐβλάβην. νῦν δὲ—οὐ γὰρ ἔστιν—ἴσως ἂν δυναίμην ἐκτεῖσαι ὑμῖν μνᾶν ἀργυρίου· τοσούτου οὖν τιμῶμαι [propose a penalty of so much].

Plato, *Apology* 38 a-b

Chapter 30 Vocabulary

Verb:
    ἀδικέω   do wrong, be unjust, wrong (someone)

Noun:
    ἀρετή, -ῆς, ἡ   excellence

Conjunction:
    ἐάν   εἰ + ἄν

CHAPTER 31

1. The indefinite relative pronoun/adjective ὅστις

This is simply the indefinite version of the relative pronoun ὅς, ἥ, ὅ (Ch. 9.5). It consists of the relative pronoun with τις added to make it indefinite; each component is fully declined.

		M	F	N
SING.	Nom.	ὅστις	ἥτις	ὅ τι
	Gen.	οὕτινος	ἧστινος	οὕτινος
	Dat.	ᾧτινι	ᾗτινι	ᾧτινι
	Acc.	ὅντινα	ἥντινα	ὅ τι
PLUR.	Nom.	οἵτινες	αἵτινες	ἅτινα
	Gen.	ὧντινων	ὧντινων	ὧντινων
	Dat.	οἷστισι(ν)	αἷστισι(ν)	οἷστισι(ν)
	Acc.	οὕστινας	ἅστινας	ἅτινα

Note: The neuter singular ὅ τι is written as two words, which helps to distinguish it from ὅτι, 'that'.

The indefinite relative pronoun means 'whoever', 'anyone who'. Like τις alone, it can also be used as an adjective, to make another noun indefinite: στρατηγὸς ὅστις, 'any general who...'. ὅστις can be used instead of τίς to introduce an indirect question (Ch. 29.1):

> ἐρωτᾷ τὸν ἄγγελον οἵτινες οἱ πρέσβεις εἰσίν.
> He asks the messenger who the ambassadors are.

It can also introduce an indefinite relative clause (section 4 below).

2. Correlative pronouns/adjectives

You have now learned most of the Greek pronouns. The following table summarizes the relationship in form and meaning among the various types. An initial π is characteristic of the interrogative forms[1], and an initial rough breathing marks the relatives.

INTERROGATIVE	INDEFINITE (ENCLITIC)	DEMONSTRATIVE	RELATIVE	INDEFINITE RELATIVE OR INDIRECT INTERROGATIVE
τίς, who?	τις, someone	οὗτος, this	ὅς, who	ὅστις, whoever
πόσος, how much?	ποσός, some amount	τοσοῦτος, this much	ὅσος, as much as	ὁπόσος, however much
ποῖος, what kind?	ποιός, some kind	τοιοῦτος, this kind	οἷος, the kind which	ὁποῖος, whatever kind

---

[1] An older labio-velar consonant k^w became π in Classical Greek before vowels formed in the back of the mouth, like o. Before front vowels like the ι in τίς, the labio-velar became τ.

3. Correlative adverbs

The same relationships in form and meaning observed among pronouns also hold for adverbs:

INTERROGATIVE	INDEFINITE (ENCLITIC)	DEMONSTRATIVE	RELATIVE	INDEFINITE RELATIVE OR INDIRECT INTERROGATIVE
ποῦ, where?	που, somewhere	ἐνταῦθα, here, there	οὗ, where	ὅπου, where, wherever
πόθεν, from where?	ποθέν, from somewhere	ἐντεῦθεν, from here	ὅθεν, from where	ὁπόθεν, from where, from wherever
ποῖ, to where?	ποι, to somewhere	ἐνταῦθα, to here, to there	οἷ, to where	ὅποι, to where, to wherever
πότε, when?	ποτέ, ever	τότε, then	ὅτε, when	ὁπότε, when, whenever
πῶς, how?	πως, somehow	οὕτως, thus	ὡς, as, how	ὅπως, how, however

4. Indefinite relative clauses

These behave just like conditional clauses, except that they are introduced by a relative pronoun or adverb instead of εἰ or ἐάν. Here are English examples of the most common types.

Whoever obeys the laws is a good man.	(cf. present general)
Whenever he comes we will begin.	(cf. future more vivid)
They always went wherever he led.	(cf. past general)
I would do whatever you wanted.	(cf. future less vivid)

An indefinite relative sentence in Greek uses the same construction as the type of condition it resembles. The relative which introduces it is usually indefinite, but not always.

The exception to this pattern is that when ὅστις (instead of ὅς) introduces a future more vivid or a present general clause, the verb in the protasis is indicative (instead of subjunctive with ἄν). This is because ὅστις already has a general indefinite meaning.

Note: When ἄν appears in the protasis (future more vivid and present general constructions), it is combined into one word with the relative adverbs ὅτε and ὁπότε: ὅταν, ὁπόταν. Following other relative adverbs and pronouns it is written as a separate word.

PRACTICE A. Identify the following constructions:

1. ὃς ἂν πείθηται τοῖς νόμοις ἀγαθός ἐστιν.
    ὅστις πείθεται τοῖς νόμοις ἀγαθός ἐστιν.
    Whoever obeys the laws is good.

2. πιστεύσομεν ὅς ἂν πείθηται τοῖς νόμοις.
    We will trust whoever obeys the laws.
    (As in English, the relative is in the nominative; its function as subject of the relative clause is more important than its function as object of the main clause.)

3. ποιήσω ὅ τι ἂν βούλῃ.
    I will do whatever you want.

4. ὅστις πείθοιτο τοῖς νόμοις ἀγαθὸς ἦν.
    Whoever obeyed the laws was good.

5. πιστεύοιμεν ἂν ὅστις πείθοιτο τοῖς νόμοις.
    We would trust whoever obeyed the laws.

5. Temporal clauses with ἕως and μέχρι

Temporal clauses describe the time-frame of an action. They are introduced by the conjunctions ἕως and μέχρι, 'as long as', 'while', 'until'. After a secondary tense main verb, the verb in the subordinate clauses is indicative because it refers to a definite time. After a primary tense main verb, the most common construction is ἕως or μέχρι + ἄν + subjunctive, referring to an indefinite future time. This construction resembles the future more vivid condition; the negative is μή.

> ἐμείναμεν ἕως ἦλθον.
> We waited until they came.

> ἐμείναμεν μέχρι οἱ βάρβαροι παρῆσαν.
> We waited as long as/while the foreigners were present.

> μενοῦμεν ἕως ἂν οἱ βάρβαροι ἀπέρχωνται.
> We will wait until the foreigners go away.

Construction Summary

secondary tense main verb:	ἕως/μέχρι + indicative (negative οὐ)
primary tense main verb:	ἕως/μέχρι + ἄν + subjunctive (negative μή)

6. Temporal clauses with πρίν

The conjunction πρίν has two possible senses. When it means 'until', it is followed by an imperfect or aorist indicative, whichever is appropriate. It can only be used in this sense if the main clause is negative; otherwise, Greek uses ἕως or μέχρι.

When πρίν means 'before', it is followed by an infinitive. The subject of the infinitive is in the accusative case if it is not the subject of the sentence. πρίν can only be used in this sense if the main clause is positive.

> οὐκ ἐλίπομεν πρὶν ἦλθον.
> We did not leave until they came.

> ἦλθον πρὶν ἡμᾶς λιπεῖν.
> They came before we left.

Construction Summary

negative main clause:	πρίν + imperfect or aorist indicative	means 'until'
positive main clause:	πρίν + infinitive	means 'before'

EXERCISE 155.

1. ὅ τι ἂν λέγῃ ὁ ῥήτωρ, πιστεύσομεν αὐτῷ.
2. ἐποίμεθα ἂν ὅποι κελεύσαι ὁ ἡγεμών.
3. οἵτινες μὴ θύσαιεν τοῖς θεοῖς οὐκ ἐλάμβανον δῶρα ἀπ᾽ αὐτῶν.
4. ἕξεις ἵππον ὁποῖον ἂν βούλῃ.
5. ἐξῆλθεν ὁ πρέσβυς πρὶν λέγειν τὸν Σωκράτη.
6. ὅστις μὴ πείθοιτο τοῖς νόμοις, οὐκ ἂν ποιοῖμεν ἄρχοντα.
7. ὁπόσα ἂν χρήματα ἔχητε, οὐκ ἀσφαλεῖς ἐστε.
8. ὁ δοῦλος μενεῖ σὺν τοῖς βουσὶν ἕως ἂν ὁ δεσπότης μεταπέμψηται ἑαυτόν.
9. ὁπόθεν ἔλθοι βοήθεια, ἡδέως ἂν δεχοίμεθα αὐτήν.
10. οὐ προσεβάλλομεν τοῖς πολεμίοις πρὶν ἐκέλευσεν ἡμᾶς ὁ στρατηγός.

EXERCISE 156.

1. Whenever the children left the city, their fathers were afraid.
2. I will not listen to you, however many words you speak.
3. The animals always followed that shepherd to wherever he led them.
4. It is necessary for the gods to have whatever kind of gifts they demand.
5. Whoever has the most weapons will win the war.
6. The general arrived before the cavalry attacked.
7. Anyone whom the general saw was ordered to fight.
8. The prisoners did not answer until the king freed them.
9. Whenever we see a storm coming, we hasten into the house.
10. The king of Persia would send soldiers to wherever he should wish.

Chapter 31 Vocabulary

Verb:

ἕπομαι (+ *dat.*)   follow
   ἕψομαι, ἑσπόμην

Pronouns:

οἷος, -α, -ον	the kind which	ποῖος, -α, -ον	what kind?
ὁποῖος, -α, -ον	whatever kind	ποιός, -ά, -όν	some kind
ὅσος, -η, -ον	as much/many as	πόσος, -η, -ον	how much/many?
ὅστις, ὅ τι	anyone who, anything which	ποσός, -ή, -όν	some amount

Adverbs:

ἐνταῦθα	here, there, to here to there	ὁπότε	whenever
		ὅπως	how
ἐντεῦθεν	from here, from there	ὅτε	when
ὅθεν	from where	οὗ	where
οἷ	to where	πότε	when?
ὁπόθεν	from wherever	ποτέ	ever, sometime

Conjunctions:

ἕως	as long as, while, until	πρίν	before, until
μέχρι	as long as, while, until		

CHAPTER 32

Χρόνος δίκαιον ἄνδρα δείκνυσιν μόνος.
—Menander, Sententiae 1.829

ἐκ παντὸς ἄν τις πράγματος δισσῶν λόγων
ἀγῶνα θεῖτ' ἄν, εἰ λέγειν εἴη σοφός.
—Euripides, fr. 189.1 (Nauck)

1. Athematic (-μι) verbs, first principal part

So far, almost all the verbs you have learned are *thematic* verbs; that is, many of their forms incorporate the thematic vowel. -μι verbs, on the other hand, are *athematic*. In place of the thematic vowel, each verb stem has its own vowel. The indicative middle/passive endings are identical to those of thematic verbs; in the active, there are some differences. The present and imperfect indicative endings are as follows:

	Singular	Plural		Singular	Plural
PRESENT	**Active**			**Middle/Passive**	
1st	-μι	-μεν		-μαι	-μεθα
2nd	-ς	-τε		-σαι	-σθε
3rd	-σι	-ᾱσι		-ται	-νται
IMPERFECT					
1st	-ν	-μεν		-μην	-μεθα
2nd	-ς	-τε		-σο	-σθε
3rd	——	-σαν		-το	-ντο

2. Athematic (-μι) verbs, first principal part (δείκνυμι, τίθημι, ἵστημι, δίδωμι)

The simplest type of **-μι** verb has a stem ending in υ, as in δείκνυμι, 'show'. Three common **-μι** verbs have more complicated present and aorist systems. The principal parts of τίθημι, 'I put', ἵστημι, 'I stand', and δίδωμι, 'I give' are as follows.

PRESENT	FUTURE A/M	AORIST A/M	PERFECT A	PERFECT M/P	AORIST P
δείκνυμι	δείξω	ἔδειξα	δέδειχα	δέδειγμαι	ἐδείχθην
τίθημι	θήσω	ἔθηκα	τέθηκα	τέθειμαι	ἐτέθην
ἵστημι	στήσω	ἔστησα, ἔστην[1]	ἕστηκα	ἕσταμαι	ἐστάθην
δίδωμι	δώσω	ἔδωκα	δέδωκα	δέδομαι	ἐδόθην

---

[1] ἔστησα is transitive ('I made x stand'); ἔστην is intransitive ('I stood').

The first principal part of the last three verbs above is reduplicated, with the vowel ι standing between the repeated consonants. This is clearest in δίδωμι. In τίθημι, the reduplicated θ becomes τ, because Greek never begins two syllables in a row with an aspirated consonant. In ἵστημι the initial σ was weak and dropped out, leaving a rough breathing.

The present system of all four verbs is shown here. Each uses its own stem vowel throughout, where thematic verbs would use the thematic vowel. For δείκνυμι the stem vowel is υ, for τίθημι it is ε, for ἵστημι it is α, and for δίδωμι it is ο. In the indicative active this vowel is long in the singular, short in the plural forms.

Note: In the subjunctive and optative, the stem vowel α, ε and ο must contract with the ending, as happens in contract verbs (Ch. 18); the stem vowel υ does not contract.

PRESENT ACTIVE SYSTEM

		show	put	stand	give
INDICATIVE					
Present					
SING.	1st	δείκνυμι	τίθημι	ἵστημι	δίδωμι
	2nd	δείκνυς	τίθης	ἵστης	δίδως
	3rd	δείκνυσι(ν)	τίθησι(ν)	ἵστησι(ν)	δίδωσι(ν)
PLUR.	1st	δείκνυμεν	τίθεμεν	ἵσταμεν	δίδομεν
	2nd	δείκνυτε	τίθετε	ἵστατε	δίδοτε
	3rd	δεικνύασι(ν)	τιθέασι(ν)	ἱστᾶσι(ν)	διδόασι(ν)
Imperfect					
SING.	1st	ἐδείκνυν	ἐτίθην	ἵστην	ἐδίδουν
	2nd	ἐδείκνυς	ἐτίθης	ἵστης	ἐδίδους
	3rd	ἐδείκνυ	ἐτίθη	ἵστη	ἐδίδου
PLUR.	1st	ἐδείκνυμεν	ἐτίθεμεν	ἵσταμεν	ἐδίδομεν
	2nd	ἐδείκνυτε	ἐτίθετε	ἵστατε	ἐδίδοτε
	3rd	ἐδείκνυσαν	ἐτίθεσαν	ἵστασαν	ἐδίδοσαν
SUBJUNCTIVE					
SING.	1st	δεικνύω	τιθῶ	ἱστῶ	διδῶ
	2nd	δεικνύῃς	τιθῇς	ἱστῇς	διδῷς
	3rd	δεικνύῃ	τιθῇ	ἱστῇ	διδῷ
PLUR.	1st	δεικνύωμεν	τιθῶμεν	ἱστῶμεν	διδῶμεν
	2nd	δεικνύητε	τιθῆτε	ἱστῆτε	διδῶτε
	3rd	δεικνύωσι(ν)	τιθῶσι(ν)	ἱστῶσι(ν)	διδῶσι(ν)
OPTATIVE					
SING.	1st	δεικνύοιμι	τιθείην	ἱσταίην	διδοίην
	2nd	δεικνύοις	τιθείης	ἱσταίης	διδοίης
	3rd	δεικνύοι	τιθείη	ἱσταίη	διδοίη
PLUR.	1st	δεικνύοιμεν	τιθεῖμεν	ἱσταῖμεν	διδοῖμεν
	2nd	δεικνύοιτε	τιθεῖτε	ἱσταῖτε	διδοῖτε
	3rd	δεικνύοιεν	τιθεῖεν	ἱσταῖεν	διδοῖεν

IMPERATIVE

		show	put	stand	give
SING.	2nd	δείκνυ	τίθει	ἵστη	δίδου
	3rd	δεικνύτω	τιθέτω	ἱστάτω	διδότω
PLUR.	2nd	δείκνυτε	τίθετε	ἵστατε	δίδοτε
	3rd	δεικνύντων	τιθέντων	ἱστάντων	διδόντων

INFINITIVE   δεικνύναι   τιθέναι   ἱστάναι   διδόναι

PARTICIPLE   δεικνύς, -ῦσα,   τιθείς, -εῖσα,   ἱστάς, -ᾶσα,   διδούς, -οῦσα,
                -ύν   -έν   -άν   -όν
                δεικνύντος, etc.   τιθέντος, etc.   ἱστάντος, etc.   διδόντος, etc.

PRESENT MIDDLE/PASSIVE SYSTEM

		show	put	stand	give
INDICATIVE					
Present					
SING.	1st	δείκνυμαι	τίθεμαι	ἵσταμαι	δίδομαι
	2nd	δείκνυσαι	τίθεσαι	ἵστασαι	δίδοσαι
	3rd	δείκνυται	τίθεται	ἵσταται	δίδοται
PLUR.	1st	δεικνύμεθα	τιθέμεθα	ἱστάμεθα	διδόμεθα
	2nd	δείκνυσθε	τίθεσθε	ἵστασθε	δίδοσθε
	3rd	δείκνυνται	τίθενται	ἵστανται	δίδονται
Imperfect					
SING.	1st	ἐδεικνύμην	ἐτιθέμην	ἱστάμην	ἐδιδόμην
	2nd	ἐδείκνυσο	ἐτίθεσο	ἵστασο	ἐδίδοσο
	3rd	ἐδείκνυτο	ἐτίθετο	ἵστατο	ἐδίδοτο
PLUR.	1st	ἐδεικνύμεθα	ἐτιθέμεθα	ἱστάμεθα	ἐδιδόμεθα
	2nd	ἐδείκνυσθε	ἐτίθεσθε	ἵστασθε	ἐδίδοσθε
	3rd	ἐδείκνυντο	ἐτίθεντο	ἵσταντο	ἐδίδοντο
SUBJUNCTIVE					
SING.	1st	δεικνύωμαι	τιθῶμαι	ἱστῶμαι	διδῶμαι
	2nd	δεικνύῃ	τιθῇ	ἱστῇ	διδῷ
	3rd	δεικνύηται	τιθῆται	ἱστῆται	διδῶται
PLUR.	1st	δεικνώμεθα	τιθώμεθα	ἱστώμεθα	διδώμεθα
	2nd	δεικνύησθε	τιθῆσθε	ἱστῆσθε	διδῶσθε
	3rd	δεικνύωνται	τιθῶνται	ἱστῶνται	διδῶνται
OPTATIVE					
SING.	1st	δεικνοίμην	τιθείμην	ἱσταίμην	διδοίμην
	2nd	δεικνύοι	τιθεῖο	ἱσταῖο	διδοῖο
	3rd	δεικνύοιτο	τιθεῖτο	ἱσταῖτο	διδοῖτο
PLUR.	1st	δεικνυοίμεθα	τιθείμεθα	ἱσταίμεθα	διδοίμεθα
	2nd	δεικνύοισθε	τιθεῖσθε	ἱσταῖσθε	διδοῖσθε
	3rd	δεικνύοιντο	τιθεῖντο	ἱσταῖντο	διδοῖντο

		show	put	stand	give
IMPERATIVE					
SING.	2nd	δείκνυσο	τίθεσο	ἵστασο	δίδοσο
	3rd	δεικνύσθω	τιθέσθω	ἱστάσθω	διδόσθω
PLUR.	2nd	δείκνυσθε	τίθεσθε	ἵστασθε	δίδοσθε
	3rd	δεικνύσθων	τιθέσθων	ἱστάσθων	διδόσθων
INFINITIVE		δείκνυσθαι	τιθέσθαι	ἱστάσθαι	διδόσθαι
PARTICIPLE		δεικνύμενος,	τιθέμενος,	ἱστάμενος,	διδόμενος,
		-η, -ον	-η, -ον	-η, -ον	-η, -ον
		δεικνυμένου,etc	τιθεμένου, etc.	ἱσταμένου, etc.	διδομένου, etc.

3. Athematic verbs, 3rd principal part

δείκνυμι has a regular thematic weak aorist, ἔδειξα, which is conjugated normally. ἵστημι has both a weak and a strong aorist. The weak aorist ἔστησα is transitive ('I stood the book on its end') and has regular thematic forms. The strong aorist is intransitive ('I stood on the bridge'). The aorist forms of τίθημι and δίδωμι and the strong aorist of ἵστημι (conjugated like ἔβην, Ch. 21.6, 29.3) are presented here.

Note: Many of the aorist forms resemble the present, except that they are not reduplicated.

AORIST ACTIVE SYSTEM

		put	stand	give
INDICATIVE				
SING.	1st	ἔθηκα	ἔστην	ἔδωκα
	2nd	ἔθηκας	ἔστης	ἔδωκας
	3rd	ἔθηκε	ἔστη	ἔδωκε
PLUR.	1st	ἔθεμεν	ἔστημεν	ἔδομεν
	2nd	ἔθετε	ἔστητε	ἔδοτε
	3rd	ἔθεσαν	ἔστησαν	ἔδοσαν
SUBJUNCTIVE				
SING.	1st	θῶ	στῶ	δῶ
	2nd	θῇς	στῇς	δῷς
	3rd	θῇ	στῇ	δῷ
PLUR.	1st	θῶμεν	στῶμεν	δῶμεν
	2nd	θῆτε	στῆτε	δῶτε
	3rd	θῶσι(ν)	στῶσι(ν)	δῶσι(ν)
OPTATIVE				
SING.	1st	θείην	σταίην	δοίην
	2nd	θείης	σταίης	δοίης
	3rd	θείη	σταίη	δοίη
PLUR.	1st	θεῖμεν	σταῖμεν	δοῖμεν
	2nd	θεῖτε	σταῖτε	δοῖτε
	3rd	θεῖεν	σταῖεν	δοῖεν

IMPERATIVE

SING.	2nd	θές	στῆθι	δός
	3rd	θέτω	στήτω	δότω
PLUR.	2nd	θέτε	στῆτε	δότε
	3rd	θέντων	στάντων	δόντων

INFINITIVE   θεῖναι   ἱστάναι   δοῦναι

PARTICIPLE   θείς, -εῖσα, -έν   στάς, -ᾶσα, -άν   δούς, -οῦσα, -όν
                   θέντος, etc.   στάντος, etc.   δόντος, etc.

AORIST MIDDLE SYSTEM

		put	give
INDICATIVE			
SING.	1st	ἐθέμην	ἐδόμην
	2nd	ἔθεσο	ἔδου
	3rd	ἔθετο	ἔδοτο
PLUR.	1st	ἐθέμεθα	ἐδόμεθα
	2nd	ἔθεσθε	ἔδοσθε
	3rd	ἔθεντο	ἔδοντο
SUBJUNCTIVE			
SING.	1st	θῶμαι	δῶμαι
	2nd	θῇ	δῷ
	3rd	θῆται	δῶται
PLUR.	1st	θώμεθα	δώμεθα
	2nd	θῆσθε	δῶσθε
	3rd	θῶνται	δῶνται
OPTATIVE			
SING.	1st	θείμην	δοίμην
	2nd	θεῖο	δοῖο
	3rd	θεῖτο	δοῖτο
PLUR.	1st	θείμεθα	δοίμεθα
	2nd	θεῖσθε	δοῖσθε
	3rd	θεῖντο	δοῖντο
IMPERATIVE			
SING.	2nd	θοῦ	δοῦ
	3rd	θέσθω	δόσθω
PLUR.	2nd	θέσθε	δόσθε
	3rd	θέσθων	δόσθων
INFINITIVE		θέσθαι	δόσθαι
PARTICIPLE		θέμενος, -η, -ον	δόμενος, -η, -ον
		θεμένου, etc.	δομένου, etc.

PRACTICE A. Identify the following forms:

1. διδόναι	7. ἑστήκαμεν	13. ἵστασαν
2. ἔδοτο	8. τιθείσας	14. δόντα
3. σταῖμεν	9. δομένων	15 ἔθηκας
4. στήσει	10. διδοίη	16. τιθῶμαι
5. ἐδόθητε	11. ἔθου	17. διδῷ
6. θῇς	12. ἐτιθέμεθα	18. ἱσταῖντο

4. ἵημι

This athematic verb, of the ε-stem type, is not irregular. However, contracting vowels sometimes obscure the regular pattern. The rough breathing helps to distinguish its forms from those of εἰμί, 'be' and εἶμι, 'go'.

PRESENT	FUTURE A/M	AORIST A/M		PERFECT A	PERFECT M/P	AORIST P
ἵημι	ἥσω	ἧκα	εἷκα		εἷμαι	εἵθην

PRESENT SYSTEM

	SINGULAR	PLURAL	SINGULAR	PLURAL
INDICATIVE	**Active**		**Middle/Passive**	
Present				
1st	ἵημι	ἵεμεν	ἵεμαι	ἱέμεθα
2nd	ἵης	ἵετε	ἵεσαι	ἵεσθε
3rd	ἵησι(ν)	ἱᾶσι(ν)	ἵεται	ἵενται
Imperfect				
1st	ἵην	ἵεμεν	ἱέμην	ἱέμεθα
2nd	ἵεις	ἵετε	ἵεσο	ἵεσθε
3rd	ἵει	ἵεσαν	ἵετο	ἵεντο
SUBJUNCTIVE				
1st	ἱῶ	ἱῶμεν	ἱῶμαι	ἱώμεθα
2nd	ἱῇς	ἱῆτε	ἱῇ	ἱῆσθε
3rd	ἱῇ	ἱῶσι(ν)	ἱῆται	ἱῶνται
OPTATIVE				
1st	ἱείην	ἱεῖμεν/ἱείημεν	ἱείμην	ἱείμεθα
2nd	ἱείης	ἱεῖτε/ἱείητε	ἱεῖο	ἱεῖσθε
3rd	ἱείη	ἱεῖεν/ἱείησαν	ἱεῖτο	ἱεῖντο
IMPERATIVE				
2nd	ἵει	ἵετε	ἵεσο	ἵεσθε
3rd	ἱέτω	ἱέντων	ἱέσθω	ἱέσθων
INFINITIVE	ἱέναι		ἵεσθαι	
PARTICIPLE	ἱείς, ἱεῖσα, ἱέν ἱέντος, etc.		ἱέμενος, -μένη, -μενον ἱεμένου, etc.	

AORIST SYSTEM

	SINGULAR	PLURAL	SINGULAR	PLURAL
INDICATIVE	**Active**		**Middle**	
1st	ἧκα	εἷμεν	εἵμην	εἵμεθα
2nd	ἧκας	εἷτε	εἷο	εἷσθε
3rd	ἧκε(ν)	εἷσαν	εἷτο	εἷντο
SUBJUNCTIVE				
1st	ὧ	ὧμεν	ὧμαι	ὥμεθα
2nd	ἧς	ἧτε	ἧ	ἧσθε
3rd	ἧ	ὧσι(ν)	ἧται	ὧνται
OPTATIVE				
1st	εἵην	εἷμεν/εἵημεν	εἵμην	εἵμεθα
2nd	εἵης	εἷτε/εἵητε	εἷο	εἷσθε
3rd	εἵη	εἷεν/εἵησαν	εἷτο	εἷντο
IMPERATIVE				
2nd	ἕς	ἕτε	οὗ	ἕσθε
3rd	ἕτω	ἕντων	ἕσθω	ἕσθων
INFINITIVE	εἷναι		ἕσθαι	
PARTICIPLE	εἵς, εἷσα, ἕν		ἕμενος, -η, -ον	
	ἕντος, etc.		ἑμένου, etc.	

EXERCISE 157.

1. ἐθέλει δῶρόν τι δοῦναι ἐκείνῳ τῷ θεῷ.
2. ἧλθεν ἵνα τὰ χρήματα θείη εἰς τὴν οἰκίαν.
3. τῶν στρατιωτῶν στάντων ἐπὶ τοῦ τείχους, οἱ πολέμιοι οὐχ οἷοί τ᾽ ἧσαν προχωρεῖν.
4. ὁρᾷς τὸν παῖδα ἱέντα λίθον εἰς τὸν ποταμόν;
5. οἱ στρατηγοὶ ἔστησαν τοὺς αἰχμαλώτους ἐν τῇ νήσῳ.
6. τοσαῦτα χρήματα δέδωκα τῷ πατρὶ ὥστε οὐδὲν νῦν ἔχω.
7. ποῦ ἐστιν ὁ ἰχθὺς ὃς ἐτέθη εἰς τὴν ναῦν;
8. εἰ δοίης αὐτὸ τῷ παιδὶ λάβοι ἂν αὐτό.
9. σταίην ἂν ἡδέως ἐν τῇ γῇ ἢ δέδωκεν ἡμῖν τὸν Σωκράτη.
10. ἐὰν θῇς ταύτην τὴν στρατιὰν ἐπὶ τοῦ ὄρους, ἥσουσι τὰ ὅπλα ἐπὶ τοὺς πολεμίους.

EXERCISE 158.

1. We were putting the books in the ship.
2. He stood the sword on the ground.
3. They gave many gifts to each other.
4. I placed the soldiers on the wall.
5. The man to whom he threw [use ἵημι] the money is a sailor.
6. They have been placed in very great danger.
7. The cities in Greece were given to the enemy.
8. He says that he will throw the slaves into the harbor.
9. If you placed your men on the wall, you would conquer the enemy.
10. If we place them there we will be able to find them.

Chapter 32 Vocabulary

Verbs:

δείκνυμι	show	ἵστημι	stand
δίδωμι	give	τίθημι	put, place
ἵημι	throw		

Summary of Forms

DEFINITE ARTICLE

| | | SINGULAR | | | PLURAL | |
	M	F	N	M	F	N
Nom.	ὁ	ἡ	τό	οἱ	αἱ	τά
Gen.	τοῦ	τῆς	τοῦ	τῶν	τῶν	τῶν
Dat.	τῷ	τῇ	τῷ	τοῖς	ταῖς	τοῖς
Acc.	τόν	τήν	τό	τούς	τάς	τά

NOUNS

FIRST DECLENSION

		honor (F)	country (F)	Muse (F)	bridge (F)	judge (M)	young man (M)
SING.	Nom.	τιμή	χώρᾱ	Μοῦσᾰ	γέφυρᾰ	κριτής	νεανίας
	Gen.	τιμῆς	χώρᾱς	Μούσης	γεφύρᾱς	κριτοῦ	νεανίου
	Dat.	τιμῇ	χώρᾳ	Μούσῃ	γεφύρᾳ	κριτῇ	νεανίᾳ
	Acc.	τιμήν	χώρᾱν	Μοῦσᾰν	γέφυρᾰν	κριτήν	νεανίαν
	Voc.	τιμή	χώρᾱ	Μοῦσᾰ	γέφυρᾰ	κριτά	νεανία
PLUR.	Nom.	τιμαί	χῶραι	Μοῦσαι	γέφυραι	κριταί	νεανίαι
	Gen.	τιμῶν	χωρῶν	Μουσῶν	γεφυρῶν	κριτῶν	νεανιῶν
	Dat.	τιμαῖς	χώραις	Μούσαις	γεφύραις	κριταῖς	νεανίαις
	Acc.	τιμάς	χώρας	Μούσας	γεφύρας	κριτάς	νεανίας
	Voc.	τιμαί	χῶραι	Μοῦσαι	γέφυραι	κριταί	νεανίαι

SECOND DECLENSION

		word (M)	island (F)	yoke (N)
SING.	Nom.	λόγος	νῆσος	ζυγόν
	Gen.	λόγου	νήσου	ζυγοῦ
	Dat.	λόγῳ	νήσῳ	ζυγῷ
	Acc.	λόγον	νῆσον	ζυγόν
	Voc.	λόγε	νῆσε	ζυγόν
PLUR.	Nom.	λόγοι	νῆσοι	ζυγά
	Gen.	λόγων	νήσων	ζυγῶν
	Dat.	λόγοις	νήσοις	ζυγοῖς
	Acc.	λόγους	νήσους	ζυγά
	Voc.	λόγοι	νῆσοι	ζυγά

THIRD DECLENSION (Stems in -κ, dentals)

		herald (M)	body (N)	love (M)	torch (F)	grace (F)	child (M/F)
SING.	Nom.	κῆρυξ	σῶμα	ἔρως	λαμπάς	χάρις	παῖς
	Gen.	κήρυκος	σώματος	ἔρωτος	λαμπάδος	χάριτος	παιδός
	Dat.	κήρυκι	σώματι	ἔρωτι	λαμπάδι	χάριτι	παιδί
	Acc.	κήρυκα	σῶμα	ἔρωτα	λαμπάδα	χάριν	παῖδα
	Voc.	κῆρυξ	σῶμα	ἔρως	λαμπάς	χάρις	παῖ

THIRD DECLENSION (Stems in -κ, dentals)

		herald (M)	body (N)	love (M)	torch (F)	grace (F)	child (M/F)
PLUR.	Nom.	κήρυκες	σώματα	ἔρωτες	λαμπάδες	χάριτες	παῖδες
	Gen.	κηρύκων	σωμάτων	ἐρώτων	λαμπάδων	χαρίτων	παίδων
	Dat.	κήρυξι(ν)	σώμασι(ν)	ἔρωσι(ν)	λαμπάσι(ν)	χάρισι(ν)	παισί(ν)
	Acc.	κήρυκας	σώματα	ἔρωτας	λαμπάδας	χάριτας	παῖδας
	Voc.	κήρυκες	σώματα	ἔρωτες	λαμπάδες	χάριτες	παῖδες

THIRD DECLENSION (Stems in -κτ, -ντ)

		giant (M)	tooth (M)	night (F)	lion (M)
SING.	Nom.	γίγας	ὀδούς	νύξ	λέων
	Gen.	γίγαντος	ὀδόντος	νυκτός	λέοντος
	Dat.	γίγαντι	ὀδόντι	νυκτί	λέοντι
	Acc.	γίγαντα	ὀδόντα	νύκτα	λέοντα
	Voc.	(γίγαν)	ὀδούς	νύξ	(λέον)
PLUR.	Nom.	γίγαντες	ὀδόντες	νύκτες	λέοντες
	Gen.	γιγάντων	ὀδόντων	νυκτῶν	λεόντων
	Dat.	γίγᾱσι(ν)	ὀδοῦσι(ν)	νυξί(ν)	λέουσι(ν)
	Acc.	γίγαντας	ὀδόντας	νύκτας	λέοντας
	Voc.	γίγαντες	ὀδόντες	νύκτες	λέοντες

THIRD DECLENSION (Stems in -ρ)

		orator (M)	wild beast (M)	mother (F)	father (M)	man (M)
SING.	Nom.	ῥήτωρ	θήρ	μήτηρ	πατήρ	ἀνήρ
	Gen.	ῥήτορος	θηρός	μητρός	πατρός	ἀνδρός
	Dat.	ῥήτορι	θηρί	μητρί	πατρί	ἀνδρί
	Acc.	ῥήτορα	θῆρα	μητέρα	πατέρα	ἄνδρα
	Voc.	ῥῆτορ	θήρ	μῆτερ	πάτερ	ἄνερ
PLUR.	Nom.	ῥήτορες	θῆρες	μητέρες	πατέρες	ἄνδρες
	Gen.	ῥητόρων	θηρῶν	μητέρων	πατέρων	ἀνδρῶν
	Dat.	ῥήτορσι(ν)	θηρσί(ν)	μητράσι(ν)	πατράσι(ν)	ἀνδράσι(ν)
	Acc.	ῥήτορας	θῆρας	μητέρας	πατέρας	ἄνδρας
	Voc.	ῥήτορες	θῆρες	μητέρες	πατέρες	ἄνδρες

THIRD DECLENSION (Stems in -ν)

		Greek (M)	contest (M)	shepherd (M)	leader (M)	dolphin (M)
SING.	Nom.	Ἕλλην	ἀγών	ποιμήν	ἡγεμών	δελφίς
	Gen.	Ἕλληνος	ἀγῶνος	ποιμένος	ἡγεμόνος	δελφῖνος
	Dat.	Ἕλληνι	ἀγῶνι	ποιμένι	ἡγεμόνι	δελφῖνι
	Acc.	Ἕλληνα	ἀγῶνα	ποιμένα	ἡγεμόνα	δελφῖνα
	Voc.	Ἕλλην	ἀγών	ποιμήν	ἡγεμών	δελφίς
PLUR.	Nom.	Ἕλληνες	ἀγῶνες	ποιμένες	ἡγεμόνες	δελφῖνες
	Gen.	Ἑλλήνων	ἀγώνων	ποιμένων	ἡγεμόνων	δελφίνων
	Dat.	Ἕλλησι(ν)	ἀγῶσι(ν)	ποιμέσι(ν)	ἡγεμόσι(ν)	δελφῖσι(ν)
	Acc.	Ἕλληνας	ἀγῶνας	ποιμένας	ἡγεμόνας	δελφῖνας
	Voc.	Ἕλληνες	ἀγῶνες	ποιμένες	ἡγεμόνες	δελφῖνες

THIRD DECLENSION (Stems in -σ, -ι, -υ)

		trireme (F)	wall (N)	city (F)	elder (M)	town (N)	fish (M)
SING.	Nom.	τριήρης	τεῖχος	πόλις	πρέσβυς	ἄστυ	ἰχθύς
	Gen.	τριήρους	τείχους	πόλεως	πρέσβεως	ἄστεως	ἰχθύος
	Dat.	τριήρει	τείχει	πόλει	πρέσβει	ἄστει	ἰχθύϊ
	Acc.	τριήρη	τεῖχος	πόλιν	πρέσβυν	ἄστυ	ἰχθύν
	Voc.	(τριῆρες)	τεῖχος	πόλι	πρέσβυς	ἄστυ	ἰχθύ
PLUR.	Nom.	τριήρεις	τείχη	πόλεις	πρέσβεις	ἄστη	ἰχθύες
	Gen.	τριήρων	τειχῶν	πόλεων	πρέσβεων	ἄστεων	ἰχθύων
	Dat.	τριήρεσι(ν)	τείχεσι(ν)	πόλεσι(ν)	πρέσβεσι(ν)	ἄστεσι(ν)	ἰχθύσι(ν)
	Acc.	τριήρεις	τείχη	πόλεις	πρέσβεις	ἄστη	ἰχθύας, ἰχθῦς
	Voc.	τριήρεις	τείχη	πόλεις	πρέσβεις	ἄστη	ἰχθύες

THIRD DECLENSION (Stems in diphthongs, irregular)

		woman (F)	ship (F)	water (N)	king (M)	ox (M/F)	old woman (F)
SING.	Nom.	γυνή	ναῦς	ὕδωρ	βασιλεύς	βοῦς	γραῦς
	Gen.	γυναικός	νεώς	ὕδατος	βασιλέως	βοός	γρᾱός
	Dat.	γυναικί	νηΐ	ὕδατι	βασιλεῖ	βοΐ	γρᾱΐ
	Acc.	γυναῖκα	ναῦν	ὕδωρ	βασιλέᾱ	βοῦν	γραῦν
	Voc.	γύναι	ναῦ	ὕδωρ	βασιλεῦ	βοῦ	γραῦ
PLUR.	Nom.	γυναῖκες	νῆες	ὕδατα	βασιλεῖς/ -ῆς	βόες	γρᾶες
	Gen.	γυναικῶν	νεῶν	ὑδάτων	βασιλέων	βοῶν	γρᾱῶν
	Dat.	γυναιξί(ν)	ναυσί(ν)	ὕδασι(ν)	βασιλεῦσι(ν)	βουσί(ν)	γραυσί(ν)
	Acc.	γυναῖκας	ναῦς	ὕδατα	βασιλέᾱς	βοῦς	γραῦς
	Voc.	γυναῖκες	νῆες	ὕδατα	βασιλεῖς/ -ῆς	βόες	γρᾶες

ADJECTIVES
FIRST AND SECOND DECLENSION

		wise			friendly		
		M	F	N	M	F	N
SING.	Nom.	σοφός	σοφή	σοφόν	φίλιος	φιλία	φίλιον
	Gen.	σοφοῦ	σοφῆς	σοφοῦ	φιλίου	φιλίας	φιλίου
	Dat.	σοφῷ	σοφῇ	σοφῷ	φιλίῳ	φιλίᾳ	φιλίῳ
	Acc.	σοφόν	σοφήν	σοφόν	φίλιον	φιλίαν	φίλιον
	Voc.	σοφέ	σοφή	σοφόν	φίλιε	φιλία	φίλιον
PLUR.	Nom.	σοφοί	σοφαί	σοφά	φίλιοι	φίλιαι	φίλια
	Gen.	σοφῶν	σοφῶν	σοφῶν	φιλίων	φιλίων	φιλίων
	Dat.	σοφοῖς	σοφαῖς	σοφοῖς	φιλίοις	φιλίαις	φιλίοις
	Acc.	σοφούς	σοφάς	σοφά	φιλίους	φιλίας	φίλια
	Voc.	σοφοί	σοφαί	σοφά	φίλιοι	φίλιαι	φίλια

FIRST AND SECOND DECLENSION (Contract)

silver

		M	F	N
SING.	Nom.	ἀργυροῦς (-έος)	ἀργυρᾶ (-έα)	ἀργυροῦν (-έον)
	Gen.	ἀργυροῦ	ἀργυρᾶς	ἀργυροῦ
	Dat.	ἀργυρῷ	ἀργυρᾷ	ἀργυρῷ
	Acc.	ἀργυροῦν	ἀργυρᾶν	ἀργυροῦν
	Voc.	ἀργυροῦς	ἀργυρᾶ	ἀργυροῦν
PLUR.	Nom.	ἀργυροῖ	ἀργυραῖ	ἀργυρᾶ
	Gen.	ἀργυρῶν	ἀργυρῶν	ἀργυρῶν
	Dat.	ἀργυροῖς	ἀργυραῖς	ἀργυροῖς
	Acc.	ἀργυροῦς	ἀργυρᾶς	ἀργυρᾶ
	Voc.	ἀργυροῖ	ἀργυραῖ	ἀργυρᾶ

THIRD DECLENSION

		kindly		well-born	
		M/F	N	M/F	N
SING.	Nom.	εὔφρων	εὔφρον	εὐγενής	εὐγενές
	Gen.	εὔφρονος	εὔφρονος	εὐγενοῦς	εὐγενοῦς
	Dat.	εὔφρονι	εὔφρονι	εὐγενεῖ	εὐγενεῖ
	Acc.	εὔφρονα	εὔφρον	εὐγενῆ	εὐγενές
	Voc.	εὖφρον	εὖφρον	εὐγενές	εὐγενές
PLUR.	Nom.	εὔφρονες	εὔφρονα	εὐγενεῖς	εὐγενῆ
	Gen.	εὐφρόνων	εὐφρόνων	εὐγενῶν	εὐγενῶν
	Dat.	εὔφροσι(ν)	εὔφροσι(ν)	εὐγενέσι(ν)	εὐγενέσι(ν)
	Acc.	εὔφρονας	εὔφρονα	εὐγενεῖς	εὐγενῆ
	Voc.	εὔφρονες	εὔφρονα	εὐγενεῖς	εὐγενῆ

FIRST AND THIRD DECLENSION

		sweet			all		
		M	F	N	M	F	N
SING.	Nom.	ἡδύς	ἡδεῖα	ἡδύ	πᾶς	πᾶσα	πᾶν
	Gen.	ἡδέος	ἡδείας	ἡδέος	παντός	πάσης	παντός
	Dat.	ἡδεῖ	ἡδείᾳ	ἡδεῖ	παντί	πάσῃ	παντί
	Acc.	ἡδύν	ἡδεῖαν	ἡδύ	πάντα	πᾶσαν	πᾶν
	Voc.	ἡδύς	ἡδεῖα	ἡδύ	πᾶς	πᾶσα	πᾶν
PLUR.	Nom.	ἡδεῖς	ἡδεῖαι	ἡδέα	πάντες	πᾶσαι	πάντα
	Gen.	ἡδέων	ἡδειῶν	ἡδέων	πάντων	πασῶν	πάντων
	Dat.	ἡδέσι(ν)	ἡδείαις	ἡδέσι(ν)	πᾶσι(ν)	πάσαις	πᾶσι(ν)
	Acc.	ἡδεῖς	ἡδείας	ἡδέα	πάντας	πάσας	πάντα
	Voc.	ἡδεῖς	ἡδεῖαι	ἡδέα	πάντες	πᾶσαι	πάντα

wretched

		M	F	N
SING.	Nom.	τάλας	τάλαινα	τάλαν
	Gen.	τάλανος	ταλαίνης	τάλανος
	Dat.	τάλανι	ταλαίνη	τάλανι
	Acc.	τάλανα	τάλαιναν	τάλαν
	Voc.	τάλαν	τάλαινα	τάλαν
PLUR.	Nom.	τάλανες	τάλαιναι	τάλανα
	Gen.	ταλάνων	ταλαινῶν	ταλάνων
	Dat.	τάλασι(ν)	ταλαίναις	τάλασι(ν)
	Acc.	τάλανας	ταλαίνας	τάλανα
	Voc.	τάλανες	τάλαιναι	τάλανα

IRREGULAR

		big			much, many		
		M	F	N	M	F	N
SING.	Nom.	μέγας	μεγάλη	μέγα	πολύς	πολλή	πολύ
	Gen.	μεγάλου	μεγάλης	μεγάλου	πολλοῦ	πολλῆς	πολλοῦ
	Dat.	μεγάλῳ	μεγάλη	μεγάλῳ	πολλῷ	πολλῇ	πολλῷ
	Acc.	μέγαν	μεγάλην	μέγα	πολύν	πολλήν	πολύ
	Voc.	μεγάλε	μεγάλη	μέγα	πολύς	πολλή	πολύ
PLUR.	Nom.	μεγάλοι	μεγάλαι	μεγάλα	πολλοί	πολλαί	πολλά
	Gen.	μεγάλων	μεγάλων	μεγάλων	πολλῶν	πολλῶν	πολλῶν
	Dat.	μεγάλοις	μεγάλαις	μεγάλοις	πολλοῖς	πολλαῖς	πολλοῖς
	Acc.	μεγάλους	μεγάλας	μεγάλα	πολλούς	πολλάς	πολλά
	Voc.	μεγάλοι	μεγάλαι	μεγάλα	πολλοί	πολλαί	πολλά

PARTICIPLES
REGULAR THEMATIC VERBS

		PRESENT ACTIVE			PRESENT MIDDLE/PASSIVE		
		M	F	N	M	F	N
SING.	Nom.	λύων	λύουσα	λῦον	λυόμενος	λυομένη	λυόμενον
	Gen.	λύοντος	λυούσης	λύοντος	λυομένου	λυομένης	λυομένου
	Dat.	λύοντι	λυούση	λύοντι	λυομένῳ	λυομένη	λυομένῳ
	Acc.	λύοντα	λύουσαν	λῦον	λυόμενον	λυομένην	λυόμενον
	Voc.	λύων	λύουσα	λῦον	λυόμενος	λυομένη	λυόμενον
PLUR.	Nom.	λύοντες	λύουσαι	λύοντα	λυόμενοι	λυόμεναι	λυόμενα
	Gen.	λυόντων	λυουσῶν	λυόντων	λυομένων	λυομένων	λυομένων
	Dat.	λύουσι(ν)	λυούσαις	λύουσι(ν)	λυομένοις	λυομέναις	λυομένοις
	Acc.	λύοντας	λυούσας	λύοντα	λυομένους	λυομένας	λυόμενα
	Voc.	λύοντες	λύουσαι	λύοντα	λυόμενοι	λυόμεναι	λυόμενα

FIRST AORIST ACTIVE / FIRST AORIST MIDDLE

		M	F	N	M	F	N
SING.	Nom.	λύσας	λύσασα	λῦσαν	λυσάμενος	λυσαμένη	λυσάμενον
	Gen.	λύσαντος	λυσάσης	λύσαντος	λυσαμένου	λυσαμένης	λυσαμένου
	Dat.	λύσαντι	λυσάσῃ	λύσαντι	λυσαμένῳ	λυσαμένῃ	λυσαμένῳ
	Acc.	λύσαντα	λύσασαν	λῦσαν	λυσάμενον	λυσαμένην	λυσάμενον
	Voc.	λύσας	λύσασα	λῦσαν			
PLUR.	Nom.	λύσαντες	λύσασαι	λύσαντα	λυσάμενοι	λυσάμεναι	λυσάμενα
	Gen.	λυσάντων	λυσασῶν	λυσάντων	λυσαμένων	λυσαμένων	λυσαμένων
	Dat.	λύσασι(ν)	λυσάσαις	λύσασι(ν)	λυσαμένοις	λυσαμέναις	λυσαμένοις
	Acc.	λύσαντας	λυσάσας	λύσαντα	λυσαμένους	λυσαμένας	λυσάμενα
	Voc.	λύσαντες	λύσασαι	λύσαντα	λυσάμενοι	λυσάμεναι	λυσάμενα

SECOND AORIST ACTIVE / SECOND AORIST MIDDLE

		M	F	N	M	F	N
SING.	Nom.	λιπών	λιποῦσα	λιπόν	λιπόμενος	λιπομένη	λιπόμενον
	Gen.	λιπόντος	λιπούσης	λιπόντος	λιπομένου	λιπομένης	λιπομένου
	Dat.	λιπόντι	λιπούσῃ	λιπόντι	λιπομένῳ	λιπομένῃ	λιπομένῳ
	Acc.	λιπόντα	λιποῦσαν	λιπόν	λιπόμενον	λιπομένην	λιπόμενον
	Voc.	λιπών	λιποῦσα	λιπόν	λιπόμενος	λιπομένη	λιπόμενον
PLUR.	Nom.	λιπόντες	λιποῦσαι	λιπόντα	λιπόμενοι	λιπόμεναι	λιπόμενα
	Gen.	λιπόντων	λιπουσῶν	λιπόντων	λιπομένων	λιπομένων	λιπομένων
	Dat.	λιποῦσι(ν)	λιπούσαις	λιποῦσι(ν)	λιπομένοις	λιπομέναις	λιπομένοις
	Acc.	λιπόντας	λιπούσας	λιπόντα	λιπομένους	λιπομένας	λιπόμενα
	Voc.	λιπόντες	λιποῦσαι	λιπόντα	λιπόμενοι	λιπόμεναι	λιπόμενα

PERFECT ACTIVE / PERFECT MIDDLE/PASSIVE

		M	F	N	M	F	N
SING.	Nom.	λελυκώς	λελυκυῖα	λελυκός	λελυμένος	λελυμένη	λελυμένον
	Gen.	λελυκότος	λελυκυίας	λελυκότος	λελυμένου	λελυμένης	λελυμένου
	Dat.	λελυκότι	λελυκυίᾳ	λελυκότι	λελυμένῳ	λελυμένῃ	λελυμένῳ
	Acc.	λελυκότα	λελυκυῖαν	λελυκός	λελυμένον	λελυμένην	λελυμένον
	Voc.	λελυκός	λελυκυῖα	λελυκός	λελυμένος	λελυμένη	λελυμένον
PLUR.	Nom.	λελυκότες	λελυκυῖαι	λελυκότα	λελυμένοι	λελυμέναι	λελυμένα
	Gen.	λελυκότων	λελυκυιῶν	λελυκότων	λελυμένων	λελυμένων	λελυμένων
	Dat.	λελυκόσι(ν)	λελυκυίαις	λελυκόσι(ν)	λελυμένοις	λελυμέναις	λελυμένοις
	Acc.	λελυκότας	λελυκυίας	λελυκότα	λελυμένους	λελυμένας	λελυμένα
	Voc.	λελυκότες	λελυκυῖαι	λελυκότα	λελυμένοι	λελυμέναι	λελυμένα

AORIST PASSIVE

		M	F	N
Sing.	Nom.	λυθείς	λυθεῖσα	λυθέν
	Gen.	λυθέντος	λυθείσης	λυθέντος
	Dat.	λυθέντι	λυθείσῃ	λυθέντι
	Acc.	λυθέντα	λυθεῖσαν	λυθέν
	Voc.	λυθείς	λυθεῖσα	λυθέν
Plur.	Nom.	λυθέντες	λυθεῖσαι	λυθέντα
	Gen.	λυθέντων	λυθεισῶν	λυθέντων
	Dat.	λυθεῖσι(ν)	λυθείσαις	λυθεῖσι(ν)
	Acc.	λυθέντας	λυθείσας	λυθέντα
	Voc.	λυθέντες	λυθεῖσαι	λυθέντα

CONTRACT THEMATIC VERBS

PRESENT ACTIVE   PRESENT MIDDLE/PASSIVE
φιλέω

		M	F	N	M	F	N
Sing.	Nom	φιλῶν	φιλοῦσα	φιλοῦν	φιλούμενος	φιλουμένη	φιλούμενον
	Gen.	φιλοῦντος	φιλούσης	φιλοῦντος	φιλουμένου	φιλουμένης	φιλουμένου
	Dat.	φιλοῦντι	φιλούσῃ	φιλοῦντι	φιλουμένῳ	φιλουμένῃ	φιλουμένῳ
	Acc.	φιλοῦντα	φιλοῦσαν	φιλοῦν	φιλούμενον	φιλουμένην	φιλούμενον
	Voc.	φιλῶν	φιλοῦσα	φιλοῦν	φιλούμενος	φιλουμένη	φιλούμενον
Plur.	Nom.	φιλοῦντες	φιλοῦσαι	φιλοῦντα	φιλούμενοι	φιλούμεναι	φιλούμενα
	Gen.	φιλούντων	φιλουσῶν	φιλούντων	φιλουμένων	φιλουμένων	φιλουμένων
	Dat.	φιλοῦσι(ν)	φιλούσαις	φιλοῦσι(ν)	φιλουμένοις	φιλουμέναις	φιλουμένοις
	Acc.	φιλοῦντας	φιλούσας	φιλοῦντα	φιλουμένους	φιλουμένας	φιλούμενα
	Voc.	φιλοῦντες	φιλοῦσαι	φιλοῦντα	φιλούμενοι	φιλούμεναι	φιλούμενα

τιμάω

		M	F	N	M	F	N
Sing.	Nom.	τιμῶν	τιμῶσα	τιμῶν	τιμώμενος	τιμωμένη	τιμώμενον
	Gen.	τιμῶντος	τιμώσης	τιμῶντος	τιμωμένου	τιμωμένης	τιμωμένου
	Dat.	τιμῶντι	τιμώσῃ	τιμῶντι	τιμωμένῳ	τιμωμένῃ	τιμωμένῳ
	Acc.	τιμῶντα	τιμῶσαν	τιμῶν	τιμώμενον	τιμωμένην	τιμώμενον
	Voc.	τιμῶν	τιμῶσα	τιμῶν	τιμώμενος	τιμωμένη	τιμώμενον
Plur.	Nom.	τιμῶντες	τιμῶσαι	τιμῶντα	τιμώμενοι	τιμώμεναι	τιμώμενα
	Gen.	τιμώντων	τιμωσῶν	τιμώντων	τιμωμένων	τιμωμένων	τιμωμένων
	Dat.	τιμῶσι(ν)	τιμώσαις	τιμῶσι(ν)	τιμωμένοις	τιμωμέναις	τιμωμένοις
	Acc.	τιμῶντας	τιμώσας	τιμῶντα	τιμωμένους	τιμωμένας	τιμώμενα
	Voc.	τιμῶντες	τιμῶσαι	τιμῶντα	τιμώμενοι	τιμώμεναι	τιμώμενα

PRESENT ACTIVE   PRESENT MIDDLE/PASSIVE

δηλόω

	M	F	N	M	F	N
SING.						
Nom.	δηλῶν	δηλοῦσα	δηλοῦν	δηλούμενος	δηλουμένη	δηλούμενον
Gen.	δηλοῦντος	δηλούσης	δηλοῦντος	δηλουμένου	δηλουμένης	δηλουμένου
Dat.	δηλοῦντι	δηλούσῃ	δηλοῦντι	δηλουμένῳ	δηλουμένῃ	δηλουμένῳ
Acc.	δηλοῦντα	δηλοῦσαν	δηλοῦν	δηιλούμενον	δηλουμένην	δηλούμενον
Voc.	δηλῶν	δηλοῦσα	δηλοῦν	δηιλούμενος	δηλουμένη	δηλούμενον
PLUR.						
Nom.	δηλοῦντες	δηλοῦσαι	δηιλοῦντα	δηλούμενοι	δηλούμεναι	δηλούμενα
Gen.	δηλούντων	δηλουσῶν	δηλούντων	δηλουμένων	δηλουμένων	δηλουμένων
Dat.	δηλοῦσι(ν)	δηλούσαις	δηλοῦσι(ν)	δηλουμένοις	δηλουμέναις	δηλουμένοις
Acc.	δηλοῦντας	δηλούσας	δηλοῦντα	δηλουμένους	δηλουμένας	δηλούμενα
Voc.	δηλοῦντες	δηλοῦσαι	δηλοῦντα	δηλούμενοι	δηλούμεναι	δηλούμενα

PRONOUNS

PERSONAL AND INTENSIVE

		1st (I)	2nd (you)	3rd (he/she/it)		
				M	F	N
SING.	Nom.	ἐγώ	σύ	αὐτός	αὐτή	αὐτό
	Gen.	ἐμοῦ, μου	σοῦ, σου	αὐτοῦ	αὐτῆς	αὐτοῦ
	Dat.	ἐμοί μοι	σοί σοι	αὐτῷ	αὐτῇ	αὐτῷ
	Acc.	ἐμέ, με	σέ, σε	αὐτόν	αὐτήν	αὐτό
PLUR.	Nom.	ἡμεῖς	ὑμεῖς	αὐτοί	αὐταί	αὐτά
	Gen.	ἡμῶν	ὑμῶν	αὐτῶν	αὐτῶν	αὐτῶν
	Dat.	ἡμῖν	ὑμῖν	αὐτοῖς	αὐταῖς	αὐτοῖς
	Acc.	ἡμᾶς	ὑμᾶς	αὐτούς	αὐτάς	αὐτά

RECIPROCAL (each other)

	M	F	N
Gen.	ἀλλήλων	ἀλλήλων	ἀλλήλων
Dat.	ἀλλήλοις	ἀλλήλαις	ἀλλήλοις
Acc.	ἀλλήλους	ἀλλήλας	ἄλληλα

REFLEXIVE

		1st (myself)		2nd (yourself)		3rd (himself/herself/itself)		
		M	F	M	F	M	F	N
SING.	Gen.	ἐμαυτοῦ	ἐμαυτῆς	σεαυτοῦ	σεαυτῆς	ἑαυτοῦ	ἑαυτῆς	ἑαυτοῦ
	Dat.	ἐμαυτῷ	ἐμαυτῇ	σεαυτῷ	σεαυτῇ	ἑαυτῷ	ἑαυτῇ	ἑαυτῷ
	Acc.	ἐμαυτόν	ἐμαυτήν	σεαυτόν	σεαυτήν	ἑαυτόν	ἑαυτήν	ἑαυτό
PLUR.	Gen.	ἡμῶν αὐτῶν	ἡμῶν αὐτῶν	ὑμῶν αὐτῶν	ὑμῶν αὐτῶν	ἑαυτῶν	ἑαυτῶν	ἑαυτῶν
	Dat.	ἡμῖν αὐτοῖς	ἡμῖν αὐταῖς	ὑμῖν αὐτοῖς	ὑμῖν αὐταῖς	ἑαυτοῖς	ἑαυταῖς	ἑαυτοῖς
	Acc.	ἡμᾶς αὐτούς	ἡμᾶς αὐτάς	ὑμᾶς αὐτούς	ὑμᾶς αὐτάς	ἑαυτούς	ἑαυτάς	ἑαυτά

DEMONSTRATIVE

		this			that		
		M	**F**	**N**	**M**	**F**	**N**
SING.	Nom.	οὗτος	αὕτη	τοῦτο	ἐκεῖνος	ἐκείνη	ἐκεῖνο
	Gen.	τούτου	ταύτης	τούτου	ἐκείνου	ἐκείνης	ἐκείνου
	Dat.	τούτῳ	ταύτῃ	τούτῳ	ἐκείνῳ	ἐκείνῃ	ἐκείνῳ
	Acc.	τοῦτον	ταύτην	τοῦτο	ἐκεῖνον	ἐκείνην	ἐκεῖνο
PLUR.	Nom.	οὗτοι	αὗται	ταῦτα	ἐκεῖνοι	ἐκεῖναι	ἐκεῖνα
	Gen.	τούτων	τούτων	τούτων	ἐκείνων	ἐκείνων	ἐκείνων
	Dat.	τούτοις	ταύταις	τούτοις	ἐκείνοις	ἐκείναις	ἐκείνοις
	Acc.	τούτους	ταύτας	ταῦτα	ἐκείνους	ἐκείνας	ἐκεῖνα

		this		
		M	**F**	**N**
SING.	Nom.	ὅδε	ἥδε	τόδε
	Gen.	τοῦδε	τῆσδε	τοῦδε
	Dat.	τῷδε	τῇδε	τῷδε
	Acc.	τόνδε	τήνδε	τόδε
PLUR.	Nom.	οἵδε	αἵδε	τάδε
	Gen.	τῶνδε	τῶνδε	τῶνδε
	Dat.	τοῖσδε	ταῖσδε	τοῖσδε
	Acc.	τούσδε	τάσδε	τάδε

INTERROGATIVE AND INDEFINITE

		who?/what?		someone/something	
		M/F	**N**	**M/F**	**N**
SING.	Nom.	τίς	τί	τις	τι
	Gen.	τίνος	τίνος	τινός	τινός
	Dat.	τίνι	τίνι	τινί	τινί
	Acc.	τίνα	τί	τινά	τι
PLUR.	Nom.	τίνες	τίνα	τινές	τινά
	Gen.	τίνων	τίνων	τινῶν	τινῶν
	Dat.	τίσι	τίσι	τισί	τισί
	Acc.	τίνας	τίνα	τινάς	τινά

RELATIVE

		who/what			anyone who		
		M	**F**	**N**	**M**	**F**	**N**
SING.	Nom.	ὅς	ἥ	ὅ	ὅστις	ἥτις	ὅ τι
	Gen.	οὗ	ἧς	οὗ	οὗτινος	ἧστινος	οὗτινος
	Dat.	ᾧ	ᾗ	ᾧ	ᾧτινι	ᾗτινι	ᾧτινι
	Acc.	ὅν	ἥν	ὅ	ὅντινα	ἥντινα	ὅ τι
PLUR.	Nom.	οἵ	αἵ	ἅ	οἵτινες	αἵτινες	ἅτινα
	Gen.	ὧν	ὧν	ὧν	ὧντινων	ὧντινων	ὧντινων
	Dat.	οἷς	αἷς	οἷς	οἷστισι(ν)	αἷστισι(ν)	οἷστισι(ν)
	Acc.	οὕς	ἅς	ἅ	οὕστινας	ἅστινας	ἅτινα

NUMBERS

CARDINAL AND ORDINAL

1	εἷς, μία, ἕν	πρῶτος, -η, -ον
2	δύο	δεύτερος, -α, -ον
3	τρεῖς, τρία	τρίτος, -η, -ον
4	τέσσαρες, τέσσαρα	τέταρτος, -η, -ον
5	πέντε	πέμπτος, -η, -ον
6	ἕξ	ἕκτος, -η, -ον
7	ἑπτά	ἕβδομος, -η, -ον
8	ὀκτώ	ὄγδοος, -η, -ον
9	ἐννέα	ἔνατος, -η, -ον
10	δέκα	δέκατος, -η, -ον
11	ἕνδεκα	ἑνδέκατος, -η, -ον
12	δώδεκα	δωδέκατος, -η, -ον
13	τρεῖς καὶ δέκα	τρίτος, -η, -ον καὶ δέκατος, -η, -ον
14	τέσσαρες καὶ δέκα	τέταρτος, -η, -ον καὶ δέκατος, -η, -ον
15	πεντεκαίδεκα	πέμπτος, -η, -ον καὶ δέκατος, -η, -ον
16	ἐκκαίδεκα	ἕκτος, -η, -ον καὶ δέκατος, -η, -ον
17	ἑπτακαίδεκα	ἕβδομος, -η, -ον καὶ δέκατος, -η, -ον
18	ὀκτωκαίδεκα	ὄγδοος, -η, -ον καὶ δέκατος, -η, -ον
19	ἐννεακαίδεκα	ἔνατος, -η, -ον καὶ δέκατος, -η, -ον
20	εἴκοσι(ν)	εἰκοστός, -ή, -όν
21	εἷς καὶ εἴκοσι, εἴκοσι καὶ εἷς	πρῶτος, -η, -ον καὶ εἰκοστός, -ή, -όν
30	τριάκοντα	τριακοστός, -ή, -όν
40	τεσσαράκοντα	τεσσαρακοστός, -ή, -όν
50	πεντήκοντα	πεντηκοστός, -ή, -όν
60	ἑξήκοντα	ἑξηκοστός, -ή, -όν
70	ἑβδομήκοντα	ἑβδομηκοστός, -ή, -όν
80	ὀγδοήκοντα	ὀγδοηκοστός, -ή, -όν
90	ἐνενήκοντα	ἐνενηκοστός, -ή, -όν
100	ἑκατόν	ἑκατοστός, -ή, -όν
200	διακόσιοι, -αι, -α	διακοσιοστός, -ή, -όν
300	τριακόσιοι, -αι, -α	τριακοσιοστός, -ή, -όν
400	τετρακόσιοι, -αι, -α	τετρακοσιοστός, -ή, -όν
500	πεντακόσιοι, -αι, -α	πεντακοσιοστός, -ή, -όν
600	ἑξακόσιοι, -αι, -α	ἑξακοσιοστός, -ή, -όν
700	ἑπτακόσιοι, -αι, -α	ἑπτακοσιοστός, -ή, -όν
800	ὀκτακόσιοι, -αι, -α	ὀκτακοσιοστός, -ή, -όν
900	ἐνακόσιοι, -αι, -α	ἐνακοσιοστός, -ή, -όν
1000	χίλιοι, -αι, -α	χιλιοστός, -ή, -όν

DECLENSION OF NUMBERS 1 to 4:

	one			two	three		four	
	M	F	N	M/F/N	M/F	N	M/F	N
Nom.	εἷς	μία	ἕν	δύο	τρεῖς	τρία	τέσσαρες	τέσσαρα
Gen.	ἑνός	μιᾶς	ἑνός	δυοῖν	τριῶν	τριῶν	τεσσάρων	τεσσάρων
Dat.	ἑνί	μιᾷ	ἑνί	δυοῖν	τρισί(ν)	τρισί(ν)	τέσσαρσι(ν)	τέσσαρσι(ν)
Acc.	ἕνα	μίαν	ἕν	δύο	τρεῖς	τρία	τέσσαρας	τέσσαρα
Voc.	εἷς	μία	ἕν	δύο	τρεῖς	τρία	τέσσαρες	τέσσαρα

REGULAR THEMATIC VERBS

PRESENT SYSTEM

		SINGULAR	PLURAL	SINGULAR	PLURAL
		Active		**Middle/Passive**	
INDICATIVE					
Present					
	1st	λύω	λύομεν	λύομαι	λυόμεθα
	2nd	λύεις	λύετε	λύῃ / -ει	λύεσθε
	3rd	λύει	λύουσι(ν)	λύεται	λύονται
Imperfect					
	1st	ἔλυον	ἐλύομεν	ἐλυόμην	ἐλυόμεθα
	2nd	ἔλυες	ἐλύετε	ἐλύου	ἐλύεσθε
	3rd	ἔλυε(ν)	ἔλυον	ἐλύετο	ἐλύοντο
SUBJUNCTIVE					
	1st	λύω	λύωμεν	λύωμαι	λυώμεθα
	2nd	λύῃς	λύητε	λύῃ	λύησθε
	3rd	λύῃ	λύωσι(ν)	λύηται	λύωνται
OPTATIVE					
	1st	λύοιμι	λύοιμεν	λυοίμην	λυοίμεθα
	2nd	λύοις	λύοιτε	λύοιο	λύοισθε
	3rd	λύοι	λύοιεν	λύοιτο	λύοιντο
IMPERATIVE					
	2nd	λύε	λύετε	λύου	λύεσθε
	3rd	λυέτω	λυόντων	λυέσθω	λυέσθων
INFINITIVE		λύειν		λύεσθαι	
PARTICIPLE		λύων, λύουσα, λῦον		λυόμενος, -μένη, -μενον	

FUTURE SYSTEM

	SINGULAR	PLURAL	SINGULAR	PLURAL	SINGULAR	PLURAL
	Active		**Middle**		**Passive**	
INDICATIVE						
1st	λύσω	λύσομεν	λύσομαι	λυσόμεθα	λυθήσομαι	λυθησόμεθα
2nd	λύσεις	λύσετε	λύσῃ / -ει	λύσεσθε	λυθήσῃ / -ει	λυθήσεσθε
3rd	λύσει	λύσουσι(ν)	λύσεται	λύσονται	λυθήσεται	λυθήσονται
OPTATIVE						
1st	λύσοιμι	λύσοιμεν	λυσοίμην	λυσοίμεθα	λυθησοίμην	λυθησοίμεθα
2nd	λύσοις	λύσοιτε	λύσοιο	λύσοισθε	λυθήσοιο	λυθήσοισθε
3rd	λύσοι	λύσοιεν	λύσοιτο	λύσοιντο	λυθήσοιτο	λυθήσοιντο
INFINITIVE	λύσειν		λύσεσθαι		λυθήσεσθαι	
PARTICIPLE	λύσων, -ουσα, -ον		λυσόμενος, -μένη, -μενον		λυθησόμενος, -μένη, -μενον	

AORIST SYSTEM (WEAK)

	SINGULAR	PLURAL	SINGULAR	PLURAL	SINGULAR	PLURAL
	Active		**Middle**		**Passive**	
INDICATIVE						
1st	ἔλυσα	ἐλύσαμεν	ἐλυσάμην	ἐλυσάμεθα	ἐλύθην	ἐλύθημεν
2nd	ἔλυσας	ἐλύσατε	ἐλύσω	ἐλύσασθε	ἐλύθης	ἐλύθητε
3rd	ἔλυσε(ν)	ἔλυσαν	ἐλύσατο	ἐλύσαντο	ἐλύθη	ἐλύθησαν
SUBJUNCTIVE						
1st	λύσω	λύσωμεν	λύσωμαι	λυσώμεθα	λυθῶ	λυθῶμεν
2nd	λύσῃς	λύσητε	λύσῃ	λύσησθε	λυθῇς	λυθῆτε
3rd	λύσῃ	λύσωσι(ν)	λύσηται	λύσωνται	λυθῇ	λυθῶσι(ν)
OPTATIVE						
1st	λύσαιμι	λύσαιμεν	λυσαίμην	λυσαίμεθα	λυθείην	λυθεῖμεν
2nd	λύσαις	λύσαιτε	λύσαιο	λύσαισθε	λυθείης	λυθεῖτε
3rd	λύσαι	λύσαιεν	λύσαιτο	λύσαιντο	λυθείη	λυθεῖεν
IMPERATIVE						
2nd	λῦσον	λύσατε	λῦσαι	λύσασθε	λύθητι	λύθητε
3rd	λυσάτω	λυσάντων	λυσάσθω	λυσάσθων	λυθήτω	λυθέντων
INFINITIVE	λῦσαι		λύσασθαι		λυθῆναι	
PARTICIPLE	λύσας, -ασα, -αν		λυσάμενος, -μένη, -μενον		λυθείς, -θεῖσα, -θέν	

AORIST SYSTEM (STRONG)

	SINGULAR	PLURAL	SINGULAR	PLURAL	SINGULAR	PLURAL
	Active		**Middle**		**Passive**	
INDICATIVE						
1st	ἔλαβον	ἐλάβομεν	ἐλαβόμην	ἐλαβόμεθα	ἐλήφθην	ἐλήφθημεν
2nd	ἔλαβες	ἐλάβετε	ἐλάβου	ἐλάβεσθε	ἐλήφθης	ἐλήφθητε
3rd	ἔλαβε(ν)	ἔλαβον	ἐλάβετο	ἐλάβοντο	ἐλήφθη	ἐλήφθησαν
SUBJUNCTIVE						
1st	λάβω	λάβωμεν	λάβωμαι	λαβώμεθα	λαβῶ	λαβῶμεν
2nd	λάβῃς	λάβητε	λάβῃ	λάβησθε	λαβῇς	λαβῆτε
3rd	λάβῃ	λάβωσι(ν)	λάβηται	λάβωνται	λαβῇ	λαβῶσι(ν)
OPTATIVE						
1st	λάβοιμι	λάβοιμεν	λαβοίμην	λαβοίμεθα	ληφθείην	ληφθεῖμεν
2nd	λάβοις	λάβοιτε	λάβοιο	λάβοισθε	ληφθείης	ληφθεῖτε
3rd	λάβοι	λάβοιεν	λάβοιτο	λάβοιντο	ληφθείη	ληφθεῖεν
IMPERATIVE						
2nd	λάβε	λάβετε	λαβοῦ	λάβεσθε	λήφθητι	λήφθητε
3rd	λαβέτω	λαβόντων	λαβέσθω	λαβέσθων	ληφθέτω	ληφθέντων
INFINITIVE	λαβεῖν		λαβέσθαι		ληφθῆναι	
PARTICIPLE	λαβών, -ουσα, -ον		λαβόμενος, -μένη, -μενον		ληφθείς, -θεῖσα, -θέν	

PERFECT SYSTEM

	SINGULAR	PLURAL	SINGULAR	PLURAL
	Active		**Middle/Passive**	
INDICATIVE				
Perfect				
1st	λέλυκα	λελύκαμεν	λέλυμαι	λελύμεθα
2nd	λέλυκας	λελύκατε	λέλυσαι	λέλυσθε
3rd	λέλυκε	λελύκασι(ν)	λέλυται	λέλυνται
Pluperfect				
1st	ἐλελύκην	ἐλελύκεμεν	ἐλελύμην	ἐλελύμεθα
2nd	ἐλελύκης	ἐλελύκετε	ἐλέλυσο	ἐλέλυσθε
3rd	ἐλελύκει(ν)	ἐλελύκεσαν	ἐλέλυτο	ἐλέλυντο
SUBJUNCTIVE				
1st	λελυκώς ὦ	λελυκότες ὦμεν	λελυμένος ὦ	λελυμένοι ὦμεν
2nd	λελυκώς ᾖς	λελυκότες ἦτε	λελυμένος ᾖς	λελυμένοι ἦτε
3rd	λελυκώς ᾖ	λελυκότες ὦσι(ν)	λελυμένος ᾖ	λελυμένοι ὦσι(ν)
OPTATIVE				
1st	λελυκώς εἴην	λελυκότες εἶμεν	λελυμένος εἴην	λελυμένοι εἶμεν
2nd	λελυκώς εἴης	λελυκότες εἶτε	λελυμένος εἴης	λελυμένοι εἶτε
3rd	λελυκώς εἴη	λελυκότες εἶεν	λελυμένος εἴη	λελυμένοι εἶεν
IMPERATIVE				
2nd	λελυκώς ἴσθι	λελυκότες ἔστε	λέλυσο	λέλυσθε
3rd	λελυκώς ἔστω	λελυκότες ἔστων	λελύσθω	λελύσθων
INFINITIVE	λελυκέναι		λελύσθαι	
PARTICIPLE	λελυκώς, -κυῖα, -κός		λελυμένος, -μένη, -μενον	

CONTRACT THEMATIC VERBS

PRESENT SYSTEM

	SINGULAR		PLURAL	
	Active		**Middle/Passive**	

φιλέω

INDICATIVE

Present

	Active		Middle/Passive	
1st	φιλῶ	φιλοῦμεν	φιλοῦμαι	φιλούμεθα
2nd	φιλεῖς	φιλεῖτε	φιλεῖ	φιλεῖσθε
3rd	φιλεῖ	φιλοῦσι(ν)	φιλεῖται	φιλοῦνται

Imperfect

1st	ἐφίλουν	ἐφιλοῦμεν	ἐφιλούμην	ἐφιλούμεθα
2nd	ἐφίλεις	ἐφιλεῖτε	ἐφιλοῦ	ἐφιλεῖσθε
3rd	ἐφίλει	ἐφίλουν	ἐφιλεῖτο	ἐφιλοῦντο

SUBJUNCTIVE

1st	φιλῶ	φιλῶμεν	φιλῶμαι	φιλώμεθα
2nd	φιλῇς	φιλῆτε	φιλῇ	φιλῆσθε
3rd	φιλῇ	φιλῶσι(ν)	φιλῆται	φιλῶνται

OPTATIVE

1st	φιλοίην	φιλοῖμεν / φιλοίημεν	φιλοίμην	φιλοίμεθα
2nd	φιλοίης	φιλοῖτε / φιλοίητε	φιλοῖο	φιλοῖσθε
3rd	φιλοίη	φιλοῖεν / φιλοίησαν	φιλοῖτο	φιλοῖντο

IMPERATIVE

2nd	φίλει	φιλεῖτε	φιλοῦ	φιλεῖσθε
3rd	φιλείτω	φιλούντων	φιλείσθω	φιλείσθων

INFINITIVE	φιλεῖν	φιλεῖσθαι
PARTICIPLE	φιλῶν, -οῦσα, -οῦν	φιλούμενος, -μένη, -μενον

τιμάω

INDICATIVE

Present

	Active		Middle/Passive	
1st	τιμῶ	τιμῶμεν	τιμῶμαι	τιμώμεθα
2nd	τιμᾷς	τιμᾶτε	τιμᾷ	τιμᾶσθε
3rd	τιμᾷ	τιμῶσι(ν)	τιμᾶται	τιμῶνται

Imperfect

1st	ἐτίμων	ἐτιμῶμεν	ἐτιμώμην	ἐτιμώμεθα
2nd	ἐφίλεις	ἐτιμᾶτε	ἐτιμῶ	ἐτιμᾶσθε
3rd	ἐφίλει	ἐτίμων	ἐτιμᾶτο	ἐτιμῶντο

SUBJUNCTIVE

1st	τιμῶ	τιμῶμεν	τιμῶμαι	τιμώμεθα
2nd	τιμᾷς	τιμᾶτε	τιμᾷ	τιμᾶσθε
3rd	τιμᾷ	τιμῶσι(ν)	φιλῆται	τιμῶνται

OPTATIVE

1st	τιμῴην	τιμῷμεν / τιμῴημεν	τιμῴμην	τιμῴμεθα
2nd	τιμῴης	τιμῷτε / τιμῴητε	τιμῷ	τιμῷσθε
3rd	τιμῴη	τιμῷεν / τιμῴησαν	τιμῷτο	τιμῷντο

IMPERATIVE

2nd	τίμα	τιμᾶτε	τιμῶ	τιμᾶσθε
3rd	τιμάτω	τιμώντων	τιμάσθω	τιμάσθων

INFINITIVE   τιμᾶν   τιμᾶσθαι

PARTICIPLE   τιμῶν, -οῦσα, -ῶν   τιμώμενος, -μένη, -μενον

δηλόω

INDICATIVE

Present

1st	δηλῶ	δηλοῦμεν	δηλοῦμαι	δηλούμεθα
2nd	δηλοῖς	δηλοῦτε	δηλοῖ	δηλοῦσθε
3rd	δηλοῖ	δηλοῦσι(ν)	δηλοῦται	δηλοῦνται

Imperfect

1st	ἐδήλουν	ἐδηλοῦμεν	ἐδηλούμην	ἐδηλούμεθα
2nd	ἐδήλους	ἐδηλοῦτε	ἐδηλοῦ	ἐδηλοῦσθε
3rd	ἐδήλου	ἐδήλουν	ἐδηλοῦτο	ἐδηλοῦντο

SUBJUNCTIVE

1st	δηλῶ	δηλῶμεν	δηλῶμαι	δηλώμεθα
2nd	δηλῷς	δηλῶτε	δηλῷ	δηλῶσθε
3rd	δηλῷ	δηλῶσι(ν)	δηλῶται	δηλῶνται

OPTATIVE

1st	δηλοίην	δηλοῖμεν / δηλοίημεν	δηλοίμην	δηλοίμεθα
2nd	δηλοίης	δηλοῖτε / δηλοίητε	δηλοῖο	δηλοῖσθε
3rd	δηλοίη	δηλοῖεν / δηλοίησαν	δηλοῖτο	δηλοῖντο

IMPERATIVE

2nd	δήλου	δηλοῦτε	δηλοῦ	δηλοῦσθε
3rd	δηλούτω	δηλούντων	δηλούσθω	δηλούσθων

INFINITIVE   δηλοῦν   δηλοῦσθαι

PARTICIPLE   δηλῶν, οῦσα, -οῦν   δηλούμενος, -μένη, -μενον

REGULAR ATHEMATIC VERBS

PRESENT SYSTEM

	SINGULAR	PLURAL	SINGULAR	PLURAL
	Active		**Middle/Passive**	
		δείκνυμι		

INDICATIVE

Present

	SINGULAR	PLURAL	SINGULAR	PLURAL
1st	δείκνυμι	δείκνυμεν	δείκνυμαι	δεικνύμεθα
2nd	δείκνυς	δείκνυτε	δείκνυσαι	δείκνυσθε
3rd	δείκνυσι(ν)	δεικνύασι(ν)	δείκνυται	δείκνυνται

Imperfect

1st	ἐδείκνυν	ἐδείκνυμεν	ἐδεικνύμην	ἐδεικνύμεθα
2nd	ἐδείκνυς	ἐδείκνυτε	ἐδείκνυσο	ἐδείκνυσθε
3rd	ἐδείκνυ	ἐδείκνυσαν	ἐδείκνυτο	ἐδείκνυντο

SUBJUNCTIVE

1st	δεικνύω	δεικνύωμεν	δεικνύωμαι	δεικνυώμεθα
2nd	δεικνύῃς	δεικνύητε	δεικνύῃ	δεικνύησθε
3rd	δεικνύῃ	δεικνύωσι(ν)	δεικνύηται	δεικνύωνται

OPTATIVE

1st	δεικνύοιμι	δεικνύοιμεν	δεικνυοίμην	δεικνυοίμεθα
2nd	δεικνύοις	δεικνύοιτε	δεικνύοιο	δεικνύοισθε
3rd	δεικνύοι	δεικνύοιεν	δεικνύοιτο	δεικνύοιντο

IMPERATIVE

2nd	δείκνυ	δείκνυτε	δείκνυσο	δείκνυσθε
3rd	δεικνύτω	δεικνύντων	δεικνύσθω	δεικνύσθων

INFINITIVE	δεικνύναι		δεικνύσθαι	
PARTICIPLE	δεικνύς, -νῦσα, -νύν		δεικνύμενος, -μένη, -μενον	

τίθημι

INDICATIVE

Present

	SINGULAR	PLURAL	SINGULAR	PLURAL
1st	τίθημι	τίθεμεν	τίθεμαι	τιθέμεθα
2nd	τίθης	τίθετε	τίθεσαι	τίθεσθε
3rd	τίθησι(ν)	τιθέασι(ν)	τίθεται	τίθενται

Imperfect

1st	ἐτίθην	ἐτίθεμεν	ἐτιθέμην	ἐτιθέμεθα
2nd	ἐτίθης	ἐτίθετε	ἐτίθεσο	ἐτίθεσθε
3rd	ἐτίθη	ἐτίθεσαν	ἐτίθετο	ἐτίθεντο

SUBJUNCTIVE

1st	τιθῶ	τιθῶμεν	τιθῶμαι	τιθώμεθα
2nd	τιθῇς	τιθῆτε	τιθῇ	τιθῆσθε
3rd	τιθῇ	τιθῶσι(ν)	τιθῆται	τιθῶνται

OPTATIVE

1st	τιθείην	τιθεῖμεν/τιθείημεν	τιθείμην	τιθείμεθα
2nd	τιθείης	τιθεῖτε/τιθείητε	τιθεῖο	τιθεῖσθε
3rd	τιθείη	τιθεῖεν/τιθείησαν	τιθεῖτο	τιθεῖντο

IMPERATIVE

2nd	τίθει	τίθετε	τίθεσο	τίθεσθε
3rd	τιθέτω	τιθέντων	τιθέσθω	τιθέσθων

INFINITIVE   τιθέναι   τιθέσθαι

PARTICIPLE   τιθείς, τιθεῖσα, τιθέν   τιθέμενος, -μένη, -μενον
τιθέντος, etc.   τιθεμένου, etc.

ἵστημι

INDICATIVE

Present

1st	ἵστημι	ἵσταμεν	ἵσταμαι	ἱστάμεθα
2nd	ἵστης	ἵστατε	ἵστασαι	ἵστασθε
3rd	ἵστησι(ν)	ἱστᾶσι(ν)	ἵσταται	ἵστανται

Imperfect

1st	ἵστην	ἵσταμεν	ἱστάμην	ἱστάμεθα
2nd	ἵστης	ἵστατε	ἵστασο	ἵστασθε
3rd	ἵστη	ἵστασαν	ἵστατο	ἵσταντο

SUBJUNCTIVE

1st	ἱστῶ	ἱστῶμεν	ἱστῶμαι	ἱστώμεθα
2nd	ἱστῇς	ἱστῆτε	ἱστῇ	ἱστῆσθε
3rd	ἱστῇ	ἱστῶσι(ν)	ἱστῆται	ἱστῶνται

OPTATIVE

1st	ἱσταίην	ἱσταῖμεν/ἱσταίημεν	ἱσταίμην	ἱσταίμεθα
2nd	ἱσταίης	ἱσταῖτε/ἱσταίητε	ἱσταῖο	ἱσταῖσθε
3rd	ἱσταίη	ἱσταῖεν/ἱσταίησαν	ἱσταῖτο	ἱσταῖντο

IMPERATIVE

2nd	ἵστη	ἵστατε	ἵστασο	ἵστασθε
3rd	ἱστάτω	ἱστάντων	ἱστάσθω	ἱστάσθων

INFINITIVE   ἱστάναι   ἱστάσθαι

PARTICIPLE   ἱστάς, ἱστᾶσα, ἱστάν   ἱστάμενος, -μένη, -μενον
ἱστάντος, etc.   ἱσταμένου, etc.

δίδωμι

INDICATIVE

Present

1st	δίδωμι	δίδομεν	δίδομαι	διδόμεθα
2nd	δίδως	δίδοτε	δίδοσαι	δίδοσθε
3rd	δίδωσι(ν)	διδόασι(ν)	δίδοται	δίδονται

Imperfect

1st	ἐδίδουν	ἐδίδομεν	ἐδιδόμην	ἐδιδόμεθα
2nd	ἐδίδους	ἐδίδοτε	ἐδίδοσο	ἐδίδοσθε
3rd	ἐδίδου	ἐδίδοσαν	ἐδίδοτο	ἐδίδοντο

SUBJUNCTIVE

1st	διδῶ	διδῶμεν	διδῶμαι	διδώμεθα
2nd	διδῷς	διδῶτε	διδῷ	διδῶσθε
3rd	διδῷ	διδῶσι(ν)	διδῶται	διδῶνται

	SINGULAR	PLURAL	SINGULAR	PLURAL
	Active		**Middle/Passive**	
		δίδωμι		

OPTATIVE

1st	διδοίην	διδοῖμεν/διδοίημεν	διδοίμην	διδοίμεθα
2nd	διδοίης	διδοῖτε/διδοίητε	διδοῖο	διδοῖσθε
3rd	διδοίη	διδοῖεν/διδοίησαν	διδοῖτο	διδοῖντο

IMPERATIVE

2nd	δίδου	δίδοτε	δίδοσο	δίδοσθε
3rd	διδότω	διδόντων	διδόσθω	διδόσθων

INFINITIVE   διδόναι   διδόσθαι

PARTICIPLE   διδούς, διδοῦσα, διδόν   διδόμενος, -μένη, -μενον
               διδόντος, etc.   διδομένου, etc.

ἵημι

INDICATIVE

Present

1st	ἵημι	ἵεμεν	ἵεμαι	ἱέμεθα
2nd	ἵης	ἵετε	ἵεσαι	ἵεσθε
3rd	ἵησι(ν)	ἱᾶσι(ν)	ἵεται	ἵενται

Imperfect

1st	ἵην	ἵεμεν	ἱέμην	ἱέμεθα
2nd	ἵεις	ἵετε	ἵεσο	ἵεσθε
3rd	ἵει	ἵεσαν	ἵετο	ἵεντο

SUBJUNCTIVE

1st	ἱῶ	ἱῶμεν	ἱῶμαι	ἱώμεθα
2nd	ἱῇς	ἱῆτε	ἱῇ	ἱῆσθε
3rd	ἱῇ	ἱῶσι(ν)	ἱῆται	ἱῶνται

OPTATIVE

1st	ἱείην	ἱεῖμεν/ἱείημεν	ἱείμην	ἱείμεθα
2nd	ἱείης	ἱεῖτε/ἱείητε	ἱεῖο	ἱεῖσθε
3rd	ἱείη	ἱεῖεν/ἱείησαν	ἱεῖτο	ἱεῖντο

IMPERATIVE

2nd	ἵει	ἵετε	ἵεσο	ἵεσθε
3rd	ἱέτω	ἱέντων	ἱέσθω	ἱέσθων

INFINITIVE   ἱέναι   ἵεσθαι

PARTICIPLE   ἱείς, ἱεῖσα, ἱέν   ἱέμενος, -μένη, -μενον

AORIST SYSTEM

		SINGULAR	PLURAL	SINGULAR	PLURAL
		Active		**Middle**	
		τίθημι			
INDICATIVE					
	1st	ἔθηκα	ἔθεμεν	ἐθέμην	ἐθέμεθα
	2nd	ἔθηκας	ἔθετε	ἔθου	ἔθεσθε
	3rd	ἔθηκε(ν)	ἔθεσαν	ἔθετο	ἔθεντο
SUBJUNCTIVE					
	1st	θῶ	θῶμεν	θῶμαι	θώμεθα
	2nd	θῇς	θῆτε	θῇ	θῆσθε
	3rd	θῇ	θῶσι(ν)	θῆται	θῶνται
OPTATIVE					
	1st	θείην	θεῖμεν/θείημεν	θείμην	θείμεθα
	2nd	θείης	θεῖτε/θείητε	θεῖο	θεῖσθε
	3rd	θείη	θεῖεν/θείησαν	θεῖτο	θεῖντο
IMPERATIVE					
	2nd	θές	θέτε	θοῦ	θέσθε
	3rd	θέτω	θέντων	θέσθω	θέσθων
INFINITIVE		θεῖναι		θέσθαι	
PARTICIPLE		θείς, θεῖσα, θέν θέντος, etc.		θέμενος, -μένη, -μενον θεμένου, etc.	

ἵστημι (Strong Aorist)

		SINGULAR	PLURAL
		Active	
INDICATIVE			
	1st	ἔστην	ἔστημεν
	2nd	ἔστης	ἔστητε
	3rd	ἔστη	ἔστησαν
SUBJUNCTIVE			
	1st	στῶ	στῶμεν
	2nd	στῇς	στῆτε
	3rd	στῇ	στῶσι(ν)
OPTATIVE			
	1st	σταίην	σταῖμεν/σταίημεν
	2nd	σταίης	σταῖτε/σταίητε
	3rd	σταίη	σταῖεν/σταίησαν
IMPERATIVE			
	2nd	στῆθι	στῆτε
	3rd	στήτω	στάντων
INFINITIVE		στῆναι	
PARTICIPLE		στάς, στᾶσα, στάν στάντος, etc.	

	SINGULAR	PLURAL	SINGULAR	PLURAL
	Active		**Middle**	

δίδωμι

		SINGULAR	PLURAL	SINGULAR	PLURAL
INDICATIVE					
	1st	ἔδωκα	ἔδομεν	ἐδόμην	ἐδόμεθα
	2nd	ἔδωκας	ἔδοτε	ἔδου	ἔδοσθε
	3rd	ἔδωκε(ν)	ἔδοσαν	ἔδοτο	ἔδοντο
SUBJUNCTIVE					
	1st	δῶ	δῶμεν	δῶμαι	δώμεθα
	2nd	δῷς	δῶτε	δῷ	δῶσθε
	3rd	δῷ	δῶσι(ν)	δῶται	δῶνται
OPTATIVE					
	1st	δοίην	δοῖμεν/δοίημεν	δοίμην	δοίμεθα
	2nd	δοίης	δοῖτε/δοίητε	δοῖο	δοῖσθε
	3rd	δοίη	δοῖεν/δοίησαν	δοῖτο	δοῖντο
IMPERATIVE					
	2nd	δός	δότε	δοῦ	δόσθε
	3rd	δότω	δόντων	δόσθω	δόσθων

INFINITIVE　　δοῦναι　　　　　　　δόσθαι

PARTICIPLE　　δούς, δοῦσα, δόν　　　δόμενος, -μένη, -μενον
　　　　　　　　δόντος, etc.　　　　　δομένου, etc.

ἵημι

		SINGULAR	PLURAL	SINGULAR	PLURAL
INDICATIVE					
	1st	ἧκα	εἷμεν	εἵμην	εἵμεθα
	2nd	ἧκας	εἷτε	εἷο	εἷσθε
	3rd	ἧκε(ν)	εἷσαν	εἷτο	εἷντο
SUBJUNCTIVE					
	1st	ὦ	ὦμεν	ὦμαι	ὥμεθα
	2nd	ᾖς	ἧτε	ᾖ	ἧσθε
	3rd	ᾖ	ὦσι(ν)	ἧται	ὦνται
OPTATIVE					
	1st	εἵην	εἷμεν/εἵημεν	εἵμην	εἵμεθα
	2nd	εἵης	εἷτε/εἵητε	εἷο	εἷσθε
	3rd	εἵη	εἷεν/εἵησαν	εἷτο	εἷντο
IMPERATIVE					
	2nd	ἕς	ἕτε	οὗ	ἕσθε
	3rd	ἕτω	ἕντων	ἕσθω	ἕσθων

INFINITIVE　　εἷναι　　　　　　　ἕσθαι

PARTICIPLE　　εἵς, εἷσα, ἕν　　　　ἕμενος, -μένη, -μενον

IRREGULAR -μι VERBS

	SINGULAR	PLURAL	SINGULAR	PLURAL
	εἰμί, be		**εἶμι, go**	
INDICATIVE				
Present				
1st	εἰμί	ἐσμεν	εἶμι	ἴμεν
2nd	εἶ	ἐστέ	εἶ(ς)	ἴτε
3rd	ἐστί(ν)	εἰσί(ν)	εἶσι(ν)	ἴᾱσι(ν)
Imperfect				
1st	ἦν	ἦμεν	ἦα/ἤειν	ἦμεν
2nd	ἦσθα	ἦτε	ἤεισθα	ἦτε
3rd	ἦν	ἦσαν	ἤειν/ἤει	ἦσαν/ἤεσαν
SUBJUNCTIVE				
1st	ὦ	ὦμεν	ἴω	ἴωμεν
2nd	ᾖς	ἦτε	ἴῃς	ἴητε
3rd	ᾖ	ὦσι(ν)	ἴῃ	ἴωσι(ν)
OPTATIVE				
1st	εἴην	εἶμεν/εἴημεν	ἴοιμι	ἴοιμεν
2nd	εἴης	εἶτε/εἴητε	ἴοις	ἴοιτε
3rd	εἴη	εἶεν/εἴησαν	ἴοι	ἴοιεν
IMPERATIVE				
2nd	ἴσθι	ἔστε	ἴθι	ἴτε
3rd	ἔστω	ἔστων/ὄντων	ἴτω	ἰόντων
INFINITIVE	εἶναι		ἰέναι	
PARTICIPLE	ὤν, οὖσα, ὄν		ἰών, ἰοῦσα, ἰόν	

	SINGULAR	PLURAL	SINGULAR	PLURAL
	οἶδα		**φημί**	

INDICATIVE

Perfect   **Present**

1st	οἶδα	ἴσμεν	φημί	φαμέν
2nd	οἶσθα	ἴστε	φής	φατέ
3rd	οἶδε(ν)	ἴσᾱσι(ν)	φησί(ν)	φᾱσί(ν)

Pluperfect   **Imperfect**

1st	ᾔδη/ᾔδειν	ᾖσμεν/ᾔδεμεν	ἔφην	ἔφαμεν
2nd	ᾔδησθα/ᾔδεις	ᾖστε/ᾔδετε	ἔφησθα/ἔφης	ἔφατε
3rd	ᾔδει(ν)	ᾖσαν/ᾔδεσαν	ἔφη	ἔφασαν

SUBJUNCTIVE

1st	εἰδῶ	εἰδῶμεν	φῶ	φῶμεν
2nd	εἰδῇς	εἰδῆτε	φῇς	φῆτε
3rd	εἰδῇ	εἰδῶσι(ν)	φῇ	φῶσι(ν)

OPTATIVE

1st	εἰδείην	εἰδεῖμεν/εἰδείημεν	φαίην	φαῖμεν/φαίημεν
2nd	εἰδείης	εἰδεῖτε/εἰδείητε	φαίης	φαῖτε/φαίητε
3rd	εἰδείη	εἰδεῖεν/εἰδείησαν	φαίη	φαῖεν/φαίησαν

IMPERATIVE

2nd	ἴσθι	ἴστε	φάθι, φαθί	φάτε
3rd	ἴστω	ἴστων	φάτω	φάντων

INFINITIVE   εἰδέναι   φάναι

PARTICIPLE   εἰδώς, εἰδυῖα, εἰδός   φάς, φᾶσα, φάν

VERB ENDING CHART (REGULAR VERBS)

PRESENT

	Indicative		Subjunctive		Optative	
	A	M/P	A	M/P	A	M/P
I	-ω	-ομαι	-ω	-ωμαι	-οιμι	-οιμην
you (s.)	-εις	-η/-ει	-ης	-η	-οις	-οιο
he	-ει	-εται	-η	-ηται	-οι	-οιτο
we	-ομεν	-ομεθα	-ωμεν	-ωμεθα	-οιμεν	-οιμεθα
you (pl.)	-ετε	-εσθε	-ητε	-ησθε	-οιτε	-οισθε
they	-ουσι	-ονται	-ωσι	-νται	-οιεν	-οιντο
inf.	-ειν	-εσθαι				
part.	-ων	-ομενος				

FUTURE

	Indicative						Optative		
	A	M	P				A	M	P
I	-σω	-σομαι	-θησομαι	——	——	——	-σοιμι	-σοιμην	-θησοιμην
you (s.)	-σεις	-ση/-ει	-θηση/-ει	——	——	——	-σοις	-σοιο	-θησοιο
he/she/it	-σει	-σεται	-θησεται	——	——	——	-σοι	-σοιτο	-θησοιτο
we	-σομεν	-σομεθα	-θησομεθα	——	——	——	-σοιμεν	-σοιμεθα	-θησοιμεθα
you (pl.)	-σετε	-σεσθε	-θησεσθε	——	——	——	-σοιτε	-σοισθε	-θησοισθε
they	-σουσι	-σονται	-θησονται	——	——	——	-σοιεν	-σοιντο	-θησοιντο
inf.	-σειν	-σεσθαι	-θησεσθαι	——	——	——			
part.	-σων	-σομενος	-θησομενος	——	——	——			

AORIST

	Indicative			Subjunctive			Optative		
	A	M	P	A	M	P	A	M	P
I	-σα	-σαμην	-θην	-σω	-σωμαι	-θω	-σαιμι	-σαιμην	-θειην
you (s.)	-σας	-σω	-θης	-σης	-ση	-θης	-σαις	-σαιο	-θειης
he/she/it	-σε	-σατο	-θη	-ση	-σηται	-θη	-σαι	-σαιτο	-θειη
we	-σαμεν	-σαμεθα	-θημεν	-σωμεν	-σωμεθα	-θωμεν	-σαιμεν	-σαιμεθα	-θειμεν
you (pl.)	-σατε	-σασθε	-θητε	-σητε	-σησθε	-θητε	-σαιτε	-σαισθε	-θειτε
they	-σαν	-σαντο	-θησαν	-σωσι	-σωνται	-θωσι	-σαιεν	-σαιντο	-θειεν
inf.	-σαι	-σασθαι	-θηναι						
part.	-σας	-σαμενος	-θεις						

PERFECT

	Indicative		Subjunctive		Optative	
	A	M/P	A	M/P	A	M/P
I	.ε. -κα	.ε. -μαι	-κως ὦ	-μενος ὦ	-κως εἴην	-μενος εἴην
you (s.)	.ε. -κας	.ε. -σαι	-κως ῇς	-μενος ῇς	-κως εἴης	-μενος εἴης
he	.ε. -κε	.ε. -ται	-κως ῇ	-μενος ῇ	-κως εἴη	-μενος εἴη
we	.ε. -καμεν	.ε. -μεθα	-κοτες ὦμεν	-μενοι ὦμεν	-κοτες εἶμεν	-μενοι εἶμεν
you (pl.)	.ε. -κατε	.ε. -σθε	-κοτες ἦτε	-μενοι ἦτε	-κοτες εἶτε	-μενοι εἶτε
they	.ε. -κασι	.ε. -νται	-κοτες ὦσι	-μενοι ὦσι	-κοτες εἶεν	-μενοι εἶεν
inf.	.ε. -κεναι	.ε. -σθαι				
part.	.ε. -κως	.ε. -μενος				

INDICATIVE

	Present A	Present M/P	Imperfect A	Imperfect M/P	Future A	Future M	Future P	Aorist A	Aorist M	Aorist P	Perfect A	Perfect M/P
I	-ω	-ομαι	-ον	-ομην	-σω	-σομαι	-θησομαι	-σα	-σαμην	-θην	ε.-κα	ε.-μαι
you (s.)	-εις	-ῃ/-ει	-ες	-ου	-σεις	-σῃ/-σει	-θησῃ/-θησει	-σας	-σω	-θης	ε.-κας	ε.-ῤσαι
he/she/it	-ει	-εται	-ε	-ετο	-σει	-σεται	-θησεται	-σε	-σατο	-θη	ε.-κε	ε.-ται
we	-ομεν	-ομεθα	-ομεν	-ομεθα	-σομεν	-σομεθα	-θησομεθα	-σαμεν	-σαμεθα	-θημεν	ε.-καμεν	ε.-μεθα
you (pl.)	-ετε	-εσθε	-ετε	-εσθε	-σετε	-σεσθε	-θησεσθε	-σατε	-σασθε	-θητε	ε.-κατε	ε.-σθε
they	-ουσι	-ονται	-ον	-οντο	-σουσι	-σονται	-θησονται	-σαν	-σαντο	-θησαν	ε.-κασι	ε.-νται
	loose	ransom/ am loosed	was loosing	was ransoming/ was being loosed	will loose	will ransom	will be ransomed	loosed	ransomed	was loosed	have loosed	have ransomed/ have been loosed

SUBJUNCTIVE

	Present A	Present M/P	Imperfect A	Imperfect M/P	Future A	Future M	Future P	Aorist A	Aorist M	Aorist P	Perfect A	Perfect M/P
I	-ω	-ωμαι	—	—	—	—	—	-σω	-σωμαι	-θω	ε.-κως ὦ	ε.-μενος ὦ
you (s.)	-ῃς	-ῃ	—	—	—	—	—	-σῃς	-σῃ	-θῃς	ε.-κως ῃς	ε.-μενος ῃς
he/she/it	-ῃ	-ηται	—	—	—	—	—	-σῃ	-σηται	-θῃ	ε.-κως ῃ	ε.-μενος ῃ
we	-ωμεν	-ωμεθα	—	—	—	—	—	-σωμεν	-σωμεθα	-θωμεν	ε.-κοτες ὦμεν	ε.-μενοι ὦμεν
you (pl.)	-ητε	-ησθε	—	—	—	—	—	-σητε	-σησθε	-θητε	ε.-κοτες ῃτε	ε.-μενοι ῃτε
they	-ωσι	-ωνται	—	—	—	—	—	-σωσι	-σωνται	-θωσι	ε.-κοτες ὦσι	ε.-μενοι ὦσι

OPTATIVE

	Present		Imperfect		Future			Aorist			Perfect	
	A	M/P	A	M/P	A	M	P	A	M	P	A	M/P
I	-οιμι	-οιμην	——	——	-σοιμι	-σοιμην	-θησοιμην	-σαιμι	-σαιμην	-θειην	ἐ. -κως εἴην	ἐ. -μενος εἴην
you (s.)	-οις	-οιο	——	——	-σοις	-σοιο	-θησοιο	-σαις	-σαιο	-θειης	ἐ. -κως εἴης	ἐ. -μενος εἴης
he/she/it	-οι	-οιτο	——	——	-σοι	-σοιτο	-θησοιτο	-σαι	-σαιτο	-θειη	ἐ. -κως εἴη	ἐ. -μενος εἴη
we	-οιμεν	-οιμεθα	——	——	-σοιμεν	-σοιμεθα	-θησοιμεθα	-σαιμεν	-σαιμεθα	-θειημεν	ἐ. -κοτες εἴημεν	ἐ. -μενοι εἴημεν
you (pl.)	-οιτε	-οισθε	——	——	-σοιτε	-σοισθε	-θησοισθε	-σαιτε	-σαισθε	-θειτε	ἐ. -κοτες εἴτε	ἐ. -μενοι εἴτε
they	-οιεν	-οιντο	——	——	-σοιεν	-σοιντο	-θησοιντο	-σαιεν	-σαιντο	-θειεν	ἐ. -κοτες εἶεν	ἐ. -μενοι εἶεν

INFINITIVE / PARTICIPLE

	Present		Imperfect		Future			Aorist			Perfect	
	A	M/P	A	M/P	A	M	P	A	M	P	A	M/P
infinitive	-ειν	-εσθαι	——	——	-σειν	-σεσθαι	-θησεσθαι	-σαι	-σασθαι	-θηναι	ἐ. -κεναι	ἐ. -σθαι
participle	-ων	-ομενος	——	——	-σων	-σομενος	-θησομενος	-σας	-σαμενος	-θεις	ἐ. -κως	ἐ. -μενος

Greek–English Vocabulary

The first appearance of a word in a lesson vocabulary is given in parentheses. Words that appear only in reading exercises are not so marked. Principal parts are given for simple verbs; they are only given for compounds when the uncompounded version is not in the vocabulary. A dash preceding a form indicates that the form only exists in compounds.

ἀγαθός, -ή, -όν, good (7)

ἄγαλμα, -ατος, τό, statue, image

Ἀγαμέμνων, -ονος, ὁ, Agamemnon

ἀγγεῖον, -ου, τό, vessel

ἀγγέλλω, ἀγγελῶ, ἤγγειλα, ἤγγελκα, ἤγγελμαι, ἠγγέλθην, announce (7)

ἄγγελος, -ου, ὁ, messenger (20)

ἄγκιστρον, -ου, τό, hook

ἀγορά, -ᾶς, ἡ, marketplace (3)

ἄγω, ἄξω, ἤγαγον, ἦχα, ἦγμαι, ἤχθην, lead, bring (2)

ἀγών, -ῶνος, ὁ, contest, game (10)

ἀδικέω, ἀδικήσω, etc., do wrong, be unjust, wrong (someone) (30)

ἀδικία, -ας, ἡ, injustice, wrongdoing

Ἄδμητος, -ου, ὁ, Admetus (12)

ἀδύνατος, -ον, impossible

ἀεί, always (4)

ἀείδω, ἀείσομαι, ᾖσα (*part.* ἀείσας), ᾖσμαι, ᾔσθην, sing

Ἀθήναζε, to Athens (12)

Ἀθῆναι, -ῶν, αἱ, Athens (4)

Ἀθηναῖος, -ου, ὁ, an Athenian (5)

Ἀθήνη, -ης, ἡ, Athene (4)

Ἀθήνηθεν, from Athens (12)

ἆθλον, -ου, τό, prize (16)

ἀθροίζω, ἀθροίσω, ἤθροισα, ἤθροικα, ἤθροισμα, ἠθροίσθην, collect

ἀθυμέω, be disheartened

ἀθυμία, -ας, ἡ, despondency

Αἴγινα, -ης, ἡ, Aegina

Αἰγινήτης, -ου, ὁ, an Aeginetan

Αἰγύπτιος, -ου, ὁ, an Egyptian (26)

Αἴγυπτος, -ου, ἡ, Egypt

αἴθω, burn

αἴξ, αἰγός, ὁ/ἡ, goat (10)

αἱρέω, αἱρήσω, εἷλον, ᾕρηκα, ᾕρημαι, ᾑρέθην, take, capture (21)

αἰσθάνομαι, αἰσθήσομαι, ᾐσθόμην, ᾔσθημαι, perceive (28)

αἴσχιστος, -η, -ον, *sup. of* αἰσχρός (22)

αἰσχίων, αἴσχιον, more shameful, *comp. of* αἰσχρός (22)

αἰσχρός, -ά, -όν, shameful, disgraceful (16)

αἰτέω, αἰτήσω, ᾔτησα, ᾔτηκα, ᾔτημαι, ask for, demand (26)

αἰχμάλωτος, -ου, ὁ, prisoner (of war) (11)

αἰχμή, -ῆς, ἡ, spear, spear point

ἀκούω, ἀκούσομαι, ἤκουσα, ἀκήκοα, ἤκουσμαι, ἠκούσθην, hear, listen to, (+ *acc. thing,* + *gen. person*) (10)

ἄκρου, -ου, τό, peak

ἀκρόπολις, -εως, ἡ, acropolis, citadel (28)

ἀκτή, -ῆς, ἡ, shore

ἄλγος, -ους, τό, pain, grief

ἀληθής, -ές, true (19)

ἀληθῆ, τά, the truth (19)

ἁλιεύς, -έως, ὁ, fisherman (19)

Ἁλικαρνασσεύς, -εως, ὁ, a Halicarnassian

Ἄλκηστις, -ιδος, ἡ, Alcestis (15)

ἀλλά, but (2)

ἀλλήλων, -ων, -ων, each other (23)

ἄλλος, -η, -ο, other, another (9); ὁ ἄλλος, the rest (of)

ἄλλως, otherwise

Ἅλυς, -υος, ὁ, Halys river

ἅμα, at the same time

ἄμαξα, -ης, ἡ, wagon (3)

Ἄμασις, -ιος, ὁ, Amasis (19)

ἀμείνων, ἄμεινον, better, *comp. of* ἀγαθός (22)

ἄμιλλα, -ης, ἡ, contest (3)

ἀμφίβληστρον, -ου, τό, net (26)

ἀμφότερος, -α, -ον, both

ἄν, conditional particle (11)

ἀναβαίνω, mount, climb (up) (12)

ἀναγιγνώσκω, read
ἀναγκάζω, ἀναγκάσω, ἠνάγκασα, ἠνάγκακα,
   ἠνάγκασμαι, ἠναγκάσθην, compel (10)
ἀναγκαῖος, -α, -ον, necessary (21)
ἀνάγκη, -ης, ἡ, necessity
ἀναγνωρίζω, recognize
ἀνάγω, put out to sea
ἀναλαμβάνω, take up
ἀναλίσκω, ἀναλώσω, ἀνήλωσα, ἀνήλωκα,
   ἀνήλωμαι, ἀνηλώθην, spend (money) (21)
ἀναξυρίδες, -ων, αἱ, trousers
ἀναχωρέω, retreat (22)
ἀνδράποδον, -ου, τό, slave
ἀνδρεία, -ας, ἡ, courage, bravery (13)
ἀνδρεῖος, -α, -ον, brave (7)
ἀνδρείως, bravely
ἄνεμος, -ου, ὁ, wind
ἀνεξέταστος, -ον, unexamined
ἄνευ, without (+ gen.)
ἀνήρ, ἀνδρός, ὁ, man, husband (10)
ἄνθρωπος, -ου, ὁ, man, human (7)
ἀνόσιος, -α, -ον, wicked, unholy
ἀνταιτέω, ask for in return
ἀντέχω, hold out, resist
ἀντί, instead of (+ gen.)
ἄνω, above
ἄξιος, -α, -ον, worthy (9)
ἀπάγω, lead away, bring back (12)
ἀπαλλάσσομαι, get rid of (+ gen.)
ἀπειθέω, disobey (+ dat.)
ἄπειμι (εἰμί, 'be'), be absent (11)
ἄπειμι (εἶμι, 'go'), go away
ἀπελαύνω, drive away (11), march away
ἀπέρχομαι, depart (25)
ἀπιστία, -ας, ἡ, disbelief
ἀπό, from (+ gen.) (4)
ἀποβαίνω, go away, disembark
ἀποβάλλω, throw away (23);
   ἀποβάλλομαι, be lost, be thrown away
ἀποθανεῖν, aor. inf. of ἀποθνήσκω (16)
ἀποθήκη, -ης, ἡ, storehouse, store
ἀποθνήσκω, ἀποθανοῦμαι, ἀπέθανον, die, be
   killed (9)
ἀποικία, -ας, ἡ, colony (10)
ἀποκρίνομαι, ἀποκρινοῦμαι, ἀπεκρινάμην,
   answer, reply (28)
ἀποκρύπτω, hide away (13)
ἀποκτείνω, ἀποκτενῶ, ἀπέκτεινα, kill (9)
ἀπολαμβάνω, cut off

ἀπολείπω, abandon (28)
Ἀπόλλων, -ωνος, ὁ, Apollo (23)
ἀποπέμπω, send away (20)
ἀποπλέω, sail away (25)
ἀπορέω, ἀπορήσω, ἠπόρησα, be at a loss
   (20)
ἀπορία, -ας, ἡ, difficulty, want (of something)
ἀποτέμνω, cut off
ἀποφαίνω, display
ἀποφεύγω, flee away, escape (10)
ἀποχωρέω, go away (20)
ἄπρακτος, -ον, unsuccessful
ἆρα, interrogative particle (23)
ἆρα οὐ, ἆρα μή, surely (introducing questions) (23)
Ἀργεῖοι, -ων, οἱ, Argives
ἀργύριον, -ου, τό, money
ἄργυρος, -ου, ὁ, silver
ἀργυροῦς, -ᾶ, -οῦν, of silver (16)
ἀρέσκω, ἀρέσω, ἤρεσα, ἠρέσθην, please
ἀρετή, -ῆς, ἡ, excellence (30)
ἀριθμός, -οῦ, ὁ, number
ἄριστα, best, sup. of εὖ (14)
Ἀρισταγόρας, -ου, ὁ, Aristagoras (26)
ἀριστεύω, ἀριστεύσω, etc., be best, be
   superior
ἄριστος, -η, -ον, best, sup. of ἀγαθός (14)
Ἀρίων, -ονος, ὁ, Arion (26)
Ἀρμενία, -ας, ἡ, Armenia (20)
Ἀρμένιος, -ου, ὁ, an Armenian (16)
ἁρπάζω, ἁρπάσω, ἥρπασα, ἥρπακα,
   ἥρπασμαι, ἡρπάχθην/ ἡρπάσθην, snatch
   (10)
Ἀρτεμβάρης, -ους, ὁ, Artembares
Ἀρτεμισία, -ας, ἡ, Artemisia (17)
ἀρχαῖος, -α, -ον, ancient (15)
ἀρχή, -ῆς, ἡ, rule, empire, command (19)
ἄρχω, ἄρξω, ἦρξα, ἦρχα, ἦργμαι, ἤρχθην,
   rule, command (+ gen.) (10)
ἄρχων, -οντος, ὁ, ruler, chief, magistrate
ἀσθενής, -ές, weak (19)
Ἀσία, -ας, ἡ, Asia
ἀσμένως, gladly
ἀσπίς, -ίδος, ἡ, shield (9)
ἄστυ, -εως, τό, town (13)
Ἀστυάγης, -ους, ὁ, Astyages
ἀσφαλής, -ές, safe (19)
ἀτάσθαλος, -η, -ον, presumptuous, reckless

ἀτιμάω, slight, dishonor
Ἀττική, -ῆς, ἡ, Attica (11)
Ἀττικός, -ή, -όν, Attic
αὖθις, again
αὐξάνω, αὐξήσω, ηὔξησα, ηὔξηκα, ηὔξημαι, ηὐξήθην, increase; αὐξάνομαι, grow
αὐτόμολος, -ου, ὁ, deserter
αὐτός, -ή, -ό, self (8); *in oblique cases*, him, her, it, them (8); ὁ αὐτός, the same (23)
ἄφθογγος, -ον, speechless
ἀφικνέομαι, ἀφίξομαι, ἀφικόμην, ἀφῖγμαι, arrive, reach (+ εἰς) (25)

Βαβυλών, -ῶνος, ἡ, Babylon (22)
Βαβυλώνιοι, -ων, οἱ, Babylonians
βαθύς, -εῖα, -ύ, deep (19)
βαίνω, βήσομαι, ἔβην, βέβηκα, go, walk (21)
βάλλω, βαλῶ, ἔβαλον, βέβληκα, βέβλημαι, ἐβλήθην, throw (21)
βάρβαρος, -ου, ὁ, foreigner (7)
βαρύς, -εῖα, -ύ, heavy (19)
βασίλεια, -ας, ἡ, queen
βασίλεια, -ων, τά, palace (26)
βασιλεύς, -έως, ὁ, king; *without article*, the king of Persia (14)
βασιλεύω, βασιλεύσω, ἐβασίλευσα, βεβασίλευκα, reign, be king (+ *gen.*) (4)
βέβαιος, -α, -ον, sure, trusty (15)
βία, -ας, ἡ, force; πρὸς βίαν, by force
βίβλος, -ου, ἡ, book (5)
βίος, -ου, ὁ, life (18)
βιωτός, -ή, -όν, worth living
βλάπτω, βλάψω, ἔβλαψα, βέβλαφα, βέβλαμμαι, ἐβλάβην, harm, injure, damage (6)
βλέπω, βλέψω, ἔβλεψα, βέβλεφα, βέβλεμμαι, ἐβλέφθην, look
βοάω, βοήσω/βοήσομαι, ἐβόησα, βεβόηκα, βεβόημαι, ἐβοήθην, shout (18)
βοή, -ῆς, ἡ, shout
βοήθεια, -ας, ἡ, help (20)
βοηθέω, βοηθήσω, ἐβοήθησα, βεβοήθηκα, βεβοήθημαι, ἐβοήθην, help (+ *dat.*) (18)
Βορέας, -ου, ὁ, North Wind (4)
βουκόλος, -ου, ὁ, herdsman
βουλεύω, βουλεύσω, ἐβούλευσα, βεβούλευκα, βεβούλευμαι, ἐβουλεύθην, plan (20); βουλεύομαι, deliberate (16)

βουλή, -ῆς, ἡ, plan (18)
βούλομαι, βουλήσομαι, ἐβουλησάμην, βεβούλημαι, ἐβουλήθην, want, wish, be willing (19)
βοῦς, βοός, ὁ/ἡ, ox (14)
βραδύς, -εῖα, -ύ, slow (19)
βράχιστος, -η, -ον, shortest, *sup. of* βραχύς (22)
βραχίων, βράχιον, shorter, *comp. of* βραχύς (22)
βραχύς, -εῖα, -ύ, short (19)

γάρ, for, because (*postpos.*) (8)
γαστήρ, γαστρός, ἡ, belly
γείτων, -ονος, ὁ, neighbor
Γέλων, -ωνος, ὁ, Gelon (28)
γέρων, -οντος, ὁ, old man (9)
γέφυρα, -ας, ἡ, bridge (3)
γῆ, γῆς, ἡ, earth, land (6)
γίγας, -αντος, ὁ, giant (9)
γίγνομαι, γενήσομαι, ἐγενόμην, γέγονα, γεγένημαι, ἐγενήθην, become, happen (25)
γιγνώσκω, γνώσομαι, ἔγνων, ἔγνωκα, ἔγνωσμαι, ἐγνώσθην, know, perceive (28)
γλυκύς, -εῖα, -ύ, sweet (19)
γλῶσσα, -ης, ἡ, tongue (3)
γνάθος, -ου, ἡ, jaw
γνώμη, -ης, ἡ, opinion
γραῦς, γραός, ἡ, old woman (14)
γράφω, γράψω, ἔγραψα, γέγραφα, γέγραμμαι, ἐγράφην, write (2)
γυμνός, -ή, -όν, naked, lightly clad
γυνή, γυναικός, ἡ, woman, wife (14)

δάκνω, δήξομαι, ἔδακον, δέδηχα, δέδηγμαι, ἐδήχθην, bite
δακρύω, δακρύσω, ἐδάκρυσα, δεδάκρυκα, δεδάκρυμαι, weep (25)
δαρεικός, -οῦ, ὁ, daric (Persian coin)
Δαρεῖος, -ου, ὁ, Darius (10)
δέ, but, and (*postpos.*) (8)
δεῖ, it is necessary (26)
δείκνυμι, δείξω, ἔδειξα, δέδειχα, δέδειγμαι, ἐδείχθην, show (32)
δειλία, -ας, ἡ, cowardice (16)
δειλός, -ή, -όν, cowardly (8)
δεινός, -ή, -όν, strange, terrible, clever (7)
δεῖπνον, -ου, τό, dinner

δέκα, ten (12)
δεκαετής, -ές, ten years old
δέκατος, -η, -ον, tenth (12)
δελεάζω, put as bait
δελφίς, -ῖνος, ὁ, dolphin (10)
Δελφοί, -ῶν, οἱ, Delphi
δένδρον, -ου, τό, tree (6)
δεσμωτήριον, -ου, τό, prison (15)
δεσπότης, -ου, ὁ, master (of a household) (7)
δεῦρο, hither
δευτεραῖος, -α, -ον, on the second day
δεύτερος, -α, -ον, second (12)
δέχομαι, δέξομαι, ἐδεξάμην, δέδεγμαι,
    ἐδέχθην, receive (16)
δή, indeed (postpos.)
δηλόω, δηλώσω, ἐδήλωσα, δεδήλωκα,
    δεδήλωμαι, ἐδηλώθην, show (18)
δῆμος, -ου, ὁ, people (18)
Δημοσθένης, -ους, ὁ, Demosthenes (12)
διά, through (+ gen.) (8); on account of
    (+ acc.) (7)
διαβαίνω, cross (8)
διαβατός, -ή, -όν, crossable
διαβιβάζω, take across
διάγω, spend (time)
διακόσιοι, -αι, -α, two hundred (14)
διαλέγομαι, converse with (+ dat.)
διαλύομαι, destroy, break off
διατρίβω, spend (time)
διαφεύγω, escape
διαφθείρω, destroy, kill
διδάσκαλος, -ου, ὁ, teacher (17)
διδάσκω, διδάξω, ἐδίδαξα, δεδίδαχα,
    δεδίδαγμαι, ἐδιδάχθην, teach (8)
δίδωμι, δώσω, ἔδωκα, δέδωκα, δέδομαι,
    ἐδόθην, give (32)
Διηνέκης, -ους, ὁ, Dieneces
δίκαιος, -α, -ον, just (9)
δικαιοσύνη, -ης, ἡ, justice (4)
δικαιόω, think it right
διπλός, -ή, -όν, twofold, double
δισμύριοι, -αι, -α, twenty thousand
δισχίλιοι, -αι, -α, two thousand
δίψα, -ης, ἡ, thirst (3)
διώκω, διώξω, ἐδίωξα, δεδίωχα, δεδίωγμαι,
    ἐδιώχθην, pursue, seek after (2)
διῶρυξ, -υχος, ἡ, trench
δοκέω, δόξω, ἔδοξα, δεδόκηκα, δέδογμαι,
    ἐδοκήθην, seem, seem good; think

δόκιμος, -η, -ον, notable
δόξα, -ης, ἡ, glory (3)
δορυφόρος, -ου, ὁ, bodyguard
δοῦλος, -ου, ὁ, slave (5)
δουλοσύνη, -ης, ἡ, slavery
δουλόω, δουλώσω, ἐδούλωσα, δεδούλωκα,
    δεδούλωμαι, ἐδουλώθην, enslave (18)
δραχμή, ῆς, ἡ, drachma (coin worth a day's
    wage for a skilled craftsman)
δρόμος, -ου, ὁ, running, course; δρόμῳ, at the
    double
δρόσος, -ου, ἡ, dew
δύναμαι, δυνήσομαι, ἐδυνησάμην,
    δεδύνημαι, ἐδυνήθην, be able
δύναμις, -εως, ἡ, power (13)
δυνατός, -ή, -όν, powerful
δύο, two (12)
δυσμαί, -ῶν, αἱ, setting
δῶρον, -ου, τό, gift (6)

ἐάν, εἰ + ἄν (26)
ἑαυτοῦ, -ῆς, -οῦ, himself, herself, itself,
    themselves (23)
ἐάω, ἐάσω, εἴασα, εἴακα, εἴαμαι, allow
ἐγγύς, near (adv.); near (+ gen.) (16)
ἐγώ, ἐμοῦ/μου, I (17)
ἐθέλω, ἐθελήσω, ἠθέλησα, ἠθέληκα, be
    willing, wish (8)
εἰ, if (11); εἰ γάρ, if only, would that, may
    (25)
εἰδέναι, inf. of οἶδα
εἶδον, aor. of ὁράω
εἴθε, if only, would that, may (25)
εἴκοσι, twenty (12)
Εἵλως, -ωτος, ὁ, Helot (a serf of the Spartans)
εἰμί, ἔσομαι, imperf. ἦν, be (present indic.
    encl. except 2 sing.) (7)
εἶμι, go (fut. sense) (25)
εἶναι, inf. of εἰμί, 'be' (16)
εἶπον, aor. of λέγω (28)
εἰρήνη, -ης, ἡ, peace (4)
εἰς, into, onto, to (+ acc.) (3); for (a pur-
    pose) (+ acc.) (10)
εἷς, μία, ἕν, one (12)
εἰσάγω, bring in, lead in (26)
εἰσβαίνω, enter, go in, go on board
εἰσβάλλω (+ εἰς), throw into, invade, flow
    into (10)
εἰσβολή, -ῆς, ἡ, (mountain) pass (10)

εἴσειμι (εἶμι, 'go'), enter (25)
εἰσέρχομαι, come in, go in, enter (26)
εἴσοδος, -ου, ἡ, entrance
εἶτα, then
εἴτε...εἴτε (εἰ + τε), either...or, whether...or
ἐκ, ἐξ, out of, from (+ *gen*.) (3)
ἑκάς, far
ἕκαστος, -η, -ον, each, every
ἑκάτερος, -α, -ον, each of two
ἑκατέρωθεν, on both sides
ἑκατόν, one hundred (12)
ἐκβαίνω, go out
ἐκβάλλω, throw out
ἐκεῖ, there (11)
ἐκεῖνος, -η, -ο, that (23)
ἐκείνως, in that way (23)
ἐκεῖσε, to that place (26)
ἐκκλησία, -ας, ἡ, assembly (8)
ἐκκομίζω, bring out
ἐκλέπω, ἐκλέψω, hatch
ἐκπηδάω, ἐκπηδήσομαι, ἐξεπήδησα,
  ἐκπεπήδηκα, leap out (26)
ἐκπλήσσω, ἐκπλήξω, ἐξέπληξα, ἐκπέπληγα,
  ἐκπέπληγμαι, ἐξεπλήγην, scare, startle
ἐκπολιορκέω, ἐκπολιορκήσω, etc., capture by
  siege
ἔκπωμα, -ατος, τό, drinking-cup
ἐκτίνω, ἐκτείσω, ἐξέτεισα, ἐκτέτεικα,
  ἐκτέτεισμαι, ἐξετείσθην, pay in full
ἕκτος, -η, -ον, sixth (12)
ἐλάσσων, ἔλασσον, less, smaller, fewer,
  comp. of μικρός, ὀλίγος (22)
ἐλαύνω, ἐλῶ, ἤλασα, -ελήλακα, ἐλήλαμαι,
  ἠλάθην, drive (8)
ἐλάχιστος, -η, -ον, least, smallest, fewest,
  sup. of μικρός, ὀλίγος (22)
ἐλέγχω, ἐλέγξω, etc., convict
ἐλεύθερος, -α, -ον, free (9)
ἐλευθερόω, ἐλευθερώσω, ἠλευθέρωσα, etc.,
  free (18)
Ἐλεφαντίνη, -ης, ἡ, Elephantine (city in
  Egypt)
ἐλθεῖν, *aor. inf. of* ἔρχομαι
ἕλκω, ἕλξω, εἵλκυσα / εἷλξα, ——,
  -εἵλκυσμαι, -εἱλκύσθην, drag (3)
Ἑλλάς, -άδος, ἡ, Greece (9)
Ἕλλην, -ηνος, ὁ, a Greek (10)
Ἑλλήσποντος, -ου, ὁ, Hellespont

ἕλος, -ους, τό, marsh
ἐλπίζω, ἐλπιῶ, ἤλπισα, ἤλπικα, ἤλπισμαι,
  ἠλπίσθην, hope, expect (+ *fut. inf.*) (17)
ἐλπίς, -ίδος, ἡ, hope, expectation (9)
ἐμαυτοῦ, -ῆς, myself (23)
ἐμβάλλω, ram (+ *dat.*)
ἐμβολή, -ῆς, ἡ, invasion, entrance
ἐμός, -ή, -όν, my (17)
ἔμπροσθε(ν), in front of (+ *gen.*)
ἐν, in, on, (+ *dat.*) (3); among (+ *dat.*) (6);
  ἐν τούτῳ, meanwhile
ἐνάγω, lead on, urge
ἔνδον, inside
ἔνειμι (εἰμί, 'be'), be in, be among (28)
ἕνεκα, for the sake of (+ *gen.; past pos.*)
ἐνθάδε, here
ἐννέα, nine (12)
ἐνταῦθα, here, there, to here, to there (31)
ἐντεῦθεν, from here, from there (31)
ἐξ, out of, from (+ *gen.*) (3)
ἕξ, six (12)
ἐξάγω, lead out, bring out
ἐξάλλομαι, ἐξαλοῦμαι, ἐξηλάμην, leap out
ἔξεστι, it is possible
ἐξετάζω, ἐξετάσω, etc., examine
ἐξηγέομαι, ἐξηγήσομαι, ἐξηγησάμην,
  ἐξήγημαι, explain, recount
ἑξήκοντα, sixty (12)
ἔξω, outside (+ *gen.*) (16)
ἑορτή, -ῆς, ἡ, feast (18)
ἐπάγω, lead against
ἐπανέρχομαι, return (25)
ἐπεί, when, since, as (23)
ἐπείγομαι, ἐπείξομαι, etc., hasten
ἔπειμι (εἰμί, 'be'), be upon (+ *gen.*)
ἔπειμι (εἶμι, 'go'), attack (+ *dat.*)
ἔπειτα, then, next
ἐπί, against, on to (+ *acc.*) (8); on, upon
  (+ *gen.*) (26); on (+ *dat.*); ἐπὶ τούτῳ, on
  this condition
ἐπιβάτης, -ου, ὁ, marine (fighting man on a
  ship)
ἐπιβιβάζω, put on board
ἐπιβουλεύω, plot
ἐπίκειμαι, ἐπικείσομαι, etc., lie opposite
  (+ *dat.*)
ἐπιπίπτω, fall upon
ἐπιστάτης, -ου, ὁ, overseer

ἐπιστολή, -ῆς, ἡ, letter (3)
ἐπιτήδειος, -α, -ον, fit, suitable
ἐπιτρέπω, entrust (19)
ἐπιφαίνομαι, appear (25)
ἐπιχειρέω, make an attempt
ἕπομαι, ἕψομαι, ἑσπόμην, follow (+ *dat.*)
    (31)
ἐποτρύνω, ἐποτρυνῶ, ἐπώτρυνα, urge on
ἑπτά, seven (12)
ἑπτακαίδεκα, seventeen (12)
ἐργάζομαι, ἐργάσομαι, ἠργασάμην,
    εἴργασμαι, ἠργάσθην, work, earn by
    working
ἔργον, -ου, τό, work, deed (6)
ἐρέτης, -ου, ὁ, rower (14)
ἔρυμα, -ατος, τό, fort
ἔρχομαι, ἐλεύσομαι, ἦλθον, ἐλήλυθα, come,
    go (25)
ἔρως, -τος, ὁ, love, desire (9)
ἐρωτάω, ἐρωτήσω, ἠρώτησα/ἠρόμην,
    ἠρώτηκα, ἠρώτημαι, ἠρωτήθην ask (29)
ἐσθίω, ἔδομαι, ἔφαγον, ἐδήδοκα, -εδήδεσμαι,
    eat
ἑσπέρα, -ας, ἡ, evening (3)
ἔσχατος, -η, -ον, last; ἔσχατα, -ων, τά,
    outskirts
ἔσω, inside
ἕτερος, -α, -ον, other
ἔτι, still, yet (11); ἔτι δέ; still more
ἑτοῖμος, -η, -ον, ready (9)
ἔτος, -ους, τό, year (12)
εὖ, well (10)
εὐγενής, -ές, well-born (19)
εὐδαίμων, εὔδαιμον, happy (19)
εὐεργέτης, -ου, ὁ, benefactor
εὐθύς, immediately, at once (16)
εὔνοια, -ας, ἡ, kindness
εὔνους, -ουν, kindly (22)
εὐπορία, -ας, ἡ, plenty
εὑρίσκω, εὑρήσω, ηὗρον/εὗρον, ηὕρηκα/
    εὕρηκα, ηὕρημαι/εὕρημαι, ηὑρέθην, find,
    find out (8)
Εὐρυβιάδης, -ου, ὁ, Eurybiades
εὐρύς, -εῖα, -ύ, wide (19)
Εὐρώπη, -ης, ἡ, Europe
εὐτυχέω, εὐτυχήσω, etc., prosper
εὐτυχής, -ές, fortunate (19)
εὐτυχία, -ας, ἡ, good fortune, prosperity
Εὐφράτης, -ου, ὁ, Euphrates

εὔφρων, -ον, kindly (19)
ἔφη, *aor.* of φημί
ἐχθίων, ἔχθιον, more hostile, *comp. of* ἐχθρός
    (22)
ἔχθιστος, -η, -ον, most hostile, *sup. of* ἐχθρός
    (22)
ἐχθρός, -ά, -όν, hostile (7)
ἔχω, ἕξω/σχήσω, ἔσχον, ἔσχηκα, ἔσχημαι,
    have (2); hold, keep
ἕως, until, as long as, while (31)

ζάω, ζήσω, ἔζην, ἔζηκα, live
Ζεύς, Διός, ὁ, Zeus (14)
ζητέω, ζητήσω, etc., seek (18)
ζυγόν, -οῦ, τό, yoke (6)
ζῷον, -ου, τό, animal (6)
ζωός, -ή, -όν, alive

ἤ, or, than; ἤ...ἤ, either...or (15)
ᾗ, where
ἡγεμονεύω, ἡγεμονεύσω, etc., command
    (+ *gen.*)
ἡγεμονία, -ας, ἡ, leadership
ἡγεμών, -όνος, ὁ, leader, guide (10)
ἡδέως, gladly (22)
ἤδη, already (7)
ἤδη, *pluperf. of* οἶδα
ἥδιστος, -η, ον, sweetest, *sup. of* ἡδύς (22)
ἡδίων, ἥδιον, sweeter, *comp. of* ἡδύς (22)
ἥδομαι, ἡσθήσομαι, ἥσθην, enjoy oneself; be
    pleased with (+ *dat.*)
ἡδύς, -εῖα, -ύ, sweet, pleasant (19)
ἥκω, ἥξω, have come (10)
ἦλθον, *aor. of* ἔρχομαι
ἥλιος, -ου, ὁ, sun (13)
ἡμεῖς, ἡμῶν, we (17)
ἡμέρα, -ας, ἡ, day (3)
ἡμέτερος, -α, -ον, our (17)
ἡμῶν αὐτῶν, ourselves (23)
ἤπειρος, -ου, ἡ, mainland, continent
Ἡρακλῆς, -έους, ὁ, Herakles (15)
ἠρόμην, *aor. of* ἐρωτάω
ᾐσθόμην, *aor. of* αἰσθάνομαι
ἥσσων, ἧσσον, less, weak, inferior, *irregular
    comp. of* κακός
ἡσυχάζω, ἡσυχάσω, etc., rest, remain quiet
    (12)
ἡσυχίαν ἄγω, keep quiet

θάλασσα, -ης, ἡ, sea (3)
θάνατος, -ου, ὁ, death (10)
θάπτω, θάψω, etc., bury (10)
θάσσων, θᾶσσον, faster, *comp. of* ταχύς (22)
θαῦμα, -ατος, τό, wonder
θαυμάζω, θαυμάσομαι, etc., wonder (at), admire, wonder (8)
θεά, -ᾶς, ἡ, goddess (3)
Θεμιστοκλῆς, -έους, ὁ, Themistocles (13)
θεός, -οῦ, ὁ, god (9)
θεράπαινα, -ης, ἡ, (female) servant
θεραπεύω, θεραπεύσω, etc., honor, worship (3); heal, cure, tend (5)
θεράπων, -οντος, ὁ, (male) servant (19)
Θερμοπύλαι, -ῶν, αἱ, Thermopylae
θερμός, -ή, -όν, warm
θέρος, -ους, τό, summer (12)
θέω, θεύσομαι, run
Θῆβαι, -ῶν, αἱ, Thebes
θῆλυς, -εια, -υ, female
θήρ, θηρός, ὁ, wild beast (10)
θηρευτής, -οῦ ὁ, hunter
θηρεύω, θηρεύσω, etc., hunt (3)
θηρίον, -ου, τό, beast
θησαυρός, -οῦ, ὁ, treasure-house
Θήχης, -ου, ὁ Theches (mountain in Armenia)
θνῄσκω / θανοῦμαι, ἔθανον, τέθνηκα, die (20)
θόρυβος, -ου, ὁ, uproar
θρόνος, -ου, ὁ, throne
θυγάτηρ, -τρός, ἡ, daughter (10)
θύρα, -ας, ἡ, door (3)
θύω, θύσω, ἔθυσα, τέθυκα, τέθυμαι, ἐτύθην, sacrifice (2)
θώραξ, -ακος, ὁ, breastplate (8)

ἰατρός, -οῦ, ὁ, doctor (5)
ἰδέα, -ας, ἡ, appearance
ἰδών, *aor. part. of* ὁράω
ἱερεύς, -έως, ὁ, priest (14)
ἱερόν, -οῦ, τό, temple (17)
ἱερός, -ά, -όν, sacred (25)
ἵημι, ἥσω, ἧκα, εἷκα, εἷμαι, εἵθην, throw (32)
ἱκετεύω, ἱκετεύσω, ἱκέτευσα, entreat, supplicate (10)
ἱμάτιον, -ου, τό, cloak
ἵνα, in order (to, that), so that (26)
ἱππεύς, -έως, ὁ, cavalryman; *plur.*, cavalry (14)

Ἱππίας, -ου, ὁ, Hippias
ἵππος, -ου, ὁ, horse (5)
ἵππος, -ου, ἡ, cavalry (*always singular*)
Ἰσθμός, -οῦ, ὁ, Isthmus (of Corinth)
ἵστημι, στήσω, ἔστησα/ἔστην, ἔστηκα, ἔσταμαι, ἐστάθην, stand (32)
ἰσχυρός, -ά, -όν, strong (7)
ἴσως, perhaps
Ἰταλία, -ας, ἡ, Italy (28)
ἰχθύς, -ύος, ὁ, fish (13)
Ἴωνες, -ων, οἱ, Ionians (26)

καθεύδω, καθευδήσω, sleep (26)
καθίζω, καθιῶ, ἐκάθισα, sit
καί, and, also, even (2)
καίπερ, although (20)
καιρός, -οῦ, ὁ, right time, opportunity
καίω, καύσω, ἔκαυσα, -κέκαυκα, κέκαυμαι, ἐκαύθην, burn, kindle
κάκιστος, -η, -ον, worst, *sup. of* κακός (22)
κακίων, κάκιον, worse, *comp. of* κακός (22)
κακός, -ή, -όν, bad (7)
κακῶς, badly (11)
κάλαμος, -ου, ὁ, reed
καλέω, καλήσω, ἐκάλεσα, κέκληκα, κέκλημαι, ἐκλήθην, call, summon
Καλλίμαχος, -ου, ὁ, Callimachus
κάλλιστος, -η, -ον, most beautiful, finest, *sup. of* καλός (22)
καλλίων, κάλλιον, more beautiful, finer, *comp. of* καλός (22)
καλός, -ή, -όν, beautiful, fine (7)
καλύπτω, καλύψω, ἐκάλυψα, κεκάλυμμαι, ἐκαλύφθην, cover
κάμηλος, -ου, ὁ/ἡ, camel (10)
καρπός, -οῦ, ὁ, fruit (6)
Καρχηδόνιος, -ου, ὁ, a Carthaginian
κατά, under (+ gen.); by way of, (+ acc.) (23); κατὰ γῆν, by land (23)
καταβαίνω, go down
καταβάλλω, throw down
καταδύω, καταδύσω, etc., sink (18)
κατακαίω, burn down
καταλαμβάνω, capture; *of events*, happen to
καταλείπω, leave behind (13)
καταλύω, destroy (10)
καταμένω, stay behind
καταπίνω, swallow down

κατασκευάζω, κατασκευάσω, etc., build

κατέστρεφω, καταστρέψω, κατέστρεψα,
    κατέστραμμαι, κατεστρέφθην/
    κατεστράφην, overturn; καταστρέφομαι,
    subdue

κατάστρωμα, -ατος, τό, deck

καταφεύγω, flee for refuge

κάτω, underneath

κελεύω, κελεύσω, etc., order (8); κελεύω
    χαίρειν, bid farewell

κενός, -ή, -όν, empty

κέρας, -ατος, τό, wing (of army)

κεφαλή, -ῆς, ἡ, head (29)

κῆρυξ, -υκος, ὁ, herald (8)

κιθάρα, -ας, ἡ, harp

κιθαρῳδός, -οῦ, ὁ, harpist

κινδυνεύω, κινδυνεύσω, etc., run risks (5)

κίνδυνος, -ου, ὁ, danger (7)

κινέω, κινήσω, etc., move

Κλεομένης, -ου, ὁ, Cleomenes

κλέπτω, κλέψω, etc., steal

Κλέων, -ωνος, ὁ, Cleon (22)

κλῖμαξ, -ακος, ἡ, ladder

κλίνη, -ης, ἡ, couch

κοινόν, -οῦ, τό, public treasury

κοίτη, -ης, ἡ, bed

κολάζω, κολάσω, etc., punish (20)

κολωνός, -οῦ, ὁ, cairn

κομίζω, κομιῶ, ἐκόμισα, κεκόμικα,
    κεκόμισμαι, ἐκομίσθην, convey (17);
    κομίζομαι, recover

κόπτω, κόψω, etc., cut, cut down (6)

Κορίνθιος, -ου, ὁ, a Corinthian (19)

Κορίνθιος, -α, -ον, Corinthian

Κόρινθος, -ου, ἡ, Corinth

κόρυς, -υθος, ἡ, helmet (9)

κοσμέω, κοσμήσω, etc., adorn

κοῦφος, -η, -ον, light (in weight)

κρατέω, κρατήσω, etc., conquer, become
    master of (+ gen.)

κραυγή, -ῆς, ἡ, shout

κριτής, -οῦ, ὁ, judge (4)

Κροῖσος, -ου, ὁ, Croesus (16)

κροκόδειλος, -ου, ὁ, crocodile (26)

κρύπτω, κρύψω, etc., hide (13)

κτῆμα, -ατος, τό, possession

κυβερνήτης, -ου, ὁ, helmsman

κυρβασία, -ας, ἡ, turban

κύριος, -α, -ον, appointed

Κῦρος, -ου, ὁ, Cyrus (10)

κωλύω, κωλύσω, etc., hinder, prevent (2);
    κωλύω ἀπό, keep (someone) from (+ gen.)
    (4)

κώμη, -ης, ἡ, village (3)

κώνωψ, -ωπος, ὁ, gnat (26)

λάθρα, secretly

Λακεδαιμόνιος, -ου, ὁ, a Spartan (8)

λαμβάνω, λήψομαι, ἔλαβον, εἴληφα,
    εἴλημμαι, ἐλήφθην, take, capture, catch,
    arrest (8)

λαμπάς, -άδος, ἡ, torch (9)

λανθάνω, λήσω, ἔλαθον, λέληθα, -λέλησμαι,
    (escape the notice of) (+ part.) (21)

λέγω, λέξω, ἔλεξα/εἶπον, εἴρηκα, λέλεγμαι,
    ἐλέχθην, say, speak, tell (8)

λειμών, -ῶνος, ὁ, meadow (10)

λείπω, λείψω, ἔλιπον, λέλοιπα, λέλειμμαι,
    ἐλείφθην, leave (13)

Λέσβιος, -ου, ὁ, a Lesbian

λέων, -οντος, ὁ, lion (9)

Λεωνίδας, -ου, ὁ, Leonidas (10)

λίθινος, -η, -ον, of stone

λίθος, -ου, ὁ, stone (13)

λιμήν, -ένος, ὁ, harbor (10)

λίμνη, -ης, ἡ, marsh, lake (23)

λόγος, -ου, ὁ, word (5)

λοιπός, -ή, -όν, rest, remaining

λοχαγός, -οῦ, ὁ, captain (16)

Λυδός, -οῦ, ὁ, a Lydian

λύω, λύσω, ἔλυσα, λέλυκα, λέλυμαι, ἐλύθην,
    loose, set free (2); λύομαι, ransom (16)

μακρός, -ά, -όν, long (7)

μάλα, very, much (22)

μάλιστα, very much, sup. of μάλα (22)

μᾶλλον, more, comp. of μάλα (22)

μανθάνω, μαθήσομαι, ἔμαθον, μεμάθηκα,
    learn (21)

μαντεῖον, -ου, τό, oracle

Μαραθών, -ῶνος, ὁ, Marathon

μάστιξ, -ιγος, ὁ, whip

μάτην, in vain (10)

μάχη, -ης, ἡ, battle (3)

μάχομαι, μαχοῦμαι, ἐμαχεσάμην, μεμάχημαι,
    fight (+ dat.) (16)

μέγας, μεγάλη, μέγα, big, great, large (19)

μέγεθος, -ους, τό, size

μέγιστος, -η, -ον, biggest, *sup. of* μέγας (22)

μείζων, μεῖζον, bigger, *comp. of* μέγας (22)

μείων, μεῖον, less, fewer, *comp. of* ὀλίγος (22)

μέλλω, μελλήσω, etc., be about to, intend (+ *fut. inf.*) (17)

μέμνημαι, remember, perf. mid. of μιμνήσκω (+ *gen.*)

μέν, sets up contrast with δέ (*postpos.*) (8)

μέντοι, however (*postpos.*)

μένω, μενῶ, ἔμεινα, μεμένηκα, stay, remain (8), wait for (12)

μέρος, -ους, τό, part

μεσογεία, -ας, ἡ, interior

μέσος, -η, -ον, middle

Μεσσήνιος, -ου, ὁ, a Messenian

μετά, with (+ *gen.*); after (+ *acc.*) (10)

μέταλλον, -ου, τό, mine

μεταξύ, between; ἐν τῷ μεταξύ, meanwhile

μεταπέμπομαι, send for (26)

μέχρι, until, as long as, while (31)

μή, not (8)

μηδέ, and not

μηδείς, μηδεμία, μηδέν, no, not one (*adj.*) (12); no one, nothing (*pronoun*) (12)

Μῆδος, -ου, ὁ, a Mede

μηκέτι, no longer

μήν, μηνός, ὁ, month (12)

μήποτε, never

μήτε...μήτε, neither...nor

μήτηρ, μητρός, ἡ, mother (10)

μία, *fem. of* εἷς

μικρός, -ά, -όν, small (8)

Μιλήσιος, -α, -ον, Milesian, of Miletus

Μίλητος, -ου, ἡ, Miletus

Μιλτιάδης, -ου, ὁ, Miltiades (18)

μισθόομαι, μισθώσομαι, etc., hire

μνᾶ, μνᾶς, ἡ, mina (coin worth 100 drachmas)

μνημόσυμον, -ου, τό, memorial, reminder

μοῖρα, -ας, ἡ, part, share

μόνον, only (14)

μόνος, -η, -ον, alone, only

Μοῦσα, -ης, ἡ, Muse (3)

μύζω, μύξω, suck

μωρία, -ας, ἡ, folly

μωρός, -ά, -όν, foolish (10)

ναυμαχία, -ας, ἡ, sea battle (14)

ναῦς, νεώς, ἡ, ship (14)

ναύτης, -ου, ὁ, sailor (4)

ναυτικόν, -οῦ, τό, fleet, navy (13)

νεανίας, -ου, ὁ, young man (4)

νῆσος, -ου, ἡ, island (5)

νικάω, νικήσω, ἐνίκησα, νενίκηκα, νενίκημαι, ἐνικήθην, win; conquer, defeat (18)

νίκη, -ης, ἡ, victory (7)

Νικίας, -ου, ὁ, Nicias

νομίζω, νομιῶ, ἐνόμισα, νενόμικα, νενόμισμαι, ἐνομίσθην, think (15)

νόμος, -ου, ὁ, law (16)

νόος, -ου, ὁ, mind

νόσος, -ου, ἡ, illness, plague (5)

νῦν, now (9)

νύξ, νυκτός, ἡ, night (9)

νῶτον, -ου, τό, back; κατὰ νώτου, in the rear

ξενίζω, ξενίσω, ἐξένισα, entertain

ξένος, -ου, ὁ, friend, stranger, guest

Ξενοφῶν, -ῶντος, ὁ, Xenophon (9)

Ξέρξης, -ου, ὁ, Xerxes (4)

ξίφος, -ους, τό, sword (22)

ξύλινος, -η, -ον, of wood, wooden (20)

ξύλον, -ου, τό, wood, firewood

ὁ, ἡ, τό, the (4); οἱ μέν...οἱ δέ, some...others (8)

ὅδε, ἥδε, τόδε, this (23)

ὀδμή, -ῆς, ἡ, smell

ὁδός, -οῦ, ἡ, road, way, journey (5)

ὀδούς, ὀδόντος, ὁ, tooth (9)

Ὀδυσσεύς, -έως, ὁ, Odysseus (15)

ὅθεν, from where (31)

οἷ, to where (31)

οἶδα, know (28)

οἴκαδε, homeward (12)

οἰκεῖος, -α, -ον, related

οἰκέτης, -ου, ὁ, member of the household, slave

οἰκέω, οἰκήσω, etc., live; inhabit

οἰκία, -ας, ἡ, house (3)

οἰκίζω, οἰκιῶ, ᾤκισα, ᾤκισμαι, ᾠκίσθην, found (a colony) (10)

οἴκοθεν, from home (12)

οἰκτείρω, οἰκτερῶ, ᾤκτειρα, pity (11)

οἶνος, -ου, ὁ, wine (10)

οἷος, -α, -ον, the kind which, of such a kind (31); οἷός τέ εἰμι, be able, can (8) ὀκτώ, eight (12)

ὀλίγος, -η, -ον, little, few (12)

ὅλος, -η, -ον, whole

ὁμαίμων, -ον, related by blood

ὄνομα, -ατος, τό, name (8)

ὀνομάζω, ὀνομάσω, etc., name, call by name (10)

ὀξύς, -εῖα, -ύ, sharp (19)

ὄπισθε(ν), behind (+ *gen.*) (10)

ὅπλα, -ων, τά, arms, weapons (6)

ὁπλίζω, ὁπλίσω, etc., arm (8)

ὁπλίτης, -ου, ὁ, hoplite (heavy-armed soldier) (9)

ὁπόθεν, from wherever (31)

ὅποι, to where, to wherever (29)

ὁποῖος, -α, -ον, whatever kind (31)

ὁπόσος, -η, -ον, as much/many as, how much/many (29)

ὅπου, where, wherever (29)

ὅπως, in order (to, that), so that (26); how (31)

ὁράω, ὄψομαι, εἶδον, ἑώρακα, ἑώραμαι, ὤφθην, see (18)

ὀργή, -ῆς, ἡ, anger

ὀργίζομαι, ὀργιοῦμαι, ὤργισμαι, ὠργίσθην, grow angry

ὁρμάομαι, ὁρμήσομαι, etc., start, set out

ὄρνις, -ιθος, ὁ/ἡ, bird (9)

ὄρος, -ους, τό, mountain (12)

ὀρυκτός, -ή, -όν, dug out

ὀρύσσω, ὀρύξω, ὤρυξα, -ορώρυχα, ὀρώρυγμαι, ὠρύχθην, dig

ὅς, ἥ, ὅ, who, which (9)

ὅσος, -η, -ον, as much/many as (31)

ὅστις, ἥτις, ὅ τι, whoever, whatever (31)

ὅτε, when (31)

ὅτι, because (9); that (28)

οὐ, οὐκ (*before smooth breathing*), οὐχ (*before rough breathing*), not (2)

οὗ, where (31)

οὐδέ, and not, nor

οὐδείς, οὐδεμία, οὐδέν, no, not one (*adj.*) (12); no one, nothing (*pronoun*) (12)

οὐκέτι, no longer (27)

οὖν, therefore (*postpos.*) (8)

οὔποτε, never (17)

οὔπω, not yet (15)

οὖς, ὠτός, τό, ear

οὔτε...οὔτε, neither...nor (8)

οὗτος, αὕτη, τοῦτο, this (23)

οὕτω(ς), thus, in this way, *adv. of* οὗτος (23); so (27)

ὀφθαλμός, -οῦ, ὁ, eye

ὄψις, ὄψεως, ἡ, sight, presence

παιδεύω, παιδεύσω, ἐπαίδευσα, πεπαίδευκα, πεπαίδευμαι, ἐπαιδεύθην, educate, teach, train (4)

παίζω, παίσω, etc., play

παῖς, παιδός, ὁ/ἡ, child, boy, girl (9)

πάλαι, of old, long ago (11)

πάλιν, back

πανσέληνος, -ου, ἡ, full moon

πανταχοῦ, everywhere

παρά, from (+ *gen.*); beside (+ *dat.*) (16); to, to the presence of (+ *acc.*)

παρακαλέω, summon

παραλαμβάνω, invite

παρασκευάζω, παρασκευάσω, etc., prepare (12)

πάρειμι (εἰμί, 'be'), be present (17)

παρέχω, produce, cause, provide (4)

πᾶς, πᾶσα, πᾶν, all, every, whole (20)

πάσχω, πείσομαι, ἔπαθον, πέπονθα, suffer (21)

πατήρ, πατρός, ὁ, father (10)

πατρίς, -ίδος, ἡ, fatherland, own country (9)

παύω, παύσω, ἔπαυσα, πέπαυκα, πέπαυμαι, ἐπαύθην, stop (3); παύομαι, cease from (+ *gen.*) (16)

πέδη, -ης, ἡ, fetter

πεζός, -οῦ, ὁ, footsoldier; *plur.*, infantry

πείθω, πείσω, ἔπεισα, πέπεικα, πέπεισμαι, ἐπείσθην, persuade (2); *perf.* πέποιθα, trust (12); πείθομαι, πείσομαι, ἐπιθόμην, obey (+ *dat.*) (16)

Πεισίστρατος, -ου, ὁ, Pisistratus

πέλαγος, -ους, τό, sea

Πελοποννήσιος, -ου, ὁ, a Peloponnesian

πελταστής, -οῦ, ὁ, targeteer (soldier with light shield)

πέμπτος, -η, -ον, fifth (12)

πέμπω, πέμψω, ἔπεμψα, πέπομφα, πέπεμμαι, ἐπέμφθην, send (2)

πέντε, five (12)

πεντήκοντα, fifty (12)

πεντηκόντερος, -ου, ὁ, ship with fifty oars
περί, about, concerning (+ *gen.*) (13);
   around (+ *acc.*) (25)
Περίανδρος, -ου, ὁ, Periander
περιβάλλω, embrace
περιέπω, treat, handle
περιέρχομαι, *with inf.* περιιέναι (εἶμι, 'go'),
   go around
Περικλῆς, -κλέους, ὁ, Pericles (13)
περίοδος, -ου, ἡ, map
περιπέμπω, send around (10)
περιπλέω, sail around
Πέρσης, -ου, ὁ, a Persian (4)
Περσικός, -ή, -όν, Persian
πηλός, -οῦ, ὁ, mud, clay
πῆχυς, -εως, ὁ, cubit (about 18 inches)
πιέζω, πιέσω, ἐπίεσα, weigh down
πιθέσθαι, *aor. inf. of* πείθομαι (see πείθω)
πίναξ, -ακος, ὁ, tablet
πίνω, πίομαι, ἔπιον, πέπωκα, πέπομαι,
   ἐπόσθην, drink (18)
πίπτω, πεσοῦμαι, ἔπεσον, πέπτωκα, fall (11)
πιστεύω, πιστεύσω, ἐπίστευσα, πεπίστευκα,
   πεπίστευμαι, ἐπιστεύθην, trust, believe
   (+ *dat.*) (4)
πιστός, -ή, -όν, faithful (9)
πλεῖστος, -η, -ον, very much, very many,
   most, *sup. of* πολύς (22)
πλείων, πλεῖον, more, *comp. of* πολύς (22)
πλέω, πλεύσομαι, ἔπλευσα, πέπλευκα,
   πέπλευσμαι, ἐπλεύσθην sail (25)
πληγή, -ῆς, ἡ, blow
πλήν, except (+ *gen.*)
πληρόω, πληρώσω, etc., fill, man
πλοῖον, -ου, τό, boat
πλούσιος, -α, -ον, rich (7)
πλοῦτος, -ου, ὁ, wealth
πόθεν, from where? (24)
ποθέν, from somewhere (*encl.*) (24)
ποῖ, to where? (24)
ποι, to somewhere (*encl.*) (24)
ποιέω, ποιήσω, etc., make, do; treat (18)
ποίημα, -ατος, τό, poem (20)
ποιητής, -οῦ, ὁ, poet (4)
ποιμήν, -ένος, ὁ, shepherd (10)
ποῖος, -α, -ον, what kind? (31)
ποιός, -ά, -όν, some kind (*encl.*) (31)
πολεμέω, πολεμήσω, etc., make war on
πολέμιοι, -ων, οἱ, enemy (group) (6)

πολέμιος, -α, -ον, hostile (22)
πόλεμος, -ου, ὁ, war (5)
πολιορκέω, πολιορκήσω, etc., besiege
πόλις, -εως, ἡ, city (13)
πολίτης, -ου, ὁ, citizen (4)
πολλάκις, often
πολλῷ, by much, far
Πολυκράτης, -ους, ὁ, Polycrates (19)
πολύς, πολλή, πολύ, much, many (19)
πονέω, πονήσω, etc., toil
πορεύομαι, πορεύσομαι, etc., march, journey
   (16)
πόσος, -η, -ον, how much?, how many? (31)
ποσός, -ή, -όν, some amount (*encl.*) (31)
ποταμός, -οῦ, ὁ, river (5)
πότε, when? (31)
ποτέ, once, ever (*encl.*) (9); sometime, ever
   (*encl.*) (31)
πότερον, whether (29)
πότερος, -α, -ον, which of two? (29)
ποῦ, where? (24)
που, somewhere (*encl.*) (24)
πούς, ποδός, ὁ, foot (29)
πρᾶγμα, -ατος, τό, matter, affair
πράσσω, πράξω, ἔπραξα, πέπραχα,
   πέπραγμαι, ἐπράχθην, do, manage; fare
   (*with perf. act.* πέπραγα) (10)
πρέσβυς, -εως, ὁ, elder; *plur.*, ambassadors
   (13)
πρίν, before (*adv.*); before, until (31)
πρό, before, in front of (+ *gen.*) (16)
προδότης, -ου, ὁ, traitor (18)
προκαλέομαι, invite
προπέμπω, send forth (10)
πρός, in addition to (+ *dat.*); to, toward,
   against (+ *acc.*) (4); πρὸς βίαν, by force
προσάγω, move (something) toward
προσαιρέομαι, choose as colleague
προσβάλλω, attack (+ *dat.*) (22)
προσειλόμην, *aor. of* προσαιρέομαι
προσέρχομαι, approach
προσπίπτω, attack, fall upon (+ *dat.*)
προστάσσω, order
πρόσωπον, -ου, τό, face
πρότερον, before, formerly (18)
προχωρέω, advance (20)
πρύμνα, -ης, ἡ, stern
πρωτεύω, πρωτεύσω, etc., hold the first place
πρῶτον, first, at first

πρῶτος, -η, -ον, first
Πυθία, -ας, ἡ, Pythia, priestess of Apollo
πύλη, -ης, ἡ, gate (3)
Πύλος, -ου, ἡ, Pylos (28)
πυνθάνομαι, πεύσομαι, ἐπυθόμην, πέπυσμαι,
    learn, ascertain
πῦρ, πυρός, τό, fire
πύργος, -ου, ὁ, tower
πῶς, how? (24)
πως, somehow (encl.) (24)

ῥᾴδιος, -α, -ον, easy (8)
ῥᾷστος, -η, -ον, easiest, sup. of ῥᾴδιος (22)
ῥᾴων, ῥᾷον, easier, comp. of ῥᾴδιος (22)
ῥεῖθρον, -ου, τό, river, river bed
ῥήτωρ, -ορος, ὁ, orator (10)

Σαλαμίς, -ῖνος, ἡ, Salamis (19)
σάλπιγξ, -γγος, ἡ, trumpet (8)
Σάμιος, -ου, ὁ, a Samian
Σάμος, -ου, ἡ, Samos
σαφής, -ές, clear (19)
σεαυτοῦ, -ῆς, -οῦ, yourself (23)
σελήνη, -ης, ἡ, moon (12)
σημαίνω, σημανῶ, ἐσήμηνα, σεσήμασμαι,
    ἐσημάνθην, signify, mean, signal
σήμερον, today (25)
σιγάω, σιγήσω, etc., keep silent
Σικελία, -ας, ἡ, Sicily (19)
Σίκιννος, -ου, ὁ, Sicinnus (24)
σῖτος, -ου, ὁ, food (6)
σκευή, -ῆς, ἡ, dress, attire
σκηνή, -ῆς, ἡ, tent
σκιά, -ᾶς, ἡ, shade
σμάραγδος, -ου, ὁ, smaragdus, a precious
    stone of green color
σός, σή, σόν, your (sing.) (17)
Σοῦσα, -ων, τά, Susa
σοφία, -ας, ἡ, wisdom (3)
Σοφοκλῆς, -έους, ὁ, Sophocles (18)
σοφός, -ή, -όν, wise (7)
Σπάρτη, -ης, ἡ, Sparta (4)
σπεύδω, σπεύσω, ἔσπευσα, ἔσπευσμαι,
    hasten, hurry (15)
σπονδαί, -ῶν αἱ, truce
στέγη, -ης, ἡ, roof
στενός, -ή, -όν, narrow (17)
στέφανος, -ου, ὁ, crown
στόμα, -ατος, τό, mouth, entrance

στράτευμα, -ατος, τό, army (8)
στρατεύω, στρατεύσω, etc., march (3)
στρατηγός, -οῦ, ὁ, general (5)
στρατιά, -ᾶς, ἡ, army (3)
στρατιώτης, -ου, ὁ, soldier (4)
στρατοπεδεύομαι, στρατοπεδεύσομαι, etc.,
    encamp (16)
στρατόπεδον, -ο, τό, army camp (6)
στρατός, -οῦ, ὁ, army (21)
Στρυμών, -όνος, ὁ, Strymon
σύ, σοῦ/σου, you (sing.) (17)
συγγιγνώσκω, pardon (+ dat.)
συλάω, συλήσω, etc., ravage (19)
συλλαμβάνω, arrest
συμβουλεύω, advise (+ dat.) (10)
συμμαχία, -ας, ἡ, alliance
σύμμαχος, -ου, ὁ, ally (8)
συμφορά, -ᾶς, ἡ, misfortune, disaster
σύν, with (+ dat.) (10)
συνάγω, lead together, assemble
Συρακόσιος, -ου, ὁ, a Syracusan
Συράκουσαι, -ῶν, αἱ, Syracuse
συχνός, -ή, -όν, plur., many
Σφακτηρία, -ας, ἡ, Sphacteria
σφραγίς, -ῖδος, ἡ, ring (19)
σχίζω, σχίσω, etc., split
σῴζω, σώσω, ἔσωσα, σέσωκα, σέσω(σ)μαι,
    ἐσώθην, save (8); protect (26); σῴζομαι,
    get safely back
Σωκράτης, -ους, ὁ, Socrates (12)
σῶμα, -ατος, τό, body (8)
σωτηρία, -ας, ἡ, safety (17)
σώφρων, -ον, prudent (19)

τάλας, τάλαινα, τάλαν, wretched (19)
ταμίας, -ου, ὁ, steward (4)
Τάρας, -αντος, ὁ, Tarentum
ταράσσω, ταράξω, ἐτάραξα, τετάραχα,
    τετάραγμαι, ἐταράχθην, throw into
    confusion (10)
τάσσω, τάξω, ἔταξα, τέταχα, τέταγμαι,
    ἐτάχθην, draw up (10)
τάφος, -ου, ὁ, tomb (21)
τάφρος, -ου, ἡ, ditch
ταχέως, quickly
ταχθείς, -εῖσα, -έν, aor. part. of τάσσω
τάχιστος, -η, -ον, fastest, sup. of ταχύς (22)
ταχύς, -εῖα, -ύ, swift, quick (19)
τε, and (encl.); τε...καί, both...and (8)

τειχίζω, τειχίσω, etc., fortify (28)
τείχισμα, -ατος, τό, fortification
τεῖχος, -ους, τό, wall (12)
τέκνον, -ου, τό, child (6)
τέλος, at last (18)
τέμνω, τεμῶ, ἔτεμον, τέτμηκα, τέτμημαι,
   ἐτμήθην, cut
τέσσαρες, -α, four (12)
τέταρτος, -η, -ον, fourth (12)
τέχνη, -ης, ἡ, skill
τί, why? (24)
τίθημι, θήσω, ἔθηκα, τέθηκα, τέθημαι, ἐτέθην,
   put, place (32)
τίκτω, τέξομαι, ἔτεκον, τέτοκα, breed, lay
   (eggs), give birth
τιμάω, τιμήσω, ἐτίμησα, τετίμηκα, τετίμημαι,
   ἐτιμήθην, honor (18); τιμάομαι, propose
   a penalty
τιμή, -ῆς, ἡ, honor (3)
τίς, τί, who?, what? (24)
τις, τι, someone/thing, anyone/thing (encl.)
   (24)
τοίνυν, therefore (postpos.)
τοιοῦτος, τοιαύτη, τοιοῦτο, such, this kind
   (23)
τολμάω, τολμήσω, etc., dare
τόξευμα, -ατος, τό, arrow
τοξεύω, τοξεύσω, etc., shoot (with arrows)
   (2)
τόξον, -ου, τό, bow (9)
τοξότης, -ου, ὁ, archer
τόπος, -ου, ὁ, place (17)
τοσοῦτος, τοσαύτη, τοσοῦτο, so much, so
   great; plur. so many (23)
τότε, then (15)
τράπεζα, -ης, ἡ, table (3)
τρεῖς, τρία, three (12)
τρέπω, τρέψω, ἔτρεψα, τέτροφα, τέτραμμαι,
   ἐτρέφθην/ἐτράπην, turn, rout
τρέφω, θρέψω, ἔθρεψα, τέτροφα, τέθραμμαι,
   ἐτράφην, feed, nourish (21)
τρέχω, δραμοῦμαι, ἔδραμον, δεδράμηκα, run
   (17)
τριακόσιοι, -αι, -α, three hundred (12)
τριήραρχος, -ου, ὁ, captain of a trireme
τριήρης, -ους, ἡ, trireme (12)
Τροιζήν, -ῆνος, ἡ, Troezen
τρόπος, -ου, ὁ, way

τυγχάνω, τεύξομαι, ἔτυχον, τετύχηκα, happen
   to (+ part.) (21)
τύπτω, τύψω/τυπτήσω, ἔτυψα/ἔτυπον,
   τέτυμμαι, ἐτύπην, strike, hit (13)
τύραννος, -ου, ὁ, tyrant (10)
τύχῃ, by chance

ὑβρίζω, ὑβριῶ, ὕβρισα, ὕβρικα, ὕβρισμαι,
   ὑβρίσθην, insult
ὕδωρ, ὕδατος, τό, water (14)
υἱός, -οῦ, ὁ, son (16)
ὕλη, -ης, ἡ, wood, forest (9)
ὑμεῖς, ὑμῶν, you (plur.) (17)
ὑμέτερος, -α, -ον, your (plur.) (17)
ὑμῶν αὐτῶν, yourselves (23)
ὑπείκω, ὑπείξω, ὑπεῖξα, yield, give in
ὑπέρ, on behalf of, for (+ gen.) (9); beyond
   (+ acc.)
ὑπερβαίνω, climb over (27)
ὑπερβάλλω, cross
ὑπισχνέομαι, ὑποσχήσομαι, ὑπεσχόμην,
   ὑπέσχημαι, promise
ὑπό, by (+ gen.) (14); under (+ gen., dat.); of
   cause, from, by reason of
ὑποζύγιον, -ου, τό, beast of burden
ὑπολαμβάνω, take on one's back
ὑπολείπω, leave behind
ὑπομένω, stand firm
ὗς, ὑός, ὁ/ἡ, pig
ὕστερον, later
ὑψηλός, -ή, -όν, high (12)

φαίνομαι, φανοῦμαι, πέφασμαι, ἐφάνθην/
   ἐφάνην, seem, appear (16)
φανερός, -ά, -όν, visible
φανερῶς, obviously
Φεραί, -ῶν, αἱ, Pherae
φέρω, οἴσω, ἤνεγκον, ἐνήνοχα, ἐνήνεγμαι,
   ἠνέχθην, carry, bear (2); φέρομαι, win
   (a prize) (16)
φεύγω, φεύξομαι, ἔφυγον, πέφευγα, flee (2)
φημί, imperf. ἔφην, say (present indic. encl.
   except 2 sing.) (28)
φθάνω, φθήσομαι, ἔφθασα, ἔφθακα, (outstrip, anticipate) (+ part.) (21)
φθείρω, φθερῶ, ἔφθειρα, ἔφθαρκα, ἔφθαρμαι,
   ἐφθάρην, lay waste
φθονέω, φθονήσω, etc., be jealous

φιάλη, -ης, ἡ, drinking bowl

φιλέω, φιλήσω, ἐφίλησα, πεφίληκα,
   πεφίλημαι, ἐφιλήθην, love (18)

φιλία, -ας, ἡ, friendship (6)

φίλιος, -α, -ον, friendly (7)

Φιλιππίδης, -ου, ὁ, Philippides

φίλος, -ου, ὁ, friend (20)

φοβέομαι, φοβήσομαι, ἐφοβησάμην,
   πεφόβημαι, ἐφοβήθην, fear, be afraid (23)

φόβος, -ου, ὁ, fear

Φοῖνιξ, -ικος, ὁ, a Phoenician

Φοίνισσα (fem. adj.), Phoenician

φορέω, φορήσω, etc., wear

φυγάς, -άδος, ὁ/ἡ, exile (a person) (9)

φυλακή, -ῆς, ἡ, custody, watch

φυλακτήριον, -ου, τό, guardpost

φύλαξ, -ακος, ὁ, guard (8)

φυλάσσω, φυλάξω, ἐφύλαξα, πεφύλαχα,
   πεφύλαγμαι, ἐφυλάχθην, guard (2)

φωνή, -ῆς, ἡ, voice (3)

χαίρω, χαιρήσω, etc., rejoice (20); κελεύω
   χαίρειν, bid farewell

χαλεπαίνω, χαλεπανῶ, ἐχαλέπηνα,
   ἐχαλεπάνθην, grow annoyed

χαλεπός, -ή, -όν, difficult, dangerous, harsh
   (7)

χαλκοῦς, -ῆ, -οῦν, of bronze

χαρίζομαι, χαριοῦμαι, ἐχαρισάμην,
   κεχάρισμαι, ἐχαρίσθην, curry favor with
   (+ dat.)

χάρις, -ιτος, ἡ, grace, thanks (9); χάριν ἔχω,
   feel grateful (9)

χειμών, -ῶνος, ὁ, storm, winter (10)

χείρ, χειρός, ἡ, hand; εἰς χεῖρας ἐλθεῖν, come
   to grips

χήν, χηνός, ἡ, goose

χίλιοι, -αι, α, one thousand

χιλός, -οῦ, ὁ, grass

χιών, -όνος, ἡ, snow (18)

χορεύω, χορεύσω, etc., dance

χράομαι, χρήσομαι, etc., use (+ dat.)

χρῆμα, -ατος, τό, thing; plur., money (8)

χρήσιμος, -η, -ον, useful (8)

χρόνος, -ου, ὁ, time (12)

χρυσόδετος, -ον, bound with gold, set in gold

χρυσός, -οῦ, ὁ, gold

χρυσοῦς, -ῆ, -οῦν, of gold (16)

χώρα, -ας, ἡ, country (3)

χωρέω, χωρήσω, etc., advance, withdraw

χωρίον, -ου, τό, place

ψευδής, -ές, false (19)

ψεύδω, ψεύσω, ἔψευσα, ἔψευσμαι, ἐψεύσθην,
   tell a lie (10)

ψηφίζομαι, ψηφιοῦμαι, ἐψηφισάμην,
   ἐψήφισμαι, ἐψηφίσθην, vote (for)

ψιλοί, -ῶν, οἱ, light-armed troops

ψυχή, -ῆς, ἡ, soul, life

ὦ, (used with voc.) (3)

ὧδε, thus, in this way (23)

ὦμος, -ου, ὁ, shoulder

ᾠόν, -οῦ, τό, egg

ὥρα, -ας, ἡ, right time, season, hour

ὡς, when; since, because (18); as (18); in
   order (to, that), so that (26); that (after
   verbs of 'saying') (28); to (a person)
   (+ acc.) (21)

ὡς + sup., as...as possible (22)

ὥσπερ, just as

ὥστε, (so) that, (so) as to (27)

ὦτα, acc. of οὖς

English–Greek Vocabulary

abandon, ἀπολείπω (28)

able, be, οἷός τέ εἰμι (8)

about to, be, μέλλω (+ *fut. inf.*) (17)

about (concerning), περί (+ *gen.*) (13)

absent, be, ἄπειμι (εἰμί, 'be') (11)

accomplish, πράσσω (10)

account of, on, διά (+ *acc.*) (7)

acropolis, Ἀκρόπολις, -εως, ἡ (28)

act, πράσσω (10)

Admetus, Ἄδμητος, -ου, ὁ (12)

admire, θαυμάζω (8)

advance, προχωρέω (20)

advise, συμβουλεύω (+ *dat.*) (10)

affair, πρᾶγμα; the affairs of, τά (+ *gen.*) (11)

afraid, be, φοβέομαι (23)

after, μετά (+ *acc.*) (10)

against, ἐπί (+ *acc.*) (8)

ago, long, πάλαι (11)

Alcestis, Ἄλκηστις, -ιδος, ἡ (15)

all, πᾶς, πᾶσα, πᾶν (20)

ally, σύμμαχος, -ου, ὁ (8)

already, ἤδη (7)

also, καί (2)

although, καίπερ (20)

always, ἀεί (4)

Amasis, Ἄμασις, -ιος, ὁ (19)

ambassadors, plur. of πρέσβυς, -εως, ὁ (13)

among, ἐν (+ *dat.*) (6)

among, be, ἔνειμι (28)

ancient, ἀρχαῖος, -α, -ον (15)

and, καί (2); δέ (8); τε (8)

animal, ζῷον, -ου, τό (6)

announce, ἀγγέλλω (7)

another, ἄλλος, -η, -ο (9)

answer, ἀποκρίνομαι (28)

(anticipate), φθάνω (+ *part.*) (21)

anyone, τις, τι (*encl.*) (24)

anyone who, anything which, ὅστις, ὅ τι (31)

Apollo, Ἀπόλλων, -ωνος, ὁ (23)

appear, φαίνομαι (16); ἐπιφαίνομαι (25)

Arion, Ἀρίων, -ονος, ὁ (26)

Aristagoras, Ἀρισταγόρας, -ου, ὁ (26)

Armenia, Ἀρμένια, -ας, ἡ (20)

Armenian, an, Ἀρμένιος, -ου, ὁ, (16)

arm, ὁπλίζω (8)

arms, ὅπλα, -ων, τά (6)

army, στράτευμα, -ατος, τό (8); στρατιά, -ᾶς, ἡ (3); στρατός, -οῦ, ὁ (21)

army camp, στρατόπεδον, -ο, τό (6)

around, περί (+ *acc.*) (25)

arrive, ἀφικνέομαι (+ εἰς) (25)

Artemisia, Ἀρτεμισία, -ας, ἡ (17)

as (since), ἐπεί (23); ὡς (18)

as...as possible, ὡς + *sup.* (22)

ask, ἐρωτάω (29)

ask for, αἰτέω (26)

assembly, ἐκκλησία, -ας, ἡ (8)

at, ἐν (+ *dat.*) (3)

Athena, Ἀθήνη, -ης, ἡ (4)

Athenian, an, Ἀθηναῖος, -ου, ὁ (5)

Athens, Ἀθῆναι, -ῶν, αἱ (4); to Athens, Ἀθήναζε (12); from Athens, Ἀθήνηθεν (12)

attack, προσβάλλω (+ *dat.*) (22)

Attica, Ἀττική, -ῆς, ἡ (11)

Babylon, Βαβυλών, -ῶνος, ἡ (22)

bad, κακός, -ή, -όν (7)

badly, κακῶς (11)

battle, μάχη, -ης, ἡ (3)

be, εἰμί (7)

bear, φέρω (2)

beast, θήρ, θηρός (10)

beautiful, καλός, -ή, -όν (7); *comp.* καλλίων, κάλλιον (22); *sup.* κάλλιστος, -η, -ον (22)

because, γάρ (postpos.) (8); ὅτι (9); ὡς (18)

because of, διά (+ *acc.*) (7)

become, γίγνομαι (25)

before, πρό (+ *gen.*) (16); (*adv.*) πρότερον (18); (*conj.*) πρίν (31)

behalf of, on, ὑπέρ (+ *gen.*) (9)

behind, ὄπισθε(ν) (+ *gen.*) (10)

behind, leave, καταλείπω

believe, πιστεύω (+ *dat.*) (4)

beside, παρά (+ *dat.*) (16)

best, ἄριστος, -η, -ον (14)

better, ἀμείνων, ἄμεινον (22)

big, μέγας, μεγάλη, μέγα (19); *comp.* μείζων, μεῖζον (22); *sup.* μέγιστος, -η, -ον (22)

bird, ὄρνις, -ιθος, ὁ/ἡ (9)

body, σῶμα, -ατος, τό (8)
book, βίβλος, -ου, ἡ (5)
both...and, τε καί (8)
bow, τόξον, -ου, τό (9)
boy, παῖς, παιδός, ὁ (9)
brave, ἀνδρεῖος, -α, -ον (7)
bravery, ἀνδρεία, -ας, ἡ (13)
breastplate, θώραξ, -ακος, ὁ (8)
bridge, γέφυρα, -ας, ἡ (3)
bring, ἄγω (2); bring back, ἀπάγω (12);
  bring in, εἰσάγω (26)
broad, εὐρύς, -εῖα, -ύ (19)
bury, θάπτω (10)
but, ἀλλά (2); δέ (postpos.) (8)
by (agent), ὑπό (+ gen.) (14)
by land, κατὰ γῆν (23)
by way of, κατά (+ acc.) (23)

call, ὀνομάζω (10)
camel, κάμηλος, -ου, ὁ/ἡ (10)
camp, army, στρατόπεδον, -ο, τό (6)
can (be able), οἷός τέ εἰμι (8)
captain, λοχαγός, -οῦ, ὁ (16)
capture, λαμβάνω (8); αἱρέω (21)
carry, φέρω (2)
catch, λαμβάνω (8)
cause, παρέχω (4)
cavalry, plur. of ἱππεύς, -έως, ὁ (14); ἵππος,
  -ου, ἡ
cavalryman, ἱππεύς, -έως, ὁ (14)
cease from, παύομαι (+ gen.) (16)
child, τέκνον, -ου, τό (6); παῖς, παιδός, ὁ/ἡ
  (9)
citizen, πολίτης, -ου, ὁ (4)
city, πόλις, -εως, ἡ (13)
clear, σαφής, -ές (19)
Cleon, Κλέων, -ωνος, ὁ (22)
clever, δεινός, -ή, -όν (7)
climb (up), ἀναβαίνω (12)
climb over, ὑπερβαίνω (27)
colony, ἀποικία, -ας, ἡ (10)
come, ἔρχομαι (25); have come, ἥκω (10)
come in, εἰσέρχομαι (26)
command, ἄρχω (+ gen.) (10)
command, ἀρχή, -ῆς, ἡ (19)
compel, ἀναγκάζω (10)
concerning, περί (+ gen.) (13)
confusion, throw into, ταράσσω (10)
conquer, νικάω (18)

contest, ἅμιλλα, -ης, ἡ (3); ἀγών, -ῶνος, ὁ
  (10)
convey, κομίζω (17)
Corinthian, a, Κορίνθιος, -ου, ὁ (19)
country, χώρα, -ας, ἡ (3); own country,
  fatherland, πατρίς, -ίδος, ἡ (9)
courage, ἀνδρεία, -ας, ἡ (13)
cowardice, δειλία, -ας, ἡ (16)
cowardly, δειλός, -ή, -όν (8)
crocodile, κροκόδειλος, -ου, ὁ (26)
Croesus, Κροῖσος, -ου, ὁ (16)
cross, διαβαίνω (8)
cure, θεραπεύω (5)
cut, cut down, κόπτω (6)
Cyrus, Κῦρος, -ου, ὁ (10)

damage, βλάπτω (6)
danger, κίνδυνος, -ου, ὁ (7)
dangerous, χαλεπός, -ή, -όν (7)
Darius, Δαρεῖος, -ου, ὁ (10)
daughter, θυγάτηρ, -τρός, ἡ (10)
day, ἡμέρα, -ας, ἡ (3)
death, θάνατος, -ου, ὁ (10)
deed, ἔργον, -ου, τό (6)
deep, βαθύς, -εῖα, -ύ (19)
defeat, νικάω (18)
deliberate, βουλεύομαι (16)
demand, αἰτέω (26)
Demosthenes, Δημοσθένης, -ους, ὁ (12)
depart, ἀπέρχομαι (25)
desire, ἔρως, -τος, ὁ (9)
destroy, καταλύω (10)
die, ἀποθνῄσκω (9), θνῄσκω (20)
difficult, χαλεπός, -ή, -όν (7)
discover, εὑρίσκω (8)
do, πράσσω (10); ποιέω (18)
do wrong, ἀδικέω (30)
doctor, ἰατρός, -οῦ, ὁ (5)
dolphin, δελφίς, -ῖνος, ὁ (10)
door, θύρα, -ας, ἡ (3)
drag, ἕλκω (3)
draw up, τάσσω (10)
drink, πίνω (18)
drive, ἐλαύνω (8); drive away, ἀπελαύνω
  (11)

each other, ἀλλήλων, -ων, -ων (23)
earth, γῆ, γῆς, ἡ (6)
easily, ῥᾳδίως (8)

easy, ῥᾴδιος, -α, -ον (8); *comp.* ῥᾴων, ῥᾷον (22); *sup.* ῥᾷστος, -η, -ον (22)

educate, παιδεύω (4)

Egyptian, an, Αἰγύπτιος, -ου, ὁ (26)

either...or, ἤ...ἤ (15)

elder, πρέσβυς, -εως, ὁ (13)

empire, ἀρχή, -ῆς, ἡ (19)

encamp, στρατοπεδεύομαι (16)

enemy (group), πολέμιοι, -ων, οἱ (6)

enslave, δουλόω (18)

enter, εἴσειμι (εἶμι, 'go') (25); εἰσέρχομαι (26)

entreat, ἱκετεύω (10)

entrust, ἐπιτρέπω (19)

escape, ἀποφεύγω (10)

(escape the notice of), λανθάνω (+ *part.*) (21)

even, καί (2)

evening, ἑσπέρα, -ας, ἡ (3)

ever, ποτέ (*encl.*) (9)

every, πᾶς, πᾶσα, πᾶν (20)

excellence, ἀρετή, -ῆς, ἡ (30)

exile (a person), φυγάς, -άδος, ὁ/ἡ (9)

expect, ἐλπίζω (+ *fut. inf.*) (17)

expectation, ἐλπίς, -ίδος, ἡ (9)

faithful, πιστός, -ή, -όν (9)

fall, πίπτω (11)

false, ψευδής, -ές (19)

fare, πράσσω *with perf.* πέπραγα (10)

fast, ταχύς, -εῖα, -ύ (19); *comp.* θάσσων, θᾶσσον (22); *sup.* τάχιστος, -η, -ον (22)

faster (*adv.*), θᾶσσον (22)

father, πατήρ, πατρός, ὁ (10)

fatherland, πατρίς, -ίδος, ἡ (9)

fear, φοβέομαι (23)

feast, ἑορτή, -ῆς, ἡ (18)

feed, τρέφω (21)

feel grateful, χάριν ἔχω (9)

few, *plur. of* ὀλίγος, -η, -ον (12); *comp. plur. of* ἐλάσσων, ἔλασσον (22); *plur. of* μείων, μεῖον (22); *sup. plur. of* ἐλάχιστος, -η, -ον (22); *plur. of* ὀλίγιστος, -η, -ον (22)

fight, μάχομαι (+ *dat.*) (16)

find, find out, εὑρίσκω (8)

fine, καλός, -ή, -όν (7); *comp.* καλλίων, κάλλιον (22); *sup.* κάλλιστος, -η, -ον (22)

fish, ἰχθύς, -ύος, ὁ (13)

fisherman, ἁλιεύς, -έως, ὁ (19)

five, πέντε (12)

flee, φεύγω (2); flee away, ἀποφεύγω (10)

fleet, ναυτικόν, -οῦ, τό (13)

follow, ἕπομαι (+ *dat.*) (31)

food, σῖτος, -ου, ὁ (6)

foolish, μωρός, -ά, -όν (10)

foot, πούς, ποδός, ὁ (29)

for (because), γάρ (8)

for (on account of), διά (+ *acc.*) (7)

for (on behalf of), ὑπέρ (+ *gen.*) (9)

for (a purpose), εἰς (+ *acc.*) (10)

foreigner, βάρβαρος, -ου, ὁ (7)

forest, ὕλη, -ης, ἡ (9)

formerly, πρότερον (18)

fortify, τειχίζω (28)

fortunate, εὐτυχής, -ές (19)

found (a colony), οἰκίζω (10)

fourth, τέταρτος, -η, -ον (12)

free, ἐλευθερόω (18)

free, ἐλεύθερος, -α, -ον (9)

friend, φίλος, -ου, ὁ (20)

friendly, φίλιος, -α, -ον (7)

friendship, φιλία, -ας, ἡ (6)

front of, in, πρό (+ *gen.*) (16)

from, ἀπό (+ *gen.*) (4); ἐκ, ἐξ (+ *gen.*) (3)

fruit, καρπός, -οῦ, ὁ (6)

game, ἀγών, -ῶνος, ὁ (10)

gate, πύλη, -ης, ἡ (3)

general, στρατηγός, -οῦ, ὁ (5)

giant, γίγας, -αντος, ὁ (9)

gift, δῶρον, -ου, τό (6)

girl, παῖς, παιδός, ἡ (9)

give, δίδωμι (32)

gladly, ἡδέως (22)

glory, δόξα, -ης, ἡ (3)

gnat, κώνωψ, -ωπος, ὁ (26)

go, βαίνω (21), ἔρχομαι (25), εἶμι (*fut. sense*) (25); go away, ἀπέρχομαι (28), ἀποχωρέω (20)

goat, αἴξ, αἰγός, ὁ/ἡ (10)

god, θεός, -οῦ, ὁ (9)

goddess, θεά, -ᾶς, ἡ (3)

gold, of, χρυσοῦς, -ῆ, -οῦν (16)

good, ἀγαθός, -ή, -όν (7)

grace, χάρις, -ιτος, ἡ (9)

grateful, feel, χάριν ἔχω (9)

great, μέγας, μεγάλη, μέγα (19); *comp.*
  μείζων, μεῖζον (22); *sup.* μέγιστος, -η, -ον
  (22)
Greece, Ἑλλάς, -άδος, ἡ (9)
Greek, a, Ἕλλην, -ηνος, ὁ (10)
guard, φυλάσσω (2)
guard, φύλαξ, -ακος, ὁ (8)
guide, ἡγεμών, -όνος, ὁ (10)

happen, γίγνομαι (25)
happen to, τυγχάνω (+ *part.*) (21)
happy, εὐδαίμων, εὔδαιμον (19)
harbor, λιμήν, -ένος, ὁ (10)
harm, βλάπτω (6)
harsh, χαλεπός, -ή, -όν (7)
hasten, σπεύδω (20)
have, ἔχω (2)
head, κεφαλή, -ῆς, ἡ (29)
heal, θεραπεύω (5)
hear, ἀκούω (+ *acc. thing*, + *gen. person*)
  (10)
heavy, βαρύς, -εῖα, -ύ (19)
helmet, κόρυς, -υθος, ἡ (9)
help, βοηθέω (+ dat.) (18)
help, βοήθεια, -ας, ἡ (20)
her, *oblique cases of* αὐτή (8)
her (*possessive*), αὐτῆς (8); her own, ἑαυτῆς
  (23)
Herakles, Ἡρακλῆς, -έους, ὁ (15)
herald, κῆρυξ, -υκος, ὁ (8)
here, ἐνθάδε; ἐνταῦθα (31); from here,
  ἐντεῦθεν (31)
herself (*intensive*), αὐτή (8)
herself (*reflexive*), ἑαυτῆς (23)
hide, κρύπτω (13); hide away, ἀποκρύπτω
  (13)
high, ὑψηλός, -ή, -όν (12)
him, *oblique cases of* αὐτός (8)
himself, herself, itself, themselves (*intensive*),
  αὐτός, -ή, -ό (8)
himself, herself, itself, themselves (*reflexive*),
  ἑαυτοῦ, -ῆς, -οῦ (23)
hinder, κωλύω (2)
his, αὐτοῦ (8)
his own, ἑαυτοῦ (23)
hit, τύπτω (13)
home, from, οἴκοθεν (12)
homeward, οἴκαδε (12)
honor, θεραπεύω (3); τιμάω (18)

honor, τιμή, -ῆς, ἡ (3)
hope, ἐλπίζω (+ *fut. inf.*) (17)
hope, ἐλπίς, -ίδος, ἡ (9)
hoplite, ὁπλίτης, -ου, ὁ (9)
horse, ἵππος, -ου, ὁ (5)
hostile, ἐχθρός, -ά, -όν (7); *comp.* ἐχθίων,
  ἔχθιον (22); *sup.* ἔχθιστος, -η, -ον (22);
  πολέμιος, -α, -ον (22)
house, οἰκία, -ας, ἡ (3)
how?, πῶς (24)
how, ὅπως (31)
how much/many?, πόσος, -η, -ον (31)
how much/many, ὁπόσος, -η, -ον (29); πόσος,
  -η, -ον (31)
human, ἄνθρωπος, -ου, ὁ (7)
hundred, ἑκατόν (12)
hunt, θηρεύω (3)
hurry, σπεύδω (15)
husband, ἀνήρ, ἀνδρός, ὁ (10)

I, ἐγώ, ἐμοῦ/μου (17)
if, εἰ (29)
if only, εἴθε, εἰ γάρ (25)
ill, be, νοσέω (28)
illness, νόσος, -ου, ἡ (5)
immediately, εὐθύς (16)
in, ἐν (3)
in, be, ἔνειμι (εἰμί, 'be') (28)
in order (to, that), ἵνα, ὡς, ὅπως (26)
injure, βλάπτω (6)
intend, μέλλω (+ *fut. inf.*) (17)
into, εἰς (+ *acc.*) (3)
invade, εἰσβάλλω (+ εἰς) (10)
island, νῆσος, -ου, ἡ (5)
it, *oblique cases of* αὐτός (8)
Italy, Ἰταλία, -ας, ἡ (28)
itself (intensive), αὐτό (8)
itself (reflexive), ἑαυτοῦ (23)

journey, πορεύομαι (16)
journey, ὁδός, -οῦ, ἡ (5)
judge, κριτής, -οῦ, ὁ (4)
just, δίκαιος, -α, -ον (9)
justice, δικαιοσύνη, -ης, ἡ (4)

keep (someone) from, κωλύω ἀπό (+ *gen.*)
  (4)
kill, ἀποκτείνω (9)
killed, be, ἀποθνῄσκω (9)

kind, some, ποιός, -ά, -όν (*encl.*) (31)

kind, what?, ποῖος, -α, -ον (31)

kind, whatever, ὁποῖος, -α, -ον (31)

kind which, οἷος, -α, -ον (31)

kindly, εὔφρων, -ον, (19); εὔνους, -ουν (22)

king, be, βασιλεύω (+ *gen.*) (4)

king, βασιλεύς, -έως, ὁ (14)

king of Persia, βασιλεύς, -έως without article (14)

know, γιγνώσκω (28), οἶδα (28)

lake, λίμνη, -ης, ἡ (23)

land, γῆ, γῆς, ἡ (6); land, by, κατὰ γῆν (23)

large, μέγας, μεγάλη, μέγα (19)

last, at, τέλος (18)

law, νόμος, -ου, ὁ (16)

lead, ἄγω (2); lead away, ἀπάγω (12); lead in, εἰσάγω (26)

leader, ἡγεμών, -όνος (10)

leap out, ἐκπηδάω (26)

learn, μανθάνω (21)

leave, λείπω (13); leave behind, καταλείπω (13)

Leonidas, Λεωνίδας, -ου, ὁ (10)

letter, ἐπιστολή, -ῆς, ἡ (3)

lie, tell a, ψεύδω (10)

life, βίος, -ου, ὁ (18)

lion, λέων, -οντος, ὁ (9)

listen to, ἀκούω (+ *acc. thing*, + *gen. person*) (10)

little, ὀλίγος, -η, -ον (12); *comp.* ἐλάσσων, ἔλασσον (22); μείων, μεῖον (22); *sup.* ἐλάχιστος, -η, -ον (22); ὀλίγιστος, -η, ον (22)

long, μακρός, -ά, -όν (7)

long ago, πάλαι (11)

long as, as, ἕως, μέχρι (31)

loose, λύω (2)

loss, be at a, ἀπορέω (20)

love, φιλέω (18)

love, ἔρως, -τος, ὁ (9)

make, ποιέω (18)

man (male), ἀνήρ, ἀνδρός, ὁ (10)

man (human), ἄνθρωπος, -ου, ὁ (7)

manage, πράσσω (10)

many, *plur. of* πολύς, πολλή, πολύ (19); *comp.* πλείων, -ον (22); *sup.* πλεῖστος, -η, -ον (22)

many as, as, *plur. of* ὅσος, -η, -ον (31)

march, στρατεύω (3); πορεύομαι (16)

market-place, ἀγορά, -ᾶς, ἡ (3)

marsh, λίμνη, -ης, ἡ (23)

master (of a household), δεσπότης, -ου, ὁ (7)

may, εἰ γάρ, εἴθε (25)

meadow, λειμών, -ῶνος, ὁ (10)

messenger, ἄγγελος, -ου, ὁ (20)

Miltiades, Μιλτιάδης, -ου, ὁ (18)

money, *plur. of* χρῆμα, -ατος, τό (8)

month, μήν, μηνός, ὁ (12)

moon, σελήνη, -ης, ἡ (12)

more, πλείων, πλεῖον (22)

more (*adv.*), μᾶλλον (22)

most, πλεῖστος, -η, -ον (22)

mother, μήτηρ, μητρός, ἡ (10)

mount, ἀναβαίνω (12)

mountain, ὄρος, -ους, τό, (12)

(mountain) pass, εἰσβολή, -ῆς, ἡ (10)

much, πολύς, πολλή, πολύ (19)

much as, as, ὅσος, -η, -ον (31)

Muse, Μοῦσα, -ης, ἡ (3)

my, ἐμός, -ή, -όν (17)

my own, ἐμαυτοῦ, -ῆς (23)

myself, ἐμαυτοῦ, -ῆς (23)

name, ὀνομάζω (10)

name, ὄνομα, -ατος, τό (8)

narrow, στενός, -ή, -όν (17)

navy, ναυτικόν, -οῦ, τό (13)

near, ἐγγύς (+ *gen.*) (16)

necessary, ἀναγκαῖος, -α, -ον (21)

neither...nor, οὔτε...οὔτε (8); μήτε...μήτε

net, ἀμφίβληστρον, -ου, τό (26)

never, οὔποτε (17); μήποτε

night, νύξ, νυκτός, ἡ (9)

no (*adj.*), οὐδείς, οὐδεμία, οὐδέν (12); μηδείς, μηδεμία, μηδέν (12)

no longer, οὐκέτι (27)

no one, nothing, οὐδείς, οὐδεμία, οὐδέν (12); μηδείς, μηδεμία, μηδέν (12)

North Wind, Βορέας, -ου, ὁ (4)

not, οὐ, οὐκ (*before smooth breathing*), οὐχ (*before rough breathing*) (2); μή

not one (*adj.*), οὐδείς, οὐδεμία, οὐδέν (12); μηδείς, μηδεμία, μηδέν (12)

not yet, οὔπω (15)

nothing, οὐδέν (12); μηδέν (12)

notice, escape (someone's), λανθάνω (21)

nourish, τρέφω (21)
now, νῦν (9)

obey, πείθομαι (+ *dat.*) (16)
Odysseus, Ὀδυσσεύς, -έως, ὁ (15)
of old, πάλαι (11)
old man, γέρων, -οντος, ὁ (9)
old woman, γραῦς, γραός, ἡ (14)
on, ἐν (+ *dat.*) (3); ἐπί (+ *gen.*) (26)
once, ποτέ (*encl.*) (9)
once, at, εὐθύς (16)
one, εἷς, μία, ἕν (12)
only (*adv.*), μόνον (14)
onto, εἰς (+ *acc.*) (3); ἐπί (+ *acc.*) (8)
or, ἤ (15)
orator, ῥήτωρ, -ορος, ὁ (10)
order, κελεύω (8)
order that, in, ἵνα, ὡς, ὅπως (26)
other, ἄλλος, -η, -ο (9)
our, ἡμέτερος, -α, -ον (17)
ourselves, ἡμῶν αὐτῶν (23)
out of, ἐκ, ἐξ (+ *gen.*) (3)
outside, ἔξω (+ *gen.*) (16)
(outstrip), φθάνω (+ *part.*) (21)
overcome, νικάω (18)
ox, βοῦς, βοός, ὁ/ἡ (14)

palace, βασίλεια, -ων, τά (26)
pass (mountain), εἰσβολή, -ῆς, ἡ (10)
peace, εἰρήνη, -ης, ἡ (4)
perceive, αἰσθάνομαι (28); γιγνώσκω (28)
Pericles, Περικλῆς, -κλέους, ὁ (13)
Persian, a, Πέρσης, -ου, ὁ (4)
persuade, πείθω (2)
pity, οἰκτείρω (11)
place, τίθημι (32)
place, τόπος, -ου, ὁ (17)
place, to that, ἐκεῖσε (26)
plague, νόσος, -ου, ἡ (5)
plan, βουλεύω (20)
plan, βουλή, -ῆς, ἡ (18)
pleasant, ἡδύς, -εῖα, -ύ (19)
poem, ποίημα, -ατος, τό (20)
poet, ποιητής, -οῦ, ὁ (4)
Polycrates, Πολυκράτης, -ους, ὁ (19)
power, δύναμις, -εως, ἡ (13)
prepare, παρασκευάζω (12)
present, be, πάρειμι (εἰμί, 'be') (17)
prevent, κωλύω (2)

priest, ἱερεύς, -έως, ὁ (14)
prison, δεσμωτήριον, -ου, τό (15)
prisoner (of war), αἰχμάλωτος, -ου, ὁ (11)
prize, ἆθλον, -ου, τό (16)
produce, παρέχω (4)
protect, σῴζω (26)
provide, παρέχω (4)
prudent, σώφρων, -ον (19)
punish, κολάζω (20)
pursue, διώκω (2)
put, τίθημι (32)
Pylos, Πύλος, -ου, ἡ (28)

quick, ταχύς, -εῖα, -ύ (19); *comp.* θάσσων,
    -ον (22); *sup.* τάχιστος, -η, -ον (22)
quiet, remain, ἡσυχάζω (12)

ransom, λύομαι (16)
ravage, συλάω (19)
reach, ἀφικνέομαι (+ εἰς) (25)
ready, ἑτοῖμος, -η, -ον (9)
receive, δέχομαι, (16)
reign, βασιλεύω (+ *gen.*) (4)
rejoice, χαίρω (20)
remain, μένω (8)
remain quiet, ἡσυχάζω (12)
reply, ἀποκρίνομαι (28)
rest, ἡσυχάζω (12)
retreat, ἀναχωρέω (22)
return, ἐπανέρχομαι (25)
rich, πλούσιος, -α, -ον (7)
ring, σφραγίς, -ῖδος, ἡ (19)
river, ποταμός, -οῦ, ὁ (5)
road, ὁδός, -οῦ, ἡ (5)
rower, ἐρέτης, -ου, ὁ (14)
rule, ἄρχω (+ *gen.*) (10)
rule, ἀρχή, -ῆς, ἡ (19)
run, τρέχω (17)
run risks, κινδυνεύω (5)

sacred, ἱερός, -ά, -όν (25)
sacrifice, θύω (2)
safe, ἀσφαλής, -ές (19)
safety, σωτηρία, -ας, ἡ (17)
sail, πλέω (25); sail away, ἀποπλέω (25)
sailor, ναύτης, -ου, ὁ (4)
Salamis, Σαλαμίς, -ῖνος, ἡ (19)
same, the, ὁ αὐτός (23)
save, σῴζω (8)

say, λέγω (8); φημί (28)

sea, θάλασσα, -ης, ἡ (3)

sea battle, ναυμαχία, -ας, ἡ (14)

second, δεύτερος, -α, -ον (12)

see, ὁράω (18)

seek, ζητέω (18); seek after, διώκω (2)

seem, φαίνομαι (16)

self, αὐτός, -ή, -ό (8)

send, πέμπω (2); send around, περιπέμπω (10); send away, ἀποπέμπω (20); send for, μεταπέμπομαι (26); send forth, προπέμπω (10)

servant (male), θεράπων, -οντος, ὁ (19)

set free, λύω (2)

seven, ἑπτά (12)

shameful, αἰσχρός, -ά, -όν (16); comp. αἰσχίων, -ον (22); sup. αἴσχιστος, -η, -ον (22)

sharp, ὀξύς, -εῖα, -ύ (19)

shepherd, ποιμήν, -ένος, ὁ (10)

shield, ἀσπίς, -ίδος, ἡ (9)

ship, ναῦς, νεώς, ἡ (14)

shoot (with arrows), τοξεύω (2)

short, βραχύς, -εῖα, -ύ (19); comp. βραχίων, βράχιον (22); sup. βράχιστος, -η, -ον (22)

shout, βοάω (18)

show, δηλόω (18); δείκνυμι (32)

Sicily, Σικελία, -ας, ἡ (19)

Sicinnus, Σίκιννος, -ου, ὁ (24)

silver, of, ἀργυροῦς, -οῦν (16)

since, ἐπεί (23); ὡς (18)

sink, καταδύω (18)

six, ἕξ (12)

sixty, ἑξήκοντα (12)

slave, δοῦλος, -ου, ὁ (5)

sleep, καθεύδω (26)

slow, βραδύς, -εῖα, -ύ (19)

small, μικρός, -ά, -όν (8); comp. ἐλάσσων, ἔλασσον (22); μικρότερος, -α, -ον (15); sup. ἐλάχιστος, -η, -ον (22); μικρότατος, -η, -ον (15)

snatch, ἁρπάζω (10)

snow, χιών, -όνος, ἡ (18)

so, οὕτω(ς) (27)

so great, τοσοῦτος, τοσαύτη, τοσοῦτο (23)

so many, plur. of τοσοῦτος, τοσαύτη, τοσοῦτο (23)

so much, τοσοῦτος, τοσαύτη, τοσοῦτο (23)

so that, ἵνα, ὡς, ὅπως (26)

Socrates, Σωκράτης, -ους, ὁ (12)

soldier, στρατιώτης, -ου, ὁ (4)

some...others, οἱ μὲν...οἱ δέ (8)

somehow, πως (encl.) (24)

someone/thing, τις, τι (encl.) (24)

sometime, ποτέ (encl.) (31)

somewhere, που (encl.) (24)

somewhere, from, ποθέν (encl.) (24)

somewhere, to, ποι (encl.) (24)

son, υἱός, -οῦ, ὁ (16)

Sophocles, Σοφοκλῆς, -έους, ὁ (18)

Sparta, Σπάρτη, -ης, ἡ (4)

Spartan, a, Λακεδαιμόνιος, -ου, ὁ (8)

speak, λέγω (8)

spend (money), ἀναλίσκω (21)

stand, ἵστημι (32)

stay, μένω (8)

steward, ταμίας, -ου, ὁ (4)

still, ἔτι (11)

stone, λίθος, -ου, ὁ (13)

stop, παύω (3)

storm, χειμών, -ῶνος, ὁ (10)

strange, δεινός, -ή, -όν (7)

strike, τύπτω (13)

strong, ἰσχυρός, -ά, -όν (7)

such, τοιοῦτος, τοιαύτη, τοιοῦτο (23)

suffer, πάσχω (21)

summer, θέρος, -ους, τό (12)

sun, ἥλιος, -ου, ὁ (13)

supplicate, ἱκετεύω (10)

sure, βέβαιος, -α, -ον (15)

surely (introducing questions), ἆρα οὐ, ἆρα μή (23)

sweet, γλυκύς, -εῖα, -ύ (19); ἡδύς, -εῖα, -ύ (19); comp. ἡδίων, ἥδιον (22); sup. ἥδιστος, -η, ον (22)

swift, ταχύς, -εῖα, -ύ (19); comp. θάσσων, θάσσον (22); sup. τάχιστος, -η, -ον (22)

sword, ξίφος, -ους, τό (22)

table, τράπεζα, -ης, ἡ (3)

take, λαμβάνω (8); αἱρέω (21)

teach, παιδεύω (4); διδάσκω (8)

teacher, διδάσκαλος, -ου, ὁ (17)

tell, λέγω (8)

tell a lie, ψεύδω (10)

temple, ἱερόν, -οῦ, τό (17)

ten, δέκα, (12)

tend, θεραπεύω (5)
tenth, δέκατος, -η, -ον (12)
terrible, δεινός, -ή, -όν (7)
than, ἤ (15)
thanks, χάρις, -ιτος, ἡ (9)
that, ἐκεῖνος, -η, -ο (23)
that (*after verbs of saying*) ὅτι, ὡς (28)
the, ὁ, ἡ, τό (4)
them, *oblique cases of* αὐτός (8)
Themistocles, Θεμιστοκλῆς, -έους, ὁ (13)
themselves, *plur. of* ἑαυτοῦ, -ῆς, -οῦ (23)
then, τότε (15)
there, ἐκεῖ (11); ἐνταῦθα (31)
there, from, ἐντεῦθεν (31)
there, to, ἐνταῦθα (31)
therefore, οὖν (*postpos.*) (8)
thing, χρῆμα, -ατος, τό (8)
think, νομίζω (15)
thirst, δίψα, -ης, ἡ (3)
this, ὅδε, ἥδε, τόδε (23); οὗτος, αὕτη, τοῦτο
    (23)
this kind, τοιοῦτος, τοιαύτη, τοιοῦτο (23)
three, τρεῖς, τρία (12)
three hundred, τριακόσιοι, -αι, -α (12)
through, διά (+ *gen.*) (8)
throw, βάλλω (21); ἵημι (32); throw away,
    ἀποβάλλω (23); throw into, εἰσβάλλω
    (+ εἰς) (10)
throw into confusion, ταράσσω (10)
thus, οὕτω(ς) (23); ὧδε (23)
time, χρόνος, -ου, ὁ (12)
to, *dative case* (3); εἰς (+ *acc.*) (3); πρός
    (+ *acc.*) (4); with persons, ὡς (+ *acc.*) (21)
today, σήμερον (25)
tomb, τάφος, -ου, ὁ (21)
tongue, γλῶσσα, -ης, ἡ (3)
tooth, ὀδούς, ὀδόντος, ὁ (9)
torch, λαμπάς, -άδος, ἡ (9)
toward, πρός (+ *acc.*) (4)
town, ἄστυ, -εως, τό (13)
train, παιδεύω (4)
traitor, προδότης, -ου, ὁ (18)
treat, ποιέω (18)
tree, δένδρον, -ου, τό (6)
trireme, τριήρης, -ους, ἡ (12)
true, ἀληθής, -ές (19)
trumpet, σάλπιγξ, -γγος, ἡ (8)
trust, πιστεύω (+ *dat.*) (4); *perf.* πέποιθα
    from πείθω (12)

trusty, βέβαιος, -α, -ον (15)
truth, τὰ ἀληθῆ (19)
twenty, εἴκοσι (12)
two, δύο (12)
two hundred, διακόσιοι, -αι, -α (14)
tyrant, τύραννος, -ου, ὁ (10)

unjust, be, ἀδικέω (30)
until, ἕως, μέχρι, πρίν (31)
upon, ἐπί (+ *gen.*) (26)
useful, χρήσιμος, -η, -ον (8)

vain, in, μάτην (10)
very, μάλα (22)
very much, μάλιστα (22)
victory, νίκη, -ης, ἡ (7)
village, κώμη, -ης, ἡ (3)
voice, φωνή, -ῆς, ἡ (3)

wagon, ἅμαξα, -ης, ἡ (3)
wait for, μένω (12)
walk, βαίνω (21)
wall, τεῖχος, -ους, τό (12)
want, ἐθέλω (8); βούλομαι (19)
want (of something), ἀπορία, -ας, ἡ (19)
war, πόλεμος, -ου, ὁ (5)
water, ὕδωρ, ὕδατος, τό (14)
way (journey), ὁδός, -οῦ, ἡ (5)
we, ἡμεῖς, ἡμῶν (17)
weak, ἀσθενής, -ές (19)
weapons, ὅπλα, -ων, τά (6)
weep, δακρύω (25)
well, εὖ (10)
well-born, εὐγενής, -ές (19)
what?, τί (24)
whatever, ὅ τι (31)
whatever kind, ὁποῖος, -α, -ον (31)
when?, πότε (31)
when, ἐπεί (23); ὅτε (31)
where?, ποῦ (24)
where, ὅπου (29); οὗ (31)
where?, from, πόθεν (24)
where, from, ὅθεν (31)
where?, to, ποῖ (24)
where, to, ὅποι (29); οἷ (31)
wherever, ὅπου (29)
wherever, from, ὁπόθεν (31)
wherever, to, ὅποι (29)
whether, πότερον (29)

which, ὅς, ἥ, ὅ (9)
which (of two)?, πότερος, -α, -ον (29)
while, ἕως, μέχρι (31)
who?, what?, τίς, τί (24)
who, ὅς, ἥ, ὅ (9)
whoever, whatever, ὅστις, ἥτις, ὅ τι (31)
whole, πᾶς, πᾶσα, πᾶν (20)
why?, τί (24)
wide, εὐρύς, -εῖα, -ύ (19)
wife, γυνή, γυναικός, ἡ (14)
wild beast, θήρ, θηρός, ὁ (10)
willing, be, ἐθέλω (8); βούλομαι (19)
win (a prize), φέρομαι (16)
win (conquer), νικάω (18)
wine, οἶνος, -ου, ὁ (10)
winter, χειμών, -ῶνος, ὁ (10)
wisdom, σοφία, -ας, ἡ (3)
wise, σοφός, -ή, -όν (7)
wish, ἐθέλω (8); βούλομαι (19)
with, μετά (+ gen.) (10); σύν (+ dat.) (10)
woman, γυνή, γυναικός, ἡ (14)
wonder, wonder at, θαυμάζω (8)
wood (forest), ὕλη, -ης, ἡ (9)
wooden, of wood ξόλινος, -η, ον (20)
word, λόγος, -ου, ὁ (5)
work, ἔργον, -ου, τό (6)

worse, κακίων, κάκιον (22)
worship, θεραπεύω (3)
worst, κάκιστος, -η, -ον (22)
worthy, ἄξιος, -α, -ον (9)
would that, εἴθε, εἰ γάρ (25)
wretched, τάλας, τάλαινα, τάλαν (19)
write, γράφω (2)
wrong, ἀδικέω (30)
wrong, do, ἀδικέω (30)

Xenophon, Ξενοφῶν, -ῶντος, ὁ (9)
Xerxes, Ξέρξης, -ου, ὁ (4)

year, ἔτος, -ους, τό (12)
yet, ἔτι (11)
yoke, ζυγόν, -οῦ, τό (6)
you (sing.), σύ, σοῦ/σου (17)
you (plur.), ὑμεῖς, ὑμῶν (17)
young man, νεανίας, -ου, ὁ (4)
your (sing.), σός, σή, σόν (17)
your (plur.), ὑμέτερος, -α, -ον (17)
yourself, σεαυτοῦ, -ῆς, -οῦ (23)
yourselves, ὑμῶν αὐτῶν (23)

Zeus, Ζεύς, Διός, ὁ (14)

ESSENTIAL READINGS IN

COMPARATIVE

POLITICS   FOURTH EDITION

PATRICK H. O'NEIL
RONALD ROGOWSKI

W. W. NORTON & COMPANY
New York • London

Editor: Ann Shin
Associate Editor: Jake Schindel
Project Editor: Diane Cipollone
Electronic Media Editor: Lorraine Klimowich
Electronic Media Assistant Editor: Jennifer Barnhardt
Editorial Assistant: Caitlin Cummings
Marketing Manager, Political Science: Sasha Levitt
Production Manager: Eric Pier-Hocking
Photo Editor: Michael Fodera
Permissions Manager: Megan Jackson
Permissions Assistant: Bethany Salminen
Text Design: Faceout Studio
Art Director: Hope Miller Goodell, Chris Welch
Composition: Jouve North America—Brattleboro, VT
Manufacturing: Quad Graphics—Taunton, MA

Library of Congress Cataloging-in-Publication Data

Essential readings in comparative politics / edited by Patrick H. O'Neil and Ronald Rogowski. — 4th ed.
    p. cm.
  Includes bibliographical references.

  ISBN 978-0-393-91280-7 (pbk.)

  1. Comparative government.   I. O'Neil, Patrick H., 1966–   II. Rogowski, Ronald.
JF51.E77 2012
320.3—dc23

                                                      2012020081

W. W. Norton & Company, Inc., 500 Fifth Avenue, New York, N.Y. 10110
www.wwnorton.com

W. W. Norton & Company Ltd., Castle House, 75/76 Wells Street, London W1T 3QT

4 5 6 7 8 9 0

CONTENTS

PREFACE ix

1. ## WHAT IS COMPARATIVE POLITICS? 1

MARK I. LICHBACH AND ALAN S. ZUCKERMAN
Research Traditions and Theory in Comparative Politics: An Introduction, from *Comparative Politics* 3

GARY KING, ROBERT O. KEOHANE, AND SIDNEY VERBA
The *Science* in Social Science, from *Designing Social Inquiry* 7

LARRY M. BARTELS
Some Unfulfilled Promises of Quantitative Imperialism 13

RONALD ROGOWSKI
How Inference in the Social (But Not the Physical) Sciences Neglects Theoretical Anomaly 17

2. ## THE STATE 24

FRANCIS FUKUYAMA
The Necessity of Politics, from *The Origins of Political Order* 26

MAX WEBER
Politics as a Vocation 39

JEFFREY HERBST
War and the State in Africa 45

ROBERT I. ROTBERG
The New Nature of Nation-State Failure 60

STEPHEN D. KRASNER
Sovereignty 68

3. NATIONS AND SOCIETY 75

ERIC HOBSBAWM
Nationalism, from *The Age of Revolution* 77

JAMES D. FEARON AND DAVID D. LAITIN
Ethnicity, Insurgency, and Civil War 86

ALBERTO ALESINA AND ELIANA LA FERRARA
Ethnic Diversity and Economic Performance 96

KATE BALDWIN AND JOHN D. HUBER
Economic Versus Cultural Differences: Forms of Ethnic Diversity and Public Goods Provision 114

4. POLITICAL ECONOMY 134

ADAM SMITH
An Inquiry into the Nature and Causes of the Wealth of Nations 137

DOUGLASS C. NORTH
Institutions 143

DARON ACEMOGLU
Root Causes: A Historical Approach to Assessing the Role of Institutions in Economic Development 155

ABHIJIT BANERJEE AND LAKSHMI IYER
History, Institutions, and Economic Performance: The Legacy of Colonial Land Tenure Systems in India 160

N. GREGORY MANKIW
The Trilemma of International Finance 184

5. DEMOCRATIC REGIMES 186

FAREED ZAKARIA
A Brief History of Human Liberty, from *The Future of Freedom* 188

PHILIPPE C. SCHMITTER AND TERRY LYNN KARL
What Democracy Is . . . and Is Not   203

AREND LIJPHART
Constitutional Choices for New Democracies   213

ROBERT D. PUTNAM
Tuning In, Tuning Out: The Strange Disappearance of Social Capital in America   222

ALFRED STEPAN, JUAN J. LINZ, AND YOGENDRA YADAV
The Rise of "State-Nations"   250

6. NONDEMOCRATIC REGIMES   265

JUAN J. LINZ AND ALFRED STEPAN
Modern Nondemocratic Regimes, from *Problems of Democratic Transition and Consolidation*   267

ERIKA WEINTHAL AND PAULINE JONES LUONG
Combating the Resource Curse: An Alternative Solution to Managing Mineral Wealth   279

LARRY DIAMOND
The Rule of Law Versus the Big Man   294

STEVEN LEVITSKY AND LUCAN A. WAY
The Rise of Competitive Authoritarianism   303

7. POLITICAL VIOLENCE   314

THEDA SKOCPOL
France, Russia, China: A Structural Analysis of Social Revolutions   316

MARTHA CRENSHAW
The Causes of Terrorism   333

TIMUR KURAN
Now Out of Never: The Element of Surprise in the East European Revolution of 1989   349

JACK GOLDSTONE
Understanding the Revolutions of 2011: Weakness and Resilience in Middle Eastern Autocracies 366

MAX ABRAHMS
What Terrorists Really Want: Terrorist Motives and Counterterrorism Strategy 372

8. ADVANCED DEMOCRACIES 395

ALEXIS DE TOCQUEVILLE
Author's Introduction, from *Democracy in America* 398

DARON ACEMOGLU, SIMON JOHNSON, JAMES A. ROBINSON, AND PIERRE YARED
Income and Democracy 405

ADAM PRZEWORSKI
Conquered or Granted? A History of Suffrage Extensions 411

MAURICE DUVERGER
The Number of Parties, from *Political Parties* 436

TORBEN IVERSEN AND DAVID SOSKICE
Electoral Institutions and the Politics of Coalitions: Why Some Democracies Redistribute More than Others 440

MARGARITA ESTÉVEZ-ABE, TORBEN IVERSEN, AND DAVID SOSKICE
Social Protection and the Formation of Skills: A Reinterpretation of the Welfare State 450

9. COMMUNISM AND POSTCOMMUNISM 467

KARL MARX AND FRIEDRICH ENGELS
Manifesto of the Communist Party 469

VALERIE BUNCE AND SHARON WOLCHIK
Conclusions: Democratizing Elections, International Diffusion, and U.S. Democracy Assistance, from *Defeating Authoritarian Leaders in Postcommunist Countries* 481

IVAN KRASTEV
Paradoxes of the New Authoritarianism   502

BAOGANG HE AND MARK E. WARREN
Authoritarian Deliberation: The Deliberative Turn in Chinese Political Development   509

AZAR GAT
The Return of Authoritarian Great Powers   539

10. LESS-DEVELOPED AND NEWLY INDUSTRIALIZING COUNTRIES   545

WILLIAM EASTERLY
To Help the Poor, from *The Elusive Quest for Growth*   547

PAUL COLLIER AND JAN WILLEM GUNNING
Why Has Africa Grown Slowly?   553

PAUL KRUGMAN
The Myth of Asia's Miracle   571

WAYNE ARNOLD
Vietnam Holds Its Own within China's Vast Economic Shadow   580

DARON ACEMOGLU AND SIMON JOHNSON
Disease and Development: The Effect of Life Expectancy on Economic Growth   582

11. GLOBALIZATION   588

RICHARD FLORIDA
The World Is Spiky: Globalization Has Changed the Economic Playing Field,
But Hasn't Leveled It   590

DANI RODRIK
Is Global Governance Feasible? Is It Desirable?, from *The Globalization Paradox*   595

THE ECONOMIST
Leviathan Stirs Again   609

MIN JIANG
Authoritarian Informationalism: China's Approach to Internet Sovereignty   613

CREDITS   628

PREFACE

One of the greatest problems in comparative politics is that it lacks an agreed upon core. While this problem can be found across political science as a whole, the study of comparative politics has been plagued by disagreements over what merits study and how to go about this study. Whereas the study of international relations (political relations between countries) draws upon a set of key ideas and scholarship, not until recently has there been some similar consensus within comparative politics. Even now, scholars vary widely in the questions, approaches, and evidence that they bring to bear. It was this very problem that led to the creation of the *Essentials* set of texts in comparative politics.

Bringing together the "essentials" of comparative politics in a volume of manageable dimensions presented us with a serious challenge, but also, in our view, an irresistible opportunity. Where textbooks inevitably only summarize the original literature, if they discuss it at all, we have long thought it crucial—not least in our own teaching—to expose our students to the key works and original ideas and to show how they fit together in a larger and more generous understanding of comparative politics. Thus when Ann Shin and Roby Harrington suggested, on behalf of Norton, that we collaborate on a set of original readings to complement *Essentials of Comparative Politics*, we quickly overcame our initial trepidation and took up the challenge.

The readings have been chosen and organized to serve a number of purposes. On most topics, we have combined one or more "classic" pieces—widely recognized as having shaped the present field—with more recent influential contributions. Other works provide valuable surveys of changes in the field over time. Where possible, we have juxtaposed contending views on a topic, giving readers the opportunity to weigh the merits of competing arguments. Finally, we have sought to include a number of shorter and contemporary pieces that help link theory to current political events and developments. The headnotes to each chapter explain more fully our rationale for including the readings we did. The chapters of this volume parallel those of *Essentials of Comparative Politics*, often tying directly to concepts addressed in that textbook. They are also meant to flesh out ideas and developments addressed in *Cases in Comparative Politics*.

The reader begins with an overview of some of the ideas and debates concerning the study of comparative politics itself. From there, we investigate the key concepts of the state and sovereignty, and how scholars have thought about its rise, fall, and failure. We then consider national and ethnic identities and their relationship to political stability and violent conflict. Our discussion of political economy helps trace the relationship between states, markets, and property, while the chapters on democratic and nondemocratic regimes consider how democracies emerge, the foundations of nondemocratic rule, and the prospects for democracy and democratization around the world. This discussion then leads to the chapter on political violence, with its particular focus on terrorism and revolution—particularly pertinent in light of the Arab Spring. From here, we lay out readings on advanced, less-developed and newly industrializing, and communist and postcommunist countries, attempting to apply some of the ideas addressed in the chapters above in understanding these parts of the world. Finally, our chapter on globalization considers the ways in which this process may—or may not—shape the role and place of domestic and international politics in the future, and what this means for the future study of comparative politics. Hopefully, this material will provide the reader a sense of the core issues and ideas within comparative political scholarship, and its relationship to real world issues. The readings also build upon and often reference each other, giving the reader a sense of how they are interconnected as a single body of scholarship. While comparative politics may be diverse and even fractious, the readings underscore the perennial questions and concepts that drive our teaching and research.

While this collection is addressed primarily to undergraduates who are deepening their knowledge of comparative politics, we intend it also as a contribution—and in our view a highly necessary one— to *intra*disciplinary professional dialogue. Far too many graduate students and practicing scholars, in our view, are forgetting or ignoring the impressive depth and breadth of comparative politics. We thus intend this volume as both an introduction and a remedy. Now in its fourth edition, we have refined and improved our selections, seeking to strike a balance between complexity and accessibility.

We owe deep and extensive thanks to the various individuals who contributed to this work. Ann Shin played a critical role in initiating this project, reviewing our choices and helping us maintain order in the face of constant changes, updates, and second thoughts. Aaron Javsicas took the lead on the third edition, and Jake Schindel helped expand and improve our offerings in this fourth edition. Our thanks, too, to those external reviewers who considered our selections and provided important suggestions on how the reader might be improved. Finally, thanks to all those students with whom we have shared these readings in the past. Their responses, tacit and explicit, greatly influenced our selections and rationale. We hope that this range of materials can serve comparative politics courses across a range of levels, and that students and faculty alike will find them both wide-ranging and compelling.

Patrick O'Neil
Ron Rogowski
May 2012

1

WHAT IS COMPARATIVE POLITICS?

The ancestry of comparative politics can be traced back to ancient Greece and Aristotle and to the classic social theorists of the Renaissance and Enlightenment. From its modern revival in the late nineteenth century until the mid-1950s, it was a predominantly legalistic, normative, and descriptive enterprise. It focused on legal texts; it argued about how institutions should be, rather than analyzing their actual characteristics; and it described—often in numbing detail—how countries' institutions worked. However, comparison of countries' institutions was usually limited to two cases (most often, the United Kingdom and the United States), and political scientists demonstrated scant interest in what we would now call the comparative method.

All of this changed with stunning rapidity in the late 1950s and the 1960s, when leading comparativists rediscovered the "grand tradition" in social theory, particularly the works of Karl Marx and Max Weber. Also, through such works as Anthony Downs's *An Economic Theory of Democracy* (1957) and Seymour Martin Lipset's *Political Man* (1960), political scientists explored the possibilities of quantitative, game-theoretic, and economic approaches. From the early 1970s on, an increasing share of scholarly articles used quantitative methods; and during the 1980s and 1990s, the *rational-choice* perspective came to underlie some of the most significant work in comparative politics.

In a work that has already become a modern classic, *Research Traditions and Theory in Comparative Politics: An Introduction* (1997), Mark Lichbach and Alan Zuckerman give a brilliant capsule history of these developments and focus our attention on what they and many others regard as the three major theories that have emerged in the field of comparative politics: the cultural, the structural, and the rational-choice approaches. Lichbach and Zuckerman trace the intellectual antecedents of these approaches, examine the reasons for their ascendance, and address the research questions that each theory pushes to the fore.

Lichbach and Zuckerman also note that, despite their disagreements, today's comparativists agree on the need for comparison and explanation. Most would also agree with the great sociologist Max Weber (1864–1920) that social-scientific explanation is best achieved by what we now call a model—or, as Weber put it, a conjecture or hypothesis about people's behavior that (1) "makes sense" in terms of what we already know about how people think; (2) is "fertile," meaning that it logically implies predictions about behavior that we are not immediately studying; and (3) is "testable," particularly in a comparative setting.

We can also divide comparativists into those who emphasize area studies—close knowledge of a country or region (the Middle East, Latin America, Africa, China, Nigeria)—and those who stress the "science" in "social science," seeking general laws of political behavior and institutions that would apply in all areas of the world. In Lichbach and Zuckerman's terms, almost all culturalists fall into the first category, and almost all rationalists into the second. Structuralists divide between the two, often focusing on a close comparison of similar cases (for example, major revolutions or civil wars). Increasingly, these distinctions are being overshadowed by the one between "quantitative" and "qualitative" scholars. Although almost all rationalists and most structuralists use quantitative (or, more rarely, experimental) methods in their empirical work, culturalists are more likely to conduct qualitative or multi-method research.

King, Keohane, and Verba's pathbreaking textbook, *Designing Social Inquiry* (1994), set itself the ambitious goal of bridging the divides between qualitative and quantitative, and between cultural/structural and rational-choice, work in comparative politics. The difference, KKV (King-Keohane-Verba) contended, was stylistic, not fundamental. Whether one studied a few cases (or even just one) in depth, or many more on only a few dimensions, the same standards of scientific inference must (and, indeed, among practitioners usually did) apply. Exactly as Lichbach and Zuckerman (and, long before them, Weber) had argued, KKV insisted that good comparative theory must be fertile, testable, and tentative, and must seek to simplify complexity.

Yet the KKV framing of the issue failed to command wide assent, and indeed some of it was seen by qualitative scholars as condescending. It is interesting to note that some of that volume's main problems were exposed not by qualitative scholars but by ones working in the rational-choice and quantitative traditions from which KKV emerged.

The last two excerpts included here illustrate the issues. Larry Bartels, among the best and most innovative of quantitative scholars, accused KKV of "quantitative imperialism," contending that (1) some of the best work in the comparative tradition had been nonquantitative; and (2) KKV glossed too readily over some of the obstacles (measurement error, unit homogeneity) to quantitative work. Ronald Rogowski, who had uniformly employed the rational-choice approach in his own work on legitimacy and trade-based coalitions, observed that KKV's overly quantitative standard allowed no room for the kind of crucial experiments that are typical of the natural sciences. (A current example is the frenzied search for the Higgs boson, or "god particle," at the Large Hadron Collider in Switzerland.)

In practice, comparativists today choose freely among methods. Although quantitative ones predominate, they are often supplemented by qualitative work, including examining documents, interviews, and news reports. Crucial experiments, such as those on the effectiveness of a theoretically important intervention, are sometimes performed. And although the rational-choice perspective is by far the dominant one, all practicing comparativists are aware of that approach's limits: cultural taboos or resentments, for example, may trump economic self-interest (a point to which we return in examining nationalism and ethnicity).

Mark I. Lichbach and Alan S. Zuckerman
RESEARCH TRADITIONS AND THEORY IN COMPARATIVE POLITICS: AN INTRODUCTION

The Common Heritage of Comparative Politics

Comparativists inherit their dream of theorizing about politics from the founders of social theory. Their intellectual forebears represent the pantheon of Western thought. In the classic survey of the field's intellectual origins, Harry Eckstein (1963) highlights the past masters.

> Comparative politics . . . has a particular right to claim Aristotle as an ancestor because of the primacy that he assigned to politics among the sciences and because the problems he raised and the methods he used are similar to those still current in political studies (Eckstein 1963: 3).

Machiavelli and Montesquieu, Hobbes and Smith are the progenitors who lived during the Renaissance and the Enlightenment. The classic theorists of social science—Karl Marx, Max Weber, Emile Durkheim, Vilfredo Pareto, Gaetano Mosca, and Roberto Michels—established the field's research agenda, mode of analysis, and contrasting theoretical visions. Several seminal theorists of contemporary political science—Harry Eckstein, David Apter, Robert Dahl, Seymour Lipset, Karl Deutsch, Gabriel Almond, and Sidney Verba—drew on this heritage to rebuild and reinvigorate the field of comparative politics. A shared, grand intellectual vision motivates comparativists.

From *Comparative Politics: Rationality, Culture, and Structure* (New York: Cambridge University Press, 1997), pp. 3–8.

Comparativists want to understand the critical events of the day, a position that ensures that dreams of theory address the political world as it exists, not formal abstractions or utopias. Just as Marx and Weber responded to the fundamental transformations associated with the rise of capitalism, just as Marx developed a general strategy for a socialist revolution and Weber grappled with the theoretical and normative demands of the bureaucratic state, and just as Mosca, Pareto, and Michels strove to understand the possibilities and limits of democratic rule, students of comparative politics examine pressing questions in the context of their immediate political agenda. The contemporary study of comparative politics therefore blossomed in response to the political problems that followed World War II. New forms of conflict emerged: Communist threats; peasant rebellions and revolutions; social movements, urban riots, student upheavals, military coups, and national liberation struggles swept the world. Government decisions replaced markets as foci for economic development. New states followed the disintegration of colonial empires, and the worldwide movement toward democratic rule seemed to resume after the fascist tragedies. The challenges of the current era—domestic conflict, state-building, the political bases of economic growth, and democratization, to note but a few—stand at the center of today's research, indicating that the need to respond to contemporary issues guides the field.

Comparative politics therefore asserts an ambitious scope of inquiry. No political phenomenon is foreign to it; no level of analysis is irrelevant, and no time period beyond its reach. Civil war in

Afghanistan; voting decisions in Britain; ethnic conflict in Quebec, Bosnia, and Burundi; policy interactions among the bureaucracies of the European Union in Brussels, government agencies in Rome, regional offices in Basilicata, and local powers in Potenza; the religious bases of political action in Iran, Israel, and the United States; the formation of democracies in Eastern Europe and the collapse of regimes in Africa; and global economic patterns are part of the array of contemporary issues that stand before the field. Questions about the origins of capitalism; the formation of European states; the rise of fascism and the collapse of interwar democracies; and the transition to independence after colonial rule are some of the themes of past eras that still command our attention.

Second, comparativists assert an ambitious intellectual vision in that they approach these substantive concerns with general questions in mind. Anyone who studies the politics of a particular country—whether Germany or Ghana, the United Arab Emirates or the United States of America—so as to address abstract issues, does comparative politics. Anyone who is interested in who comes to power, how, and why—the names, places, and dates of politics in any one place or other—in order to say something about the politics of succession or the determinants of vote choice, is a comparativist. In other words, students of comparative politics examine a case to reveal what it tells us about a larger set of political phenomena, or they relate the particulars of politics to more general theoretical ideas about politics.

Comparativists therefore insist that analysis requires explicit comparisons. Because events of global historical significance affect so many countries in so short a period of time, studies of single countries and abstract theorizing are woefully inadequate to capture epoch-shaping developments. More than three decades ago, when the founders of the contemporary field of comparative politics initiated the most recent effort to merge theory and data in the study of politics, they therefore established another of the field's guiding principles: The proper study of politics requires systematic comparisons.[1]

Finally, comparativists assert a grand intellectual vision in that their generalizations are situated in the context of the Big Questions of social thought: Who rules? How are interests represented? Who wins and who loses? How is authority challenged? Why are some nations "developed"? These questions have produced much contemporary theorizing about the connections among social order, the state, civil society, and social change, especially in democracies. Comparativists engage the basic issues that inform social and political thought.

In sum, comparative politics follows the lead of the grand masters in their approach to substantive issues, to the scope of inquiry, to the nature of theory-building, and to the enduring problems of social thought. As comparativists address politically significant matters, explore a range of political phenomena, propose general explanatory propositions based on systematic evidence from multiple cases, and address Big Questions, they move along a path first marked by the founders of social science.

The Competing Traditions in Comparative Politics

In spite of this shared dream, long-standing disagreements separated the field's forebears and contrasting research schools characterize current efforts to build theories in comparative politics. When many of today's senior scholars were graduate students, their training included courses that compared psychological and culturalist approaches, institutional studies of political organizations, structural-functional and systems analyses, cybernetics and modes of information theory, pluralist, elitist, and Marxist analyses, modernization theory and its alternatives of dependency and world-systems theories, and rational choice theory, to name the most obvious. Most of these perspectives have disappeared and some have formed new combinations. Today, rational choice theories, culturalist approaches, and structural analyses stand as the principal competing theoretical schools in comparative politics. Rational choice theorists follow a path laid out by Hobbes, Smith, and Pareto; culturalists continue work begun by Montesquieu and developed by Weber and Mosca; and structuralists build on Marx's foundations and add to Weber's edifice. The themes and debates of contemporary comparative politics are therefore rooted in the enduring questions of social thought. They continue to lie at the center of work in all the social sciences.

Rationalists begin with assumptions about actors who act deliberately to maximize their advantage. This research school uses the power of mathematical reasoning to elaborate explanations with impressive scope. Analysis begins at the level of the individual and culminates in questions about collective actions, choices, and institutions. Following the path first charted by Downs (1957), Olson (1968), and Riker (1962), rational choice theory has spread to address diverse problems: from electoral choice to revolutionary movements, from coalitions to political economy, and from institution formation to state-building. Here, the clarity of mathematical reasoning takes pride of place; powerful abstract logics facilitate a shared understanding among the members of the research school.

As comparativists engage in fieldwork in diverse societies, they grapple with the need to understand varied ways of life, systems of meaning, and values. As students who cut their teeth on the abstractions of modernization and dependency theory encounter the realities of particular villages, political parties, and legislatures, they seek to ground their observations in the politics that is being analyzed. Following the lead of social and cultural anthropologists, many comparativists adhere to Geertz's (1973) admonition to provide "thick descriptions." Culturalists therefore provide nuanced and detailed readings of particular cases, frequently drawn from fieldwork, as they seek to understand the phenomena being studied. This stance usually joins strong doubts about both the ability to generalize to abstract categories and the ability to provide explanations that apply to more than the case at hand.

Structuralists draw together long-standing interests in political and social institutions. Many emphasize the formal organizations of governments; some retain Marx's concern with class relations; some study political parties and interest groups; some combine these into analyses of how states and societies interact; and some emphasize the themes of political economy. Although these scholars display diverse patterns of reasoning, from mathematical models to verbal arguments, and many modes of organizing empirical evidence, they continue to follow Marx's and Weber's contention that theory and data guide social analysis.

* * * These research traditions take strong positions on the methodological issues that divide comparativists.[2] Rational choice theorists seek to maximize the ability to provide universal laws that may be used in nomothetic explanations. They consider problems of reliability—the concern with the evidence required to support generalizations from the particular to sets of cases—as a challenge to research design. Cultural interpreters maximize the importance of reliability as they describe the constellations of particular cases and minimize the value of generalist research expectations. They interpret particular events, decisions, and patterns, eschewing any need to tie explanations to general principles. Structural analysts who follow Marx offer universal theories that include causal accounts. At the same time, they struggle to tie reliable descriptions into powerful generalizations; they grapple self-consciously with the requirements of case selection and how best to move from the particular analysis to the set of cases about which they seek to theorize. Comparativists' long-standing debates over method thus reappear in the three research traditions.

However, * * * the dispute among the schools goes beyond the ideographic-nomothetic divide. The traditions differ with respect to ontology: Rationalists study how actors employ reason to satisfy their interests, culturalists study rules that constitute individual and group identities, and structuralists explore relations among actors in an institutional context. Reasons, rules, and relations are the various starting points of inquiry. The traditions also differ with respect to explanatory strategy: Rationalists perform comparative static experiments, culturalists produce interpretive understandings, and structuralists study the historical dynamics of real social types. Positivism, interpretivism, and realism are the possible philosophies of social science.

Moreover, * * * no school displays a rigid and uniform orthodoxy. Rationalists debate the utility of relaxing the core assumption that defines individuals as maximizers of their self-interest. They differ as well over the proper form of explanation, some seeking covering laws and others proposing causal accounts, as they debate the necessity of transforming formal models into accounts of events. Continuing the debate initiated by Marx and Weber, structuralists differ over the ontological status of their concepts: Are social class, ethnicity, state, and other concepts that characterize this research school natural types? Are political processes best seen as determined and closed ended or probabilistic and open-ended processes? Structuralists differ as well over the utility of nomothetic and causal explanations. Culturalists disagree over the theoretical importance of generalizations drawn from their fieldwork. May one derive or test general propositions from the analysis of a particular village? Do public opinion surveys provide an adequate picture of people's goals, values, and identities? They differ over the nature of explanation in comparative politics as well. Some culturalists reject any form of covering law or causal accounts, offering only interpretations of political life in particular places; others move toward the mainstream of comparative politics, incorporating values and systems of meaning into theories that adhere to the standard forms of explanation. In short, as Lichbach makes clear in his essay, ideal-type rationalists, culturalists, and structuralists need to be identified so that we may recognize how practicing comparativists employ a battery of ideal-type strategies in their concrete empirical work.

Comparative politics is dominated today by rationalist, culturalist, and structuralist approaches. What explains the imperialist expansion of these schools and the disappearance of earlier approaches? [For one thing, t]hese schools share an ontological and epistemological symmetry. They offer—indeed force—choices along the same dimensions. Furthermore, at a more fundamental level, the themes of the research schools rest at the heart of the human sciences. Reason, rules, and relations are unique to social theory. Focusing on these themes sets research in the social sciences apart from the physical sciences, providing a fundamental basis on which to theorize about political phenomena. Rationalist, culturalist, and structuralist theories are thus embedded in strong research communities, scholarly traditions, and analytical languages.

NOTES

1. Classic works that appeared to herald the emergence of comparative politics as a subdiscipline of political science include Almond and Coleman (1960), Almond and Verba (1963), Beer and Ulam (1958), Dahl (1966; 1971), Eckstein and Apter (1963), Holt and Turner (1970), Huntington (1968), La Palombara and Weiner (1966), Lipset and Rokkan (1967), Moore (1966), Przeworski and Teune (1970); Pye and Verba (1965), Riker (1962), and Sartori (1970). At the same time, two journals, *Comparative Politics* and *Comparative Political Studies*, appeared, helping to institutionalize the subfield.

2. There is also a long-standing debate in comparative politics about methodology. As comparativists propose explanations that cover sets of cases, perhaps based on causal accounts, they grapple with questions that relate to theory-building, concept formation, and case selection: How do concepts carry across cases? What is the value of treating concepts as variables that are measured by indicators? What is the proper use of case-specific information in theories that cover many cases? How does the choice of cases affect the general propositions offered? Are there requirements that define the number of cases that need to be included in an analysis? What is the

relevance of single case studies to the development of theory? How can single case studies be used to speak to general sets of phenomena? Is it possible or desirable to include all relevant instances in the analysis? Is it possible to devise an adequate methodology that permits powerful generalizations based on the observation of a small number of cases? These questions raise problems of external validity, the ability to generalize beyond the case being observed.

Nearly thirty years ago, Sartori (1970) drew attention to fundamental questions of concept formation. At that same time, Lijphart (1971) and Przeworski and Teune (1970) initiated a controversy about the proper methodology of comparative research, in which Eckstein (1975), Ragin (1987), Ragin and Becker (1992), and Skocpol and Somers (1980) have offered significant alternative positions (see Collier 1993 for a review of this literature). Most recently, Collier and Mahon (1993), Collier (1993), and Sartori (1994) illustrate further developments concerning the proper formation of concepts, and King, Keohane, and Verba (1994; 1995) initiated a productive debate over issues of research design in comparative politics. On the latter, see especially Bartels (1995), Brady (1995), Caporaso (1995), Collier (1995), Laitin (1995), Mohr (1996), Rogowski (1995), and Tarrow (1995). There is a natural affinity between studies of research design and comparative method that is frequently overlooked. King, Keohane, and Verba (1994; 1995) argue that there is only one scientific method. Hence, their strictures resemble those proposed by Cook and Campbell (1979).

Gary King, Robert O. Keohane, and Sidney Verba
THE *SCIENCE* IN SOCIAL SCIENCE

■   ■   ■

For several decades, political scientists have debated the merits of case studies versus statistical studies, area studies versus comparative studies, and "scientific" studies of politics using quantitative methods versus "historical" investigations relying on rich textual and contextual understanding. Some quantitative researchers believe that systematic statistical analysis is the only road to truth in the social sciences. Advocates of qualitative research vehemently disagree. This difference of opinion leads to lively debate; but unfortunately, it also bifurcates the social sciences into a quantitative-systematic-generalizing branch and a qualitative-humanistic-discursive branch. As the former becomes more and more sophisticated in the analysis of statistical data (and their work becomes less comprehensible to those who have not studied the techniques), the latter becomes more and more convinced of the irrelevance of such analyses to the seemingly nonreplicable and nongeneralizable events in which its practitioners are interested.

A major purpose of this book is to show that the differences between the quantitative and qualitative traditions are only stylistic and are methodologically and substantively unimportant. All good research can be understood—indeed, is best understood—to derive from the same underlying logic of inference. Both quantitative and qualitative research can be systematic and scientific. Historical research can be analytical, seeking to evaluate alternative

From *Designing Social Inquiry: Scientific Interest in Qualitative Research* (Princeton: Princeton University Press, 1994), pp. 3–12.

explanations through a process of valid causal inference. History, or historical sociology, is not incompatible with social science (Skocpol 1984: 374–86).

Breaking down these barriers requires that we begin by questioning the very concept of "qualitative" research. We have used the term in our title to signal our subject matter, not to imply that "qualitative" research is fundamentally different from "quantitative" research, except in style.

Most research does not fit clearly into one category or the other. The best often combines features of each. In the same research project, some data may be collected that is amenable to statistical analysis, while other equally significant information is not. Patterns and trends in social, political, or economic behavior are more readily subjected to quantitative analysis than is the flow of ideas among people or the difference made by exceptional individual leadership. If we are to understand the rapidly changing social world, we will need to include information that cannot be easily quantified as well as that which can. Furthermore, all social science requires comparison, which entails judgments of which phenomena are "more" or "less" alike in degree (i.e., quantitative differences) or in kind (i.e., qualitative differences).

* * * Neither quantitative nor qualitative research is superior to the other, regardless of the research problem being addressed. Since many subjects of interest to social scientists cannot be meaningfully formulated in ways that permit statistical testing of hypotheses with quantitative data, we do not wish to encourage the exclusive use of quantitative techniques. We are not trying to get all social scientists out of the library and into the computer center, or to replace idiosyncratic conversations with structured interviews. Rather, we argue that nonstatistical research will produce more reliable results if researchers pay attention to the rules of scientific inference—rules that are sometimes more clearly stated in the style of quantitative research. Precisely defined statistical methods that undergird quantitative research represent abstract formal models applicable to all kinds of research, even that for which variables cannot be measured quantitatively. The very abstract, and even unrealistic, nature of statistical models is what makes the rules of inference shine through so clearly.

The rules of inference that we discuss are not relevant to all issues that are of significance to social scientists. Many of the most important questions concerning political life—about such concepts as agency, obligation, legitimacy, citizenship, sovereignty, and the proper relationship between national societies and international politics—are philosophical rather than empirical. But the rules are relevant to all research where the goal is to learn facts about the real world. Indeed, the distinctive characteristic that sets social science apart from casual observation is that social science seeks to arrive at valid inferences by the systematic use of well-established procedures of inquiry. Our focus here on empirical research means that we sidestep many issues in the philosophy of social science as well as controversies about the role of postmodernism, the nature and existence of truth, relativism, and related subjects. We assume that it is possible to have some knowledge of the external world but that such knowledge is always uncertain.

Furthermore, nothing in our set of rules implies that we must run the perfect experiment (if such a thing existed) or collect all relevant data before we can make valid social scientific inferences. An important topic is worth studying even if very little information is available. The result of applying any research design in this situation will be relatively uncertain conclusions, but so long as we honestly report our uncertainty, this kind of study can be very useful. Limited information is often a necessary feature of social inquiry. Because the social world changes rapidly, analyses that help us understand those changes require that we describe them and seek to understand them contemporaneously, even when uncertainty about our conclusions is high. The urgency of a problem may be so great that data gathered by the most useful scientific methods might be obsolete before it can be accumulated. If a distraught person is running at us swinging an ax, administering a five-page questionnaire on psychopathy may not be the best strategy. Joseph Schumpeter once cited Albert Einstein, who said "as far as our propositions are certain, they do not say anything about reality, and as far as they do say anything about reality, they are not certain" (Schumpeter [1936] 1991:298–99). Yet even though certainty is unattainable, we can improve the reliability, validity, certainty, and honesty of our conclusions by paying attention to the rules of scientific inference. The social science we espouse seeks to make descriptive and causal inferences about the world. Those who do not share the assumptions of partial and imperfect knowability and the aspiration for descriptive and causal understanding will have to look elsewhere for inspiration or for paradigmatic battles in which to engage.* * *

1.1.2 Defining Scientific Research in the Social Sciences

Our definition of "scientific research" is an ideal to which any actual quantitative or qualitative research, even the most careful, is only an approximation. Yet, we need a definition of good research, for which we use the word "scientific" as our descriptor.[1] This word comes with many connotations that are unwarranted or inappropriate or downright incendiary for some qualitative researchers. Hence, we provide an explicit definition here. As should be clear, we do not regard quantitative research to be any more scientific than qualitative research. Good research, that is, scientific research, can be quantitative or qualitative in style. In design, however, scientific research has the following four characteristics:

1. **The goal is inference.** Scientific research is designed to make descriptive or explanatory *inferences* on the basis of empirical information about the world. Careful descriptions of specific phenomena are often indispensable to scientific research, but the accumulation of facts alone is not sufficient. Facts can be collected (by qualitative or quantitative researchers) more or less systematically, and the former is obviously better than the latter, but our particular definition of science requires the additional step of attempting to infer beyond the immediate data to something broader that is not directly observed. That something may involve *descriptive inference*—using observations from the world to learn about other unobserved facts. Or that something may involve *causal inference*—learning about causal effects from the data observed. The domain of inference can be restricted in space and time—voting behavior in American elections since 1960, social movements in Eastern Europe since 1989—or it can be extensive—human behavior since the invention of agriculture. In either case, the key distinguishing mark of scientific research is the goal of making inferences that go beyond the particular observations collected.

2. **The procedures are public.** Scientific research uses explicit, codified, and *public* methods to generate and analyze data whose reliability can therefore be assessed. Much social research in the qualitative style follows fewer precise rules of research procedure or of inference. As Robert K. Merton ([1949] 1968:71–72) put it, "The sociological analysis of qualitative data often resides in a private world of penetrating but unfathomable insights and ineffable understandings. . . . [However,] science . . . is public, not private." Merton's statement is not true of all qualitative researchers (and it is unfortunately still true of some quantitative analysts), but many proceed as if they had no method—sometimes as if the use of explicit methods would diminish their creativity. Nevertheless they cannot help but use some method. Somehow they observe phenomena, ask questions, infer information about the world from these observations, and make inferences about cause and effect. If the

method and logic of a researcher's observations and inferences are left implicit, the scholarly community has no way of judging the validity of what was done. We cannot evaluate the principles of selection that were used to record observations, the ways in which observations were processed, and the logic by which conclusions were drawn. We cannot learn from their methods or replicate their results. Such research is not a *public* act. Whether or not it makes good reading, it is not a contribution to social science.

All methods—whether explicit or not—have limitations. The advantage of explicitness is that those limitations can be understood and, if possible, addressed. In addition, the methods can be taught and shared. This process allows research results to be compared across separate researchers and research projects studies to be replicated, and scholars to learn.

3. **The conclusions are uncertain.** By definition, inference is an imperfect process. Its goal is to use quantitative or qualitative data to learn about the world that produced them. Reaching perfectly certain conclusions from uncertain data is obviously impossible. Indeed, uncertainty is a central aspect of all research and all knowledge about the world. Without a reasonable estimate of uncertainty, a description of the real world or an inference about a causal effect in the real world is uninterpretable. A researcher who fails to face the issue of uncertainty directly is either asserting that he or she knows everything perfectly or that he or she has no idea how certain or uncertain the results are. Either way, inferences without uncertainty estimates are not science as we define it.

4. **The content is the method.** Finally, scientific research adheres to a set of rules of inference on which its validity depends. Explicating the most important rules is a major task of this book.[2] The content of "science" is primarily the methods and rules, not the subject matter, since we can use these methods to study virtually anything. This point was recognized over a century ago when Karl Pearson (1892:16) explained that "the field of science is unlimited; its material is endless; every group of natural phenomena, every phase of social life, every stage of past or present development is material for science. The unity of all science consists alone in its method, not in its material."

These four features of science have a further implication: science at its best is a *social enterprise.* Every researcher or team of researchers labors under limitations of knowledge and insight, and mistakes are unavoidable, yet such errors will likely be pointed out by others. Understanding the social character of science can be liberating since it means that our work need not be beyond criticism to make an important contribution—whether to the description of a problem or its conceptualization, to theory or to the evaluation of theory. As long as our work explicitly addresses (or attempts to redirect) the concerns of the community of scholars and uses public methods to arrive at inferences that are consistent with rules of science and the information at our disposal, it is likely to make a contribution. And the contribution of even a minor article is greater than that of the "great work" that stays forever in a desk drawer or within the confines of a computer.

1.1.3 Science and Complexity

Social science constitutes an attempt to make sense of social situations that we perceive as more or less complex. We need to recognize, however, that what we perceive as complexity is not entirely inherent in phenomena: the world is not naturally divided into simple and complex sets of events. On the contrary, the perceived complexity of a situation depends in part on how well we can simplify reality, and our capacity to simplify depends on whether we can specify outcomes and explanatory variables in a coherent way. Having more observations may assist us in this process but is usually insufficient. Thus *"complexity" is partly conditional on the state of our theory.*

Scientific methods can be as valuable for intrinsically complex events as for simpler ones. Complexity is likely to make our inferences less certain but should *not* make them any less scientific. Uncertainty and limited data should not cause us to abandon scientific research. On the contrary: the biggest payoff for using the rules of scientific inference occurs precisely when data are limited, observation tools are flawed, measurements are unclear, and relationships are uncertain. With clear relationships and unambiguous data, method may be less important, since even partially flawed rules of inference may produce answers that are roughly correct.

Consider some complex, and in some sense unique, events with enormous ramifications. The collapse of the Roman Empire, the French Revolution, the American Civil War, World War I, the Holocaust, and the reunification of Germany in 1990 are all examples of such events. These events seem to be the result of complex interactions of many forces whose conjuncture appears crucial to the event having taken place. That is, independently caused sequences of events and forces converged at a given place and time, their interaction appearing to bring about the events being observed (Hirschman 1970). Furthermore, it is often difficult to believe that these events were inevitable products of large-scale historical forces: some seem to have depended, in part, on idiosyncrasies of personalities, institutions, or social movements. Indeed, from the perspective of our theories, chance often seems to have played a role: factors outside the scope of the theory provided crucial links in the sequences of events.

One way to understand such events is by seeking generalizations: conceptualizing each case as a member of a *class of events* about which meaningful generalizations can be made. This method often works well for ordinary wars or revolutions, but some wars and revolutions, being much more extreme than others, are "outliers" in the statistical distribution. Furthermore, notable early wars or revolutions may exert such a strong impact on subsequent events of the same class—we think again of the French Revolution—that caution is necessary in comparing them with their successors, which may be to some extent the product of imitation. Expanding the class of events can be useful, but it is not always appropriate.

Another way of dealing scientifically with rare, large-scale events is to engage in counterfactual analysis: "the mental construction of a course of events which is altered through modifications in one or more 'conditions'" (Weber [1905] 1949:173). The application of this idea in a systematic, scientific way is illustrated in a particularly extreme example of a rare event from geology and evolutionary biology, both historically oriented natural sciences. Stephen J. Gould has suggested that one way to distinguish systematic features of evolution from stochastic, chance events may be to imagine what the world would be like if all conditions up to a specific point were fixed and then the rest of history were rerun. He contends that if it were possible to "replay the tape of life," to let evolution occur again from the beginning, the world's organisms today would be a completely different (Gould 1989).

A unique event on which students of evolution have recently focused is the sudden extinction of the dinosaurs 65 million years ago. Gould (1989:318) says, "we must assume that consciousness would not have evolved on our planet if a cosmic catastrophe had not claimed the dinosaurs as victims." If this statement is true, the extinction of the dinosaurs was as important as any historical event for human beings; however, dinosaur extinction does not fall neatly into a class of events that could be studied in a systematic, comparative fashion through the application of general laws in a straightforward way.

Nevertheless, dinosaur extinction can be studied scientifically: alternative hypotheses can be developed and tested with respect to their observable implications. One hypothesis to account for dinosaur extinction, developed by Luis Alvarez and collaborators at Berkeley in the late 1970s (Alvarez 1990), posits a cosmic collision: a meteorite crashed into the earth at about 72,000 kilometers an hour, creating a blast greater than that from a full-scale nuclear war. If this hypothesis is correct, it would have the observable implication that iridium (an element common in meteorites but rare on earth) should be found in the particular layer of the earth's crust that corresponds to sediment laid down sixty-five million years ago; indeed, the discovery of iridium at predicted layers in the earth has been taken as partial confirming evidence for the theory. Although this is an unambiguously unique event, there are many other observable implications. For one example, it should be possible to find the meteorite's crater somewhere on Earth (and several candidates have already been found).[3]

The issue of the cause(s) of dinosaur extinction remains unresolved, although the controversy has generated much valuable research. For our purposes, the point of this example is that scientific generalizations are useful in studying even highly unusual events that do not fall into a large class of events. The Alvarez hypothesis cannot be tested with reference to a set of common events, but it does have observable implications for other phenomena that can be evaluated. We should note, however, that a hypothesis is not considered a reasonably certain explanation until it has been evaluated empirically and passed a number of demanding tests. At a minimum, its implications must be consistent with our knowledge of the external world; at best, it should predict what Imre Lakatos (1970) refers to as "new facts," that is, those formerly unobserved.

The point is that even apparently unique events such as dinosaur extinction can be studied scientifically if we pay attention to improving theory, data, and our use of the data. Improving our theory through conceptual clarification and specification of variables can generate more observable implications and even test causal theories of unique events such as dinosaur extinction. Improving our data allows us to observe more of these observable implications, and improving our use of data permits more of these implications to be extracted from existing data. That a set of events to be studied is highly complex does not render careful research design irrelevant. Whether we study many phenomena or few—or even one—the study will be improved if we collect data on as many observable implications of our theory as possible.

NOTES

1. We reject the concept, or at least the word, "quasi-experiment." Either a research design involves investigator control over the observations and values of the key causal variables (in which case it is an experiment) or it does not (in which case it is nonexperimental research). Both experimental and nonexperimental research have their advantages and drawbacks; one is not better in all research situations than the other.

2. Although we do cover the vast majority of the important rules of scientific inference, they are not complete. Indeed, most philosophers agree that a complete, exhaustive inductive logic is impossible, even in principle.

3. However, an alternative hypothesis, that extinction was caused by volcanic eruptions, is also consistent with the presence of iridium, and seems more consistent than the meteorite hypothesis with the finding that all the species extinctions did not occur simultaneously.

REFERENCES

Alvarez, Walter, and Frank Asaro. 1990. "An Extraterrestrial Impact." *Scientific American* (October): 78–84.

Gould, Stephen J. 1989. *Wonderful Life: The Burgess Shale and the Nature of History.* New York: Norton.

Hirschmann, Albert O. 1970. "The Search for Paradigms as a Hindrance to Understanding." *World Politics* 22, no. 3 (April): 329–43.

Lakatos, Imre. 1970. "Falsification and the Methodology of Scientific Research Programs." In I. Lakatos and A. Musgrave, eds. *Criticism and the Growth of Knowledge.* Cambridge: Cambridge University Press.

Merton, Robert K. [1949] 1968. *Social Theory and Social Structure.* Reprint. New York: Free Press.

Schumpeter, Joseph A. [1936] 1991. "Can Capitalism Survive?" In Richard Swedberg, ed. *The Economics of Sociology and Capitalism,* Princeton: Princeton University Press.

Skocpol, Theda. 1984. "Emerging Agendas and Recurrent Strategies in Historical Sociology." In Theda Skocpol, ed. *Vision and Method in Historical Sociology.* New York: Cambridge University Press.

Weber, Max. [1905] 1949. "Critical Studies in the Logic of the Cultural Sciences." In Max Weber, ed. *The Methodology of the Social Sciences.* Translated and edited by Edward A. Shils and Henry A. Fluch. New York: Free Press.

Larry M. Bartels

SOME UNFULFILLED PROMISES OF QUANTITATIVE IMPERIALISM

King, Keohane, and Verba's *Designing Social Inquiry: Scientific Inference in Qualitative Research* (hereafter *DSI*) is an important addition to the literature on research methodology in political science and throughout the social sciences. It represents a systematic effort by three of the most eminent figures in our discipline to codify the basic precepts of quantitative inference and apply them with uncommon consistency and self-consciousness to the seemingly distinct style of qualitative research that has produced most of the science in most of the social sciences over most of their history. The book seems to me to be remarkably interesting and useful both for its successes, which are considerable, and for its failures, which are also, in my view, considerable.

Here I shall touch only briefly upon one obvious and very important contribution of the book, and upon one respect in which the authors' argument seems to me to be misguided. The rest of my discussion will be devoted to identifying some of the author's more notable unfulfilled promises—not because they are somehow characteristic of the book as a whole, but because they are among the more important unfulfilled promises of our entire discipline. If *DSI* stimulates progress on some of these fronts, as I hope and believe it will, the book will turn out to represent a very significant contribution to qualitative methodology.

The Contribution and a Shortcoming

Anyone who thinks about social research primarily in terms of quantitative and statistical inference, as I do, has probably thought—and perhaps even said out loud—that the world would be a happier place if only qualitative researchers would learn and respect the basic rudiments of quantitative reasoning. By presenting those rudiments clearly, engagingly, and with

From Henry E. Brady and David Collier, eds., *Rethinking Social Inquiry: Diverse Tools, Shared Standards*, 2nd Edition (Lanham, MD: Rowman & Littlefield Publishers, 2010), pp. 69–74.

a minimum of technical apparatus, *DSI* has helped shine the light of basic methodological knowledge into many rather dark corners of the social sciences. For that we owe its authors profound thanks.

At another level *DSI*'s argument seems to be misguided, although in a way that seems unlikely to have significant practical consequences. It is hard to doubt that "all qualitative and quantitative researchers would benefit by more explicit attention to this logic [i.e., the logic "explicated and formalized clearly in discussions of quantitative research methods"] in the course of designing research" (3). However, it simply does not seem to follow that "all good research can be understood—indeed, is best understood—to derive from the same underlying logic of inference" (4). Even if we set aside theorizing of every sort, from Arrow's (1951) theorem on the incoherence of liberal preference aggregation to Collier and Levitsky's (1997) conceptual analysis of scores of distinct types and subtypes of "democracy," it seems pointless to attempt to force "all good [empirical] research" into the procrustean bed of "scientific inference" set forth by *DSI*. Would it be fruitful—or even feasible—to recast such diverse works as Michels's *Political Parties* (1915), Polanyi's *The Great Transformation* (1944), Lane's *Political Ideology* (1962), Thompson's *The Making of the English Working Class* (1963), and Fenno's *Home Style* (1978) in the concepts and language of quantitative inference? Or are these not examples of "good research"?

The authors of *DSI* attempt to skirt the limitations of their focus by conceding that "analysts should simplify their descriptions only after they attain an understanding of the richness of history and culture—[R]ich, unstructured knowledge of the historical and cultural context of the phenomena with which they want to deal in a simplified and scientific way is usually a requisite for avoiding simplifications that are simply wrong" (43). But since they provide no scientific criteria for recognizing "understanding" and "unstructured knowledge" when we have it, the system of inference they offer is either too narrow or radically incomplete. Perhaps it doesn't really matter whether we speak of the process of "attain[ing] an understanding" as a poorly understood but indispensable requirement for doing science or as a poorly understood but indispensable part of the scientific process itself. I prefer the latter formulation, but the authors' apparent insistence upon the former will not keep anyone from relying upon—or aspiring to produce—"understanding" and "unstructured knowledge."

Omissions and an Agenda for Research

Most importantly, I am struck by what *DSI* leaves out of its codification of good inferential practice. I emphasize these limitations because they seem to suggest (though apparently unintentionally) an excellent agenda for the future development of qualitative and quantitative methodology. As is often the case in scientific work, the silences and failures of the best practitioners may point the way toward a discipline's subsequent successes. Here I shall provide four examples drawn from *DSI*'s discussions of uncertainty, qualitative evidence, measurement error, and multiplying observations.

Uncertainty

One of *DSI*'s most insistent themes concerns the importance of uncertainty in scientific inference. Its authors proclaim that "inferences without uncertainty estimates are not science as we define it" (9), and implore qualitative researchers to get on the scientific bandwagon by including estimates of uncertainty in their research reports (9 and elsewhere). But how, exactly, should well-meaning qualitative researchers implement that advice? Should they simply attempt to report their own subjective uncertainty about their conclusions? How should they attempt to reason from uncertainty about various separate aspects of their research to uncertainty about the end results of that research, if not by the standard quantitative calculus of probability? What sorts of checks on subjective reports of uncertainty about qualitative inferences might be feasible, when even the systematic policing mechanism enshrined in the quantitative approach to inference is routinely abused to the point of absurdity (Learner 1978, 1983; Freedman 1983)? Since *DSI* offers so little in the way of concrete guidance, its emphasis on uncertainty can do little more than sensitize researchers to the general limitations of inference in the qualitative mode without providing the tools to overcome those limitations. As far as I know, such tools do not presently exist; but their development should be high on the research agenda of qualitative methodologists.

Qualitative Evidence

DSI's discussions of the respective roles and merits of quantitative and qualitative evidence is equally sketchy. While its authors rightly laud Lisa Martin's (1992) *Coercive Cooperation* and Robert Putnam's (1993) *Making Democracy Work* for combining quantitative and qualitative evidence in especially fruitful ways (5), their discussion provides no clear account of *how*, exactly, Martin's or Putnam's juxtaposition of quantitative and qualitative evidence bolsters the force of their conclusions. Martin's work is rushed precipitously off the stage (as most of *DSI*'s concrete examples are), while Putnam's work only reappears—other than in an unrelated discussion of using alternative quantitative indicators of a single underlying theoretical concept (223–24)—in a discussion of qualitative immersion as a source of *hypotheses* rather than *evidence*. This in turn leads to the rather patronizing conclusion that "any definition of science that does not include room for ideas regarding the generation of hypotheses is as foolish as an interpretive account that does not care about discovering truth" (38).

There is more going on here than a simpleminded distinction between (qualitative) hypothesis generation and (quantitative) hypothesis testing, or a simpleminded faith that two kinds of evidence are better than one. Qualitative evidence does more than suggest hypotheses, and analyses combining quantitative and qualitative evidence can and

sometimes do ar [...] their parts. The a [...] nate those facts. P [...] point is that nobe [...] the "persuasive for [...] science as V. O. Ke [...] *tics in State and Natio* [...] *American Soldier*, and B [...] *ing* "is not easily explained [...] cal theory even today" (Achen [...] the persuasive force of these and [...] works convincingly accounted for th [...] interpretive, ethnographic, historical, or [...] brand of qualitative inquiry.

With reference to both uncertainty and qu[...] tative evidence, the limitations of *DSI*'s analysis faithfully reflect the limitations of the existing methodological literature on qualitative inference. Other gaps in *DSI*'s account are attributable to the limitations of the theory of quantitative inference it offers as a model for qualitative research. As a quantitative methodologist—and the coauthor of a rather optimistic survey of the recent literature in quantitative political methodology (Bartels and Brady 1993)—I am chagrined to notice how wobbly and incomplete are some of the inferential foundations that *DSI* claims are "explicated and formalized clearly in discussions of quantitative research methods" (3). Again, two examples will suffice to illustrate the point.

Measurement Error

The first example of the weak foundations of inferential claims is *DSI*'s treatment of measurement error, which—like much of the elementary textbook wisdom on that subject—is both incomplete and unrealistically optimistic. The authors assert that unsystematic (random) measurement error in explanatory variables "unfailingly [biases] inferences in predictable ways. Understanding the nature of these biases will help ameliorate or possibly avoid them" (155). Later, they assert more specifically that the resulting bias

m: it results in the estima-
usal relationship than is the
e end of their discussion the
edge that their analysis is based
with a single explanatory variable.
y assert that it "applies just the same
her has many explanatory variables,
one with substantial random measure-
rror," or if researchers "study the effect of
variable sequentially rather than simultane-
y" (166). Their only suggestion of potential
implications is a claim that "if one has multiple
explanatory variables and is simultaneously analyzing their effects, and if each has different kinds
of measurement error, we can only ascertain the
kinds of biases likely to arise by extending the formal analysis" (166).

DSI's assertion about the case of several explanatory variables, where only one is measured with
substantial error, is quite misleading in failing to
note that the bias in the parameter estimate associated with the one variable measured with substantial error will be propagated in complicated ways to
all of the other parameter estimates in the analysis.
This will bias them upward or downward depending on the pattern of correlations among the various explanatory variables. The book's assertion
about sequential rather than simultaneous analysis of several explanatory variables is also misleading, at least in the sense that the resulting omitted
variable bias may mitigate, exacerbate, or reverse
the bias attributable to measurement error. And
the promise of "ascertain[ing] the kinds of biases
likely to arise" in more complicated situations "by
extending the formal analysis" (DSI 166) can in
general be redeemed only if we have a good deal
of prior information about the nature and magnitudes of the various errors—information virtually
impossible to come by in all but the most well-
understood and data-rich research settings (Achen
1983; Cowden and Hartley 1993). Thus, while it
seems useful to have alerted qualitative researchers
to the fact that measurement error in explanatory
variables may lead to serious biases in parameter

estimates, it seems disingenuous to suggest that
quantitative tools offer reliable ways to "ameliorate
or possibly avoid" (155) those biases in real qualitative research.

Multiplying Observations

The second example is DSI's chapter on "Increasing the Number of Observations," which seems
equally disingenuous in asserting that "almost any
qualitative research design can be reformulated
into one with many observations, and that this can
often be done without additional costly data collection if the researcher appropriately conceptual-
izes the observable implications that have already
been gathered" (208). While it is right to emphasize the importance of "maximizing leverage" by
using the available data to test many implications
of a given theory (or even better, of several competing theories), DSI's discussion obscures the
fact that having many *implications* is not the same
thing as having many *observations*. In order for our
inferences to be valid, each of our many implications must itself be verified using a research design
that avoids the pitfall of "indeterminacy" inherent
in having more explanatory variables than relevant
observations.

What, then, is a "relevant observation"? DSI
provides the answer in its earlier, clear, and careful discussion of causal homogeneity.[1] Relevant
observations are those for which "all units with
the same value of the explanatory variables have
the same expected value of the dependent variable" (91). But the more we succeed in identifying diverse empirical implications of our theories,
the less likely it will be that those diverse implications can simply be accumulated as homogeneous
observations in a single quantitative model. Having a richly detailed case study touching upon
many implications of the same theory or theories
is no substitute for "seek[ing] homogenous units
across time or across space" (93), as DSI points
out in the subsequent discussion of "process tracing" (226–28).

The authors of *DSI* allow that "attaining [causal] homogeneity is often impossible," but go on to assert in the next sentence that "understanding the degree of heterogeneity in our units of analysis will help us to estimate the degree of uncertainty or likely biases to be attributed to our inferences" (93–94). How is that? Again, the authors do not explain. But once again, the more important point is that nobody else does either—a point I am compelled to acknowledge despite my own efforts in that direction (Bartels 1996). If we accept *DSI*'s assertion that the "generally untestable" assumption of causal homogeneity (or the related assumption of "constant causal effects") "lies at the base of all scientific research" (93), this is a loud and embarrassing silence.

Conclusion

In the end, *DSI*'s optimistic-sounding unit of quantitative and qualitative research seems t to promise a good deal more than it delivers, and good deal more than it could possibly deliver given the current state of political methodology in both its qualitative and quantitative modes. But perhaps that is the genius of the book. By presenting a bold and beguiling vision of a seamless, scientific methodology of social inquiry, *DSI* may successfully challenge all of us to make some serious progress toward implementing that vision.

NOTE

1. *DSI* (91) uses the label "unit homogeneity" for this assumption.

Ronald Rogowski

HOW INFERENCE IN THE SOCIAL (BUT NOT THE PHYSICAL) SCIENCES NEGLECTS THEORETICAL ANOMALY

Designing Social Inquiry, by King, Keohane, and Verba (hereafter *DSI*), deserves praise for many reasons. It attempts, seriously and without condescension, to bridge the gap between qualitative and quantitative political science. It reminds a new generation of students, in both traditions, of some main characteristics of good theory (testability, operationalizability, and "leverage" or deductive fertility). It clarifies, even for the profoundly mathematically challenged, some of the central strictures of quantitative inference (why one cannot have

more variables than cases or select on the dependent variable, or why it biases results if measurement of the independent variable is faulty). It abounds with practical wisdom on research design, case selection, and complementary methodologies. Perhaps most importantly, it opens a dialogue between previously isolated practitioners of these two forms of analysis and provokes worthwhile discussion.

For all of these reasons and more, the book should be, will be, and—indeed even in its *samizdat* forms—already has been widely assigned and read. It is, quite simply, the best work of its kind now available; indeed, it is very likely the best yet to have appeared.[1] At the same time, I think, *DSI* falters in its aim of evangelizing qualitative social scientists;

From Henry E. Brady and David Collier, eds., *Rethinking Social Inquiry: Diverse Tools, Shared Standards* (Lanham, MD: Rowman & Littlefield Publishers, 2010), pp. 75–83.

and it does so, paradoxically, because it attends insufficiently to the importance of problemation and deductive theorizing in the scientific enterprise.

Problemation and Deductive Theorizing

As natural scientists have long understood (see Hempel 1966), inference proceeds most efficiently by three complementary routes: (1) making clear the essential model, or process, that one hypothesizes to be at work; (2) teasing out the deductive implications of that model, focusing particularly on the implications that seem a priori least plausible; and (3) rigorously testing those least plausible implications against empirical reality.[2] The Nobel physicist and polymath Richard Feynman may have put it best:[3]

experimenters search most diligently, and with the greatest effort, in exactly those places where it seems most likely that we can prove our theories wrong. In other words we are trying to prove ourselves wrong as quickly as possible, because only in that way can we find progress. (1965:158)

The classical example is Einstein's Theory of Relativity, which: (1) uniquely provided an overarching model that could explain both the anomalies and the enduring validities of classical Newtonian mechanics, indeed could subsume it as a special case; (2) had, among its many other implications, a quite specific, rather implausible, and previously untested one about how light reflected from the planet Mercury would be deflected by the sun's gravitation; and (3) appeared at the time to be precisely accurate in this specific and implausible implication.[4] To test, however rigorously, hypotheses that challenge no deeper theory or that themselves lack deductive implications is an inefficient route of scientific inference; while theories that are precise and deductively fertile enough can often be sustained or refuted by surprisingly unelaborate

tests, including ones that involve few observations or that violate normally sacrosanct principles of selection.

DSI, I contend, emphasizes the third part of scientific inquiry, the rigorous testing of hypotheses, almost to the exclusion of the first two—the elaboration of precise models and the deduction of their (ideally, many) logical implications—and thus points us to a pure, but needlessly inefficient, path of social-scientific inquiry.

Theory and Anomaly: Some Examples

I can best illustrate these points by applying *DSI*'s strictures to some landmark works in comparative politics, often cited as worthy of emulation. Each work, it seems to me, would fail *DSI*'s tests and would be dismissed as insufficiently scientific. Yet in each case, the dismissal would be incorrect: the works illustrate—indeed epitomize—valid and efficient social-scientific inquiry; and the ways in which they do so illuminate the shortcomings in *DSI*'s analysis.

Three of the classical works that I have in mind are single-observation studies; one involves three cases, but all within a single region; one selects chiefly on the independent—but also on the dependent—variable, in ways deprecated by *DSI*; and one selects on the dependent variable. I propose: (1) to sketch each briefly; (2) to argue that the conventional wisdom is right, and *DSI* is wrong, with regard to these works' worth; and (3) to reflect on the deficiencies that these works reveal in *DSI*'s analysis.

The single-observation studies are Arend Lijphart's (1968) study of the Netherlands, *The Politics of Accommodation*; William Sheridan Allen's single-city examination, *The Nazi Seizure of Power*; and Peter Alexis Gourevitch's 1978 critique of Immanuel Wallerstein's *Modern World-System*. Each involves disconfirmation of a prevailing theory, by what Eckstein called the strategy of the "most likely" case (1975:119).

Lijphart rightly saw in the Netherlands a serious empirical challenge to David Truman's (1951) then widely accepted theory of "cross-cutting cleavages." Truman had argued, plausibly enough, that mutually reinforcing social cleavages (class coterminous with religious practice, or religion with language) impeded social agreement and made conflict more likely. Only where each deep cleavage was orthogonal to another (e.g., Switzerland, where many Catholics are German-speaking, many Francophones Protestant) was social peace likely to endure. About the Netherlands, however, two things were abundantly clear: (1) it had virtually no cross-cutting cleavages; and (2) it had about as stable and amicable a democracy as one could find. Lijphart's study was taken at the time, I believe correctly, as having refuted Truman's theory.[5]

In attempting to explain popular support for such totalitarian movements as Fascism, many social scientists had, by the 1950s, accepted a theory whose roots went back to Montesquieu and Tocqueville but whose modern version had been shaped chiefly by Lederer (1940), Arendt (1958), and—the great synthesizer of this genre—Kornhauser (1959). Again simplifying it to the point of caricature, this theory held that societies were opened to totalitarianism's Manichean zealotries by the waning (e.g., through rapid modernization) of associational life—the disappearance of those "natural" groups that afforded meaning, balance, and a sense of efficacy. Totalitarian followers were "atomized" or "mass" individuals.

Tracing the growth of the National Socialist cause in a single midsized German town where it had prospered earlier and better than the average, however, Allen (1965) found, if anything, a superabundance of associational life: singing and shooting societies, card clubs, fraternal orders, religious associations, drinking groups, and *Stammtische* of long standing, to the point that one could hardly imagine a free evening in these proto-Fascists' lives. Neither could he observe any waning of this associational activity before or during the Nazi expansion, nor were Nazis drawn disproportionately from the less active (if anything, the contrary).[6] Only *after*

Hitler came to power, with the Nazi *Gleichschaltung* of all associations, did activity decline. Allen's results were read (again, I think, rightly) as having strongly impugned an otherwise plausible theory.

A central assertion of Immanuel Wallerstein's *Modern World-System*, vol. 1 (1974), was that the "core" states of the world economy, from the sixteenth century onward, had been likeliest to develop strong states (in order to guarantee capitalist property rights and to protect trade routes) and to pursue linguistic and cultural homogeneity (in order to lower administrative and transaction costs). Yet as Gourevitch and others quickly observed, it was, in fact, a central European state of what Wallerstein had called the "semiperiphery" (i.e., Prussia) that developed arguably the strongest state in the early modern world and that came earliest to mass education and the pursuit of linguistic homogeneity (1978: esp. 423–27). The case seriously undermined this aspect of Wallerstein's theory; but Gourevitch went on to speculate—and Charles Tilly (1990) has subsequently advanced considerable argument and evidence to show—that in fact, the correlation was the reverse: The economically most advanced early modern states were often the least powerful and vice versa.

Against the record amassed by these and other single-observation studies, *DSI* contends that "[I]n general . . . the single observation is not a useful technique for testing hypotheses or theories" (211), chiefly because measurement error may yield a false negative, omitted variables may yield an unpredicted result, or social-scientific theories are insufficiently precise.[7] The authors would have us accept that the Lijphart, Allen, and Gourevitch studies—and even more the sweeping inferences that most comparativists drew from them—were bad science; as *DSI* states explicitly, falsification from a single observation "is not the way social science is or should be conducted" (103).

Rudolf Heberle's (1963, 1970) justly famous exploration of Nazi support in Schleswig-Holstein is exemplary in doing what *DSI* calls "making many observations from few" (217); yet Heberle's research, too, would presumably fail to meet *DSI*'s standard. Long before Barrington Moore, Jr. (1967) solidified the thesis, analysts had conjectured a close link between labor-repressive agriculture and susceptibility to Fascism. It occurred to Heberle that the north German state of Schleswig-Holstein offered an ideal test of the thesis, containing, as it did, three distinct agricultural regions, characterized respectively by: (1) plantation agriculture on the East Elbian, or the "Junker" model (the Hill district); (2) prosperous family farms like those of western and southwestern Germany (the Marsh); and (3) hardscrabble, quasi-subsistence farming (the *Geest*). The asserted link to feudalism would predict the earliest and strongest Nazi support in the first of these regions; but in fact the Fascist breakthrough occurred in the *Geest*, among the marginalized subsistence farmers; the family farmers came along only considerably later, and the feudal region resisted almost to the end. This brilliantly designed little study thus seriously undermined, even before its precise formulation, what has since come to be know as the "Moore thesis" about the origins of Fascism.

Like Atul Kohli's (1987) three-state study of poverty policy in India, Heberle's examination inventively exploits within-country—in Heberle's case, within-region—variation. Yet *DSI* dismisses precisely this aspect of Kohli's analysis, on the ground that the values of both the explanatory and the dependent variables were known in advance; "selection, in effect, is on both the explanatory and dependent variables" so that "the design . . . provides no information about his causal hypothesis" (145). Of course, Heberle, by confining his attention to a single state, partially constrained himself against biased selection; but Schleswig-Holstein itself might represent only random variation, and so (*DSI* would surely say) could not be taken as refuting the hypothesized causal link between feudalism and Fascism. Again, I think, *DSI*'s strictures, taken literally, would dismiss a brilliant study as bad (or at least inadequate) social science.

My final two examples raise the stakes considerably, for they represent, by common consent, the very best of recent work in comparative politics. Yet Peter Katzenstein's *Small States in World Markets* (1985), by *DSI*'s lights, inadmissibly restricts variation on the independent and dependent variables; and Robert Bates's *Markets and States in Tropical Africa* (1981) impermissibly selects on the dependent variable.

Katzenstein, contesting the conventional wisdom that only large states were independent enough to be worth studying, deliberately restricted his focus to the smaller European states and, within that set, to the smaller states that were "close to the apex of the international pyramid of success," thus "excluding Ireland, Finland, and some of the Mediterranean countries" (1985: 21). His reasons were straightforward: (1) the cases that he did study were *anomalous*, for small, price-taking countries were widely supposed to face particular challenges in an uncertain international environment; and (2) they were *forerunners*, in the sense that all countries were rapidly becoming as dependent on international markets as these small ones had long been. To examine why countries that theoretically should not succeed in fact did so (reminiscent of Lijphart's strategy) and to attempt to discern a possible path of adaptation of larger states, seemed, both to Katzenstein and to his generally enthusiastic readership, a sensible strategy. Yet *DSI*, at least as I read the book, must hold Katzenstein guilty of two cardinal sins that largely vitiate his analysis: (1) instead of choosing his cases to guarantee some range of variation on the independent variable, he restricts his analysis to small (and therefore quite trade-dependent) states; and (2) more seriously, taking economic success or failure as his dependent variable, he looks only at instances of success.

Bates's book is an even clearer case of selection on the dependent variable. Exactly as Michael Porter's *Competitive Advantage of Nations* (1990) examines only cases of economic success and thus draws withering fire from *DSI* (133–34), Bates focuses almost entirely on cases of economic failure or, more precisely, on the remarkably uniform *pattern* of economic failure among the states of post-independence Africa. He nonetheless develops an account that most readers have found compelling: (1) that the failures all resulted from an economic policy that heavily taxed agricultural exports to subsidize investment in heavily protected manufactures; and (2) that this self-destructive economic policy was the inevitable result of a political constellation in which urban groups were organized and powerful, rural ones scattered and weak. While Bates supports his analysis by observing that the two African cases of relative economic success (i.e., Kenya and Côte d'Ivoire) were characterized by export-friendly policy and politically more powerful farmers, this part of his discussion is brief and clearly tangential to his main argument.

Why, despite their seemingly egregious sins,[8] are all of these works believed by most comparativists—rightly, in my judgment—to have provided convincing inferences about their topics of study? Chiefly, I submit, for two reasons, which shed much light on the problems of *DSI*'s account: (1) all of them tested, relied on, or proposed, clear and precise *theories*; and (2) all focused on *anomalies,* either in prevailing theories or in the world—cases that contradicted received beliefs or unexpected regularities that were too pronounced to be accidental.

The theories of cross-cutting cleavages (Truman 1951), atomization (e.g., Kornhauser 1959), world-systems (Wallerstein 1974), and feudal legacy (Moore 1967) had the great advantage of being precise enough to yield implications for single, or for very few, observations. Lijphart, Allen, Gourevitch, and Heberle, respectively, took brilliant scholarly advantage of that precision: (1) to seek out anomalous cases and, usually, (2) to conjecture intelligently about a more satisfactory general theory that could avoid such anomalies.

About small states and heavy reliance on external markets there was less a prevailing theory than a prevailing prejudice—that puniness entailed constraint, insecurity, and (barring extraordinary good luck) economic trouble. By adducing seven cases of small states that had consistently prospered, Katzenstein demonstrated that insecurity and poverty were far from inevitable; by showing that their strategies, in similar circumstances, had differed, he proved that they retained considerable freedom of policy; and by analyzing their marked similarities of historical development and present-day governance, he advanced a plausible (if in this work still conjectural)[9] theory of situational requisites for highly trade-dependent states.

The African economic devastation that Bates studied was usually "explained" by a mélange of misunderstood Marxism and economic illiteracy that stressed the "dependence" of the third world on the first. By invoking standard, simple economics, Bates easily showed that local policy, and not first-world plots, must be to blame. If domestic agricultural prices were systematically suppressed, one would expect to see smuggling and rural flight; if domestic industry was protected and subsidized, one would expect cartels, uncompetitive goods, and an overvalued currency; if taxes and controls poured power and resources into the hands of bureaucrats, one would anticipate a bloated public sector and vicious competition for place and favor. In each African case, all of these in fact prevailed, and no amount of external "dependence" could so easily explain this particular concatenation of disasters.

Yet this left a riddle no less profound than the original one: why should almost all governments of the region have deliberately chosen policies so inimical to aggregate welfare and to long-term growth? Just as a psychologist might become intrigued if all but one or two of the people on a certain street began suddenly to mutilate themselves, Bates pursued a "cluster analysis" (see *DSI* 148–49) of perverse African policies and reached his highly plausible conjecture that rural weakness produced a fatal "urban bias" (see Lipton 1976) in policy.[10]

In the works of Katzenstein and Bates, then, no less than in those cited earlier, the crucial ingredient was clear, precise, powerful ("high leverage") theory with what Lave and March (1975) tellingly called a "sense of process," that is, intuitively plausible causal links. In both accounts, universally accepted economic theory underpinned the critique of received wisdom: if small, price-taking firms survived in uncertain markets, why not small, price-taking countries; if all of the symptoms of the African cases were consistent with systematic price distortions, what other diagnosis was possible? The core of Katzenstein's alternative account was a story about how democratic corporatism facilitated flexible adjustment to external markets; the core of Bates's account, a hypothesized link between power and policy. That both arguments were so clear, plausible, and precise contributed crucially to their persuasiveness.

Lessons

DSI (127), in contrast, frequently chooses as examples hypotheses that seem obvious or that lack deductive fertility. To prove, for example, that declining Communist societies were more likely to spawn mass movements of opposition the less repressive the old regime was neither contravenes received wisdom nor carries broader implications for other cases.

The aspects of larger theory and of "sense of process," consequently, seem to be sorely absent from *DSI*'s prescriptions for social inquiry. While the authors are right to fear our natural tendency to see patterns where none exist (21), they emphasize insufficiently the centrality of patterns—indeed, of "paradigms" (Kuhn 1962)—to efficient scientific inquiry. A powerful, deductive, internally consistent theory can be seriously undermined, at least in comparative politics, by even one wildly discordant observation (Lijphart's Netherlands). On the positive side, a powerful theory can, by explaining an otherwise mysterious empirical regularity (European small-state corporatism, African economic failure), gain provisional acceptance at least as a highly plausible conjecture worthy of further research. As most discussions of spurious correlation make clear, we

gain confidence in a proposed explanation to the extent that it *both* (1) fits the data *and* (2) "makes sense" in terms of its consistency with other observations and its own deductive implications. *DSI*, it seems to me, emphasizes the former at the expense of the latter. In consequence, its advice to area specialists focuses almost entirely on "increasing the number of observations" (chap. 6). Many comparativists, I think, would instead counsel: "Choose better theory, which can make better use of few or single observations."[11]

Valuable as *DSI*'s strictures are, I fear that devout attention to them may paralyze, rather than stimulate, scientific inquiry in comparative politics. The authors write eloquently and insightfully about the trade-offs between close observation of a few cases and more cursory measurement of many (chap. 2, esp. 66–68); I wish they had as perceptively discussed how better theory permits inference from fewer cases, allows restriction on the independent variable, and may even profit from judicious selection on the dependent variable.

In short, I suspect *DSI* does not mean quite as stern a message as it sends; or perhaps the authors view the studies I have discussed here in a different and more redeeming light. However, the book would have spoken more clearly to comparativists if it had specifically addressed the major literature of the less quantitative tradition.

NOTES

1. The only competition, long out of print and aimed more at the advanced undergraduate level, is probably Lave and March (1975).
2. Eckstein characterized this as the strategy of the "least-likely" case (1975: 118–19). See also Hempel (1966: 37–38).
3. I owe this citation to Mark Lichbach.
4. To quote a famous statement on this prediction in a letter of J. E. Littlewood to Bertrand Russell, written in 1919: "Dear Russell: Einstein's theory is completely confirmed. The predicted displacement

was 1″.72 and the observed 1.″75 ± .06. Yours, J. E. L." Quoted in Russell (1969: 149).

5. Lijphart went on to conjecture, on the basis of the Dutch case, about the precise circumstances in which non-cross-cutting cleavages were compatible with civic peace; but that is secondary to the point I am arguing here.

6. To be sure, *DSI* distinguishes between *cases* and *observations*; and Allen's study could be read as a single case that encompasses many observations, given that Allen examines a variety of groups and individuals. Such a reading, in my view, would fundamentally misunderstand the underlying theory, whose central independent variable is the level of association that individuals encounter. Given the theory, the town (or, at most, the class within the town) is the relevant observation; and Allen's study is therefore a single case *and* a single observation.

7. *DSI*'s strictures on the first two points are so sweeping that they must, by implication, include theories and hypotheses in the physical sciences. Hence I take it that *DSI* would also reject the confirmation of the theory of relativity and other cases alluded to by Hempel (1966: 77), which rested on single observations.

8. As regards selection on the dependent variable, *DSI* takes a particularly draconian stand: "We can . . .

learn nothing about a causal effect from a study which selects observations so that the dependent variable does not vary" (147).

9. To be sure, by looking only at successful small European states, Katzenstein had to leave open the possibilities (1) that unsuccessful small states were also governed corporatively; and (2) that small non-European states had discovered quite different recipes for success.

10. It is worth noting that Bates has pursued this conjecture *not* through any large-N study, but by close analysis of an apparently anomalous case: Colombia, where dispersed coffee farmers of modest means prevailed politically not only against city dwellers but over concentrated plantation owners of considerable wealth.

11. As I note at the outset, *DSI* does discuss—at some length and quite sensibly—some major characteristics of good theory (section 3.5). The authors seem, however, to despair that social-scientific theories can ever be precise enough to permit valid inference from few cases (210–11); and they explicitly reject parsimony as an inherently desirable property of social-scientific theory (20, 104–5). On neither point, I suspect, will most comparativists find their arguments persuasive; and they seem to me to be refuted by the examples I adduce here.

2

THE STATE

At the center of most discussions of comparative politics lies the state, the organization that wields power over people and territory. In this chapter, we will consider the ways in which we think about and measure the state and how these have changed over time. A theoretical discussion of the state is complemented by more concrete discussions of the challenges that states confront in the current international system.

We begin with a recent work, one that reaches furthest back in the study of the state. Francis Fukuyama's book *The Origins of Political Order* (2011) begins with a discussion of the importance of the state in understanding modern political development. Fukuyama rejects what he calls "fantasies of statelessness," in which technology or ideology would marginalize the state. Rather, this institution and its long historical development are crucial to understanding the central questions of comparative politics: Why are some countries democratic and others not? Why are some countries rich and others poor? A long range of history and a broad sweep across the globe are central to understanding modern politics. It is interesting that Fukuyama rejects most comparativists' historical focus on Europe as the origin of states, arguing instead for "China first."

Fukuyama and other scholars rely heavily on the work of Max Weber, often cited as one of the forefathers of modern social science. In addition to political science, the fields of sociology and economics also owe a debt to Weber. Indeed, at the time of his writing, during the late nineteenth and early twentieth century, these fields were not clearly distinguished from each other. "Politics as a Vocation" (1918) was a speech originally presented at Munich University, in which Weber sought to lay out some of the most basic ways in which he understood political power. Weber provided the modern definition of the state (a monopoly of force over territory) and from there outlined what he believed to be the central forms of political authority (traditional, charismatic, rational-legal). For Weber, the development of the modern state occurs alongside the growing domination of the bureaucracy and rational legal authority—politics as a profession, rather than a calling or an inherited role. Thus, charismatic or traditional leaders gave way to the modern professional state. In spite of the profound influence of Weber's work, by the mid-twentieth century, state-focused analysis began to lose favor, particularly in the United States. Swept up in the so-called behavioral revolution, political scientists began to concentrate more on societal factors, downplaying the degree to which the state itself was an important source of politics.

However, as Fukuyama's work suggests, over the past three decades, political scientists have returned their attention to the idea of state power and how the state's autonomy and capacity can shape such things as the emergence of democracy or economic progress (topics that we discuss in Chapters 4 and 5). Comparative politics has again become a much more state-focused field of study. A wide range of contemporary scholars has refocused on the state as an important variable in comparative politics. Jeffrey Herbst's "War and the State in Africa" (1990) draws on historical studies of state formation in Europe to consider whether we can expect a similar outcome in other parts of the world, such as Africa. In Europe, the author notes, interstate war was a critical component in the development of the modern state, helping to improve taxation, administration, and the development of symbols to establish national identity, a process that occurred over many centuries. In Africa, however, states have not formed out of a long process of warfare, but rather are the remnants of empires that once dominated the continent. These states are ill-equipped to carry out most administrative tasks and lack the kind of national unity that can help build state legitimacy. There is a terrible irony, then: the absence of interstate war across Africa has left the continent with an array of weak states that cannot secure either prosperity or security. Indeed, one could go so far as to argue that the lack of war between states has resulted in horrible wars within them, such as the civil conflicts in Liberia or the genocide in Rwanda. Herbst is skeptical that peaceful state-building policies could be an alternative to war, and though he does not suggest that war between countries should be welcomed in Africa in order to build stronger states, it is hard not to draw such an uncomfortable conclusion. In the foreseeable future, the author anticipates an Africa of "permanently weak states."

In the years since Herbst's work was written, Africa and other parts of the world have seen the rise of something worse than the weak states Herbst discusses. This is what is known as the "failed state." From the former Soviet Union to Latin America, Asia, and Africa, various countries have teetered on the edge or plunged into the abyss of state failure, where the most basic functions of the state—including the monopoly of force—have broken down, leading to civil conflict and anarchy. Failed states have become a tremendous concern, not only because of the suffering that such state failures cause but also because of the fear that failed states often provide the perfect breeding ground for terrorism. Robert Rotberg considers this in "The New Nature of Nation-State Failure" (2002). When states fail, we see greater civil conflict, weak infrastructure, inequality, corruption, and economic decline. As we learned from Herbst, it is very difficult to build a strong state; for a failed state, this task is even more difficult. Policy makers, Rotberg argues, should take more care to identify and strengthen states in danger of collapse before they are beyond assistance and become an international threat.

Scholars are concerned about not only the power of the state but also the state's future direction. In "Sovereignty" (2001), Stephen D. Krasner takes on many of the recent arguments that, in one way or another, suggest the decline of the state as a major political actor. In spite of such factors as globalization and political integration, the state is still very much alive and will continue to be the driving force in domestic and international politics. This dovetails nicely with Fukuyama's argument that the state has a long historical pedigree and an enormous impact on central questions in human development—and it is not going away anytime soon.

Francis Fukuyama
THE NECESSITY OF POLITICS

During the forty-year period from 1970 to 2010, there was an enormous upsurge in the number of democracies around the world. In 1973, only 45 of the world's 151 countries were counted as "free" by Freedom House, a nongovernmental organization that produces quantitative measures of civil and political rights for countries around the world. That year, Spain, Portugal, and Greece were dictatorships; the Soviet Union and its Eastern European satellites looked like strong and cohesive societies; China was caught up in Mao Zedong's Cultural Revolution; Africa saw the consolidation of rule by a group of corrupt "presidents for life"; and most of Latin America had fallen under military dictatorship. The following generation saw momentous political change, with democracies and market-oriented economies spreading in virtually every part of the world except for the Arab Middle East. By the late 1990s, some 120 countries around the world—more than 60 percent of the world's independent states—had become electoral democracies. This transformation was Samuel Huntington's third wave of democratization; liberal democracy as the default form of government became part of the accepted political landscape at the beginning of the twenty-first century.

Underlying these changes in political systems was a massive social transformation as well. The shift to democracy was a result of millions of formerly passive individuals around the world organizing themselves and participating in the political life of their societies. This social mobilization was driven by a host of factors: greatly expanded access to education that made people more aware of themselves and the political world around them; information technology, which facilitated the rapid spread of ideas and knowledge; cheap travel and communications that allowed people to vote with their feet if they didn't like their government; and greater prosperity, which induced people to demand better protection of their rights.

The third wave crested after the late 1990s, however, and a "democratic recession" emerged in the first decade of the twenty-first century. Approximately one in five countries that had been part of the third wave either reverted to authoritarianism or saw a significant erosion of democratic institutions. Freedom House noted that 2009 marked the fourth consecutive year in which freedom had declined around the world, the first time this had happened since it established its measures of freedom in 1973.

Political Anxieties

At the beginning of the second decade of the twenty-first century, malaise in the democratic world took several distinct forms. The first was the outright reversal of democratic gains that had occurred in countries such as Russia, Venezuela, and Iran, where elected leaders were busy dismantling democratic institutions by manipulating elections, closing down or buying independent TV and newspaper outlets, and clamping down on opposition activities. Liberal democracy is more than majority voting in elections; it is a complex set of institutions that restrain and regularize the exercise of power through law and a system of checks and balances. In many countries, official acceptance of democratic legitimacy was accompanied by the systematic removal of checks on executive power and the erosion of the rule of law.

In other cases, countries that seemed to be making a transition from authoritarian government got stuck in what the analyst Thomas Carothers has labeled a "gray zone," where they were neither fully

From Francis Fukuyama, *The Origins of Political Order* (New York: Farrar, Strauss and Giroux, 2011), pp. 3–25. Author's notes have been omitted.

authoritarian nor meaningfully democratic. Many successor states to the former Soviet Union, like Kazakhstan and Uzbekistan in Central Asia, found themselves in this situation. There had been a broad assumption in the years following the fall of the Berlin Wall in 1989 that virtually all countries were transitioning to democracy and that failures of democratic practice would be overcome with the simple passage of time. Carothers pointed out that this "transition paradigm" was an unwarranted assumption and that many authoritarian elites had no interest in implementing democratic institutions that would dilute their power.

A third category of concern has to do not with the failure of political systems to become or remain democratic but rather their failure to deliver the basic services that people demand from their governments. The mere fact that a country has democratic institutions tells us very little about whether it is well or badly governed. This failure to deliver on the promise of democracy poses what is perhaps the greatest challenge to the legitimacy of such political systems.

An example of this was Ukraine. Ukraine surprised the world in 2004 when tens of thousands of people turned up in Kiev's Maidan Square to protest manipulation of that country's presidential election. These protests, which came to be known as the Orange Revolution, triggered a new election and the rise of the reformer Viktor Yushchenko as president. Once in power, however, the Orange Coalition proved utterly feckless, and Yushchenko himself disappointed the hopes of those who supported him. The government quarreled internally, failed to deal with Ukraine's serious corruption problem, and presided over a meltdown of the economy during the 2008–2009 global financial crisis. The result was the election in early 2010 of Viktor Yanukovich, the very man accused of stealing the 2004 election that had triggered the Orange Revolution in the first place.

Many other species of governance failure plague democratic countries. It is well understood that Latin America has the highest level of economic inequality of any region in the world, in which class hierarchies often correspond to racial and ethnic ones. The rise of populist leaders like Hugo Chávez in Venezuela and Evo Morales in Bolivia is less a cause of instability than a symptom of that inequality and the feeling of social exclusion felt by many who are nominally citizens. Persistent poverty often breeds other kinds of social dysfunctions, like gangs, narcotrafficking, and a general feeling of insecurity on the part of ordinary people. In Colombia, Mexico, and El Salvador, organized criminality threatens the state itself and its basic institutions, and the failure to deal effectively with these problems has undermined the legitimacy of democracy.

India, to take another example, has been a remarkably successful democracy since its independence in 1947—an achievement all the more remarkable given its poverty, ethnic and religious diversity, and enormous size. Nonetheless, Indian democracy, like sausage making, looks less appealing the closer one gets to the process. Nearly one-third of Indian legislators, for example, are under some form of criminal indictment, some for serious crimes like murder and rape. Indian politicians often practice an overt form of patronage politics, in which votes are traded for political favors. The fractiousness of Indian democracy makes it very hard for the government to make major decisions on issues like investments in major infrastructure projects. And in many Indian cities, glittering high-tech centers of excellence exist next to African-style poverty.

The apparent chaos and corruption of democratic politics in India has frequently been contrasted to the quick and efficient decision making of China. Chinese rulers are not constrained by either a rule of law or democratic accountability; if they want to build a huge dam, bulldoze neighborhoods to make way for highways or airports, or mount a rapid economic stimulus package, they can do so far more quickly than democratic India.

A fourth broad source of political anxiety concerns the economy. Modern global capitalism has proved to be productive and wealth-creating beyond the dreams of anyone living before the year 1800. In the period following the oil crises of the 1970s, the size of the world economy almost quadrupled, and Asia, based on its openness to trade and investment, saw much of its population join the developed world. But global capitalism has not found a way to avoid high levels of volatility, particularly in the financial sector. Global economic growth has been plagued by periodic financial crises, striking Europe in the early 1990s, Asia in 1997–1998, Russia and Brazil in 1998–1999, and Argentina in 2001. This instability culminated, perhaps with poetic justice, in the great crisis that struck the United States, the home of global capitalism, in 2008–2009. Free markets are necessary to promote long-term growth, but they are not self-regulating, particularly when it comes to banks and other large financial institutions. The system's instability is a reflection of what is ultimately a political failure, that is, the failure to provide sufficient regulatory oversight both at a national and an international level.

The cumulative effect of these economic crises has not necessarily been to undermine confidence in market-based economics and globalization as engines of economic growth. China, India, Brazil, and any number of other so-called emerging market countries continue to perform well economically based on their participation in global capitalism. But it is clear that the *political* job of finding the right regulatory mechanisms to tame capitalism's volatility have not yet been found.

Political Decay

The latter point suggests an urgent but often overlooked area of concern about democracy's future. Political institutions develop, often slowly and painfully, over time, as human societies strive to organize themselves to master their environments. But political decay occurs when political systems fail to adjust to changing circumstances. There is something like a law of the conservation of institutions. Human beings are rule-following animals by nature; they are born to conform to the social norms they see around them, and they entrench those rules with often transcendent meaning and value. When the surrounding environment changes and new challenges arise, there is often a disjunction between existing institutions and present needs. Those institutions are supported by legions of entrenched stakeholders who oppose any fundamental change.

American political institutions may well be headed for a major test of their adaptability. The American system was built around a firm conviction that concentrated political power constituted an imminent danger to the lives and liberty of citizens. For this reason, the U.S. Constitution was designed with a broad range of checks and balances by which different parts of the government could prevent other parts from exercising tyrannical control. This system has served the country well, but only because at certain critical junctures in its history when strong government was necessary, it was possible to forge the consensus to bring it about through the exercise of political leadership.

There is unfortunately no institutional guarantee that the system as designed will always check tyrannical power yet allow exercises of state authority when the need arises. The latter depends in the first instance on the existence of a social consensus on political ends, and this has been lacking in American political life in recent years. The United States faces a series of large challenges, mostly related to fixing its long-term fiscal situation. Over the past generation, Americans have spent money on themselves without paying their own way through taxation, a situation that has been exacerbated by years of too-easy access to credit and overspending on both a household and governmental level. The long-term fiscal shortfall and foreign indebtedness threaten the very basis of American power around the world, as other countries like China gain in relative stature.

None of these challenges is so enormous that it cannot be resolved through timely, if painful, action. But the American political system, which should facilitate the formation of consensus, is instead contributing to the problem. The Congress has become highly polarized, making the passage of legislation extremely difficult. For the first time in modern history, the most conservative Democrat in Congress is more liberal than the most liberal Republican. The number of seats in Congress won by a margin of 10 percent or less, meaning that they are up for grabs by either party, has fallen steadily from nearly two hundred in the late nineteenth century to only a little more than fifty in the early 2000s. Both political parties have become much more ideologically homogeneous, and deliberative debate between them has deteriorated. These kinds of divisions are not historically unprecedented, but in the past they have been overcome by strong presidential leadership, which has not been forthcoming.

The future of American politics rests not just in politics but also in society. The polarization of Congress reflects a broad trend toward the growing homogenization of neighborhoods and regions, as Americans sort themselves out ideologically by where they choose to live. The trend towards associating only with like-minded people is strongly amplified by the media, where the proliferation of communication channels ends up weakening the shared experience of citizenship.

The American political system's ability to deal with its fiscal challenges is affected not just by the Left-Right polarization of Congress but also by the growth and power of entrenched interest groups. Trade unions, agribusinesses, drug companies, banks, and a host of other organized lobbies often exercise an effective veto on legislation that hurts their pocketbooks. It is perfectly legitimate and indeed expected that citizens should defend their interests in a democracy. But at a certain point this defense crosses over into the claiming of privileges, or a situation of gridlock where no one's interests may be challenged. This explains the rising levels of populist anger on both the Right and Left that contribute to polarization and reflect a social reality at odds with the country's own legitimating principles.

The complaint by Americans that the United States is dominated by elites and powerful interest groups reflects the reality of increasing income and wealth inequality in the period from the 1970s to the early 2000s. Inequality per se has never been a big problem in American political culture, which emphasizes equality of opportunity rather than of outcomes. But the system remains legitimate only as long as people believe that by working hard and doing their best, they and their children have a fair shot at getting ahead, and that the wealthy got there playing by the rules.

The fact is, however, that rates of intergenerational social mobility are far lower in the United States than many Americans believe them to be, and lower than in many other developed countries that traditionally have been regarded as rigid and stratified. Over time, elites are able to protect their positions by gaming the political system, moving their money offshore to avoid taxation, and transmitting these advantages to their children through favored access to elite institutions. Much of this was laid bare during the financial crisis of 2008–2009, when it became painfully clear that there was little relationship between compensation in the financial services sector and real contributions to the economy. The industry had used its considerable political muscle to dismantle regulation and oversight in the previous decade, and continued to fend off regulation in the crisis's aftermath. The economist Simon Johnson suggested that the power of the financial oligarchy in the United States was not too different from what exists in emerging market countries like Russia or Indonesia.

There is no automatic mechanism by which political systems adjust themselves to changing circumstances. The story of the failure to adjust, and thus the phenomenon of political decay, is told in later pages of this volume. There was no necessary reason why the Mamluk Sultanate in Egypt couldn't have adopted firearms earlier to meet rising external threats, as the Ottomans who ultimately defeated them did; nor was it inevitable that emperors in the late Ming Dynasty in China would fail to tax their citizens adequately to support an army that could defend the country from the Manchus. The problem in both cases was the enormous institutional inertia existing behind the status quo.

Once a society fails to confront a major fiscal crisis through serious institutional reform, as the French monarchy did after the failure of the Grand Parti in 1557, it is tempted to resort to a host of short-term fixes that erode and eventually corrupt its own institutions. These fixes involved giving in to various entrenched stakeholders and interest groups, who invariably represented people with wealth and power in French society. The failure to balance the country's budget led to bankruptcy and the delegitimization of the state itself, a course that finally terminated in the French Revolution.

The United States is not in nearly as serious a moral and fiscal crisis as ancien régime France. The danger, however, is that its situation will continue to worsen over time in the absence of some powerful force that will knock the system off its current dysfunctional institutional equilibrium.

Fantasies of Statelessness

A common thread links many of our contemporary anxieties about the future, from authoritarian backsliding in Russia to corruption in India, to failed states in the developing world, to entrenched interest groups in contemporary American politics. It concerns the difficulties of creating and maintaining effective political institutions, governments that are simultaneously powerful, rule bound, and accountable. This might seem like an obvious point that any fourth grader would acknowledge, and yet on further reflection it is a truth that many intelligent people fail to understand.

Let's begin with the question of the receding of the third wave and the democratic recession that has taken place around the world in the 2000s. The reasons for our disappointments in the failure of democracy to spread do not lie, I would argue, on the level of ideas at the present moment. Ideas are extremely important to political order; it is the perceived legitimacy of the government that binds populations together and makes them willing to accept its authority. The fall of the Berlin Wall marked the collapse of

one of democracy's great competitors, communism, and the rapid spread of liberal democracy as the most widely accepted form of government.

This is true up to the present, where democracy, in Amartya Sen's words, remains the "default" political condition: "While democracy is not yet universally practiced, nor indeed universally accepted, in the general climate of world opinion democratic governance has achieved the status of being taken to be generally right." Very few people around the world openly profess to admire Vladimir Putin's petronationalism, or Hugo Chávez's "twenty-first-century socialism," or Mahmoud Ahmadinejad's Islamic Republic. No important international institution endorses anything but democracy as the basis for just governance. China's rapid growth incites envy and interest, but its exact model of authoritarian capitalism is not one that is easily described, much less emulated, by other developing countries. Such is the prestige of modern liberal democracy that today's would-be authoritarians all have to stage elections and manipulate the media from behind the scenes to legitimate themselves. Not only has totalitarianism virtually disappeared from the world; authoritarians pay a compliment to democracy by pretending to be democrats.

Democracy's failure, then, lies less in concept than in execution: most people around the world would strongly prefer to live in a society in which their government was accountable *and* effective, where it delivered the sorts of services demanded by citizens in a timely and cost-effective way. But few governments are actually able to do both, because institutions are weak, corrupt, lacking capacity, or in some cases absent altogether. The passion of protesters and democracy advocates around the world, from South Africa to Korea to Romania to Ukraine, might be sufficient to bring about "regime change" from authoritarian to democratic government, but the latter will not succeed without a long, costly, laborious, and difficult process of institution building.

There is in fact a curious blindness to the importance of political institutions that has affected many people over the years, people who dream about a world in which we will somehow transcend politics. This particular fantasy is not the special province of either the Left or the Right; both have had their versions of it. The father of communism, Karl Marx, famously predicted the "withering away of the state" once the proletarian revolution had achieved power and abolished private property. Left-wing revolutionaries from the nineteeth-century anarchists on thought it sufficient to destroy old power structures without giving serious thought to what would take their place. This tradition continues up through the present, with the suggestion by antiglobalization authors like Michael Hardt and Antonio Negri that economic injustice could be abolished by undermining the sovereignty of states and replacing it with a networked "multitude."

Real-world Communist regimes of course did exactly the opposite of what Marx predicted, building large and tyrannical state structures to force people to act collectively when they failed to do so spontaneously. This in turn led a generation of democracy activists in Eastern Europe to envision their own form of statelessness, where a mobilized civil society would take the place of traditional political parties and centralized governments. These activists were subsequently disillusioned by the realization that their societies could not be governed without institutions, and when they encountered the messy compromises required to build them. In the decades since the fall of communism, Eastern Europe is democratic, but it is not thereby necessarily happy with its politics or politicians.

The fantasy of statelessness most prevalent on the Right is that the market economy will somehow make government unnecessary and irrelevant. During the dot-com boom of the 1990s, many enthusiasts argued along the lines of the former Citibank CEO Walter Wriston that the world was experiencing a "twilight of sovereignty," in which the political powers traditionally exercised by states were being undermined by new information technologies that were making borders impossible to police and rules

difficult to enforce. The rise of the Internet led activists like John Perry Barlow of the Electronic Frontier Foundation to issue a "Declaration of Independence of Cyberspace," where governments of the industrialized world were told, "You are not welcome among us. You have no sovereignty where we gather." A global capitalist economy would replace the sovereignty of democratic governments with the sovereignty of the market: if a legislature voted for excessive regulation or restricted trade, it would be punished by the bond market and forced to adopt policies deemed rational by global capital markets. Fantasies of a stateless world have always found a sympathetic audience in the United States, where hostility to the state is a staple of American political culture. Libertarians of various stripes have suggested not just rolling back an overgrown welfare state but also abolishing more basic institutions like the Federal Reserve Board and the Food and Drug Administration.

It is quite legitimate to argue that modern governments have grown excessively large, and that they thereby limit economic growth and individual freedom. People are right to complain about unresponsive bureaucracy, corrupt politicians, and the unprincipled nature of politics. But in the developed world, we take the existence of government so much for granted that we sometimes forget how important it is, and how difficult it was to create, and what the world would look like without certain basic political institutions.

It is not only that we take democracy for granted; we also take for granted the fact that we have a state at all that can carry out certain basic functions. Fairfax County, Virginia, a suburb of Washington, D.C., where I lived for many years, is one of the richest counties in the United States. Every winter, potholes appear in the county's roads as a result of the seasonal freezing and thawing after winter storms. And yet by the end of the spring, all of those potholes get magically filled so no one has to worry about breaking an axle in one. If they don't get filled, the residents of Fairfax County get angry and complain about the incompetence of local government;

no one (apart from a few specialists in public administration) ever stops to think about the complex, invisible social system that makes this possible, or why it takes longer to fill potholes in the neighboring District of Columbia, or why potholes *never* get filled in many developing countries.

Indeed, the kinds of minimal or no-government societies envisioned by dreamers of the Left and Right are not fantasies; they actually exist in the contemporary developing world. Many parts of sub-Saharan Africa are a libertarian's paradise. The region as a whole is a low-tax utopia, with governments often unable to collect more than about 10 percent of GDP in taxes, compared to more than 30 percent in the United States and 50 percent in parts of Europe. Rather than unleashing entrepreneurship, this low rate of taxation means that basic public services like health, education, and pothole filling are starved of funding. The physical infrastructure on which a modern economy rests, like roads, court systems, and police, are missing. In Somalia, where a strong central government has not existed since the late 1980s, ordinary individuals may own not just assault rifles but also rocket-propelled grenades, antiaircraft missiles, and tanks. People are free to protect their own families, and indeed are forced to do so. Nigeria has a film industry that produces as many titles as India's famed Bollywood, but films have to earn a quick return because the government is incapable of guaranteeing intellectual property rights and preventing products from being copied illegally.

The degree to which people in developed countries take political institutions for granted was very much evident in the way that the United States planned, or failed to plan, for the aftermath of its 2003 invasion of Iraq. The U.S. administration seemed to think that democracy and a market economy were default conditions to which the country would automatically revert once Saddam Hussein's dictatorship was removed, and seemed genuinely surprised when the Iraqi state itself collapsed in an orgy of looting and civil conflict. U.S. purposes have been similarly stymied in Afghanistan, where ten years of effort and the

investment of hundreds of billions of dollars have not produced a stable, legitimate Afghan state.

Political institutions are necessary and cannot be taken for granted. A market economy and high levels of wealth don't magically appear when you "get government out of the way"; they rest on a hidden institutional foundation of property rights, rule of law, and basic political order. A free market, a vigorous civil society, the spontaneous "wisdom of crowds" are all important components of a working democracy, but none can ultimately replace the functions of a strong, hierarchical government. There has been a broad recognition among economists in recent years that "institutions matter": poor countries are poor not because they lack resources, but because they lack effective political institutions. We need therefore to better understand where those institutions come from.

Getting to Denmark

The problem of creating modern political institutions has been described as the problem of "getting to Denmark," after the title of a paper written by two social scientists at the World Bank, Lant Pritchett and Michael Woolcock. For people in developed countries, "Denmark" is a mythical place that is known to have good political and economic institutions: it is stable, democratic, peaceful, prosperous, inclusive, and has extremely low levels of political corruption. Everyone would like to figure out how to transform Somalia, Haiti, Nigeria, Iraq, or Afghanistan into "Denmark," and the international development community has long lists of presumed Denmark-like attributes that they are trying to help failed states achieve.

There are any number of problems with this agenda. It does not seem very plausible that extremely poor and chaotic countries could expect to put into place complex institutions in short order, given how long such institutions took to evolve. Moreover, institutions reflect the cultural values of the societies in which they are established, and it is not clear that Denmark's democratic political order can take root in very different cultural contexts. Most people living in rich, stable developed countries have no idea how Denmark itself got to be Denmark—something that is true for many Danes as well. The struggle to create modern political institutions was so long and so painful that people living in industrialized countries now suffer from a historical amnesia regarding how their societies came to that point in the first place.

The Danes themselves are descended from the Vikings, a ferocious tribal people who conquered and pillaged much of Europe, from the Mediterranean all the way to Kiev in southern Ukraine. The Celtic peoples who first settled the British Isles, as well as the Romans who conquered them, and the Germanic barbarians who displaced the Romans, were all originally organized into tribes much like those that still exist in Afghanistan, central Iraq, and Papua New Guinea. So were the Chinese, Indians, Arabs, Africans, and virtually all other peoples on earth. They owed primary obligation not to a state but to kinfolk, they settled disputes not through courts but through a system of retributive justice, and they buried their dead on property held collectively by groups of kin.

Over the course of time, however, these tribal societies developed political institutions. First and foremost was the centralized source of authority that held an effective monopoly of military power over a defined piece of territory—what we call a state. Peace was kept not by a rough balance of power between groups of kin but by the state's army and police, now a standing force that could also defend the community against neighboring tribes and states. Property came to be owned not by groups of kinfolk but by individuals, who increasingly won the right to buy and sell it at will. Their rights to that property were enforced not by kin but by courts and legal systems that had the power to settle disputes and compensate wrongs.

In time, moreover, social rules were formalized as written laws rather than customs or informal traditions. These formal rules were used to organize the way that power was distributed in the system, regardless of the individuals who exercised power at any given time. Institutions, in other words, replaced individual leaders. Those legal systems were eventually accorded supreme authority over society, an authority that was seen to be superior to that of rulers who temporarily happened to command the state's armed forces and bureaucracy. This came to be known as the rule of law.

Finally, certain societies not only limited the power of their states by forcing rulers to comply with written law; they also held them accountable to parliaments, assemblies, and other bodies representing a broader proportion of the population. Some degree of accountability was present in many traditional monarchies, but it was usually the product of informal consultation with a small body of elite advisers. Modern democracy was born when rulers acceded to formal rules limiting their power and subordinating their sovereignty to the will of the larger population as expressed through elections.

The purpose of this book is to fill in some of the gaps of this historical amnesia, by giving an account of where basic political institutions came from in societies that now take them for granted. The three categories of institutions in question are the ones just described:

1. the state
2. the rule of law
3. accountable government

A successful modern liberal democracy combines all three sets of institutions in a stable balance. The fact that there are countries capable of achieving this balance constitutes the miracle of modern politics, since it is not obvious that they can be combined. The state, after all, concentrates and uses power, to bring about compliance with its laws on the part of its citizens and to defend itself against other states and threats. The rule of law and accountable government, on the other hand, limit the state's power, first by forcing it to use its power according to certain public and transparent rules, and then by ensuring that it is subordinate to the will of the people.

These institutions come into being in the first place because people find that they can protect their interests, and the interests of their families, through them. But what people regard as self-interest, and how they are willing to collaborate with others, depends critically on ideas that legitimate certain forms of political association. Self-interest and legitimacy thus form the cornerstones of political order.

The fact that one of these three types of institutions exists does not imply that the others do so as well. Afghanistan, for example, has held democratic elections since 2004 but has an extremely weak state and is unable to uphold laws in much of its territory. Russia, by contrast, has a strong state and holds democratic elections, but its rulers do not feel bound by a rule of law. The nation of Singapore has both a strong state and a rule of law bequeathed to it by its former British colonial masters but only an attenuated form of democratic accountability.

Where did these three sets of institutions originally come from? What were the forces that drove their creation and the conditions under which they developed? In what order were they created, and how did they relate to one another? If we could understand how these basic institutions came into being, we could then perhaps better understand the distance that separates Afghanistan or Somalia from contemporary Denmark.

The story of how political institutions developed cannot be told without understanding the complementary process of political decay. Human institutions are "sticky"; that is, they persist over time and are changed only with great difficulty. Institutions that are created to meet one set of conditions often survive even when those conditions change or disappear, and the failure to adapt appropriately entails political decay. This applies to modern liberal democracies encompassing the state, rule of law, and accountability as much as to older political systems. For there is no guarantee that any given democracy will continue to deliver what it promises to its

citizens, and thus no guarantee that it will remain legitimate in their eyes.

Moreover, the natural human propensity to favor family and friends—something I refer to as patrimonialism—constantly reasserts itself in the absence of strong countervailing incentives. Organized groups—most often the rich and powerful—entrench themselves over time and begin demanding privileges from the state. Particularly when a prolonged period of peace and stability gives way to financial and/or military crisis, these entrenched patrimonial groups extend their sway, or else prevent the state from responding adequately.

A version of the story of political development and political decay has of course been told many times before. Most high schools offer a class on the "rise of civilization," which presents a broad overview of the evolution of social institutions. A century ago, the historical account presented to most American schoolchildren was highly Euro-, and indeed, Anglocentric. It might have begun in Greece and Rome, then progressed through the European Middle Ages, the Magna Carta, the English Civil War and Glorious Revolution, and thence perhaps on to 1776 and the writing of the U.S. Constitution. Today, such curricula are far more multicultural and incorporate the experiences of non-Western societies like China and India as well, or else dwell on history's marginalized groups like indigenous peoples, women, the poor, and so on.

There are several reasons to be dissatisfied with the existing literature on the development of political institutions. First, much of it is not comparative on a sufficiently broad scale. It is only by comparing the experience of different societies that we can begin to sort through complex causal factors that explain why certain institutions emerged in some places but not in others. A lot of theorizing about modernization, from the massive studies of Karl Marx to contemporary economic historians like Douglass North, has focused heavily on the experience of England as the first country to industrialize. The English experience was exceptional in many ways but is not necessarily a good guide to development in countries differently situated.

The multicultural approaches that have displaced this narrative in recent decades are not for the most part seriously comparative. They tend to select either positive stories of how non-Western civilizations have contributed to the overall progress of humankind, or else negative ones about how they were victimized. One seldom finds serious comparative analysis of why an institution developed in one society but not in another.

The great sociologist Seymour Martin Lipset used to say that an observer who knows only one country knows no countries. Without comparison, there is no way of knowing whether a particular practice or behavior is unique to the society in question or common to many. Only through comparative analysis is it possible to link causes, like geography, climate, technology, religion, or conflict, to the range of outcomes existing in the world today. In doing so, we might be able to answer questions like the following:

- Why are Afghanistan, the jungle regions of India, the island nations of Melanesia, and parts of the Middle East still tribally organized?
- Why is China's default condition to be ruled by a strong, centralized government, while India has never seen that degree of centralization except for very brief periods over the past three millennia of its history?
- Why is it that almost all of the cases of successful authoritarian modernization—countries like South Korea, Taiwan, Singapore, and China—are clustered in East Asia, rather than in Africa or the Middle East?
- Why have democracy and a strong rule of law taken root in Scandinavia, while Russia, subject to similar climactic and geographical conditions, experienced the growth of unconstrained absolutism?
- Why have countries in Latin America been subject to high inflation and economic crises repeatedly over the past century, while the United States and Canada have not?

The historical data presented in this book are interesting precisely because they shed light on the present and explain how different political orders came to be. But human societies are not trapped by their pasts. If modern states emerged in China or Europe as a result of certain factors like the constant need to prepare for and fight wars, this does not necessarily mean that weak states in Africa today must replicate this experience if they are to modernize. The social deck is being constantly shuffled by economic growth, and international factors impinge to a much greater extent on individual societies than they did in the past. So while the historical material in this book may explain how different societies got to where they are now, their paths to the present do not determine their futures, or serve as models for other societies.

China First

The classic theories of modernization written by such towering figures as Karl Marx, Émile Durkheim, Henry Maine, Ferdinand Tönnies, and Max Weber tended to regard the experience of the West as paradigmatic of modernization as such because industrialization took place first in the West. This focus on the West is understandable since the explosion of productivity and sustained economic growth that occurred after about 1800 in Europe and North America was unprecedented and transformed the world into what it is today.

But development is not only about economics. Political institutions develop, as do social ones. Sometimes political and social development are closely related to economic change, but at other times they happen independently. This book focuses on the *political* dimension of development, the evolution of government institutions. Modern political institutions appeared far earlier in history than did the Industrial Revolution and the modern capitalist economy. Indeed, many of the elements of what we now understand to be a modern state were already in place in China in the third century B.C., some eighteen hundred years before they emerged in Europe.

It is for this reason that I begin my account of the emergence of the state in Part II with China. While classic modernization theory tended to take European development as the norm and ask why other societies diverged from it, I take China as a paradigm of state formation and ask why other civilizations didn't replicate the path it followed. This is not to say that China was better than other societies. As we will see, a modern state without rule of law or accountability is capable of enormous despotism. But China was the first to develop state institutions, and its pioneering experience is seldom referred to in Western accounts of political development.

In beginning with China, I skip over other important early societies like Mesopotamia, Egypt, Greece and Rome, and the civilizations of Meso- and South America. The decision not to cover Greece and Rome at greater length in this volume requires further explanation.

The ancient Mediterranean world set precedents that were extremely important to the subsequent development of European civilization, which from the time of Charlemagne on were self-consciously imitated by European rulers. The Greeks are commonly credited with having invented democracy, in which rulers were not hereditary but selected by ballot. Most tribal societies are also relatively egalitarian and elect their rulers, but the Greeks went beyond this by introducing a concept of citizenship that was based on political criteria rather than kinship. The form of government practiced in fifth-century Athens or under the Roman Republic is probably better described as "classical republicanism" rather than "democracy," since the franchise was given to only a limited number of citizens, and there were sharp class distinctions that excluded large numbers of people (including the numerous slaves) from political participation. These were, moreover, not liberal states but highly communitarian ones that did not respect the privacy or autonomy of their citizens.

The classical republican precedent established by Greece and Rome was copied by many later societies, including the oligarchic republics of Genoa, Venice, Novgorod, and the Dutch United Prov-

inces. But this form of government had one fatal defect that was widely recognized by later writers, including many of the American Founding Fathers who thought deeply about that tradition: classical republicanism did not scale well. It worked best in small, homogeneous societies like the city-states of fifth-century Greece, or Rome in its early years. But as these republics grew larger through conquest or economic growth, it became impossible to maintain the demanding communitarian values that bound them together. As the Roman Republic grew in size and diversity, it faced irresolvable conflicts over who should enjoy the privileges of citizenship and how to divide the spoils of empire. The Greek city-states were all eventually conquered by monarchies, and the Roman Republic, after a prolonged civil war, gave way to the Empire. Monarchy as a form of government proved superior in its ability to govern large empires and was the political system under which Rome achieved its greatest power and geographical extent.

I will return to the question of classical republicanism as a precedent for modern democracy. But there is good reason for paying closer attention to China than to Greece and Rome in studying the rise of the state, since China alone created a *modern* state in the terms defined by Max Weber. That is, China succeeded in developing a centralized, uniform system of bureaucratic administration that was capable of governing a huge population and territory when compared to Mediterranean Europe. China had already invented a system of impersonal, merit-based bureaucratic recruitment that was far more systematic than Roman public administration. While the total population of the Chinese empire in 1 A.D. was roughly comparable to that of the Roman empire, the Chinese put a far larger proportion of its people under a uniform set of rules than did the Romans. Rome had other important legacies, particularly in the domain of law. But although Greece and Rome were extremely important as precursors of modern accountable government, China was more important in the development of the state.

Among the societies to be compared with China is India. India graduated from a tribal to a state-level society at about the same time as China. But then, around twenty-five hundred years ago, it took a big detour due to the rise of a new Brahmanic religion, which limited the power that any Indian polity could achieve and in some sense paved the way for modern Indian democracy. The Middle East at the time of the Prophet Muhammad was also tribally organized; it took not just the advent of a new religion, Islam, but also a curious institution of slave-soldiers to enable certain polities in Egypt and Turkey to turn themselves into major political powers. Europe was very different from these other societies insofar as its exit from tribalism was not imposed by rulers from the top down but came about on a social level through rules mandated by the Catholic church. In Europe alone, state-level institutions did not have to be built on top of tribally organized ones.

Religion is also key to the origins of the rule of law. Religiously based law existed in ancient Israel, India, the Muslim Middle East, and also the Christian West. It was Western Europe, however, that saw the strongest development of independent legal institutions that managed to take on a secular form and survive into the present day.

The story of the rise of accountable governments is also largely a European one. But Europe was hardly uniform in this respect: accountable governments arose in England and Denmark but not in France or Spain; Russia developed a form of absolutism comparable in its power to that of China. The ability of certain societies to force accountability on their sovereigns, then, depended on a host of specific historical conditions such as the survival of certain feudal institutions into modern times.

The sequencing of political development in Western Europe was highly unusual when compared to other parts of the world. Individualism on a social level appeared centuries before the rise of either modern states or capitalism; a rule of law existed before political power was concentrated in the hands of centralized governments; and institutions

of accountability arose because modern, centralized states were unable to completely defeat or eliminate ancient feudal institutions like representative assemblies.

Once this combination of state, law, and accountability appeared, it proved to be a highly powerful and attractive form of government that subsequently spread to all corners of the world. But we need to remember how historically contingent this emergence was. China had a strong state, but without law and accountability; India had law and now has accountability, but has traditionally lacked a strong state; the Middle East had states and law, but in much of the Arab part it lost the latter tradition. Societies are not trapped by their pasts and freely borrow ideas and institutions from each other. But what they are in the present is also shaped by what they were in the past, and there is not one single path that links one to the other.

Turtles All The Way Down

The purpose of this book is less to present a history of political development than to analyze some of the factors that led to the emergence of certain key political institutions. A lot of historical writing has been characterized as ODTAA—"one damn thing after another"—without an effort to extract general rules or causal theories that can be applied in other circumstances. The same can be said of the ethnographies written by anthropologists, which are highly detailed but deliberately shy away from broad generalization. That is definitely not my approach, which compares and generalizes across many civilizations and time periods.

The overall framework for understanding political development presented here bears many resemblances to biological evolution. Darwinian evolution is built around the two principles of variance and selection: organisms experience random genetic mutation, and those best adapted to their environments survive and multiply. So too in political development: there is variation in political institutions, and those best suited to the physical and social environment survive and proliferate. But there are also many important differences between biological and political evolution: human institutions are subject to deliberate design and choice, unlike genes; they are transmitted across time culturally rather than genetically; and they are invested with intrinsic value through a variety of psychological and social mechanisms, which makes them hard to change. The inherent conservatism of human institutions then explains why political development is frequently reversed by political decay, since there is often a substantial lag between changes in the external environment that should trigger institutional change, and the actual willingness of societies to make those changes.

In the end, however, this general framework amounts to something less than a predictive theory of political development. A parsimonious theory of political change, comparable to the theories of economic growth posited by economists, is in my view simply not possible. The factors driving the development of any given political institution are multiple, complex, and often dependent on accidental or contingent events. Any causal factors one adduces for a given development are themselves caused by prior conditions that extend backward in time in an endless regression.

Let us take one example. A well-known theory of political development argues that European state building was driven by the need to wage war. The relationship between the need to wage war and the development of modern state institutions is fairly well established for early modern Europe, and as we will see applies equally well to ancient China. But before we can declare this to be a general theory of state formation, we need to answer some difficult questions: Why did some regions that experienced long-term warfare fail to develop state institutions (e.g., Melanesia)? Why did warfare in other regions seem to weaken rather than strengthen states (e.g., Latin America)? Why did some regions experience lower levels of conflict than others (e.g., India when compared to China)? Answering these questions

pushes causality back to other factors such as population density, physical geography, technology, and religion. Warfare in places that are densely populated, with good physical communications (e.g., plains or steppe) and appropriate technologies (e.g., horses) has very different political effects from war in sparsely populated mountainous, jungle, or desert regions. So the theory of war and state formation dissolves into a series of further questions about why certain forms of warfare erupt in some places and not in others.

What I am aiming for in this book is a middle-range theory that avoids the pitfalls both of excessive abstraction (the vice of economists) and excessive particularism (the problem of many historians and anthropologists). I am hoping to recover something of the lost tradition of nineteenth-century historical sociology or comparative anthropology. I do not confront the general reader with a big theoretical framework at the outset. While I engage various theories in the course of the historical chapters, I reserve the more abstract treatment of political development (including definitions of some basic terms) for the last three chapters. This includes a general account of how political development happens as well as a discussion of how political development relates to the economic and social dimensions of development.

Putting the theory after the history constitutes what I regard as the correct approach to analysis: theories ought to be inferred from facts, and not the other way around. Of course, there is no such thing as a pure confrontation with facts, devoid of prior theoretical constructs. Those who think they are empirical in that fashion are deluding themselves. But all too often social science begins with an elegant theory and then searches for facts that will confirm it. This, hopefully, is not the approach I take.

There is a perhaps apocryphal story, retold by the physicist Stephen Hawking, about a famous scientist who was giving a public lecture on cosmology when he was interrupted by an old lady at the back of the room who told him he was speaking rubbish, and that the universe was actually a flat disc balanced on the back of a turtle. The scientist thought he could shut her up by asking what the turtle was standing on. She replied, "You're very clever, young man, but it's turtles all the way down."

This then is the problem with any theory of development: the particular turtle you pick as the starting point for your story is actually standing on the back of another turtle, or else an elephant or a tiger or a whale. Most purportedly general theories of development fail because they don't take into account the multiple independent dimensions of development. They are, rather, reductionist in seeking to abstract a single causal factor out of a much more complex historical reality. And they fail to push the story back far enough historically to the conditions that explain their own starting points and premises.

I push the story back very far. Before we get to state building in China, we need to understand not just where war comes from but also how human societies originated. The surprising answer is that they didn't come from anywhere. Both society and conflict have existed for as long as there have been human beings, because human beings are by nature both social and competitive animals. The primates from which the human species evolved practiced an attenuated form of politics. To understand this, then, we need to go back to the state of nature and to human biology, which in some sense sets the framework for the whole of human politics. Biology presents a certain degree of solid ground resting below the turtles at the bottom of the stack, though even biology, as we will see, is not an entirely fixed point.

Max Weber
POLITICS AS A VOCATION

This lecture, which I give at your request, will necessarily disappoint you in a number of ways. You will naturally expect me to take a position on actual problems of the day. But that will be the case only in a purely formal way and toward the end, when I shall raise certain questions concerning the significance of political action in the whole way of life. In today's lecture, all questions that refer to what policy and what content one should give one's political activity must be eliminated. For such questions have nothing to do with the general question of what politics as a vocation means and what it can mean. Now to our subject matter.

What do we understand by politics? The concept is extremely broad and comprises any kind of *independent* leadership in action. One speaks of the currency policy of the banks, of the discounting

From H. H. Gerth and C. Wright Mills, eds., trans. From *Max Weber: Essays in Sociology* (New York: Galaxy, 1958), pp. 77–87.

policy of the Reichsbank, of the strike policy of a trade union; one may speak of the educational policy of a municipality or a township, of the policy of the president of a voluntary association, and, finally, even of the policy of a prudent wife who seeks to guide her husband. Tonight, our reflections are, of course, not based upon such a broad concept. We wish to understand by politics only the leadership, or the influencing of the leadership, of a *political* association, hence today, of a *state*.

But what is a "political" association from the sociological point of view? What is a "state"? Sociologically, the state cannot be defined in terms of its ends. There is scarcely any task that some political association has not taken in hand, and there is no task that one could say has always been exclusive and peculiar to those associations which are designated as political ones: today the state, or historically, those associations which have been the predecessors of the modern state. Ultimately, one can define the modern state sociologically only in terms of the specific *means* peculiar to it, as to every political association, namely, the use of physical force.

"Every state is founded on force," said Trotsky at Brest-Litovsk. That is indeed right. If no social institutions existed which knew the use of violence, then the concept of "state" would be eliminated, and a condition would emerge that could be designated as "anarchy," in the specific sense of this word. Of course, force is certainly not the normal or the only means of the state—nobody says that—but force is a means specific to the state. Today the relation between the state and violence is an especially intimate one. In the past, the most varied institutions—beginning with the sib—have known the use of physical force as quite normal. Today, however, we have to say that a state is a human community that (successfully) claims the *monopoly of the legitimate use of physical force* within a given territory. Note that "territory" is one of the characteristics of the state. Specifically, at the present time, the right to use physical force is ascribed to other institutions or to individuals only to the extent to which the state permits it. The state is considered the sole source of the "right" to use violence. Hence, "politics" for us means striving to share power or striving to influence the distribution of power, either among states or among groups within a state.

This corresponds essentially to ordinary usage. When a question is said to be a "political" question, when a cabinet minister or an official is said to be a "political" official, or when a decision is said to be "politically" determined, what is always meant is that interests in the distribution, maintenance, or transfer of power are decisive for answering the questions and determining the decision or the official's sphere of activity. He who is active in politics strives for power either as a means in serving other aims, ideal or egoistic, or as "power for power's sake," that is, in order to enjoy the prestige-feeling that power gives.

Like the political institutions historically preceding it, the state is a relation of men dominating men, a relation supported by means of legitimate (i.e., considered to be legitimate) violence. If the state is to exist, the dominated must obey the authority claimed by the powers that be. When and why do men obey? Upon what inner justifications and upon what external means does this domination rest?

To begin with, in principle, there are three inner justifications, hence basic *legitimations* of domination.

First, the authority of the "eternal yesterday," i.e., of the mores sanctified through the unimaginably ancient recognition and habitual orientation to conform. This is "traditional" domination exercised by the patriarch and the patrimonial prince of yore.

There is the authority of the extraordinary and personal *gift of grace* (charisma), the absolutely personal devotion and personal confidence in revelation, heroism, or other qualities of individual leadership. This is "charismatic" domination, as exercised by the prophet or—in the field of politics—by the elected war lord, the plebiscitarian ruler, the great demagogue, or the political party leader.

Finally, there is a domination by virtue of "legality," by virtue of the belief in the validity of legal statute and functional "competence" based on rationally created *rules*. In this case, obedience is expected in discharging statutory obligations. This is domination as exercised by the modern "servant of the state" and by all those bearers of power who in this respect resemble him.

It is understood that, in reality, obedience is determined by highly robust motives of fear and hope—fear of the vengeance of magical powers or of the power-holder, hope for reward in this world or in the beyond—and besides all this, by interests of the most varied sort. Of this we shall speak presently. However, in asking for the "legitimations" of this obedience, one meets with these three "pure" types: "traditional," "charismatic," and "legal."

These conceptions of legitimacy and their inner justifications are of very great significance for the structure of domination. To be sure, the pure types are rarely found in reality. But today we cannot deal with the highly complex variants, transitions, and combinations of these pure types, which problems belong to "political science." Here we are interested above all in the second of these types: domination by virtue of the devotion of those who obey the purely personal "charisma" of the "leader." For this is the root of the idea of a *calling* in its highest expression.

Devotion to the charisma of the prophet, or the leader in war, or to the great demagogue in the *ecclesia* or in parliament, means that the leader is personally recognized as the innerly "called" leader of men. Men do not obey him by virtue of tradition or statute, but because they believe in him. If he is more than a narrow and vain upstart of the moment, the leader lives for his cause and "strives for his work." The devotion of his disciples, his followers, his personal party friends is oriented to his person and to its qualities.

Charismatic leadership has emerged in all places and in all historical epochs. Most importantly in the past, it has emerged in the two figures of the magician and the prophet on the one hand, and in the elected war lord, the gang leader and *condotierre* on the other hand. *Political* leadership in the form of the free "demagogue" who grew from the soil of the city state is of greater concern to us; like the city state, the demagogue is peculiar to the Occident and especially to Mediterranean culture. Furthermore, political leadership in the form of the parliamentary "party leader" has grown on the soil of the constitutional state, which is also indigenous only to the Occident.

These politicians by virtue of a "calling," in the most genuine sense of the word, are of course nowhere the only decisive figures in the cross-currents of the political struggle for power. The sort of auxiliary means that are at their disposal is also highly decisive. How do the politically dominant powers manage to maintain their domination? The question pertains to any kind of domination, hence also to political domination in all its forms, traditional as well as legal and charismatic.

Organized domination, which calls for continuous administration, requires that human conduct be conditioned to obedience towards those masters who claim to be the bearers of legitimate power. On the other hand, by virtue of this obedience, organized domination requires the control of those material goods which in a given case are necessary for the use of physical violence. Thus, organized domination requires control of the personal executive staff and the material implements of administration.

The administrative staff, which externally represents the organization of political domination, is, of course, like any other organization, bound by obedience to the power-holder and not alone by the concept of legitimacy, of which we have just spoken. There are two other means, both of which appeal to personal interests: material reward and social honor. The fiefs of vassals, the prebends of patrimonial officials, the salaries of modern civil servants, the honor of knights, the privileges of estates, and the honor of the civil servant comprise their respective wages. The fear of losing them is the final and decisive basis for solidarity between the executive staff and the power-holder. There is honor and booty for the followers in war; for the demagogue's following, there are "spoils"—that is, exploitation of the dominated through the monopolization of office—and there are politically determined profits and premiums of vanity. All of these rewards are also derived from the domination exercised by a charismatic leader.

To maintain a dominion by force, certain material goods are required, just as with an economic organization. All states may be classified according to whether they rest on the principle that the staff of men themselves *own* the administrative means, or whether the staff is "separated" from these means of administration. This distinction holds in the same sense in which today we say that the salaried employee and the proletarian in the capitalistic enterprise are "separated" from the material means of production. The power-holder must be able to count on the obedience of the staff members, officials, or whoever else they may be. The administrative means may consist of money, building, war material, vehicles, horses, or whatnot. The question is whether or not the power-holder himself directs and organizes the administration while delegating executive power to personal servants, hired officials, or personal favorites and confidants, who are non-owners, i.e., who do not use the material means of administration in their own right but are directed by the lord. The distinction runs through all administrative organizations of the past.

These political associations in which the material means of administration are autonomously controlled, wholly or partly, by the dependent administrative staff may be called associations organized in "*estates*." The vassal in the feudal association, for instance, paid out of his own pocket for the administration and judicature of the district enfeoffed to him. He supplied his own equipment and provisions for war, and his subvassals did likewise. Of course, this had consequences for the lord's position of power, which only rested upon a relation of personal faith and upon the fact that the legitimacy of his possession of the fief and the social honor of the vassal were derived from the overlord.

However, everywhere, reaching back to the earliest political formations, we also find the lord himself directing the administration. He seeks to take the administration into his own hands by having men personally dependent upon him: slaves, household officials, attendants, personal "favorites," and prebendaries enfeoffed in kind or in money from his magazines. He seeks to defray the expenses from his own pocket, from the revenues of his patrimonium; and he seeks to create an army which is dependent upon him personally because it is equipped and provisioned out of his granaries, magazines, and armories. In the association of "estates," the lord rules with the aid of an autonomous "aristocracy" and hence shares his domination with it; the lord who personally administers is supported either by members of his household or by plebeians. These are propertyless strata having no social honor of their own; materially, they are completely chained to him and are not backed up by any competing power of their own. All forms of patriarchal and patrimonial domination, Sultanist despotism, and bureaucratic states belong to this latter type. The bureaucratic state order is especially important; in its most rational development, it is precisely characteristic of the modern state.

Everywhere the development of the modern state is initiated through the action of the prince. He paves the way for the expropriation of the autonomous and "private" bearers of executive power who stand beside him, of those who in their own right possess the means of administration, warfare, and financial organization, as well as politically usable goods of all sorts. The whole process is a complete parallel to the development of the capitalist enterprise through gradual expropriation of the independent producers. In the end, the modern state controls the total means of political organization, which actually come together under a single head. No single official personally owns the money he pays out, or the buildings, stores, tools, and war machines he controls. In the contemporary "state"—and this is essential for the concept of state—the "separation" of the administrative staff, of the administrative officials, and of the workers from the material means of administrative organization is completed. Here the most modern development begins, and we see with our own eyes the attempt to inaugurate the expropriation of this expropriator of the political means, and therewith of political power.

The revolution [of Germany, 1918] has accomplished, at least in so far as leaders have taken the place of the statutory authorities, this much: the leaders, through usurpation or election, have attained control over the political staff and the apparatus of material goods; and they deduce their legitimacy—no matter with what right—from the will of the governed. Whether the leaders, on the basis of this at least apparent success, can rightfully entertain the hope of also carrying through the expropriation within the capitalist enterprises is a different question. The direction of capitalist enterprises, despite far-reaching analogies, follows quite different laws than those of political administration.

Today we do not take a stand on this question. I state only the purely *conceptual* aspect for our consideration: the modern state is a compulsory association which organizes domination. It has been successful in seeking to monopolize the legitimate use of physical force as a means of domination within a territory. To this end the state has combined the material means of organization in the hands of its leaders, and it has expropriated all autonomous functionaries of estates who formerly controlled these means in their own right. The state has taken their positions and now stands in the top place.

During this process of political expropriation, which has occurred with varying success in all countries on earth, "professional politicians" in another sense have emerged. They arose first in the service of a prince. They have been men who, unlike the charismatic leader, have not wished to be lords themselves, but who have entered the *service* of political lords. In the struggle of expropriation, they placed themselves at the princes' disposal and by managing the princes' politics they earned, on the one hand, a living and, on the other hand, an ideal content of life. Again, it is *only* in the Occident that we find this kind of professional politician in the service of powers other than the princes. In the past, they have been the most important power instrument of the prince and his instrument of political expropriation.

Before discussing "professional politicians" in detail, let us clarify in all its aspects the state of affairs their existence presents. Politics, just as economic pursuits, may be a man's avocation or his vocation. One may engage in politics, and hence seek to influence the distribution of power within and between political structures, as an "occasional" politician. We are all "occasional" politicians when we cast our ballot or consummate a similar expression of intention, such as applauding or protesting in a "political" meeting, or delivering a "political" speech, etc. The whole relation of many people to politics is restricted to this. Politics as an avocation is today practiced by all those party agents and heads of voluntary political associations who, as a rule, are politically active only in case of need and for whom politics is, neither materially nor ideally, "their life" in the first place. The same holds for those members of state counsels and similar deliberative bodies that function only when summoned. It also holds for rather broad strata of our members of parliament who are politically active only during sessions. In

the past, such strata were found especially among the estates. Proprietors of military implements in their own right, or proprietors of goods important for the administration, or proprietors of personal prerogatives may be called "estates." A large portion of them were far from giving their lives wholly, or merely preferentially, or more than occasionally, to the service of politics. Rather, they exploited their prerogatives in the interest of gaining rent or even profits; and they became active in the service of political associations only when the overlord of their status-equals especially demanded it. It was not different in the case of some of the auxiliary forces which the prince drew into the struggle for the creation of a political organization to be exclusively at his disposal. This was the nature of the *Rate von Haus aus* [councilors] and, still further back, of a considerable part of the councilors assembling in the "Curia" and other deliberating bodies of the princes. But these merely occasional auxiliary forces engaging in politics on the side were naturally not sufficient for the prince. Of necessity, the prince sought to create a staff of helpers dedicated wholly and exclusively to serving him, hence making this their major vocation. The structure of the emerging dynastic political organization, and not only this but the whole articulation of the culture, depended to a considerable degree upon the question of where the prince recruited agents.

A staff was also necessary for those political associations whose members constituted themselves politically as (so-called) "free" communes under the complete abolition or the far-going restriction of princely power.

They were "free" not in the sense of freedom from domination by force, but in the sense that princely power legitimized by tradition (mostly religously sanctified) as the exclusive source of all authority was absent. These communities have their historical home in the Occident. Their nucleus was the city as a body politic, the form in which the city first emerged in the Mediterranean culture area. In all these cases, what did the politicians who made politics their major vocation look like?

There are two ways of making politics one's vocation: Either one lives "for" politics or one lives "off" politics. By no means is this contrast an exclusive one. The rule is, rather, that man does both, at least in thought, and certainly he also does both in practice. He who lives "for" politics makes politics his life, in an internal sense. Either he enjoys the naked possession of the power he exerts, or he nourishes his inner balance and self-feeling by the consciousness that his life has *meaning* in the service of a "cause." In this internal sense, every sincere man who lives for a cause also lives off this cause. The distinction hence refers to a much more substantial aspect of the matter, namely, to the economic. He who strives to make politics a permanent *source of income* lives "off" politics as a vocation, whereas he who does not do this lives "for" politics. Under the dominance of the private property order, some—if you wish—very trivial preconditions must exist in order for a person to be able to live "for" politics in this economic sense. Under normal conditions, the politician must be economically independent of the income politics can bring him. This means, quite simply, that the politician must be wealthy or must have a personal position in life which yields a sufficient income.

This is the case, at least in normal circumstances. The war lord's following is just as little concerned about the conditions of a normal economy as is the street crowd following of the revolutionary hero. Both live off booty, plunder, confiscations, contributions, and the imposition of worthless and compulsory means of tender, which in essence amounts to the same thing. But necessarily, these are extraordinary phenomena. In everyday economic life, only some wealth serves the purpose of making a man economically independent. Yet this alone does not suffice. The professional politician must also be economically "dispensable," that is, his income must not depend upon the fact that he constantly and personally places his ability and thinking entirely, or at least by far predominantly, in the service of economic acquisition. In the most unconditional way, the rentier is dispensable in this sense. Hence, he is a man who receives completely unearned income. He may be the territorial lord of the past or the large landowner and aristocrat of the present who receives ground rent. In Antiquity and the Middle Ages they who received slave or serf rents or in modern times rents from shares or bonds or similar sources—these are rentiers.

Neither the worker nor—and this has to be noted well—the entrepreneur, especially the modern, large-scale entrepreneur, is economically dispensable in this sense. For it is precisely the entrepreneur who is tied to his enterprise and is therefore *not* dispensable. This holds for the entrepreneur in industry far more than for the entrepreneur in agriculture, considering the seasonal character of agriculture. In the main, it is very difficult for the entrepreneur to be represented in his enterprise by someone else, even temporarily. He is as little dispensable as is the medical doctor, and the more eminent and busy he is the less dispensable he is. For purely organizational reasons, it is easier for the lawyer to be dispensable; and therefore the lawyer has played an incomparably greater, and often even a dominant, role as a professional politician. We shall not continue in this classification; rather let us clarify some of its ramifications.

The leadership of a state or of a party by men who (in the economic sense of the word) live exclusively for politics and not off politics means necessarily a "plutocratic" recruitment of the leading political strata. To be sure, this does not mean that such plutocratic leadership signifies at the same time that the politically dominant strata will not also seek to live "off" politics, and hence that the dominant stratum will not usually exploit their political domination in their own economic interest. All that is unquestionable, of course. There has never been such a stratum that has not somehow lived "off" politics. Only this is meant: that the professional politician need not seek remuneration directly for his political work, whereas every politician without means must absolutely claim this. On the other hand, we do not mean to say that the propertyless politician will pursue private economic advantages through politics, exclusively, or even predominantly. Nor do we mean that he will not think, in the first place, of "the subject matter." Nothing would be more incorrect. According to all experience, a care for the economic "security" of his existence is consciously or unconsciously a cardinal point in the whole life orientation of the wealthy man. A quite reckless and unreserved political idealism is found if not exclusively at least predominantly among those strata who by virtue of their propertylessness stand entirely outside of the strata who are interested in maintaining the economic order of a given society. This holds especially for extraordinary and hence revolutionary epochs. A non-plutocratic recruitment of interested politicians, of leadership and following, is geared to the self-understood precondition that regular and reliable income will accrue to those who manage politics.

Either politics can be conducted "honorifically" and then, as one usually says, by "independent," that is, by wealthy, men, and especially by rentiers. Or, political leadership is made accessible to propertyless men who must then be rewarded. The professional politician who lives "off" politics may be a pure "prebendary" or a salaried "official." Then the politician receives either income from fees and perquisites for specific services—tips and bribes are only an irregular and formally illegal variant of this category of income—or a fixed income in kind, a money salary, or both. He may assume the character of an "entrepreneur," like the *condottiere* or the holder of a farmed-out or purchased office, or like the American boss who considers his costs a capital investment which he brings to fruition through exploitation of his influence. Again, he may receive a fixed wage, like a journalist, a party secretary, a modern cabinet minister, or a political official. Feudal fiefs, land grants, and prebends of all sorts have been typical, in the past. With the development of the money economy, perquisites and prebends especially are the typical rewards for the following of princes, victorious conquerors, or successful party chiefs. For loyal services today, party leaders give offices of all sorts—in parties, newspapers, co-operative societies, health insurance, municipalities, as well as in the state. *All* party struggles are struggles for the patronage of office, as well as struggles for objective goals.

Jeffrey Herbst
WAR AND THE STATE IN AFRICA

Most analyses assume that in Africa, as elsewhere, states will eventually become strong. But this may not be true in Africa, where states are developing in a fundamentally new environment. Lessons drawn from the case of Europe show that war is an important cause of state formation that is missing in Africa today. The crucial role that war has played in the formation of European states has long been noted. Samuel P. Huntington argued that "war was the great stimulus to state building," and

Charles Tilly went so far as to claim that "war made the state, and the state made war."[1] Similarly, two of the most successful states in the Third World today, South Korea and Taiwan, are largely "warfare" states that have been molded, in part, by the near constant threat of external aggression. However, studies of political development and state consolidation in Africa and many other parts of the Third World have all but ignored the important role that war can play in political development.

The role of war has not been examined because the vast majority of states in Africa and elsewhere in the world gained independence without having to

From *International Security* 14, no. 4. (Spring 1990), pp. 117–39.

resort to combat and have not faced a security threat since independence.[2] Those scholars who have analyzed the military in the developing world have studied the armed forces' role in economic and political processes but have not examined the changes that war could potentially effect on a state.[3] Studying the military and studying warfare are not the same, especially in the area of state consolidation, because warfare has independent effects on economic policies, administrative structures, and the citizenry's relationship with the state that have very little to do with the military.[4] Finally, beyond the usual problem of trying to study the impact of a factor that is missing, there is a less excusable normative bias which has sometimes prevented students of politics from examining the effects of war. The question of whether it is only possible to create a nation out of "blood and iron" is apparently one that many analysts find too disturbing to examine.[5]

Comparison of the European case with that of Africa is therefore crucial to understanding whether the analogy holds. War in Europe played an important role in the consolidation of many now-developed states: war caused the state to become more efficient in revenue collection; it forced leaders to dramatically improve administrative capabilities; and it created a climate and important symbols around which a disparate population could unify. While there is little reason to believe that war would have exactly the same domestic effects in Africa today as it did in Europe several centuries ago, it is important to ask if developing countries can accomplish in times of peace what war enabled European countries to do. I conclude that they probably cannot because fundamental changes in economic structures and societal beliefs are difficult, if not impossible, to bring about when countries are not being disrupted or under severe external threat.

The next section of this article outlines how war affected state formation in Europe, with particular attention to two crucial developments: the creation of centralized and efficient structures to collect taxes, and the development of nationalism. I then compare the European experience of state building

through warfare to the relative peace that Africa has experienced since the 1960s. While African states have benefited from peace, their development has been stunted by the very problems that war helped European countries to solve. I then evaluate the possibilities that African states might develop strategies to solve these fundamental problems in times of peace. I conclude that some states will probably be unsuccessful in finding ways of building the state in times of peace and will therefore remain permanently weak. Accordingly, the international community will have to develop non-traditional policies for helping a new brand of states: those that will continue to exist but that will not develop. Other states, perceiving that peace locks them into a permanently weak position, may be tempted to use war as a means of resolving their otherwise intractable problems of state consolidation.

Effects of War on State Consolidation: The European Case

It is instructive to look at war's impact on European societies because, as will be noted below, war in Europe helped alleviate some of the problems that affect African countries today. At the most basic level, war in Europe acted as a filter whereby weak states were eliminated and political arrangements that were not viable either were reformed or disappeared. Weak states do exist in Europe today—Belgium is one example—but the near-constant threat of war did prompt most states to become stronger to survive. The contrast between this evolutionary development and the current situation in the Third World, where even states that are largely dependent on foreign aid will continue to exist for the foreseeable future, is dramatic. It is, of course, important not to generalize too much because war had many different effects over time, and even in the same period states reacted in a variety of ways to external threats. However, war did affect the ability of European states to increase taxation and contributed to the forging of national identities in many countries. It is therefore important to examine the potential impact of external threat to better understand state consolidation in the Third World.

Taxes

Perhaps the most noticeable effect of war in European history was to cause the state to increase its ability to collect significantly more revenue with greater efficiency and less public resistance. Given the freedom of European states to attack each other, those states that could raise money quickly could successfully threaten their neighbors with a war that might lead to significant damage or even complete destruction. Richard Bean writes, "Once the power to tax had been successfully appropriated by any one sovereign, once he had used that power to bribe or coerce his nobility into acquiescence, that state could face all neighboring states with the choice of being conquered or of centralizing authority and raising taxes."[6] While success in war depends on many factors including technology, tactics, and morale of the troops, raising sufficient revenue was a necessary condition to prevent defeat. States that did not raise sufficient revenue for war perished. As Michael Mann notes, "A state that wished to survive had to increase its extractive capacity to pay for professional armies and/or navies. Those that did not would be crushed on the battlefield and absorbed into others—the fate of Poland, of Saxony, of Bavaria in [the seventeenth and eighteenth centuries]. No European states were continuously at peace. It is impossible to escape the conclusion that a peaceful state would have ceased to exist even more speedily than the militarily inefficient actually did."[7]

War affects state finances for two reasons. First, it puts tremendous strains on leaders to find new and more regular sources of income. While rulers may recognize that their tax system is inadequate, a war may be the only thing that forces them to expend the necessary political capital and undertake the coercion required to gain more revenue. For instance, in Mann's study of taxation in England between 1688 and 1815, he finds that there were six major jumps in state revenue and that each corresponds with the beginning of a war.[8] The association between the need to fight and the need to collect revenue is perhaps clearest in Prussia, where the main tax collection agency was called the General War Commissariat.[9]

Second, citizens are much more likely to acquiesce to increased taxation when the nation is at war, because a threat to their survival will overwhelm other concerns they might have about increased taxation. In fact, taxation for a war can be thought of as a "lumpy" collective good: not only must the population pay to get the good, but it must also pay a considerable amount more than the current level of taxation, because a small increase in revenue is often not enough to meet the new security threat facing the state.[10] In this way, taxation for a war is like taxation for building a bridge: everyone must pay to build the bridge and a small increase in revenue will not be enough, because half a bridge, like fighting half a war, is useless.

Thus, war often causes a "ratchet effect" whereby revenue increases sharply when a nation is fighting but does not decline to the *ante bellum* level when hostilities have ceased.[11] Once governments have invested the sunken costs in expanding tax collection systems and routinized the collection of new sources of revenue, the marginal costs of continuing those structures are quite low and the resources they collect can be used for projects that will enhance the ruling group's support.

While it is not a universal rule, war in other societies at other times often played the same kind of role that war did in Europe. For instance, Joseph Smaldone writes in his study of the Sokoto Caliphate (in what is now Nigeria) between 1500 and 1800:

> War was the principal instrument for the establishment and extension of political authority over subject people and foreign territory, and for the organization, maintenance, and reinforcement of that authority. The demands of perennial war

evoked institutions to subordinate the sectors of society crucial to the interests of these militarized polities. The permanent requirement to mobilize human and material resources for military purposes [i.e., taxation] intensified tendencies toward the monopolization of power and the elaboration of auxiliary institutions of social control.[12]

Similarly, the South Korean and Taiwanese states have been able to extract so many resources from their societies in part because the demands to be constantly vigilant provoked the state into developing efficient mechanisms for collecting resources and controlling dissident groups.[13] A highly extractive state also could cloak demands for greater resources in appeals for national unity in the face of a determined enemy.

Nationalism

War also had a major impact on the development of nationalism of Europe. Indeed, the presence of a palpable external threat may be the strongest way to generate a common association between the state and the population. External threats have such a powerful effect on nationalism because people realize in a profound manner that they are under threat because of who they are as a nation; they are forced to recognize that it is only as a nation that they can successfully defeat the threat. Anthony Giddens recounts the effects of World War I: "The War canalized the development of states' sovereignty, tying this to citizenship and to nationalism in such a profound way that any other scenario [of how the international system would be ordered] came to appear as little more than idle fantasy."[14] Similarly, Michael Howard notes the visceral impact of wars on the development of nationalism throughout Europe:

> Self-identification as a Nation implies almost by definition alienation from other communities, and the most memorable incidents in the group-memory consisted in conflict with and triumph over other communities. France *was* Marengo,

Austerlitz and Jena: military triumph set the seal on the new-found national consciousness. Britain *was* Trafalgar—but it had been a nation for four hundred years, since those earlier battles Crecy and Agincourt. Russia *was* the triumph of 1812. Germany *was* Gravelotte and Sedan.[15]

In Europe there was an almost symbiotic relationship between the state's extractive capacity and nationalism: war increased both as the population was convinced by external threat that they should pay more to the state, and as, at the same time, the population united around common symbols and memories that were important components of nationalism. Fighting wars may be the only way whereby it is possible to have people pay more taxes and at the same time feel more closely associated with the state.

The Absence of Interstate War in the Modern Era

While trying to study the chaos caused by administrative disintegration, the forceful crushing of ethnic challenges, and large-scale human rights abuses, many scholars have generally assumed that poor countries today face even more external challenges than European states did in their formative periods.[16] In fact, since the end of the Second World War, very few Third World states have fought interstate wars of the type that affected the evolution of European states. The few Third World interstate wars that have occurred (e.g., India-Pakistan, Iran-Iraq, China-Vietnam) have obscured the fact that the vast majority of Third World states most of the time do not face significant external threats. States like Israel, South Korea, or Taiwan, where national survival has been a real consideration in national politics, are exceptional and even these countries have survived intact.

Even in Africa, the continent seemingly destined for war given the colonially-imposed boundaries and weak political authorities, there has not been one involuntary boundary change since the dawn of the independence era in the late 1950s, and very few countries face even the prospect of a conflict with their neighbors. Most of the conflicts in Africa that have occurred were not, as in Europe, wars of conquest that threatened the existence of other states, but conflicts over lesser issues that were resolved without threatening the existence of another state. For instance, Tanzania invaded Uganda in 1979 to overthrow Idi Amin, not to conquer Uganda. Similarly, the war in the Western Sahara is a colonial question, not a conflict between independent states. Even South Africa's destabilization efforts against its neighbors are primarily attempts to influence the policies of the majority-ruled countries, not to change the borders of the region. Lesotho or Swaziland would not exist today if South Africa had any real territorial ambitions. In the few conflicts that did have the potential to threaten fundamentally the existence of states—Somalia's attempt to invade Ethiopia in the 1970s and Libya's war against Chad in the 1970s and 1980s—the aggressor did not succeed.[17]

African states have seldom fought interstate wars and the continent has not witnessed significant boundary changes, because independent leaders have continued the system of boundary maintenance that the colonial powers first developed to regulate the scramble for Africa in the late 1800s.[18] African leaders recognized in the early 1960s that a potentially large number of groups would want to secede from the states they are presently in, to join others or create entirely new ones. In order to prevent the continent from being thrown into the chaos of large-scale boundary changes in which the stability and integrity of any state could be threatened, they created a system of explicit norms, propounded by the Organization of African Unity in 1963, which declared any change in the inherited colonial boundaries to be illegitimate. Most of the continent has, accordingly, refused to recognize boundary changes (e.g., Biafra, Eritrea) even where the principle of self-determination might have led them to do so. This system has been successful in preserving African national boundaries and has so far deterred almost all countries from initiating the

kind of conquest wars that were so common in European history. The system that maintained the inherited borders as inviolate was strengthened somewhat inadvertently, because two of the largest states on the continent (Nigeria and Zaire), which could conceivably have threatened their much smaller neighbors, faced significant secessionist threats (from the Ibo and Kataganese respectively) and therefore worked resolutely to strengthen the norm that the borders should not be changed.

The stability of new states, especially in Africa, is a remarkable development given that the vast majority of the over one hundred countries in the Third World that have gained their independence since 1945 are poor, have weak administrative structures, and consist of populations that are splintered along regional or ethnic lines. In other words, they are precisely the kind of states that before 1945 were routinely invaded and taken over by stronger states in their region or by external powers. Yet, very few states in the Third World, despite their evident military and political weaknesses, face any significant external threat.

In contrast, Tilly estimates, the "enormous majority" of states in Europe failed. Peace was the exception and long periods with no major fighting were almost unknown, as for centuries weak states were routinely defeated and populations regularly absorbed by foreign rulers.[19] The psychology of Europe in its formative centuries, where state survival was a very real issue of constant concern to leaders, is so different from the outlook facing Third World leaders today as to suggest that there has been a fundamental change in the survival prospects of weak states and that control of territory is no longer correlated with military power.[20]

Problems of State Consolidation in Africa

African states face numerous problems in their efforts to consolidate power. They are poor, short of trained manpower, and confront societies that are often fragmented and have little orientation to the state as a whole. Many other Third World nations face these same problems although they are often most extreme in Africa, given the poverty of the continent and the fragility of the states. Elites can come to power but, given the precariousness of control in countries where rules governing leadership and succession have not been institutionalized, they may be displaced. Once they lose power, or are prevented from gaining it, ambitious politicians have no other opportunity to accumulate wealth or power because the state controls the badges of status and many of the free-floating resources in the economy, such as they are.[21] Even when they do control the apex of the state, elites may feel that because of their country's vulnerability to exogenous shocks (e.g., sudden sharp drops in the price of their raw material exports) and the presence of sophisticated multinational enterprises and well-connected minority groups (e.g., Lebanese in West Africa, Indians in East Africa), they are not really in control of their own destiny and therefore are vulnerable. As a result of their gross insecurities, these "lame Leviathans"[22] try desperately to control ever-greater parts of society through outright ownership or regulation. However, since they are weak, their efforts are almost inevitably clumsy, heavy-handed, and authoritarian.

Therefore, although the average state in Africa compared to other states is small (as measured by government spending as a percentage of gross domestic product [GDP]),[23] it appears to be too large because its clumsy extractive efforts cause so much damage compared to the benefits that it delivers. Thus arises the image of so many African states as "overdeveloped" or "swollen."[24] The problems confronted by states in Africa can be illustrated by comparing their experience with European states in two areas where war had a significant impact: the state's ability to extract resources through taxes, and the degree of nationalism in the countries south of the Sahara.

A classic example of how weak state power causes the state to institute desperate and self-defeating economic policies is in the area of government revenue. Government revenue poses a major problem for all African states and many others in the Third World. These states are desperately short of revenue to fund even minimal state services (e.g., pay nurses' salaries, buy books for schools, supply transport for agricultural extension services) that their populations have long been promised. In addition to these recurrent costs, Third World countries are in need of more extensive and more efficient tax systems because the process of development requires large expenditures on infrastructure to promote economic activity throughout the country and to handle the ramifications of development, especially the large expenses incurred by urbanizing countries.[25] W. Arthur Lewis estimates that the public sector in Third World countries should be spending on the order of 20 percent of GDP on services, exclusive of defense and debt repayment.[26] However, when defense (2.5 percent of GDP) and debt repayments (3.4 percent of GDP) are subtracted, the average African country spends only 15.7 percent of its GDP on all government functions.[27] While these figures are only rough estimates given the problems associated with African economic statistics, they do illustrate the extent of the fiscal crisis facing African states.

Due to the weakness of administrative and statistical structures in Africa, many governments rely on taxation of foreign trade, because imports and exports must physically pass through a relatively small number of border posts that can be easily manned. Thus, the average African state depends on revenue from tariffs for 20.5 percent of total revenue, compared to all developing countries which, on average, gain 12.9 percent of their revenue from tariffs, and industrialized countries where tariffs account for only 1.3 percent of total revenue.[28]

Unfortunately, funding the state through indirect taxes on foreign trade damages national economies because leaders are compelled to erect ever-greater administrative controls on imports. These tariffs promote corruption, smuggling and, most importantly, overvalued exchange rates, because governments grow to rely on administrative controls rather than the market to regulate imports. Overvalued exchange rates in turn lead to widespread damage within poorer economies as exporters are universally hurt, the population is encouraged to become dependent on imported food, and black markets quickly develop to take advantage of distorted prices.[29] Beyond the immediate damage caused by a tax system dependent on imports and exports, this *type* of tax system is particularly inappropriate for Third World countries. These countries need guarantees of slow and steady increases in government revenue above the rate of economic growth in order to accomplish the tasks crucial to development: build transport and communications systems, establish utilities, and create educational systems.[30]

Another major problem facing leaders in Africa is the absence of a strong popular identity with the state. The lack of a popular consensus over national purpose both aggravates the state's clumsy efforts to extract resources and is itself exacerbated by an insecure, authoritarian elite. Indeed, the picture of African societies widely accepted today is of populations trying desperately to escape the clutches of the state, rather than becoming more involved in it, and certainly not willing to pay more taxes to it.[31] Twenty-five years after "the nationalist period," there are few signs of nationalism in most African countries despite the now *pro forma* exhortations from propaganda organs to engage in state-building. Indeed, the majority of states still have difficulty creating viable symbols to attract the loyalties of their citizens.

Not surprisingly, therefore, there are today very few attempts in African countries to forge a national consensus on major issues, much less a national identity. For instance, most formulas to decrease interethnic tension concentrate only on ameliorating the negative aspects of ethnic conflict by accomodating it through decentralized government structures and preferential policies.[32] However, formulas such as federalism often are inappropriate in countries where national institutions are not strong. Federalist solutions broke down in Sudan and Uganda, among other places, because the incentives for leaders to

attempt to gain total control were much greater than the barriers posed by recently adopted institutional arrangements.[33] Moreover, no matter how well accommodationist formulas of intra-societal conflict work, almost everyone in Africa and elsewhere in the Third World would agree that a more basic national loyalty by all societal groups would still be desirable. However, the means by which to induce a disparate society to identify more with the nation-state are unknown in Africa and few in the current era are even attempting to speculate on how to develop a national consensus.

Difficulties of State Consolidation without War

War in Europe played such an important role in the evolution of the state mechanism and society's relationship with the state because it is extraordinarily difficult, outside times of crisis, to reform elemental parts of the governmental system, such as the means of taxation, or to effect a real change in national identity. For instance, since taxes are so consequential to every business decision, the tax system over time reflects a large number of political bargains made by the state with different interest groups. Often governments find it too politically difficult to provide direct subsidies to those they want to favor, so the tax system is a convenient backdoor to aid politically important groups without incurring opprobrium. The political bargains that constitute the tax system develop a momentum of their own because individuals and businesses base their future economic decisions on the incentives and disincentives in the existing tax code. Indeed, Joseph Schumpeter called the fiscal system "a collection of hard, naked facts" and claimed that "the spirit of a people, its cultural level, its social structure, the deeds its policy may prepare — all this and more is written in its fiscal history, stripped of all phrases."[34]

Therefore, even minor changes such as alterations in the level of taxation or shifts in the tax burden, as the United States and most Western European countries have made in the last few years, engender tremendous political battles. Not only the previously favored political groups but all those that simply followed the signals sent out by government will forcefully oppose fiscal reform. Greater changes in the nature of the tax system are even more difficult. Edward Ames' and Richard Rapp's conclusion that tax systems "last until the end of the government that instituted them" and that tax systems in some European countries survived "almost intact" from the thirteenth and fourteenth centuries until the late eighteenth century may be an exaggeration, but their conclusions suggest just how much inertia a particular system for collecting government revenue can develop over time.[35] Other than war, no type of crisis demands that the state increase taxes with such forcefulness, and few other situations would impel citizens to accept those demands, or at least not resist them as strongly as they otherwise might have. It is therefore hard to counter Tilly's argument that "the formation of standing armies provided the largest single incentive to extraction and the largest single means of state coercion over the long run of European state-making."[36]

Domestic security threats, of the type African countries face so often, may force the state to increase revenue; however, these crises are almost never as grave as the type of external threat the European states had to confront, because they do not threaten the very existence of the state. In addition, domestic conflicts result in fragmentation and considerable hostility among different segments of the population. As a result, the state does not necessarily achieve the greater revenue efficiency gains engendered by an external crisis. Indeed, in a civil war—as in Nigeria in the late 1960s—parts of the state are fighting against each other, which hardly promotes efficiency in tax collection. Public acceptance of tax increases, a crucial factor in allowing European states to extract greater resources in times of war, will be a much more complicated issue in civil disputes. As Mann notes, "the growth of the

modern state, as measured by finances, is explained primarily not in domestic terms but in terms of geopolitical relations of violence."[37]

The obstacles posed by large peasant populations, significant nonmonetarized sectors, and widespread poverty are, of course, important contributors to the revenue crisis of the African state. However, these problems do not fully explain why poor states do not extract greater resources from society in a manner that is less economically harmful. Factors such as political will, administrative ability, and the population's willingness to be taxed—issues that can be affected by the decisions of political leaders—are also crucial in understanding why states are unable to achieve their potential level of taxation in a benign manner.[38] For instance, Margaret Levi successfully shows that in such diverse cases as republican Rome, France and England in the Middle Ages, eighteenth-century Britain, and twentieth-century Australia, levels of taxation were affected primarily by political constraints faced by rulers, despite the fact that most of these economies also posed significant barriers to increased tax collection.[39]

Nor has there been any success in developing means to cause the population to identify more with the state, other than fighting a war. Nationalism, which was never nearly as strong or widespread (especially outside the major cities) in Africa as many had thought, was palpable in the late colonial period because there was a "relevant other"—the colonialists—who could be easily identified as oppressors and around which a nominal national identity could be built.[40] However, since independence in most African countries, there has been no "relevant other" to oppose, so it has been extremely difficult to create nationwide symbols of identity. There has therefore been no way of generating a national identity in Africa such as wars forged in Europe. Anthony Smith writes, "the central difficulty of 'nation-building' in much of Africa and Asia is the lack of any shared historical mythology and memory on which state elites can set about 'building' the nation. The 'nation' [is built up] from the central fund of culture and symbolism and mythology provided by shared historical experiences."[41] The result is the anomie in most African countries today.

It could be argued that the lack of nationalism simply reflects the fact that African countries are artificial groupings of disparate peoples and therefore are not really nation-states. However, no "natural" nation-states are mature at birth with populations that have readily agreed to a central identity. Rather, the goal of those who want to create the nation-state is to convince different groups that they do, in fact, share a common identity. This is why even in Europe, which today seems to have nation-states that are more "natural" than Africa's, war had such a crucial role to play in the forging of common identities.

Indeed, the symbiotic relationship that war fostered in Europe between tax collection and nationalism is absent in Africa, precisely because there is no external threat to encourage people to acquiesce in the state's demands, and no challenge that causes them to respond as a nation. Instead, the African state's clumsy efforts at greater extraction are met by popular withdrawal rather than by a populace united around a common identity.

Of course, not all wars led to the strengthening of administrative institutions and greater nationalism. For example, Joseph Strayer notes that the Hundred Years War "was so exhausting for both sides that it discouraged the normal development of the apparatus of the state. There was a tendency to postpone structural reforms, to solve problems on an ad hoc basis rather than [to create] new agencies of government, to sacrifice efficiency for immediate results."[42] However, the Hundred Years War was exceptional because of its length and it therefore did not allow rulers to consolidate the gains usually achieved after facing a short period of external danger. Yet overall, the historical record suggests that war was highly efficient in promoting state consolidation in Europe, and that it would be much more difficult for states to accomplish the same tasks in peacetime.

Are There Peaceful Routes to State Consolidation?

Since African and other Third World countries need to transform important parts of their governmental systems, including their fiscal arrangements, and to promote nationalism, but do not have the traditional avenue of war to aid them, the immediate question is whether they can follow a path other than that adopted by Europe to consolidate state power and to develop new national identities to reduce the divisions between society and the state.

Once again it is interesting to focus on government revenue because the issue is so decisive in its own right and because tax systems are such a good reflection of the basic bargains in society. In an age with reduced levels of interstate war, African countries are faced with the problem of trying to increase the capacity of the state without being able to use wars to "ratchet up" the state's extractive ability. Given the evidence of European fiscal inertia, it is clear that it will be even more difficult to institute major reforms when states are operating in normal circumstances. The one clear chance African countries did have to institute major reforms was at independence, because at that moment political arrangements were in such flux that significant new initiatives could be undertaken. Indeed, some African countries (e.g., Mozambique, Angola) did make massive changes in their political economy (e.g., nationalization, collectivization); unfortunately, these particular reforms were economically ruinous because their socialist policies distorted economies even more than in most African countries. Once independence becomes the normal situation, as it has in African countries, it becomes extraordinarily difficult for leaders to make basic reforms of political arrangements, such as fiscal systems, which might hurt powerful groups. As Peter Bachrach and Morton Baratz noted in the context of American politics, dominant values, myths, rituals, and institutions quickly ossify so that crucial issues, such as fiscal reform, are not even on the agenda.[43] There appears to be no impetus from inside African countries to disrupt the current fiscal arrangements significantly. Indeed, much of the argument that there is currently a significant economic crisis in Africa, and that this crisis was caused by malfunctioning government policies, came from outside the continent.[44]

However, it could be argued that structural adjustment, pressed on African countries by the International Monetary Fund (IMF), the World Bank, and bilateral donors, could serve many state-making functions. As external actors dedicated to fundamental reforms of the economy and of the way the state operates, the IMF and other donors are not subject to the same rigidities that paralyze domestic reformers. The IMF and other actors who insist on fundamental reform could pressure African states for significant changes in their tax system. Demands from an external actor are similar to war, in that a leader can legitimately argue to its population that it has no choice in asking them to make very difficult sacrifices because it is under too much external pressure.

It would be a major mistake, however, to take too far the analogy between pressure from actors such as the IMF and the effects of war. For instance, war produced such spectacular gains in governmental efficiency because the state itself felt threatened. The IMF, or any other actor, cannot produce that feeling; indeed, structural adjustment has been least successful when it has tried to address the issues of how the state itself operates in areas such as public enterprises or fiscal arrangements.[45] The cost to the state itself in failing to adopt a structural adjustment program can be severe, but falls far short of what war would threaten. The IMF will never cause a state to disappear. At worst, a state can simply opt for the high cost of breaking off relations with the IMF.

Nor does external pressure of the type the Fund exerts produce any change in national identity. While leaders can occasionally rally people against the external threat posed by "imperialists," these sentiments usually are not long-lasting because the population may be unable to distinguish between international actors supposedly draining away the nation's funds during a structural adjustment

exercise, and those national leaders who led their country into such a spectacular economic debacle. While Europe's leaders in previous centuries hardly treated their populations well by modern standards, it was usually unambiguous that people would be better off if they won the war than if they lost.

The prospects of structural adjustment fostering some kind of nationalism based on resisting foreigners is also limited because the IMF is not really a "relevant other" to a largely peasant population, and cannot induce changes in national consciousness of the type that wars in Europe produced. Unlike a war where the entire population was threatened because of its national identity, structural adjustment will help certain groups unambiguously (e.g., peasants who grow export crops), clearly hurt some (e.g., the urban population dependent on imported food), and have ambiguous effects on many others. Further, the intensity in shared experience that a war generates simply cannot be replicated by, say, protracted negotiations over the IMF's Extended Fund Facility.

The Likelihood of War in Africa

If internal reform seems improbable and there is no other external threat that can perform quite the same role as war, the question becomes whether at some point in the future African leaders will begin to see war as a potential avenue for state-making. Some leaders may look to war simply because they are truly concerned about the fate of the nation and see no other option. Others may not be concerned particularly with nation-building, but may find that their countries have suffered economic decline for so long that the possibilities for their own personal enrichment have become severely limited, and therefore will seek to seize the assets of other countries. So far, the system that has preserved the continent's boundaries has not been significantly tested because most leaders considered it obvious that they were better off with their inherited boundaries than they would be in a chaotic war situation where sovereignty or considerable territory might be lost. However, especially in the context of decades of economic decline, it is possible that some African leaders may recalculate the benefits of a peace that locks them into perpetual weakness. Instead, they may try to increase their state's extractive ability and divert their citizens from inter-ethnic squabbles by seizing upon the multitude of provocations, always present, to provoke a fight with neighboring states. Paul Colinvaux presents the extreme case for the prospects of interstate war in Africa:

> Africa holds the greatest possibilities for the aspiring general. . . . That there will be battles between African nations as they build their African continent in a new image is as certain as anything in history. For each country there must come times when wealth, hopes, ambitions, and numbers all rise together. It then needs only access to high-quality weapons for an aggression to be an attractive undertaking.[46]

If significant interstate wars break out when provocations are small but elites realize what war could do for the state and the nation, it would not be a strikingly new development. Rather, increased interstate warfare in Africa would simply be a return to the European norm. Whether war in Africa today would actually bring about the same kind of changes that it did in Europe centuries ago is unclear, but the possibility that leaders might become so desperate that they try in some fundamental way to alter the political rules under which their nations function should not be ignored.

Many are the possible provocations that could bring about significant interstate war in Africa. Certainly, there are plenty of border disputes and fragments of ethnic groups that need to be rescued from "foreign domination" to provide enough rationalization for hostile action against other African countries. Conflicts between language blocs (e.g., English versus French),[47] disputes over control of crucial rivers and railroads (especially given the number of

land-locked countries), or the simple need to have more land for populations that double every twenty years provide many other potential reasons for war in Africa. More than a few African leaders might someday agree with Bismarck, a brilliant consolidator of a "new nation," on the only real way to unite a fragmented people:

> Prussia . . . , as a glance at the map will show, could no longer wear unaided on its long narrow figure the panoply which Germany required for its security; it must be equally distributed over all German peoples. We should get no nearer the goal by speeches, associations, decisions of majorities; we should be unable to avoid a serious contest, a contest which could only be settled by blood and iron.[48]

Although African countries had more or less equal defense capabilities at independence, the growing differential in force projection capabilities have led some to suggest that Africa will experience much greater resort to force in the future. Inventories of tanks and other armored vehicles as well as artillery, jet fighters, and naval craft have increased considerably throughout the continent. For instance, just in the period between 1966 and 1981, the number of countries in sub-Saharan Africa with tanks increased from two to eighteen, the number with field artillery went from seven to thirty-six, the number with light armor went from thirteen to thirty-six, and the number possessing jet aircraft went from six to twenty-one.[49] Countries such as Nigeria and Zaire have developed military capabilities that are far greater than their neighbors'. So far, the assurance of stability that is the central advantage of the current African state system has almost always been more attractive than whatever reasons African leaders may have had to begin conflict with their neighbors. However, as President Nyerere of Tanzania showed when he invaded Uganda to depose Idi Amin, even strong proponents of African norms can be driven to interstate conflict if they believe that the costs of not acting are high enough. In the future, African leaders may find that, despite all their efforts, economic reform cannot progress and they cannot get their citizenry to unite around national symbols; it is conceivable that then the deterrent value of the norms of sovereignty may seem much less powerful than they do now. If these norms no longer provided protection to a large number of states, they would lose all meaning throughout the African continent. While the timing of these wars is not predictable, it should be obvious that the incentives that African leaders have to incite wars for the purposes of state-making are significant and may become much stronger in the future when the futility of domestic reform during times of business as usual, that is, peace, becomes clear.

The Permanently Weak State: A New Development

Much of this discussion has focused on the potential opportunities for African states that, in a European-type state system, might have engaged in battle, won (or at least not lost too badly), and thereby used war in order to further state building. However, it should be recognized that another class of states in Africa is directly affected by the current absence of war: those states that would have lost badly and would have been absorbed by the winners. These states range from those that are just geographic anachronisms left by colonialism (e.g., The Gambia, Djibouti), and very small states in the shadow of giants (e.g., Benin and Togo, close to Nigeria, or Rwanda and Burundi bordering Zaire), to those that simply lack significant resources for development or defense (e.g., Mali, Mauritania). In Europe during the formative centuries, disintegration of weak states like these was a regular occurrence. Weak states that were defeated then became the poorer regions of richer countries, but at least they had a chance to share in the revenue and resources of a viable state. Yet the absence of a truly competitive state system that penalizes military weakness means that even those states that have no other prospects than long-term

dependence on international aid will survive in their crippled form for the foreseeable future. Perhaps the only task of state consolidation that these otherwise weak states can accomplish is to physically capture their populations within the stable boundaries of the African state system.[50]

The presence of permanently weak states that will not be eliminated is a new development in international relations and one that poses novel development challenges. All theoretical work on development so far, no matter what the ideological predisposition of the authors, has implicitly assumed that somehow the nation-states as they currently exist are viable arrangements for development, if only they follow the proper strategies and receive enough help from the international community. This assumption was appropriate for the European context where centuries of war had eliminated states that simply were not viable. However, for Africa, whose states have not been tested by an international system that severely punishes political weakness, there is little reason to believe that many of them will be able to have a favorable enough geographic position, control adequate natural resources, gain the support of a significant portion of their populations, and construct strong administrative structures to ever develop. In the long term, these states may disappear if interstate wars finally do break out in Africa.

In the meantime, what is to be done with states that exist but cannot develop? It is far too early to write off any state's prospects. We have been wrong about the development prospects of many states both in Africa (where scholars were too optimistic) and elsewhere in the world, such as East Asia.[51] It would also be morally unacceptable simply to allow these countries to gradually slide from the world's view into a twilight of perpetual poverty because nature and history have been unkind to them. However, thought must be given to nontraditional alternatives for aid to states that in previous times would simply have been defeated and absorbed by stronger neighbors in a war. For instance, the international community might consider rewarding those countries in the Third World that have taken in economic migrants from non-viable states.[52] The West could consider providing additional aid to those countries willing to engage in some kind of regional integration to mitigate the problems of unchanging boundaries, much as countries that have adopted more rational economic policies have attracted greater aid from donors. The world may simply have to recognize that a certain number of countries are locked into non-viable positions, and develop a long-term approach to their welfare rather than acting surprised every time the inevitable famine or ecological disaster occurs.

Conclusion

It is important not to glorify war. The wars that Europe went through caused immense suffering for generations and wholesale destruction of some societies. Yet it is undeniable that out of this destruction emerged stronger political arrangements and more unified populations. No one would advocate war as a solution to Africa's political and economic problems, where the costs of interstate war could be even higher than in Europe. It is doubtful that, if African countries do start fighting wars, they will undergo exactly the same processes of state consolidation that war engendered in Europe. However, it should be recognized that there is very little evidence that African countries, or many others in the Third World, will be able to find peaceful ways to strengthen the state and develop national identities. In particular, the prospects for states that will not disappear, but simply cannot develop, must be examined. At the same time, we must recognize the possibility that some African leaders in the future may come to believe that the costs of peace—limits on reform possibilities and a fragmented population—are so high that war may not seem like such an undesirable alternative. If African leaders do indeed make this calculation, the suffering that Africa has seen in the last twenty-five years may only be a prelude to much more dangerous developments.

NOTES

1. Samuel P. Huntington, *Political Order in Changing Societies* (New Haven: Yale University Press, 1968), p. 123; and Charles Tilly, "Reflections on the History of European State-Making," in Charles Tilly, ed., *The Formation of National States in Western Europe* (Princeton: Princeton University Press, 1975), p. 42. An important recent addition to this literature is Brian M. Downing, "Constitutionalism, Warfare and Political Change in Early Modern Europe," *Theory and Society*, Vol. 17, No. 1 (January 1988), pp. 7–56. The general literature on warfare's effect on society is voluminous. An early work which concentrates on some of the themes examined here is Hans Delbrück, *History of the Art of the War within the Framework of Political History*, Vol. III, trans. Walter J. Renfroe, Jr. (Westport, Conn.: Greenwood Press, 1982).

2. For instance, in Morris Janowitz's classic study of the military in the developing world, the political, social, and economic functions of the military are studied extensively but the potential effects of war, or of peace, are not analyzed. Morris Janowitz, *The Military in the Political Development of New Nations: An Essay in Comparative Analysis* (Chicago: University of Chicago Press, 1964), p. 12.

3. The literature is reviewed by Henry Bienen, "Armed Forces and National Modernization: Continuing the Debate," *Comparative Politics*, Vol. 16, No. 1 (October 1983), pp. 1–16.

4. Gabriel Ardent, "Financial Policy and Economic Infrastructure of Modern States and Nations," in Tilly, *The Formation of National States*, p. 89.

5. A useful corrective to the conventional view is provided by John A. Hall, "War and the Rise of the West," in Colin Creighton and Martin Shaw, eds., *The Sociology of the War and Peace* (London: Macmillan, 1987).

6. Richard Bean, "War and the Birth of the Nation State," *Journal of Economic History*, Vol. 33, No. 1 (March 1973), p. 220.

7. Michael Mann, "State and Society, 1130–1815: An Analysis of English State Finances," in Mann, *States,*

War and Capitalism: Studies in Political Sociology (Oxford: Basil Blackwell, 1988), p. 109.

8. Michael Mann, *The Sources of Social Power* (Cambridge: Cambridge University Press, 1986), p. 486.

9. Michael Duffy, "The Military Revolution and the State, 1500–1800," in Michael Duffy, ed., *The Military Revolution and the State, 1500–1800*, Exeter Studies in History No. 1 (Exeter, U.K.: University of Exeter, 1980), p. 5.

10. "Lumpy" goods are products which are not useful if only part is purchased. Margaret Levi, *Of Rule and Revenue* (Berkeley: University of California Press, 1988), pp. 56–57.

11. Mann, *Sources of Social Power*, pp. 483–490.

12. Joseph P. Smaldone, *Warfare in the Sokoto Caliphate: Historical and Sociological Perspectives* (Cambridge: Cambridge University Press, 1977), p. 139. The same point is made by Richard L. Roberts in his *Warriors, Merchants, and Slaves: The State and the Economy in the Middle Niger Valley, 1700–1914* (Palo Alto: Stanford University Press, 1987), p. 20.

13. Joel S. Migdal, *Strong Societies and Weak States: State-Society Relations and State Capabilities in the Third World* (Princeton: Princeton University Press, 1988), p. 274.

14. Anthony Giddens, *The Nation-State and Violence*, vol. II of *A Contemporary Critique of Historical Materialism* (Berkeley: University of California Press, 1985), p. 235.

15. Michael Howard, *War and the Nation State* (Oxford: Clarendon Press, 1978), p. 9. Emphasis in the original.

16. See, for instance, Joseph LaPalombara, "Penetration: A Crisis of Governmental Capacity," in Leonard Binder, et al., *Crises and Sequences in Political Development* (Princeton: Princeton University Press, 1971), p. 222.

17. In 1977 Somalia, as part of its irredentist project to create "Greater Somalia," invaded Ethiopia in the hope of annexing the Ogaden; the Ethiopians, with significant help from the Soviet Union and Cuba, defeated Somalia in 1978. David D. Laitin and Said S. Samatar, *Somalia: Nation in Search of a State* (Boulder, Colo.: Westview, 1987), pp. 140–143. In 1973 Libyan forces invaded Chad by moving forces into the disputed Aozou strip. The Libyan military presence gradually expanded until a dramatic series of conflicts with the Chadian government (heavily supported by France and the United States) in 1987 forced the Libyans to agree to an end to hostilities. John Wright, *Libya, Chad and the Central Sahara* (London: Hurst, 1989), pp. 126–146.

18. This argument is developed in Jeffrey Herbst, "The Creation and Maintenance of National Boundaries in Africa," *International Organization*, Vol. 43, No. 4 (Fall 1989), pp. 673–692.

19. Tilly, "Reflections on the History of European State-Making," p. 38.

20. Ibid., p. 81.

21. Richard Hodder-Williams, *An Introduction to the Politics of Tropical Africa* (London: Allen and Unwin, 1984), p. 95.

22. Thomas M. Callaghy, "The State and the Development of Capitalism in Africa: Theoretical, Historical, and Comparative Reflections," in Donald Rothchild and Naomi Chazan, eds., *The Precarious Balance: State and Society in Africa* (Boulder, Colo.: Westview, 1988), p. 82.

23. The share of total gross domestic product of sub-Saharan African states is smaller, at 21.6 percent, than the developing country average of 25.5 percent. (Both figures are from 1984.) International Monetary Fund (IMF), *Government Finance Statistics Yearbook 1988* (Washington, D.C.: IMF, 1988), p. 94.

24. See, for instance, Larry Diamond, "Class Formation in the Swollen African State," *The Journal of Modern African Studies*, Vol. 25, No. 4 (December 1987), pp. 592–596; and Nzongola-Ntalaja, "The Crisis of the State in Post-Colonial Africa," in Nzongola-Ntalaja, *Revolution and Counter-Revolution in Africa* (London: Zed Books, 1987), p. 85.

25. W. Arthur Lewis, *The Evolution of the International Economic Order* (Princeton: Princeton University Press, 1978), p. 39.

26. W. Arthur Lewis, *Development Planning: The Essentials of Economic Policy* (New York: Harper and Row, 1966), p. 115.

27. Calculated from IMF, *Government Finance Statistics Yearbook 1988*, pp. 58, 74, and 94.

28. Calculated from ibid., p. 54.

29. See World Bank, *Accelerated Development in Sub-Saharan Africa: An Agenda for Action* (Washington, D.C.: World Bank, 1981), pp. 24–30.

30. Alex Radian, *Resource Mobilization in Poor Countries: Implementing Tax Policies* (New Brunswick, NJ: Transaction Books, 1980), pp. 13–17.

31. See Rothchild and Chazan, *The Precarious Balance*.

32. See, for instance, Donald L. Horowitz, *Ethnic Groups in Conflict* (Berkeley: University of California Press, 1985), pp. 563–680.

33. Buganda had a degree of autonomy when Uganda gained independence and the Kabaka, the traditional ruler of the Buganda people, was the country's first president. However, this arrangement fell apart in 1966 when then Prime Minister Milton Obote overthrew the Kabaka and invaded Buganda. Crawford Young, *The Politics of Cultural Pluralism* (Madison: University of Wisconsin Press, 1976), pp. 149–156. In 1983, President Gaafar Mohamed Nimeiri of the Sudan effectively abrogated the Addis Ababa agreement which had given autonomy to Southern Sudan. The Sudan has been embroiled in a civil war ever since. Mansour Khalid, *Nimeiri and the Revolution of Dis-May* (London: KPI, 1985), pp. 234–240.

34. Joseph A. Schumpeter, "The Crisis of the Tax State," in Alan T. Peacock, et al., eds., *International Economic Papers*, No. 4 (London: Macmillan, 1954), pp. 6–7.

35. Edward Ames and Richard T. Rapp, "The Birth and Death of Taxes: A Hypothesis," *Journal of Economic History*, Vol. 37, No. 1 (March 1977), p. 177.

36. Tilly, "Reflections on the History of European State-Making," p. 73.

37. Mann, *Sources of Social Power*, p. 490.

38. Raja J. Chelliah, "Trends in Taxation in Developing Countries," *International Monetary Fund Staff Papers*, Vol. 18, No. 2 (July 1971), p. 312. On the possibility of changing fiscal arrangements in Africa, see Dennis Anderson, *The Public Revenue and Economic Policy in African Countries*, World Bank Discussion Paper No. 19 (Washington, D.C.: World Bank, 1987), pp. 14–15.

39. For instance, see Levi, *Of Rule and Revenue*, p. 105.

40. The importance of the "relevant other" concept in developing group cohesion is explored by Young, *The Politics of Cultural Pluralism*, p. 42.

41. Anthony D. Smith, "State-Making and Nation-Building," in John A. Hall, ed., *States in History* (Oxford: Basil Blackwell, 1986), p. 258.

42. Joseph R. Strayer, *On the Medieval Origins of the Modern State* (Princeton: Princeton University Press, 1970), p. 60.

43. Peter Bachrach and Morton S. Baratz, "Two Faces of Power," *American Political Science Review*, Vol. 56, No. 4 (December 1962), p. 950.

44. For instance, the World Bank's report, *Accelerated Development in Sub-Saharan Africa*, was crucial in noting the dimensions of Africa's economic crisis; it set the agenda for reform of African economies.

45. Jeffrey Herbst, "Political Impediments to Economic Rationality: Why Zimbabwe Cannot Reform its Public Sector," *The Journal of Modern African Studies*, Vol. 27, No. 1 (March 1989), pp. 67–85.

46. Paul Colinvaux, *The Fates of Nations: A Biological Theory of History* (London: Penguin, 1980), pp. 219–220.

47. Ibid., p. 219.

48. Otto, Prince von Bismarck, *Bismarck, the Man and the Statesman: Being the Reflections and Reminiscences of Otto, Prince von Bismarck, Written and Dictated by Himself after his Retirement from Office*, translated under the supervision of A. J. Butler, Vol. I (New York: Harper and Brothers, 1899), p. 313.

49. William G. Thom, "Sub-Saharan Africa's Changing Military Capabilities," in Bruce E. Arlinghaus and Pauline H. Baker, eds., *African Armies: Evolution and Capabilities* (Boulder, Colo.: Westview, 1986), p. 101. See also Walter L. Barrows, "Changing Military Capabilities in Black Africa," in William Foltz and Henry Bienen, eds., *Arms and the African:*

Military Influence and Africa's International Relations (New Haven: Yale University Press, 1985), p. 99 and p. 120; and Henry Bienen, "African Militaries as Foreign Policy Actors," *International Security*, Vol. 5, No. 2 (Fall 1980), p. 176.

50. See Jeffrey Herbst, "Migration, the Politics of Protest, and State Consolidation in Africa," *African Affairs*, Vol. 89, No. 355 (April 1990), pp. 183–203.

51. In the 1950s American administrations debated whether South Korea could achieve any increase in living standards and if American aid should be devoted to simply preventing the country from getting poorer. Clive Crook, "Trial and Error," *The Economist*, September 23, 1989, p. 4.

52. See Jeffrey Herbst, "Migration Helps Poorest of Poor," *Wall Street Journal*, June 15, 1988, p. 12.

Robert I. Rotberg

THE NEW NATURE OF NATION-STATE FAILURE

Nation-states fail because they can no longer deliver positive political goods to their people. Their governments lose legitimacy and, in the eyes and hearts of a growing plurality of its citizens, the nation-state itself becomes illegitimate.

Only a handful of the world's 191 nation-states can now be categorized as failed, or collapsed, which is the end stage of failure. Several dozen more, however, are weak and serious candidates for failure. Because failed states are hospitable to and harbor nonstate actors—warlords and terrorists—understanding the dynamics of nation-state failure is central to the war against terrorism. Strengthening weak nation-states in the developing world has consequently assumed new urgency.

Defining State Failure

Failed states are tense, deeply conflicted, danger-ous, and bitterly contested by warring factions. In most failed states, government troops battle armed revolts led by one or more rivals. Official authorities in a failed state sometimes face two or more insur-gencies, varieties of civil unrest, differing degrees of communal discontent, and a plethora of dissent directed at the state and at groups within the state.

The absolute intensity of violence does not define a failed state. Rather, it is the enduring charac-ter of that violence (as in Angola, Burundi, and Sudan), the direction of such violence against the existing government or regime, and the vigorous character of the political or geographical demands for shared power or autonomy that rationalize or justify that violence that identifies the failed state. Failure for a nation-state looms when violence cas-cades into all-out internal war, when standards of living massively deteriorate, when the infrastructure of ordinary life decays, and when the greed of rul-ers overwhelms their responsibilities to better their people and their surroundings.

The civil wars that characterize failed states usu-ally stem from or have roots in ethnic, religious, lin-guistic, or other intercommunal enmity. The fear of "the other" that drives so much ethnic conflict may stimulate and fuel hostilities between ruling entities

From *The Washington Quarterly* 25, no. 3 (Summer 2002), pp. 85–96.

and subordinate and less-favored groups. Avarice also propels antagonism, especially when discoveries of new, frequently contested sources of resource wealth, such as petroleum deposits or diamond fields, encourage that greed.

There is no failed state without disharmonies between communities. Yet, the simple fact that many weak nation-states include haves and have-nots, and that some of the newer states contain a heterogeneous collection of ethnic, religious, and linguistic interests, is more a contributor to than a root cause of nation-state failure. In other words, state failure cannot be ascribed primarily to the inability to build nations from a congeries of ethnic groups. Nor should it be ascribed baldly to the oppression of minorities by a majority, although such brutalities are often a major ingredient of the impulse toward failure.

In contrast to strong states, failed states cannot control their borders. They lose authority over chunks of territory. Often, the expression of official power is limited to a capital city and one or more ethnically specific zones. Indeed, one measure of the extent of a state's failure is how much of the state's geographical expanse a government genuinely controls. How nominal is the central government's sway over rural towns, roads, and waterways? Who really rules up-country, or in particular distant districts?

In most cases, driven by ethnic or other intercommunal hostility or by regime insecurity, failed states prey on their own citizens. As in Mobutu Sese Seko's Zaire or the Taliban's Afghanistan, ruling cadres increasingly oppress, extort, and harass the majority of their own compatriots while favoring a narrowly based elite. As in Zaire, Angola, Siaka Stevens's Sierra Leone, or Hassan al-Turabi's pre-2001 Sudan, patrimonial rule depends on a patronage-based system of extraction from ordinary citizens. The typical weak-state plunges toward failure when this kind of ruler-led oppression provokes a countervailing reaction on the part of resentful groups or newly emerged rebels.

Another indicator of state failure is the growth of criminal violence. As state authority weakens and fails, and as the state becomes criminal in its oppression of its citizens, so general lawlessness becomes more apparent. Gangs and criminal syndicates assume control over the streets of the cities. Arms and drug trafficking become more common. Ordinary police forces become paralyzed. Anarchy becomes more and more the norm. For protection, citizens naturally turn to warlords and other strong figures who express ethnic or clan solidarity, thus projecting strength at a time when all else, including the state itself, is crumbling.

Fewer and Fewer Political Goods

Nation-states exist to deliver political goods—security, education, health services, economic opportunity, environmental surveillance, a legal framework of order and a judicial system to administer it, and fundamental infrastructural requirements such as roads and communications facilities—to their citizens. Failed states honor these obligations in the breach. They increasingly forfeit their function as providers of political goods to warlords and other nonstate actors. In other words, a failed state is no longer able or willing to perform the job of a nation-state in the modern world.

Failed states are unable to provide security—the most central and foremost political good—across the whole of their domains. Citizens depend on states and central governments to secure their persons and free them from fear. Because a failing state is unable to establish an atmosphere of security nationwide and is often barely able to assert any kind of state power beyond a capital city, the failure of the state becomes obvious even before rebel groups and other contenders threaten the residents of central cities and overwhelm demoralized government contingents, as in contemporary Liberia and recent Sierra Leone.

Failed states contain weak or flawed institutions—that is, only the executive institution functions. If legislatures exist at all, they are rubber-stamp machines. Democratic debate is noticeably absent. The judiciary is derivative of the executive rather than being independent, and citizens know that they cannot rely on the court system for significant redress or remedy, especially against the state. The bureaucracy has long ago lost its sense of professional responsibility and exists solely to carry out the orders of the executive and, in petty ways, to oppress citizens. The military is possibly the only institution with any remaining integrity, but the armed forces of failed states are often highly politicized, without the esprit that they once exhibited.

Deteriorating or destroyed infrastructures typify failed states. Metaphorically, the more potholes (or main roads turned to rutted tracks), the more likely a state will exemplify failure. As rulers siphon funds from the state, so fewer capital resources are available for road crews, and maintaining road or rail access to distant provinces becomes less and less of a priority. Even refurbishing basic navigational aids along arterial waterways, as in the Democratic Republic of the Congo (DRC), succumbs to neglect. Where the state still controls the landline telephone system, that form of political and economic good also betrays a lack of renewal, upkeep, investment, and bureaucratic interest. Less a metaphor than a daily reality is the index of failed connections, repeated required dialing, and interminable waits for repair or service. If state monopolies have permitted private entrepreneurs to erect cell telephone towers and offer mobile telephone service, cell telephones may already have rendered the government's landline monopoly obsolete. In a state without a government, such as Somalia, the overlapping system of privately provided cell telephone systems is effective.

In failed states, the effective educational and health systems have either been privatized (with a resulting hodgepodge of shady schools and medical clinics in the cities) or have slowly slumped to increasingly desperate levels of decrepitude. Teachers, physicians, nurses, and orderlies are paid late or not at all, and absenteeism rises. Textbooks and essential medicines become scarce. X-ray machines cannot be repaired. Reports to the relevant ministries go unanswered; and parents, students, and patients—especially rural ones—slowly realize that

the state has abandoned them to the forces of nature and to their own devices. Sometimes, where a failed state is effectively split (Sudan), essential services are still provided to the favored half (northern Sudan) but not to the half engulfed by war. Most of the time, however, the weakened nation-state completely fails to perform. Literacy falls, infant mortality rises, the AIDS epidemic overwhelms any health infrastructure that exists, life expectancies plummet, and an already poor and neglected citizenry becomes even poorer and more immiserated.

Failed states provide unparalleled economic opportunity, but only for a privileged few. Those close to the ruler or the ruling oligarchy grow richer while their less-fortunate brethren starve. Immense profits can be made from currency speculation, arbitrage, and knowledge of regulatory advantages. But the privilege of making real money when everything else is deteriorating is confined to clients of the ruling elite or to especially favored external entrepreneurs. The responsibility of a nation-state to maximize the well-being and personal prosperity of all of its citizens is conspicuously absent, if it ever existed.

Corruption flourishes in failed states, often on an unusually destructive scale. Petty or lubricating corruption is widespread. Levels of venal corruption escalate, especially kickbacks on anything that can be put out to bid, including medical supplies, textbooks, bridges; unnecessarily wasteful construction projects solely for the rents they will generate; licenses for existing and nonexisting activities; the appropriating by the ruling class of all kinds of private entrepreneurial endeavors; and generalized extortion. Corrupt ruling elites invest their gains overseas, not at home. A few build numerous palaces or lavish residences with state funds. Military officers always benefit from these corrupt regimes and feed ravenously from the same illicit troughs as their civilian counterparts.

An indicator, but not a cause, of failure is declining real national and per capita levels of gross domestic product (GDP). The statistical foundations of most states in the developing world are shaky, most certainly, but failed states—even, or particularly, failed states with abundant natural resources—show overall worsening GDP figures, slim year-to-year growth rates, and greater disparities of income between the wealthiest and poorest fifths of the population. High official deficits (Zimbabwe's reached 30 percent of GDP in 2001) support lavish security spending and the siphoning of cash by elites. Inflation usually soars because the ruling elite raids the central bank and prints money. From the resulting economic insecurity, often engineered by rulers to maximize their own fortunes and their own political as well as economic power, entrepreneurs favored by the prevailing regime can reap great amounts of money. Smuggling becomes rife. When state failure becomes complete, the local currency falls out of favor, and some or several international currencies take its place. Money changers are everywhere, legal or not, and arbitrage becomes an everyday national pursuit.

Sometimes, especially if climatic disasters intervene, the economic chaos and generalized neglect that is endemic to failed states can lead to regular food scarcities and widespread hunger—even to episodes of starvation and resulting international humanitarian relief efforts. Natural calamities can overwhelm the resources even of nonfailed but weak states in the developing world. But when unscrupulous rulers and ruling elites have consciously sucked state competencies dry, unforeseen natural disasters or man-made wars can drive ignored populations over the edge of endurance into starvation. Once such populations have lost their subsistence plots or sources of income, they lose their homes, forfeit already weak support networks, and are forced into an endless cycle of migration and displacement. Failed states offer no safety nets, and the homeless and destitute become fodder for anyone who can provide food and a cause.

A nation-state also fails when it loses a basic legitimacy—when its nominal borders become irrelevant and when one or more groups seek autonomous control within one or more parts of the national territory or, sometimes, even across its borders. Once the state's capacity deteriorates and what little capacity still remains is devoted largely to the fortunes of a few or to a favored ethnicity or community, then there is every reason to expect less and less loyalty to the state on the part of the excluded and the disenfranchised. When the rulers are seen to be working for themselves and their kin, and not for the state, their legitimacy, and the state's legitimacy, plummets. The state increasingly is perceived as owned by an exclusive class or group, with all others pushed aside.

Citizens naturally become more and more conscious of the kinds of sectional or community loyalties that are their main recourse and their only source of security and economic opportunity. They transfer their allegiances to clan and group leaders, some of whom become warlords. These warlords or other local strongmen derive support from external and local supporters. In the wilder, more marginalized corners of failed states, terror can breed along with the prevailing anarchy that emerges from state breakdown and failure.

A collapsed state is an extreme version of a failed state. It has a total vacuum of authority. A collapsed state is a mere geographical expression, a black hole into which a failed polity has fallen. Dark energy exists, but the forces of entropy have overwhelmed the radiance that hitherto provided some semblance of order and other vital political goods to the inhabitants embraced by language affinities or borders. When a state such as Somalia collapses (or Lebanon and Afghanistan a decade ago and Sierra Leone in the late 1990s), substate actors take over. They control regions and subregions, build their own local security apparatuses, sanction markets or other trading arrangements, and even establish an attenuated form of international relations. By definition, they are illegitimate and unrecognized, but some may assume the trappings of a quasi-state, such as Somaliland in northern Somalia. Yet, within the collapsed state prevail disorder, anomic behavior, and the kinds of anarchic mentality and entrepreneurial pursuits— especially gun and drug running—that are compatible with networks of terror.

Contemporary State Failure

This decade's failed states are Afghanistan, Angola, Burundi, the DRC, Liberia, Sierra Leone, and Sudan. These seven states exemplify the criteria of state failure. Beyond those states is one collapsed state: Somalia. Each of these countries has typified state failure continuously since at least 1990, if not before. Lebanon was once a failed state. So were Bosnia, Tajikistan, and Nigeria. Many other modern states approach the brink of failure, some much more ominously than others. Others drift disastrously downward from weak to failing to failed.

Of particular interest is why and how states slip from endemic weakness (Haiti) toward failure, or not. The list of weak states is long, but only a few of those weak and badly governed states necessarily edge into failure. Why? Even the categorization of a state as failing—Colombia and Indonesia, among others—need not doom it unquestionably to full failure. Another critical question is, what does it take to drive a failing state into collapse? Why did Somalia not stop at failure rather than collapsing?

Not each of the classical failed and collapsed states fully fills all of the cells on the matrix of failure. To be termed a failure, however, a state certainly needs to demonstrate that it has met most of the explicit criteria. "Failure" is meant to describe a specific set of conditions and to exclude states that only meet a few of the criteria. In other words, how truly minimal are the roads, the schools, the hospitals, and the clinics? How far has GDP fallen and infant mortality risen? How far does the ambit of the central government reach? How little legitimacy remains? Most importantly, because civil conflict is decisive for state failure, can the state still provide security to its citizens and to what extent? Continuously? Only on good days and nights? Has the state lost control of large swaths of territory or only some provinces and regions?

Several test cases are interesting. Sri Lanka has been embroiled in a bitter and destructive civil war for 19 years. The rebel Liberation Tigers of Tamil Eelam (LTTE), a Tamil separatist insurgency, has at times in the last decade controlled as much as 15 percent of Sri Lanka's total land mass. Additionally, with relative impunity, the LTTE has been able to assassinate prime ministers, bomb presidents, kill off rival Tamils, and last year even wreak destruction at the nation's civil aviation terminal and main air force base. But, as unable as the Sinhala-dominated governments of Sri Lanka have been to put down the LTTE rebellion, so the nation-state has remained merely weak, never close to failure. For 80 percent of Sri Lankans, the government performs reasonably well. Since the early 1990s, too, Sri Lanka has exhibited robust levels of economic performance. The authority of successive governments, even before the recent ceasefire, extended securely to the Sinhala-speaking 80 percent of the country, and the regime recaptured some of the contested Tamil areas. Before the truce, road maintenance, educational and medical services, and the other necessary political goods continued to be delivered despite the civil war, to some limited degree even into the war-torn parts of the country. For all of these reasons, despite a consuming internal conflict founded on majority-minority discrimination and deprivation and on ethnic and religious differences, Sri Lanka has successfully escaped failure.

Indonesia is another example of weakness avoiding failure despite widespread insecurity. As the world's largest Muslim nation, its far-flung archipelago harbors the separatist wars of Aceh in the west and Papua (Irian Jaya) in the east, plus Muslim-Christian conflict in Ambon and the Mulukus, Muslim-Christian hostility in Sulawesi, and ethnic xenophobic outbursts in West Kalimantan. Given all of these conflictual situations, none of which have become less bitter since the end of Suharto's dictatorship, suggesting that Indonesia is approaching failure is easy. Yet, as one argument goes, only the insurgents in Aceh and Papua want to secede from the state; and, even in Aceh, official troops have the upper hand. Elsewhere, hostilities are intercommunal and not directed against the government or the state. Unlike the low-level war in Aceh, they do not threaten the integrity and resources of the state. Overall, most of Indonesia is still secure and is "glued" together well by an abiding sense of nationalism. The government still projects power and authority. Despite dangerous economic and other vicissitudes in the post-Suharto era, the state provides most of the other necessary political goods and remains legitimate. Indonesia need not be classified as anything other than a weak state, but the government's performance and provision of security should be monitored closely.

What about Colombia? An otherwise well-endowed, prosperous, and stable state has the second-highest murder rate per capita in the world, its politicians and businessmen wear flak jackets and travel with armed guards, and three private armies control relatively large chunks of its territory with impunity. The official defense and political establishment has effectively ceded authority in those zones to the insurgencies and to drug traffickers. Again, why should Colombia not be ranked as a failed state? Although it could deteriorate into further failure, at present the Colombian government still performs for the 70 percent of the nation that remains under official authority. It provides political goods, even some improving security, for the large part of the state under official authority. When and if the government of Colombia can reassert itself into the disputed zones and further reduce drug trafficking, the power of the state will grow and a weak, endangered state such as Colombia can move away from possible failure toward the stronger side of the equation.

Zimbabwe is an example of a once unquestionably strong African state—indeed, one of the strongest—that has fallen rapidly through weakness to the very edge of failure. All that Zimbabwe lacks in order to join the ranks of failed states is a widespread internal insurgent movement directed at the government, which could still emerge. Meanwhile, per capita GDP has receded by 10 percent annually for two years. During the same period, inflation has galloped from 30 percent to 116 percent. The local currency has fallen against the U.S. dollar from 38:1 to 400:1. Foreign and domestic investment have largely ceased. Health and educational services are almost nonexistent and shrinking further. Road maintenance and telephone service are obviously suffering. Judicial independence survives, but barely, and not in critical political cases. The state has also been preying on its own citizens for at least two years. Corruption is blatant and very much dominated by the avaricious ruling elite. Zimbabwe is an example of a state that, like Sierra Leone and the DRC at earlier moments in history, has been driven into failure by human agency.

Indonesia, Colombia, Sri Lanka, and Zimbabwe are but four among a large number of nation-states (two dozen by a recent count) that contain serious elements of failure but will probably avoid failure, especially if they receive sufficient outside assistance. They belong to a category of state that is designated weak but that encompasses and spreads into the category of failing—the precursor to true failure. Haiti, Chad, and Kyrgyzstan, from three continents, are representative examples of perpetual weakness. Argentina has recently joined an analogous rank; Russia was once a candidate. Fiji, the Solomon Islands, Tajikistan, Lebanon, Nigeria, Niger, and Burkina Faso remain vulnerable to further deterioration. Even Kenya is a weak state with some potential for definitive failure if ethnic disparities and ambitions provoke civil strife.

The list of states in weakness is longer and hardly static. Some of the potentially stronger states move in and out of weakness and nearer or farther from failure. Others are foreordained weak. Particular decisions by ruling groups would be needed to destabilize members of this second group further and drive them into failure.

The Hand of Man

State failure is man-made, not merely accidental nor—fundamentally—caused geographically, environmentally, or externally. Leadership decisions and leadership failures have destroyed states and continue to weaken the fragile polities that operate on the cusp of failure. Mobutu's kleptocratic rule extracted the marrow of Zaire/DRC and left nothing for his national dependents. Much of the resource wealth of that vast country ended up in Mobutu's or his cronies' pockets. During four decades, hardly any money was devoted to uplifting the Congolese people, improving their welfare, building infrastructures, or even providing more than rudimentary security. Mobutu's government performed only for Mobutu, not for Zaire/DRC.

Likewise, oil-rich Angola continues to fail because of three decades of war, but also because President Eduardo dos Santos and his associates have refused to let the Angolan government deliver more than basic services within the large zone that they control. Stevens (1967–1985) decapitated the Sierra Leonean state in order to strengthen his own power amid growing chaos. Sierra Leone has not yet recovered from Stevens's depredations. Nor has Liberia been resuscitated in the aftermath of the slashing neglect and unabashed greed of Samuel Doe, Prince Johnson, and Charles Taylor. In Somalia, Mohammed Siad Barre arrogated more and more power and privilege to himself and his clan. Finally, nothing was left for the other pretenders to power. The Somali state was gutted, the abilities of the Somali government to provide political goods endlessly compromised, and the descent into failure and then full collapse followed.

President Robert Gabriel Mugabe has personally led Zimbabwe from strength to the precipice of failure. His high-handed and seriously corrupt rule bled the resources of the state into his own pocket, squandered foreign exchange, discouraged domestic and international investment, subverted the courts, and this year drove his country to the very brink of starvation. In Sri Lanka, Solomon and Sirimavo Bandaranaike, one after the other, drove the LTTE into reactive combat by abrogating minority rights and vitiating the social contract on which the country called Ceylon had been created. In Afghanistan, Gulbuddin Hakmatyar and Burrhan ul-Din Rabani tried to prevent Afghans other than their fellow Pushtun and Tajik nationals from sharing the perquisites of governance; their narrowly focused, self-enriching decisions enabled the Taliban to triumph and Afghanistan to become a safe harbor for terrorists.

Preventing State Failure

Strengthening weak states against failure is far easier than reviving them after they have definitively failed or collapsed. As the problem of contemporary Afghanistan shows, reconstruction is very long, very expensive, and hardly a smooth process. Creating security and a security force from scratch, amid bitter memories, is the immediate need. Then comes the re-creation of an administrative structure—primarily re-creating a bureaucracy and finding the funds with which to pay the erstwhile bureaucrats and policemen. A judicial method is required, which means the establishment or reestablishment of a legitimate legal code and system; the training of judges, prosecutors, and defenders (as attempted recently in East Timor); and the opening of courtrooms and offices. Restarting the schools, employing teachers, refurbishing and re-equipping hospitals, building roads, and even gathering statistics—all of these fundamental chores take time, large sums of money (especially in war-shattered Afghanistan), and meticulous oversight in postconflict nations with overstretched human resources. Elections need not be an early priority, but constitutions must be written eventually and elections held in order to encourage participatory democracy.

Strengthening states prone to failure before they fail is prudent policy and contributes significantly to world order and to minimizing combat, casualties, refugees, and displaced persons. Doing so is far less expensive than reconstructing states after failure. Strengthening weak states also has the potential to eliminate the authority and power vacuums within which terror thrives.

From a policy perspective, however, these are obvious nostrums. The mechanisms for amelioration are also more obvious than obscure. In order to encourage responsible leadership and good governance, financial assistance from international lending agencies and bilateral donors must be designed to reinforce positive leadership only. Outside support should be conditional on monetary and fiscal streamlining, renewed attention to good governance, reforms of land tenure systems, and strict adherence to the rule of law. External assistance to create in-country jobs by reducing external tariff barriers (e.g., on textiles) and by supporting vital foreign direct investment is critical. So is support for innovations that can reduce importation and exportation transport expenditures for the weak nations, improve telephone and power systems through privatization, open predominantly closed economies in general, create new incentives for agricultural productivity, and bolster existing security forces through training and equipment.

All these ingredients of a successful strengthening process are necessary. The developed world can apply tough love and assist the developing and more vulnerable world to help itself in many more similarly targeted ways. In addition to the significant amounts of cash (grants are preferred over loans) that must be transferred to help the poorer nations help themselves, however, the critical ingredient is sustained interest and sustained assistance over the very long run. Nothing enduring can be accomplished instantaneously. If the world order wants to dry up the reservoirs of terror, as well as do good more broadly, it must commit itself and its powers

to a campaign of decades, not months. The refurbishment and revitalization of Afghanistan will take much more than the $4.7 billion pledged and the many years that Secretary of State Colin L. Powell has warned the U.S. people will be necessary to make Afghanistan a self-sufficient state. Strengthening Indonesia, for example, would take a concerted effort for decades. So would strengthening any of the dangerous and needy candidates in Africa or in Central Asia.

Preventing state failure is imperative, difficult, and costly. Yet, doing so is profoundly in the interest not only of the inhabitants of the most deprived and ill-governed states of the world, but also of world peace.

Satisfying such lofty goals, however — making the world much safer by strengthening weak states against failure — is dependent on the political will of the wealthy big-power arbiters of world security. Perhaps the newly aroused awareness of the dangers of terror will embolden political will in the United States, Europe, and Japan. Otherwise, the common ingredients of zero-sum leadership; ethnic, linguistic, and religious antagonisms and fears; chauvinistic ambition; economic insufficiency; and inherited fragility will continue to propel nation-states from weakness toward failure. In turn, that failure will be costly in terms of humanitarian relief and postconflict reconstruction. Ethnic cleansing episodes will recur, as will famines, and in the thin and hospitable soils of newly failed and collapsed states, terrorist groups will take root.

Stephen D. Krasner
SOVEREIGNTY

The idea of states as autonomous, independent entities is collapsing under the combined onslaught of monetary unions, CNN, the Internet, and nongovernmental organizations. But those who proclaim the death of sovereignty misread history. The nation-state has a keen instinct for survival and has so far adapted to new challenges—even the challenge of globalization.

"The Sovereign State Is Just About Dead"

Very Wrong

Sovereignty was never quite as vibrant as many contemporary observers suggest. The conventional norms of sovereignty have always been challenged. A few states, most notably the United States, have had autonomy, control, and recognition for most of their existence, but most others have not. The politics of many weaker states have been persistently penetrated, and stronger nations have not been immune to external influence. China was occupied. The constitutional arrangements of Japan and Germany were directed by the United States after World War II. The United Kingdom, despite its rejection of the euro, is part of the European Union.

Even for weaker states—whose domestic structures have been influenced by outside actors, and whose leaders have very little control over transborder movements or even activities within their own country—sovereignty remains attractive. Although sovereignty might provide little more than international recognition, that recognition guarantees

access to international organizations and sometimes to international finance. It offers status to individual leaders. While the great powers of Europe have eschewed many elements of sovereignty, the United States, China, and Japan have neither the interest nor the inclination to abandon their usually effective claims to domestic autonomy.

In various parts of the world, national borders still represent the fault lines of conflict, whether it is Israelis and Palestinians fighting over the status of Jerusalem, Indians and Pakistanis threatening to go nuclear over Kashmir, or Ethiopia and Eritrea clashing over disputed territories. Yet commentators nowadays are mostly concerned about the erosion of national borders as a consequence of globalization. Governments and activists alike complain that multilateral institutions such as the United Nations, the World Trade Organization, and the International Monetary Fund overstep their authority by promoting universal standards for everything from human rights and the environment to monetary policy and immigration. However, the most important impact of economic globalization and transnational norms will be to alter the scope of state authority rather than to generate some fundamentally new way to organize political life.

"Sovereignty Means Final Authority"

Not Anymore, If Ever

When philosophers Jean Bodin and Thomas Hobbes first elaborated the notion of sovereignty in the 16th and 17th centuries, they were concerned with establishing the legitimacy of a single hierarchy of domestic authority. Although Bodin and Hobbes accepted the existence of divine and natural law, they both

From *Foreign Policy* (January/February 2001), pp. 20–29.

(especially Hobbes) believed the word of the sovereign was law. Subjects had no right to revolt. Bodin and Hobbes realized that imbuing the sovereign with such overweening power invited tyranny, but they were predominately concerned with maintaining domestic order, without which they believed there could be no justice. Both were writing in a world riven by sectarian strife. Bodin was almost killed in religious riots in France in 1572. Hobbes published his seminal work, *Leviathan*, only a few years after parliament (composed of Britain's emerging wealthy middle class) had executed Charles I in a civil war that had sought to wrest state control from the monarchy.

This idea of supreme power was compelling, but irrelevant in practice. By the end of the 17th century, political authority in Britain was divided between king and parliament. In the United States, the Founding Fathers established a constitutional structure of checks and balances and multiple sovereignties distributed among local and national interests that were inconsistent with hierarchy and supremacy. The principles of justice, and especially order, so valued by Bodin and Hobbes, have best been provided by modern democratic states whose organizing principles are antithetical to the idea that sovereignty means uncontrolled domestic power.

If sovereignty does not mean a domestic order with a single hierarchy of authority, what does it mean? In the contemporary world, sovereignty primarily has been linked with the idea that states are autonomous and independent from each other. Within their own boundaries, the members of a polity are free to choose their own form of government. A necessary corollary of this claim is the principle of nonintervention: One state does not have a right to intervene in the internal affairs of another.

More recently, sovereignty has come to be associated with the idea of control over transborder movements. When contemporary observers assert that the sovereign state is just about dead, they do not mean that constitutional structures are about to disappear. Instead, they mean that technological change has made it very difficult, or perhaps impossible, for states to control movements across their borders of all kinds of material things (from coffee to cocaine) and not-so-material things (from Hollywood movies to capital flows).

Finally, sovereignty has meant that political authorities can enter into international agreements. They are free to endorse any contract they find attractive. Any treaty among states is legitimate provided that it has not been coerced.

"The Peace of Westphalia Produced the Modern Sovereign State"

No, It Came Later

Contemporary pundits often cite the 1648 Peace of Westphalia (actually two separate treaties, Münster and Osnabrück) as the political big bang that created the modern system of autonomous states. Westphalia—which ended the Thirty Years' War against the hegemonic power of the Holy Roman Empire—delegitimized the already waning transnational role of the Catholic Church and validated the idea that international relations should be driven by balance-of-power considerations rather than the ideals of Christendom. But Westphalia was first and foremost a new constitution for the Holy Roman Empire. The preexisting right of the principalities in the empire to make treaties was affirmed, but the Treaty of Münster stated that "such Alliances be not against the Emperor, and the Empire, nor against the Publick Peace, and this Treaty, and without prejudice to the Oath by which every one is bound to the Emperor and the Empire." The domestic political structures of the principalities remained embedded in the Holy Roman Empire. The Duke of Saxony, the Margrave of Brandenburg, the Count of Palatine, and the Duke of Bavaria were affirmed as electors who (along with the archbishops of Mainz, Trier, and Cologne) chose the emperor. They did not become or claim to be kings in their own right.

Perhaps most important, Westphalia established rules for religious tolerance in Germany. The treaties gave lip service to the principle (*cuius regio, eius religio*) that the prince could set the religion of this territory—and then went on to violate this very principle through many specific provisions. The signatories agreed that the religious rules already in effect would stay in place. Catholics and Protestants in German cities with mixed populations would share offices. Religious issues had to be settled by a majority of both Catholics and Protestants in the diet and courts of the empire. None of the major political leaders in Europe endorsed religious toleration in principle, but they recognized that religious conflicts were so volatile that it was essential to contain rather than repress sectarian differences. All in all, Westphalia is a pretty medieval document, and its biggest explicit innovation—provisions that undermined the power of princes to control religious affairs within their territories—was antithetical to the ideas of national sovereignty that later became associated with the so-called Westphalian system.

"Universal Human Rights Are an Unprecedented Challenge to Sovereignty"

Wrong

The struggle to establish international rules that compel leaders to treat their subjects in a certain way has been going on for a long time. Over the centuries the emphasis has shifted from religious toleration, to minority rights (often focusing on specific ethnic groups in specific countries), to human rights (emphasizing rights enjoyed by all or broad classes of individuals). In a few instances states have voluntarily embraced international supervision, but generally the weak have acceded to the preferences of the strong: the Vienna settlement following the Napoleonic wars guaranteed religious toleration for

Catholics in the Netherlands. All of the successor states of the Ottoman Empire, beginning with Greece in 1832 and ending with Albania in 1913, had to accept provisions for civic and political equality for religious minorities as a condition for international recognition. The peace settlements following World War I included extensive provisions for the protection of minorities. Poland, for instance, agreed to refrain from holding elections on Saturday because such balloting would have violated the Jewish Sabbath. Individuals could bring complaints against governments through a minority rights bureau established within the League of Nations.

But as the Holocaust tragically demonstrated, interwar efforts at international constraints on domestic practices failed dismally. After World War II, human, rather than minority, rights became the focus of attention. The United Nations Charter endorsed both human rights and the classic sovereignty principle of nonintervention. The 20-plus human rights accords that have been signed during the last half century cover a wide range of issues including genocide, torture, slavery, refugees, stateless persons, women's rights, racial discrimination, children's rights, and forced labor. These UN agreements, however, have few enforcement mechanisms, and even their provisions for reporting violations are often ineffective.

The tragic and bloody disintegration of Yugoslavia in the 1990s revived earlier concerns with ethnic rights. International recognition of the Yugoslav successor states was conditional upon their acceptance of constitutional provisions guaranteeing minority rights. The Dayton accords established externally controlled authority structures in Bosnia, including a Human Rights Commission (a majority of whose members were appointed by the Western European states). NATO created a de facto protectorate in Kosovo.

The motivations for such interventions—humanitarianism and security—have hardly changed. Indeed, the considerations that brought the great powers into the Balkans following the wars of the 1870s were hardly different from those that engaged NATO and Russia in the 1990s.

"Globalization Undermines State Control"

No

State control could never be taken for granted. Technological changes over the last 200 years have increased the flow of people, goods, capital, and ideas—but the problems posed by such movements are not new. In many ways, states are better able to respond now than they were in the past.

The impact of the global media on political authority (the so-called CNN effect) pales in comparison to the havoc that followed the invention of the printing press. Within a decade after Martin Luther purportedly nailed his 95 theses to the Wittenberg church door, his ideas had circulated throughout Europe. Some political leaders seized upon the principles of the Protestant Reformation as a way to legitimize secular political authority. No sovereign monarch could contain the spread of these concepts, and some lost not only their lands but also their heads. The sectarian controversies of the 16th and 17th centuries were perhaps more politically consequential than any subsequent transnational flow of ideas.

In some ways, international capital movements were more significant in earlier periods than they are now. During the 19th century, Latin American states (and to a lesser extent Canada, the United States, and Europe) were beset by boom-and-bust cycles associated with global financial crises. The Great Depression, which had a powerful effect on the domestic politics of all major states, was precipitated by an international collapse of credit. The Asian financial crisis of the late 1990s was not nearly as devastating. Indeed, the speed with which countries recovered from the Asian flu reflects how a better working knowledge of economic theories and more effective central banks have made it easier for states to secure the advantages (while at the same time minimizing the risks) of being enmeshed in global financial markets.

In addition to attempting to control the flows of capital and ideas, states have long struggled to manage the impact of international trade. The opening of long-distance trade for bulk commodities in the 19th century created fundamental cleavages in all of the major states. Depression and plummeting grain prices made it possible for German Chancellor Otto von Bismarck to prod the landholding aristocracy into a protectionist alliance with urban heavy industry (this coalition of "iron and rye" dominated German politics for decades). The tariff question was a basic divide in U.S. politics for much of the last half of the 19th and first half of the 20th centuries. But, despite growing levels of imports and exports since 1950, the political salience of trade has receded because national governments have developed social welfare strategies that cushion the impact of international competition, and workers with higher skill levels are better able to adjust to changing international conditions. It has become easier, not harder, for states to manage the flow of goods and services.

"Globalization Is Changing the Scope of State Control"

Yes

The reach of the state has increased in some areas but contracted in others. Rulers have recognized that their effective control can be enhanced by walking away from issues they cannot resolve. For instance, beginning with the Peace of Westphalia, leaders chose to surrender their control over religion because it proved too volatile. Keeping religion within the scope of state authority undermined, rather than strengthened, political stability.

Monetary policy is an area where state control expanded and then ultimately contracted. Before the 20th century, states had neither the administrative competence nor the inclination to conduct independent monetary policies. The mid-20th-century effort to control monetary affairs, which was associated with Keynesian economics, has now been reversed due to the magnitude of short-term capital flows and the inability of some states to control inflation. With the exception of Great Britain, the major European states have established a single monetary authority. Confronting recurrent hyperinflation, Ecuador adopted the U.S. dollar as its currency in 2000.

Along with the erosion of national currencies, we now see the erosion of national citizenship—the notion that an individual should be a citizen of one and only one country, and that the state has exclusive claims to that person's loyalty. For many states, there is no longer a sharp distinction between citizens and noncitizens. Permanent residents, guest workers, refugees, and undocumented immigrants are entitled to some bundle of rights even if they cannot vote. The ease of travel and the desire of many countries to attract either capital or skilled workers have increased incentives to make citizenship a more flexible category.

Although government involvement in religion, monetary affairs, and claims to loyalty has declined, overall government activity, as reflected in taxation and government expenditures, has increased as a percentage of national income since the 1950s among the most economically advanced states. The extent of a country's social welfare programs tends to go hand in hand with its level of integration within the global economy. Crises of authority and control have been most pronounced in the states that have been the most isolated, with sub-Saharan Africa offering the largest number of unhappy examples.

"NGOs Are Nibbling at National Sovereignty"

To Some Extent

Transnational nongovernmental organizations (NGOs) have been around for quite a while, especially if you include corporations. In the 18th century, the East India Company possessed political power (and even an expeditionary military force) that rivaled many national governments. Throughout the 19th century, there were transnational movements to abolish slavery, promote the rights of women, and improve conditions for workers.

The number of transnational NGOs, however, has grown tremendously, from around 200 in 1909 to over 17,000 today. The availability of inexpensive and very fast communications technology has made it easier for such groups to organize and make an impact on public policy and international law—the international agreement banning land mines being a recent case in point. Such groups prompt questions about sovereignty because they appear to threaten the integrity of domestic decision making. Activists who lose on their home territory can pressure foreign governments, which may in turn influence decision makers in the activists' own nation.

But for all of the talk of growing NGO influence, their power to affect a country's domestic affairs has been limited when compared to governments, international organizations, and multinational corporations. The United Fruit Company had more influence in Central America in the early part of the 20th century than any NGO could hope to have anywhere in the contemporary world. The International Monetary Fund and other multilateral financial institutions now routinely negotiate conditionality agreements that involve not only specific economic targets but also domestic institutional changes, such as pledges to crack down on corruption and break up cartels.

Smaller, weaker states are the most frequent targets of external efforts to alter domestic institutions, but more powerful states are not immune. The openness of the U.S. political system means that not only NGOs but also foreign governments can play some role in political decisions. (The Mexican government, for instance, lobbied heavily for the passage of the North American Free Trade Agreement.) In fact, the permeability of the American polity makes the United States a less threatening partner; nations are more willing to sign on to U.S.-sponsored international arrangements because they have some confidence that they can play a role in U.S. decision making.

"Sovereignty Blocks Conflict Resolution"

Yes, Sometimes

Rulers as well as their constituents have some reasonably clear notion of what sovereignty means—exclusive control within a given territory—even if this norm has been challenged frequently by inconsistent principles (such as universal human rights) and violated in practice (the U.S.- and British-enforced no-fly zones over Iraq). In fact, the political importance of conventional sovereignty rules has made it harder to solve some problems. There is, for instance, no conventional sovereignty solution for Jerusalem, but it doesn't require much imagination to think of alternatives: divide the city into small pieces; divide the Temple Mount vertically with the Palestinians controlling the top and the Israelis the bottom; establish some kind of international authority; divide control over different issues (religious practices versus taxation, for instance) among different authorities. Any one of these solutions would be better for most Israelis and Palestinians than an ongoing stalemate, but political leaders on both sides have had trouble delivering a settlement because they are subject to attacks by counterelites who can wave the sovereignty flag.

Conventional rules have also been problematic for Tibet. Both the Chinese and the Tibetans might be better off if Tibet could regain some of the autonomy it had as a tributary state within the traditional Chinese empire. Tibet had extensive local control but symbolically (and sometimes through tribute payments) recognized the supremacy of the emperor. Today, few on either side would even know what a tributary state is, and even if the leaders of then Tibet worked out some kind of settlement that would give their country more self-government, there would be no guarantee that they could gain the support of their own constituents.

If, however, leaders can reach mutual agreements, bring along their constituents, or are willing to use coercion, sovereignty rules can be violated in inventive ways. The Chinese, for instance, made Hong Kong a special administrative region after the transfer from British rule, allowed a foreign judge to sit on the Court of Final Appeal, and secured acceptance by other states not only for Hong Kong's participation in a number of international organizations but also for separate visa agreements and recognition of a distinct Hong Kong passport. All of these measures violate conventional sovereignty rules, since Hong Kong does not have juridical independence. Only by inventing a unique status for Hong Kong, which involved the acquiescence of other states, could China claim sovereignty while simultaneously preserving the confidence of the business community.

"The European Union Is a New Model for Supranational Governance"

Yes, But Only for the Europeans

The European Union (EU) really is a new thing, far more interesting in terms of sovereignty than Hong Kong. It is not a conventional international organization because its member states are now so intimately linked with one another that withdrawal is not a viable option. It is not likely to become a "United States of Europe"—a large federal state that might look something like the United States of America—because the interests, cultures, economies, and domestic institutional arrangements of its members are too diverse. Widening the EU to include the former communist states of Central Europe would further complicate any efforts to move toward a political organization that looks like a conventional sovereign state.

The EU is inconsistent with conventional sovereignty rules. Its member states have created supranational institutions (the European Court of Justice, the European Commission, and the Council of Ministers) that can make decisions opposed by some member states. The rulings of the court have direct effect and supremacy within national judicial systems, even though these doctrines were never explicitly endorsed in any treaty. The European Monetary Union created a central bank that now controls monetary affairs for three of the union's four largest states. The Single European Act and the Maastricht Treaty provide for majority or qualified majority, but not unanimous, voting in some issue areas. In one sense, the European Union is a product of state sovereignty because it has been created through voluntary agreements among its member states. But, in another sense, it fundamentally contradicts conventional understandings of sovereignty because these same agreements have undermined the juridical autonomy of its individual members.

The European Union, however, is not a model that other parts of the world can imitate. The initial moves toward integration could not have taken place without the political and economic support of the United States, which was, in the early years of the Cold War, much more interested in creating a strong alliance that could effectively oppose the Soviet Union than it was in any potential European challenge to U.S. leadership. Germany, one of the largest states in the European Union, has been the most consistent supporter of an institutional structure that would limit Berlin's own freedom of action, a reflection of the lessons of two devastating wars and the attractiveness of a European identity for a country still grappling with the sins of the Nazi era. It is hard to imagine that other regional powers such as China, Japan, or Brazil, much less the United States, would have any interest in tying their own hands in similar ways. (Regional trading agreements such as Mercosur and NAFTA have very limited supranational provisions and show few signs of evolving into broader monetary or political unions.) The EU is a new and unique institutional structure, but it will coexist with, not displace, the sovereign-state model.

3

NATIONS AND SOCIETY

The readings presented in this chapter address three basic issues: nationalism, the role of ethnic conflict in civil war, and whether ethnic diversity and segregation lead to worse political and economic results.

Certainly until the sixteenth century, and plausibly even until the eighteenth, nationalism in the modern sense did not exist. People were loyal to a particular lord or locality, but not to a linguistically or ethnically defined nation, and no one was surprised that the typical state or empire embraced a large variety of languages and ethnicities. How, then, did modern nationalism become so powerful a force, and why are most states today *nation-states*, that is, ones that have, or seek, a single national identity (including, in most cases, a single language)?

In his 1962 book *The Age of Revolution: 1789–1848*, the eminent historian E. J. Hobsbawm wrote what many comparativists still regard as the most convincing account of how modern nationalisms arose, with clear implications for present-day ethnic conflicts around the globe. Hobsbawm's crucial insight—that nationalism is always linked to the rapid rise of an indigenous middle class and to the spread of literacy in the native language—remains valid today and has been stressed in analyses of (among many others) Irish, Québecois, Basque, Eritrean, Catalan, and Kurdish nationalism. One should also remember, as Hobsbawm notes, that a sizeable proportion of the "national" languages claimed by such groups—among them Croatian, Romanian, Gaelic, Norwegian, Czech, and modern Hebrew—were more invented (that is, constructed out of a welter of dialects or the imagined evolution of an ossified language) than revived.

Ethnic divisions sometimes lead to violent conflict, inflicting heavy costs on societies both poor (Nigeria, Rwanda, Sri Lanka) and rich (Northern Ireland, Spain, Russia). In the 1990s, some economists held that ethnic fragmentation alone, at least in Africa, led directly to bad policies, weak trust, and continuing poverty. They thus provided a dual rationale for ethnically unified states, or for the secession of "nations" that formed within existing states.

Violence, particularly civil war, undoubtedly inhibited economic growth. But Paul Collier and other World Bank economists argued that most civil wars were a result of "greed" rather than "grievance." Conflict was often all about, and fueled by, huge and readily marketable reserves of valuable natural resources (oil, diamonds, copper ore, mahogany). In 2003, the comparativists James Fearon and David Laitin went far toward settling these questions in a famous article (excerpted here) entitled

"Ethnicity, Insurgency, and Civil War." They showed that ethnically diverse societies were no more likely than homogeneous ones to experience civil war; rather, the chief causes were poverty, political instability, and a terrain that favored insurgency. At about the same time, Alberto Alesina and Eliana La Ferrara, in their 2005 article "Ethnic Diversity and Economic Performance," reestablished that ethnic diversity, at least in poor societies, inhibited economic growth, even after other plausible causes had been taken into account. On the other hand, they pointed to the possibility, particularly in wealthy societies, that ethnic diversity could accelerate economic growth by providing complementary skills and insights.

Surprisingly, most of the early research looked only at the degree of ethnic fragmentation in societies: more precisely, the likelihood that two randomly chosen individuals would belong to different ethnic groups.[1] Yet common sense tells us that differences in the wealth of ethnic groups, or in the degree to which they are physically separate from one another, matter also. In a recent article excerpted here, Kate Baldwin and John Huber show that where ethnic groups differ radically in wealth, government services are poorly provided—one possible reason that fractionalization inhibits economic growth. Another study, by Lars-Erik Cederman and his colleagues (not included here), comes to the surprising conclusion that both the richest and poorest ethnic groups are more likely to initiate violent conflict than those in the middle, and that this effect is strongest where those groups are regionally concentrated.[2]

Nationalism and ethnicity remain among the most active research areas in comparative politics, and data on ethnicity (and on the wealth and location of ethnic groups) are becoming steadily better. Yet one deep mystery endures: How has the "nation" been able, at least for the past century and a half, to elicit the degree of loyalty and self-sacrifice that its citizens have exhibited in both interstate and civil wars?

NOTES

1. If one ethnic group constitutes 20 percent of a society, the probability that two randomly chosen citizens will both be members of this group is $(.2)^2$, or .04. If another group constitutes 30 percent of the society, the likelihood that two randomly chosen citizens will both belong to this ethnic group is .09. If the remaining half of the population belongs to a third ethnic group, the probability that the two random individuals will belong to this third group is $(.5)^2 = .25$. Thus, the probability that any two randomly chosen people will be coethnics (i.e., belong to the same group, regardless of which of the three it is) must be the sum of these probabilities: $.04 + .09 + .25 = .38$. And the probability that the two random people are *not* coethnics is just $1 - .38 = .62$. Generalizing to any number n of ethnic groups in a society, where p_i represents the share of the population that belongs to a given ethnic group, most work defines an *ethnic fractionalization index* (ELF) as $1 - \Sigma(p_i^2)$. Economists recognize this as a "Herfindahl index."

2. Lars-Erik Cederman, Nils B. Weidmann, and Kristian Skrede Gleditsch. "Horizontal Inequalities and Ethnonationalist Civil War: A Global Comparison," *American Political Science Review* 105 (2011), pp. 478–95.

Eric Hobsbawm
NATIONALISM

Every people has its special mission, which will cooperate towards the fulfilment of the general mission of humanity. That mission constitutes its nationality. Nationality is sacred.

ACT OF BROTHERHOOD OF YOUNG EUROPE, 1834

The day will come . . . when sublime Germania shall stand on the bronze pedestal of liberty and justice, bearing in one hand the torch of enlightenment, which shall throw the beam of civilization into the remotest corners of the earth, and in the other the arbiter's balance. The people will beg her to settle their disputes; those very people who now show us that might is right, and kick us with the jackboot of scornful contempt.

FROM SIEBENPFEIFFER'S SPEECH AT THE HAMBACH FESTIVAL, 1832

After 1830, as we have seen, the general movement in favour of revolution split. One product of this split deserves special attention: the self-consciously nationalist movements.

The movements which best symbolize this development are the 'Youth' movements founded or inspired by Giuseppe Mazzini shortly after the 1830 revolution: Young Italy, Young Poland, Young Switzerland, Young Germany, and Young France (1831–6) and the analogous Young Ireland of the 1840s, the ancestor of the only lasting and successful revolutionary organization on the model of the early nineteenth-century conspiratory brotherhoods, the Fenians or Irish Republican Brotherhood, better known through its executive arm of the Irish Republican Army. In themselves these movements were of no great importance; the mere presence of Mazzini would have been enough to ensure their total ineffectiveness. Symbolically they are of extreme importance, as is indicated by the adoption in subsequent nationalist movements of such labels as 'Young Czechs' or 'Young Turks.' They mark the distintegration of the European revolutionary movement into national segments. Doubtless each of these segments had much the same political programme strategy, and tactics as the others, and even much the same flag—almost invariably a tricolour of some kind. Its members saw no contradiction between their own demands and those of other nations, and indeed envisaged a brotherhood of all, simultaneously liberating themselves. On the other hand each now tended to justify its primary concern with its own nation by adopting the role of a Messiah for all. Through Italy (according to Mazzini), through Poland (according to Mickiewicz), the suffering peoples of the world were to be led to freedom; an attitude readily adaptable to conservative or indeed imperialist policies, as witness the Russian Slavophils with their championship of Holy Russia, the Third Rome, and the Germans who were subsequently to tell the world at some length that it would be healed by the German spirit. Admittedly this ambiguity of nationalism went back to the French Revolution. But in those days there had been only *one* great and revolutionary nation and it made sense (as indeed it still did) to regard it as the headquarters of all revolutions, and the necessary prime

From *The Age of Revolution* (London: Weidenfeld & Nicholson, 1962), pp. 132–45. Some of the author's notes have been omitted.

mover in the liberation of the world. To look to Paris was rational; to look to a vague "Italy," "Poland," or "Germany" (represented in practice by a handful of conspirators and emigrés) made sense only for Italians, Poles, and Germans.

If the new nationalism had been confined only to the membership of the national-revolutionary brotherhoods, it would not be worth much more attention. However, it also reflected much more powerful forces, which were emerging into political consciousness in the 1830s as the result of the double revolution. The most immediately powerful of these were the discontent of the lesser landowners or gentry and the emergence of a national middle- and even lower-middle class in numerous countries, the spokesmen for both being largely professional intellectuals.

The revolutionary role of the lesser gentry is perhaps best illustrated in Poland and Hungary. There, on the whole, the large landed magnates had long found it possible and desirable to make terms with absolutism and foreign rule. The Hungarian magnates were in general Catholic and had long been accepted as pillars of Viennese court society; very few of them were to join the revolution of 1848. The memory of the old *Rzeczpospolita* made even Polish magnates nationally minded, but the most influential of their quasi-national parties, the Czartoryski connection, now operating from the luxurious emigration of the Hotel Lambert in Paris, had always favoured the alliance with Russia and continued to prefer diplomacy to revolt. Economically they were wealthy enough to afford what they needed, short of really titanic dissipation, and even to invest enough in the improvement of their estates to benefit from the economic expansion of the age, if they chose to. Count Széchenyi, one of the few moderate liberals from this class and a champion of economic improvement, gave a year's income for the new Hungarian Academy of Sciences—some 60,000 florins. There is no evidence that his standard of life suffered from such disinterested generosity. On the other hand the numerous gentlemen who had little but their birth to distinguish them from other impoverished farmers—one in eight of the Hungarian population claimed gentlemanly status—had neither the money to make their holdings profitable nor the inclination to compete with Germans and Jews for middle-class wealth. If they could not live decently on their rents, and a degenerate age deprived them of a soldier's chances, then they might, if not too ignorant, consider the law, administration, or some intellectual position, but no bourgeois activity. Such gentlemen had long been the stronghold of opposition to absolutism, foreigners, and magnate rule in their respective countries, sheltering (as in Hungary) behind the dual buttress of Calvinism and county organization. It was natural that their opposition, discontent, and aspiration for more jobs for local gentlemen should now fuse with nationalism.

The national business classes which emerged in this period were, paradoxically, a rather less nationalist element. Admittedly in disunited Germany and Italy the advantages of a large unified national market made sense. The author of *Deutschland über Alles* apostrophized

Ham and scissors, boots and garters,
Wool and soap and yarn and beer,

because they had achieved, what the spirit of nationality had been unable to, a genuine sense of national unity through customs union. However, there is little evidence that, say, the shippers of Genoa (who were later to provide much of the financial backing for Garibaldi) preferred the possibilities of a national Italian market to the larger prosperity of trading all over the Mediterranean. And in the large multinational empires the industrial or trading nuclei which grew up in particular provinces might grumble about discrimination, but at bottom clearly preferred the great markets open to them now to the little ones of future national independence. The Polish industrialists, with all Russia at their feet, took little part as yet in Polish nationalism. When Palacky claimed on behalf of the Czechs that "if Austria did not exist, it would have to be invented," he was not merely calling on the monarchy's support against the

Germans, but also expressing the sound economic reasoning of the economically most advanced sector of a large and otherwise backward empire. Business interests were sometimes at the head of nationalism, as in Belgium, where a strong pioneer industrial community regarded itself, with doubtful reason, as disadvantaged under the rule of the powerful Dutch merchant community, to which it had been hitched in 1815. But this was an exceptional case.

The great proponents of middle-class nationalism at this stage were the lower and middle professional, administrative and intellectual strata, in other words the *educated* classes. (These are not, of course, distinct from the business classes, especially in backward countries where estate administrators, notaries, lawyers, and the like are among the key accumulators of rural wealth.) To be precise, the advance guard of middle-class nationalism fought its battle along the line which marked the educational progress of large numbers of "new men" into areas hitherto occupied by a small elite. The progress of schools and universities measures that of nationalism, just as schools and especially universities became its most conscious champions: the conflict of Germany and Denmark over Schleswig-Holstein in 1848 and again in 1864 was anticipated by the conflict of the universities of Kiel and Copenhagen on this issue in the middle 1840s.

The progress was striking, though the total number of the "educated" remained small. The number of pupils in the French state *lycées* doubled between 1809 and 1842, and increased with particular rapidity under the July monarchy, but even so in 1842 it was only just under 19,000. (The total of all children receiving secondary education then was about 70,000.) Russia, around 1850, had some 20,000 secondary pupils out of a total population of sixty-eight million. The number of university students was naturally even smaller, though it was rising. It is difficult to realize that the Prussian academic youth which was so stirred by the idea of liberation after 1806 consisted in 1805 of not much more than 1,500 young men all told; that the *Polytechnique*, the bane of the post-1815 Bourbons, trained a total

of 1,581 young men in the entire period from 1815 to 1830, i.e., an annual intake of about one hundred. The revolutionary prominence of the students in the 1848 period makes us forget that in the whole continent of Europe, including the unrevolutionary British Isles, there were probably not more than 40,000 university students in all. Still their numbers rose. In Russia it rose from 1,700 in 1825 to 4,600 in 1848. And even if they did not, the transformation of society and the universities . . . gave them a new consciousness of themselves as a social group. Nobody remembers that in 1789 there were something like 6,000 students in the University of Paris, because they played no independent part in the Revolution. But by 1830 nobody could possibly overlook such a number of young academics.

Small *elites* can operate in foreign languages; once the cadre of the educated becomes large enough, the national language imposes itself (as witness the struggle for linguistic recognition in the Indian states since the 1940s). Hence the moment when textbooks or newspapers in the national language are first written, or when that language is first used for some official purpose, measures a crucial step in national evolution. The 1830s saw this step taken over large areas of Europe. Thus the first major Czech works on astronomy, chemistry, anthropology, mineralogy, and botany were written or completed in this decade; and so, in Rumania, were the first school textbooks substituting Rumanian for the previously current Greek. Hungarian was adopted instead of Latin as the official language of the Hungarian Diet in 1840, though Budapest University, controlled from Vienna, did not abandon Latin lectures until 1844. (However, the struggle for the use of Hungarian as an official language had gone on intermittently since 1790.) In Zagreb, Gai published his *Croatian Gazette* (later: *Illyrian National Gazette*) from 1835 in the first literary version of what had hitherto been merely a complex of dialects. In countries which had long possessed an official national language, the change cannot be so easily measured, though it is interesting that after 1830 the number of

German books published in Germany (as against Latin and French titles) for the first time consistently exceeded 90 percent; the number of French ones after 1820 fell below 4 percent.[1] More generally the expansion of publishing gives us a comparable indication. Thus in Germany the number of books published remained much the same in 1821 as in 1800—about 4,000 titles a year, but by 1841 it had risen to 12,000 titles.

Of course the great mass of Europeans, and of non-Europeans, remained uneducated. Indeed, with the exception of the Germans, the Dutch, Scandinavians, Swiss, and the citizens of the USA, no people can in 1840 be described as literate. Several can be described as totally illiterate, like the Southern Slavs, who had less than one-half percent literacy in 1827 (even much later only one percent of Dalmatian recruits to the Austrian army could read and write), or the Russians, who had two percent (1840), and a great many as almost illiterate, like the Spaniards, the Portuguese (who appear to have had barely 8,000 children in all *at school* after the Peninsular War) and, except for the Lombards and Piedmontese, the Italians. Even Britain, France, and Belgium were 40 to 50 percent illiterate in the 1840s. Illiteracy is no bar to political consciousness, but there is, in fact, no evidence that nationalism of the modern kind was a powerful mass force except in countries already transformed by the dual revolution: in France, in Britain, in the USA and—because it was an economic and political dependency of Britain—in Ireland.

To equate nationalism with the literate class is not to claim that the mass of, say, Russians, did not consider themselves "Russian" when confronted with somebody or something that was not. However, for the masses in general the test of nationality was still religion: the Spaniard was defined by being Catholic, the Russian by being Orthodox. However, though such confrontations were becoming rather more frequent, they were still rare, and certain kinds of national feeling, such as the Italian, were as yet wholly alien to the great mass of the people, which did not even speak the national literary language but mutually almost incomprehensible *patois*. Even in

Germany patriotic mythology has greatly exaggerated the degree of national feeling against Napoleon. France was extremely popular in Western Germany, especially among soldiers, whom it employed freely. Populations attached to the Pope or the Emperor might express resentment against their enemies, who happened to be the French, but this hardly implied any feelings of national consciousness, let alone any desire for a national state. Moreover, the very fact that nationalism was represented by middle class and gentry was enough to make the poor man suspicious. The Polish radical-democratic revolutionaries tried earnestly—as did the more advanced of the South Italian Carbonari and other conspirators—to mobilize the peasantry even to the point of offering agrarian reform. Their failure was almost total. The Galician peasants in 1846 opposed the Polish revolutionaries even though these actually proclaimed the abolition of serfdom, preferring to massacre gentlemen and trust to the Emperor's officials.

The uprooting of peoples, which is perhaps the most important single phenomenon of the nineteenth century, was to break down this deep, age-old and localized traditionalism. Yet over most of the world up to the 1820s hardly anybody as yet migrated or emigrated, except under the compulsion of armies and hunger, or in the traditionally migratory groups such as the peasants from Central France who did seasonal building jobs in the north, or the travelling German artisans. Uprooting still meant, not the mild form of homesickness which was to become the characteristic psychological disease of the nineteenth century (reflected in innumerable sentimental popular songs), but the acute, killing *mal de pays* or *mal de cœur* which had first been clinically described by doctors among the old Swiss mercenaries in foreign lands. The conscription of the revolutionary wars revealed it, notably among the Bretons. The pull of the remote northern forests was so strong that it could lead an Estonian servant-girl to leave her excellent employers the Kügelgens in Saxony, where she was free, and return home to serfdom. Migration and emigration, of which the migration to the USA is the most convenient index, increased notably from the 1820s, though it did not reach anything like major proportions until the 1840s, when one and three-quarter millions crossed the North Atlantic (a little less than three times the figure for the 1830s). Even so, the only major migratory nation outside the British Isles was as yet the German, long used to sending its sons as peasant settlers to Eastern Europe and America, as travelling artisans across the continent and as mercenaries everywhere.

We can in fact speak of only one Western national movement organized in a coherent form before 1848 which was genuinely based on the masses, and even this enjoyed the immense advantage of identification with the strongest carrier of tradition, the Church. This was the Irish Repeal movement under Daniel O'Connell (1785–1847), a golden-voiced lawyer–demagogue of peasant stock, the first—and up to 1848 the only one—of those charismatic popular leaders who mark the awakening of political consciousness in hitherto backward masses. (The only comparable figures before 1848 were Feargus O'Connor (1794–1855), another Irishman, who symbolized Chartism in Britain, and perhaps Louis Kossuth (1802–1894), who may have acquired something of his subsequent mass prestige before the 1848 revolution, though in fact his reputation in the 1840s was made as a champion of the gentry, and his later canonization by nationalist historians makes it difficult to see his early career at all clearly.) O'Connell's Catholic Association, which won its mass support and the not wholly justified confidence of the clergy in the successful struggle for Catholic Emancipation (1829), was in no sense tied to the gentry, who were in any case Protestant and Anglo-Irish. It was a movement of peasants, and such elements of a native Irish lower-middle class as existed in that pauperized island. 'The Liberator' was borne into leadership by successive waves of a mass movement of agrarian revolt, the chief motive force of Irish politics throughout that appalling century. This was organized in secret terrorist societies which themselves helped to break down the parochialism of Irish life. However, his aim was neither revolution nor national independence, but

a moderate middle-class Irish autonomy by agreement or negotiation with the British Whigs. He was, in fact, not a nationalist and still less a peasant revolutionary but a moderate middle-class autonomist. Indeed, the chief criticism which has been not unjustifiably raised against him by later Irish nationalists (much as the more radical Indian nationalists have criticized Gandhi, who occupied an analogous position in his country's history) was that he could have raised all Ireland against the British, and deliberately refused to do so. But this does not alter the fact that the movement he led was genuinely supported by the mass of the Irish nation.

■　■　■

Outside the zone of the modern bourgeois world there were, however, movements of popular revolt against alien rule (i.e., normally understood as meaning rule by a different religion rather than a different nationality) which sometimes appear to anticipate later national movements. Such were the rebellions against the Turkish Empire, against the Russians in the Caucasus, and the fight against the encroaching British raj in and on the confines of India. It is unwise to read too much modern nationalism into these, though in backward areas populated by armed and combative peasants and herdsmen, organized in clan groups and inspired by tribal chieftains, bandit-heroes, and prophets, resistance to the foreign (or better, the unbelieving) ruler could take the form of veritable people's wars quite unlike the elite nationalist movements in less Homeric countries. In fact, however, the resistance of Mahrattas (a feudal-military Hindu group) and Sikhs (a militant religious sect) to the British in 1803–18 and 1845–49 respectively have little connection with subsequent Indian nationalism and produced none of their own.[2] The Caucasian tribes, savage, heroic, and feud-ridden, found in the puritan Islamic sect of Muridism a temporary bond of unity against the invading Russians and in Shamyl (1797–1871) a leader of major stature; but there is not to this day a Caucasian nation, but merely a congeries of small mountain peoples in small Soviet republics. (The Georgians and Armenians, who have formed nations in the modern sense, were not involved in the Shamyl movement.) The Bedouin, swept by puritan religious sects like the Wahhabi in Arabia and the Senussi in what is today Libya, fought for the simple faith of Allah and the simple life of the herdsman and raider against the corruption of taxes, pashas, and cities; but what we know as Arab nationalism—a product of the twentieth century—has come out of the cities, not the nomadic encampments.

Even the rebellions against the Turks in the Balkans, especially among the rarely subdued mountain peoples of the south and west, should not be too readily interpreted in modern nationalist terms though the bards and braves of several—the two were often the same, as among the poet-warrior bishops of Montenegro—recalled the glories of quasi-national heroes like the Albanian Skanderbeg and the tragedies like the Serbian defeat at Kossovo in the remote battles against the Turks. Nothing was more natural than to revolt, where necessary or desirable, against a local administration of a weakening Turkish Empire. However, little but a common economic backwardness united what we now know as the Yugoslavs, even those in the Turkish Empire, and the very concept of Yugoslavia was the product of intellectuals in Austro-Hungary rather than of those who actually fought for liberty.[3] The Orthodox Montenegrins, never subdued, fought the Turks, but with equal zest they fought the unbelieving Catholic Albanians and the unbelieving, but solidly Slav, Moslem Bosnians. The Bosnians revolted against the Turks, whose religion many of them shared, with as much readiness as the Orthodox Serbs of the wooded Danube plain, and with more zest than the Orthodox "old Serbs" of the Albanian frontier-area. The first of the Balkan peoples to rise in the nineteenth century were the Serbs under a heroic pig-dealer and brigand Black George (1760–1817), but the initial phase of his rising (1804–7) did not even claim to be against Turkish rule, but on the contrary for the Sultan against the abuses of the local rulers. There is little in the early history of mountain rebellion in the Western Balkans to suggest that the local Serbs, Albanians, Greeks, and others would not in the early nineteenth century have been satisfied with the sort of non-national autonomous principality which a powerful satrap, Ali Pasha "the Lion of Jannina" (1741–1822), for a time set up in Epirus.

In one and only one case did the perennial fight of the shepherding clansmen and bandit-heroes against *any* real government fuse with the ideas of middle-class nationalism and the French Revolution: in the Greek struggle for independence (1821–30). Not unnaturally Greece therefore became the myth and inspiration of nationalists and liberals everywhere. For in Greece alone did an entire people rise against the oppressor in a manner which could be plausibly identified with the cause of the European left; and in turn the support of the European left, headed by the poet Byron who died there, was of very considerable help in the winning of Greek independence.

Most Greeks were much like the other forgotten warrior-peasantries and clans of the Balkan peninsula. A part, however, formed an international merchant and administrative class also settled in colonies or minority communities throughout the Turkish Empire and beyond, and the language and higher ranks of the entire Orthodox Church, to which most Balkan peoples belonged, were Greek, headed by the Greek Patriarch of Constantinople. Greek civil servants, transmuted into vassal princes, governed the Danubian principalities (the present Rumania). In a sense the entire educated and mercantile classes of the Balkans, the Black Sea area, and the Levant, whatever their national origins, were hellenized by the very nature of their activities. During the eighteenth century this hellenization proceeded more powerfully than before, largely because of the marked economic expansion which also extended the range and contacts of the Greek diaspora. The new and thriving Black Sea grain trade took it into Italian, French, and British business centres and strengthened its links with Russia; the expansion of Balkan trade brought Greek or Grecized merchants into Central Europe. The first Greek language newspapers were published in Vienna (1784–1812). Periodic emigration and resettlement of peasant rebels further reinforced the exile communities. It was among this cosmopolitan diaspora that the ideas of the French Revolution—liberalism, nationalism, and the methods of political organization by masonic secret societies—took root. Rhigas (1760–98), the leader of an early obscure and possibly pan-Balkanist revolutionary movement, spoke French and adapted the *Marseillaise* to Hellenic conditions. The *Philiké Hetairía*, the secret patriotic society mainly responsible for the revolt of 1821, was founded in the great new Russian grain port of Odessa in 1814.

Their nationalism was to some extent comparable to the elite movements of the West. Nothing else explains the project of raising a rebellion for Greek independence in the Danube principalities under the leadership of local Greek magnates; for the only people who could be described as Greeks in these miserable serf-lands were lords, bishops, merchants, and intellectuals. Naturally enough that rising failed miserably (1821). Fortunately, however, the Hetairía had also set out to enrol the anarchy of local brigand-heroes, outlaws, and clan chieftains in the Greek mountains (especially in the Peloponnese), and with considerably greater success—at any rate after 1818—than the South Italian gentlemen Carbonari, who attempted a similar proselytization of their local banditti. It is doubtful whether anything like modern nationalism meant much to these "klephts," though many of them had their "clerks"—a respect for and interest in book-learning was a surviving relic of ancient Hellenism—who composed manifestoes in the Jacobin terminology. If they stood for anything it was for the age-old ethos of a peninsula in which the role of man was to become a hero, and the outlaw who took to the mountains to resist any government and to right the peasant's wrongs was the universal political ideal. To the rebellions of men like Kolokotrones, brigand and cattle-dealer, the nationalists of the Western type gave leadership and a pan-hellenic rather than a purely local scale. In turn they got from them that unique and awe-inspiring thing, the mass rising of an armed people.

The new Greek nationalism was enough to win independence, though the combination of middle-class leadership, klephtic disorganization, and great power intervention produced one of those petty caricatures of the Western liberal ideal which were to become so familiar in areas like Latin America. But it also had the paradoxical result of narrowing Hellenism to Hellas, and thus creating or intensifying the latent nationalism of the other Balkan peoples. While being Greek had been little more than the professional requirement of the literate Orthodox Balkan Christian, hellenization had made progress. Once it meant the political support for Hellas, it receded, even among the assimilated Balkan literate classes. In this sense Greek independence was the essential preliminary condition for the evolution of the other Balkan nationalisms.

Outside Europe it is difficult to speak of nationalism at all. The numerous Latin American republics which replaced the token Spanish and Portuguese Empires (to be accurate, Brazil became and remained an independent monarchy from 1816 to 1889), their frontiers often reflecting little more than the distribution of the estates of the grandees who had backed one rather than another of the local rebellions, began to acquire vested political interests and territorial aspirations. The original pan-American ideal of Simón Bolívar (1783–1830) of Venezuela and San Martín (1788–1850) of the Argentine was impossible to realize, though it has persisted as a powerful revolutionary current throughout all the areas united by the Spanish language, just as pan-Balkanism, the heir of Orthodox unity against Islam, persisted and may still persist today. The vast extent and variety of the continent, the existence of independent foci of rebellion in Mexico (which determined Central America), Venezuela, and Buenos Aires, and the special problem of the centre of Spanish colonialism in Peru, which was liberated from without, imposed automatic fragmentation. But the Latin American revolutions were the work of small groups of patricians, soldiers and gallicized *évolués*, leaving the mass of the Catholic poor-white population passive and the Indians indifferent or hostile. Only in Mexico was independence won by the initiative of a popular agrarian, i.e., Indian, movement marching under the banner of the Virgin of Guadalupe, and Mexico has consequently ever since followed a different and politically more advanced road from the remainder of continental Latin America. However, even among the tiny layer of the politically decisive Latin Americans it would be anachronistic in our period to speak of anything more than the embryo of Colombian, Venezuelan, Ecuadorian, etc. "national consciousness."

Something like a proto-nationalism, however, existed in various countries of Eastern Europe, but paradoxically it took the direction of conservatism rather than national rebellion. The Slavs were oppressed everywhere, except in Russia and in a few wild Balkan strongholds, but in their immediate perspective the oppressors were, as we have seen, not the absolute monarchs, but the German or Magyar landlords and urban exploiters. Nor did the nationalism of these allow any place for Slav national existence: even so radical a programme as that of the German United States proposed by the republicans and democrats of Baden (in Southwest Germany) envisaged the inclusion of an Illyrian (i.e., Croat and Slovene) republic with its capital in Italian Trieste, a Moravian one with its capital in Olomouc, and a Bohemian one led by Prague. Hence the immediate hope of the Slav nationalists lay in the emperors of Austria and Russia. Various versions of Slav solidarity expressed the Russian orientation, and attracted Slav rebels—even the anti-Russian Poles—especially in times of defeat and hopelessness as after the failure of the risings in 1846. "Illyrianism" in Croatia and a moderate Czech nationalism expressed the Austrian trend, and both received deliberate support from the Habsburg rulers, two of whose leading ministers—Kolowrat and the chief of the police system, Sedlnitzky—were themselves Czechs. Croatian cultural aspirations were protected in the 1830s, and by 1840 Kolowrat actually proposed what was later to prove so useful in the 1848 revolution, the appointment of a Croat military *ban* as chief of

Croatia, and with control over the military frontier with Hungary, as a counterweight to the obstreperous Magyars. To be a revolutionary in 1848 therefore came to be virtually identical with opposition to Slav national aspirations; and the tacit conflict between the "progressive" and the "reactionary" nations did much to doom the revolutions of 1848 to failure.

Nothing like nationalism is discoverable elsewhere, for the social conditions for it did not exist. In fact, if anything, the forces which were later to produce nationalism were at this stage opposed to the alliance of tradition, religion, and mass poverty which produced the most powerful resistance to the encroachment of Western conquerors and exploiters. The elements of a local bourgeoisie which grew up in Asian countries did so in the shelter of the foreign exploiters whose agents, intermediaries and dependants they largely were. The Parsee community of Bombay is an example. Even if the educated and "enlightened" Asian was not a *compradore* or a lesser official of some foreign ruler or firm (a situation not dissimilar to that of the Greek diaspora in Turkey), his first political task was to Westernize—i.e., to introduce the ideas of the French Revolution and of scientific and technical modernization among his people, against the united resistance of traditional rulers and traditional ruled (a situation not dissimilar to that of the gentlemen-Jacobins of Southern Italy). He was therefore doubly cut off from his people. Nationalist mythology has often obscured this divorce, partly by suppressing the link between colonialism and the early native middle classes, partly lending to earlier anti-foreign resistance the colours of a later nationalist movement. But in Asia, in the Islamic countries, and even more in Africa, the junction between the *évolués* and nationalism, and between both and the masses, was not made until the twentieth century.

Nationalism in the East was thus the eventual product of Western influence and Western conquest. This link is perhaps most evident in the one plainly Oriental country in which the foundations of what was to become the first modern colonial nationalist movement[4] were laid: in Egypt. Napoleon's conquest introduced Western ideas, methods, and techniques, whose value an able and ambitious local soldier, Mohammed Ali (Mehemet Ali), soon recognized. Having seized power and virtual independence from Turkey in the confused period which followed the withdrawal of the French, and with French support, Mohammed Ali set out to establish an efficient and Westernizing despotism with foreign (mainly French) technical aid. European left-wingers in the 1820s and '30s hailed this enlightened autocrat, and put their services at his disposal, when reaction in their own countries looked too dispiriting. The extraordinary sect of the Saint-Simonians, equally suspended between the advocacy of socialism and of industrial development by investment bankers and engineers, temporarily gave him their collective aid and prepared his plans of economic development. * * * They thus also laid the foundation for the Suez Canal (built by the Saint-Simonian de Lesseps) and the fatal dependence of Egyptian rulers on vast loans negotiated by competing groups of European swindlers, which turned Egypt into a centre of imperialist rivalry and anti-imperialist rebellion later on. But Mohammed Ali was no more a nationalist than any other Oriental despot. His Westernization, not his or his people's aspirations, laid the foundations for later nationalism. If Egypt acquired the first nationalist movement in the Islamic world and Morocco one of the last, it was because Mohammed Ali (for perfectly comprehensible geopolitical reasons) was in the main paths of Westernization and the isolated self-sealed Sherifian Empire of the Moslem far west was not, and made no attempts to be. Nationalism, like so many other characteristics of the modern world, is the child of the dual revolution.

NOTES

1. In the early eighteenth century only about 60 percent of all titles published in Germany were in the German language; since then the proportion had risen fairly steadily.
2. The Sikh movement has remained largely *sui generis* to this day. The tradition of combative Hindu resistance in Maharashtra made that area an early centre of the Indian nationalism, and provided some of its earliest—and highly traditionalist—leaders, notably B. G. Tilak; but this was at best a regional, and far from dominant strain in the movement. Something like Mahratta nationalism may exist today, but its social basis is the resistance of large Mahratta working class and underprivileged lower-middle class to the economically and until recently linguistically dominant Gujeratis.
3. It is significant that the present Yugoslav regime has broken up what used to be classed as the Serb nation into the much more realistic sub-national republics and units of Serbia, Bosnia, Montenegro, Macedonia, and Kossovo-Metohidja. By the linguistic standards of nineteenth-century nationalism most of these belonged to a single "Serb" people, except the Macedonians, who are closer to the Bulgarians, and the Albanian minority in Kosmet. But in fact they have never developed a single Serb nationalism.
4. Other than the Irish.

James D. Fearon and David D. Laitin
ETHNICITY, INSURGENCY, AND CIVIL WAR

Between 1945 and 1999, about 3.33 million battle deaths occurred in the 25 interstate wars that killed at least 1,000 and had at least 100 dead on each side. These wars involved just 25 states that suffered casualties of at least 1,000 and had a median duration of not quite 3 months. In contrast, in the same period there were roughly 127 civil wars that killed at least 1,000, 25 of which were ongoing in 1999. A conservative estimate of the total dead as a direct result of these conflicts is 16.2 million, five times the interstate toll. These civil wars occurred in 73 states—more than a third of the United Nations system—and had a median duration of roughly six years.[1] The civil conflicts in this period surely produced refugee flows far greater than their death toll and far greater than the refugee flows associated with interstate wars since 1945. Cases such as Afghanistan, Somalia, and Lebanon testify to the economic devastation that civil wars can produce. By these crude measures, civil war has been a far greater scourge than interstate war in this period, though it has been studied far less.

What explains the recent prevalence of violent civil conflict around the world? Is it due to the end of the Cold War and associated changes in the international system, or is it the result of longer-term trends? Why have some countries had civil wars while others have not? and Why did the wars break out when they did? We address these questions using data for the period 1945 to 1999 on the 161 countries that had a population of at least half a million in 1990.

The data cast doubt on three influential conventional wisdoms concerning political conflict before and after the Cold War. First, contrary to common opinion, the prevalence of civil war in the 1990s was *not* due to the end of the Cold War and associated changes in the international system. The current level of about one in six countries had already been reached prior to the breakup of the Soviet Union and resulted from a steady, gradual accumulation of civil conflicts that began immediately after World War II.

Second, it appears *not* to be true that a greater degree of ethnic or religious diversity—or indeed any particular cultural demography—by itself makes a country more prone to civil war. This finding runs contrary to a common view among journalists, policy makers, and academics, which holds "plural" societies to be especially conflict-prone due to ethnic or religious tensions and antagonisms.

Third, we find little evidence that one can predict where a civil war will break out by looking for where ethnic or other broad political grievances are strongest. Were this so, one would expect political democracies and states that observe civil liberties to be less civil war-prone than dictatorships. One would further anticipate that state discrimination against minority religions or languages would imply higher risks of civil war. We show that when comparing states at similar levels of per capita income, these expectations are not borne out.

The main factors determining both the secular trend and the cross-sectional variation in civil violence in this period are not ethnic or religious differences or broadly held grievances but, rather, conditions that favor *insurgency*. Insurgency is a technology of military conflict characterized by small, lightly armed bands practicing guerrilla warfare from rural base areas. As a form of warfare insurgency can be harnessed to diverse political

From *American Political Science Review* 97, no. 1 (2003), pp. 75–90.

agendas, motivations, and grievances. The concept is most closely associated with communist insurgency, but the methods have equally served Islamic fundamentalists, ethnic nationalists, or "rebels" who focus mainly on traffic in coca or diamonds.

We hypothesize that financially, organizationally, and politically weak central governments render insurgency more feasible and attractive due to weak local policing or inept and corrupt counterinsurgency practices. These often include a propensity for brutal and indiscriminate retaliation that helps drive noncombatant locals into rebel forces. Police and counterinsurgent weakness, we argue, is proxied by a low per capita income. Shocks to counterinsurgent capabilities can arise from political instability at the center or the sudden loss of a foreign patron. On the rebel side, insurgency is favored by rough terrain, rebels with local knowledge of the population superior to the government's, and a large population. All three aid rebels in hiding from superior government forces. Foreign base camps, financial support, and training also favor insurgency.

Our data show that measures of cultural diversity and grievances fail to postdict civil war onset, while measures of conditions that favor insurgency do fairly well. Surely ethnic antagonisms, nationalist sentiments, and grievances often motivate rebels and their supporters. But such broad factors are too common to distinguish the cases where civil war breaks out. Also, because insurgency can be successfully practiced by small numbers of rebels under the right conditions, civil war may require only a small number with intense grievances to get going.

Using data on about 45 civil wars since 1960, Collier and Hoeffler (1999, 2001) find similarly that measures of "objective grievance" fare worse as predictors than economic variables, which they initially interpreted as measures of rebel "greed" (i.e., economic motivation).[2] More recently, they argue that rebellion is better explained by "opportunity" than by grievance (cf. Eisinger 1973 and Tilly 1978) and that the main determinant of opportunity is the availability of finance and recruits for rebels. They proxy these with measures of primary commodity exports and rates of secondary-school enrollment for males. We agree that financing is one determinant of the viability of insurgency. We argue, however, that economic variables such as per capita income matter primarily because they proxy for state administrative, military, and police capabilities. We find no impact for primary commodity exports, and none for secondary schooling rates distinct from income. Our theoretical interpretation is more Hobbesian than economic. Where states are relatively weak and capricious, both fears and opportunities encourage the rise of would-be rulers who supply a rough local justice while arrogating the power to "tax" for themselves and, often, for a larger cause.

Civil War Since 1945

■ ■ ■

Trends over Time

Figure 3.1 shows the number of countries with ongoing civil wars by year from 1945 to 1999. Since the number of independent states grew sharply in this period, it also shows the proportion of countries with at least one ongoing war in each year.

The graph indicates that, contrary to popular belief, the prevalence of civil wars in the 1990s is *not* due to effects of the end of the Cold War. The 1999 level of 25 ongoing wars had already been reached by the mid 1980s. Conflicts associated with the Soviet collapse were partly responsible for the sharp increase in the early 1990s, but a marked *decline* has followed.[3]

One might conjecture that more and more civil wars are breaking out over time, thus producing the secular increase. This is incorrect. The rate of outbreak is 2.31 per year since 1945, highly variable but showing no significant trend up or down. The secular increase stems from the fact that civil wars have ended at a rate of only about 1.85 per year. The result has been a steady, almost-linear accumulation of unresolved conflicts since 1945.

Figure 3.1. Number and Percentage of Countries with Ongoing Civil Wars by Year from 1945 to 1999

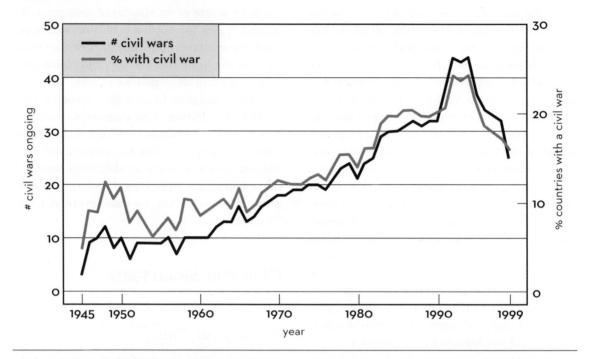

Put differently, states in the international system have been subject to a more or less constant risk of violent civil conflict over the period, but the conflicts they suffer have been difficult to end. The average duration of the civil wars in progress has increased steadily from two years in 1947 to about 15 years in 1999. From a policy perspective this suggests caution about seeing as a temporary "blip" the sorts of military and political problems Western foreign policy makers have faced recently in Kosovo, Macedonia, Bosnia, Somalia, Haiti, East Timor, Colombia, and elsewhere.

Ethnicity, Discrimination, and Grievances

During the Cold War, political scientists and sociologists often sought to trace rebellion to economic inequality (Muller 1985; Paige 1975; Russett 1964), to rapid economic growth said to destabilize traditional rural social systems (Huntington 1968; Scott 1976), or to frustrations arising from the failure to gain expected benefits of economic modernization (Gurr 1971). A few scholars argued that the real source of rebellion was often ethnic nationalism (Connor 1994), and a rich literature on the sources of nationalist mobilization developed in comparative politics (e.g., Anderson 1983, Deutsch 1953, and Gellner 1983). With the collapse of the Soviet Union and Yugoslavia, such culturalist perspectives became a dominant frame for interpreting inter- and intranational conflict (e.g., Huntington 1996).

■   ■   ■

Insurgency

If many post-1945 civil wars have been "ethnic" or "nationalist" as these terms are usually understood, then even more have been fought as *insurgencies*. Insurgency is a technology of military conflict characterized by small, lightly armed bands practicing guerrilla warfare from rural base areas. To explain why some countries have experienced civil wars in this period one needs to understand the conditions that favor insurgency, which are largely independent of cultural differences between groups and even group grievances. These conditions are best summarized by way of a brief statement of the logic of insurgency.[4]

The fundamental fact about insurgency is that insurgents are weak relative to the governments they are fighting, at least at the start of operations. If government forces knew who the rebels were and how to find them, they would be fairly easily destroyed or captured. This is true even in states whose military and police capacities are low. The total number of active rebels in many wars in which thousands of civilians have been killed (through the actions of both governments and rebels) is often in the hundreds or low thousands.

The numerical weakness of the insurgents implies that, to survive, the rebels must be able to hide from government forces. Several hypotheses follow.

H_8: The presence of (a) rough terrain, poorly served by roads, at a distance from the centers of state power, should favor insurgency and civil war. So should the availability of (b) foreign, cross-border sanctuaries and (c) a local population that can be induced not to denounce the insurgents to government agents.

Much scholarly writing holds that ethnic or class solidarity and grievances are necessary for H_{8c}, the local population's support of active rebels. In line with Kriger (1992) and some analysts of communist insurgencies (e.g., Clutterbuck 1967, Leites and Wolf 1970, and Thompson 1966), we argue that while grievances and ethnic solidarity can be helpful in this regard, they are not necessary. Instead, the key to inducing the local population not to denounce the active rebels is *local knowledge*, or information about who is doing what at the village level. Local knowledge allows the active rebels to threaten retribution for denunciation credibly.[5] Ethnic insurgents use this informational advantage to great

effect, often threatening and inflicting unimaginably harsh sanctions on "their own" people (Kalyvas 1999; Kriger 1992). The presence of an ethnic insurgency does not imply that the members of the ethnic group are of one mind in their determination to fight the state till they realize a nationalist dream. The immediate concern is how to survive in between government forces using violence to gain information or punish alleged rebel supporters and rebel forces using violence to punish alleged informants, "moderates," or government sympathizers.

An empirical implication of the importance of local knowledge is hypothesis H_{8d}: Having a *rural base* should greatly favor insurgency. In the city, anonymous denunciation is easier to get away with, giving the government an advantage in its counterinsurgent efforts.

Given the basic constraints posed by numerical weakness — the need to hide and not be denounced — various factors determine insurgents' ability to wage war. To survive, rebels need arms and matériel, money to buy them, or smugglable goods to trade for them. They need a supply of recruits to the insurgent way of life, and they may also need information and instruction in the practical details of running an insurgency.[6]

Most important for the prospects of a nascent insurgency, however, are *the government's police and military capabilities and the reach of government institutions into rural areas.* Insurgents are better able to survive and prosper if the government and military they oppose are relatively weak — badly financed, organizationally inept, corrupt, politically divided, and poorly informed about goings-on at the local level.

Effective counterinsurgency requires government forces to distinguish active rebels from noncombatants without destroying the lives and living conditions of the latter. This is an extremely difficult political, military, and organizational problem even for well-equipped and well-paid modern militaries; witness the U.S. military's failures in Vietnam (Avant 1994; Krepinevich 1986), early British efforts in Northern Ireland (Kennedy-Pipe 1997), or Soviet efforts in Afghanistan. For less well-financed and bureaucratically competent states, the problem appears to be nearly insoluble. Such states either cannot prevent the abuse of local powers by field commanders or may even permit these abuses as a sort of tax farming to the military. That is, they "pay" the soldiers with the opportunity to loot and pillage, a practice that tends to sustain rather than end insurgencies (see Keen 1998 for examples). Thus, we have the following hypothesis.

> H_9: Proxies for the relative weakness or strength of the insurgents — their odds of being killed or captured for a given level of counterinsurgent effort by the government — should be associated with the likelihood that a country develops a civil war. In particular, a *higher per capita income* should be associated with a lower risk of civil war onset because (a) it is a proxy for a state's overall financial, administrative, police, and military capabilities, and (b) it will mark more developed countries with terrain more "disciplined" by roads and rural society more penetrated by central administration.

There is an additional reason why a lower per capita income should favor the technology of insurgency: (c) Recruiting young men to the life of a guerrilla is easier when the economic alternatives are worse. Though we try below, it is difficult to find measures to distinguish among these three mechanisms associating a low per capita income with civil war onset. We believe that the strong results for per capita income reported below are due largely to its acting as a proxy for state military and police strength relative to potential insurgents (a and b in H_9). The fact that measures such as the percentage of young males and male secondary schooling rates predict less well than per capita income is consistent with this conjecture, though not definitive.

Additional factors that would be expected to affect (or proxy) the strength of an insurgent band relative to a state follow.

> H_{10}: The political and military technology of insurgency will be favored, and thus civil war

made more likely, when potential rebels face or have available the following.

(a) A newly independent state, which suddenly loses the coercive backing of the former imperial power and whose military capabilities are new and untested (Fearon 1998).

(b) Political instability at the center, which may indicate disorganization and weakness and thus an opportunity for a separatist or center-seeking rebellion.

(c) A regime that mixes democratic with autocratic features, as this is likely to indicate political contestation among competing forces and, in consequence, state incapacity. (In contrast, pure autocracy tends to reflect the successful monopolization of state coercive and administrative power by an individual or group.)

(d) A large country population, which makes it necessary for the center to multiply layers of agents to keep tabs on who is doing what at the local level and, also, increases the number of potential recruits to an insurgency for a given level of income.

(e) A territorial base separated from the state's center by water or distance — for example, East Pakistan (now Bangladesh) from West Pakistan or Angola from Portugal.

(f) Foreign governments or diasporas willing to supply weapons, money, or training.

(g) Land that supports the production of high-value, low-weight goods such as coca, opium, diamonds, and other contraband, which can be used to finance an insurgency.

(h) A state whose revenues derive primarily from oil exports. Oil producers tend to have weaker state apparatuses than one would expect given their level of income because the rulers have less need for a socially intrusive and elaborate bureaucratic system to raise revenues — a political "Dutch disease" (Chaudhry 1989; Karl 1997; Wantchekon 2000). At the same time, oil revenues raise the value of the "prize" of controlling state power.

Partially excepting f, none of these conditions crucially involves cultural differences, ethnic minority status, or group grievances. We do not claim that these factors provide no help to would-be insurgents in specific cases. But, to reiterate, grievances and ethnic differences are too common to help distinguish the countries and years that see civil wars, and in any event the technology of insurgency does not require strong popular grievances or ethnic solidarities to operate effectively. The latter point suggests a contrast to H_4–H_6.

> H_{11}: After controlling for per capita income (or other measures of state strength), neither political democracy, the presence of civil liberties, higher income inequality, nor nondiscriminatory linguistic or religious policies should associate strongly with lower odds of civil war. Given the right environmental conditions, insurgencies can thrive on the basis of small numbers of rebels without strong, widespread, popular support rooted in grievances and, hence, even in democracies.

As for measures, for "rough terrain" we use the proportion of the country that is "mountainous" according to the codings of geographer A. J. Gerard.[7] This does not pick up other sorts of rough terrain that can be favorable to guerrillas such as swamps and jungle, and it takes no account of population distributions or food availability in relation to mountains; but it is the best we have been able to do for H_{8a}. For H_9 we use Penn World Tables and World Bank data on per capita income, estimating missing values using data on per capita energy consumption.[8] For H_{10a} (new states) we mark countries in their first and second years of independence; for H_{10b} (political instability) we use a dummy variable indicating whether the country had a three-or-greater change on the Polity IV regime index in any of the three years prior to the country-year in question.[9] For countries that mix democratic and autocratic features (called "anocracies" or "semidemocracies" in the international relations literature and "praetorian regimes" by Huntington 1968) we mark regimes that score between −5 and 5 on the difference between Polity IV's democracy and autocracy measures (the difference ranges from −10 to 10). Country population (H_{10d}) is based largely on World Bank figures. For oil exporters we marked country-years in which fuel exports exceeded one-third of export revenues, using World Bank data.[10] We coded a dummy variable for states with noncontiguous territory ourselves (H_{10e}).[11]

The remaining hypotheses (H_{8b}–H_{8d}, H_{10f} and H_{10g}) present more difficult measurement challenges. Whether availability of a rural base favors civil war (H_{8d}) is better tested in a research design where ethnic groups are the unit of analysis, so that groups with different geographic concentrations can be compared.[12]

Although it is possible to code rebellions in progress for whether the rebels receive shelter and support from foreign countries (H_{8b}, H_{10f}), the potential availability of these aids to rebel strength is difficult to observe prior to the onset of fighting. In two special cases, the potential availability of support from a foreign power to *governments* is observable—in Soviet policy (the "Brezhnev doctrine") in Eastern Europe and French policy with regard to its former colonies in subSaharan Africa.[13] We would expect such support to increase the relative advantage of government forces against potential insurgents and thus associate with lower rates of civil war onset. We also consider a more tenuous measure of potential support to rebels—the number of civil wars ongoing in neighboring countries—which might yield more easily available weapons, training, or the presence of experienced guerrillas.[14]

Empirical Analysis

Our central hypotheses concern the relationship between ethnic and religious diversity or structure, on the one hand, and the susceptibility of a country to civil war, on the other. Several multivariate analyses of the country-year data are presented below, but the main story emerging from them is made clear by the contour plot in Figure 3.2.

Figure 3.2. Probability of Civil War Onset per Five-Year Period

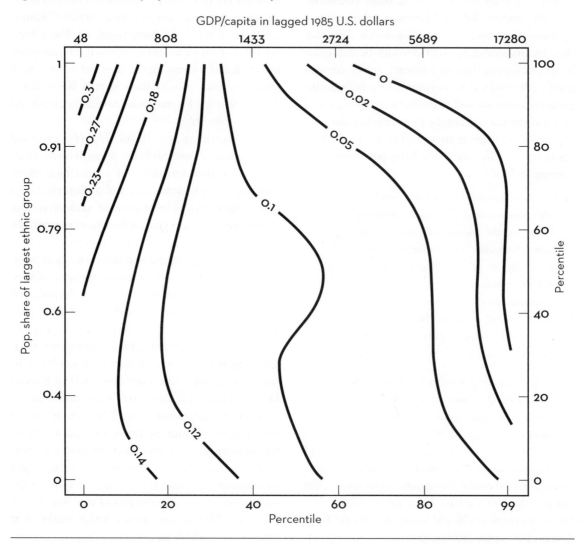

Are More Diverse Countries Prone to Civil War?

Figure 3.2 shows how probabilities of civil war onset vary at different percentiles for country income (on the *x* axis, measured in lagged 1985 dollars) and ethnic homogeneity (on the *y* axis, measured by the population share of the largest ethnic group). The lines in the plot show the probability of war onset in the next five years for a country at the given level of income and ethnic homogeneity. For example, countries at the twentieth percentile in terms of the size of their largest ethnic group—thus quite ethnically *diverse*—but at the eightieth percentile on income have had about a 5% chance of civil war outbreak in the next five years. In contrast, countries at the eightieth percentile on ethnic homogeneity and at the twentieth percentile on income had a 15% chance of war in the next five years.[15]

Note that *for any level of ethnic diversity*, as one moves up the income scale (in Figure 3.2), the odds of civil war decrease, by substantial factors in all cases and dramatically among the most homogeneous countries. The richest fifth is practically immune regardless of ethnic composition. In contrast, for given levels of country income, no consistent effect is associated with variation in ethnic homogeneity (i.e., moving up or down the figure). Among the poorest countries where we observe the highest rates of civil war, the data indicate a tendency for *more homogeneous* countries to be more civil war-prone. Among the richest countries there may be a weak tendency for the most homogeneous countries to have fewer civil wars, but the size of the effect, if any, is small.

The empirical pattern is thus inconsistent with * * * the common expectation that ethnic diversity is a major and direct cause of civil violence. Nor is there strong evidence in favor of [the hypothesis that] ethnic strife [is] activated as modernization advances. Ethnic diversity could still cause civil war *indirectly*, if it causes a low per capita income (Easterly and Levine 1997) or a weak state. But then the mechanisms that actually produce the violence would more likely be those of the insurgency perspective than the culturalist arguments.

■   ■   ■

Conclusion

The prevalence of internal war in the 1990s is mainly the result of an accumulation of protracted conflicts since the 1950s rather than a sudden change associated with a new, post–Cold War international system. Decolonization from the 1940s through the 1970s gave birth to a large number of financially, bureaucratically, and militarily weak states. These states have been at risk for civil violence for the whole period, almost entirely in the form of insurgency, or rural guerrilla warfare. Insurgency is a mode of military practice that can be harnessed to various political agendas, be it communism in Southeast Asia and Latin America, Islamic fundamentalism in Afghanistan, Algeria,

or Kashmir, right-wing "reaction" in Nicaragua, or ethnic nationalism in a great many states. The conditions that favor insurgency—in particular, state weakness marked by poverty, a large population, and instability—are better predictors of which countries are at risk for civil war than are indicators of ethnic and religious diversity or measures of grievances such as economic inequality, lack of democracy or civil liberties, or state discrimination against minority religions or languages.

How could democracy and cultural or religious homogeneity fail to associate with civil peace across countries? Viewing "ethnic wars" as a species of insurgency may help explain this paradoxical result. If, under the right environmental conditions, just 500 to 2,000 active guerrillas can make for a long-running, destructive internal war, then the average level of grievance in a group may not matter that much. What matters is whether active rebels can hide from government forces and whether economic opportunities are so poor that the life of a rebel is attractive to 500 or 2,000 young men. Grievance may favor rebellion by leading nonactive rebels to help in hiding the active rebels. But all the guerrillas really need is superior local knowledge, which enables them to threaten reprisal for denunciation.

If our analysis is correct, then policy makers should not assume that civil wars and the "failed states" they sometimes produce are temporary phenomena of the immediate post–Cold War world. Nor should policy makers or academics infer that ethnic diversity is the root cause of civil conflict when they observe insurgents in a poor country who mobilize fighters along ethnic lines. Instead, the civil wars of the period have structural roots, in the combination of a simple, robust military technology and decolonization, which created an international system numerically dominated by fragile states with limited administrative control of their peripheries.

Regarding policy implications, the spread of democracy and tolerance for ethnic and religious minorities should be major foreign policy goals because they are desirable for their own sake, but not with the expectation that they are "magic bullets" for the prevention or resolution of civil war. Sometimes recommended as a general international policy for resolving ethnic civil wars (e.g., Kaufmann 1996), ethnic partitions should be viewed as having large international implications and high costs. International support for partition would increase the expected benefits for rebels, who, we have argued, may be able to get a nasty civil war going on the basis of small numbers when the conditions for insurgency are right.

Policies to redress grievances, or, in the limit, partition, *could* be important to resolve ongoing conflicts. We cannot say on the basis of this research, which focused on civil war onset rather than termination. We find little evidence that civil war is predicted by large cultural divisions or broadly held grievances. But it seems quite clear that intense grievances *are produced by* civil war—indeed, this is often a central objective of rebel strategy. These could well pose obstacles to settlement.

Regarding prevention, our analysis suggests that while economic growth may correlate with fewer civil wars, the causal mechanism is more likely a well-financed and administratively competent government. In specific terms, international and nongovernmental organizations should develop programs that improve legal accountability within developing world militaries and police, and make aid to governments fighting civil wars conditional on the state observing counterinsurgency practices that do not help rebels recruit militias. Governments that follow horrible, war-perpetuating counterinsurgency practices or are so corrupt as to be helpless should be left on their own or, when there are major implications for regional stability or international terrorism, be viewed as candidates for "neotrusteeship" under the United Nations or regional military and political organizations such as NATO and the European Union. The latter system, which we already see operating, in effect, in Bosnia, Kosovo, and East Timor, should be rationalized so as to improve internal coordination among the many players involved in such operations.

NOTES

1. The interstate war data derive from Singer and Small 1994, updated to include the Kargil and Eritrean wars. The bases for the civil war estimates are discussed below.

2. There are 79 wars in their sample, but they lose about 34 due to missing values on explanatory variables, which are mainly economic. Standard economic data tend to be missing for countries that are poor and civil war-torn. This highly nonrandom listwise deletion may account for some of the differences between our results.

3. Gurr (2000) notes the late-1990s decline in ethic war and argues that the trend reflects improved management strategies by states and international organizations. The basic pattern in Figure 3.1 is not an artifact of the way we have coded "civil war"; it is observed in a broad range of other data sets on violent domestic conflict for this period (e.g., Gleditsch et al. 2002).

4. Though our formulations differ, we have been influenced here by Stathis Kalyvas's work on the Greek civil war. The literature on guerrilla warfare is extensive; see, for examples, Desai and Eckstein 1990, Griffith 1961, and Laqueur 1976.

5. A "second-order" mechanism by which ethnicity may favor insurgency is that ethnic minorities are sometimes marked by dense social networks that are isolated from dominant group networks, thus giving an informational advantage to local rebels (Fearon and Laitin 1996). But such an advantage does not require ethnic distinctiveness.

6. In the case literature one frequently finds either that rebels leaders have spent time at guerrilla training camps in, for example, Libya, Afghanistan, Lebanon, or Mozambique (in the 1970s) or that they gained guerrilla experience in one insurgency that apply in pursuing another.

7. Gerard produced this measure for the DECRG project on civil wars at the World Bank. Our sample of

countries differs slightly, so we estimated values for 21 missing countries using the difference between the highest and the lowest point of elevation in each country, which is well correlated with the mountains measure (0.78 in logs).

8. We used income growth rates from the World Development Indicators 2001 to extend the estimates in the Penn World Tables 5.6 and then used the per capita energy consumption estimates provided by the COW project to estimate additional missing values. For details see Fearon and Laitin 2003.

9. For this variable, "transition periods" and "interruptions" (which indicate a "complete collapse of central authority") are coded as instability; foreign occupations are treated as missing.

10. The data are for five-year intervals beginning in 1960; we interpolated for years after 1960, set the value to that in 1960 for years prior to 1960, and used country-specific sources for a few countries without World Bank coverage.

11. Countries with territory holding at least 10,000 people and separated from the land area containing the capital city either by land or by 100 km of water were coded as "noncontiguous." Ignoring the colonial empires, 25 of our 161 countries meet this criterion at some time since 1945.

12. Using the Phase III Minorities at Risk (MAR) data, Fearon and Laitin (1999) found that groups without a rural base area were far less likely to be engaged in violent conflict with the state, even after controlling for various country- and group-specific factors. Toft (1996) was the first to note and examine the strong bivariate relationship in the MAR data.

13. U.S. support to rightist regimes in Latin America during the Cold War might also qualify, although this was perhaps more offset by support for armed insurgency in this area from the Soviet Union and Cuba.

14. The presence of valuable minerals or the suitability of land for the cultivation of narcotics is also codable in principle, but at present we lack such measures (H_{10c}). Nor do we have measures for the comparative

disadvantage of governments in access to village-level information (H_{8c}).

15. The figure was produced using R's locfit package, with a smoothing parameter of 0.9, and transforming annual probabilites of outbreak to five-year equivalents. The figure looks highly similar if we use other measures of ethnic diversity, such as fractionalization.

REFERENCES

Anderson, Benedict. 1983. *Imagined Communities.* London: Verso.

Collier, Paul, and Anke Hoeffler. 1999. "Justice Seeking and Loot-seeking in Civil War," World Bank. Typescript. http://econ.worldbank.org/programs/conflict/library (November 18, 2002).

Collier, Paul, and Anke Hoeffler. 2001. "Greed and Grievance in Civil War." World Bank. Typescript. http://econ.worldbank.org/programs/library (November 18, 2002).

Connor, Walker. 1994. *Ethnonationalism.* Princeton, NJ: Princeton University Press.

Deutsch, Karl W. 1953. *Nationalism and Social Communication.* Cambridge, MA: MIT Press.

Easterly, William, and Ross Levine. 1997. "Africa's Growth Tragedy: Policies and Ethnic Divisions." *Quarterly Journal of Economics* 112 (4): 1203–50.

Eisinger, Peter. 1973. "The Conditions of Protest Behavior in American Cities." *American Political Science Review* 67: 11–28.

Gellner, Ernest. 1983. *Nations and Nationalism.* Ithaca, NY: Cornell University Press.

Gleditsch, Nils, Havard Strand, Mikael Eriksson, Margareta Sollenberg, and Peter Wallensteen. 2002. "Armed Conflict 1946–2001: A New Dataset." *Journal of Peace Research* 39 (5): 615–37.

Gurr, Ted R. 1971. *Why Men Rebel.* Princeton, NJ: Princeton University Press.

Gurr, Ted R. 2000. *Peoples versus States.* Washington, DC: United States Institute of Peace Press.

Huntington, Samuel P. 1968. *Political Order in Changing Societies.* New Haven, CT: Yale University Press.

Huntington, Samuel P. 1996. *The Clash of Civilizations and the Remaking of World Order.* New York: Simon & Schuster.

Kaufmann, Chaim. 1996. "Possible and Impossible Solutions to Ethnic Civil Wars." *International Security* 20 (4): 136–75.

Muller, Edward N. 1985. "Income Inequality, Regime Repressiveness, and Political Violence." *American Sociological Review* 50: 47–61.

Paige, Jeffery M. 1975. *Agrarian Revolution.* New York: Free Press.

Russett, Bruce M. 1964. "Inequality and Instability." *World Politics* 16: 442–54.

Scott, James C. 1976. *The Moral Economy of the Peasant.* New Haven: Yale University Press.

Singer, J. David and Melvin H. Small. 1994. " Correlates of War Project: International and Civil War Data, 1816–1992." ICPSR 9905, April.

Tilly, Charles. 1978. *From Mobilization to Revolution.* Reading, MA: Addison-Wesley.

Alberto Alesina and Eliana La Ferrara
ETHNIC DIVERSITY AND ECONOMIC PERFORMANCE

1. Introduction

New York and Los Angeles are among the two most troubled American cities in terms of racial relations; at the same time they are constant producers of innovation in the arts and business. The United States itself is an economically successful melting pot, but many of its social problems are related to racial and ethnic cleavages. The "tragedy of Africa" is, according to many, largely a result of ethnic conflict, which is indeed pervasive in many parts of the developing world. So, what are the pros and cons of "diversity," being that racial, ethnic, religious, or linguistic?

The potential costs of diversity are fairly evident. Conflict of preferences, racism, and prejudices often lead to policies that are at the same time odious and counterproductive for society as a whole. The oppression of minorities may lead to political

From *Journal of Economic Literature* 43 (September 2005), pp. 762–800.

unrest or even civil wars. But a diverse ethnic mix also brings about variety in abilities, experiences, and cultures that may be productive and may lead to innovation and creativity. In what follows, we try to highlight the trade-off between the benefits of "diversity" and the costs of heterogeneity of preferences in a diverse multiethnic society.

■   ■   ■

So, is diversity "good" or "bad"? Fragmented societies are often more prone to poor policy management and pose more politico-economic challenges than homogenous ones; it is easy to find rather voluminous evidence on this point. However, to the extent that not all diverse societies are a failure but in fact some work much better than others, and in fact rather well, it is important to understand why and how. We propose a simple theoretical framework in which the skills of individuals from different ethnic groups are complementary in the production process for a private good, implying that more diversity translates into increased productivity. On the other hand, individual utility also depends on the consumption of a shared public good and, since different ethnic groups may have different preferences on the type of public good to provide, increased diversity lowers the utility from public good consumption. The size of the public sector and the number of ethnic groups are determined by the trade-off between these two forces. We verify the consistency of this theory using repeated cross-sectional data on countries * * * and we find that, while *ceteris paribus* increases in ethnic diversity are associated with lower growth rates, the interaction between diversity and the income level of the community under study is positive. This suggests that ethnic diversity can be beneficial (or at least less detrimental) at higher levels of development. One potential explanation for this effect is that the productivity benefits of skill complementarities are realized only when the production process is sufficiently diversified, as in advanced economies. Another — possibly complementary — explanation is that richer societies have developed institutional features that allow them to better cope with the conflict element intrinsic in diversity and isolate or moderate its negative effects. From the micro to the macro level, in fact, the importance of adequate "rules of the game" to manage diversity is stressed by all disciplines.

* * * [W]e need to clarify what we, and the literature which we review, mean by various terms like diversity, fractionalization, ethnicity, race, etc. The empirical literature on cross-country studies has typically used various measures of ethno-linguistic fractionalization. An "ethno-linguistic group" (often referred for brevity as "ethnic group") is identified by a language only in some cases and in other cases by language and skin color or other physically attributes; a variety of indexes have been suggested and we will discuss below similarity and differences. * * * We will use the terms "fractionalization" and "diversity" when we want to be generic and not refer to any particular type of identifying characteristics of

the groups; we will use ethnic, racial, religious fragmentation, and diversity when we want to be more specific. With the term "diverse society" . . . we mean a nonhomogenous place. The term fractionalization, on the other hand, will be directly related to a specific measure of number and size of groups: specifically, a more fractionalized place is one in which the probability the two randomly drawn individuals belong to the same group is lower. In surveying the existing literature, we do not touch on the question of what identifies an ethnic group and we take the classifications adopted by the authors as given.

■   ■   ■

2. Theories on Diversity

The goal of this section is to briefly highlight some basic economic forces underlying the relationship between ethnic diversity and economic performance.

■   ■   ■

2.1 Some "Microfoundations"

First diversity can affect economic choices by directly entering individual *preferences*. Early work on social identity theory has established that patterns of intergroup behavior can be understood considering that individuals may attribute positive utility to the well being of members of their own group and negative utility to that of members of other groups (see e.g., Henri Tajfel, Michael Billig, Robert Bundy, and Claude Flament 1971). A recent formalization of this concept is the analysis of group participation by Alesina and La Ferrara (2000), where the population is heterogeneous and individual utility from joining a group depends positively on the share of group members of one's own type and negatively on the share of different types.[1]

Second, diversity can affect economic outcomes by influencing the *strategies* of individuals.

Even when individuals have no taste for or against homogeneity, it may be optimal from an efficiency point of view to transact preferentially with members of one's own type if there are market imperfections. For example, Avner Greif (1993) argues that traders in Medieval times formed coalitions along ethnic lines in order to monitor agents by exchanging information on their opportunistic behavior. Ethnic affiliation helped sustain a reputation mechanism in the presence of asymmetric information. But strategies can be conditional on one's ethnic identity also in the presence of perfect information.

■ ■ ■

Finally, diversity may enter the *production* function. People differ in their productive skills and, more fundamentally, in the way they interpret problems and use their cognitive abilities to solve them. This can be considered the origin of the relationship between individual heterogeneity and innovation or productivity. An elegant formalization of this concept is provided by Lu Hong and Scott Page (1998), who prove two key results on this point. First, a group of "cognitively diverse" problem solvers can find optimal solutions to difficult problems; second, under certain conditions, a more diverse group of people with limited abilities can outperform a more homogeneous group of high-ability problem solvers. The intuition is that an individual's likelihood of improving decisions depends more on her having a different perspective from other group members than on her own high expected score.

■ ■ ■

2.2.3 SUMMING UP THE IMPLICATIONS OF THE THEORY

The potential benefits of heterogeneity come from variety in production. The costs come from the inability to agree on common public goods and public policies. One testable implication is that more heterogeneous societies may exhibit higher productivity in private goods but lower taxation and lower provision of public goods (in relative terms). The benefits in production from variety in skills are more likely to be relevant for more advanced societies. While in poor economies ethnic diversity may not be beneficial from the point of view of productivity, it may be so in rich ones. The more unwilling to share public goods or resources are the different groups, the smaller the size of jurisdictions.[2] The larger the benefits in production from variety, the larger the size. If variety in production can be achieved without sharing public goods, different groups will want to create smaller jurisdictions to take advantage of homogeneity in the enjoyment of the public good.

■ ■ ■

3. The Consequences of Fragmentation

3.1 Countries

3.1.1 EFFECTS ON PRODUCTIVITY AND INCOME LEVEL

Economists have started to pay attention to the effects of racial fragmentation across countries at least since a paper by William Easterly and Ross Levine (1997) who argued that, *ceteris paribus*, more racially fragmented countries grow less and that this factor is a major determinant of Africa's poor economic performance.[3] Several subsequent papers confirmed these results in the context of cross-country growth regressions. In their overview of Africa's problems, Collier and Jan Gunning (1999) also place much emphasis on ethno–linguistic fractionalization (coupled with low political rights) as a major explanation for the lack of social capital, productive public goods, and other growth enhancing policies.

Easterly and Levine's paper, and much of the literature that followed, used as a measure of fragmentation the probability that two randomly drawn individuals from the unit of observation (say, country) belong to two different groups. Their ethno–linguistic fractionalization (ELF) measure is a Herfindahl-based index defined as follows:

$$ELF = 1 - \sum_i s_{t_i}^2$$

where s_i is the share of group i over the total of the population. This index represents the probability that two randomly drawn individuals from the population belong to different ethnic groups. The source used by Easterly and Levine to construct the ethno–linguistic groups is the Atlas Narodov Mira, originally compiled by Soviet researchers. Apart from issues of measurement (to which we return below), the robustness of Easterly and Levine's results has been called into question by Jean-Louis Arcand, Patrick Guillaumont, and Sylviane Guillaumont Jeanneney (2000) due to problems of data missingness.[4] Despite the criticisms, subsequent estimates have taken Easterly and Levine's results as a benchmark, and have confirmed them.

Using the updated data set of Alesina, Arnaud Devleeschauwer, Easterly, Sergio Kurlat, and Wacziarg (2003), we now test whether the negative correlation between ethnic fragmentation and growth holds irrespective of the level of economic development or, as our model suggests, is mitigated when the benefits of heterogeneity for productivity are taken into account. Alesina et al. (2003) construct two indices with the same structure as above but using two different (although closely related) characterizations of groups. One is more comprehensive, is labeled ELF, and extends the Easterly and Levine index by differentiating groups that may speak the same language but have different ethnicity based upon certain physical characteristics. A striking example would be blacks and whites in the United States, or various ethnic groups in Latin America all speaking the same language, often that of a former colonizer.[5] The second index relies exclusively on language spoken.

Table 3.1 shows some standard growth regressions adopting the baseline specification of Alesina et al. (2003). The dependent variable is the growth rate of GDP per capita from 1960 to 2000 and we use a SUR method in four ten-year periods. The first two columns use the more comprehensive index of fractionalization (which we label ELF), while columns 3 and 4 use the one based solely on language. Columns 1 and 3 show a baseline regression with very few controls: regional dummies, initial income, and schooling. Columns 2 and 4 include additional controls, such as measures of political stability and quality of policy. One may argue (and in fact we explore this point below) that the effect of fractionalization on growth may go through exactly these variables; therefore by controlling for these variables one may underestimate the effects of fractionalization on growth. Overall, table 3.1 shows considerable support for the negative effects of fractionalization on growth.[6] In terms of magnitude, the estimates in column 1 suggest that, *ceteris paribus*, going from perfect homogeneity to maximum heterogeneity (i.e., increasing ELF from 0 to 1) would reduce a country's growth rate by 2 percentage points per year. Increasing ethnic fractionalization by one standard deviation would reduce growth by 0.6 percentage points per year. These are quite sizeable effects. All the other controls have signs consistent with the vast literature on growth.

An important question is whether or not these negative effects from ethnic fractionalization on growth depend on the level of income or other features of society. * * * Table 3.2 adds to all the regressions of table 1 an interaction term between fractionalization and GDP per capita. In all four regressions, the interaction of initial GDP per capita and fractionalization has the expected (positive) sign, suggesting that indeed fractionalization has more negative effects at lower levels of income. In two out of four regressions, this effect is strongly statistically significant.

Table 3.1. *Fractionalization and Long-Run Growth (dependent variable is growth of per capita GDP)*

Variable	ETHNIC		LANGUAGE	
	1	2	3	4
Dummy for the 1960s	0.059 (3.357)	0.153 (5.144)	0.065 (3.563)	0.156 (5.248)
Dummy for the 1970s	0.057 (3.093)	0.158 (5.222)	0.062 (3.280)	0.161 (5.333)
Dummy for the 1980s	0.036 (1.940)	0.141 (4.601)	0.042 (2.213)	0.145 (4.725)
Dummy for Sub-Saharian Africa	-0.008 (-1.630)	-0.016 (2.853)	-0.009 (-2.026)	-0.014 (-2.595)
Dummy for Latin America and the Caribbean	-0.016 (-4.458)	-0.011 (-2.923)	-0.019 (-5.252)	-0.018 (-4.201)
Log of initial income	-0.004 (-1.499)	-0.018 (-3.767)	-0.004 (-1.660)	-0.018 (-3.724)
Log of schooling	0.012 (2.767)	0.005 (1.092)	0.011 (2.627)	0.008 (1.669)
Assassinations		-21.342 (2.212)		-13.988 (-1.010)
Financial Depth		0.012 (1.798)		0.010 (1.652)
Black Market premium		-0.021 (4.738)		-0.022 (-4.953)
Fiscal Surplus/GDP		(0.128) 3.369		0.132 (3.474)
Log of telephones per worker		(0.006) 2.078		0.004 (1.488)
Fractionalization	-0.020 (-3.005)	-0.014 (-1.795)	-0.019 (-2.979)	-0.021 (-2.881)
No of Observations	82; 88; 94	40; 69; 66	82; 86; 92	39; 68; 65
R-squared	.23; .17; .35	.32; .43; 54	.21; .21; .30	.36; .47; .52

(t-statistics in parentheses)
Estimated using Seemingly Unrelated Regressions: a separate regression for each ten year period.

Table 3.2. Fractionalization and Long-Run Growth (dependent variable is growth of per capita GDP)

	ETHNIC		LANGUAGE	
Variable	1	2	3	4
Dummy for the 1960s	0.064 (2.522)	0.220 (5.116)	0.098 (3.910)	0.253 (6.827)
Dummy for the 1970s	0.061 (2.369)	0.226 (5.179)	0.096 (3.735)	0.260 (6.897)
Dummy for the 1980s	0.041 (1.542)	0.209 (4.757)	0.077 (2.951)	0.245 (6.411)
Dummy for Sub-Saharian Africa	−0.007 (−1.574)	−0.014 (−2.479)	−0.007 (−1.478)	−0.011 (−2.138)
Dummy for Latin America and the Caribbean	−0.016 (−4.386)	−0.013 (−3.233)	−0.021 (−5.517)	−0.019 (−4.787)
Log of initial income	−0.005 (−1.297)	−0.027 (−4.253)	−0.008 (−2.420)	−0.031 (−5.523)
Log of schooling	0.012 (2.775)	0.006 (1.112)	0.011 (2.599)	0.009 (1.966)
Assassinations		−21.880 (−2.311)		−16.919 (−1.303)
Financial Depth		0.011 (1.649)		0.008 (1.385)
Black Market premium		−0.021 (−4.736)		−0.020 (−4.729)
Fiscal Surplus/GDP		0.136 (3.618)		0.146 (4.048)
Log of telephones per worker		0.007 (2.532)		0.005 (1.969)
Fractionalization	−0.031 (−0.655)	−0.129 (−2.319)	−0.083 (−1.851)	−0.214 (−4.382)
Fractionalization * log of initial income	0.001 (0.227)	0.015 (2.084)	0.008 (1.279)	0.025 (3.977)
No of Observations	82; 88; 94	40; 69; 66	80; 86; 92	39; 68; 65
R-squared	.23; .18; .35	.27; .48; .55	.22; .25; .28	.36; .55; .56

(t-statistics in parentheses)
Estimated using Seemingly Unrelated Regressions: a separate regression for each ten year period.

Collier (2000) argues that fractionalization has negative effects on growth and productivity only in nondemocratic regimes, while democracies manage to cope better with ethnic diversity. This is an important result worth exploring further. It is well known that per capita GDP and democracy are positively correlated: richer countries are more democratic. From a statistical point of view, this high correlation makes it quite difficult to disentangle the effects of democracy from the effects of the level of income on any dependent variable that might be affected by either one or both.[7] Table 3.3 considers the effects of the interaction of ethnic and language fractionalization with the Gastil index of democracy. This index is *decreasing* in the level of democracy so the expected sign on the interaction with fractionalization is negative. The estimates in table 3 are consistent with Collier's findings that fractionalization has less negative effects in democracies.

Table 3.4 uses the two basic specifications to try and disentangle the effects of income and democracy. Since we are adding several variables with interactions, we use the simpler specification. Overall, the effect of income seems more robust and more precisely estimated than the effect of democracy. However, these results have to be taken cautiously given the high correlation between democracy and GDP per capita.

The punch line is that rich democracies are more capable of "handling" productively ethnic diversity. Note, however, that as argued above, the variable "democracy" may be endogenous to ethnic diversity. It may be the case that racially fragmented societies that choose democratic institutions are also those in which ethnic cleavages are less deep and/or the power distribution of groups is such that none can impose a nondemocratic rule.

Related to the issue of how democracy interacts with ethnic conflict and with the level of development is the role played by institutions in general. Easterly (2001) constructs an index of institutional quality aggregating Stephen Knack and Philip Keefer's (1995) data on contract repudiation,

expropriation, rule of law, and bureaucratic quality. He finds that the negative effect of ethnic diversity is significantly mitigated by the presence of "good" institutions and the marginal effect of ethnic diversity at the maximum level of institutional development is actually zero. Again, the institutional variables used as explanatory factors are likely not exogenous and more work needs to be done to assess the marginal impact of institutional arrangements. Nonetheless, it seems important to take into account that, whatever the mechanisms relating ethnic diversity to economic growth, channeling diversity toward productive uses may require a particular set of "rules of the game."

3.1.2 EFFECTS ON PUBLIC POLICIES

An important prediction of our model is that the propensity to supply true public goods should be lower in more ethnically fragmented societies.

■   ■   ■

Rafael La Porta, Florencio Lopez-de-Silanes, Andrei Shleifer, and Robert Vishny (1999) and Alesina et al. (2003) show that ethnic fragmentation is negatively correlated with measures of infrastructure quality, literacy, and school attainment and positively correlated with infant mortality. These correlations are very strong in regressions without income per capita (that may be endogenous to ethnic fragmentation). They lose some of their significance in regressions where on the right hand side one controls for GDP per capita.[8] In any case, neither of these studies argues that ethnic fragmentation is the only cause of "poor quality of government": La Porta et al. (1999), for instance, argue that legal origins are at least as important.

An interesting related question regards the size of public transfers rather than public goods. For a large sample of countries, Alesina, Glaeser, and Bruce Sacerdote (2001) show an inverse relationship between the size of government social spending and transfers relative to GDP on the one hand, and ethnic fractionalization on the other. One explanation

Table 3.3. Fractionalization, Democracy and Long-Run Growth (dependent variable is growth of per capita GDP)

Variable	ETHNIC		LANGUAGE	
	1	2	3	4
Dummy for the 1960s	0.059 (3.290)	0.153 (5.090)	0.073 (3.897)	0.159 (5.331)
Dummy for the 1970s	0.056 (2.869)	0.155 (4.983)	0.069 (3.418)	0.162 (5.220)
Dummy for the 1980s	0.035 (1.790)	0.137 (4.358)	0.050 (2.420)	0.146 (4.632)
Dummy for Sub-Saharian Africa	−0.008 (−1.628)	−0.014 (−2.493)	−0.006 (−1.371)	−0.010 (−1.805)
Dummy for Latin America and the Caribbean	−0.016 (−4.521)	−0.012 (−3.017)	−0.020 (−5.324)	−0.017 (−4.087)
Log of initial income	−0.004 (−1.619)	−0.019 (−3.933)	−0.006 (−2.274)	−0.019 (−4.029)
Log of schooling	0.012 (2.842)	0.007 (1.351)	0.013 (3.108)	0.010 (1.959)
Assassinations		−23.495 (−2.423)		−14.057 (−1.045)
Financial Depth		0.012 (1.951)		0.012 (1.897)
Black Market premium		−0.021 (−4.828)		−0.023 (−5.169)
Fiscal Surplus/GDP		0.117 (3.060)		0.131 (3.520)
Log of telephones per worker		0.006 (2.185)		0.004 (1.610)
Fractionalization	−0.014 (−1.856)	−0.002 (−0.233)	−0.017 (−2.187)	−0.008 (−0.877)
Democracy	0.001 (0.867)	0.003 (1.833)	0.002 (1.390)	0.002 (2.064)
Fractionalization * Democracy	−0.002 (−1.230)	−0.005 (−1.871)	−0.003 (−1.885)	−0.005 (−2.489)
No of Observations	82; 87; 93	40; 69; 66	80; 85; 90	39; 68; 65
R-squared	.23; .19; .34	.33; .46; .53	.21; .26; .27	.35; .52; .52

(t-statistics in parentheses)
Estimated using Seemingly Unrelated Regressions: a separate regression for each ten year period.

Table 3.4. Fractionalization, Democracy and Long-Run Growth (dependent variable is growth of per capita GDP)

Variable	ETHNIC 1	LANGUAGE 3
Dummy for the 1960s	0.118 (4.689)	0.138 (5.593)
Dummy for the 1970s	0.115 (4.356)	0.135 (5.197)
Dummy for the 1980s	0.096 (3.562)	0.117 (4.426)
Dummy for Sub-Saharian Africa	-0.005 (-1.053)	-0.003 (-0.668)
Dummy for Latin America and the Caribbean	-0.017 (-4.793)	-0.020 (-5.267)
Log of initial income	-0.012 (-3.398)	-0.014 (-4.247)
Log of schooling	0.012 (2.878)	0.012 (2.979)
Fractionalization	-0.149 (-3.510)	-0.170 (-4.135)
Fractionalization * log of initial income	0.017 (3.233)	0.020 (3.769)
Democracy	0.001 (0.665)	0.001 (1.228)
Fractionalization * Democracy	-0.002 (-1.067)	-0.003 (-1.944)
No of Observations	82; 87; 93	80; 85; 90
R-squared	.21; .33; .30	.20; .39; .25

(t-statistics in parentheses)
Estimated using Seemingly Unrelated Regressions: a separate regression for each ten year period.

is that altruism does not travel well across ethnic lines. Relating this point to the model above, one can view redistributive policies as a "public good" in a society that values equality as a public benefit. On this point, a comparison between United States and Europe seems especially suggestive. In the United States, welfare spending and redistributive policies are much smaller than in Europe, consistent with the fact that the United States is much more racially and ethnically diverse than most countries in Continental Europe, a point explored in much detail by Alesina and Glaeser (2004). One implication of this analysis is that, to the extent that Western European countries will become more ethnically fragmented, their welfare systems will be under stress.

■　■　■

A line of research by Alesina and Spolaore (1997, 2003), Alesina, Spolaore, and Wacziarg (2000), and Spolaore and Wacziarg (2002) emphasizes the role of racial conflict as a determinant of the number and size of countries. The argument is as follows. The size of a country emerges from a trade-off between the benefits of scale (broadly defined) and the cost of heterogeneity of preferences in the population. Benefits of size include economies of scale in the production of some public goods, internalization of policy externalities, the size of the market, defense and protection from foreign aggression, and regional insurance schemes. The costs of heterogeneity arise because, in large and diverse countries, individuals with different preferences have to share common policies so the average utility of these policies is decreasing with heterogeneity. Empirically, racial fragmentation is often associated with differences in preferences, so racial cleavages are a major determinant of the determination of borders, secessions, and various centrifugal forces.[9]

A potentially testable implication of this approach is that, as the benefits of size diminish, then it becomes more likely that countries can split into more homogenous smaller political entities. One building bloc of this argument is of course that openness to trade is particularly beneficial for small countries. Results by Ades and Glaeser (1999), Alesina, Spolaore, and Wacziarg (2000), and Alcala and Ciccone (2004) suggest that, as freedom of trade increases, the benefit of size for economic growth diminishes. In a completely autarkic world, the political size of a country also determines its economic size; in a world of free trade they become

more disjoint. That is, from an "economic" point of view (our production of private goods in the simple model above), trade makes economic size "larger." On the other hand, since countries can retain their independence while trading, they do not have to share common public policies on which there are differences of opinions. In ethnically diverse societies, then, increased economic integration should make it more likely that conflicts are resolved with breakdown of countries. Some insights on this issue can be gathered from the political science literature on partition as a solution to ethnic civil war, supported among others by Chaim Kaufmann (1996, 1998). A critical assessment of the view that separation is the best solution for civil wars generated by ethnic conflict is provided by Nicholas Sambanis (2000), who uses a cross sectional data set of all civil wars since 1944 and estimates the probability of partition as a function of the type of civil war (ethnic/religious as opposed to ideological) and of several socioeconomic factors, among which ethnic heterogeneity of the population.

The relationship between ethnic heterogeneity and the likelihood of country breakdowns is also mediated by the role of natural resources, and this is a particularly relevant issue for developing countries. Natural resource discoveries tend to be located in remote areas at the periphery of a country, as resources more centrally located have likely been discovered already. It is often the case that people living in peripheral areas have ethnic identities that do not coincide with the majority of the country as a whole. The availability of new natural resources makes these regions more economically viable on their own and therefore increases pressure for separation or autonomy.[10]

In addition to economies of scale, another benefit of country size is defense and protection from aggressions, so as the world becomes more peaceful one should observe centrifugal forces. Alesina and Spolaore (2003) discuss historical evidence, arguing that this implication is consistent with the data concerning the evolution of country size, international trade, and threats of conflicts. Recently, the collapse of the Soviet Union, by reducing the threat of an East–West conflict, has certainly facilitated political separatism in Eastern Europe. Huntington (1998) notes how the end of the Cold War allowed the realignment of peoples into countries that better reflected homogenous "civilizations." In most cases, this movement meant breakdown of countries and in a few cases movement toward reunification.

Finally, an important issue is the relationship between ethnic heterogeneity, country formation, and democracy. Alesina and Spolaore (2003) discuss the effect of authoritarian systems on measured racial, linguistic, or religious fragmentation and country size. Dictators prefer large countries for several reasons. One is that they can extract rents from larger populations, another one is that they can support with size their bellicose attitudes. Historically, one of the main problems of dictators has been to repress ethnic conflict in an attempt to create artificially homogeneous countries—an issue to which we return below when we discuss the endogeneity of the notion of fragmentation. In fact, dictators often use racial hatred to create support for the dominance of one group over others, a result consistent with models and empirical evidence by Glaeser (2002). One of the implications of this artificial repression of diversity is that centrifugal forces typically explode when dictators fall, as happened for example in the Soviet Union, Spain, Yugoslavia, and Iraq. Fearon (1998) provides an insightful game theoretic model of civil wars that follow the collapse of dictators.

6. Conclusions and Policy Implications

We proposed a model in which public good provisions was lower in fragmented societies while productivity may be positively related to variety. Is the evidence consistent with it? We certainly found overwhelming evidence supporting the first part of the preposition. As for the productivity effects of diversity, the picture is complex. It is somehow easy to point to economic failures of fractionalized societies, but this is not a general phenomenon. Rich democratic societies work well with diversity, in the case of the United States very well in terms of growth and productivity. Even within the developing world, similar levels of ethnic diversity are associated with very different degrees of conflict and interethnic cooperation. Useful theoretical progress would incorporate in a model like this more realistic institutional features that would distinguish cases in which the economy manages to actually take advantage more or less well of the potential benefits of variety in production.

What are the policy implications of all of the above? The issue is quite difficult and politically charged and it is relevant in at least two areas: immigration policies and local policies that may increase or decrease racial integration. The implication of promoting racial homogeneity is unappealing and probably incorrect both in the short and in the long run. Laitin (1994) provides an interesting example concerning language in Ghana. After independence, this country faced the question of which language to adopt as the official one. Using English had the advantage of being understood by most and of not favoring one ethnic group over another. On the other hand, it was the language of a colonizer. Laitin argues that a solution with multiple languages may dominate that of a single homogenous language. The benefit of homogeneity had to be traded off against other considerations (national pride, ethnic balance, etc.).[11] On the other hand, peaceful separation and country breakdown may be perfectly reasonable solutions to racial or cultural diversity.

Globalization also has important implications for ethnic politics. To the extent that small countries can prosper in a world of free trade, then peaceful separatism of certain minorities should not be viewed as threatening, at least from an economic point of view. As far as domestic social policy is concerned, the question is to what extent favoring racial mixing (say with affirmative action) promotes harmony, an issue that would require an entirely separate paper. The starting point would be Arend

Lijphart's (1977) seminal contribution that provides a notion of power sharing denoted as "consociational democracy." The key features of this type of democracy should be a coalition government in which "all significant segments of the plural society" are represented, with a proportionality system, a mutual veto, and a federalist structure.[12] He highlights the conditions under which power sharing is likely to succeed, namely, a relative balance of power and economic equality among the different groups. Most importantly, he argues that different groups are most likely to find an agreement when they have to face *external* threats. This makes power sharing schemes difficult to implement and ultimately unstable in some developing countries (e.g., Africa) where most threats to the state come from within. Among recent examples of power sharing agreements that have failed due to internal conflicts are those of Angola and Rwanda. On the other hand, South Africa and Somaliland have managed to successfully implement consociationalist schemes. Ian S. Spears (2002) reports that, in addition to the presence of an "external" threat (Mogadishu), in the case of Somaliland a deeply rooted tradition of power sharing among the elders of local clans may have contributed to the viability of such schemes. However, this calls into question the effectiveness of power sharing as a means of *generating* interethnic cooperation: indeed power sharing may well be the *result* of preexisting attitudes toward interethnic cooperation. Aghion, Alesina, and Trebbi (2004a) in fact report that racial and ethnic fractionalization are empirically inversely related to forms of consociativism and widespread proportional representation.[13]

The issue of multiethnicity is especially relevant for current Europe. In fact, while the United States has been a melting pot throughout most of its history, Western European countries have been much more ethnically homogeneous. However, with the opening of borders within the European Union and its expansion to the East, in addition to increasing migration from Africa and other neighboring areas, members countries of the European Union will become less and less homogeneous; in fact the issue of multiethnicity will be one of the major challenges for Europe in the near future.

With this survey, we have tried to assess the costs and benefits of ethnic fragmentation and the policy issues arising in diverse societies. In a more and more integrated world, the question of how different people can peacefully interact is the critical problem for the next many decades.

NOTES

1. A "business counterpart" of the preference element in diversity may be seen in the theories of "customer discrimination." According to these theories, businesses whose employees reflect the ethnic mix of the communities in which they operate perform better than those who do not, as customer satisfaction increases from interacting with service providers similar to themselves.

2. In principle, various ethnic groups could segregate within the same jurisdiction and use different public goods. However, segregation is often imperfect, may entail other costs, and some public goods are by nature jurisdiction wide.

3. An early and never published paper by David Canning and Marianne Fay (1993) used ethnic fractionalization as an instrument for growth.

4. Arcand, Guillaumont, and Guillaumont Jeanneney (2000) note that African countries constitute only 27 of the 172 observations in Easterly and Levine's main regression, and highlight the potential sample selection bias generated by the fact that the data is missing precisely for those countries (in Africa) that have experienced slower growth.

5. In fact, several countries in Latin America appear as more fractionalized compared to Easterly and Levine's classification using this more comprehensive index. See Alesina et al. (2003) for more details.

6. These results are very similar to those reported by Alesina et al. (2003). The only difference is that they use both a linear and a quadratic term for initial per capita income. We use only the linear

one because below we explore interactions of the initial level of income with other variables and we want to keep a simpler specification. In any case results with a quadratic term for initial income are very similar for our variables of interest.

7. This is a well known and common stumbling block for anybody who has tried to estimate empirically the costs and benefit of democracy on economic variables, a vast literature that we do not review here; see Jose Tavares and Wacziarg (2001) for one of the most recent and careful contributions.

8. Another variable that is correlated with racial fragmentation is "latitude" and this high correlation makes it sometimes difficult to disentangle the two effects separately, although it is unclear why latitude per se (leaving aside its possible effects on GDP per capita) should affect public policies. Often both variables (latitude and fragmentation) used together are insignificant while they are significant if used separately.

9. Patrick Bolton and Gerard Roland (1997) explore how income differences and redistribution may lead to break down of countries.

10. We are grateful to a referee for suggesting this point.

11. For a recent application to language diversity in the European Union and a measure of the "disenfranchisement" that would arise from a reduction in the number of EU working languages, see Victor Ginsburgh, Ignacio Ortuno-Ortin, and Shlomo Weber (forthcoming).

12. Lijphart (1977), p. 25.

13. Note that while proportional representation and consociationalist schemes may diffuse racial tension, their presence is also empirically associated with difficulties in pursuing adequate fiscal policies, larger budget deficits, and macroeconomic policy instability. For extensive empirical evidence, see Torsten Persson and Guido Tabellini (2003).

REFERENCES

Ades, Alberto F., and Edward L. Glaeser. 1995. "Trade and Circuses: Explaining Urban Giants." *Quarterly Journal of Economics*, 110(1): 195–227.

Ades, Alberto F., and Edward L. Glaeser. 1999. "Evidence on Growth, Increasing Returns, and the Extent of the Market." *Quarterly Journal of Economics*, 114(3): 1025–45.

Aghion, Philippe, Alberto Alesina, and Francesco Trebbi. 2004a. "Endogenous Political Institutions." *Quarterly Journal of Economics*, 119(2): 565–611.

Aghion, Philippe, Alberto Alesina, and Francisco Trebbi. 2004b. "Choosing Electoral Rules: Evidence from US Cities." Unpublished.

Alcala, Francisco, and Antonio Ciccone. 2004. "Trade and Productivity." *Quarterly Journal of Economics*, 119(2): 613–46.

Alesina, Alberto, Reza Baqir, and William Easterly. 1999. "Public Goods and Ethnic Divisions." *Quarterly Journal of Economics*, 114(4): 1243–84.

Alesina, Alberto, Reza Baqir, and William Easterly. 2000. "Redistributive Public Employment." *Journal of Urban Economics*, 48(2): 219–41.

Alesina, Alberto, Reza Baqir, and Caroline Hoxby. 2004. "Political Jurisdictions in Heterogeneous Communities." *Journal of Political Economy*, 112(2): 348–96.

Alesina, Alberto, Robert J. Barro, and Silvana Tenreyro. 2002. "Optimal Currency Areas," in *NBER Macroeconomics Annual 2002.* Mark Gertler and Kenneth Rogoff, eds. Cambridge: MIT Press, 301–55.

Alesina, Alberto, Arnaud Devleeschauwer, William Easterly, Sergio Kurlat, and Romain Wacziarg. 2003. "Fractionalization." *Journal of Economic Growth*, 8(2): 155–94.

Alesina, Alberto, and Edward L. Glaeser. 2004. *Fighting Poverty in the US and Europe: A World of Difference.* Oxford and New York: Oxford University Press.

Alesina, Alberto, Edward Glaeser, and Bruce Sacerdote. 2001. "Why Doesn't the United States Have a European-Style Welfare State?" *Brookings Papers on Economic Activity*, 2: 187–254.

Alesina, Alberto, and Eliana La Ferrara. 2000. "Participation in Heterogeneous Communities." *Quarterly Journal of Economics*, 115(3): 847–904.

Alesina, Alberto, and Eliana La Ferrara. 2002. "Who Trusts Others?" *Journal of Public Economics*, 85(2): 207–34.

Alesina, Alberto, and Enrico Spolaore. 1997. "On the Number and Size of Nations." *Quarterly Journal of Economics*, 112(4): 1027–56.

Alesina, Alberto, and Enrico Spolaore. 2003. *The Size of Nations.* Cambridge: MIT Press.

Alesina, Alberto, Enrico Spolaore, and Romain Wacziarg. 2000. "Economic Integration and Political Disintegration." *American Economic Review*, 90(5): 1276–96.

Alesina, Alberto, and Romain Wacziarg. 1998. "Openness, Country Size and Government." *Journal of Public Economics*, 69(3): 305–21.

Anderson, Benedict. 1983. *Imagined Communities.* London: Verso.

Arcand, Jean-Louis, Patrick Guillaumont, and Sylviane Guillaumont Jeanneney. 2000. "How to Make a Tragedy: On the Alleged Effect of Ethnicity on Growth." *Journal of International Development*, 12(7): 925–38.

Bannon, Alicia, Edward Miguel, and Daniel Posner. 2004. "Sources of Ethnic Identification in Africa." University of California at Los Angeles. Mimeo.

Barr, Abigail. 2003. "Trust and Expected Trustworthiness: Experimental Evidence from Zimbabwean Villages." *Economic Journal*, 113(489): 614–30.

Bates, Robert H. 2000. "Ethnicity and Development in Africa: A Reappraisal." *American Economic Review*, 90(2): 131–34.

Berman, Eli. 2000. "Sect, Subsidy, and Sacrifice: An Economist's View of Ultra-Orthodox Jews." *Quarterly Journal of Economics*, 115(3): 905–53.

Bernard, Tanguy, Alain de Janvry, and Elisabeth Sadoulet. 2004. "Social Resistance to Institutional Change: Explaining the Emergence of Differentiating Organizations in Rural Senegal." University of California at Berkeley. Mimeo.

Biggs, Tyler, Mayank Raturi, and Pradeep Srivastava. 2002. "Ethnic Networks and Access to Credit: Evidence from the Manufacturing Sector in Kenya." *Journal of Economic Behavior and Organization*, 49(4): 473–86.

Bigsten, Arne, Peter Kimuyu, and Karl Lundvall. 2000. "Informality, Ethnicity, and Productivity: Evidence from Small Manufacturers in Kenya." Göteborg University Department of Economics Working Paper No. 27.

Blanchard, Olivier Jean, and Lawrence F. Katz. 1992. "Regional Evolutions." *Brookings Papers on Economic Activity* 1: 1–61.

Bloch, Francis, and Vijayendra Rao. 2001. "Statistical Discrimination and Social Assimilation." *Economics Bulletin*, 10(2): 1–5.

Bolton, Patrick, and Gerard Roland. 1997. "The Breakup of Nations: A Political Economy Analysis." *Quarterly Journal of Economics*, 112(4): 1057–90.

Bossert, Walter, Conchita D'Ambrosio, and Eliana La Ferrara. 2005. "A Generalized Index of Fractionalization." Bocconi University and University of Montreal. Mimeo.

Bossert, Walter, Prasanta K. Pattanaik, and Yongsheng Xu. 2003. "Similarity of Options and the Measurement of Diversity." *Journal of Theoretical Politics*, 15(4): 405–21.

Brender, Adi. 2004. "Ethnic Segregation and the Quality of Local Governments in the Minority's Localities: Local Tax Collection in the Israeli–Arab Municipalities." Unpublished.

Buchanan, James M., and Roger L. Faith. 1987. "Secession and the Limits of Taxation: Toward a Theory of Internal Exit." *American Economic Review*, 77(5): 1023–31.

Burns, Nancy. 1994. *The Formation of American Local Governments: Private Values in Public Institutions.* New York: Oxford University Press.

Calabrese, Stephen, Glenn Cassidy, and Dennis Epple. 2002. "Local Governments, Fiscal Structure, and Metropolitan Consolidation." *Brookings–Wharton Papers on Urban Affairs 2002*: 1–32.

Canning, David, and Marianne Fay. 1993. "The Role of Infrastructures in Economic Growth." Unpublished.

Caselli, Francesco, and Wilbur J. Coleman. 2002. "On the Theory of Ethnic Conflict." Harvard University. Unpublished.

Collier, Paul. 2000. "Ethnicity, Politics, and Economic Performance." *Economics and Politics*, 12(3): 225–45.

Collier, Paul. 2001. "Implications of Ethnic Diversity." *Economic Policy*, 32(16): 127–66.

Collier, Paul, and Jan Willem Gunning. 1999. "Explaining African Economic Performance." *Journal of Economic Literature*, 37(1): 64–111.

Costa, Dora L., and Matthew E. Kahn. 2003a. "Civic Engagement and Community Heterogeneity: An Economist's Perspective." *Perspectives on Politics*, 1(1): 103–11.

Costa, Dora L., and Matthew E. Kahn. 2003b. "Understanding the Decline in American Social Capital, 1952–1998." *Kyklos*, 56(1): 17–46.

Dayton-Johnson, Jeff. 2000. "The Determinants of Collective Action on the Local Commons: A Model with Evidence from Mexico." *Journal of Development Economics*, 62(1): 181–208.

Demange, Gabrielle. 2005. "Group Formation: The Interaction of Increasing Returns and Preferences Diversity." In *Group Formation in Economics: Networks, Clubs, and Coalitions.* Gabrielle Demange and Myrna Wooders, eds. Cambridge: Cambridge University Press.

Demange, Gabrielle, and Myrna Wooders. 2005. *Group Formation in Economics: Networks, Clubs, and Coalitions.* Cambridge: Cambridge University Press.

Dudley, Geoff. 1991. "Scale, Aggregation, and the Modifiable Area Unit Problem." *The Operational Geographer*, 9(3): 28–33.

Easterly, William. 2001. "Can Institutions Resolve Ethnic Conflict?" *Economic Development and Cultural Change*, 49(4): 687–706.

Easterly, William, and Ross Levine. 1997. "Africa's Growth Tragedy: Policies and Ethnic Divisions." *Quarterly Journal of Economics*, 112(4): 1203–50.

Ellickson, Bryan, Birgit Grodal, Suzanne Scotchmer, and William R. Zame. 1999. "Clubs and the Market." *Econometrica*, 67(5): 1185–1217.

Epple, Dennis, and Thomas Romer. 1991. "Mobility and Redistribution." *Journal of Political Economy*, 99(4): 828–58.

Esteban, Joan, and Debraj Ray. 1994. "On the Measurement of Polarization." *Econometrica*, 62(4): 819–51.

Fafchamps, Marcel. 2000. "Ethnicity and Credit in African Manufacturing." *Journal of Development Economics*, 61(1): 205–35.

Fafchamps, Marcel. 2004. *Market Institutions in Sub-Saharan Africa: Theory and Evidence.* Cambridge: MIT Press.

Fearon, James D. 1998. "Commitment Problems and the Spread of Ethnic Conflict," in *The International Spread of Ethnic Conflict: Fear, Diffusion, and Escalation.* David Lake and Donald Rothschild, eds. Princeton: Princeton University Press, 107–26.

Fearon, James D. 1999. "Why Ethnic Politics and 'Pork' Tend to Go Together." Stanford University. Unpublished.

Fearon, James D. 2002. "Fractionalization and Civil Wars." Stanford University. Unpublished.

Fearon, James D. 2003. "Ethnic and Cultural Diversity by Country." *Journal of Economic Growth*, 8(2): 195–222.

Fearon, James D., and David D. Laitin. 1996. "Explaining Interethnic Cooperation." *American Political Science Review*, 90(4): 715–35.

Fearon, James D., and David D. Laitin. 2003. "Ethnicity, Insurgency, and Civil War." *American Political Science Review*, 97(1): 75–90.

Fisman, Raymond J. 1999. "Trade Credit and Productive Efficiency in Developing Economies." Columbia University. Mimeo.

Fisman, Raymond J. 2003. "Ethnic Ties and the Provision of Credit: Relationship-Level Evidence from African Firms." *Advances in Economic Analysis and Policy*, 3(1): Article 4.

Florida, Richard. 2002a. "Bohemia and Economic Geography." *Journal of Economic Geography*, 2(1): 55–71.

Florida, Richard. 2002b. "The Economic Geography of Talent." *Annals of the Association of American Geographers*, 92(4): 743–55.

Friedman, David. 1977. "A Theory of the Size and Shape of Nations." *Journal of Political Economy*, 85(1): 59–77.

Garfinkel, Michelle. 2004. "On the Stability of Group Formation: Managing the Conflict Within." *Conflict Management and Peace Science*, 21(1): 43–68.

Ginsburgh, Victor, Ignacio Ortuno-Ortin, and Shlomo Weber. Forthcoming. "Disenfranchisement in Linguistically Diverse Societies: The Case of the European Union." *Journal of the European Economic Association.*

Glaeser, Edward L. 2002. "The Political Economy of Hatred." Harvard University. Unpublished.

Glaeser, Edward L., David Laibson, Jose A. Scheinkman, and Christine L. Soutter. 2000. "Measuring Trust." *Quarterly Journal of Economics*, 115(3): 811–46.

Glaeser, Edward L., Jose A. Scheinkman, and Andrei Shleifer. 1995. "Economic Growth in a Cross-Section of Cities." *Journal of Monetary Economics*, 36(1): 117–43.

Goldin, Claudia, and Lawrence F. Katz. 1999. "Human Capital and Social Capital: The Rise of Secondary School in America, 1910 to 1940." *Journal of Interdisciplinary History*, 29(4): 683–723.

Greif, Avner. 1993. "Contract Enforceability and Economic Institutions in Early Trade: the Maghribi Traders' Coalition." *American Economic Review*, 83(3): 525–48.

Gurr, Ted. 1996. *Minorities at Risk Dataset*. University of Maryland.

Habyarimana, James, Macartan Humphreys, Daniel Posner, and Jeremy Weinstein. 2004. "Ethnic Identifiability: An Experimental Approach." University of California, Los Angeles. Mimeo.

Hong, Lu, and Scott E. Page. 1998. "Diversity and Optimality," Santa Fe Institute Working Paper 98-08-077.

Horowitz, Donald L. 1985. *Ethnic Groups in Conflict*. Berkeley: University of California Press.

Horowitz. Donald L. 2001. *The Deadly Ethnic Riot*. Berkeley: University of California Press.

Humphreys, Macartan, and Habaye ag Mohamed. 2002. "Senegal and Mali: A Comparative Study of Rebellions in West Africa." Paper presented at the World Bank/Center for United Nations Studies Conference, Yale University, 12–15 April 2002.

Humphreys, Macartan, Daniel M. Posner, and Jeremy M. Weinstein. 2002. "Ethnic Identity, Collective Action, and Conflict: An Experimental Approach." Harvard University and UCLA. Unpublished.

Huntington, Samuel P. 1998. *The Clash of Civilizations and the Remaking of the World Order*. New York: Simon and Schuster.

Jackson, Susan E. and Marian N. Ruderman, eds. 1996. *Diversity in Work Teams: Research Paradigms for a Changing Workplace*. Washington, D.C.: American Psychological Association.

Jehiel, Philippe, and Suzanne Scotchmer. 2001. "Constitutional Rules of Exclusion in Jurisdiction Formation." *Review of Economic Studies*, 68(2): 393–413.

Karlan, Dean S. 2003. "Social Capital and Group Banking." Princeton University. Mimeo.

Katzenstein, Peter J. 1985. *Small States in World Markets: Industrial Policy in Europe*. Ithaca: Cornell University Press.

Kaufmann, Chaim D. 1996. "Possible and Impossible Solutions to Ethnic Civil Wars." *International Security*, 20(4): 136–75.

Kaufmann, Chaim D. 1998. "When All Else Fails: Ethnic Population Transfers and Partitions in the Twentieth Century." *International Security*, 23(2): 120–56.

Keefer, Philip, and Stephen Knack. 2000. "Polarization, Politics, and Property Rights: Links between Inequality and Growth," World Bank Policy Research Working Paper 2418.

Khwaja, Asim I. 2000. "Can Good Projects Succeed in Bad Communities? Collective Action in the Himalayas." Harvard University. Mimeo.

Kochan, Thomas, Katerina Bezrukova, Robin Ely, Susan Jackson, Aparna Joshi, Karen Jehn, Jonathan Leonard, David Levine, and David Thomas. 2002. "The Effects of Diversity on Business Performance: Report of the Diversity Research Network." MIT Sloan School of Management. Mimeo.

Kyriacou, Andreas P. 2005. "Rationality, Ethnicity and Institutions: A Survey of Issues and Results." *Journal of Economic Surveys*, 19(1): 23–42.

La Ferrara, Eliana. 2002a. "Inequality and Group Participation: Theory and Evidence from Rural Tanzania." *Journal of Public Economics*, 85(2): 235–73.

La Ferrara, Eliana. 2002b. "Self-Help Groups and Income Generation in the Informal Settlements of Nairobi." *Journal of African Economies*, 11(1): 61–89.

La Ferrara, Eliana. 2003a. "Kin Groups and Reciprocity: A Model of Credit Transactions in Ghana." *American Economic Review*, 93(5): 1730–51.

La Ferrara, Eliana. 2003b. "Solidarity in Heterogeneous Communities," in *Cultural Diversity vs. Economic Solidarity*. Philippe van Parjis, ed. Brussels: DeBoeck University.

La Ferrara, Eliana, and Angelo Mele. 2003. "Racial Segregation and Public School Expenditure." Bocconi University. Mimeo.

La Porta, Rafael, Florencio Lopez-de-Silanes, Andrei Shleifer and Robert Vishny. 1999. "The Quality of Government." *Journal of Law, Economics, and Organization*, 15(1): 222–79.

Laitin, David D. 1994. "The Tower of Babel as a Coordination Game: Political Linguistics in Ghana." *American Political Science Review*, 88(3): 622–34.

Laitin, David D. 1995. "Marginality: A Microperspective." *Rationality and Society*, 7(1): 31–57.

Laitin, David D. 1998. *Identity in Formation: The Russian-Speaking Populations in the Near Abroad.* Ithaca: Cornell University Press.

Laitin, David D. 2000. "What is a Language Community?" *American Journal of Political Science*, 44(1): 142–54.

Lazear, Edward P. 1999a. "Globalisation and the Market for Team-Mates." *Economic Journal*, 109(454): C15–40.

Lazear, Edward P. 1999b. "Culture and Language." *Journal of Political Economy*, 107(6): S95–126.

Levinson, David. 1998. *Ethnic Groups Worldwide: A Ready Reference Handbook.* Phoenix: Oryx Press.

Lijphart, Arend. 1977. *Democracy in Plural Societies: A Comparative Exploration.* New Haven: Yale University Press.

Lijphart, Arend. 1999. *Patterns of Democracy.* New Haven: Yale University Press.

Luttmer, Erzo F. P. 2001. "Group Loyalty and the Taste for Redistribution." *Journal of Political Economy*, 109(3): 500–528.

Macours, Karen. 2003. "Ethnic Divisions, Interlinkages and Search Costs in the Guatemalan Land Rental Market." Johns Hopkins University. Unpublished.

Madison, James. 1787. "Federalist Papers n. 11."

Massey, Douglas S., and Nancy A. Denton. 1988. "The Dimensions of Racial Segregation." *Social Forces*, 67(2): 281–315.

McMillan, Margaret. 2003. *Paris 1919: Six Months that Changed the World.* New York: Random House.

Miguel, Edward, and Mary Kay Gugerty. Forthcoming. "Ethnic Diversity, Social Sanctions, and Public Goods in Kenya." *Journal of Public Economics.*

Milchtaich, Igal, and Eyal Winter. 2002. "Stability and Segregation in Group Formation." *Games and Economic Behavior*, 38(2): 318–46.

Montalvo, José García, and Martha Reynal-Querol. 2002. "Why Ethnic Fractionalization? Polarization, Ethnic Conflict and Growth." Universitat Pompeu Fabra. Unpublished.

Nopo, Hugo, Jaime Saavedra, and Maximo Torero. 2002. "Ethnicity and Earnings in Urban Peru." GRADE. Mimeo.

Okten, Cagla, and Una Okonkwo Osili. 2004. "Contributions in Heterogeneous Communities: Evidence from Indonesia." *Journal of Population Economics*, 17(4): 603–26.

Olson, Mancur. 1965. *The Logic of Collective Action.* Cambridge: Harvard University Press.

Openshaw, Stan, and Peter J. Taylor. 1979. "A Million or So Correlation Coefficients: Three Experiments on the Modifiable Area Unit Problem," in *Statistical Applications in the Spatial Sciences.* N. Wrigley, ed. London: Pion, 127–44.

O'Reilly, Charles L., Katherine Y. Williams, and Sigal G. Barsade. 1997. "Demography and Group Performance." Unpublished.

Ottaviano, Gianmarco, and Giovanni Peri. 2003. "The Economic Value of Cultural Diversity: Evidence from US Cities." University of California, Davis. Unpublished.

Ottaviano, Gianmarco and Giovanni Peri. 2004. "Cities and Cultures." Unpublished.

Persson, Torsten, and Guido Tabellini. 2003. *The Economic Effects of Constitutions.* Cambridge: MIT Press.

Posner, Daniel N. 2004a. "Measuring Ethnic Fractionalization in Africa." *American Journal of Political Science*, 48(4): 849–63.

Posner, Daniel N. 2004b. "The Political Salience of Cultural Difference: Why Chewas and Tumbukas are Allies in Zambia and Adversaries in Malawi." *American Political Science Review*, 98(4): 529–45.

Poterba, James M. 1997. "Demographic Structure and the Political Economy of Public Education." *Journal of Policy Analysis and Management*, 16(1): 48–66.

Prat, Andrea. 2002. "Should a Team Be Homogeneous?" *European Economic Review*, 46(7): 1187–1207.

Rappaport, Jordan. 1999. "Local Growth Empirics." CID Working Paper, Harvard University, No. 23.

Rauch, James E. 2001. "Business and Social Networks in International Trade." *Journal of Economic Literature*, 39(4): 1177–1203.

Rauch, James E., and Alessandra Casella, eds. 2001. *Networks and Markets.* New York: Russell Sage Foundation.

Rauch, James E., and Alessandra Casella. 2003. "Overcoming Informational Barriers to International Resource Allocation: Prices and Ties." *Economic Journal*, 113(484): 21–42.

Ray, Debraj, and Rajiv Vohra. 1999. "A Theory of Endogenous Coalition Structures." *Games and Economic Behavior*, 26(2): 286–336.

Ray, Debraj, and Rajiv Vohra. 2001. "Coalitional Power and Public Goods." *Journal of Political Economy*, 109(6): 1355–84.

Richard, Orlando, Thomas Kochan, and Amy McMillan-Capehart. 2002. "The Impact of Visible Diversity on Organizational Effectiveness: Disclosing the Contents in Pandora's Black Box." *Journal of Business and Management*, 8(3): 265–92.

Rogowski, Ronald. 1987. "Trade and the Variety of Democratic Institutions." *International Organization*, 41(2): 203–23.

Sambanis, Nicholas. 2000. "Partition as a Solution to Ethnic War: An Empirical Critique of the Theoretical Literature." *World Politics*, 52(4): 437–83.

Sethi, Rajiv, and Rohini Somanathan. 2004. "Inequality and Segregation." *Journal of Political Economy*, 112(6): 1296–1321.

Spears, Ian S. 2002. "Africa: The Limits of Power Sharing." *Journal of Democracy*, 13(3): 123–36.

Spolaore, Enrico, and Romain T. Wacziarg. 2002. "Borders and Growth." NBER Working Paper 9223.

Srinivas, Mysore Narasimhachar. 1966. *Social Change in Modern India.* Berkeley: University of California Press.

Tajfel, Henri, Michael Billig, Robert P. Bundy, and Claude Flament. 1971. "Social Categorization and Intergroup Behavior." *European Journal of Social Psychology*, 1: 149–78.

Tavares, Jose, and Romain Wacziarg. 2001. "How Democracy Affects Growth." *European Economic Review*, 45(8): 1341–78.

Tiebout, Charles M. 1956. "A Pure Theory of Local Public Expenditure." *Journal of Political Economy*, 64(5): 416–24.

Vigdor, Jacob L. 2004. "Community Composition and Collective Action: Analyzing Initial Mail Response to the 2000 Census." *Review of Economics and Statistics*, 86(1): 303–12.

Weitzman, Martin L. 1992. "On Diversity." *Quarterly Journal of Economics*, 107(2): 363–405.

Wilkinson, Steven. 2002. "Memo on Developing Better Indicators of Ethnic and Non-Ethnic Identities," Paper presented at the LICEP 5th Meeting, Stanford University.

Williams, Katherine Y., and Charles A. O'Reilly, III. 1998. "Demography and Diversity in Organizations: A Review of 40 Years of Research," in *Research in Organizational Behavior: An Annual Series of Analytical Essays and Critical Reviews, Volume 20.* B. M. Staw and L. L. Cummings, eds. Greenwich, Conn.: JAI Press, 77–140.

Kate Baldwin and John D. Huber

ECONOMIC VERSUS CULTURAL DIFFERENCES: FORMS OF ETHNIC DIVERSITY AND PUBLIC GOODS PROVISION

Ethnic diversity is widely held to make governance more difficult. Such diversity is associated with low production of public goods; poor economic growth; and high levels of corruption, violence, and civil conflict. But diversity hardly sentences a country to poor political and economic outcomes. Latvia, for example, has better governance indicators than Brazil, and Zambia has better governance indicators than Nigeria, even though these pairs of countries have similar levels of ethnolinguistic fractionalization (ELF). Why, then, do some countries cope more successfully with ethnic diversity than others?

This article addresses this question by focusing on the nature of substantive differences between groups. The vast majority of cross-national evidence about ethnic diversity and governance uses the standard measure of ELF (e.g., Alesina et al. 2003; Alesina and La Ferrara 2005; Collier 2000; Easterly and Levine 1997; La Porta et al. 1999). This measure contains information about the identity and size of groups but incorporates no other information about groups' substantive characteristics. Existing arguments about how ethnic diversity affects governance, however, are typically grounded in the assumption that groups differ from each other in substantively important ways, and posit that these differences underlie governance problems in multiethnic societies.

From *American Political Science Review* 104, no. 4 (November 2010), pp. 644–62.

This article examines two important types of differences between groups—cultural and economic. Our goal is to understand the empirical relationship between such differences and public goods provision across countries. Is diversity more problematic for governance in countries when this diversity is based on strong cultural or economic differences between groups? Do standard empirical results about ethnolinguistic fractionalization still hold when controlling for the cultural or economic differences between groups?

The focus on cultural differences has received substantial attention in the literature on ethnic diversity. Scholars argue that such differences make it more difficult for individuals to cooperate across groups. This may be true for a number of reasons, as Habyarimana et al. (2009) describe. One reason is that ethnic similarities make it easier for individuals to communicate with each other (e.g., Bacharach and Gambetta 2001; Deutsch 1966). The shared languages and social networks of ethnically similar individuals allow them to assess each other's intentions and trustworthiness, and to communicate goals and necessary actions. These individuals experience lower transaction costs when cooperating toward common ends. In addition, ethnically similar individuals should find it easier to sanction each other for failing to cooperate (e.g., Fearon and Laitin 1996; Greif 1994; Miguel and Gugerty 2005). Thus, as the cultural differences between groups in a country grow, public goods should be harder to produce. Although these arguments have been subject to limited cross-national empirical research, a recent paper by Desmet, Ortuo, and Weber (2009) shows that redistribution by the government is lower in countries that have higher levels of linguistic diversity, which is a key indicator of cultural differences.

Economic differences between groups have received less attention in the literature, in part because empirical measures of group-based economic differences across countries have not existed. However, there are good reasons to expect that such differences will affect governance. Group-based economic differences can lead to different group needs with respect to public goods, feelings of alienation or discrimination by some groups, different attitudes toward redistribution across groups, and different "class" identities by different groups. The effect of group economic differences on the policy preferences of group members are likely to be particularly important in affecting governance. If the different economic statuses of groups lead them to prioritize different public goods, then it will be difficult for these groups to reach agreement on which public goods to provide (e.g., Alesina, Baqir, and Easterly 1999; Alesina and Spolaore 1997; Alesina and Drazen 1991). Under these circumstances, politicians may try to win reelection by providing private goods for each group, especially when the number of groups is not too large (Fernández and Levy 2008).

This article demonstrates that it is possible to measure differences in the economic well-being of groups using existing cross-national surveys of citizens. Specifically, we use between-group inequality (BGI), which is a weighted average of the differences in mean incomes across groups in a country, as a measure of economic differences between groups. We then argue that between-group inequality can be satisfactorily measured using surveys such as the Afrobarometer, the World Values Survey (WVS), and the Comparative Study of Electoral Systems (CSES). We combine the measure of between-group inequality with existing measures of ELF and with existing measures of cultural differences between groups that are based on language differences (Desmet, Ortuo, and Weber 2009; Fearon 2003). The data show that these variables measure different things and that the choice between them has an important impact on our understanding of which countries are most ethnically diverse.

Which measure of ethnic diversity shows the strongest association with public goods provision? We do not find a robust empirical relationship between either the standard ELF measure or measures of cultural difference and public goods provision. However, the tests do reveal that between-group inequality has a large, robust negative relationship with public goods provision. Countries with higher levels of inequality between groups have lower levels of public goods, a finding that has important implications for understanding the pathways by which ethnic diversity creates governance problems.

The article is organized as follows. The next section introduces the measures of ethnic differences—cultural fractionalization (CF) and between-group inequality—that are central to the analysis. Because cross-national measures of between-group inequality do not currently exist, the following section describes how they can be created from cross-national surveys. We then compare the measures of cultural fractionalization, between-group inequality, and ethnolinguistic fractionalization with each other. Our main empirical tests follow. We first treat each country as a unit of analysis and use ordinary least squares (OLS) models to test the relationships between each measure and public goods provision. The results show that only BGI has a robust relationship. Between-group economic differences, however, can be caused by policies related to public goods. We therefore also estimate models [not included here] aimed at exploring whether BGI has a causal effect on public goods provision. The final section concludes the article.

Measures of Cultural and Economic Differences Between Groups

The well-known index of ethnolinguistic fractionalization, or *ELF*, measures the probability that two randomly chosen individuals will belong to different groups. It is written as

$$ELF = 1 - \sum_{i=1}^{n} p_i^2,$$

where p_i is the proportion of individuals who belong to group i and n is the number of groups in society.[1] As noted previously, ELF does not include information on the extent of cultural or economic differences across groups. But ELF can be altered to incorporate information about group-based differences.

To measure cultural differences, one approach is to consider language differences between ethnic groups. The importance of language to cultural identity has been emphasized by many scholars (Gellner 1983; Laitin 1994, 1998). Linguistic differences can lead to divergent preferences on linguistic and educational policy; in addition, they make communication between individuals more difficult and are often correlated with social networks (Milroy 1987). As a result, a version of ELF that incorporates information about the extent of linguistic differences between ethnic groups provides a useful measure of the level of cultural differences between groups.

To measure cultural differences, we use a measure first proposed by Greenberg (1956). This measure is a variation on ELF that captures the expected linguistic similarity between two randomly selected individuals in a society, and it has been used by Fearon (2003) to measure cultural fractionalization within societies. * * *

We use Fearon's (2003) measure of linguistic similarity, which he constructed based on the distance between different languages in language trees. Linguists use language trees to classify languages into

families, and then within each family, they subclassify languages into different branches. Fearon's measure is based on the premise that the more branches two languages have in common, the more similar the languages are to each other. In Spain, for example, Spanish and Basque are very different because they come from two different language families (Indo-European and Basque). In contrast, Spanish and Catalan are quite similar, only branching apart from each other at the eighth junction in their language tree.[2] * * * If two groups speak the same language, $r_{ij} = l = 1$, and if two groups speak languages from different linguistic trees, $r_{ij} = l = 0$; otherwise, r_{ij} takes a value between 0 and 1 that is increasing in the number of shared branches of the two group's languages. Desmet, Ortuño-Ortín, and Weber (2009) construct a similar measure but give less weight to having large numbers of shared branches within language trees as compared to being part of the same language tree. We are agnostic about which of these measures is more appropriate and thus include both Fearon's and Desmet, Ortuño-Ortín, and Weber's measures.[3]

Although factors other than language may create cultural barriers between groups, focusing on language differences has considerable merit because it employs an objective criterion that can be measured consistently across countries. It is possible to imagine factors unrelated to language that lead to cultural differences in a country; however, it is more difficult to describe such factors in a way that is as amenable to the level of objectivity and cross-national measurement reliability as the linguistic measures. Cultural fractionalization is therefore a good proxy for the underlying level of cultural differences across groups in a society.

Next consider the measurement of group economic differences. A straightforward and easily interpretable measure of group-based income differences is BGI. This measure is based on the familiar Gini index, but instead of calculating inequality based on each individual's income, it assigns each group's mean income to every member of that group. It can be interpreted as the expected difference in the mean income of the ethnic groups of any two randomly selected individuals. * * *

Although not widely familiar to political scientists, between-group inequality has been studied by economists interested in decomposing inequality into its different components.[4] Milanovic (2005) uses the BGI formula as a proxy for global inequality; his second measure of international inequality calculates a Gini in which each country's mean income is weighted by its population. Mancini, Stewart, and Brown 2008 (see also Mancini 2008) advocate the use of BGI as a measure of group differences in their studies of communal violence. The measure is also similar to the grouped version of the Generalized Ethno-linguistic Fractionalization (GELF) measure that Bossert, D'Ambrosio, and La Ferrara (n.d.) developed and applied to the United States.[5]

Both the Gini and BGI have interpretations related to the Lorenz curve. The Lorenz curve is a graphical illustration of the cumulative distribution of a society's income over different ranges of the income distribution. To draw a Lorenz curve based on individual income differences, each person in society is ranked according to their individual income. The points on the Lorenz curve indicate that y percentage of the society's income accrues to the bottom x percentage of people in the income distribution. In a perfectly equal society, where the "bottom" 10% of people control 10% of the society's income, the "bottom" 20% of people control 20% of the society's income, and so on, the Lorenz curve is equal to the 45-degree line. In any society where there is not perfect equality, the Lorenz curve is typically a convex curve below the 45-degree line. The Gini index is equal to two times the area between the Lorenz curve and the 45-degree line.

BGI is based on a ranking of people *not* by their individual income, but by their ethnic groups' mean income, and thus ignores information about income differences within groups. Each group member is ranked according to the mean income of their ethnic group. Because BGI is based on the proportion of income held by each group, the Lorenz curve for BGI will be a series of straight lines meeting at points where members of one group end and members of the next group begin. BGI is equal to two times the area between the group-based Lorenz curve and the 45-degree line.

Figure 3.3 illustrates BGI using the Lorenz curve for three hypothetical societies, each divided into three groups—group 1, group 2, and group 3—with 35, 40, and 25 members, respectively. Each society has 100 units of income to distribute among these groups. In a completely equal society, group 1 will receive 35 units of wealth, group 2 will receive 40 units of wealth, and group 3 will receive 25 units of wealth. The Lorenz curve will be a straight line because the group occupying the "bottom" 35% of the income distribution controls 35% of the income, the groups occupying the "bottom" 75% of the income distribution control 75% of the income, and so on. This case is depicted by the solid black line. BGI in this case is 0.

In an unequal society, the wealthiest group will control more income per person than the poorest group. The middle line draws the Lorenz curve if group 1 controls only 20% of the income, group 2 controls only 30% of the income, and group 3 controls 50% of the income. In this case, the group occupying the bottom 35% of the income distribution control only 20% of the income, and the two groups occupying the bottom 75% of the income distribution control only 50% of the income. The BGI in this case is 0.275. The bottom line depicts the Lorenz curve in an even more unequal society in which group 1 controls just 5% of the income, group 2 controls 20%, and group 3 controls 75%. In this case, the bottom 75% of the income distribution controls only 25% of the society's income and BGI is 0.55.

Like the Gini, BGI ranges from 0 to 1. It takes on its minimum value of 0 when the average incomes of all groups in society are the same, and it takes on its maximum value of 1 when one infinitely small group controls all the income in society. Put another way, for any level of ELF, BGI will be 0 if all groups have the same mean income. Holding ELF constant, BGI is increasing in the income differences between

Figure 3.3. Graphical Illustration of BGI

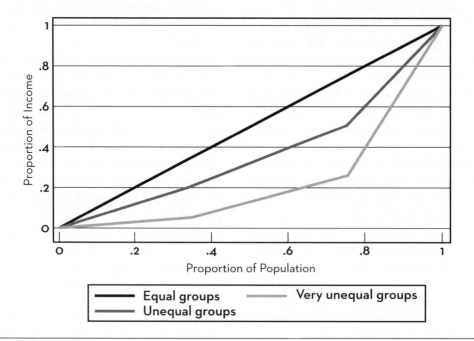

groups. The effect of income differences across groups on BGI will be largest when ELF is largest. BGI will take its largest values when there are many equally sized groups (as with ELF) and when the income differences between the groups are large. Between-group inequality, then, can be viewed as an extension of the ELF that allows income differences between groups to vary. Conversely, ELF can be viewed as a restriction on between-group inequality that holds differences between all groups constant at 1.

Measuring Between-Group Inequality Using Existing Surveys

The main empirical challenge in analyzing the effects of between-group economic differences is constructing national-level measures of BGI for a large set of countries. A number of different scholars have con-structed ELF measures (Alesina et al. 2003; Fearon 2003), and Fearon (2003) and Desmet, Ortuño-Ortín, and Weber (2009) have created measures of cultural fractionalization for almost all the countries in the world. But existing cross-national data sets do not include measures of between-group inequality, in part because BGI requires information on the economic well-being of groups that is not readily available from secondary sources. The construction of BGI for a particular country requires information on both the size of ethnic groups within the coun-try and the economic well-being of these groups. [Fortunately,] existing cross-national surveys—the Afrobarometer, the WVS, and the CSES—can be used to create BGI measures.

The Afrobarometer, WVS, and CSES surveys all contain instruments that make it possible to iden-tify the "ethnicity" of respondents. However, ethnic categories often nest inside broader categories, and as Posner (2004) demonstrates, choices about which groups to include can have a significant impact on the conclusions one draws about the relationship between group diversity and outcomes. A decision rule is therefore necessary to decide which groups are most relevant in a particular country. In this article, we follow the identification of groups made by Fearon (2003) as closely as possible because we believe that Fearon's work is the most careful and theoretically motivated classification of groups that has been completed to date. His seven criteria emphasize groups that are understood as "descent groups" and that are locally viewed as socially or politically consequential. Depending on the country, Fearon's identification of groups may be based on race (e.g., the US), language (e.g., Belgium), religion (e.g., France), tribe (e.g., many African countries), or even some combination of these factors. He draws on a range of secondary sources to identify the size of each group for the vast majority of countries in the world, and the resulting data set provides both a guide for the creation of the BGI measure and a benchmark against which to judge it.

In classifying survey respondents into groups, we mirror as closely as possible the groups used by Fearon. In the US, for example, Fearon identifies four ethnic groups: whites, blacks, Hispanics, and Asians. Variable x051 in the WVS has seven categories: white, black, Hispanic, other, central Asian, south Asian, and east Asian. We convert this sevenfold variable to the Fearon groups by recoding the three Asian groups to "Asian" and dropping "Other." It is not always possible to place all respondents into one of the Fearon groups. In France, for example, he identifies the groups as French, Muslim, and Bretons. Using the CSES, we cannot identify the Bretons, but we can identify the French and Muslims.

* * * We focus on democracies because dictators have little incentive to provide public goods regardless of the ethnic diversity of their countries (Olson 1993; Sen 1999), and the effect of ELF on governance has been found to differ in democratic and authoritarian countries (Collier 2000). We therefore consider only countries that have a Polity 2 score of 1 or higher. Some countries have more than one

survey, and when this occurs, we average BGI scores across the surveys for that country. The resulting 46 countries included in the analysis are listed in Table 3.5.

* * * Is the correlation between the survey data ELF and the Fearon ELF strong? Figure 3.4 plots this relationship for the 46 countries. The survey-based ELF, which takes the average value within countries when there is more than one survey in a country, is obviously very closely related to the Fearon ELF. The Fearon-based measures typically take higher values, particularly at low levels of fractionalization, but the overall correlation is an impressive 0.96 [which is higher than the correlation between Fearon's measures of ELF and Alesina et al.'s (2003) measures of ELF].

The next challenge is measuring group economic well-being. Ideally, one would construct the BGI measure using fine-grained, individual-level income or consumption data, aggregated by group. There currently do not exist a large number of multinational surveys that contain this type of data with appropriate information about group identity, but the Afrobarometer, WVS, and CSES surveys contain coarse measures of each respondents' economic well-being that can be used to evaluate the relative well-being of different groups. Even coarse data on group income differences provides information that can be used to measure BGI.

Each survey measures respondents' income or consumption using a different metric. For example, the WVS survey asks the respondent to answer the following question:

> Here is a scale of incomes and we would like to know in what group your household is, counting all wages, salaries, pension, and other incomes that come in. Just give the letter of the group your household falls into, after taxes and other deductions.

The respondent is given a country-specific scale, typically with 8 to 10 categories, created to be meaningful within each country. Each CSES country survey asks a similar question to the WVS, but

Table 3.5. Countries in Study

Survey	Region					
	Western Europe	Other Europe	Asia	Latin America	Africa	Other
WVS only	Belgium Germany Ireland Netherlands Switzerland	Estonia Georgia Latvia Macedonia Moldova	Bangladesh Indonesia India	Colombia Dominican Republic Uruguay Venezuela		
CSES only	Finland France	Bulgaria Czech Republic Hungary Lithuania Romania Russia Slovenia Ukraine				
Both CSES and WVS	Spain			Brazil Mexico		Australia Canada New Zealand US
Afrobarometer					Benin Botswana Kenya Madagascar Malawi Mali Mozambique Namibia Nigeria Senegal South Africa Zambia	
Total countries	8	13	3	6	12	4

CSES, Comparative Study of Electoral Systems: WVS, World Values Survey.

Figure 3.4. Comparing Ethnolinguistic Fractionalizations (ELFs): Fearon Data versus Survey Data

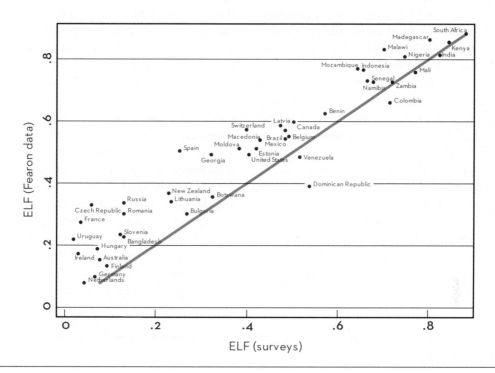

the CSES reports only the income quintiles of the respondents.

The Afrobarometer survey, like most surveys in developing parts of the world, does not have an income variable. For many individuals in these countries, such a question would be meaningless because the individuals have little or no cash income. Instead, the common strategy in such surveys is to ask respondents questions about their access to things crucial to their basic needs. For the Afrobarometer, each survey asks respondents a number of questions of the following type:

Over the past year, how often, if ever, have you or anyone in your family gone without food?

In addition to asking about food, the survey asks about water, medical care, cooking fuel, and cash income. Each variable is coded on a five-point

scale (from 0 to 4) according to how often the respondent has gone without the item. The sum of the responses from these five questions can be used to create an economic well-being metric that ranges from 0 (maximal unmet needs) to 20 (no unmet needs). This index is obviously most useful in distinguishing differences among the least well-off, masking differences that exist among the more well-to-do.

These "income" variables, along with the group identity variables, make it possible to calculate BGI for each survey. In cases where we have multiple surveys for a given country, we average across surveys to create a score for each country.[6] * * * It is reassuring to note that in the survey, whites are richer than Mulattos who are richer than blacks in Brazil; Bulgarians are richer than Turks in Bulgaria; the Flemish are wealthier than the French in Belgium; whites are wealthier than Mestizos and blacks in the

Dominican Republic; Muslims are poorer than the "French" in France; and whites are richer than blacks and Hispanics in the US. In the African countries, where the income measures are most limited in that they only distinguish between differences among the poor, the data still capture the fact that whites and people of mixed race background are wealthier than other ethnic groups in Namibia, the Ibo and Yoruba are richer than the Hausa in Nigeria, and whites, coloureds, and Asians are richer than blacks in South Africa. Thus, in these cases where the income relationships between groups are known, there is considerable face validity in the way that the data rank the relative incomes of groups.

The problem, of course, is that data on between-group economic differences has not been previously collected on a large scale, so little is known about the economic differences between many other groups.

As [another] strategy for exploring how the Afrobarometer's focus on income differences among the poor affect measures of BGI, we conducted simulations. As described in more detail in Appendix 1, the simulated data set contains thousands of societies made up of individuals whose exact income was known. To replicate the Afrobarometer coarsening technique, we assigned all people above a fixed poverty line in the simulated income data to the richest category and then divided the poor into different income levels based on their absolute level of deprivation. We then constructed measures of BGI for each society based on the "true" income variable and the "coarsened" income variable.

Figure 3.5 plots the true BGI (based on the fine-grained income distribution) against the coarsened income data (where income differences exist only at low income levels, as in the Afrobarometer). The dark *xs* represent societies where there are minimal

Figure 3.5. Simulating the Effect of Afrobarometer Data on Estimates of Between-Group Inequality (BGI)

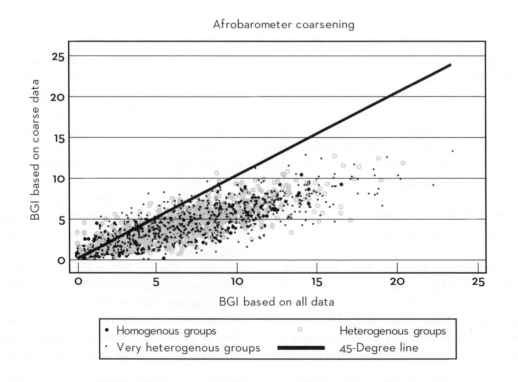

income differences *within* ethnic groups (homogenous groups), the solid gray dots represent societies where there are some income differences *within* ethnic groups (heterogenous groups), and the open gray circles represent societies where there are large income differences *within* ethnic groups (very heterogenous groups). Figure 3.5 also depicts the 45-degree line, making it easy to identify whether "coarsening" leads to overestimates (points above the line) or underestimates (points below the line) of the true BGI. Not surprisingly, we can see that for any assumption about group income heterogeneity and for any of the three coarsening techniques, on average, the coarsened metrics underestimate the true level of between-group inequality. But we also find that the correlation between the true BGI and the BGI based on the coarsened data is very strong, ranging from 0.76 (when groups are most heterogenous) to 0.87 (when groups are most homogenous).

Thus, despite the fact that the Afrobarometer suppresses information about income differences among the nonpoor, it provides measures of BGI that are highly correlated with finer measures of BGI. Furthermore, the Afrobarometer measures are biased in the "right" direction to the extent that they systematically underestimate the true BGI. This should make it more difficult to find differential results of ELF and BGI on public goods provision.

Comparing Ethnolinguistic Fractionalization, Cultural Fractionalization, and Between-Group Inequality

ELF, CF, and BGI measure theoretically distinct concepts. But are the three measures also empirically distinct? Are the countries with the greatest linguistic differences between ethnic groups different from the countries with the greatest economic differences between groups?

Figure 3.6 depicts the relationships between the three measures of ethnic diversity, with each of the measures standarized to have a mean of 0 and a standard deviation of 1. First, consider the relationship between CF and ELF, which is also discussed in Fearon (2003). For his full set of countries, he found that the two measures are highly correlated ($r = 0.79$), with the largest differences occurring in sub-Saharan Africa and Latin America. In our subset of 46 countries, the correlation between ELF and CF is 0.64, somewhat lower than in Fearon's full data set. The top panel in Figure 3.6 shows that the correlation between the two variables is relatively strong throughout the range of ELF, but definitely weakens as ELF grows. A number of countries with high ELF—particularly those in Latin America—have groups that use similar languages. The countries whose diversity rankings are most affected by the switch from ELF to CF are listed in Table 3.6. Colombia ranks 13th in ELF and only 43rd in CF because the various ethnic groups in Colombia all speak Spanish. Madagascar is the second most diverse country in the data using ELF. But all groups in Madagascar speak Malagasy or a closely related language, so Madagascar's CF score ranks only 30th in the data. Russia and Estonia, in contrast, move in the other direction, each increasing 13 places in the country rankings when one switches from ELF to CF. This is because the main language groups in these countries are from different language families.

Second, consider the relationship between ELF and BGI, which is depicted in the middle panel of Figure 3.6. As with the previous comparison, there is a strong correlation between the two variables ($r = 0.62$), but for many countries, their relative ranking depends substantially on which measure is used. Among the low BGI countries, there is a wide range of ELF scores, and among the high ELF scores, there is a wide range of BGI scores. Table 3.7 lists the countries whose diversity rankings are most affected by the change from ELF to BGI. Indonesia is the country that declines the most: it is ranked 7th using ELF but only 23rd using BGI. The

Figure 3.6. Ethnolinguistic Fractionalization (ELF), Cultural Fractionalization (CF), and Between-Group Inequality (BGI) in 46 Countries

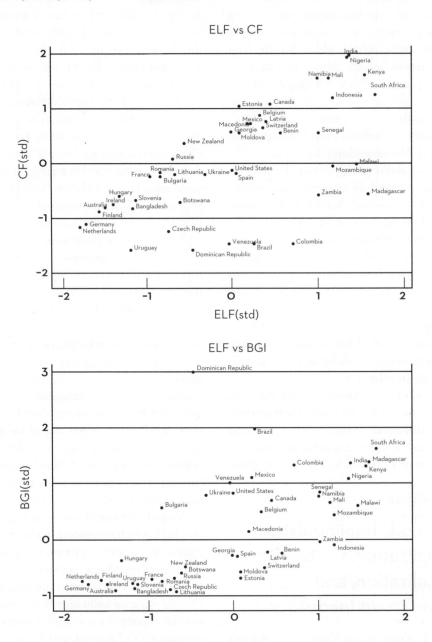

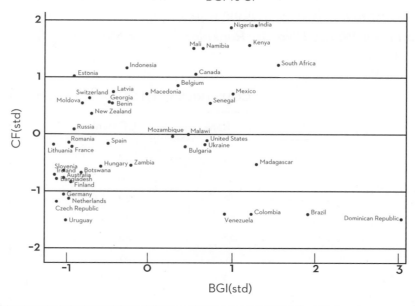

BGI vs CF

Dominican Republic moves sharply in the opposite direction: it is ranked only 29th using ELF but has the highest BGI in the data set.

The bottom panel in Figure 3.6 examines the relationship between CF and BGI. The correlation between these two variables ($r = 0.17$) is quite weak. As is clear in Figure 3.6, a number of countries, particularly in Latin America, have very high levels of between-group inequality but low levels of language difference. Furthermore, there are a number of countries, particularly in eastern and central Europe, where language differences are large, but between-group economic differences are relatively small.

The analysis therefore demonstrates that the three diversity measures, although related, are clearly distinct. The relative rankings of the countries change, at times dramatically, across the different measures. Incorporating information about cultural fractionalization or the economic well-being of groups therefore alters how we understand the relative ethnic diversity of countries.

Group Differences and Public Goods Provision

Although the three measures differ, do the differences matter for understanding the relationship between diversity and public goods provision? Does one of the measures have a stronger relationship with public goods provision than the others, suggesting that it may be the more important factor driving the relationship between ethnic diversity and poor governance outcomes? This section presents results from a series of regression models that analyze the relationship between the measures of diversity and public goods provision.

The models in this section treat a country as the unit of analysis. As noted previously, the survey data used to construct the BGI measures are from the 1996 to 2006 time period. When multiple surveys exist for a given country, we average across the surveys, minimizing measurement error that may be associated with particular surveys. We also average the World Bank's World Development Indicators

Table 3.6. Countries Whose Diversity Rankings Change Most When Switching from ELF to CF

	COUNTRIES WITH LARGEST DECLINE IN RANK		
Country	ELF Rank	CF Rank	Δ Rank
Colombia	13	43	–30
Madagascar	2	30	–28
Brazil	19	42	–23
Zambia	11	31	–20
Venezuela	27	44	–17
Malawi	4	21	–17
Dominican Republic	29	46	–17

	COUNTRIES WITH LARGEST INCREASE IN RANK		
Country	ELF Rank	CF Rank	Δ Rank
Russia	33	20	13
Estonia	22	9	13
Romania	35	24	11
Georgia	26	15	11
New Zealand	30	19	11

CF, cultural fractionalization; ELF, ethnolinguistic fractionalization.

(WDIs) used to measure public goods over the 1996 to 2006 period, which is important given that the WDIs are often missing in particular years. Because ELF and CF are constant over time, the strategy of using a country as a unit of analysis also facilitates comparison of the correlations between the various measures of diversity and public goods provision.

To measure public goods provision, we rely on ten variables in the World Bank's WDIs, each related to government-provided public goods, such as public health, education, public infrastructure,

and the government's taxing capacity. There are a larger number of candidate variables in the WDI data set, but many have large numbers of missing values. We averaged the country values for each variable for the period 1996–2006, and then retained only those variables such that (1) none of the 46 countries had more than 3 missing, and (2) no variable was missing for more than 7 of the 46 countries. The resulting ten variables used in the analysis, with the number of missing countries in brackets, are as follows:

Table 3.7. Countries Whose Diversity Rankings Change Most When Switching from ELF to BGI

	COUNTRIES WITH LARGEST DECLINE IN RANK		
Country	ELF Rank	BGI Rank	Δ Rank
Indonesia	7	23	–16
Lithuania	32	46	–14
Switzerland	17	30	–13
Malawi	4	16	–13
Mozambique	8	20	–12

	COUNTRIES WITH LARGEST INCREASE IN RANK		
Country	ELF Rank	BGI Rank	Δ Rank
Dominican Republic	29	1	28
Bulgaria	36	18	18
Brazil	19	2	17
Venezuela	27	10	17
Ukraine	28	13	15

BGI, between-group inequality; ELF, ethnolinguistic fractionalization.

- Expenditure per student, primary (% of GDP per capita) [7]
- Public spending on education, total (% of GDP) [1]
- Immunization, measles (% of children aged 12–23 months) [0]
- Immunization, DPT (% of children aged 12–23 months) [0]
- Improved sanitation facilities (% of population with access) [7]
- Improved water source (% of population with access) [6]
- Roads, paved (% of total roads) [0]
- Procedures to enforce a contract (number) [0]
- Tax revenue (% of GDP) [4]
- Telephone lines (number per 100 people) [0]

Each variable alone is a noisy predictor of the overall level of public goods provision in a country, susceptible to measurement error that is likely idiosyncratic to particular countries. Therefore, rather than choosing one or more specific variables for analysis, we use the information from all ten variables to create a single measure of the overall level of public goods provision. To this end, we conduct a factor analysis on all ten variables. We then use the

Table 3.8. Factor Analysis of Public Goods Variables

Variable	Factor 1
Primary school spending	0.47
Total public spending on education	0.52
Measles immunizations	0.82
DPT immunizations	0.88
Sanitation facilities	0.91
Water source	0.86
Roads	0.70
Contract enforcement	-0.58
Tax revenue	0.41
Telephone lines	0.85

Eigenvalue of factor 1: 5.21
Proportion of variance explained by factor 1: 0.69

We estimate OLS models with robust standard errors using Public Goods as the dependent variable. The models include several controls. One is the level of economic development [*GDP/capita* (*ln*), measured using purchasing power parity], which is known to have a very strong relationship with the level of public goods provision. Scholars have also emphasized the importance of democracy for public goods provision (e.g., Lake and Baum 2001), and although we focus on countries that are in some sense democratic (achieving Polity 2 scores of greater than or equal to 1), there is considerable variation within our data set regarding the development of democratic institutions and practices. We therefore include *Polity 2* as a control for the level of democratic institutionalization. It is also important to take into account the population of a country. If there are economies of scale, then public goods provision may be largest in the most populous countries. But if the most populous countries present the most challenges to governance, public goods provision may be negatively correlated with population. In the regression models, we standardize each continuous right-hand-side variable to have a mean of 0 and a standard deviation of 1. This makes it straightforward to compare the size of the effects of the different variables. The parentheses in the tables provide the p values for the estimated coefficients.

In Table 3.9, models 1 to 4 include the controls and one of the measures of diversity. Model 1 includes ELF. Consistent with previous research, the coefficient for ELF is in the expected negative direction and is very precisely estimated. Model 2 uses Fearon's cultural fractionalization measure of diversity. The coefficient is in the expected negative direction but is very small and estimated with considerable error. Model 3 uses the Desmet, Ortuño, and Weber measure of cultural fractionalization instead of Fearon's measure. The coefficient has the wrong sign and is also estimated with considerable error. Finally, in model 4, the coefficient for BGI is negative and very precisely estimated. In models including only one measure of ethnic diversity, then,

first dimension of the factor analysis to create the dependent variable, which we call *Public Goods*. The results for the first factor in this factor analysis are shown in Table 3.8. All ten of the variables load strongly on the first factor. The variables with the strongest relationship to the underlying factor, and which therefore receive the greatest weight in the construction of the public goods variable, are immunizations, sanitation, water, and telephone lines, all with factor loadings greater than 0.8. Two variables have a loading that is less than 0.5—Tax Revenue and Primary School Spending—but each variable still has a relatively strong relationship with the underlying factor. The first factor explains 69% of the variance in these ten variables. Figure 3.7 plots Public Goods against the log of GDP per capita (measured in purchasing power parity). The two variables are obviously strongly correlated, but at any level of economic development, and in particular at lower levels of development, there exists variation in the level of public goods.

Figure 3.7. Public Goods Provision and National Wealth

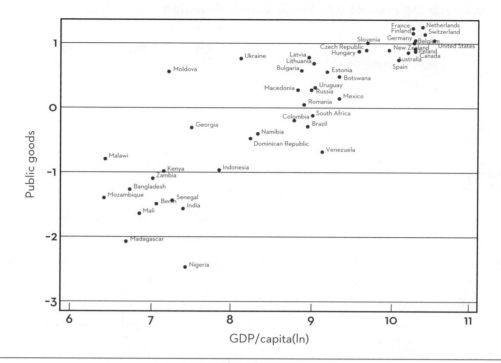

ELF and BGI have a clear relationship to public goods provision, but cultural differences do not.

Next we examine the results when we include measures of each form of diversity in the same model. Model 5 uses the Fearon measure of cultural fractionalization, and model 6 uses the Desmet, Ortuño, and Weber measure. In both models, the coefficient for cultural fractionalization is very imprecisely estimated and has the wrong sign. The models also show that when BGI and ELF are included in the same model, the relationship between ELF and Public Goods disappears. The ELF coefficient now has the wrong sign and is estimated with large error, whereas the coefficient from BGI remains negatively and rather precisely estimated, especially in model 6.

We have estimated a wide range of additional models, and the results for cultural fractionalization are consistently estimated with very large error and often have the wrong sign. Because there is no empirical support for including this variable and it

is strongly correlated with ELF, model 7 presents results when only BGI and ELF are included (along with the controls). ELF is positive, although it is estimated with considerable error, and the coefficient for BGI remains negative and precisely estimated. These results from Table 3.9 therefore suggest the possibility that in previous research claiming a correlation between ELF and public goods provision, the relationship was actually being driven by between-group economic differences. * * *

Conclusion

The empirical analysis tells a clear story. First, and most important, we find a strong and robust relationship between the level of public goods provision and between-group inequality. In contrast, neither traditional measures of ELF nor cultural differences between groups (measured using information about

Table 3.9. Group Differences and Public Goods Provision I

	(1)	(2)	(3)	(4)	(5)	(6)	(7)
ELF	−0.210	—	—	—	0.009	0.072	0.096
	(0.005)				(0.950)	(0.473)	(0.327)
CF-Fearon	—	−0.007	—	—	0.089	—	—
		(0.928)			(0.383)		
CF-Desmet	—	—	−0.024	—	—	0.069	—
			(0.764)			(0.326)	
BGI	—	—	—	−0.137	−0.133	−0.166	−0.168
				(0.041)	(0.093)	(0.023)	(0.026)
GDP(ln)	0.635	0.733	0.737	0.492	0.474	0.461	0.506
	(0.000)	(0.000)	(0.000)	(0.007)	(0.007)	(0.008)	(0.004)
Population	−0.140	−0.173	−0.168	−0.200	−0.237	−0.240	−0.216
	(0.004)	(0.002)	(0.001)	(0.001)	(0.000)	(0.000)	(0.001)
Polity 2	0.123	0.159	0.149	0.172	0.207	0.224	0.190
	(0.351)	(0.272)	(0.265)	(0.146)	(0.094)	(0.074)	(0.124)
Afrobarometer	—	—	—	−0.620	−0.684	−0.761	−0.676
				(0.038)	(0.038)	(0.025)	(0.036)
WVS	—	—	—	−0.043	−0.015	−0.061	−0.015
				(0.747)	(0.911)	(0.679)	(0.916)
CSES	—	—	—	0.141	0.177	0.145	0.196
				(0.447)	(0.327)	(0.461)	(0.287)
Constant	0.000	0.000	0.000	0.149	0.149	0.192	0.143
	(1.000)	(1.000)	(1.000)	(0.282)	(0.277)	(0.177)	(0.293)
Adj. R squared	0.787	0.761	0.761	0.832	0.829	0.829	0.830
N	46	46	46	46	46	46	46

Notes: P value based on robust standard errors are in parentheses. BGI between-group inequality; CF, cultural fractionalization; CSES, Comparative Study of Electoral Systems; ELF, ethnolinguistic fractionalization; GDP, gross domestic product; WVS, World Values Survey.

the languages groups speak) has such a relationship. Second, although there are clear limits on how hard we can push our data, we have suggestive evidence that between-group economic differences lead to lower public goods provision, particularly in the less established democracies. Third, we find that when controlling for group economic differences, the overall level of inequality itself has no impact on public goods provision. The analysis therefore strongly suggests that paying more attention to group economic differences will yield strong dividends in efforts to understand the impacts of ethnic diversity and inequality on governance.

Several avenues for future research are worth pursuing. Although the BGI data employed in this article provide useful information about group economic differences, it is important to continue the search for more fine-grained measures of group income to estimate BGI. It is equally important to explore the possibility of measuring cultural differences using factors other than language, such as religion. Additional insight could also be achieved by exploring other definitions of groups in efforts to determine how robust the results are to alternative categorizations of the ethnic groups themselves.

Second, the analysis here assumes that the effect of between-group differences on governance is the same across political systems. But do some institutional forms for governance mitigate or exacerbate the effect of BGI on outcomes? We find, for example, that the negative effect of BGI is largest when the most well-developed democracies are eliminated from the data set, suggesting that there may be an interaction between the level of democracy and BGI. And it may be the case that particular forms of democracy may mediate the effect of BGI. Does federalism, for example, soften the impact of between-group differences on governance by giving groups autonomy to provide the public goods they most value?

Finally, we have provided some evidence that BGI has a causal impact on public goods provision. But as we noted, there are good reasons to suspect that public goods policy also affects between-group inequality. It is certainly possible—perhaps even likely—that these two variables are mutually and negatively reinforcing: low public goods provision exacerbates group economic differences, which impedes public goods provision, which exacerbates group-based inequality, and so forth. We cannot use our data to explore this issue, but it is clear that group-based economic differences do not arise by chance—they are the result of political processes that unfold over time, and that are reinforced or ameliorated by government policy decisions. Between-group inequality might therefore be rightly construed as a measure of group-based discrimination, and the level of such discrimination clearly varies across countries with similar levels of ethnic or cultural fractionalization. Why, then, do some countries have higher levels of group-based inequality than others? And what role does public goods provision play in answering this question? In light of the findings in this study, addressing this question should play a large role in improving our understanding of how between-group economic differences affect policy making.

NOTES

1. The measure of ELF used in this article is from Fearon (2003) and is based on data from the early 1990s. We discuss his system for identifying groups later.

2. Both languages follow these seven branches: Indo-European, Italic, Romance, Italo-Western, Western, Gallo-Iberian, Ibero-Romance. At this point, they diverge in their linguistic classification, with Spanish on the West-Iberian branch and Catalan on the East-Iberian branch.

3. The main difference between these measures is the α they use in calculating cultural fractionalization; however, they also rely on different data to identify ethnic groups. Fearon uses his classification of ethnic groups, based on data from the early 1990s, and Desmet, Ortuño, and Weber (2009) use data from the 2005 *Ethnologue*.

4. On the decomposition of the Gini into its between, within, and overlap components, see Pyatt (1976) and Yitzhaki and Lerman (1991).

5. The innovation of the GELF is that it does not *require* one to impose *ex ante* group partitions onto the data. However, in research where scholars are interested in comparing exogenously defined groups, GELF is very similar to BGI. The GELF equivalent of BGI would be based on a "similarity matrix," where individuals from the same ethnic group have the same income and where the similarity between members of any two different ethnic groups is a function of the distance between the mean incomes of the two ethnic groups (normalized to range from 0 to 1).

6. There are three usable WVS surveys from African countries, each of which also has an Afrobarometer survey. Because the Afrobarometer measure of "income" is quite different than the measure of income from WVS, and because we are taking averages when we have multiple surveys, we do not include these three WVS surveys in our analysis. When these three WVS surveys are included, the results are not affected. For WVS and CSES, we impute missing values for income using standard demographic variables. There are few missing values for the relevant variables in the Afrobarometer surveys.

REFERENCES

Alesina, Alberto, Reza Baqir, and William Easterly. 1999. "Public Goods and Ethnic Divisions." *Quarterly Journal of Economics* 114 (4): 1243–84.

Alesina, Alberto, Arnaud Devleeschauwer, William Easterly, Sergio Kurlat, and Romain Wacziarg. 2003. "Fractionalization." *Journal of Economic Growth* 8 (2): 155–94.

Alesina, Alberto, and Allen Drazen. 1991. "Why Are Stabilizations Delayed?" *American Economic Review* 81 (5): 1170–88.

Alesina, Alberto, and Eliana La Ferrara. 2005. "Ethnic Diversity and Economic Performance." *Journal of Economic Literature* 43 (3): 762–800.

Alesina, Alberto, and Enrico Spolaore. 1997. "On the Number and Size of Nations." *Quarterly Journal of Economics* 112 (4): 1027–56.

Bacharach, Michael, and Diego Gambetta. 2001. "Trust as Type Detection." In *Trust and Deception in Virtual Societies*, eds. Christiano Castelfranchi and Yao-Hua Tan. Norwell, MA: Kluwer Academic, 1–26.

Bardhan, Pranab. 2000. "Irrigation and Cooperation: An Empirical Analysis of 48 Irrigation Communities in South India." *Economic Development and Cultural Change* 48: 847–65.

Bossert, Walter, Conchita D'Ambrosio, and Eliana La Ferrara. n.d. "A Generalized Index of Fractionalization." *Economica*. Forthcoming.

Collier, Paul. 2000. "Ethnicity, Politics and Economic Performance." *Economics and Politics* 12 (3): 222–45.

Dayton-Johnson, Jeff. 2000. "The Determinants of Collective Action on the Local Commons: A Model with Evidence from Mexico." *Journal of Development Economics* 62 (1): 181–208.

Desmet, Klaus, Ignacio Ortuño-Ortín, and Shlomo Weber. 2009. "Linguistic Diversity and Redistribution." *Journal of the European Economic Association* 7 (6): 1291–318.

Deutsch, Karl. 1966. *Nationalism and Social Communication*. Cambridge: MIT Press.

Easterly, William, and Ross Levine. 1997. "Africa's Growth Tragedy: Policies and Ethnic Divisions." *Quarterly Journal of Economics* 112 (4): 1203–50.

Fearon, James. 2003. "Ethnic and Cultural Diversity by Country." *Journal of Economic Growth* 8 (2): 195–222.

Fearon, James, and David Laitin. 1996. "Explaining Interethnic Cooperation." *American Political Science Review* 90 (4): 715–35.

Fernández, Raquel, and Gilat Levy. 2008. "Diversity and Redistribution." *Journal of Public Economics* 92: 925–43.

Gellner, Ernest. 1983. *Nations and Nationalism*. Ithaca, NY: Cornell University Press.

Greenberg, Joseph H. 1956. "The Measurement of Linguistic Diversity." *Language* 32: 109–15.

Greif, Avner. 1994. "Cultural Beliefs and the Organization of Society." *Journal of Political Economy* 102 (5): 912–50.

Habyarimana, James, Macartan Humphreys, Daniel Posner, and Jeremy Weinstein. 2009. *Coethnicity: Diversity and Dilemmas of Collective Action*. New York: Russell Sage Press.

Khwaja, Asim. 2009. "Can Good Projects Succeed in Bad Communities?" *Journal of Public Economics* 93 (7–8): 899–916.

Knack, Stephen, and Philip Keefer. 1997. "Does Social Capital Have an Economic Payoff? A Cross-Country Investigation." *Quarterly Journal of Economics* 112 (4): 1251–88.

Laitin, David. 1994. "The Tower of Babel as a Coordination Game: Political Linguistics in Ghana." *American Political Science Review* 88 (3): 622–34.

Laitin, David. 1998. *Identity in Formation: The Russian-Speaking Population in the Near Abroad*. Ithaca, NY: Cornell University Press.

Lake, David, and Matthew Baum. 2001. "The Invisible Hand of Democracy: Political Control and the Provision of Public Services." *Comparative Political Studies* 34 (6): 587–621.

La Porta, Rafael, Florencio Lopez-de-Silanes, Andrei Shleifer, and Robert W. Vishny. 1999. "The Quality of Government." *The Journal of Law, Economics, and Organization* 15 (1): 22–79.

Mancini, Luca. 2008. "Horizontal Inequality and Communal Violence: Evidence from Indonesian Districts." In *Horizontal Inequalities and Conflict: Understanding Group Violence in Multiethnic Societies*, ed. Frances Stewart. London: Palgrave, 106–35.

Mancini, Luca, Frances Stewart, and Graham K. Brown. 2008. "Approaches to the Measurement of Horizontal Inequalities." In *Horizontal Inequalities and Conflict: Understanding Group Violence in Multiethnic Societies*, ed. Francis Stewart. London: Palgrave McMillan, 85–101.

Massey, Douglas S., and Nancy A. Denton. 1988. "The Dimensions of Residential Segregation." *Social Forces* 67(2): 281–315.

Miguel, Edward, and Mary Kay Gugerty. 2005. "Ethnic Diversity, Social Sanctions, and Public Goods in Kenya." *Journal of Public Economics* 89 (11–12): 2325–68.

Milanovic, Branko. 2005. *Worlds Apart: Measuring International and Global Inequality*. Princeton, NJ: Princeton University Press.

Milroy, Lesley. 1987. *Language and Social Networks*. Oxford: Wiley-Blackwell.

Olson, Mancur. 1993. "Dictatorship, Democracy and Development." *American Political Science Review* 87 (3): 567–76.

Posner, Daniel. 2004. "Measuring Ethnic Fractionalization in Africa." *American Journal of Political Science* 48 (4): 849–63.

Pyatt, Graham. 1976. "On the Interpretation and Disaggregation of Gini Coefficients." *The Economic Journal* 86: 243–55.

Sen, Amartya. 1999. *Development as Freedom*. New York: Anchor Books.

Solt, Frederick. 2009. "Standardizing the World Income Inequality Database." *Social Science Quarterly* 90 (2): 231–42.

Uslaner, Eric M. 2002. *The Moral Foundations of Trust*. New York: Cambridge University Press.

Uslaner, Eric M. 2008. *Corruption, Inequality, and the Rule of Law: The Bulging Pocket Makes the Easy Life*. New York: Cambridge University Press.

Yitzhaki, Shlomo, and Robert Lerman. 1991. "Income Stratification and Income Inequality." *Review of Income and Wealth* 37 (3): 313–29.

4 POLITICAL ECONOMY

Comparative political economy (and its close cousin, international political economy) is among the liveliest areas of research and theorizing in present-day comparative politics. Given the importance and the state of the global economy, that should not surprise us. Among the principal questions this subfield addresses are: (1) what policies and institutions are best for economic growth; (2) how do choices of economic institutions affect the functioning of democracies; and (3) what options are open to domestic governments in their policies toward the international economy.

Early political economists overwhelmingly favored a minimalist government. Indeed, the field of political economy, the concept of laissez-faire economic liberalism, and the modern discipline of economics are all generally considered to have originated with Adam Smith's *The Wealth of Nations*, published in 1776. Many of Smith's most important ideas, particularly the division and specialization of labor, were already familiar to literate Europeans from earlier works, including Bernard Mandeville's witty and enduring poem *The Fable of the Bees*, first published in 1705, and the French *Encyclopédie* of the 1750s. But it was Smith who, through plain examples and seemingly irrefutable logic, convinced three generations of European and American elites that free markets and minimal government would maximize economic growth. The excerpts from *The Wealth of Nations* included here encapsulate Smith's arguments on the division of labor, the self-regulating nature of capitalism (the "invisible hand"), the advantages of free trade, and the importance of limited but effective government. These ideas remain crucial in understanding what kinds of government policies favor, or impede, economic growth and prosperity.

Perhaps the most fundamental, and certainly the most counterintuitive, argument in political economy is that free international trade (an absence of tariffs, quotas, or other restrictions) benefits all countries, and particularly poorer countries.[1] Virtually every serious student of political economy today, as well as political theorists and practitioners of almost all ideological persuasions—liberals, conservatives, social democrats, and most Marxists[2]—from poor and rich countries alike, believe in free trade and expanding world markets. Mercantilists of the Right and Left—usually xenophobes in the former case and antiglobalization activists in the latter—have constituted, at least until recently, a small "nut fringe" on the ends of the political spectrum and have been derided by virtually every serious student of politics or economics.

If the classical laissez-faire endorsement of free trade remains almost universally accepted, another major tenet—that of the minimalist state—does not. In the classical analyses of Adam Smith, to most nineteenth-century thinkers, and even to Libertarians today, government taxation and expenditure always entail "deadweight costs," and are justified only to provide collective goods that voluntary or market-based action would undersupply: defense against foreign enemies, enforcement of contracts, maintenance of roads and harbors, and public education.[3] Yet in modern times, government expenditures in advanced economies have grown enormously, apparently at little cost to growth or productivity (see more on this in Chapter 7). Meanwhile, efforts to establish flourishing free-market economies in post-Communist and developing countries have frequently failed, not least because of deficient or perverse government institutions.

So how important are institutions? What kinds matter most? And why do so many countries end up with weak or bad institutions? In a pathbreaking 1991 article, "Institutions," the economic historian and Nobel laureate Douglass North brought history and logic to bear on these questions: What institutions are most essential to make markets work? Why do they sometimes fail to develop? And to what extent can that failure be reversed? North contended that "path dependence," including a country's colonial experience (for example, the seemingly clear difference between former Spanish and former English colonies in North America), played a large role.

Some critics held that geography mattered more than institutions: a tropical climate, or wide distances between major ports and trade routes, would inhibit development no matter how good institutions were. But in fundamental papers by Daron Acemoglu, Simon Johnson, and James Robinson in 2001 and 2002 (summarized here in Acemoglu's "Root Causes," 2003), the geographical argument was refuted, and the sources of institutional difference were clarified. Precisely the regions of the world that were now poorest, they demonstrated, were often richest around 1500, when the European wave of colonization began. Because Europeans sought to plunder those richer regions, they established predatory institutions (rapacious governments, insecure property rights) that have often survived down to the present day. When Europeans colonized originally poorer and less densely settled regions (Australia, North America), and especially where the climate was more favorable to European survival, they could augment wealth only by attracting settlers, minimizing the burdens of government, and establishing clear property rights. The result had been a "reversal of fortune," in which originally poor regions wound up with good institutions, rapid economic growth, and ultimate wealth, while originally rich regions inherited bad institutions that impoverished them.

If this view is right, then the specific kinds of institutions that colonialists imposed should have had a lasting effect. This is exactly what Bannerjee and Iyer (2005) find in their pioneering article on the heritage of colonialism in India. By a historical accident, British rule in India imposed two kinds of landownership institutions: up to about 1830, under largely Conservative administrations, one that favored traditional owners of large estates; after that, under largely Liberal administrations, the promotion of a small-holding "yeomanry" that entailed the breaking up of large estates.

Bannerjee and Iyer show that, by sheer historical accident, the two kinds of areas had no significant differences in features like quality of soil or annual rainfall. Yet even today, the "yeoman" areas provide significantly better public services (education, clean water, roads, etc.) than the "landlord" areas. It appears that, much as Thomas Jefferson argued, family farmers are politically powerful and assertive in a way that tenant farmers or landless laborers cannot be; and that the pattern of land-ownership, once established, may change very little over centuries.

Increasingly, international institutions and policies matter in political economy. Domestic institutions obviously affect the ability of countries to attract foreign investment, but they cannot be the whole story. Among the most important policy choices for domestic governments in the international economy is whether to adopt fixed or floating exchange rates.[4] To attract foreign investment and encourage domestic exporters, governments may well prefer the predictability of a fixed exchange rate. Yet they also want to keep their capital markets open (that is, allow easy movement of funds from or to their country) and maintain monetary autonomy (the ability to raise interest rates in a boom, or to cut them in a recession). As the eminent Harvard economist Greg Mankiw reiterates in "The Trilemma of International Finance," we have known since the 1950s that only two of those objectives can actually be attained at once. Because it has proven almost impossible in present-day conditions to impose capital controls (limitations on the movement of funds between countries), and since most nations want to maintain monetary autonomy, this "trilemma" has in practice forced almost all countries to adopt floating exchange rates, with large consequences—most significant, that central banks, rather than elected officials, control most macroeconomic policy.

NOTES

1. This is not the same thing as saying that every *person* benefits in every country. When the United States trades with China, skilled U.S. workers gain but unskilled U.S. workers lose, whereas in China, at least initially, unskilled workers gain but skilled workers lose. Nonetheless, the gains of skilled U.S. workers far outweigh American unskilled workers' losses, just as the gains of low-skill Chinese workers exceed the losses of skilled Chinese workers.

2. Karl Marx himself was as avid a supporter of free trade as Adam Smith had been, and every early Marxist party in Europe was free-trading. Social Democrats today, in all developed countries, are among the strongest supporters of trade expansion. The late Communist regimes walled themselves off from world markets, but in this—as in many other aspects—they were diametrically opposed to original Marxism.

3. Even Adam Smith endorsed governmental support for education, since the social gain (the overall productivity gain to the economy from a person's acquiring greater skills) exceeds the private return (the increase in the educated person's earnings), meaning that purely private schooling will always undersupply education.

4. Where the exchange rate is fixed, the government guarantees that, for example, one Hong Kong dollar will always exchange for one U.S. dollar. Where the exchange rate floats, as for example the Euro does

versus the dollar, the exchange rate is determined by actual trading of the currencies and can vary from day to day, and even hour to hour. Thus the Euro at its inception (2001) traded at 85 U.S. cents; by 2007 it had risen to $1.60; and now (2012) is worth about $1.30.

Adam Smith
AN INQUIRY INTO THE NATURE AND CAUSES OF THE WEALTH OF NATIONS

Of the Division of Labour[1]

The greatest improvement[2] in the productive powers of labour, and the greater part of the skill, dexterity, and judgment with which it is any where directed, or applied, seem to have been the effects of the division of labour.

The effects of the division of labour, in the general business of society, will be more easily understood, by considering in what manner it operates in some particular manufactures.

■   ■   ■

To take an example, therefore,[3] from a very trifling manufacture; but one in which the division of labour has been very often taken notice of, the trade of the pin-maker; a workman not educated to this business (which the division of labour has rendered a distinct trade),[4] nor acquainted with the use of the machinery employed in it (to the invention of which the same division of labour has probably given occasion), could scarce, perhaps, with his utmost industry, make one pin in a day, and certainly could not make twenty. But in the way in which this business is now carried on, not only the whole work is a peculiar trade, but it is divided into a number of branches, of which the greater part are likewise peculiar trades. One man draws out the wire, another straights it, a third cuts it, a fourth points it, a fifth grinds it at the top for receiving the head; to make the head requires two or three distinct operations; to put it on, is a peculiar business, to whiten the pins is another; it is even a trade by itself to put them into the paper; and the important business of making a pin is, in this manner, divided into about eighteen distinct operations, which, in some manufactories, are all performed by distinct hands, though in others the same man will sometimes perform two or three of them.[5] I have seen a small manufactory of this kind where ten men only were employed, and where some of them consequently performed two or three distinct operations. But though they were very poor, and therefore but indifferently accommodated with the necessary machinery, they could, when they exerted themselves, make among them about twelve pounds of pins in a day. There are in a pound upwards of four thousand pins of a middling size. Those ten persons, therefore, could make among them upwards of forty-eight thousand pins in a day. Each person, therefore, making a tenth part of forty-eight thousand pins, might be considered as making

From Edwin Cannan, ed., Adam Smith, *An Inquiry into the Nature and Causes of the Wealth of Nations* (Chicago: The University of Chicago Press, 1976. Originally published in 1776.) Book I, pp. 7–19, Book IV, pp. 474–81, 208–9. Some notes have been omitted; those that follow are Cannan's.

four thousand eight hundred pins in a day. But if they had all wrought separately and independently, and without any of them having been educated to this peculiar business, they certainly could not each of them have made twenty, perhaps not one pin in a day; that is, certainly, not the two hundred and fortieth, perhaps not the four thousand eight hundredth part of what they are at present capable of performing, in consequence of a proper division and combination of their different operations.

In every other art and manufacture, the effects of the division of labour are similar to what they are in this very trifling one; though, in many of them, the labour can neither be so much subdivided, nor reduced to so great a simplicity of operation. The division of labour, however, so far as it can be introduced, occasions, in every art, a proportionable increase of the productive powers of labour. The separation of different trades and employments from one another, seems to have taken place, in consequence of this advantage. This separation too is generally carried furthest in those countries which enjoy the highest degree of industry and improvement; what is the work of one man in a rude state of society, being generally that of several in an improved one.

■   ■   ■

This great increase of the quantity of work which, in consequence of the division of labour, the same number of people are capable of performing,[6] is owing to three different circumstances; first to the increase of dexterity in every particular workman; secondly, to the saving of the time which is commonly lost in passing from one species of work to another; and lastly, to the invention of a great number of machines which facilitate and abridge labour, and enable one man to do the work of many.[7]

■   ■   ■

It is the great multiplication of the productions of all the different arts, in consequence of the divi-

sion of labour, which occasions, in a well-governed society, that universal opulence which extends itself to the lowest ranks of the people. Every workman has a great quantity of his own work to dispose of beyond what he himself has occasion for; and every other workman being exactly in the same situation, he is enabled to exchange a great quantity of his own goods for a great quantity, or, what comes to the same thing, for the price of a great quantity of theirs. He supplies them abundantly with what they have occasion for, and they accommodate him as amply with what he has occasion for, and a general plenty diffuses itself through all the different ranks of the society.

■   ■   ■

Of the Principle which gives Occasion to the Division of Labour

This division of labour, from which so many advantages are derived, is not originally the effect of any human wisdom, which foresees and intends that general opulence to which it gives occasion.[8] It is the necessary, though very slow and gradual, consequence of a certain propensity in human nature which has in view no such extensive utility; the propensity to truck, barter, and exchange one thing for another.

* * * [T]his propensity * * * is common to all men, and to be found in no other race of animals, which seem to know neither this nor any other species of contracts. * * *

Nobody ever saw a dog make a fair and deliberate exchange of one bone for another with another dog.[9] Nobody ever saw one animal by its gestures and natural cries signify to another, this is mine, that yours; I am willing to give this for that.

■   ■   ■

But man has almost constant occasion for the help of his brethren, and it is in vain for him to expect it from their benevolence only. He will be more likely to prevail if he can interest their self-love in his favour, and show them that it is for their own advantage to do for him what he requires of them. Whoever offers to another a bargain of any kind, proposes to do this. Give me that which I want, and you shall have this which you want, is the meaning of every such offer; and it is in this manner that we obtain from one another the far greater part of those good offices which we stand in need of. It is not from the benevolence of the butcher, the brewer, or the baker, that we expect our dinner, but from their regard to their own interest. We address ourselves, not to their humanity but to their self-love, and never talk to them of our own necessities but of their advantages. Nobody but a beggar chuses to depend chiefly upon the benevolence of his fellow-citizens.

■　■　■

As it is by treaty, by barter, and by purchase, that we obtain from one another the greater part of those mutual good offices which we stand in need of, so it is this same trucking disposition which originally gives occasion to the division of labour. In a tribe of hunters or shepherds a particular person makes bows and arrows, for example, with more readiness and dexterity than any other. He frequently exchanges them for cattle or for venison with his companions; and he finds at last that he can in this manner get more cattle and venison, than if he himself went to the field to catch them. From a regard to his own interest, therefore, the making of bows and arrows grows to be his chief business, and he becomes a sort of armourer. Another excels in making the frames and covers of their little huts or moveable houses. He is accustomed to be of use in this way to his neighbours, who reward him in the same manner with cattle and with venison, till at last he finds it his interest to dedicate himself entirely to this employment, and to become a sort of house-carpenter. In the same manner a third becomes a smith or a bra-zier; a fourth a tanner or dresser of hides or skins, the principal part of the clothing of savages. And thus the certainty of being able to exchange all that surplus part of the produce of his own labour, which is over and above his own consumption, for such parts of the produce of other men's labour as he may have occasion for, encourages every man to apply himself to a particular occupation, and to cultivate and bring to perfection whatever talent or genius he may possess for that particular species of business.[10]

■　■　■

Of Restraints upon the Importation from Foreign Countries of such Goods as can be Produced at Home

■　■　■

No regulation of commerce can increase the quantity of industry in any society beyond what its capital can maintain. It can only divert a part of it into a direction into which it might not otherwise have gone; and it is by no means certain that this artificial direction is likely to be more advantageous to the society than that into which it would have gone of its own accord.

Every individual is continually exerting himself to find out the most advantageous employment for whatever capital he can command. It is his own advantage, indeed, and not that of the society which he has in view. But the study of his own advantage naturally, or rather necessarily leads him to prefer that employment which is most advantageous to the society.

■　■　■

. . . [E]very individual . . . necessarily endeavours so to direct that industry, that its produce may be of the greatest possible value.

The produce of industry is what it adds to the subject or materials upon which it is employed. In proportion as the value of this produce is great or small, so will likewise be the profits of the employer. But it is only for the sake of profit that any man employs a capital in the support of industry; and he will always, therefore, endeavour to employ it in the support of that industry of which the produce is likely to be of the greatest value, or to exchange for the greatest quantity either of money or of other goods.

But the annual revenue of every society is always precisely equal to the exchangeable value of the whole annual produce of its industry, or rather is precisely the same thing with that exchangeable value. As every individual, therefore, endeavours as much as he can both to employ his capital in the support of domestic industry, and so to direct that industry that its produce may be of the greatest value; every individual necessarily labours to render the annual revenue of the society as great as he can. He generally, indeed, neither intends to promote the public interest, nor knows how much he is promoting it. By preferring the support of domestic to that of foreign industry, he intends only his own security; and by directing that industry in such a manner as its produce may be of the greatest value, he intends only his own gain, and he is in this, as in many other cases, led by an invisible hand to promote an end which was no part of his intention. Nor is it always the worse for the society that it was no part of it. By pursuing his own interest he frequently promotes that of the society more effectually than when he really intends to promote it. I have never known much good done by those who affected to trade for the public good. It is an affectation, indeed, not very common among merchants, and very few words need be employed in dissuading them from it.

What is the species of domestic industry which his capital can employ, and of which the produce is likely to be of the greatest value, every individual, it is evident, can, in his local situation, judge much better than any statesman or lawgiver can do for him. The statesman, who should attempt to direct private people in what manner they ought to employ their capitals, would not only load himself with a most unnecessary attention, but assume an authority which could safely be trusted, not only to no single person, but to no council or senate whatever, and which would no-where be so dangerous as in the hands of a man who had folly and presumption enough to fancy himself fit to exercise it.

To give the monopoly of the home-market to the produce of domestic industry, in any particular art or manufacture, is in some measure to direct private people in what manner they ought to employ their capitals, and must, in almost all cases, be either a useless or a hurtful regulation. If the produce of domestic can be brought there as cheap as that of foreign industry, the regulation is evidently useless. If it cannot, it must generally be hurtful. It is the maxim of every prudent master of a family, never to attempt to make at home what it will cost him more to make than to buy. The taylor does not attempt to make his own shoes, but buys them of the shoemaker. The shoemaker does not attempt to make his own clothes, but employs a taylor. The farmer attempts to make neither the one nor the other, but employs those different artificers. All of them find it for their interest to employ their whole industry in a way in which they have some advantage over their neighbours, and to purchase with a part of its produce, or what is the same thing, with the price of a part of it, whatever else they have occasion for.

What is prudence in the conduct of every private family, can scarce be folly in that of a great kingdom. If a foreign country can supply us with a commodity cheaper than we ourselves can make it, better buy it of them with some part of the produce of our own industry, employed in a way in which we have some advantage. The general industry of the country, being always in proportion to the capital which employs it, will not thereby be diminished, no more than that of the above-mentioned artificers; but only left to find out the way in which it can be employed with the greatest advantage. It is certainly not employed to the greatest advantage, when it is thus directed towards an object which it can buy cheaper than it can make.

The value of its annual produce is certainly more or less diminished, when it is thus turned away from producing commodities evidently of more value than the commodity which it is directed to produce. According to the supposition, that commodity could be purchased from foreign countries cheaper than it can be made at home. It could, therefore, have been purchased with a part only of the commodities, or what is the same thing, with a part only of the price of the commodities, which the industry employed by an equal capital would have produced at home, had it been left to follow its natural course. The industry of the country, therefore, is thus turned away from a more, to a less advantageous employment, and the exchangeable value of its annual produce, instead of being increased, according to the intention of the lawgiver, must necessarily be diminished by every such regulation.

■   ■   ■

The natural advantages which one country has over another in producing particular commodities are sometimes so great, that it is acknowledged by all the world to be in vain to struggle with them. By means of glasses, hotbeds, and hotwalls, very good grapes can be raised in Scotland, and very good wine too can be made of them at about thirty times the expence for which at least equally good can be brought from foreign countries. Would it be a reasonable law to prohibit the importation of all foreign wines, merely to encourage the making of claret and burgundy in Scotland? But if there would be a manifest absurdity in turning towards any employment, thirty times more of the capital and industry of the country, than would be necessary to purchase from foreign countries an equal quantity of the commodities wanted, there must be an absurdity, though not altogether so glaring, yet exactly of the same kind, in turning towards any such employment a thirtieth, or even a three hundredth part more of either. Whether the advantages which one country has over another, be natural or acquired, is in this respect of no consequence. As long as the one

country has those advantages, and the other wants them, it will always be more advantageous for the latter, rather to buy of the former than to make. It is an acquired advantage only, which one artificer has over his neighbour, who exercises another trade; and yet they both find it more advantageous to buy of one another, than to make what does not belong to their particular trades.

■   ■   ■

All systems either of preference or of restraint, therefore, being thus completely taken away, the obvious and simple system of natural liberty establishes itself of its own accord. Every man, as long as he does not violate the laws of justice, is left perfectly free to pursue his own interest his own way, and to bring both his industry and capital into competition with those of any other man, or order of men. The sovereign is completely discharged from a duty, in the attempting to perform which he must always be exposed to innumerable delusions, and for the proper performance of which no human wisdom or knowledge could ever be sufficient; the duty of superintending the industry of private people, and of directing it towards the employments most suitable to the interest of the society. According to the system of natural liberty, the sovereign has only three duties to attend to; three duties of great importance, indeed, but plain and intelligible to common understandings: first, the duty of protecting the society from the violence and invasion of other independent societies; secondly, the duty of protecting, as far as possible, every member of the society from the injustice or oppression of every other member of it, or the duty of establishing an exact administration of justice; and, thirdly, the duty of erecting and maintaining certain public works and certain public institutions, which it can never be for the interest of any individual, or small number of individuals, to erect and maintain; because the profit could never repay the expence to any individual or small number of individuals, though it may frequently do much more than repay it to a great society.

The proper performance of those several duties of the sovereign necessarily supposes a certain expence; and this expence again necessarily requires a certain revenue to support it.

■   ■   ■

NOTES

1. This phrase, if used at all before this time, was not a familiar one. Its presence here is probably due to a passage in Mandeville, *Fable of the Bees*, pt. ii. (1729), dial. vi., p. 335: 'Cleo. . . . When once men come to be governed by written laws, all the rest comes on apace . . . No number of men, when once they enjoy quiet, and no man needs to fear his neighbour, will be long without learning to divide and subdivide their labour. Hor. I don't understand you. Cleo. Man, as I have hinted before, naturally loves to imitate what he sees others do, which is the reason that savage people all do the same thing: this hinders them from meliorating their condition, though they are always wishing for it: but if one will wholly apply himself to the making of bows and arrows, whilst another provides food, a third builds huts, a fourth makes garments, and a fifth utensils, they not only become useful to one another, but the callings and employments themselves will, in the same number of years, receive much greater improvements, than if all had been promiscuously followed by every one of the five. Hor. I believe you are perfectly right there; and the truth of what you say is in nothing so conspicuous as it is in watch-making, which is come to a higher degree of perfection than it would have been arrived at yet, if the whole had always remained the employment of one person; and I am persuaded that even the plenty we have of clocks and watches, as well as the exactness and beauty they may be made of, are chiefly owing to the division that has been made of that art into many branches.' The index contains, 'Labour, The usefulness of dividing and subdividing it'. Joseph Harris, *Essay upon Money and Coins*, 1757, pt. i., §

12, treats of the 'usefulness of distinct trades,' or 'the advantages accruing to mankind from their betaking themselves severally to different occupations,' but does not use the phrase 'division of labour'.

2. Ed. 1 reads 'improvements'.

3. Another and perhaps more important reason for taking an example like that which follows is the possibility of exhibiting the advantage, of division of labour in statistical form.

4. This parenthesis would alone be sufficient to show that those are wrong who believe Smith did not include the separation of employments in 'division of labour'.

5. In Adam Smith's *Lectures*, p. 164, the business is, as here, divided into eighteen operations. This number is doubtless taken from the *Encyclopédie*, tom. v. (published in 1755), *s.v.* Épingle. The article is ascribed to M. Delaire, 'qui décrivait la fabrication de l'épingle dans les ateliers même des ouvriers,' p. 807. In some factories the division was carried further. E. Chambers, *Cyclopædia*, vol. ii., 2nd ed., 1738, and 4th ed., 1741, *s.v.* Pin, makes the number of separate operations twenty-five.

6. Ed. 1 places 'in consequence of the division of labour' here instead of in the line above.

7. 'Pour la célérité du travail et la perfection de l'ouvrage, elles dépendent entièrement de la multitude des ouvriers rassemblés. Lorsqu'une manufacture est nombreuse, chaque opération occupe un homme différent. Tel ouvrier ne fait et ne fera de sa vie qu'une seule et unique chose; tel autre une autre chose: d'où il arrive que chacune s'exécute bien et promptement, et que l'ouvrage le mieux fait est encore celui qu'on a à meilleur marché. D'ailleurs le goût et la façon se perfectionment nécessairement entre un grand nombre d'ouvriers, parce qu'il est difficile qu'il ne s'en rencontre quelques-uns capables de réfléchir, de combiner, et de trouver enfin le seul moyen qui puisse les mettre audessus de leurs semblables; le moyen ou d'épargner la matière, ou d'allonger le temps, ou de surfaire l'industrie, soit par une machine nouvelle, soit par une manœuvre plus commode.' —*Encyclopédie*, tom i. (1751), p. 717, *s.v.* Art. All three advantages mentioned in the text above are included here.

8. *I.e.*, it is not the effect of any conscious regulation by the state or society, like the 'law of Sesostris,' that every man should follow the employment of his father, referred to in the corresponding passage in *Lectures*, p. 168. The denial that it is the effect of individual wisdom recognising the advantage of exercising special natural talents comes lower down, p. 19.

9. It is by no means clear what object there could be in exchanging one bone for another.

10. This is apparently directed against Harris, *Money and Coins*, pt. i., § II, and is in accordance with the view of Hume, who asks readers to 'consider how nearly equal all men are in their bodily force, and even in their mental powers and faculties, ere cultivated by education'. — 'Of the Original Contract,' in *Essays, Moral and Political*, 1748, p. 291.

Douglass C. North
INSTITUTIONS

Institutions are the humanly devised constraints that structure political, economic and social interaction. They consist of both informal constraints (sanctions, taboos, customs, traditions, and codes of conduct), and formal rules (constitutions, laws, property rights). Throughout history, institutions have been devised by human beings to create order and reduce uncertainty in exchange. Together with the standard constraints of economics they define the choice set and therefore determine transaction and production costs and hence the profitability and feasibility of engaging in economic activity. They evolve incrementally, connecting the past with the present and the future; history in consequence is largely a story of institutional evolution in which the historical performance of economies can only be understood as a part of a sequential story. Institutions provide the incentive structure of an economy; as that structure evolves, it shapes the direction of economic change towards growth, stagnation, or decline. In this essay I intend to elaborate on the role of institutions in the performance of economies and illustrate my analysis from economic history.

What makes it necessary to constrain human interaction with institutions? The issue can be most succinctly summarized in a game theoretic context. Wealth-maximizing individuals will usually find it worthwhile to cooperate with other players when the play is repeated, when they possess complete information about the other player's past performance, and when there are small numbers of players. But turn the game upside down. Cooperation is difficult to sustain when the game is not repeated (or there is an endgame), when information on the other players is lacking, and when there are large numbers of players.

These polar extremes reflect contrasting economic settings in real life. There are many examples of simple exchange institutions that permit low cost transacting under the former conditions. But institutions that permit low cost transacting and producing in a world of specialization and division of labor require solving the problems of human cooperation under the latter conditions.

From *Journal of Economic Perspectives* 5, no. 1 (Winter 1991), pp. 97–112.

It takes resources to define and enforce exchange agreements. Even if everyone had the same objective function (like maximizing the firm's profits), transacting would take substantial resources; but in the context of individual wealth-maximizing behavior and asymmetric information about the valuable attributes of what is being exchanged (or the performance of agents), transaction costs are a critical determinant of economic performance. Institutions and the effectiveness of enforcement (together with the technology employed) determine the cost of transacting. Effective institutions raise the benefits of cooperative solutions or the costs of defection, to use game theoretic terms. In transaction cost terms, institutions reduce transaction and production costs per exchange so that the potential gains from trade are realizeable. Both political and economic institutions are essential parts of an effective institutional matrix.

The major focus of the literature on institutions and transaction costs has been on institutions as efficient solutions to problems of organization in a competitive framework (Williamson, 1975; 1985). Thus market exchange, franchising, or vertical integration are conceived in this literature as efficient solutions to the complex problems confronting entrepreneurs under various competitive conditions. Valuable as this work has been, such an approach assumes away the central concern of this essay: to explain the varied performance of economies both over time and in the current world.

How does an economy achieve the efficient, competitive markets assumed in the foregoing approach? The formal economic constraints or property rights are specified and enforced by political institutions, and the literature simply takes those as a given. But economic history is overwhelmingly a story of economies that failed to produce a set of economic rules of the game (with enforcement) that induce sustained economic growth. The central issue of economic history and of economic development is to account for the evolution of political and economic institutions that create an economic environment that induces increasing productivity.

Institutions to Capture the Gains from Trade

Many readers will be at least somewhat familiar with the idea of economic history over time as a series of staged stories. The earliest economies are thought of as local exchange within a village (or even within a simple hunting and gathering society). Gradually, trade expands beyond the village: first to the region, perhaps as a bazaar-like economy; then to longer distances, through particular caravan or shipping routes; and eventually to much of the world. At each stage, the economy involves increasing specialization and division of labor and continuously more productive technology. This story of gradual evolution from local autarky to specialization and division of labor was derived from the German historical school. However, there is no implication in this paper that the real historical evolution of economies necessarily paralleled the sequence of stages of exchange described here.[1]

I begin with local exchange within the village or even the simple exchange of hunting and gathering societies (in which women gathered and men hunted). Specialization in this world is rudimentary and self-sufficiency characterizes most individual households. Small-scale village trade exists within a "dense" social network of informal constraints that facilitates local exchange, and the costs of transacting in this context are low. (Although the basic societal costs of tribal and village organization may be high, they will not be reflected in additional costs in the process of transacting.) People have an intimate understanding of each other, and the threat of violence is a continuous force for preserving order because of its implications for other members of society.[2]

As trade expands beyond a single village, however, the possibilities for conflict over the exchange grow. The size of the market grows and transaction costs increase sharply because the dense social network is replaced; hence, more resources must be devoted to measurement and enforcement. In the absence of a state that enforced contracts, religious precepts usually imposed standards of conduct on the players. Needless to say, their effectiveness in lowering the costs of transacting varied widely, depending on the degree to which these precepts were held to be binding.

The development of long-distance trade, perhaps through caravans or lengthy ship voyages, requires a sharp break in the characteristics of an economic structure. It entails substantial specialization in exchange by individuals whose livelihood is confined to trading and the development of trading centers, which may be temporary gathering places (as were the early fairs in Europe) or more permanent towns or cities. Some economies of scale—for example, in plantation agriculture—are characteristic of this world. Geographic specialization begins to emerge as a major characteristic and some occupational specialization is occurring as well.

The growth of long distance trade poses two distinct transaction cost problems. One is a classical problem of agency, which historically was met by use of kin in long-distance trade. That is, a sedentary merchant would send a relative with the cargo to negotiate sale and to obtain a return cargo. The costliness of measuring performance, the strength of kinship ties, and the price of "defection" all determined the outcome of such agreements. As the size and volume of trade grew, agency problems became an increasingly major dilemma.[3] A second problem consisted of contract negotiation and enforcement in alien parts of the world, where there is no easily available way to achieve agreement and enforce contracts. Enforcement means not only such enforcement of agreements but also protection of the goods and services en route from pirates, brigands, and so on.

The problems of enforcement en route were met by armed forces protecting the ship or caravan or by the payment of tolls or protection money to local coercive groups. Negotiation and enforcement in alien parts of the world entailed typically the development of standardized weights and measures, units of account, a medium of exchange, notaries, consuls, merchant law courts, and enclaves of foreign merchants protected by foreign princes in return for revenue. By lowering information costs and providing incentives for contract fulfillment this complex of institutions, organizations, and instruments made possible transacting and engaging in long-distance trade. A mixture of voluntary and semi-coercive bodies, or at least bodies that effectively could cause ostracism of merchants that didn't live up to agreements, enabled long-distance trade to occur.[4]

This expansion of the market entails more specialized producers. Economies of scale result in the beginnings of hierarchical producing organizations, with full-time workers working either in a central place or in a sequential production process. Towns and some central cities are emerging, and occupational distribution of the population now shows, in addition, a substantial increase in the proportion of the labor force engaged in manufacturing and in services, although the traditional preponderance in agriculture continues. These evolving stages also reflect a significant shift towards urbanization of the society.

Such societies need effective, impersonal contract enforcement, because personal ties, voluntaristic constraints, and ostracism are no longer effective as more complex and impersonal forms of exchange emerge. It is not that these personal and social alternatives are unimportant; they are still significant even in today's interdependent world. But in the absence of effective impersonal contracting, the gains from "defection" are great enough to forestall the development of complex exchange. Two illustrations deal with the creation of a capital market and with the interplay between institutions and the technology employed.

A capital market entails security of property rights over time and will simply not evolve where political rulers can arbitrarily seize assets or radically alter their value. Establishing a credible commitment to secure property rights over time requires either a ruler who exercises forebearance and restraint in using coercive force, or the shackling of the ruler's power to prevent arbitrary seizure of assets. The first alternative was seldom successful for very long in the face of the ubiquitous fiscal crises of rulers (largely as a consequence of repeated warfare). The latter entailed a fundamental restructuring of the polity such as occurred in England as a result of the Glorious Revolution of 1688, which resulted in parliamentary supremacy over the crown.[5]

The technology associated with the growth of manufacturing entailed increased fixed capital in plant and equipment, uninterrupted production, a disciplined labor force, and a developed transport network; in short, it required effective factor and product markets. Undergirding such markets are secure property rights, which entail a polity and judicial system to permit low costs contracting, flexible laws permitting a wide latitude of organizational structures, and the creation of complex governance structures to limit the problems of agency in hierarchical organizations.[6]

In the last stage, the one we observe in modern western societies, specialization has increased, agriculture requires a small percentage of the labor force, and markets have become nationwide and worldwide. Economies of scale imply large-scale organization, not only in manufacturing but also in agriculture. Everyone lives by undertaking a specialized function and relying on the vast network of interconnected parts to provide the multitude of goods and services necessary to them. The occupational distribution of the labor force shifts gradually from dominance by manufacturing to dominance, eventually, by what are characterized as services. Society is overwhelmingly urban.

In this final stage, specialization requires increasing percentages of the resources of the society to be engaged in transacting, so that the transaction sector rises to be a large percentage of gross national product. This is so because specialization in trade, finance, banking, insurance, as well as the simple coordination of economic activity, involves an increasing proportion of the labor force.[7] Of necessity, therefore, highly specialized forms of transaction organizations emerge. International specialization and division of labor requires institutions and organizations to safeguard property rights across international boundaries so that capital markets (as well as other kinds of exchange) can take place with credible commitment on the part of the players.

These very schematic stages appear to merge one into another in a smooth story of evolving cooperation. But do they? Does any necessary connection move the players from less complicated to more complicated forms of exchange? At stake in this evolution is not only whether information costs and economies of scale together with the development of improved enforcement of contracts will permit and indeed encourage more complicated forms of exchange, but also whether organizations have the incentive to acquire knowledge and information that will induce them to evolve in more socially productive directions.

In fact, throughout history, there is no necessary reason for this development to occur. Indeed, most of the early forms of organization that I have mentioned in these sections still exist today in parts of the world. There still exist primitive tribal societies; the Suq (bazaar economies engaged in regional trade) still flourishes in many parts of the world; and while the caravan trade has disappeared, its demise (as well as the gradual undermining of the other two forms of "primitive" exchange) has reflected external forces rather than internal evolution. In contrast, the development of European long-distance trade initiated a sequential development of more complex forms of organization.

The remainder of this paper will examine first some seemingly primitive forms of exchange that failed to evolve and then the institutional evolution that occurred in early modern Europe. The concluding section of the paper will attempt to enunciate why some societies and exchange institutions evolve and others do not, and to apply that framework in the context of economic development in the western hemisphere during the 18th and 19th centuries.

When Institutions Do Not Evolve

In every system of exchange, economic actors have an incentive to invest their time, resources, and energy in knowledge and skills that will improve their material status. But in some primitive institutional settings, the kind of knowledge and skills that will pay off will not result in institutional evolution towards more productive economies. To illustrate this argument, I consider three primitive types of exchange—tribal society, a regional economy with bazaar trading, and the long-distance caravan trade—that are unlikely to evolve from within.

As noted earlier, exchange in a tribal society relies on a dense social network. Elizabeth Colson (1974, p. 59) describes the network this way:

> The communities in which all these people live were governed by a delicate balance of power, always endangered and never to be taken for granted: each person was constantly involved in securing his own position in situations where he had to show his good intentions. Usages and customs appear to be flexible and fluid given that judgement on whether or not someone has done rightly varies from case to case. . . . But this is because it is the individual who is being judged and not the crime. Under these conditions, a flouting of generally accepted standards is tantamount to a claim to illegitimate power and becomes part of the evidence against one.

The implication of Colson's analysis as well as that of Richard Posner in his account of primitive institutions (1980) is that deviance and innovation are viewed as threats to group survival.

A second form of exchange that has existed for thousands of years, and still exists today in North Africa and the Middle East is that of the Suq, where widespread and relatively impersonal exchange and relatively high costs of transacting exist.[8] The basic characteristics are a multiplicity of small-scale enter-prises with as much as 40 to 50 percent of the town's labor force engaged in this exchange process; low fixed costs in terms of rent and machinery; a very finely drawn division of labor; an enormous number of small transactions, each more or less independent of the next; face to face contacts; and goods and services that are not homogeneous.

There are no institutions devoted to assembling and distributing market information; that is, no price quotations, production reports, employment agencies, consumer guides, and so on. Systems of weights and measures are intricate and incompletely standardized. Exchange skills are very elaborately developed, and are the primary determinant of who prospers in the bazaar and who does not. Haggling over terms with respect to any aspect or condition of exchange is pervasive, strenuous, and unremitting. Buying and selling are virtually undifferentiated, essentially a single activity; trading involves a continual search for specific partners, not the mere offers of goods to the general public. Regulation of disputes involves testimony by reliable witnesses to factual matters, not the weighting of competing, juridical principles. Governmental controls over marketplace activity are marginal, decentralized, and mostly rhetorical.

To summarize, the central features of the Suq are (1) high measurement costs; (2) continuous effort at clientization (the development of repeat-exchange relationships with other partners, however imperfect); and (3) intensive bargaining at every margin. In essence, the name of the game is to raise the costs of transacting to the other party to exchange. One makes money by having better information than one's adversary.

It is easy to understand why innovation would be seen to threaten survival in a tribal society but harder to understand why these "inefficient" forms of bargaining would continue in the Suq. One would anticipate, in the societies with which we are familiar, that voluntary organizations would evolve to insure against the hazards and uncertainties of such information asymmetries. But that is precisely the issue. What is missing in the Suq are the fundamental underpinnings of institutions that would make such voluntary organizations viable and profitable. These include an effective legal structure and court system to enforce contracts which in turn depend on the development of political institutions that will create such a framework. In their absence there is no incentive to alter the system.

The third form of exchange, caravan trade, illustrates the informal constraints that made trade possible in a world where protection was essential and no organized state existed. Clifford Geertz (1979, p. 137) provides a description of the caravan trades in Morocco at the turn of the century:

> In the narrow sense, a zettata (from the Berber TAZETTAT, 'a small piece of cloth') is a passage toll, a sum paid to a local power . . . for protection when crossing localities where he is such a power. But in fact it is, or more properly was, rather more than a mere payment. It was part of a whole complex of moral rituals, customs with the force of law and the weight of sanctity—centering around the guest-host, client-patron, petitioner-petitioned, exile-protector, suppliant-divinity relations—all of which are somehow of a package in rural Morocco. Entering the tribal world physically, the outreaching trader (or at least his agents) had also to enter it culturally.
>
> Despite the vast variety of particular forms through which they manifest themselves, the characteristics of protection in the Berber societies of the High and Middle Atlas are clear and constant. Protection is personal, unqualified, explicit, and conceived of as the dressing of one man in the reputation of another. The reputation may be political, moral, spiritual, or even idiosyncratic, or, often enough, all four at once. But the essential transaction is that a man who counts 'stands up and says' (quam wa qal, as the classical tag has it) to those to whom he counts: 'this man is mine; harm him and you insult me; insult me and you will answer for it.' Benediction (the famous baraka), hospitality, sanctuary, and safe passage are

alike in this: they rest on the perhaps somewhat paradoxical notion that though personal identity is radically individual in both its roots and its expressions, it is not incapable of being stamped onto the self of someone else.

While tribal chieftains found it profitable to protect merchant caravans they had neither the military muscle nor the political structure to extend, develop, and enforce more permanent property rights.

Institutional Evolution in Early Modern Europe

In contrast to many primitive systems of exchange, long distance trade in early modern Europe from the 11th to the 16th centuries was a story of sequentially more complex organization that eventually led to the rise of the western world. Let me first briefly describe the innovations and then explore some of their underlying sources.[9]

Innovations that lowered transaction costs consisted of organizational changes, instruments, and specific techniques and enforcement characteristics that lowered the costs of engaging in exchange over long distances. These innovations occurred at three cost margins: (1) those that increased the mobility of capital, (2) those that lowered information costs, and (3) those that spread risk. Obviously, the categories are overlapping, but they provide a useful way to distinguish cost-reducing features of transacting. All of these innovations had their origins in earlier times; most of them were borrowed from medieval Italian city states or Islam or Byzantium and then elaborated upon.

Among the innovations that enhanced the mobility of capital were the techniques and methods evolved to evade usury laws. The variety of ingenious ways by which interest was disguised in loan contracts ranged from "penalties for late payment," to exchange rate manipulation (Lopez and Raymond, 1955, p. 163), to the early form of the mortgage; but all increased the costs of contracting. The costliness of usury laws was not only that they made the writing of contracts to disguise interests complex and cumbersome, but also that enforceability of such contracts became more problematic. As the demand for capital increased and evasion became more general, usury laws gradually broke down and rates of interest were permitted. In consequence, the costs of writing contracts and the costs of enforcing them declined.

A second innovation that improved the mobility of capital, and the one that has received the most attention, was the evolution of the bill of exchange (a dated order to pay, say 120 days after issuance, conventionally drawn by a seller against a purchaser of goods delivered) and particularly the development of techniques and instruments that allowed for its negotiability as well as for the development of discounting methods. Negotiability and discounting in turn depended on the creation of institutions that would permit their use and the development of centers where such events could occur: first in fairs, such as the Champagne fairs that played such a prominent part in economic exchange in 12th and 13th century Europe; then through banks; and finally through financial houses that could specialize in discounting. These developments were a function not only of specific institutions but also of the scale of economic activity. Increasing volume obviously made such institutional developments possible. In addition to the economies of scale necessary for the development of the bills of exchange, improved enforceability of contracts was critical, and the interrelationship between the development of accounting and auditing methods and their use as evidence in the collection of debts and in the enforcement of contracts was an important part of this process (Yamey, 1949; Watts and Zimmerman, 1983).

Still a third innovation affecting the mobility of capital arose from the problems associated with maintaining control of agents involved in long distance trade. The traditional resolution of this problem in medieval and early modern times was the use of kinship and family ties to bind agents to principals. However, as the size and scope of merchant trading empires grew, the extension of discretionary behavior to others than kin of the principal required the development of more elaborate accounting procedures for monitoring the behavior of agents.

The major developments in the area of information costs were the printing of prices of various commodities, as well as the printing of manuals that provided information on weights, measures, customs, brokerage fees, postal systems, and, particularly, the complex exchange rates between monies in Europe and the trading world. Obviously these developments were primarily a function of the volume of international trade and therefore a consequence of economies of scale.

The final innovation was the transformation of uncertainty into risk. By uncertainty, I mean here a condition wherein one cannot ascertain the probability of an event and therefore cannot arrive at a way of insuring against such an occurrence. Risk, on the other hand, implies the ability to make an actuarial determination of the likelihood of an event and hence insure against such an outcome. In the modern world, insurance and portfolio diversification are methods for converting uncertainty into risks and thereby reducing, through the provision of a hedge against variability, the costs of transacting. In the medieval and early modern world, precisely the same conversion occurred. For example, marine insurance evolved from sporadic individual contracts covering partial payments for losses to contracts issued by specialized firms. As De Roover (1945, p. 198) described:

> By the fifteenth century marine insurance was established on a secure basis. The wording of the policies had already become stereotyped and changed very little during the next three or four hundred years. . . . In the sixteenth century it was already current practice to use printed forms provided with a few blank spaces for the name of the ship, the name of the master, the amount of the insurance, the premium, and a few other items that were apt to change from one contract to another.

Another example of the development of actuarial, ascertainable risk was the business organization that spread risk through either portfolio diversification or institutions that permitted a large number of investors to engage in risky activities. For example, the commenda was a contract employed in long distance trade between a sedentary partner and an active partner who accompanied the goods. It evolved from its Jewish, Byzantine, and Muslim origins (Udovitch, 1962) through its use at the hands of Italians to the English Regulated Company and finally the Joint Stock Company, thus providing an evolutionary story of the institutionalization of risk.

These specific innovations and particular institutional instruments evolved from interplay between two fundamental economic forces: the economies of scale associated with a growing volume of trade, and the development of improved mechanisms to enforce contracts at lower costs. The causation ran both ways. That is, the increasing volume of long distance trade raised the rate of return to merchants of devising effective mechanisms for enforcing contracts. In turn, the development of such mechanisms lowered the costs of contracting and made trade more profitable, thereby increasing its volume.

The process of developing new enforcement mechanisms was a long one. While a variety of courts handled commercial disputes, it is the development of enforcement mechanisms by merchants themselves that is significant. Enforceability appears to have had its beginnings in the development of internal codes of conduct in fraternal orders of guild merchants; those who did not live up to them were threatened with ostracism. A further step was the evolution of mercantile law. Merchants carried with them in long distance trade mercantile codes of conduct, so that Pisan laws passed into the sea codes of Marseilles; Oleron and Lubeck gave laws to the north of Europe, Barcelona to the south of Europe; and from Italy came the legal principle of insurance and bills of exchange (Mitchell, 1969, p. 156).

The development of more sophisticated accounting methods and of notarial records provided evidence for ascertaining facts in disputes. The gradual

blending of the voluntaristic structure of enforcement of contracts via internal merchant organizations with enforcement by the state is an important part of the story of increasing the enforceability of contracts. The long evolution of merchant law from its voluntary beginnings and the differences in resolutions that it had with both the common and Roman law are a part of the story.

The state was a major player in this whole process, and there was continuous interplay between the state's fiscal needs and its credibility in its relationships with merchants and the citizenry in general. In particular, the evolution of capital markets was critically influenced by the policies of the state, since to the extent the state was bound by commitments that it would not confiscate assets or use its coercive power to increase uncertainty in exchange, it made possible the evolution of financial institutions and the creation of more efficient capital markets. The shackling of arbitrary behavior of rulers and the development of impersonal rules that successfully bound both the state and voluntary organizations were a key part of this whole process. The development of an institutional process by which government debt could be circulated, become a part of a regular capital market, and be funded by regular sources of taxation was also a key part (Tracy, 1985; North and Weingast, 1989).

It was in the Netherlands, Amsterdam specifically, that these diverse innovations and institutions were combined to create the predecessor of the efficient modern set of markets that make possible the growth of exchange and commerce. An open immigration policy attracted businessmen. Efficient methods of financing long distance trade were developed, as were capital markets and discounting methods in financial houses that lowered the costs of underwriting this trade. The development of techniques for spreading risk and transforming uncertainty into actuarial, ascertainable risks as well as the creation of large scale markets that allowed for lowering the costs of information, and the development of negotiable government indebtedness all were a part of this story (Barbour, 1949).

Contrasting Stories of Stability and Change

These contrasting stories of stability and change go to the heart of the puzzle of accounting for changes in the human economic condition. In the former cases, maximizing activity by the actors will not induce increments to knowledge and skills which will modify the institutional framework to induce greater productivity; in the latter case, evolution is a consistent story of incremental change induced by the private gains to be realized by productivity-raising organizational institutional changes.

What distinguished the institutional context of western Europe from the other illustrations? The traditional answer of economic historians has been competition among the fragmented European political units accentuated by changing military technology which forced rulers to seek more revenue (by making bargains with constituents) in order to survive (North and Thomas, 1973; Jones, 1981; Rosenberg and Birdzell, 1986). That is surely part of the answer; political competition for survival in early modern Europe was certainly more acute than in other parts of the world. But it is only a partial answer. Why the contrasting results within western Europe? Why did Spain, the great power of 16th century Europe, decline while the Netherlands and England developed?

To begin to get an answer (and it is only a beginning), we need to dig deeper into two key (and related) parts of the puzzle: the relationship between the basic institutional framework, the consequent organizational structure, and institutional change; and the path dependent nature of economic change that is a consequence of the increasing returns characteristic of an institutional framework.

In the institutional accounts given earlier, the direction and form of economic activity by individuals and organizations reflected the opportunities thrown up by the basic institutional framework of customs, religious precepts, and formal rules (and the effectiveness of enforcement). Whether we examine the organization of trade in the Suq or that in the Champagne Fairs, in each case the trader was constrained by the institutional framework, as well as the traditional constraints common to economic theory.

In each case the trader would invest in acquiring knowledge and skills to increase his wealth. But in the former case, improved knowledge and skills meant getting better information on opportunities and having greater bargaining skills than other traders, since profitable opportunities came from being better informed and being a more skilled bargainer than other traders. Neither activity induced alteration in the basic institutional framework. On the other hand, while a merchant at a medieval European fair would certainly gain from acquiring such information and skills, he would gain also from devising ways to bond fellow merchants, to establish merchant courts, to induce princes to protect goods from brigandage in return for revenue, to devise ways to discount bills of exchange. His investment in knowledge and skills would gradually and incrementally alter the basic institutional framework.

Note that the institutional evolution entailed not only voluntary organizations that expanded trade and made exchange more productive, but also the development of the state to take over protection and enforcement of property rights as impersonal exchange made contract enforcement increasingly costly for voluntary organizations which lacked effective coercive power. Another essential part of the institutional evolution entails a shackling of the arbitrary behavior of the state over economic activity.

Path dependence is more than the incremental process of institutional evolution in which yesterday's institutional framework provides the opportunity set for today's organizations and individual entrepreneurs (political or economic). The institutional matrix consists of an interdependent web of institutions and consequent political and economic organizations that are characterized by massive increasing returns.[10] That is, the organizations owe their existence to the opportunities provided by the institutional framework. Network externalities arise because of the initial setup costs (like the de novo creation of the U.S. Constitution in 1787), the learning effects described above, coordination effects via contracts with other organizations, and adaptive expectations arising from the prevalence of contracting based on the existing institutions.

When economies do evolve, therefore, nothing about that process assures economic growth. It has commonly been the case that the incentive structure provided by the basic institutional framework creates opportunities for the consequent organizations to evolve, but the direction of their development has not been to promote productivity-raising activities. Rather, private profitability has been enhanced by creating monopolies, by restricting entry and factor mobility, and by political organizations that established property rights that redistributed rather than increased income.

The contrasting histories of the Netherlands and England on the one hand and Spain on the other hand reflected the differing opportunity sets of the actors in each case. To appreciate the pervasive influence of path dependence, let us extend the historical account of Spain and England to the economic history of the New World and the striking contrast in the history of the areas north and south of the Rio Grande River.

In the case of North America, the English colonies were formed in the century when the struggle between Parliament and the Crown was coming to a head. Religious and political diversity in the mother country was paralleled in the colonies. The general development in the direction of local political control and the growth of assemblies was unambiguous. Similarly, the colonist carried over free and common socage tenure of land (fee simple ownership rights) and secure property rights in other factor and product markets.

The French and Indian War from 1755–63 is a familiar breaking point in American history. British efforts to impose a very modest tax on colonial subjects, as well as curb westward migration, produced a violent reaction that led via a series of steps, by individuals and organizations, to the Revolution,

the Declaration of Independence, the Articles of Confederation, the Northwest Ordinance, and the Constitution, a sequence of institutional expressions that formed a consistent evolutionary pattern despite the precariousness of the process. While the American Revolution created the United States, post-revolutionary history is only intelligible in terms of the continuity of informal and formal institutional constraints carried over from before the Revolution and incrementally modified (Hughes, 1989).

Now turn to the Spanish (and Portuguese) case in Latin America. In the case of the Spanish Indies, conquest came at the precise time that the influence of the Castilian Cortes (parliament) was declining and the monarchy of Castile, which was the seat of power of Spain, was firmly establishing centralized bureaucratic control over Spain and the Spanish Indies.[11] The conquerors imposed a uniform religion and a uniform bureaucratic administration on an already existing agricultural society. The bureaucracy detailed every aspect of political and economic policy. There were recurrent crises over the problem of agency. Wealth-maximizing behavior by organizations and entrepreneurs (political and economic) entailed getting control of, or influence over, the bureaucratic machinery. While the nineteenth century Wars of Independence in Latin America turned out to be a struggle for control of the bureaucracy and consequent policy as between local colonial control and imperial control, nevertheless the struggle was imbued with the ideological overtones that stemmed from the American and French revolutions. Independence brought U.S.-inspired constitutions, but the results were radically different. In contrast to those of the United States, Latin American federal schemes and efforts at decentralization had one thing in common after the Revolutions. None worked. The gradual country-by-country reversion to centralized bureaucratic control characterized Latin America in the 19th century.[12]

The divergent paths established by England and Spain in the New World have not converged despite the mediating factors of common ideological influences. In the former, an institutional framework has evolved that permits complex impersonal exchange necessary to political stability as well as to capture the potential economic benefits of modern technology. In the latter, "personalistic" relationships are still the key to much of the political and economic exchange. They are the consequence of an evolving institutional framework that has produced erratic economic growth in Latin America, but neither political nor economic stability, nor realization of the potential of modern technology.

The foregoing comparative sketch probably raises more questions than it answers about institutions and the role that they play in the performance of economies. Under what conditions does a path get reversed, like the revival of Spain in modern times? What is it about informal constraints that gives them such a pervasive influence upon the long-run character of economies? What is the relationship between formal and informal constraints? How does an economy develop the informal constraints that make individuals constrain their behavior so that they make political and judicial systems effective forces for third party enforcement? Clearly we have a long way to go for complete answers, but the modern study of institutions offers the promise of dramatic new understanding of economic performance and economic change.

NOTES

1. In an article written many years ago (North, 1955), I pointed out that many regional economies evolved from the very beginning as export economies and built their development around the export sector. This is in comparison and in contrast to the old stage theory of history derived from the German historical school, in which the evolution was always from local autarky to gradual evolution of specialization and division of labor. It is this last pattern that is described here, even though it may not characterize the particular evolution that in fact has occurred.

2. For an excellent summary of the anthropological literature dealing with trade in tribal societies, see Elizabeth Colson (1974).

3. Jewish traders in the Mediterranean in the 11th century "solved" the agency problem as a result of close community relationships amongst themselves that lowered information costs and enabled them to act as a group to ostracize and retaliate against agents who violated their commercial code. See Avner Greif (1989).

4. Philip Curtin's *Cross Cultural Trade in World History* (1984) summarizes a good deal of the literature, but is short on analysis and examination of the mechanisms essential to the structure of such trade. The Cambridge Economic History, Volume III (1966), has more useful details on the organization of such trade.

5. North and Weingast (1989) provide a history and analysis of the political institutions of 17th century England leading up to the Revolution of 1688 and of the consequences for the development of the English capital market.

6. See North (1981), particularly chapter 13, and Chandler (1977). Joseph Stiglitz's (1989) essay, "Markets, Market Failures, and Development," details some of the theoretical issues.

7. The transaction sector (that proportion of transaction costs going through the market and therefore measureable) of the U.S. economy was 25 percent of GNP in 1870 and 45 percent of GNP in 1970 (Wallis and North, 1986).

8. There is an extensive literature on the Suq. A sophisticated analysis (on which I have relied) focused on the Suq in Sefrou, Morocco is contained in Geertz, Geertz, and Rosen (1979).

9. For a much more detailed description and analysis of the evolution of European trade see Tracy (forthcoming), particularly Volume II. For a game theoretic analysis of one aspect of this trade revival see Milgrom, North and Weingast (1990).

10. The concept of path dependence was developed by Brian Arthur (1988, 1989) and Paul David (1985) to explore the path of technological change. I believe the concept has equal explanatory power in

helping us understand institutional change. In both cases increasing returns are the key to path dependence, but in the case of institutional change the process is more complex because of the key role of political organizations in the process.

11. The subsequent history of Spanish rise and decline is summarized in North and Thomas (1973).

12. For a summary account of the Latin American experience, see Veliz (1980) or Glade (1969).

REFERENCES

Arthur, W. Brian, "Self-Reinforcing Mechanisms in Economics." In Anderson, Phillip W., Kenneth J. Arrow, and David Pines, eds., *The Economy as an Evolving Complex System.* Reading, MA: Addison-Wesley, 1988.

Arthur, W. Brian, "Competing Technologies, Increasing Returns, and Lock-In by Historical Events," *Economic Journal*, 1989, *99*, 116–31.

Barbour, Violet, "Capitalism in Amsterdam in the Seventeenth Century," *Johns Hopkins University Studies in Historical and Political Science*, Volume LXVIII. Baltimore: The Johns Hopkins University Press, 1949.

The Cambridge Economic History. Cambridge: Cambridge University Press, 1966.

Chandler, Alfred, *The Visible Hand.* Cambridge: The Belknap Press, 1977.

Colson, Elizabeth, *Tradition and Contract: The Problem of Order.* Chicago: Adeline Publishing, 1974.

Curtin, Philip D., *Cross-Cultural Trade in World History.* Cambridge: Cambridge University Press, 1984.

David, Paul, "Clio and the Economics of QWERTY," *American Economic Review*, 1985, *75*, 332–37.

De Roover, F. E., "Early Examples of Marine Insurance," *Journal of Economic History*, November 1945, *5*, 172–200.

Geertz, C., H. Geertz, and L. Rosen, *Meaning and Order in Moroccan Society.* Cambridge: Cambridge University Press, 1979.

Glade, W. P., *The Latin American Economies: A Study of Their Institutional Evolution.* New York: American Book, 1969.

Greif, Avner, "Reputation and Economic Institutions in Medieval Trade: Evidences from the Geniza Documents," *Journal of Economic History*, 1989.

Hughes, J. R. T., "A World Elsewhere: The Importance of Starting English." In Thompson, F. M. L., ed., *Essays in Honor of H. J. Habakkuk.* Oxford: Oxford University Press, 1989.

Jones, E. L., *The European Miracle: Environments, Economies, and Geopolitics in the History of Europe and Asia.* Cambridge: Cambridge University Press, 1981.

Kalt, J. P. and M. A. Zupan, "Capture and Ideology in the Economic Theory of Politics," *American Economic Review*, 1984, *74*, 279–300.

Lopez, Robert S., and Irving W. Raymond, *Medieval Trade in the Mediterranean World.* New York: Columbia University Press, 1955.

Milgrom, P. R., D. C. North, and B. R. Weingast, "The Role of Institutions in the Revival of Trade: The Medieval Law Merchant," *Economics and Politics*, March 1990, *II*.

Mitchell, William, *An Essay on the Early History of the Law Merchant.* New York: Burt Franklin Press, 1969.

Nelson, Douglas, and Eugene Silberberg, "Ideology and Legislator Shirking," *Economic Inquiry*, January 1987, *25*, 15–25.

North, Douglass C., "Location Theory and Regional Economic Growth," *Journal of Political Economy*, June 1955, *LXIII*, 243–258.

North, Douglass C., *Structure and Change in Economic History.* New York: Norton, 1981.

North, Douglass C., and Robert Thomas, *The Rise of the Western World: A New Economic History.* Cambridge: Cambridge University Press, 1973.

North, Douglass C., and Barry R. Weingast, "The Evolution of Institutions Governing Public Choice in 17th Century England," *Journal of Economic History*, November 1989, *5*, 172–200.

Posner, Richard, "A Theory of Primitive Society, with Special Reference to the Law," *Journal of Law and Economics*, April 1980, *XXIII*, 1–54.

Rosenberg, Nathan, and L. E. Bridzell, *How the West Grew Rich: The Economic Transformation of the Industrial World.* New York: Basic Books, 1986.

Stiglitz, Joseph, "Markets, Market Failures, and Development," *American Economic Review*, 1989, *79*, 197–203.

Tracy, James, *A Financial Revolution in the Hapsburg Netherlands: Renters and Rentiers in the Country of Holland, 1515–1565*. Berkeley: University of California Press, 1985.

Tracy, James, *The Rise of Merchant Empires*. Cambridge: Cambridge University Press, 1990.

Udovitch, Abraham, "At the Origins of the Western Commenda: Islam, Israel, Byzanteum?" *Speculum*, April 1962, *XXXVII*, 198–207.

Veliz, C., *The Centralist Tradition of Latin America*. Princeton: Princeton University Press, 1980.

Wallis, John J., and Douglass C. North, "Measuring the Transaction Sector in the American Economy, 1870–1970." In Engermann, Stanley, and Robert Gallman, eds., *Income and Wealth: Long-Term Factors in American Economic Growth*. Chicago: University of Chicago Press, 1986.

Watts, R., and J. Zimmerman, "Agency Problems, Auditing, and the Theory of the Firm: Some Evidence," *Journal of Law and Economics*, October 1983, *XXVI*, 613–633.

Williamson, Oliver E., *Markets and Hierarchies: Analysis and Antitrust Implications*. New York: Free Press, 1975.

Williamson, Oliver E., *The Economic Institutions of Capitalism*. New York: Free Press, 1985.

Yamey, B. S., "Scientific Bookkeeping and the Rise of Capitalism," *Economic History Review*, Second Series, 1949, *II*, 99–113.

Daron Acemoglu

ROOT CAUSES: A HISTORICAL APPROACH TO ASSESSING THE ROLE OF INSTITUTIONS IN ECONOMIC DEVELOPMENT

Tremendous differences in incomes and standards of living exist today between the rich and the poor countries of the world. Average per capita income in sub-Saharan Africa, for example, is less than one-twentieth that in the United States. Explanations for why the economic fortunes of countries have diverged so much abound. Poor countries, such as those in sub-Saharan Africa, Central America, or South Asia, often lack functioning markets, their populations are poorly educated, and their machinery and technology are outdated or nonexistent. But these are only *proximate* causes of poverty, begging the question of why these places don't have better markets, better human capital, more investments, and better machinery and technology. There must be some *fundamental* causes leading to these outcomes, and via these channels, to dire poverty.

From *Finance & Development* (June 2003), pp. 27–30.

The two main candidates to explain the fundamental causes of differences in prosperity between countries are geography and institutions. The *geography hypothesis*, which has a large following both in the popular imagination and in academia, maintains that the geography, climate, and ecology of a society shape both its technology and the incentives of its inhabitants. It emphasizes forces of nature as a primary factor in the poverty of nations. The alternative, the *institutions hypothesis*, is about human influences. According to this view, some societies have good institutions that encourage investment in machinery, human capital, and better technologies, and, consequently, these countries achieve economic prosperity.

Good institutions have three key characteristics: enforcement of property rights for a broad cross section of society, so that a variety of individuals have incentives to invest and take part in economic life; constraints on the actions of elites, politicians, and other powerful groups, so that these people cannot expropriate the incomes and investments of others or create a highly uneven playing field; and some degree of equal opportunity for broad segments of society, so that individuals can make investments, especially in human capital, and participate in productive economic activities. These good institutions contrast with conditions in many societies of the world, throughout history and today, where the rule of law is applied selectively; property rights are nonexistent for the vast majority of the population; the elites have unlimited political and economic power, and only a small fraction of citizens have access to education, credit, and production opportunities.

Geography's Influence

If you want to believe that geography is the key, look at a world map. Locate the poorest places in the world where per capita incomes are less than one-twentieth those in the United States. You will find almost all of them close to the equator, in very hot regions that experience periodic torrential rains and where, by definition, tropical diseases are widespread.

However, this evidence does not establish that geography is a primary influence on prosperity. It is true there is a *correlation* between geography and prosperity. But correlation does not prove causation. Most important, there are often omitted factors driving the associations we observe in the data.

Similarly, if you look around the world, you'll see that almost no wealthy country achieves this position without institutions protecting the property rights of investors and imposing some control over the government and elites. Once again, however, this correlation between institutions and economic development could reflect omitted factors or reverse causality.

To make progress in understanding the relative roles of geographic and institutional factors, we need to find a source of exogenous variation in institutions—in other words, a natural experiment where institutions change for reasons unrelated to potential omitted factors (and geographic factors remain constant, as they almost always do).

The colonization of much of the globe by Europeans starting in the fifteenth century provides such a natural experiment. The colonization experience transformed the institutions in many lands conquered or controlled by Europeans but, by and large, had no effect on their geographies. Therefore, if geography is the key factor determining the economic potential of an area or a country, the places that were rich before the arrival of the Europeans should have remained rich after the colonization experience and, in fact, should still be rich today. In other words, since the key determinant of prosperity remains the same, we should see a high degree of persistence in economic outcomes. If, on the other hand, it is institutions that are central, then those places where good institutions were introduced or developed should be richer than those in which Europeans introduced or maintained extractive institutions to plunder resources or exploit the non-European population.

Historical evidence suggests that Europeans indeed pursued very different colonization strategies, with very different associated institutions, in various colonies. At one extreme, Europeans set up exclusively extractive institutions, exemplified by the Belgian colonization of the Congo, slave plantations in the Caribbean, and forced labor systems in the mines of Central America. These institutions neither protected the property rights of regular citizens nor constrained the power of elites. At the other extreme, Europeans founded a number of colonies where they created settler societies, replicating—and often improving—the European form of institutions protecting private property. Primary examples of this mode of colonization include Australia, Canada, New Zealand, and the United States. The settlers in these societies also managed to place significant constraints on elites and politicians, even if they had to fight to achieve this objective.

Reversal of Fortune

So what happened to economic development after colonization? Did places that were rich before colonization remain rich, as suggested by the geography hypothesis? Or did economic fortunes change systematically as a result of the changes in institutions?

The historical evidence shows no evidence of the persistence suggested by the geography hypothesis. On the contrary, there is a remarkable *reversal of fortune* in economic prosperity. Societies like the Mughals in India and the Aztecs and the Incas in America that were among the richest civilizations in 1500 are among the poorer societies of today. In contrast, countries occupying the territories of the less developed civilizations in North America, New Zealand, and Australia are now much *richer* than those in the lands of the Mughals, the Aztecs, and the Incas. Moreover, the reversal of fortune is not confined to this comparison. Using various proxies for prosperity before modern times, we can show that the reversal is a much more widespread phenomenon. For example, before industrialization,

Shifting prosperity

Countries that were rich in 1500 are among the less-well-off societies today.

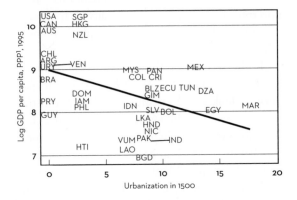

Source: Author.

Note: ARG = Argentina, AUS = Australia, BGD = Bangladesh, BLZ = Belize, BOL = Bolivia, BRA = Brazil, CAN = Canada, CHL = Chile, COL = Colombia, CRI = Costa Rica, DOM = Dominican Republic, DZA = Albania, ECU = Ecuador, EGY = Egypt, GTM = Guatemala, GUY = Guyana, JAM = Jamaica, HKG = Hong Kong SAR, HND = Honduras, HTI = Haiti, IDN = Idonesia, IND = India, LAO = Lao People's Democratic Republic, LKA = Sri Lanka, MAR = Morocco, MEX = Mexico, MYS = Malaysia, NIC = Nicaragua, NZL = New Zealand, PAK = Pakistan, PAN = Panama, PER = Peru, PHL = Philippines, PRY = Paraguay, SGP = Singapore, SLV = El Salvador, TUN = Tunisia, URY = Uruguay, USA = United States, VEN = Venezuela, VNM = Vietnam
[1]Purchasing power parity.

only relatively developed societies could sustain significant urbanization, so urbanization rates are a relatively good proxy for prosperity before European colonization. The chart here shows a strong negative relationship between urbanization rates in 1500 and income per capita today. That is, the former European colonies that are relatively rich today are those that were poor before the Europeans arrived.

This reversal is *prima facie* evidence against the most standard versions of the geography hypothesis discussed above: it cannot be that the climate, ecology, or disease environments of the tropical areas have condemned these countries to poverty today, because these same areas with the same climate, ecology, and disease environment were richer than the temperate areas 500 years ago. Although it is possible that the reversal may be related to geographic factors whose effects on economic prosperity vary over time—for example, certain characteristics that first cause prosperity then condemn nations to poverty—there is no evidence of any such factor or any support for sophisticated geography hypotheses of this sort.

Is the reversal of fortune consistent with the institutions hypothesis? The answer is yes. In fact, once we look at the variation in colonization strategies, we see that the reversal of fortune is exactly what the institutions hypothesis predicts. European colonialism made Europeans the most politically powerful group, with the capability to influence institutions more than any indigenous group was able to at the time. In places where Europeans did not settle and cared little about aggregate output and the welfare of the population, in places where there was a large population that could be coerced and employed cheaply in mines or in agriculture or simply taxed, in places where there were resources to be extracted, Europeans pursued the strategy of setting up extractive institutions or taking over existing extractive institutions and hierarchical structures. In those colonies, there were no constraints on the power of the elites (which were typically the Europeans themselves and their allies) and no civil or property rights for the majority of the population; in fact, many of them were forced into labor or enslaved. Contrasting with this pattern, in colonies where there was little to be extracted, where most of the land was empty, where the disease environment was favorable, Europeans settled in large numbers and developed laws and institutions to ensure that they themselves were protected, in both their political and their economic lives. In these colonies, the institutions were therefore much more conducive to investment and economic growth.

This evidence does not mean that geography does not matter at all, however. Which places were rich and which were poor before Europeans arrived might have been determined by geographic factors. These geographic factors also likely influenced the institutions that Europeans introduced. For example,

the climate and soil quality in the Caribbean made it productive to grow sugar there, encouraging the development of a plantation system based on slavery. What the evidence shows instead is that geography neither condemns a nation to poverty nor guarantees its economic success. If you want to understand why a country is poor today, you have to look at its institutions rather than its geography.

No Natural Gravitation

If institutions are so important for economic prosperity, why do some societies choose or end up with bad institutions? Moreover, why do these bad institutions persist long after their disastrous consequences are apparent? Is it an accident of history or the result of misconceptions or mistakes by societies or their policymakers? Recent empirical and theoretical research suggests that the answer is no: there are no compelling reasons to think that societies will naturally gravitate toward good institutions. Institutions not only affect the economic prospects of nations but are also central to the distribution of income among individuals and groups in society—in other words, institutions not only affect the size of the social pie, but also how it is distributed.

This perspective implies that a potential change from dysfunctional and bad institutions toward better ones that will increase the size of the social pie may nonetheless be blocked when such a change significantly reduces the slice that powerful groups receive from the pie and when they cannot be credibly compensated for this loss. That there is no natural gravitation toward good institutions is illustrated by the attitudes of the landed elites and the emperors in Austria-Hungary and in Russia during the nineteenth century. These elite groups blocked industrialization and even the introduction of railways and protected the old regime because they realized capitalist growth and industrialization would reduce their power and their privileges.

Similarly, European colonists did not set up institutions to benefit society as a whole. They chose good institutions when it was in their interests to do so, when they would be the ones living under the umbrella of these institutions, as in much of the New World. In contrast, they introduced or maintained existing extractive institutions when it was in their interest to extract resources from the non-European populations of the colonies, as in much of Africa, Central America, the Caribbean, and South Asia. Furthermore, these extractive institutions showed no sign of evolving into better institutions, either under European control or once these colonies gained independence. In almost all cases, we can link the persistence of extractive institutions to the fact that, even after independence, the elites in these societies had a lot to lose from institutional reform. Their political power and claim to economic rents rested on the existing extractive institutions, as best illustrated by the Caribbean plantation owners whose wealth directly depended on slavery and extractive institutions. Any reform of the system, however beneficial for the country as a whole, would be a direct threat to the owners.

European colonialism is only one part of the story of the institutions of the former colonies, and many countries that never experienced European colonialism nonetheless suffer from institutional problems (while certain other former European colonies have arguably some of the best institutions in the world today). Nevertheless, the perspective developed in this article applies to these cases as well: institutional problems are important in a variety of instances, and, in most of these, the source of institutional problems and the difficulty of institutional reform lie in the fact that any major change creates winners and losers, and the potential losers are often powerful enough to resist change.

The persistence of institutions and potential resistance to reform do not mean that institutions are unchanging. There is often significant institutional evolution, and even highly dysfunctional institutions can be successfully transformed. For example, Botswana managed to build a functioning democracy after its independence from Britain and become the fastest-growing country in the world. Institutional change will happen either when groups that favor change become powerful enough to impose it on the potential losers, or when societies can strike a bargain with potential losers so as to credibly compensate them after the change takes place or, perhaps, shield them from the most adverse consequences of these changes. Recognizing the importance of institutions in economic development and the often formidable barriers to beneficial institutional reform is the first step toward significant progress in jump-starting rapid growth in many areas of the world today.

Abhijit Banerjee and Lakshmi Iyer

HISTORY, INSTITUTIONS, AND ECONOMIC PERFORMANCE: THE LEGACY OF COLONIAL LAND TENURE SYSTEMS IN INDIA

*** We compare the present-day economic performance of different districts of India, which were placed under different land revenue systems by British colonial rulers as a result of certain historical accidents. We show that districts in India where the collection of land revenue from the cultivators was assigned to a class of landlords systematically underperform the districts where this type of intermediation was avoided, after controlling for a wide range of geographical differences. The differences show up in agricultural investment and yields, in various measures of public investment in education and health, as well as in health and educational outcomes. For example, the average yield of wheat is 23 percent higher and infant mortality is 40 percent lower in non-landlord districts. The non-landlord effect remains significant even when we restrict our data analysis to a set of 35 districts, chosen so that a landlord district always borders a non-landlord district. Finally, in all the data we have from the earlier period, i.e., from the nineteenth and early twentieth centuries, there is no evidence of landlord districts being at a disadvantage.

An obvious advantage of focusing on one specific institution in one particular country is that it makes it easy to locate the source of the difference, relative to the case where there is a complex of institutions that are all different. Another advantage is that we have access to a very detailed history of how the insti-

tutional variation came about, which makes it easier to argue for exogeneity of specific pieces of the variation. In particular, we will argue, based on historical facts, that areas where the land revenue collection was taken over by the British between 1820 and 1856 (but not before or after) are much more likely to have a non-landlord system, for reasons that have nothing to do with factors that directly influence agricultural investment and yields. We will therefore use the fact of being conquered in this period as an instrument for having a non-landlord system. We allow for the possibility that areas that were conquered in this period may have had a different experience simply because, for example, they were conquered later than most other areas, by including controls for the length of British rule. The instrumental variable estimates confirm the OLS results.

A third advantage of this particular experiment is that the land revenue systems introduced by the British departed with the British: there are no direct taxes on agricultural incomes in independent India. Our results therefore tell us that the system for land revenue collection established by the British 150 years ago or more continues to have an effect, long after it was abolished. We therefore have a pure example of institutional overhang, underscoring how hard it is to reform the institutional environment.[1]

The one disadvantage of a very specific experiment like ours is the suspicion that it reflects the peculiarity of the Indian experience. In other words, our results would be more interesting if we could

From *American Economic Review* 95, no. 4 (2005), pp. 1190–213.

identify the reasons for this extreme persistence. While our data do not allow us to identify exactly the channel through which the historical land revenue system continues to have an effect, there are a number of clues. When the British left, areas where landlords collected the revenue had an elite class that had enjoyed a great deal of economic and political power for over a century; there was no counterpart to this class in the non-landlord areas. This meant that these areas inherited a more unequal land distribution at the time of independence, and a very specific set of social cleavages, absent elsewhere.

Our data suggest, however, that in the post-independence period there is substantial convergence in inequality between the landlord and non-landlord areas, probably because states with landlord-dominated areas tend to enact a greater number of land reforms. This makes it unlikely that the persistence of the landlord effect is mainly through its effect on the contemporaneous land distribution.

On the other hand, it seems that, despite the abolition of the format structure of landlordism, the class-based antagonism that it created within the communities in these areas persisted well into the post-independence period. The conflictual environment this created is likely to have limited the possibility of collective action in these areas. This collective action-based view is consistent with the fact that the gap between the non-landlord and landlord districts grows particularly fast in the period 1965–1980 when there is extensive public investment in rural areas. We find that states with a higher proportion of landlord districts have much lower levels of public development expenditures and that a substantial part of the gap between landlord and non-landlord districts in health, education, and agricultural technology investments can be explained by this difference in public spending. This suggests that the key to what happened may lie in the relative inability of the landlord districts to claim their fair share of public investment.

■   ■   ■

I. Historical Background

A. British Political Control

The British Empire in India lasted for nearly two hundred years.

■   ■   ■

B. Pre-British and British Systems of Land Revenue

■   ■   ■

All cultivable land in British India fell under one of three alternative systems: (a) a landlord-based system (also known as *zamindari* or *malguzari*), (b) an individual cultivator-based system (*raiyatwari*), and (c) a village-based system (*mahalwari*). Table 4.1 gives the number of districts in each category for the states in our data. Map 4.1 illustrates the geographic distribution of these areas.

In the landlord areas, the revenue liability for a village or a group of villages lay with a single landlord. The landlord was free to set the revenue terms for the peasants under his jurisdiction and to dispossess any peasants who did not pay the landlord what they owed him.[2] Whatever remained after paying the British revenue demand was for the landlord to keep. These revenue-collecting rights could be bequeathed, as well as bought and sold (Kumar, 1982). In this sense, the landlord effectively had property rights on the land. Landlord systems were established mainly in Bengal, Bihar, Orissa, the Central Provinces (modern Madhya Pradesh state), and some parts of Madras Presidency (modern Tamil Nadu and Andhra Pradesh states). In some of these areas, the British declared the landlords' revenue commitments to the government to be fixed in perpetuity (the "Permanent Settlement" of 1793). In other areas, a "temporary" settlement was implemented whereby the revenue

Table 4.1. State-Wise Distribution of Landlord and Non-Landlord Districts

| | | CLASSIFICATION OF REVENUE SYSTEMS | | | | |
| | | | | VILLAGE BODIES | | |
State	Mean non-landlord proportion	Landlord based	Individual based	Landlord	Non-landlord	Total districts
Andhra Pradesh	0.66	2	8	0	0	10
Bihar	0.00	12	0	0	0	12
Gujarat	1.00	0	7	0	0	7
Haryana	0.85	0	0	0	5	5
Karnataka	1.00	0	15	0	0	15
Madhya Pradesh	0.10	14	1	0	0	15
Maharashtra	0.78	4	14	0	0	18
Orissa	0.32	6	2	0	0	8
Punjab	0.87	0	0	0	6	6
Rajasthan	0.00	1	0	0	0	1
Tamil Nadu	0.75	2	9	0	0	11
Uttar Pradesh	0.42	0	0	12	35	47
West Bengal	0.00	11	0	0	0	11
Total	0.51	52	56	12	46	166

Notes: This table lists only districts that used to be part of British India. Areas where the British did not set up the land revenue system are excluded. Districts of British India currently in Pakistan, Bangladesh, or Burma are excluded. The table also excludes the states of Assam and Kerala, for which agricultural data are not available in the World Bank dataset. The table lists 1960 districts, some of which were split into two or more districts over time. We use unsplit districts in all our analyses.

was fixed for a certain number of years, after which it was subject to revision.

In most areas of Madras and Bombay Presidencies, and in Assam, the *raiyatwari* system was adopted under which the revenue settlement was made directly with the individual *raiyat* or cultivator. In these areas, an extensive cadastral survey of the land was done and a detailed record-of-rights was prepared, which served as the legal title to the land for the cultivator. Unlike the Permanent Settlement areas, the revenue commitment was not fixed; it was

usually calculated as the money value of a share of the estimated average annual output. This share typically varied from place to place, was different for different soil types, and was adjusted periodically in response to changes in the productivity of the land.

In the North-West Provinces and Panjab, the village-based (*mahalwari*) system was adopted in which village bodies which jointly owned the village were responsible for the land revenue. Village bodies could be in charge of varying areas, from part of a village to several villages. The composition of the

Map 4.1 Map of India

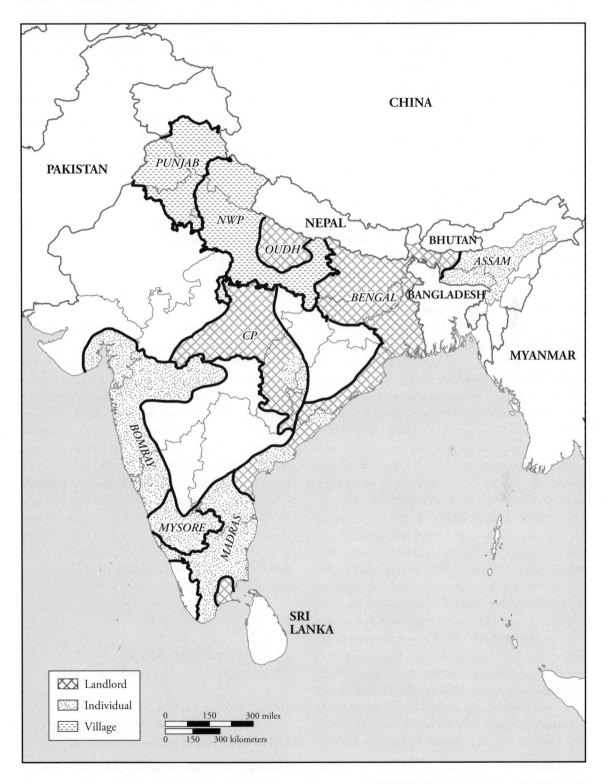

village body also varied from place to place. In some areas it was a single person or family that made up the village body and hence was very much like the Bengal landlord system (*zamindari*), while in other areas the village body had a large number of members with each person being responsible for a fixed share of the revenue. * * *

C. Choice of Land Revenue System

Why did the British choose different systems in different areas? It is broadly agreed that their major motivation was to ensure a large and steady source of revenue for the government, while maintaining a certain political equilibrium. It is also clear, however, that they often faced a lack of hard information and based their decision on a priori arguments. For instance, Sir Thomas Munro argued for the establishment of an individual cultivator system in Madras on the grounds that it would raise agricultural productivity by improving incentives; that the cultivators would be less subject to arbitrary expropriation than under a landlord; that they would have a measure of insurance (via government revenue remissions in bad times); that the government would be assured of its revenue (since small peasants are less able to resist paying their dues); and that this was the mode of land tenure prevailing in South India from ancient times. The Madras Board of Revenue, in its turn, used more or less the same arguments (in reverse, of course) for favoring landlords. Large landlords would have the capacity to invest more and therefore productivity would be higher; the peasants' long-term relationship with the landlord would result in less expropriation than the short-term one with a government official; a big landlord would provide insurance for small farmers; a steady revenue would be assured because the landlords would be wealthy and could make up an occasional shortfall from their own resources; and this was the mode of tenure prevailing from ancient times (Nilmani Mukherjee, 1962)! While the British often invoked history to justify the choices they made, they frequently misread history. For example, one reason they favored landlords in

Bengal is because they found landlords in Bengal when they arrived. As has been pointed out by a number of scholars,[3] however, these landlords were really local chieftains and not the large farmers that the British had thought them to be.

Decisions were therefore often taken on the basis of some general principle, and the ideology of the individual decision maker and contemporary economic doctrines played an important role in combination with the exigencies of the moment.

■   ■   ■

Areas that came under British revenue administration at later dates were in general more likely to have non-landlord systems.

■   ■   ■

Landlord-based systems required much less administrative machinery to be set up by the British, and so areas conquered in the early periods of British rule were likely to have landlord-based systems. Once a landlord-based system was established, however, it was costly to change and hence the landlord system survived. Also, the increasing popularity of dealing directly with the peasant mirrored shifts in the views of economists and others in Britain. In the 1790s, under the shadow of the French Revolution across the Channel, the British elites were inclined to side with the landlords. In the 1820s, with peasant power long defeated and half forgotten, they were more inclined to be sympathetic to the utilitarians and others who were arguing for dealing directly with peasants.[4, 5]

■   ■   ■

D. Post-Independence Developments in Land Policy

Under the constitution of independent India, states were granted the power to enact land reforms. Several states passed legislation in the early 1950s, formally abolishing landlords and other intermediaries between the government and the cultivator. Other laws have also been passed by different states at different times regarding tenancy reform, ceiling on land holdings, and land consolidation measures. Besley and Burgess (2000) provide a good review of these laws and their impact on state-level poverty rates.

II. Why Should the Historical Land System Matter?

Why would we expect productivity and investment (including public investment in infrastructure) to differ between areas having a greater or lesser extent of landlord control? Why would these differences persist and not be wiped out as soon as the landlord class is formally abolished? In this section, we list some potential answers to these questions, postponing to Section VI any discussion of the empirical plausibility of these answers.

A. Differences in the Distribution of Wealth

Under landlord-based systems, the landlords were given a more or less free hand to set the terms for the tenants[6] and, as a result, they were in a position to appropriate most of the gains in productivity. Moreover, landlord areas were also the only areas subject to the Permanent Settlement of 1793 (which fixed the landlord's dues permanently in nominal terms), and even where the settlement was not permanent, the political power of the landlord class made it less likely that their rates would be raised when their surplus grew. As the nineteenth century was a period of significant productivity growth and inflation, the landlord class grew rich over this period and inequality went up. By contrast, in the individual cultivator areas, rents were raised frequently by the British in an attempt to extract as much as possible from the tenant. There was, as a result, comparatively little differentiation

within the rural population of these areas until, in the latter years of the nineteenth century, the focus of the British moved away from extracting as much as they could from the peasants. At this point, there was indeed increasing differentiation within the peasant class, but overall one would expect less inequality in the non-landlord areas.

In fact, this is what the limited historical data we have suggest. The provinces with a higher non-landlord proportion have lower Gini measures of land inequality in 1885 (Figure 4.2A). Further, the differences in inequality persist until the end of the colonial period. In 1948, the districts of Uttar Pradesh that had a higher landlord proportion had a much higher proportion of land revenue being paid by very large landlords and a correspondingly higher measure of inequality (Figure 4.2B).

The distribution of wealth is important for three reasons: first, because it determines the size of the group within the peasantry that has enough land and other wealth to be able to make the many somewhat lumpy and/or risky investments necessary to raise productivity;[7] second, because it affects the balance between those who cultivate mainly their own land and those who cultivate other people's land (as is well-known, cultivating other people's land generates incentive problems, which reduces investment and productivity); finally, because it made it likely that the political interests of the rural masses would diverge substantially from that of the elite. In particular, it made it very tempting for the peasants to support political programs that advocate expropriating the assets of the rich. To the extent that the differences in the land distribution still persist, this would be one mechanism through which historical differences in the land tenure system could continue to affect productivity today.

B. Differences in the Political Environment

The right to set the land revenue rates and to penalize those who did not pay gave the landlords a substantial degree of political power over the rest

Figure 4.2 Land Tenure and Land Inequality

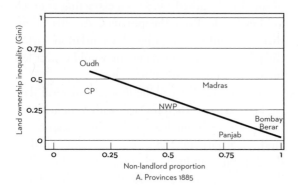

A. Provinces 1885

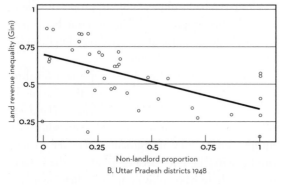

B. Uttar Pradesh districts 1948

period.[8] Those familiar with post-independence India will recognize, for example, that the areas most associated with Maoist peasant uprisings (known as "Naxalite" movements)—clearly the most extreme form of the politics of class conflict in India—are West Bengal, Bihar, and the Srikakulam district of Andhra Pradesh, all landlord areas. Paul R. Brass (1994, pp. 326–27) argues explicitly that these peasant movements had their roots in the history of exploitation and oppression of peasants by landlords. Moreover, these class-based conflicts go back to the colonial period. Kathleen Gough (1974) studies 77 peasant struggles from the end of the Mughal era until today and suggests that at least a third of these originated in Bengal, the oldest and best established of the landlord areas. Along the same lines, Partha Chatterjee (1984) has argued, based on the pattern of voting on the Tenancy Act Amendment in the Bengal Legislative Council in 1928, that the representatives of the peasants voted largely in a block against the landlords, and vice versa.

Given this history, it is no surprise that the elites and the masses in these areas rarely shared the trust that is essential for being able to act together in the collective interest.[9] It is quite plausible that, in the post-independence period, the political energies of the masses were directed more toward expropriating from the rich (via land reforms, for example) than toward trying to get more public goods (schools, tap water, electricity) from the state, while the political energies of the rich were aimed at trying to ensure that the poor did not get their way.[10] Moreover, it was not uncommon for the rural elites in the landlord areas to be quite disassociated from the actual business of agriculture, since they typically were more likely to be rent collectors than farmers, and even the rent collection rights were often leased out. This would tend to weaken the political pressure on the state to deliver public goods that were important to farmers. Moreover, they were often physically absent, preferring to live in the city and simply collect their rents, and as a result had only rather limited stakes in improving the living conditions in rural areas.

of the population in their domain. One possible consequence of this may be that peasant property was relatively insecure in the landlord areas. Investments that made the land more productive were discouraged because of the risk of expropriation by the landlord. In contrast, in the *raiyatwari* areas, the proprietary rights of peasants were based on an explicit, typically written, contract with the colonial state, which the colonial state was broadly committed to honor. This may have resulted in better incentives for the peasants in the non-landlord areas in the colonial period.

The exercise of this type of more or less arbitrary power by the landlord over the property and not, infrequently, the body of the peasant, created a political ethos of class-based resentment in these areas, which persisted well into the post-independence

C. Differences in the Relationship with the Colonial State

Since it was easier for the colonial government to raise rents in non-landlord areas, it meant that the state could capture some of the productivity gains from these areas, and hence had more reason to invest in irrigation, railways, schools, and other infrastructure in these areas during the colonial period.[11] In this context, we should note that almost all canals constructed by the British were in non-landlord areas. If, indeed, these areas had better public goods when the British left, it is plausible that they could continue to have some advantage even now.

III. Data

We use a combination of historical and recent data for our analysis. All data are at the district level, a district in India being an administrative unit within a state. In 1991, India had 415 districts in 17 major states, a district on average having an area of 7,500 square kilometers and a population of 1.5 million.

■   ■   ■

Using district-level data gives us a larger sample size. The drawback is that we are limited in the kind of data that we can get. For instance, we do not have measures of GDP or average income per capita at the district level. We will thus be using other correlates or proxies of economic prosperity for which we have data at the district level: agricultural investment outcomes (the proportion of irrigated gross cropped area, quantity of fertilizer used per hectare of gross cropped area, and the proportion of area sown with high-yielding varieties (HYV) of rice, wheat, and other cereals); agricultural productivity (crop yields); and the stock of health and education infrastructure (schools and health centers).

The district-level data on agricultural investments and productivity come from the India Agriculture and Climate Data Set assembled by the World Bank and cover the period 1956–1987. This dataset has information on 271 districts in 13 major states.[12] All data are at the 1961 district level, aggregating over subsequent splits in districts. We also have data for health and education infrastructure from the 1981 Census. We matched each modern district to an older British district using old and new maps, and retained only the districts where the land tenure system was established by the British, because we do not have detailed information on the land systems in districts that were under native princes or tribal chiefs.[13] For each district of British India,[14] we then proceed to compute a measure of non-landlord control in the colonial period as follows: for many areas (the states of Andhra Pradesh, Madhya Pradesh, Panjab, Tamil Nadu, and Uttar Pradesh), we have district-level information on the proportion of villages, estates, or land area, not under the revenue liability of landlords; for other areas where we do not have the exact proportion (Bihar, Karnataka, Maharashtra, Orissa, West Bengal), we assign the non-landlord measure as being either zero or one, depending on the dominant land revenue system. In all cases, the measure of non-landlord control is computed based on data from the 1870s or 1880s.

■   ■   ■

IV. Empirical Approach

We will compare agricultural investments and productivity between landlord and non-landlord areas by running regressions of the form

$$(1) \qquad y_{it} = constant + \alpha_t + \beta \mathrm{NL}_i + X_{it} \gamma + \varepsilon_{it}$$

where y_{it} is our outcome variable of interest (investment, productivity, etc.) in district i and year t, α_t is a year-fixed effect, NL_i is the historical measure of the non-landlord control in district i, and X_{it} are other control variables. Our coefficient of interest is β, which captures the average difference between a non-landlord district and a landlord district in the post-independence period.

In all our regressions, we control for such geographic variables as latitude, altitude, soil type, mean annual rainfall, and a dummy for whether the district is on the coast or not. In addition, we also control for the length of time under British rule (or, equivalently, the date of British conquest), which may have independent effects, because early British rule was particularly rapacious or because the best (or the worst) districts fell to the British first. Note that we do not include district fixed effects in this regression, since NL_i is fixed for district i over time (it is the historical land arrangement), * * * [and] the modern states were formed at a later date than our non-landlord proportion. We would like to see how far historical factors can account for the widely varied performance of Indian states in the post-independence period.

As mentioned in the introduction, we will try to deal with concerns about exogeneity, first by looking only at the difference between neighboring districts, and second by adopting an instrumental variables approach. After establishing the robustness of the differences in investment and productivity between landlord and non-landlord areas, we estimate some additional specifications. First we re-estimate the yield equations after controlling for various measures of investment in agriculture (fertilizer use, irrigation, etc.) to check whether there is a non-landlord effect over and above the effect on investment. Then we allow the non-landlord coefficient to vary over time to see whether we can demonstrate how the gap between landlord and non-landlord areas has evolved over time.

V. The Impact on Agricultural Outcomes

A. Differences in Geography and Other Differences

There are significant geographical differences between landlord areas and non-landlord areas. Landlord areas have somewhat lower altitudes, higher rainfall, and fewer areas with black soil as compared to non-landlord areas. In particular, we note that landlord areas have a greater depth of topsoil, which together with the greater rainfall and lower altitudes seems to indicate that these areas might be inherently more fertile and productive. Landlord areas have a slightly higher total population and a significantly higher population density than non-landlord areas. This is consistent with the fact they seem to be more fertile areas. * * *

We have very limited historical data on yields. Looking at data for rice yields in ten districts of Madras Presidency, and rice and wheat yields for 17 districts of Uttar Pradesh during the colonial period, we see in Figure 4.3 that yields were in fact *lower* in non-landlord areas during this period.[15] Given the size of the sample, we cannot hope to control for geographical differences between the districts. These yield differences may therefore reflect differences in geography. The only point we are making here is that the landlord districts did not start with a disadvantage.

B. Differences in Agricultural Investments and Productivity

We mainly investigate investment and productivity differences in the 1956–1985 period. Table 4.2 documents large and significant differences in measures of agricultural investments and productivity between landlord and non-landlord areas in the post-independence period. Each entry in this table represents the regression coefficient from a regression of the dependent variable on the non-landlord proportion, controlling for year fixed effects, geographical variables (latitude, altitude, mean annual rainfall, and soil types), length of British rule, and within-district clustering of errors. Our base specification in column (1) shows that non-landlord districts have a 24-percent-higher proportion of irrigated area and 43-percent-higher levels of fertilizer use. They have a 27-percent-higher proportion of rice area and 18 percent more

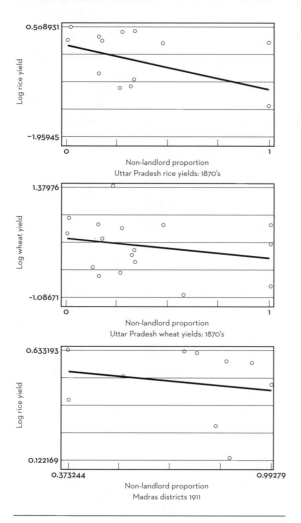

Figure 4.3 Agricultural Yields in Colonial Period

(plots)

Uttar Pradesh rice yields: 1870's

Uttar Pradesh wheat yields: 1870's

Madras districts 1911

It is worth noting that these differences are driven neither by substitution away from agriculture in landlord districts nor by a greater shift toward crops other than rice or wheat. Landlord areas have a higher proportion of their working population engaged in farming, and they also devote a lower proportion of area to growing cash crops.

■   ■   ■

D. Results Using Neighboring Districts

Obviously, our interpretation of these results has to be tempered by the possibility that the non-landlord gap might reflect omitted variables. One strategy to control for possible omitted variables is to consider an extremely restricted sample: we consider only those districts that happen to be geographical neighbors (i.e., share a common border), but that happened to have different historical land systems. We expect that there would be fewer differences in omitted variables, if any, in this sample of geographic neighbors than in our overall sample, and we verify that there are no significant differences in our observed geographic and demographic variables between these districts.

Even when we restrict our sample to this small set of 35 geographically neighboring districts, we still see large and significant differences between landlord and non-landlord districts in agricultural investments and outcomes (Table 4.4, panel A, column 1). In particular, total yields are 15 percent higher and wheat yields 25 percent higher in non-landlord areas than in landlord areas. These estimates are very close to the estimates in our base specification. The differences in fertilizer use and HYV adoption for wheat are also fairly close to the magnitudes obtained in our base specification. These results serve to confirm that our original results were not caused primarily by some unobserved district characteristics.

wheat area under high-yielding varieties. Overall agricultural yields are 16 percent higher, rice yields are 17 percent higher, and wheat yields are 23 percent higher. Further, column 2 shows that these differences arc slightly bigger if we exclude the states of West Bengal and Bihar, the two states that have the highest proportion of landlord districts and the first to be conquered by the British. (We wanted to be sure that something idiosyncratic about these states was not driving our results.)

Table 4.2. Differences in Agricultural Investments and Yields (Mean non-landlord proportion = 0.5051 (s.d. = 0.4274))

Dependent variable	Mean of dependent variable	Coefficient on non-landlord proportion	
		OLS Full sample (1)	OLS Excluding Bengal and Bihar (2)
Agricultural investments			
Proportion of gross cropped area irrigated	0.276	0.065*	0.066*
		(0.034)	(0.035)
Fertilizer use (kg/ha)	24.64	10.708***	10.992***
		(3.345)	(3.406)
Proportion of rice area under HYV	0.298	0.079*	0.094**
		(0.044)	(0.043)
Proportion of wheat area under HYV	0.518	0.092**	0.119***
		(0.046)	(0.045)
Proportion of other cereals area under HYV	0.196	0.057*	0.084***
		(0.031)	(0.024)
Agricultural productivity			
log (yield of 15 major crops)		0.157**	0.152**
		(0.071)	(0.074)
log (rice yield)		(0.071)**	0.195**
		(0.081)	(0.081)
log (wheat yield)		0.229***	0.228***
		(0.067)	(0.070)
No. of districts		166	143
Year fixed effects		YES	YES
Geographic controls		YES	YES
Date of British land revenue control		YES	YES

Notes: Standard errors in parentheses, corrected for district-level clustering. * Significant at 10-percent level; ** significant at 5-percent level; *** significant at 1-percent level. Each cell represents the coefficient from a regression of the dependent variable on the measure of non-landlord control. Data are from 1956 to 1987. Data for area under high-yielding varieties (HYV) is after 1965. Geographic controls are altitude, latitude, mean annual rainfall, and dummies for soil type and coastal regions. The non-landlord dummy is assigned as follows: the dummy equals one for all individual-based districts and all village-based districts except those in Oudh. For landlord-based districts and the village-based districts of Oudh, the dummy is zero.

E. Results Using Instrumental Variables

As discussed above, our results might also be biased if the British decision regarding which land tenure system to adopt depended on other characteristics of the area in systematic ways. We would like to highlight a few facts in this regard. First, we do not expect the choice of land tenure system to be very highly correlated with local district characteristics, since the choice of land tenure system was made for large contiguous areas at the same time and was often based on very little information regarding local conditions. Second, as explained earlier, places that were conquered earlier tended to have landlord-based systems. If British annexation policy was selectively directed toward the more productive places,[16] then landlord-controlled areas are likely to be inherently more productive. Third, *zamindari* areas were usually highly fertile areas which created enough rent to support a landlord-tenant-laborer hierarchy (Roy, 2000). In some areas, where landlord defaults were excessive, these were later changed to different forms of settlement. Therefore, areas that ended up with non-landlord systems are more likely to be inherently less productive, or at least were less productive in colonial times. Another way to deal with this potential problem of omitted variables is to use an instrumental variables strategy. This has the additional advantage of helping us deal with the problem of measurement error in our non-landlord proportion variable, caused by district boundary changes and the fact that the historical record tends to be impressionistic (in any case, reflects the impression of one observer at one point of time).

Our instrumental variables strategy is based on the observation, mentioned in Section I, that areas that came under British revenue administration after 1820 have predominantly non-landlord systems.

the characteristics of the district, and a dummy for the date of conquest being between 1820 and 1856 is a valid instrument for the non-landlord proportion, especially after we control for the date of British conquest to take into account any direct effects of a longer period of British rule.[17]

Figure 4.4 demonstrates the basis for our instrumental variable strategy. In this figure, we plot the kernel regression of the non-landlord proportion and the mean log agricultural yield against the date of conquest. It is clear that there is a good fit in the shape of the two graphs and that both curves are highly nonlinear. Therefore, the co-movement in the two graphs is not driven by the fact that both are trending up or down, making it less likely that the relation between the two reflects the direct effect of the date of conquest. The figure also demonstrates that the non-landlord proportion is significantly higher for areas conquered between 1820 and 1856 compared to areas conquered earlier or later. This is exactly what we would have expected given the discussion above.[18] Panel B in Table 4.4 shows the first-stage coefficients of our IV strategy; we should note that the first-stage relationship remains significant even when we include a quadratic control for the length of British rule, as well as when we include state fixed effects.

Our IV results confirm that non-landlord systems indeed have a large and significant impact on current outcomes (Table 4.3, panel A, column 2). In fact, all the IV coefficients are larger than their OLS counterparts, although the difference between the two estimates is not statistically significant.[19] The standard errors for the IV estimates are also larger than the OLS standard errors, but the non-landlord effect remains statistically significant in the case of HYV adoption, as well as in fertilizer usage and wheat yields. Rice yields are significantly greater.

■   ■   ■

The fact that areas conquered between 1820 and 1856 got non-landlord systems does not depend on

■   ■   ■

The fact that the IV results are larger than the OLS results suggests that the OLS results are biased

Table 4.3. Robustness of OLS Results

Panel A: Robustness checks

	Coefficient on non-landlord proportion	
Dependent variable	OLS Neighbors only (1)	IV Full sample (2)
Agricultural investments		
Proportion of gross cropped area irrigated	0.101**	0.216
	(0.041)	(0.137)
Fertilizer use (kg/ha)	10.589**	26.198**
	(4.979)	(13.244)
Proportion of rice area under HYV	–0.015	0.411**
	(0.083)	(0.163)
Proportion of wheat area under HYV	0.078**	0.584***
	(0.034)	(0.163)
Proportion of other cereals area under HYV	–0.025	0.526***
	(0.024)	(0.129)
Agricultural productivity		
log (yield of 15 major crops)	0.145**	0.409
	(0.061)	(0.261)
leg (rice yield)	0.126	0.554*
	(0.098)	(0.285)
log (wheat yield)	0.253***	0.706***
	(0.084)	(0.214)
No. of districts	35	166
Year fixed effects	YES	YES
Geographic controls	YES	YES
Date of British land revenue control	YES	YES

Panel B: First-stage regressions for IV

Dependent variable: Non-landlord proportion

Coefficient on	(1)	(2)	(3)
Instrument (= 1 if date of British revenue control is between 1820 and 1856)	0.331*** (0.086)	0.430*** (0.092)	0.419*** (0.087)
R-squared	0.40	0.43	0.63
No. of observations	166	166	166

(Continued

Table 4.3. Robustness of OLS Results (Continued)

Geographic controls	YES	YES	YES
Date of British land revenue control	YES	YES	YES
Date of British land revenue control squared	NO	YES	NO
State fixed effects	NO	NO	YES

Notes: Standard errors in parentheses, corrected for district-level clustering. * Significant at 10-percent level; ** significant at 5-percent level; *** significant at 1-percent level. Each cell in Panel A represents the coefficient from a regression of the dependent variable on the non-landlord proportion. Data are from 1956–1987. Data for area under high-yielding varieties (HYV) is after 1965. Geographic controls are altitude, latitude, mean annual rainfall, and dummies for soil type and coastal regions. Instrument is a dummy that equals one if the date of British revenue control is after 1820 and before 1856.

Figure 4.4. Instrumental Variables Strategy

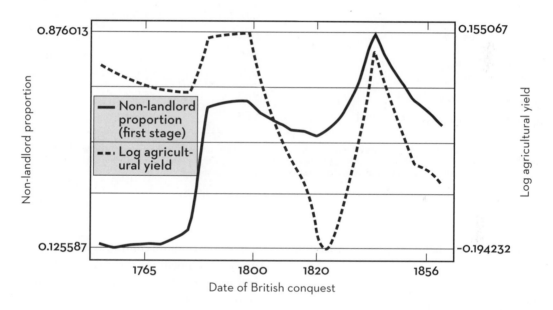

downward. This is the direction of bias we would have expected, given our discussion above, especially the fact that landlord areas, which were not productive enough to sustain a landlord class, tended to become non-landlord.

■ ■ ■

Our IV results, together with the results on neighboring districts and the historical data, lead us to conclude that our OLS results are not biased upward due to omitted district characteristics. Because of the possibility of upward bias in the IV estimates, however, we will continue to treat the OLS results as benchmark estimates of the

Table 4.4. Are Yields Explained by Investments?

	Dependent variables		
	Log total yield OLS (1)	Log rice yield OLS (2)	Log wheat yield OLS (3)
Proportion non-landlord	0.035	0.070	0.109
	(0.053)	(0.063)	(0.063)
Proportion of gross cropped area irrigated	0.693**	0.439**	0.435**
	(0.112)	(0.096)	(0.117)
Fertilizer use (kg/ha)	0.007**	0.004**	0.001
	(0.001)	(0.001)	(0.001)
Percent area under HYV	4.274**	0.580**	0.618**
	(1.122)	(0.063)	(0.070)
Adjusted R-squared	0.60	0.52	0.56
No. of districts	166	166	166
Year fixed effects	YES	YES	YES
Geographic controls	YES	YES	YES
Date of British land revenue control	YES	YES	YES

Notes: Standard errors in parentheses, corrected for district-level clustering. * Significant at 10-percent level; ** significant at 5-percent level; *** significant at 1-percent level. Data are from 1956–1987. Data for area under high-yielding varieties (HYV) is after 1965. Geographic controls are altitude, latitude, mean annual rainfall, and dummies for soil type and coastal regions.

difference between landlord and non-landlord districts.

F. Does Land Tenure Have an Independent Effect on Productivity?

We have established large and robust differences between landlord and non-landlord districts in terms of agricultural investments and productivity, with the non-landlord districts showing better performance in all of these measures. In Table 4.4, we argue that the differences in productivity are due largely to differences in investments. We do this by regressing productivity measures on the propor-

tion of non-landlord control, as well as on the measures of investment. All the measures of investment (irrigation, fertilizer use, and adoption of HYV) are positive and strongly significant, as we would expect. The addition of these measures reduces the coefficient on the non-landlord proportion by 78 percent for total yields, 59 percent for rice yields, and 52 percent for wheat yields. The non-landlord variable is also no longer statistically significant.

G. When Do the Differences Arise?

As shown before, non-landlord districts were not more productive than landlord-based districts in the

Figure 4.5 Investment and Productivity Time Series

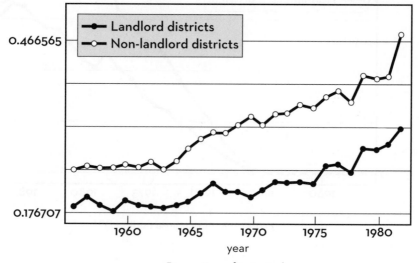

Proportion of irrigated area

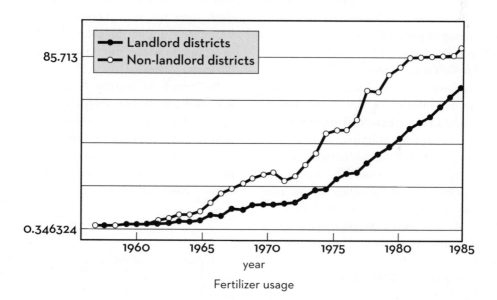

Fertilizer usage

colonial period. Figure 4.5 indicates that the differences in investments (irrigation, fertilizer) and yields widen in the mid-1960s. Table 4.5 (panel A) formally establishes that the gap between landlord and non-landlord areas is larger after 1965 than in the 1956–1965 period.

VI. Why do the Landlord Districts Fall Behind?

The period after 1965 saw the state in India becoming much more active in rural areas, through the Intensive Rural Development Programs, the

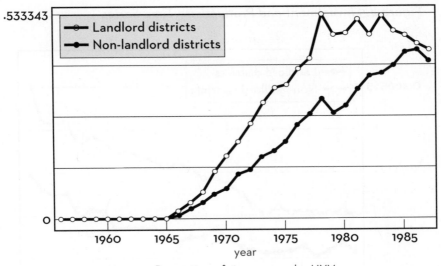

.533343

Landlord districts
Non-landlord districts

0

1960   1965   1970   1975   1980   1985

year

Proportion of rice area under HYV

efforts to disseminate new high-yielding varieties of crops (resulting in the "Green Revolution"), and the building of public infrastructure (including fertilizer delivery systems) in rural areas under the 1971 *Garibi Hatao* (poverty alleviation) program. As we have seen, the landlord areas were slower in the adoption of high-yielding varieties. They also seem to have benefited less from the growth in public investment in irrigation, though our numbers do not distinguish between public and private irrigation facilities. Why were landlord areas unable to take advantage of the new opportunities that presented themselves after the mid-1960s? We discussed some potential answers in Section II, and we assess their empirical relevance here.

Of the three alternative classes of explanations discussed earlier, the explanation based on differential investment by the colonial state is probably the least compelling, given that the major differences between the landlord and non-landlord areas arose after 1965 (Table 4.5). In principle, one could still argue that the advantage they got from these early public investments continues to help them in the post-independence period.[20] The fact that the main source of the non-landlord advantage does not come

from the *mahalwari* districts of northern India,[21] which were the main beneficiaries of the canal construction during the colonial period, makes it harder to believe that this is the source of the entire difference.

We noted in Section II that the landlord-controlled areas had higher levels of land inequality in the colonial period. It therefore comes as no surprise that the major landlord-dominated states enacted an average of 6.5 land reform measures in the period between 1957 and 1992, while non-landlord states had an average of 3.5.[22]

■   ■   ■

The biggest piece of the story is probably the differences in the political environment. If the effect of the political environment operated mainly through the insecurity of peasant property in the landlord areas, however, we would have observed convergence rather than divergence after independence, since peasant property clearly became less insecure once the landlords lost their formal authority. This suggests that the important difference in the political environment probably has to do with the nature of collective action in the two areas. We find that in

Table 4.5. When Do the Differences Appear?

Panel A: Full sample

Dependent variable	Coefficient on non-landlord proportion		
	1956–1965 (1)	After 1965 (2)	Difference (3)
Agricultural investments			
Proportion of gross cropped area irrigated	0.046	0.079**	0.033**
	(0.033)	(0.036)	(0.016)
Fertilizer use (kg/ha)	1.026**	15.581***	14.55***
	(0.425)	(4.763)	(4.44)
Agricultural productivity			
log (yield of 15 major crops)	0.066	0.201***	0.135***
	(0.065)	(0.076)	(0.033)
log (rice yield)	0.108	0.196**	0.088**
	(0.069)	(0.089)	(0.044)
log (wheat yield)	0.146**	0.268***	0.122*
	(0.058)	(0.079)	(0.063)
No. of districts	166	166	166
Year fixed effects	YES	YES	YES
Geographic controls	YES	YES	YES
Date of British land revenue control	YES	YES	YES

Panel B: Rice yields for Tamil Nadu districts

Sample: 10 districts of Tamil Nadu. Data are for 1870, 1901, 1911, 1917, 1919, and five-yearly intervals from 1922 to 1982.

Dependent variable	Coefficient on non-landlord proportion		
	Before 1965	After 1965	Difference
Log rice yield	–0.099	0.415	0.514**
	(0.172)	(0.366)	(0.217)
No. of districts	10	10	10
Year fixed effects	YES	YES	YES

Notes: Standard errors in parentheses, corrected for district-level clustering. * Significant at 10-percent level; ** significant at 5-percent level; *** significant at 1-percent level, Data are from 1956–1987. Geographic controls are altitude, latitude, mean annual rainfall, and dummies for soil type and coastal regions. Estimates in column (3) are computed from a regression of the dependent variable on the interaction of the non-landlord proportion and a dummy for year > 1965, after controlling for the main effects of these variables, as well as geographic controls.

addition to placing a greater emphasis on land reform measures, states with a higher proportion of landlord areas spent less on development expenditure. Between 1960 and 1965, the landlord states spent 13 rupees per capita on development expenditure, compared to 19 rupees in the non-landlord states. This spending gap is higher in the post-1965 period, just when new technologies were appearing in the agricultural sector: landlord states spent 29 rupees per capita, while the non-landlord states spent a much higher 49 rupees per capita (Table 4.6). This is not simply because of lack of resources: development expenditure as a proportion of state domestic product is also lower in the landlord states, and the difference

Table 4.6. Impact of State Policy

| | | Coefficient on non-landlord proportion | | |
Dependent variables	Mean of dependent variable	OLS Base specification (1)	OLS Control for state dev exp per capita (2)	OLS State FE (3)
Panel A: Agricultural investments				
Proportion of gross cropped area irrigated	0.276	0.065*	0.074**	0.028
		(0.034)	(0.035)	(0.036)
Fertilizer use (kg/ha)	24.64	10.708***	10.805***	4.297
		(3.345)	(3.717)	(3.308)
Proportion of rice area under HYV	0.298	0.079*	0.007	0.000
		(0.044)	(0.040)	(0.042)
Proportion of wheat area under HYV	0.518	0.092**	0.061	0.028
		(0.046)	(0.047)	(0.039)
Proportion of other cereals area under HYV	0.196	0.057*	0.025	0.043*
		(0.031)	(0.030)	(0.026)
Panel B: Agricultural productivity				
log (yield of 15 major crops)		0.157**	0.174**	0.059
		(0.071)	(0.076)	(0.072)
log (rice yield)		0.171**	0.083	0.016
		(0.081)	(0.082)	(0.078)
log (wheat yield)		0.229***	0.243***	0.150***
		(0.067)	(0.072)	(0.045)

(Continued)

Table 4.6. Impact of State Policy (Continued)

Dependent variables	Mean of dependent variable	Coefficient on non-landlord proportion		
		OLS Base specification (1)	OLS Control for state dev exp per capita (2)	OLS State FE (3)
Panel C: Education and health investments, 1981				
Proportion of villages having:				
Primary school	0.745	0.154***	0.062*	0.102***
		(0.036)	(0.037)	(0.039)
Middle school	0.204	0.125***	0.093***	0.064***
		(0.023)	(0.021)	(0.018)
High school	0.082	0.052***	0.019	0.030***
		(0.018)	(0.014)	(0.013)
Primary health center	0.023	0.011***	0.002	0.012***
		(0.004)	(0.004)	(0.004)
Primary health subcenter	0.031	0.033***	0.011	0.006
		(0.011)	(0.009)	(0.006)
Panel D: Education and health outcomes				
Literacy rate (1961, 1971. 1981, 1991)	0.2945	0.0524**	0.0290*	0.0241
		(0.0190)	(0.0171)	(0.0176)
Infant mortality rate (1991)	82.17	−32.71***	−25.43***	−15.81***
		(5.38)	(5.28)	(5.40)
State fixed effects		NO	NO	YES
Year fixed effects		YES	YES	YES
Geographic controls		YES	YES	YES
Date of British land revenue control		YES	YES	YES

Notes: Standard errors in parentheses, corrected for district-level clustering. * Significant at 10-percent level; ** significant at 5-percent level; *** significant at 1-percent level. Geographic controls are altitude, latitude, mean annual rainfall, and dummies for soil type and coastal regions.

in per capita spending persists even after controlling for state domestic product per capita. Given that the difference in the number of land reforms is also mainly from the post-1965 period, one way to characterize the difference in the nature of public action is to say that landlord-dominated states were busy carrying out land reform exactly when the non-landlord states started focusing on development.

This difference in public spending turns out to be important in explaining our results. When we add development expenditure per capita as an explanatory variable in our base regressions, we find that it sharply reduces the magnitude of the non-landlord coefficient for the measures of HYV adoption (Table 4.7, column 2). The idea of state policy priorities as the major channel of influence is consistent with what we find when we estimate the investment and yield equations after including a fixed effect for each state. This reduces the estimated coefficient on the non-landlord share substantially (by 50 percent or so), though the signs are unaltered and several remain significant (Table 4.7, column 3).[23] The differences in state policies are also reflected in the substantial difference between landlord and non-landlord areas in the provision of educational and health facilities: landlord areas had 21 percent fewer villages (15 percentage points) equipped with primary schools, while the gap in middle school and high school availability are 61 percent and 63 percent, respectively. Given these differences in investments, it is not surprising that literacy rates are 5 percentage points higher in non-landlord areas, while infant mortality rates are 40 percent lower; both these differences are statistically significant (Table 4.7, panel D).[24] A large part of these differences can be attributed to the difference in state development expenditure (column 2).

Why are the political priorities so different in these two areas? As already suggested in Section II, the masses in the landlord areas, with their memories of an oppressive and often absentee landlord class, may perceive their interests as being opposed to that of the local elite, while those in the non-landlord areas may be more interested in working with that elite. The existence of a highly conflictual environment is consistent with our results on crime rates. Landlord districts have significantly higher levels of violent crime (such as murder, rape, kidnap, armed robbery, and riots), but not of economic crimes like cheating or counterfeiting.

The perception of a large divergence of interests between the masses and the elite in landlord areas may not, however, be necessarily correct. The final empirical exercise in this paper compares poverty reduction in the landlord and non-landlord areas. While the head count ratio falls in both areas between 1972 and 1987 (the mean reduction is about 11 percentage points), the decline in poverty according to our OLS estimates is about seven percentage points higher in non-landlord areas. The difference in poverty reduction is five percentage points for the sample of neighboring districts and is robust to the inclusion of a state fixed effect. * * * In sum, there is no evidence that the masses fare better in the landlord areas, and there is some evidence that they do worse. If we were prepared to attribute the change in poverty to the differences in political priorities and the resulting differences in policies, these results would suggest that the masses could perhaps have done a little better, or at least no worse, by focusing on what they had in common with the elites.

NOTES

1. This distinguishes this work from the recent empirical literature on the effects of current land reform on current economic outcomes (see Banerjee et al., 2002; Timothy Besley and Robin Burgess, 2000; Justin Y. Lin, 1992, among others).
2. Some measures for protecting the rights of tenants and subproprietors were introduced in later years.
3. See Tirthankar Roy (2000) and Ratnalekha Ray (1979).
4. James Mill actually worked for the East India Company, and George Wingate, who helped set up the

individual-cultivator system in Bombay, was heavily influenced by him.

5. For a discussion of the role of ideology and economic doctrines in the formation of the land revenue systems, see Ranajit Guha (1963) and Eric Stokes (1959, 1978a).

6. Under the *Haftam* regulation of 1799 and the *Panjam* regulation of 1812.

7. See Banerjee and Andrew F. Newman (1993) and Oded Galor and Joseph Zeira (1993) for theoretical models of the link between income distribution and long-run development.

8. See Sugato Bose (1993) for an account of the rise of class-based agrarian politics in colonial Bengal (a landlord area) and its subsequent influence on the politics of independent West Bengal.

9. See Alberto Alesina and Dani Rodrik (1994) and Torsten Persson and Guido Tabellini (1994) for models where collective action fails in the presence of groups with misaligned interests.

10. For instance, the rich could undercut democratic processes and resist public policies that would empower the poor, very much along the lines taken by the Latin American elites (see Engerman and Sokoloff, 2002).

11. Amiya K. Bagchi (1976) also makes this point.

12. The states included in the dataset are Andhra Pradesh, Bihar, Gujarat, Haryana, Karnataka, Madhya Pradesh, Maharashtra, Orissa, Punjab, Rajasthan, Tamil Nadu, Uttar Pradesh, and West Bengal. Assam, Himachal Pradesh, Jammu and Kashmir, and Kerala are the large states not covered.

13. This usually corresponds to the areas under direct British administrative control, with one exception. In the princely state of Mysore (part of modern Karnataka state), the British took over the administration in 1831 and ruled for 50 years, before reinstating the royal family in 1881. During this time, the British instituted an individual-based land revenue system, which the ruler was obliged to continue after his reinstatement.

14. We dropped districts currently in Pakistan and Bangladesh.

15. The yield data for Uttar Pradesh come from the same settlement reports of the 1870s and 1880s that we use to calculate our non-landlord proportion. Very few of the reports contain data on yields, resulting in a very small sample. We also have data for ten Tamil Nadu districts from Haruka Yanagisawa (1996).

16. See Iyer (2005) for some evidence in support of this hypothesis.

17. By "date of conquest," we mean the date when the district came under British land revenue administration. The two dates are usually the same, with two exceptions. The first is the kingdom of Mysore, which was under British administration for the period when the land revenue systems were put in place, but was never part of the British Empire. The second is the kingdom of Nagpur, which was formally annexed in 1854, but had been under British revenue control in 1818.

18. The other "hump" (or mode) on the left is mainly due to the districts of Madras Presidency, which were conquered fairly early, but which switched over to a non-landlord system after 1820.

19. A Hausman test does not reject the null hypothesis that the OLS and IV coefficients are equal.

20. Tirthankar Roy (2002) makes the argument that the areas that gained from the Green Revolution were those that showed improvements during the colonial period as well.

21. Table 4.3, column 4, shows that leaving them out makes the non-landlord coefficient larger for some of the outcomes.

22. Data on state-level land reforms comes from Besley and Burgess (2000). We classify Bihar, Madhya Pradesh, Orissa, Rajasthan, Uttar Pradesh, and West Bengal as "landlord" states, and Andhra Pradesh, Assam, Gujarat, Karnataka, Kerala, Maharashtra, Punjab, and Tamil Nadu as "non-landlord" states.

23. We need to be a little cautious when interpreting these results. Adding state fixed effects effectively drops the states that have no within-state variation in non-landlord proportion. These states (Bihar, Gujarat, Karnataka, Rajasthan, and West Bengal) account for about one-fourth of our sample, so putting in state fixed effects results in a lack of power in our estimation.

24. IV estimates of these differences are larger in magnitude than the OLS estimates for literacy, infant mortality, and primary school provision (results not shown).

REFERENCES

Acemoglu, Daron; Johnson, Simon and Robinson, James A. "The Colonial Origins of Comparative Development: An Empirical Investigation." *American Economic Review*, 2001, *91*(5), pp. 1369–1401.

Acemoglu, Daron; Johnson, Simon and Robinson, James A. "Reversal of Fortune; Geography and Institutions in the Making of the Modern World Income Distribution." *Quarterly Journal of Economics*, 2002, *117*(4), pp. 1231–94.

Alesina, Alberto and Rodrik, Dani. "Distributive Politics and Economic Growth." *Quarterly Journal of Economics*, 1994, *109*(2), pp. 465–90.

Baden-Powell, Baden H. *The land-systems of British India*, 3 Volumes. Oxford: Clarendon Press, 1892.

Bagchi, Amiya K. "Reflections on Patterns of Regional Growth in India under British Rule." *Bengal Past and Present*, 1976, *95*(1), pp. 247–89.

Banerjee, Abhijit V.; Gertler, Paul J. and Ghatak, Maitreesh. "Empowerment and Efficiency: Tenancy Reform in West Bengal." *Journal of Political Economy*, 2002, *110*(2), pp. 239–80.

Banerjee, Abhijit V. and Newman, Andrew F. "Occupational Choice and the Process of Development." *Journal of Political Economy*, 1993, *101*(2), pp. 274–98.

Besley, Timothy and Burgess, Robin. "Land Reform, Poverty Reduction, and Growth: Evidence from India." *Quarterly Journal of Economics*, 2000, *115*(2), pp. 389–430.

Binswanger, Hans P. and Rosenzweig, Mark R. "Behavioural and Material Determinants of Production Relations in Agriculture." *Journal of Development Studies*, 1986, *22*(3), pp. 503–39.

Bose, Sugato. *Peasant labour and colonial capital: Rural Bengal since 1770*. Cambridge: Cambridge University Press, 1993.

Brass, Paul R. *The Politics of India since independence*. Cambridge: Cambridge University Press, 1994.

Chatterjee, Partha. *Bengal 1920–1947, Vol. 1: The land question*. Calcutta: K. P. Bagchi and South Asia Books, 1984.

Engerman, Stanley L. and Sokoloff, Kenneth L. "Factor Endowments, Institutions, and Differential Paths of Growth among New World Economies: A View from Economic Historians of the United States," in Steven Haber, ed., *How Latin America fell behind: Essays on the economic histories of Brazil and Mexico, 1800–1914*. Stanford: Stanford University Press, 1997, pp. 260–304.

Engerman, Stanley L. and Sokoloff, Kenneth L. "Factor Endowments, Inequality, and Paths of Development among New World Economies." *Economia: Journal of the Latin American and Caribbean Economic Association*, 2002, *3*(1), pp. 41–88.

Galor, Oded and Zeira, Joseph. "Income Distribution and Macroeconomics." *Review of Economic Studies*, 1993, *60*(1), pp. 35–52.

Gough, Kathleen. "Indian Peasant Uprisings." *Economic and Political Weekly*, 1974, *9*(13), pp. 1391–1412.

Guha, Ranajit. *A rule of property for Bengal: An essay on the idea of permanent settlement*. Paris: Mouton & Co., 1963.

Gupta, Rai M. N. *Land system of Bengal*. Calcutta: University of Calcutta, 1940.

Iyer, Lakshmi. "The Long-Term Impact of Colonial Rule: Evidence from India." Harvard University, Harvard Business School Working Papers: No. 05-041, 2005.

Kane, Thomas J.; Rouse, Cecilia Elena and Staiger, Douglas. "Estimating Returns to Schooling When Schooling Is Misreported." National Bureau of Economic Research, Inc., NBER Working Papers: No. 7235, 1999.

Kumar, Dharma. *The Cambridge economic history of India, Vol. 2:c. 1757-c. 1970*. Cambridge: Cambridge University Press, 1982.

La Porta, Rafael; López de Silanes, Florencio; Shleifer, Andrei and Vishny, Robert. "Law and Finance." *Journal of Political Economy*, 1998, *106*(6), pp. 1113–55.

La Porta, Rafael; López de Silanes, Florencio; Shleifer, Andrei and Vishny, Robert. "The Quality of

Government." *Journal of Law, Economics, and Organization*, 1999, *15*(1), pp. 222–79.

La Porta, Rafael; López de Silanes, Florencio; Shleifer, Andrei and Vishny, Robert. "Investor Protection and Corporate Governance." *Journal of Financial Economics*, 2000, *58*(1-2), pp. 3–27.

Lin, Justin Y. "Rural Reforms and Agricultural Growth in China." *American Economic Review*, 1992, *82*(1), pp. 34–51.

Misra, Baba Ram. *Land revenue policy in the united provinces under British rule*. Benares: Nand Kishore & Brothers, 1942.

Mukherjee, Nilmani. *The Ryotwari system in Madras 1792–1827*. Calcutta: Firma K. L. Mukhopadhyay, 1962.

Patel, Govindlal Dalsukhbhai. *The land problem of re-organized Bombay State*. Bombay: N. M. Tripathi Pvt. Ltd., 1957.

Persson, Torsten and Tabellini, Guido. "Is Inequality Harmful for Growth?" *American Economic Review*, 1994, *84*(3), pp. 600–21.

Porter, F. W. *Final settlement report of the Allahabad district*. Allahabad: North-Western Provinces and Oudh Government Press, 1878.

Ray, Ratnalekha. *Change in Bengal agrarian society 1760–1850*. New Delhi: Manohar, 1979.

Roy, Tirthankar. *The economic history of India, 1857–1947*. Oxford: Oxford University Press, 2000.

Roy, Tirthankar. "Economic History and Modern India: Redefining the Link." *Journal of Economic Perspectives*, 2002, *16*(3), pp. 109–30.

Smith, W. H. *Final report on the revision of settlement in the district of Aligarh*. Allahabad: North-Western Provinces and Oudh Government Press, 1882.

Sokoloff, Kenneth L. and Engerman, Stanley L. "Institutions, Factor Endowments, and Paths of Development in the New World." *Journal of Economic Perspectives*, 2000, *14*(3), pp. 217–32.

Stokes, Eric. *The English utilitarians and India*. Oxford: Clarendon Press, 1959.

Stokes, Eric. "The Land Revenue Systems of the North-Western Provinces and Bombay Deecan 1830–1948: Ideology and the Official Mind," in Eric Stokes, ed., *The peasant and the Raj: Studies in agrarian society and peasant rebellion in colonial India*. Cambridge: Cambridge University Press, 1978a.

Stokes, Eric. "The Structure of Landholding in Uttar Pradesh 1860–1948," in Eric Stokes, ed., *The peasant and the Raj: Studies in agrarian society and peasant rebellion in colonial India*. Cambridge: Cambridge University Press, 1978b, ch. 9.

Yanagisawa, Haruka. *A century of change: Caste and irrigated lands in Tamil Nadu 1860's–1870's*. New Delhi: Manohar, 1996.

N. Gregory Mankiw

THE TRILEMMA OF INTERNATIONAL FINANCE

As the world economy struggles to recover from its various ailments, the international financial order is coming under increased scrutiny. Currencies and exchange rates, in particular, are getting a hard look.

Various pundits and politicians, including President Obama himself, have complained that the Chinese renminbi is undervalued and impeding a global recovery. The problems in Greece have caused many people to wonder whether the euro is a failed experiment and whether Europe's nations would have been better off maintaining their own currencies.

In thinking about these issues, the place to start is what economists call the fundamental trilemma of international finance. Yes, trilemma really is a word. It has been a term of art for logicians since the 17th century, according to the Oxford English Dictionary, and it describes a situation in which someone faces a choice among three options, each of which comes with some inevitable problems.

What is the trilemma in international finance? It stems from the fact that, in most nations, economic policy makers would like to achieve these three goals:

- *Make the country's economy open to international flows of capital.* Capital mobility lets a nation's citizens diversify their holdings by investing abroad. It also encourages foreign investors to bring their resources and expertise into the country.
- *Use monetary policy as a tool to help stabilize the economy.* The central bank can then increase the money supply and reduce interest rates when the economy is depressed, and reduce money growth and raise interest rates when it is overheated.
- *Maintain stability in the currency exchange rate.* A volatile exchange rate, at times driven by speculation, can be a source of broader economic volatility. Moreover, a stable rate makes it easier for households and businesses to engage in the world economy and plan for the future.

But here's the rub: You can't get all three. If you pick two of these goals, the inexorable logic of economics forces you to forgo the third.

In the United States, we have picked the first two. Any American can easily invest abroad, simply by sending cash to an international mutual fund, and foreigners are free to buy stocks and bonds on domestic exchanges. Moreover, the Federal Reserve sets monetary policy to try to maintain full employment and price stability. But a result of this decision is volatility in the value of the dollar in foreign exchange markets.

By contrast, China has chosen a different response to the trilemma. Its central bank conducts monetary policy and maintains tight control over the exchange value of its currency. But to accomplish these two goals, it has to restrict the international flow of capital, including the ability of Chinese citizens to move their wealth abroad. Without such restrictions, money would flow into and out of the country, forcing the domestic interest rate to match those set by foreign central banks.

Most of Europe's nations have chosen the third way. By using the euro to replace the French franc, the German mark, the Italian lira, the Greek drachma and other currencies, these countries have

From *The New York Times* (January 10, 2010).

eliminated all exchange-rate-movements within their zone. In addition, capital is free to move among nations. Yet the cost of making these choices has been to give up the possibility of national monetary policy.

The European Central Bank sets interest rates for Europe as a whole. But if the situation in one country—Greece, for example—differs from that in the rest of Europe, that country no longer has its own monetary policy to address national problems.

Is there a best way to deal with this trilemma? Perhaps not surprisingly, many American economists argue for the American system of floating exchange rates determined by market forces. This preference underlies much of the criticism of China's financial policy. It also led to skepticism when Europe started down the path toward a common currency in the early 1990s. Today, those euro skeptics feel vindicated by the problems in Greece.

But economists should be cautious when recommending exchange-rate policy, because it is far from obvious what is best. In fact, Americans' embrace of floating exchange rates is relatively recent. From World War II to the early 1970s, the United States participated in the Bretton Woods system, which fixed exchange rates among the major currencies. Moreover, in 1998, as much of Asia was engulfed in a financial crisis, Robert E. Rubin, then the Treasury secretary, praised China's exchange-rate policy as an "island of stability" in a turbulent world.

Even the euro experiment is based in part on an American model. Anyone taking a trip across the United States doesn't need to change money with every crossing of a state border. A common currency among the 50 states has served Americans well. Europeans were aspiring for [sic] similar benefits.

To be sure, Europe is different from the United States, which has a large central government that can redistribute resources among regions as needed. More important, our common language and heritage allow labor to move freely among regions in a way that will always be harder in Europe. The United States of Europe may have been too much to hope for.

Without doubt, the world financial system presents policy makers with difficult tradeoffs. Americans shouldn't be too harsh when other nations facing the trilemma reach conclusions different from ours. In this area of economic policy, as well as many others, there is room for reasonable nations to disagree.

5

DEMOCRATIC REGIMES

If democracy is something positive to be striven for, how does it come about, and what are its necessary components? The readings in this chapter try to address these questions by considering the origins and institutions of democracy as well as the dangers that democracy faces. Much of this work has emerged in the past fifteen years, following the end of the Cold War and the subsequent wave of democratization throughout much of the world.

Fareed Zakaria's "Brief History of Human Liberty" (2003) builds on our earlier discussion of the state in Chapter 2 to help us understand why modern democracy first emerged in Europe. With the collapse of the Roman Empire, Europe dissolved into an enormous number of rival political units, leading to diversity, competition, and interstate conflict that eventually helped forge the modern state. These early states were often highly decentralized, with power in the hands of a local elite that could check a monarch's ability to gather absolute power. At the same time, the early division of church and state also weakened the ability of any leader to claim both spiritual and earthly authority, something reinforced by the Protestant Reformation. This decentralization of power allowed for greater individual liberties, helping to foster both capitalist development and the idea of democratic control. In the end, Zakaria concludes that democracy requires the development of the entrenched habits of liberty — individual rights supported by the rule of law — something not easily or intentionally created. His comments in many ways reflect Levitsky and Way's discussion of competitive authoritarianism in Chapter 6.

While Zakaria focuses on the origins of democracy, other scholars are concerned with how its institutions are actually constructed, and to what effect. In their widely cited work "What Democracy Is . . . and Is Not" (1991), Philippe C. Schmitter and Terry Lynn Karl provide an overview of some of the most important elements, among them government accountability, public competition, and the mechanisms of elections and majority rule. Democracy is not just a set of mechanisms, however; it is also a set of agreed-on principles promising that the members of the democracy will abide by the competitive outcome. But beyond these basic elements is a wide array of democratic types, differing in such areas as how majorities are structured, the nature of executive power, the kinds of checks and balances that will be used to stabilize power, and the way power is decentralized. There is no one necessary mix for democracy, and how these institutions are combined or modified depends on the historical circumstances and the contemporary challenges of the country in question.

However, some scholars do believe that certain kinds of democratic combinations are more stable or responsive than others. Arend Lijphart (1996) investigates two of the most important differences among democracies: presidential versus parliamentary rule, and proportional representation (PR) versus plurality (also known as single-member district plurality or "first past the post") elections. Presidentialism and plurality elections promote majoritarian or a "winner-take-all" form of government; proportional representation tends to generate more consensus in politics. Is one better than the other? Lijphart concludes that in terms of minority rights, participation, and economic equality, the parliamentary PR system is superior to the presidential plurality system of the United States.

What about the centralization of state power? Is unitary or federal government more democratic? This may depend on the diversity of the nation. In "The Rise of 'State-Nations,'" (2010) Stepan, Linz, and Yadav note that in many countries around the world, states and nations do not cohere as neatly as the term *nation-state* implies. Instead, we often find what the authors term "state-nations." In contrast to nation-states, whose dominant national identity is linked to the state, state-nations contain several national groups whose strong identities and competing interests may lead to conflicts that undermine democracy and state integrity. The authors argue that in these cases, stability is possible where such varied identities are embraced by and embodied in state institutions, from religion to multilingualism. Of particular interest is their discussion of asymmetric federalism: the uneven devolution of power among subnational units in order to meet the demands of different ethnic or religious groups. Inclusive and idiosyncratic crafting of state institutions can make multinationalism work, and many political scientists cite India as an example of a country which, perhaps against all odds, has made diversity work.

Finally, we turn to a consideration of social capital and participation. The concept of social capital has become widely discussed in political science and policy circles, due largely to the work of Robert Putnam in his 2000 book, *Bowling Alone*. Drawing from research conducted in both the United States and Italy (which appeared in an earlier work entitled *Making Democracy Work*), Putnam has described the notion of social capital as networks and "norms of reciprocity" that make people active participants in democratic life. Where social capital is strong, Putnam argues, democracy is sustained by this web of interconnections that promotes civic life. In the United States (and perhaps elsewhere), however, civic organization is declining, he argues. If social capital continues to erode, what will this mean for the future of democracy? Is democracy viable if few members of the public are active participants in civil life?

Fareed Zakaria

A BRIEF HISTORY OF HUMAN LIBERTY

It all started when Constantine decided to move. In A.D. 324 the leader of the greatest empire in the world went east, shifting his capital from Rome to Byzantium, the old Greek colony, at the mouth of the Black Sea, which he promptly renamed Constantinople. Why abandon Rome, the storied seat of the empire? Constantine explained that he did it "on command of God." You can't really argue with that kind of logic, though vanity and ambition surely played some part as well. Constantine desperately wanted to leave behind a grand legacy and, short of winning a war, what better way to do so than to build a new capital city? The move was also politically smart. Constantinople was closer to the great cultural and economic centers of the day, such as Athens, Thessalonika, and Antioch. (Rome in those days was considered a backwater.) And Constantinople was a more strategic point from which to defend the empire against its enemies, mainly Germanic tribes and Persian armies. In the fourth century, the pivots of history lay in the east.

Emperors don't travel light, and Constantine was no exception. He shifted not just the capital but tens of thousands of its inhabitants and commandeered immense quantities of food and wine from Egypt, Asia Minor, and Syria to feed his people. He sent his minions across the empire to bring art for the "new Rome." Such was the pillage that the historian Jacob Burckhardt described it as "the most disgraceful and extensive thefts of art in all history . . . committed for the purpose of decorating [Constantinople]."[1] Senators and other notables were given every inducement to move; exact replicas of their homes were waiting for them in the new city. But although

he took most of his court, Constantine left one person behind: the bishop of Rome. This historic separation between church and state was to have fateful, and beneficial, consequences for humankind.

Although the bishop of Rome had nominal seniority—because the first holder of that office, Peter, was the senior apostle of Christ—Christianity had survived by becoming a de-centralized religion, comprising a collection of self-governing churches. But Rome was now distant from the imperial capital. Other important priests, such as the bishop of Byzantium and those of nearby Antioch, Jerusalem, and Alexandria, now lived in the shadow of the emperor and quickly became appendages of state authority. But, far from palace power and intrigue, the Roman church flourished, asserting an independence that eventually allowed it to claim the mantle of spiritual leadership of the Christian peoples. As a result of this separation, the great English classical scholar Ernest Barker observed, the East (Byzantium) fell under the control of the state and the West (Rome) came under the sovereignty of religion. It would be more accurate to say that in the West sovereignty was contested; for 1,500 years after Constantine's move, European history was marked by continual strife between church and state. From the sparks of those struggles came the first fires of human liberty.

Liberty, Old and New

Obviously it is an oversimplification to pick a single event to mark the beginnings of a complex historical phenomenon—in this case, the development of human liberty—but stories have to start somewhere. And the rise of the Christian Church is, in my view, the first important source of

From *The Future of Freedom* (New York: W. W. Norton, 2003), pp. 29–58. Some of the author's notes have been omitted.

liberty in the West—and hence the world. It highlights the central theme of this chapter, which is that liberty came to the West centuries before democracy. Liberty led to democracy and not the other way around. It also highlights a paradox that runs through this account: whatever the deeper structural causes, liberty in the West was born of a series of power struggles. The consequences of these struggles—between church and state, lord and king, Protestant and Catholic, business and the state—embedded themselves in the fabric of Western life, producing greater and greater pressures for individual liberty, particularly in England and, by extension, in the United States.

Some might contest this emphasis on the Christian Church, pointing fondly to ancient Greece as the seedbed of liberty. They will think of Pericles' famous funeral oration, delivered in 431 B.C., which conjured a stirring vision of the Athens of his day, dedicated to freedom, democracy, and equality. For much of the nineteenth century British and German university curricula assumed that the greatest flowering of human achievement took place in the city-states of Greece around the fifth century B.C. (The study of ancient Greece and Rome at Oxford and Cambridge is still colloquially called "Greats.") But the Victorian obsession with Greece was part fantasy. Ancient Greece was an extraordinary culture, fertile in philosophy, science, and literature. It was the birthplace of democracy and some of its associated ideas, but these were practiced in only a few, small city-states for at most a hundred years and died with the Macedonian conquest of Athens in 338 B.C. Over a millennium later, Greece's experiment became an inspiration for democrats, but in the intervening centuries, it left no tangible or institutional influences on politics in Europe.

More to the point, Greece was not the birthplace of liberty as we understand it today. Liberty in the modern world is first and foremost the freedom of the individual from arbitrary authority, which has meant, for most of history, from the brute power of the state. It implies certain basic human rights: freedom of expression, of association, and of worship,

and rights of due process. But ancient liberty, as the enlightenment philosopher Benjamin Constant explained, meant something different: that everyone (actually, every male citizen) had the right to participate in the governance of the community. Usually all citizens served in the legislature or, if this was impractical, legislators were chosen by lottery, as with American juries today. The people's assemblies of ancient Greece had unlimited powers. An individual's rights were neither sacred in theory nor protected in fact. Greek democracy often meant, in Constant's phrase, "the subjection of the individual to the authority of the community."[2] Recall that in the fourth century B.C. in Athens, where Greek democracy is said to have found its truest expression, the popular assembly—by democratic vote—put to death the greatest philosopher of the age because of his teachings. The execution of Socrates was democratic but not liberal.

If the Greek roots of Western liberty are often overstated, the Roman ones are neglected. When Herodotus wrote that the Greeks were "a free people" he meant that they were not slaves under foreign conquest or domination—an idea we would today call "national independence" or "self-determination." (By this definition, the North Koreans today are a free people.) The Romans emphasized a different aspect of freedom: that all citizens were to be treated equally under the law. This conception of freedom is much closer to the modern Western one, and the Latin word for it, *libertas*, is the root of ours. Whereas Greece gave the world philosophy, literature, poetry, and art, Rome gave us the beginnings of limited government and the rule of law. The Roman Republic, with its divided government (three branches), election of officials to limited terms, and emphasis on equality under law has been a model for governments ever since, most consciously in the founding of the American Republic. To this day Roman political concepts and terms endure throughout the Western world: senate, republic, constitution, prefecture. Western law is so filled with Roman legacies that until the early twentieth century, lawyers had to be well versed in

Latin. Most of the world's laws of contract, property, liability, defamation, inheritance, and estate and rules of procedure and evidence are variations on Roman themes. For Herbert Asquith, the gifted amateur classicist who became prime minister of the United Kingdom, Rome's greatest gift to the ages was that "she founded, developed and systematized the jurisprudence of the world."[3]

The gaping hole in Roman law, however, was that as a practical matter, it didn't apply to the ruling class, particularly as the republic degenerated into a monarchy by the first century. Emperors such as Nero, Vitellius, and Galba routinely sentenced people to death without trial, pillaged private homes and temples, and raped and murdered their subjects. Caligula famously had his horse appointed senator, an act that probably violated the implicit, if not explicit, rules of that once-august body. Traditions of law that had been built carefully during Rome's republican years crumbled in the decadence of empire. The lesson of Rome's fall is that, for the rule of law to endure, you need more than the good intentions of the rulers, for they may change (both the intentions and the rulers). You need institutions within society whose strength is independent of the state. The West found such a countervailing force in the Catholic Church.

The Paradox of Catholicism

Rome's most concrete legacy has been the Roman Catholic Church, which the English philosopher Thomas Hobbes called "the ghost of the deceased Roman Empire sitting crowned upon [its] grave."[4] The culture of Rome became the culture of Catholicism. Through the church were transmitted countless traditions and ideas—and, of course, Latin which gave educated people all over Europe a common language and thus strengthened their sense of being a single community. To this day the ideas and structure of the Catholic Church—its universalism, its hierarchy, its codes and laws—bear a strong resemblance to those of the Roman Empire.

The Catholic Church might seem an odd place to begin the story of liberty. As an institution it has not stood for freedom of thought or even, until recently, diversity of belief. In fact, during the Middle Ages, as it grew powerful, it became increasingly intolerant and oppressive, emphasizing dogma and unquestioning obedience and using rather nasty means to squash dissent (recall the Spanish Inquisition). To this day, its structure remains hierarchical and autocratic. The church never saw itself as furthering individual liberty. But from the start it tenaciously opposed the power of the state and thus placed limits on monarchs' rule. It controlled crucial social institutions such as marriage and birth and death rites. Church properties and priests were not subject to taxation—hardly a small matter since at its height the church owned one-third of the land in Europe. The Catholic Church was the first major institution in history that was independent of temporal authority and willing to challenge it. By doing this it cracked the edifice of state power, and in nooks and crannies individual liberty began to grow.

The struggles between church and state began just over fifty years after Constantine's move. One of Constantine's successors, the emperor Theodosius, while in a nasty dispute with the Thessalonians, a Greek tribe, invited the whole tribe to Milan—and orchestrated a blood-curdling massacre of his guests: men, women, and children. The archbishop of Milan, a pious priest named Ambrose, was appalled and publicly refused to give the emperor Holy Communion. Theodosius protested, resorting to a biblical defense. He was guilty of homicide, he explained, but wasn't one of the Bible's heroic kings, David, guilty not just of homicide but of adultery as well? The archbishop was unyielding, thundering back, in the English historian Edward Gibbon's famous account, "You have imitated David in his crime, imitate then his repentance."[5] To the utter amazement of all, for the next eight months the emperor, the most powerful man in the world, periodically dressed like a beggar (as David had in the biblical tale) and stood outside the cathedral at Milan to ask forgiveness of the archbishop.

As the Roman Empire crumbled in the East, the bishop of Rome's authority and independence grew. He became first among the princes of the church, called "Il Papa," the holy father. In 800, Pope Leo III was forced to crown the Frankish ruler Charlemagne as Roman emperor. But in doing so, Leo began the tradition of "investiture," whereby the church had to bless a new king and thus give legitimacy to his reign. By the twelfth century, the pope's power had grown, and he had become a pivotal player in Europe's complex political games. The papacy had power, legitimacy, money, and even armies. It won another great symbolic battle against Holy Roman Emperor Henry IV, who in 1077 challenged—unsuccessfully—Pope Gregory VII's expansion of the power of investiture. Having lost the struggle, Henry, so the legend goes, was forced to stand barefoot in the snow at Canossa to seek forgiveness from the holy father. Whether or not that tale is true, by the twelfth century the pope had clearly become, in power and pomp, a match for any of Europe's kings, and the Vatican had come to rival the grandest courts on the continent.

The Geography of Freedom

The church gained power in the West for a simple reason: after the decline of the Roman Empire, it never again faced a single emperor of Europe. Instead, the Catholic Church was able to play one European prince against another, becoming the vital "swing vote" in the power struggles of the day. Had one monarch emerged across the continent, he could have crushed the church's independence, turning it into a handmaiden of state power. That is what happened to the Greek Orthodox Church and later the Russian Orthodox Church (and, for that matter, to most religions around the world). But no ruler ever conquered all of Europe, or even the greater part of it. Over the millennia only a few tried—Charlemagne, Charles V, Napoleon, Kaiser Wilhelm, and Hitler. All were thwarted, most fairly quickly.

What explains this? Probably mountains and rivers. Europe is riven with barriers that divide its highlands into river valleys bordered by mountain ranges. Its rivers flow into sheltered, navigable bays along the long, indented Mediterranean coastline—all of which means that small regions could subsist, indeed thrive, on their own. Hence Europe's long history of many independent countries. They are hard to conquer, easy to cultivate, and their rivers and seas provide ready trade routes. Asia, by contrast, is full of vast flatlands—the steppes in Russia, the plains in China—through which armies could march unhindered. Not surprisingly, these areas were ruled for millennia by centralized empires.

Europe's topography made possible the rise of communities of varying sizes—city-states, duchies, republics, nations, and empires. In 1500 Europe had within it more than 500 states, many no larger than a city. This variety had two wondrous effects. First, it allowed for diversity. People, ideas, art, and even technologies that were unwelcome or unnoticed in one area would often thrive in another. Second, diversity fueled constant competition between states, producing innovation and efficiency in political organization, military technology, and economic policy. Successful practices were copied; losing ways were cast aside. Europe's spectacular economic and political success—what the economic historian Eric Jones has termed "the European miracle"—might well be the result of its odd geography.[6]

Lords and Kings

Geography and history combined to help shape Europe's political structure. The crumbling of the Roman Empire and the backwardness of the German tribes that destroyed it resulted in decentralized authority across the continent; no ruler had the administrative capacity to rule a far-flung kingdom comprising so many independent tribes. By contrast, in their heyday, Ming and Manchu China, Mughal India, and the Ottoman Empire controlled vast lands and diverse peoples. But in Europe local landlords and chieftains governed their territories and developed close ties with their tenants. This became the distinctive feature of European feudalism — that its great landowning classes were independent. From the Middle Ages until the seventeenth century, European sovereigns were distant creatures who ruled their kingdoms mostly in name. The king of France, for example, was considered only a duke in Brittany and had limited authority in that region for hundreds of years. In practice if monarchs wanted to do anything — start a war, build a fort — they had to borrow and bargain for money and troops from local chieftains, who became earls, viscounts, and dukes in the process.

Thus Europe's landed elite became an aristocracy with power, money, and legitimacy — a far cry from the groveling and dependent courtier-nobles in other parts of the world. This near-equal relationship between lords and kings deeply influenced the course of liberty. As Guido de Ruggiero, the great historian of liberalism, wrote, "Without the effective resistance of particular privileged classes, the monarchy would have created nothing but a people of slaves."[7] In fact monarchs did just that in much of the rest of the world. In Europe, on the other hand, as the Middle Ages progressed, the aristocracy demanded that kings guarantee them certain rights that even the crown could not violate. They also established representative bodies — parliaments, estates general, diets — to give permanent voice to their claims. In these medieval bargains lie the foundations of what we today call "the rule of law." Building on Roman traditions, these rights were secured and strengthened by the power of the nobility. Like the clash between church and state, the conflict between the aristocracy and the monarchy is the second great power struggle of European history that helped provide, again unintentionally, the raw materials of freedom.

The English aristocracy was the most independent in Europe. Lords lived on their estates, governing and protecting their tenants. In return, they extracted taxes, which kept them both powerful and rich. It was, in one scholar's phrase, "a working aristocracy": it maintained its position not through elaborate courtly rituals but by taking part in politics and government at all levels.[8] England's kings, who consolidated their power earlier than did most of their counterparts on the continent, recognized that their rule depended on co-opting the aristocracy — or at least some part of it. When monarchs pushed their luck they triggered a baronial backlash. Henry II, crowned king in 1154, extended his rule across the country, sending judges to distant places to enforce royal decrees. He sought to unify the country and create a common, imperial law. To do this he had to strip the medieval aristocracy of its powers and special privileges. His plan worked but only up to a point. Soon the nobility rose up in arms — literally — and after forty years of conflict, Henry's son, King John, was forced to sign a truce in 1215 in a field near Windsor Castle. That document, Magna Carta, was regarded at the time as a charter of baronial privilege, detailing the rights of feudal lords. It also had provisions guaranteeing the freedom of the church and local autonomy for towns. It came out (in vague terms) against the oppression of any of the king's subjects. Over time the document was interpreted more broadly by English judges, turning it into a quasi constitution that enshrined certain individual rights. But even in its day, Magna Carta was significant, being the first written limitation on royal authority in Europe. As such, the historian Paul Johnson noted, it is "justly classified as the first of the English Statutes of the Realm, from which English, and thus American, liberties can be said to flow."[9]

Rome versus Reform

After church versus state and king versus lord, the next great power struggle, between Catholics and Protestants, was to prove the longest and bloodiest, and once again it had accidental but revolutionary implications for freedom. Its improbable instigator was a devout German monk who lived in a small backwater town called Wittenberg. It was the early sixteenth century, and across Europe there was already great dissatisfaction with the papacy, which had become extraordinarily powerful and corrupt. Rome's most scandalous practice was the widespread sale of indulgences: papal certificates absolving the buyer of sins, even those not yet committed. The money financed the church's never-ending extravagance, which even by the glittering standards of the Baroque era was stunning. Its newest project was the largest, grandest cathedral ever known to man—St. Peter's in Rome. Even today, when one walks through the acres of marble in the Vatican, gazing at gilt, jewels, tapestries, and frescos from wall to wall and floor to ceiling, it is easy to imagine the pious rage of Martin Luther.

There had been calls for reform before Luther—Erasmus, for one, had urged a simpler, stripped down form of worship—but none had frontally challenged the authority of the church. Luther did so in ninety-five tightly reasoned theses, which he famously nailed to the door of the Castle Church in Wittenberg on the morning of October 31, 1517. Luther may have had right on his side, but he also had luck. His heresy came at an opportune moment in the history of technology. By the time the Catholic Church reacted and responded to his action, strictly forbidding the dissemination of his ideas, the new printing presses had already circulated Luther's document all over Europe. The Reformation had begun. One hundred and fifty bloody years later, almost half of Europe was Protestant.

Were Martin Luther to see Protestantism today, with its easygoing doctrines that tolerate much and require little, he would probably be horrified. Luther was not a liberal. On the contrary, he had accused the Vatican of being too lax in its approach to religion. In many ways he was what we would today call a fundamentalist, demanding a more literal interpretation of the Bible. Luther's criticisms of the papacy were quite similar to those made today by Islamic fundamentalists about the corrupt, extravagant regimes of the Middle East that have veered from the true, devout path. Luther was attacking the pope from the conservative end of the theological spectrum. In fact some have said that the clash between Catholicism and Protestantism illustrates the old maxim that religious freedom is the product of two equally pernicious fanaticisms, each canceling the other out.

Most of the sects that sprang up as a consequence of the Reformation were even more puritanical than Lutheranism. The most influential of them was a particularly dour creed, Calvinism, which posited the wretched depravity of man and the poor chances of salvation for all but a few, already chosen by God. But the various Protestant sects converged in rejecting the authority of the papacy and, by implication, all religious hierarchy. They were part of a common struggle against authority and, although they didn't know it at the time, part of the broader story of liberty.

For all their squabbles, these small Protestant sects in northern Europe opened up the possibility of a personal path to truth, unmediated by priests. To the extent that they imagined any clergy at all, it was to be elected by a self-governing congregation. Often minority sects within a larger community, they fought for the rights of all minorities to believe and worship as they chose. Together, they opened up the space for religious freedom in the Western world. They helped shape modern ideas about not only freedom of conscience and of speech but also critical scientific inquiry, first of religious texts such as the Bible, then of all received wisdom. Science, after all, is a constant process of challenging authority and contesting dogma. In that sense modern science owes an unusual debt to sixteenth-century religious zealots.

The more immediate, political effect of Protestantism was to give kings and princes an excuse to wrest power away from the increasingly arrogant Vatican, something they were looking to do anyway. The first major assault took place not in support of

Protestant ideals but for the less-exalted reason that a restless monarch wanted an heir. Henry VIII of England asked Pope Clement VII to annul his marriage to Catherine of Aragon because she had not produced an heir to the throne. (Not for lack of effort: in eight years she had given birth to one daughter and five infants who had died, and had miscarried twice.) The pope refused and King Henry broke with the Vatican, proclaiming himself head of the Church of England. Henry had no doctrinal dispute with the Catholic Church. In fact he had defended the pope against Luther in an essay, for which the Vatican honored him as "Defender of the Faith," a title his successor, strangely, bears to this day. The newly independent Anglican Church was thus Catholic in doctrine—except for the small matter of the pope.

The English break was the first and most prominent of a series of religious revolts and wars against the Vatican involving virtually every state in Europe and lasting almost 150 years after Luther's act of defiance. The wars resulting from the Reformation came to an end in 1648. The Peace of Westphalia, as it was called, ended the Thirty Years' War among the Germans and rendered unto Caesar that which was Caesar's—plus a good bit of that which used to be God's (actually, the pope's). It revived a 1555 idea— *cuius regio eius religio* (whoever's domain, his religion prevails)—that princes could choose their state religions, and it explicitly permitted religious toleration and migration. The year 1648 is not a clean point of separation between church and state, but it does symbolize an important shift in Western history. Westphalia laid to rest the idea that Europe was one great Christian community—"Christendom"—governed spiritually by the Catholic Church and temporally by the holy Roman emperor. The future belonged to the state.

The Enlightened State

By the seventeenth century, the real challenge to princely power came not from religion but from local authorities: the princes, dukes, barons, and counts.

But over the course of this century the prince would best his rivals. He strengthened his court and created a central government—a state—that dwarfed its local rivals. The state triumphed for several reasons: technological shifts, heightened military competition, the stirrings of nationalism, and the ability to centralize tax collection. One consequence, however, is worth noting. The strengthening of the state was not good for liberty. As the power of monarchs grew, they shut down most of the medieval parliaments, estates, assemblies, and diets. When France's Estates General were summoned in the spring of 1789—on the eve of the revolution—it was their first assembly in 175 years! The newly powerful royals also began abolishing the multilayered system of aristocratic privileges, regional traditions, and guild protections in favor of a uniform legal code, administered by the monarch. The important exception was the English Parliament, which actually gained the upper hand in its struggle with the monarchy after the Glorious Revolution of 1688.[10]

On the face of it the weakening of the aristocracy might seem a victory for equality under law, and it was presented as such at the time. As Enlightenment ideas swept through seventeenth century Europe, philosophers such as Voltaire and Diderot fantasized about the "rationalization" and "modernization" of government. But in practice these trends meant more power for the central government and the evisceration of local and regional authority. "Enlightened absolutism," as it was later called, had some progressive elements about it. Rulers such as Frederick II of Prussia, Catherine II of Russia, and Joseph II of Austria tolerated religious dissent, enacted legal reforms, and lavished money and attention on artists, musicians, and writers (which might help explain the good press they received). But the shift in power weakened the only groups in society capable of checking royal authority and excess. Liberty now depended on the largesse of the ruler. When under pressure from abroad or at home, even the most benign monarch—and his not-so-benign successors—abandoned liberalization and squashed dissent. By the end of the eighteenth century, with war, revolution, and domestic rebellion disturbing the tranquility of Europe, enlightened absolutism became more absolutist than enlightened.

The monarchy reached its apogee in France under Louis XIV. Feudalism in France had always been different from that in England. Sandwiched between hostile neighbors, France was perpetually mobilizing for war, which kept its central government strong. (Louis XIV was at war for thirty of his fifty-four years of rule.) The monarchy exploited these geopolitical realities to keep the nobles distant from their power base, which was their land. Building on the foundation laid by the brilliant Cardinal Richelieu, Louis XIV edged nobles out of local administration and put in their place his own regional officials. He also downgraded regional councils and assemblies. Louis was called the "Sun King" not because of his gilded possessions, as is often thought, but because of his preeminent position in the country. All other forces paled in comparison. Louis XIV brought France's aristocrats to Paris permanently, luring them with the most glittering court in Europe. His purpose was to weaken them. The legendary excess of the French monarchy—the ceaseless games, balls, hunts, and court rituals, the wonder of Versailles—was at one level a clever political device to keep the lords in a gilded cage. Behind the sumptuous silks and powdered wigs, the French aristocracy was becoming powerless and dependent.[11]

The French Revolution (1789) changed much in the country, but not these centripetal tendencies. Indeed, the revolution only centralized the country further. In contrast to England's Glorious Revolution (1688), which had strengthened the landed aristocracy, the French Revolution destroyed it. It also crippled the church and weakened local lords, parishes, and banks. As the great nineteenth century scholar-politician Lord Acton observed, the revolution was not so much about the limitation of central power as about the abrogation of all other powers that got in the way. The French, he noted, borrowed from Americans "their theory of revolution not their theory of government—their cutting but not their

sewing." Popular sovereignty took on all the glory and unchecked power of royal sovereignty. "The people" were supreme, and they proclaimed their goals to be *liberté, égalité, fraternité*. Once dependent on royal largesse, liberty now depended on the whims of "the citizens," represented of course by the leaders of the revolution.

But there was another model of liberty and it took a Frenchman to see it. Montesquieu—actually Charles-Louis de Secondat, baron de La Brède et de Montesquieu—like many Enlightenment liberals in the eighteenth century admired England for its government. But Montesquieu went further, identifying the genius of the English system: that it guaranteed liberty in fact rather than proclaiming it in theory. Because government was divided between the king, aristocrats (House of Lords), and commoners (House of Commons), no one branch could grow too strong. This "separation of powers" ensured that civil liberties would be secure and religious dissent tolerated. Montesquieu did not put blind faith in the mechanics of government and constitutions; his major work was titled, after all, *The Spirit of the Laws*.

In fact, over the centuries, the British monarch's powers had been so whittled away that by the late eighteenth century, Britain, although formally a monarchy, was really an aristocratic republic, ruled by its landed elite. Montesquieu's flattering interpretation strongly influenced the British themselves. The preeminent English jurist of the era, William Blackstone, used Montesquieu's ideas when writing his commentaries on English law. The American political philosopher Judith Shklar pointed out that during the founding of the American Republic "Montesquieu was an oracle." James Madison, Thomas Jefferson, John Adams, and others consciously tried to apply his principles in creating a new political system. He was quoted by them more than any modern author (only the Bible trumped him). His appeal was so widespread, noted Shklar, that "both those who supported the new constitution and those who opposed it relied heavily on Montesquieu for their arguments."[12]

The Consequences of Capitalism

By the eighteenth century, Britain's unusual political culture gained a final, crucial source of strength: capitalism. If the struggles between church and state, lords and kings, and Catholics and Protestants cracked open the door for individual liberty, capitalism blew the walls down. Nothing has shaped the modern world more powerfully than capitalism, destroying as it has millennia-old patterns of economic, social, and political life. Over the centuries it has destroyed feudalism and monarchism with their emphasis on bloodlines and birth. It has created an independent class of businesspeople who owe little to the state and who are now the dominant force in every advanced society in the world. It has made change and dynamism—rather than order and tradition—the governing philosophy of the modern age. Capitalism created a new world, utterly different from the one that had existed for millennia. And it took root most firmly in England.

It started elsewhere. By the fourteenth century, trade and commerce, frozen during much of the Middle Ages, was once again thriving in parts of Europe. A revolution in agricultural technology was producing surpluses of grain, which had to be sold or bartered. Market towns and port cities—Antwerp, Brussels, Venice, Genoa—became centers of economic activity. Double-entry bookkeeping, the introduction of Arabic numerals, and the rise of banking turned money-making from an amateur affair into a systematic business. Soon the commercial impulse spread inland from the port cities, mostly in the Low Countries and later in England, where it was applied to all kinds of agriculture, crafts, manufacturing, and services. Why capitalism spread to these areas first is still debated, but most economic historians agree that a competent state that protected private property was an important factor. Where capitalism succeeded it was "in the main due to the type of property rights created," write the leading historians on the subject, Douglass North and Robert Thomas.[13] By the sixteenth century a consensus was developing across Europe that "Property belongs to the family, sovereignty to the prince and his magistrates." A fifteenth-century jurist in Spain had explained, "To the king is confided solely the administration of the kingdom and not dominion over things."[14] Only in England, however, was a king (Charles I) actually executed, in large part for levying arbitrary taxes.

The systematic protection of property rights transformed societies. It meant that the complex web of feudal customs and privileges—all of which were obstacles to using property efficiently—could be eliminated. The English landed elite took a leading role in modernizing agriculture. Through the enclosures system, a brutal process of asserting their rights over the pastures and commons of their estates, they forced the peasants and farmers who had lived off these lands into more specialized and efficient labors. The pastures were then used for grazing sheep, to service the highly profitable wool trade. By adapting to the ongoing capitalist revolution, the English landed classes secured their power but also helped modernize their society. The French aristocrats, in contrast, were absentee landlords who did little to make their properties more productive and yet continued to extract hefty feudal dues from their tenants. Like many continental aristocracies, they disdained commerce.

Beyond enterprising nobles, capitalism also created a new group of wealthy and powerful men who owed their riches not to land grants from the crown but to independent economic activity. Ranging from minor aristocrats to enterprising peasants, these English "yeomen" were, in the words of one historian, "a group of ambitious, aggressive small capitalists."[15] They were the first members of the bourgeoisie, the industrious property-owning class that Karl Marx defined as "the owners of the means of production of a society and employer of its laborers." Marx accurately recognized that this class was the vanguard of political liberalization in Europe. Since its members benefited greatly from capitalism, the rule of law, free markets, and the rise of professionalism and meritocracy, they supported gradual reforms that furthered these trends. In a now-legendary work of social science, the Harvard scholar Barrington Moore, Jr., studied the pathways to democracy and dictatorship around the world and presented his central conclusion in four words: "No bourgeoisie, no democracy."[16]

British politics was revolutionized as entrepreneurial activity became the principal means of social advancement. The House of Commons, which had wrested power from the king in the seventeenth century and ran the country, now swelled with newly rich merchants and traders. The number of titled nobles in Britain was always tiny: fewer than 200 by the end of the eighteenth century.[17] But beneath them lay a broad class, often called the "English gentry." The gentry usually had some connection to the aristocracy and often took on responsibilities in local government, but it ultimately drew its prestige and power from business, professional work, or efficient farming. Many of these men entered public life, and with a healthy distance from the old order, pushed for progressive reforms such as free trade, free markets, individual rights, and freedom of religion.

The three most powerful British prime ministers of the nineteenth century—Robert Peel, William Gladstone, and Benjamin Disraeli—all came from the ranks of the gentry. This newly powerful class adopted many of the traits of the aristocracy—manor houses, morning coats, hunting parties—but it was more fluid. "Gentlemen" were widely respected and, even more than lords, became the trendsetters of their society. Indeed, by the eighteenth century, the English gentleman became an almost mythic figure toward which society aspired. A nurse is said to have asked King James I to make her son a gentleman. The monarch replied, "A gentleman I could never make him, though I could make him a lord." A visiting Frenchman ridiculed the tendency of the English aristocracy to ape the gentry: "At London, masters dress like their valets and duchesses copy after their chambermaids."[18] Today the English gentleman is remembered mostly as a dandy, whose aesthetic sensibility is marketed worldwide by Ralph Lauren. But his origins are intimately connected with the birth of English liberty.

Anglo-America

Despite the rise of capitalism, limited government, property rights, and constitutionalism across much of Europe by the eighteenth century, England was seen as unique. It was wealthier, more innovative, freer, and more stable than any society on the continent. As Guido de Ruggiero noted, "The liberties of the individual, especially security of person and property, were solidly assured. Administration was decentralized and autonomous. The judiciary bodies were wholly independent of the central government. The prerogatives of the crown were closely restricted. . . . [P]olitical power was concentrated in the hands of Parliament. What similar spectacle could the continent offer?" Many observers at the time drew similar conclusions, praising England's constitution and national character. Some focused more specifically on economics. For Voltaire, "commerce which has enriched the citizens of England has helped make them free . . . that liberty has in turn expanded commerce." Rather than cultivating the decadent pleasures of its nobility, the observant French clergyman Abbe Coyer remarked, the English government had helped "the honest middle class, that precious portion of nations."[19] Free markets helped enrich the middle class, which then furthered the cause of liberty. It seemed a virtuous circle.

The lands most like England were its colonies in America. The colonists had established governments that closely resembled those they had left behind in Tudor England. In 1776, when they rebelled against George III, the colonists couched their revolution as a call for the return of their rights as Englishmen. As they saw it, their long-established liberties had been usurped by a tyrannical monarch, forcing them to declare independence. In some ways it was a replay of England's own Glorious Revolution, in which Parliament rebelled against an arbitrary monarch whose chief sin was also to have raised taxes without the consent of the governed—or rather, the taxed. The winners in both 1688 and 1776 were the progressive, modernizing, and commercially minded elites. (The losers, in addition to the king, were the old Tories, who remained loyal to the crown both in seventeenth-century England and eighteenth-century America.)

But if England was exceptional, America was a special case of a special case. It was England without feudalism. Of course America had rich, landed families, but they were not titled, had no birthrights, and were not endowed with political power comparable to that of the members of the House of Lords. To understand eighteenth-century America, the historian Richard Hofstadter wrote, one had to imagine that unique possibility, "a middle class world."[20] Aristocratic elements in the economy and society, though present, rarely dominated. In the North, they began to wane by the close of the eighteenth century. The historian Gordon Wood noted, "In the 1780s we can actually sense the shift from a pre-modern society to a modern one where business interests and consumer tastes of ordinary people were coming to dominate." The American Revolution, which produced, in Wood's words, "an explosion of entrepreneurial power," widened the gulf between America and Europe.[21] America was now openly bourgeois and proud of it. Days after arriving in the United States in 1831, Tocqueville noted in his diary that in America "the whole society seems to have melted into a middle class."

The American path to liberal democracy was exceptional. Most countries don't begin their national experience as a new society without a feudal past. Free of hundreds of years of monarchy and aristocracy, Americans needed neither a powerful central government nor a violent social revolution to overthrow the old order. In Europe liberals feared state power but also fantasized about it. They sought to limit it yet needed it to modernize their societies. "The great advantage of the Americans," Tocqueville observed famously, "is that they have arrived at a state of democracy without having to endure a democratic revolution. . . . [T]hey are born equal without having to become equal."

By the early nineteenth century in the United Kingdom and the United States, for the most part, individual liberty flourished and equality under law ruled. But neither country was a democracy. Before the Reform Act of 1832, 1.8 percent of the adult population of the United Kingdom was eligible to vote. After the law that figure rose to 2.7 percent. After further widening of the franchise in 1867, 6.4 percent could vote, and after 1884, 12.1 percent.[22] Only in 1930, once women were fully enfranchised, did the United Kingdom meet today's standard for being democratic: universal adult suffrage. Yet it was widely considered the model of a constitutional liberal state—one that protected liberty and was governed by law.

The United States was more democratic than the United Kingdom, but not by as much as people think. For its first few decades, only white male property owners were eligible to vote—a system quite similar to that in the country whose rule it had just thrown off. In 1824—48 years after independence—only 5 percent of adult Americans cast a ballot in the presidential election. That number rose dramatically as the Jacksonian revolution spread and property qualifications were mostly eliminated. But not until the eve of the Civil War could it even be said that every white man in the United States had the right to vote. Blacks were enfranchised in theory in 1870, but in fact not until a century later in the South. Women got the vote in 1920. Despite this lack of democracy, for most of the nineteenth century, the United States and its system of laws and rights were the envy of the world. And with time, constitutional liberalism led to democracy, which led to further liberty, and so it went.

The rest of Europe followed a more complex path to liberal democracy than did the United Kingdom and the United States, but it eventually got there. What happened in Britain and America slowly and (mostly) peacefully happened on the continent in a jerky and bloody fashion (as will be discussed in the next chapter). Still, most became liberal democracies by the late 1940s and almost all the rest have done so since 1989, with consolidation taking place fast and firmly. The reason is clear: all Western countries shared a history that, for all its variations, featured the building of a constitutional liberal tradition. The English case is what scholars call the "ideal type," which makes it useful to highlight. But by the eighteenth century, even the most retrograde European power was a liberal regime when compared with its counterparts in Asia or Africa. Citizens had explicit rights and powers that no non-Western subject could imagine. Monarchs were restrained by law and tradition. A civil society of private enterprise, churches, universities, guilds, and associations flourished without much interference from the state. Private property was protected and free enterprise flowered. Often these freedoms were stronger in theory than in practice, and frequently they were subject to abuse by autocratic monarchs. But compared with the rest of the world the West was truly the land of liberty.

Culture as Destiny

This brief history of liberty might seem a discouraging guide. It suggests that any country hoping to become a liberal democracy should probably relocate to the West. And without a doubt, being part of the Western world—even if on the periphery— is a political advantage. Of all the countries that gained independence after the Soviet empire collapsed, those that have shared what one might call "the Western experience"—the old lands of the Austrian and German empires—have done best at liberal democracy. The line that separated Western and Eastern Christendom in 1500 today divides successful liberal regimes from unsuccessful, illiberal ones. Poland, Hungary, and the Czech Republic, which were most securely a part of Europe, are furthest along in consolidating their democracies; the Baltic states are next in line. Even in the Balkans, Slovenia and Croatia, which fall on the western side

of that East-West line, are doing well while Serbia and Albania (on the east) are having a far more troubled transition.

Does this mean that culture is destiny? This powerful argument has been made by distinguished scholars from Max Weber to Samuel Huntington. It is currently a trendy idea. From business consultants to military strategists, people today talk about culture as the easy explanation to most puzzles. Why did the U.S. economy boom over the last two decades? It's obvious: our unique entrepreneurial culture. Why is Russia unable to adapt to capitalism? Also obvious: it has a feudal, antimarket culture. Why is Africa mired in poverty? And why is the Arab world breeding terrorists? Again, culture.

But these answers are too simple. After all, American culture also produced stagflation and the Great Depression. And the once-feudal cultures of Japan and Germany seem to have adapted to capitalism well, having become the second- and third-richest countries in the world, respectively. A single country can succeed and fail at different times, sometimes just a few decades apart, which would suggest that something other than its culture—which is relatively unchanging—is at work.

Singapore's brilliant patriarch Lee Kuan Yew once explained to me that if you want to see how culture works, compare the performance of German workers and Zambian workers anywhere in the world. You will quickly come to the conclusion that there is something very different in the two cultures that explains the results. Scholars make similar arguments: in his interesting work *Tribes*, Joel Kotkin argues that if you want to succeed economically in the modern world, the key is simple—be Jewish, be Indian, but above all, be Chinese.

Lee and Kotkin are obviously correct in their observation that certain groups—Chinese, Indians, Jews—do superbly in all sorts of settings. (In fact I find this variant of the culture theory particularly appealing, since I am of Indian origin.) But if being Indian is a key to economic success, what explains the dismal performance of the Indian economy over the first four decades after its independence in 1947—or, for that matter, for hundreds of years before that? Growing up in India I certainly did not think of Indians as economically successful. In fact I recall the day a legendary member of the Indian parliament, Piloo Mody, posed the following question to Indira Gandhi during the prime minister's "question hour" in New Delhi: "Can the prime minister explain why Indians seem to thrive economically under every government in the world except hers?"

Similar questions might be asked of China, another country that did miserably in economic terms for hundreds of years until two decades ago. If all you need are the Chinese, China has billions of them. As for Jews, although they have thrived in many places, the one country where they are a majority, Israel, was also an economic mess until recently. Interestingly, the economic fortunes of all three countries (India, China, Israel) improved markedly around the 1980s. But this was not because they got themselves new cultures, but because their governments changed specific policies and created a more market-friendly system. China is today growing faster than India, but that has more to do with the fact that China is reforming its economy more extensively than India is, than with any supposed superiority of the Confucian ethic over the Hindu mind-set.

It is odd that Lee Kuan Yew is such a fierce proponent of cultural arguments. Singapore is culturally not very different from its neighbor Malaysia. It is more Chinese and less Malay but compared to the rest of the world, the two countries share much in common. But much more than its neighbors, Singapore has had an effective government that has pursued wise economic policies. That surely, more than innate cultural differences, explains its success. The key to Singapore's success, in other words, is Lee Kuan Yew, not Confucius. The point is not that culture is unimportant; on the contrary it matters greatly. It represents the historical experience of a people, is embedded in their institutions, and shapes their attitudes and expectations about the world. But culture can change. German culture in 1939 was very different from what it became in 1959, just twenty years later. Europe, once the heartland of hyperna-

tionalism, is now postnationalist, its states willing to cede power to supranational bodies in ways that Americans can hardly imagine. The United States was once an isolationist republic with a deep suspicion of standing armies. Today it is a hegemon with garrisons around the world. The Chinese were once backward peasants; now they are smart merchants. Economic crises, war, political leadership—all these things change culture.

A hundred years ago, when East Asia seemed immutably poor, many scholars—most famously Max Weber—argued that Confucian-based cultures discouraged all the attributes necessary for success in capitalism.[23] A decade ago, when East Asia was booming, scholars had turned this explanation on its head, arguing that Confucianism actually emphasized the traits essential for economic dynamism. Today the wheel has turned again and many see in "Asian values" all the ingredients of crony capitalism. In his study Weber linked northern Europe's economic success to its "Protestant ethic" and predicted that the Catholic south would stay poor. In fact, Italy and France have grown faster than Protestant Europe over the last half-century. One may use the stereotype of shifty Latins and a *mañana* work ethic to explain the poor performance of some countries, but then how does one explain Chile? Its economy is doing as well as that of the strongest of the Asian "tigers." Its success is often attributed to another set of Latin values: strong families, religious values, and determination.

In truth we cannot find a simple answer to why certain societies succeed at certain times. When a society does succeed it often seems inevitable in retrospect. So we examine successful societies and search within their cultures for the seeds of success. But cultures are complex; one finds in them what one wants. If one wants to find cultural traits of hard work and thrift within East Asia, they are there. If you want instead to find a tendency toward blind obedience and nepotism, these too exist. Look hard enough and you will find all these traits in most cultures.

Culture is important. It can be a spur or a drag, delaying or speeding up change. It can get codified in institutions and practices, which are often the real barriers to success. Indian culture may or may not hurt its chances for economic growth, but Indian bureaucracy certainly does. The West's real advantage is that its history led to the creation of institutions and practices that, although in no sense bound up with Western genes, are hard to replicate from scratch in other societies. But it can be done.

The East Asian Model

Looking at the many non-Western transitions to liberal democracy over the last three decades one can see that the countries that have moved furthest toward liberal democracy followed a version of the European pattern: capitalism and the rule of law first, and then democracy. South Korea, Taiwan, Thailand, and Malaysia were all governed for decades by military juntas or single-party systems. These regimes liberalized the economy, the legal system, and rights of worship and travel, and then, decades later, held free elections. They achieved, perhaps accidentally, the two essential attributes of good government that James Madison outlined in the Federalist Papers. First, a government must be able to control the governed, then it must be able to control itself. Order plus liberty. These two forces will, in the long run, produce legitimate government, prosperity, and liberal democracy. Of course, it's easier said than done.

In the 1950s and 1960s, most Western intellectuals scorned East Asia's regimes as reactionary, embracing instead popular leaders in Asia and Africa who were holding elections and declaring their faith in the people—for example in Ghana, Tanzania, and Kenya. Most of these countries degenerated into dictatorships while East Asia moved in precisely the opposite direction. It should surely puzzle these scholars and intellectuals that the best-consolidated democracies in Latin America and East Asia—Chile, South Korea, and Taiwan—were for a long while ruled by military juntas. In East Asia, as in western

Europe, liberalizing autocracies laid the groundwork for stable liberal democracies.

In almost every case the dictatorships opened the economy slowly and partially, but this process made the government more and more liberal. "An unmistakable feature in East Asia since World War II," wrote a leading scholar of East Asia, Minxin Pei,

> is the gradual process of authoritarian institutionalization. . . . At the center of this process was the slow emergence of modern political institutions exercising formal and informal constraining power through dominant parties, bureaucracies, semi-open electoral procedures, and a legal system that steadily acquired a measure of autonomy. The process had two beneficial outcomes—a higher level of stability and security of property rights (due to increasing constraints placed on rulers by the power of market forces and new political norms)."[24]

East Asia is still rife with corruption, nepotism, and voter fraud—but so were most Western democracies, even fifty years ago. Elections in Taiwan today are not perfect but they are probably more free and fair than those in the American South in the 1950s (or Chicago in the 1960s). Large conglomerates (*chaebols*) have improper influence in South Korean politics today, but so did their equivalents in Europe and the United States a century ago. The railroads, steel companies, shipbuilders, and great financiers of the past were probably more powerful than any East Asian tycoon today. They dominated America during its late-nineteenth-century Gilded Age. (Can you even name the political contemporaries of J. P. Morgan, E. H. Harriman, and John D. Rockefeller?) One cannot judge new democracies by standards that most Western countries would have flunked even thirty years ago. East Asia today is a mixture of liberalism, oligarchy, democracy, capitalism, and corruption—much like the West in, say, 1900. But most of East Asia's countries are considerably more liberal and democratic than the vast majority of other non-Western countries.

An even more striking proof that a constitutional liberal past can produce a liberal democratic present was identified by the late political scientist Myron Weiner in 1983. He pointed out that, as of then, "every single country in the Third World that emerged from colonial rule since the Second World War with a population of at least one million (and almost all the smaller colonies as well) with a continuous democratic experience is a former British colony."[25] British rule meant not democracy—colonialism is almost by definition undemocratic—but limited constitutional liberalism and capitalism. There are now other Third World democracies but Weiner's general point still holds. To say this is not to defend colonialism. Having grown up in a postcolonial country I do not need to be reminded of the institutionalized racism and the abuse of power that was part of the imperial legacy. But it is an undeniable fact that the British Empire left behind a legacy of law and capitalism that has helped strengthen the forces of liberal democracy in many of its former colonies—though not all. France, by contrast, encouraged little constitutionalism or free markets in its occupied lands, but it did enfranchise some of its colonial populations in northern Africa. Early democratization in all those cases led to tyranny.

The Western path has led to liberal democracy far from the Western world. But the sequence and timing of democratization matter. Most Third World countries that proclaimed themselves democracies immediately after their independence, while they were poor and unstable, became dictatorships within a decade. As Giovanni Sartori, Columbia University's great scholar of democracy, noted about the path from constitutional liberalism to democracy, "the itinerary is not reversible." Even European deviations from the Anglo-American pattern—constitutionalism and capitalism first, only then democracy—were far less successful in producing liberal democracy. To see the complications produced by premature democratization, we could return to the heart of Europe—back in time to the early twentieth century.

NOTES

1. Jacob Burckhardt, *The Age of Constantine the Great*, tr. Moses Hadas (Berkeley: University of California Press, 1983), 351.

2. Benjamin Constant, "The Liberty of the Ancients Compared with That of the Moderns" (1819), in *Benjamin Constant: Political Writings*, Biancamaria Fontana, ed. (New York: Cambridge University Press, 1988).

3. Herbert Asquith, "Introduction," in Ernest Barker, *The Legacy of Rome* (Oxford, Clarendon Press, 1923), vii.

4. Quoted in David Gress, *From Plato to NATO: The Idea of the West and Its Opponents* (New York: Free Press, 1998), 125. I am particularly indebted to this fascinating and important book for its discussion of Rome and the Catholic Church.

5. Edward Gibbon, *The Decline and Fall of the Roman Empire*, vol. 3, chapter 27, part 4. Again, thanks to David Gress for this story and source.

6. E. L. Jones, *The European Miracle: Environments, Economies, and Geopolitics in the History of Europe and Asia* (New York: Cambridge University Press, 1981). This is a wonderfully broad and suggestive book, but Jones places greater weight on culture than I do.

7. Guido de Ruggiero, *The History of European Liberalism* (Oxford: Oxford University Press, 1927). A wonderful book that deserves to be a classic.

8. Daniel A. Baugh, ed., *Aristocratic Government and Society in Eighteenth Century England* (New York: New Viewpoints, 1975).

9. Paul Johnson, "Laying Down the Law," *Wall Street Journal*, March 10, 1999.

10. In the historian J. H. Plumb's words, "the Revolution of 1688 was a monument raised by the gentry to its own sense of independence." J. H. Plumb, *The Growth of Political Stability in England, 1675–1725* (London: Macmillan, 1967), 29–30.

11. Jacques Barzun, *From Dawn to Decadence: 1500 to the Present* (New York: HarperCollins, 2000), 287–89.

12. Judith Shklar, *Montesquieu* (New York: Oxford University Press, 1987), 121.

13. Douglass North and Robert Thomas, *The Rise of the Western World: A New Economic History* (Cambridge: Cambridge University Press, 1973), x.

14. Richard Pipes, *Property and Freedom* (New York: Knopf, 1999), 111.

15. Mildred Campbell, *The English Yeomen under Elizabeth and the Early Stuarts* (New York: A. M. Kelley, 1968), cited in Barrington Moore, *Social Origins of Dictatorship and Democracy: Lord and Peasant in the Making of the Modern World* (Boston: Beacon Press, 1966).

16. Moore, *Social Origins*, 418. The original says "bourgeois" not "bourgeoisie," but it is often quoted as the latter, which is what I have done.

17. J. M. Roberts, *The Penguin History of the World* (New York: Penguin, 1997), 553.

18. E. J. Hobsbawm, *Industry and Empire* (New York: Penguin, 1969), 26.

19. Hobsbawm, *Industry*, 48.

20. Richard Hofstadter, *America at 1750: A Social Portrait* (New York: Knopf, 1971), 131.

21. Gordon Wood, *The Radicalism of the American Revolution* (New York: Random House, 1993), 348.

22. Voting percentages calculated using B. R. Mitchell, *Abstract of British Historical Statistics* (Cambridge: Cambridge University Press, 1962); The Great Britain Historical G.I.S., University of Essex, available at www.geog.port.ac.uk/gbhgis/db; and E. J. Evans, *The Forging of the Modern Industrial State: Early Industrial Britain, 1783–1870* (New York: Longman, 1983). Also see Gertrude Himmelfarb, "The Politics of Democracy: The English Reform Act of 1867," *Journal of British Studies* 6 (1966).

23. Max Weber, *The Protestant Ethic and the Spirit of Capitalism* (New York: Scribner's, 1958).

24. Minxin Pei, "Constructing the Political Foundations for Rapid Economic Growth," in Henry Rowen, ed., *Behind East Asia's Growth: The Political and Social Foundations of an Economic Miracle* (London: Routledge, 1997), 39–59.

25. Myron Weiner, "Empirical Democratic Theory," in Myron Weiner and Ergun Ozbudun, eds., *Competitive Elections in Developing Countries* (Durham, N.C.: Duke University Press, 1987), 20.

Philippe C. Schmitter and Terry Lynn Karl
WHAT DEMOCRACY IS . . . AND IS NOT

For some time, the word democracy has been circulating as a debased currency in the political marketplace. Politicians with a wide range of convictions and practices strove to appropriate the label and attach it to their actions. Scholars, conversely, hesitated to use it—without adding qualifying adjectives—because of the ambiguity that surrounds it. The distinguished American political theorist Robert Dahl even tried to introduce a new term, "polyarchy," in its stead in the (vain) hope of gaining a greater measure of conceptual precision. But for better or worse, we are "stuck" with democracy as the catchword of contemporary political discourse. It is the word that resonates in people's minds and springs from their lips as they struggle for freedom and a better way of life; it is the word whose meaning we must discern if it is to be of any use in guiding political analysis and practice.

From *Journal of Democracy* (Summer 1991), pp. 67–73.

The wave of transitions away from autocratic rule that began with Portugal's "Revolution of the Carnations" in 1974 and seems to have crested with the collapse of communist regimes across Eastern Europe in 1989 has produced a welcome convergence toward [a] common definition of democracy.[1] Everywhere there has been a silent abandonment of dubious adjectives like "popular," "guided," "bourgeois," and "formal" to modify "democracy." At the same time, a remarkable consensus has emerged concerning the minimal conditions that polities must meet in order to merit the prestigious appellation of "democratic." Moreover, a number of international organizations now monitor how well these standards are met; indeed, some countries even consider them when formulating foreign policy.[2]

What Democracy Is

Let us begin by broadly defining democracy and the generic *concepts* that distinguish it as a unique system for organizing relations between rulers and the ruled. We will then briefly review *procedures*, the rules and arrangements that are needed if democracy is to endure. Finally, we will discuss two operative *principles* that make democracy work. They are not expressly included among the generic concepts or formal procedures, but the prospect for democracy is grim if their underlying conditioning effects are not present.

One of the major themes of this essay is that democracy does not consist of a single unique set of institutions. There are many types of democracy, and their diverse practices produce a similarly varied set of effects. The specific form democracy takes is contingent upon a country's socioeconomic conditions as well as its entrenched state structures and policy practices.

Modern political democracy is a system of governance in which rulers are held accountable for their actions in the public realm by citizens, acting indirectly through the competition and cooperation of their elected representatives.[3]

A *regime or system of governance* is an ensemble of patterns that determines the methods of access to the principal public offices; the characteristics of the actors admitted to or excluded from such access; the strategies that actors may use to gain access; and the rules that are followed in the making of publicly binding decisions. To work properly, the ensemble must be institutionalized—that is to say, the various patterns must be habitually known, practiced, and accepted by most, if not all, actors. Increasingly, the preferred mechanism of institutionalization is a written body of laws undergirded by a written constitution, though many enduring political norms can have an informal, prudential, or traditional basis.[4]

For the sake of economy and comparison, these forms, characteristics, and rules are usually bundled together and given a generic label. Democratic is one; others are autocratic, authoritarian, despotic, dictatorial, tyrannical, totalitarian, absolutist, traditional, monarchic, oligarchic, plutocratic, aristocratic, and sultanistic.[5] Each of these regime forms may in turn be broken down into subtypes.

Like all regimes, democracies depend upon the presence of *rulers*, persons who occupy specialized authority roles and can give legitimate commands to others. What distinguishes democratic rulers from nondemocratic ones are the norms that condition how the former come to power and the practices that hold them accountable for their actions.

The *public realm* encompasses the making of collective norms and choices that are binding on the society and backed by state coercion. Its content can vary a great deal across democracies, depending upon preexisting distinctions between the public and the private, state and society, legitimate coercion and voluntary exchange, and collective needs and individual preferences. The liberal conception of democracy advocates circumscribing the public realm as narrowly as possible, while the socialist or social-democratic approach would extend that realm through regulation, subsidization, and, in some cases, collective ownership of property. Neither is intrinsically more democratic than the other—just *differently* democratic. This implies that measures aimed at "developing the private sector" are no more democratic than those aimed at "developing the public sector." Both, if carried to extremes, could undermine the practice of democracy, the former by destroying the basis for satisfying collective needs and exercising legitimate authority; the latter by destroying the basis for satisfying individual preferences and controlling illegitimate government actions. Differences of opinion over the optimal mix of the two provide much of the substantive content of political conflict within established democracies.

Citizens are the most distinctive element in democracies. All regimes have rulers and a public realm, but only to the extent that they are democratic do they have citizens. Historically, severe restrictions on citizenship were imposed in most emerging or partial democracies according to criteria of age, gender, class, race, literacy, property ownership, tax-paying status, and so on. Only a small part of the total population was eligible to vote or run for office. Only restricted social categories were allowed to form, join, or support political associations. After protracted struggle—in some cases involving violent domestic upheaval or international war—most of these restrictions were lifted. Today, the criteria for inclusion are fairly standard. All native-born adults are eligible, although somewhat higher age limits may still be imposed upon candidates for certain offices. Unlike the early American and European democracies of the nineteenth century, none of the recent democracies in southern Europe, Latin America, Asia, or Eastern Europe has even attempted to impose formal restrictions on the franchise or eligibility to office. When it comes to informal restrictions on the effective exercise of citizenship rights, however, the story can be quite different. This explains the central importance (discussed below) of procedures.

Competition has not always been considered an essential defining condition of democracy. "Classic" democracies presumed decision making based on direct participation leading to consensus. The assembled citizenry was expected to agree on a common course of action after listening to the alternatives and weighing their respective merits and demerits. A tradition of hostility to "faction," and "particular interests" persists in democratic thought, but at least since *The Federalist Papers* it has become widely accepted that competition among factions is a necessary evil in democracies that operate on a more-than-local scale. Since, as James Madison argued, "the latent causes of faction are sown into the nature of man," and the possible remedies for "the mischief of faction" are worse than the disease, the best course is to recognize them and to attempt to control their effects.[6] Yet while democrats may agree on the inevitability of factions, they tend to disagree about the best forms and rules for governing factional competition. Indeed, differences over the preferred modes and boundaries of competition contribute most to distinguishing one subtype of democracy from another.

The most popular definition of democracy equates it with regular *elections*, fairly conducted and honestly counted. Some even consider the mere fact of elections—even ones from which specific parties or candidates are excluded, or in which substantial portions of the population cannot freely participate—as a sufficient condition for the existence of democracy. This fallacy has been called "electoralism" or "the faith that merely holding elections will channel political action into peaceful contests among elites and accord public legitimacy to the winners"—no matter how they are conducted or what else constrains those who win them.[7] However central to democracy, elections occur intermittently and only allow citizens to choose between the highly aggregated alternatives offered by political parties, which can, especially in the early stages of a democratic transition, proliferate in a bewildering variety. During the intervals between elections, citizens can seek to influence public policy through a wide variety of other intermediaries: interest associations, social movements, locality groupings, clientelistic arrangements, and so forth. *Modern democracy, in other words, offers a variety of competitive processes and channels for the expression of interests and values— associational as well as partisan, functional as well as territorial, collective as well as individual. All are integral to its practice.*

Another commonly accepted image of democracy identifies it with *majority rule*. Any governing body that makes decisions by combining the votes of more than half of those eligible and present is said to be democratic, whether that majority emerges within an electorate, a parliament, a committee, a city council, or a party caucus. For exceptional purposes (e.g., amending the constitution or expelling a member), "qualified majorities" of more than 50 percent may be required, but few would deny that democracy must involve some means of aggregating the equal preferences of individuals.

A problem arises, however, when *numbers* meet *intensities*. What happens when a properly assembled majority (especially a stable, self-perpetuating one) regularly makes decisions that harm some minority (especially a threatened cultural or ethnic group)? In these circumstances, successful democracies tend to qualify the central principle of majority rule in order to protect minority rights. Such qualifications can take the form of constitutional provisions that place certain matters beyond the reach of majorities (bills of rights); requirements for concurrent majorities in several different constituencies (confederalism); guarantees securing the autonomy of local or regional governments against the demands of the central authority (federalism); grand coalition governments that incorporate all parties (consociationalism); or the negotiation of social pacts between major social groups like business and labor (neocorporatism). The most common and effective way of protecting minorities, however, lies in the everyday operation of interest associations and social movements. These reflect (some would say, amplify) the different intensities of preference that exist in the population and bring them to bear on democratically elected decision makers. Another way of putting this intrinsic tension between numbers and intensities would be to say that "in modern democracies, votes may be counted, but influences alone are weighted."

Cooperation has always been a central feature of democracy. Actors must voluntarily make collective decisions binding on the polity as a whole.

They must cooperate in order to compete. They must be capable of acting collectively through parties, associations, and movements in order to select candidates, articulate preferences, petition authorities, and influence policies.

But democracy's freedoms should also encourage citizens to deliberate among themselves, to discover their common needs, and to resolve their differences without relying on some supreme central authority. Classical democracy emphasized these qualities, and they are by no means extinct, despite repeated efforts by contemporary theorists to stress the analogy with behavior in the economic marketplace and to reduce all of democracy's operations to competitive interest maximization. Alexis de Tocqueville best described the importance of independent groups for democracy in his *Democracy in America*, a work which remains a major source of inspiration for all those who persist in viewing democracy as something more than a struggle for election and re-election among competing candidates.[8]

In contemporary political discourse, this phenomenon of cooperation and deliberation via autonomous group activity goes under the rubric of "civil society." The diverse units of social identity and interest, by remaining independent of the state (and perhaps even of parties), not only can restrain the arbitrary actions of rulers, but can also contribute to forming better citizens who are more aware of the preferences of others, more self-confident in their actions, and more civic-minded in their willingness to sacrifice for the common good. At its best, civil society provides an intermediate layer of governance between the individual and the state that is capable of resolving conflicts and controlling the behavior of members without public coercion. Rather than overloading decision makers with increased demands and making the system ungovernable,[9] a viable civil society can mitigate conflicts and improve the quality of citizenship—without relying exclusively on the privatism of the marketplace.

Representatives—whether directly or indirectly elected—do most of the real work in modern democracies. Most are professional politicians who orient their careers around the desire to fill key offices. It is doubtful that any democracy could survive without such people. The central question, therefore, is not whether or not there will be a political elite or even a professional political class, but how these representatives are chosen and then held accountable for their actions.

As noted above, there are many channels of representation in modern democracy. The electoral one, based on territorial constituencies, is the most visible and public. It culminates in a parliament or a presidency that is periodically accountable to the citizenry as a whole. Yet the sheer growth of government (in large part as a byproduct of popular demand) has increased the number, variety, and power of agencies charged with making public decisions and not subject to elections. Around these agencies there has developed a vast apparatus of specialized representation based largely on functional interests, not territorial constituencies. These interest associations, and not political parties, have become the primary expression of civil society in most stable democracies, supplemented by the more sporadic interventions of social movements.

The new and fragile democracies that have sprung up since 1974 must live in "compressed time." They will not resemble the European democracies of the nineteenth and early twentieth centuries, and they cannot expect to acquire the multiple channels of representation in gradual historical progression as did most of their predecessors. A bewildering array of parties, interests, and movements will all simultaneously seek political influence in them, creating challenges to the polity that did not exist in earlier processes of democratization.

Procedures That Make Democracy Possible

The defining components of democracy are necessarily abstract, and may give rise to a considerable variety of institutions and subtypes of democracy. For democracy to thrive, however, specific procedural norms must be followed and civic rights must be respected. Any polity that fails to impose such restrictions upon itself, that fails to follow the "rule of law" with regard to its own procedures, should not be considered democratic. These procedures alone do not define democracy, but their presence is indispensable to its persistence. In essence, they are necessary but not sufficient conditions for its existence.

Robert Dahl has offered the most generally accepted listing of what he terms the "procedural minimal" conditions that must be present for modern political democracy (or as he puts it, "polyarchy") to exist:

1. Control over government decisions about policy is constitutionally vested in elected officials.
2. Elected officials are chosen in frequent and fairly conducted elections in which coercion is comparatively uncommon.
3. Practically all adults have the right to vote in the election of officials.
4. Practically all adults have the right to run for elective offices.
5. Citizens have a right to express themselves without the danger of severe punishment on political matters broadly defined. . . .
6. Citizens have a right to seek out alternative sources of information. Moreover, alternative sources of information exist and are protected by law.
7. . . . Citizens also have the right to form relatively independent associations or organizations, including independent political parties and interest groups.[10]

These seven conditions seem to capture the essence of procedural democracy for many theorists, but we propose to add two others. The first might be thought of as a further refinement of item (1), while the second might be called an implicit prior condition to all seven of the above.

1. Popularly elected officials must be able to exercise their constitutional powers without being subjected to overriding (albeit informal)

opposition from unelected officials. Democracy is in jeopardy if military officers, entrenched civil servants, or state managers retain the capacity to act independently of elected civilians or even veto decisions made by the people's representatives. Without this additional caveat, the militarized polities of contemporary Central America, where civilian control over the military does not exist, might be classified by many scholars as democracies, just as they have been (with the exception of Sandinista Nicaragua) by U.S. policy makers. The caveat thus guards against what we earlier called "electoralism"—the tendency to focus on the holding of elections while ignoring other political realities.

2. The polity must be self-governing; it must be able to act independently of constraints imposed by some other overarching political system. Dahl and other contemporary democratic theorists probably took this condition for granted since they referred to formally sovereign nation-states. However, with the development of blocs, alliances, spheres of influence, and a variety of "neocolonial" arrangements, the question of autonomy has been a salient one. Is a system really democratic if its elected officials are unable to make binding decisions without the approval of actors outside their territorial domain? This is significant even if the outsiders are relatively free to alter or even end the encompassing arrangement (as in Puerto Rico), but it becomes especially critical if neither condition [pertains] (as in the Baltic states).

Principles That Make Democracy Feasible

Lists of component processes and procedural norms help us to specify what democracy is, but they do not tell us much about how it actually functions. The simplest answer is "by the consent of the people"; the more complex one is "by the contingent consent of politicians acting under conditions of bounded uncertainty."

In a democracy, representatives must at least informally agree that those who win greater electoral support or influence over policy will not use their temporary superiority to bar the losers from taking office or exerting influence in the future, and that in exchange for this opportunity to keep competing for power and place, momentary losers will respect the winners' right to make binding decisions. Citizens are expected to obey the decisions ensuing from such a process of competition, provided its outcome remains contingent upon their collective preferences as expressed through fair and regular elections or open and repeated negotiations.

The challenge is not so much to find a set of goals that command widespread consensus as to find a set of rules that embody contingent consent. The precise shape of this "democratic bargain," to use Dahl's expression,[11] can vary a good deal from society to society. It depends on social cleavages and such subjective factors as mutual trust, the standard of fairness, and the willingness to compromise. It may even be compatible with a great deal of dissensus on substantive policy issues.

All democracies involve a degree of uncertainty about who will be elected and what policies they will pursue. Even in those polities where one party persists in winning elections or one policy is consistently implemented, the possibility of change through independent collective action still exists, as in Italy, Japan, and the Scandinavian social democracies. If it does not, the system is not democratic, as in Mexico, Senegal, or Indonesia.

But the uncertainty embedded in the core of all democracies is bounded. Not just any actor can get into the competition and raise any issue he or she pleases—there are previously established rules that must be respected. Not just any policy can be adopted—there are conditions that must be met. Democracy institutionalizes "normal," limited political uncertainty. These boundaries vary from country to country. Constitutional guarantees of property, privacy, expression, and other rights

are a part of this, but the most effective boundaries are generated by competition among interest groups and co-operation within civil society.
Whatever the rhetoric (and some polities appear
to offer their citizens more dramatic alternatives
than others), once the rules of contingent consent have been agreed upon, the actual variation
is likely to stay within a predictable and generally
accepted range.

This emphasis on operative guidelines contrasts
with a highly persistent, but misleading theme
in recent literature on democracy—namely, the
emphasis upon "civic culture." The principles we
have suggested here rest on rules of prudence, not
on deeply ingrained habits of tolerance, moderation, mutual respect, fair play, readiness to compromise, or trust in public authorities. Waiting for
such habits to sink deep and lasting roots implies
a very slow process of regime consolidation—
one that takes generations—and it would probably
condemn most contemporary experiences *ex hypothesi* to failure. Our assertion is that contingent consent and bounded uncertainty can emerge from the
interaction between antagonistic and mutually suspicious actors and that the far more benevolent and
ingrained norms of a civic culture are better thought
of as a *product* and not a producer of democracy.

How Democracies Differ

Several concepts have been deliberately excluded from
our generic definition of democracy, despite the fact
that they have been frequently associated with it in
both everyday practice and scholarly work. They are,
nevertheless, especially important when it comes to
distinguishing subtypes of democracy. Since no single
set of actual institutions, practices, or values embodies
democracy, polities moving away from authoritarian
rule can mix different components to produce different democracies. It is important to recognize that
these do not define points along a single continuum
of improving performance, but a matrix of potential
combinations that are *differently* democratic.

1. *Consensus*: All citizens may not agree on the
substantive goals of political action or on the
role of the state (although if they did, it would
certainly make governing democracies much
easier).
2. *Participation*: All citizens may not take an
active and equal part in politics, although it
must be legally possible for them to do so.
3. *Access*: Rulers may not weigh equally the preferences of all who come before them, although
citizenship implies that individuals and groups
should have an equal opportunity to express
their preferences if they choose to do so.
4. *Responsiveness*: Rulers may not always follow
the course of action preferred by the citizenry.
But when they deviate from such a policy, say
on grounds of "reason of state" or "overriding
national interest," they must ultimately be held
accountable for their actions through regular
and fair processes.
5. *Majority rule*: Positions may not be allocated
or rules may not be decided solely on the
basis of assembling the most votes, although
deviations from this principle usually must be
explicitly defended and previously approved.
6. *Parliamentary sovereignty*: The legislature may not
be the only body that can make rules or even the
one with final authority in deciding which laws
are binding, although where executive, judicial,
or other public bodies make that ultimate choice,
they too must be accountable for their actions.
7. *Party government*: Rulers may not be nominated,
promoted, and disciplined in their activities by
well-organized and programmatically coherent
political parties, although where they are not,
it may prove more difficult to form an effective
government.
8. *Pluralism*: The political process may not be
based on a multiplicity of overlapping, voluntaristic, and autonomous private groups.
However, where there are monopolies of representation, hierarchies of association, and obligatory memberships, it is likely that the interests
involved will be more closely linked to the state

and the separation between the public and private spheres of action will be much less distinct.

9. *Federalism*: The territorial division of authority may not involve multiple levels and local autonomies, least of all ones enshrined in a constitutional document, although some dispersal of power across territorial and/or functional units is characteristic of all democracies.

10. *Presidentialism*: The chief executive officer may not be a single person and he or she may not be directly elected by the citizenry as a whole, although some concentration of authority is present in all democracies, even if it is exercised collectively and only held indirectly accountable to the electorate.

11. *Checks and Balances*: It is not necessary that the different branches of government be systematically pitted against one another, although governments by assembly, by executive concentrations, by judicial command, or even by dictatorial fiat (as in time of war) must be ultimately accountable to the citizenry as a whole.

While each of the above has been named as an essential component of democracy, they should instead be seen either as indicators of this or that type of democracy, or else as useful standards for evaluating the performance of particular regimes. To include them as part of the generic definition of democracy itself would be to mistake the American polity for the universal model of democratic governance. Indeed, the parliamentary, consociational, unitary, corporatist, and concentrated arrangements of continental Europe may have some unique virtues for guiding polities through the uncertain transition from autocratic to democratic rule.[12]

What Democracy Is Not

We have attempted to convey the general meaning of modern democracy without identifying it with some particular set of rules and institutions or restricting it to some specific culture or level of development. We have also argued that it cannot be reduced to the regular holding of elections or equated with a particular notion of the role of the state, but we have not said much more about what democracy is not or about what democracy may not be capable of producing.

There is an understandable temptation to load too many expectations on this concept and to imagine that by attaining democracy, a society will have resolved all of its political, social, economic, administrative, and cultural problems. Unfortunately, "all good things do not necessarily go together."

First, democracies are not necessarily more efficient economically than other forms of government. Their rates of aggregate growth, savings, and investment may be no better than those of nondemocracies. This is especially likely during the transition, when propertied groups and administrative elites may respond to real or imagined threats to the "rights" they enjoyed under authoritarian rule by initiating capital flight, disinvestment, or sabotage. In time, depending upon the type of democracy, benevolent long-term effects upon income distribution, aggregate demand, education, productivity, and creativity may eventually combine to improve economic and social performance, but it is certainly too much to expect that these improvements will occur immediately—much less that they will be defining characteristics of democratization.

Second, democracies are not necessarily more efficient administratively. Their capacity to make decisions may even be slower than that of the regimes they replace, if only because more actors must be consulted. The costs of getting things done may be higher, if only because "payoffs" have to be made to a wider and more resourceful set of clients (although one should never underestimate the degree of corruption to be found within autocracies). Popular satisfaction with the new democratic government's performance may not even seem greater, if only because necessary compromises often please no one completely, and because the losers are free to complain.

Third, democracies are not likely to appear more orderly, consensual, stable, or governable than the autocracies they replace. This is partly a byproduct of democratic freedom of expression, but it is also a reflection of the likelihood of continuing disagreement over new rules and institutions. These products of imposition or compromise are often initially quite ambiguous in nature and uncertain in effect until actors have learned how to use them. What is more, they come in the aftermath of serious struggles motivated by high ideals. Groups and individuals with recently acquired autonomy will test certain rules, protest against the actions of certain institutions, and insist on renegotiating their part of the bargain. Thus the presence of antisystem parties should be neither surprising nor seen as a failure of democratic consolidation. What counts is whether such parties are willing, however reluctantly, to play by the general rules of bounded uncertainty and contingent consent.

Governability is a challenge for all regimes, not just democratic ones. Given the political exhaustion and loss of legitimacy that have befallen autocracies from sultanistic Paraguay to totalitarian Albania, it may seem that only democracies can now be expected to govern effectively and legitimately. Experience has shown, however, that democracies too can lose the ability to govern. Mass publics can become disenchanted with their performance. Even more threatening is the temptation for leaders to fiddle with procedures and ultimately undermine the principles of contingent consent and bounded uncertainty. Perhaps the most critical moment comes once the politicians begin to settle into the more predictable roles and relations of a consolidated democracy. Many will find their expectations frustrated; some will discover that the new rules of competition put them at a disadvantage; a few may even feel that their vital interests are threatened by popular majorities.

Finally, democracies will have more open societies and polities than the autocracies they replace, but not necessarily more open economies. Many of today's most successful and well-established democracies have historically resorted to protectionism and closed borders, and have relied extensively upon public institutions to promote economic development. While the long-term compatibility between democracy and capitalism does not seem to be in doubt, despite their continuous tension, it is not clear whether the promotion of such liberal economic goals as the right of individuals to own property and retain profits, the clearing function of markets, the private settlement of disputes, the freedom to produce without government regulation, or the privatization of state-owned enterprises necessarily furthers the consolidation of democracy. After all, democracies do need to levy taxes and regulate certain transactions, especially where private monopolies and oligopolies exist. Citizens or their representatives may decide that it is desirable to protect the rights of collectivities from encroachment by individuals, especially propertied ones, and they may choose to set aside certain forms of property for public or cooperative ownership. In short, notions of economic liberty that are currently put forward in neoliberal economic models are not synonymous with political freedom—and may even impede it.

Democratization will not necessarily bring in its wake economic growth, social peace, administrative efficiency, political harmony, free markets, or "the end of ideology." Least of all will it bring about "the end of history." No doubt some of these qualities could make the consolidation of democracy easier, but they are neither prerequisites for it nor immediate products of it. Instead, what we should be hoping for is the emergence of political institutions that can peacefully compete to form governments and influence public policy, that can channel social and economic conflicts through regular procedures, and that have sufficient linkages to civil society to represent their constituencies and commit them to collective courses of action. Some types of democracies, especially in developing countries, have been unable to fulfill this promise, perhaps due to the circumstances of their transition from authoritarian rule.[13] The democratic wager is that such a regime, once established, will not only persist by reproducing itself within its initial confining conditions, but will eventually expand beyond them.[14] Unlike authoritarian regimes, democracies have the capacity to modify their rules and institutions consensually in response to changing circumstances. They may not immediately produce all the goods mentioned above, but they stand a better chance of eventually doing so than do autocracies.

NOTES

1. For a comparative analysis of the recent regime changes in southern Europe and Latin America, see Guillermo O'Donnell, Philippe C. Schmitter, and Laurence Whitehead, eds., *Transitions from Authoritarian Rule*, 4 vols. (Baltimore: Johns Hopkins University Press, 1986). For another compilation that adopts a more structural approach see Larry Diamond, Juan Linz, and Seymour Martin Lipset, eds., *Democracy in Developing Countries*, vols. 2, 3, and 4 (Boulder, Colo.: Lynne Rienner, 1989).

2. Numerous attempts have been made to codify and quantify the existence of democracy across political systems. The best known is probably Freedom House's *Freedom in the World: Political Rights and Civil Liberties*, published since 1973 by Greenwood Press and since 1988 by University Press of America. Also see Charles Humana, *World Human Rights Guide* (New York: Facts on File, 1986).

3. The definition most commonly used by American social scientists is that of Joseph Schumpeter: "that institutional arrangement for arriving at political decisions in which individuals acquire the power to decide by means of a competitive struggle for the people's vote." *Capitalism, Socialism, and Democracy* (London: George Allen and Unwin, 1943), 269. We accept certain aspects of the classical procedural approach to modern democracy, but differ primarily in our emphasis on the accountability of rulers to citizens and the relevance of mechanisms of competition other than elections.

4. Not only do some countries practice a stable form of democracy without a formal constitution (e.g., Great Britain and Israel), but even more countries have constitutions and legal codes that offer no guarantee of reliable practice. On paper, Stalin's 1936 constitution for the USSR was a virtual model of democratic rights and entitlements.

5. For the most valiant attempt to make some sense out of this thicket of distinctions, see Juan Linz, "Totalitarian and Authoritarian Regimes" in *Handbook of Political Science*, eds. Fred I. Greenstein and Nelson W. Polsby (Reading, Mass.: Addison Wesley, 1975), 175–411.

6. "Publius" (Alexander Hamilton, John Jay, and James Madison), *The Federalist Papers* (New York: Anchor Books, 1961). The quote is from Number 10.

7. See Terry Karl, "Imposing Consent? Electoralism versus Democratization in El Salvador," in *Elections and Democratization in Latin America, 1980–1985*, eds. Paul Drake and Eduardo Silva (San Diego: Center for Iberian and Latin American Studies, Center for US/Mexican Studies, University of California, San Diego, 1986), 9–36.

8. Alexis de Tocqueville, *Democracy in America*, 2 vols. (New York: Vintage Books, 1945).

9. This fear of overloaded government and the imminent collapse of democracy is well reflected in the work of Samuel P. Huntington during the 1970s. See especially Michel Crozier, Samuel P. Huntington, and Joji Watanuki, *The Crisis of Democracy* (New York: New York University Press, 1975). For Huntington's (revised) thoughts about the prospects for democracy, see his "Will More Countries Become Democratic?," *Political Science Quarterly* 99 (Summer 1984): 193–218.

10. Robert Dahl, *Dilemmas of Pluralist Democracy* (New Haven: Yale University Press, 1982), 11.

11. Robert Dahl, *After the Revolution: Authority in a Good Society* (New Haven: Yale University Press, 1970).

12. See Juan Linz, "The Perils of Presidentialism," *Journal of Democracy* 1 (Winter 1990): 51–69, and the ensuing discussion by Donald Horowitz, Seymour Martin Lipset, and Juan Linz in *Journal of Democracy* 1 (Fall 1990): 73–91.

13. Terry Lynn Karl, "Dilemmas of Democratization in Latin America" *Comparative Politics* 23 (October 1990): 1–23.

14. Otto Kirchheimer, "Confining Conditions and Revolutionary Breakthroughs," *American Political Science Review* 59 (1965): 964–974.

Arend Lijphart
CONSTITUTIONAL CHOICES
FOR NEW DEMOCRACIES

Two fundamental choices that confront architects of new democratic constitutions are those between plurality elections and proportional representation (PR) and between parliamentary and presidential forms of government. The merits of presidentialism and parliamentarism were extensively debated by Juan J. Linz, Seymour Martin Lipset, and Donald L. Horowitz in the Fall 1990 issue of the *Journal of Democracy*.[1] I strongly concur with Horowitz's contention that the electoral system is an equally vital element in democratic constitutional design, and therefore that it is of crucial importance to evaluate these two sets of choices in relation with each other. Such an analysis, as I will try to show, indicates that the combination of parliamentarism with proportional representation should be an especially attractive one to newly democratic and democratizing countries.

The comparative study of democracies has shown that the type of electoral system is significantly related to the development of a country's party system, its type of executive (one-party vs. coalition cabinets), and the relationship between its executive and legislature. Countries that use the plurality method of election (almost always applied, at the national level, in single-member districts) are likely to have two-party systems, one-party governments, and executives that are dominant in relation to their legislatures. These are the main characteristics of the Westminster or *majoritarian* model of democracy, in which power is concentrated in the hands of the major-

ity party. Conversely, PR is likely to be associated with multiparty systems, coalition governments (including, in many cases, broad and inclusive coalitions), and more equal executive-legislative power relations. These latter characteristics typify the *consensus* model of democracy, which, instead of relying on pure and concentrated majority rule, tries to limit, divide, separate, and share power in a variety of ways.[2]

Three further points should be made about these two sets of related traits. First, the relationships are mutual. For instance, plurality elections favor the maintenance of a two-party system; but an existing two-party system also favors the maintenance of plurality, which gives the two principal parties great advantages that they are unlikely to abandon. Second, if democratic political engineers desire to promote either the majoritarian cluster of characteristics (plurality, a two-party system, and a dominant, one-party cabinet) or the consensus cluster (PR, multipartism, coalition government, and a stronger legislature), the most practical way to do so is by choosing the appropriate electoral system. Giovanni Sartori has aptly called electoral systems "the most specific manipulative instrument of politics."[3] Third, important variations exist among PR systems. Without going into all the technical details, a useful distinction can be made between *extreme* PR, which poses few barriers to small parties, and *moderate* PR. The latter limits the influence of minor parties through such means as applying PR in small districts instead of large districts or nationwide balloting, and requiring parties to receive a minimum percentage of the vote in order to gain representation, such as the 5-percent threshold in Germany. The Dutch, Israeli, and Italian systems

From Larry Diamond and Marc F. Plattner, eds., *The Global Resurgence of Democracy* (Baltimore: Johns Hopkins University Press, 1996), pp. 162–74.

exemplify extreme PR and the German and Swedish systems, moderate PR.

The second basic constitutional choice, between parliamentary and presidential forms of government, also affects the majoritarian or consensus character of the political system. Presidentialism yields majoritarian effects on the party system and on the type of executive, but a consensus effect on executive-legislative relations. By formally separating the executive and legislative powers, presidential systems generally promote a rough executive-legislative balance of power. On the other hand, presidentialism tends to foster a two-party system, as the presidency is the biggest political prize to be won, and only the largest parties have a chance to win it. This advantage for the big parties often carries over into legislative elections as well (especially if presidential and legislative elections are held simultaneously), even if the legislative elections are conducted under PR rules. Presidentialism usually produces cabinets composed solely of members of the governing party. In fact, presidential systems concentrate executive power to an even greater degree than does a one-party parliamentary cabinet—not just in a single *party* but in a single *person*.

Explaining Past Choices

My aim is not simply to describe alternative democratic systems and their majoritarian or consensus characteristics, but also to make some practical recommendations for democratic constitutional engineers. What are the main advantages and disadvantages of plurality and PR and of presidentialism and parliamentarism? One way to approach this question is to investigate why contemporary democracies made the constitutional choices they did.

Figure 5.1 illustrates the four combinations of basic characteristics and the countries and regions where they prevail. The purest examples of the combination of presidentialism and plurality are the United States and democracies heavily influenced by the United States, such as the Philippines and Puerto Rico. Latin American countries have overwhelmingly opted for presidential-PR systems. Parliamentary-plurality systems exist in the United Kingdom and many former British colonies, including India, Malaysia, Jamaica, and the countries of the so-called Old Commonwealth (Canada, Australia, and New Zealand). Finally, parliamentary-PR systems are concentrated in Western Europe. Clearly, the overall pattern is to a large extent determined by

Figure 5.1 Four Basic Types of Democracy

	Presidential	Parliamentary
Plurality Elections	United States Philippines	United Kingdom Old Commonwealth India Malaysia Jamaica
Proportional Representation	Latin America	Western Europe

geographic, cultural, and colonial factors—a point to which I shall return shortly.

Very few contemporary democracies cannot be accommodated by this classification. The major exceptions are democracies that fall in between the pure presidential and pure parliamentary types (France and Switzerland), and those that use electoral methods other than pure PR or plurality (Ireland, Japan, and, again, France).[4]

Two important factors influenced the adoption of PR in continental Europe. One was the problem of ethnic and religious minorities; PR was designed to provide minority representation and thereby to counteract potential threats to national unity and political stability. "It was no accident," Stein Rokkan writes, "that the earliest moves toward proportional representation (PR) came in the ethnically most heterogeneous countries." The second factor was the dynamic of the democratization process. PR was adopted "through a convergence of pressures from below and from above. The rising working class wanted to lower the thresholds of representation in order to gain access to the legislatures, and the most threatened of the old-established parties demanded PR to protect their position against the new waves of mobilized voters created by universal suffrage."[5] Both factors are relevant for contemporary constitution making, especially for the many countries where there are deep ethnic cleavages or where new democratic forces need to be reconciled with the old antidemocratic groups.

The process of democratization also originally determined whether parliamentary or presidential institutions were adopted. As Douglas V. Verney has pointed out, there were two basic ways in which monarchical power could be democratized: by taking away most of the monarch's personal political prerogatives and making his cabinet responsible to the popularly elected legislature, thus creating a parliamentary system; or by removing the hereditary monarch and substituting a new, democratically elected "monarch," thus creating a presidential system.[6]

Other historical causes have been voluntary imitations of successful democracies and the dominant influence of colonial powers. As Figure 5.1 shows very clearly, Britain's influence as an imperial power has been enormously important. The U.S. presidential model was widely imitated in Latin America in the nineteenth century. And early in the twentieth century, PR spread quickly in continental Europe and Latin America, not only for reasons of partisan accommodation and minority protection, but also because it was widely perceived to be the most democratic method of election and hence the "wave of the democratic future."

This sentiment in favor of PR raises the controversial question of the *quality* of democracy achieved in the four alternative systems. The term "quality" refers to the degree to which a system meets such democratic norms as representativeness, accountability, equality, and participation. The claims and counterclaims are too well-known to require lengthy treatment here, but it is worth emphasizing that the differences between the opposing camps are not as great as is often supposed. First of all, PR and plurality advocates disagree not so much about the respective effects of the two electoral methods as about the weight to be attached to these effects. Both sides agree that PR yields greater proportionality and minority representation and that plurality promotes two-party systems and one-party executives. Partisans disagree on which of these results is preferable, with the plurality side claiming that only in two-party systems can clear accountability for government policy be achieved.

In addition, both sides argue about the *effectiveness* of the two systems. Proportionalists value minority representation not just for its democratic quality but also for its ability to maintain unity and peace in divided societies. Similarly, proponents of plurality favor one-party cabinets not just because of their democratic accountability but also because of the firm leadership and effective policy making that they allegedly provide. There also appears to be a slight difference in the relative emphasis that the two sides place on quality and effectiveness.

Proportionalists tend to attach greater importance to the *representativeness* of government, while plurality advocates view the *capacity to govern* as the more vital consideration.

Finally, while the debate between presidentialists and parliamentarists has not been as fierce, it clearly parallels the debate over electoral systems. Once again, the claims and counterclaims revolve around both quality and effectiveness. Presidentialists regard the direct popular election of the chief executive as a democratic asset, while parliamentarists think of the concentration of executive power in the hands of a single official as less than optimally democratic. But here the question of effectiveness has been the more seriously debated issue, with the president's strong and effective leadership role being emphasized by one side and the danger of executive-legislative conflict and stalemate by the other.

Evaluating Democratic Performance

How can the actual performance of the different types of democracies be evaluated? It is extremely difficult to find quantifiable measures of democratic performance, and therefore political scientists have rarely attempted a systematic assessment. The major exception is G. Bingham Powell's pioneering study evaluating the capacity of various democracies to maintain public order (as measured by the incidence of riots and deaths from political violence) and their levels of citizen participation (as measured by electoral turnout).[7] Following Powell's example, I will examine these and other aspects of democratic performance, including democratic representation and responsiveness, economic equality, and macroeconomic management.

Due to the difficulty of finding reliable data outside the OECD countries to measure such aspects of performance, I have limited the analysis to the advanced industrial democracies. In any event, the Latin American democracies, given their lower levels of economic development, cannot be considered

comparable cases. This means that one of the four basic alternatives—the presidential-PR form of democracy prevalent only in Latin America—must be omitted from our analysis.

Although this limitation is unfortunate, few observers would seriously argue that a strong case can be made for this particular type of democracy. With the clear exception of Costa Rica and the partial exceptions of Venezuela and Colombia, the political stability and economic performance of Latin American democracies have been far from satisfactory. As Juan Linz has argued, Latin American presidential systems have been particularly prone to executive-legislative deadlock and ineffective leadership.[8] Moreover, Scott Mainwaring has shown persuasively that this problem becomes especially serious when presidents do not have majority support in their legislatures.[9] Thus the Latin American model of presidentialism combined with PR legislative elections remains a particularly unattractive option.

The other three alternatives—presidential-plurality, parliamentary-plurality, and parliamentary-PR systems—are all represented among the firmly established Western democracies. I focus on the 14 cases that unambiguously fit these three categories. The United States is the one example of presidentialism combined with plurality. There are four cases of parliamentarism-plurality (Australia, Canada, New Zealand, and the United Kingdom), and nine democracies of the parliamentary-PR type (Austria, Belgium, Denmark, Finland, Germany, Italy, the Netherlands, Norway, and Sweden). Seven long-term, stable democracies are excluded from the analysis either because they do not fit comfortably into any one of the three categories (France, Ireland, Japan, and Switzerland), or because they are too vulnerable to external factors (Israel, Iceland, and Luxembourg).

Since a major purpose of PR is to facilitate minority representation, one would expect the PR systems to outperform plurality systems in this respect. There is little doubt that this is indeed the case. For instance, where ethnic minorities have formed ethnic political parties, as in Belgium and Finland, PR has enabled them to gain virtually perfect proportional representation. Because there are so many different kinds of ethnic and religious minorities in the democracies under analysis, it is difficult to measure systematically the *degree* to which PR succeeds in providing more representatives for minorities than does plurality. It is possible, however, to compare the representation of women — a minority in political rather than strictly numerical terms — systematically across countries. The first column of Table 5.1 shows the percentages of female members in the lower (or only) houses of the national legislatures in these 14 democracies during the early 1980s. The 16.4-percent average for the parliamentary-PR systems is about four times higher than the 4.1 percent for the United States or the 4.0-percent average for the parliamentary-plurality countries. To be sure, the higher social standing of women in the four Nordic countries accounts for part of the difference, but the average of 9.4 percent in the five other parliamentary-PR countries remains more than twice as high as in the plurality countries.

Does higher representation of women result in the advancement of their interests? Harold L. Wilensky's careful rating of democracies with regard to the innovativeness and expansiveness of their family policies — a matter of special concern to women — indicates that it does.[10] On a 13-point scale (from a maximum of 12 to a minimum of 0), the scores of these countries range from 11 to 1. The differences among the three groups (as shown in the second column of Table 5.1) are striking: the PR countries have an average score of 7.89, whereas the parliamentary-plurality countries have an average of just 2.50, and the U.S. only a slightly higher score of 3.00. Here again, the Nordic countries have the highest scores, but the 6.80 average of the non-Nordic PR countries is still well above that of the plurality countries.

Table 5.1 Women's Legislative Representation, Innovative Family Policy, Voting Turnout, Income Inequality, and the Dahl Rating of Democratic Quality

	Women's Repr. 1980–82	Family Policy 1976–80	Voting Turnout 1971–80	Income Top 20% 1985	Dahl Rating 1969
Pres.-Plurality (N=1)	4.1	3.00	54.2%	39.9%	3.0
Parl.-Plurality (N=4)	4.0	2.50	75.3	42.9	4.8
Parl.-PR (N=9)	16.4	7.89	84.5	39.0	2.2

Note: The one presidential-plurality democracy is the United States; the four parliamentary-plurality democracies are Australia, Canada, New Zealand, and the United Kingdom; and the nine parliamentary-PR democracies are Austria, Belgium, Denmark, Finland, Germany, Italy, the Netherlands, Norway, and Sweden.

Sources: Based on Wilma Rule, "Electoral Systems, Contextual Factors and Women's Opportunity for Election to Parliament in Twenty-Three Democracies," *Western Political Quarterly* 40 (September 1987): 483; Harold L. Wilensky, "Common Problems, Divergent Policies: An 18-Nation Study of Family Policy," *Public Affairs Report* 31 (May 1990): 2; personal communication by Harold L. Wilensky to the author, dated 18 October 1990; Robert W. Jackman, "Political Institutions and Voter Turnout in the Industrial Democracies," *American Political Science Review* 81 (June 1987): 420; World Bank, *World Development Report 1989* (New York: Oxford University Press, 1989), 223; Robert A. Dahl, *Polyarchy: Participation and Opposition* (New Haven: Yale University Press, 1971), 232.

The last three columns of Table 5.1 show indicators of democratic quality. The third column lists the most reliable figures on electoral participation (in the 1970s); countries with compulsory voting (Australia, Belgium, and Italy) are not included in the averages. Compared with the extremely low voter turnout of 54.2 percent in the United States, the parliamentary-plurality systems perform a great deal better (about 75 percent). But the average in the parliamentary-PR systems is still higher, at slightly above 84 percent. Since the maximum turnout that is realistically attainable is around 90 percent (as indicated by the turnouts in countries with compulsory voting), the difference between 75 and 84 percent is particularly striking.

Another democratic goal is political equality, which is more likely to prevail in the absence of great economic inequalities. The fourth column of Table 5.1 presents the World Bank's percentages of total income earned by the top 20 percent of households in the mid-1980s.[11] They show a slightly less unequal distribution of income in the parliamentary-PR than in the parliamentary-plurality systems, with the United States in an intermediate position.

Finally, the fifth column reports Robert A. Dahl's ranking of democracies according to ten indicators of democratic quality, such as freedom of the press, freedom of association, competitive party systems, strong parties and interest groups, and effective legislatures.[12] The stable democracies range from a highest rating of 1 to a low of 6. There is a slight pro-PR bias in Dahl's ranking (he includes a number-of-parties variable that rates multiparty systems somewhat higher than two-party systems), but even when we discount this bias we find striking differences between the parliamentary-PR and parliamentary-plurality countries: six of the former are given the highest score, whereas most of the latter receive the next to lowest score of 5.

No such clear differences are apparent when we examine the effect of the type of democracy on the maintenance of public order and peace. Parliamentary-plurality systems had the lowest incidence of riots during the period 1948–77, but the highest incidence of political deaths; the lat-

ter figure, however, derives almost entirely from the high number of political deaths in the United Kingdom, principally as a result of the Northern Ireland problem. A more elaborate statistical analysis shows that societal division is a much more important factor than type of democracy in explaining variation in the incidence of political riots and deaths in the 13 parliamentary countries.[13]

A major argument in favor of plurality systems has been that they favor "strong" one-party governments that can pursue "effective" public policies. One key area of government activity in which this pattern should manifest itself is the management of the economy. Thus advocates of plurality systems received a rude shock in 1987 when the average per capita GDP in Italy (a PR and multiparty democracy with notoriously uncohesive and unstable governments) surpassed that of the United Kingdom, typically regarded as the very model of strong and effective government. If Italy had discovered large amounts of oil in the Mediterranean, we would undoubtedly explain its superior economic performance in terms of this fortuitous factor. But it was not Italy but Britain that discovered the oil!

Economic success is obviously not solely determined by government policy. When we examine economic performance over a long period of time, however, the effects of external influences are minimized, especially if we focus on countries with similar levels of economic development. Table 5.2 presents OECD figures from the 1960s through the 1980s for the three most important aspects of macroeconomic performance—average annual economic growth, inflation, and unemployment rates.

Although Italy's economic growth has indeed been better than that of Britain, the parliamentary-plurality and parliamentary-PR countries as groups do not differ much from each other or from the United States. The slightly higher growth rates in the parliamentary-PR systems cannot be considered significant. With regard to inflation, the United States has the best record, followed by the parliamentary-PR systems. The most sizable differences appear in unemployment levels; here the

Table 5.2 Economic Growth, Inflation, and Unemployment (in percent)

	Economic Growth 1961–88	Inflation 1961–88	Unemployment 1965–88
Pres.-Plurality (N=1)	3.3	5.1	6.1
Parl.-Plurality (N=4)	3.4	7.5	6.1
Parl.-PR (N=9)	3.5	6.3	4.4

Sources: OECD Economic Outlook, No. 26 (December 1979), 131; No. 30 (December 1981), 131, 140, 142; No. 46 (December 1989), 166, 176, 182.

parliamentary-PR countries perform significantly better than the plurality countries.[14] Comparing the parliamentary-plurality and parliamentary-PR countries on all three indicators, we find that the performance of the latter is uniformly better.

Lessons for Developing Countries

Political scientists tend to think that plurality systems such as the United Kingdom and the United States are superior with regard to democratic quality and governmental effectiveness—a tendency best explained by the fact that political science has always been an Anglo-American-oriented discipline. This prevailing opinion is largely contradicted, however, by the empirical evidence presented above. Wherever significant differences appear, the parliamentary-PR systems almost invariably post the best records, particularly with respect to representation, protection of minority interests, voter participation, and control of unemployment.

This finding contains an important lesson for democratic constitutional engineers: the parliamentary-PR option is one that should be given serious consideration. Yet a word of caution is also in order,

since parliamentary-PR democracies differ greatly among themselves. Moderate PR and moderate multipartism, as in Germany and Sweden, offer more attractive models than the extreme PR and multiparty systems of Italy and the Netherlands. As previously noted, though, even Italy has a respectable record of democratic performance.

But are these conclusions relevant to newly democratic and democratizing countries in Asia, Africa, Latin America, and Eastern Europe, which are trying to make democracy work in the face of economic underdevelopment and ethnic divisions? Do not these difficult conditions require strong executive leadership in the form of a powerful president or a Westminster-style, dominant one-party cabinet?

With regard to the problem of deep ethnic cleavages, these doubts can be easily laid to rest. Divided societies, both in the West and elsewhere, need peaceful coexistence among the contending ethnic groups. This requires conciliation and compromise, goals that in turn require the greatest possible inclusion of representatives of these groups in the decision-making process. Such power sharing can be arranged much more easily in parliamentary and PR systems than in presidential and plurality systems. A president almost inevitably belongs to one ethnic group, and hence presidential systems are particularly inimical to ethnic power sharing. And while Westminster-style parliamentary systems feature collegial cabinets, these tend not to be ethnically inclusive, particularly when there is a majority ethnic group. It is significant that the British government, in spite of its strong majoritarian traditions, recognized the need for consensus and power sharing in religiously and ethnically divided Northern Ireland. Since 1973, British policy has been to try to solve the Northern Ireland problem by means of PR elections and an inclusive coalition government.

As Horowitz has pointed out, it may be possible to alleviate the problems of presidentialism by requiring that a president be elected with a stated minimum of support from different groups, as in Nigeria.[15] But this is a palliative that cannot compare with the advantages of a truly collective and inclusive executive. Similarly, the example of Malaysia shows that a parliamentary system can have a broad multiparty and multiethnic coalition cabinet in spite of plurality elections, but this requires elaborate preelection pacts among the parties. These exceptions prove the rule: the ethnic power sharing that has been attainable in Nigeria and Malaysia only on a limited basis and through very special arrangements is a natural and straightforward result of parliamentary-PR forms of democracy.

PR and Economic Policy Making

The question of which form of democracy is most conducive to economic development is more difficult to answer. We simply do not have enough cases of durable Third World democracies representing the different systems (not to mention the lack of reliable economic data) to make an unequivocal evaluation. However, the conventional wisdom that economic development requires the unified and decisive leadership of a strong president or a Westminster-style dominant cabinet is highly suspect. First of all, if an inclusive executive that must do more bargaining and conciliation were less effec-

tive at economic policy making than a dominant and exclusive executive, then presumably an authoritarian government free of legislative interference or internal dissent would be optimal. This reasoning—a frequent excuse for the overthrow of democratic governments in the Third World in the 1960s and 1970s—has now been thoroughly discredited. To be sure, we do have a few examples of economic miracles wrought by authoritarian regimes, such as those in South Korea or Taiwan, but these are more than counterbalanced by the sorry economic records of just about all the nondemocratic governments in Africa, Latin America, and Eastern Europe.

Second, many British scholars, notably the eminent political scientist S. E. Finer, have come to the conclusion that economic development requires not so much a *strong* hand as a *steady* one. Reflecting on the poor economic performance of post-World War II Britain, they have argued that each of the governing parties indeed provided reasonably strong leadership in economic policy making but that alternations in governments were too "absolute and abrupt," occurring "between two sharply polarized parties each eager to repeal a large amount of its predecessor's legislation." What is needed, they argue, is "greater stability and continuity" and "greater moderation in policy," which could be provided by a shift to PR and to coalition governments much more likely to be centrist in orientation.[16] This argument would appear to be equally applicable both to developed and developing countries.

Third, the case for strong presidential or Westminster-style governments is most compelling where rapid decision making is essential. This means that in foreign and defense policy parliamentary-PR systems may be at a disadvantage. But in economic policy making speed is not particularly important—quick decisions are not necessarily wise ones.

Why then do we persist in distrusting the economic effectiveness of democratic systems that engage in broad consultation and bargaining aimed at a high degree of consensus? One reason is that multiparty and coalition governments *seem* to be messy, quarrelsome, and inefficient in contrast to the clear authority of strong presidents and strong one-party cabinets. But we should not let ourselves be deceived by these superficial appearances. A closer look at presidential systems reveals that the most successful cases—such as the United States, Costa Rica, and pre-1970 Chile—are at least equally quarrelsome and, in fact, are prone to paralysis and deadlock rather than steady and effective economic policy making. In any case, the argument should not be about governmental aesthetics but about actual performance. The undeniable elegance of the Westminster model is not a valid reason for adopting it.

The widespread skepticism about the economic capability of parliamentary-PR systems stems from confusing governmental strength with effectiveness. In the short run, one-party cabinets or presidents may well be able to formulate economic policy with greater ease and speed. In the long run, however, policies supported by a broad consensus are more likely to be successfully carried out and to remain on course than policies imposed by a "strong" government against the wishes of important interest groups.

To sum up, the parliamentary-PR form of democracy is clearly better than the major alternatives in accommodating ethnic differences, and it has a slight edge in economic policy making as well. The argument that considerations of governmental effectiveness mandate the rejection of parliamentary-PR democracy for developing countries is simply not tenable. Constitution makers in new democracies would do themselves and their countries a great disservice by ignoring this attractive democratic model.

NOTES

1. Donald L. Horowitz, "Comparing Democratic Systems," Seymour Martin Lipset, "The Centrality of Political Culture," and Juan J. Linz, "The Virtues of Parliamentarism," *Journal of Democracy* 1 (Fall 1990): 73–91. A third set of important decisions concerns institutional arrangements that are related to the difference between federal and unitary forms of government: the degree of government centralization, unicameralism or bicameralism, rules for constitutional amendment, and judicial review. Empirical analysis shows that these factors tend to be related: federal countries are more likely to be decentralized, to have significant bicameralism, and to have "rigid" constitutions that are difficult to amend and protected by judicial review.

2. For a fuller discussion of the differences between majoritarian and consensus government, see Arend Lijphart, *Democracies: Patterns of Majoritarian and Consensus Government in Twenty-One Countries* (New Haven: Yale University Press, 1984).

3. Giovanni Sartori, "Political Development and Political Engineering," in *Public Policy* vol. 17, eds. John D. Montgomery and Alfred O. Hirschman (Cambridge: Harvard University Press, 1968), 273.

4. The first scholar to emphasize the close connection between culture and these constitutional arrangements was G. Bingham Powell, Jr. in his *Contemporary Democracies Participation, Stability, and Violence* (Cambridge: Harvard University Press, 1982), 67. In my previous writings, I have sometimes classified Finland as a presidential or semipresidential system, but I now agree with Powell (pp. 56–57) that, although the directly elected Finnish president has special authority in foreign policy, Finland operates like a parliamentary system in most other respects. Among the exceptions, Ireland is a doubtful case; I regard its system of the single transferable vote as mainly a PR method, but other authors have classified it as a plurality system. And I include Australia in the parliamentary-plurality group, because its alternative-vote system, while not identical with plurality, operates in a similar fashion.

5. Stein Rokkan, *Citizens, Elections, Parties: Approaches to the Comparative Study of the Processes of Development* (Oslo: Universitetsforlaget, 1970), 157.

6. Douglas V. Verney, *The Analysis of Political Systems* (London: Routledge and Kegan Paul, 1959), 18–23, 42–43.

7. Powell, op. cit., esp. 12–29 and 111–74.

8. Juan J. Linz, "The Perils of Presidentialism," *Journal of Democracy* 1 (Winter 1990), 51–69.

9. Scott Mainwaring, "Presidentialism in Latin America," *Latin American Research Review* 25 (1990), 167–70.

10. Wilensky's ratings are based on a five-point scale (from 4 to 0) "for each of three policy clusters: existence and length of maternity and parental leave, paid and unpaid; availability and accessibility of public daycare programs and government effort to expand daycare; and flexibility of retirement systems. They measure government action to assure care of children and maximize choices in balancing work and family demands for everyone." See Harold L. Wilensky, "Common Problems, Divergent Policies: An 18-Nation Study of Family Policy," *Public Affairs Report* 31 (May 1990), 2.

11. Because of missing data, Austria is not included in the parliamentary-PR average.

12. Robert A. Dahl, *Polyarchy: Participation and Opposition* (New Haven: Yale University Press, 1971), 231–45.

13. This multiple-correlation analysis shows that societal division, as measured by the degree of organizational exclusiveness of ethnic and religious groups, explains 33 percent of the variance in riots and 25 percent of the variance in political deaths. The additional explanation by type of democracy is only 2 percent for riots (with plurality countries slightly more orderly) and 13 percent for deaths (with the PR countries slightly more peaceful).

14. Comparable unemployment data for Austria, Denmark, and New Zealand are not available, and these countries are therefore not included in the unemployment figures in Table 5.2.

15. Horowitz, op. cit., 76–77.

16. S. E. Finer, "Adversary Politics and Electoral Reform," in *Adversary Politics and Electoral Reform*, ed. S. E. Finer (London: Anthony Wigram, 1975), 30–31.

Robert D. Putnam

TUNING IN, TUNING OUT: THE STRANGE DISAPPEARANCE OF SOCIAL CAPITAL IN AMERICA

It is a daunting honor to deliver the inaugural Pool Lecture. Ithiel de Sola Pool was a brilliant, broad-gauged scholar whose interests ranged from the Nazi elite to direct satellite broadcasting, from the first rigorous computer simulation of electoral behavior to the development of network theory, from which he invented "small world" research. He helped found the field of political communications. A graduate of the University of Chicago's political

science department during its classic golden age, and first chair of the MIT political science department, Pool must also have been a remarkable teacher, for his students continue to contribute to our understanding of technology, communications, and political behavior. When I accepted this honor, I did not guess how close my own inquiry would lead me to Pool's own professional turf. I shall return to the contemporary relevance of Pool's insights at the conclusion of this talk.

For the last year or so, I have been wrestling with a difficult mystery. It is, if I am right, a puzzle of

From *PS: Political Science & Politics* (December 1995), pp. 664–83.

some importance to the future of American democracy. It is a classic brain-teaser, with a corpus delicti, a crime scene strewn with clues, and many potential suspects. As in all good detective stories, however, some plausible miscreants turn out to have impeccable alibis, and some important clues hint at portentous developments that occurred long before the curtain rose. Moreover, like Agatha Christie's *Murder on the Orient Express*, this crime may have had more than one perpetrator, so that we shall need to sort out ringleaders from accomplices. Finally, I need to make clear at the outset that I am not yet sure that I have solved the mystery. In that sense, this lecture represents work-in-progress. I have a prime suspect that I am prepared to indict, but the evidence is not yet strong enough to convict, so I invite your help in sifting clues.

Theories and Measures of Social Capital

Allow me to set the scene by saying a word or two about my own recent work.[1] Several years ago I conducted research on the arcane topic of local government in Italy (Putnam 1993). That study concluded that the performance of government and other social institutions is powerfully influenced by citizen engagement in community affairs, or what (following Coleman 1990) I termed *social capital*. I am now seeking to apply that set of ideas and insights to the urgent problems of contemporary American public life.

By "social capital," I mean features of social life—networks, norms, and trust—that enable participants to act together more effectively to pursue shared objectives. Whether or not their shared goals are praiseworthy is, of course, entirely another matter. To the extent that the norms, networks, and trust link substantial sectors of the community and span underlying social cleavages—to the extent that the social capital is of a "bridging" sort—then the enhanced cooperation is likely to serve broader interests and to be widely welcomed. On the other

hand, groups like the Michigan militia or youth gangs also embody a kind of social capital, for these networks and norms, too, enable members to cooperate more effectively, albeit to the detriment of the wider community.

Social capital, in short, refers to social connections and the attendant norms and trust. Who benefits from these connections, norms, and trust—the individual, the wider community, or some faction within the community—must be determined empirically, not definitionally.[2] Sorting out the multiple effects of different forms of social capital is clearly a crucial task, although it is not one that I can address here. For present purposes, I am concerned with forms of social capital that, generally speaking, serve civic ends.

Social capital in this sense is closely related to political participation in the conventional sense, but these terms are not synonymous. Political participation refers to our relations with political institutions. Social capital refers to our relations with one another. Sending a check to a PAC is an act of political participation, but it does not embody or create social capital. Bowling in a league or having coffee with a friend embodies and creates social capital, though these are not acts of political participation. (A grassroots political movement or a traditional urban machine is a social capital-intensive form of political participation.) I use the term "civic engagement" to refer to people's connections with the life of their communities, not merely with politics. Civic engagement is correlated with political participation in a narrower sense, but whether they move in lock-step is an empirical question, not a logical certitude. Some forms of individualized political participation, such as check-writing, for example, might be rising at the same time that social connectedness was on the wane. Similarly, although social trust—trust in other people—and political trust—trust in political authorities—might be empirically related, they are logically quite distinct. I might well trust my neighbors without trusting city hall, or vice versa.

The theory of social capital presumes that, generally speaking, the more we connect with other people, the more we trust them, and vice versa. At least in the contexts I have so far explored, this presumption generally turns out to be true: social trust and civic engagement are strongly correlated. That is, with or without controls for education, age, income, race, gender, and so on, people who join are people who trust.[3] Moreover, this is true across different countries, and across different states in the United States, as well as across individuals, and it is true of all sorts of groups.[4] Sorting out which way causation flows—whether joining causes trusting or trusting causes joining—is complicated both theoretically and methodologically, although John Brehm and Wendy Rahn (1995) report evidence that the causation flows mainly from joining to trusting. Be that as it may, civic connections and social trust move together. Which way are they moving?

Bowling Alone: Trends in Civic Engagement

Evidence from a number of independent sources strongly suggests that America's stock of social capital has been shrinking for more than a quarter century.

- Membership records of such diverse organizations as the PTA, the Elks club, the League of Women Voters, the Red Cross, labor unions, and even bowling leagues show that participation in many conventional voluntary associations has declined by roughly 25% to 50% over the last two to three decades (Putnam 1995, 1996).
- Surveys of the time budgets of average Americans in 1965, 1975, and 1985, in which national samples of men and women recorded every single activity undertaken during the course of a day, imply that the time we spend on informal socializing and visiting is down (perhaps by one quarter) since 1965, and that the time we devote to clubs and organizations is

down even more sharply (probably by roughly half) over this period.[5]

- While Americans' interest in politics has been stable or even growing over the last three decades, and some forms of participation that require moving a pen, such as signing petitions and writing checks, have increased significantly, many measures of collective participation have fallen sharply (Rosenstone and Hansen 1993; Putnam 1996), including attending a rally or speech (off 36% between 1973 and 1993), attending a meeting on town or school affairs (off 39%), or working for a political party (off 56%).
- Evidence from the General Social Survey demonstrates, at all levels of education and among both men and women, a drop of roughly one-quarter in group membership since 1974 and a drop of roughly one-third in social trust since 1972.[6] Moreover, as Figure 5.2 illustrates, slumping membership has afflicted all sorts of groups, from sports clubs and professional associations to literary discussion groups and labor unions.[7] Only nationality groups, hobby and garden clubs, and the catch-all category of "other" seem to have resisted the ebbing tide. Furthermore, Gallup polls report that church attendance fell by roughly 15% during the 1960s and has remained at that lower level ever since, while data from the National Opinion Research Center suggest that the decline continued during the 1970s and 1980s and by now amounts to roughly 30% (Putnam 1996).

Each of these approaches to the problem of measuring trends in civic engagement has advantages and drawbacks. Membership records offer long-term coverage and reasonable precision, but they may underrepresent newer, more vibrant organizations. Time budgets capture real investments of time and energy in both formal and informal settings, not merely nominal membership, but the available data are episodic and drawn from relatively small samples that are not entirely comparable across time. Surveys

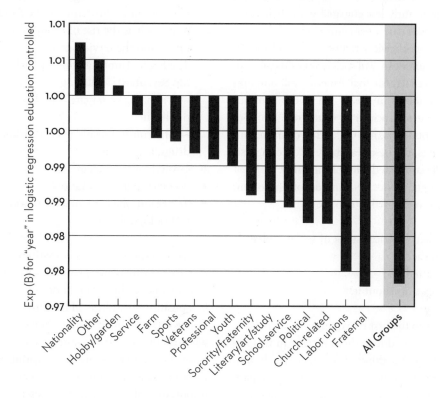

Source: General Social Survey, 1974–1994.

are more comprehensive in their coverage of various types of groups, but (apart from church attendance) comparable trend data are available only since the mid-1970s, a decade or more after the putative downturn began, so they may understate the full decline. No single source is perfect for testing the hypothesized decline in social connectedness, although the consistency across different measuring rods is striking.

A fuller audit of American social capital would need to account for apparent countertrends.[8] Some observers believe, for example, that support groups and neighborhood watch groups are proliferating, and few deny that the last several decades have witnessed explosive growth in interest groups represented in Washington. The growth of "mailing list" organizations, like the American Association of

Retired People or the Sierra Club, although highly significant in political (and commercial) terms, is not really a counter-example to the supposed decline in social connectedness, however, since these are not really associations in which members meet one another. Their members' ties are to common symbols and ideologies, but not to each other. These organizations are sufficiently different from classical "secondary" associations as to deserve a new rubric—perhaps "tertiary" associations. Similarly, although most secondary associations are not-for-profit, most prominent nonprofits (from Harvard University to the Metropolitan Opera) are bureaucracies, not secondary associations, so the growth of the "Third Sector" is not tantamount to a growth in social connectedness. With due regard to various kinds of counter-evidence, I believe that the weight of the available evidence confirms that Americans today are significantly less engaged with their communities than was true a generation ago.

Of course, lots of civic activity is still visible in our communities. American civil society is not moribund. Indeed, evidence suggests that America still outranks many other countries in the degree of our community involvement and social trust (Putnam 1996). But if we compare ourselves, not with other countries but with our parents, the best available evidence suggests that we are less connected with one another.

This prologue poses a number of important questions that merit further debate:

- Is it true that America's stock of social capital has diminished?
- Does it matter?
- What can we do about it?

The answer to the first two questions is, I believe, "yes," but I cannot address them further in this setting. Answering the third question—which ultimately concerns me most—depends, at least in part, on first understanding the *causes* of the strange malady afflicting American civic life. This is the mystery I seek to unravel here: Why, beginning in the 1960s and accelerating in the 1970s and 1980s, did the fabric of American community life begin to fray? Why are more Americans bowling alone?

Explaining the Erosion of Social Capital

Many possible answers have been suggested for this puzzle:

- Busyness and time pressure
- Economic hard times (or, according to alternative theories, material affluence)
- Residential mobility
- Suburbanization
- The movement of women into the paid labor force and the stresses of two-career families

- Disruption of marriage and family ties
- Changes in the structure of the American economy, such as the rise of chain stores, branch firms, and the service sector
- The Sixties (most of which actually happened in the Seventies), including
  —Vietnam, Watergate, and disillusion with public life
  —The cultural revolt against authority (sex, drugs, and so on)
- Growth of the welfare state
- The civil rights revolution
- Television, the electronic revolution, and other technological changes

Most respectable mystery writers would hesitate to tally up this many plausible suspects, no matter how energetic the fictional detective. I am not yet in a position to address all these theories—certainly not in any definitive form—but we must begin to winnow the list. To be sure, a social trend as pervasive as the one we are investigating probably has multiple causes, so our task is to assess the relative importance of such factors as these.

A solution, even a partial one, to our mystery must pass several tests.

Is the proposed explanatory factor correlated with trust and civic engagement? If not, it is difficult to see why that factor should even be placed in the lineup. For example, many women have entered the paid labor force during the period in question, but if working women turned out to be more engaged in community life than housewives, it would be harder to attribute the downturn in community organizations to the rise of two-career families.

Is the correlation spurious? If parents, for example, were more likely to be joiners than childless people, that might be an important clue. However, if the correlation between parental status and civic engagement turned out to be entirely spurious, due to the effects of (say) age, we would have to remove the declining birth rate from our list of suspects.

Is the proposed explanatory factor changing in the relevant way? Suppose, for instance, that people who often move have shallower community roots. That could be an important part of the answer to our mystery *only if* residential mobility itself had risen during this period.

Is the proposed explanatory factor vulnerable to the claim that it might be the result *of civic disengagement, not the cause?* For example, even if newspaper readership were closely correlated with civic engagement across individuals and across time, we would need to weigh the possibility that reduced newspaper circulation is the result (not the cause) of disengagement.

Against that set of benchmarks, let us consider various potential influences on social capital formation.

Education

Human capital and social capital are closely related, for education has a very powerful effect on trust and associational membership, as well as many other forms of social and political participation. Education is by far the strongest correlate that I have discovered of civic engagement in all its forms, including social trust and membership in many different types of groups.[9] In fact, as Figure 5.3 illustrates, the relationship between education and civic engagement is a curvilinear one of increasing returns. The last two years of college make twice as much difference to trust and group membership as the first two years of high school. The four years of education between 14 and 18 total years have *ten times more impact* on trust and membership than the first four years of formal education. The same basic pattern applies to both men and women, and to all races and generations. Education, in short, is an extremely powerful predictor of civic engagement.

Sorting out just why education has such a massive effect on social connectedness would require a book, not a mere lecture.[10] Education is in part a proxy for social class and economic differences, but when income, social status, and education are used together to predict trust and group member-

ship, education continues to be the primary influence. (Income and satisfaction with one's personal financial situation both have a significant independent effect.) In short, highly educated people are much more likely to be joiners and trusters, partly because they are better off economically, but mostly because of the skills, resources, and inclinations that were imparted to them at home and in school.

It is widely recognized that Americans today are better educated than our parents and grandparents. It is less often appreciated how massively and rapidly this trend has transformed the educational composition of the adult population during just the last two decades. Since 1972, the proportion of all adults with fewer than 12 years of education has been cut in half, falling from 40% to 18%, while the proportion with more than 12 years has nearly doubled, rising from 28% to 50%, as the generation of Americans educated around the turn of this century (most of whom did not finish high school) passed from the scene and were replaced by the baby boomers and their successors (most of whom attended college).

Thus, education boosts civic engagement sharply, and educational levels have risen massively. Unfortunately, these two undeniable facts only deepen our central mystery. By itself, the rise in educational levels should have *increased* social capital during the last 20 years by 15–20%, even assuming that the effects of education were merely linear. (Taking account of the curvilinear effect in Figure 5.2, the rise in trusting and joining should have been even greater, as Americans moved up the accelerating curve.) By contrast, however, the actual GSS figures show a net *decline* since the early 1970s of roughly the same magnitude (trust by about 20–25%, memberships by about 15–20%). The relative declines in social capital are similar *within* each educational category—roughly 25% in group memberships and roughly 30% in social trust since the early 1970s, and probably even more since the early 1960s.

Thus, this first investigative foray leaves us more mystified than before. We may nevertheless draw

Figure 5.3 Social Trust and Group Membership by Years of Education

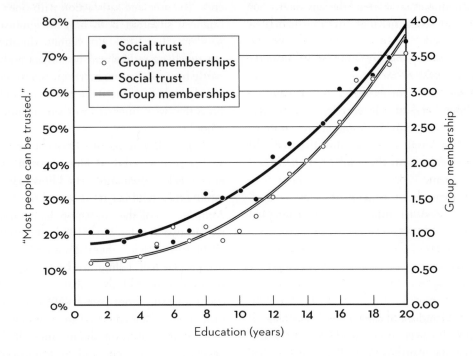

Source: General Social Survey, 1972–1994.

two useful conclusions from these findings, one methodological and one substantive:

1. Since education has such a powerful effect on civic engagement and social trust, we need to take account of educational differences in our exploration of other possible factors, in order to be sure that we do not confuse the consequences of education with the possible effects of other variables.[11]

2. Whatever forces lie behind the slump in civic engagement and social trust, those forces have affected all levels in American society.[12] Social capital has eroded among the one in every twelve Americans who have enjoyed the advantages (material and intellectual) of graduate study; it has eroded among the one in every eight Americans who did not even make it into high school; and it has eroded among all the

strata in between. The mysterious disengagement of the last quarter century seems to have afflicted all echelons of our society.

Pressures of Time and Money

Americans certainly *feel* busier now than a generation ago: the proportion of us who report feeling "always rushed" jumped by half between the mid-1960s and the mid-1990s (Robinson and Godbey 1995). Probably the most obvious suspect behind our tendency to drop out of community affairs is pervasive busyness. And lurking nearby in the shadows are those endemic economic pressures so much discussed nowadays—job insecurity and declining real wages, especially among the lower two-thirds of the income distribution.

Yet, however culpable busyness and economic insecurity may appear at first glance, it is hard to find any incriminating evidence. In fact, the balance of the evidence argues that pressures of time and money are apparently *not* important contributors to the puzzle we seek to solve.

In the first place, time budget studies do *not* confirm the thesis that Americans are, on average, working longer than a generation ago. On the contrary, Robinson and Godbey (1995) report a five-hour per week *gain* in free time for the average American between 1965 and 1985, due partly to reduced time spent on housework and partly to earlier retirement. Their claim that Americans have more leisure time now than several decades ago is, to be sure, contested by other observers. Schor (1991), for example, reports evidence that our work hours are lengthening, especially for women. Whatever the resolution of that controversy, however, the thesis that attributes civic disengagement to longer workdays is rendered much less plausible by looking at the correlation between work hours, on the one hand, and social trust and group membership, on the other.

The available evidence strongly suggests that, in fact, long hours on the job are *not* associated with lessened involvement in civic life or reduced social trust. Quite the reverse: results from the General Social Survey show that employed people belong to somewhat *more* groups than those outside the paid labor force. Even more striking is the fact that among workers, longer hours are linked to *more* civic engagement, not less.[13] This surprising discovery is fully consistent with evidence from the time budget studies. Robinson (1990a) reports that, unsurprisingly, people who spend more time at work do feel more rushed, and these harried souls do spend less time eating, sleeping, reading books, engaging in hobbies, and just doing nothing. Compared to the rest of the population, they also spend a lot less time watching television—almost 30% less. However, they do *not* spend less time on organizational activity. In short, those who work longer forego *Nightline*, but not the Kiwanis club, *ER*, but not the Red Cross.

I do not conclude from the positive correlation between group membership and work hours that working longer actually *causes* greater civic involvement—there are too many uncontrolled variables here for that—but merely that hard work does not *prevent* civic engagement. Moreover, the nationwide falloff in joining and trusting is perfectly mirrored among full-time workers, among part-time workers, and among those outside the paid labor force. So if people are dropping out of community life, long hours do not seem to be the reason.

If time pressure is not the culprit we seek, how about financial pressures? It is true that people with lower incomes and those who feel financially strapped are less engaged in community life and less trusting than those who are better off, even holding education constant. On the other hand, the downtrends in social trust and civic engagement are entirely visible at all levels in the income hierarchy, with no sign whatever that they are concentrated among those who have borne the brunt of the economic distress of the last two decades. Quite the contrary, the declines in engagement and trust are actually somewhat greater among the more affluent segments of the American public than among the poor and middle-income wage-earners. Furthermore, controlling for both real income and financial satisfaction does little to attenuate the fall in civic engagement and social trust. In short, neither objective nor subjective economic well-being has inoculated Americans against the virus of civic disengagement; if anything, affluence has slightly exacerbated the problem.

I cannot absolutely rule out the possibility that some part of the erosion of social capital in recent years might be linked to a more generalized sense of economic insecurity that may have affected all Americans, nor do I argue that economic distress *never* causes disengagement. Studies of the unemployed during and after the Great Depression (Jahoda, Lazarsfeld, and Zeisel 1933; Ginzberg 1943; Wilcock and Franke 1963) have described a tendency for them to disengage from community life. However, the basic patterns in the contemporary evidence are inconsistent with any simple economic explanation for our central puzzle. Pressures of time and money may be a part of the backdrop, but neither can be a principal culprit.[14]

Mobility and Suburbanization

Many studies have found that residential stability and such related phenomena as homeownership are associated with greater civic engagement. At an earlier stage in this investigation (Putnam 1995, 30), I observed that "mobility, like frequent repotting of plants, tends to disrupt root systems, and it takes time for an uprooted individual to put down new roots." I must now report, however, that further inquiry fully exonerates residential mobility from any responsibility for our fading civic engagement. Data from the U.S. Bureau of the Census 1995 (and earlier years) show that rates of residential mobility have been remarkably constant over the last half century. In fact, to the extent that there has been any change at all, both long-distance and short-distance mobility have *declined* over the last five decades. During the 1950s, 20% of Americans changed residence each year and 6.9% annually moved across county borders; during the 1990s, the comparable figures are 17% and 6.6%. Americans, in short, are today slightly *more* rooted residentially than a generation ago. If the verdict on the economic distress interpretation had to be nuanced, the verdict on mobility is unequivocal. This theory is simply wrong.

But if moving itself has not eroded our social capital, what about the possibility that we have moved to places—especially the suburbs—that are less congenial to social connectedness? To test this theory, we must first examine the correlation between place of residence and social capital. In fact, social connectedness does differ by community type, but the differences turn out to be modest and in directions that are inconsistent with the theory.

Controlling for such demographic characteristics as education, age, income, work status, and race, citizens of the nation's 12 largest metropolitan areas (particularly their central cities, but also their suburbs) are roughly 10% less trusting and report 10–20% fewer group memberships than residents of other cities and towns (and their suburbs). Meanwhile, residents of very small towns and rural areas are (in accord with some hoary stereotypes) slightly more trusting and civically engaged than other Americans. Unsurprisingly, the prominence of different *types* of groups does vary significantly by location: major cities have more political and nationality clubs; smaller cities more fraternal, service, hobby, veterans, and church groups; and rural areas more agricultural organizations. But overall rates of associational memberships are not very different.

Moreover, this pallid pattern cannot account for our central puzzle. In the first place, there is virtually no correlation between gains in population and losses in social capital, either across states or across localities of different sizes. Even taking into account the educational and social backgrounds of those who have moved there, the suburbs have faintly higher levels of trust and civic engagement than their respective central cities, a fact that *ceteris paribus* should have produced growth, not decay, in social capital over the last generation. The central point, however, is that the downtrends in trusting and joining are virtually identically everywhere—in cities, big and small, in suburbs, in small towns, and in the countryside.

There are, of course, suburbs and suburbs. Evanston is not Levittown is not Sun City. The evidence available does not allow us to determine whether different types of suburban living have different effects on civic connections and social trust. However, these data do rule out the thesis that suburbanization per se has caused the erosion of America's social capital. In this respect, size of place is like mobility—a cross-sectional correlate that cannot explain our trend. Both where we live and how long we've lived there matter for social capital, but neither explains why it is eroding everywhere.

The Changing Role of Women

Most of our mothers were housewives, and most of them invested heavily in social capital formation—a jargony way of referring to untold, unpaid hours in church suppers, PTA meetings, neighborhood coffee klatches, and visits to friends and relatives. The movement of women out of the home and into the paid labor force is probably the most portentous social change of the last half century. However welcome and overdue the feminist revolution may be, it is hard to believe that it has had no impact on social connectedness. Could this be the primary reason for the decline of social capital over the last generation?

Some patterns in the available survey evidence seem to support this claim. All things considered, women belong to somewhat fewer voluntary associations than men (Edwards, Edwards, and Watts 1984 and the sources cited there; more recent GSS data confirm this finding). On the other hand, time budget studies suggest that women spend more time on those groups and more time in informal social connecting than men (Robinson and Godbey 1995). Although the absolute declines in joining and trusting are approximately equivalent among men and women, the relative declines are somewhat greater among women. Controlling for education, memberships among men have declined at a rate of about 10–15% a decade, compared to about 20–25% a decade for women. The time budget data, too, strongly suggest that the decline in organizational involvement in recent years is concentrated among women. These sorts of facts, coupled with the obvious transformation in the professional role of women over this same period, led me in previous work to suppose that the emergence of two-career families might be the most important single factor in the erosion of social capital.

As we saw earlier, however, work status itself seems to have little net impact on group membership or on trust. Housewives belong to different types of groups than do working women (more PTAs, for example, and fewer professional associations), but in the aggregate working women are actually members of slightly more voluntary associations.[15] Moreover, the overall declines in civic engagement are somewhat greater among housewives than among employed women. Comparison of time budget data between 1965 and 1985 (Robinson and Godbey 1995) seems to show that

employed women as a group are actually spending more time on organizations than before, while nonemployed women are spending less. This same study suggests that the major decline in informal socializing since 1965 has also been concentrated among nonemployed women. The central fact, of course, is that the overall trends are down for all categories of women (and for men, too—even bachelors), but the figures suggest that women who work full-time actually may have been more resistant to the slump than those who do not.

Thus, although women appear to have borne a disproportionate share of the decline in civic engagement over the last two decades, it is not easy to find any micro-level data that tie that fact directly to their entry into the labor force. It is hard to control for selection bias in these data, of course, because women who have chosen to enter the workforce doubtless differ in many respects from women who have chosen to stay home. Perhaps one reason that community involvement appears to be rising among working women and declining among housewives is that precisely the sort of women who, in an earlier era, were most involved with their communities have been disproportionately likely to enter the workforce, thus simultaneously lowering the average level of civic engagement among the remaining homemakers and raising the average among women in the workplace. Obviously, we have not been running a great national controlled experiment on the effects of work on women's civic engagement, and in any event the patterns in the data are not entirely clear. Contrary to my own earlier speculations, however, I can find little evidence to support the hypothesis that the movement of women into the workplace over the last generation has played a major role in the reduction of social connectedness and civic engagement. On the other hand, I have no clear alternative explanation for the fact that the relative declines are greater among women than among men. Since this evidence is at best circumstantial, perhaps the best interim judgment here is the famous Scots verdict: not proven.

Marriage and Family

Another widely discussed social trend that more or less coincides with the downturn in civic engagement is the breakdown of the traditional family unit—mom, dad, and the kids. Since the family itself is, by some accounts, a key form of social capital, perhaps its eclipse is part of the explanation for the reduction in joining and trusting in the wider community. What does the evidence show?

First of all, evidence of the loosening of family bonds is unequivocal. In addition to the century-long increase in divorce rates (which accelerated in the mid-1960s to the mid-1970s and then leveled off), and the more recent increase in single-parent families, the incidence of one-person households has more than doubled since 1950, in part because of the rising number of widows living alone (Caplow, Bahr, Modell, and Chadwick 1991, 47, 106, 113). The net effect of all these changes, as reflected in the General Social Survey, is that the proportion of all American adults who are currently unmarried climbed from 28% in 1974 to 48% in 1994.

Second, married men and women do rank somewhat higher on both our measures of social capital. That is, controlling for education, age, race, and so on, single people—both men and women, divorced, separated, and never-married—are significantly less trusting and less engaged civically than married people.[16] Roughly speaking, married men and women are about a third more trusting and belong to about 15–25% more groups than comparable single men and women. (Widows and widowers are more like married people than single people in this comparison.)

In short, successful marriage (especially if the family unit includes children) is statistically associated with greater social trust and civic engagement. Thus, some part of the decline in both trust and membership is tied to the decline in marriage. To be sure, the direction of causality behind this correlation may be complicated, since it is conceivable that loners and paranoids are harder to live with. If so, divorce may in some degree be the conse-quence, not the cause, of lower social capital. Probably the most reasonable summary of these arrays of data, however, is that the decline in successful marriage is a significant, though modest part of the reason for declining trust and lower group membership. On the other hand, changes in family structure cannot be a major part of our story, since the overall declines in joining and trusting are substantial even among the happily married. My own verdict (based in part on additional evidence to be introduced later) is that the disintegration of marriage is probably an accessory to the crime, but not the major villain of the piece.

The Rise of the Welfare State

Circumstantial evidence, particularly the timing of the downturn in social connectedness, has suggested to some observers (for example, Fukuyama 1995, 313–314) that an important cause—perhaps even *the* cause—of civic disengagement is big goverment and the growth of the welfare state. By "crowding out" private initiative, it is argued, state intervention has subverted civil society. This is a much larger topic than I can address in detail here, but a word or two may be appropriate.

On the one hand, some government policies have almost certainly had the effect of destroying social capital. For example, the so-called "slum clearance" policies of the 1950s and 1960s replaced physical capital, but destroyed social capital, by disrupting existing community ties. It is also conceivable that certain social expenditures and tax policies may have created disincentives for civic-minded philanthropy. On the other hand, it is much harder to see which government policies might be responsible for the decline in bowling leagues and literary clubs.

One empirical approach to this issue is to examine differences in civic engagement and public policy across different political jurisdictions to see whether swollen government leads to shriveled social capital. Among the U.S. states, however, differences in social capital appear essentially uncorrelated with various measures of welfare spending or government size.[17] Citizens in free-spending states are no less trusting or engaged than citizens in frugal ones. Cross-national comparison can also shed light on this question. Among 19 OECD countries for which data on social trust and group membership are available from the 1990–1991 World Values Survey, these indicators of social capital are, if anything, *positively* correlated with the size of the state.[18] This simple bivariate analysis, of course, cannot tell us whether social connectedness encourages welfare spending, whether the welfare state fosters civic engagement, or whether both are the result of some other unmeasured factor(s). Sorting out the underlying causal connections would require much more thorough analysis. However, even this simple finding is not easily reconciled with the notion that big government undermines social capital.

Race and the Civil Rights Revolution

Race is such an absolutely fundamental feature of American social history that nearly every other feature of our society is connected to it in some way. Thus, it seems intuitively plausible that race might somehow have played a role in the erosion of social capital over the last generation. In fact, some observers (both black and white) have noted that the decline in social connectedness and social trust began just after the greatest successes of the civil rights revolution of the 1960s. To some, that coincidence has suggested the possibility of a kind of sociological "white flight," as legal desegregation of civic life led whites to withdraw from community associations.

Like the theory about the welfare state, this racial interpretation of the destruction of social capital is highly controversial and can hardly be settled within the compass of these brief remarks. Nevertheless, the basic facts are these.

First, racial differences in associational membership are not large. At least until the 1980s, control-

ling for educational and income differences, blacks actually belonged to more associations on average than whites, essentially because they were more likely than comparably situated whites to belong to religious and ethnic organizations and no less likely to belong to any other type of group.[19] On the other hand, racial differences in social trust are very large indeed, even taking into account differences in education, income, and so on. On average, during the 1972–94 period, controlling for educational differences, about 17% of blacks endorsed the view that "most people can be trusted," as compared to about 45% of whites, and about 27% of respondents of other races.[20] These racial differences in social trust, of course, reflect not collective paranoia, but real experiences over many generations.

Second, the erosion of social capital has affected all races. In fact, during the 1980s the downturns in both joining and trusting were even greater among blacks (and other racial minorities) than among the white majority. This fact is inconsistent with the thesis that "white flight" is a significant cause of civic disengagement, since black Americans have been dropping out of religious and civic organizations at least as rapidly as white Americans. Even more important, the pace of disengagement among whites has been uncorrelated with racial intolerance or support for segregation. Avowedly racist or segregationist whites have been no quicker to drop out of community organizations during this period than more tolerant whites. Figure 5.4 presents illustrative evidence, its three parallel slopes showing that the decline in group membership is essentially identical among whites who favor segregation, whites who oppose it, and blacks.[21]

This evidence is far from conclusive, of course, but it does shift the burden of proof onto those who believe that racism is a primary explanation for growing civic disengagement over the last quarter century, however virulent racism continues to be in American society.[22] This evidence also suggests that reversing the civil rights gains of the last 30 years would do nothing to reverse the social capital losses.

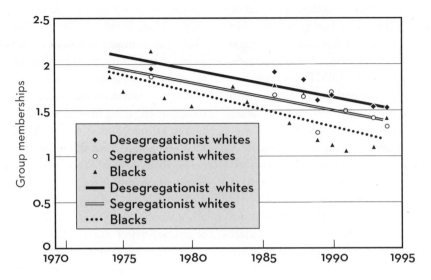

Figure 5.4 Group Membership by Race and Racism, 1974–1994 (education controlled)

Source: General Social Survey, 1972–1994.
Equal weighting of three educational categories.
White segregationism measured by support for racial segregation in social club.

Generational Effects

Our efforts thus far to localize the sources of civic disengagement have been singularly unfruitful. The downtrends are uniform across the major categories of American society—among men and among women; in central cities, in suburbs, and in small towns; among the wealthy, the poor, and the middle class; among blacks, whites, and other ethnic groups; in the North, in the South, on both coasts and in the heartland. One notable exception to this uniformity, however, involves age. In all our statistical analyses, age is second only to education as a predictor of all forms of civic engagement and trust. Older people belong to more organizations than young people, and they are less misanthropic. Older Americans also vote more often and read newspapers more frequently, two other forms of civic engagement closely correlated with joining and trusting.

Figure 5.5 shows the basic pattern—civic involvement appears to rise more or less steadily from early adulthood toward a plateau in middle age, from which it declines only late in life. This humpback pattern, familiar from many analyses of social participation, including time-budget studies (Robinson and Godbey 1995), seems naturally to represent the arc of life's engagements. Most observers have interpreted this pattern as a life cycle phenomenon, and so, at first, did I.

Evidence from the General Social Survey (GSS) enables us to follow individual cohorts as they age. If the rising lines in Figure 5.5 represent deepening civic engagement with age, then we should be able to track this same deepening engagement as we follow, for example, the first of the baby boomers—born in 1947—as they aged from 25 in 1972 (the first year of the GSS) to 47 in 1994 (the latest year available). Startlingly, however, such an analysis, repeated for successive birth cohorts, produces virtually no evidence of such life cycle changes in civic engagement. In fact, as various generations moved through the period between 1972 and 1994, their

Figure 5.5 Civic Engagement by Age (education controlled)

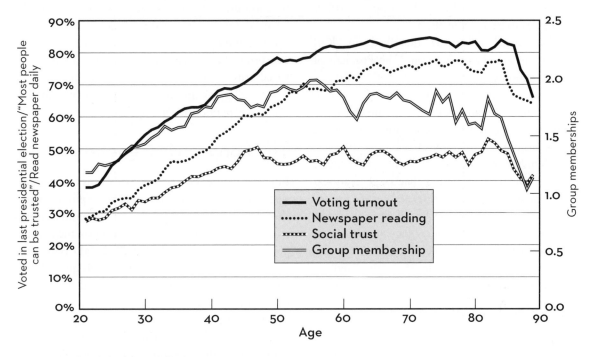

Source: General Social Survey, 1972–1994.
Respondents aged 21–89. Three-year moving averages.
Equal weighting of three educational categories.

levels of trust and membership more often fell than rose, reflecting a more or less simultaneous decline in civic engagement among young and old alike, particularly during the second half of the 1980s. But that downtrend obviously cannot explain why, throughout the period, older Americans were always more trusting and engaged. In fact, the only reliable life cycle effect visible in these data is a withdrawal from civic engagement very late in life, as we move through our 80s.

The central paradox posed by these patterns is this: Older people are consistently more engaged and trusting than younger people, yet we do not become more engaged and trusting as we age. What's going on here?

Time and age are notoriously ambiguous in their effects on social behavior. Social scientists have learned to distinguish three contrasting phenomena:

1. *Life-cycle effects* represent differences attributable to stage of life. In this case individuals change as they age, but since the effects of aging are, in the aggregate, neatly balanced by the "demographic metabolism" of births and deaths, life cycle effects produce no aggregate change. Everyone's close-focus eyesight worsens as we age, but the aggregate demand for reading glasses changes little.

2. *Period effects* affect all people who live through a given era, regardless of their age.[23] Period effects can produce both individual and aggregate change, often quickly and enduringly, without any age-related differences. The sharp drop in trust in government between 1965 and 1975, for example, was almost entirely this sort of period effect, as Americans of all ages changed their minds about their leaders' trustworthiness.

Similarly, as just noted, a modest portion of the decline in social capital during the 1980s appears to be a period effect.

3. *Generational effects*, as described in Karl Mannheim's classic essay on "The Problem of Generations," represent the fact that "[i]ndividuals who belong to the same generation, who share the same year of birth, are endowed, to that extent, with a common location in the historical dimension of the social process" (Mannheim 1952, 290). Like life cycle effects (and unlike typical period effects), generational effects show up as disparities among age groups at a single point in time, but like period effects (and unlike life cycle effects) generational effects produce real social change, as successive generations, enduringly "imprinted" with divergent outlooks, enter and leave the population. In pure generational effects, no individual ever changes, but society does.

At least since the landmark essay by Converse (1976), social scientists have recognized that to sort out life cycle, period, and generational effects requires sensitivity to a priori plausibility, "side knowledge," and parsimony, not merely good data and sophisticated math. In effect, cohort analysis inevitably involves more unknowns than equations. With some common sense, some knowledge of history, and some use of Ockham's razor, however, it is possible to exclude some alternatives and focus on more plausible interpretations.

Returning to our conundrum, how could older people today be more engaged and trusting, if they did not become more engaged and trusting as they aged? The key to this paradox, as David Butler and Donald Stokes (1974) observed in another context, is to ask, not *how old people are*, but *when they were young*. Figure 5.6 addresses this reformulated question, displaying various measures of civic engagement according to the respondents' year of birth.[24] (Figure 5.6 includes data on voting from the National Election Studies, since Miller 1992 and Miller and Shanks 1995 have drawn on that data to demonstrate powerful generational effects on turnout, and it is instructive to see how parallel are the patterns that they discovered for voting turnout and the patterns for civic engagement that concern us here.[25] The figure also includes data on social trust from the National Election Studies, which will prove useful in parsing generational, life cycle, and period interpretations.)

The Long Civic Generation

In effect, Figure 5.6 lines up Americans from left to right according to their date of birth, beginning with those born in the last third of the nineteenth century and continuing across to the generation of their great-grandchildren, born in the last third of the twentieth century. As we begin moving along this queue from left to right—from those raised around the turn of the century to those raised during the Roaring Twenties, and so on—we find relatively high and unevenly rising levels of civic engagement and social trust. Then rather abruptly, however, we encounter signs of reduced community involvement, starting with men and women born in the early 1930s. Remarkably, this downward trend in joining, trusting, voting, and newspaper reading continues almost uninterruptedly for nearly 40 years. The trajectories for the various different indicators of civic engagement are strikingly parallel: each shows a high, sometimes rising plateau for people born and raised during the first third of the century; each shows a turning point in the cohorts born around 1930; and each then shows a more or less constant decline down to the cohorts born during the 1960s.[26]

By any standard, these intergenerational differences are extraordinary. Compare, for example, the generation born in the early 1920s with the generation of their grandchildren born in the late 1960s. Controlling for educational disparities, members of the generation born in the 1920s belong to almost twice as many civic associations as those born in the late 1960s (roughly 1.9 memberships per capita, compared to roughly 1.1 memberships per capita). The grandparents are more than twice as likely to

Figure 5.6 Social Capital and Civic Engagement by Generation (education controlled)

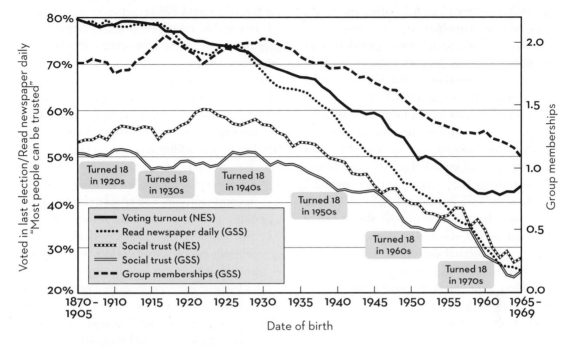

Source: General Social Survey (GSS), 1972–1994, and National Election Studies (NES), 1952–1992.
Respondents aged 25–80. Five-year moving averages.
Equal weighting of three educational categories.

trust other people (50–60%, compared with 25% for the grandchildren). They vote at nearly double the rate of the most recent cohorts (roughly 75% compared with 40–45%), and they read newspapers almost three times as often (70–80% read a paper daily compared with 25–30%). And bear in mind that we have found no evidence that the youngest generation will come to match their grandparents' higher levels of civic engagement as they grow older.

Thus, read not as life cycle effects, but rather as generational effects, the age-related patterns in our data suggest a radically different interpretation of our basic puzzle. Deciphered with this key, Figure 5.6 depicts a long "civic" generation, born roughly between 1910 and 1940, a broad group of people substantially more engaged in community affairs and substantially more trusting than those younger than they.[27] The culminating point of this civic

generation is the cohort born in 1925–1930, who attended grade school during the Great Depression, spent World War II in high school (or on the battle-field), first voted in 1948 or 1952, set up housekeeping in the 1950s, and watched their first television when they were in the late twenties. Since national surveying began, this cohort has been exceptionally civic: voting more, joining more, reading newspapers more, trusting more. As the distinguished sociologist Charles Tilly (born in 1928) said in commenting on an early version of this essay, "we are the last suckers."

To help in interpreting the historical contexts within which these successive generations of Americans matured, Figure 5.6 also indicates the decade within which each cohort came of age. Thus, we can see that each generation who reached adulthood since the 1940s has been less engaged in community affairs than its immediate predecessor.

Further confirmation of this *generational* interpretation comes from a comparison of the two parallel lines that chart responses to an identical question about social trust, posed first in the National Election Studies (mainly between 1964 and 1976) and then in the General Social Survey between 1972 and 1994.[28] If the greater trust expressed by Americans born earlier in the century represented a *life cycle* effect, then the graph from the GSS surveys (conducted when these cohorts were, on average, 10 years older) should have been some distance *above* the NES line. In fact, the GSS line lies about 5–10% *below* the NES line. That downward shift almost surely represents a *period* effect that depressed social trust among all cohorts during the 1980s.[29] That downward period effect, however, is substantially more modest than the large generational differences already noted.

In short, the most parsimonious interpretation of the age-related differences in civic engagement is that they represent a powerful reduction in civic engagement among Americans who came of age in the decades after World War II, as well as some modest additional disengagement that affected all cohorts during the 1980s. These patterns hint that being raised after World War II was a quite different experience from being raised before that watershed. It is as though the postwar generations were exposed to some mysterious X-ray that permanently and increasingly rendered them less likely to connect with the community. Whatever that force might have been, *it*—rather than anything that happened during the 1970s and 1980s—accounts for most of the civic disengagement that lies at the core of our mystery.

But if this reinterpretation of our puzzle is correct, why did it take so long for the effects of that mysterious X-ray to become manifest? If the underlying causes of civic disengagement can be traced to the 1940s and 1950s, why did the effects become conspicuous in PTA meetings and Masonic lodges, in the volunteer lists of the Red Cross and the Boy Scouts, and in polling stations and church pews and bowling alleys across the land only during the 1960s, 1970s, and 1980s?

The visible effects of this generational disengagement were delayed for several decades by two important factors:

1. The postwar boom in college enrollments boosted massive numbers of Americans up the sloping curve of civic engagement traced in Figure 5.3. Miller and Shanks (1995) observe that the postwar expansion of educational opportunities "forestalled a cataclysmic drop" in voting turnout, and it had a similar delaying effect on civic disengagement more generally.

2. The full effects of generational developments generally appear several decades after their onset, because it takes that long for a given generation to become numerically dominant in the adult population. Only after the mid-1960s did significant numbers of the "post-civic generation" reach adulthood, supplanting older, more civic cohorts. Figure 5.7 illustrates this generational accounting. The long civic generation (born between 1910 and 1940) reached its zenith in 1960, when it comprised 62% of those who chose between John Kennedy and Richard Nixon. By the time that Bill Clinton was elected president in 1992, that cohort's share in the electorate had been cut precisely in half. Conversely, over the last two decades (from 1974 to 1994) boomers and X-ers (that is, Americans born after 1946) have grown as a fraction of the adult population from 24% to 60%.

In short, the very decades that have seen a national deterioration in social capital are the same decades during which the numerical dominance of a trusting and civic generation has been replaced by the dominion of "post-civic" cohorts. Moreover, although the long civic generation has enjoyed unprecedented life expectancy, allowing its members to contribute more than their share to American social capital in recent decades, they are now passing from the scene. Even the youngest members of

Figure 5.7 The Rise and Decline of a "Civic" Generation

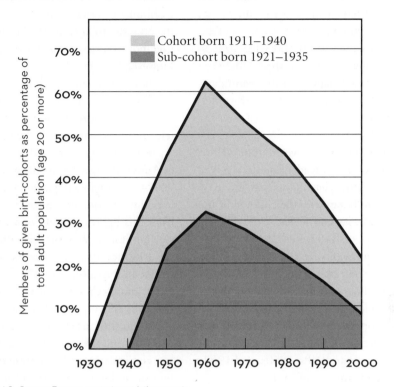

Legend:
- Cohort born 1911–1940
- Sub-cohort born 1921–1935

Y-axis: Members of given birth-cohorts as percentage of total adult population (age 20 or more)

Source: Calculated from U.S. Census Bureau, current population reports.

that generation will reach retirement age within the next few years. Thus, a generational analysis leads almost inevitably to the conclusion that the national slump in trust and engagement is likely to continue, regardless of whether the more modest "period effect" depression of the 1980s continues.

More than two decades ago, just as the first signs of disengagement were beginning to appear in American politics, Ithiel de Sola Pool (1973, 818–21) observed that the central issue would be—it was then too soon to judge, as he rightly noted—whether the development represented a temporary change in the weather or a more enduring change in the climate. It now appears that much of the change whose initial signs he spotted did in fact reflect a climatic shift. Moreover, just as the erosion of the ozone layer was detected only many years after the proliferation of the chlorofluorocarbons that caused

it, so too the erosion of America's social capital became visible only several decades after the underlying process had begun. Like Minerva's owl that flies at dusk, we come to appreciate how important the long civic generation has been to American community life just as its members are retiring. Unless America experiences a dramatic upward boost in civic engagement (a favorable "period effect") in the next few years, Americans in 2010 will join, trust, and vote even less than we do today.

The Puzzle Reformulated

To say that civic disengagement in contemporary America is in large measure generational merely reformulates our central puzzle. We now know that much of the cause of our lonely bowling probably dates to the 1940s and 1950s, rather than to the 1960s and 1970s. What could have been the mysterious anti-civic "X-ray" that affected Americans who came of age after World War II and whose effects progressively deepened at least into the 1970s?[30]

A number of superficially plausible candidates fail to fit the timing required by this new formulation of our mystery.

- Family instability seems to have an ironclad alibi for what we have now identified as the critical period, for the generational decline in civic engagement began with the children of the maritally stable 1940s and 1950s.[31] The divorce rate in America actually fell after 1945, and the sharpest jump in the divorce rate did not occur until the 1970s, long after the cohorts who show the sharpest declines in civic engagement and social trust had left home. Similarly, working mothers are exonerated by this re-specification of our problem, for the plunge in civicness among children of the 1940s, 1950s, and 1960s happened while mom was still at home.

- Our new formulation of the puzzle opens the possibility that the *Zeitgeist* of national unity and patriotism that culminated in 1945 might have reinforced civic-mindedness. On the other hand, it is hard to assign any consistent role to the Cold War and the Bomb, since the anti-civic trend appears to have deepened steadily from the 1940s to the 1970s, in no obvious harmony with the rhythms of world affairs. Nor is it easy to construct an interpretation of Figure 5.6 in which the cultural vicissitudes of "the Sixties" could play a significant role.

- Neither economic adversity nor affluence can easily be tied to the generational decline in civic engagement, since the slump seems to have affected in equal measure those who came of age in the placid Fifties, the booming Sixties, and the busted Seventies.

I have discovered only one prominent suspect against whom circumstantial evidence can be mounted, and in this case, it turns out, some directly incriminating evidence has also turned up. This is not the occasion to lay out the full case for the prosecution, nor to review rebuttal evidence for the defense. However, I want to illustrate the sort of evidence that justifies indictment. The culprit is television.

First, the timing fits. The long civic generation was the last cohort of Americans to grow up without television, for television flashed into American society like lightning in the 1950s. In 1950 barely 10% of American homes had television sets, but by 1959 90% did, probably the fastest diffusion of a technological innovation ever recorded. The reverberations from this lightning bolt continued for decades, as viewing hours per capita grew by 17–20% during the 1960s and by an additional 7–8% during the 1970s. In the early years, TV watching was concentrated among the less educated sectors of the population, but during the 1970s the viewing time of the more educated sectors of the population began to converge upward. Television viewing increases with age, particularly upon retirement, but each generation since the introduction of television has begun its life cycle at a higher starting point. By 1995, viewing per TV household was more than 50% higher than it had been in the 1950s.[32]

Most studies estimate that the average American now watches roughly four hours per day.[33] Robinson (1990b), using the more conservative time-budget technique for determining how people allocate their time, offers an estimate closer to three hours per day, but concludes that as a primary activity, television absorbs 40% of the average American's free time, an increase of about one-third since 1965. Moreover, multiple sets have proliferated: by the late 1980s, three quarters of all U.S. homes had more than one set (Comstock 1989), and these numbers too are rising steadily, allowing ever more private viewing. In short, as Robinson and Godbey 1995 conclude, "television is the 800-pound gorilla of leisure time." This massive change in the way Americans spend our days and nights occurred precisely during the years of generational civic disengagement.

Evidence of a link between the arrival of television and the erosion of social connections is, however, not merely circumstantial. The links between civic engagement and television viewing can instructively be compared with the links between civic engagement and newspaper reading. The basic contrast is straightforward: newspaper reading is associated with high social capital, TV viewing with low social capital.

Controlling for education, income, age, race, place of residence, work status, and gender, TV viewing is strongly and negatively related to social trust and group membership, whereas the same correlations with newspaper reading are positive. Figure 5.8 shows that within every educational category, heavy readers are avid joiners, whereas Figure 5.9 shows that heavy viewers are more likely to be loners.[34] Viewing and reading are themselves uncorrelated—some people do lots of both, some do little of either—but Figure 5.10 shows that (controlling for education, as always) "pure readers" (that is, people who watch less TV than average and read more newspapers than average) belong to 76% more civic organizations than "pure viewers." Precisely the same pattern applies to other indicators of civic engagement, including social trust and voting turnout. "Pure readers," for example, are 55% more trusting than "pure viewers."[35]

In other words, each hour spent viewing television is associated with less social trust and less group membership, while each hour reading a newspaper is associated with more. An increase in television viewing of the magnitude that the United States has experienced in the last four decades might directly account for as much as one-quarter to one-half of the total drop in social capital, even without taking into account, for example, the indirect effects of television viewing on newspaper readership or the cumulative effects of "life-time" viewing hours.[36]

Figure 5.8 Group Membership by Newspaper Readership and Education

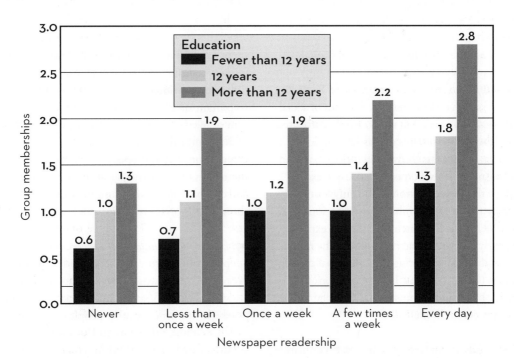

Source: General Social Survey, 1974–1994.

Figure 5.9 Group Membership by Television Viewing and Education

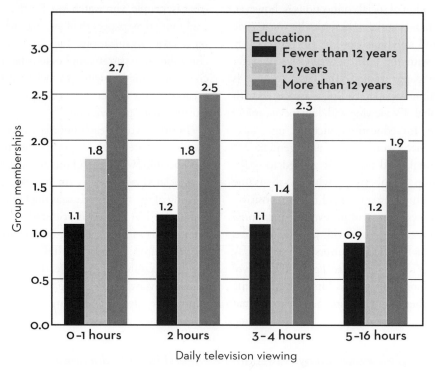

Source: General Social Survey, 1974–1994.

How might television destroy social capital?

- *Time displacement.* Even though there are only 24 hours in everyone's day, most forms of social and media participation are positively correlated. People who listen to lots of classical music are more likely, not less likely, than others to attend Cubs games. Television is the principal exception to this generalization—the only leisure activity that seems to inhibit participation outside the home. TV watching comes at expense of nearly every social activity outside the home, especially social gatherings and informal conversations (Comstock et al 1978; Comstock 1989; Bower 1985; and Robinson and Godbey 1995). TV viewers are homebodies.

Most studies that report a negative correlation between television watching and community involve-

ment (including my Figure 5.8) are ambiguous with respect to causality, because they merely compare different individuals at a single time. However, one important quasi-experimental study of the introduction of television in three Canadian towns (Williams 1986) found the same pattern at the aggregate level across time: a major effect of television's arrival was the reduction in participation in social, recreational, and community activities among people of all ages. In short, television is privatizing our leisure time.

- *Effects on the outlooks of viewers.* An impressive body of literature, gathered under the rubric of the "mean world effect," suggests that heavy watchers of TV are unusually skeptical about the benevolence of other people—overestimating crime rates, for example. This body of literature has generated much debate about the underlying causal patterns, with skeptics

Figure 5.10 Group Membership by Media Usage (education controlled)

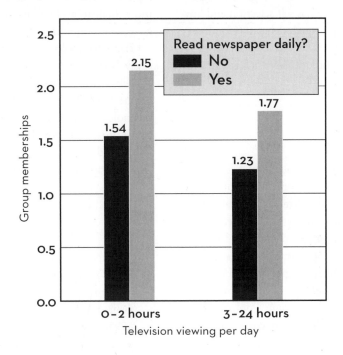

Read newspaper daily?
- No
- Yes

Group memberships (y-axis)

0–2 hours: No = 1.54, Yes = 2.15
3–24 hours: No = 1.23, Yes = 1.77

Television viewing per day (x-axis)

Source: General Social Survey, 1974–1994.
Entries based on three equally weighted educational categories.

suggesting that misanthropy may foster couch-potato behavior rather than the reverse. While awaiting better experimental evidence, however, a reasonable interim judgment is that heavy television watching may well increase pessimism about human nature (Gerbner et al 1980; Dobb and MacDonald 1979; Hirsch 1980; Hughes 1980; and Comstock 1989, 265–69). Perhaps, too, as social critics have long argued, both the medium and the message have more basic effects on our ways of interacting with the world and with one another. Television may induce passivity, as Postman (1985) has claimed, and it may even change our fundamental physical and social perceptions, as Meyrowitz (1985) has suggested.

- *Effects on children.* TV occupies an extraordinary part of children's lives—consuming about 40 hours per week on average. Viewing is especially high among pre-adolescents, but it remains high among younger adolescents: time-budget studies (Carnegie Council on Adolescent Development 1993, 5, citing Timmer et al. 1985) suggest that among youngsters aged 9–14 television consumes as much time as *all other discretionary activities combined*, including playing, hobbies, clubs, outdoor activities, informal visiting, and just hanging out. The effects of television on childhood socialization have, of course, been hotly debated for more than three decades. The most reasonable conclusion from a welter of sometimes conflicting results appears to be that heavy television watching probably increases aggressiveness (although perhaps not actual violence), that it probably reduces school achievement, and that it is statistically associated with "psychosocial malfunctioning," although how much of this effect is self-selection and how much causal remains much debated (Condry, 1993). The evidence is, as I have said, not yet enough to convict, but the defense has a lot of explaining to do.

Conclusion

Ithiel de Sola Pool's posthumous book, *Technologies Without Borders* (1990), is a prescient work, astonishingly relevant to our current national debates about the complicated links among technology, public policy, and culture. Pool defended what he called "soft technological determinism." Revolutions in communications technologies have profoundly affected social life and culture, as the printing press helped bring on the Reformation. Pool concluded that the electronic revolution in communications technology, whose outlines he traced well before most of us were even aware of the impending changes, was the first major technological advance in centuries that would have a profoundly decentralizing and fragmenting effect on society and culture.

Pool hoped that the result might be "community without contiguity." As a classic liberal, he welcomed the benefits of technological change for individual freedom, and, in part, I share that enthusiasm. Those of us who bemoan the decline of community in contemporary America need to be sensitive to the liberating gains achieved during the same decades. We need to avoid an uncritical nostalgia for the Fifties. On the other hand, some of the same freedom-friendly technologies whose rise Pool predicted may indeed be undermining our connections with one another and with our communities. I suspect that Pool would have been open to that argument, too, for one of Pool's most talented protégés, Samuel Popkin (1991, 226–31) has argued that the rise of television and the correlative decline of social interaction have impaired American political discourse. The last line in Pool's last book (1990, 262) is this: "We may suspect that [the techno-logical trends that we can anticipate] will promote individualism and will make it harder, not easier, to govern and organize a coherent society."

Pool's technological determinism was "soft" precisely because he recognized that social values can condition the effects of technology. In the end this perspective invites us not merely to consider how technology is privatizing our lives—if, as it seems to me, it is—but to ask whether we entirely like the result, and if not, what we might do about it. But that is a topic for another day.

NOTES

1. I wish to thank several researchers for sharing valuable unpublished work on related themes: John Brehm and Wendy Rahn (1995); Warren Miller and Merrill Shanks (1995), John Robinson and Geoffrey Godbey (1995); and Eric Uslaner (1995). Professor Uslaner was generous in helping track down some elusive data and commenting on an earlier draft. I also wish to thank a fine team of research assistants, including Jay Braatz, Maryann Barakso, Karen Ferree, Archon Fung, Louise Kennedy, Jeff Kling, Kimberly Lochner, Karen Rothkin, and Mark Warren. Support for the research project from which this study derives has been provided by the Aspen Institute, Carnegie Corporation, the Ford, Kovler, Norman, and Rockefeller foundations, and Harvard University.

2. In this respect I deviate slightly from James Coleman's "functional" definition of social capital. See Coleman (1990): 300–21.

3. The results reported in this paragraph and throughout the paper, unless otherwise indicated, are derived from the General Social Survey. These exceptionally useful data derive from a series of scientific surveys of the adult American population, conducted nearly every year since 1972 by the National Opinion Research Center, under the direction of James A. Davis and Tom W. Smith. The cumulative sample size is approximately 32,000, although the questions on trust and group membership that are at the focus of our inquiry have not been asked of all respondents in all years. Our

measure of trust derives from this question: "Generally speaking, would you say that most people can be trusted, or that you can't be too careful in dealing with people": for this question, N = 22390. For evidence confirming the power of this simple measure of social trust, see Uslaner (1995). Our measure of group membership derives from this question: "Now we would like to know something about the groups or organizations to which individuals belong. Here is a list of various organizations. Could you tell me whether or not you are a member of each type?" The list includes fraternal groups, service clubs, veterans' groups, political clubs, labor unions, sports groups, youth groups, school service groups, hobby or garden clubs, social fraternities or sororities, nationality groups, farm organizations, literary, arts, discussion or study groups, professional or academic societies, church-affiliated groups, and any other groups. For this question, N = 19326. Neither of these questions, of course, is a perfect measure of social capital. In particular, our measure of multiple memberships refers not to total groups, but to total *types* of groups. On the other hand, "noise" in data generally depresses observed correlations below the "true" value, so our findings are more likely to understate than to exaggerate patterns in the "real world."

4. Across the 35 countries for which data are available from the World Values Survey (1990–91), the correlation between the average number of associational memberships and endorsement of the view that "most people can be trusted" is r .65. Across the 42 states for which adequate samples are available in the General Social Survey (1972–1994), the comparable correlation is r .71. Across individuals in the General Social Survey (1972–1994), controlling for education, race, and age, social trust is significantly and separately correlated with membership in political clubs, literary groups, sports clubs, hobby and garden clubs, youth groups, school service groups, and other associations. The correlation with social trust is insignificant only for veterans' groups, labor unions, and nationality groups.

5. The 1965 sample, which was limited to nonretired residents of cities between 30,000 and 280,000 population, was not precisely equivalent to the later national samples, so appropriate adjustments need to be made to ensure comparability. For the 1965–1975 comparison, see Robinson (1981, 125). For the 1975–1985 comparison (but apparently without adjustment for the 1965 sampling peculiarities), see Cutler (1990). Somewhat smaller declines are reported in Robinson and Godbey (1995), although it is unclear whether they correct for the sampling differences. Additional work to refine these cross-time comparisons is required and is currently underway.

6. Trust in political authorities—and indeed in many social institutions—has also declined sharply over the last three decades, but that is conceptually a distinct trend. As we shall see later, the etiology of the slump in social trust is quite different from the etiology of the decline in political trust.

7. For reasons explained below, Figure 5.2 reports trends for membership in various types of groups, *controlling for* the respondent's education level.

8. Some commentaries on "Bowling Alone" have been careless, however, in reporting apparent membership growth. *The Economist* (1995, 22), for example, celebrated a recent rebound in total membership in parent-teacher organizations, without acknowledging that this rebound is almost entirely attributable to the growing number of children. The fraction of parents who belong to PTAs has regained virtually none of the 50% fall that this metric registered between 1960 and 1975. Despite talk about the growth of "support groups," another oft-cited counter-example. I know of no statistical substantiation for this claim. One might even ask whether the vaunted rise in neighborhood watch groups might not represent only a partial, artificial replacement for the vanished social capital of traditional neighborhoods—a kind of sociological Astroturf, suitable only where you can't grow the real thing. See also Glenn (1987, S124) for survey evidence of "an increased tendency for individuals to withdraw allegiance from . . . anything outside of themselves."

9. The only exceptions are farm groups, labor unions, and veterans' organizations, whose members have slightly less formal education than the average American. Interestingly, sports clubs are *not* an exception; college graduates are nearly three times more likely to

belong to a sports group than are high school drop-outs. Education is uncorrelated with church attendance, but positively correlated with membership in church-related groups.

10. For a thorough recent investigation of the role of education in accounting for differences in political participation, see Verba, Schlozman, and Brady (1995).

11. As a practical matter, all subsequent statistical presentations here implement this precept by equally weighing respondents from three broad educational categories—those with fewer than 12 years formal schooling, those with exactly 12 years, and those with more than 12 years. Conveniently, this categorization happens to slice the 1972–1994 GSS sample into nearly equal thirds. The use of more sophisticated mathematical techniques to control for educational differences would alter none of the central conclusions of this essay.

12. The downturns in both joining and trusting seem to be somewhat greater among Americans on the middle rungs of the educational ladder—high school graduates and college dropouts—than among those at the very top and bottom of the educational hierarchy, but the differences are not great, and the trends are statistically significant at all levels.

13. This is true with or without controls for education and year of survey. The patterns among men and women on this score are not identical, for women who work part-time appear to be somewhat more civically engaged and socially trusting than either those who work full-time or those who do not work outside the home at all. Whatever we make of this intriguing anomaly, which apparently does not appear in the time budget data (Robinson and Godbey 1995) and which has no counterpart in the male half of the population, it cannot account for our basic puzzle, since female part-time workers constitute a relatively small fraction of the American population, and the fraction is growing, not declining. Between the first half of the 1970s and the first half of the 1990s, according to the GSS data, the fraction of the total adult population constituted by female part-time workers rose from about 8% to about 10%.

14. Evidence on generational differences presented below reinforces this conclusion.

15. Robinson and Godbey (1995); however, report that nonemployed women still spend more time on activity in voluntary associations than their employed counterparts.

16. Multivariate analysis hints that one major reason why divorce lowers connectedness is that it lowers family income, which in turn reduces civic engagement.

17. I have set aside this issue for fuller treatment in later work. However, I note for the record that (1) state-level differences in social trust and group membership are substantial, closely intercorrelated and reasonably stable, at least over the period from the 1970s to the 1990s, and (2) those differences are surprisingly closely correlated (R^2 = .52) with the measure of "state political culture" invented by Elazar (1966), and refined by Sharkansky (1969), based on descriptive accounts of state politics during the 1950s and traceable in turn to patterns of immigration during the nineteenth century and before.

18. Public expenditure as a percentage of GDP in 1989 is correlated r − .29 with 1990–1991 trust and r − .48 with 1990–1991 associational memberships.

19. For broadly similar conclusions, see Verba, Schlozman, and Brady (1995, 241–47) and the sources cited there.

20. As elsewhere in this essay, "controlling for educational differences" here means averaging the average scores for respondents with fewer than 12 years of schooling, with exactly 12 years, and with more than 12 years, respectively.

21. White support for segregation in Figure 5.4 is measured by responses to this question in the General Social Survey: "If you and your friends belonged to a social club that would not let Blacks join, would you try to change the rules so that Blacks could join?" Essentially identical results obtain if we measure white racism instead by support for antimiscegenation laws or for residential segregation.

22. As we shall see in a moment, much civic disengagement actually appears to be generational, affecting people born after 1930, but not those born before. If this phenomenon represented white flight from integrated community life after the civil rights revolution,

it is difficult to see why the trend should be so much more marked among those who came of age in the more tolerant 1960s and 1970s, and hardly visible at all among those who came of age in the first half of the century, when American society was objectively more segregated and subjectively more racist.

23. Period effects that affect only people of a specific age shade into generational effects, which is why Converse, when summarizing these age-related effects, refers to "two-and-a-half" types, rather than the conventional three types.

24. To exclude the life cycle effects in the last years of life, Figure 5.6 excludes respondents over 80. To avoid well-known problems in reliably sampling young adults, as discussed by Converse (1976), Figure 5.6 also excludes respondents aged under 25. To offset the relatively small year-by-year samples and to control for educational differences, Figure 5.6 charts five-year moving averages across the three educational categories used in this essay.

25. I learned of the Miller/Shanks argument only after discovering generational differences in civic engagement in the General Social Survey data, but their findings and mine are strikingly consistent.

26. Too few respondents born in the late nineteenth century appear in surveys conducted in the 1970s and 1980s for us to discern differences among successive birth cohorts with great reliability. However, those scant data (not broken out in Figure 5.6) suggest that the turn of the century might have been an era of rising civic engagement. Similarly, too few respondents born after 1970 have yet appeared in national surveys for us to be confident about their distinctive generational profile, although the slender results so far seem to suggest that the 40-year generational plunge in civic engagement might be bottoming out. However, even if this turns out to be true, it will be several decades before that development could arrest the aggregate drop in civic engagement, for reasons subsequently explained in the text.

27. Members of the 1910–1940 generation also seem more civic than their elders, at least to judge by the outlooks of the relatively few men and women born in the late nineteenth century who appeared in our samples.

28. The question on social trust appeared biennially in the NES from 1964 to 1976 and then reappeared in 1992. I have included the 1992 NES interviews in the analysis in order to obtain estimates for cohorts too young to have appeared in the earlier surveys.

29. Additional analysis of indicators of civic engagement in the GSS, not reported in detail here, confirms this downward shift during the 1980s.

30. I record here one theory attributed variously to Robert Salisbury (1985), Gerald Gamm, and Simon and Garfunkel. Devotees of our national pastime will recall that Joe DiMaggio signed with the Yankees in 1936, just as the last of the long civic generation was beginning to follow the game, and he turned center field over to Mickey Mantle in 1951, just as the last of "the suckers" reached legal maturity. Almost simultaneously, the Braves, the Athletics, the Browns, the Senators, the Dodgers, and the Giants deserted cities that had been their homes since the late nineteenth century. By the time Mantle in turn left the Yankees in 1968, much of the damage to civic loyalty had been done. This interpretation explains why Mrs. Robinson's plaintive query that year about Joltin' Joe's whereabouts evoked such widespread emotion. A deconstructionist analysis of social capital's decline would highlight the final haunting lamentation, "our nation turns its *lonely* eyes to you" [emphasis added].

31. This exoneration applies to the possible effects of divorce on children, not to its effects on the couple themselves, as discussed earlier in this essay.

32. For introductions to the massive literature on the sociology of television, see Bower (1985), Comstock et al. (1978), Comstock (1989), and Grabner (1993). The figures on viewing hours in the text are from Bower (1985, 33) and *Public Perspective* (1995, 47). Cohort differences are reported in Bower 1985, 46.

33. This figure excludes periods in which television is merely playing in the background. Comstock (1989, 17)

reports that "on any fall day in the late 1980s, the set in the average television owning household was on for about eight hours.")

34. In fact, multiple regression analysis, predicting civic engagement from television viewing and education, suggests that heavy TV watching is one important reason *why* less educated people are less engaged in the life of their communities. Controlling for differential TV exposure significantly reduces the correlation between education and engagement.

35. Controlling for education, 45% of respondents who watch TV two hours or less a day and read newspapers daily say that "most people can be trusted," as compared to 29% of respondents who watch TV three hours or more a day and do not read a newspaper daily.

36. Newspaper circulation (per household) has dropped by more than half since its peak in 1947. To be sure, it is not clear which way the tie between newspaper reading and civic involvement works, since disengagement might itself dampen one's interest in community news. But the two trends are clearly linked.

REFERENCES

Bower, Robert T. 1985. *The Changing Television Audience in America*. New York: Columbia University Press.

Brehm, John, and Wendy Rahn. 1995. "An Audit of the Deficit in Social Capital." Durham, NC: Duke University. Unpublished manuscript.

Butler, David, and Donald Stokes. 1974. *Political Change in Britain: The Evolution of Electoral Choice*, 2nd ed. New York: St. Martin's.

Caplow, Theodore, Howard M. Bahr, John Modell, and Bruce A. Chadwick. 1991. *Recent Social Trends in the United States: 1960–1990*. Montreal: McGill-Queen's University Press.

Carnegie Council on Adolescent Development. 1993. *A Matter of Time: Risk and Opportunity in the Nonschool Hours: Executive Summary*. New York: Carnegie Corporation of New York.

Coleman, James. 1990. *Foundations of Social Theory*. Cambridge, MA: Harvard University Press.

Comstock, George, Steven Chaffee, Natan Katzman, Maxwell McCombs, and Donald Roberts. 1978. *Television and Human Behavior*. New York: Columbia University Press.

Comstock, George. 1989. *The Evolution of American Television*. Newbury Park, CA: Sage.

Condry, John. 1993. "Thief of Time, Unfaithful Servant: Television and the American Child," *Daedalus* 122 (Winter): 259–78.

Converse, Philip E. 1976. *The Dynamics of Party Support: Cohort-Analyzing Party Identification*. Beverly Hills, CA: Sage.

Cutler, Blaine. 1990. "Where Does the Free Time Go?" *American Demographics* (November): 36–39.

Davis, James Allan, and Tom W. Smith. *General Social Surveys. 1972–1994*. [machine readable data file]. Principal Investigator, James A. Davis; Director and Co-Principal Investigator, Tom W. Smith. NORC ed. Chicago: National Opinion Research Center, producer, 1994; Storrs, CT: The Roper Center for Public Opinion Research, University of Connecticut, distributor.

Dobb, Anthony N., and Glenn F. Macdonald. 1979. "Television Viewing and Fear of Victimization: Is the Relationship Causal?" *Journal of Personality and Social Psychology* 37: 170–79.

The Economist. 1995. "The Solitary Bowler." 334 (18 February): 21–22.

Edwards, Patricia Klobus, John N. Edwards, and Ann DeWitt Watts, "Women, Work, and Social Participation." *Journal of Voluntary Action Research* 13 (January–March, 1984), 7–22.

Elazar, Daniel J. 1966. *American Federalism: A View from the States*. New York: Crowell.

Fukuyama, Francis. 1995. *Trust: The Social Virtues and the Creation of Prosperity*. New York: The Free Press.

Gerbner, George, Larry Gross, Michael Morgan, and Nancy Signorielli. 1980. "The 'Mainstreaming' of America: Violence Profile No. 11," *Journal of Communication* 30 (Summer): 10–29.

Ginzberg, Eli. *The Unemployed*. 1943. New York: Harper and Brothers.

Glenn, Norval D. 1987. "Social Trends in the United States: Evidence from Sample Surveys." *Public Opinion Quarterly* 51: S109–S126.

Grabner, Doris A. 1993. *Mass Media and American Politics*. Washington, D.C.: CQ Press.

Hirsch, Paul M. 1980. "The 'Scary World' of the Non-viewer and Other Anomalies: A Re-analysis of Gerbner et al.'s Findings on Cultivation Analysis, Part I," *Communication Research* 7 (October): 403–56.

Hughes, Michael. 1980. "The Fruits of Cultivation Analysis: A Re-examination of the Effects of Television Watching on Fear of Victimization, Alienation, and the Approval of Violence." *Public Opinion Quarterly* 44: 287–303.

Jahoda, Marie, Paul Lazarsfeld, and Hans Zeisel. 1933. *Marienthal*. Chicago: Aldine-Atherton.

Mannheim, Karl. 1952. "The Problem of Generations." In *Essays on the Sociology of Knowledge*, ed. Paul Kecsckemeti. New York: Oxford University Press: 276–322.

Meyrowitz, Joshua. 1985. *No Sense of Place: The Impact of Electronic Media on Social Behavior*. New York: Oxford University Press.

Miller, Warren E. 1992. "The Puzzle Transformed: Explaining Declining Turnout." *Political Behavior* 14: 1–43.

Miller, Warren E., and J. Merrill Shanks. 1995. *The American Voter Reconsidered*. Tempe, AZ: Arizona State University. Unpublished manuscript.

Pool, Ithiel de Sola. 1973. "Public Opinion." In *Handbook of Communication*, ed. Ithiel de Sola Pool et al. Chicago: Rand McNally: 779–835.

Pool, Ithiel de Sola. 1990. *Technologies Without Boundaries: On Telecommunications in a Global Age*. Cambridge, MA: Harvard University Press.

Popkin, Samuel L. 1991. *The Reasoning Voter*. Chicago: University of Chicago Press.

Postman, Neil. 1985. *Amusing Ourselves to Death: Public Discourse in the Age of Show Business*. New York: Viking-Penguin Books.

Public Perspective. 1995. "People, Opinion, and Polls: American Popular Culture." 6 (August/September): 37–48.

Putnam, Robert D. 1993. *Making Democracy Work: Civic Traditions in Modern Italy*. Princeton, NJ: Princeton University Press.

Putnam, Robert D. 1995. "Bowling Alone, Revisited," *The Responsive Community* (Spring): 18–33.

Putnam, Robert D. 1996. "Bowling Alone: Democracy in America at the End of the Twentieth Century," forthcoming in a collective volume edited by Axel Hadenius. New York: Cambridge University Press.

Robinson, John. 1981. "Television and Leisure Time: A New Scenario," *Journal of Communication* 31 (Winter): 120–30.

Robinson, John. 1990a. "The Time Squeeze." *American Demographics* (February).

Robinson, John. 1990b. "I Love My TV." *American Demographics* (September): 24–27.

Robinson, John, and Geoffrey Godbey, 1995. *Time for Life*. College Park, MD: University of Maryland. Unpublished manuscript.

Rosenstone, Steven J., and John Mark Hansen. 1993. *Mobilization, Participation, and Democracy in America*. New York: Macmillan.

Salisbury, Robert H. 1985. "Blame Dismal World Conditions on . . . Baseball. *Miami Herald* (May 18): 27A.

Schor, Juliet. 1991. *The Overworked American*. New York: Basic Books.

Sharkansky, Ira. 1969. "The Utility of Elazar's Political Culture." *Polity* 2: 66–83.

Timmer, S. G., J. Eccles, and I. O'Brien. 1985. "How Children Use Time." In *Time, Goods, and Well-Being*, ed. F. T. Juster and F. B. Stafford. Ann Arbor, MI: University of Michigan, Institute for Social Research.

U.S. Bureau of the Census. 1995 (and earlier years). *Current Population Reports*. Washington, D.C.

Uslaner, Eric M. 1995. "Faith, Hope, and Charity: Social Capital, Trust, and Collective Action." College Park, MD: University of Maryland. Unpublished manuscript.

Verba, Sidney, Kay Lehman Schlozman, and Henry E. Brady. 1995. *Voice and Equality: Civic Volunteerism in American Politics*. Cambridge, MA: Harvard University Press.

Wilcock, Richard, and Walter H. Franke. 1963. *Unwanted Workers*. New York: Free Press of Glencoe.

Williams, Tannis Macbeth, ed. 1986. *The Impact of Television: A Natural Experiment in Three Communities*. New York: Academic Press.

Alfred Stepan, Juan J. Linz, and Yogendra Yadav
THE RISE OF "STATE-NATIONS"

One of the most urgent conceptual, normative, and political tasks of our day is to think anew about how polities that aspire to be democracies can accommodate great sociocultural and even multinational diversity within one state. The need to think anew arises from a mismatch between the political realities of the world we live in and an old political wisdom that we have inherited. The old wisdom holds that the territorial boundaries of a state must coincide with the perceived cultural boundaries of a nation. Thus, this understanding requires that every state must contain within itself one and not more than one culturally homogenous nation, that every state should be a nation, and that every nation should be a state. Given the reality of sociocultural diversity in many of the world's polities, this widespread belief seems to us to be misguided and indeed dangerous since, as we shall argue, many successful democratic states in the world today do not conform to this expectation.

All independent democratic states have a degree of cultural diversity, but for comparative purposes we can say that states may be divided into three broad categories:

1) States that have strong cultural diversity, some of which is territorially based and politically articulated by significant groups with leaders who advance claims of independence in the name of nationalism and self-determination.
2) States that are culturally quite diverse, but whose diversity is nowhere organized by territorially based, politically significant groups that mobilize nationalist demands for independence.

3) States in which a community that is culturally homogeneous enough to consider itself a nation dominates the state, and no other significant group articulates similar claims.

We call countries in the first category "robustly multinational" societies. Canada (owing to Quebec), Spain (especially owing to the Basque Country and Catalonia), and Belgium (owing to Flanders) are all "robustly multinational." India, owing to the Kashmir Valley alone, merits classification in this category. The Sikh-led Khalistan movement in the Punjab, the Mizo independence movement in the northeast, and the Dravidian secessionist movement in southern India strengthen the multinational dimension of the Indian polity.

Switzerland and the United States are both sociologically diverse and multicultural. Yet since neither has significant territorially based groups mobilizing claims for independence, both countries clearly fall into the second and not the first category.

Finally, Japan, Portugal, and most of the Scandinavian countries fall into the third category.

What political implications do these three very different situations have for reconciling democracy with diversity? If a polity has only one significant group which sees itself as a nation, and there exists a relatively common sense of history and religion and a shared language throughout the territory, the building of a nation-state and the building of democracy can reinforce each other.

Yet if competitive elections are inaugurated under conditions that are already "robustly multinational," the logic of nation-state building and the logic of democracy building will come into conflict. This is so because only one of the polity's "nations" will be privileged in the state-building effort, while the other "nations" will go unrecognized and may even be marginalized. But before

From *Journal of Democracy* 21, no. 3 (July 2010), pp. 50–68.

examining alternatives to the nation-state, we first need to attempt to explain its normative and political power.

The belief that every state should be a nation reflects perhaps the most widely accepted normative vision of a modern democratic state—that is, the "nation-state." After the French Revolution, and especially in the latter part of the nineteenth century, France pursued many policies devoted to creating a unitary nation-state in which all French citizens would have only one cultural and political identity. These policies included a package of incentives and disincentives to ensure that French increasingly became the only acceptable language in the state. Political mechanisms to allow the recognition and expression of regional cultural differences were so unacceptable to French nation-state builders that advocacy of federalism was at one time a capital offense. Throughout France, state schools at any given hour were famously teaching the same curriculum with identical syllabi by teachers who had been trained and certified by the same Ministry of Education. Numerous state policies, such as universal military conscription, were designed to create a common French identity and a country that was robustly assimilationist.[1]

Some very successful contemporary democracies such as Sweden, Japan, and Portugal are close to the ideal type of a unitary nation-state. Some federal states such as Germany and Australia have also become nation-states. In our view, if at the time a polity adopts a state-directed program of "nation-state" building sociocultural differences have not acquired political salience, and if most politically aware citizens have a strong sense of shared history, policies designed to build a nation-state should not create problems for the achievement of an inclusive democracy. In fact, the creation of such a national identity and relative homogeneity in the nineteenth century was identified with democratization and was possible in consolidated states.

In the twentieth century, however, attempts to create nation-states via state policies encountered growing difficulties, even in such old states as Spain.

Thus if a polity has significant and politically salient cultural or linguistic diversity (as a large number of polities do), then its leaders need to think about, craft, and normatively legitimate a type of polity with the characteristics of a "state-nation."

Identities and Boundaries

Two of the authors of the present essay, Juan Linz and Alfred Stepan, introduced the concept of the state-nation in 1996, but only in a paragraph (and one figure), citing states that "are multicultural, and [which] sometimes even have significant multinational components, [but] which nonetheless still manage to engender strong identification and loyalty from their citizens, an identification and loyalty that proponents of homogeneous nation states perceive that only nation states can engender." They went on to say that neither Switzerland nor India was

> strictly speaking [in the French sense] a nation state, but we believe both can now be called state nations. Under Jawaharlal Nehru, India made significant gains in managing multinational tensions through skillful and consensual usage of numerous consociational practices. Through this process India became in the 1950s and the early 1960s a democratic state-nation.[2]

"Nation-state" policies stand for a political-institutional approach that tries to make the political boundaries of the state and the presumed cultural boundaries of the nation match. Needless to say, the cultural boundaries are far from obvious in most cases. Thus the creation of a nation-state involves privileging *one* sociocultural identity over other potential or actual sociocultural cleavages that can be politically mobilized. "Nation-state" policies have been pursued historically by following a variety of routes that range from relatively soft to downright brutal. These may include: (1) creating or arousing a special kind of allegiance or common cultural identity among those living in a state; (2) encouraging the voluntary assimilation into the nation-state's

Table 5.3 Two Contrasting Ideal Types: "Nation-State" and "State-Nation"

	NATION-STATE	STATE-NATION
Preexisting Conditions		
Sense of belonging or "we-ness"	There is general attachment to one major cultural civilizational tradition. This cultural identity corresponds to existing state boundaries with minor exceptions.	There is attachment to more than one cultural civilizational tradition within the existing boundaries. However, these attachments do not preclude identification with a common state.
State Policy		
Cultural policies	There are homogenizing attempts to foster one core cultural identity, particularly one official language. Multiplicity of cultures is not recognized. The goal is unity in oneness.	There is recognition and support of more than one cultural identity (and more than one official language) within a frame of some common polity-wide symbols. The goal is unity in diversity.
Institutions		
Territorial division of power	The state is unitary or, if a federation, it is mononational and symmetrical.	There is normally a federal system, and it is often asymmetrical. The state can be unitary if aggressive nation-state policies are not pursued and de facto multilingualism is accepted. Federacies are possible.
Politics		
Ethnocultural or territorial cleavages	Such splits are not too salient.	Such splits are salient, but are recognized as such and democratically managed.
Autonomist or secessionist parties	Autonomist parties are normally not "coalitionable." Secessionist parties are outlawed or marginalized in democratic electoral politics.	Autonomist parties can govern in federal units and are "coalitionable" at the center. Nonviolent secessionist parties can sometimes participate in democratic political processes.

Table 5.3 (Continued)

	NATION-STATE	STATE-NATION
	Citizen Orientation	
Political identity	Citizens feel that they belong to the state and to the same cultural nation at the same time.	Many citizens have multiple but complementary identities.
Obedience and loyalty	Citizens believe in obedience to the state and loyalty to the nation.	Citizens feel obedience to the state and identification with its institutions; none of this is based on a single national identity.

identity of those who do not share that initial allegiance or cultural identity; (3) various forms of social pressure and coercion to achieve this and to prevent the emergence of alternative cultural identities or to erode them if they exist; and (4) coercion that might, in the more extreme cases, even involve ethnic cleansing.

By contrast, "state-nation" policies stand for a political-institutional approach that respects and protects *multiple but complementary* sociocultural identities. "State-nation" policies recognize the legitimate public and even political expression of active sociocultural cleavages, and they include mechanisms to accommodate competing or conflicting claims without imposing or privileging in a discriminatory way any one claim. "State-nation" policies involve creating a sense of belonging (or "we-feeling") with respect to the statewide political community, while simultaneously creating institutional safeguards for respecting and protecting politically salient sociocultural diversities. The "we-feeling" may take the form of defining a tradition, history, and shared culture in an inclusive manner, with all citizens encouraged to feel a sense of attachment to common symbols of the state and some form of "constitutional patriotism."

In democratic societies, the institutional safeguards constitutive of "state-nation" policies will most likely take the form of federalism, and often specifically *asymmetrical* federalism, possibly combined with consociational practices.[3] Virtually every longstanding and relatively peaceful contemporary democracy with more than one territorially concentrated, politically mobilized, linguistic-cultural group forming a majority in some significant part of its territory is not only federal, but "asymmetrically federal" (Belgium, Canada, India) or is a unitary nation-state with a "federacy."[4] As we discuss later, a federacy is a distinct cultural-political unit within an otherwise unitary state that relates to the central government via a set of asymmetrical federal arrangements. This means that such a polity, at a certain point in its history, decided that it could "hold together" within a single democratic system only by constitutionally embedding special cultural and historical prerogatives for some of the member units—prerogatives that respond to those units' distinct linguistic-cultural aspirations, security situations, or historical identities.

We believe that if political leaders in India, Belgium, Spain, and Canada had attempted to force one language and culture on their respective countries, and had insisted on imposing homogenizing nation-state policies reminiscent of the French Third Republic, the cause of social peace, inclusionary democracy, and individual rights would have been poorly served. For in each of these countries, more than one territorially based, linguistic-cultural cleavage had already been activated. The strategic question, therefore, was whether to attempt to *repress* or to *accommodate* this preexisting, politically activated diversity.

"State-nation" is a term that we introduce to help us think about democratic states that do not—and cannot—fit well into the classic French-style "nation-state" model based on a "we-feeling" resulting from an existing or forged homogeneity. For a summary of the difference between the "nation-state" and "state-nation" as opposing ideal types that shape policies, norms, and institutions for recognizing and accommodating diversity, see Table 5.3 below.

As a diverse polity approximates the state-nation ideal type, we expect it to have the following four empirically verifiable patterns: First, despite multiple cultural identities among its citizens, there will be a high degree of *positive identification* with the state and pride in being citizens of that state. Second, citizens will have *multiple but complementary* political identities and loyalties. Third, there will be a high degree of *institutional trust* in the most important constitutional, legal, and administrative components of the state. Fourth, by world standards, there will be a comparatively high degree of positive support for democracy among all the diverse groups of citizens in the country, and this will include support for the specific statewide democratic institutions through which the polity is governed.

To be sure, these patterns do not simply exist right from the beginning. It all depends on crafting and is very much an outcome of deliberate policies and designs. We turn now to the question of how such "state-nation" behavior and values can be crafted and supported.

State-Nation Policies

On both theoretical and empirical grounds, we contend that there can be a nested set of policy and institutional choices which reinforce each other and help to facilitate the emergence and persistence of a state-nation. This set includes:

1. An asymmetrical, "holding-together" federal state, but *not* a symmetrical, "coming-together" federal state or a unitary state;
2. Both individual rights *and* collective recognition;
3. Parliamentary *instead of* presidential or semi-presidential government;
4. Polity-wide *and* "centric-regional" parties and careers;
5. Politically integrated but *not* culturally assimilated populations;
6. Cultural nationalists in power mobilizing *against* secessionist nationalists;
7. A pattern of multiple *but* complementary identities.

We describe these policies as "nested" because each one tends to depend for its success on the adoption of the ones preceding it. Thus the second policy, "group recognition," is normally nested within the first, federalism (especially asymmetrical federalism). The fourth policy, which has to do with having the kinds of parties and politicians who are ready to form coalitions, is greatly facilitated if the choice of the third policy is parliamentarism because under that form of government the executive is a "shareable good." And the success of the seventh policy, multiple but complementary identities, relies heavily on the prior success of the previous six.

Each of the recommended choices requires some explanation. To begin with, a federal as opposed to a unitary state is appropriate for a state-nation because federal structures will allow a large and territorially concentrated cultural group with serious nationalist aspirations to attain self-governance within that territory. But why do these federal arrangements need to be asymmetrical? In a symmetrical federal system, all units have identical rights and obligations. It is possible, however, that some culturally distinct and territorially concentrated groups might have acquired prerogatives that they wish to retain or reacquire. It is also possible, for example, that some tribal groups controlling large territories (such as the Mizos in India's northeast) would agree to join the federation only if some of their unique land-use laws were respected. Bargains and compromises on these issues, which might be necessary for peace and voluntary membership in the political community, are negotiable in an asymmetrical system, but are normally unacceptable in a symmetrical system.

Second, why does a state-nation need both individual rights and collective recognition? A polity cannot be democratic unless throughout its whole extent the rights of individuals are constitutionally inviolable and protected by the state. This necessary function of central government cannot be devolved. But certain territorially concentrated cultural groups, even nations, may need some collective recognition for rights that go beyond classic liberal rights (or what Michael Walzer calls "Liberalism 2") in order for members of those groups to be able to thrive culturally or even possibly to exercise fully their classic individual liberal rights.[5] Walzer argues that Liberalism 2 "allows for a state committed to the survival and flourishing of . . . a (limited) set of nations, cultures and religions—so long as the basic rights of citizens who have different commitments or no such commitments are protected."[6] There may well be concrete moments in the crafting of a democracy when individuals cannot develop and exercise their full rights until they are active members of a group that struggles and wins some collective goods common to most members of the group. These group rights might be most easily accommodated by a federal system that is asymmetrical. For example, if a large territorially concentrated group speaks a distinct language, some official recognition of the privileged right of that language to be used in government institutions, schools, and the media might be necessary to enable the members of this group to act upon their own individual rights.

If there are territorially concentrated minority religions in the polity, the identification of their practitioners with the center may well be reduced if there is only one established religion throughout the territory. In such cases, identity with the state-nation may be encouraged if, instead, all religions are officially recognized and possibly even financially supported. The financial support of religions, majority and minority, is of course a violation of classic U.S. or French doctrines of separation of church and state, but it is not a violation of any person's individual human rights.[7]

Third, why the need for parliamentarism? In a presidential or semipresidential system, the highest executive office is an "indivisible good"—it can only be held by one person, from one nationality, for a fixed term. A parliamentary system, by contrast, creates the possibility of a "shareable good." That is, there is a possibility that other parties, composed of other nationalities, could help to constitute the ruling coalition. If no single party has a majority, parliamentarism is coalition-requiring. Also, because the government may collapse unless it constantly bargains to retain the support of its coalition partners, parliamentarism often displays coalition-sustaining qualities as well. These "shareable" and "coalition-friendly" aspects of a parliamentary executive might be useful in a robustly multinational society.

If almost all parties draw the vast bulk of their votes from their own respective ethnoterritorial units, the sense of trust in and identification with the center will probably be low. Many analysts would call such parties "regional-secessionist." Yet if there are major polity-wide parties that regularly need allies from regional parties to help form a government at the center, and if the polity-wide parties often help their regional-party allies to form a majority in their own ethnofederal units, then the logic of incentives makes these allegedly "regional-secessionist" parties actually "centric-regional" parties, because they regularly share in rule at the center. This coalitional pattern is possible only if both the polity-wide and the regional parties are "nested" in a system that is both federal and parliamentary.

The importance of "polity-wide careers" can be grasped by considering India as an example. There, English serves as an all-India *lingua franca* that makes it possible for educated members of regional groups who do not speak the majority language (Hindi) to pursue careers in law, communications, business, and the federal civil service. Citizens whose careers are "polity-wide" rather than regional will likely feel strong incentives not to "exit" from the polity-wide networks that such careers open up for them, and upon which their careers in turn depend.[8]

Fifth, it is important that political integration be able to go forward independent of cultural integration. In a state-nation, many cultural and especially ethnonational groups will be educated and self-governing in their own language. They will thus probably never be fully culturally assimilated to the dominant culture in the polity. This is a reality of "state-nations." If the ethnofederal group sees the polity-wide state as having helped to put a "roof of rights" over its head, however, and if the "centric-regional" parties are "coalitionable" with polity-wide parties and regularly help to form the government at the center, and if many individuals from the ethnofederal group enjoy polity-wide careers, then it is a good bet that the ethnofederal group and its members will be politically well-integrated into the state-nation.

Sixth, what do we mean by saying that cultural nationalists in power will mobilize against nationalists who embrace secession? Ernest Gellner forcefully articulated the position of many theorists of the nation-state when he famously asserted: "Nationalism is primarily a political principle, which holds that the political and the national unit should be congruent . . . Nationalist *sentiment* is the feeling of anger aroused by the violation of the principle . . . A nationalist *movement* is one actuated by a sentiment of this kind."[9]

Thus, we are constantly admonished not to advocate state-nation policies because all nationalism inevitably becomes "secessionist nationalism,"

with eventual demands for independence. Yet there can be a situation in which a "cultural nationalist" movement, nested within an asymmetrically federal and parliamentary system, wins democratic political control of a federal territorial unit; educates the citizens of this territory in the language, culture, and history of their own nation; and also stands ready to join coalitions at the center. If such a cultural nationalist group in power is challenged by secessionist nationalists who use force or threaten its use to pursue independence, the ruling nationalist group faces the loss of treasured resources. Under such circumstances, the "cultural nationalists" will likely mobilize the political and security resources under their control to defeat the "secessionist nationalists."[10]

Finally, what do we mean by talking about multiple but complementary identities? In the polity-wide system produced by the six nested policies and norms that we have just discussed, it is possible that citizens could strongly identify with and be loyal to *both* their culturally powerful ethnofederal unit *and* the polity-wide center. They would have these complementary identities because the center has recognized and defended many of their cultural demands and, in addition, has helped to structure and protect their full participation in the larger political life of the country. Such citizens are also likely to have strong trust in the center because they see it (or the institutions historically associated with it) as having helped to deliver some valued collective goods such as independence from a colonial power, security from threatening neighbors, or possibly even a large and growing common market. Thus the pattern of multiple but complementary identities that is likely to obtain is no accident, but an outcome earned by deliberately crafted policies.

The Case of India

India would seem to present one of the most difficult tests for our argument that multiple and complementary identities, as well as democratic state-nation loyalties, are possible even in a polity with robustly multinational dimensions and a plethora of intense linguistic and religious differences. Let us briefly document how extensive these diversities actually are.

One of the greatest points of conflict in multicultural and multinational polities, whether federal or not, is language. When India gained independence in 1947, it had in addition to its most widely spoken single language (Hindi), ten additional languages that were used by at least 13 million people each. Many had their own unique scripts.[11] Added to this linguistic complexity was an enormous diversity of religious beliefs and practices that alone would make the country a case of special interest to students of comparative democratization. India has large communities of almost every world religion, including Hinduism, Buddhism, Sikhism, Christianity, and Islam. In 2009, India's Muslim minority amounted to about 161 million people, the world's third-largest Islamic population, exceeded only by those of Indonesia and Pakistan.[12] At a time when too many scholars and political activists see Islam as being in deep cultural conflict with democracy, it is worth pausing to reflect that the world's largest Islamic community with extensive democratic experience is in multicultural, multinational, federal, and consociational India.

India's longstanding democracy enhances the "scope value" of the state-nation concept by showing that the model can be applied not only to rich but also to very poor countries. Of the world's four longstanding multinational federal democracies— Belgium, Canada, and Spain are the others—only India lacks an advanced industrial economy. To put it in rough terms, in 2008 Belgium, Canada, and Spain all had purchasing-power parity (PPP) per capita Gross National Income of more than US$30,000 per year. The comparable figure for India was a bit less than a tenth of that.[13] Given its extraordinarily deep diversity, India could never have created a French-style democratic nation-state. But it has managed to craft a democratic state-nation, supported by all religions, all socioeconomic groups, and many states that once experienced secessionist movements. In our forthcoming book, we devote the better part of three chapters to showing how Indians imagined, negotiated, and crafted their longstanding democratic state-nation. What follows here is an abbreviated discussion of three key paths followed by India's emerging democratic communities; their long and creative political, ethical, and constitutional search for policy formulas more appropriate than the classical nation-state model for reconciling deep diversity and democracy; their choice of asymmetrical federalism to help them solve the problem of self-governance in the context of many languages and the special needs of tribal populations; and their creation of a new model of secularism as a way of accommodating India's religious heterogeneity and its great intensity of religious practice.

The building of a state-nation in India was no accident or afterthought. The state-nation model was implicit in the idea of India forged by modern Indian political thinkers, nurtured by the freedom movement, enshrined in the Indian Constitution, sustained by the first generation of postindependence leadership, and institutionalized in competitive politics. In that sense, our "state-nation" model is best seen not only as a new analytic ideal type, but also as a theoretical defense of what political thinkers and practitioners in India knew for more than a century. Here we can only illustrate this with reference to an early episode in India's long and creative search for institutional designs more appropriate than the classical nation-state model for reconciling deep diversity with democracy.

By the mid-1920s, more than two decades before independence, the Indian National Congress (INC) had already begun to look in detail at the question of which political institutions and practices would best serve a self-governing India. The INC rejected the British-drafted Simon Commission Report, and appointed its own committee under the leadership of Motilal Nehru, the father of Jawaharlal Nehru, to outline a constitution for a free India. The Nehru Report, approved by the All Parties Conference in Lucknow in 1928, foreshadowed many provisions of the Indian Constitution of 1950. The definition of citizenship in the Nehru Report was very state-nation–friendly in that it was absolutely inclusive and territorial: "The word 'citizen,' wherever it occurs in this constitution, means every person who was born, or whose father was either born or naturalized, within the territorial limits of the commonwealth" (Article 3). The Nehru Report also laid down that independent India would have parliamentary government (Article 5) and a bicameral, federal system (Articles 8 and 9). All this was incorporated into the Indian Constitution. As we argued above, a parliamentary federal system is the most supportive combination for the emergence of "centric-regional" parties that may be a useful alternative to "exit" for parties with different linguistic majorities.

The radical "state-nation" reconfiguration of India that allowed each large linguistic community to have a state of its own and to govern itself in its local majority language did not fully occur until 1957; however, it was strongly supported at the 1921 INC meeting in Madras and endorsed in the Nehru Report, which held that "the redistribution of provinces should take place on a linguistic basis on the demand of the majority of the population of the area concerned" (Article 86). This formula allowed independent India to respond democratically to the presence within its borders of numerous territorially based linguistic majorities. (At present, 22 languages enjoy "official" constitutional status.) This is a classic feature of the state-nation style of "holding-together" federalism, and by that token unthinkable in a U.S.-style "coming-together" federation. Also supportive of a relatively strong "holding-together" federalism (and again, quite unlike U.S. practice) was the Nehru Committee provision (Article 49) that gave the Supreme Court of the Union "original jurisdiction" in almost all matters. The choice of asymmetrical federalism also allowed for the creation of some small states with tribal majorities, like Mizoram, to preserve tribal cultures by means of special, constitutionally embedded prerogatives that allowed only Mizos to vote in local elections or to buy land. These prerogatives were crucial to

the 1986 Mizo Accord that not only helped to end a secessionist war but contributed as well to the building of the "multiple and complementary" identities that our surveys reveal.

On the all-important question of religion, the Nehru Report was also supportive of state-nation policies. Under the section on "Fundamental Rights," it clearly rules out an established religion and supported a religiously impartial state, but unlike the U.S. Constitution, it also implied the admissibility of state aid for religious educational establishments (Article 4). The Indian Constitution duly reflected this spirit. The relationship between religion and the state that the Indian Constituent Assembly crafted later was a highly original creation with strong affinities to our state-nation model. All religious communities were recognized and respected by the state. All religious communities, for example, could run schools, organizations, and charities eligible for state financial support. The norms and practices of this model are now so pervasive that even when the Bharatiya Janata Party (BJP), the party of Hindu nationalism, headed the government coalition, it did not dare break with the tradition of paying extensive state subsidies to help Muslim citizens make the *hajj* (pilgrimage) to Mecca. Every single nation-state in Western Europe has some paid compulsory public holidays for the majority Christian religion (Sweden, Denmark, Norway, and Germany alone have 39) but none of them has a single compulsory public holiday for a non-Christian minority religion. India has five such holidays for the majority Hindu religion, but ten for minority religions, including five for Islam.[14]

Thus, when the Constituent Assembly formally set about its tasks in 1946, there was little doubt that it would adopt provisions for the protection of linguistic, cultural, and religious diversity. The institutional structures and norms that the Constituent Assembly agreed upon facilitated a broad set of policies conducive to the crafting of a robust state-nation on the Indian subcontinent.

India's Experience: Examining the Evidence

Was the "idea of India" described above confined merely to the high traditions of political theory and legal constitutional texts? Or did this idea find resonance among ordinary Indian citizens across different religions, regions, communities, and classes? Fortunately, we can begin to answer this question about ordinary citizens' attitudes because India has been included in all four rounds of the World Values Survey. In addition, the Centre for the Study of Developing Societies (CSDS) in Delhi regularly carries out some of the world's largest social-scientific surveys of political opinions and attitudes. The latest such survey, the National Election Study of 2009, had a nationwide sample of 36,169 people.[15]

In our book, we present in detail and in comparative perspective the Indian evidence on diversity and democracy as seen in the mirror of public opinion. In particular, we look at the four empirical attributes mentioned above that we expect from a successful state-nation: the degree of *positive identification* with the state and pride in being its citizens; the existence of *multiple but complementary* political identities and loyalties; the degree of *institutional trust* in the most important constitutional, legal, and administrative components of the state; and the degree of positive *support for democracy and for polity-wide democratic institutions* among all the diverse groups of citizens in the country.

We do not shy away from many of the continuing problems of India's development that can and must be better addressed: Nearly half of India's women are illiterate, and half its children are underweight; a quarter or more of the population lives below the official "poverty line," with this proportion being higher among Muslims. We analyze human-rights violations and the still unresolved secessionist conflicts in Kashmir and Nagaland. We discuss the lethal Hindu-nationalist program that swept the state of Gujarat in 2002, and we consider the Naxalite movement. Notwithstanding these failures on the developmental and human-rights fronts, the evidence regarding the four measures of state-nation success is highly impressive indeed. A large majority of citizens, despite their great linguistic, religious, and cultural diversity, positively identify with and trust the Indian central state while supporting India's democracy.

For example, let us compare the level of national pride in India with the attitudes of the citizens of the other ten longstanding federal democracies (Argentina, Australia, Austria, Belgium, Brazil, Canada, Germany, Spain, Switzerland, and the United States). The World Values Survey routinely asks citizens whether they feel "great," "some," "little," or "no" pride in being a member of their country. In 2002, 67 percent of Indians expressed "great pride," a figure exceeded only in the United States (71 percent) and Australia (70 percent). Another important state-nation indicator is whether citizens, despite a possible strong sense of identification with an ethnic, linguistic, or cultural minority unit of the federation, nonetheless still trust the central government. Only Switzerland recorded a higher level of trust in the central government (50 percent) than did India (48 percent). It is crucial in a multinational, multilingual, multicultural polity that citizens trust the overall legal system; the three countries in our set of eleven whose citizens were most prone to express trust in the legal system were India (67 percent), Switzerland (65 percent), and Austria (58 percent).[16]

A Few Questions

A classic and frequently used battery of questions concerning democracy asks respondents which of the following three statements is closest to their own opinion: 1) "Democracy is preferable to any other kind of government"; 2) "Under some circumstances, an authoritarian government can be preferable to a democratic one"; or 3) "For people like me, it does not matter whether we have a democratic or a nondemocratic regime." If a respondent opts for the second or third statement, it is coded as an explicitly authoritarianism-accepting response. The percentage of respondents who gave such a response in India (12) is far lower than the comparable figure from five other countries that feature prominently in the democratization literature: Brazil (47), Chile (46), South Korea (38), Uruguay (18), and Spain (17).[17] Using the National Election Study of 2004, which had more than three-thousand Muslim respondents, we were able to evaluate how similar or dissimilar Muslims were from Hindus in this respect. The shares of Indian Muslims and Hindus who chose as their response "Democracy is preferable to any other kind of government" were virtually the same at 87 and 88 percent, respectively.[18]

Some political observers fear that growing religiosity among Hindus and Muslims alike will create new challenges for democracy in India. We tested this by creating a low-medium-high index of "the intensity of religious practice" that we could place alongside an index measuring "support for democracy." We found that for Hindus and Muslims alike, the greater the reported intensity of religious practice, the greater the professed support for democracy.[19] This evidence not only robustly disconfirms the proposition that religious intensity threatens Indian democracy, but also suggests that the Indian state-nation is currently holding its own even in the arena of the greatest contestation of our times, religion.

Let us now shift from surveys and attitudes to policies and outcomes. Let us specifically contrast how India, following state-nation policies, politically integrated its Tamil population in the south, and how nearby Sri Lanka, which pursued nation-state policies toward the Tamil population in its own northeast, barely avoided state disintegration and has just terminated by force a civil war in which approximately a hundred-thousand people were killed.

Sri Lanka provides a counterfactual example that we analyze at length in our book. The main point can be summarized here. India arguably started in a more difficult position in this nearly "matched pair" because the Indian Tamils were involved with the Dravidian movement, which briefly flirted with the idea of secession from India. Indeed, there had been a long series of conflicts between Brahmins and non-Brahmins in what is now the state of Tamil Nadu at India's southern tip. We can thus say that there was a robust multinational dimension to politics in Tamil Nadu, although many Tamils felt great attachment to the polity-wide independence movement led by the INC.[20]

In comparative terms, Sri Lanka actually started in an easier position vis-à-vis its Tamil minority. For a century before independence in 1948, there had been no politically significant riots between Sinhalese, who were largely Buddhists, and the Tamils, who were primarily Hindu. In fact, the first president of the Ceylon Congress Party was a Tamil. Tamils had done well in English-language civil-service exams in Ceylon, and though they were interested in greater power-sharing, it is still true to say that at independence there had been no Tamil demands for devolution or federalism, much less independence. Ceylon also had a much higher per capita income than India, and could have made modest side payments to some Sinhalese groups, especially the Buddhists, who had been marginalized during the period of British colonial rule.

Yet 35 years after independence, the potential issue of Tamil separatism in India had become a nonissue, while the Sri-Lankan nonissue had become a bloody civil war for secession that raged for a quarter of a century. What explains such sharply different outcomes?

Much of the explanation, we believe, is related to the radically differential application of the nested policies that we discussed earlier. Table 5.4 highlights the state-integrating state-nation policies followed by India and the state-disintegrating nation-state policies followed by Sri Lanka.

Extending the Argument

Let us conclude by touching upon three questions that we have not yet addressed. First, can some state-nation policies be of use in unitary states that are not nation-states? We believe that this is quite possible, for we can imagine geopolitical and domestic contexts where *neither* full state-nation policies *nor* full nation-state policies offer plausible ways to manage the multinational dimensions of a polity. Why?

There may be some geopolitical contexts, especially in a country bordering a powerful state that has some irredentist tendencies toward said country, in which asymmetrical federalism (or indeed any type of federalism) would present dangers for the nurturing of a new democratic political community via this classic state-nation policy. The safest solution might be a unitary state. At the same time, if the domestic context includes politically significant populations deeply divided over cultural policies (for example, large territorially concentrated parts of the state where most of the populace hews to a distinct language and culture), it would be democratically dangerous and politically implausible to try to impose such classic nation-state policies as a single language. Trouble, even violence, would be the likely result.

If such a combination of geopolitical and domestic factors exists, classic state-nation federal policies will not work. Yet some elements of state-nation policies nonetheless seem a must. But is it possible to follow state-nation policies in a unitary state? We believe that some such policies can be employed. In the hypothetical example above, a key state-nation policy that might be appropriate would be to allow the different cultural or linguistic zones to use their own respective languages at the start of the democratization process.

In our book we analyze the case of Ukraine, which upon its independence from the USSR in 1991 found itself a multinational society, but not a robustly multinational polity. If it had pursued aggressive nation-state policies, such as legally permitting only the Ukrainian language to be used in schools or communications with public officials, Russophones in eastern Ukraine who self-identified as Russians—and especially some of their political leaders—would most likely have become secession-ists (much as the Tamils had in Sri Lanka). Some Russians in the east and Crimea could well have requested, and received, Russian military backing for their breakaway efforts.

A second question asks if a democratic, unitary nation-state can use constitutionally embedded federal guarantees in order to respond to the presence of a territorially concentrated minority that has radical cultural differences with the majority population. We propose a revised theory of *federacy* to tackle this situation. Our new ideal-type definition of a federacy holds it to be a political-administrative unit in an independent unitary state with exclusive power (including some legislative power) in certain areas that is constitutionally or quasi-constitutionally embedded and cannot be changed unilaterally, but whose inhabitants have full citizenship rights in the otherwise unitary state.

In the penultimate chapter of our forthcoming book, we examine how this formula has actually been applied to the democratic management of robustly multinational problems by the otherwise unitary nation-states of Finland (in the case of the Åland Islands) and Denmark (in the cases of both Greenland and the Faroe Islands). We also show that the "scope value" of these kinds of arrangements has extended to the postwar reconstruction of Italy with regard to the once-separatist South Tyrol region (with an 86 percent German-speaking population), as well as to the revolutionary context of 1975 Portugal and its efforts to deal with an emerging secessionist movement in the Azores. The federacy formula also proved useful in negotiating the August 2005 Helsinki Agreement that brought a relatively consensual, peaceful, and inclusionary end to the civil war in Aceh in Indonesia. We also argue that if China ever were to become democratic, a federacy formula could conceivably be of use with regard to Tibet, Hong Kong, and possibly even Taiwan.

Finally, why have we had so little to say about the still-influential federal model presented by the United States? The founders of the United States did not see that country as a multinational

Table 5.4 Contrasting Strategies of India and Sri Lanka Toward Their Respective Tamil Minorities

Policy	India	Sri Lanka
1. An Asymmetrically Federal, but not a Unitary or Symmetrically Federal State	The constituent assembly creates an asymmetrical federal system that enables state boundaries to be redrawn and eventually allows regional cultural majorities to rule these states in their own languages. A Tamil-speaking state called Tamil Nadu is carved out of Madras State.	No constituent assembly is held, but the parliament approves a constitution that declares Sri Lanka a unitary state. After 1956, the Sinhalese-Buddhist majority increasingly advances majoritarian state policies. No significant devolutionary policies are ever implemented.
2. Individual Rights and Collective Recognition	Language: In 1965, after intense mobilizations and political negotiations, plans for implementing Hindi as the official language of the Indian Union are abandoned. Tamil becomes the domain of a "three-language" formula. Tamil becomes the official language of Tamil Nadu, and the state is not obliged to use Hindi in its communications with the Union. / Religion: All major religions are constitutionally recognized, and minority institutions are eligible for state funds.	Language: In 1956, Sinhalese is made the only official language and English and Tamil are no longer accepted. / Religion: Article 9 of the 1978 Constitution assigns Buddhism "the foremost place" among religions. State subsidies favor Buddhists.
3. Parliamentary instead of Semipresidential or Presidential Systems	Parliamentarism makes the executive a "shareable good," which allows regional, even potentially secessionist, parties to help form ruling coalitions at the center. Since the late 1970s, the ruling coalition at the center has included one of the Dravidian parties from Tamil Nadu.	In 1978, Sri Lanka creates a semipresidential system in which the president has more powers than in France. From then until now, no northern-based Tamil party joins any coalition at the center.
4. Polity-Wide and "Centric-Regional" Parties (and Careers)	Tamil-centric regional parties, due to their great coalitional ability with polity-wide parties, enjoy substantial presence in the Indian parliament and a disproportionate share of powerful ministries. After the mid-1970s, no significant "regional-separatist" parties exist, and all Tamil parties become "centric regional."	Tamils, especially after 1956, lose virtually all their coalitional ability in polity-wide politics and government formation. No elected Tamil from the north becomes a federal minister after 1957. After the mid-1970s, no major "centric-regional" Tamil parties exist, and all subsequent major Tamil parties are "regional separatist."
5. Politically Integrated but not Culturally Assimilated Minorities	Tamils integrate politically into the Indian polity but maintain strong pride in Tamil culture. Different governments in Tamil Nadu aggressively take up the promotion of Tamil language and culture, including in state schools and educational curricula.	In 1948, "Indian Tamils" are disenfranchised. In 1983, all members of pro-autonomist Tamil parties must leave parliament. By the mid-1980s, Sri Lanka is "politically multinational" with Tamil guerrilla leaders beyond hope of integration.
6. Cultural Nationalists vs. Territorial Nationalists	Cultural nationalists achieve many of their goals. Territorial nationalists, advocating separatist goals, virtually disappear.	By the late 1970s, violent nationalist guerrillas with explicitly separatist goals become the leaders of the Tamil community in the northeast.
7. Earned Pattern of Complementary and Multiple Identities	Strong Tamil identities remain, but polity-wide Indian identity grows. Trust in the central government is higher in the state of Tamil Nadu than it is in the rest of the country.	Marginalized in electoral politics, and facing growing state discrimination and repression, Tamils in the northeast opt for conflict. The ensuing civil war kills 100,000 (most of them Tamils) before ending with the Tamils' defeat in 2009.

polity, and crafted a constitution for what they saw as an emerging nation-state. Indeed, they constitutionally embedded features that make the U.S. model particularly ill-suited to the flexible policy management of robustly multinational societies. Symmetrical U.S.-style federalism would be of no help in managing small, territorially concentrated religious or linguistic minorities such as those found in the Indian state of Mizoram. And U.S.-style presidentialism lacks the coalition-facilitating qualities of parliamentarism, which have often been crucial, as in Tamil Nadu, in helping to promote the evolution of regional-separatist parties into "centric-regional" parties that can join polity-wide coalitions.

Symmetrical federalism and presidentialism have been enormously successful in maintaining stable democratic rule in the United States, a country that, although composed of immigrants from many lands, is not robustly multinational: For all its diversity, the United States does not contain territorially based, politically significant groups mobilizing nationalist demands for independence. But many of the world's democracies are unavoidably confronted with the task of governing robustly multinational societies, and these countries have much more to learn from the experience of India than from that of the United States.

NOTES

1. See the classic account of these policies in Eugen Weber, *Peasants into Frenchmen: The Modernization of Rural France, 1870–1914* (Stanford: Stanford University Press, 1976). Most nineteenth-century progressives and democrats, particularly those associated with the French Revolution, were profoundly opposed to federalism.
2. See the chapter titled "Stateness, Nationalism, and Democratization," in Juan J. Linz and Alfred Stepan, *Problems of Democratic Transition and Consolidation: Southern Europe, South America, and Post-Communist Europe* (Baltimore: Johns Hopkins University Press, 1996), 34, as well as Figure 2.1.
3. We accept Robert A. Dahl's definition of federalism as "a system in which some matters are exclusively *within* the competence of certain local units— cantons, states, provinces—and are constitutionally *beyond* the scope of the authority of the national government; and where certain other matters are constitutionally outside the scope of the authority of the smaller units." Robert A. Dahl, "Federalism and the Democratic Process," in *Democracy, Liberty, and Equality* (Oslo: Norwegian University Press, 1986), 114.
4. For more details on "asymmetrical" and "holding-together" federalism, see Alfred Stepan, "Federalism and Democracy: Beyond the U.S. Model," *Journal of Democracy* 10 (October 1999): 19–34.
5. See Charles Taylor, "The Politics of Recognition," in Amy Gutmann, ed., *Multiculturalism: Examining the Politics of Recognition* (Princeton: Princeton University Press, 1994).
6. The quote from Michael Walzer is from Gutmann, *Multiculturalism*, 99.
7. See Alfred Stepan, "The World's Religious Systems and Democracy: Crafting the 'Twin Tolerations'" in his *Arguing Comparative Politics* (Oxford: Oxford University Press, 2001), 213–54.
8. However, the systematic effort by an ethnocultural group to monopolize access to careers, even in their own ethnofederal unit, runs counter to the nurturing and preservation of a state-nation.
9. All quotes are from the influential opening paragraphs of Ernest Gellner's *Nations and Nationalism* (Ithaca: Cornell University Press, 1983), 1. Emphasis in the original.
10. At the same time, a convergence between cultural and secessionist nationalists on some issues cannot be ruled out if the secessionists come into conflict with the central state over the use of force.
11. For an analytic discussion of these figures, see Jyotirindra Das Gupta, *Language Conflict and National Development: Group Politics and National Language Policy in India* (Berkeley: University of California Press, 1970), 31–68.

12. Pew Forum on Religion in Public Life, "Mapping the Global Muslim Population: A Report on the Size and Distribution of the World's Muslim Population," 7 October 2009, 14. Available at *http://pewforum.org/docs/?DocID=450*.

13. See the World Bank's World Development Indicators Database.

14. For the Indian model in comparative perspective and the question of paid holidays, see Alfred Stepan, "Multiple Secularisms of Modern Democratic and Non-Democratic Regimes," in Craig Calhoun and Mark Juergensmeyer, eds., *Rethinking Secularism* (New York: Oxford University Press, 2010).

15. Survey archives at the CSDS go back to 1965. Yogendra Yadav, one of the authors, has been involved with directing, designing, and analyzing these surveys, including the National Election Study series. Since 2003, the other two authors have worked with the CSDS team to design some questions for the surveys. For an overview of the CSDS tradition of survey research, see Lokniti Team, "National Election Study 2004: An Introduction," *Economic and Political Weekly*, 18 December 2004, 5373–82.

16. All the data for these 11 longstanding federal democracies come from various rounds of the World Values Survey coordinated by Ronald Inglehart and his colleagues at the Inter-University Consortium for Political and Social Research, University of Michigan.

17. Data on Latin America come from the 2008 Latinobarómetro, on Spain from the 1992 Eurobarometer, on Korea from the 2004 Korea Democracy Barometer, and on India from the previously cited 2004 National Election Study.

18. According to a Pearson's chi-square test, the findings for all religious communities are statistically significant (p-value < .001). Thus, the probability of this occurring by chance is less than one in a thousand.

19. Full methodological details will appear in the forthcoming book from which the present essay is adapted. Our regression indicates that a one-unit increase in the index of religiosity (controlling for other factors) predicts approximately a 3.5 percent increase in the probability of support for democracy.

20. For excellent discussions of some secessionist tendencies in what is now Tamil Nadu, see Narendra Subramanian, *Ethnicity and Populist Mobilization: Political Parties, Citizens and Democracy in South India* (Oxford: Oxford University Press, 1999).

6 NONDEMOCRATIC REGIMES

When we think about different kinds of regimes around the world, we tend to think only in terms of democracy or authoritarianism. In democratic societies, authoritarianism is often viewed almost as a temporary aberration until a subject people is able to throw off its fetters and join the free world. Thus, it might seem less important to understand the complexities of authoritarianism than to concentrate on how countries make the transition from there to democracy. But authoritarianism is a much more diverse and entrenched form of politics. Remember that democracy is the newcomer to political life, having been established relatively recently in human history.

Juan J. Linz and Alfred Stepan's chapter on nondemocratic regimes is in many ways a culmination of research these two scholars have been conducting since the 1960s. For them, to understand how countries become democratic, it is important to understand the regime type that precedes democracy. Linz and Stepan lay out a comprehensive analysis of the difference between totalitarianism and authoritarianism and describe how each has an impact on the most basic facets of nondemocratic rule. Why does this matter? Linz and Stepan argue that the type of authoritarian or totalitarian regime strongly affects how and if democracy will replace it. The institutions of nondemocratic rule will shape the path to democracy in the future. This kind of analysis, sometimes called "path dependent," has grown in recent years in the study of comparative politics and is consistent with a greater focus on institutions as actors in their own right. Stepan and Linz, with Yogendra Yadav, also authored "The Rise of State-Nations," which we covered in Chapter 5. In that work they observe that their discussion of state-nations was first broached in this article, as they considered how the interaction of regime type and social institutions can shape the prospects for political change.

Stepan and Linz's work reflects much of the literature from the 1980s and 1990s, which has been described as belonging to a "transition paradigm." In other words, this scholarship emphasized paths of change from authoritarianism and the institutional or other factors that shape how those changes come about. By the last decade, however, political scientists grew more skeptical of their emphasis on this type of research, when many authoritarian regimes failed to give way or seemingly democratizing states became instead new, hybrid forms of nondemocratic rule. Accordingly, scholars turned their attention to these semidemocratic or illiberal systems as regimes in their own right rather than simply transitions to democracy that had not yet come to fruition. Levitsky and Way's "Rise of Competitive Authoritarianism" (2002) provides a succinct overview of the practices of hybrid regimes, which combine formal participatory mechanisms (such as elections) with institutions and policies designed to hinder challenges to power. This can include biased media coverage, harassment of opposition candidates, weak legislatures, and corrupt judiciaries. Competitive authoritarianism may be a more tenacious form of nondemocratic rule, given its ostensibly democratic mechanisms, meant to channel and divide opposition. However, the authors note the inherent tension in such a system, in which participatory mechanisms, even when largely powerless, create the spaces in which challenges to those in power may emerge. Finally, the argument regarding hybrid regimes also notes that democracies themselves can slowly erode into illiberalism, with participatory institutions losing power as that power is concentrated into the hands of an elite.

Many of the discussions noted above are rooted in experiences in Latin America, Eastern Europe, and the former Soviet Union. But of course, they have applications elsewhere. Larry Diamond's "Rule of Law Versus the Big Man" (2008) builds on many of the above ideas as they relate to Africa. There, many competitive authoritarian systems rely on particular highly centralized presidencies and clientelism—a patron-client relationship based on personal connections and benefits. Such a system generates a highly personal, corrupt, and largely unaccountable form of rule. In Africa, such a system is often dominated by a "big man," as such a leader is called, who solidifies his power with this network of patronage. Following Levitsky and Way, we might conclude that such regimes, though unstable, are not easily dislodged and simply transfer from one big man to another. However, Diamond is more optimistic, suggesting that in Africa civil society is a growing challenge to competitive authoritarianism. Moreover, he emphasizes that international actors can play an important role in bolstering society while holding authoritarian rulers accountable, a point also made by Levitsky and Way.

Whether international or domestic actors have leverage over those in power may depend in part on the economic resources the state is able to wield. In Weinthal and Luong's "Combatting the Resource Curse," the authors explain the paradox that a country rich in resources can wind up both undemocratic and poor. It is commonly argued that democracy emerges when those who rule are compelled to share their power with a rising middle class. The state exchanges political power (representation) for economic resources (taxes). But in countries where significant wealth lies in the ground, the equation changes. Those in power can rely on oil or mineral wealth to support themselves and buy off or suppress the public. Natural-resource wealth also tends to crowd out private business, leading to a smaller middle class less able to demand greater participation. Here again, the international community can play a role in helping to move natural resources out of state hands. But this is only part of the solution, and a challenging part at that.

Juan J. Linz And Alfred Stepan
MODERN NONDEMOCRATIC REGIMES

Democratic transition and consolidation involve the movement from a nondemocratic to a democratic regime. However, specific polities may vary immensely in the *paths* available for transition and the unfinished *tasks* the new democracy must face before it is consolidated. Our central endeavor in the next two chapters is to show how and why much—though of course not all—of such variation can be explained by prior regime type.

For over a quarter of a century the dominant conceptual framework among analysts interested in classifying the different political systems in the world has been the tripartite distinction between democratic, authoritarian, and totalitarian regimes. New paradigms emerge because they help analysts see commonalities and implications they had previously overlooked. When Juan Linz wrote his 1964 article "An Authoritarian Regime: Spain," he wanted to call attention to the fact that between what then were seen as the two major stable political poles—the democratic pole and the totalitarian pole—there existed a form of polity that had its own internal logic and was a steady regime type. Though this type was nondemocratic, Linz argued that it was fundamentally different from a totalitarian regime on four key dimensions—pluralism, ideology, leadership, and mobilization. This was of course what he termed an *authoritarian regime*. He defined them as: "political systems with limited, not responsible, political pluralism, without elaborate and guiding ideology, but with distinctive mentalities, without extensive nor intensive political mobilization, except at some points in their development, and in which a leader or occasionally a small group exercises power

From *Problems of Democratic Transition and Consolidation: Southern Europe, South America, and Post-Communist Europe* (Baltimore: Johns Hopkins University Press, 1996), pp. 38–54. Some of the authors' notes have been omitted.

within formally ill-defined limits but actually quite predictable ones."[1]

In the 1960s, as analysts attempted to construct categories with which to compare and contrast all the systems in the world, the authoritarian category proved useful. As the new paradigm took hold among comparativists, two somewhat surprising conclusions emerged. First, it became increasingly apparent that more regimes were "authoritarian" than were "totalitarian" or "democratic" combined. Authoritarian regimes were thus the modal category of regime type in the modern world. Second, authoritarian regimes were not necessarily in transition to a different type of regime. As Linz's studies of Spain in the 1950s and early 1960s showed, the four distinctive dimensions of an authoritarian regime—limited pluralism, mentality, somewhat constrained leadership, and weak mobilization—could cohere for a long period as a reinforcing and integrated system that was relatively stable.

Typologies rise or fall according to their analytic usefulness to researchers. In our judgment, the existing tripartite regime classification has not only become less useful to democratic theorists and practitioners than it once was, it has also become an obstacle. Part of the case for typology change proceeds from the implications of the empirical universe we need to analyze. Very roughly, if we were looking at the world of the mid-1980s, how many countries could conceivably be called "democracies" of ten years' duration? And how many countries were very close to the totalitarian pole for that entire period?

Answers have, of course, an inherently subjective dimension, particularly as regards the evaluation of the evidence used to classify countries along the different criteria used in the typology. Fortunately, however, two independently organized studies attempt to measure most of the countries in the world as to their political rights and civil liberties. The criteria used in the studies are explicit, and there is a very high degree of agreement in the results. If we use these studies and the traditional tripartite regime type distinction, it turns out that more than 90 percent of modern nondemocratic regimes would have to share the same typological space—"authoritarian."[2] Obviously, with so many heterogenous countries sharing the same typological "starting place," this typology of regime type cannot tell us much about the extremely significant range of variation in possible transition paths and consolidation tasks that we believe in fact exists. Our purpose in the rest of this chapter is to reformulate the tripartite paradigm of regime type so as to make it more helpful in the analysis of *transition paths* and *consolidation tasks*. We propose therefore a revised typology, consisting of "democratic," "authoritarian," "totalitarian," "post-totalitarian," and "sultanistic" regimes.

Democracy

To start with the democratic type of regime, there are of course significant variations within democracy. However, we believe that such important categories as "consociational democracy" and "majoritarian democracy" are subtypes of democracy and not different regime types. Democracy as a regime type seems to us to be of sufficient value to be retained and not to need further elaboration at this point in the book.

Totalitarianism

We also believe that the concept of a totalitarian regime as an ideal type, with some close historical approximations, has enduring value. If a regime has eliminated almost all pre-existing political, economic, and social pluralism, has a unified, articulated, guiding, utopian ideology, has intensive and extensive mobilization, and has a

leadership that rules, often charismatically, with undefined limits and great unpredictability and vulnerability for elites and nonelites alike, then it seems to us that it still makes historical and conceptual sense to call this a regime with strong totalitarian tendencies.

If we accept the continued conceptual utility of the democratic and totalitarian regime types, the area in which further typological revision is needed concerns the regimes that are clearly neither democratic nor totalitarian. By the early 1980s, the number of countries that were clearly totalitarian or were attempting to create such regimes had in fact been declining for some time. As many Soviet-type regimes began to change after Stalin's death in 1953, they no longer conformed to the totalitarian model, as research showed. This change created conceptual confusion. Some scholars argued that the totalitarian category itself was wrong. Others wanted to call post-Stalinist regimes authoritarian. Neither of these approaches seems to us fully satisfactory. Empirically, of course, most of the Soviet-type systems in the 1980s were not totalitarian. However, the "Soviet type" regimes, with the exception of Poland * * *, could not be understood in their distinctiveness by including them in the category of an authoritarian regime.

The literature on Soviet-type regimes correctly drew attention to regime characteristics that were no longer totalitarian and opened up promising new studies of policy-making. One of these perspectives was "institutional pluralism." However, in our judgment, to call these post-Stalinist polities *pluralistic* missed some extremely important features that could hardly be called pluralistic. Pluralist democratic theory, especially the "group theory" variant explored by such writers as Arthur Bentley and David Truman, starts with *individuals in civil society* who enter into numerous freely formed interest groups that are relatively autonomous and often criss-crossing. The many groups in civil society attempt to aggregate their interests and compete against each other in political society to influence state policies. However, the "institutional pluralism" that some writers discerned in the Soviet Union was radically different, in that almost all the pluralistic conflict occurred in *regime-created organizations within the party-state* itself. Conceptually, therefore, this form of competition and conflict is actually closer to what political theorists call *bureaucratic politics* than it is to *pluralistic politics*.

Rather than forcing these Soviet-type regimes into the existing typology of totalitarian, authoritarian, and democratic regimes, we believe we should expand that typology by explicating a distinctive regime type that we will call *post-totalitarian*.[3] Methodologically, we believe this category is justified because on each of the four dimensions of regime type—pluralism, ideology, leadership, and mobilization—there can be a post-totalitarian ideal type that is different from a totalitarian, authoritarian, or democratic ideal type. Later in this chapter we will also rearticulate the argument for considering sultanism as a separate ideal-type regime.

To state our argument in bold terms, we first present a schematic presentation of how the five ideal-type regimes we propose—democratic, totalitarian, post-totalitarian, authoritarian, and sultanistic—differ from each other on each one of the four constituent characteristics of regime type (Table 6.1). In the following chapter we make explicit what we believe are the implications of each regime type for democratic transition paths and the tasks of democratic consolidation.

Post-Totalitarianism

Our task here is to explore how, on each of the four dimensions of regime type, post-totalitarianism is different from totalitarianism, as well as different from authoritarianism. Where appropriate we will also call attention to some under-theorized characteristics of both totalitarian and post-totalitarian regimes that produce dynamic pressures for out-of-

type change. We do not subscribe to the view that either type is static.

Post-totalitarianism, as Table 6.1 implies, can encompass a continuum varying from "early post-totalitarianism," to "frozen post-totalitarianism," to "mature post-totalitarianism." Early post-totalitarianism is very close to the totalitarian ideal type but differs from it on at least one key dimension, normally some constraints on the leader. There can be frozen post-totalitarianism in which, despite the persistent tolerance of some civil society critics of the regime, almost all the other control mechanisms of the party-state stay in place for a long period and do not evolve (e.g., Czechoslovakia, from 1977 to 1989). Or there can be mature post-totalitarianism in which there has been significant change in all the dimensions of the post-totalitarian regime except that politically the leading role of the official party is still sacrosanct (e.g., Hungary from 1982 to 1988, which eventually evolved by late 1988 very close to an out-of-type change).

Concerning *pluralism*, the defining characteristic of totalitarianism is that there is no political, economic, or social pluralism in the polity and that pre-existing sources of pluralism have been uprooted or systematically repressed. In an authoritarian regime there is some limited political pluralism and often quite extensive economic and social pluralism. In an authoritarian regime, many of the manifestations of the limited political pluralism and the more extensive social and economic pluralism predate the authoritarian regime. How does pluralism in post-totalitarian regimes contrast with the near absence of pluralism in totalitarian regimes and the limited pluralism of authoritarian regimes?

In mature post-totalitarianism, there is a much more important and complex play of institutional pluralism within the state than in totalitarianism. Also, in contrast to totalitarianism, post-totalitarianism normally has a much more significant degree of social pluralism, and in mature post-totalitarianism there is often discussion of a "second culture" or a "parallel culture." Evidence of this is found in such

Table 6.1 Major Modern Regime Ideal Types and Their Defining Characteristics

Characteristic	Democracy	Authoritarianism	Totalitarianism	Post-totalitarianism	Sultanism
Pluralism	Responsible political pluralism reinforced by extensive areas of pluralist autonomy in economy, society, and internal life of organizations. Legally protected pluralism consistent with "societal corporatism" but not "state corporatism."	Political system with limited, not responsible political pluralism. Often quite extensive social and economic pluralism. In authoritarian regimes most of pluralism had roots in society before the establishment of the regime. Often some space for semiopposition.	No significant economic, social, or political pluralism. Official party has *de jure* and *de facto* monopoly of power. Party has eliminated almost all pretotalitarian pluralism. No space for second economy or parallel society.	Limited, but not responsible social, economic, and institutional pluralism. Almost no political pluralism because party still formally has monopoly of power. May have "second economy," but state still the overwhelming presence. Most manifestations of pluralism in "flattened polity" grew out of tolerated state structures or dissident groups consciously formed in opposition to totalitarian regime. In mature post-totalitarianism opposition often creates "second culture" or "parallel society."	Economic and social pluralism does not disappear but is subject to unpredictable and despotic intervention. No group or individual in civil society, political society, or the state is free from sultan's exercise of despotic power. No rule of law. Low institutionalization. High fusion of private and public.
Ideology	Extensive intellectual commitment to citizenship and procedural rules of contestation. Not teleological. Respect for rights of minorities, state of law, and value of individualism.	Political system without elaborate and guiding ideology but with distinctive mentalities.	Elaborate and guiding ideology that articulates a reachable utopia. Leaders, individuals, and groups derive most of their sense of mission, legitimation, and often specific policies from their commitment to some holistic conception of humanity and society.	Guiding ideology still officially exists and is part of the social reality. But weakened commitment to or faith in utopia. Shift of emphasis from ideology to programmatic consensus that presumably is based on rational decision-making and limited debate without too much reference to ideology.	Highly arbitrary manipulation of symbols. Extreme glorification of ruler. No elaborate or guiding ideology or even distinctive mentalities outside of despotic personalism. No attempt to justify major initiatives on the basis of ideology. Pseudo-ideology not believed by staff, subjects, or outside world.
Mobilization	Participation via autonomously generated organization of civil society and competing parties of political society guaranteed by a system of law. Value is on low regime mobilization but high citizen participation. Diffuse effort by regime to induce good citizenship and patriotism. Toleration of peaceful and orderly opposition.	Political system without extensive or intensive political mobilization except at some points in their development.	Extensive mobilization into a vast array of regime-created obligatory organizations. Emphasis on activism of cadres and militants. Effort at mobilization of enthusiasm. Private life is decried.	Progressive loss of interest by leaders and nonleaders involved in organizing mobilization. Routine mobilization of population within state-sponsored organizations to achieve a minimum degree of conformity and compliance. Many "cadres" and "militants" are mere careerists and opportunists. Boredom, withdrawal, and ultimately privatization of population's values become an accepted fact.	Low but occasional manipulative mobilization of a ceremonial type by coercive or clientelistic methods without permanent organization. Periodic mobilization of parastate groups who use violence against groups targeted by sultan.

Characteristic	Democracy	Authoritarianism	Totalitarianism	Post-totalitarianism	Sultanism
Leadership	Top leadership produced by free elections and must be exercised within constitutional limits and state of law. Leadership must be periodically subjected to and produced by free elections.	Political system in which a leader or occasionally a small group exercises power within formally ill-defined but actually quite predictable norms. Effort at cooptation of old elite groups. Some autonomy in state careers and in military.	Totalitarian leadership rules with undefined limits and great unpredictability for members and nonmembers. Often charismatic. Recruitment to top leadership highly dependent on success and commitment in party organization.	Growing emphasis by post-totalitarian political elite on personal security. Checks on top leadership via party structures, procedures, and "internal democracy." Top leaders are seldom charismatic. Recruitment to top leadership restricted to official party but less dependent upon building a career within party's organization. Top leaders can come from party technocrats in state apparatus.	Highly personalistic and arbitrary. No rational-legal constraints. Strong dynastic tendency. No autonomy in state careers. Leader unencumbered by ideology. Compliance to leaders based on intense fear and personal rewards. Staff of leader drawn from members of his family, friends, business associates, or men directly involved in use of violence to sustain the regime. Staff's position derives from their purely personal submission to the ruler.

things as a robust underground *samizdat* literature with multi-issue journals of the sort not possible under totalitarianism.[4] This growing pluralism is simultaneously a dynamic source of vulnerability for the post-totalitarian regime and a dynamic source of strength for an emerging democratic opposition. For example, this "second culture" can be sufficiently powerful that, even though leaders of the second culture will frequently be imprisoned, in a mature post-totalitarian regime opposition leaders can generate substantial followings and create enduring oppositional organizations in civil society. At moments of crisis, therefore, a mature post-totalitarian regime can have a cadre of a democratic opposition based in civil society with much greater potential to form a democratic political opposition than would be available in a totalitarian regime. A mature post-totalitarian regime can also feature the coexistence of a state-planned economy with extensive partial market experiments in the state sector that can generate a "red bourgeoisie" of state sector managers and a growing but subordinate private sector, especially in agriculture, commerce and services.

However, in a post-totalitarian regime this social and economic pluralism is different in degree and kind from that found in an authoritarian regime. It is different in degree because there is normally more social and economic pluralism in an authoritarian regime (in particular there is normally a more autonomous private sector, somewhat greater religious freedom, and a greater amount of above-ground cultural production). The difference in kind is typologically even more important. In a post-totalitarian society, the historical reference both for the power holders of the regime and the opposition is the previous totalitarian regime. By definition, the existence of a previous totalitarian regime means that most of the pre-existing sources of responsible and organized pluralism have been eliminated or repressed and a totalitarian order has been established. There is therefore an active effort at "detotalitarianization" on the part of oppositional currents in civil society. Much of the emotional and organizational drive of the opposition in civil society is thus consciously crafted to forge alternatives to the political, economic, and social structures created by the totalitarian regime, structures that still play a major role in the post-totalitarian society. Much of the second culture therefore is not traditional in form but is found in new movements that arise out of the totalitarian experience. There can also be a state-led detotalitarianization in which the regime itself begins to eliminate some of the most extreme features of the monist experience. Thus, if there is growing "institutional pluralism," or a growing respect for procedure and law, or a newly tolerated private sector, it should be understood as a kind of pluralism that emerges *out of* the previous totalitarian regime.

However, it is typologically and politically important to stress that there are significant limits to pluralism in post-totalitarian societies. In contrast to an authoritarian regime, there is *no* limited and relatively autonomous pluralism in the explicitly political realm. The official party in all post-totalitarian regimes is still legally accorded the leading role in the polity. The institutional pluralism of a post-totalitarian regime should not be confused with political pluralism; rather, institutional pluralism is exercised within the party-state or within the newly tolerated second economy or parallel culture. The pluralism of the parallel culture or the second culture should be seen as a *social* pluralism that may have political implications. But we must insist that the party and the regime leaders in post-totalitarian regimes, unless they experience out-of-type change, accord *no* legitimacy or responsibility to nonofficial political pluralism.[5] Even the formal pluralism of satellite parties becomes politically relevant only in the final stages of the regime after the transition is in progress.

When we turn to the dimension of *leadership*, we also see central tendencies that distinguish totalitarian from authoritarian leadership. Totalitarian leadership is unconstrained by laws and procedures and is often charismatic. The leadership can come from the revolutionary party or movement, but members of this core are as vulnerable to the sharp policy and ideological changes enunciated by the leader (even more so in terms of the possibility of losing their lives) as the rest of the population. By contrast, in the Linzian scheme, authoritarian leadership is characterized by a political system in which a leader or occasionally a small group exercises power within

formally ill-defined but actually quite predictable norms. There are often extensive efforts to co-opt old elite groups into leadership roles, and there is some autonomy in state careers and in the military.

As in a totalitarian regime, post-totalitarian leadership is still exclusively restricted to the revolutionary party or movement. However, in contrast to a totalitarian regime, post-totalitarian leaders tend to be more bureaucratic and state technocratic than charismatic. The central core of a post-totalitarian regime normally strives successfully to enhance its security and lessen its fear by reducing the range of arbitrary discretion allowed to the top leadership.

In contrast to those who say that the totalitarian regime concept is static, we believe that, when an opportunity presents itself (such as the death of the maximum leader), the top elite's desire to reduce the future leader's absolute discretion is predictably a dynamic source of pressure for out-of-type regime change from totalitarianism to post-totalitarianism. The post-totalitarian leadership is thus typologically closer in this respect to authoritarian leadership, in that the leader rules within unspecified but in reality reasonably predictable limits. However, the leadership in these two regime types still differs fundamentally. Post-totalitarian leadership is exclusively recruited from party members who develop their careers in the party organization itself, the bureaucracy, or the technocratic apparatus of the state. They all are thus recruited from the structures created by the regime. In sharp contrast, in most authoritarian regimes, the norm is for the regime to co-opt much of the leadership from groups that have some power, presence, and legitimacy that does not derive directly from the regime itself. Indeed, the authoritarian regime has often been captured by powerful fragments of the pre-existing society. In some authoritarian regimes, even access to top positions can be established not by political loyalties as much as by some degree of professional and technical expertise and some degree of competition through examinations that are open to the society as a whole. In mature post-totalitarian regimes, technical competence becomes increasingly important, but we should remember that the original access to professional training was controlled by political criteria. Also, the competences that are accepted or recognized in post-totalitarian systems are technical or managerial but do not include skills developed in a broader range of fields such as the law, religious organizations, or independent business or labor.

The limited party-bureaucratic-technocratic pluralism under post-totalitarianism does not give the regime the flexibility for change within the regime that co-optation of nonregime elites can give to many authoritarian regimes. The desire to resist the personalized leadership of the First Secretary–ideologue can be a source of change from totalitarian to post-totalitarian, but it can also lead eventually to the oligarchic leadership of aging men supported by the nomenklatura. Attempts at rejuvenation at the top by including or co-opting new men and women from the outside are normally very limited. In extreme cases (i.e., the GDR and post-1968 Czechoslovakia), frozen post-totalitarianism shows geriatric tendencies. Under crisis circumstances, the inability to renovate leadership, not so paradoxically, is a potential source of dynamic change in that a frozen post-totalitarian regime, with its old and narrow leadership base, has a very limited capacity to negotiate. Such a leadership structure, if it is not able to repress opponents in a crisis, is particularly vulnerable to *collapse*. One of the reasons why midlevel cadres in the once all-powerful coercive apparatus might, in time of crisis, let the regime collapse rather than fire upon the democratic opposition has to do with the role of ideology in post-totalitarianism.

The contrast between the role of *ideology* in a totalitarian system and in a post-totalitarian system is sharp, but it is more one of behavior and belief than one of official canon. In the area of ideology, the dynamic potential for change from a totalitarian to a post-totalitarian regime, both on the part of the cadres and on the part of the society, is the growing empirical disjunction between official ideological claims and reality. This disjunction produces lessened ideological commitment on the part of the cadres and growing criticism of the regime by groups in civil society. In fact, many of the new critics in civil society emerge out of the ranks of former true believers, who argue that the regime does not—or, worse, cannot—advance its own goals. The pressures created by this tension between doctrine and reality often contributes to an out-of-type shift from a totalitarian regime effort to mobilize enthusiasm to a post-totalitarian effort to maintain acquiescence. In the post-totalitarian phase, the elaborate and guiding ideology created under the totalitarian regime still exists as the official state canon, but among many leaders there is a weakened commitment to and faith in utopia. Among much of the population, the official canon is seen as an obligatory ritual, and among groups in the "parallel society" or "second culture," there is constant reference to the first culture as a "living lie." This is another source of weakness, of the "hollowing out" of the post-totalitarian regime's apparent strength.

The role of ideology in a post-totalitarian regime is thus diminished from its role under totalitarianism, but it is still quite different from the role of ideology in an authoritarian regime. Most authoritarian regimes have diffuse nondemocratic mentalities, but they do not have highly articulated ideologies concerning the leading role of the party, interest groups, religion, and many other aspects of civil society, political society, the economy, and the state that still exist in a regime we would call post-totalitarian. Therefore, a fundamental contrast between a post-totalitarian and authoritarian regime is that in a post-totalitarian regime there is an important ideological legacy that cannot be ignored and that cannot be questioned officially. The state-sanctioned ideology has a *social presence* in the organizational life of the post-totalitarian polity. Whether it expresses itself in the extensive array of state-sponsored organizations or in the domain of incipient but still officially controlled organizations, ideology is part of the social reality of a post-totalitarian regime to a greater degree than in most authoritarian regimes.

The relative de-ideologization of post-totalitarian regimes and the weakening of the belief in utopia as a foundation of legitimacy mean that, as in many authoritarian regimes, there is a growing effort in a post-totalitarian polity to legitimate the regime on the basis of performance criteria. The gap between the original utopian elements of the ideology and the increasing legitimation efforts on the basis of efficacy, particularly when the latter fails, is one of the sources of weakness in post-totalitarian regimes. Since democracies base their claim to obedience on the procedural foundations of democratic citizenship, as well as performance, they have a layer of insulation against weak performance not available to most post-totalitarian or authoritarian regimes. The weakening of utopian ideology that is a characteristic of post-totalitarianism thus opens up a new dynamic of regime vulnerabilities—or, from the perspective of democratic transition, new opportunities—that can be exploited by the democratic opposition. For example, the discrepancy between the constant reiteration of the importance of ideology and the ideology's growing irrelevance to policymaking or, worse, its transparent contradiction with social reality contribute to undermining the commitment and faith of the middle and lower cadres in the regime. Such a situation can help contribute to the rapid collapse of the regime if mid-level functionaries of the coercive apparatus have grave doubts about their right to shoot citizens who are protesting against the regime and its ideology, as we shall see when we discuss events in 1989 in East Germany and Czechoslovakia.

The final typological difference we need to explore concerns *mobilization*. Most authoritarian regimes never develop complex, all-inclusive networks of association whose purpose is the mobilization of the population. They may have brief periods of intensive mobilization, but these are normally less intensive than in a totalitarian regime and less extensive than in a post-totalitarian regime. In totalitarian regimes, however, there is extensive and intensive mobilization of society into a vast array of regime-created organizations and activities. Because utopian goals are intrinsic to the regime, there is a great effort to mobilize enthusiasm to activate cad-

res, and most leaders emerge out of these cadres. In the totalitarian system, "privatized" bourgeois individuals at home with their family and friends and enjoying life in the small circle of their own choosing are decried.

In post-totalitarian regimes, the extensive array of institutions of regime-created mobilization vehicles still dominate associational life. However, they have lost their intensity. Membership is still generalized and obligatory but tends to generate more boredom than enthusiasm. State-technocratic employment is an alternative to cadre activism as a successful career path, as long as there is "correct" participation in official organizations. Instead of the mobilization of enthusiasm that can be so functional in a totalitarian regime, the networks of ritualized mobilization in a post-totalitarian regime can produce a "cost" of time away from technocratic tasks for professionals and a cost of boredom and flight into private life by many other people. When there is no structural crisis and especially when there is no perception of an available alternative, such privatization is not necessarily a problem for a post-totalitarian regime. Thus, Kadar's famous saying, "Those who are not against us are for us," is a saying that is conceivable only in a post-totalitarian regime, not in a totalitarian one. However, if the performance of a post-totalitarian as opposed to a totalitarian regime is so poor that the personal rewards of private life are eroded, then privatization and apathy may contribute to a new dynamic—especially if alternatives are seen as possible—of crises of "exit," "voice," and "loyalty."[6]

Let us conclude our discussion of post-totalitarianism with a summary of its political and ideological weaknesses. We do this to help enrich the discussion of why these regimes collapsed so rapidly once they entered into prolonged stagnation and the USSR withdrew its extensive coercive support.

Totalitarianism, democracy, and even many authoritarian regimes begin with "genetic" legitimacy among their core supporters, given the historical circumstances that led to the establishment of these regimes. By contrast, post-totalitarianism regimes do not have such a founding genetic legitimacy because they emerge out of the routinization, decay, or elite fears of the totalitarian regime. Post-totalitarian regimes, because of coercive resources they inherit and the related weaknesses of organized opposition, can give the appearance of as much or more stability than authoritarian regimes; if external support is withdrawn, however, their inner loss of purpose and commitment make them vulnerable to collapse.

Post-totalitarian politics was a result in part of the moving away from Stalinism, but also of social changes in Communist societies. Post-totalitarian regimes did away with the worst aspects of repression but at the same time maintained most mechanisms of control. Although less bloody than under Stalinism, the presence of security services — like the Stasi in the GDR — sometimes became more pervasive. Post-totalitarianism could have led to moderate reforms in the economy, like those discussed at the time of the Prague Spring, but the Brezhnev restoration stopped dynamic adaptation in the USSR and in most other Soviet-type systems, except for Hungary and Poland.

Post-totalitarianism had probably less legitimacy for the ruling elites and above all the middle-level cadres than had a more totalitarian system. The loss of the utopian component of the ideology and the greater reliance on performance (which after some initial success did not continue) left the regimes vulnerable and ultimately made the use of massive repression less justifiable. Passive compliance and careerism opened the door to withdrawal into private life, weakening the regime so that the opposition could ultimately force it to negotiate or to collapse when it could not rely on coercion.

The weakness of post-totalitarian regimes has not yet been fully analyzed and explained but probably can be understood only by keeping in mind the enormous hopes and energies initially associated with Marxism-Leninism that in the past explained the emergence of totalitarianism and its appeal.[7] Many distinguished and influential Western intellectuals admired or excused Leninism and in the 1930s even Stalinism, but few Western intellectuals on the left could muster enthusiasm for post-totalitarianism in the USSR or even for perestroika and glasnost.

The emergence and evolution of post-totalitarianism can be the result of three distinct but often interconnected processes: (1) deliberate policies of the rulers to soften or reform the totalitarian system (detotalitarianism by choice), (2) the internal "hollowing out" of the totalitarian regimes' structures and an internal erosion of the cadres' ideological belief in the system (detotalitarianism by decay), and (3) the creation of social, cultural, and even economic spaces that resist or escape totalitarian control (detotalitarianism by societal conquest).

"Sultanism"

A large group of polities, such as Haiti under the Duvaliers, the Dominican Republic under Trujillo, the Central African Republic under Bokassa, the Philippines under Marcos, Iran under the Shah, Romania under Ceauşescu, and North Korea under Kim Il Sung, have had strong tendencies toward an extreme form of patrimonialism that Weber called *sultanism*. For Weber,

> *patrimonialism* and, in the extreme case, *sultanism* tend to arise whenever traditional domination develops an administration and a military force which are purely personal instruments of the master. . . . Where domination . . . operates primarily on the basis of discretion, it will be called *sultanism* . . . The non-traditional element is not, however, rationalized in impersonal terms, but consists only in the extreme development of the ruler's discretion. It is this which distinguishes it from every form of rational authority.[8]

Weber did not intend the word *sultanism* to imply religious claims to obedience. In fact, under Ottoman rule, the ruler held two distinct offices and titles, that of sultan and that of caliph. Initially, the Ottoman ruler was a sultan, and only after the conquest of Damascus did he assume the title of caliph, which entailed religious authority. After the defeat of Turkey in World War I and the proclamation of the republic, the former ruler lost his title of sultan but retained his religious title of caliph until Atatürk eventually forced him to relinquish even that title. Our point is that the secular and religious dimensions of his authority were conceptually and historically distinguished. Furthermore, the term *sultan* should not be analytically bound to the Middle East. Just as there are mandarins in New Delhi and Paris as well as in Peking and there is a macho style of politics in the Pentagon as well as in Buenos Aires, there are sultanistic rulers in Africa and the Caribbean as well as in the Middle East. What we do want the term *sultanism* to connote is a generic style of domination and regime rulership that is, as Weber says, an extreme form of patrimonialism. In sultanism, the private and the public are fused, there is a strong tendency toward familial power and dynastic succession, there is no distinction between a state career and personal service to the ruler, there is a lack of rationalized impersonal ideology, economic success depends on a personal relationship to the ruler, and, most of all, the ruler acts only according to his own unchecked discretion, with no larger, impersonal goals.

Table 6.1 gives substantial details on what a sultanistic type is in relation to pluralism, ideology, mobilization, and leadership. In this section we attempt to highlight differences between sultanism, totalitarianism, and authoritarianism because, while we believe they are distinct ideal types, in any concrete case a specific polity could have a mix of some sultanistic and some authoritarian tendencies (a combination that might open up a variety of transition options) or a mix of sultanistic and totalitarian tendencies (a combination that would tend to eliminate numerous transition options).

In his long essay, "Totalitarian and Authoritarian Regimes," Juan Linz discussed the special features that make sultanism a distinctive type of nondemocratic regime.[9] Since the sultanistic regime type has not been widely accepted in the literature, we believe it will be useful for us to highlight systematically its distinctive qualities so as to make more clear the implications of this type of regime for the patterns of democratic resistance and the problems of democratic consolidation.

In sultanism, there is a high fusion by the ruler of the private and the public. The sultanistic polity becomes the personal domain of the sultan. In this domain there is no rule of law and there is low institutionalization. In sultanism there may be extensive social and economic pluralism, but almost never political pluralism, because political power is so directly related to the ruler's person. However, the essential reality in a sultanistic regime is that all individuals, groups, and institutions are permanently subject to the unpredictable and despotic intervention of the sultan, and thus all pluralism is precarious.

In authoritarianism there may or may not be a rule of law, space for a semi-opposition, or space for regime moderates who might establish links with opposition moderates, and there are normally extensive social and economic activities that function within a secure framework of relative autonomy. Under sultanism, however, there is no rule of law, no space for a semiopposition, no space for regime moderates who might negotiate with democratic moderates, and no sphere of the economy or civil society that is not subject to the despotic exercise of the sultan's will. As we demonstrate in the next chapter, this critical difference between pluralism in authoritarian and sultanistic regimes has immense implications for the types of transition that are *available* in an authoritarian regime but *unavailable* in a sultanistic regime.

There is also a sharp contrast in the function and consequences of ideology between totalitarian and sultanistic regimes. In a totalitarian regime not only is there an elaborate and guiding ideology, but ideology has the function of legitimating the regime, and rulers are often somewhat constrained by their own value system and ideology. They or their followers, or both, believe in that ideology as a point of reference and justification for their actions. In contrast, a sultanistic ruler characteristically has no elaborate and guiding ideology. There may be highly personalistic statements with pretensions of being an ideology, often named after the sultan, but this ideology is elaborated after the ruler has assumed power, is subject to extreme manipulation, and, most importantly, is not believed to be constraining on the ruler and is relevant only as long as he practices it. Thus, there could be questions raised as to whether Stalin's practices and statements were consistent with Marxism-Leninism, but there would be no reason for anyone to debate whether Trujillo's statements were consistent with Trujilloism. The contrast between authoritarian and sultanistic regimes is less stark over ideology; however, the distinctive mentalities that are a part of most authoritarian alliances are normally more constraining on rulers than is the sultan's idiosyncratic and personal ideology.

The extensive and intensive mobilization that is a feature of totalitarianism is seldom found in a sultanistic regime because of its low degree of institutionalization and its low commitment to an overarching ideology. The low degree of organization means that any mobilization that does occur is uneven and sporadic. Probably the biggest difference between sultanistic mobilization and authoritarian mobilization is the tendency within sultanism (most dramatic in the case of the Duvaliers' Tonton Macoutes in Haiti) to use para-state groups linked to the sultan to wield violence and terror against anyone who opposes the ruler's will. These para-state groups are not modern bureaucracies with generalized norms and procedures; rather, they are direct extensions of the sultan's will. They have no significant institutional autonomy. As Weber stressed, they are purely "personal treatments of the master."

Finally, how does leadership differ in sultanism, totalitarianism, and authoritarianism? The essence of sultanism is *unrestrained personal rulership*. This personal rulership is, as we have seen, unconstrained by ideology, rational-legal norms, or any balance of power. "Support is based not on a coincidence of interest between preexisting privileged social groups and the ruler but on interests created by his rule, rewards he offers for loyalty, and the fear of his vengeance."[10]

In one key respect leadership under sultanism and totalitarianism is similar. In both regimes the leader rules with undefined limits on his power and there is great unpredictability for elites and non-elites alike. In this respect, a Stalin and a Somoza are alike. However, there are important differences. The elaborate ideology, with its sense of nonpersonal and public mission, is meant to play an important legitimating function in totalitarian regimes. The ideological pronouncements of a totalitarian leader are taken seriously not only by his followers and cadres, but also by the society and intellectuals, including—in the cases of Leninism, Stalinism, and Marxism (and even fascism)—by intellectuals outside the state in which the leader exercises control. This places a degree of organizational, social, and ideological constraint on totalitarian leadership that is not present in sultanistic leadership. Most importantly, the intense degree to which rulership is personal in sultanism makes the *dynastic* dimension of rulership normatively acceptable and empirically common, whereas the public claims of totalitarianism make dynastic ambition, if not unprecedented, at least aberrant.

The leadership dimension shows an even stronger contrast between authoritarianism and sultanism. As Linz stated in his discussion of authoritarianism, leadership is exercised in an authoritarian regime "with formally ill-defined but actually quite predictable" norms.[11] In most authoritarian regimes some bureaucratic entities play an important part. These bureaucratic entities often retain or generate their own norms, which imply that there are procedural and normative limits on what leaders can ask them to do in their capacity as, for example, military officers, judges, tax officials, or police officers. However, a sultanistic leader simply "demands unconditional administrative compliance, for the official's loyalty to his office is not an impersonal commitment to impersonal tasks that define the extent and content of his office, but rather a servant's loyalty based on a strictly personal relationship to the ruler and an obligation that in principle permits no limitation."[12]

We have now spelled our the central tendencies of five ideal-type regimes in the modern world, four of which are nondemocratic. We are ready for the next step, which is to explore why and how the *type* of prior nondemocratic regime has an important effect on the democratic transition paths available and the tasks to be addressed before democracy can be consolidated.

NOTES

1. Juan J. Linz, "An Authoritarian Regime: The Case of Spain," in Erik Allardt and Yrjö Littunen, eds., *Cleavages, Ideologies and Party Systems* (Helsinki: Transactions of the Westermarck Society, 1964), 291–342. Reprinted in Erik Allardt and Stein Rokkan, eds., *Mass Politics: Studies in Political Sociology* (New York: Free Press, 1970). The definition is found on 255.

2. We arrive at this conclusion in the following fashion. The annual survey coordinated by Raymond D. Gastil employs a 7-point scale of the political rights and civil liberties dimensions of democracy. With the help of a panel of scholars, Gastil, from 1978 to 1987, classified annually 167 countries on this scale. For our purposes if we call the universe of democracies those countries that from 1978 to 1987 never received a score of lower than 2 on the Gastil scale for political rights and 3 for civil liberty, we come up with 42 countries. This is very close to the number of countries that Coppedge and Reinicke classify as "full polyarchies" in their independent study of the year 1985. Since our interest is in how countries become democracies we will exclude those 42 countries from our universe of analysis. This would leave us with 125 countries in the universe we want to explore.

   If we then decide to call long-standing "totalitarian" regimes those regimes that received the lowest possible score on political rights and civil liberties on the Gastil scale for each year in the 1978–1987 period, we would have a total of nine countries that fall into the totalitarian classification. Thus, if one used the traditional typology, the Gastil scale would imply that 116 of 125 countries, or 92.8 percent of the universe under analysis, would have to be placed in the same typological space. See Gastil, *Freedom in the World*, 54–65.

3. Juan Linz, in his "Totalitarian and Authoritarian Regimes," in Fred I. Greenstein and Nelson W. Polsby, eds., *Handbook of Political Science* (Reading, Mass.: Addison-Wesley Publishing Co., 1975), 3:175–411, analyzed what he called "post-totalitarian authoritarian regimes," see 336–50. Here, with our focus on the available paths to democratic transition and the tasks of democratic consolidation, it seems to both of us that it is more useful to treat post-totalitarian regimes not as a subtype of authoritarianism, but as an ideal type in its own right.

4. For example, in mature post-totalitarian Hungary the most influential *samizdat* publication, *Beszélő*, from 1982 to 1989, was issued as a quarterly with publication runs of 20,000. Information supplied to Alfred Stepan by the publisher and editorial board member, Miklós Haraszti. Budapest, August 1994.

5. Hungary in 1988–89 represents a mature post-totalitarian regime which, by engaging in extensive detotalitarianization and by increasingly recognizing the legitimacy of other parties, had experienced significant out-of-type changes even before the Communist Party lost power. * * *

6. The reference, of course, is to Albert Hirschman, *Exit, Voice and Loyalty* (Cambridge: Harvard University Press, 1970), 59. For a fascinating discussion of this dynamic in relation to the collapse of the GDR, see Hirschman, "Exit, Voice and the Fate of the German Democratic Republic: An Essay on Conceptual History," *World Politics* 45:2 (January 1993): 173–202.

7. On the ideological and moral attractiveness of revolutionary Marxist-Leninism as a total system and the "vacuum" left in the wake of its collapse, see Ernest Gellner, "Homeland of the Unrevolution," *Daedalus* (Summer 1993): 141–54.

8. Max Weber, *Economy and Society: An Outline of Interpretive Sociology*, ed. Guenther Roth and Claus Wittich (Berkeley: University of California Press, 1978), 1:231, 232. Italics in the original.

9. Linz, "*Totalitarian and Authoritarian Regimes*," 259–63.

10. Ibid., 260.

11. Ibid., 255.

12. Ibid., 260.

Erika Weinthal and Pauline Jones Luong

COMBATING THE RESOURCE CURSE: AN ALTERNATIVE SOLUTION TO MANAGING MINERAL WEALTH

The race to find new sources of petroleum has been ongoing since commercially viable oil was discovered in Titusville, Pennsylvania in 1859. Almost a century and a half later, the discovery of new oil wealth in several parts of the world, including Azerbaijan, Kazakhstan, East Timor, Chad, and Sudan has muffled increasingly popular cries that world oil production would ultimately peak by the middle of this decade.[1]

For most industrial countries heavily dependent upon fossil fuels for economic growth, these new petroleum sources were a welcome blessing that could delay an impending global energy shortage. Europe's reliance upon imported oil and gas is expected to increase dramatically over the next few decades, especially as oil production in the North Sea declines from approximately seven million barrels per day to less than four million barrels per day by 2020.[2] Similarly, the United States has become increasingly dependent upon foreign petroleum sup-

plies since 1998 when petroleum imports surpassed the 50 percent barrier for the first time.[3] These new petroleum discoveries are even more vital for meeting the rising energy demand in the world's fastest growing economies of developing Asia including China and India.[4]

For the countries where these discoveries were made, however, new concerns arose over whether they could avoid the curse associated with mineral wealth. Countless studies document the correlation between abundant mineral resources (for example, oil, gas, diamonds, copper, and gold) and a series of negative economic and political outcomes, including poor economic performance and authoritarian regimes, across the developing world.[5] There are also numerous empirical examples of countries that have squandered their mineral wealth and actually made their citizens worse off. Nigeria (the world's seventh largest oil producer) provides a notorious one. Its government has accrued $350 billion in oil revenues since independence, and yet its economy has shrunk; in purchasing power parity (PPP) terms, Nigeria's per capita GDP was $1,113 in 1970 but only $1,084 in 2000, and during this

From *Perspectives on Politics* 4, no. 1 (March 2008), pp. 35–53.

same period, its poverty rate, "measured as the share of the population subsisting on less than US$1 per day increased from close to 36 percent to just under 70 percent."[6] Thus, despite its vast oil wealth, Nigeria is among the 15 poorest nations in the world.

The disappointing experience of mineral-rich countries has generated a large body of scholarship aimed at explaining this empirical correlation and a list of prescriptions for combating the resource curse. The most popular solutions emphasize macroeconomic policies, economic diversification, natural resource funds, transparency and accountability, and direct distribution as mechanisms for managing mineral wealth wisely. While many mineral-rich countries in the developing world have implemented one or more of these solutions, their success has been limited to only a few exceptional cases (for example, Botswana, Chile, and Malaysia). We contend that this is because these solutions either presuppose strong state institutions, which are widely absent in the developing world, or assume state ownership over mineral wealth and thus the need for external actors to constrain the state.

Despite the emerging consensus that robust political institutions are the determining factor in successful efforts to disrupt the link between mineral wealth and the aforementioned negative outcomes, we know little about how to build such institutions. We suggest one possible way—domestic private ownership. Domestic private ownership is rarely discussed in the literature and, when discussed, it often is maligned. Our research indicates, however, that it would foster institutions that more effectively constrain state leaders, encourage them to invest in institution building, and enable them to respond more successfully to commodity booms and busts.

The Paradox of Mineral Wealth

The central paradox that has inspired innumerable studies of mineral-rich countries in the developing world is that, since the 1970s, they have consistently underperformed their mineral-poor counterparts on a variety of economic and political indicators, including economic performance, good governance, income equality, and democracy.

It has been well established that—controlling for income—the more intense a country's reliance on mineral exports (measured as a percentage of GDP) during this time period, the more slowly its economy grew.[7] From 1960 to 1990, GDP per capita in mineral-rich countries increased 1.7 percent compared to 2.5–3.5 percent in mineral-poor countries; similarly, from 1970–1993, mineral-rich countries grew by only 0.8 percent PCGDP compared to 2.1–3.7 percent in mineral-poor countries.[8] A prominent illustration of this surprising result are the "tigers" in mineral-poor East Asia (Hong Kong, Korea, Singapore and Taiwan), whose economies maintained phenomenal growth rates from the early 1960s to the 1990s while the economies of mineral-rich Latin America stagnated or declined.[9] Also during this period (roughly 1965–1998), members of the Organization of Petroleum Exporting Countries (OPEC) experienced nearly universally low or negative annual growth rates.[10]

Mineral exporters were also more likely to incur greater debt, even as world prices soared, and thus forced to commit a significant percentage of their shrinking GDP to debt servicing.[11] The World Bank classifies 12 of the world's most mineral-dependent countries and six of the world's most oil-dependent countries as "highly indebted poor countries."[12] Six out of the top 10 most indebted countries in Africa are major fuel exporters.[13] Outside Africa, similar patterns emerge; although Ecuador is one of the smallest countries in South America, in 2002 it ranked seventh in the region for external indebtedness— just below Brazil, Argentina, and Venezuela—and had the highest debt per capita.[14]

Related to these economic problems is the consistent finding that mineral wealth is strongly correlated with poor governance and high levels of corruption— all the more so if the primary commodity is oil.[15] Mineral exporters in the developing world find themselves ranked at the bottom of the list among countries included in both the World Bank Governance

Research Indicators[16] and the Transparency International's Corruption Perception Index (CPI).[17]

Mineral-exporting states also fare much worse when it comes to standards of living and the condition of the poor. Citizens living in such countries are subjected to high levels of poverty, child mortality, and income inequality.[18]

Finally, mineral-dependent countries tend to have authoritarian regimes. Several studies exploring this relationship have found that mineral wealth not only impedes democratic transitions but also prevents the consolidation of democracies,[19] and conversely, promotes the consolidation of authoritarian regimes.[20] Oil wealth in particular has been identified as inhibiting democratization, especially in oil-poor and low-income countries—thus indicating that even a little "oil *does* hurt democracy."[21] Of the 20 major oil exporters in 2000, only Mexico and Venezuela—both of which have previously experienced long periods of dictatorship—could be classified as democracies.

That mineral-abundant countries in the developing world are more prone to poor economic performance, unbalanced growth, corruption, income inequality, and authoritarian regimes is certainly alarming, especially given the initial optimism about their future prospects. In the 1950s and 1960s many development economists argued that these countries would grow much faster than their resource-poor counterparts precisely because their mineral wealth would provide them with the necessary capital to industrialize and diversify their exports.[22] Economic growth, in turn, was widely believed to promote the degree of social change and income equality necessary for democratization.[23] What is even more striking, then, is that by the 1990s a scholarly consensus emerged that these countries' vast wealth is the root cause of their severe political and economic problems—often referred to as the "resource curse."

These scholars emphasize two main aspects of the resource curse: first, the economic consequences that rapid booms and the volatility of commodity markets have for sustained growth; and second, the negative impact that reliance on external rents has on governance, state capacity, and democracy, which is exacerbated by boom and bust cycles. We review these briefly below.

Windfalls and Economic Growth

The most prevalent cause attributed to poor rates of economic growth in mineral-rich countries is Dutch Disease—a term originally coined to refer to the short-lived problems that the Netherlands faced when it discovered huge gas reserves off its northern coast in 1959. Yet, the direct effects of export booms—whether due to a rapid rise in exports or commodity prices—is a common source of economic stagnation across mineral-rich states. Simply put, these windfalls lead to an appreciation of the real exchange rate (that is, the rate of exchange between currencies adjusted for inflation) by shifting production inputs (capital and labor) to the booming mineral sector and non-tradable sector (that is, retail trade, services, and construction), thereby reducing the competitiveness of the non-booming exports sectors (for example, agriculture and manufacturing) and hence precipitating their collapse. The shift into the non-tradable sector accelerates domestic inflation, which is responsible for the rise in the real exchange rate.

These short-term macro-adjustment problems result in long-term effects on growth by reducing the country's economic diversity and increasing its reliance on exports from its natural resource sector. Equatorial Guinea—one of Africa's newest oil producers—is illustrative of how fast Dutch Disease effects can transform the domestic economy: cocoa and coffee have declined from approximately 60 percent of GDP in 1991 to less than 9 percent of GDP in 2001.[24]

The decline of the manufacturing sector also retards economic growth by decreasing both the demand for and supply of skilled labor, which in turn, affects the level of income inequality and educational opportunities.[25] A number of recent studies have found, for example, that school enrollment at all levels and public expenditures on education relative to national income are inversely related to natural resource abundance.

The phenomenon of Dutch Disease, however, is not the only mechanism whereby economic growth is negatively affected by windfalls. Perhaps equally important are the incentives that windfalls create for unproductive investments, rent-seeking, and corruption.

First, the export boom exerts pressure on governments to share increased revenues with the public, often by investing in unproductive public work projects that are motivated by politics rather than profit (that is, "white elephants") or subsidizing food, fuel, failing industries and even government jobs. There is no shortage of prominent examples, such as the Ajaokuta steel mill that Nigeria built in the 1970s to appease the Yoruba region, which "has absorbed over US$3 billion,"[26] and yet, "has still not produced a commercial ton of steel."[27] In addition to squandering the proceeds from their most precious commodities on failed investment programs, countries also suffer from spiraling inflation, the collapse of private savings and investment, and economic stagnation.

Second, many argue that because windfall rents are concentrated and easily obtained, they exert pressure to engage in rent-seeking and corruption — both of which harm economic growth. Windfalls can shift the focus to competition over rents, leading to a "feeding frenzy"[28] and thereby distract both individuals and governments from long-term developmental goals. For example, in the late 1960s and early 1970s Indonesia's state oil company, Pertamina, accrued large windfalls that generated rent-seeking opportunities for actors closely tied to the state; these mineral rents became a source of patronage for the Indonesian military.[29] The long-term effects on Indonesia's economy are evident in the lack of foreign investment in new energy projects over the last decade and its unique distinction of becoming OPEC's first member to import oil in 2004.[30]

Validity and Economic Growth

Another chief concern is the effect that the extreme volatility of commodities, also known as "boom and bust" cycles, can have on economic growth. Although market volatility is a problem for all exporters of primary commodities, it especially plagues oil exporters because the economic importance of oil makes this particular commodity both a valuable and an attractive political weapon.

The economic impact includes, first and foremost, unpredictable revenue streams because widely fluctuating export revenues lead to fluctuating levels in overall government revenues.[31] These "frequent upward or downward adjustments of fiscal expenditures are costly" because they simultaneously discourage private investment and wreak havoc on the government's budget, thereby impeding its ability to sustain investment and public goods provision.[32] Moreover, once expenditures become entrenched, it is harder for governments to make budget cuts; rather than reversing their spending patterns during busts, they often opt to borrow, and hence, incur huge debt burdens.[33]

Excessive borrowing also occurs during booms. Many countries have followed the ill-advised strategy of "borrow[ing] on the strength of their booms."[34] For example, although it experienced "only a small oil windfall in 1979–81," Mexico "borrowed abroad against future oil earnings to boost expenditures by a further 1.8 percent of non-oil GDP."[35] In fact, oil exporters "built up more debt during the 1970s" — that is, as oil revenues were rising the fastest.[36]

Political Consequences of Reliance on External Rents

The main political consequences of relying on external rents[37] are weakly institutionalized states and skewed state-societal relations. Relying on an external source of revenue fosters weakly institutionalized states because the ease of financing state expenditures provides no incentives for government officials to build strong institutions. More specifically, countries rich in minerals, particularly petroleum, fail to develop a robust central bureaucracy because their ability to rely on an external revenue source engenders rigid and myopic decision making. This includes, most importantly, the failure to build a viable tax regime because rulers do not feel compelled to extract revenue from domestic sources to fill their coffers.

In short, mineral-rich states inevitably become rentier states. Rentier states seek to exert social and political control over their populations by creating and maintaining economic dependencies through their sole authority to allocate and redistribute income obtained from natural resource rents. This has three critical implications for state-societal relations.

First, the freedom to rely on external rather than internal sources of income both enfeebles the state and impairs the development of societal opposition because it reduces both the need for leaders to be accountable to the public and popular demands for representation. Indeed, the lack of a viable tax regime has been consistently identified with not only impeding broad economic growth but also undermining state capacity and democratization.

Second, rentier states bolster their autonomy from societal forces by exploiting their fiscal independence to engage in discretionary spending. Large sums of money are spent on sustaining patronage networks and/or providing huge subsidies to the population to garner social and political support, rather than on developing institutionalized mechanisms of responsiveness. The Kuwaiti government, for example, employed 75 percent of the workforce in 1975, but most were "underqualified and underutilized."[38] In short, these states are characterized by the "progressive substitution of public spending for statecraft."[39]

Third, rentier states are subject to state capture and high levels of corruption. While the majority of the population is effectively disenfranchised, those who run the natural resource sector are able to exert disproportionate influence over government policies. There are primarily two reasons for this. First, the highly concentrated nature of the mineral sector enables the small number of firms that occupy it to form a united front to pressure the state. Second, the sheer economic impact of the mineral sector fosters a tendency for the state to conflate this sector's interest with its own.[40] The Gulf states, where the oil sector and the ruling families are nearly indistinguishable, represent the most extreme illustration.[41] As a result, both sides have a vested interest in nontransparent transactions, thereby ensuring state autonomy vis-à-vis the broader population and enabling those with access to mineral rents (first and foremost, government officials) to enrich themselves at society's expense.

The cumulative impact of external rent reliance, therefore, is not just weakly institutionalized states and skewed state-societal relations but also corrupt, authoritarian regimes. With unfettered access to huge rents, incumbents have such a disproportionate advantage over their opponents so that they can remain in office almost indefinitely. These regimes also sustain themselves by simultaneously creating a strong deterrent to popular mobilization—either because they successfully preempt social discontent with populist policies or because they possess effective internal security forces. The result is that only very few developing countries, such as the Republic of Congo and Venezuela, have been able to channel their oil wealth into creating the socioeconomic and political conditions conducive to democratic transition.

Boom and bust cycles also play a role by aggravating the effects of external rents reliance. Booms exacerbate both state spending and rent-seeking behavior, thus reinforcing the dynamic of weakly institutionalized states and corrupt, authoritarian regimes.[42] They also further enfeeble the state by actually creating a disincentive for state leaders to build strong institutions that might interfere with their ability to allocate rents to supporters.[43] Weakly institutionalized states, in turn, are unable to respond to busts, either because their bureaucracies are too centralized and bloated to adjust, sectoral interests have captured the policy-making process, or some combination.[44] * * *

The Missing Link: Private Ownership and State Capacity

In sum, these existing solutions have largely failed because making the state a better "manager" of its mineral wealth requires institutions that promote transparency, accountability, and oversight—that is, institutions that are widely absent in developing countries.[45] In contrast, we propose a solution that deliberately addresses the core problem of weak institutions—private domestic ownership.

Robust institutions are the product of both supply and demand; governments must have an incentive to supply them and societal actors must have both the interest and ability to make a credible demand for them. In the majority of mineral-rich states in the developing world, however, neither condition is met. State ownership in particular creates a distinctive for supplying institutions that would limit the government's fiscal independence or discretionary decision-making power. It also undermines the development of societal actors that are either powerful enough to challenge the state or have a keen interest in limiting its power. Not surprisingly, then, the vast majority of mineral-rich countries exercised state ownership over their mineral reserves from the late 1960s to the early 1990s—the very historical time period on which most of the literature on the resource curse focuses.* * *

By taking resource rents out of the state's direct control, privatization to domestic owners simultaneously fosters the conditions under which governments have an incentive to build strong fiscal and regulatory institutions and creates a new set of societal actors with the potential to demand these institutions. Because these private owners benefit directly from the production and export of the country's mineral reserves, they have a vested interest in secur-

ing both their property rights and a stable revenue stream as well as the means to bring state actors to the bargaining table. At the same time, because the state has less control over how these resources are extracted and utilized, it is more likely to invest in institution building that enables it to extract revenue from private owners, regulate the private sector, and generate other sources of revenue outside the natural resource sector. Thus, privatization to domestic actors offers an alternative path out of the "resource curse" because it creates an incentive for both state and societal actors to bargain over and eventually establish the formal rules of the game.

Russia provides a powerful illustration of this proposition. In the mid-1990s, Russia began privatizing its oil sector to domestic investors but retained state control over the gas sector.[46] Since then, the degree of reform and economic promise in these two leading sectors has diverged significantly. By the end of 1990s, the majority of the oil industry was privatized to multiple owners, substantially deregulated, and had undergone significant internal restructuring. Under private ownership, the Russian oil industry has successfully expanded production and seen its net profits jump to $25 billion in 2003.[47] In addition, the domestic owners that emerged from this process have increasingly pressured the Russian government not only to support greater liberalization within the energy sector itself, but also to develop institutions outside the energy sector to promote greater transparency and fiscal stability. The gas sector, in contrast, continues to be dominated by the primarily state-owned monopoly Gazprom, which has resisted any structural reform, amassed substantial foreign debt, and remained chronically undercapitalized, translating into direct losses to the Russian economy and indirect losses to the institutional capacity of the Russian state.

Why Ownership Matters

Why should we expect state and private ownership to result in such distinct institutional outcomes? In short, because they foster a very different relationship between the main actors they generate. While both sets of actors under state ownership (that is, state elites and bureaucrats) and private ownership (that is, state elites and domestic owners) are *relatively* symmetrical in their ability to exert influence over the other, the boundaries between them are blurred and clear, respectively. These boundaries, in turn, promote very different incentives for institution building because they impose very different transaction and monitoring costs for the actors involved.

Under state ownership, the boundary between the main actors—state elites and bureaucrats—is blurred because there is no clearly identifiable principal. Rather, the population as a whole is the nominal principal whose interests are ostensibly served by a multitude of agents. At the same time, because the control structure is not clearly defined and there are no objective criteria for determining managerial performance, these agents often act like principals such that administrative tasks and political goals also become blurred. The relative power between state elites and bureaucrats is symmetrical because both have direct access to the proceeds from mineral exploitation. They also both have exclusive access to information about the income—as well as the misdeeds—of the other.

In the case of the Russian gas sector, for example, it is difficult to distinguish the management from the government. For most of the 1990s, Gazprom's president and board of directors not only controlled their own shares but also were entrusted with the government's shares. Thus, they openly ran the company as if they owned it. Then, as now, the Gazprom CEO is a presidential appointee and Gazprom's managers and government representatives form a majority on the board of directors. As a result, some have suggested that it has been hard to determine where "Gazprom ends and the Russian state begins."[48]

Blurred boundaries reduce transaction and monitoring costs by making revenue readily available to multiple principals, all of whom are charged with managing this revenue but none of whom can

benefit directly when it is generated efficiently. In most developing countries, for example, petroleum resources are managed through a state oil company. Bureaucrats are assigned to run the company on behalf of the state, with the understanding that the company—and most importantly, its income—ultimately falls under the jurisdiction of the state elites.[49] These bureaucrats not only have a greater opportunity to steal from the company but also a greater incentive to do so because, as de facto government employees, they are not compensated for performance. Because they have no direct claim to the residual (or profits), they also have a greater incentive to operate the company without regard for profitability.[50] This is reinforced by soft budget constraints—that is, continued access to state revenue, regardless of whether or not the company is profitable.

As a result, state elites and bureaucrats share incentives for building or sustaining weak institutions. Both prefer greater discretionary power, and thus, institutions that are unlikely to constrain their behavior in any meaningful or predictable way. Neither side has an incentive to support the development of institutions that foster internal and external oversight mechanisms, increase transparency, or impose hard budget constraints. Rather, because both sides have direct access to the proceeds from the exploitation of the energy sector, they prefer greater discretionary power and informal agreements over the allocation and use of these proceeds. This encourages a form of implicit bargaining whereby each side tacitly agrees to either undermine existing institutions that might pose a threat to their discretionary authority, for example, by increasing transparency and accountability, or to maintain the status quo, and thus neglect institution building altogether. These tendencies are likely to be exacerbated, moreover, by an exogenous shock or economic crisis because time horizons shorten and opportunities for rent-seeking expand.

The blurred boundary between the state and Gazprom, for example, has benefited both sides. On the one hand, it has empowered the gas sector to operate with very little internal or external scrutiny over its transactions. For example, during most of the 1990s, the Russian Audit Chamber did not demand an official audit of Gazprom's finances. This lack of oversight is evident in Gazprom's notorious mismanagement of investment funds and arbitrary transfer of assets to board members and relatives during Boris Yeltsin's presidency. Gazprom's integrated structure also provides the company with a relatively costless and effortless way of hiding its profits, and thus lining its managers' pockets.

On the other hand, this blurred boundary has enabled the Russian government to utilize its leverage as the ultimate owner to fulfill its domestic fiscal and spending requirements. Gazprom remains subjected to price controls and delivery requirements for nonpaying domestic customers, which account for a large portion of its implicit tax burden. As a result, Gazprom is forced to sell most of the gas it produces (70 percent) on the domestic market for approximately 15 percent of the price it would receive on the global market. Combined with the high rate of tariff arrears in Russia among industrial and household consumers alike, therefore, it is not surprising that Gazprom operates at a loss. Nonetheless, the government has refused to lower Gazprom's explicit tax burden, contributing further to its well-earned position as Russia's largest taxpayer. Gazprom's explicit tax burden has actually increased following the August 1998 financial crisis and the adoption of a new tax code in 2000–2001. Meanwhile, its implicit tax burden has also steadily increased as government officials utilize Gazprom's budget for social and political goals such as financing election campaigns.

Yet, the long-term costs of weak fiscal, regulatory, and supervisory institutions outweigh the short-term benefits to each side. In sum, the blurred boundary has created and reinforced an informal agreement whereby Gazprom's managers accept a high tax burden in exchange for the ability to line their own pockets and the government accepts less transparency and accountability for virtually unlimited access to Gazprom's coffers. This has resulted in a net economic loss for both Gazprom as a company and the Russian economy as a whole. "Years of asset stripping and lack of transparency," for example, are responsible for Gazprom's gross undercapitalization.

Under private domestic ownership, in contrast, the boundary between the main actors—state elites and domestic owners—is clear because there is a clearly identifiable principle. Because the control structure is clearly defined and there are objective criteria for evaluating managerial performance, agents do not conflate administrative tasks with political goals. Rather, they are punished and rewarded based on their ability, for example, to maximize efficiency, increase profits and market capitalization, and expanded market share. Their relative power is symmetrical because each has an independent source of authority over the other. Domestic owners possess the rights to revenue from mineral exploitation, and thus, are a critical source of tax revenue for the state. State elites possess the authority to revoke property rights and reduce revenue streams through demanding excessive taxation. In short, they need each other not just to survive, but also to thrive.

Clear boundaries increase transaction and monitoring costs by simultaneously making it more difficult for state elites to extract revenue and for private owners to hide their income. During Yeltsin's presidency (1991–98), for example, the government was forced to either confiscate revenue from the oil companies or to engage in continuous bargaining over revenue burdens. Also during this period, the Russian oil companies (hereafter, ROCs) devised several legal and semi-legal schemes to reduce their profitability on paper that eventually proved too costly—not only because it required expending effort and finances on nonproductive activities but also because it earned them a lower stock market valuation.

Clear boundaries also make it less rational to steal. Unlike state companies, in private companies managers are compensated based on performance and the owners have a direct claim to profits, and thus, both owners and managers are primarily concerned with profitability. Owners—including shareholders with a minority stake (that is, 25 percent of the shares)[51]—also have a vested interest in ensuring that both their managers and employees do not steal or otherwise jeopardize the company's financial health. When these minority shareholders are multinational corporations (MNCs), moreover, they can also provide further defense against state predation because they carry the added weight of access to capital, international arbitration, and foreign governments to both deter and challenge such practices.

Nor can private companies necessarily rely on the state to bail them out if they are operating at a loss. Hard budget constraints and the fear of bankruptcy thus reinforce the desire of owners and managers to run the company efficiently. As a result, they are unlikely to invest in unproductive public work projects or provide subsidies—tasks that a government often demands of state-owned companies to promote its own social and political objectives.

High transaction and monitoring costs, therefore, promote mutual incentives for building stable, effective, and far-reaching institutions—that is, strong institutions. Both state elites and private actors, for example, prefer a tax regime that is stable, so as to ensure fiscal predictability, and one that is broad-based, so as to decrease the state's fiscal reliance on the mineral sector. Both also prefer regulatory institutions that will effectively monitor companies' profits and employees. The main actors' interests concerning institution building thus converge. Yet, their preferences over the exact content of these institutions (for example, tax rates, number of audits, and so forth) will vary based on their specific interests. Combined with the fact that their relative power is symmetrical (that is, neither can impose their preferred outcome on the other), this variation in preferences over content encourages these two sets of actors to engage in explicit bargaining to formulate strong institutions. The mutual desire for formal guarantees is likely to be reinforced, moreover, by an exogenous shock or economic crisis because both actors will feel vulnerable and their continued survival will depend more acutely on the actions of the other.

The mutual desire for fiscal predictability following the August 1998 financial crisis, for example,

provided the impetus for the Russian government and private domestic oil companies to negotiate a broad-based tax code that was enacted between 1999–2002.[52] By most accounts, this new tax code exceeds Western standards—not only because it sets lower tax rates than the OECD recommends but also because it is much simpler and clearer than the previous one. Most important, the new tax code has resulted in an increase in the contribution of the personal income tax to the budget.[53] Foreign and domestic financial and political analysts alike have also praised the new tax code for the inclusive nature of tax benefits, and thus, its potentially positive impact on the Russian economy as a whole. The increased tax collection rates since the new code was put into effect support this optimism. In 2004 alone, for example, Russia's federal budget recorded a 17.7 percent increase in tax revenue.[54]

The financial crisis also motivated the ROCs to alter significantly their prior behavior and to design forward-looking development strategies.[55] Whereas governments across mineral-rich countries in which the oil sector is under state ownership commonly respond to economic crises linked to sharp declines in the market price of petroleum (or commodity "busts") by increasing production to make up for budgetary shortfalls, thereby lowering their profits, and/or by borrowing against future expected revenues,[56] the ROCs did neither. Nor did they pool their lobbying efforts or resources to seek state protection or "capture" the policy process, as Michael Shafer[57] and others would have predicted.[58] Rather, the ROCs consciously and successfully adjusted to the current bust and prepared for future booms by concentrating their efforts on cleaning up their internal operations so as to get their finances in order and finding ways to increase both production and profits over the long-term.

A central component of this adjustment strategy consisted of building foreign partnerships through attracting minority shareholders from abroad and/or bringing in foreign management.[59] This has had several undeniably positive effects on the development of the Russian oil industry. First, the ROCs' desire to attract foreign capital, and consequently to increase share prices, bolstered their commitment to greater transparency and corporate governance. Indeed, hiring foreign managers was a conscious attempt to signal this commitment to shareholders, as well as the Russian government. Second, bringing foreign expertise and capital directly into their respective enterprises enabled the ROCs to invest in new technology to increase production by tapping into old (brown) wells—a strategy that was both technologically impossible and highly unpopular among *neftyaniki* (oilmen) during the late Soviet period. Several of the ROC representatives and foreign investors we interviewed commented that Soviet-trained oilmen viewed this practice as "unmanly," preferring to open up new wells when oil did not easily flow from existing ones. Some of the ROCs also viewed foreign expertise and capital as a means to realize their ambitions to build new pipelines that would open up new markets—especially China—and provide an alternative to government-controlled pipelines as a prelude to investment in exploring and developing new wells. Finally, many ROCs deliberately sought foreign partnerships in order to simultaneously expand their operations at home—in particular to the Northern Territories where exploration requires both more capital and advanced technology—and abroad so as to reduce their future dependence on domestic reserves. By 2001, for example, Lukoil had already teamed up with Conoco International to explore oil in Russia's Timan-Pechora region[60] and had approximately 40 percent of its operations in foreign markets.[61]

Thus while some Western analysts have criticized the ROCs failure to invest in exploration, and hence, the development of new oil wells,[62] these efforts suggest a different picture. Combined, they indicate a strategy that is aimed not only at long-term investment but also at securing multiple sources of oil and access to new markets. On the one hand, these analysts and others have downplayed the ROCs attempts to explore new fields in the Far East, for which present production-sharing agreement (PSA) legislation privileges foreign investors.[63] On the other, they have overlooked the fact that the ROCs eventually want to be able to compete on the same playing field as other multinational oil companies, which requires looking beyond domestic production and existing markets.

Conclusion

In a recent op-ed, Joseph Stiglitz writes, "Abundant natural resources can and should be a blessing, not a curse. We know what must be done. What is missing is the political will to make it so."[64] Scholars and policy makers alike have become increasingly convinced that it is possible to combat the resource curse through a broad array of policies that include natural resource funds, economic diversification, transparency and accountability, and direct distribution. These solutions, however, rely on a degree of institutional capacity that is widely absent in mineral-rich countries, and thus they are prone to suffer from the aforementioned negative economic, political, and social outcomes.

In contrast, we offer a solution that directly addresses the pervasive problem of weak institutions in mineral-rich states—privatization to domestic owners. By taking resource rents out of the state's direct control, domestic privatization simultaneously fosters the conditions under which governments have an incentive to build strong fiscal and regulatory institutions and creates a new set of societal actors with the potential to demand these institutions.

Domestic privatization, however, is not a short-term remedy for institutional weakness. Building institutions is a lengthy process, involving numerous conflicts between the government and domestic capitalists over their respective roles in the economy and the rules that define them. This process is also a highly political one and, as such, is often mired in the political priorities of the moment, which can temporarily derail economic ones.

Russia again serves to illustrate. In June 2003 various agencies within the Russian government launched an increasingly fierce assault against Yukos, which had become the largest and most profitable ROC by 2002 owing to the aforementioned strategic changes.[65] This assault culminated in the arrest of Yukos's former CEO, Mikhail Khodorkovsky, and the forced sale of its most valuable subsidiary and covetable asset—Yuganskneftegaz[66]—on December 19, 2004, to cover unsubstantiated tax claims exceeding the company's revenue. Yet, while many analysts have interpreted the government's assault against Yukos as the death knell of private ownership in the oil sector, and thus, a calculated move toward regaining control over the country's most important economic assets, the overwhelming evidence indicates that the primary motivation was political and personal.[67]

First, Khodorkovsky openly flaunted his economic success—most notably through arranging the first shipments of Russian crude oil to the United States in the summer of 2002 and financially sponsoring opposition parties in the 2003 parliamentary elections—and used it to launch his own political career, suggesting that he would run for president in 2008. The state prosecutor's recent decision in March 2005 not to demand additional jail terms for Khodorkovsky and Platon Lebedev, Yukos's second largest shareholder, for their role in the illegal purchase of shares in *Apatit*, a fertilizer company, in 1994 has reinforced the political nature of government's case, given that in addition to alleged tax fraud, this was the main reason underlying their arrest.[68]

Second, the assault on Yukos has thus far been unique, both in form and content. It has not amounted to the renationalization of the oil sector, but rather, the *partial* dismantling of Yukos. As of the spring of 2005, no concrete action had been taken against Yukos's other subsidiaries, Tomskneft and Samaraneftegaz. If Yukos managers to retain these two subsidiaries, it would still be a major contender in the Russian oil industry.[69] At the same time, other ROCs—particularly those with a formidable MNC partner[70]—have escaped the degree of government predation that Yukos has experienced. While minority foreign ownership, perhaps because it only constituted 10 percent of the shares,

did not prevent the government's assault against Yukos, minority shareholders in both this company and its single largest domestic investor, Menatep Bank, played a key role in foiling the Russian government's plan to buy Yuganskneftegaz outright via Gazprom's winning bid and seem to have stalled any further legal action against the company.[71]

Finally, the government has remained committed to private ownership and securing property rights, as evidenced by its decision to sell its remaining shares in Lukoil in 2004[72] and Putin's recent initiative to provide legal protection for the various "insider privatizations" that occurred in the mid-1990s by reducing the statute of limitations on them from 10 years to three years.[73] That this commitment is credible is evidenced by the fact that, despite the assault against Yukos, other ROCs have continued to increase their domestic investments.[74]

Domestic privatization is also not universally applicable. Like any policy prescription, the domestic context can be more or less conducive to its feasibility. First, state leaders are more likely to privatize their mineral sector where they are both able to rely on an alternative source of export revenue in the short-term and feel threatened by the emergence of a rival political cleavage.[75] Transferring ownership of these resources from the state to private domestic actors thus becomes a way to bolster existing supporters and/or appease emerging rivals without the immediate need for attracting foreign capital. When privatization occurs in this manner, moreover, it is more likely to lead to the establishment of clear boundaries between those who own the resource (that is, domestic capitalists) and those who regulate it (that is, the state). Second, domestic privatization is more likely to succeed where domestic entrepreneurs have an interest in developing the mineral sector, as is clearly the case in Russia today as well as the United States in the late 1800s and Romania during the interwar period.[76]

While Stiglitz and others tend to view the problem of mineral wealth as a matter of political will alone, our research suggests that this approach fails to take the broader picture into account. Political will, like institutional capacity, is the product of incentives. Thus, even though domestic privatization can be a highly contentious process, it remains the only solution that can generate the incentives for governments in mineral-rich countries to both acquire the will and build the capacity to manage their resources effectively. Precisely because domestic capitalists own its mineral resources, rather than the state, Russia has the potential to build a brighter future than its mineral-rich counterparts in the developing world. International actors and organizations would therefore be well advised to advocate privatization to domestic owners as another possible solution for combating the resource curse, especially for new producers of mineral wealth like Azerbaijan, Kazakhstan, East Timor, Chad, and Sudan. With time and international support, they can pursue domestic privatization as a strategy and thereby create the necessary institutions to turn their mineral wealth into a blessing rather than a curse.

NOTES

1. See, for example, Deffeyes 2003, Campbell 1997.
2. Gault 2002.
3. Klare 2004.
4. U.S. Department of Energy, Energy Information Administration (DoE/EIA) 2004.
5. Davis 1995 is the only exception.
6. Sala-i-Martin and Subramanian 2003, 3.
7. See, for example, Auty 1993, Auty and Gelb 2001, Sachs and Warner 1995.
8. Auty and Mikesell 1998.
9. See, for example, Wade 1990, World Bank 1993.
10. World Bank 2001.
11. See, for example, Lewis 1984, Philip 1994.
12. World Bank 2004.
13. CIA 2003, World Bank 2004.
14. CIA 2003.
15. See, for example, Gylfason 2001, Leite and Weidmann 1999.
16. This includes six indicators (Voice and Accountability, Political Stability and Lack of Violence,

Government Effectiveness, Regulatory Quality, Rule of Law, and Control of Corruption) "based on 25 separate data sources at 18 different organizations, including the World Bank itself, Gallup International, the Economist Intelligence Unit, IMD, DRI/McGraw-Hill, Columbia University, Freedom House, Afrobarometer, Latinobarometro, the World Economic Forum, and Reporters Without Borders." World Bank 2003. Data available at http://www .worldbank.org/wbi/governance/data.html.
17. World Bank 2002, Transparency International 2004. CPI ranks countries according to the degree to which corruption is perceived to exist among public officials and politicians, ranging between 10 (highly clean) and 0 (highly corrupt). For more information, see http://www.transparency.org/ surveys/index.html#cpi.
18. See, for example, Ross 2001b.
19. See, for example, Jensen and Wantchekon 2004.
20. See, for example, Wantchekon 1999, Smith 2004.
21. Ross 2001a, 356. Herb 2005, in contrast, argues that the negative effects of oil rents on democracy have been overestimated.
22. See, for example, Baldwin 1966, Hirschman 1958.
23. See, for example, Lipset 1960, Deutsch 1961.
24. Gary and Karl 2003, 41.
25. See, for example, Sachs and Warner 1995.
26. Ascher 1999, 179.
27. Sala-i-Martin and Subramanian 2003, 13.
28. Lane and Tornell 1997.
29. Ascher 1999, 62.
30. Bradsher 2005.
31. Mikesell 1997.
32. Katz et al. 2004, 9–10.
33. Katz et al. 2004, 10, McMahon 1997.
34. Sarraf and Jiwanji 2001, 7.
35. Gelb 1985, 76.
36. Philip 1994, 12.
37. A rent is "a return in excess of a resource owner's opportunity costs" (Tollison 1982, 575); in the case of mineral-exporting countries, these returns are thus generated from foreign sources.
38. Crystal 1989, 434.

39. Karl 1997, 16.

40. Shafer 1994.

41. Crystal 1989.

42. Karl 1997, 139.

43. Ascher 1999, Ross 2001a.

44. Karl 1997, Shafer 1994, Chaudhry 1989.

45. It is worth mentioning here that our portrayal of effective state institutions differs from the large and distinguished literature on the "developmental state." The latter focuses on the need for a competent state bureaucracy for promoting industrialization and export-led growth. See, for example, Wade 1990, Evans 1995, Kohli 2004.

46. Comparing the oil and gas sector within Russia (as opposed to oil sectors in two different countries) also allows us to control for national level variation, and thus to isolate ownership structure as the key explanatory variable.

47. *Russia Journal*, May 19, 2004.

48. Rutland 1997, 8.

49. This is not the case where state oil companies are effectively monitored by a third party, such as the parliament or an independent regulatory agency, as is the case with Statoil in Norway. These institutions tend to either not exist or be ineffective, however, in developing countries.

50. On "residual claimant" theory, see Alchian and Demsetz 1972.

51. The 25 percent threshold is crucial because it allows them to block any major decision, such as the transfer of assets.

52. See Jones Luong and Weinthal 2004 for details.

53. Aslund 2001, 22.

54. *Russia Journal*, January 25, 2005.

55. Authors' interviews with representatives from both Russian and foreign oil and gas companies, Russian government officials, and Russian and foreign financial and energy experts, Moscow, September 2001 and July 2002.

56. It is interesting to note that many scholars attribute this common failure to respond to busts to *weak institutions* in resource-rich states. See, for example, Chaudhry 1989 and Shafer 1994.

57. Shafer, 1994.

58. See Jones Luong and Weinthal 2004 for details. Although they have similar interests, as direct competitors and possibly intense rivals, private owners are unlikely to rely on collusion to exert influence. In attempting to work together in order to pressure the government for favorable policies, therefore, even a small number of actors face a considerable collective action problem—particularly in a fluid context such as Russia. See, for example, Olson 1982.

59. Authors' interviews (op. cit.).

60. Authors' interview with Eric Bell, President, Conoco International Petroleum Company, Moscow, September 20, 2001.

61. Author's interview with Konstantin Reznikov, Alfa Bank, Senior Oil and Gas Analyst, Moscow, September 19, 2001.

62. See, for example, Dienes 2004, Hill 2004.

63. Authors' interviews (op. cit.).

64. Stiglitz 2004.

65. See Weinthal and Jones Luong forthcoming for details.

66. Yuganskneftegaz accounts for two-thirds of Yukos's and approximately 11 percent of Russia's total oil production.

67. Indeed, our comprehensive survey of the Russian language press from June 2003 to August 2004, which we do not have the space to present here, indicates that this is the consensus among Russian analysts.

68. In his decision, the state prosecutor cited the 100-year statute of limitations. Faulconbridge 2005.

69. Korchagina 2004.

70. This is true, for example, of the ROC Tyumenskaia Neftianaia Kompaaniia (TNK), which partnered with British Petroleum in 2003.

71. The fear of a lengthy (and high-profile) legal battle propelled a consortium of international banks to withdraw their financial support for Gazprom's bid and the Russian government to come up with an elaborate scheme to find another Kremlin-friendly buyer. See, for example, Belton 2004.

72. *Radio Free Europe/Radio Liberty (RFE/RL)*; back issues can be accessed at http://search.rferl.org/. September 29, 2004.

73. Granville and Lissovolik 2005. Russia's "insider privatization" refers to its controversial privatization program in the 1990s that allowed those with close ties to the Kremlin to gain control over the state's most important strategic resources.

74. *Moscow Times*, April 7, 2005.

75. See Jones Luong and Weinthal 2001 for details.

76. In contrast, domestic capitalists in Colombia refused the government's offer to take on the development of oilfields (Kline 1995). In Venezuela they quickly sold off their oil fields to foreign companies in order to pursue other economic interests (Lieuwen 1954).

REFERENCES

Alchian, Arman A., and Harold Demsetz. 1972. Production, information costs, and economic organization. *American Economic Review* 62 (5): 777–95.

Ascher, William. 1999. *Why governments waste natural resources: Policy failures in developing countries.* Baltimore: Johns Hopkins University Press.

Aslund, Anders. 2001. Russia. *Foreign Policy.* July/August: 20–25.

Auty, Richard M., and Raymond F. Mikesell. 1998. *Sustainable development in mineral economies.* Oxford: Clarendon Press.

Baldwin, Robert E. 1966. *Economic development and export growth.* Berkeley: University of California Press.

Belton, Catherine. 2004. Yukos accused of "filthy theft." *Moscow Times*, December 14.

Bradsher, Keith. 2005. Oil wealth wasting away in Indonesia. *New York Times*, March 19.

Campbell, Colin J. 1997. *The coming oil crisis.* Essex, UK: Multi-Science Publishing.

Central Intelligence Agency (CIA). 2003. *World Factbook 2003.* Washington, DC: Central Intelligence Agency.

Chaudhry, Kiren Aziz. 1989. The price of wealth: Business and state in labor remittance and oil economies. *International Organization* 43 (1): 101–45.

Crystal, Jill. 1989. Coalitions in oil monarchies: Kuwait and Qatar. *Comparative Politics* 21 (4): 427–43.

Davis, Graham. 1995. Learning to love the Dutch disease: Evidence from the mineral economies. *World Development* 23 (10): 1765–79.

Deffeyes, Kenneth S. 2003. *Hubbert's peak: The impending world oil shortage.* Princeton: Princeton University Press.

Deutsch, Karl W. 1961. Social mobilization and political development. *American Political Science Review* 55 (3): 493–514.

Dienes, Leslie. 2004. Observations on the problematic potential of Russian oil and the complexities of Siberia. *Eurasian Geography and Economics* 45 (5): 319–45.

Evans, Peter. 1995. *Embedded autonomy: State and industrial transformation.* Princeton: Princeton University Press.

Faulconbridge, Guy. 2005. Prosecutors go for the full 10 years. *Moscow Times*, March 30.

Friends of the Earth. 2002. Oil funds: Answer to the paradox of plenty? November.

Gary, Ian, and Terry Karl. 2003. *Bottom of the barrel: Africa's oil boom and the poor.* Catholic Relief Services.

Gault, John. 2002. The European Union: Energy security and the periphery. *Occasional Paper Series, No. 40.* Geneva Centre for Security Policy. http://www.gcsp.ch/e/publications/Other-pubs/Occ-papers/2002/40-Gault.pdf

Gelb, Alan H. 1985. Adjustment to windfall gains: A comparative study of oil-exporting countries. In *Natural resources and the macroeconomy*, eds. J. Peter Neary and Sweder van Wijnbergen, 54–95. Cambridge: MIT Press.

Gelb, Alan H., and Associates. 1988. *Oil windfalls: Blessing or curse?* New York: Oxford University Press.

Granville, Christopher, and Yaroslav Lissovolik. 2005. Dusting off a difficult amnesty. *Moscow Times*, March 30.

Gylfason, Thorvaldur. 2001. Nature, power, and growth. *Journal of Political Economy* 48 (5): 558–88.

Herb, Michael. 2005. No representation without taxation? Rents, development, and democracy. *Comparative Politics* 37 (3): 297–317.

Hill, Fiona. 2004. *Energy empire: Oil, gas, and Russia's revival.* London: Foreign Policy Centre.

Hirschman, Albert O. 1958. *The strategy of economic development*. New Haven: Yale University Press.

Jensen, Nathan, and Leonard Wantchekon. 2004. Resource wealth and political regimes in Africa. *Comparative Political Studies* 37 (7): 816–41.

Jones Luong, Pauline, and Erika Weinthal. 2001. Prelude to the resource curse: Explaining oil and gas development strategies in the Soviet successor states and beyond. *Comparative Political Studies* 34 (4): 367–99.

Karl, Terry Lynn. 1987. Petroleum and political pacts: The transition to democracy in Venezuela. *Latin American Research Review* 22 (1): 63–94.

Karl, Terry Lynn. 1997. *The paradox of plenty: Oil booms and petro-states*. Berkeley: University of California Press.

Katz, Menachem, Ulrich Bartsch, Harinder Malothra, and Milan Cuc. 2004. *Lifting the oil curse: Improving petroleum revenue management in Sub-Saharan Africa*. Washington, DC: IMF.

Klare, Michael T. 2004. *Blood and oil: The dangers and consequences of America's growing dependency on imported petroleum*. New York: Metropolitan Books.

Kline, Harvey. 1995. *Colombia democracy under assault*. Boulder: Westview Press.

Kohli, Atul. 2004. *State-directed development: Political power and industrialization in the global periphery*. Cambridge: Cambridge University Press.

Korchagina, Valeria. 2004. Kagalovsky makes new Yukos offer. *Moscow Times*, December 15.

Lane, Philip R., and Aaron Tornell. 1997. Voracity and growth. *Discussion Paper 1807*. Harvard Institute of Economic Research, Harvard University, Cambridge, MA.

Leite, Carlos, and Jens Weidmann. 1999. Does mother nature corrupt? Natural resources, corruption, and economic growth. *IMF Working Paper 99/85*.

Lewis, Stephen R. 1984. Development problems of the mineral-rich countries. In *Economic structure and performance*, eds. Moshe Syrquin, Lance Taylor, and Larry E. Westphal, 157–77. New York: Academic Press.

Lieuwen, Edwin. 1954. *Petroleum in Venezuela: A history*. Berkeley: University of California Press.

Lipset, Seymour Martin. 1960. *Political man: The social bases of politics*. Garden City, NY: Doubleday.

McMahon, Gary. 1997. The natural resource curse: Myth or reality? Mimeo, World Bank Institute.

Mikesell, Raymond F. 1997. Explaining the resource curse, with specific reference to mineral exporting countries. *Resources Policy* 23 (4): 191–99.

Olson, Mancur. 1982. *The rise and decline of nations: Economic growth, stagflation, and social rigidities*. New Haven: Yale University Press.

Philip, George. 1994. *The political economy of international oil*. Edinburgh: Edinburgh University Press.

Ross, Michael L. 2001a. Does oil hinder democracy? *World Politics* 53 (3): 325–61.

———. 2001b. *Extractive sectors and the poor: An Oxfam America report*. Boston, MA: Oxfam America.

Rutland, Peter. 1997. Lost opportunities: Energy and politics in Russia. *NBR Analysis* 8 (5).

Sachs, Jeffrey D., and Andrew M. Warner. 1995. Natural resource abundance and economic growth. *NBER Working Paper 5398*.

Sala-i-Martin, Xavier, and Arvind Subramanian. 2003. Addressing the natural resource curse: An illustration from Nigeria. *IMF Working Paper WP/03/139*.

Sarraf, Maria, and Moortaza Jiwanji. 2001. Beating the resource curse: The case of Botswana. *Environmental Economics Series, Paper 83*, World Bank.

Shafer, D. Michael. 1994. *Winners and losers: How sectors shape the developmental prospects of states*. Ithaca: Cornell University Press.

Shleifer, Andrei, and Robert Vishny. 1994. Politicians and firms. *Quarterly Journal of Economics* 109 (4): 995–1025.

Smith, Benjamin. 2004. Oil wealth and regime survival in the developing world, 1960–1999. *American Journal of Political Science* 48 (2): 232–46.

Stiglitz, Joseph. 2004. We can now cure Dutch disease. *The Guardian*, August 18.

Tollison, Robert D. 1982. Rent-seeking: A survey. *Kyklos* 35: 575–602.

U.S. Department of Energy, Energy Information Administration (DoE/EIA). 2004. *International energy outlook 2004*. Washington, DC: DoE/EIA. http://www.eia.doe.gov/oiaf/ieo/index.html.

Wade, Robert. 1990. *Governing the market: Economic theory and the role of government in East Asia industrialization*. Princeton: Princeton University Press.

Wantchekon, Leonard. 1999. Why do resource dependent countries have authoritarian governments? *Leitner Working Paper 1999–11*. New Haven: Yale Center for International and Area Studies.

Weinthal, Erika, and Pauline Jones Luong. 2001. Energy wealth and tax reform in Russia and Kazakhstan. *Resources Policy* 27 (4): 215–23.

———. Forthcoming. The paradox of energy sector reform in Russia. In *The state after communism:*

Governance in the new Russia, eds. Timothy Colton and Stephen Holmes.

World Bank. 1993. *The East Asian miracle: Economic growth and public policy*. Washington, DC: World Bank Group and Oxford University Press.

———. 2001. *World development indicators 2000*. Washington, DC: World Bank.

———. 2002. *Worldwide governance research indicators dataset 2002*. Washington, DC: World Bank.

———. 2003. Measuring the quality of governance. *Development News*, July 14.

———. 2004. *World development indicators 2003*. Washington, DC: World Bank.

Larry Diamond

THE RULE OF LAW VERSUS THE BIG MAN

As the articles in this cluster make clear, governance in Africa is in a state of transition, or some would say, suspension. Two powerful trends vie for dominance. One is the longstanding organization of African politics and states around autocratic personal rulers; highly centralized and overpowering presidencies; and steeply hierarchical, informal networks of patron-client relations that draw their symbolic and emotional glue from ethnic bonds. The other is the surge since 1990 of democratic impulses, principles, and institutions. Of course, the formal institutions of democracy—including free, fair, and competitive elections—can coexist with the informal practices of clientelism, corruption, ethnic mobilization, and personal rule by largely unchecked presidents. Indeed, much of the story of African politics over the last two decades has been the contest between these two approaches to power—even in countries that are formally democratic. But slowly, democracy, with its norms of freedom, participation, accountability, and transparency, is giving rise to new and more vigorous horizontal forms of organization, in both the state and civil society.

According to Freedom House, fully half the 48 states of sub-Saharan Africa (hereafter "Africa") are democracies today, but analysts will inevitably differ on whether the glass is half-full or half-empty. I am more worried than Richard Joseph that democratization is starting to lose momentum in Africa. Certainly Kenya's calamitous December 2007 election, which triggered horrific violence and ethnic cleansing that few analysts fully anticipated, shows that nothing can be taken for granted. As Joseph and Kwasi Prempeh note, even the high-profile democracies

From *Journal of Democracy* 19, n. 2 (April 2008), pp. 138–49.

in South Africa and Ghana are showing worrisome trends. Moreover, it is possible to argue that a number of the African countries Freedom House classifies as electoral democracies are really better scored as "competitive authoritarian states."[1]

Nevertheless, even if some of Africa's "democracies" hover in a gray zone between democracy and pseudodemocracy, the larger picture still represents historic progress. In the half-century since decolonization began, there have never been so many democracies and so much public pressure on democracy's behalf. Civil society has never been stronger, mass publics have never been so questioning and vigilant, and the natural impulse toward the reassertion of predatory personal rule has never faced so many constraints. Prempeh is right that these constraints remain weak relative to their counterparts in Europe and now parts of Asia and Latin America that are much more economically developed and better educated. Yet if we take Africa's history of abusive government as our measure, significant progress is evident.

Part of this progress is taking place at the level of specific democratic institutions. As Joel Barkan notes in his comparative analysis of six African legislatures, under certain circumstances, we see (even in Uganda's nondemocracy) the emergence of legislative coalitions for reform. These comprise legislators who (for varying motives) want to enhance their own branch's power relative to that of the executive. Doing so, he writes, entails institutional (and even constitutional) changes to give African legislatures significantly more resources, and more financial independence. The same is true for African judiciaries and other institutions of horizontal accountability, such as ombudsmen and anticorruption commissions. When these bodies have serious leaders, significant resources, and independent legal authority, they can begin to cut away at seemingly impregnable dynamics of predatory corruption and abuse of power. With leadership, resources, and authority, Joseph notes, the Economic and Financial Crimes Commission of Nigeria made unprecedented progress in prosecuting venal governors and other prominent public officials—until the country's new president reassigned the Commission's chairman in late 2007.

When Africa's "second liberation" began in 1990, the continent was home to just three countries that could be called democracies (Botswana, Mauritius, and the Gambia) with a total population of only about three million. Between that year and 2008, more than twenty African countries made transitions to democracy or something near it.[2] Today, of the 24 African countries that Freedom House rates as democracies, eight are relatively "liberal," meaning that they score no worse than a 2 on FH's scales of political rights and civil liberties (where 1 is the most free and 7 the most repressive).

Between 2001 and 2007, twenty-two African countries experienced a net improvement in their freedom scores (though some were by a small margin from a very authoritarian starting point), while only nine countries suffered declines. In 2007 itself, however, eight African countries declined in freedom while only four gained. The most recent trend is moving slightly downward, then, but over the last six years African countries have continued improving in their levels of freedom and democracy, more than a decade after the onset of this democratic wave.

The picture looks worse, however, if we focus on Africa's biggest countries, the seven with populations above thirty million. South Africa is still a liberal democracy. None of the other six—Congo (Kinshasa), Ethiopia, Kenya, Nigeria, Sudan, and Tanzania—can be said to be a democracy at all.

Still, the general transformation of African politics has been extraordinary. Many of the electoral democracies that emerged after 1990—such as those in Benin, Mali, and South Africa—have persisted for more than a decade. Following two decades of rule under coupmaker Jerry Rawlings, Ghana has emerged as one of Africa's most liberal and vibrant democracies, reclaiming a leading position like that of its early postindependence years.

The positive trend is all the more remarkable when one looks at the many unlikely democratizers.

They include four of the six poorest countries on the Human Development Index (Mali, Mozambique, Niger, and Sierra Leone) and several others in the bottom twenty (such as Benin, Burundi, Malawi, and Zambia), as well as four countries (Burundi, Liberia, Mozambique, and Sierra Leone) where democratization followed murderous civil conflicts, including the one in Burundi that left 200,000 dead.

Across Africa, the formal constitutional rules governing how leaders acquire and leave power are coming to matter more than ever before. As Daniel Posner and Daniel Young have shown in these pages, Africa's politics have grown less violent and more institutionalized since 1990.[3] Between that year and 2005, six presidents, including Uganda's Yoweri Museveni, succeeded in eviscerating term limits. But these cases were the minority. Powerful presidents such as Ghana's Rawlings and Kenya's Daniel Arap Moi, joined eventually by ten others, ran into term-limit provisions that forced them to step down. After more than two decades in power, Rawlings and Moi were tempted to hang on, but yielded to domestic and international pressure. Three African leaders—including President Olusegun Obasanjo in Nigeria—tried hard and failed to extend their presidencies. Further, from the 1960s through the 1980s, more than two-thirds of African leaders left power violently—usually, as a result of a coup or assassination. During the 1990s, Posner and Young find, peaceful exits—principally as a result of electoral defeat or voluntary resignation—became the norm. Between 2000 and 2005, roughly four out of five African leaders were replaced this way.

Even more decisive than the rise of democracy has been the end of the one-party state. Since the 1990s, African elections have become increasingly regular and frequent, and almost all of them have been contested. As has been the case in Nigeria—and in Ethiopia, the Gambia, Kenya, Uganda, and Zimbabwe, among others—many of these elections have been brutally fought and outrageously rigged. But the sight of a ruling party or a "big man" losing is no longer quite so odd. Whereas only one African president was defeated at the polls between 1960 and 1990, incumbent presidents lost one out of every seven tries at reelection between 1990 and 2005.[4] Moreover, electoral alternation has significant positive effects on public support for and confidence in democracy.[5]

Why do African presidents feel more constrained now? Posner and Young advance two intriguing explanations. One is greater sensitivity to international pressure. The median level of foreign aid (relative to the overall economy) in countries where presidents did not attempt to secure third terms was almost twice as high as in those countries where the presidents did (and often succeeded). The other explanation points to public opinion. The nine African presidents who declined to seek a third term had narrower electoral mandates than the nine who did, suggesting a greater sensitivity to public opinion.

Building from the Bottom Up

This points to another positive trend in Africa, with potentially lasting consequences: the growth of civil society.[6] As wide varieties of associations independent of ruling parties have begun to engage in political dialogue and advocacy, demands for increased political accountability gain force, challenging and at times even preempting presidents inclined to flirt with the idea of staying in power. Some of these organizations—including many student associations, trade unions, religious bodies, and interest groups based on commercial, professional, and ethnic solidarities—date back to colonial days or the era just after independence. Yet active as well is a new generation of groups devoted explicitly to promoting democracy and good governance: think tanks, bar associations, human rights organizations, women's and civic-education groups, election-monitoring networks, and local as well as national-level development organizations.

More than ever, the building of democracy in Africa is a bottom-up affair. Nongovernmental organizations are teaching people their rights and duties as citizens, giving them the skills and confidence to demand answers from their rulers, to expose and challenge corruption, to resolve conflicts peacefully, to promote accommodation among ethnic and religious groups, to monitor government budgets and spending, to promote community development, and to recruit and train new political leaders. Civic groups and think tanks are also working at the national level to monitor elections, government budgets, and parliamentary deliberations; to expose waste, fraud, and abuses of power; and to lobby for legal reforms and institutional innovations to control corruption and improve the quality and transparency of governance.

These organizations draw strength not only from the funding and advice that international foundations and donors give them, but more importantly from their increasingly dense interactions with one another. The African Democracy Forum now links dozens of organizations from thirty countries on the basis of a common desire to advance the related causes of democracy and good governance.[7] Some African civil society organizations, most notably the Institute for Democracy in South Africa (IDASA), have reached a point of institutional maturity where they are now assisting democratic development elsewhere on the continent.

Also significant has been the growth of independent media and new information and communication technologies in Africa. The long tradition of independent daily newspapers has been enriched by a proliferation of newsweeklies and community and cross-border radio stations. Many of the community stations focus on local-development and health issues, from agriculture to HIV/AIDS, but they also address political issues and compensate for their low-wattage signals with high-voltage independence. And some broadcast from exile as the last sources of credible information about the deplorable conditions in their own home countries. One of the best is SW Radio Africa. Accurately self-billed as the "Independent Voice of Zimbabwe," it left the air when the Mugabe regime succeeded in suppress-

ing its signal with Chinese-provided jamming gear. Undaunted, the station then turned to live streaming and posting on the Internet.

Perhaps most revolutionary are the ways that digital technology is being used in Africa, even where few computers (not to mention broadband Internet access) can be found. One nonprofit organization, kiwanja.net, is making available free software—FrontlineSMS—that can be used by charities and NGOs to facilitate text-messaging via short-message service (SMS) on everything from crop, weather, and road conditions to health news and politics. "Originally developed for conservationists to keep in touch with communities in National Parks in South Africa, the system allows mass-messaging to mobile phones and crucially the ability [for recipients] to reply to a central computer."[8]

Then there is the mobile phone, whose beauty is its versatility and astonishingly rapid empowerment of even poor individuals. Today, more than 30 million Nigerians (nearly one in every four) own a mobile phone. In Africa as a whole, the number of mobile users is believed to be approaching 300 million.[9] This rapid spread has enabled quantum leaps forward in election monitoring. In Nigeria in April 2007, millions of ordinary citizens instantly became election monitors by reporting what they saw (much of it bad, unfortunately) at the polls. The profusion of evidence did not stop massive rigging, but it may be helping to provide the legal basis for court challenges to overturn some of the cheating's effects.

The abovementioned FrontlineSMS technology is the brainchild of intrepid British anthropologist and programmer Ken Banks. Now being revised with support from the MacArthur Foundation, FrontlineSMS has also served to facilitate feedback to community radio programs in South Africa, to monitor voting in the Philippines, to send "security alerts to fieldworkers in Afghanistan [and] market prices to smallholder farmers in Aceh, and to circumvent government restrictions in countries including Zimbabwe and Pakistan."[10] Increasingly in Africa, and around the world, text-messaging will give citizens, NGOs, and community radio stations a powerful tool not only to extend their reach and connect people in ways that enhance development, but to monitor what governments do, document human rights abuses as they happen, and facilitate civic organization and demonstrations.

As text-messaging gains momentum in Africa, it will probably encounter a technological challenge from its biggest global nemesis, the communist regime in China. The rulers of the People's Republic are continually and desperately looking for ways to contain and disrupt any uncontrolled citizen activity that takes on a political edge. African dictatorships can be expected to call on Beijing for help in fighting this new tool for promoting democratic mobilization. African civil societies, meanwhile, can be expected to look for ways around the control mechanisms—one hopes with plenty of technical support from sympathetic actors in international civil society.

Coinciding with the flowering of civil society has been a visible public demand for and appreciation of democracy. When surveyed by the Afrobarometer in 2005 and 2006, an average of 62 percent of the public in eighteen countries said that "democracy is preferable to any other kind of government."[11] Levels of support for democracy ran as high as 75 percent in Ghana, Kenya, and Senegal, and reached 65 percent or higher in ten of the countries surveyed. In fact, in only a few African countries can one find much of an avowed appetite for any specific form of authoritarian rule, and never does it rise above a fifth of the population. Moreover, this is not just an abstract commitment to democracy in general. Four out of five Africans surveyed believe that "regular, open, and honest elections" are the only way to choose their country's leaders, and two-thirds agree that elected assemblies (not the president) should make the laws in the country, even if the president disagrees with them.[12] Only about one in six Africans, on average, expresses a positive preference for an authoritarian option such as military or one-party rule. And a slight majority (52 percent) actively rejects all three authoritarian options offered.

Africans' support for democracy seems to flow from something other than a naïve sense that democracy must spell quick economic progress. When asked to define what democracy means to them, "a majority of Africans interviewed (54 percent) regard it in procedural terms by referring to the protection of civil liberties, participation in decision making, voting in elections, and governance reforms."[13] And when asked whether they felt that their system of electoral democracy "should be given more time to deal with inherited problems" or instead, if it "cannot produce results soon, we should try another form of government," 56 percent of Africans in 2005–2006 chose to give democracy more time. This represents a significant increase in patience with democracy since 2000.

Michael Bratton notes that while the demand for democracy is proving fairly resilient in Africa, the perceived supply is more questionable. For example, while 81 percent of Africans want free and fair elections that can remove incumbents, only 47 percent think they are getting this in their countries. Two-thirds of Africans want their president to be subject to the rule of law, but barely a third (36 percent) thinks that he is.[14] Clearly, Africans value and demand democracy—but African parties and politicians are not meeting citizens' aspirations.

Consequently, disillusionment is rising. Between 2000 and 2005, satisfaction with the way democracy works declined an average of 13 percentage points (from 58 to 45 percent) across the countries surveyed. While satisfaction rose in a few relatively well-functioning democracies such as Ghana and South Africa, it declined in eight of the twelve countries surveyed both times. Nevertheless, even on the supply side there are cautious grounds for optimism. The perception that one's own country is a democracy has held constant at around 50 percent, and 54 percent think it is likely that their country will remain a democracy.[15] Nor are the problematic numbers set in stone. On the contrary, there is evidence that actually delivering democracy can dramatically improve citizen attitudes and perceptions. Analyzing the 2005 data, Bratton found that respondents' perception of the most recent national election as free and fair was the most powerful predictor of their readiness to agree that their countries were democracies. In other words, the ruler's performance is no longer enough to satisfy the public—formal institutions are starting to matter more than informal ones.[16]

The Deadening Hand of Personal Rule

These trends, hopeful as they are, nonetheless tell only part of the story. Countries such as Cameroon, Eritrea, Ethiopia, Gabon, Sudan, and Togo remained trapped in longstanding patterns of authoritarian rule. Nigeria, Uganda under the increasingly corrupt Museveni, and now Kenya have been slipping backwards. And in Zimbabwe, deepening repression is morphing into a psychosis of authoritarian misrule under an aging dictator, Robert Mugabe, who seems increasingly detached from reality as his country's economy collapses amid hyperinflation that his policies have bred.

No less worrisome are the poor governance, persistent corruption, and stubborn personalism that so often continue to beset Africa's democracies. Of the six measures that the World Bank Institute uses to gauge the quality of governance in a country, the one known as "voice and accountability" (which includes freedom of expression and citizen participation in selecting the government) is a rough and partial surrogate for democracy. The others measure political stability and the absence of violence; the effectiveness of public services and administration; whether or not public regulations "permit and promote private sector development"; the rule of law (including the quality of policing and the courts); and control of corruption.

Africa does poorly on all these measures. On average, it ranks in the thirtieth percentile—a little better on the political measures of accountability and stability, but slightly worse on the measures of rule of law, corruption control, regulatory quality, and governmental effectiveness. On these latter four measures, which I collect together as a gauge of "state quality," Africa's mean percentile ranking, twenty-eighth, trails well behind Eastern Europe (fifty-ninth), Latin America and East Asia (forty-seventh), the Middle East (forty-second), and even South Asia (thirty-sixth).

Save for South Africa, the other six largest countries in Africa rank very low in their quality of governance. Five of the six have worse governance than the continent as a whole, and three of them dismally so. Across all six measures, Nigeria ranks in the thirteenth percentile. On rule of law plus control of corruption and political stability plus control of violence, only 5 percent of countries score worse. Ethiopia ranks in the eighteenth percentile, Sudan in the fifth, Congo (Kinshasa) in the third. Kenya and Tanzania do better, at the twenty-sixth and thirty-sixth percentiles, respectively, but Kenya still scores below the African average.

Underlying these painful figures is the continuing neopatrimonial character of politics in Africa. Experts call postcolonial African states *neo*patrimonial because they combine the forms of a modern bureaucratic state—constrained in theory by laws, constitutions, and other impersonal rules and standards—with the informal reality of personalized, unaccountable power and pervasive patron-client ties. These ties radiate out and down from the biggest "big man"—the autocratic president—to his lieutenants and allies, who in turn serve as patrons to lower-level power brokers, and down to the fragmented mass of ordinary citizens, who are trapped by their dependence on local political patrons.

In such systems, the informal always trumps the formal. Subordinates owe loyalty to their personal patrons, not to laws and institutions. Presidents and their minions use state resources as a personal slush fund to maintain political dominance, giving their clients state offices, jobs, licenses, contracts, vehicles, bribes, and other access to illicit rents, while getting unconditional support in return.[17] State offices at every level become permits to loot, either for an individual or a somewhat wider network of family members, ethnic kin, political clients, and business cronies.[18] Corruption, clientelism, and personal rule thus seep into the culture, making the system even more resilient. In Africa, contending patron-client networks organize along ethnic or subethnic lines, and the president sees his ethnic kin as the most reliable loyalists in the struggle for power. This makes the system particularly unstable, as conflicts over pelf, power, and identity mix in a volatile, even explosive brew.[19] The typical African pattern of concentrating extreme power in the presidency makes politics even more of a tense, zero-sum game. This helps to explain how a single rigged election can ignite the paroxysms of violence and ethnic cleansing that a horrified world has been watching lately in Kenya, where ethnic groups that have been shut out of the presidency ever since independence nurse deep anger.

The fundamental purpose of neopatrimonial governments is not to produce *public* goods—roads, bridges, markets, irrigation, education, health care, public sanitation, clean drinking water, effective legal systems—that increase productivity, improve human capital, stimulate investment, and generate development. The point of neopatrimonialism, rather, is to produce *private* goods for those with access to power. Contracts are granted not on the basis of who can deliver the best service for the lowest price, but rather on who will pay the biggest bribe. Budgets are steered to projects that can readily generate bribes. Government funds disappear into the overseas accounts of officeholders. Public payrolls are swollen with the ranks of phantom workers and soldiers whose pay goes into the pockets of higher-ups.

One thing that can arrest the decay and refresh the system is a change in leadership. But a key feature of the neopatrimonial system is the way the "king of the hill" hangs on and on. In 2005, Uganda's President Museveni, whose original claim to his office was being the top general of the strongest private army in his conflict-wracked homeland, "openly bribed members of parliament, blackmailed and intimidated others to amend the constitution and remove term limits on the presidency so that he can run again, and again, and again."[20] In the run-up to the February 2006 election, he stepped up his harassment of the independent media and those elements of civil society that he had not already coopted. Then he jailed the main opposition presidential candidate, before finally claiming a highly suspect first-round victory through apparent manipulation of the vote count.[21]

Museveni's two decades in power hardly make him Africa's longest-serving president, however. Omar Bongo of small but oil-rich Gabon in West Africa has ruled for nearly four decades. Robert Mugabe's merciless reign in Zimbabwe has stretched past a quarter-century. In Angola, Cameroon, and Guinea, presidents have also ruled for well over twenty years, and in Burkina Faso for nearly that. Sudan's Hassan al-Bashir has held power for eighteen years, and Meles Zenawi in Ethiopia and Yahya Jammeh in the Gambia for more than a decade each. None of them shows any sign of surrendering office. Of course, such prolonged personal reigns are hardly new in Africa—witness the late Mobutu Sese Seko's 32 years in power in Zaire, now Congo (Kinshasa)—but they have always been associated with national decline, if not disaster.

If Africa is now suspended between democracy and personal rule, what can tip it toward democracy? The deciding factor will not be economic development. For probably decades to come, much of Africa will remain well below the high level of development that seems to assure democratic survival. Steady economic growth can help to give people more confidence in democracy, building up its long-term legitimacy. But sustainable development has been stymied by the same factor that has undermined democracy itself: bad governance. If both democracy and development are to have a future in Africa, the core priority must be to improve the quality of governance.

Social scientists often lament their lack of adequate understanding of the policy challenges of our time, calling for more research. We do need to understand better how winning coalitions can be generated and sustained for the kinds of institutional reforms that will gain traction on Africa's core problem of bad, corrupt, abusive governance. But broadly, we know where the answers lie. Countervailing institutions of power—the judiciary, the legislature, and the whole apparatus of countercorruption, audit, human rights, and other oversight bodies that are sometimes called a "fourth branch of government"—must be greatly strengthened in their political autonomy, statutory authority, and financial and human resources. Power and resources must be decentralized down to elected lower levels of government, ideally (in any large country) through a federal system (the one saving grace that has held Nigeria together). Political parties must themselves be democratized internally and made more effective as organizations, independent of ethnicity or personal ties. Elections must be truly free and fair, and thus electoral administrations must be made up of career civil-service professionals who, as in India, have the training, resources, autonomy, and *esprit de corps* to resist partisan pressures. State economic ownership and control must be diminished, but the state must be strengthened in its capacity to deliver its essential mission of managing the economy and generating the public goods (such as schools, roads, courts, markets, and other infrastructure) needed for development. And citizens must have the freedom to monitor and report on what government does, and to organize to challenge it and pursue their interests.

It is not difficult to find, in African civil societies and in the state itself, numerous actors ready to rise to the challenge. The problem is that African leaders are not generally to be found among these coalitions for reform, because they calculate that their own interests lie not in reform, but in building or reinforcing monopolies of power and wealth. Of course, in the absence of democracy, it is always the monopolists who triumph. But democracy in itself is no guarantee against the resurgence of many bad practices.

For much of the last half-century (and well before that of course, under colonial rule), the missing link has been the international community, which has been only too happy to embrace any African despot in the quest for resources and strategic advantage. Idealists, by contrast, have thought that the answer lies in "foreign aid," which is supposed to make up for the vast shortages of financial resources needed to deliver health, education, and roads. About US$600 billion later, we know (or at least we *should* know) that pouring more aid unconditionally on bad governments is like pouring gasoline on a fire. In the circumstances of predatory rule in Africa, aid functions like the revenue that gushes in from oil exports—it is just another source of external rents that enables rulers to float on a cushion above their societies, controlling the state without having to answer to their own people.

Certainly Richard Joseph is correct that the entry of China into the "great game" of aid, investment, and resources in Africa creates a new context, in some ways akin to the superpower competition of the Cold War. And the "new cold war" against international terrorism has not helped. Both developments have given African authoritarian regimes new alternatives and new forms of leverage against Western pressure for democratic reform. But this is not the 1960s or 1970s. African societies are informed and autonomously organized as never before. Africans are aware of their political rights and demanding of democracy as never before. And together, Europe and the United States still provide the vast bulk of aid and investment in Africa.

Most of all, principled pressure is needed from international actors, tying substantial flows of development assistance to concrete institutional improvements in governance. Donors can also provide generous financial and technical assistance to the institutions of governance—African legislatures, judiciaries, countercorruption commissions, and other agencies of horizontal accountability—that must work well if the balance is to tip from autocracy to democracy. It is the very fluidity of things on the continent today—so powerfully evoked by Joseph's concept of "frontier Africa"—that makes so much possible. From the experience of a small but growing number of better-functioning African democracies, we know that the continent is not condemned to perpetual misrule. The challenge now is for the international donors to join with Africans in demanding that their governments be truly accountable.

NOTES

1. Steven Levitsky and Lucan Way, *Competitive Authoritarianism: International Linkage. Organizational Power, and the Fare of Hybrid Regimes* (Cambridge University Press, forthcoming). They classify countries on the basis of their respective regimes during the period 1990–95, and then track their evolution. On this basis, they classify Benin, Malawi, Mozambique, and Zambia all as competitive authoritarian regimes, whereas other analyses (including that of Freedom House) often have considered them democracies. I exclude the Central African Republic because of its very poor freedom score, average 5 on the two seven-point scales of Freedom House.

2. The Gambia, whose politics had been dominated for almost thirty years by one leader and his party, slipped entirely from democratic ranks after a military coup in 1994. Retrospectively, some analysts have questioned just how democratic the Gambia was at that point.

3. Daniel Posner and Daniel Young, "The Institutionalization of Political Power in Africa," *Journal of Democracy* 18 (July 2007): 126–40.

4. Posner and Young, "Institutionalization of Political Power in Africa," 131.

5. Michael Bratton, "The 'Alternation Effect' in Africa," *Journal of Democracy* 15 (October 2004): 147–58.

6. The evidence and arguments here are developed at greater length in Larry Diamond, *Developing Democracy: Toward Consolidation* (Baltimore: Johns Hopkins University Press, 1999), ch. 6.

7. See *www.africandemocracyforum.org*.

8. "Texts Monitor Nigerian Elections," BBC News, 20 April 2007. Available at *http://news.bbc.co.uk/2/hi/technology/6570919.stm*.

9. This would probably represent something like 30 percent of the roughly 750 million people in sub-Saharan Africa, even allowing for some people owning multiple devices.

10. From *http://frontlinesms.kiwanja.net*.

11. Most of the data presented here from the Afrobarometer is available in the publications of the project, at *www.afrobarometer.org/publications.html*. See in particular, "The Status of Democracy, 2005–2006: Findings from Afrobarometer Round 3 for 18 Countries," Afrobarometer Briefing Paper no. 40, June 2006.

12. Michael Bratton, "Formal vs. Informal Institutions in Africa," *Journal of Democracy* 18 (July 2007): 96–110.

13. Michael Bratton, Robert Mattes, and E. Gyimah-Boadi, *Public Opinion, Democracy, and Market Reform in Africa* (Cambridge: Cambridge University Press, 2005), 69–70.

14. Bratton, "Formal vs. Informal Institutions," Figure 2, 106.

15. Bratton, "Formal vs. Informal Institutions," 102.

16. Bratton, "Formal vs. Informal Institutions," Table 2, 107.

17. Michael Bratton and Nicolas van de Walle, *Democratic Experiments in Africa: Regime Transitions in Comparative Perspective* (Cambridge: Cambridge University Press, 1997), 61–68; Robert H. Jackson and Carl G. Rosberg, *Personal Rule in Black Africa: Prince, Autocrat, Prophet, Tyrant* (Berkeley: University of California Press, 1982), 38–42.

18. Drawing on Max Weber, Joseph has called such systems "prebendal." Richard A. Joseph, *Democracy and Prebendal Politics in Nigeria: The Rise and Fall of the Second Republic* (Cambridge: Cambridge University Press, 1987), 6; see also 55–68 for elaboration of the concept and its relationship to clientelism.

19. Joseph, *Democracy and Prebendal Politics in Nigeria,* 8. This work develops these themes at length,

20. Andew Mwenda, "Please Stop Helping Us," paper presented to the Novartis Foundation, 12 August 2006, 3.

21. Andrew Mwenda, "Personalizing Power in Uganda," *Journal of Democracy* 18 (July 2007): 23–37.

Steven Levitsky and Lucan A. Way

THE RISE OF COMPETITIVE AUTHORITARIANISM

The post–Cold War world has been marked by the proliferation of hybrid political regimes. In different ways, and to varying degrees, polities across much of Africa (Ghana, Kenya, Mozambique, Zambia, Zimbabwe), postcommunist Eurasia (Albania, Croatia, Russia. Serbia, Ukraine), Asia (Malaysia, Taiwan), and Latin America (Haiti, Mexico, Paraguay, Peru) combined democratic rules with authoritarian governance during the 1990s. Scholars often treated these regimes as incomplete or transitional forms of democracy. Yet in many cases these expectations (or hopes) proved overly optimistic. Particularly in Africa and the former Soviet Union, many regimes have either remained hybrid or moved in an authoritarian direction. It may therefore be time to stop thinking of these cases in terms of transitions to democracy and to begin thinking about the specific types of regimes they actually are.

In recent years, many scholars have pointed to the importance of hybrid regimes. Indeed, recent academic writings have produced a variety of labels for mixed cases, including not only "hybrid regime" but also "semidemocracy," "virtual democracy," "electoral democracy," "pseudodemocracy," "illiberal democracy," "semi-authoritarianism," "soft authoritarianism," "electoral authoritarianism," and Freedom House's "Partly Free."[1] Yet much of this literature suffers from two important weaknesses. First, many studies are characterized by a democratizing bias. Analyses frequently treat mixed regimes as partial or "diminished" forms of democracy,[2] or as undergoing prolonged transitions to democracy. Such characterizations imply that these cases are moving in a democratic direction. Yet as both Jeffrey Herbst and Thomas Carothers have recently argued, this is often not the case.[3] Although some hybrid regimes (Mexico, Senegal, Taiwan) underwent democratic transitions in the 1990s, others (Azerbaijan, Belarus) moved in a distinctly authoritarian direction. Still others either remained stable or moved in multiple directions (Malaysia, Russia, Ukraine, Zambia, Zimbabwe), making the unidirectional implications of the word "transitional" misleading.

Second, terms like "semidemocratic," "semi-authoritarian," and "Partly Free" are often used as residual categories and tend to gloss over important differences among regime types. For example, El Salvador, Latvia, and Ukraine were all hybrid regimes in the early 1990s, and each received a combined political rights and civil liberties score of six—or "Partly Free"—from Freedom House in 1992–93. Yet these regimes differed in fundamental ways. Whereas in Latvia the principal undemocratic

From *Journal of Democracy* 13, no. 2 (April 2002), pp. 51–65.

feature was the absence of citizenship rights for people of Russian descent, in El Salvador the main undemocratic features included substantial human rights violations and the absence of civilian control over the military. Ukraine possessed both universal citizenship rights and a civilian-controlled military, but civil liberties were frequently violated and incumbents routinely abused or manipulated democratic procedures. Hence, although each of these cases could be categorized as "hybrid," "semidemocratic," or "partly free," such labels obscure crucial differences—differences that may have important causal implications. Different mixes of authoritarian and democratic features have distinct historical roots, and they may have different implications for economic performance, human rights, and the prospects for democracy.

Defining Competitive Authoritarianism

This article examines one particular type of "hybrid" regime: *competitive authoritarianism.* In competitive authoritarian regimes, formal democratic institutions are widely viewed as the principal means of obtaining and exercising political authority. Incumbents violate those rules so often and to such an extent, however, that the regime fails to meet conventional minimum standards for democracy. Examples include Croatia under Franjo Tudjman, Serbia under Slobodan Milošević, Russia under Vladimir Putin, Ukraine under Leonid Kravchuk and Leonid Kuchma, Peru under Alberto Fujimori, and post-1995 Haiti, as well as Albania, Armenia, Ghana, Kenya, Malaysia, Mexico, and Zambia through much of the 1990s. Although scholars have characterized many of these regimes as partial or "diminished" forms of democracy, we agree with Juan Linz that they may be better described as a (diminished) form of authoritarianism.[4]

Competitive authoritarianism must be distinguished from democracy on the one hand and full-scale authoritarianism on the other. Modern democratic regimes all meet four minimum criteria: (1) Executives and legislatures are chosen through elections that are open, free, and fair; (2) virtually all adults possess the right to vote; (3) political rights and civil liberties, including freedom of the press, freedom of association, and freedom to criticize the government without reprisal, are broadly protected; and (4) elected authorities possess real authority to govern, in that they are not subject to the tutelary control of military or clerical leaders.[5] Although even fully democratic regimes may at times violate one or more of these criteria, such violations are not broad or systematic enough to seriously impede democratic challenges to incumbent governments. In other words, they do not fundamentally alter the playing field between government and opposition.[6]

In competitive authoritarian regimes, by contrast, violations of these criteria are both frequent enough and serious enough to create an uneven playing field between government and opposition. Although elections are regularly held and are generally free of massive fraud, incumbents routinely abuse state resources, deny the opposition adequate media coverage, harass opposition candidates and their supporters, and in some cases manipulate electoral results. Journalists, opposition politicians, and other government critics may be spied on, threatened, harassed, or arrested. Members of the opposition may be jailed, exiled, or—less frequently—even assaulted or murdered. Regimes characterized by such abuses cannot be called democratic.

Competitive authoritarianism must therefore be distinguished from unstable, ineffective, or otherwise flawed types of regimes that nevertheless meet basic standards of democracy, and this includes what Guillermo O'Donnell has called "delegative democracies."[7] According to O'Donnell, delegative democracies are characterized by low levels of horizontal accountability (checks and balances) and therefore exhibit powerful, plebiscitarian, and occasionally abusive executives. Yet such regimes meet minimum standards for democracy. Delegative democracy thus applies to such cases as Argentina and Brazil in the early 1990s, but not to Peru after Fujimori's 1992 presidential self-coup.

Yet if competitive authoritarian regimes fall short of democracy, they also fall short of full-scale authoritarianism. Although incumbents in competitive authoritarian regimes may routinely manipulate formal democratic rules, they are unable to eliminate them or reduce them to a mere façade. Rather than openly violating democratic rules (for example, by banning or repressing the opposition and the media), incumbents are more likely to use bribery, co-optation, and more subtle forms of persecution, such as the use of tax authorities, compliant judiciaries, and other state agencies to "legally" harass, persecute, or extort cooperative behavior from critics. Yet even if the cards are stacked in favor of autocratic incumbents, the persistence of meaningful democratic institutions creates arenas through which opposition forces may—and frequently do—pose significant challenges. As a result, even though democratic institutions may be badly flawed, both authoritarian incumbents and their opponents must take them seriously.

In this sense, competitive authoritarianism is distinct from what might be called "façade" electoral regimes—that is, regimes in which electoral institutions exist but yield no meaningful contestation for power (such as Egypt, Singapore, and Uzbekistan in the 1990s). Such regimes have been called "pseudodemocracies," "virtual democracies," and "electoral authoritarian" regimes. In our view, they are cases of full-scale authoritarianism.[8] The line between this type of regime and competitive authoritarianism can be hard to draw, and noncompetitive electoral institutions may one day become competitive (as occurred in Mexico). It is essential, however, to distinguish regimes in which democratic institutions offer an important channel through which the opposition may seek power from those regimes in which democratic rules simply serve as to legitimate an existing autocratic leadership.

Finally, competitive authoritarianism must be distinguished from other types of hybrid regimes. Regimes may mix authoritarian and democratic features in a variety of ways, and competitive authoritarianism should not be viewed as encompassing all of these regime forms. Other hybrid regime types include "exclusive republics"[9] (regimes with strong democratic institutions but highly restrictive citizenship laws) and "tutelary" or "guided" democracies—competitive regimes in which nondemocratic actors such as military or religious authorities wield veto power.

Four Arenas of Democratic Contestation

Due to the persistence of meaningful democratic institutions in competitive authoritarian regimes, arenas of contestation exist through which opposition forces may periodically challenge, weaken, and occasionally even defeat autocratic incumbents. Four such arenas are of particular importance: (1) the electoral arena; (2) the legislature; (3) the judiciary; and (4) the media.

(1) The electoral arena. The first and most important arena of contestation is the electoral arena. In authoritarian regimes, elections either do not exist or are not seriously contested. Electoral competition is eliminated either de jure, as in Cuba and China, or de facto, as in Kazakhstan and Uzbekistan. In the latter, opposition parties are routinely banned or disqualified from electoral competition, and opposition leaders are often jailed. In addition, independent or outside observers are prevented from verifying results via parallel vote counts, which creates widespread opportunities for vote stealing. As a result, opposition forces do not present a serious electoral threat to incumbents, and elections are, for all intents and purposes, noncompetitive. Thus Kazakhstani president Nursultan Nazarbayev was reelected in 1999 with 80 percent of the vote, and in Uzbekistan, President Islam Karimov was

reelected in 2000 with 92 percent of the vote. (As a rule of thumb, regimes in which presidents are reelected with more than 70 percent of the vote can generally be considered noncompetitive.) In such cases, the death or violent overthrow of the president is often viewed as a more likely means of succession than his electoral defeat.

In competitive authoritarian regimes, by contrast, elections are often bitterly fought. Although the electoral process may be characterized by large-scale abuses of state power, biased media coverage, (often violent) harassment of opposition candidates and activists,[10] and an overall lack of transparency, elections are regularly held, competitive (in that major opposition parties and candidates usually participate), and generally free of massive fraud. In many cases, the presence of international observers or the existence of parallel vote-counting procedures limits the capacity of incumbents to engage in large-scale fraud. As a result, elections may generate considerable uncertainty, and autocratic incumbents must therefore take them seriously. For example, Russian president Boris Yeltsin in 1996 and Ukrainian president Leonid Kuchma in 1999 faced strong electoral challenges from former communist parties. Despite concerted efforts to use blackmail and other techniques to secure votes,[11] Kuchma won only 35 percent of the vote in the first round of the 1999 presidential elections and 56 percent in the second round. In Kenya, longtime autocrat Daniel arap Moi won reelection with bare pluralities in 1992 and 1997, and in Zimbabwe, the opposition Movement for Democratic Change nearly won the 2000 parliamentary elections. In several cases, opposition forces have managed to defeat autocratic incumbents or their hand-picked candidates, as occurred in Nicaragua in 1990, Zambia in 1991, Malawi and Ukraine in 1994, Albania in 1997, and Ghana in 2000.

Although incumbents may manipulate election results, this often costs them dearly and can even bring them down. In Peru, for example, Fujimori was able to gain reelection in 2000 but was forced to resign amid scandal months later. Similarly, efforts by Milošević to falsify Serbian election results in 2000 led to a regime crisis and the president's removal. Regime crises resulting from electoral fraud also occurred in Mexico in 1988 and Armenia in 1996.

(2) The legislative arena. A second arena of contestation is the legislature. In most full-scale authoritarian regimes, legislatures either do not exist or are so thoroughly controlled by the ruling party that conflict between the legislature and the executive branch is virtually unthinkable. In competitive authoritarian regimes, legislatures tend to be relatively weak, but they occasionally become focal points of opposition activity. This is particularly likely in cases in which incumbents lack strong majority parties. In both Ukraine and Russia in the 1990s, for example, presidents were faced with recalcitrant parliaments dominated by former communist and other left-wing parties. The Ukrainian parliament repeatedly blocked or watered down economic reform legislation proposed by President Kuchma, and in 2000–2001, despite Kuchma's threats to take "'appropriate" measures if it did not cooperate, parliament blocked the president's effort to call a referendum aimed at reducing the powers of the legislature. Although incumbents may attempt to circumvent or even shut down the legislature (as in Peru in 1992 and Russia in 1993), such actions tend to be costly, particularly in the international arena. Thus both Fujimori and Yeltsin held new legislative elections within three years of their "self-coups," and Yeltsin continued to face opposition from the post-1993-coup parliament.

Even where incumbent executives enjoy large legislative majorities, opposition forces may use the legislature as a place for meeting and organizing and (to the extent that an independent media exists) as a public platform from which to denounce the regime. In Peru, despite the fact that opposition parties exerted little influence over the legislative process between 1995 and 2000, anti-Fujimori legislators used congress (and media coverage of it) as a place to air their views. In Ukraine in November 2000, opposition deputy Aleksandr Moroz used parliament to accuse the president of murder and to distribute damaging tapes of the president to the press.

(3) The judicial arena. A third arena of potential contestation is the judiciary. Governments in competitive authoritarian regimes routinely attempt to subordinate the judiciary, often via impeachment, or, more subtly, through bribery, extortion, and other mechanisms of co-optation, In Peru, for example, scores of judges—including several Supreme Court justices—were entwined in the web of patronage, corruption, and blackmail constructed by Fujimori's intelligence chief, Vladimiro Montesinos. In Russia, when the Constitutional Court declared Yeltsin's 1993 decree disbanding parliament to be unconstitutional, Yeltsin cut off the Court's phone lines and took away its guards. In some cases, governments resort to threats and violence. In Zimbabwe, after the Supreme Court ruled that occupations of white-owned farmland—part of the Mugabe government's land-redistribution policy—were illegal, independent justices received a wave of violent threats from pro-government "war veterans." Four justices, including Chief Justice Anthony Gubbay, opted for early retirement in 2001 and were replaced by justices with closer ties to the government.

Yet the combination of formal judicial independence and incomplete control by the executive can give maverick judges an opening. In Ukraine, for example, the Constitutional Court stipulated that President Kuchma's referendum to reduce the powers of the legislature was not binding. In Slovakia, the Constitutional Court prevented Vladimír Mečiar's government from denying the opposition seats in parliament in 1994, and in Serbia, the courts legitimized local opposition electoral victories in 1996. Courts have also protected media and opposition figures from state persecution. In Croatia, the courts acquitted an opposition weekly that had been charged with falsely accusing President Tudjman of being a devotee of Spain's Francisco Franco. Similarly, in Malaysia in 2001, a High Court judge released two dissidents who had been jailed under the regime's Internal Security Act and publicly questioned the need for such a draconian law.[12]

Although competitive authoritarian governments may subsequently punish judges who rule against them, such acts against formally independent judiciaries may generate important costs in terms of domestic and international legitimacy. In Peru, for example, the pro-Fujimori congress sacked three members of the Constitutional Tribunal in 1997 after they attempted to block Fujimori's constitutionally dubious bid for a third presidential term. The move generated sharp criticism both domestically and abroad, however, and the case remained a thorn in the regime's side for the rest of the decade.

(4) The media. Finally, the media are often a central point of contention in competitive authoritarian regimes. In most full-blown autocracies, the media are entirely state-owned, heavily censored, or systematically repressed. Leading television and radio stations are controlled by the government (or its close allies), and major independent newspapers and magazines are either prohibited by law (as in Cuba) or de facto eliminated (as in Uzbekistan and Turkmenistan). Journalists who provoke the ire of the government risk arrest, deportation, and even assassination. In competitive authoritarian regimes, by contrast, independent media outlets are not only legal but often quite influential, and journalists—though frequently threatened and periodically attacked—often emerge as important opposition figures. In Peru, for example, independent newspapers such as *La República* and *El Comercio* and weekly magazines such as *Sí* and *Caretas* operated freely throughout the 1990s. In Ukraine, newspapers such as *Zerkalo nedeli*, *Den*, and, more recently, *Vicherni visti* functioned as important sources of independent views on the Kuchma government.

Independent media outlets often play a critical watchdog role by investigating and exposing government malfeasance. The Peruvian media uncovered a range of government abuses, including the 1992 massacre of students at La Cantuta University and the forgery of the signatures needed for Fujimori's party to qualify for the 2000 elections. In Russia, Vladimir Gusinsky's Independent TV was an important source of criticism of the Yeltsin government, particularly with respect to its actions in Chechnya. In Zimbabwe, the *Daily News* played an important role in exposing the abuses of the Mugabe government. Media outlets may also serve as mouthpieces for opposition forces. In Serbia, the Belgrade radio station B-92 served as a key center of opposition to Milošević in the second half of the 1990s. Newspapers played an important role in supporting opposition forces in Panama and Nicaragua in the late 1980s.

Executives in competitive authoritarian regimes often actively seek to suppress the independent media, using more subtle mechanisms of repression than their counterparts in authoritarian regimes. These methods often include bribery, the selective allocation of state advertising, the manipulation of debts and taxes owed by media outlets, the fomentation of conflicts among stockholders, and restrictive press laws that facilitate the prosecution of independent and opposition journalists. In Russia, the government took advantage of Independent TV's debts to the main gas company, Gazprom, to engineer a takeover by government-friendly forces. In Peru, the Fujimori government gained de facto control over all of the country's privately owned television stations through a combination of bribery and legal shenanigans, such as the invalidation of Channel 2 owner Baruch Ivcher's citizenship. Governments also make extensive use of libel laws to harass or persecute independent newspapers "legally." In Ghana, for example, the Jerry Rawlings government used colonial-era libel statutes to imprison several newspaper editors and columnists in the 1990s, and in Croatia, the Open Society Institute reported in 1997 that major independent newspapers had been hit by more than 230 libel suits. Similarly, Armenia's government used libel suits to quiet press criticism after the country's controversial 1996 elections.[13]

Yet efforts to repress the media may be costly to incumbents in competitive authoritarian regimes. For example, when in 1996 the Tudjman government in Croatia tried to revoke the license of Radio 101, a popular independent station in the capital, the massive protests that broke out both galvanized the opposition and temporarily split the ruling party. In Ukraine in 2000, charges that President Kuchma had sought the killing of an opposition journalist led to large domestic protests and partial isolation from the West. In Peru, the persecution and exiling of Ivcher provoked substantial protest at home and became a focal point of criticism abroad.

Inherent Tensions

Authoritarian governments may coexist indefinitely with meaningful democratic institutions. As long as incumbents avoid egregious (and well-publicized) rights abuses and do not cancel or openly steal elections, the contradictions inherent in competitive authoritarianism may be manageable. Using bribery, co-optation, and various forms of "legal" persecution, governments may limit opposition challenges without provoking massive protest or international repudiation.

Yet the coexistence of democratic rules and autocratic methods aimed at keeping incumbents in power creates an inherent source of instability. The presence of elections, legislatures, courts, and an independent media creates periodic opportunities for challenges by opposition forces. Such challenges create a serious dilemma for autocratic incumbents. On the one hand, repressing them is costly, largely because the challenges tend to be both formally legal and widely perceived (domestically and internationally) as legitimate. On the other hand, incumbents could lose power if they let democratic challenges run their course.[14] Periods of serious democratic contestation thus bring out the contradictions inherent in competitive authoritarianism, forcing autocratic incumbents to choose between egregiously violating democratic rules, at the cost of international isolation and domestic conflict, and allowing the challenge to proceed, at the cost of possible defeat. The result is often some kind of regime crisis, as occurred in Mexico in 1988; Nicaragua in 1990; Zambia in 1991; Russia in 1993; Armenia in 1996; Albania in 1997; Ghana, Peru, Serbia, and Ukraine in 2000; and Zambia (again) in 2001. A similar crisis appears likely to emerge in Zimbabwe surrounding the March 2002 presidential election.

In some cases, such as those of Kenya, Malaysia, Russia, and Ukraine, autocratic incumbents weathered the storm. In several of these countries, the regime cracked down and dug in deeper. In other cases, such as Nicaragua in 1990, Zambia in 1991, and Ghana and Mexico in 2000, competitive authoritarian governments failed to crack down and lost power. In still other cases, including Peru and Serbia, autocrats attempted to crack down but, in doing so, were badly weakened and eventually fell.

But succession is not democratization. Although in many cases (Croatia, Nicaragua, Peru, Slovakia, Serbia) incumbent turnover resulted in democratic transitions, in other cases, including Albania, Zambia, Ukraine, and Belarus, newly elected leaders continued or even intensified many of the authoritarian practices of their predecessors. Hence, while the removal of autocratic elites creates an important *opportunity* for regime change and even democratization, it does not ensure such an outcome.

Although it is beyond the scope of this article to explain variations in the capacity of competitive authoritarian regimes to survive crises brought about by episodes of democratic contestation, one pattern is worth noting.[15] In regions with closer ties to the West, particularly Latin America and Central Europe, the removal of autocratic incumbents has generally resulted in democratization in the post–Cold War period. In Latin America, for example, four out of five competitive authoritarian regimes democratized after 1990 (the Dominican Republic, Mexico, Nicaragua, and Peru, but

not Haiti). Similarly, during the same period four out of five competitive authoritarian regimes in Central Europe democratized (Croatia, Serbia, Slovakia, and Romania, but not Albania). By contrast, the record of competitive authoritarian regimes in Africa and the former Soviet Union is strikingly different. Among former Soviet republics, only one competitive authoritarian regime (Moldova) democratized in the 1990s.

This evidence suggests that proximity to the West may have been an important factor shaping the trajectory of competitive authoritarian regimes in the 1990s. Linkages to the West—in the form of cultural and media influence, elite networks, demonstration effects, and direct pressure from Western governments—appear to have raised the costs of authoritarian entrenchment, making the democratization of competitive authoritarian regimes more likely. Where Western linkages were weaker, or where alternative, nondemocratic hegemons (such as Russia or China) exerted substantial influence, competitive authoritarian regimes were more likely either to persist or to move in a more authoritarian direction.

Paths to Competitive Authoritarianism

Although competitive authoritarian regimes are not a new phenomenon (historical examples include parts of East Central Europe in the 1920s and Argentina under Perón from 1946 to 1955), they have clearly proliferated in recent years. Competitive authoritarianism emerged out of three different regime paths during the 1990s. One path was the decay of a full-blown authoritarian regime. In these cases, established authoritarian regimes were compelled—often by a combination of domestic and international pressure—either to adopt formal democratic institutions or to adhere seriously to what had previously been façade democratic institutions. Yet due to the weakness of opposition movements, transitions fell short of democracy, and incumbents proved adept at manipulating or selectively adhering to the new democratic rules. Transitions of this type occurred across much of sub-Saharan Africa, where economic crisis and international pressure compelled established autocrats to call multiparty elections, but where many transitions fell short of democratization and many autocrats retained power.

A second path to competitive authoritarianism was the collapse of an authoritarian regime, followed by the emergence of a new, competitive authoritarian regime. In these cases, weak electoral regimes emerged, more or less by default, in the wake of an authoritarian breakdown. Although the absence of democratic traditions and weak civil societies created opportunities for elected governments to rule autocratically, these governments lacked the capacity to consolidate authoritarian rule. This path was followed by such postcommunist countries as Armenia, Croatia, Romania, Russia, Serbia, and Ukraine, as well as by Haiti after 1994.

A third path to competitive authoritarianism was the decay of a democratic regime. In these cases, deep and often longstanding political and economic crises created conditions under which freely elected governments undermined democratic institutions—either via a presidential "self-coup" or through selective, incremental abuses—but lacked the will or capacity to eliminate them entirely. Examples of such transitions include Peru in the early 1990s and perhaps contemporary Venezuela.

The roots of this recent proliferation lie in the difficulties associated with consolidating both democratic *and* authoritarian regimes in the immediate post–Cold War period. Notwithstanding the global advance of democracy in the 1990s (and the democratic optimism that it inspired among scholars), in much of the world democratic regimes remained difficult to establish or sustain. A large number of transitions took place in countries with high levels of poverty, inequality, and illiteracy; weak states and civil societies; institutional instability; contested national borders; and—in parts of the former communist world—continued domination by the state of the economy, major religious institutions, and other areas of social activity.

Yet if the prospects for full-scale democratization remained bleak in much of the post–Cold War world, so too were the prospects for building and sustaining full-scale authoritarian regimes.[16] In large part, this change was a product of the post–Cold War international environment. Western liberalism's triumph and the Soviet collapse undermined the legitimacy of alternative regime models and created strong incentives for peripheral states to adopt formal democratic institutions. As Andrew Janos has argued, periods of liberal hegemony place a "web of constraints" on nondemocratic governments that seek to maintain international respectability and viability. Thus, during the brief period of liberal hegemony that followed World War I, relatively authoritarian governments in Central Europe faced strong pressure to tolerate a semi-free press, regular scrutiny from opposition members of parliament, and a quasi-independent judiciary.[17] When Western liberal states are challenged by authoritarian counter-hegemonic powers, however, these "webs of constraints" tend to disappear. Counter-hegemonic powers provide alternative sources of legitimacy and military and economic assistance, thereby weakening the incentive for governing elites to maintain formal democratic institutions. Thus the emergence of Nazi Germany and Soviet Russia as regional powers contributed to the collapse of Central European hybrid regimes in the 1930s, and the strength of the Soviet Union facilitated the establishment of Leninist dictatorships across much of the Third World during the Cold War. When Western powers face a challenger to their hegemony, they are more likely to tolerate autocracies that can present themselves as buffers against their rivals.

The 1990s marked a period of Western liberal hegemony similar to that of the 1920s but much broader in scope. International influences took many forms, including demonstration effects, conditionality (as in the case of European Union membership), direct state-to-state pressure (in the form of sanctions, behind-the-scenes diplomacy, and even direct military intervention), and the activities of emerging transnational actors and institutions. In this new context, the liberal democratic model gained unprecedented acceptance among postcommunist and Third World elites. Perhaps more importantly, the absence of alternative sources of military and economic aid increased the importance of being on good terms with Western governments and institutions. Although the effect of international pressure varied considerably across regions (and even across countries), for most governments in most poorer and middle-income countries, the benefits of adopting formal democratic institutions—and the costs of maintaining overtly authoritarian ones—rose considerably in the 1990s.

Emerging and potential autocrats also confronted important domestic impediments to the consolidation of authoritarian regimes. To consolidate a fully closed regime, authoritarian elites must eliminate all major sources of contestation through the systematic repression or co-optation of potential opponents. Such action requires both elite cohesion and a minimally effective—and financially solvent—state apparatus. Resource scarcity has made it more difficult for leaders to sustain the patronage networks that previously undergirded authoritarian state structures. In addition, uncertain hierarchical control over repressive organs, while heightening the risk of civil war, has also increased the difficulty of consolidating authoritarian rule. Finally, in many postcommunist regimes the dispersal of control over different state and economic resources among different groups made it difficult for any single leader to establish complete control, resulting in a kind of pluralism by default.

A substantial number of regimes *were* able to overcome the domestic and international obstacles to authoritarian rule in the 1990s. Some benefited from pockets of permissiveness in the international system, due in large part to economic or security issues that trumped democracy promotion on Western foreign policy agendas. Others benefited from state control over revenues from valuable commodi-

ties (such as oil), which undermined the development of an autonomous civil society and gave rulers the means to co-opt potential opponents, and still others took advantage of quasi-traditional elite networks that facilitated the establishment of neopatrimonial regimes (as in Central Asia).

Yet in much of Africa, Latin America, and postcommunist Eurasia in the 1990s, emerging or potential autocrats lacked these advantages. Due to a combination of international pressure, state weakness, and elite fragmentation, many incumbents found the cost of co-opting or repressing opponents to be prohibitively high. As a result, even some highly autocratic leaders were unable to eliminate important arenas of contestation. The sources of authoritarian weakness varied across cases. In Albania and Haiti, for example, international factors were probably decisive in preventing full-scale authoritarian rule. In Africa, a contraction of resources caused by the end of Cold War sponsorship and the conditionality imposed by international financial institutions left some governments too weak to co-opt or repress even relatively feeble opposition challenges.[18] In post-Soviet countries such as Moldova, Russia, and Ukraine, the fragmentation of control over state and economic resources generated political competition even where civil society remained weak. What is common to virtually all of these cases, however, is that pluralism and democratic contestation persisted less because elites wanted them than because elites simply could not get rid of them.

In the 1990s, then, competitive authoritarian regimes were most likely to emerge where conditions were unfavorable to the consolidation of either democratic or authoritarian regimes. It must be noted, of course, that such conditions do not necessarily result in competitive authoritarianism. In some cases, including El Salvador, Mali, and Mongolia, democracy may take hold in spite of highly unfavorable conditions. In other cases, the breakdown of authoritarian rule may result in state collapse and civil war, as occurred in Liberia, Sierra Leone, and Somalia.

Conceptualizing Nondemocracies

We conclude by echoing Thomas Carothers' call to move beyond what he calls the "transition paradigm."[19] It is now clear that early hopes for democratization in much of the world were overly optimistic. Many authoritarian regimes have survived the "third wave" of democratization. In other cases, the collapse of one kind of authoritarianism yielded not democracy but a new form of nondemocratic rule. Indeed, a decade after the collapse of the Soviet Union, the majority of the world's independent states remained nondemocratic. Yet whereas an extensive literature has emerged concerning the causes and consequences of democratization, emerging types of democracy, and issues of democratic consolidation, remarkably little research has been undertaken on the emergence or persistence of nondemocratic regimes.

The post–Cold War Western liberal hegemony, global economic change, developments in media and communications technologies, and the growth of international networks aimed at promoting democracy and human rights all have contributed to reshaping the opportunities and constraints facing authoritarian elites. As a result, some forms of authoritarianism, such as totalitarianism and bureaucratic authoritarianism, have become more difficult to sustain. At the same time, however, several new (or partially new) nondemocratic regime types took on greater importance in the 1990s, including competitive authoritarianism. A range of other nondemocratic outcomes also gained in importance, including other types of hybrid regimes, postcommunist patrimonial dictatorships, and cases of sustained state collapse ("chaosocracy").[20] Research on these nondemocratic outcomes is critical to gaining a better understanding of the full (rather than hoped for) set of alternatives open to post–Cold War transitional regimes.

NOTES

The authors thank Jason Brownlee, Timothy Colton, Michael Coppedge, Keith Darden, Jorge Domínguez, Steve Hanson, Marc Morjé Howard, Rory MacFarquhar, Mitch Orenstein, Maria Popova, Andreas Schedler, Oxana Shevel, and Richard Snyder for their comments on earlier drafts of this article.

1. Terry Lynn Karl, "The Hybrid Regimes of Central America," *Journal of Democracy* 6 (July 1995): 72–87; William Case, "Can the 'Halfway House' Stand? Semidemocracy and Elite Theory in Three Southeast Asian Countries," *Comparative Politics* 28 (July 1996): 437–64; Richard A. Joseph, "Africa, 1990–1997: From *Abertura* to Closure," *Journal of Democracy* 9 (April 1998): 3–17; Larry Diamond, *Developing Democracy: Toward Consolidation* (Baltimore: Johns Hopkins University Press, 1999); Fareed Zakaria, "The Rise of Illiberal Democracy," *Foreign Affairs* 76 (November–December 1997): 22–41; Thomas Carothers, *Aiding Democracy Abroad: The Learning Curve* (Washington, D.C.: Carnegie Endowment for International Peace, 1999); Gordon P. Means, "Soft Authoritarianism in Malaysia and Singapore," *Journal of Democracy* 7 (October 1996): 103–17; Andreas Schedler, "Mexico's Victory: The Democratic Revelation," *Journal of Democracy* 11 (October 2000): 5–19; and M. Steven Fish, "Authoritarianism Despite Elections: Russia in Light of Democratic Theory and Practice," paper prepared for delivery at the 2001 Annual Meeting of the American Political Science Association, San Francisco, 30 August–2 September 2001.

2. See David Collier and Steven Levitsky, "Democracy with Adjectives: Conceptual Innovation in Comparative Research," *World Politics* 49 (April 1997): 430–51.

3. See Jeffrey Herbst, "Political Liberalization in Africa after Ten Years," *Comparative Politics* 33 (April 2001): 357–75; Thomas Carothers, "The End of

the Transition Paradigm," *Journal of Democracy* 13 (January 2002): 5–21.

4. Juan J. Linz, *Totalitarian and Authoritarian Regimes* (Boulder, Colo.: Lynne Rienner, 2000), 34.

5. See Scott Mainwaring, Daniel Brinks, and Aníbal Pérez Linan, "Classifying Political Regimes in Latin America, 1945–1999," *Studies in Comparative International Development* 36 (Spring 2001). This definition is consistent with what Larry Diamond calls "mid-range" conceptions of democracy (Larry Diamond, *Developing Democracy*, 13–15).

6. Obviously, the exact point at which violations of civil and political rights begin to fundamentally alter the playing field is difficult to discern and will always be open to debate. However, the problem of scoring borderline cases is common to all regime conceptualizations.

7. Guillermo O'Donnell, "Delegative Democracy," *Journal of Democracy* 5 (January 1994): 55–69.

8. Larry Diamond, *Developing Democracy*, 15–16; Richard Joseph, "Africa, 1990–1997"; Jason Brownlee, "Double Edged Institutions: Electoral Authoritarianism in Egypt and Iran," paper presented at the 2001 Annual Meeting of the American Political Science Association, San Francisco, 30 August–2 September 2001.

9. Philip G. Roeder, "Varieties of Post-Soviet Authoritarian Regimes," *Post-Soviet Affairs* 10 (January–March 1994): 61–10.

10. In Kenya, government-backed death squads were responsible for large-scale violence, particularly in ethnic minority areas. See Joel Barkan and Njuguna Ng'ethe, "Kenya Tries Again," in Larry Diamond and Marc F. Planner, eds., *Democratization in Africa* (Baltimore: Johns Hopkins University Press, 1999), 185. Substantial violence against opposition forces was also seen in Serbia and Zimbabwe in the 1990s.

11. See Keith Darden, "Blackmail as a Tool of State Domination: Ukraine Under Kuchma," *East European Constitutional Review* 10 (Spring–Summer 2001): 67–71.

12. *The Economist*, 14 July 2001, 37.

13. H. Kwasi Prempeh, "A New Jurisprudence for Africa," *Journal of Democracy* 10 (July 1999): 138; Nebojsa Bjelakovic and Sava Tatic, "Croatia: Another Year of Bleak Continuities," *Transitions-on-Line*, http://archive.tol.cz/countries/croar97.html (1997); Mikhail Diloyen, "Journalists Fall through the Legal Cracks in Armenia," *Eurasia Insight* (June 2000).

14. These dilemmas are presented in an insightful way in Andreas Schedler, "The Nested Game of Democratization by Elections," *International Political Science Review* 23 (January 2002).

15. For a more developed explanation, see Steven Levitsky and Lucan A. Way, "Competitive Authoritarianism: Hybrid Regime Change in Peru and Ukraine in Comparative Perspective," Studies in Public Policy Working Paper No. 355 (Glasgow: University of Strathclyde Center for the Study of Public Policy, 2001).

16. On obstacles to authoritarianism in the former Soviet Union, see Philip G. Roeder, "The Rejection of Authoritarianism," in Richard Anderson, M. Stephen Fish, Stephen E. Hanson, and Philip G. Roeder, *Postcommunism and the Theory of Democracy* (Princeton: Princeton University Press, 2001).

17. Andrew Janos, *East Central Europe in the Modern World: The Politics of Borderlands From Pre- to Postcommunism* (Stanford, Calif.: Stanford University Press, 2000), 97–99.

18. Michael Bratton and Nicolas van de Walle, *Democratic Experiments in Africa: Regime Transitions in Comparative Perspective* (New York: Cambridge University Press, 1997), 100.

19. Thomas Carothers, "The End of the Transition Paradigm."

20. See Richard Snyder, "Does Lootable Wealth Breed Disorder? States, Regimes, and the Political Economy of Extraction," paper presented at the 2001 Annual Meeting of the American Political Science Association, San Francisco, 30 August–2 September 2001. See also Juan J. Linz, *Totalitarian and Authoritarian Regimes*, 37.

7

POLITICAL VIOLENCE

In this chapter we look at violence against states and peoples that is not carried out by states themselves. Recall from Chapter 2 that the state is commonly defined as the monopoly of violence over a territory. States use this force at the domestic level to generate stability through such institutions as the law and police. At the international level, armies and diplomacy help generate peace. But at times, the monopoly of force may escape state control, as in the case of revolutions and terrorism.

In some circumstances, the public may seek to overthrow the current regime through revolution. Theda Skocpol transformed political science with her piece, "France, Russia, China: A Structural Analysis of Social Revolutions" (1976). Expanded in her 1979 book *States and Social Revolutions*, Skocpol's thinking on revolution contributed to political science by returning our attention to the state, and *States and Social Revolutions* went on to become one of the most cited works in the field. Why do revolutions, sweeping transformations in existing regime and state institutions, occur? In each case, Skocpol believes that a particular set of conditions in the state and society is necessary to set such revolutions in motion. Her analysis, influenced by Marx, is structural—that is, institutions are central (if not decisive) in shaping the likelihood of dramatic political change.

Such institutional arguments make a great deal of sense, and we shall see in Chapter 8 how institutions such as educational systems can help explain the paths of Communist collapse. However, these same theories are less helpful in understanding why revolution occurs when it does. Few expected communism's fall in 1989, or the Arab Spring in 2011. Timur Kuran's "Now Out of Never: The Element of Surprise in the East European Revolution of 1989" (1991), attempts to analyze "the element of surprise" in communism's demise, is an important contribution in this regard. Though accepting the importance of institutional forces, Kuran argues that understanding revolution requires an understanding of individual motivations that will bring a public that is quiescent on one day out on the streets the next. A central point he emphasizes is preference falsification. In authoritarian systems, individuals might express in private preferences for political change that differs widely from those they express in public. This difference leads to a wide divergence between what behavior is observed within the community (by those in the community or on the outside) and what potential for political change lies beneath the surface.

In the case of Eastern Europe, Kuran notes such important factors as the existence of organized opposition combined with signals from the Soviet Union that certain types of political reform would be tolerated. Such factors helped shift private preferences to the public sphere. People felt safe enough to express their grievances publicly with relatively little fear of reprisal, and organized oppositions helped "push the bandwagon into motion," so to speak. Kuran concludes that this interaction between private preferences and structural factors means that revolutions will continue to surprise us in the future—just as the Arab Spring did.

Goldstone's "Understanding the Revolutions of 2011" helps bring these ideas and arguments into the present. Goldstone, a longtime scholar of revolution, reviews the factors that must be in place for a revolution to succeed, noting the "striking resemblance" between the revolutions of 2011 and those before them. But he also argues that there are important institutional differences as well. In particular, he notes that in the Middle East (as elsewhere) authoritarianism has commonly taken a sultanistic form, in which power and wealth are monopolized by a dictatorship that keeps state institutions weak. The result is a system that ostensibly promotes modernization, but due to corruption blocks opportunities for the population (especially the young) to advance. Sultanism can fall to revolution, but the legacy of sultanism is a badly functioning state that poses a major challenge to institutionalizing democracy.

Whereas the above works debate the central factors surrounding revolution, related work tackles the puzzle of what causes terrorism. Some scholars and observers have assumed that terrorism is primarily a result of institutional factors, such as authoritarianism or poverty. However, the research tends not to support such arguments. Martha Crenshaw's 1981 piece, "The Causes of Terrorism," focuses more on individual motivations that lead people to resort to terrorist acts. Crenshaw notes that certain structural preconditions can foster terrorism, but they are not enough to explain its use or growth. More central is the role of a minority or elite group: their grievances and perceived lack of alternatives and the internal culture they foster. In recent years some scholars have rejected these arguments, asserting that terrorism should be understood best simply as a strategic tool that actors use because it generates the results they desire. Max Abrahms's 2008 piece, "What Terrorists Really Want," takes issue with this argument. There is little evidence that terrorists achieve their stated goals, he argues, or that ideology necessarily drives terrorism. Rather, Abrahms builds on Crenshaw's work to suggest that individual factors are key. Marginalized individuals are drawn to terrorist organizations because of the social bonds they provide, not because of the cause. This would seem to go against the common conception of terrorists as people so committed to a cause or idea that they can justify killing civilians and often themselves. But like revolution, the very act of political rebellion can be a powerful source of solidarity, even if the vision of change is far from clear. Just as revolutions come out of nowhere, the sources of terrorism similarly emerge from individual motivations not easily captured by social science.

Theda Skocpol

FRANCE, RUSSIA, CHINA: A STRUCTURAL ANALYSIS OF SOCIAL REVOLUTIONS

A revolution," writes Samuel P. Huntington in *Political Order in Changing Societies*, "is a rapid, fundamental, and violent domestic change in the dominant values and myths of a society, in its political institutions, social structure, leadership, and government activities and policies."[1] In *The Two Tactics of Social Democracy in the Democratic Revolution*, Lenin provides a different, but complementary perspective: "Revolutions," he says, "are the festivals of the oppressed and the exploited. At no other time are the masses of the people in a position to come forward so actively as creators of a new social order."[2]

Together these two quotes delineate the distinctive features of *social revolutions*. As Huntington points out, social revolutions are rapid, basic transformations of socio-economic and political institutions, and — as Lenin so vividly reminds us — social revolutions are accompanied and in part effectuated through class upheavals from below. It is this combination of thoroughgoing structural transformation and massive class upheavals that sets social revolutions apart from coups, rebellions, and even political revolutions and national independence movements.

If one adopts such a specific definition, then clearly only a handful of successful social revolutions have ever occurred. France, 1789, Russia, 1917, and China, 1911–49, are the most dramatic and clear-cut instances. Yet these momentous upheavals have

helped shape the fate of the majority of mankind, and their causes, consequences, and potentials have preoccupied many thoughtful people since the late eighteenth century.

Nevertheless, recently, social scientists have evidenced little interest in the study of social revolutions as such. They have submerged revolutions within more general categories — such as "political violence," "collective behavior," "internal war," or "deviance" — shorn of historical specificity and concern with large-scale social change.[3] The focus has been mostly on styles of behavior common to wide ranges of collective incidents (ranging from riots to coups to revolutions, from panics to hostile outbursts to "value-oriented movements," and from ideological sects to revolutionary parties), any of which might occur in any type of society at any time or place. Revolutions tend increasingly to be viewed not as "locomotives of history," but as extreme forms of one or another sort of behavior that social scientists, along with established authorities everywhere, find problematic and perturbing.

Why this avoidance by social science of the specific problem of social revolution? Ideological bias might be invoked as an explanation, but even if it were involved, it would not suffice. An earlier generation of American social scientists, certainly no more politically radical than the present generation, employed the "natural history" approach to analyze handfuls of cases of great revolutions.[4] In large part, present preoccupation with broader categories can be understood as a reaction against this natural history approach, deemed by its critics too "historical" and "a-theoretical."

From *Comparative Studies in Society and History* 18, no. 2 (April 1976), pp. 175–203. Some of the author's notes have been omitted.

In the "Introduction" to a 1964 book entitled *Internal War*, Harry Eckstein defines "a theoretical subject" as a "set of phenomena about which one can develop informative, testable generalizations that hold for all instances of the subject, and some of which apply to those instances alone."[5] He goes on to assert that while "a statement about two or three cases is certainly a generalization in the dictionary sense, a generalization in the methodological sense must usually be based on more; it ought to cover a number of cases large enough for certain rigorous testing procedures like statistical analysis to be used."[6] Even many social scientists who are not statistically oriented would agree with the spirit of this statement: theory in social science should concern itself only with general phenomena; the "unique" should be relegated to "narrative historians."

Apparently it directly follows that no theory specific to social revolution is possible, that the *explanandum* of any theory which sheds light on social revolutions must be something more general than social revolution itself. Hence the efforts to conceptualize revolution as an extreme instance of patterns of belief or behavior which are also present in other situations or events.

This approach, however, allows considerations of technique to define away substantive problems. Revolutions are not just extreme forms of individual or collective behavior. They are distinctive conjunctures of socio-historical structures and processes. One must comprehend them as complex wholes — however few the cases — or not at all.

Fortunately social science is not devoid of a way of confronting this kind of problem. Social revolutions *can* be treated as a "theoretical subject." To test hypotheses about them, one may employ the comparative method, with national historical trajectories as the units of comparison. As many students of society have noted, the comparative method is nothing but that mode of multivariate analysis to which sociologists necessarily resort when experimental manipulations are not possible and when there are "too many variables and not enough cases" — that is, not enough cases for statistical testing of hypotheses.[7] According to this method, one looks for concomitant variations, contrasting cases where the phenomena in which one is interested are present with cases where they are absent, controlling in the process for as many sources of variation as one can, by contrasting positive and negative instances which otherwise are as similar as possible.

Thus, in my inquiry into the conditions for the occurrence and short-term outcomes of the great historical social revolutions in France, Russia and China, I have employed the comparative historical method, specifically contrasting the positive cases with (a) instances of non-social revolutionary modernization, such as occurred in Japan, Germany and Russia (up to 1904), and with (b) instances of abortive social revolutions, in particular Russia in 1905 and Prussia/Germany in 1848. These comparisons have helped me to understand those aspects of events and of structures and processes which distinctively rendered the French, Chinese and Russian Revolutions successful social revolutions. In turn, the absence of conditions identified as positively crucial in France, Russia and China constitutes equally well an explanation of why social revolutions have not occurred, or have failed, in other societies. In this way, hypotheses developed, refined, and tested in the comparative historical analysis of a handful of cases achieve a potentially general significance.

Explaining the Historical Cases: Revolution in Modernizing Agrarian Bureaucracies

Social revolutions in France, Russia and China occurred, during the earlier world-historical phases of modernization, in agrarian bureaucratic societies situated within, or newly incorporated into, international fields dominated by more economically modern nations abroad. In each case, social revolution was a conjuncture of three developments: (1) the collapse or incapacitation of central administrative and military machineries; (2) widespread peasant rebellions; and (3) marginal elite political movements. What each social revolution minimally "accomplished" was the extreme rationalization and centralization of state institutions, the removal of a traditional landed upper class from intermediate (regional and local) quasi-political supervision of the peasantry, and the elimination or diminution of the economic power of a landed upper class.

In the pages that follow, I shall attempt to explain the three great historical social revolutions, first, by discussing the institutional characteristics of agrarian states, and their special vulnerabilities and potentialities during the earlier world-historical phases of modernization, and second, by pointing to the peculiar characteristics of old regimes in France, Russia and China, which made them uniquely vulnerable among the earlier modernizing agrarian states to social-revolutionary transformations. Finally, I shall suggest reasons for similarities and differences in the outcomes of the great historical social revolutions.

An agrarian bureaucracy is an agricultural society in which social control rests on a division of labor and a coordination of effort between a semi-bureaucratic state and a landed upper class.[8] The landed upper class typically retains, as an adjunct to its landed property, considerable (though varying in different cases) undifferentiated local and regional authority over the peasant majority of the population. The partially bureaucratic central state extracts taxes and labor from peasants either indirectly through landlord intermediaries or else directly, but with (at least minimal) reliance upon cooperation from individuals of the landed upper class. In turn, the landed upper class relies upon the backing of a coercive state to extract rents and/or dues from the peasantry. At the political center, autocrat, bureaucracy, and army monopolize decisions, yet (in varying degrees and modes) accommodate the regional and local power of the landed upper class and (again, to varying degrees) recruit individual members of this class into leading positions in the state system.

Agrarian bureaucracies are inherently vulnerable to peasant rebellions. Subject to claims on their surpluses, and perhaps their labor, by landlords and state agents, peasants chronically resent both. To the extent that the agrarian economy is commercialized, merchants are also targets of peasant hostility. In all agrarian bureaucracies at all times, and in France, Russia and China in non-revolutionary times, peasants have had grievances enough to warrant, and recurrently spur, rebellions. Economic crises (which are endemic in semi-commercial agrarian economies anyway) and/or increased demands from above for rents or taxes might substantially enhance the likelihood of rebellions at particular times. But such events ought to be treated as short-term precipitants of peasant unrest, not fundamental underlying causes.

Modernization is best conceived not only as an *intra*societal process of economic development accompanied by lagging or leading changes in non-economic institutional spheres, but also as a world-historic *inter*societal phenomenon. Thus,

> a necessary condition of a society's modernization is its incorporation into the historically unique network of societies that arose first in Western Europe in early modern times and today encompasses enough of the globe's population for the world to be viewed for some purposes as if it consisted of a single network of societies.[9]

Of course, societies have always interacted. What was special about the modernizing intersocietal network that arose in early modern Europe was, first, that it was based upon trade in commodities and manufactures, as well as upon strategic politico-military competition between independent states,[10] and, second, that it incubated the "first (self-propelling) industrialization" of England after she had gained commercial hegemony within the Western European-centered world market.[11]

In the wake of that first commercial-industrial breakthrough, modernizing pressures have reverberated throughout the world. In the first phase of world modernization, England's thoroughgoing commercialization, capture of world market hegemony, and expansion of manufactures (both before and after the technological Industrial Revolution which began in the 1780s), transformed means and stakes in the traditional rivalries of European states and put immediate pressure for reforms, if only to facilitate the financing of competitive armies and navies, upon the other European states and especially upon the ones with less efficient fiscal machineries.[12] In the second phase, as Europe modernized and further expanded its influence around the globe, similar militarily compelling pressures were brought to bear on those non-European societies which escaped immediate colonization, usually the ones with pre-existing differentiated and centralized state institutions.

During these phases of global modernization, independent responses to the dilemmas posed by incorporation into a modernizing world were possible and (in some sense) necessary for governmental elites in agrarian bureaucracies. Demands for more and more efficiently collected taxes; for better and more generously and continuously financed militaries; and for "guided" national economic development, imitating the available foreign models, were voiced within these societies especially by bureaucrats and the educated middle strata. The demands were made compelling by international military competition and threats. At the same time, governmental leaders did have administrative machineries, however rudimentary, at their disposal for the implementation of whatever modernizing reforms seemed necessary and feasible (at given moments in world history). And their countries had not been incorporated into dependent economic and political positions in a world stratification system dominated by a few fully industrialized giants.

But agrarian bureaucracies faced enormous difficulties in meeting the crises of modernization. Governmental leaders' realm of autonomous action tended to be severely limited, because few fiscal or economic reforms could be undertaken which did not encroach upon the advantages of the traditional landed upper classes which constituted the major social base of support for the authority and functions of the state in agrarian bureaucracies. Only so much revenue could be squeezed out of the peasantry, and yet landed upper classes could often raise formidable obstacles to rationalization of tax systems. Economic development might mean more tax revenues and enhanced military prowess, yet it channelled wealth and manpower away from the agrarian sector. Finally, the mobilization of mass popular support for war tended to undermine the traditional, local authority of landlords or landed bureaucrats upon which agrarian bureaucratic societies partly relied for the social control of the peasantry.

Agrarian bureaucracies could not indefinitely "ignore" the very specific crises, in particular fiscal and martial, that grew out of involvement with a modernizing world, yet they could not adapt without undergoing fundamental structural changes. Social revolution helped accomplish "necessary" changes in some but was averted by reform or "revolution from above" in others. Relative stagnation, accompanied by subincorporation into international power spheres, was still another possibility (e.g., Portugal, Spain?). Social revolution was never deliberately "chosen." Societies only "backed into" social revolutions.

All modernizing agrarian bureaucracies have peasants with grievances and face the unavoidable challenges posed by modernization abroad. So, in some sense, potential for social revolution has been built into all modernizing agrarian bureaucracies. Yet, only a handful have succumbed. Why? A major part of the answer, I believe, lies in the insight that "not oppression, but weakness, breeds revolution."[13] It is the breakdown of a societal mode of social control which allows and prompts social revolution to unfold. In the historical cases of France, Russia and China, the unfolding of social revolution depended upon the emergence of revolutionary crises occasioned by the incapacitation of administrative and military organizations. That incapacitation, in turn, is best explained not as a function of mass discontent and mobilization, but as a function of a combination of pressures on state institutions from more modernized countries abroad, and (in two cases out of three) built-in structural incapacities to mobilize increased resources in response to those pressures. France, Russia and China were also special among all agrarian bureaucracies in that their agrarian institutions afforded peasants not only the usual grievances against landlords and state agents but also "structural space" for autonomous collective insurrection. Finally, once administrative/military breakdown occurred in agrarian bureaucracies with such especially insurrection-prone peasantries, then, and only then, could organized revolutionary leaderships have great impact upon their societies' development—though not necessarily in the ways they originally envisaged.

Breakdown of Societal Controls: Foreign Pressures and Administrative/Military Collapse

If a fundamental cause and the crucial trigger for the historical social revolutions was the incapacitation of administrative and military machineries in modernizing agrarian bureaucracies, then how and why did this occur in France, Russia and China? What differentiated these agrarian bureaucracies which succumbed to social revolution from others which managed to respond to modernizing pressures with reforms from above? Many writers attribute differences in response to qualities of will or ability in governmental leaders. From a sociological point of view, a more satisfying approach might focus on the interaction between (a) the magnitude of foreign pressures brought to bear on a modernizing agrarian bureaucracy, and (b) the particular structural characteristics of such societies that underlay contrasting performances by leaders responding to foreign pressures and internal unrest.

Overwhelming foreign pressures on an agrarian bureaucracy could cut short even a generally successful government program of reforms and industrialization "from above." Russia is the obvious case in point. From at least the 1890s onward, the Czarist regime was committed to rapid industrialization, initially government-financed out of resources squeezed from the peasantry, as the only means of rendering Russia militarily competitive with Western nations. Alexander Gerschenkron argues that initial government programs to promote heavy industry had succeeded in the 1890s to such an extent that, when the government was forced to reduce its direct financial and administrative role after 1904, Russia's industrial sector was nevertheless capable of autonomously generating further growth (with the aid of foreign capital investments).[14] Decisive steps to modernize agriculture and free peasant labor for permanent urban migration were taken after the unsuccessful Revolution of 1905.[15] Had she been able to sit out World War I, Russia might have recapitulated the German experience of industrialization facilitated by bureaucratic guidance.

But participation in World War I forced Russia to fully mobilize her population including her restive peasantry. Army officers and men were subjected to years of costly fighting, and civilians to mounting economic privations—all for nought. For, given Russia's "industrial backwardness . . . enhanced by the fact that Russia was very largely blockaded . . . ," plus the "inferiority of the Russian military machine to the German in everything but sheer numbers . . . , military defeat, with all of its inevitable consequences for the internal condition of the country, was very nearly a foregone conclusion."[16] The result was administrative demoralization and paralysis, and the disintegration of the army. Urban insurrections which brought first middle-strata moderates and then the Bolsheviks to power could not be suppressed, owing to the newly-recruited character and war weariness of the urban garrisons.[17] Peasant grievances were enhanced, young peasant men were politicized through military experiences, and, in consequence, spreading peasant insurrections from the spring of 1917 on could not be controlled.

It is instructive to compare 1917 to the Revolution of 1905. Trotsky called 1905 a "dress rehearsal" for 1917, and, indeed, many of the same social forces with the same grievances and similar political programs took part in each revolutionary drama. *What accounts for the failure of the Revolution of 1905 was the Czarist regime's ultimate ability to rely upon the army to repress popular disturbances.* Skillful tactics were involved: the regime bought time to organize repression and assure military loyalty with well-timed liberal concessions embodied in the October Manifesto of 1905 (and later largely retracted). Yet, it was of crucial importance that the futile 1904–05 war with Japan was, in comparison with the World War I morass, circumscribed, geographically peripheral, less demanding of resources and manpower, and quickly concluded once defeat was apparent.[18] The peace treaty was signed by late 1905, leaving the Czarist government free to bring military reinforcements back from the Far East into European Russia.

The Russian Revolution occurred in 1917 because Russia was too inextricably entangled with foreign powers, friend and foe, economically and militarily more powerful than she. Foreign entanglement must be considered not only to explain the administrative and military incapacitation of 1917, but also entry into World War I. That involvement cannot be considered "accidental." Nor was it "voluntary" in the same sense as Russia's entry into the 1904 war with Japan.[19] Whatever leadership "blunders" were involved, the fact remains that in 1914 both the Russian state and the Russian economy depended heavily on Western loans and capital. Moreover, Russia was an established part of the European state system and could not remain neutral in a conflict that engulfed the whole of that system.[20]

Foreign pressures and involvements so inescapable and overwhelming as those that faced Russia in 1917 constitute an extreme case for the earlier modernizing agrarian bureaucracies we are considering here. For France and China the pressures were surely no more compelling than those faced by agrarian bureaucracies such as Japan, Germany and Russia (1858–1914) which successfully adapted through reforms from above that facilitated the extraordinary mobilization of resources for economic and military development. Why were the Bourbon and Manchu regimes unable to adapt? Were there structural blocks to effective response? First, let me discuss some general characteristics of all agrarian states, and then point to a peculiar structural characteristic shared by Bourbon France and Manchu China which I believe explains these regimes' inability to meet snow-balling crises of modernization until at last their feeble attempts triggered administrative and military disintegration, hence revolutionary crises.

Weber's ideal type of bureaucracy may be taken as an imaginary model of what might logically be the most effective means of purposively organizing social power. According to the ideal type, fully developed bureaucracy involves the existence of an hierarchically arrayed officialdom, where officials are oriented to superior authority in a disciplined manner because they are dependent for jobs, livelihood, status and career-advancement on resources and decisions channeled through that superior authority. But in preindustrial states, monarchs found it difficult to channel sufficient resources through the "center" to pay simultaneously for wars, culture and court life on the one hand, and a fully bureaucratic officialdom on the other. Consequently, they often had to make do with "officials" recruited from wealthy backgrounds, frequently, in practice, landlords. In addition, central state jurisdiction rarely touched local peasants or communities directly; governmental functions were often delegated to landlords in their "private" capacities, or else to nonbureaucratic authoritative organizations run by local landlords.

Inherent in all agrarian bureaucratic regimes were tensions between, on the one hand, state elites interested in preserving, using, and extending the powers of armies and administrative organizations and, on the other hand, landed upper classes interested in defending locally and regionally based social networks, influence over peasants, and powers and privileges associated with the control of land and agrarian surpluses. Such tensions were likely to be exacerbated once the agrarian bureaucracy was forced to adapt to modernization abroad because foreign military pressures gave cause, while foreign economic development offered incentives and models, for state elites to attempt reforms which went counter to the class interests of traditional, landed upper strata. Yet there were important variations in the ability of semi-bureaucratic agrarian states to respond to modernizing pressures with reforms which sharply and quickly increased resources at the disposal of central authorities. What can account for the differences in response?

■   ■   ■

The Manchu Dynasty proved unable to mobilize resources sufficient to meet credibly the challenges posed by involvement in the modernizing world. "[T]he problem was not merely the very real one of the inadequate resources of the Chinese economy as a whole. In large measure the financial straits in which the Peking government found itself were due to . . . [inability to] command such financial capacity as there was in its empire."[21] Part of the explanation for this inability lay in a characteristic which the Chinese state shared with other agrarian states: lower and middle level officials were recruited from the landed gentry, paid insufficient salaries, and allowed to engage in a certain amount of "normal" corruption, withholding revenues collected as taxes from higher authorities.[22] Yet, if the Manchu Dynasty had encountered the forces of modernization at the height of its powers (say in the early eighteenth century) rather than during its declining phase, it might have controlled or been able to mobilize sufficient resources to finance modern industries and equip a centrally controlled modern army. In that case, officials would never have been allowed to serve in their home provinces, and thus local and regional groups of gentry would

have lacked institutional support for concerted opposition against central initiatives. But, as it happened, the Manchu Dynasty was forced to try to cope with wave after wave of imperialist intrusions, engineered by foreign industrial or industrializing nations anxious to tap Chinese markets and finances, immediately after a series of massive mid-nineteenth-century peasant rebellions. The Dynasty had been unable to put down the Taiping Rebellion on its own, and the task had fallen instead to local, gentry-led, self-defense associations and to regional armies led by complexly interrelated gentry who had access to village resources and recruits. In consequence of the gentry's role in putting down rebellion, governmental powers formerly accruing to central authorities or their bureaucratic agents, including, crucially, rights to collect and allocate various taxes, devolved upon local, gentry-dominated, sub-district governing associations and upon provincial armies and officials increasingly aligned with the provincial gentry against the center.[23]

Unable to force resources from local and regional authorities, it was all Peking could do simply to meet foreign indebtedness, and after 1895 even that proved impossible.

> Throughout the period from 1874 to 1894, the ministry [of Revenue in Peking] was engaged in a series of largely unsuccessful efforts to raise funds in order to meet a continuing series of crises—the dispute over Ili with Russia, the Sino-French War [1885], floods and famines, the Sino-Japanese War [1895]. . . . After 1895 the triple pressure of indemnity payments, servicing foreign loans, and military expenditures totally wrecked the rough balance between income and outlay which Peking had maintained [with the aid of foreign loans] until that time.[24]

The Boxer Rebellion of 1900, and subsequent foreign military intervention, only further exacerbated an already desperate situation.

Attempts by dynastic authorities to remedy matters through a series of "reforms" implemented after

1900—abolishing the Confucian educational system and encouraging modern schools;[25] organizing the socalled "New Armies" (which actually formed around the nuclei of the old provincial armies);[26] transferring local governmental functions to provincial bureaus;[27] and creating a series of local and provincial gentry-dominated representative assemblies[28]—only exacerbated the sorry situation, right up to the 1911 breaking point. "Reform destroyed the reforming government."[29] With each reform, dynastic elites thought to create powers to counterbalance entrenched obstructive forces, but new officials and functions were repeatedly absorbed into pre-existing local and (especially) regional cliques of gentry.[30] The last series of reforms, those that created representative assemblies, ironically provided cliques of gentry with legitimate representative organs from which to launch the liberal, decentralizing "Constitutionalist movement" against the Manchus.

What ultimately precipitated the "revolution of 1911" was a final attempt at reform by the central government, one that directly threatened the financial interests of the gentry power groups for the purpose of strengthening central government finances and control over national economic development:

> The specific incident that precipitated the Revolution of 1911 was the central government's decision to buy up a [railroad] line in Szechwan in which the local gentry had invested heavily. . . . The Szechwan uprising, led by the moderate constitutionalists of the Railway Protection League, sparked widespread disturbances that often had no connection with the railway issue. . . .[31]

Conspiratorial groups affiliated with Sun Yat Sen's T'eng Meng Hui, and mainly composed of Western-educated students and middle-rank New Army officers, joined the fray to produce a series of military uprisings. Finally,

> . . . the lead in declaring the independence of one province after another was taken by two principal elements: the military governors who commanded the New Army forces and the gentry-official-merchant leaders of the provincial assemblies. These elements had more power and were more conservative than the youthful revolutionarists of the T'eng Meng Hui.[32]

The Chinese "Revolution of 1911" irremediably destroyed the integument of civilian elite ties—traditionally maintained by the operation of Confucian educational institutions and the central bureaucracy's policies for recruiting and deploying educated officials so as to strengthen "cosmopolitan" orientations at the expense of local loyalties—which had until that time provided at least the semblance of unified governance for China. "Warlord" rivalries ensued as gentry interests attached themselves to regional military machines, and this condition of intra-elite disunity and rivalry (only imperfectly and temporarily overcome by Chiang Kai-Shek's regime between 1927 and 1937)[33] condemned China to incessant turmoils and provided openings (as well as cause) for lower-class, especially peasant, rebellions and for Communist attempts to organize and channel popular unrest.

Peasant Insurrections

If administrative and military breakdown in a modernizing agrarian bureaucracy were to inaugurate social revolutionary transformations, rather than merely an interregnum of intra-elite squabbling, then widespread popular revolts had to coincide with and take advantage of the hiatus of governmental supervision and sanctions. Urban insurrections provided indispensable support during revolutionary interregnums to radical political elites vying against other elites for state power: witness the Parisian *sans culottes'* support for the Jacobins;[34] the Chinese workers' support for the Communists (between 1920 and 1927);[35] and the Russian industrial workers' support for the Bolsheviks. But fundamentally more important in determining final outcomes were the peasant insurrections which in France, Russia and China constituted irreversible attacks on the powers and privileges of the traditional landed upper classes.

Agrarian bureaucracy has been the only historical variety of complex society with differentiated, centralized government that has, in certain instances, incubated a lower-class stratum that was *simultaneously strategic* in the society's economy and polity (as surplus producer, payer of rents and taxes, and as provider of corvée and military manpower), and yet *organizationally autonomous* enough to allow the "will" and "tactical space" for collective insurrection against basic structural arrangements.

How have certain agrarian bureaucracies exemplified such special propensity to peasant rebellion? As Eric Wolf has pointed out, "ultimately, the decisive factor in making a peasant rebellion possible lies in the relation of the peasantry to the field of power which surrounds it. A rebellion cannot start from a situation of complete impotence. . . ."[36] If they are to act upon, rather than silently suffer, their omnipresent grievances, peasants must have "internal leverage" or "tactical mobility." They have this to varying degrees according to their position in the total agrarian social structure. Institutional patterns which relate peasants to landlords and peasants to each other seem to be the co-determinants of degrees of peasant "tactical mobility." Sheer amounts of property held by peasants gain significance only within institutional contexts. If peasants are to be capable of self-initiated rebellion against landlords and state officials, they must have (a) some institutionally based collective solidarity, and (b) autonomy from direct, day-to-day supervision and control by landlords in their work and leisure activities. Agricultural regimes featuring large estates worked by serfs or laborers tend to be inimical to peasant rebellion—witness the East Elbian Junker regime[37]—but the reason is not that serfs and landless laborers are economically poor, rather that they are subject to close and constant supervision and discipline by landlords or their agents. If large-estate agriculture is lacking, an agrarian bureaucracy may still be relatively immune to widespread peasant rebellion if landlords control sanctioning machineries,[38] such as militias and poor relief agencies, at local levels. On the other hand, landlords as a class, and the "system" as a whole, will be relatively vulnerable to peasant rebellion if: (a) sanctioning machineries are centralized; (b) agricultural work and peasant social life are controlled by peasant families and communities themselves. These conditions prevailed in France and Russia and meant that, with the incapacitation of central administrative and military bureaucracies, these societies became susceptible to the spread and intensification of peasant revolts which in more normal circumstances could have been contained and repressed.

It is worth emphasizing that peasant actions in revolutions are not intrinsically different from peasant actions in "mere" rebellions or riots. When peasants "rose" during historical social revolutionary crises, they did so in highly traditional rebellious patterns: bread riots, "defense" of communal lands or customary rights, riots against "hoarding" merchants or landlords, "social banditry." Peasants initially drew upon traditional cultural themes to justify rebellion. Far from becoming revolutionaries through adoption of a radical vision of a desired new society, "revolutionary" peasants have typically been "backward-looking" rebels incorporated by circumstances beyond their control into political processes occurring independently of them, at the societal "center."[39]

■   ■   ■

Historians agree that the Russian Emancipation of the serfs in 1861, intended by the Czar as a measure to stabilize the agrarian situation, actually enhanced the rebellious potential of the ex-serfs. Heavy redemption payments and inadequate land allotments fuelled peasant discontent. More important, legal reinforcement of the *obshchina's* (peasant commune's) authority over families and individuals fettered ever-increasing numbers of peasants to the inadequate lands, reinforced collective solidarity, retarded the internal class differentiation of the peas-antry, and left communes largely free to run their own affairs subject only to the collective fulfillment of financial obligations to the state.[40] Estate owners were deprived of most direct authority over peasant communities.[41]

Not surprisingly, given this agrarian situation, widespread peasant rebellions erupted in Russia in 1905, when the Czarist regime simultaneously con-fronted defeat abroad and an anti-autocratic move-ment of the middle classes, the liberal gentry, and the working classes at home. "Economic hardship created a need for change; peasant tradition, as well as revolutionary propaganda, suggested the remedy [i.e., attacks on landlords and land seizures]; official preoccupation and indecisiveness invited the storm; and soon the greatest disturbance since the days of Pugachev was under way."[42]

In the wake of the unsuccessful Revolution of 1905, the Czarist regime abandoned its policy of shoring up the peasant commune. It undertook the break-up of repartitional lands into private hold-ings and implemented measures to facilitate land sales by poorer peasants and purchases by richer ones.[43] Between 1905 and 1917, these measures, in tandem with general economic developments, did something to alleviate agrarian stagnation, promote permanent rural migration to urban industrial areas, and increase class differentiation and individual-ism in the countryside.[44] However, by 1917, little enough had been accomplished—only one-tenth of all peasant families had been resettled on individual holdings[45]—that peasant communities engaged in solidary actions against both landlords and any rich peasant "separators" who did not join their struggle.

"Any shrewd observer of Russian conditions who weighed the lessons of the agrarian disorders of 1905 could have foreseen that a breakdown of cen-tral power and authority was almost certain to bring an even greater upheaval in its train."[46] And, indeed, between the spring and the autumn of 1917, "side by side with the mutiny of the Russian army marched a second great social revolutionary movement: the seizure of the landed estates by the peasantry."[47]

The peasant movement of 1917 was primarily a drive of the peasantry against the *pomyeschik* class. Among the cases of agrarian disturbance, violent and peaceful, 4,954, overwhelming the larg-est number, were directed against landlords, as against 324 against the more well-to-do peasants, 235 against the Government and 211 against the clergy.[48]

The broad general result of the wholesale peasant land seizure of 1917 was a sweeping levelling in Russian agriculture. The big latifundia, even the small estate, ceased to exist. On the other hand landless or nearly landless peasants obtained larger allotments.[49]

For the peasants simply applied traditional communal repartitional procedures to lands seized from the landlords. Their revolt, together with the Bolsheviks' victory, ". . . sealed forever the doom of the old landed aristocracy."[50]

The Chinese case presents decisive contrasts with France and Russia but nevertheless confirms our general insight about the importance of structurally conditioned "tactical space" for peasant insurrection as a crucial factor in the translation of administrative/military breakdown into social revolution.

Except in infertile and marginal highland areas, Chinese peasants, though mostly family smallhold-ers or tenants,[51] did not live in their own village communities clearly apart from landlords.

The Chinese peasant . . . was a member of two communities: his village and the marketing system to which his village belonged ["typically includ-ing fifteen to twenty-five villages . . ." dependent on one of 45,000 market towns]. An important feature of the larger marketing community was its elaborate system of stratification. . . . Those who provided *de facto* leadership within the marketing community *qua* political system and those who gave it collective representation at its interface with larger polities were gentrymen—landed, leisured, and literate. . . . It was artisans, merchants, and other full-time economic specialists, not peasants, who sustained the heartbeat of periodic marketing that kept the community alive. It was priests backed by gentry temple managers . . . who gave religious meaning to peasants' local world.[52]

Voluntary associations, and clans where they flourished, were likewise contained within marketing communities, headed and economically sustained by gentry. Thus kinship, associational and client-age ties cut across class distinctions between peasants and landlords in traditional China. Gentry controlled at local levels a variety of sanctioning machineries, including militias and other organizations which functioned *de facto* as channels of poor relief.[53]

Not surprisingly, therefore, settled Chinese peasant agriculturalists did not initiate class-based revolts against landlords, either in pre-modern or in revolutionary (1911–49) times. Instead, peasant rebellion manifested itself in the form of accelerating rural, violence and social banditry, spreading outward from the mountainous "border areas" at the edges of the empire or at the intersections of provincial boundaries. Social banditry invariably blossomed during periods of central administrative weakness or collapse and economic deflation and catastrophe. Precisely because normal traditional Chinese agrarian-class relations were significantly commercialized, local prosperity depended upon overall administrative stability, and peasants were not cushioned against economic dislocations by kin or village communal ties. During periods of dynastic decline, local (marketing) communities "closed in" upon themselves normatively, economically, and coercively,[54] and poorer peasants, especially in communities without well-to-do local landed elites, lost property and livelihood, and were forced to migrate. Such impoverished migrants often congregated as bandits or smugglers operating out of "border area" bases and raiding settled communities. Ultimately they might provide (individual or group) recruits for rebel armies led by marginal elites vying for imperial power.[55]

The nineteenth and the first half of the twentieth centuries constituted a period of dynastic decline and interregnum in China, complicated in quite novel ways by Western and Japanese economic and military intrusions. Peasant impoverishment, local community closure, spreading social banditry and military conflicts among local militias, bandit groups, and warlord and/or "ideological" armies, characterized the entire time span, and peaked during the mid-nineteenth and mid-twentieth centuries.

The Communist movement originated as a political tendency among a tiny fraction of China's nationalist and pro-modern intellectual stratum and created its first mass base among Chinese industrial workers concentrated in the treaty ports and to a lesser degree among students and southeast Chinese peasants. But after 1927, the Chinese Communists were forced out of China's cities and wealthier agrarian regions by Kuomintang military and police repression. Would-be imitators of the Bolsheviks were thus forced to come to terms with the Chinese agrarian situation. This they did initially (between 1927 and 1942) by recapitulating the experiences and tactics of traditional rebel elite contenders for imperial power in China. Scattered, disorganized and disoriented Communist leaders, along with military units (which had split off from KMT or warlord armies) of varying degrees of loyalty, retreated to mountainous border areas, there often to ally with already existing bandit groups.[56] Gradually the fruits of raiding expeditions, plus the division and weakness of opposing armies, allowed the "Communist" base areas to expand into administrative regions.

Only after a secure and stable administrative region had finally been established in Northwest China (after 1937) could the Communists finally turn to the intra-market-area and intra-village political organizing that ultimately bypassed and then eliminated the gentry, and so made their drive for power unique in China's history. Before roughly 1940, ideological appeals, whether "Communist" or "Nationalist" played little role in mediating Communist elites' relations to peasants, and spontaneous class struggle, fuelled from below, played virtually no role in achieving whatever (minimal) changes in agrarian class *relations* were accomplished in Communist base areas.[57] To be sure, ideology was important in integrating the Party, an elite organization, and in mediating its relationship with the Red Army. But until Party and Army established relatively secure and stable military and administrative control over a region, Communist cadres were not in a position to penetrate local communities in order to provide organization, leadership, and encouragement for peasants themselves to expropriate land. This finally occurred in North China in the 1940s.[58] Once provided with military and organizational protection from landlord sanctions and influence, peasants often reacted against landlords with a fury that exceeded even what Party policy desired. Perhaps Communist ideological appeals were partially responsible for peasant insurrection. More likely, even at this stage, the Communist organizations' important input to local situations was not a sense of grievances, or their ideological articulation, but rather simply *protection* from traditional social controls: William Hinton's classic *Fanshen: A Documentary of Revolution in a Chinese Village* vividly supports such an interpretation.[59]

Even to gain the military strength they needed to defeat the Kuomintang, the Chinese Communists had to shove aside—or encourage and allow peasants to shove aside—the traditional landed upper class and establish a more direct link to the Chinese peasantry than had ever before been established between an extra-local Chinese rebel movement and local communities.[60] The Chinese Communists also established more direct links to peasants than did radical elites in Russia or France. The Chinese Revolution, at least in its closing stages, thus has more of the aspect of an elite/mass movement than the other great historical social revolutions. Yet the reasons for this peasant mass-mobilizing aspect have little to do with revolutionary ideology (except in retrospect) and everything to do with the "peculiarities" (from a European perspective) of the Chinese agrarian social structure. That structure did not afford settled Chinese peasants institutional autonomy and solidarity

against landlords, yet it did, in periods of political-economic crisis, generate marginal poor-peasant outcasts whose activities exacerbated the crises and whose existence provided potential bases of support for oppositional elite-led rebellions or, in the twentieth-century world context, a revolutionary movement. Thus Chinese Communist activities after 1927 and ultimate triumph in 1949 depended directly upon *both* the insurrectionary potentials and the blocks to peasant insurrection built into the traditional Chinese social structure.

Radical Political Movements and Centralizing Outcomes

Although peasant insurrections played a decisive role in each of the great historical social revolutions, nevertheless an exclusive focus on peasants—or on the peasant situation in agrarian bureaucracies—cannot provide a complete explanation for the occurrence of social revolutions, Russia and China were recurrently rocked by massive peasant rebellions,[61] yet peasant uprisings did not fuel structural transformations until the late eighteenth century and after. Obviously agrarian bureaucracies were exposed to additional and unique strains and possibilities once English and then European commercialization-industrialization became a factor in world history and development. The stage was set for the entry of marginal elites animated by radical nationalist goals.

Who were these marginal elites? What sectors of society provided the social bases for nationalist radicalisms? *Not* the bourgeoisie proper: merchants, financiers and industrialists. These groups have had surprisingly little *direct* effect upon the politics of modernization in any developing nation, from England to the countries of the Third World today. Instead, their activities, commerce and manufacturing, have created and continuously transformed, indeed revolutionized, the national and international *contexts* within which bureaucrats, professionals, politicians, landlords, peasants, and proletarians have engaged in the decisive political struggles. To be sure, in certain times and places, the "bourgeois" commercial or industrial context has been pervasive enough virtually to determine political outcomes, even without the overt political participation of bourgeois actors. But such was not the case in the earlier modernizing agrarian bureaucracies, including France, Russia and China.

Instead, nationalist radicals tended to "precipitate out" of the ranks of those who possessed specialized skills and were oriented to state activities or employments, but either lacked traditionally prestigious attributes such as nobility, landed wealth, or general humanist education, or else found themselves in situations where such attributes were no longer personally or nationally functional. Their situations in political and social life were such as to make them, especially in times of political crises, willing to call for such radical reforms as equalization of mobility opportunities, political democracy, and (anyway, before the revolution) extension of civil liberties. Yet the primary orientation of these marginal elites was toward a broad goal that they shared with all those, including traditionally prestigious bureaucrats, whose careers, livelihoods, and identities were intertwined with state activities: the goal of extension and rationalization of state powers in the name of national welfare and prestige.

■ ■ ■

In Russia, by 1917, the revolutionary sects, such as the Bolsheviks and the Left Social Revolutionaries, constituted the surviving politically organized representatives of what had earlier been an out-look much more widespread among university-educated Russians: extreme alienation, disgust at Russia's backwardness, preoccupation with public events and yet refusal to become involved in the round of civil life.[62] As Russia underwent rapid industrialization after 1890, opportunities for university education were extended beyond the nobility—a circumstance which helped to ensure that universities would be hotbeds of political radicalism—yet,

before long, opportunities for professional and other highly skilled employments also expanded. Especially in the wake of the abortive 1905 Revolution, Russia's university-educated moved toward professional employments and liberal politics.[63] Yet when events overtook Russia in 1917, organized radical leadership was still to be found among the alienated intelligentsia.

In China, as in Russia, radical nationalist modernizers came from the early student generations of university-educated Chinese.[64] Especially at first, most were the children of traditionally wealthy and prestigious families, but urban and "rich peasant" backgrounds, respectively, came to be overrepresented in the (pre-1927) Kuomintang and the Communist elites.[65] With the abolition of the Confucian educational system in 1904, and the collapse of the imperial government in 1911, even traditionally prestigious attributes and connections lost their meaning and usefulness. At the same time, neither warlord regimes, nor the Nationalist government after 1927 offered much scope for modern skills or credentials; advancement in these regimes went only to those with independent wealth or personal ties to military commanders. Gradually, the bulk of China's modern-educated, and especially the young, came to support the Communist movement, some through active commitment in Yenan, others through passive political support in the cities.[66]

Two considerations help to account for the fact that radical leadership in social revolutions came specifically from the ranks of skilled and/or university-educated marginal elites oriented to state employments and activities. First, agrarian bureaucracies are "statist" societies. Even before the era of modernization official employments in these societies constituted both an important route for social mobility and a means for validating traditional status and supplementing landed fortunes. Second, with the advent of economic modernization in the world, state activities acquired greater-than-ever objective import in the agrarian bureaucratic societies which were forced to adapt to modernization abroad. For the concrete effects of modernization abroad first impinged upon the state's sphere, in the form of sharply and suddenly stepped up military competition or threats from more developed nations abroad. And the cultural effects of modernization abroad first impinged upon the relatively highly educated in agrarian bureaucracies, that is upon those who were mostly either employed by the state or else connected or oriented to its activities.

■   ■   ■

The earlier modernizing agrarian bureaucracies that (to varying degrees) successfully adapted to challenges from abroad did so either through revolution, or basic reforms "from above" or social revolution "from below." Either traditional bureaucrats successfully promoted requisite reforms or else their attempts precipitated splits within the upper class which could, if the peasantry were structurally insurrection-prone, open the door to social revolution. In the context of administrative/military disorganization and spreading peasant rebellions, tiny, organized radical elites that never could have created revolutionary crises on their own gained their moments in history. As peasant insurrections undermined the traditional landed upper classes, and the old regime officials and structures tied to them, radical elites occupied center stage, competing among themselves to see who could seize and build upon the foundations of central state power.

"A complete revolution," writes Samuel Huntington, ". . . involves . . . the creation and institutionalization of a new political order."[67] A social revolution was consummated when one political elite succeeded in creating or capturing political organizations—a revolutionary army, or a revolutionary party controlling an army—capable of restoring minimal order and incorporating the revolutionary masses, especially the peasantry, into national life. No political elite not able or willing to accept the peasants' revolutionary economic gains could hope to emerge victorious from the intra-elite or inter-party conflicts that marked revolutionary interregnums. Elites with close social or

politico-military ties to traditional forms of landed upper-class institutional power (i.e., the privileged rentier bourgeoisie of France, the Kerensky regime in Russia, the [post-1927] Kuomintang in China) invariably lost out.

The historical social revolutions did not culminate in more liberal political arrangements. At opening stages of the French, Russian (1905) and Chinese revolutions, landed upper-class/middle-strata political coalitions espoused "parliamentary liberal" programs.[68] But events pushed these groups and programs aside, for the organized elites who provided the ultimately successful leadership in all social revolutions ended up responding to popular turmoil—counterrevolutionary threats at home and abroad, peasant anarchist tendencies, and the international crises faced by their societies—by creating *more* highly centralized, bureaucratized and rationalized state institutions than those that existed prior to the revolutions. This response, moreover, was entirely in character for elites adhering to world views which gave consistent primacy to organized political action in human affairs.[69]

■   ■   ■

Let me sum up what this essay has attempted to do. To explain the great historical social revolutions, I have, first, conceptualized a certain type of society, the agrarian bureaucracy, in which social control of the lower strata (mainly peasants) rests with institutions locally and regionally controlled by landed upper classes, together with administrative and military machineries centrally controlled; and second, I have discussed differences between agrarian bureaucracies which did and those which did not experience social revolutions in terms of (a) institutional structures which mediate landed upper-class relations to state apparatuses and peasant relations to landed upper classes and (b) types and amounts of international political and economic pressures (especially originating with more developed nations) impinging upon agrarian bureaucracies newly incorporated into the modernizing world. According to my analysis, social revolutions occurred in those modernizing agrarian bureaucracies—France, Russia and China—which *both* incubated peasantries structurally prone to autonomous insurrection *and* experienced severe administrative and military disorganization due to the direct or indirect effects of military competition or threats from more modern nations abroad.

In the process of elucidating this basic argument, I have at one point or another alluded to evidence concerning Prussia (Germany), Japan (and Turkey), and Russia in 1905. Obviously the coverage of these and other "negative" cases has been far from complete. Yet partial explanations have been offered for the avoidance of social revolution by Prussia/Germany, Japan and Russia through 1916. Japan and Russia escaped administrative/military collapse in the face of moderate challenges from abroad because their traditional governmental elites were significantly differentiated from landed upper classes. Prussia lacked a structurally autonomous, insurrection-prone peasantry, and therefore when, in 1848, the King hesitated for a year to use his armies to repress popular disturbances, the Junker-led army, manned by peasants from the estates east of the Elbe, remained loyal and intact until it was finally used to crush the German Revolutions during 1849–50.

This comparative historical analysis has been meant to render plausible a theoretical approach to explaining revolutions which breaks with certain long-established sociological proclivities. While existing theories of revolution focus on discontent, and its articulation by oppositional programs or ideologies, as the fundamental cause of revolutions, I have emphasized mechanisms and dynamics of societal social control through political and class domination. Moreover, while other theories view the impact of modernization (as a cause of revolution) in terms of the effects of processes of economic development on class structures, "system equilibrium," or societal members' levels of satisfaction, my approach focuses on the effects of modernization—viewed also as an intersocietal politico-strategic process—upon adaptive capacities of the agrarian bureaucratic states and upon the opportunities open to political elites who triumph in revolutions.

Obviously, thorough testing of these ideas will require more precise delineation of concepts and the extension of hypotheses derived from this analysis to new cases. But I have made a start. And I hope that especially those who disagree with my conclusions will themselves turn to historical evidence to argue their cases. Social science can best grow through the interplay of theory and historical investigation, and comparative historical analysis represents one indispensable tool for achieving this.

NOTES

1. Samuel P. Huntington, *Political Order in Changing Societies* (New Haven: Yale University Press, 1968), p. 264.

2. Stephan T. Possony, ed., *The Lenin Reader* (Chicago: Henry Regnery Company, 1966), p. 349.

3. For important examples see: Ted Robert Gurr, *Why Men Rebel* (Princeton, New Jersey: Princeton University Press, 1970); Neil J. Smelser, *Theory of Collective Behavior* (New York: The Free Press of Glencoe, 1963); and Harry Eckstein, "On the Etiology of Internal Wars," *History and Theory* 4(2) (1965).

4. Crane Brinton, *The Anatomy of Revolution* (New York: Vintage Books, 1965; original edition, 1938); Lyford P. Edwards, *The Natural History of Revolution* (Chicago: University of Chicago Press, 1971; originally published in 1927); George Sawyer Petee, *The Process of Revolution* (New York: Harper and Brothers, 1938); and Rex D. Hopper, "The Revolutionary Process," *Social Forces* 28 (March, 1950): 270–9.

5. Harry Eckstein, ed., *Internal War* (New York: The Free Press, 1964), p. 8.

6. *Ibid.*, p. 10.

7. See: Ernest Nagel, ed., *John Stuart Mill's Philosophy of Scientific Method* (New York: Hafner Publishing

Co., 1950); Marc Bloch, "Toward a Comparative History of European Societies," in Frederic C. Lane and Jelle C. Riemersma, eds., *Enterprise and Secular Change* (Homewood, Illinois: The Dorsey Press, 1953), pp. 494–521; William H. Sewell, Jr., "Marc Bloch and the Logic of Comparative History," *History and Theory* 6(2) (1967): 208–18; Neil J. Smelser, "The Methodology of Comparative Analysis," (unpublished draft); and S. M. Lipset, *Revolution and Counterrevolution* (New York: Anchor Books, 1970), part I.

8. In formulating the "agrarian bureaucracy" societal type concept, I have drawn especially upon the work and ideas of S. N. Eisenstadt in *The Political Systems of Empires* (New York: The Free Press, 1963); Barrington Moore, Jr., in *Social Origins of Dictatorship and Democracy* (Boston: Beacon Press, 1967); and Morton H. Fried, "On the Evolution of Social Stratification and the State," pp. 713–31 in Stanley Diamond, ed., *Culture in History* (New York: Columbia University Press, 1960). The label "agrarian bureaucracy" is pilfered from Moore. Clear-cut instances of agrarian bureaucratic societies were China, Russia, France, Prussia, Austria, Spain, Japan, Turkey.

9. Terence K. Hopkins and Immanuel Wallerstein, "The Comparative Study of National Societies," *Social Science Information* 6 (1967), 39.

10. See Immanuel Wallerstein, *The Modern World System: Capitalist Agriculture and the Origins of the European World-Economy in the Sixteenth Century* (New York and London: Academic Press, 1974).

11. E. J. Hobsbawm, *Industry and Empire* (Baltimore, Md.: Penguin Books, 1969).

12. See Walter L. Dorn, *Competition for Empire, 1740–1763* (New York: Harper and Row, 1963; originally, 1940).

13. Christopher Lasch, *The New Radicalism in America* (New York: Vintage Books, 1967), p. 141.

14. Alexander Gerschenkron, "Problems and Patterns of Russian Economic Development," pp. 42–72 in Cyril E. Black, ed., *The Transformation of Russian Society* (Cambridge, Mass.: Harvard University Press, 1960).

15. Geroid Tanquary Robinson, *Rural Russia Under the Old Regime* (Berkeley and Los Angeles: University of California Press, 1969; originally published in 1932), Chap. 11.

16. William Henry Chamberlin, *The Russian Revolution*, Volume I (New York: Grosset and Dunlap, 1963; originally published in 1935), pp. 64–65.

17. Katharine Chorley, *Armies and the Art of Revolution* (London: Faber and Faber, 1943), Chap. 6.

18. *Ibid.*, pp. 118–9.

19. In 1904, "[t]he Minister of Interior, von Plehve, saw a desirable outlet from the [turbulent domestic] situation in a 'little victorious war'" (Chamberlin, op. cit., p. 47).

20. See: Leon Trotsky, *The Russian Revolution* (selected and edited by F. W. Dupee) (New York: Anchor Books, 1959; originally published in 1932), Volume I, Chap. 2; and Roderick E. McGrew, "Some Imperatives of Russian Foreign Policy," pp. 202–29 in Theofanis George Stavrou, ed., *Russia Under the Last Tsar* (Minneapolis: University of Minnesota Press, 1969).

21. Albert Feuerwerker, *China's Early Industrialization* (New York: Atheneum, 1970; originally published in 1958), p. 41.

22. Chung-li Chang, *The Chinese Gentry* (Seattle: University of Washington Press, 1955); Ping-ti Ho, *The Ladder of Success in Imperial China* (New York: Columbia University, Press, 1962); and Franz Michael, "State and Society in Nineteenth Century China," *World Politics* 7 (April, 1955): 419–33.

23. Philip Kuhn, *Rebellion and Its Enemies in Late Imperial China* (Cambridge, Mass.: Harvard University Press, 1970).

24. Feuerwerker, *op. cit.*, pp. 40–41.

25. Mary C. Wright, ed., *China in Revolution: The First Phase, 1900–1913* (New Haven: Yale University Press, 1968), pp. 24–26.

26. Yoshiro Hatano, "The New Armies," pp. 365–82 in Wright, ed., *op. cit.*; and John Gittings, "The Chinese Army," pp. 187–224 in Jack Gray, ed., *Modern China's Search for a Political Form* (London: Oxford University Press, 1969).

27. John Fincher, "Political Provincialism and the National Revolution," in Wright, ed., *op. cit.*, p. 202.

28. Fincher, *op. cit.*; and P'eng-yuan Chang, "The Constitutionalists," in Wright, ed., *op. cit.*

29. Wright, ed., *op. cit.*, p. 50.

30. Fincher, *op. cit.*

31. Wright, ed., *loc. cit.*

32. John King Fairbank, *The United States and China* (Third Edition) (Cambridge, Mass.: Harvard University Press, 1971), p. 132.

33. Martin C. Wilbur, "Military Separatism and the Process of Reunification Under the Nationalist Regime, 1922–1937," pp. 203–63 in Ping-ti Ho and Tang Tsou, eds., *China in Crisis*, Volume I, Book I (Chicago: University of Chicago Press, 1968).

34. Albert Soboul, *The Sans Culottes* (New York: Anchor Books, 1972; originally published in French in 1968); and George Rudé, *The Crowd in the French Revolution* (London: Oxford University Press, 1959).

35. Jean Chesneaux, *The Chinese Labor Movement, 1919–1927* (Stanford: Stanford University Press, 1968).

36. Eric R. Wolf, *Peasant Wars of the Twentieth Century* (New York: Harper and Row, 1969), p. 290.

37. In 1848 the East Elbian region of "Germany" escaped general peasant insurrection, and the Prussian armies that crushed the German Revolutions of 1848 were recruited from the East Elbian estates, officers and rank-and-file alike. See: Theodore Hamerow, *Restoration, Revolution, Recreation* (Princeton, N.J.: Princeton University Press, 1958); and Hajo Holborn, *A History of Modern Germany*, 1648–1840 (New York: Alfred A. Knopf, 1963).

38. "Sanctioning machineries" are organizations which control forceful or remunerative sanctions. "Social control" also involves normative pressures, but to be truly binding, especially in hierarchical situations, these must typically be "backed up" by application or credible threat of application of force or manipulation of needed remuneration.

39. See Wolf, *op. cit.*, "Conclusion"; and Moore, *op. cit.*, Chap. 9 and "Epilogue."

40. Terence Emmons, "The Peasant and the Emancipation," and Francis M. Watters, "The Peasant and the Village Commune," both in Wayne S. Vucinich, ed., *The Peasant in Nineteenth-Century Russia* (Stanford: Stanford University Press, 1968); and Robinson, *op. cit.*

41. Jerome Blum, *Lord and Peasant in Russia* (Princeton, New Jersey: Princeton University Press, 1961), pp. 598–9; and Robinson, *op. cit.*, pp. 78–79.

42. Robinson, *op. cit.*, p. 155.

43. *Ibid.*, pp. 188–207.

44. Gerschenkron, *op. cit.*, pp. 42–72.

45. Robinson, *op. cit.*, pp. 225–6.

46. Chamberlin, *op. cit.*, p. 257.

47. *Ibid.*, p. 242.

48. *Ibid.*, p. 252.

49. *Ibid.*, p. 256.

50. *Ibid.*, p. 256.

51. R. H. Tawney, *Land and Labour in China* (Boston: Beacon Press, 1966; originally published in 1932), Chap. 2.

52. G. William Skinner, "Chinese Peasants and the Closed Community: An Open and Shut Case," *Comparative Studies in Society and History* 13(3) (July, 1971), pp. 272–3.

53. Kuhn, *op. cit.*, *passim.*

54. Skinner, *op. cit.*, 278ff.

55. See: Skinner, *op. cit.*, Kuhn, *op. cit.*; and George E. Taylor, "The Taiping Rebellion: Its Economic Background and Social Theory," *Chinese Social and Political Science Review* 16 (1933): 545–614.

56. See: Mark Selden, *The Yenan Way in Revolutionary China* (Cambridge, Mass.: Harvard University Press, 1971), Chaps. 1–2; Dick Wilson, *The Long March 1935* (New York: Avon Books, 1971); and Agnes Smedly, *The Great Road: The Life and Times of Chu Teh* (New York: Monthly Review Press, 1956).

57. Selden, op. cit.; Franz Schurmann, *Ideology and Organization in Communist China* (second edition) (Berkeley and Los Angeles: University of California Press, 1968), pp. 412–37; Ilpyong J. Kim, "Mass Mobilization Policies and Techniques Developed in the Period of the Chinese Soviet Republic," pp. 78–98 in A. Doak Barnett, ed., *Chinese Communist Politics in Action* (Seattle: University of Washington Press, 1969).

58. Selden, *op. cit.*; and Schurmann, *op. cit.*

59. William Hinton, *Fanshen: A Documentary of Revolution in a Chinese Village* (New York: Vintage Books, 1968; first published in 1966).

60. Schurmann, *op. cit.*, pp. 425–31.

61. See, for example, Roland Mousnier, *Peasant Uprisings in the Seventeenth Century: France, Russia and China* (New York: Harper and Row, 1972; originally published in French, 1967).

62. George Fischer, "The Intelligentsia and Russia," pp. 253–73 in Black, ed., *op. cit.*

63. George Fischer, "The Russian Intelligentsia and Liberalism," pp. 317–36 in Hugh McLean, Martin Malia and George Fischer, eds., *Russian Thought and Politics — Harvard Slavic Studies, Volume IV* (Cambridge, Mass.: Harvard University Press, 1957); and Donald W. Treadgold, "Russian Radical Thought, 1894–1917," pp. 69–86 in Stavrou, ed., *op. cit.*

64. John Israel, "Reflections on the Modern Chinese Student Movement," *Daedalus* (Winter, 1968):

229–53; and Robert C. North and Ithiel de Sola Pool, "Kuomintang and Chinese Communist Elites," pp. 319–455 in Harold D. Lasswell and Daniel Lerner, eds., *World Revolutionary Elites* (Cambridge, Mass.: The M.I.T. Press, 1966).

65. North and Pool, *op. cit.*

66. John Israel, *Student Nationalism in China: 1927–1937* (Stanford: Hoover Institute Publications, 1966).

67. Huntington, *op. cit.*, p. 266.

68. See: Hampson, *A Social History . . . ,* Chap. 2; Sidney Harcave, *The Russian Revolution of 1905* (London: Collier Books, 1970; first published in 1964); and P'eng-yuan Chang, "The Constitutionalists," pp. 143–83 in Wright, ed., *op. cit.*

69. On the Bolsheviks, see Robert V. Daniels, "Lenin and the Russian Revolutionary Tradition," pp. 339–54 in McLean, Malia and Fischer, eds., *op. cit.* Daniels argues that "the more autocratic societies like pre-revolutionary Russia . . . prompted historical theories which put a premium on individual will, power and ideas . . . ," p. 352.

Martha Crenshaw
THE CAUSES OF TERRORISM

Terrorism occurs both in the context of violent resistance to the state as well as in the service of state interests. If we focus on terrorism directed against governments for purposes of political change, we are considering the premeditated use or threat of symbolic, low-level violence by conspiratorial organizations. Terrorist violence communicates a political message; its ends go beyond damaging an enemy's material resources.[1] The victims or objects of terrorist attack have little intrinsic value to the terrorist group but represent a larger human audience whose reaction the terrorists seek. Violence characterized by spontaneity, mass participation, or a primary intent of physical destruction can therefore be excluded from our investigation.

The study of terrorism can be organized around three questions: why terrorism occurs, how the process of terrorism works, and what its social and political effects are. Here the objective is to outline an approach to the analysis of the causes of terrorism, based on comparison of different cases of terrorism, in order to distinguish a common pattern of causation from the historically unique.

The subject of terrorism has inspired a voluminous literature in recent years. However, nowhere

From *Comparative Politics* 13, no. 4 (July 1981), pp. 379–99.

among the highly varied treatments does one find a general theoretical analysis of the causes of terrorism. This may be because terrorism has often been approached from historical perspectives, which, if we take Laqueur's work as an example, dismiss explanations that try to take into account more than a single case as "exceedingly vague or altogether wrong."[2] Certainly existing general accounts are often based on assumptions that are neither explicit nor factually demonstrable. We find judgments centering on social factors such as the permissiveness and affluence in which Western youth are raised or the imitation of dramatic models encouraged by television. Alternatively, we encounter political explanations that blame revolutionary ideologies, Marxism-Leninism or nationalism, governmental weakness in giving in to terrorist demands, or conversely government oppression, and the weakness of the regime's opponents. Individual psychopathology is often cited as a culprit.

Even the most persuasive of statements about terrorism are not cast in the form of testable propositions, nor are they broadly comparative in origin or intent. Many are partial analyses, limited in scope to revolutionary terrorism from the Left, not terrorism that is a form of protest or a reaction to political or social change. A narrow historical or geographical focus is also common; the majority of explanations concern modern phenomena. Some focus usefully on terrorism against the Western democracies.[3] In general, propositions about terrorism lack logical comparability, specification of the relationship of variables to each other, and a rank-ordering of variables in terms of explanatory power.

We would not wish to claim that a general explanation of the sources of terrorism is a simple task, but it is possible to make a useful beginning by establishing a theoretical order for different types and levels of causes. We approach terrorism as a form of political behavior resulting from the deliberate choice of a basically rational actor, the terrorist organization. A comprehensive explanation, however, must also take into account the environment in which terrorism occurs and address the question of whether broad political, social, and economic conditions make terrorism more likely in some contexts than in others. What sort of circumstances lead to the formation of a terrorist group? On the other hand, only a few of the people who experience a given situation practice terrorism. Not even all individuals who share the goals of a terrorist organization agree that terrorism is the best means. It is essential to consider the psychological variables that may encourage or inhibit individual participation in terrorist actions. The analysis of these three levels of causation will center first on situational variables, then on the strategy of the terrorist organization, and last on the problem of individual participation.

This paper represents only a preliminary set of ideas about the problem of causation; historical cases of terrorism are used as illustrations, not as demonstrations of hypotheses. The historical examples referred to here are significant terrorist campaigns since the French Revolution of 1789; terrorism is considered as a facet of secular modern politics, principally associated with the rise of nationalism, anarchism, and revolutionary socialism.[4] The term *terrorism* was coined to describe the systematic inducement of fear and anxiety to control and direct a civilian population, and the phenomenon of terrorism as a challenge to the authority of the state grew from the difficulties revolutionaries experienced in trying to recreate the mass uprisings of the French Revolution. Most references provided here are drawn from the best-known and most-documented examples: Narodnaya Volya and the Combat Organization of the Socialist-Revolutionary party in Russia, from 1878 to 1913; anarchist terrorism of the 1890s in Europe, primarily France; the Irish Republican Army (IRA) and its predecessors and successors from 1919 to the present; the Irgun Zwai Leumi in Mandate Palestine from 1937 to 1947; the Front de Libération Nationale (FLN) in Algeria from 1954 to 1962; the Popular Front for the Liberation of Palestine from 1968 to the present;

the Rote Armee Fraktion (RAF) and the 2nd June Movement in West Germany since 1968; and the Tupamaros of Uruguay, 1968–1974.

The Setting for Terrorism

An initial obstacle to identification of propitious circumstances for terrorism is the absence of significant empirical studies of relevant cross-national factors. There are a number of quantitative analyses of collective violence, assassination, civil strife, and crime,[5] but none of these phenomena is identical to a campaign of terrorism. Little internal agreement exists among such studies, and the consensus one finds is not particularly useful for the study of terrorism.[6] For example, Ted Robert Gurr found that "modern" states are less violent than developing countries and that legitimacy of the regime inhibits violence. Yet, Western Europe experiences high levels of terrorism. Surprisingly, in the 1961–1970 period, out of 87 countries, the United States was ranked as having the highest number of terrorist campaigns.[7] Although it is impractical to borrow entire theoretical structures from the literature on political and criminal violence, some propositions can be adapted to the analysis of terrorism.

To develop a framework for the analysis of likely settings for terrorism, we must establish conceptual distinctions among different types of factors. First, a significant difference exists between *preconditions*, factors that set the stage for terrorism over the long run, and *precipitants*, specific events that immediately precede the occurrence of terrorism. Second, a further classification divides preconditions into enabling or permissive factors, which provide opportunities for terrorism to happen, and situations that directly inspire and motivate terrorist campaigns. Precipitants are similar to the direct causes of terrorism.[8] Furthermore, no factor is neatly compartmentalized in a single nation-state; each has a transnational dimension that complicates the analysis.

First, modernization produces an interrelated set of factors that is a significant permissive cause of terrorism, as increased complexity on all levels of society and economy creates opportunities and vulnerabilities. Sophisticated networks of transportation and communication offer mobility and the means of publicity for terrorists. The terrorists of Narodnaya Volya would have been unable to operate without Russia's newly established rail system, and the Popular Front for the Liberation of Palestine could not indulge in hijacking without the jet aircraft. In Algeria, the FLN only adopted a strategy of urban bombings when they were able to acquire plastic explosives. In 1907, the Combat Organization of the Socialist-Revolutionary party paid 20,000 rubles to an inventor who was working on an aircraft in the futile hope of bombing the Russian imperial palaces from the air.[9] Today we fear that terrorists will exploit the potential of nuclear power, but it was in 1867 that Nobel's invention of dynamite made bombings a convenient terrorist tactic.

Urbanization is part of the modern trend toward aggregation and complexity, which increases the number and accessibility of targets and methods. The popular concept of terrorism as "urban guerilla warfare" grew out of the Latin American experience of the late 1960s.[10] Yet, as Hobsbawn has pointed out, cities became the arena for terrorism after the urban renewal projects of the late nineteenth century, such as the boulevards constructed by Baron Haussman in Paris, made them unsuitable for a strategy based on riots and the defense of barricades.[11] In preventing popular insurrections, governments have exposed themselves to terrorism. P. N. Grabosky has recently argued that cities are a significant cause of terrorism in that they provide an opportunity (a multitude of targets, mobility, communications, anonymity, and audiences) and a recruiting ground among the politicized and volatile inhabitants.[12]

Social "facilitation," which Gurr found to be extremely powerful in bringing about civil strife in general, is also an important permissive factor. This concept refers to social habits and historical traditions that sanction the use of violence against the government, making it morally and politically justifiable, and even dictating an appropriate form, such as demonstrations, coups, or terrorism. Social myths, traditions, and habits permit the development of terrorism as an established political custom. An excellent example of such a tradition is the case of Ireland, where the tradition of physical force dates from the eighteenth century, and the legend of Michael Collins in 1919–21 still inspires and partially excuses the much less discriminate and less effective terrorism of the contemporary Provisional IRA in Northern Ireland.

Moreover, broad attitudes and beliefs that condone terrorism are communicated transnationally. Revolutionary ideologies have always crossed borders with ease. In the nineteenth and early twentieth centuries, such ideas were primarily a European preserve, stemming from the French and Bolshevik Revolutions. Since the Second World War, Third World War revolutions—China, Cuba, Algeria—and intellectuals such as Frantz Fanon and Carlos Marighela[13] have significantly influenced terrorist movements in the developed West by promoting the development of terrorism as routine behavior.

The most salient political factor in the category of permissive causes is a government's inability or unwillingness to prevent terrorism. The absence of adequate prevention by police and intelligence services permits the spread of conspiracy. However, since terrorist organizatons are small and clandestine, the majority of states can be placed in the permissive category. Inefficiency or leniency can be found in a broad range of all but the most brutally efficient dictatorships, including incompetent authoritarian states such as tsarist Russia on the eve of the emergence of Narodnaya Volya as well as modern liberal democratic states whose desire to protect civil liberties constrains security measures. The absence of effective security measures is a necessary cause, since our limited information on the subject indicates that terrorism does not occur in the communist dictatorships; and certainly repressive military regimes in Uruguay, Brazil, and Argentina have crushed ter-

rorist organizations. For many governments, however, the cost of disallowing terrorism is too high.

Turning now to a consideration of the direct causes of terrorism, we focus on background conditions that positively encourage resistance to the state. These instigating circumstances go beyond merely creating an environment in which terrorism is possible; they provide motivation and direction for the terrorist movement. We are dealing here with reasons rather than opportunities.

The first condition that can be considered a direct cause of terrorism is the existence of concrete grievances among an identifiable subgroup of a larger population, such as an ethnic minority discriminated against by the majority. A social movement develops in order to redress these grievances and to gain either equal rights or a separate state; terrorism is then the resort of an extremist faction of this broader movement. In practice, terrorism has frequently arisen in such situations: in modern states, separatist nationalism among Basques, Bretons, and Québecois has motivated terrorism. In the colonial era, nationalist movements commonly turned to terrorism.

This is not to say, however, that the existence of a dissatisfied minority or majority is a necessary or a sufficient cause of terrorism. Not all those who are discriminated against turn to terrorism, nor does terrorism always reflect objective social or economic deprivation. In West Germany, Japan, and Italy, for example, terrorism has been the chosen method of the privileged, not the downtrodden. Some theoretical studies have suggested that the essential ingredient that must be added to real deprivation is the perception on the part of the deprived that this condition is not what they deserve or expect, in short, that discrimination is unjust. An attitude study, for example, found that "the idea of justice or fairness may be more centrally related to attitudes toward violence than are feelings of deprivation. It is the perceived injustice underlying the deprivation that gives rise to anger or frustration."[14] The intervening variables, as we have argued, lie in the terrorists' perceptions. Moreover, it seems likely that for terrorism to occur the government must be singled out to blame for popular suffering.

The second condition that creates motivations for terrorism is the lack of opportunity for political participation. Regimes that deny access to power and persecute dissenters create dissatisfaction. In this case, grievances are primarily political, without social or economic overtones. Discrimination is not directed against any ethnic, religious, or racial subgroup of the population. The terrorist organization is not necessarily part of a broader social movement; indeed, the population may be largely apathetic. In situations where paths to the legal expression of opposition are blocked, but where the regime's repression is inefficient, revolutionary terrorism is doubly likely, as permissive and direct causes coincide. An example of this situation is tsarist Russia in the 1870s.

Context is especially significant as a direct cause of terrorism when it affects an elite, not the mass population. Terrorism is essentially the result of elite disaffection; it represents the strategy of a minority, who may act on behalf of a wider popular constituency who have not been consulted about, and do not necessarily approve of, the terrorists' aims or methods. There is remarkable relevance in E. J. Hobsbawm's comments on the political conspirators of post-Napoleonic Europe: "All revolutionaries regarded themselves, with some justification, as small elites of the emancipated and progressive operating among, and for the eventual benefit of, a vast and inert mass of the ignorant and misled common people, which would no doubt welcome liberation when it came, but could not be expected to take much part in preparing it."[15] Many terrorists today are young, well-educated, and middle class in background. Such students or young professionals, with prior political experience, are disillusioned with the prospects of changing society and see little chance of access to the system despite their privileged status. Much terrorism has grown out of student unrest; this was the case in nineteenth century Russia as well as post–World War II West Germany, Italy, the United States, Japan, and Uruguay.

Perhaps terrorism is most likely to occur precisely where mass passivity and elite dissatisfaction coincide. Discontent is not generalized or severe enough to provoke the majority of the populace to action against the regime, yet a small minority, without access to the bases of power that would permit overthrow of the government through coup d'état or subversion, seeks radical change. Terrorism may thus be a sign of a stable society rather than a symptom of fragility and impending collapse. Terrorism is the resort of an elite when conditions are not revolutionary. Luigi Bonanate has blamed terrorism on a "blocked society" that is strong enough to preserve itself (presumably through popular inertia) yet resistant to innovation. Such self-perpetuating "immobilisme" invites terrorism.[16]

The last category of situational factors involves the concept of a precipitating event that immediately precedes outbreaks of terrorism. Although it is generally thought that precipitants are the most unpredictable of causes, there does seem to be a common pattern of government actions that act as catalysts for terrorism. Government use of unexpected and unusual force in response to protest or reform attempts often compels terrorist retaliation. The development of such an action-reaction syndrome then establishes the structure of the conflict between the regime and its challengers. There are numerous historical examples of a campaign of terrorism precipitated by a government's reliance on excessive force to quell protest or squash dissent. The tsarist regime's severity in dealing with the populist movement was a factor in the development of Narodaya Volya as a terrorist organization in 1879. The French government's persecution of anarchists was a factor in subsequent anarchist terrorism in the 1890s. The British government's execution of the heros [sic] of the Easter Rising set the stage for Michael Collins and the IRA. The Protestant violence that met the Catholic civil rights movement in Northern Ireland in 1969 pushed the Provisional IRA to retaliate. In West Germany, the death of Beno Ohnesorg at the hands of the police in a demonstration against the Shah of Iran in 1968 contributed to the emergence of the RAF.

This analysis of the background conditions for terrorism indicates that we must look at the terrorist organization's perception and interpretation of the situation. Terrorists view the context as permissive, making terrorism a viable option. In a material sense, the means are placed at their disposal by the environment. Circumstances also provide the terrorists with compelling reasons for seeking political change. Finally, an event occurs that snaps the terrorists' patience with the regime. Government action is now seen as intolerably unjust, and terrorism becomes not only a possible decision but a morally acceptable one. The regime has forfeited its status as the standard of legitimacy. For the terrorist, the end may now excuse the means.

The Reasons for Terrorism

Significant campaigns of terrorism depend on rational political choice. As purposeful activity, terrorism is the result of an organization's decision that it is a politically useful means to oppose a government. The argument that terrorist behavior should be analyzed as "rational" is based on the assumption that terrorist organizations possess internally consistent sets of values, beliefs, and images of the environment. Terrorism is seen collectively as a logical means to advance desired ends. The terrorist organization engages in decision-making calculations that an analyst can approximate. In short, the terrorist group's reasons for resorting to terrorism constitute an important factor in the process of causation.[17]

Terrorism serves a variety of goals, both revolutionary and subrevolutionary. Terrorists may be revolutionaries (such as the Combat Organization of the Socialist-Revolutionary Party in the nineteenth century or the Tupamaros of the twentieth); nationalists fighting against foreign occupiers (the Algerian FLN, the IRA of 1919–21, or the Irgun); minority separatists combatting indigenous regimes (such as the Corsican, Breton, and Basque movements, and the Provisional IRA); reformists (the bombing of nuclear construction sites, for example, is meant to halt nuclear power, not to overthrow governments); anarchists or millenarians (such as the original anarchist movement of the nineteenth century and modern millenarian groups such as the Red Army faction in West Germany, the Italian Red Brigades, and the Japanese Red Army); or reactionaries acting to prevent change from the top (such as the Secret Army Organization during the Algerian war or the contemporary Ulster Defence Association in Northern Ireland).[18]

Saying that extremist groups resort to terrorism in order to acquire political influence does not mean that all groups have equally precise objectives or that the relationship between means and ends is perfectly clear to an outside observer. Some groups are less realistic about the logic of means and ends than others. The leaders of Narodnaya Volya, for example, lacked a detailed conception of how the assassination of the tsar would force his successor to permit the liberalization they sought. Other terrorist groups are more pragmatic: the IRA of 1919–21 and the Irgun, for instance, shrewdly foresaw the utility of a war of attrition against the British. Menachem Begin, in particular, planned his campaign to take advantage of the "glass house" that Britain operated in.[19] The degree of skill in relating means to ends seems to have little to do with the overall sophistication of the terrorist ideology. The French anarchists of the 1890s, for example, acted in light of a well-developed philosophical doctrine but were much less certain of how violence against the bourgeoisie would bring about freedom. It is possible that anarchist or millenarian terrorists are so preoccupied with the splendor of the future that they lose sight of the present. Less theoretical nationalists who concentrate on the short run have simpler aims but sharper plans.

However diverse the long-run goals of terrorist groups, there is a common pattern of proximate or short-run objectives of a terrorist strategy. Proximate objectives are defined in terms of the reactions that terrorists want to achieve in their different audiences.[20] The most basic reason for terrorism is to gain recognition or attention—what Thornton called advertisement of the cause. Violence and bloodshed always excite human curiosity, and the theatricality, suspense, and threat of danger inherent in terrorism enhance its attention-getting qualities. In fact, publicity may be the highest goal of some groups. For example, terrorists who are fundamentally protesters might be satisfied with airing their grievances before the world. Today, in an interdependent world, the need for international recognition encourages transnational terrorist activities, with escalation to ever more destructive and spectacular violence. As the audience grows larger, more diverse, and more accustomed to terrorism, terrorists must go to extreme lengths to shock.

Terrorism is also often designed to disrupt and discredit the processes of government, by weakening it administratively and impairing normal operations. Terrorism as a direct attack on the regime aims at the insecurity and demoralization of government officials, independent of any impact on public opinion. An excellent example of this strategy is Michael Collins's campaign against the British intelligence system in Ireland in 1919–21. This form of terrorism often accompanies rural guerrilla warfare, as the insurgents try to weaken the government's control over its territory.

Terrorism also affects public attitudes in both a positive and a negative sense, aiming at creating either sympathy in a potential constituency or fear and hostility in an audience identified as the "enemy." These two functions are interrelated, since intimidating the "enemy" impresses both sympathizers and the uncommitted. At the same time, terrorism may be used to enforce obedience in an audience from whom the terrorists demand allegiance. The FLN in Algeria, for example, claimed more Algerian than French victims. Fear and respect were not incompatible with solidarity against the French.[21] When terrorism is part of a struggle between incumbents and challengers, polarization of public opinion undermines the government's legitimacy.

Terrorism may also be intended to provoke a counterreaction from the government, to increase publicity for the terrorists' cause and to demonstrate to the people that their charges against the regime are well founded. The terrorists mean to force the state to show its true repressive face, thereby driving the people into the arms of the challengers. For example, Carlos Marighela argued that the way to win popular support was to provoke the regime to measures of greater repression and persecution.[22] Provocative terrorism is designed to bring about revolutionary conditions rather than to exploit them. The FLN against the French, the Palestinians against Israel, and the RAF against the Federal Republic all appear to have used terrorism as provocation.

In addition, terrorism may serve internal organizational functions of control, discipline, and morale building within the terrorist group and even become an instrument of rivalry among factions in a resistance movement. For example, factional terrorism has frequently characterized the Palestinian resistance movement. Rival groups have competed in a vicious game where the victims are Israeli civilians or anonymous airline passengers, but where the immediate goal is influence within the resistance movement rather than the intimidation of the Israeli public or international recognition of the Palestinian cause.

Terrorism is a logical choice when oppositions have such goals and when the power ratio of government to challenger is high. The observation that terrorism is a weapon of the weak is hackneyed but apt. At least when initially adopted, terrorism is the strategy of a minority that by its own judgment lacks other means. When the group perceives its options as limited, terrorism is attractive because it is a relatively inexpensive and simple alternative, and because its potential reward is high.

Weakness and consequent restriction of choice can stem from different sources. On the one hand, weakness may result from the regime's suppression of opposition. Resistance organizations who lack the means of mounting more extensive violence may then turn to terrorism because legitimate expression of dissent is denied. Lack of popular support at the outset of a conflict does not mean that the terrorists' aims lack general appeal. Even though they cannot immediately mobilize widespread and active support, over the course of the conflict they may acquire the allegiance of the population. For example, the Algerian FLN used terrorism as a significant means of mobilizing mass support.[23]

On the other hand, it is wrong to assume that where there is terrorism there is oppression. Weakness may mean that an extremist organization deliberately rejects nonviolent methods of opposition open to them in a liberal state. Challengers then adopt terrorism because they are impatient with time-consuming legal methods of eliciting support or advertising their cause, because they distrust the regime, or because they are not capable of, or interested in, mobilizing majority support. Most terrorist groups operating in Western Europe and Japan in the past decade illustrate this phenomenon. The new millenarians lack a readily identifiable constituency and espouse causes devoid of mass appeal. Similarly, separatist movements represent at best only a minority of the total population of the state.

Thus, some groups are weak because weakness is imposed on them by the political system they operate in, others because of unpopularity. We are therefore making value judgments about the potential legitimacy of terrorist organizations. In some cases resistance groups are genuinely desperate, in others they have alternatives to violence. Nor do we want to forget that nonviolent resistance has been chosen in other circumstances, for example, by Gandhi and by Martin Luther King. Terrorists may argue that they had no choice, but their perceptions may be flawed.[24]

In addition to weakness, an important rationale in the decision to adopt a strategy of terrorism is impatience. Action becomes imperative. For a variety of reasons, the challenge to the state cannot be left to the future. Given a perception of limited means, the group often sees the choice as between action as survival and inaction as the death of resistance.

One reason for haste is external: the historical moment seems to present a unique chance.

For example, the resistance group facing a colonial power recently weakened by a foreign war exploits a temporary vulnerability: the IRA against Britain after World War I, the Irgun against Britain after World War II, and the FLN against France after the Indochina war. We might even suggest that the stalemate between the United States and North Vietnam stimulated the post-1968 wave of anti-imperialist terrorism, especially in Latin America. There may be other pressures or catalysts provided by the regime, such as the violent precipitants discussed earlier or the British decision to introduce conscription in Ireland during World War I.

A sense of urgency may also develop when similar resistance groups have apparently succeeded with terrorism and created a momentum. The contagion effect of terrorism is partially based on an image of success that recommends terrorism to groups who identify with the innovator. The Algerian FLN, for example, was pressured to keep up with nationalists in Tunisia and Morocco, whose violent agitation brought about independence in 1956. Terrorism spread rapidly through Latin America in the post-1968 period as revolutionary groups worked in terms of a continental solidarity.

Dramatic failure of alternative means of obtaining one's ends may also fuel a drive toward terrorism. The Arab defeat in the 1967 war with Israel led Palestinians to realize that they could no longer depend on the Arab states to further their goals. In retrospect, their extreme weakness and the historical tradition of violence in the Middle East made it likely that militant nationalists should turn to terrorism. Since international recognition of the Palestinian cause was a primary aim (given the influence of outside powers in the region) and since attacks on Israeli territory were difficult, terrorism developed into a transnational phenomenon.

These external pressures to act are often intensified by internal politics. Leaders of resistance groups act under constraints imposed by their followers. They are forced to justify the organization's existence, to quell restlessness among the cadres, to satisfy demands for revenge, to prevent splintering of the movement, and to maintain control. Pressures may also come from the terrorists' constituency.

In conclusion, we see that terrorism is an attractive strategy to groups of different ideological persuasions who challenge the state's authority. Groups who want to dramatize a cause, to demoralize the government, to gain popular support, to provoke regime violence, to inspire followers, or to dominate a wider resistance movement, who are weak vis-à-vis the regime, and who are impatient to act, often find terrorism a reasonable choice. This is especially so when conditions are favorable, providing opportunities and making terrorism a simple and rapid option, with immediate and visible payoff.

Individual Motivation and Participation

Terrorism is neither an automatic reaction to conditions nor a purely calculated strategy. What psychological factors motivate the terrorist and influence his or her perceptions and interpretations of reality? Terrorists are only a small minority of people with similar personal backgrounds, experiencing the same conditions, who might thus be expected to reach identical conclusions based on logical reasoning about the utility of terrorism as a technique of political influence.

The relationship between personality and politics is complex and imperfectly understood.[25] Why individuals engage in political violence is a complicated problem, and the question why they engage in terrorism is still more difficult.[26] As most simply and frequently posed, the question of a psychological explanation of terrorism is whether or not there is a "terrorist personality," similar to the authoritarian personality, whose emotional traits we can specify with some exactitude.[27] An identifiable pattern of attitudes and behavior in the terrorism-prone individual would result from a combination of ego-defensive needs, cognitive processes, and socialization, in interaction with a specific situation.

In pursuing this line of inquiry, it is important to avoid stereotyping the terrorist or oversimplifying the sources of terrorist actions. No single motivation or personality can be valid for all circumstances.

What limited data we have on individual terrorists (and knowledge must be gleaned from disparate sources that usually neither focus on psychology nor use a comparative approach) suggest that the outstanding common characteristic of terrorists is their normality. Terrorism often seems to be the connecting link among widely varying personalities. Franco Venturi, concentrating on the terrorists of a single small group, observed that "the policy of terrorism united many very different characters and mentalities" and that agreement on using terrorism was the cement that bound the members of Narodnaya Volya together.[28] The West German psychiatrist who conducted a pretrial examination of four members of the RAF concluded that they were "intelligent," even "humorous," and showed no symptoms of psychosis or neurosis and "no particular personality type."[29] Psychoanalysis might penetrate beneath superficial normality to expose some unifying or pathological trait, but this is scarcely a workable research method, even if the likelihood of the existence of such a characteristic could be demonstrated.

Peter Merkl, in his study of the pre-1933 Nazi movement—a study based on much more data than we have on terrorists—abandoned any attempt to classify personality types and instead focused on factors like the level of political understanding.[30] An unbiased examination of conscious attitudes might be more revealing than a study of subconscious predispositions or personalities. For example, if terrorists perceive the state as unjust, morally corrupt, and violent, then terrorism may seem legitimate and justified. For example, Blumenthal and her coauthors found that "the stronger the perception of an act as violence, the more violence is thought to be an appropriate response."[31] The evidence also indicates that many terrorists are activists with prior political experience in nonviolent opposition to the state. How do these experiences in participation influence later attitudes? Furthermore, how do terrorists view their victims? Do we find extreme devaluation, depersonalization, or stereotyping? Is there "us versus them" polarization or ethnic or religious prejudice that might sanction or prompt violence toward an out-group? How do terrorists justify and rationalize violence? Is remorse a theme?

The questions of attitudes toward victims and justifications for terrorism are especially important because different forms of terrorism involve various degrees of selectivity in the choice of victims. Some acts of terrorism are extremely discriminate, while others are broadly indiscriminate. Also, some terrorist acts require more intimate contact between terrorist and victim than others. Thus, the form of terrorism practiced—how selective it is and how much personal domination of the victim it involves—would determine the relevance of different questions.

Analyzing these issues involves serious methodological problems. As the Blumenthal study emphasizes, there are two ways of analyzing the relationship between attitudes and political behavior.[32] If our interest is in identifying potential terrorists by predicting behavior from the existence of certain consciously held attitudes and beliefs, then the best method would be to survey a young age group in a society determined to be susceptible. If terrorism subsequently occurred, we could then see which types of individuals became terrorists. (A problem is that the preconditions would change over time and that precipitants are unpredictable.) The more common and easier way of investigating the attitudes-behavior connection is to select people who have engaged in a particular behavior and ask them questions about their opinions. Yet attitudes may be adopted subsequent, rather than prior, to behavior, and they may serve as rationalizations for behavior engaged in for different reasons, not as genuine motivations. These problems would seem to be particularly acute when the individuals concerned have engaged in illegal forms of political behavior.

Another problem facing the researcher interested in predispositions or attitudes is that terrorists are recruited in different ways. Assuming that people who are in some way personally attracted to terrorism actually engage in such behavior supposes that potential terrorists are presented with an appropriate opportunity, which is a factor over which they have little control.[33] Moreover, terrorist groups often discourage or reject potential recruits who are openly seeking excitement or danger for personal motives. For instance, William Mackey Lomasney, a member of the Clan na Gael or American Fenians in the nineteenth century (who was killed in 1884 in an attempt to blow up London Bridge) condemned the "disgraceful" activities of the hotheaded and impulsive Jeremiah O'Donovan Rossa:

> Were it not that O'Donovan Rossa has openly and unblushingly boasted that he is responsible for those ridiculous and futile efforts . . . we might hesitate to even suspect that any sane man, least of all one professedly friendly to the cause, would for any consideration or desire for notoriety take upon himself such a fearful responsibility, and, that having done so, he could engage men so utterly incapable of carrying out his insane designs.[34]

Lomasney complained that the would-be terrorists were:

> such stupid blundering fools that they make our cause appear imbecile and farcical. When the fact becomes known that those half-idiotic attempts have been made by men professing to be patriotic Irishmen what will the world think but that Irish revolutionists are a lot of fools and ignoramuses, men who do not understand the first principles of the art of war, the elements of chemistry or even the amount of explosive material necessary to remove or destroy an ordinary brick or stone wall. Think of the utter madness of men who have no idea of accumulative and destructive forces undertaking with common blasting powder to scare and shatter the Empire.[35]

Not only do serious terrorists scorn the ineptitude of the more excitable, but they find them a serious security risk. Rossa, for example, could not be trusted not to give away the Clan na Gael's plans for terrorism in his New York newspaper articles. In a similar vein, Boris Savinkov, head of the Combat Organization of the Socialist-Revolutionary party in Russia, tried to discourage an aspirant whom he suspected of being drawn to the adventure of terrorism:

> I explained to him that terrorist activity did not consist only of throwing bombs; that it was much more minute, difficult and tedious than might be imagined; that a terrorist is called upon to live a rather dull existence for months at a time, eschewing meeting his own comrades and doing most difficult and unpleasant work—the work of systematic observation.[36]

Similar problems in analyzing the connection between attitudes and behavior are due to the fact that there are role differentiations between leaders and followers. The degree of formal organization varies from the paramilitary hierarchies of the Irgun or the IRA to the semi-autonomous coexistence of small groups in contemporary West Germany or Italy or even to the rejection of central direction in the nineteenth century anarchist movement in France. Yet even Narodnaya Volya, a self-consciously democratic group, observed distinctions based on authority. There are thus likely to be psychological or background differences between leaders and cadres. For example, a survey of contemporary terrorist movements found that leaders are usually older than their followers, which is not historically unusual.[37] In general, data are scant on individual terrorist leaders, their exercise of authority, the basis for it, and their interactions with their followers.[38] Furthermore, if there is a predisposition to terrorism, the terrorism-prone individual who obtains psychic gratification from the experience is likely to be a follower, not a leader who commands but does not perform the act.

An alternative approach to analyzing the psychology of terrorism is to use a deductive method based on what we know about terrorism as an activity, rather than an inductive method yielding general propositions from statements of the particular. What sort of characteristics would make an individual suited for terrorism? What are the role requirements of the terrorist?

One of the most salient attributes of terrorist activity is that it involves significant personal danger.[39] Furthermore, since terrorism involves premediated, not impulsive, violence, the terrorist's awareness of the risks is maximized. Thus, although terrorists may simply be people who enjoy or disregard risk,[40] it is more likely that they are people who tolerate high risk because of intense commitment to a cause. Their commitment is strong enough to make the risk of personal harm acceptable and perhaps to outweigh the cost of society's rejection, although defiance of the majority may be a reward in itself. In either case, the violent activity is not gratifying per se.

It is perhaps even more significant that terrorism is a group activity, involving intimate relationships among a small number of people. Interactions among members of the group may be more important in determining behavior than the psychological predispositions of individual members. Terrorists live and make decisions under conditions of extreme stress. As a clandestine minority, the members of a terrorist group are isolated from society, even if they live in what Menachem Begin called the "open underground."[41]

Terrorists can confide in and trust only each other. The nature of their commitment cuts them off from society; they inhabit a closed community that is forsaken only at great cost. Isolation and the perception of a hostile environment intensify shared belief and commitment and make faith in the cause imperative. A pattern of mutual reassurance, solidarity, and comradeship develops, in which the members of the group reinforce each other's self-righteousness, image of a hostile world, and sense of mission. Because of the real danger terrorists confront, the strain they live under, and the moral conflicts they undergo, they value solidarity highly.[42] Terrorists are not necessarily people who seek "belonging" or personal integration through ideological commitment, but once embarked on the path of terrorism, they desperately need the group and the cause. Isolation and internal consensus explain how the beliefs and values of a terrorist group can be so drastically at odds with those of society at large. An example of such a divorce from social and political reality is the idea of the RAF that terrorism would lead to a resurgence of Nazism in West Germany that would in turn spark a workers' revolt.[43]

In their intense commitment, separation from the outside world, and intolerance of internal dissent, terrorist groups resemble religious sects or cults. Michael Barkun has explained the continued commitment of members of millenarian movements, a conviction frequently expressed in proselytizing in order to validate beliefs, in terms of the reinforcement and reassurance of rightness that the individual receives from other members of the organization. He also notes the frequent practice of initiation rites that involve violations of taboos, or "bridge-burning acts," that create guilt and prevent the convert's return to society. Thus the millenarian, like the terrorist group, constitutes "a community of common guilt."[44] J. Bowyer Bell has commented on the religious qualities of dedication and moral fervor characterizing the IRA: "In the Republican Movement, the two seemingly opposing traditions, one of the revolution and physical force, and the other of pious and puritanical service, combine into a secular vocation."[45]

If there is a single common emotion that drives the individual to become a terrorist, it is vengeance on behalf of comrades or even the constituency the terrorist aspires to represent. (At the same time, the demand for retribution serves as public justification or excuse.) A regime thus encourages terrorism when it creates martyrs to be avenged. Anger at what is perceived as unjust persecution inspires demands for revenge, and as the regime responds to terrorism with greater force, violence escalates out of control.

There are numerous historical demonstrations of the central role vengeance plays as motivation for terrorism. It is seen as one of the principal causes of anarchist terrorism in France in the 1890s. The infamous Ravachol acted to avenge the "martyrs of Clichy," two possibly innocent anarchists who were beaten by the police and sentenced to prison. Subsequent bombings and assassinations, for instance that of President Carnot, were intended to avenge Ravachol's execution.[46] The cruelty of the sentences imposed for minor offenses at the "Trial of the 193," the hanging of eleven southern revolutionaries after Soloviev's unsuccessful attack on the tsar in 1879, and the "Trial of the 16" in 1880 deeply affected the members of Narodnaya Volya. Kravchinski (Stepniak) explained that personal resentment felt after the Trial of the 193 led to killing police spies; it then seemed unreasonable to spare their employers, who were actually responsible for the repression. Thus, intellectually the logic first inspired by resentment compelled them to escalate terrorism by degrees.[47] During the Algerian war, the French execution of FLN prisoners; in Northern Ireland, British troops firing on civil rights demonstrators; in West Germany, the death of a demonstrator at the hands of the police—all served to precipitate terrorism as militants sought to avenge their comrades.

The terrorists' willingness to accept high risks may also be related to the belief that one's death will be avenged. The prospect of retribution gives the act of terrorism and the death of the terrorist meaning and continuity, even fame and immortality. Vengeance may be not only a function of anger but of a desire for transcendence.

Shared guilt is surely a strong force in binding members of the terrorist group together. Almost all terrorists seem compelled to justify their behavior, and this anxiety cannot be explained solely by reference to their desire to create a public image of virtuous sincerity. Terrorists usually show acute concern for morality, especially for sexual purity, and believe that they act in terms of a higher good. Justifications usually focus on past suffering, on the glorious future to be created, and on the regime's illegitimacy and violence, to which terrorism is the only available response. Shared guilt and anxiety increase the group's interdependence and mutual commitment and may also make followers more dependent on leaders and on the common ideology as sources of moral authority.

Guilt may also lead terrorists to seek punishment and danger rather than avoid it. The motive of self-sacrifice notably influenced many Russian terrorists of the nineteenth century. Kaliayev, for example, felt that only his death could atone for the murder he committed. Even to Camus, the risk of death for the terrorist is a form of personal absolution.[48] In other cases of terrorism, individuals much more pragmatic than Kaliayev, admittedly a religious mystic, seemed to welcome capture because it brought release from the strains of underground existence and a sense of content and fulfillment. For example, Meridor, a member of the Irgun High Command, felt "high spirits" and "satisfaction" when arrested by the British because he now shared the suffering that all fighters had to experience. He almost welcomed the opportunity to prove that he was prepared to sacrifice himself for the cause. In fact, until his arrest he had felt "morally uncomfortable," whereas afterwards he felt "exalted."[49] Menachem Begin expressed similar feelings. Once, waiting as the British searched the hotel where he was staying, he admitted anxiety and fear, but when he knew there was "no way out," his "anxious thoughts evaporated." He "felt a peculiar serenity mixed with incomprehensible happiness" and waited "composedly," but the police passed him by.[50]

Vera Figner, a leader of the Narodnaya Volya, insisted on physically assisting in acts of terrorism, even though her comrades accused her of seeking personal satisfaction instead of allowing the organization to make the best use of her talents. She found it intolerable to bear a moral responsibility for acts that endangered her comrades. She could not encourage others to commit acts she would not herself commit; anything less than full acceptance of the consequences of her decisions would be cowardice.[51]

It is possible that the willingness to face risk is related to what Robert J. Lifton has termed "survivor-guilt" as well as to feelings of group solidarity or of guilt at harming victims.[52] Sometimes individuals who survive disaster or escape punishment when others have suffered feel guilty and may seek relief by courting a similar fate. This guilt may also explain why terrorists often take enormous risks to rescue imprisoned comrades, as well as why they accept danger or arrest with equanimity or even satisfaction.

It is clear that once a terrorist group embarks on a strategy of terrorism, whatever its purpose and whatever its successes or failures, psychological factors make it very difficult to halt. Terrorism as a process gathers its own momentum, independent of external events.

Conclusions

Terrorism per se is not usually a reflection of mass discontent or deep cleavages in society. More often it represents the disaffection of a fragment of the elite, who may take it upon themselves to act on the behalf of a majority unaware of its plight, unwilling to take action to remedy grievances, or unable to express dissent. This discontent, however subjective in origin or minor in scope, is blamed on the government and its supporters. Since the sources of terrorism are manifold, any society or polity that permits opportunities for terrorism is vulnerable. Government reactions that are inconsistent, wavering between tolerance and repression, seem most likely to encourage terrorism.

Given some source of disaffection—and in the centralized modern state with its faceless bureaucracies, lack of responsiveness to demands is ubiquitous—terrorism is an attractive strategy for small organizations of diverse ideological persuasions who want to attract attention for their cause, provoke the government, intimidate opponents, appeal for sympathy, impress an audience, or promote the adherence of the faithful. Terrorists perceive an absence of choice. Whether unable or unwilling to perceive a choice between terrorist and nonterrorist action, whether unpopular or prohibited by the government, the terrorist group reasons that there is no alternative. The ease, simplicity, and rapidity with which terrorism can be implemented and the prominence of models of terrorism strengthen its appeal, especially since terrorist groups are impatient to act. Long-standing social traditions that sanction terrorism against the state, as in Ireland, further enhance its attractiveness.

There are two fundamental questions about the psychological basis of terrorism. The first is why the individual takes the first step and chooses to engage in terrorism: why join? Does the terrorist possess specific psychological predispositions, identifiable in advance, that suit him or her for terrorism? That terrorists are people capable of intense commitment tells us little, and the motivations for terrorism vary immensely. Many individuals are potential terrorists, but few actually make that commitment. To explain why terrorism happens, another question is more appropriate: Why does involvement continue? What are the psychological mechanisms of group interaction? We are not dealing with a situation in which certain types of personalities suddenly turn to terrorism in answer to some inner call. Terrorism is the result of a gradual growth of commitment and opposition, a group development that furthermore depends on government action. The psychological relationships within the terrorist group—the interplay of commitment, risk, solidarity, loyalty, guilt, revenge, and isolation—discourage terrorists from changing the direction they have taken. This may explain why—even if objective circumstances change when, for example, grievances are satisfied, or if the logic of the situation changes when, for example, the terrorists are offered other alternatives for the expression of opposition—terrorism may endure until the terrorist group is physically destroyed.

NOTES

1. For discussions of the meaning of the concept of terrorism, see Thomas P. Thornton, "Terror as a Weapon of Political Agitation," in Harry Eckstein, ed. *Internal War* (New York, 1964), pp. 71–99; Martha Crenshaw Hutchinson, "The Concept of Revolutionary Terrorism," *Revolutionary Terrorism: The FLN in Algeria, 1954–1962* (Stanford: The Hoover Institution Press, 1978) chap. 2; and E. Victor Walter, *Terror and Resistance* (New York, 1969).

2. Walter Laqueur, "Interpretations of Terrorism—Fact, Fiction and Political Science," *Journal of Contemporary History*, 12 (January 1977), 1–42. See also his major work *Terrorism* (London: Weidenfeld and Nicolson, 1977).

3. See, for example, Paul Wilkinson, *Terrorism and the Liberal State* (London: Macmillan, 1977), or J. Bowyer Bell, *A Time of Terror: How Democratic Societies Respond to Revolutionary Violence* (New York, 1978).

4. This is not to deny that some modern terrorist groups, such as those in West Germany, resemble premodern millenarian movements. See specifically Conor Cruise O'Brien, "Liberty and Terrorism," *International Security*, 2 (1977), 56–67. In general, see Norman Cohn, *The Pursuit of the Millennium* (London: Secker and Warburg, 1957), and E. J. Hobsbawm, *Primitive Rebels: Studies in Archaic Forms of Social Movement in the 19th and 20th Centuries* (Manchester: Manchester University Press, 1971).

5. A sampling would include Douglas Hibbs, Jr., *Mass Political Violence: A Cross-National Causal Analysis* (New York, 1973); William J. Crotty, ed. *Assassinations and the Political Order* (New York, 1971); Ted Robert Gurr, *Why Men Rebel* (Princeton, 1971), and Gurr, Peter N. Grabosky, and Richard C. Hula, *The Politics of Crime and Conflict* (Beverly Hills, 1977).

6. For a summary of these findings, see Gurr, "The Calculus of Civil Conflict," *Journal of Social Issues*, 28 (1972), 27–47.

7. Gurr, "Some Characteristics of Political Terrorism in the 1960s," in Michael Stohl, ed. *The Politics of Terrorism* (New York, 1979), pp. 23–50 and 46–47.

8. A distinction between preconditions and precipitants is found in Eckstein, "On the Etiology of

Internal Wars," *History and Theory*, 4 (1965), 133–62. Kenneth Waltz also differentiates between the framework for action as a permissive or underlying cause and special reasons as immediate or efficient causes. In some cases we can say of terrorism, as he says of war, that it occurs because there is nothing to prevent it. See *Man, the State and War* (New York, 1959), p. 232.

9. Boris Savinkov, *Memoirs of a Terrorist*, trans. Joseph Shaplen (New York: A. & C. Boni, 1931), pp. 286–87.

10. The major theoreticians of the transition from the rural to the urban guerrilla are Carlos Marighela, *For the Liberation of Brazil* (Harmondsworth: Penguin Books, 1971), and Abraham Guillen, *Philosophy of the Urban Guerrilla: The Revolutionary Writings of Abraham Guillen*, trans. and edited by Donald C. Hodges (New York, 1973).

11. Hobsbawm, *Revolutionaries: Contemporary Essays* (New York, 1973), pp. 226–27.

12. Grabosky, "The Urban Context of Political Terrorism," in Michael Stohl, ed., pp. 51–76.

13. See Amy Sands Redlick, "The Transnational Flow of Information as a Cause of Terrorism," in Yonah Alexander, David Carlton, and Wilkinson, eds. *Terrorism: Theory and Practice* (Boulder, 1979), pp. 73–95. See also Manus I. Midlarsky, Martha Crenshaw, and Fumihiko Yoshida, "Why Violence Spreads: The Contagion of International Terrorism," *International Studies Quarterly*, 24 (June 1980), 262–98.

14. Monica D. Blumenthal, et al., *More About Justifying Violence: Methodological Studies of Attitudes and Behavior* (Ann Arbor: Survey Research Center, Institute for Social Research, University of Michigan, 1975), p. 108. Similarly, Peter Lupsha, "Explanation of Political Violence: Some Psychological Theories Versus Indignation," *Politics and Society*, 2 (1971), 89–104, contrasts the concept of "indignation" with Gurr's theory of relative deprivation, which holds that expectations exceed rewards (see *Why Men Rebel*, esp. pp. 24–30).

15. Hobsbawm, *Revolutionaries*, p. 143.

16. Luigi Bonanate, "Some Unanticipated Consequences of Terrorism," *Journal of Peace Research*, 16 (1979), 197–211. If this theory is valid, we then need to identify such blocked societies.

17. See Barbara Salert's critique of the rational choice model of revolutionary participation in *Revolutions and Revolutionaries* (New York, 1976). In addition, Abraham Kaplan discusses the distinction between reasons and causes in "The Psychodynamics of Terrorism," *Terrorism—An International Journal*, 1, 3 and 4 (1978), 237–54.

18. For a typology of terrorist organizations, see Wilkinson, *Political Terrorism* (New York, 1975). These classes are not mutually exclusive, and they depend on an outside assessment of goals. For example, the Basque ETA would consider itself revolutionary as well as separatist. The RAF considered itself a classic national liberation movement, and the Provisional IRA insists that it is combatting a foreign oppressor, not an indigenous regime.

19. Bell presents a succinct analysis of Irgun strategy in "The Palestinian Archetype: Irgun and the Strategy of Leverage," in *On Revolt: Strategies of National Liberation* (Cambridge [Ma.], 1976), chap. 3.

20. See Thornton's analysis of proximate goals in "Terror as a Weapon of Political Agitation," in Eckstein, ed. pp. 82–88.

21. Walter's discussion of the concept of "forced choice" explains how direct audiences, from whom the victims are drawn, may accept terrorism as legitimate; see *Terror and Resistance*, pp. 285–89.

22. See Marighela, *For the Liberation of Brazil*, pp. 94–95. The West German RAF apparently adopted the idea of provocation as part of a general national liberation strategy borrowed from the Third World.

23. See Hutchinson, *Revolutionary Terrorism*, chap. 3, pp. 40–60.

24. See Michael Walzer's analysis of the morality of terrorism in *Just and Unjust Wars* (New York, 1977), pp. 197–206. See also Bernard Avishai, "In Cold Blood," *The New York Review of Books*, March 8, 1979, pp. 41–44, for a critical appraisal of the failure of recent works on terrorism to discuss moral issues. The question of the availability of alternatives to terrorism

is related to the problem of discrimination in the selection of victims. Where victims are clearly responsible for a regime's denial of opportunity, terrorism is more justifiable than where they are not.

25. See Fred I. Greenstein, *Personality and Politics: Problems of Evidence, Inference, and Conceptualization* (Chicago, 1969).

26. See Jeffrey Goldstein, *Aggression and Crimes of Violence* (New York, 1975).

27. A study of the West German New Left, for example, concludes that social psychological models of authoritarianism do help explain the dynamics of radicalism and even the transformation from protest to terrorism. See S. Robert Lichter, "A Psychopolitical Study of West German Male Radical Students," *Comparative Politics*, 12 (October 1979), pp. 27–48.

28. Franco Venturi, *Roots of Revolution: A History of the Populist and Socialist Movements in Nineteenth Century Russia* (London: Weidenfeld and Nicolson, 1960), p. 647.

29. Quoted in *Science*, 203, 5 January 1979, p. 34, as part of an account of the proceedings of the International Scientific Conference on Terrorism held in Berlin, December, 1978. Advocates of the "terrorist personality" theory, however, argued that terrorists suffer from faulty vestibular functions in the middle ear or from inconsistent mothering resulting in dysphoria. For another description see John Wykert, "Psychiatry and Terrorism," *Psychiatric News*, 14 (February 2, 1979), 1 and 12–14. A psychologist's study of a single group, the Front de Libération du Québec, is Gustav Morf, *Terror in Quebec: Case Studies of the FLQ* (Toronto: Clarke, Irvin, and Co., 1970).

30. Peter Merkl, *Political Violence Under the Swastika: 581 Early Nazis* (Princeton, 1974), 33–34.

31. Blumenthal, et al., p. 182.

32. Ibid., p. 12. Lichter also recognizes this problem.

33. Ibid., pp. 12–13.

34. William O'Brien and Desmond Ryan, eds. *Devoy's Post Bag*, vol. II (Dublin: C. J. Fallon, Ltd., 1953), p. 51.

35. Ibid., p. 52.

36. Savinkov, *Memoirs*, p. 147.

37. Charles A. Russell and Bowman H. Miller, "Profile of a Terrorist," *Terrorism—An International Journal*, 1 (1977), reprinted in John D. Elliott and Leslie K. Gibson, eds. *Contemporary Terrorism: Selected Readings* (Gaithersburg, Md.: International Association of Chiefs of Police, 1978), pp. 81–95.

38. See Philip Pomper's analysis of the influence of Nechaev over his band of followers: "The People's Revenge," *Sergei Nechaev* (New Brunswick [N.J.], 1979), chap. 4.

39. A Rand Corporation study of kidnappings and barricade-and-hostage incidents concluded that such tactics are not necessarily perilous, while admitting that drawing statistical inferences from a small number of cases in a limited time period (August, 1968 to June, 1975) is hazardous. See Brian Jenkins, Janera Johnson, and David Ronfeldt, *Numbered Lives: Some Statistical Observations from 77 International Hostage Episodes*, Rand Paper P-5905 (Santa Monica: The Rand Corporation, 1977).

40. Psychiatrist Frederick Hacker, for example, argues that terrorists are by nature indifferent to risk; see *Crusaders, Criminals and Crazies* (New York, 1976), p. 13.

41. Menachem Begin, *The Revolt* (London: W. H. Allen, 1951).

42. J. Glenn Gray, "The Enduring Appeals of Battle," *The Warriors: Reflections on Men in Battle* (New York, 1970), chap. 2, describes similar experiences among soldiers in combat.

43. Statements of the beliefs of the leaders of the RAF can be found in *Textes des prisonniers de la Fraction armée rouge et dernières lettres d'Ulrike Meinhof* (Paris: Maspéro, 1977).

44. Michael Barkun, *Disaster and the Millennium* (New Haven, 1974), pp. 14–16. See also Leon Festinger, et al., *When Prophecy Fails* (New York, 1964).

45. Bell, *The Secret Army* (London: Anthony Blond, 1970), p. 379.

46. Jean Maitron, *Histoire du mouvement anarchiste en France (1880–1914)* (Paris: Societé universitaire d'éditions et de librairie, 1955), pp. 242–43.

47. S. Stepniak (pseudonym for Kravchimski), *Underground Russia: Revolutionary Profiles and Sketches from Life* (London: Smith, Elder, and Co., 1882), pp. 36–37; see also Venturi, pp. 639 and 707–08.

48. See "Les meurtriers délicats" in *L'Homme Révolté* (Paris: Gallimard, 1965), pp. 571–79.

49. Ya'acov Meridor, *Long is the Road to Freedom* (Tujunga [Ca.]: Barak Publications, 1961), pp. 6 and 9.

50. Begin, p. 111.

51. Vera Figner, *Mémoires d'une révolutionnaire*, trans. Victor Serge (Paris: Gallimard, 1930), pp. 131 and 257–62.

52. Such an argument is applied to Japanese Red Army terrorist Kozo Okamoto by Patricia Steinhof in "Portrait of a Terrorist," *Asian Survey*, 16 (1976), 830–45.

Timur Kuran

NOW OUT OF NEVER: THE ELEMENT OF SURPRISE IN THE EAST EUROPEAN REVOLUTION OF 1989

I. United in Amazement

"Our jaws cannot drop any lower," exclaimed Radio Free Europe one day in late 1989. It was commenting on the electrifying collapse of Eastern Europe's communist regimes.[1] The political landscape of the entire region changed suddenly, astonishing even the most seasoned political observers. In a matter of weeks entrenched leaders were overthrown, the communist monopoly on power was abrogated in one country after another, and persecuted critics of the communist system were catapulted into high office.

In the West the ranks of the stunned included champions of the view that communist totalitarianism is substantially more stable than ordinary authoritarianism.[2] "It has to be conceded," wrote a leading proponent of this view in early 1990, "that

those of us who distinguish between the two nondemocratic types of government underestimated the decay of Communist countries and expected the collapse of totalitarianism to take longer than has actually turned out to be the case."[3] Another acknowledged her bewilderment through the title of a new book: *The Withering Away of the Totalitarian State . . . And Other Surprises.*[4]

Even scholars who had rejected the concept of a frozen and immobile region were amazed by the events of 1989. In 1987 the American Academy of Arts and Sciences invited a dozen specialists, including several living in Eastern Europe, to prepare interpretive essays on East European developments. As the *Daedalus* issue featuring these essays went to press, the uprisings took off, prompting many authors to change "whole sentences and paragraphs in what were once thought to be completed essays." *Daedalus* editor Stephen Graubard remarks in his preface to the issue: "A quarterly journal has been obliged to adapt, inconveniently, but in some measure necessarily, the techniques of a weekly or even a daily newspaper."[5] Graubard proudly points out

From *World Politics*, 44 (October 1991), pp. 7–48. Some of the author's notes have been omitted.

that even before the last-minute revisions the essays offered remarkable insights into the intellectual, social, and political stirrings that were transforming the region. But he concedes that neither he nor his essayists foresaw what was to happen. Recalling that in a planning session he had asked whether anything could be done to avoid publishing "an issue that will seem 'dated' three years after publication," he continues: "Was this passage a premonition of all that was to follow? One wishes that one could claim such extraordinary prescience. Regrettably, it did not really exist."[6]

■ ■ ■

While the collapse of the post–World War II political order of Eastern Europe stunned the world, in retrospect it appears as the inevitable consequence of a multitude of factors. In each of the six countries the leadership was generally despised, lofty economic promises remained unfulfilled, and freedoms taken for granted elsewhere existed only on paper. But if the revolution was indeed inevitable, why was it not foreseen? Why did people overlook signs that are clearly visible after the fact? One of the central arguments of this essay is precisely that interacting social and psychological factors make it inherently difficult to predict the outcome of political competition. I shall argue that the East European Revolution was by no means inevitable. What *was* inevitable is that we would be astounded if and when it arrived.

"The victim of today is the victor of tomorrow,/ And out of Never grows Now!"[7] Brecht's couplet captures perfectly our central paradox: seemingly unshakable regimes saw public sentiment turn against them with astonishing rapidity, as tiny oppositions mushroomed into crushing majorities. Currently popular theories of revolution offer little insight into this stunning pace; nor for that matter do they shed light on the element of surprise in previous revolutions. All lay claim to predictive power, yet none has a track record at veritable prediction. The next section briefly critiques the pertinent

scholarly literature. Without denying the usefulness of some received theories at explaining revolutions of the past, I go on to present a theory that illuminates both the process of revolutionary mobilization and the limits of our ability to predict where and when mobilizations will occur. Subsequent sections apply this argument to the case at hand.

The term *revolution* is used here in a narrow sense to denote a mass-supported seizure of political power that aims to transform the social order. By this definition it is immaterial whether the accomplished transfer of power brings about significant social change. With regard to the East European Revolution, it is too early to tell whether the post-revolutionary regimes will succeed in reshaping the economy, the legal system, international relations, and individual rights—to mention just some of the domains on the reformist agenda. But even if the ongoing reforms all end in failure, the upheavals of 1989 can continue to be characterized as a region-wide revolution.

II. Received Theories of Revolution and Their Predictive Weaknesses

In her acclaimed book *States and Social Revolutions*, Theda Skocpol treats social revolutions as the product of structural and situational conditions.[8] Specifically, she argues that a revolution occurs when two conditions coalesce: (1) a state's evolving relations with other states and local classes weaken its ability to maintain law and order, and (2) the elites harmed by this situation are powerless to restore the status quo ante yet strong enough to paralyze the government. Through their obstructionism the elites generate a burst of antielite sentiment, which sets in motion an uprising aimed at transforming the social order. The appeal of Skocpol's theory lies in its invocation of structural causes to explain shifts in the structure of political power. It does not depend on such "subjective" factors as beliefs, expectations, attitudes, preferences, intentions, and goals, although these do creep into structuralist case studies, including those of Skocpol herself.

Tracking emotions and mental states is a treacherous business, which is why the structuralist school considers it a virtue to refrain from appealing to them. Social structures are ostensibly easier to identify, which would seem to endow the structuralist theory with predictive superiority over "voluntarist" theories based on "rational choice." Theories that fall under the rubric of rational choice have certainly been unsuccessful at predicting mass upheavals. What they explain well is the rarity of popular uprisings.[9] The crucial insight of the rational-choice school is that an individual opposed to the incumbent regime is unlikely to participate in efforts to remove it, since the personal risk of joining a revolutionary movement could outweigh the personal benefit that would accrue were the movement a success. It is generally in a person's self-interest to let others make the sacrifices required to secure the regime's downfall, for a revolution constitutes a "collective good"—a good he can enjoy whether or not he has contributed to its realization. With most of the regime's opponents choosing to free ride, an upheaval may fail to materialize even if the potential revolutionaries constitute a substantial majority. Yet from time to time revolution does break out, and this presents a puzzle that the standard theory of rational choice cannot solve. The standard theory simply fails to make sense of why the first people to challenge the regime choose selflessly to gamble with their lives.[10]

With respect to the East European Revolution in particular, the standard theory illuminates why, for all their grievances, the nations of the region were remarkably quiescent for so many years. It does not explain why in 1989 their docility suddenly gave way to an explosive demand for change. For its part, the structuralist theory elucidates why the revolution broke out at a time when the Soviet Union was emitting increasingly convincing signals that it would not use force to try to preserve the East European status quo. But it explains neither why the old order collapsed so suddenly in several countries at once nor why the events of 1989 outdistanced all expectations.

Neither school has come to terms with its predictive weaknesses. That granted, can the deficiencies in question be overcome by incorporating additional relationships into these theories? It would seem, on the basis of reasons developed below, that perfect predictability is an unachievable objective. The theory developed here accommodates some of the major features and implications of these two theories, with the added virtue, however, of illuminating why major revolutions come as a surprise and why, even so, they are quite easily explained *after the fact*.

■ ■ ■

If one bête noire of the structuralist school is the rational-choice approach to the study of revolutions, another is the relative-deprivation approach. According to this third approach revolutions are propelled by economic disappointments, that is, by outcomes that fall short of expectations. If the consequent discontent becomes sufficiently widespread, the result is a revolt.[11] With respect to the major revolutions she investigates, Skocpol correctly observes that they began at times when levels of discontent were by historical standards not unusual. More evidence against the relative-deprivation theory comes from Charles Tilly and his associates, who find that in France the level of collective violence has been uncorrelated with the degree of mass discontent.[12] Thus, the relative-deprivation theory neither predicts nor explains. The reason is simple. While relative deprivation is doubtless a factor in every revolution in history, it is too common in politically stable societies to provide a complete explanation for every observed instability. By implication, to treat relative deprivation as an unmistakable sign of impending revolution is to subject oneself to a continuous string of alarms, mostly false.

III. Preference Falsification and Revolutionary Bandwagons

So mass discontent does not necessarily generate a popular uprising against the political status quo. To understand when it does, we need to identify the conditions under which individuals will display antagonism toward the regime under which they live. After all, a mass uprising results from multitudes of individual choices to participate in a movement for change; there is no actor named "the crowd" or "the opposition." The model presented here is in agreement with the rational-choice school on this basic methodological point, although it departs in important ways from the standard fare in rational-choice modeling.

Consider a society whose members are indexed by i. Each individual member must choose whether to support the government in public or oppose it; depending on his public acts and statements, each person is perceived as either a friend of the government or an enemy, for the political status quo or against. In private, of course, a person may feel torn between the government and the opposition, seeing both advantages and disadvantages to the existing regime. I am thus distinguishing between an individual's *private preference* and *public preference*. The former is effectively fixed at any given instant, the latter a variable under his control. Insofar as his two preferences differ—that is, the preference he expresses in public diverges from that he holds in private—the individual is engaged in *preference falsification.*

Let S represent the size of the public opposition, expressed as a percentage of the population. Initially it is near 0, implying that the government commands almost unanimous public support. A revolution, as a mass-supported seizure of political power, may be treated as an enormous jump in S.

Now take a citizen who wants the government overthrown. The likely impact of his own public preference on the fate of the government is negligible: it is unlikely to be a decisive factor in whether the government stands or falls. But it may bring him personal rewards and impose on him personal punishments. If he chooses to oppose the government, for instance, he is likely to face persecution, though in the event the government falls his outspokenness may be rewarded handsomely. Does this mean that our individual will base his public preference solely on the potential rewards and punishments flowing from the two rival camps? Will his private antipathy to the regime play no role whatsoever in his decision? This does not seem reasonable, for history offers countless examples of brave individuals who stood up for a cause in the face of the severest pressures, including torture.

On what, then, will our disaffected individual's choice depend? I submit that it will depend on a trade-off between two payoffs, one external and the other internal.[13]

The external payoff to siding with the opposition consists of the just-discussed personal rewards and punishments. In net terms, this payoff is apt to become increasingly favorable (or increasingly less unfavorable) with S. The larger S, the smaller the individual dissenter's chances of being persecuted for his identification with the opposition and the fewer hostile supporters of the government he has to face. The latter relationship reflects the fact that government supporters, even ones privately sympathetic to the opposition, participate in the persecution of the government's opponents, as part of their personal efforts to establish convincing progovernment credentials. This relationship implies that a rise in S leaves fewer people seeking to penalize members of the public opposition.

The internal payoff is rooted in the psychological cost of preference falsification. The suppression of one's wants entails a loss of personal autonomy, a sacrifice of personal integrity. It thus generates lasting discomfort, the more so the greater the lie. This relationship may be captured by postulating that person i's internal payoff for supporting the opposition varies positively with his private preference, x^i. The higher his x^i, the more costly he finds it to suppress his antigovernment feelings.

So *i*'s public preference depends on S and x^i. As the public opposition grows, with his private preference constant, there comes a point where his external cost of joining the opposition falls below his internal cost of preference falsification. This switching point may be called his *revolutionary threshold*, T^i. Since a threshold represents a value of S, it is a number between 0 and 100.

If x^i should rise, T^i will fall. In other words, if the individual becomes more sympathetic to the opposition, it will take a smaller public opposition to make him take a stand against the government. The same will be true if the government becomes less efficient, or the opposition becomes more efficient, at rewarding its supporters and punishing its rivals. In fact, anything that affects the relationship between S and the individual's external payoff for supporting the opposition will change his revolutionary threshold. Finally, T^i will fall if i develops a greater need to stand up and be counted, for the internal cost of preference falsification will then come to dominate the external benefit at a lower S.[14]

This simple framework offers a reason why a person may choose to voice a demand for change even when the price of dissent is very high and the chances of a successful uprising very low. If his private opposition to the existing order is intense and/or his need for integrity is quite strong, the suffering he incurs for dissent may be outweighed by the satisfaction he derives from being true to himself. In every society, of course, there are people who go against the social order of the day. Joseph Schumpeter once observed that in capitalist societies this group is dominated by intellectuals. Their position as "onlookers" and "outsiders" with much time for deep reflection causes them to develop a "critical attitude" toward the status quo. And because of the high value they attach to self-expression, they are relatively unsusceptible to social pressures.[15] The same argument applies to noncapitalist societies. As a case in point, a disproportionately large share of the East European dissidents were intellectuals.

Returning to the general model, we can observe that individuals with different private preferences and psychological constitutions will have different revolutionary thresholds. Imagine a ten-person society featuring the *threshold sequence*

$$A = \{0, 20, 20, 30, 40, 50, 60, 70, 80, 100\}.$$

Person 1 ($T^1 = 0$) supports the opposition regardless of its size, just as person 10 ($T^{10} = 100$) always supports the government. The remaining eight people's preferences are sensitive to S: depending on its level, they opt for one camp or the other. For instance, person 5 ($T^5 = 40$) supports the government if $0 \le S < 40$ but joins the opposition if $40 \le S \le 100$. Let us assume that the opposition consists initially of a single person, or 10 percent of the population, so $S = 10$. Because the nine other individuals have thresholds above 10, this S is self-sustaining; that is, it constitutes an *equilibrium*.

This equilibrium happens to be vulnerable to a minor change in A. Suppose that person 2 has an unpleasant encounter at some government ministry. Her alienation from the regime rises, pushing her threshold down from 20 to 10. The new threshold sequence is

$$A' = \{0, 10, 20, 30, 40, 50, 60, 70, 80, 100\}.$$

Person 2's new threshold happens to equal the existing S of 10, so she switches sides, and S becomes 20. Her move into the opposition takes the form of tossing an egg at the country's long-standing leader during a government-organized rally. The new S of 20 is not self-sustaining but self-augmenting, as it drives person 3 into the opposition. The higher S of 30 then triggers a fourth defection, raising S to 40, and this process continues until S reaches 90—a new equilibrium. Now the first nine individuals are in opposition, with only the tenth supporting the government. A slight shift in one individual's threshold has thus generated a *revolutionary bandwagon*, an explosive growth in public opposition.[16]

Now consider the sequence

$$B = \{0, 20, 30, 30, 40, 50, 60, 70, 80, 100\},$$

which differs from A only in its third element: 30 as opposed to 20. As in the previous illustration, let T^2 fall from 20 to 10. The resulting sequence is

$$B' = \{0, 10, 30, 30, 40, 50, 60, 70, 80, 100\}.$$

Once again, the incumbent equilibrium of 10 becomes unsustainable, and S rises to 20. But the opposition's growth stops there, for the new S *is* self-sustaining. Some government supporters privately enjoy the sight of the leader's egg-splattered face, but none follows the egg thrower into public opposition. We see that a minor variation in thresholds may drastically alter the effect of a given perturbation. And in particular, an event that causes a revolution in one setting may in a slightly different setting produce only a minor decline in the government's popularity.

Neither private preferences nor the corresponding thresholds are common knowledge. So a society can come to the brink of a revolution without anyone knowing this, not even those with the power to unleash it. In sequence A, for instance, person 2 need not recognize that she has the ability to set off a revolutionary bandwagon. Even if she senses the commonness of preference falsification, she simply cannot know whether the actual threshold sequence is A or B. Social psychologists use the term *pluralistic ignorance* to describe misperceptions concerning distributions of individual characteristics.[17] In principle, pluralistic ignorance can be mitigated through polls that accord individuals anonymity. But it is easier to offer people anonymity than to convince them that the preferences they reveal will remain anonymous and never be used against them. In any case, an outwardly popular government that knows preference falsification to be pervasive has no interest in publicizing the implied fragility of its support, because this might inspire the disaffected to bring their antigovernment feelings into the open. It has an incentive to discourage independent polling and discredit surveys that reveal unflattering information.

We have already seen that the threshold sequence is not fixed. Anything that affects the distribution of private preferences may alter it, for instance, an economic recession, contacts with other societies, or intergenerational replacement. But whatever the underlying reason, private preferences and, hence, the threshold sequence can move dramatically against the government without triggering a revolution. In the sequence

$$C = \{0, 20, 20, 20, 20, 20, 20, 20, 60, 100\}$$

the average threshold is 30, possibly because most people sympathize with the opposition. Yet $S = 10$ remains an equilibrium. It is true, of course, that a revolution is more likely under C than under A. C features seven individuals with thresholds of 20, A only one. A ten-unit fall in any one of the seven thresholds would trigger a revolution.

The point remains that widespread disapproval of the government is not sufficient to mobilize large numbers for revolutionary action. Antigovernment feelings can certainly bring a revolution within the realm of possibility, but other conditions must come together to set it off. By the same token, a revolution may break out in a society where private preferences, and therefore individual thresholds, tend to be relatively unfavorable to the opposition. Reconsider the sequence A', where the average threshold is 46, as opposed to 30 in C. Under A' public opposition darts from 10 to 90, whereas under C it remains stuck at 10. This simple comparison shows why the relative-deprivation theory of revolution has not held up under empirical testing. By treating the likelihood of revolution as the sum of the individual levels of discontent, the relative-deprivation theory overlooks the significance of the distribution of discontent. As our comparison between A' and C indicates, one sufficiently disaffected person with a threshold of 10 may do more for a revolution than seven individuals with thresholds of 20.

Imagine now that a superpower long committed to keeping the local government in power suddenly rescinds this commitment, declaring that it will cease meddling in the internal affairs of other countries. This is precisely the type of change to which the structuralist theory accords revolutionary significance. In the present framework, such a change will not necessarily ignite a revolution. The outcome depends on both the preexisting distribution of thresholds and the consequent shifts. Since the postulated change in international relations is likely to lower the expected cost of joining the opposition, people's thresholds are likely to fall. Let us say that every threshold between 10 and 90 drops by 10 units. If the preexisting threshold sequence were A, B, or C, the result would be an explosion in S from 10 to 90. But suppose that it were

$$D = \{0, 30, 30, 30, 30, 30, 30, 30, 30, 100\}.$$

The structural shock turns this sequence into

$$D' = \{0, 20, 20, 20, 20, 20, 20, 20, 20, 100\}.$$

Fully four-fifths of the population is now willing to switch over to the opposition but *only if someone else goes first.* No one does, leaving S at 10.

Structural factors are thus part of the story, yet by no means the whole story. While they certainly affect the likelihood of revolution, they cannot possibly deliver infallible predictions. A single person's reaction to an event of global importance may make all the difference between a massive uprising and a *latent bandwagon* that never takes off. So to suggest, as the structuralists do, that revolutions are brought about by deep historical forces with individuals simply the passive bearers of these forces is to overlook the potentially crucial importance of individual characteristics of little significance in and of themselves. It is always a conjunction of factors, many of them intrinsically unimportant and thus unobserved, if not unobservable, that determines the flow of events. A major global event can produce drastically different outcomes in two settings that differ trivially. Structuralism and individualism are not rival and mutually incompatible approaches to the study of revolu-

tion, as Skocpol would have it. They are essential components of a single story.

We can now turn to the question of why with hindsight an unanticipated revolution may appear as the inevitable consequence of monumental forces for change. A successful revolution brings into the open long-repressed grievances. Moreover, people who were relatively content with the old regime embrace the new regime, and they are apt to attribute their former public preferences to fears of persecution.

Reconsider the threshold sequence

$$A' = \{0, 10, 20, 30, 40, 50, 60, 70, 80, 100\}.$$

The relatively high thresholds in A' are likely to be associated with private preferences more favorable to the government than to the opposition.[18] Person 9 ($T^9 = 80$) is much more satisfied with the government than, say, person 3 ($T^3 = 20$). As such she has little desire to join a movement aimed at toppling it. Remember that public opposition settles at 90, she being the last to jump on the revolutionary bandwagon. The important point is this: person 9 changes her public preference only after the opposition snowballs into a crushing majority, making it imprudent to remain a government supporter.

Having made the switch, she has every reason to feign a long-standing antipathy to the toppled government. She will not admit that she yearns for the status quo ante, because this would contradict her new public preference. Nor will she say that her change of heart followed the government's collapse, because this might render her declared sympathy for the revolution unconvincing. She will claim that she has long had serious misgivings about the old order and has sympathized with the objectives of the opposition. An unintended effect of this distortion is to make it seem as though the toppled government enjoyed even less genuine support than it actually did.

This illusion is rooted in the very phenomenon responsible for making the revolution a surprise: preference falsification. Having misled everyone into seeing a revolution as highly unlikely, preference falsification now conceals the forces that were working against it. One of the consequences of post-revolutionary preference falsification is thus to make even less comprehensible why the revolution was unforeseen.

■   ■   ■

Before moving to the East European Revolution, it may be useful to comment on how the foregoing argument relates to three sources of controversy in the literature on revolutions: the continuity of social change, the power of the individual, and the significance of unorganized crowds.

The proposed theory treats continuous and discontinuous change as a single, unified process. Private preferences and the corresponding thresholds may change gradually over a long period during which public opposition is more or less stable. If the cumulative movement establishes a latent bandwagon, a minor event may then precipitate an abrupt and sharp break in the size of the public opposition. This is not to say that private preferences change *only* in small increments. A major blunder on the part of the government may suddenly turn private preferences against it.

Such a shift could also occur in response to an initial, possibly modest, increase in public opposition. The underlying logic was expressed beautifully by Alexis de Tocqueville: "Patiently endured so long as it seemed beyond redress, a grievance comes to appear intolerable once the possibility of removing it crosses men's minds."[19] In terms of our model, Tocqueville suggests that the threshold sequence is itself dependent on the size of the public opposition. If so, a revolutionary bandwagon may come about as the joint outcome of two mutually reinforcing trends: a fall in thresholds and a rise in public opposition. Imagine that public opposition rises sufficiently to convince those privately sympathetic to the government that a revolution might be in the making. This realization induces many of them to think about possible alternatives to the status quo. Their thinking starts a chain reaction through which private preferences shift swiftly and dramatically against the government. The consequent changes in the threshold sequence cause the revolutionary bandwagon to accelerate.

The theory depicts the individual as both powerless and potentially very powerful. The individual is powerless because a revolution requires the mobilization of large numbers, but he is also potentially very powerful because under the right circumstances he may set off a chain reaction that generates the necessary mobilization. Not that the individual can know precisely when his own choice can make a difference. Although he may sense that his chances of sparking a wildfire are unusually great, he can never be certain about the consequences of his own opposition. What is certain is that the incumbent regime will remain in place unless someone takes the lead in moving into the opposition.

As we saw in the previous section, the standard theory of rational choice depicts the potential revolutionary as paralyzed by the realization of his powerlessness. Many social thinkers who, like the present author, accept the logic of collective action have struggled with the task of explaining how mass mobilizations get started. One of the proposed explanations rests on a cognitive illusion: the individual overestimates his personal political influence. Another invokes an ethical commitment: the individual feels compelled to do his fair share for the attainment of a jointly desired outcome.[20] The approach used here, which is not incompatible with these explanations, places the burden of sparking the mobilization process on the individual's need to be true to himself. This approach is consistent with the fact that revolutionary leaders tend to be surprised when their goals materialize. The cognitive-illusion explanation is not: people who challenge the government out of an overestimation of their personal ability to direct the course of history will not be surprised when their wishes come true. The approach of this essay is also consistent with the fact that some people risk their lives for a revolution even as the vast majority of the potential beneficiaries refrain from doing their own fair share.

Finally, the outlined theory accords organized pressure groups and unorganized crowds complementary roles in the overthrow of the government.

Organized oppositions enhance the external payoff to dissent, both by providing the individual dissenter with a support network and by raising the likelihood of a successful revolution. They also help shatter the appearance of the invulnerability of the status quo, and through propaganda, they shift people's private preferences in favor of change. Charles Tilly is therefore right to draw attention to the structural and situational factors that govern a society's pattern of political organization.[21] But as Pamela Oliver warns, we must guard against overemphasizing the role of organization at the expense of the role of the unorganized crowd. A small difference in the resources at the disposal of an organized opposition may have a tremendous impact on the outcome of its efforts.[22] This observation makes perfect sense in the context of the theory developed here. Where a small pressure group fails to push a bandwagon into motion a *slightly better organized* or *slightly larger* one might.

IV. East European Communism and the Wellspring of Its Stability

Communist parties came to power in Russia, and then in Eastern Europe and elsewhere, with the promise that "scientific socialism" would pioneer new dimensions of freedom, eliminate exploitation, vest political power in the masses, eradicate nationalism, and raise standards of living to unprecedented heights—all this, while the state was withering away. They did not deliver on any of these promises. Under their stewardship, communism came to symbolize repression, censorship, ethnic chauvinism, militarism, red tape, and economic backwardness.

The failures of communism prompted a tiny number of Soviet and East European citizens to criticize official policies and established institutions. Such dissidents expressed their frustrations through clandestine self-publications (*samizdat*) and writings published in the West (*tamizdat*). Given the chasm between the rhetoric of communism and its

achievements, the existence of an opposition is easily understood. Less comprehensible is the rarity of public opposition—prior, that is, to 1989. The few uprisings that were crushed—notably, East Berlin in 1953, Hungary in 1956, and Czechoslovakia in 1968—are the exceptions that prove the rule. For most of several decades, most East Europeans displayed a remarkable tolerance for tyranny and inefficiency. They remained docile, submissive, and even outwardly supportive of the status quo.

This subservience is attributable partly to punishments meted out by the communist establishment to its actual and imagined opponents. In the heyday of communism a person speaking out against the leadership or in favor of some reform could expect to suffer harassment, lose his job, and face imprisonment—in short, he could expect to be denied the opportunity to lead a decent life. Even worse horrors befell millions of suspected opponents. Just think of the forced-labor camps of the Gulag Archipelago and of the liquidations carried out under the pretext of historical necessity. "We can only be right with and by the Party," wrote a leading theoretician of communism, "for history has provided no other way of being in the right."[23] Such thinking could, and did, serve to justify horrible crimes against nonconformists.

Yet official repression is only one factor in the endurance of communism. The system was sustained by a general willingness to support it in public: people routinely applauded speakers whose message they disliked, joined organizations whose mission they opposed, and signed defamatory letters against people they admired, among other manifestations of consent and accommodation. "The lie," wrote the Russian novelist Alexander Solzhenitsyn in the early 1970s, "has been incorporated into the state system as the vital link holding everything together, with billions of tiny fasteners, several dozen to each man."[24] If people stopped lying, he asserted, communist rule would break down instantly. He then asked rhetorically, "What does it mean, *not to lie*?" It means "*not saying what you don't think*, and that includes not whispering, not opening your mouth, not raising your hand, not casting your vote, not feigning a smile, not lending your presence, not standing up, and not cheering."[25]

In "The Power of the Powerless," Havel speaks of a greengrocer who places in his window, among the onions and carrots, the slogan "Workers of the World, Unite!" Why does the greengrocer do this, Havel wonders.

> Is he genuinely enthusiastic about the idea of unity among the workers of the world? Is his enthusiasm so great that he feels an irrepressible impulse to acquaint the public with his ideals? Has he really given more than a moment's thought to how such a unification might occur and what it would mean?

Havel's answer is worth quoting at length:

> The overwhelming majority of shopkeepers never think about the slogans they put in their windows, nor do they use them to express their real opinions. That poster was delivered to our greengrocer from the enterprise headquarters along with the onions and carrots. He put them all into the window simply because it has been done that way for years, because everyone does it, and because that is the way it has to be. If he were to refuse, there could be trouble. He could be reproached for not having the proper "decoration" in his window; someone might even accuse him of disloyalty. He does it because these things must be done if one is to get along in life. It is one of the thousands of details that guarantee him a relatively tranquil life in "harmony with society," as they say.[26]

So our greengrocer puts up the assigned slogan to communicate not a social ideal but his preparedness to conform. And the reason the display conveys a message of submission is that every submissive greengrocer has exhibited the same slogan for years. By removing the poster—or worse, replacing it with one that reads "Workers of the World, Eat Onions and Carrots!"—our greengrocer would expose himself to the charge of subversion. He therefore displays the required slogan faithfully and

fends off trouble. In the process, he reinforces the perception that society is solidly behind the Party. His own prudence thus becomes a factor in the willingness of other greengrocers to promote the unity of the world's workers. Moreover, it pressures farmers, miners, bus drivers, artists, journalists, and bureaucrats to continue doing and saying the things expected of *them*.

Let us return to the story of the greengrocer. Havel asks us to "imagine that one day something in our greengrocer snaps and he stops putting up the slogans." The greengrocer also "stops voting in elections he knows are a farce"; he "begins to say what he really thinks at political meetings"; and he "even finds the strength in himself to express solidarity with those whom his conscience commands him to support." In short, he makes "an attempt to *live within the truth.*"[27] Here are the likely consequences of this revolt:

> [The greengrocer] will be relieved of his post as manager of the shop and transferred to the warehouse. His pay will be reduced. His hopes for a holiday in Bulgaria will evaporate. His children's access to higher education will be threatened. His superiors will harass him and his fellow workers will wonder about him. Most of those who apply these sanctions, however, will not do so from any authentic inner conviction but simply under pressure from conditions, the same conditions that once pressured the greengrocer to display the official slogans. They will persecute the greengrocer either because it is expected of them, or to demonstrate their loyalty, or simply as part of the general panorama, to which belongs an awareness that this is how situations of this sort are dealt with, that this, in fact, is how things are always done, particularly if one is not to become suspect oneself.[28]

The brilliance of this vignette lies in its insights into the pressures that kept East Europeans outwardly loyal to their inefficient, tyrannical regimes. Official repression met with the approval of ordinary citizens and indeed was predicated on their complicity. By falsifying their preferences and helping to discipline dissenters, citizens jointly sustained a system that many considered abominable. According to Havel, the crucial "line of conflict" ran not between the Party and the people but "through each person," for in one way or another everyone was "both a victim and a supporter of the system."[29]

■ ■ ■

So processes rooted in preference falsification kept private opposition to communism far from unanimous. This does not negate the fact that vast numbers remained outwardly loyal to communist rule primarily out of fear. But for widespread preference falsification, the communist regimes of Eastern Europe would have faced severe public opposition, very possibly collapsing before 1989. In view of its profound impact on both private and public sentiment, preference falsification may be characterized as the wellspring of the communist system's stability.

V. The Revolution

The foregoing argument has two immediate implications. First, the regimes of Eastern Europe were substantially more vulnerable than the subservience and quiescence of their populations made them seem. Millions were prepared to stand up in defiance if ever they sensed that this was sufficiently safe. The people's solidarity with their leaders would then have been exposed as illusory, stripping the veneer of legitimacy from the communist monopoly on power. Second, even the support of those genuinely sympathetic to the status quo was rather thin. Though many saw no alternative to socialism, their many grievances predisposed them to the promise of fundamental change. Were public discourse somehow to turn against socialism, they would probably awaken to the possibility that their lives could be improved.

But what would catalyze the process of revolutionary mobilization? With hindsight it appears that the push came from the Soviet Union. In the mid-1980s festering economic problems, until then

officially denied, convinced the top Soviet leadership to call for *perestroika* (restructuring) and *glasnost* (public openness). Repressed grievances burst into the open, including dissatisfaction with communist rule itself. And with Mikhail Gorbachev's rise to the helm in 1985, the Soviet Union abandoned its longstanding policy of confrontation with the West, to seek accommodation and cooperation.[30] In Eastern Europe these changes kindled hopes of greater independence and meaningful social reform.

Lest it appear that these developments provided a clear signal of the coming revolution, remember that Havel dismissed a Czechoslovak crowd's jubilation over Gorbachev as a sign of naïveté. He was hardly alone in his pessimism. Even if Gorbachev wanted to liberate Eastern Europe, a popular argument went, it was anything but obvious that he could. Surely, the military and hard-line conservatives would insist on retaining the Soviet Union's strategic buffer against an attack from the West.

■ ■ ■

As Gorbachev was trying to restructure the Soviet Union, Poland was testing the limits of its freedom from Moscow. The struggle to legalize Solidarity had already given the country a taste of pluralism, and government censorship was being relaxed in fits and starts. Everyone recognized that this softening enjoyed Gorbachev's approval. Yet few informed people put much faith in Gorbachev's ability to push the liberation of Eastern Europe substantially forward, and once again it was not clear that he intended to try. "Dissidents throughout Europe," wrote the *Economist* in mid-1987, sound "sceptical" when talking about Gorbachev. "This is not because they question [his] reforming zeal. It is simply that many thinking people in Eastern Europe have come to believe that real change in Communist countries cannot be imposed from the top—or from outside—but must emerge from below."[31] Plenty of events lent credence to this reasoning. For instance, Gorbachev did not prevent the East German regime from falsifying the results of local elections held in the spring of 1989 or from endorsing China's massacre at Tiananmen Square that summer. Nor did he keep the East German regime from using force to disperse small demonstrations against these two acts.[32]

■　■　■

The point remains that the Soviet reform movement fueled expectations of a freer Eastern Europe, reducing for growing numbers the perceived risk of challenging the status quo. In terms of the model described in Section III, the movement lowered the revolutionary thresholds of East Europeans, making it increasingly easy to set in motion a revolutionary bandwagon. But no one could see that a revolution was in the making, not even the Soviet leader whose moves were helping to establish the still-latent bandwagon.

Recall that revolutionary thresholds are influenced also by people's private preferences. Since private preferences are governed to a considerable extent by public discourse, the dissent generated by Soviet glasnost probably pushed the private preferences of East Europeans against communism and communist rule. The East German surveys discussed above provide dramatic evidence to this effect. They show that after 1985 East German attachment to socialism steadily deteriorated. By October 1989 only 15 percent of the surveyed trade school students endorsed the statement "I am a devoted citizen of the German Democratic Republic," down from 46 percent in 1983. Fully 60 percent endorsed it with reservations and 25 percent rejected it. In the same month as few as 3 percent continued to believe that "socialism will triumph throughout the world," down from 50 percent in 1984. Just 27 percent agreed with reservations and a whopping 70 percent disagreed.[33] The contrast between the figures for 1989 and those for 1983–84 is striking. It points to a massive rise in discontent in the second half of the decade, a rise that must have lowered the revolutionary thresholds of millions of individual East Germans.

What specific events set the revolutionary bandwagon in motion? One must recognize that attempting to answer this question is akin to trying to identify the spark that ignited a forest fire or the cough responsible for the flu epidemic. There were many turning points in the East European Revolution, any one of which might have derailed it.

One turning point came in early October, when East German officials refused to carry out Party leader Honecker's order to open fire on street demonstrators. On October 7 Gorbachev was in Berlin for celebrations marking the fortieth anniversary of the German Democratic Republic. With scores of foreign reporters looking on, crowds took to the streets, chanting, "Gorby! Gorby!" And the police clubs went into action. West German television immediately played these events back to the rest of East Germany. The scenes alerted disgruntled citizens in every corner of the country to the pervasiveness of discontent, while the government's weak response revealed its vulnerability. A peaceful protest broke out in Leipzig on October 9. Honecker ordered the regional Party secretary to block the demonstration, by force if necessary. But bloodshed was averted when Egon Krenz, a Politburo member in charge of security, flew to Leipzig and encouraged the security forces to show restraint. Local leaders — some of whom had already appealed for restraint — accepted this contravention of Honecker's order, and tens of thousands marched without interference. Sensing the shifting political winds, more and more East Germans throughout the country took to the streets. The East German uprising was now in full swing. As the regime tried to stem the tide through a string of concessions, the swelling crowds began to make increasingly bold demands. Within a month the Berlin Wall would be breached, and in less than a year the German Democratic Republic would become part of a unified, democratic Germany.[34]

Another turning point came on October 25, during Gorbachev's state visit to Finland. Two months earlier a solidarity official had formed Poland's first noncommunist government since the 1940s, following the Communist Party's stunning defeat at the polls. A legislative deputy to Gorbachev had declined detailed comment on the grounds that the developments were a domestic matter for the Poles.[35] The communists were in retreat in Hungary, too. In meetings with dissident groups the Hungarian Communist Party had endorsed free parliamentary elections. Then, in the belief that its candidates would do poorly running under the banner of communism, it had transformed itself into the Hungarian Socialist Party.[36] This was the first time that a ruling communist party had formally abandoned communism. With the world wondering whether the Soviet Union had reached the limits of its tolerance, Gorbachev declared in Finland that his country had no moral or political right to interfere in the affairs of its East European neighbors. Defining this position as "the Sinatra doctrine," his spokesman jokingly asked reporters whether they knew the Frank Sinatra song "I Did It My Way." He went on to say that "Hungary and Poland are doing it their way." Using the Western term for the previous Soviet policy of armed intervention to keep the governments of the Warsaw Pact in communist hands, he added, "I think the Brezhnev doctrine is dead."[37] Coming on the heels of major communist retreats in Poland and Hungary, these comments offered yet another indication that Gorbachev would not try to silence East European dissent.

If one effect of this signal was to embolden the opposition movements of Eastern Europe, another must have been to discourage the governments of Eastern Europe from resorting to violence unilaterally. This is not to say that Gorbachev enunciated his Sinatra doctrine with the intention of encouraging East European oppositions to grab for power. Nor is it to say that the revolution would have petered out in the absence of this move. By the time Gorbachev renounced the Soviet Union's right to intervene, opposition movements in Poland, East Germany, and Hungary already commanded mass support, and it is unlikely that anything short of massive brutality would have broken their momentum and restored the status quo ante. Nonetheless, some incumbent communist leaders were seriously considering a military solution, and the proclamation of the Sinatra doctrine may well have tipped the balance against the use

of force. Had even one East European government resorted to force at this stage, the result may well have been a series of bloody and protracted civil wars.

■ ■ ■

VI. The Predictability of Unpredictability

Unexpected as they were, these developments now seem as though they could easily have been predicted. Was it not obvious that the economic failures of communism had sown the seeds of a massive revolt? Was it not self-evident that the East Europeans were just waiting for an opportunity to topple their despised dictators? Did not the severe domestic problems of the Soviet Union necessitate its withdrawal from Eastern Europe, to concentrate its resources on economic reforms? Retrospective accounts of 1989 offer a panoply of such reasons why the East European Revolution was inevitable. "It is no accident that Mikhail Gorbachev declined to intervene," writes one commentator[38]—this, in a volume peppered with comments on how 1989 surprised one and all.

This essay has shown that the warning signs of the revolution remained cloudy until it was all over. Moreover, the unobservability of private preferences and revolutionary thresholds concealed the latent bandwagons in formation and also made it difficult to appreciate the significance of events that were pushing these into motion. The explanation for this predictive failure transcends the particularities of Eastern Europe: this is after all hardly the first time a major social uprising has come as a big surprise.

The French Revolution of 1789 shocked not only Louis XVI and his courtiers but also outside observers and the rioters who helped end his reign. Yet it had many deep causes—all expounded at great length in literally thousands of volumes. This paradox is one of the central themes of Tocqueville's *Old Régime and the French Revolution*. "Chance played no part whatever in the outbreak of the revolution," he observes.

"Though it took the world by surprise, it was the inevitable outcome of a long period of gestation, the abrupt and violent conclusion of a process in which six generations played an intermittent part."[39]

■   ■   ■

Should we conclude, along with John Dunn, that revolutions are inelectable "facts of nature," events that fail "to suggest the dominance of human reason in any form"?[40] In other words, is the culprit human irrationality? The argument developed in this paper does not point in this direction. It suggests, on the contrary, that predictive failure is entirely consistent with calculated, purposeful human action. Underlying an explosive shift in public sentiment are multitudes of individual decisions to switch political allegiance, each undertaken in response to changing incentives. So just as a failure to predict a rainstorm does not imply that the clouds obey no physical laws, a failure to predict some revolution does not imply individual irrationality.

Dunn also suggests that revolutions have too many determinants to make them amenable to a grand, comprehensive theory. Shunning the futile exercise of constructing a theory with universal applicability, we ought to focus, he says, on the particularities of each situation. Although I agree that revolutions are complex events brought on by a symphony of interacting variables, I depart from Dunn on the usefulness of general theorizing: obstacles to forecasting particular revolutions do not preclude userful insights into the *process* of revolution. Even if we cannot predict the time and place of the next big uprising, we may prepare ourselves mentally for the mass mobilization that will bring it about. Equally important, we can understand why it may surprise us. There are other spheres of knowledge where highly useful theories preclude reliable predictions of specific outcomes. The Darwinian theory of biological evolution illuminates the process whereby species evolve but without enabling us to predict the future evolution of the gazelle. Sophisticated theories of the weather elucidate why it is in perpetual flux but without making it possible to say with much confidence whether it will rain in Rome a week from next Tuesday.

Such general theories have a common virtue: they reveal the source of their predictive limitations. The reason they cannot predict infallibly is not simply that they contain large numbers of variables. In each theory variables are related to one another *nonlinearly*; that is, a *small* perturbation in one variable, which normally produces *small* changes in other variables, may under the right set of circumstances have *large* consequences. Consider the theory of climatic turbulence developed by Edward Lorenz. It shows that a sparrow flapping its wings in Istanbul—an intrinsically insignificant event—can generate a hurricane in the Gulf of Mexico. This is because the weather at any given location is related to its determinants nonlinearly. In other words, its sensitivity to other variables, and their sensitivities to one another, are themselves *variable*. Accordingly, variable x may be impervious to a jump in y from 20 to 200, yet exhibit hypersensitivity if y rises a bit higher, say, to 202. It may then start to grow explosively, effectively feeding on itself. The notion that small events may unleash huge forces goes against much of twentieth-century social thought, with its emphasis on linearity, continuity, and gradualism. But in contexts as different as technological diffusion and cognitive development it is the key to understanding a host of otherwise inexplicable phenomena.

What endows intrinsically insignificant events with potentially explosive power in the context of political change is that public preferences are interdependent. Because of this interdependence, the equilibrium levels of the public opposition are related to the underlying individual characteristics nonlinearly. A massive change in private preferences may leave the incumbent equilibrium undisturbed, only to be followed by a tiny change that destroys the status quo, setting off a bandwagon that will culminate in a very different equilibrium. Partly because of preference falsification, the nature of the interdependence is *imperfectly observable*. This is why a massive rise in public opposition may catch everyone by surprise.

Because preference falsification afflicts politics in every society, major revolutions are likely to come again and again as a surprise. This is not to assert the impossibility of accurate prediction. If we possessed a reliable technique for measuring people's revolutionary thresholds, we would see what it would take to get a revolution started. And if we understood the determinants of these thresholds, we would know when the required conditions were about to be met. For all practical purposes, however, such information is available only in highly incomplete form. In any case, there is an irremovable political obstacle to becoming sufficiently knowledgeable: vulnerable regimes can block the production and dissemination of information potentially harmful to their own survival. Censorship and the regulation of opinion surveys—both widely practiced in prerevolutionary Eastern Europe—are two of the policies that serve these objectives.

I have deliberately characterized the source of unpredictability as *imperfect* observability, as opposed to *un*observability. The degree of imperfection obviously constitutes a continuum. Societies with strong democratic traditions exhibit less imperfection than ones with nonexistent or fragile democratic freedoms. This is because there is less preference falsification in the former group, at least with respect to the political system itself. Accordingly, one can track the course of antigovernment or antiregime sentiment more confidently for Norway, Switzerland, or France than for Pakistan, Brazil, or Ghana. This is why developments in Pakistan are more likely to catch the world off guard than are developments in Norway; by implication, Norway's political future can be predicted with greater confidence than can that of Pakistan. Most countries of the world lie closer to Pakistan than to Norway as regards the significance of preference falsification in sustaining their political regimes.

This emphasis on unpredictability should not be considered offensive to the scientific spirit: accepting the limits of what we can expect from science is not an admission of defeat. On the contrary, establishing these limits of knowledge is itself a contri-

bution to the pool of useful knowledge. It is also a necessary step toward charting a realistic scientific agenda. "To act as if we possessed scientific knowledge enabling us to transcend [the absolute obstacles to the prediction of specific events]," wrote Friedrich Hayek in his Nobel Memorial Lecture, "may itself become a serious obstacle to the advance of the human intellect."[41]

The prediction of unpredictability is not to be confused with the unfalsifiability of the underlying theory. The theory developed in this essay is fully falsifiable. It implies that political revolutions will continue to surprise us, so a string of successful predictions would render it suspect. Simply put, it can be falsified by developing some theory of revolution that forecasts accurately. In principle, if not in practice, the presented theory can also be falsified by showing that preference falsification was not a factor in unanticipated revolutions of the past.

NOTES

1. Bernard Gwertzman and Michael T. Kaufman, eds., *The Collapse of Communism, by the Correspondents of "The New York Times"* (New York: Times Books, 1990), vii.

2. For an early statement of this thesis, see Hannah Arendt, *The Origins of Totalitarianism*, 2d ed. (1951; reprint, New York: World Publishing, 1958), pt. 3. Arendt suggested that communism weakens interpersonal bonds rooted in family, community, religion, and profession, a situation that makes individuals terribly dependent on the goodwill of the state and thus blocks the mobilization of an anticommunist revolt.

3. Richard Pipes, "Gorbachev's Russia: Breakdown or Crackdown?" *Commentary*, March 1990, p. 16.

4. Jeane J. Kirkpatrick, *The Withering Away of the Totalitarian State, . . . And Other Surprises* (Washington, D.C.: AEI Press, 1990). A decade earlier Kirkpatrick had articulated a variant of Arendt's thesis, insisting that the communist system is incapable of self-propelled evolution. See Kirkpatrick,

"Dictatorships and Double Standards," *Commentary*, November 1979, pp. 34–45.

5. Graubard, "Preface to the Issue 'Eastern Europe . . . Central Europe . . . Europe,'" *Daedalus* (Winter 1990), vi.

6. Ibid., ii.

7. Bertolt Brecht, "Lob der Dialectic" (In praise of dialectics, 1933), in *Gedichte* (Frankfurt: Suhrkt-amp Verlag, 1961), 3:73; poem translated by Edith Anderson.

8. Skocpol, *States and Social Revolutions: A Comparative Analysis of France, Russia, and China* (Cambridge: Cambridge University Press, 1979).

9. The seminal contribution is Mancur Olson, *The Logic of Collective Action: Public Goods and the Theory of Groups* (1965; rev. ed., Cambridge: Harvard University Press, 1971).

10. This point is developed by Michael Taylor, "Rationality and Revolutionary Action," in Taylor, ed., *Rationality and Revolution* (Cambridge: Cambridge University Press, 1988), 63–97. Taylor also offers an illuminating critique of structuralism.

11. For two of the major contributions to this approach, see James C. Davies, "Toward a Theory of Revolution," *American Sociological Review* 27 (February 1962), 5–19; and Ted R. Gurr, *Why Men Rebel* (Princeton: Princeton University Press, 1970).

12. David Snyder and Charles Tilly, "Hardship and Collective Violence in France, 1830 to 1960," *American Sociological Review* 37 (October 1972), 520–32; and Charles Tilly, Louise Tilly, and Richard Tilly, *The Rebellious Century: 1830–1930* (Cambridge: Harvard University Press, 1975). For much additional evidence against the theory of relative deprivation, see Steven E. Finkel and James B. Rule, "Relative Deprivation and Related Psychological Theories of Civil Violence: A Critical Review," in Louis Kriesberg, ed., *Research in Social Movements, Conflicts and Change* (Greenwich, Conn.: JAI Press, 1986), 9:47–69.

13. For a detailed analysis of this trade-off, see Timur Kuran, "Private and Public Preferences," *Economics and Philosophy* 6 (April 1990), 1–26,

14. The theory outlined in this section is developed more fully in Timur Kuran, "Sparks and Prairie Fires: A Theory of Unanticipated Political Revolution," *Public Choice* 61 (April 1989), 41–74. A summary of the present formulation was delivered at the annual convention of the American Economic Association, Washington, D.C., December 28–30, 1990. This presentation appeared under the title "The East European Revolution of 1989: Is It Surprising That We Were Surprised?" in the *American Economic Review, Papers and Proceedings* 81 (May 1991), 121–25.

15. Schumpeter, *Capitalism, Socialism and Democracy*, 3d ed. (1950; reprint, New York: Harper Torch-books, 1962), chap. 13.

16. Lucid analyses of bandwagon processes include Mark Granovetter, "Threshold Models of Collective Behavior," *American Journal of Sociology* 83 (May 1978), 1420–43; and Thomas C. Schelling, *Micromotives and Macrobehavior* (New York: W. W. Norton, 1978).

17. Under the term *impression of universality*, the concept was introduced by Floyd H. Allport, *Social Psychology* (Boston: Houghton, Mifflin, 1924), 305–9. The term *pluralistic ignorance* was first used by Richard L. Schanck, "A Study of a Community and Its Groups and Institutions Conceived of as Behavior of Individuals," *Psychological Monographs* 43-2 (1932), 101.

18. Relatively high thresholds may also be associated with relatively great vulnerability to social pressure.

19. Tocqueville, *The Old Régime and the French Revolution* (1856), trans. Stuart Gilbert (Garden City, N.Y.: Doubleday, 1955), 177.

20. Each of these is developed by Steven E. Finkel, Edward N. Muller, and Karl-Dieter Opp, "Personal Influence, Collective Rationality, and Mass Political Action," *American Political Science Review* 83 (September 1989), 885–903.

21. Tilly, *From Mobilization to Revolution* (Reading, Mass.: Addison-Wesley, 1978).

22. Oliver, "Bringing the Crowd Back In: The Non-organizational Elements of Social Movements," in

Louis Kriesberg, ed., *Research in Social Movements, Conflict and Change* (Greenwich, Conn.: JAI Press, 1989): 11:1–30.

23. The words of Leon Trotsky, cited by Arendt (n. 2), 307.

24. Solzhenitsyn, "The Smatterers" (1974), in Solzhenitsyn et al., *From under the Rubble*, trans. A. M. Brock et al. (Boston: Little, Brown, 1975), 275.

25. Ibid., 276; emphasis in original.

26. Havel, "The Power of the Powerless" (1979), in Havel et al., *The Power of the Powerless: Citizens against the State in Central-Eastern Europe*, ed. John Keane and trans. Paul Wilson (Armonk, N.Y.: M. E. Sharpe, 1985), 27–28.

27. Ibid., 39; emphasis in original.

28. Ibid., 39.

29. Ibid., 37.

30. For details, see Robert C. Tucker, *Political Culture and Leadership in Soviet Russia: From Lenin to Gorbachev* (New York: W. W. Norton, 1987), chap. 7.

31. *Economist*, July 18, 1987, p. 45.

32. Timothy Garton Ash, "Germany Unbound," *New York Review of Books*, November 22, 1990, p. 12.

33. "Daten des Zentralinstituts für Jugendforschung Leipzig" (Mimeograph), Tables 1 and 2. These tables were compiled by Walter Friedrich, the director of the institute, and distributed to the participants at a conference held in Ladenburg in February 1991, under the auspices of the Gottlieb Daimler and Karl Benz Foundation. Elisabeth Noelle-Neumann brought the document to my attention; John Ahouse translated it into English.

34. This account draws on Timothy Garton Ash, "The German Revolution," New York Review of Books, December 21, 1989; Edith Anderson, "Town Mice and Country Mice: The East German Revolution," in William M. Brinton and Alan Rinzler, eds., *Without Force or Lies: Voices from the Revolution of Central Europe in 1989–90* (San Francisco: Mercury House, 1990), 170–92; and the *New York Times* reports compiled in Gwertzman and Kaufman (n. 1), 158–60, 166–84, 216–22.

35. *New York Times*, August 18, 1989, p. 1.

36. Ibid., October 8, 1989, p. 1. For a fuller account of the transformation, see Elie Abel, *The Shattered Bloc: Behind the Upheaval in Eastern Europe* (Boston: Houghton Mifflin, 1990), chap. 2.

37. *New York Times*, October 26, 1989, p. 1.

38. William M. Brinton, "Gorbachev and the Revolution of 1989–90," in Brinton and Rinzler (n. 34), 373.

39. Tocqueville (n. 19), 20.

40. Dunn, *Modern Revolutions: An Introduction to the Analysis of a Political Phenomenon*, 2d ed. (New York: Cambridge University Press, 1989), 2–3.

41. Hayek, "The Pretence of Knowledge" (1974), *American Economic Review* 79 (December 1989), 6.

Jack Goldstone

UNDERSTANDING THE REVOLUTIONS OF 2011: WEAKNESS AND RESILIENCE IN MIDDLE EASTERN AUTOCRACIES

The wave of revolutions sweeping the Middle East bears a striking resemblance to previous political earthquakes. As in Europe in 1848, rising food prices and high unemployment have fueled popular protests from Morocco to Oman. As in Eastern Europe and the Soviet Union in 1989, frustration with closed, corrupt, and unresponsive political systems has led to defections among elites and the fall of once powerful regimes in Tunisia, Egypt, and perhaps Libya. Yet 1848 and 1989 are not the right analogies for this past winter's events. The revolutions of 1848 sought to overturn traditional monarchies, and those in 1989 were aimed at toppling communist governments. The revolutions of 2011 are fighting something quite different: "sultanistic" dictatorships. Although such regimes often appear unshakable, they are actually highly vulnerable, because the very strategies they use to stay in power make them brittle, not resilient. It is no coincidence that although popular protests have shaken much of the Middle East, the only revolutions to succeed so far—those in Tunisia and Egypt—have been against modern sultans.

For a revolution to succeed, a number of factors have to come together. The government must appear so irremediably unjust or inept that it is widely viewed as a threat to the country's future; elites (especially in the military) must be alienated from the state and no longer willing to defend it; a broad-based section of the population, spanning ethnic and religious groups and socioeconomic classes, must mobilize; and international powers must either refuse to step in to defend the government or constrain it from using maximum force to defend itself.

Revolutions rarely triumph because these conditions rarely coincide. This is especially the case in traditional monarchies and one-party states, whose leaders often manage to maintain popular support by making appeals to respect for royal tradition or nationalism. Elites, who are often enriched by such governments, will only forsake them if their circumstances or the ideology of the rulers changes drastically. And in almost all cases, broad-based popular mobilization is difficult to achieve because it requires bridging the disparate interests of the urban and rural poor, the middle class, students, professionals, and different ethnic or religious groups. History is replete with student movements, workers' strikes, and peasant uprisings that were readily put down because they remained a revolt of one group, rather than of broad coalitions. Finally, other countries have often intervened to prop up embattled rulers in order to stabilize the international system.

Yet there is another kind of dictatorship that often proves much more vulnerable, rarely retaining power for more than a generation: the sultanistic regime. Such governments arise when a national leader expands his personal power at the expense of formal institutions. Sultanistic dictators appeal to no ideology and have no purpose other than maintaining their personal authority. They may preserve some of the formal aspects of democracy—elections, political parties, a national assembly, or a constitution—but they rule above them by installing compliant supporters in key positions and sometimes by declaring states of emergency, which they justify by appealing to fears of external (or internal) enemies.

From *Foreign Affairs* 90, no. 3 (May/June 2011), pp. 8–16.

Behind the scenes, such dictators generally amass great wealth, which they use to buy the loyalty of supporters and punish opponents. Because they need resources to fuel their patronage machine, they typically promote economic development, through industrialization, commodity exports, and education. They also seek relationships with foreign countries, promising stability in exchange for aid and investment. However wealth comes into the country, most of it is funneled to the sultan and his cronies.

The new sultans control their countries' military elites by keeping them divided. Typically, the security forces are separated into several commands (army, air force, police, intelligence)—each of which reports directly to the leader. The leader monopolizes contact between the commands, between the military and civilians, and with foreign governments, a practice that makes sultans essential for both coordinating the security forces and channeling foreign aid and investment. To reinforce fears that foreign aid and political coordination would disappear in their absence, sultans typically avoid appointing possible successors.

To keep the masses depoliticized and unorganized, sultans control elections and political parties and pay their populations off with subsidies for key goods, such as electricity, gasoline, and foodstuffs. When combined with surveillance, media control, and intimidation, these efforts generally ensure that citizens stay disconnected and passive.

By following this pattern, politically adept sultans around the world have managed to accumulate vast wealth and high concentrations of power. Among the most famous in recent history were Mexico's Porfirio Díaz, Iran's Mohammad Reza Shah Pahlavi, Nicaragua's Somoza dynasty, Haiti's Duvalier dynasty, the Philippines' Ferdinand Marcos, and Indonesia's Suharto.

But as those sultans all learned, and as the new generation of sultans in the Middle East—including Bashar al-Assad in Syria, Omar al-Bashir in Sudan, Zine el-Abidine Ben Ali in Tunisia, Hosni Mubarak in Egypt, Muammar al-Qaddafi in Libya,

and Ali Abdullah Saleh in Yemen—has discovered, power that is too concentrated can be difficult to hold on to.

Paper Tigers

For all their attempts to prop themselves up, sultanistic dictatorships have inherent vulnerabilities that only increase over time. Sultans must strike a careful balance between self-enrichment and rewarding the elite: if the ruler rewards himself and neglects the elite, a key incentive for the elite to support the regime is removed. But as sultans come to feel more entrenched and indispensable, their corruption frequently becomes more brazen and concentrated among a small inner circle. As the sultan monopolizes foreign aid and investment or gets too close to unpopular foreign governments, he may alienate elite and popular groups even further.

Meanwhile, as the economy grows and education expands under a sultanistic dictator, the number of people with higher aspirations and a keener sensitivity to the intrusions of police surveillance and abuse increases. And if the entire population grows rapidly while the lion's share of economic gains is hoarded by the elite, inequality and unemployment surge as well. As the costs of subsidies and other programs the regime uses to appease citizens rise, keeping the masses depoliticized places even more stress on the regime. If protests start, sultans may offer reforms or expand patronage benefits—as Marcos did in the Philippines in 1984 to head off escalating public anger. Yet as Marcos learned in 1986, these sops are generally ineffective once people have begun to clamor for ending the sultan's rule.

The weaknesses of sultanistic regimes are magnified as the leader ages and the question of succession becomes more acute. Sultanistic rulers have sometimes been able to hand over leadership to younger family members. This is only possible when the government has been operating effectively and has maintained elite support (as in Syria in 2000, when President Hafez al-Assad handed power to his son

Bashar) or if another country backs the regime (as in Iran in 1941, when Western governments promoted the succession from Reza Shah to his son Mohammad Reza Pahlavi). If the regime's corruption has already alienated the country's elites, they may turn on it and try to block a dynastic succession, seeking to regain control of the state (which is what happened in Indonesia in the late 1990s, when the Asian financial crisis dealt a blow to Suharto's patronage machine).

The very indispensability of the sultan also works against a smooth transfer of power. Most of the ministers and other high officials are too deeply identified with the chief executive to survive his fall from power. For example, the shah's 1978 attempt to avoid revolution by substituting his prime minister, Shahpur Bakhtiar, for himself as head of government did not work; the entire regime fell the next year. Ultimately, such moves satisfy neither the demands of the mobilized masses seeking major economic and political change nor the aspirations of the urban and professional class that has taken to the streets to demand inclusion in the control of the state.

Then there are the security forces. By dividing their command structure, the sultan may reduce the threat they pose. But this strategy also makes the security forces more prone to defections in the event of mass protests. Lack of unity leads to splits within the security services; meanwhile, the fact that the regime is not backed by any appealing ideology or by independent institutions ensures that the military has less motivation to put down protests. Much of the military may decide that the country's interests are better served by regime change. If part of the armed forces defects—as happened under Díaz, the shah of Iran, Marcos, and Suharto—the government can unravel with astonishing rapidity. In the end, the befuddled ruler, still convinced of his indispensability and invulnerability, suddenly finds himself isolated and powerless.

The degree of a sultan's weakness is often visible only in retrospect. Although it is easy to identify states with high levels of corruption, unemployment, and personalist rule, the extent to which elites oppose the regime and the likelihood that the military will defect often become apparent only once large-scale protests have begun. After all, the elite and military officers have every reason to hide their true feelings until a crucial moment arises, and it is impossible to know which provocation will lead to mass, rather than local, mobilization. The rapid unraveling of sultanistic regimes thus often comes as a shock.

In some cases, of course, the military does not immediately defect in the face of rebellion. In Nicaragua in the early 1970s, for example, Anastasio Somoza Debayle was able to use loyal troops in Nicaragua's National Guard to put down the rebellion against him. But even when the regime can draw on loyal sectors of the military, it rarely manages to survive. It simply breaks down at a slower pace, with significant bloodshed or even civil war resulting along the way. Somoza's success in 1975 was short-lived; his increasing brutality and corruption brought about an even larger rebellion in the years that followed. After some pitched battles, even formerly loyal troops began to desert, and Somoza fled the country in 1979.

International pressure can also turn the tide. The final blow to Marcos' rule was the complete withdrawal of U.S. support after Marcos dubiously claimed victory in the presidential election held in 1986. When the United States turned away from the regime, his remaining supporters folded, and the nonviolent People Power Revolution forced him into exile.

Rock the Casbah

The revolutions unfolding across the Middle East represent the breakdown of increasingly corrupt sultanistic regimes. Although economies across the region have grown in recent years, the gains have bypassed the majority of the population, being amassed instead by a wealthy few. Mubarak and his family reportedly built up a fortune of between $40 billion and $70 billion, and 39 officials and businessmen close to Mubarak's son Gamal are alleged to have made fortunes averaging more than $1 billion each. In Tunisia, a 2008 U.S. diplomatic cable released by the whistleblower Web site WikiLeaks noted a spike in corruption, warning that Ben Ali's family was becoming so predatory that new investment and job creation were being stifled and that his family's ostentation was provoking widespread outrage.

Fast-growing and urbanizing populations in the Middle East have been hurt by low wages and by food prices that rose by 32 percent in the last year alone, according to the United Nations' Food and Agriculture Organization. But it is not simply such rising prices, or a lack of growth, that fuels revolutions; it is the persistence of widespread and unrelieved poverty amid increasingly extravagant wealth.

Discontent has also been stoked by high unemployment, which has stemmed in part from the surge in the Arab world's young population. The percentage of young adults—those aged 15–29 as a fraction of all those over 15—ranges from 38 percent in Bahrain and Tunisia to over 50 percent in Yemen (compared to 26 percent in the United States). Not only is the proportion of young people in the Middle East extraordinarily high, but their numbers have grown quickly over a short period of time. Since 1990, youth population aged 15–29 has grown by 50 percent in Libya and Tunisia, 65 percent in Egypt, and 125 percent in Yemen.

Thanks to the modernization policies of their sultanistic governments, many of these young people have been able to go to university, especially in recent years. Indeed, college enrollment has soared across the region in recent decades, more than tripling in Tunisia, quadrupling in Egypt, and expanding tenfold in Libya.

It would be difficult, if not impossible, for any government to create enough jobs to keep pace. For the sultanistic regimes, the problem has been especially difficult to manage. As part of their patronage strategies, Ben Ali and Mubarak had long provided state subsidies to workers and families through such programs as Tunisia's National Employment Fund—which trained workers, created jobs, and issued loans—and Egypt's policy of guaranteeing job placement for college graduates. But these safety nets were phased out in the last decade to reduce expenditures. Vocational training, moreover, was weak, and access to public and many private jobs was tightly controlled by those connected to the regime. This led to incredibly high youth unemployment across the Middle East: the figure for the region hit 23 percent, or twice the global average, in 2009. Unemployment among the educated, moreover, has been even worse: in Egypt, college graduates are ten times as likely to have no job as those with only an elementary school education.

In many developing economies, the informal sector provides an outlet for the unemployed. Yet the sultans in the Middle East made even those activities difficult. After all, the protests were sparked by the self-immolation of Mohamed Bouazizi, a 26-year-old Tunisian man who was unable to find formal work and whose fruit cart was confiscated by the police. Educated youth and workers in Tunisia and Egypt have been carrying out local protests and strikes for years to call attention to high unemployment, low wages, police harassment, and state corruption. This time, their protests combined and spread to other demographics.

These regimes' concentration of wealth and brazen corruption increasingly offended their militaries. Ben Ali and Mubarak both came from the professional military; indeed, Egypt had been ruled by former officers since 1952. Yet in both countries, the military had seen its status eclipsed. Egypt's military leaders controlled some local businesses, but they fiercely resented Gamal Mubarak, who was Hosni Mubarak's heir apparent. As a banker, he preferred to build his influence through business and political cronies rather than through the military, and those connected to him gained huge profits from government monopolies and deals with foreign investors. In Tunisia, Ben Ali kept the military at arm's length to ensure that it would not harbor political ambitions. Yet he let his wife and her relatives shake down Tunisian businessmen and build seaside mansions. In both countries, military resentments made the military less likely to crack down on mass protests; officers and soldiers would not kill their country-men just to keep the Ben Ali and Mubarak families and their favorites in power.

A similar defection among factions of the Libyan military led to Qaddafi's rapid loss of large territo-ries. As of this writing, however, Qaddafi's use of mercenaries and exploitation of tribal loyalties have prevented his fall. And in Yemen, Saleh has been kept afloat, if barely, by U.S. aid given in support of his opposition to Islamist terrorists and by the tribal and regional divisions among his opponents. Still, if the opposition unites, as it seems to be doing, and the United States becomes reluctant to back his increasingly repressive regime, Saleh could be the next sultan to topple.

The Revolutions' Limits

As of this writing, Sudan and Syria, the other sul-tanistic regions in the region, have not seen major popular protests. Yet Bashir's corruption and the concentration of wealth in Khartoum have become brazen. One of the historic rationales for his regime—keeping the whole of Sudan under north-ern control—recently disappeared with southern Sudan's January 2011 vote in favor of indepen-dence. In Syria, Assad has so far retained national-ist support because of his hard-line policies toward Israel and Lebanon. He still maintains the massive state employment programs that have kept Syrians passive for decades, but he has no mass base of sup-port and is dependent on a tiny elite, whose corrup-tion is increasingly notorious. Although it is hard to say how staunch the elite and military support for Bashir and Assad is, both regimes are probably even weaker than they appear and could quickly crumble in the face of broad-based protests.

The region's monarchies are more likely to retain power. This is not because they face no calls for change. In fact, Morocco, Jordan, Oman, and the Persian Gulf kingdoms face the same demographic, educational, and economic challenges that the sul-tanistic regimes do, and they must reform to meet them. But the monarchies have one big advantage: their political structures are flexible. Modern mon-archies can retain considerable executive power while ceding legislative power to elected parlia-ments. In times of unrest, crowds are more likely to protest for legislative change than for abandonment of the monarchy. This gives monarchs more room to maneuver to pacify the people. Facing protests in 1848, the monarchies in Germany and Italy, for example, extended their constitutions, reduced the absolute power of the king, and accepted elected legislatures as the price of avoiding further efforts at revolution.

In monarchies, moreover, succession can result in change and reform, rather than the destruction of the entire system. A dynastic succession is legitimate and may thus be welcomed rather than feared, as in a typical sultanistic state. For example, in Morocco in 1999, the public greeted King Mohammed VI's ascension to the throne with great hopes for change. And in fact, Mohammed VI has investigated some of the regime's previous legal abuses and worked to somewhat strengthen women's rights. He has calmed recent protests in Morocco by promising major constitutional reforms. In Bahrain, Jordan, Kuwait, Morocco, Oman, and Saudi Arabia, rul-ers will likely to be able to stay in office if they are willing to share their power with elected officials or hand the reins to a younger family member who heralds significant reforms.

The regime most likely to avoid significant change in the near term is Iran. Although Iran has been called a sultanistic regime, it is different in sev-eral respects: unlike any other regime in the region, the ayatollahs espouse an ideology of anti-Western Shiism and Persian nationalism that draws consid-erable support from ordinary people. This makes it more like a party-state with a mass base of support. Iran is also led by a combination of several strong leaders, not just one: Supreme Leader Ali Khamenei, President Mahmoud Ahmadinejad, and Parliamen-tary Chair Ali Larijani. So there is no one corrupt or inefficient sultan on which to focus dissent. Finally, the Iranian regime enjoys the support of the Basij, an ideologically committed militia, and the Revolutionary Guards, which are deeply intertwined with the government. There is little chance that these forces will defect in the face of mass protests.

After the Revolutions

Those hoping for Tunisia and Egypt to make the transition to stable democracy quickly will likely be disappointed. Revolutions are just the beginning of a long process. Even after a peaceful revolution, it generally takes half a decade for any type of stable regime to consolidate. If a civil war or a counterrevolution arises (as appears to be happening in Libya), the reconstruction of the state takes still longer.

In general, after the post-revolutionary honeymoon period ends, divisions within the opposition start to surface. Although holding new elections is a straightforward step, election campaigns and then decisions taken by new legislatures will open debates over taxation and state spending, corruption, foreign policy, the role of the military, the powers of the president, official policy on religious law and practice, minority rights, and so on. As conservatives, populists, Islamists, and modernizing reformers fiercely vie for power in Tunisia, Egypt, and perhaps Libya, those countries will likely face lengthy periods of abrupt government turnovers and policy reversals—similar to what occurred in the Philippines and many Eastern European countries after their revolutions.

Some Western governments, having long supported Ben Ali and Mubarak as bulwarks against a rising tide of radical Islam, now fear that Islamist groups are poised to take over. The Muslim Brotherhood in Egypt is the best organized of the opposition groups there, and so stands to gain in open elections, particularly if elections are held soon, before other parties are organized. Yet the historical record of revolutions in sultanistic regimes should somewhat alleviate such concerns. Not a single sultan overthrown in the last 30 years—including in Haiti,

the Philippines, Romania, Zaire, Indonesia, Georgia, and Kyrgyzstan—has been succeeded by an ideologically driven or radical government. Rather, in every case, the end product has been a flawed democracy—often corrupt and prone to authoritarian tendencies, but not aggressive or extremist.

This marks a significant shift in world history. Between 1949 and 1979, every revolution against a sultanistic regime—in China, Cuba, Vietnam, Cambodia, Iran, and Nicaragua—resulted in a communist or an Islamist government. At the time, most intellectuals in the developing world favored the communist model of revolution against capitalist states. And in Iran, the desire to avoid both capitalism and communism and the increasing popularity of traditional Shiite clerical authority resulted in a push for an Islamist government. Yet since the 1980s, neither the communist nor the Islamist model has had much appeal. Both are widely perceived as failures at producing economic growth and popular accountability—the two chief goals of all recent anti-sultanistic revolutions.

Noting that high unemployment spurred regime change, some in the United States have called for a Marshall Plan for the Middle East to stabilize the region. But in 1945, Europe had a history of prior democratic regimes and a devastated physical infrastructure that needed rebuilding. Tunisia and Egypt have intact economies with excellent recent growth records, but they need to build new democratic institutions. Pouring money into these countries before they have created accountable governments would only fuel corruption and undermine their progress toward democracy.

What is more, the United States and other Western nations have little credibility in the Middle East given their long support for sultanistic dictators. Any efforts to use aid to back certain groups or influence electoral outcomes are likely to arouse suspicion. What the revolutionaries need from outsiders is vocal support for the process of democracy, a willingness to accept all groups that play by democratic rules, and a positive response to any requests for technical assistance in institution building.

The greatest risk that Tunisia and Egypt now face is an attempt at counterrevolution by military conservatives, a group that has often sought to claim power after a sultan has been removed. This occurred in Mexico after Díaz was overthrown, in Haiti after Jean-Claude Duvalier's departure, and in the Philippines after Marcos' fall. And after Suharto was forced from power in Indonesia, the military exerted its strength by cracking down on independence movements in East Timor, which Indonesia had occupied since 1975.

In the last few decades, attempted counterrevolutions (such as those in the Philippines in 1987–88 and Haiti in 2004) have largely fizzled out. They have not reversed democratic gains or driven post-sultanistic regimes into the arms of extremists—religious or otherwise.

However, such attempts weaken new democracies and distract them from undertaking much-needed reforms. They can also provoke a radical reaction. If Tunisia's or Egypt's military attempts to claim power or block Islamists from participating in the new regime, or the region's monarchies seek to keep their regimes closed through repression rather than open them up via reforms, radical forces will only be strengthened.

As one example, the opposition in Bahrain, which had been seeking constitutional reforms, has reacted to Saudi action to repress its protests by calling for the overthrow of Bahrain's monarchy instead of its reform. Inclusiveness should be the order of the day.

The other main threat to democracies in the Middle East is war. Historically, revolutionary regimes have hardened and become more radical in response to international conflict. It was not the fall of the Bastille but war with Austria that gave the radical Jacobins power during the French Revolution. Similarly, it was Iran's war with Iraq that gave Ayotallah Ruhollah Khomeini the opportunity to drive out Iran's secular moderates. In fact, the one event that may cause radicals to hijack the Middle Eastern revolutions is if Israeli anxiety or Palestinian provocations escalate hostility between Egypt and Israel, leading to renewed war.

That said, there is still reason for optimism. Prior to 2011, the Middle East stood out on the map as the sole remaining region in the world virtually devoid of democracy. The Jasmine and Nile Revolutions look set to change all that. Whatever the final outcome, this much can be said: the rule of the sultans is coming to an end.

Max Abrahms

WHAT TERRORISTS REALLY WANT: TERRORIST MOTIVES AND COUNTERTERRORISM STRATEGY

What do terrorists want? No question is more fundamental for devising an effective counterterrorism strategy. The international community can-not expect to make terrorism unprofitable and thus scarce without knowing the incentive structure of its practitioners.[1] The strategic model—the dominant paradigm in terrorism studies—posits that terrorists are rational actors who attack civilians for political ends. According to this view, terrorists are political

From *International Security* 32, no. 4 (Spring 2008), pp. 78–105.

utility maximizers; people use terrorism when the expected political gains minus the expected costs outweigh the net expected benefits of alternative forms of protest.[2] The strategic model has widespread currency in the policy community; extant counterterrorism strategies are designed to defeat terrorism by reducing its political utility. The most common strategies are to mitigate terrorism by decreasing its political benefits via a strict no concessions policy; decreasing its prospective political benefits via appeasement; or decreasing its political benefits relative to nonviolence via democracy promotion.

Are any of these counterterrorism strategies likely to work? Can terrorism be neutralized by withholding political concessions, granting political concessions, or providing peaceful outlets for political change? In other words, does the solution to terrorism reside in diminishing its political utility? The answer depends on whether the strategic model is externally valid, that is, on whether terrorists are in fact rational people who attack civilians for political gain. If the model is empirically grounded, then the international community can presumably combat terrorism by rendering it an ineffective or unnecessary instrument of coercion. If the model is unfounded, however, then current strategies to reduce terrorism's political utility will not defuse the terrorism threat.

Despite its policy relevance, the strategic model has not been tested. This is the first study to comprehensively examine its empirical validity.[3] The strategic model rests on three core assumptions: (1) terrorists are motivated by relatively stable and consistent political preferences; (2) terrorists evaluate the expected political payoffs of their available options, or at least the most obvious ones; and (3) terrorism is adopted when the expected political return is superior to those of alternative options.

Does the terrorist's decisionmaking process conform to the strategic model? The answer appears to be no. The record of terrorist behavior does not adhere to the model's three core assumptions. Seven common tendencies of terrorist organizations flatly contradict them. Together, these seven terrorist tendencies represent important empirical puzzles for

the strategic model, posing a formidable challenge to the conventional wisdom that terrorists are rational actors motivated foremost by political ends. Major revisions in the dominant paradigm in terrorism studies and the policy community's basic approach to fighting terrorism are consequently in order.

This article has four main sections. The first section summarizes the strategic model's core assumptions and the empirical evidence that would disconfirm them.[4] The second section demonstrates the empirical weakness of the strategic model. In this section, I present the seven puzzles—based on the records of dozens of terrorist organizations from the late 1960s to the present, supplemented with theoretical arguments from the bargaining and coercion literatures—that cannot be reconciled with the model's underlying assumptions. The third section develops an alternative explanation for terrorism. The argument is not that terrorists are crazy or irrational; as Louise Richardson notes, psychiatric profiles of terrorists are "virtually unanimous" that their "primary shared characteristic is their normalcy."[5] Rather, I contend that the strategic model misspecifies terrorists' incentive structure; the preponderance of empirical and theoretical evidence reveals that terrorists are rational people who use terrorism primarily to develop strong affective ties with fellow terrorists.[6] If terrorists generally attach utmost importance to the social benefits of using terrorism, then extant strategies to reduce its political benefits will fail to counter the terrorism threat. In the final section, I suggest a reorientation of counterterrorism strategy in light of what terrorists really seem to want.

The Strategic Model

In classical economic theory, rational agents (1) possess stable and consistent preferences; (2) compare the costs and benefits of all available options; and (3) select the optimal option, that is, the one that maximizes output.[7] Modern decision theory recognizes that decisionmakers face cognitive and informational constraints. Rational actor models therefore typically relax each assumption such that the rational agent must only (1) possess relatively stable and consistent goals; (2) weigh the expected costs and benefits of the most obvious options; and (3) select the option with the optimal expected utility.[8] The strategic model is explicitly predicated on this trio of assumptions.

First, the strategic model assumes that terrorists are motivated by relatively stable and consistent political goals, which are encoded in the political platform of the terrorist organization. That West Germany's Red Army Faction (RAF) identified itself as Marxist, for example, implies that RAF members participated in the organization to achieve its stated revolutionary agenda.[9] Disconfirming evidence would therefore reveal that the RAF expressed a protean set of political objectives, fought mainly against other groups with its identical political platform, or continued using terrorism after its stated political grievances had been resolved.

Second, the strategic model assumes that terrorism is a "calculated course of action" and that "efficacy is the primary standard by which terrorism is compared with other methods of achieving political goals."[10] Specifically, the model assumes that terrorist groups weigh their political options and resort to terrorism only after determining that alternative political avenues are blocked.[11] Disconfirming evidence would therefore demonstrate that terrorism is not a strategy of last resort and that terrorist groups reflexively eschew potentially promising nonviolent political alternatives.

Third, the strategic model assumes that the decision to use terrorism is based on "the logic of consequence," that is, its political effectiveness relative to alternative options.[12] Specifically, it is assumed that terrorist organizations achieve their political platforms at least some of the time by attacking civilians; that they possess "reasonable expectations" of the political consequences of using terrorism based on its prior record of coercive effectiveness; and that they abandon the armed struggle when it consistently fails to coerce policy concessions or when manifestly superior political options arise.[13] Disconfirming evidence would therefore reveal that terrorist organizations do not achieve their political platforms by attacking civilians; that they do not renounce terrorism in spite of consistent political failure or manifestly superior political options; or that they do not even use terrorism in a manner that could potentially coerce policy concessions from the target country. Below I identify and then describe seven tendencies of terrorist organizations that challenge the strategic model with disconfirming evidence of its core assumptions.

The Seven Puzzling Tendencies of Terrorist Organizations

Seven empirical puzzles vitiate the strategic model's premise that terrorists are rational people who are motivated mainly to achieve their organization's stated political goals. The seven puzzles contradicting the strategic model are (1) terrorist organizations do not achieve their stated political goals by attacking civilians; (2) terrorist organizations never use terrorism as a last resort and seldom seize opportunities to become productive nonviolent political parties; (3) terrorist organizations reflexively reject compromise proposals offering significant policy concessions by the target government; (4) terrorist organizations have protean political platforms; (5) terrorist organizations generally carry out anonymous attacks, precluding target countries from making policy concessions; (6) terrorist organizations with identical political platforms routinely attack each other more than their mutually professed enemy; and (7) terrorist organizations resist disbanding when they consistently fail to achieve their political platforms or when their stated political grievances have been resolved and hence are moot.

Puzzle #1: Coercive Ineffectiveness

In the strategic model, people participate in a terrorist organization because they are deeply committed to achieving its political platform. The strategic model is explicit that success for a terrorist organization requires the attainment of its stated political goals.[14] Even if all other strategies are blocked, terrorism is not based on the logic of consequence and is thus irrational according to the model unless organizations achieve their political platforms at least some of the time by attacking civilians.[15] A major puzzle for the model then is that although terrorism is by definition destructive and scary, organizations rarely if ever attain their policy demands by targeting civilians.[16]

The Rand Corporation reported in the 1980s that "terrorists have been unable to translate the consequences of terrorism into concrete political gains.... In that sense terrorism has failed. It is a fundamental failure."[17] Martha Crenshaw remarked at the time that terrorist organizations do not obtain "the long-term ideological objectives they claim to seek, and therefore one must conclude that terrorism is objectively a failure."[18] Thomas Schelling reached the same conclusion in the 1990s, noting that terrorist attacks "never appear to accomplish anything politically significant."[19] In a study assessing terrorism's coercive effectiveness, I found that in a sample of twenty-eight well-known terrorist campaigns, the terrorist organizations accomplished their stated policy goals zero percent of the time by attacking civilians.[20] Although several political scientists have developed theoretical models predicated on the notion that terrorism is an effective coercive instrument, their research fails to identify a single terrorist organization that has achieved its political platform by attacking civilians.[21]

Terrorist organizations may not realize their policy demands by targeting civilians, but do these attacks generally advance their political cause? Walter Laqueur notes that for terrorist organizations, the political consequences of their violence is nearly always "negative."[22] Polls show, for example, that after the Irish Republican Army (IRA) attacked the British public, the British people became significantly less likely to favor withdrawing from Northern Ireland.[23] Similar trends in public opinion have been registered after groups attacked civilians in Egypt,

Indonesia, Israel, Jordan, the Philippines, and Russia.[24] Although the international community frequently appeals for target countries to appease terrorists, terrorist attacks on civilians have historically empowered hard-liners who oppose, as a matter of principle, accommodating the perpetrators. For this reason, numerous studies have shown that terrorist attacks tend to close—not open—the bargaining space between what terrorist groups demand and what target governments are willing to offer.[25] In sum, the strategic model posits that rational people participate in terrorist organizations to achieve their stated political goals. In practice, however, terrorism does not accomplish them. Predictably, terrorism's political ineffectiveness has led scholars to question its rationality and motives.[26]

Puzzle #2: Terrorism as the First Resort

The strategic model assumes that groups turn to terrorism only after weighing their political options and determining they are blocked. In the parlance of the model, the decision to use terrorism is a "last resort," a "constrained choice" imposed by the absence of political alternatives.[27] In reality, terrorist groups do not embrace terrorism as a last resort and seldom elect to abandon the armed struggle to become nonviolent political parties.

Terrorist groups never lack political alternatives.[28] Large-*n* studies show, first, that only the most oppressive totalitarian states have been immune from terrorism, and second, that the number of terrorist organizations operating in a country is positively associated with its freedom of expression, assembly, and association—conditions conducive to effecting peaceful political change.[29] The "paradox of terrorism" is that terrorist groups tend to target societies with the greatest number of political alternatives, not the fewest.[30] Case studies on terrorist organizations confirm that the decision to use terrorism is not a last resort.[31] In their study of Italian terrorist organizations in the mid-1960s and early

1970s, for example, Donatella Della Porta and Sidney Tarrow found that terrorism was "part of the protest repertoire from the very beginning," even though opportunity abounded for nonviolent, constitutionally protected political protest.[32] More generally, the authors concluded that terrorism "tended to appear from the very beginning of the protest cycle" for the dozens of terrorist organizations operating in Western Europe during this period.[33]

Relatively few terrorist organizations have elected to abandon the armed struggle to become normal political parties.[34] More commonly, terrorist organizations toil alongside peaceful parties, refuse to lay down their arms after participating in national elections, or sabotage open elections that would have yielded major political gains for the group, such as today's militant Sunni groups in Iraq.[35] In many instances, nonviolent strategies are believed to be more policy effective, but terrorist organizations tend to retain, in one form or another, the path of armed resistance.[36]

For these reasons, Crenshaw has sensibly asked, "Why use terrorism when it cannot be justified . . . as a last resort?"[37] The answer of most terrorism experts is that terrorist groups seem to possess "an innate compulsion" to engage in terrorism and an "unswerving belief" in its desirability over nonviolence, contradicting the strategic model's assumption that groups employ terrorism only as a last resort upon evaluating their political options.[38]

Puzzle #3: Reflexively Uncompromising Terrorists

As a rule, terrorist organizations do not compromise with the target country. Bruce Hoffman has observed that terrorist organizations are notorious for their "resolutely uncompromising demands."[39] Crenshaw has likewise noted that terrorist organizations are characterized by "an intransigent refusal to compromise."[40] It is far more common for them to derail negotiations by ramping up their attacks.[41] In fact, no peace process has transformed a major terrorist organization into a completely nonviolent political party.[42] Proponents of the strategic model claim that terrorists are acting rationally in opposing compromise because their policy preferences are inherently extreme, precluding a mutually acceptable bargain solution with the target country.[43] This argument is empirically and theoretically flawed.

First, terrorism is an extremism of means, not ends.[44] Many terrorist organizations profess surprisingly moderate political positions. Russian terrorist groups of the mid-nineteenth century were known as "liberals with a bomb" because they sought a constitution with elementary civil freedoms.[45] The expressed goal of the al-Aqsa Martyrs Brigades is to achieve a Palestinian state in the West Bank and Gaza Strip—a policy preference held by most of the international community. Robert Pape points out that even in his sample of contemporary suicide terrorist organizations, "the terrorists' political aims, if not their methods, are often more mainstream than observers realize; they generally reflect quite common, straightforward nationalist self-determination claims of their community . . . goals that are typically much like those of other nationalists within their community."[46] Yet terrorist organizations rarely commit to negotiations, even when these would satisfy a significant portion of their stated political grievances. The al-Aqsa Martyrs Brigades, for example, responded with an unprecedented wave of terror to Israeli Prime Minister Ehud Barak's January 2001 offer of the Gaza Strip and most of the West Bank.[47]

Second, even when terrorist groups are motivated by extreme policy preferences, a negotiated settlement is always preferable to political deadlock, according to the logic of the strategic model.[48] Most bargaining theorists do not accept "issue indivisibility" between rational adversaries as a viable explanation for conflict because contested issues are typically complex and multidimensional, enabling the warring parties to find linkages and side payments that create a mutually beneficial bargain solution.[49] Hamas, for example, has opposed surrendering claims to all of historic Palestine, but the Islamist group professes to value the West Bank and

Gaza Strip. If acting solely to optimize its political platform, Hamas would therefore be expected to accept the Palestinian territories in exchange for peace. Hamas, however, acts as a spoiler, depriving its members of policy goals that the organization purports to support. In sum, bargaining theory dictates that the rational course of action is for terrorist organizations to compromise—even if that means securing only partial concessions over continued deadlock—but they rarely do. The tendency for terrorist organizations to reflexively oppose compromise undercuts the strategic model's assumptions that terrorists weigh the most obvious political options and select terrorism because of its relative political effectiveness.

Puzzle #4: Protean Political Platforms

The strategic model assumes that terrorists are motivated by relatively stable and consistent goals reflected in their organization's political platform. But terrorist organizations often have protean political platforms.[50] The Rand Corporation described France's Action Directe in the 1980s as a "chameleon organization" that "rapidly refocused" on a host of faddish policy issues, from opposing Israel to nuclear energy to the Catholic Church.[51] For Ely Karmon, Action Directe's hodgepodge of stated goals reflected the organization's inability to agree on basic ideological principles.[52] Action Directe was an unusually capricious terrorist organization, but even the crucial case of al-Qaida has purported to support a highly unstable set of political goals.[53] In "The Protean Enemy," Jessica Stern charts al-Qaida's transitory political agenda, as the movement morphed rapidly and unpredictably from waging defensive jihad against the Soviets in Afghanistan to fighting local struggles in Bosnia, the Philippines, Russia, Spain, and in Muslim countries to its eventual targeting of the "far enemy" in the late 1990s. The marked fluidity of al-Qaida's political rationale is reflected in the fatwas Osama bin Laden issued throughout the 1990s, which contain a litany of

disparate grievances against Muslims.[54] Only in his fourth call to arms on October 7, 2001, did he emphasize the Israeli occupation, which is known in policy circles as his "belated concern."[55] Al-Qaida members have frequently criticized the inconsistency of their organization's jihadi message. The al-Qaida military strategist, Abul-Walid, complained that with its "hasty changing of strategic targets," al-Qaida was engaged in nothing more than "random chaos."[56] Other disgruntled al-Qaida members have reproached the organization for espousing political objectives that "shift with the wind."[57] Not surprisingly, the "opportunistic" nature of al-Qaida's political platform has led scholars to question the movement's dedication to achieving it.[58]

Some of the most important terrorist organizations in modern history have pursued policy goals that are not only unstable but also contradictory. The Basque separatist group ETA, for example, is criticized for failing to produce "a consistent ideology," as its political goals have wavered from fighting to overturn the Franco dictatorship in Spain to targeting the emergent democratic government—a progression similar to that of the Shining Path, Peru's most notorious terrorist organization.[59] The Kurdistan Workers' Party—Turkey's most dangerous contemporary terrorist group (known by the Kurdish acronym PKK)—has likewise vacillated between advocating jihad, a Marxist revolution, and a Kurdish homeland governed without Islamist or Marxist principles.[60] The Abu Nidal Organization staged countless attacks against Syria in the 1980s and then "almost overnight switched allegiance" by becoming a Syrian proxy.[61] According to Leonard Weinberg, the most feared international terrorist group of the 1980s was willing to carry out a terrorist attack "on behalf of any cause," even conflicting ones.[62] Similarly, Laqueur points out that many well-known groups that began on the extreme right—such as the Argentine Montoneros, Colombian M-19, and the Popular Front for the Liberation of Palestine—ended up on the left as far as their phraseology was concerned.[63] Hoffman has likewise noted that in the 1980s, right-wing terrorist groups in West Germany temporarily adopted left-wing rhetoric and began attacking targets that are the traditional choice of left-wing groups. Predictably, the police initially suspected that dozens of their attacks were the work of communist groups.[64] That terrorist organizations often pursue unstable, even inconsistent, political goals undermines the assumption that terrorist members are motivated by a stable and consistent utility function encoded in their organization's political platform.

Puzzle #5: Anonymous Attacks

The strategic model assumes that terrorism is based on the logic of consequence, specifically, its ability to coerce policy concessions from the target country by conveying the costs of noncompliance. For this reason, proponents of the model describe terrorism as a form of "credible signaling" or "costly signaling."[65] A basic principle of coercion, however, is that the coercer must convey its policy demands to the coerced party.[66] A puzzle for the strategic model is that most of the time terrorist organizations neither issue policy demands nor even take credit for their attacks.

Since the emergence of modern terrorism in 1968, 64 percent of worldwide terrorist attacks have been carried out by unknown perpetrators. Anonymous terrorism has been rising, with three out of four attacks going unclaimed since September 11, 2001.[67] Anonymous terrorism is particularly prevalent in Iraq, where the U.S. military has struggled to determine whether the violence was perpetrated by Shiite or Sunni groups with vastly different political platforms.[68]

Policy demands are rarely forthcoming, even when the terrorist organization divulges its identity to the target country.[69] In the early 1990s, Schelling captured this point: "Usually there is nothing to negotiate. A soldier is killed in a disco in Germany. A bomb explodes in front of an Israeli consulate. Japanese Black Septembrists unpack automatic weapons in the Lod airport and start shooting. The perpetrators don't ask anything, demand anything."[70] The tendency for terrorist organizations to refrain from issuing policy demands increased in the late 1990s, leading Hoffman to conclude that the coercive logic of terrorism is "seriously flawed."[71] After the attacks of September 11, David Lake also observed that the terrorists "did not issue prior demands," and therefore a theory premised on coercion "would seem ill-suited to explaining such violence."[72] In sum, the strategic model assumes that terrorism is an effective coercive instrument. Yet terrorist groups rarely convey through violence their policy preferences to the target country, precluding even the possibility of successful coercion.

Puzzle #6: Terrorist Fratricide

The strategic model assumes that terrorists are motivated by a consistent utility function reflected in their organization's political platform, but terrorist organizations with the same political platform routinely undercut it in wars of annihilation against each other. Particularly in the early stages of their existence, terrorist organizations purporting to fight for a common cause frequently attack each other more than their mutually declared enemy.

The Tamil Tigers, for example, did not target the Sinhalese government in the mid-1980s. Instead, it engaged in a "systematic annihilation" of other Tamil organizations "espousing the same cause" of national liberation.[73] Pape observes that the "apparent implication" of the Tigers' target selection is that the violence had "little to do with the political grievances of Tamil society or the relationship between the Tamils and their Sinhalese opponents."[74] Ami Pedahzur alludes to the fact that the Tigers' target selection is difficult to reconcile with the strategic model: "In contrast to what might be expected from a guerrilla or a terrorist organization whose [expressed] goals were national liberation, the first violent actions initiated by the Tigers were not aimed at any army forces or Sinhalese politicians. . . . The Tigers systematically liquidated leaders and sometimes activists of other [Tamil] organizations."[75] Similarly, in the early years of the Algerian War, the

National Algerian Movement (known by the French acronym MNA) and the National Liberation Front (FLN) mainly attacked each other, not their French occupiers.[76] Proponents of the strategic model might reason that the MNA and the FLN were battling to determine the political future of Algeria. Benjamin Stora points out, however, that "for both organizations the nature of the future independent Algerian society was not at issue."[77] Predictably, the interorganizational violence had a "devastating" effect on the mutually expressed goal of the MNA and the FLN to end the French occupation.[78] Terrorist organizations also undermined their political platforms by targeting each other more than their mutually declared enemy in the violent clashes in Aden between the Liberation of Occupied South Yemen and the National Liberation Front in 1967; in Argentina between Marxist terrorist organizations in the late 1970s; and in the Gaza Strip between Palestinian groups "fighting for a common cause" during the first intifada.[79] In recent years, the same phenomenon has been endemic in terrorist hot spots. In Chechnya, local terrorist organizations have been terrorizing each other despite their joint political platform to establish Chechen independence. And in southern Iraq, Shiite militias with a shared ideological stance have been mainly blowing each other up, to the obvious benefit of the Sunnis.[80] That terrorist organizations frequently undercut their stated political agenda is puzzling for the strategic model because terrorists are presumed to be primarily motivated to achieving it.

Puzzle #7: Never-Ending Terrorism

The strategic model assumes that terrorist organizations disband or renounce terrorism when it continuously fails to advance their political platforms.[81] To act otherwise, Pape says, is "deeply irrational" because "that would not constitute learning."[82] Yet terrorist organizations survive for decades, notwithstanding their political futility.[83]

The primary explanation for war in the bargaining literature is that rational actors miscalculate the capability and resolve of their opponents.[84] Propo-

nents of the strategic model might speculate that terrorist organizations are acting rationally; they simply overestimate the likelihood that attacking civilians will coerce their governments into making policy concessions. The problem with this argument is that informational explanations provide a poor account of protracted conflict. James Fearon has shown that after a few years of war, fighters on both sides are expected to develop accurate understandings of their relative capabilities and resolve.[85] The idea that terrorists misjudge the coercive effectiveness of their violence therefore does not obtain because terrorist organizations exist for decades despite their political hopelessness. As Loren Lomasky observes, the strategic model "impute[s] to terrorists no lesser rationality than that which social analysts routinely ascribe to other actors. . . . Rational agents are not systematically unable to distinguish efficacious from inefficacious activity."[86] The longevity of terrorist organizations relative to their political accomplishments therefore conflicts with the strategic model's assumption that terrorism is based on the logic of consequence.

Conversely, the strategic model assumes that because terrorists are motivated by relatively stable policy aims, the violence will cease when the organization's stated grievances have been lifted.[87] A puzzle for the model then is that terrorist organizations resist disbanding when their political rationales have become moot.[88] Pape's research demonstrates that contemporary guerrilla campaigns have coerced major policy concessions from target countries; yet none of the organizations that also use terrorism have disbanded.[89] Hezbollah, for example, remains an operational terrorist group, despite the fact that its guerrilla attacks on the Israel Defense Forces achieved the stated goal of liberating southern Lebanon in May 2000. When their political rationale is losing relevance, terrorist organizations commonly invent one. Klaus Wasmund's case study of the RAF shows, for example, that the German terrorists were "aggravated" when the Vietnam War ended because they suddenly faced a "dilemma of finding a suitable revolutionary subject." Instead of abandoning the armed struggle, the RAF turned overnight into a militant advocate of the Palestinian cause.[90] Similarly, the 9/11 commission explains that upon discovering in April 1988 that the Soviets were planning to withdraw from Afghanistan, the mujahideen made the collective decision to remain intact while they hunted for a new political cause.[91] In this way, terrorist organizations contrive a new political raison d'être, belying the assumption that terrorists are motivated by relatively stable policy preferences reflected in their organizations' political platforms.

What Terrorists Really Want

These seven puzzles challenge the strategic model with disconfirming evidence of its core assumptions that terrorists (1) are motivated by relatively consistent and stable political goals issued by the terrorist organization; (2) weigh the expected political costs and benefits of the most obvious options; and (3) opt for a strategy of terrorism because of its expected political effectiveness (see Figure 7.1). The puzzles suggest that the strategic model is flawed in one of two ways: either terrorists are irrational people who minimize their utility or the model misspecifies their incentive structure. Psychiatric studies reveal that terrorists are not

irrational.[92] This implies that the foremost objective of terrorists may not be to achieve their organization's political platform.

The tremendous number and variation of terrorist organizations in the world preclude a single causal explanation for terrorism that obtains in every situation. The equifinality of terrorism ensures that any causal explanation is necessarily probabilistic, not deterministic.[93] This section demonstrates, however, that an alternative incentive structure has superior explanatory power. There is comparatively strong theoretical and empirical evidence that people become terrorists not to achieve their organization's declared political agenda, but to develop strong affective ties with other terrorist members. In other words, the preponderance of evidence is that people participate in terrorist organizations for the social solidarity, not for their political return.

Organization theories are potentially useful for explaining terrorist motives because nearly all terrorist attacks are perpetrated by members of terrorist organizations.[94] The natural systems model, a leading approach in organization theory, posits that people participate in organizations not to achieve their official goals, but to experience social solidarity with other members. After briefly describing the natural systems model, I demonstrate its applicability to understanding terrorists' motives.[95]

Figure 7.1 The Empirical Weakness of the Strategic Model

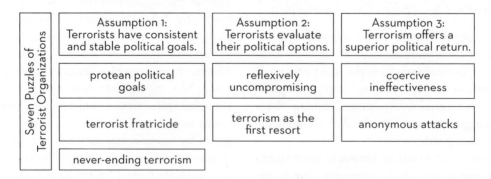

Note: The strategic model's assumptions are obviously interrelated; there is no implication that each puzzle violates only one of them.

The Natural Systems Model

Organization theory has been dominated by two dueling models since the 1930s: the classical model and the natural systems model, which counts many more adherents.[96] Classical organization theorists such as Max Weber and Frederick Taylor conceived of the organization as a set of arrangements oriented toward maximizing output. In the classical model, members participate in an organization solely to achieve its stated goals. According to this view, the effectiveness and rationality of an organization therefore depend entirely on the degree to which its actions advance its official aims.[97] In assuming that terrorists are motivated to achieving their organizations' stated political goals, the strategic model is predicated on the antiquated views of the classical model, which faced almost immediate opposition.

Chester Barnard, the father of the natural systems model, exposed the classical fallacy of equating the official goals of an organization with the goals of its members. Barnard demonstrated that most individuals engage in a cost-benefit analysis of whether to participate in an organization based on its personal inducements, which have little if any connection to the organization's stated goals. For Barnard, the most important incentive is what he called the "condition of communion," the sense of solidarity from participating in a social collectivity.[98]

The natural systems model stresses that there is often a disconnect between the official goals of an organization and the latent social goals governing its behavior. The loose coupling of organizational practices with official goals implies that the failure to achieve them may be entirely satisfactory from the perspective of its members.[99] In fact, the model emphasizes that organizations will act to perpetuate their existence—even when doing so undermines their official goals—whenever members attach utmost importance to the social benefits of the organization.[100]

If people participate in terrorist organizations primarily to achieve social solidarity, one would therefore expect to find (1) evidence at the individ-ual level that people are mainly attracted to terrorist organizations not to achieve their official political platforms, but to develop strong affective ties with other terrorist members; and (2) evidence at the organizational level that terrorist groups consistently engage in actions to preserve the social unit, even when these impede their official political agendas. There is compelling evidence at both levels of analysis.

Terrorists As Social Solidarity Seekers

Empirical evidence is accumulating in terrorism studies and political psychology that individuals participate in terrorist organizations not to achieve their political platforms, but to develop strong affective ties with fellow terrorists.

First, psychologist Jeff Victoroff has concluded in a précis of the terrorism literature that "the claim that no individual factors identify those at risk for becoming terrorists is based on completely inadequate research."[101] Terrorist organizations appeal disproportionately to certain psychological types of people, namely, the socially alienated. Melvin Seeman defines alienation broadly as the feeling of loneliness, rejection, or exclusion from valued relationships, groups, or societies.[102] Demographic data show that the vast majority of terrorist organizations are composed of unmarried young men or widowed women who were not gainfully employed prior to joining them.[103] Other demographic studies show that terrorist organizations are frequent repositories for people undergoing dislocation from their native homeland who are therefore detached from family, friends, and the host society they are attempting to join. Marc Sageman's study of 172 global Salafi jihadists demonstrates that these risk factors are particularly prevalent among the crucial case of al-Qaida members, 80 percent of whom are "cultural outcasts living at the margins of society" as unassimilated first- or second-generation immigrants in non-Muslim countries.[104] Analysts who study al-Qaida are increasingly finding that European

Muslims are unassimilated in their host countries and represent a core constituency of al-Qaida, whereas Muslims in the United States are comparatively assimilated and detached from the al-Qaida network.[105] Variation on the independent variable of alienation or social isolation can therefore explain variation on the dependent variable for joining al-Qaida. The high correlation of what Albert Bandura calls "conducive social conditions" among the hundreds of terrorist members for whom data exist is consistent with my argument that most individuals participate in terrorist organizations to achieve social solidarity.[106]

Second, members from a wide variety of terrorist groups—including ETA, the IRA, the Italian Communist Party, the RAF, the Red Brigades, Turkish terrorist organizations, and the Weather Underground—say that they joined these armed struggles not because of their personal attachment to their political or ideological agendas, but to maintain or develop social relations with other terrorist members.[107] These are not the statements of a small number of terrorists; in the Turkish sample, for instance, the 1,100 terrorists interviewed were ten times more likely to say that they joined the terrorist organization "because their friends were members" than because of the "ideology" of the group.[108]

Third, recent studies on al-Qaida, Fatah, Hamas, Hezbollah, Palestinian Islamic Jihad, and Turkish terrorists have found that the key scope condition for their joining the terrorist organization was having a friend or relative in it—a conclusion consistent with prior research on ETA, the IRA, and both Italian and German right-wing and Marxist terrorist groups.[109] These findings are also consistent with a fascinating July 2007 study of Guantanamo Bay detainees. Researchers from West Point's Combating Terrorism Center found in their sample of 516 detainees that knowing an al-Qaida member was a significantly better predictor than believing in the jihad for turning to terrorism—even when a militant definition of jihad was used and other variables were held constant.[110] The strategic model cannot explain why the vast majority of politically discon-tented people do not use terrorism. Yet the requirement of social linkages to the terrorist organization can explain the difference between the large pool of socially isolated people and the relatively small number who become terrorists.[111]

Fourth, case studies of al-Qaida, Aum Shinrikyo, Hezbollah, the IRA, the RAF, the Weather Underground, and Chechen and Palestinian terrorist groups have concluded that most of the terrorists in these groups participated in the armed struggle to improve their relationships with other terrorists or to reduce their sense of alienation from society, usually both.[112] These studies emphasize that social bonds preceded ideological commitment, which was an effect, not a cause, of becoming a terrorist member.[113]

Fifth, many terrorist foot soldiers and even their leaders never develop a basic understanding of their organization's political purpose. This finding strengthens the argument that ideological commitment enters through the back door, if at all, of terrorist organizations. In his study of the IRA, for example, Robert White found that nearly half of the terrorists he interviewed were unaware of the discrimination in Northern Ireland against Catholics, despite the salience of this issue in IRA communiqués.[114] According to Olivier Roy, Mia Bloom, and a former mujahideen, al-Qaida foot soldiers and their leaders are often ignorant about the basic tenets of Islam, if not bin Laden's political vision.[115] Al-Qaida is unexceptional in this regard; Richardson's research shows that "a striking and quite surprising" aspect of terrorism is that the leaders of "very different terrorist movements" are unable to explain their basic political purpose.[116] When asked to describe the society that their organizations hoped to achieve, the leader of the Shining Path conceded, "We have not studied the question sufficiently"; the founder of the RAF responded, "That is not our concern"; the leader of the Japanese Red Army replied, "We really do not know what it will be like"; and the spokesman for the Revolutionary Armed Forces of Colombia acknowledged, "I must admit that we have yet to define this aspect."[117] Audrey Cronin has found that leaders of both left-wing and anarchist terrorist groups are also "notorious for their inability to articulate a clear vision of their [political] goals."[118] That even terrorist leaders frequently cannot explain their organizations' political purpose suggests that members have a different motive for participating in them.[119]

Sixth, terrorist organizations focus their recruitment on the socially isolated, not on people with a demonstrable commitment to their given political cause. Pedahzur's research, for example, shows that Hezbollah, the PKK, and Chechen and Palestinian groups recruit young, unemployed men "who have never found their place in the community," not fervent nationalists committed to political change.[120] Similarly, Peter Merkl shows that Marxist terrorist groups have historically recruited unemployed youth with "failed personal lives" who lacked "political direction."[121] Gregory Johnsen likewise suggests that al-Qaida, at least in Yemen, focuses its recruitment not on committed jihadists, but on "young and largely directionless" socially marginalized Muslim men.[122]

Seventh, terrorist organizations are particularly attractive outlets for those seeking solidarity. According to political psychologists, terrorist groups are far more tight-knit than other voluntary associations because of the extreme dangers and costs of participation, as well as their tendency to violate societal expectations.[123] This observation may account for the fact that even when terrorist organizations fail to achieve their political platforms, committing acts of terrorism tends to generate new recruits, boost membership morale, and otherwise strengthen the social unit.[124]

Eighth, terrorists seem to prefer participating in terrorist groups and activities most conducive to developing strong affective ties with fellow terrorists. Jacob Shapiro has found that within the al-Qaida network, terrorists prefer operating in more centralized, cohesive clusters of cliques.[125] Indeed, since the emergence of modern international terrorism, terrorists have flocked to where other terrorists—regardless of their political orientation—were gathered. In the 1970s, thousands of terrorists from dozens of countries and organizations descended on training camps run by the Palestine Liberation Organization; in the 1980s and mid-1990s, the locus of terrorist activity shifted first to Afghanistan to train with the Afghan mujahideen and then to al-Qaida camps. Based on her interviews with terrorists, Jessica Stern has likened these adventures to an "Outward Bound" experience for young men seeking challenges, excitement, and above all "friendship" with fellow terrorists of diverse political backgrounds.[126] First-hand accounts from these camps confirm that the terrorists often had little idea or preference where they would fight upon completing their training.[127]

Ninth, there is circumstantial evidence that terrorist organizations collapse when they cease to be perceived as desirable social collectivities worth joining. David Rapoport's research demonstrates that throughout history terrorist organizations have disbanded when their members grew old, tired of waging the armed struggle, and their group failed to appeal to the younger generation.[128] Cronin's research on the decline of terrorist groups also lists "generational transition failure" as their leading cause of death.[129] The tendency for terrorist groups to die out in the course of a "human life cycle"—irrespective of the state of their political grievances—suggests that they appeal to new members primarily for social, not political, reasons.

The research landscape is constrained by the limited reliable demographic data on terrorists, representative samples, and controlled studies to firmly establish causation. In the aggregate, however, there is mounting empirical evidence that people may participate in terrorist organizations mainly to achieve social solidarity, not their official political agendas. This incentive structure is testable. The natural systems model posits that when members attach utmost importance to an organization's social benefits, the organization will seek to prolong its existence, even when doing so impedes its official goals. This is precisely the way terrorist organizations typically behave.

The Puzzles Revisited

The seven puzzles are perplexing for the strategic model because they demonstrate that terrorist organizations behave more as social solidarity maximizers than as political maximizers. The puzzles are easily resolved from the vantage of organization theory. The natural systems model predicts that terrorist organizations will routinely engage in actions to perpetuate and justify their existence, even when these undermine their official political agendas. True to the model, terrorist organizations (1) prolong their existence by relying on a strategy that hardens target governments from making policy concessions; (2) ensure their continued viability by resisting opportunities to peacefully participate in the democratic process; (3) avoid disbanding by reflexively rejecting negotiated settlements that offer significant policy concessions; (4) guarantee their survival by espousing a litany of protean political goals that can never be fully satisfied;[130] (5) avert organization-threatening reprisals by conducting anonymous attacks, even though they preclude the possibility of coercing policy concessions; (6) annihilate ideologically identical terrorist organizations that compete for members, despite the adverse effect on their stated political cause; and (7) refuse to split up after the armed struggle has proven politically unsuccessful for decades or its political rationale has become moot.

None of these common tendencies of terrorist organizations advances their official political agendas, but all of them help to ensure the survival of the social unit. Together, they reveal the operating decision rules of terrorist members. Whereas the strategic model locates the motives of terrorists in the official goals of the terrorist organization, the trade-offs it makes provides direct insight into its members' incentive structure. Just as economists measure utility functions through revealed preferences, terrorism scholars need not make comparisons among utilities.[131] The seven puzzles discussed above contradict the strategic model because terrorists already make such trade-offs by regularly prioritizing the maintenance of the terrorist organization over the advancement of its official political agenda as predicted by the natural systems model.[132]

In sum, the seven puzzles for the strategic model challenge the prevailing view that terrorists are rational people who use terrorism for political ends. The preponderance of theoretical and empirical evidence is that people participate in terrorist organizations not to achieve their official political platforms, but to develop strong affective ties with fellow terrorists—an incentive structure reflected in the trade-offs terrorist organizations typically make to maintain their survival. If terrorists generally attach greater importance to the social benefits than to the political benefits of using terrorism, then extant counterterrorism strategies require fundamental change.

Counterterrorism Implications

The most common counterterrorism strategies are designed to reduce terrorism by divesting it of its political utility. The predominant strategy is to deter terrorism by decreasing its political utility via a strict no concessions policy.[133] Like most heads of state, President George W. Bush believes that terrorism will desist when its practitioners realize that "these crimes only hurt their [political] cause."[134] Although target governments rarely appease terrorists, there is also a widespread belief in the international community that they can be defused through political accommodation.[135] Proponents of this second strategy urge rekindling stalled peace processes, for example, to deny prospective political benefits from using terrorism. The third most common counterterrorism strategy is democracy promotion, which is intended to decrease terrorism's utility by empowering citizens to peacefully address their country's political problems.[136] All three strategies have poor track records. As I have shown, terrorist organizations often resist disbanding in the face of consistent political failure, in spite of the ending of their immediate political grievances, and even when presented with peaceful alternatives for political gain.

Why does withholding political concessions, granting political concessions, or providing nonviolent political alternatives fail so often to eradicate terrorism? The strategic model's premise that terrorists are political maximizers is empirically weak. Strategies to dry up the demand for terrorism by minimizing its political utility are misguided and hence unlikely to work on any systematic basis. The evidence is stronger that terrorists tend to think and act more as social solidarity maximizers, which requires a different counterterrorism approach.

Both supply-side and demand-side counterterrorism strategies must be informed by the terrorist's incentive structure. Supply-side strategies can help law enforcement identify potential terrorists, unravel covert networks, and even thwart terrorist attacks by exploiting the knowledge that people tend to participate in terrorist groups to develop strong affective ties with fellow terrorists. There is no single "terrorist personality," but certain communities are prone to terrorism. Law enforcement must pay greater attention to the socially marginalized than to the politically downtrodden. This includes diaspora communities in Western countries that host large unassimilated, dislocated populations such as the Maghrebin in France; single, unemployed, Islamist men residing in comparatively secular Muslim countries such as in Pakistan; restive, youthful populations that feel estranged from the state such as in Saudi Arabia; and prison populations, which, by definition, are home to the socially isolated and dislocated. These are impossibly large groups of people to monitor. Law enforcement can tighten the noose considerably by exploiting the fact that terrorist groups are composed of networks of friends and family members, and that knowing one of them is the key scope condition for entry into the group. Governments should utilize this knowledge to aggressively boost funding of social network analysis (SNA) research. SNA is a mathematical method for mapping and studying relationships between people, with untapped counterterrorism potential. The basic idea is to trace the social relations or "links" emanating from known terrorists or

suspects, and then connect the dots between these "nodes" of people, to estimate the probability of their involvement in the terrorist network. People who email, talk on the phone, or intentionally meet with terrorists or their close friends are statistically more likely to be complicit. In this way, SNA can help law enforcement identify and then surveil the inner circle. Because acquaintances can also play a critical role in the network, greater data-mining power and accuracy need to be developed to expose these weak ties without undue infringements on civil liberties.[137]

Demand-side strategies should focus on divesting terrorism's social utility, in two ways. First, it is vital to drive a wedge between organization members. Since the advent of modern terrorism in the late 1960s, the sole counterterrorism strategy that was a clear-cut success attacked the social bonds of the terrorist organization, not its utility as a political instrument. By commuting prison sentences in the early 1980s in exchange for actionable intelligence against their fellow Brigatisti, the Italian government infiltrated the Red Brigades, bred mistrust and resentment among the members, and quickly rolled up the organization.[138] Similar deals should be cut with al-Qaida in cases where detainees' prior involvement in terrorism and their likelihood of rejoining the underground are minor. Greater investment in developing and seeding double agents will also go a long way toward weakening the social ties under-girding terrorist organizations and cells around the world. Second, counterterrorism strategies must reduce the demand for at-risk populations to turn to terrorist organizations in the first place. To lessen Muslims' sense of alienation from democratic societies, these societies must improve their records of cracking down on bigotry, supporting hate-crime legislation, and most crucially, encouraging moderate places of worship—an important alternative for dislocated youth to develop strong affective ties with politically moderate peers and mentors. In authoritarian countries, an abrupt transition to democracy risks empowering extremists.[139] These regimes must, however, permit the development of civil society to provide opportunities for the socially disenfranchised to bond in peaceful voluntary associations. Counterterrorism operations must also redouble their efforts to minimize collateral damage, which invariably creates dislocation, social isolation, and calls for revenge. Such policies will help reduce the incentive and therefore incidence of terrorism by diminishing its social benefits, which are what its practitioners apparently value most.

NOTES

1. See Louise Richardson, *What Terrorists Want: Understanding the Enemy, Containing the Threat* (New York: Random House, 2006), p. 44.

2. Martha Crenshaw refers to what I call the strategic model as the "instrumental model." For summaries of this model, see Crenshaw, "Theories of Terrorism: Instrumental and Organizational Approaches," in David C. Rapoport, ed., *Inside Terrorist Organizations* (New York: Columbia University Press, 1988), pp. 13–31; Crenshaw, "The Logic of Terrorism: Terrorist Behavior as a Product of Strategic Choice," in Walter Reich, ed., *Origins of Terrorism: Psychologies, Ideologies, Theologies, States of Mind* (New York: Cambridge University Press, 1990), pp. 7–24; Gordon H. McCormick, "Terrorist Decision Making," *Annual Review of Political Science*, Vol. 6 (June 2003), p. 482; and Gary C. Gambill, "The Balance of Terror: War by Other Means in the Contemporary Middle East," *Journal of Palestine Studies*, Vol. 28, No. 1 (Autumn 1998), pp. 51–66. For applications of the strategic model, see Robert A. Pape, *Dying to Win: The Strategic Logic of Suicide Terrorism* (New York: Random House, 2005); Max Abrahms, "Why Terrorism Does Not Work," *International Security*, Vol. 31, No. 2 (Fall 2006), pp. 42–78; Andrew H. Kydd and Barbara F. Walter, "The Strategies of Terrorism," *International Security*, Vol. 31, No. 1 (Summer 2006), pp. 49–80; and James DeNardo, *Power in Numbers: The Political*

Strategy of Protest and Rebellion (Princeton, N.J.: Princeton University Press, 1985), p. 3.

3. Martha Crenshaw has raised important questions about the strategic model's empirical validity. See, for example, Crenshaw's "Theories of Terrorism" and "The Logic of Terrorism."

4. There is a debate within the social sciences about whether a hypothesis's assumptions need to be empirically valid. Milton Friedman famously argued that the merit of a hypothesis depends strictly on its predictive power, whereas many other theorists believe that the core assumptions of a hypothesis must also be grounded in reality. For a summary of this theoretical debate, see Jack Melitz, "Friedman and Machlup on the Significance of Testing Economic Assumptions," *Journal of Political Economy*, Vol. 73, No. 1 (February 1965), pp. 37–60. In the field of international relations, most theory testing takes the assumptions as exogenous, but this is not always the case. For two important exceptions that criticize realism because of its assumption of anarchy, see David A. Baldwin, ed., *Neorealism and Neoliberalism: The Contemporary Debate* (New York: Columbia University Press, 1993); and Alexander Wendt, "Anarchy Is What States Make of It: The Social Construction of Power Politics," *International Organization*, Vol. 46, No. 2 (Spring 1992), pp. 391–425.

5. Richardson, *What Terrorists Want*, p. 14.

6. Sociologists routinely treat social objectives as rational. See, for example, Jeffrey Pfeffer, *Organizations and Organization Theory* (Boston: Pitman, 1982), pp. 9, 42–43, 62, 72, 256. Rational choice theorists in economics and political science also frequently treat social objectives as rational. See, for example, Jon Elster, "Introduction," in Elster, ed., *Rational Choice* (Oxford: Basil Blackwell, 1986), p. 1; Gary Becker, "The Economic Approach to Human Behavior," in Elster, *Rational Choice*, pp. 115, 119; and John C. Harsanyi, "Rational Choice Models of Political Behavior vs. Functionalist and Conformist

Theories," *World Politics*, Vol. 21, No. 4 (July 1969), pp. 513–538.

7. See David M. Kreps, *A Course in Microeconomic Theory* (Princeton, N.J.: Princeton University Press, 1990), p. 480; Elster, "Introduction," pp. 4,16; Sidney Verba, "Assumptions of Rationality and Non-Rationality in Models of the International System," *World Politics*, Vol. 14, No. 1 (October 1961), pp. 93–117; and Graham Allison and Philip Zelikow, *Essence of Decision: Explaining the Cuban Missile Crisis*, 2d ed. (New York: Longman, 1999), pp. 17–18.

8. Elster, "Introduction," p. 5; and Allison and Zelikow, *Essence of Decision*, p. 18.

9. See McCormick, "Terrorist Decision Making," p. 482; and Crenshaw, "Theories of Terrorism," pp. 15, 27.

10. McCormick, "Terrorist Decision Making," p. 481.

11. Crenshaw, "Theories of Terrorism," p. 16. See also Alex P. Schmid and Albert J. Jongman, *Political Terrorism* (Amsterdam: North-Holland, 1988), pp. 122–123.

12. See James G. March, *A Primer on Decision Making: How Decisions Happen* (New York: Free Press, 1994), pp. 2–3. See also Crenshaw, "The Logic of Terrorism," p. 20.

13. See Pape, *Dying to Win*, p. 62. See also Crenshaw, "Theories of Terrorism," p. 16; and Schmid and Jongman, *Political Terrorism*, pp. 122–123.

14. Crenshaw, "Theories of Terrorism," p. 15.

15. Sun-Ki Chai, "An Organizational Economics Theory of Antigovernment Violence," *Comparative Politics*, Vol. 26, No. 1 (October 1993), p. 100.

16. The strategic model focuses on strategic terrorism, not redemptive terrorism. The former aims to coerce a government into changing its policies, whereas the latter is intended solely to obtain specific human or material resources such as prisoners or money. On this distinction, see Abrahms, "Why Terrorism Does Not Work," p. 46.

17. Bonnie Cordes, Bruce Hoffman, Brian M. Jenkins, Konrad Kellen, Sue Moran, and William Sater, *Trends in International Terrorism, 1982 and 1983* (Santa Monica, Calif.: RAND, 1984), p. 49.

18. Crenshaw, "Theories of Terrorism," p. 15.

19. Thomas C. Schelling, "What Purposes Can 'International Terrorism' Serve?" in R. G. Frey and Christopher W. Morris, eds., *Violence, Terrorism, and Justice* (New York: Cambridge University Press, 1991), p. 20.

20. Abrahms, "Why Terrorism Does Not Work," pp. 42–78.

21. Proponents of the strategic model claim that terrorism is an effective coercive instrument. Yet their confirming examples are limited to successful guerrilla campaigns, which are directed against military and diplomatic—not civilian—targets. See, for example, Pape, *Dying to Win*, p. 39; and Kydd and Walter, "'The Strategies of Terrorism," p. 49. On the distinction between terrorist and guerrilla campaigns, see Abrahms, "Why Terrorism Does Not Work," pp. 44–46.

22. Walter Laqueur, *Terrorism* (Boston: Little, Brown, 1977), p. 117.

23. Peter R. Neumann and Mike Smith, "Strategic Terrorism: The Framework and Its Fallacies," *Journal of Strategic Studies*, Vol. 28, No. 4 (August 2005), p. 587.

24. See, for example, John Mueller, *Overblown: How Politicians and the Terrorism Industry Inflate National Security Threats, and Why We Believe Them* (New York: Free Press, 2006), p. 184; and Claude Berrebi and Esteban F. Klor, "On Terrorism and Electoral Outcomes: Theory and Evidence from the Israeli-Palestinian Conflict," *Journal of Conflict Resolution*, Vol. 50, No. 6 (Spring 2006), pp. 899–925.

25. See, for example, Alan B. Krueger, *What Makes a Terrorist: Economics and the Roots of Terrorism* (Princeton, N.J.: Princeton University Press, 2007), pp. 130–131; and Christopher Hewitt, *Consequences of Political Violence* (Sudbury, Mass.: Dartmouth, 1993), pp. 80, 97–98.

26. See Ariel Merari, "Terrorism as a Strategy of Insurgency," *Terrorism and Political Violence*, Vol. 5,

No. 4 (Winter 1993), p. 229; Richardson, *What Terrorists Want*, p. 75; and Martha Crenshaw, "How Terrorists Think: What Psychology Can Contribute to Understanding Terrorism," in Lawrence Howard, ed., *Terrorism: Roots, Impact, Responses* (New York: Praeger, 1992), p. 75.

27. See McCormick, "Terrorist Decision Making," p. 483; Crenshaw, "How Terrorists Think," p. 72; and DeNardo, *Power in Numbers*, p. 242.

28. Crenshaw, "How Terrorists Think," p. 71.

29. See, for example, William L. Eubank and Leonard B. Weinberg, "Does Democracy Encourage Terrorism?" *Terrorism and Political Violence*, Vol. 6, No. 4 (Winter 1994), pp. 417–443; and Leonard B. Weinberg and William L. Eubank, "Terrorism and Democracy: What Recent Events Disclose," *Terrorism and Political Violence*, Vol. 10, No. 1 (Spring 1998), pp. 108–118. See also Laqueur, *Terrorism*, p. 220.

30. Bonnie Cordes, "When Terrorists Do the Talking: Reflections on Terrorist Literature," in Rapoport, *Inside Terrorist Organizations*, p. 150. See also Walter Laqueur, "Interpretations of Terrorism: Fact, Fiction, and Political Science," *Journal of Contemporary History*, Vol. 12, No. 1 (January 1977), p. 1.

31. Laqueur, "Interpretations of Terrorism," p. 1; and Laqueur, *Terrorism*, p. 80.

32. Donatella Della Porta and Sidney Tarrow, "Unwanted Children: Political Violence and the Cycle of Protest in Italy, 1966–1973," *European Journal of Political Research*, Vol. 14, Nos. 5–6 (November 1986), p. 616. See also Peter H. Merkl, ed., *Political Violence and Terror: Motifs and Motivations* (Los Angeles: University of California Press, 1986), p. 146.

33. Della Porta and Tarrow, "Unwanted Children," pp. 14, 53.

34. Paul Wilkinson, *Terrorism versus Democracy: The Liberal State Response* (London: Frank Cass, 2000), p. 59.

35. Examples of the first point include the dozens of United States- and European-based Marxist terrorist organizations from the late 1960s to the late 1980s, such as Action Directe, the Communist Combatant Cells, the RAF, the Red Brigades, and the Weather Underground. Examples of the second point, including terrorist organizations overtly aligned with a "parent" political wing, are Aum Shinrikyo, the Communist Party of Nepal, the Communist Party of the Philippines, Dev Sol, ETA, Fatah, Hamas, Harakat ul-Mujahidin, Hezbollah, the IRA, the Japanese Red Army, Kach, the PKK, the Revolutionary Armed Forces of Colombia, and the Revolutionary United Front. On the relationship between terrorist organizations and political parties, see Leonard Weinberg and Ami Pedahzur, *Political Parties and Terrorist Groups* (London: Routledge, 2003).

36. See Maria Stephan and Erica Chenoweth, "Does Terrorism Work? Comparing Strategies of Asymmetric Warfare," presentation to the Centre for Defence Studies, King's College, London, March 2007. See also Crenshaw, "How Terrorists Think," p. 71; and Laqueur, "Interpretations of Terrorism," p. 1.

37. Crenshaw, "How Terrorists Think," p. 72.

38. Bruce Hoffman, *Inside Terrorism* (New York: Columbia University Press, 1998), p. 174; and Audrey Kurth Cronin, "How al-Qaida Ends: The Decline and Demise of Terrorist Groups," *International Security*, Vol. 31, No. 1 (Summer 2006), p. 11. See also Laqueur, *Terrorism*, p. 119.

39. Hoffman, *Inside Terrorism*, p. 128.

40. Martha Crenshaw, "An Organizational Approach to the Analysis of Political Terrorism," *Orbis*, Vol. 29, No. 3 (Fall 1985), p. 481.

41. See Andrew Kydd and Barbara F. Walter, "Sabotaging the Peace: The Politics of Extremist Violence," *International Organization*, Vol. 56, No. 2 (Spring 2002), pp. 263–296. See also Stephen John Stedman, "Spoiler Problems in Peace Processes," *International Security*, Vol. 22, No. 2 (Fall 1997), pp. 5–53.

42. Wilkinson, *Terrorism versus Democracy*, p. 59.

43. See, for example, David A. Lake, "Rational Extremism: Understanding Terrorism in the Twenty-first Century," *Dialog-IO*, Vol. 1, No. 1 (Spring 2002), pp. 15–29.

44. Anthony Oberschall, "Explaining Terrorism: The Contribution of Collective Action Theory," *Sociological Theory*, Vol. 22, No. 1 (March 2004), p. 26. On the types of political demands that terrorist organizations make, see Abrahms, "Why Terrorism Does Not Work," pp. 53–54.

45. Laqueur, *Terrorism*, p. 37.

46. Pape, *Dying to Win*, p. 43.

47. See Dennis Ross, *The Missing Peace: The Inside Story of the Fight for Middle East Peace* (New York Farrar, Straus and Giroux, 2004). See also Robert Malley, "Israel and the Arafat Question," *New York Review of Books*, Vol. 51, No. 15 (October 7, 2004), pp. 19–23.

48. See DeNardo, *Power in Numbers*, p. 90; and Navin A. Bapat, "State Bargaining with Transnational Terrorist Groups," *International Studies Quarterly*, Vol. 50, No. 1 (March 2006), p. 214. For a seminal work on compromise from a rationalist bargaining perspective, see Robert Powell, "Bargaining Theory and International Conflict," *Annual Review of Political Science*, Vol. 5 (June 2002), pp. 1–30.

49. See James D. Fearon, "Rationalist Explanations for War," *International Organization*, Vol. 49, No. 3 (Summer 1995), pp. 382, 390; and Robert Powell, "War as a Commitment Problem," *International Organization*, Vol. 60, No. 1 (Winter 2006), pp. 176–178, 180. For a contrarian perspective on issue indivisibility, see Monica Duffy Toft, "Issue Indivisibility and Time Horizons as Rationalist Explanations for War," *Security Studies*, Vol. 15, No. 1 (January–March 2006), pp. 34–69.

50. See Crenshaw, "Theories of Terrorism," p. 20. See also Cordes et al., *Trends in International Terrorism*, p. 50.

51. Quoted in Crenshaw, "Theories of Terrorism," p. 20.

52. Ely Karmon, *Coalitions between Terrorist Organizations: Revolutionaries, Nationalists, and Islamists* (Leiden, The Netherlands: Koninkliijke Brill, 2005), p. 141.

53. For an excellent recent study on al-Qaida's protean nature, see Vahid Brown, "Cracks in the Foundation: Leadership Schisms in al-Qaida from 1989–2006," CTC Report (West Point, N.Y.: Combating Terrorism Center, September 2007), p. 2.

54. Jessica Stern, "The Protean Enemy," *Foreign Affairs*, Vol. 82, No. 4 (July/August 2003), p. 1.

55. Samuel R. Berger and Mona Sutphen, "Commandeering the Palestinian Cause: Bin Laden's Belated Concern," in James F. Hoge Jr. and Gideon Rose, eds., *How Did This Happen? Terrorism and the New War* (New York: Public Affairs, 2001), p. 123.

56. Quoted in Brown, "Cracks in the Foundation," p. 10.

57. Omar Nasiri, *Inside the Jihad: My Life with Al Qaeda, A Spy's Story* (New York: Basic Books, 2006), p. 295.

58. Cronin, "How al-Qaida Ends," pp. 41–42.

59. Crenshaw, "An Organizational Approach to the Analysis of Political Terrorism," p. 71.

60. See Ami Pedahzur, *Suicide Terrorism* (Cambridge: Polity, 2005), pp. 87, 89. See also Mia Bloom, *Dying to Kill: The Allure of Suicide Terror* (New York: Columbia University Press, 2005), p. 112.

61. Walter Laqueur, *The Age of Terrorism* (Boston: Little, Brown, 1987), pp. 287–288.

62. Leonard Weinberg, *Global Terrorism: A Beginner's Guide* (Oxford: Oneworld, 2005), p. 83.

63. Laqueur, *The Age of Terrorism*, p. 205.

64. Bruce Hoffman, "Right-Wing Terrorism in West Germany," No. P-7270 (Santa Monica, Calif.: RAND, 1986), pp. 8–15.

65. Pape, *Dying to Win*, p. 29; and Kydd and Walter, "Strategies of Terrorism," p. 50.

66. Robert J. Art and Patrick M. Cronin, eds., *The United States and Coercive Diplomacy* (Washington, D.C: United States Institute of Peace Press, 2003), p. 371.

67. Author's calculations from RAND's MIPT data set, http://www.tkb.org.

68. See Pedahzur, *Suicide Terrorism*, pp. 114–115.

69. See Eqbal Ahmad, "Comprehending Terror," *MERIP*, No. 140 (May–June 1986), p. 3; and Bonnie Cordes, "Euroterrorists Talk about Themselves: A Look at the Literature," in Paul

Wilkinson and Alasdair M. Stewart, eds., *Contemporary Research on Terrorism* (Aberdeen, Scotland: Aberdeen University Press, 1987), p. 331.

70. Shelling, "What Purposes Can 'International Terrorism' Serve?", p. 24.

71. Bruce Hoffman, "Why Terrorists Don't Claim Credit," *Terrorism and Political Violence*, Vol. 9, No. 1 (Spring 1997), p. 1. See also Mark Juergensmeyer, "The Logic of Religious Violence," in Rapoport, *Inside Terrorist Organizations*, p. 172.

72. Lake, "Rational Extremism," p. 15.

73. Shri D. R. Kaarthikeyan, "Root Causes of Terrorism? A Case Study of the Tamil Insurgency and the LTTE," in Tore Bjorgo, ed., *Root Causes of Terrorism: Myths, Reality, and Ways Forward* (New York: Routledge, 2006), p. 134.

74. Pape, *Dying to Win*, pp. 139–140.

75. Pedahzur, *Suicide Terrorism*, pp. 81–82.

76. Martha Crenshaw, ed., *Terrorism in Context* (University Park: Penn State University Press, 1995), p. 483.

77. Benjamin Stora, *Algeria, 1830–2000: A Short History*, trans. Jane Marie Todd (Ithaca, N.Y.: Cornell University Press, 2001), p. 59.

78. Crenshaw, *Terrorism in Context*, p. 484.

79. Pedahzur, *Suicide Terrorism*, p. 44. See also Jonathan Schanzer, "Palestinian Uprisings Compared," *Middle East Quarterly*, Vol. 9, No. 3 (Summer 2002), pp. 27–38; and Peter H. Merkl, "Approaches to the Study of Political Violence," in Merkl, *Political Violence and Terror*, p. 45.

80. Ann Scott Tyson, "Attacks in Iraq Continue to Decline," *Washington Post*, October 31, 2007; and Anthony H. Cordesman, "Still Losing? The June 2007 Edition of 'Measuring Stability in Iraq,'" Working Paper (Washington, D.C: Center for Strategic and International Studies, June 20, 2007), http://www.thewashingtonnote.com/archives/IraqStab&Security06-20%5B1%5D.htm.

81. See Bruce Hoffman and Gordon H. McCormick, "Terrorism, Signaling, and Suicide Attack," *Studies in Conflict and Terrorism*, Vol. 27, No. 4 (July

2004), p. 252, See also Crenshaw, "Theories of Terrorism," p. 16.

82. Pape, *Dying to Win*, pp. 63–64.

83. Abrahms, "Why Terrorism Does Not Work," p. 47. See also Martha Crenshaw, "How Terrorism Declines," in Clark McCauley, ed., *Terrorism Research and Public Policy* (London: Frank Cass, 1991), p. 79.

84. Erik Gartzke, "War Is in the Error Term," *International Organization*, Vol. 53, No. 3 (Summer 1999), p. 573.

85. James D. Fearon, "Why Do Some Civil Wars Last So Much Longer than Others?" *Journal of Peace Research*, Vol. 41, No. 3 (May 2004), p. 290. See also Branislav L. Slantchev, "The Power to Hurt: Costly Conflict with Completely Informed States," *American Political Science Review*, Vol. 97, No. 1 (February 2003), p. 123.

86. Loren E. Lomasky, "The Political Significance of Terrorism," in Frey and Morris, *Violence, Terrorism, and Justice*, p. 90.

87. See Pape, *Dying to Win*, p. 94.

88. See Crenshaw, "How Terrorism Ends," p. 80. See also Martha Crenshaw, "The Causes of Terrorism," *Comparative Politics*, Vol. 13, No. 4 (July 1981), p. 397.

89. Pape, *Dying to Win*, p. 109.

90. Klaus Wasmund, "The Political Socialization of West German Terrorists," in Merkl, *Political Violence and Terror*, p. 221. See also Hoffman, *Inside Terrorism*, p. 179.

91. *The 9/11 Commission Report: Final Report of the National Commission on Terrorist Attacks upon the United States* (New York: W. W. Norton, 2004), p. 56.

92. Richardson, *What Terrorists Want*, p. 14. See also Marc Sageman, *Understanding Terror Networks* (Philadelphia: University of Pennsylvania Press, 2004), p. 81.

93. Karen Rasler, "Review Symposium: Understanding Suicide Terror," *Perspectives on Politics*, Vol. 5, No. 1 (February 2007), p. 118. See also Krueger, *What Makes a Terrorist*, p. x.

94. See Christopher Hewitt, *Understanding Terrorism in America: From the Klan to al-Qaida* (London: Routledge, 2003), p. 57. See also Krueger, *What Makes a Terrorist*, p. 71.

95. In the select cases where terrorism scholars have explicitly employed a variant of organization theory, they invariably present it as a secondary lens to complement—not contest—the strategic model. See, for example, Bloom, *Dying to Kill*, p. 3; Richardson, *What Terrorists Want*, p. 79; and Pedahzur, *Suicide Terrorism*, pp. 11, 25.

96. See Charles Perrow, *Complex Organizations: A Critical Essay* (Glenview, Ill.: Scott, Foresman, 1972), p, 75; and Pfeffer, *Organizations and Organization Theory*, p. 72.

97. Gibson Burrell and Gareth Morgan, *Sociological Paradigms and Organisational Analysis* (London: Heinemann, 1988), p. 149; Paul S. Goodman and Johannes M. Pennings, eds., *New Perspectives on Organizational Effectiveness* (London: Jossey-Bass, 1981), p. 3; and W. Richard Scott, "Effectiveness of Organizational Effectiveness Studies," in Goodman and Pennings, *New Perspectives on Organizational Effectiveness*, p. 75.

98. Chester I. Barnard, *The Functions of the Executive* (Cambridge, Mass.: Harvard University Press, 1938), pp. 17, 85, 145–146, 148.

99. Ibid., pp. 145–146, 148. See also W. Richard Scott, *Organizations: Rational Natural, and Open Systems*, 3d ed. (Englewood Cliffs, N.J.: Prentice Hall, 1992), pp. 5, 51; and Walter W. Powell, "Expanding the Scope of Institutional Analysis," in Walter W. Powell and Paul J. DiMaggio, eds., *The New Institutionalism in Organizational Analysis* (Chicago: University of Chicago Press, 1991), p. 183.

100. See David M. Austin, "The Political Economy of Social Benefit Organizations: Redistributive Services and Merit Goods," in Herman D. Stein, ed., *Organization and the Human Services: Cross-Disciplinary Reflections* (Philadelphia: Temple University Press, 1981), p. 170, See also David L. Clark, "Emerging Paradigms: In Organizational Theory and Research," in Yvonna S. Lincoln, ed., *Organizational Theory and Inquiry: The Paradigm Revolution* (Beverly Hills, Calif.: Sage, 1985), p. 59.

101. See Jeff Victoroff, "The Mind of the Terrorist: A Review and Critique of Psychological Approaches," *Journal of Conflict Resolution*, Vol. 49, No. 1 (February 2005), p. 34.

102. Melvin Seeman, "Alienation and Engagement," in Angus Campbell and Philip E. Converse, eds., *The Human Meaning of Social Change* (New York: Russell Sage, 1972), pp. 472–473.

103. For research on the prevalence of these demographic characteristics in a wide variety of terrorist organizations, see Pedahzur, *Suicide Terrorism*, pp. 151–152; Alex P. Schmid, "Why Terrorism? Root Causes, Some Empirical Findings, and the Case of 9/11," presentation to the Council of Europe, Strasbourg, France, April 26–27, 2007, p. 12; Ariel Merari, "Social, Organizational, and Psychological Factors in Suicide Terrorism," in Bjorgo, *Root Causes of Terrorism*, p. 75; Sageman, *Understanding Terror Networks*, p. 95; Rex A. Hudson, "The Sociology and Psychology of Terrorism" (Washington, D.C.: Federal Research Division, Library of Congress, September 1999); Charles A. Russell and Bowman A. Miller, "Profile of a Terrorist," in John D. Elliott and Leslie K. Gibson, eds., *Contemporary Terrorism: Selected Readings* (Gaithersburg, Md.: International Association of Chiefs of Police, 1978), pp. 81–95; and Stern, "The Protean Enemy," p. 6. In Sageman's sample, many of the jihadists are married, but most researchers believe that the jihadist population is overwhelmingly single.

104. Sageman, *Understanding Terror Networks*, p. 92. See also Olivier Roy, "Terrorism and Deculturation," in Louise Richardson, ed., *The Roots of Terrorism* (New York: Routledge, 2006), pp. 159–160; Stern, "The Protean Enemy," p. 7; and *The 9/11 Commission Report*, p. 231.

105. See Roy, "Terrorism and Deculturation," p. 166.

106. Albert Bandura, "Psychological Mechanisms of Aggression," in Mario von Cranach, ed., *Human*

Ethology: Claims and Limits of a New Discipline (Cambridge: Cambridge University Press, 1979). Proponents of the strategic model reject the idea that individuals turn to terrorism because they are socially alienated; their evidence, ironically, is that people who join a terrorist organization are sometimes embraced, even celebrated, by their surrounding communities. See, for example, Pape, *Dying to Win*, chap, 10.

107. See, for example, Schmid, "Why Terrorism?" p. 11; Robert W. White, "Political Violence by the Nonaggrieved," in Donatella Della Porta, ed., *International Social Movement Research*, Vol. 4 (Greenwich, Conn.: Jai Press, 1992), p. 92; Wasmund, "The Political Socialization of West German Terrorists," pp. 209–212; Hudson, "The Sociology and Psychology of Terrorism," p. 37; and Richard G. Braungart and Margaret M. Braungart, "From Protest to Terrorism: The Case of the SDS and the Weathermen," in Della Porta, *International Social Movement Research*, p. 73.

108. See Schmid, "Why Terrorism?" p. 11.

109. See, for example, White, "Political Violence by the Nonaggrieved," p. 93; Jerrold M. Post, Ehud Sprinzak, and Laurita M. Denny, "The Terrorists in Their Own Words: Interviews with 35 Incarcerated Middle Eastern Terrorists," *Terrorism and Political Violence*, Vol. 15, No. 1 (March 2003), pp. 171–184; Sageman, *Understanding Terror Networks*, p. 92; and Schmid, "Why Terrorism?" p. 11.

110. Joseph Felter and Jarret Brachman, "An Assessment of 516 Combatant Status Review Tribunal Unclassified Summaries," CTC Report (West Point, N.Y: Combating Terrorism Center, July 15, 2007), pp. 24–25, 34.

111. For discussion of the fundamental problem of specificity in terrorism studies, see Sageman, *Understanding Terror Networks*, chap. 4. See also Weinberg, *Global Terrorism*, p. 82.

112. See, for example, Hudson, "The Sociology and Psychology of Terrorism," p. 148; Sageman, *Understanding Terror Networks*, p. 95; Merkl, "Approaches to the Study of Political Violence,"

p. 42; Jerrold M. Post, "The Socio-cultural Underpinnings of Terrorist Psychology: 'When Hatred Is Bred in the Bone,'" in Bjorgo, *Root Causes of Terrorism*, p. 55; *The 9/11 Commission Report*, p. 231; and Braungart and Braungart, "From Protest to Terrorism," p. 68.

113. The studies on suicide terrorists devote extra attention to this point. One explanation for why suicide terrorists appear relatively apolitical is that organization leaders prefer expending members with no prior connection to the organization or its political cause. See Pedahzur, *Suicide Terrorism*, pp. 126, 131–133, 152–154. See also Sageman, *Understanding Terror Networks*, pp. 93, 135.

114. White, "Political Violence by the Nonaggrieved," p. 83. See also Christopher Dobson and Ronald Payne, *The Terrorists: Their Weapons, Leaders, and Tactics* (New York: Facts on File, 1981), p. 32.

115. Roy, "Terrorism and Deculturation," pp. 159–160; Mia Bloom, "The Transformation of Suicide Bombing Campaigns: Sectarian Violence and Recruitment in Pakistan, Afghanistan, and Iraq," paper presented at the "Terrorist Organizations: Social Science Research on Terrorism" conference, University of California, San Diego, May 4, 2007; and Nasiri, *Inside the Jihad*, p. 279.

116. Richardson, *What Terrorists Want*, pp. 85–86. See also Laqueur, *Terrorism*, p, 81.

117. Quoted in Richardson, *What Terrorists Want*, pp. 86–87.

118. Cronin, "How al-Qaida Ends," p. 23. See also Hoffman, *Inside Terrorism*, p. 172.

119. That terrorist members often appear uninterested and uninformed regarding their organization's official political agenda is actually not surprising. Terrorists—be it al-Qaida operatives, Red Brigadists, RAF members, the Weathermen, or the Tupamaros of Uruguay—have rarely hailed from the constituencies they claim to represent; many terrorist organizations do not train or indoctrinate their members in any ideology; and terrorists are often "walk-ins" who have no prior association with the terrorist organization or its political cause before volunteering for an operation. See *The 9/11*

Commission Report, pp. 228, 232; Dipak K. Gupta, "Exploring Roots of Terrorism," in Bjorgo, *Root Causes of Terrorism*, p. 19; Pedahzur, *Suicide Terrorism*, pp. 132–133; Crenshaw, *Terrorism in Context*, p. 15; and Crenshaw, "How Terrorists Think," p. 73.

120. Pedahzur, *Suicide Terrorism*, pp. 137–138, 168.

121. Merkl, *Political Violence and Terror*, p. 42.

122. Gregory Johnsen, "Securing Yemen's Cooperation in the Second Phase of the War on al-Qa'ida," *CTC Sentinel*, Vol. 1, No. 1 (December 2007), p. 34.

123. Crenshaw, "How Terrorists Think," p. 73; and Crenshaw, "The Psychology of Political Terrorism," in M. G. Hermann, ed., *Political Psychology: Contemporary Problems and Issues* (San Francisco, Calif.: Jossey-Bass, 1986), p. 394. See also Shira Fishman, "Perceptions of Closeness as a Function of Group Importance," University of Maryland, 2007.

124. See Richardson, *What Terrorists Want*, p. 301; Bloom, *Dying to Kill*, pp. 19, 39; and Hoffman, *Inside Terrorism*, pp. 73–75.

125. Jacob N. Shapiro, "The Terrorist's Challenge: Security, Efficiency, Control," paper presented at the "Terrorist Organizations: Social Science Research on Terrorism" conference.

126. Stem, *Terror in the Name of God*, p. 5.

127. Nasiri, *Inside the Jihad*, pp. 151, 178, 217.

128. David C. Rapoport, "The Fourth Wave: September 11 in the History of Terrorism," *Current History*, Vol. 100, No. 650 (December 2001), pp. 419–424. See also David C. Rapoport, "Generations and Waves: The Keys to Understanding Rebel Terror Movements," paper presented at the "Seminar on Global Affairs," Ronald W. Burkie Center for International Affairs, University of California, Los Angeles, November 7, 2003, http://www.international.ucla.edu/cms/files/David_Rapoport_Waves_of_Terrorism.pdf.

129. Cronin's superb study identifies seven reasons why terrorist organizations have historically gone out of business. More terrorist organizations suffered from the failure to make the "generational transition" than from any of the other six reasons explored. It should be noted that Cronin does not purport to categorize the universe of terrorist groups. See Cronin, "How al-Qaida Ends," p. 19.

130. The tendency for terrorist organizations to issue protean political demands may dissuade target countries from making policy concessions. See Paul Wilkinson, "Security Challenges in the New Reality," paper presented at the 33d IFPA-Fletcher Conference on National Security Strategy and Policy, Washington, D.C., October 16, 2002, http://www.ifpafletcherconference.com/oldtranscripts/2002/wilkinson.htm.

131. For a similar argument unrelated to terrorist motivations, see Jeffrey Pfeffer, "Usefulness of the Concept," in Goodman and Pennings, *New Perspectives on Organizational Effectiveness*, p. 137. On revealed preferences, see Amartya Sen, "Behaviour and the Concept of Preference," in Elster, *Rational Choice*, pp. 61, 67.

132. In this way, the role of social solidarity is very different in terrorist organizations than in conventional armies. In the military, training is designed to foster in-group cohesion not as the end goal, but as a means to enhance battlefield performance. Unlike terrorist organizations, conventional armies therefore do not regularly sacrifice their political goals for the social benefit of the fighting unit. On the complementary relationship between small unit cohesion and military performance, see James Griffith, "Institutional Motives for Serving in the U.S. Army National Guard," *Armed Forces and Society*, Vol. 20, No. 10 (May 2007), pp. 1–29; and Guy L. Siebold, "The Essence of Military Group Cohesion," *Armed Forces and Society*, Vol. 33, No. 2 (January 2007), pp. 286–295.

133. See Martha Crenshaw, *Terrorism, Legitimacy, and Power: The Consequences of Political Violence* (Middletown, Conn.: Wesleyan University Press, 1983), p. 10.

134. Quoted in Alan M. Dershowitz, *Why Terrorism Works: Understanding the Threat, Responding to the Challenge* (New Haven, Conn.: Yale University Press, 2002), p. 17.

135. Laqueur, *Terrorism*, p. 5.

136. See George W. Bush, "President Discusses War on Terror," National Defense University, Washington, D.C., March 8, 2005, http://www.whitehouse.gov/news/releases/2005/03/20050308-3.html.

137. For a useful primer on SNA, see Patrick Radden Keefe, "Can Network Theory Thwart Terrorists?" *New York Times*, March 12, 2006. See also

Sageman, *Understanding Terror Networks*, pp. 163, 169, 178.

138. See Bruce Hoffman, "Foreword," in Cindy C. Combs, *Twenty-first Century Terrorism* (New York: Prentice Hall, 1996), pp. v–18.

139. F. Gregory Gause III, "Can Democracy Stop Terrorism?" *Foreign Affairs*, Vol. 84, No. 5 (September/October 2005), pp. 62–76.

8

ADVANCED DEMOCRACIES

This chapter explores some of the aspects and challenges of advanced democracies, countries that have stable democratic regimes, a high level of economic development, and extensive civil rights and liberties. It focuses specifically on three questions:

1. What enables advanced democracies to emerge and thrive?
2. How do institutional differences among advanced democracies affect their politics and policies?
3. Can advanced democracies continue to promote equality—for example, through generous welfare states—in the twenty-first century?

By many measures, the United States was the first advanced democracy. Universal male suffrage—albeit almost always restricted to free white males—had been enacted by the 1830s in almost all U.S. states, whereas in Britain, even the 1832 Reform Act extended the franchise to only about one in five adult males. Institutionalization was advanced, and per capita income (according to the economic historian Angus Maddison) already exceeded that of contemporary France. The liberal French nobleman, intellectual, and politician Alexis de Tocqueville visited the United States in 1831 and set out to explain to his European compatriots why and how American democracy worked. He came to two firm conclusions, well set out in his own introduction to his 1835 classic, *Democracy in America*: (1) social equality led inevitably to democracy; and (2) equality, at least in Europe and America, was everywhere increasing.

Tocqueville saw economic growth and prosperity as but one of the causes of social equalization, and thus of democracy. However, the sociologist and political scientist Seymour Martin Lipset, in his classic *Political Man* (1960), first perceived what is now taken as a commonplace: that although other factors still matter, richer countries are highly likely to be both more equal and more democratic. Wealth alone, through a series of processes that Lipset explored, leads normally to democracy.

Lipset's theory thus predicted that as countries become richer, they also become more democratic. But as Daron Acemoglu and his associates showed in "Income and Democracy" (2008), that seems not to be true, except in the very long run. The cross-sectional, or "snapshot," correlation between wealth and democracy is thus spurious: both wealth and democracy are caused by some other factor, most likely (these authors argue) earlier institutions and property rights.

If wealth led automatically to democracy, we might also expect democracy to be readily granted: much as our standard story of England has it, enlightened rulers would find it in their own interest to broaden the franchise step by step. And some theories in comparative politics model the development of democracy in exactly this way, whereas others (including that of Acemoglu) suggest that the vote would be extended only under threat of revolution. Adam Przeworski, in "Conquered or Granted?" (2008), finds strong evidence for the latter viewpoint: elites mostly granted democracy only under strong popular pressure, often including unrest (demonstrations, violence). To put things in present-day perspective, the Arab Spring (and such earlier transformations as the Czech Velvet Revolution) is more representative of democratic transitions in general than were the British or U.S. experiences.

As we saw in Chapter 5, democracies divide between "majoritarian" and "proportional" (PR) electoral systems. Advanced democracies also differ on this dimension: the United States, the United Kingdom, Canada, Australia, France, and Japan are majoritarian (or mostly so), whereas most of the other advanced democracies (including virtually all of the smaller ones) use PR. An interesting sidelight is that several of the advanced democracies have recently changed their electoral systems: France used PR for one election in 1986, then reverted to a majoritarian system; in the early 1990s Italy and Japan changed from mostly proportional systems to mostly majoritarian ones. At almost the same time, New Zealand replaced a "first-past-the-post" majoritarian system with PR, and Italy has since shifted back to a mostly PR system.

What are countries actually choosing when they adopt (or retain) one electoral system or another? As Chapter 5 emphasized, a majoritarian system normally (as in the United States) allows only two major parties to survive, whereas PR encourages a multiplicity of parties. This regularity is so powerful and has such strong causal properties that it is called, after its discoverer, Duverger's Law—one of the very few causal laws in political science. Duverger's original 1951 explanation of it has never really been surpassed, and its essence is presented here. Note particularly how Duverger shows that, in a majoritarian system, the rise of a new "third" party (e.g., Labour in Britain between 1900 and 1930) normally dooms the old "second" party (in this case, the Liberals) to insignificance, and how the introduction of PR has often rescued the declining second party from that fate.

Since Duverger, numerous studies have shown PR to have one other very important effect, this one on policy: PR is associated with much higher levels of welfare spending, greater redistribution of income, and hence greater equality. But why? Perhaps voters in PR countries just happen to prefer higher levels of welfare spending. As early as 2002, the comparativist Bingham Powell showed that this was unlikely to be true: rather, given identical voter preferences, majoritarian systems were likely to produce more right-wing (i.e., less redistributionist) policies, whereas paradoxically PR would more reliably produce the policy that voters (or, more precisely, the median voter) actually wanted, which generally entailed greater redistribution and welfare spending. In a yet more fundamental contribution, reproduced here in abridged form, Torben Iversen and David Soskice (2006) advanced powerful logic and evidence about how exactly this result came about: given identical voter preferences, a PR system was far likelier to produce a "center-left" coalition, a majoritarian one a "center-right" government, with the latter adopting far less redistributionist policies and lower levels of welfare expenditure. As they note, fully three-quarters of the governments chosen under PR systems in the postwar period have been center-left, whereas three-quarters of those elected under majoritarian systems have been center-right.[1]

We commonly imagine that generous welfare states curb incentives and slow economic growth. But, as their leading student Peter Lindert has shown, welfare states seem to be almost "a free lunch": they are *not* associated with slower growth or less efficiency.[2] A deeper reason that welfare states work, and may even make their societies *more* competitive, is suggested by Margarita Estévez-Abe and her coauthors in their contribution to the seminal *Varieties of Capitalism* (2001). Many of the most globally competitive economies, they suggest, depend on high-quality, specialized production that requires well-trained workers with firm- or sector-specific skills. They contend that workers will invest in acquiring those skills only if generous policies of social insurance buffer them against transient market downturns or permanent obsolescence. Hence generous welfare states (such as Sweden) tend to have workers with highly specialized skills, whereas less generous ones (such as the United States) have workforces with more general, transferable skills. As logical side effects, the generous welfare states are economically more equal and encourage greater achievement by less talented youth; paradoxically, the less redistributionist countries encourage greater gender equality.

NOTES

1. In a forthcoming book (*The Long Shadow of the Industrial Revolution: Political Geography and the Representation of the Left*), the Stanford political scientist Jonathan Rodden develops an elegant theory and much supporting evidence to explain this phenomenon: supporters of Left parties, in almost all countries, are heavily concentrated in industrial districts. Hence, even seemingly neutral drawing of district lines leaves Left parties with overwhelming majorities in relatively few districts, whereas parties of the Right win slimmer majorities in many districts. Hence the Left typically wins a smaller share of seats in majoritarian systems than it does of votes, whereas in PR systems its share of seats must closely reflect its share of the vote.

2. Peter Lindert, *Growing Public: Social Spending and Economic Growth since the Eighteenth Century*, 2 vols. (Cambridge: Cambridge University Press, 2004).

Alexis De Tocqueville
AUTHOR'S INTRODUCTION

Among the novel objects that attracted my attention during my stay in the United States, nothing struck me more forcibly than the general equality of condition among the people. I readily discovered the prodigious influence that this primary fact exercises on the whole course of society; it gives a peculiar direction to public opinion and a peculiar tenor to the laws; it imparts new maxims to the governing authorities and peculiar habits to the governed.

I soon perceived that the influence of this fact extends far beyond the political character and the laws of the country, and that it has no less effect on civil society than on the government; it creates opinions, gives birth to new sentiments, founds novel customs, and modifies whatever it does not produce. The more I advanced in the study of American society, the more I perceived that this equality of condition is the fundamental fact from which all others seem to be derived and the central point at which all my observations constantly terminated.

I then turned my thoughts to our own hemisphere, and thought that I discerned there something analogous to the spectacle which the New World presented to me. I observed that equality of condition, though it has not there reached the extreme limit which it seems to have attained in the United States, is constantly approaching it; and that the democracy which governs the American communities appears to be rapidly rising into power in Europe.

Hence I conceived the idea of the book that is now before the reader.

It is evident to all alike that a great democratic revolution is going on among us, but all do not look at it in the same light. To some it appears to be novel but accidental, and, as such, they hope it may still be checked; to others it seems irresistible, because it is the most uniform, the most ancient, and the most permanent tendency that is to be found in history.

I look back for a moment on the situation of France seven hundred years ago, when the territory was divided among a small number of families, who were the owners of the soil and the rulers of the inhabitants; the right of governing descended with the family inheritance from generation to generation; force was the only means by which man could act on man; and landed property was the sole source of power.

Soon, however, the political power of the clergy was founded and began to increase: the clergy opened their ranks to all classes, to the poor and the rich, the commoner and the noble; through the church, equality penetrated into the government, and he who as a serf must have vegetated in perpetual bondage took his place as a priest in the midst of nobles, and not infrequently above the heads of kings.

The different relations of men with one another became more complicated and numerous as society gradually became more stable and civilized. Hence the want of civil laws was felt; and the ministers of law soon rose from the obscurity of the tribunals and their dusty chambers to appear at the court of the monarch, by the side of the feudal barons clothed in their ermine and their mail.

While the kings were ruining themselves by their great enterprises, and the nobles exhausting their resources by private wars, the lower orders were enriching themselves by commerce. The influence of money began to be perceptible in state affairs. The transactions of business opened a new road to power, and the financier rose to a station of political influence in which he was at once flattered and despised.

From *Democracy in America* (New York: A. A. Knopf, 1945), pp. 3–16. Author's notes have been omitted.

Gradually enlightenment spread, a reawakening of taste for literature and the arts became evident; intellect and will contributed to success; knowledge became an attribute of government, intelligence a social force; the educated man took part in affairs of state.

The value attached to high birth declined just as fast as new avenues to power were discovered. In the eleventh century, nobility was beyond all price; in the thirteenth, it might be purchased. Nobility was first conferred by gift in 1270, and equality was thus introduced into the government by the aristocracy itself.

In the course of these seven hundred years it sometimes happened that the nobles, in order to resist the authority of the crown or to diminish the power of their rivals, granted some political power to the common people. Or, more frequently, the king permitted the lower orders to have a share in the government, with the intention of limiting the power of the aristocracy.

In France the kings have always been the most active and the most constant of levelers. When they were strong and ambitious, they spared no pains to raise the people to the level of the nobles; when they were temperate and feeble, they allowed the people to rise above themselves. Some assisted democracy by their talents, others by their vices. Louis XI and Louis XIV reduced all ranks beneath the throne to the same degree of subjection; and finally Louis XV descended, himself and all his court, into the dust.

As soon as land began to be held on any other than a feudal tenure, and personal property could in its turn confer influence and power, every discovery in the arts, every improvement in commerce of manufactures, created so many new elements of equality among men. Henceforward every new invention, every new want which it occasioned, and every new desire which craved satisfaction were steps towards a general leveling. The taste for luxury, the love of war, the rule of fashion, and the most superficial as well as the deepest passions of the human heart seemed to cooperate to enrich the poor and to impoverish the rich.

From the time when the exercise of the intellect became a source of strength and of wealth, we see that every addition to science, every fresh truth, and every new idea became a germ of power placed within the reach of the people. Poetry, eloquence, and memory, the graces of the mind, the fire of imagination, depth of thought, and all the gifts which Heaven scatters at a venture turned to the advantage of democracy; and even when they were in the possession of its adversaries, they still served its cause by throwing into bold relief the natural greatness of man. Its conquests spread, therefore, with those of civilization and knowledge; and literature became an arsenal open to all, where the poor and the weak daily resorted for arms.

In running over the pages of our history, we shall scarcely find a single great event of the last seven hundred years that has not promoted equality of condition.

The Crusades and the English wars decimated the nobles and divided their possessions: the municipal corporations introduced democratic liberty into the bosom of feudal monarchy; the invention of firearms equalized the vassal and the noble on the field of battle; the art of printing opened the same resources to the minds of all classes; the post brought knowledge alike to the door of the cottage and to the gate of the palace; and Protestantism proclaimed that all men are equally able to find the road to heaven. The discovery of America opened a thousand new paths to fortune and led obscure adventures to wealth and power.

If, beginning with the eleventh century, we examine what has happened in France from one half-century to another, we shall not fail to perceive that at the end of each of these periods a twofold revolution has taken place in the state of society. The noble has gone down the social ladder, and the commoner has gone up; the one descends as the other rises. Every half-century brings them nearer to each other, and they will soon meet.

Nor is this peculiar to France. Wherever we look, we perceive the same revolution going on throughout the Christian world.

The various occurrences of national existence have everywhere turned to the advantage of democracy: all men have aided it by their exertions, both those who have intentionally labored in its cause and those who have served it unwittingly; those who have fought for it and even those who have declared themselves its opponents have all been driven along in the same direction, have all labored to one end; some unknowingly and some despite themselves, all have been blind instruments in the hands of God.

The gradual development of the principle of equality is, therefore, a providential fact. It has all the chief characteristics of such a fact: it is universal, it is lasting, it constantly eludes all human interference, and all events as well as all men contribute to its progress.

Would it, then, be wise to imagine that a social movement the causes of which lie so far back can be checked by the efforts of one generation? Can it be believed that the democracy which has overthrown the feudal system and vanquished kings will retreat before tradesmen and capitalists? Will it stop now that it has grown so strong and its adversaries so weak?

Whither, then, are we tending? No one can say, for terms of comparison already fail us. There is greater equality of condition in Christian countries at the present day than there has been at any previous time, in any part of the world, so that the magnitude of what already has been done prevents us from foreseeing what is yet to be accomplished.

The whole book that is here offered to the public has been written under the influence of a kind of religious awe produced in the author's mind by the view of that irresistible revolution which has advanced for centuries in spite of every obstacle and which is still advancing in the midst of the ruins it has caused.

It is not necessary that God himself should speak in order that we may discover the unquestionable signs of his will. It is enough to ascertain what is the habitual course of nature and the constant tendency of events. I know, without special revelation, that the planets move in the orbits traced by the Creator's hand.

If the men of our time should be convinced, by attentive observation and sincere reflection, that the gradual and progressive development of social equality is at once the past and the future of their history, this discovery alone would confer upon the change the sacred character of a divine decree. To attempt to check democracy would be in that case to resist the will of God; and the nations would then be constrained to make the best of the social lot awarded to them by Providence.

The Christian nations of our day seem to me to present a most alarming spectacle; the movement which impels them is already so strong that it cannot be stopped, but it is not yet so rapid that it cannot be guided. Their fate is still in their own hands; but very soon they may lose control.

The first of the duties that are at this time imposed upon those who direct our affairs is to educate democracy, to reawaken, if possible, its religious beliefs; to purify its morals; to mold its actions; to substitute a knowledge of statecraft for its inexperience, and an awareness of its true interest for its blind instincts, to adapt its government to time and place, and to modify it according to men and to conditions. A new science of politics is needed for a new world.

This, however, is what we think of least; placed in the middle of a rapid stream, we obstinately fix our eyes on the ruins that may still be descried upon the shore we have left, while the current hurries us away and drags us backward towards the abyss.

In no country in Europe has the great social revolution that I have just described made such rapid progress as in France; but it has always advanced without guidance. The heads of the state have made no preparation for it, and it has advanced without their consent or without their knowledge. The most powerful, the most intelligent, and the most moral classes of the nation have never attempted to control it in order to guide it. Democracy has consequently been abandoned to its wild instincts, and it has grown up like those children who have no parental guidance, who receive their education in the public streets, and who are acquainted only with the vices and wretchedness of society. Its existence was seemingly unknown when suddenly it acquired supreme power. All then servilely submitted to its caprices; it was worshipped as the idol of strength; and when afterwards it was enfeebled by its own excesses, the legislator conceived the rash project of destroying it, instead of instructing it and correcting its vices. No attempt was made to fit it to govern, but all were bent on excluding it from the government.

The result has been that the democratic revolution has taken place in the body of society without that concomitant change in the laws, ideas, customs, and morals which was necessary to render such a revolution beneficial. Thus we have a democracy without anything to lessen its vices and bring out its natural advantages; and although we already perceive the evils it brings, we are ignorant of the benefits it may confer.

While the power of the crown, supported by the aristocracy, peaceably governed the nations of Europe, society, in the midst of its wretchedness, had several sources of happiness which can now scarcely be conceived or appreciated. The power of a few of his subjects was an insurmountable barrier to the tyranny of the prince; and the monarch, who felt the almost divine character which he enjoyed in the eyes of the multitude, derived a motive for the just use of his power from the respect which he inspired. The nobles, placed high as they were above the people, could take that calm and benevolent interest in their fate which the shepherd feels towards his flock; and without acknowledging the poor as their equals, they watched over the destiny of those whose welfare Providence had entrusted to their care. The people, never having conceived the idea of a social condition different from their own, and never expecting to become equal to their leaders, received benefits from them without discussing their rights. They became attached to them when they were clement and just and submitted to their exactions without resistance or servility, as to the inevitable visitations of the Deity. Custom and usage, more-

over, had established certain limits to oppression and founded a sort of law in the very midst of violence.

As the noble never suspected that anyone would attempt to deprive him of the privileges which he believed to be legitimate, and as the serf looked upon his own inferiority as a consequence of the immutable order of nature, it is easy to imagine that some mutual exchange of goodwill took place between two classes so differently endowed by fate. Inequality and wretchedness were then to be found in society, but the souls of neither rank of men were degraded.

Men are not corrupted by the exercise of power or debased by the habit of obedience, but by the exercise of a power which they believe to be illegitimate, and by obedience to a rule which they consider to be usurped and oppressive.

On the one side were wealth, strength, and leisure, accompanied by the pursuit of luxury, the refinements of taste, the pleasures of wit, and the cultivation of the arts; on the other were labor, clownishness, and ignorance. But in the midst of this coarse and ignorant multitude it was not uncommon to meet with energetic passions, generous sentiments, profound religious convictions, and wild virtues.

The social state thus organized might boast of its stability, its power, and, above all, its glory.

But the scene is now changed. Gradually the distinctions of rank are done away with; the barriers that once severed mankind are falling; property is divided, power is shared by many, the light of intelligence spreads, and the capacities of all classes tend towards equality. Society becomes democratic, and the empire of democracy is slowly and peaceably introduced into institutions and customs.

I can conceive of a society in which all men would feel an equal love and respect for the laws of which they consider themselves the authors; in which the authority of the government would be respected as necessary, and not divine; and in which the loyalty of the subject to the chief magistrate would not be a passion, but a quiet and rational persuasion. With every individual in the possession of rights which he is sure to retain, a kind of manly confidence and reciprocal courtesy would arise between all classes, removed alike from pride and servility. The people, well acquainted with their own true interests, would understand that, in order to profit from the advantages of the state, it is necessary to satisfy its requirements. The voluntary association of the citizens might then take the place of the individual authority of the nobles, and the community would be protected from tyranny and license.

I admit that, in a democratic state thus constituted, society would not be stationary. But the impulses of the social body might there be regulated and made progressive. If there were less splendor than in an aristocracy, misery would also be less prevalent; the pleasures of enjoyment might be less excessive, but those of comfort would be more general; the sciences might be less perfectly cultivated, but ignorance would be less common; the ardor of the feelings would be constrained, and the habits of the nation softened; there would be more vices and fewer crimes.

In the absence of enthusiasm and ardent faith, great sacrifices may be obtained from the members of a commonwealth by an appeal to their understanding and their experience; each individual will feel the same necessity of union with his fellows to protect his own weakness; and as he knows that he can obtain their help only on condition of helping them, he will readily perceive that his personal interest is identified with the interests of the whole community. The nation, taken as a whole, will be less brilliant, less glorious, and perhaps less strong; but the majority of the citizens will enjoy a greater degree of prosperity, and the people will remain peaceable, not because they despair of a change for the better, but because they are conscious that they are well off already.

If all the consequences of this state of things were not good or useful, society would at least have appropriated all such as were useful and good; and having once and forever renounced the social advantages of aristocracy, mankind would enter into possession of all the benefits that democracy can offer.

But here it may be asked what we have adopted in the place of those institutions, those ideas, and those customs of our forefathers which we have abandoned.

The spell of royalty is broken, but it has not been succeeded by the majesty of the laws. The people have learned to despise all authority, but they still fear it; and fear now extorts more than was formerly paid from reverence and love.

I perceive that we have destroyed those individual powers which were able, single-handed, to cope with tyranny; but it is the government alone that has inherited all the privileges of which families, guilds, and individuals have been deprived; to the power of a small number of persons, which if it was sometimes oppressive was often conservative, has succeeded the weakness of the whole community.

The division of property has lessened the distance which separated the rich from the poor; but it would seem that, the nearer they draw to each other, the greater is their mutual hatred and the more vehement the envy and the dread with which they resist each other's claims to power; the idea of right does not exist for either party, and force affords to both the only argument for the present and the only guarantee for the future.

The poor man retains the prejudices of his forefathers without their faith, and their ignorance without their virtues; he has adopted the doctrine of self-interest as the rule of his actions without understanding the science that puts it to use; and his selfishness is no less blind than was formerly his devotion to others.

If society is tranquil, it is not because it is conscious of its strength and its well-being, but because it fears its weakness and its infirmities; a single effort may cost it its life. Everybody feels the evil, but no one has courage or energy enough to seek the cure. The desires, the repinings, the sorrows, and the joys of the present time lead to nothing visible or permanent, like the passions of old men, which terminate in impotence.

We have, then, abandoned whatever advantages the old state of things afforded, without receiving any compensation from our present condition; we have destroyed an aristocracy, and we seem inclined to survey its ruins with complacency and to accept them.

The phenomena which the intellectual world presents are not less deplorable. The democracy of France, hampered in its course or abandoned to its lawless passions, has overthrown whatever crossed its path and has shaken all that it has not destroyed. Its empire has not been gradually introduced or peaceably established, but it has constantly advanced in the midst of the disorders and the agitations of a conflict. In the heat of the struggle each partisan is hurried beyond the natural limits of his opinions by the doctrines and the excesses of his opponents, until he loses sight of the end of his exertions, and holds forth in a way which does not correspond to his real sentiments or secret instincts. Hence arises the strange confusion that we are compelled to witness.

I can recall nothing in history more worthy of sorrow and pity than the scenes which are passing before our eyes. It is as if the natural bond that unites the opinions of man to his tastes, and his actions to his principles, was now broken; the harmony that has always been observed between the feelings and the ideas of mankind appears to be dissolved and all the laws of moral analogy to be abolished.

Zealous Christians are still found among us, whose minds are nurtured on the thoughts that pertain to a future life, and who readily espouse the cause of human liberty as the source of all moral greatness. Christianity, which has declared that all men are equal in the sight of God, will not refuse to acknowledge that all citizens are equal in the eye of the law. But, by a strange coincidence of events, religion has been for a time entangled with those institutions which democracy destroys; and it is not infrequently brought to reject the equality which it loves, and to curse as a foe that cause of liberty whose efforts it might hallow by its alliance.

By the side of these religious men I discern others whose thoughts are turned to earth rather than to heaven. These are the partisans of liberty, not only as the source of the noblest virtues, but more especially as the root of all solid advantages; and they sincerely desire to secure its authority, and to impart its blessings to mankind. It is natural that they should hasten to invoke the assistance of religion, for they must know that liberty cannot be established without morality, nor morality without faith. But they have seen religion in the ranks of their adversaries, and they inquire no further; some of them attack it openly, and the rest are afraid to defend it.

In former ages slavery was advocated by the venal and slavish-minded, while the independent and the warm-hearted were struggling without hope to save the liberties of mankind. But men of high and generous character are now to be met with, whose opinions are directly at variance with their inclinations, and who praise that servility and meanness which they have themselves never known. Others, on the contrary, speak of liberty as if they were able to feel its sanctity and its majesty, and loudly claim for humanity those rights which they have always refused to acknowledge.

There are virtuous and peaceful individuals whose pure morality, quiet habits, opulence, and talents fit them to be the leaders of their fellow men. Their love of country is sincere, and they are ready to make the greatest sacrifices for its welfare. But civilization often finds them among its opponents; they confound its abuses with its benefits, and the idea of evil is inseparable in their minds from that of novelty.

Near these I find others whose object is to materialize mankind, to hit upon what is expedient without heeding what is just, to acquire knowledge without faith, and prosperity apart from virtue; claiming to be the champions of modern civilization, they place themselves arrogantly at its head, usurping a place which is abandoned to them, and of which they are wholly unworthy.

Where are we, then?

The religionists are the enemies of liberty, and the friends of liberty attack religion; the high-minded and the noble advocate bondage, and the meanest and most servile preach independence; honest and enlightened citizens are opposed to all progress, while men without patriotism and without principle put themselves forward as the apostles of civilization and intelligence.

Has such been the fate of the centuries which have preceded our own? and has man always inhabited a world like the present, where all things are not in their proper relationships, where virtue is without genius, and genius without honor; where the love of order is confused with a taste for oppression, and the holy cult of freedom with a contempt of law; where the light thrown by conscience on human actions is dim, and where nothing seems to be any longer forbidden or allowed, honorable or shameful, false or true?

I cannot believe that the Creator made man to leave him in an endless struggle with the intellectual wretchedness that surrounds us. God destines a calmer and a more certain future to the communities of Europe. I am ignorant of his designs, but I shall not cease to believe in them because I cannot fathom them, and I had rather mistrust my own capacity than his justice.

There is one country in the world where the great social revolution that I am speaking of seems to have nearly reached its natural limits. It has been effected with ease and simplicity; say rather that this country is reaping the fruits of the democratic revolution which we are undergoing, without having had the revolution itself.

The emigrants who colonized the shores of America in the beginning of the seventeenth century somehow separated the democratic principle from all the principles that it had to contend with in the old communities of Europe, and transplanted it alone to the New World. It has there been able to spread in perfect freedom and peaceably to determine the character of the laws by influencing the manners of the country.

It appears to me beyond a doubt that, sooner or later, we shall arrive, like the Americans, at an almost complete equality of condition. But I do not conclude from this that we shall ever be necessarily led to draw the same political consequences which the Americans have derived from a similar social organization. I am far from supposing that they have chosen the only form of government which a democracy may adopt; but as the generating cause of laws and manners in the two countries is the same, it is of immense interest for us to know what it has produced in each of them.

It is not, then, merely to satisfy a curiosity, however legitimate, that I have examined America; my wish has been to find there instruction by which we may ourselves profit. Whoever should imagine that I have intended to write a panegyric would be strangely mistaken, and on reading this book he will perceive that such was not my design; nor has it been my object to advocate any form of government in particular, for I am of the opinion that absolute perfection is rarely to be found in any system of laws. I have not even pretended to judge whether the social revolution, which I believe to be irresistible, is advantageous or prejudicial to mankind. I have acknowledged this revolution as a fact already accomplished, or on the eve of its accomplishment; and I have selected the nation, from among those which have undergone it, in which its development has been the most peaceful and the most complete, in order to discern its natural consequences and to find out, if possible, the means of rendering it profitable to mankind. I confess that in America I saw more than America; I sought there the image of democracy itself, with its inclinations, its character, its prejudices, and its passions, in order to learn what we have to fear or to hope from its progress.

In the first part of this work I have attempted to show the distinction that democracy, dedicated to its inclinations and tendencies and abandoned almost without restraint to its instincts, gave to the laws the course it impressed on the government, and in general the control which it exercised over affairs of state. I have sought to discover the evils and the advantages which it brings. I have examined the safeguards used by the Americans to direct it, as well as those that they have not adopted, and I have undertaken to point out the factors which enable it to govern society.

My object was to portray, in a second part, the influence which the equality of conditions and democratic government in America exercised on civil society, on habits, ideas, and customs; but I grew less enthusiastic about carrying out this plan. Before I could have completed the task which I set for myself, my work would have become purposeless. Someone else would before long set forth to the public the principal traits of the American character and, delicately cloaking a serious picture, lend to the truth a charm which I should not have been able to equal.

I do not know whether I have succeeded in making known what I saw in America, but I am certain that such has been my sincere desire, and that I have never, knowingly, molded facts to ideas, instead of ideas to facts.

Whenever a point could be established by the aid of written documents, I have had recourse to the original text, and to the most authentic and reputable works. I have cited my authorities in the notes, and anyone may verify them. Whenever opinions, political customs, or remarks on the manners of the country were concerned, I have endeavored to consult the most informed men I met with. If the point in question was important or doubtful, I was not satisfied with one witness, but I formed my opinion on the evidence of several witnesses. Here the reader must necessarily rely upon my word. I could frequently have cited names which either are known to him or deserve to be so in support of my assertions; but I have carefully abstained from this practice. A stranger frequently hears important truths at the fireside of his host, which the latter would perhaps conceal from the ear of friendship; he consoles himself with his guest for the silence to which he is restricted, and the shortness of the traveler's stay takes away all fear of an indiscretion. I carefully noted every conversation of this nature as soon as it occurred, but these notes will never leave my writing-case. I had rather injure the success of my statements than add my name to the list of those strangers who repay generous hospitality they have received by subsequent chagrin and annoyance.

■　■　■

Daron Acemoglu, Simon Johnson, James A. Robinson, and Pierre Yared
INCOME AND DEMOCRACY

One of the most notable empirical regularities in political economy is the relationship between income per capita and democracy. Today, all OECD countries are democratic, while many of the nondemocracies are in the poor parts of the world, for example sub-Saharan Africa and Southeast Asia. The positive cross-country relationship between income and democracy in the 1990s is depicted in

Figure 8.1, which shows the association between the Freedom House measure of democracy and log income per capita in the 1990s.[1] This relationship is not confined solely to a cross-country comparison. Most countries were nondemocratic before the modern growth process took off at the beginning of the nineteenth century. Democratization came together with growth. Robert J. Barro (1999, 160), for example, summarizes this as follows: "Increases in various measures of the standard of living forecast a gradual rise in democracy. In contrast, democracies

From *American Economic Review* 98, no. 3 (2008), pp. 808–42.

Figure 8.1 Democracy and Income, 1990s

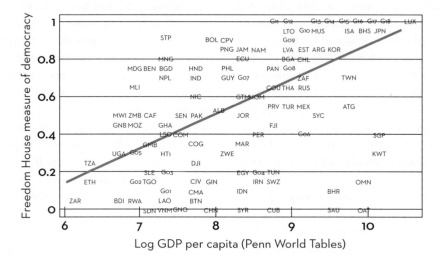

Notes: Values are averaged by country from 1990 to 1999. GDP per capita is in PPP terms. The regression represented by the fitted line yields a coefficient of 0.181 (standard error = 0.019), $N = 147$, and $R^2 = 0.35$. The "G" prefix corresponds to the average for groups of countries. G01 is AGO and MRT; G02 is NGA and TCD; G03 is KEN and KHM; G04 is DZA and LBN; G05 is BFA, NER, and YEM; G06 is GAB and MYS; G07 is DOM and SLV; G08 is BRA and VEN; G09 is BWA, DMA, POL, and VCT; G10 is HUN and URY; G11 is CRI and GRD; G12 is BLZ and LCA; G13 is KNA and TTO; G14 is GRC and MLT; G15 is BRB, CYP, ESP, and PRT; G16 is FIN, GBR, IRL, and NZL; G17 is AUS, AUT, BEL, CAN, DEU, DNK, FRA, ISL, ITA, NLD, NOR, and SWE; and G18 is CHE and USA.

---

that arise without prior economic development . . . tend not to last."[2]

This statistical association between income and democracy is the cornerstone of the influential modernization theory. Lipset (1959) suggested that democracy was both created and consolidated by a broad process of "modernization" which involved changes in "the factors of industrialization, urbanization, wealth, and education [which] are so closely interrelated as to form one common factor. And the factors subsumed under economic development carry with it the political correlate of democracy" (80). The central tenet of the modernization theory, that higher income per capita causes a country to be democratic, is also reproduced in most major works on democracy (e.g., Robert A. Dahl 1971; Samuel P. Huntington 1991; Dietrich Rusechemeyer, John D. Stephens, and Evelyn H. Stephens 1992).

In this paper, we revisit the relationship between income per capita and democracy. Our starting point is that existing work, which is based on cross-country relationships, does not establish causation. First, there is the issue of reverse causality; perhaps democracy causes income rather than the other way around. Second, and more important, there is the potential for omitted variable bias. Some other factor may determine both the nature of the political regime and the potential for economic growth.

We utilize two strategies to investigate the causal effect of income on democracy. Our first strategy is to control for country-specific factors affecting both income and democracy by including country fixed effects. While fixed effect regressions are not a panacea for omitted variable biases,[3] they are well suited to the investigation of the relationship between income and democracy, especially in the postwar era. The major source of potential bias in a regression of democracy on income per capita is country-specific, historical factors influencing both political and economic development. If these omitted characteristics are, to a first approximation, time-invariant, the inclusion of fixed effects will remove them and this source of bias. Consider, for example, the comparison of the United States and Colombia. The United States is both richer and more democratic, so a simple cross-country comparison, as well as the existing empirical strategies in the literature, which do not control for fixed country effects, would suggest that higher per capita income causes democracy. The idea of fixed effects is to move beyond this comparison and investigate the "within-country variation," that is, to ask whether Colombia is more likely to *become* (relatively) democratic as it *becomes* (relatively) richer. In addition to improving inference on the causal effect of income on democracy, this approach is more closely related to modernization theory as articulated by Lipset (1959), which emphasizes that individual countries should become more democratic if they are richer, not simply that rich countries should be democratic.

Our first result is that once fixed effects are introduced, the positive relationship between income per capita and various measures of democracy disappears. Figures 8.2 and 8.3 show this diagrammatically by plotting changes in our two measures of democracy, the Freedom House and Polity scores for each country between 1970 and 1995 against the change in GDP per capita over the same period. These figures confirm that there is no relationship between *changes* in income per capita and *changes* in democracy.

This basic finding is robust to using various different indicators for democracy, to different econometric specifications and estimation techniques, in different subsamples, and to the inclusion of additional covariates. The absence of a significant relationship between income and democracy is *not* driven by large standard errors. On the contrary, the relationship between income and democracy is estimated relatively precisely. In many cases, two-standard-error bands include only very small effects of income on democracy and often exclude the OLS

Figure 8.2 Change in Democracy and Income, 1970–1995

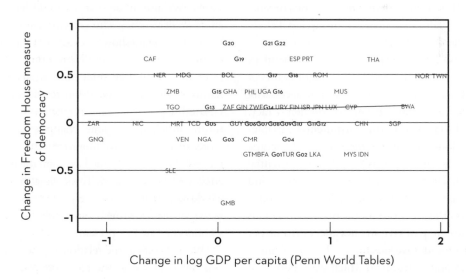

Change in log GDP per capita (Penn World Tables)

Notes: Changes are total difference between 1970 and 1995. Countries are included if they were independent by 1970. Start and end dates are chosen to maximize the number of countries in the cross section. The regression represented by the fitted line yields a coefficient of 0.032 (standard error = 0.058), $N = 102$, $R^2 = 0.00$. The "G" prefix corresponds to the average for groups of countries. G01 is FJI and KEN; G02 is COL and IND; G03 is IRN, JAM, and SLV; G04 is CHL and DOM; G05 is CIV and RWA; G06 is CHE, CRI, and NZL; G07 is DZA and SWE; G08 is AUS, DNK, MAR, and NLD; G09 is BEL, CAN, FRA, and GBR; G10 is AUT, EGY, ISL, ITA, PRY, and USA; G11 is BRB, NOR, and TUN; G12 is IRL and SYR; G13 is BDI and TZA; G14 is GAB, MEX, and TTO; G15 is PER and SEN; G16 is HTI and JOR; G17 is LSO and NPL; G18 is BRA and COG; G19 is ARG and HND; G20 is BEN and MLI; G21 is GRC, MWI, and PAN; and G22 is ECU and HUN.

Figure 8.3 Change in Democracy and Income, 1970–1995

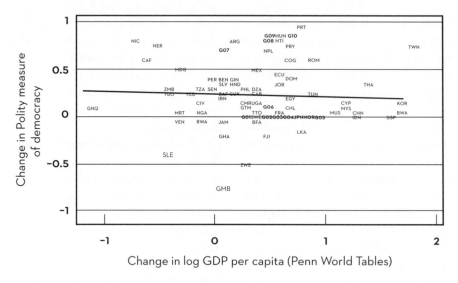

Change in Polity measure of democracy *(y-axis)*

Change in log GDP per capita (Penn World Tables) *(x-axis)*

Notes: See notes to Figure 2. The regression represented by the fitted line yields a coefficient of –0.024 (standard error = 0.063), N = 98, R^2 = 0.00. G01 is CHE, CRI, and NZL; G02 is AUS, DNK, and NLD; G03 is BEL, CAN, FIN, GBR, and TUR; G04 is AUT, COL, IND, ISL, ISR, ITA, and USA; G05 is IRL and SYR; G06 is KEN, MAR, and URY; G07 is BOL and MLI; G08 is MWI and PAN; G09 is GRC and LSO; and G10 is BRA and ESP.

estimates. These results, therefore, shed considerable doubt on the claim that there is a strong causal effect of income on democracy.[4]

While the fixed effects estimation is useful in removing the influence of long-run determinants of both democracy and income, it does not necessarily estimate the causal effect of income on democracy. Our second strategy is to use instrumental-variables (IV) regressions to estimate the impact of income on democracy.[5] We experiment with two potential instruments. The first is to use past savings rates, and the second is to use changes in the incomes of trading partners. The argument for the first instrument is that variations in past savings rates affect income per capita but should have no direct effect on democracy. The second instrument, which we believe is of independent interest, creates a matrix of trade shares and constructs predicted income for each country using a trade-share-weighted average income of other countries. We show that this predicted income has considerable explanatory power for income per

capita. We also argue that it should have no direct effect on democracy. Our second major result is that both IV strategies show no evidence of a causal effect of income on democracy. We recognize that neither instrument is perfect, since there are reasonable scenarios in which our exclusion restrictions could be violated (e.g., saving rates might be correlated with future anticipated regime changes; or democracy scores of a country's trading partners, which are correlated with their income levels, might have a direct effect on its democracy). To alleviate these concerns, we show that the most likely sources of correlation between our instruments and the error term in the second stage are not present.

We also look at the relationship between income and democracy over the past 100 years using fixed effects regressions and again find no evidence of a positive impact of income on democracy. These results are depicted in Figure 8.4, which plots the change in Polity score for each country between 1900 and 2000 against the change in GDP per capita over

Figure 8.4 Change in Democracy and Income, 1900–2000

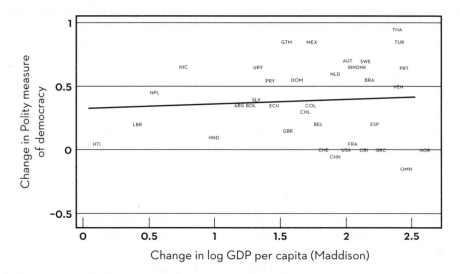

Notes: Log GDP per capita is from Angus Maddison (2003). Changes are total difference between 1900 and 2000. Countries are included if they are in the 1900–2000 balanced 50-year panel discussed in Section V of the text. The regression represented by the fitted line yields a coefficient of 0.035 (standard error = 0.049), $N = 37$, $R^2 = 0.00$.

the same period. This figure confirms that there is no relationship between income and democracy conditional on fixed effects.

These results naturally raise the following important question: why is there a cross-sectional correlation between income and democracy? In other words, why are rich countries democratic today? At a statistical level, the answer is clear: even though there is no relationship between changes in income and democracy in the postwar era or over the past 100 years or so, there is a positive association over the past 500 years. Most societies were non-democratic 500 years ago and had broadly similar income levels. The positive cross-sectional relationship reflects the fact that those that have become more democratic over this time span are also those that have grown faster. One possible explanation for the positive cross-sectional correlation is, therefore, that there is a causal effect of income on democracy, but it works at *much* longer horizons than the existing literature has posited. Although the lack of a relationship over 50 or 100 years sheds

some doubt on this explanation, this is a logical possibility.

We favor another explanation for this pattern. Even in the absence of a simple causal link from income to democracy, political and economic development paths are interlinked and are jointly affected by various factors. Societies may embark on *divergent political-economic development paths*, some leading to relative prosperity and democracy, others to relative poverty and dictatorship. Our hypothesis is that the positive cross-sectional relationship and the 500-year correlation between changes in income and democracy are caused by the fact that countries have embarked on divergent development paths at some *critical junctures* during the past 500 years.[6]

We provide support for this hypothesis by documenting that the positive association between changes in income and democracy over the past 500 years is largely accounted for by a range of historical variables. In particular, for the whole world sample, the positive association is considerably weakened when we control for date of independence, early constraints on the executive, and religion.[7] We then turn to the sample of former European colonies, where we have better proxies for factors that have influenced the development paths of nations. Acemoglu, Johnson, and Robinson (2001, 2002) and Engerman and Sokoloff (1997) argue that differences in European colonization strategies have been a major determinant of the divergent development paths of colonial societies. This reasoning suggests that in this sample, the critical juncture for most societies corresponds to their experience under European colonization. Furthermore, Acemoglu, Johnson, and Robinson (2002) show that the density of indigenous populations at the time of colonization has been a particularly important variable in shaping colonization strategies, and provide estimates of population densities in the year 1500 (before the advent of colonization). When we use information on population density, as well as on independence year and early constraints on the executive, the 500-year relationship between changes in income and democracy in the former colonies sample disappears. This pattern is consistent with the hypothesis that the positive cross-sectional relationship between income and democracy today is the result of societies embarking on divergent development paths at certain critical junctures during the past 500 years (although other hypotheses might account for these patterns).

A related question is whether income has a separate causal effect on transitions to, and away from, democracy. * * * Using both linear regression models and double-hazard models that simultaneously estimate the process of entry into, and exit from, democracy, we find no evidence that income has a causal effect on the transitions either to or from democracy.

NOTES

1. All figures use the three-letter World Bank country codes to identify countries, except when multiple countries are clustered together. When such clustering happens, countries are grouped together, the averages for the group are plotted in the figure, and the countries in each group are identified in the footnote to the corresponding figure.

2. See also, among others, Seymour Martin Lipset (1959), John B. Londregan and Keith T. Poole (1996), Adam Przeworski and Fernando Limongi (1997), Barro (1997), Przeworski et al. (2000), and Elias Papaioannou and Gregorios Siourounis (2006).

3. Fixed effects would not help inference if there are time-varying omitted factors affecting the dependent variable and correlated with the right-hand-side variables (see the discussion below). They may, in fact, make problems of measurement error worse because they remove a significant portion of the variation in the right-hand-side variables. Consequently, fixed effects are certainly no substitute for instrumental-variables or structural estimation with valid exclusion restrictions.

4. It remains true that over time there is a general tendency toward greater incomes and greater democracy throughout the world. In our regressions, time effects capture these general (world-level) tendencies. Our estimates suggest that these world-level movements in democracy are unlikely to be driven by the causal effect of income on democracy.

5. A recent creative attempt is by Edward Miguel, Shankar Satyanath, and Ernest Sergenti (2004), who use weather conditions as an instrument for income in Africa to investigate the impact of income on civil wars. Unfortunately, weather conditions are a good instrument only for relatively short-run changes in income, thus not ideal to study the relationship between income and democracy.

6. See, among others, Douglass C. North and Robert P. Thomas (1973), North (1981), Eric L. Jones (1981), Stanley L. Engerman and Kenneth L. Sokoloff (1997), and Acemoglu, Johnson, and Robinson (2001, 2002) for theories that emphasize the impact of certain historical

factors on development processes during critical junctures, such as the collapse of feudalism, the age of industrialization, or the process of colonization.

7. See Max Weber (1930), Huntington (1991), and Steven M. Fish (2002) for the hypothesis that religion might have an important effect on economic and political development.

Adam Przeworski

CONQUERED OR GRANTED? A HISTORY OF SUFFRAGE EXTENSIONS

The Principal of my Reform is to prevent the necessity of revolution. . . . I am reforming to preserve, not to overthrow.

EARL GREY SPEAKING IN THE 1831 PARLIAMENTARY DEBATE ON EXTENDING SUFFRAGE.

When first established—in England, the United States, France, Spain, and the newly independent Latin American republics—representative government was not a "democracy" as we would define the term now, nor was it seen as such by its founders.[1] In spite of their egalitarian pronouncements, the "founders," pretty much everywhere, sought to construct representative government for the propertied while protecting it from the poor. As a result, political rights were everywhere restricted to wealthy males.

In all these societies suffrage was subsequently extended to poorer males and to women, while the newly emerging countries tended to immediately grant rights more broadly, so that political rights are now universal in almost all countries that have any kind of elections. Yet the road from representative government to mass democracy took a long time to traverse. As of 1900, one country had fully universal suffrage, while seventeen enfranchised all

males. Only during the second half of the twentieth century, more than 150 years after representative institutions were first established, did universal suffrage become an irresistible norm.

Why would people who monopolize political power ever decide to put their interests or values at risk by sharing it with others? Specifically, why would those who hold political rights in the form of suffrage decide to extend these rights to anyone else?

The question is sufficiently puzzling to have received intense attention. The classical explanation of extensions is the one offered by Earl Grey: "reform to preserve." This explanation was echoed by Bendix and Rokkan,[2] who observed that "following the French Revolution many if not most European countries have undergone a process of popular agitation demanding that extension of rights, some pattern of resistance to this agitation by the privileged and established sections of the population, and an eventual accommodation through a new definition of rights." Przeworski and Cortés[3] as well as Freeman

From *British Journal of Political Science*, 39 (2008), pp. 291–32.

Figure 8.5 Proportion of countries with universal suffrage, by year

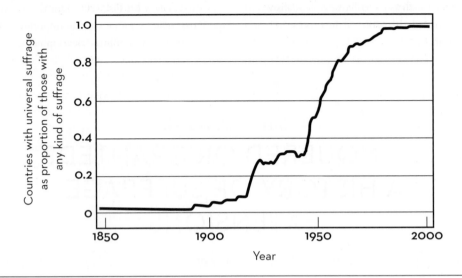

and Snidal[4] developed models in which elites extend franchise as a response to the declining viability or legitimacy of the political system. In turn, Conley and Temini argued that extensions of franchise occur when the interests of the enfranchised and disenfranchised groups conflict and the disenfranchised group presents a credible threat.[5] Albeit in different languages, the generic argument runs as follows: (1) Being excluded is a source of deprivation of some kind. (2) At some time, the excluded threaten to revolt (the political system suffers a "deficit of legitimacy"). (3) Even if sharing political rights may have consequences that are costly for the incumbent elite, the elite prefers to bear these costs rather than risk a revolution. (4) Once admitted, the new citizens use their rights within the system, abandoning the insurrectionary strategy (they become "encapsulated," "co-opted," or "integrated"). Hence, *extensions of rights are a response of the incumbent holders of rights to revolutionary threats by the excluded.*

This general argument is subject to a twist, recently provided by Acemoglu and Robinson.[6] In their model, when the elite is confronted by a revolutionary threat of a sufficient magnitude, it calculates that it would be better off making economic concessions than risking that a revolution would damage their property. But if the threat is ephemeral, that is, if the capacity of the masses to revolt is not due to their permanent organization but only to some transient circumstances, a promise by the elite that it would maintain these concessions when the threat evaporates is not credible and the masses would revolt even if granted economic concessions. The only credible response is to change the identity of the pivotal decision maker by extending suffrage. Hence, suffrage extensions are to be expected when the elite faces a *transient* insurrectionary threat, a sporadic outburst of political unrest.

In these explanations rights are conquered by the excluded, in the sense that the elite concedes these rights only when it fears that those excluded may reach for power by the only means available to them, namely revolution. Yet this story is not without rivals, arguments that claim that franchise was granted voluntarily, in the self-interest of the elite in singular or a majority within it.

Lizzeri and Persico argued that extending suffrage changes the political equilibrium from one of redistribution to one where redistribution is curtailed in favor of providing public goods.[7] This is because those currently disenfranchised value transfers less than members of the extant elite. Hence, when suffrage is extended the value of transfers becomes diluted and they become less attractive in relation to public goods. *What precipitates extensions, therefore, are exogenous changes in the evaluation of public goods by the incumbent elite.* Specifically, Lizzeri and Persico, who focus on nineteenth-century Britain, argue that the precipitating factor was the rapid growth of cities, which generated demand for sanitation and for roads.

Ticchi and Vindigni claimed, in turn, that if an elite wants to induce men to engage in acts as costly as fighting and perhaps women to take men's place in the factories, it must offer them a *quid pro quo* in terms of political rights.[8] This argument dates back to Machiavelli's *Discourses*, where he argued that governments must extend benefits to the people in anticipation that they would need their cooperation in times of adversity.[9] Once an enemy is at the gates, concessions are not credible and thus ineffective:

> For the people as a whole will consider that they owe this benefit not to you, but rather to your enemies, and, since they cannot but fear that, when the need has passed, you may deprive them of what you have been compelled to give, will in no way feel obliged to you.

Justification of suffrage in terms of conscription was indeed a frequent argument in the nineteenth century: a slogan in Sweden was "one man, one vote, one gun." *Hence, franchise is extended when elites prepare for wars.*

Finally, if the elite is divided, a majority within it may want to extend suffrage for partisan reasons.[10] These reasons may be narrowly electoral, just a search for votes, but they may also entail looking for allies in pursuit of economic interests. Note that Acemoglu and Robinson considered but rejected the possibility that extensions were driven by partisan reasons in the cases they studied, while Lizzeri and Persico ruled out electoral considerations by an assump-

tion. Yet Llavador and Oxoby think that a party of industrialists would extend suffrage to workers in order to obtain a mandate for pursuing industrialization policies, while a party of landowners may want to block such policies by enfranchising peasants in addition to workers.[11] Their model, however, focuses on whether extensions were partial or universal, rather than on whether they occur at all, and I do not consider their theory below.

Hence, in one class of stories, franchise is extended only in response to revolutionary threats: this is the sense in which political rights are *conquered* by the insurgent masses. In turn, in other models elites *grant* suffrage voluntarily, in their own interest, either because they prefer public goods over transfers or because they need to prepare for war or because they want to obtain an electoral mandate for particular economic policies. True, one might claim that in either case the elite extends suffrage only if it would be better off as a result of an extension than without it and that suffrage is thus always granted. But while extensions precipitated by a threat of revolution make the elite better off than they would have been if the revolution were to be successful, preventing revolution by means of extending political rights results in a redistribution of income in favor of the newly included, thus rendering the elite worse off than it was under the status quo. In contrast, extensions are voluntary when they make the elite or at least a majority thereof better off, for any of the reasons evoked in the particular stories. Those excluded conquer political rights when the elite realizes that, although the extension will make it worse off, its fate without an extension would be, or at least might be, even worse. In turn, the excluded are not protagonists when the elite faces the choice only between the status quo or enhancing its own welfare by extending suffrage. To put it in a nutshell, rights are conquered when their extension makes the elite worse off than under the status quo; they are granted when extensions make the elite better off.

Since some of these stories focus on redistribution of income while others evoke demand for public goods or preparations for war, they may be applicable to different types of extensions. Specifically, one could think that revolutionary threat is more likely to induce extensions along class lines, while increasing demand for public goods should lead to increasing the electorate without changing its class composition. Put differently, since the revolutionary threat theory focuses on redistribution of income, it must apply at least to extensions along class lines.[12] In turn, since extensions along a pure gender line are more neutral with regard to redistribution, the Lizzeri-Persico model should hold at least for extensions to women alone.

The purpose of this article is to adjudicate empirically among these alternative explanations. While the literature on extensions of suffrage is by now extensive, the historical material adduced in support of different theories is limited to a few—almost exclusively Western European—cases, with an obsessive focus on the English reform of 1832. This evidence consists either of narratives about particular extensions or of analyses of their fiscal consequences. The first type of evidence is loose and sometimes tendentious, at least insofar as the same reforms are cited to support different theories. The second type of evidence assumes that the consequences were the same as motivations, which may or may not be true.[13]

The data analyzed here (see the Appendix) cover 187 countries or dependent territories from the time they established first national electoral institutions until year 2000, yielding 14,604 annual observations of franchise rules. Suffrage qualifications are distinguished by twenty-one categories that combine class and gender criteria. These distinctions generate 348 franchise extensions, of which sixty-three occurred in Western Europe. Since different explanations may apply to different types of extensions, the extensions are further distinguished by the criteria by which the newly incorporated groups were defined, namely, class, gender, or both.

The article is organized as follows. The next section presents statistical analyses. Focusing on the distinction between extensions by class and by sex, the fourth section brings other additional materials to bear on the question formulated in the title. A brief conclusion closes the text.

■   ■   ■

Statistical Analyses

Testing theories systematically entails several difficulties, some insurmountable. We have only one variable that speaks directly to the threat of revolution theory: *unrest*,[14] which is the sum of strikes, demonstrations, and riots lagged one year, from Banks.[15] Moreover, this variable is available only for the period following the end of World War I and only for independent countries. We do have, however, relatively extensive information about the number of military personnel, *milper*, for several countries going back as far as 1816 (from Banks). In turn, following Lizzeri and Persico, to indicate the demand for public goods I use the proportion of the population in cities of 25,000 or more, a variable called *urban* (from Banks 1996). One could also think that public goods, specifically sanitation or vaccination, are more in demand when infant mortality, *infmor* (from Mitchell),[16] is higher.[17] Hence, their theory is tested using *urban* and *infmor*. Finally, to test the modernization theory (about which see Przeworski and Limongi),[18] which claims that democratization is an automatic consequence of economic development, I use per capita income, *gdpcap*, from Maddison.[19]

Several theories of democratization also derive conclusions concerning the impact of income inequality. A widely shared view is that higher inequality impedes or retards extensions. The typical reasoning is that democracy is costlier to the incumbent elite when income inequality is higher, since the median voter is then relatively poorer and opts for a higher degree of redistribution.[20] Acemoglu and Robinson, however, assume that revolution can occur only above some level of inequality, so that extensions are more likely in unequal societies. While the data for income inequality are available only for the post-1960 period, the relevant asset during most of the period under consideration was land and, following Therborn[21] as well as Engerman and Sokoloff,[22] I consider the effect of the proportion of farms owned and operated by family units, *family farms*, from Vanhanen.[23] (1996).

While all the theories discussed above refer to any kind of extensions, they may apply differently to extensions by class, by gender, and by both criteria. Note that each type of extension is conditioned on a different status quo: (1) pure class extensions cannot occur if suffrage is universal for males, (2) extensions by gender alone can occur only if women cannot vote already at the same basis as men, (3) extensions by class and gender can occur only if not all males and females can vote already. I show in Table 8.1 results obtained by probits applied to each type of extension at a time, with the appropriate conditioning.[24] Since numbers of observations and of extensions dwindle rapidly when more than two variables are considered simultaneously, I can examine them only one at a time.

In agreement with the revolutionary threat theories, unrest (which is lagged one year) has a strongly positive effect on the probability of extensions by class and a weaker but still significant effect on extensions by gender. The proportion of men under arms does not influence the probability of any kind of extensions.[25] The impact of urbanization on extensions entailing to women supports the Lizzeri and Persico model, but the sign of infant mortality is wrong from their point of view.[26] Equality of land distribution promotes inclusions of women. Finally, per capita income has a positive effect only on extensions by class. The impact of urbanization vanishes, however, when it is considered (in a smaller sample) together with infant mortality. In turn, infant mortality is negatively correlated with the proportion of family farms, and when they are both introduced into the specification only one remains significant. I am inclined to believe that mortality is an effect of inequality and to attribute the causal effect to the latter. Unfortunately, considering more than two variables at a time reduces rapidly the number of observations and of extensions among them.

To complete the analysis, we need to examine the effect of wars. According to Ticchi and Vindigni, concessions of suffrage are necessary to induce men to fight and perhaps women to replace them in production. Hence, extensions should occur when countries prepare for wars. Note that, perhaps informed by history, Ticchi and Vindigni stretch their argument to cover their aftermath, claiming to explain "political reforms implemented in several European countries during and *in the aftermath* of the two World Wars."[27] But in their aftermath, the wars had already occurred, so that inducements to fight or to replace men in factories are no longer needed. If extensions occur after wars end, it must be for other reasons: perhaps it is just "gratitude" but more plausibly because soldiers returning from wars are dangerous to their rulers: they believe they deserve rights and they know how to fight.

As always, there are some instances that support the theory. The French Revolution gave the right to vote to every Frenchman "qui aura fait la guerre de la liberté," will *have* fought in the war (Decree of 3 August 1792 of the Legislative Assembly).[28] This provision was maintained through the Consulate and the Empire. Tadeusz Kościuszko in Poland made vague promises to peasants to induce them to join the anti-Russian insurrection in 1794; Simon Bolivar made at one moment interracial appeals to recruit for the war against Spain;[29] Bismarck wrote in his memoirs that the acceptance of general suffrage was a weapon in the struggle against Austria and the rest of foreign powers.[30] But an overwhelming number of extensions occurred after, not before, wars. Except for Italy, where the 1912 extension was made as part of building support for the war against Libya, none of the countries that would become belligerents in World War I extended suffrage on its eve. In turn, nine belligerents extended suffrage at home between 1918 and 1922, while the United Kingdom also extended it in three of its colonies. The same happened around World War II. No suffrage extensions occurred during preparations for war; in fact, elections were abolished in the axis countries on the eve of the war. During the war,

Table 8.1 Effect on the Probability of Particular Types of Extensions (Marginal Effects, Probit Estimates)

	Any	Class	Gender	Both
unrest	0.0060***	0.0057***	0.0038*	
	(0.0011; 60)	(0.0014; 15)	(0.0019; 39)	
milper	-1.1297	-0.2022	-0.4138	-1.5009
	(0.6919; 175)	(0.5629; 49)	(0.3933; 45)	(0.8011; 26)
urban	0.0044**	0.0005	0.0045***	0.0049*
	(0.0019; 166)	(0.0025; 85)	(0.0010; 47)	(0.0028; 34)
infmor	0.0040***	0.0023***	-0.0024***	-0.0094***
	(0.0009; 91)	(0.0006; 35)	(0.0006; 35)	(0.0027; 21)
farms	0.0068***	0.0029	0.0039***	0.0058***
	(0.0024; 140)	(0.0024; 61)	(0.0010; 49)	(0.0010; 49)
gdpcap	-0.0010	0.0053**	0.0003	0.0018
	(0.0014; 159)	(0.0026; 58)	(0.0010; 56)	(0.0050; 45)
condition	Franchise lag < 72	First digit lag < 7	Second digit lag < 2	First digit lag < 7 second digit lag <2

Note: The first number in parentheses is the country-clustered standard error of the estimate, while the second number is the count of extensions of a given type in the particular subset of data. Empty cell indicates insufficient number of observations.

Figure 8.6 Diffusion effects: impact of the proportion of countries with universal suffrage on the probability of extensions

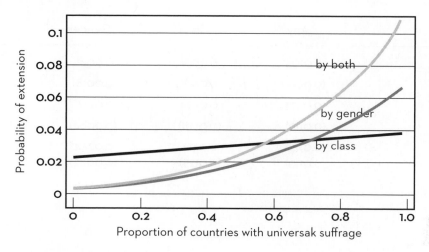

Note: Probabilities estimated by multinomial logit.

suffrage reforms occurred in Barbados, Jamaica, and Guyana. In turn, eight belligerents extended suffrage at home between 1945 and 1949, while at the same time suffrage was extended in twenty-one colonial territories.

Systematic evidence concerning international wars covered by the Correlates of War Project (see the Appendix) shows that of the 226 extensions covered by this data set, twenty occurred during five years preceding wars (of which in eight cases these were also years after another war ended), twelve occurred during wars, and thirty-five in the five years following an end of a war (of which in eight cases these were also years before another war began). As shown in Table 8.2, periods before wars do not differ from all other periods, while extensions involving women were much more likely after international wars.

Finally, another factor, not considered in any of the models, that plays an obvious role, are international norms concerning political rights. To examine this impact, I consider the effect of the proportion of countries with universal suffrage in a particular year on the probability of an extension during this year. While these diffusion effects are relatively weaker for

extensions by class, they are overwhelming for extensions involving women. The function that relates the probability of an extension by class and gender in any particular country to the proportion of countries that already had universal suffrage shows that when almost all countries reached universal suffrage, the pressure on a country that still did not have it was so overwhelming that the probability this country would yield in a particular year was 0.10. The effect on pure extensions to women may appear smaller, but it is only because countries that did not have universal male suffrage felt pressured to extend it both to all males and females simultaneously.

To put these findings together, consider a specification in which periods before and after wars[31] as well as international conditions are first considered alone (the coefficients in Table 8.2 are based on the specification with only these three variables) and then each of the other variables is added one at a time (the signs and significance levels of the first three variables are never affected by these additions).

Let me highlight only negative findings.[32] The Lizzeri and Persico model, according to which

Table 8.2 Final Specifications of Extensions (Marginal Effects, Probit Estimates)

Extension	Any	Class	Gender	Both
Before war	−0.0103	0.0084	−0.0041	−0.0005
	(0.0081)	(0.0122)	(0.0018)	(0.0017)
After war	0.0393***	0.0074	0.0197***	0.0214***
	(0.0119)	(0.0148)	(0.0064)	(0.0102)
Proportion universal	0.0742***	0.0412***	0.0244***	0.0311***
	(0.0113)	(0.0125)	(0.0042)	(0.0102)
Other variables				
unrest	+ + +	+ + +	+ +	
milper	○	○	○	○
urban	− −	○	○	+
infmor	− −	−	○	−
family farms	+	○	+	+ + +
gdpcap	− −	○	○	○

Note: For the dichotomous variables, the effects are the difference in probability between the two values. The analyses are conditioned in the same way as in Table 8.1. "Before" stands for five years preceding an international war, "After" for five years following one. Country clustered standard errors are in parentheses. "Proportion Universal" is the proportion of countries with any kind of suffrage that had universal suffrage in a given year. The coefficients and the standard errors are based on the specification with these three variables alone. "Other Variables" show the sign and the level of significance of other variables when they are added one-at-a-time to the first three factors, where three signs indicate $p < 0.01$, two signs $0.01 < p < 0.05$, and one sign $0.05 < p < 0.10$.

extensions are driven by increased demand for public goods, is persistently rejected by the data: urbanization has no effect or it is not robust, while infant mortality has a wrong sign whenever it is significant. Obviously, it is possible that the data are not reliable or that these variables do not provide a valid operationalization of the theory. Moreover, the public goods motivation may have been important in extending suffrage at the municipal level, emphasized by Lizzeri and Persico. But with these caveats the conclusion concerning this explanation must be negative.[33] The Ticchi and Vindigni story about preparations for wars fares poorly insofar as the proportion of men under arms is never significant, while extensions including women follow rather than precede wars. Finally, modernization theory—the idea that democracy is secreted by economic development—fails here, as it does in other contexts.[34] In contrast, the revolutionary threat theory goes a long way to explain extensions by class and perhaps by gender. Note, however, that Acemoglu and Robinson appear to be wrong about the impact of inequality, at least insofar as extensions by gender and by both class and gender are more likely when land distribution is more equal.

Granted or Conquered?

Since history is replete with instances in which good theories were thrown out by bad data, and the data available here are scarce and often unreliable, any conclusions are subject to this caveat. Yet, in spite of all the limitations of the data, the explanation in terms of revolutionary threats, and even more narrowly the Acemoglu-Robinson emphasis on unexpected mobilization of the excluded, makes good sense of extensions by class. Enfranchisement of women, however, is subject to different dynamics.

Extension of Citizenship to Lower Classes

To put these findings in context, note first that theories of enfranchisement assume that those excluded treat political rights as instrumental for their economic objectives, rather than as a goal in itself. The poor want political rights not because they want to be recognized as equals but only because these rights would advance their economic objectives. The assumption that political rights were merely instrumental may or may not be true, or perhaps may have been true with regard to the working class movements but not with regard to women's movements. But if it is not true, then purely economic concessions would have not sufficed to diffuse the threat of revolution. Hence, the argument that elites extend suffrage only in response to sporadic outbursts of political mobilization, while reverting to economic concessions when the poor are sufficiently well organized to think concessions are durable, is predicated on the assumption that the "masses," in fact the working-class movement and in some countries the peasant movements, treated political rights as purely instrumental.

One may wonder why the elites would wait for the threat to manifest itself in the form of unrest rather than appease the potentially revolutionary masses by extending suffrage. But if extensions of political rights do neutralize the threat of revolution and if they are more costly than economic conces-

sions, then there is a reason for the elite to wait until an extension becomes inevitable. One would thus expect, and Acemoglu and Robinson claim it to be true, that countries that developed social programs earlier waited longer for the advent of manhood (or universal) suffrage. Yet except for the Danish pension law of 1891 and Lloyd George's social policies of 1908–1914,[35] such concessions occurred only after at least manhood suffrage was already in place.[36] Hence, if the elites staved off revolutions by means other than enfranchisement, these means were more plausibly repression rather than concession.

Finally, it is not obvious that extending suffrage to the poor was sufficient to mitigate their revolutionary ardor. While from the moment of their formation, socialist parties demanded universal suffrage, for quite a long time they were ambivalent how to use it. Only after years of heated discussions[37] did Social Democrats become fully committed to electoral politics, adopting a stance sharply articulated in 1919 by J. McGurk, the chairman of the Labour Party:

> We are either constitutionalists or we are not constitutionalists. If we are constitutionalists, if we believe in the efficacy of the political weapon (and we are, or why do we have a Labour Party?) then it is both unwise and undemocratic because we fail to get a majority at the polls to turn around and demand that we should substitute industrial action.[38]

Yet in countries where no single party was able to organize and discipline the new entrants, workers or peasants, extensions of suffrage to the lower classes were not sufficient to prevent disruptive political conflicts.

Hence, the argument that the elites extended suffrage to the lower classes only when they confronted visible signs of revolutionary threat is predicated on tenuous assumptions: that the poor treated political rights as merely instrumental, that they would be appeased by economic concessions, and that they would be deradicalized once they conquered the right to participate in electoral politics. Yet the effect of unrest on extensions is large and robust in the sample for which the data are available. Moreover, as seen in Table 8.3, while the incidence of unrest lagged one year has a strong effect on the probability of extensions, all tests indicate that earlier unrest plays no role: in the presence of the first, higher lags do not matter; a four-year moving average of unrest preceding the first lag has a positive but not a significant sign; and a difference between the observed incidence of the first lag and its value predicted by the four-year average of earlier unrest predicts extensions even better than its actual value.

Finally, as seen in Figure 8.7, which shows the average intensity of unrest in years immediately preceding and following extensions, waves of mobilization peaked one year before extensions were granted and extensions reduced unrest. Hence, every possible test shows that unexpected mobilization of the masses induced elites to respond immediately with extending suffrage.

The story told by Verney about the advent of universal suffrage to Sweden in 1918 may be a caricature, but caricatures only exaggerate the truth:[39]

No progress was made when Parliament assembled. . . . On 11 November they [Left Social-

Table 8.3A Probability of Extensions as a Function of Successive Lags of Unrest (Probit Estimates, Marginal Effects)

Lag	Derivative	s.e.
1	0.0066***	0.0009
2	0.0006	0.0022
3	−0.0002	0.0028
4	0.0010	0.0024
5	−0.0020	0.0029

Table 8.3B Probability of Extensions as a Function of Past Unrest (Probit Estimates, Marginal Effects)

Variable	Model 1	Model 2	Model 3
MA(4)	0.0013*	−0.0001	0.0011
	(0.0007)	(0.0008)	(0.0008)
unrest_1		0.0068***	
		(0.0010)	
unrest_1_dev			0.0068***
			(0.0010)

Note: MA(4) is a four year average of the second through the fifth lag. unrest_1 is the first lag. unrest_1_dev is the deviation of the observed value of the first lag from its value predicted by the four preceding lags. Standard errors are country clustered.

Figure 8.7 Average intensity of unrest years before and after extensions

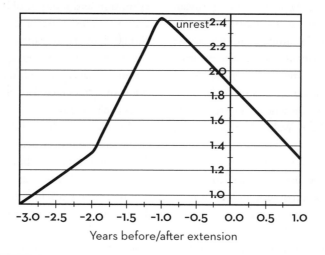

Years before/after extension

ists] had issued a communique calling for workers' and soldiers' soviets, the end of the monarchy and the First Chamber, a constituent National Assembly, land division, control of industry by the workers and preparations for a general strike. . . . The People's House [lower chamber of the parliament] was filled . . . Between speeches the crowd sung the Marseillaise and the Internationale. Branting was able to announce the new proposal by the Government promising universal suffrage. . . . Two days later the danger of revolution was over.

The open question is whether this theory also holds for the period and for the countries for which systematic data are not available. Acemoglu and Robinson cite anecdotal evidence about the United Kingdom in 1832 and 1867, France and Germany in 1848, and Sweden in 1866, 1909, and 1918. Their list can be easily extended. The largest number of extensions before 1919 occurred in 1848, a year of revolutionary upheavals throughout Europe. Massive strikes or demonstrations preceded the extension of suffrage in Austria in 1907,[40] in Belgium in 1894,[41] in New Zealand in 1889,[42] and in Finland in 1906.[43] Yet selecting cases in favor of a theory is a tendentious operation and proponents of

alternative explanations are as good in finding cases that support their model, at times referring to the same extensions.

The strongest evidence in favor of the argument that suffrage was extended to the poor under the threat of revolution comes, however, not from the events themselves but from voices of the historical protagonists. Indeed, these voices were often so explicit that one does not need to impute the motivations. A Connecticut representative, Samuel Dana, thought it was quite proper that the society was to be divided into "the rich, the few, the rulers" and "the poor, the many, the ruled."[44] The drafter of the French Constitution of 1795, Boissy d'Anglas, declared, "We must be ruled by the best . . . a country governed by property-owners is within the social order, that which is dominated by non-property owners is in a state of nature."[45] The consensus in mid-nineteenth century Colombia was: "We want enlightened democracy, a democracy in which intelligence and property direct the destinies of the people; we do not want a barbarian democracy in which the proletarianism and ignorance drown the seeds of happiness and bring the society to confusion and disorder."[46] "The right to make laws belongs to the most intelligent, to the aristocracy of knowledge, created by nature," a Peruvian constitutionalist, Bartolomé Herrera, declared in 1846;[47] the Peruvian theorist José María Pando maintained that "a perpetual aristocracy . . . is an imperative necessity"; the Chilean Andrés Bello wanted rulers to constitute "a body of wise men (*un cuerpo de sabios*)"; while the Spanish conservative thinker Donoso Cortés juxtaposed the sovereignty of the wise to sovereignty of the people.[48] Still by 1867, Walter Bagehot (1963: 277) would warn:[49]

> It must be remembered that a political combination of the lower classes, as such and for their own objects, is an evil of the first magnitude; that a permanent combination of them would make them (now that many of them have the suffrage) supreme in the country; and that their supremacy, in the state they now are, means the supremacy of ignorance over instruction and of numbers over knowledge.

As a result, the right to elect one's representatives was limited almost everywhere to wealthy males. While the prevalence of *suffrage censitaire* may appear to contradict the norm of suppressing all distinctions in society and to be incompatible with the principle of political equality, suffrage restrictions were portrayed by their proponents as serving the common good of all. The French Declaration of Rights qualified its recognition of equality in the sentence that immediately followed: "Men are born equal and remain free and equal in rights. Social distinctions may be founded only upon the general good." The argument for restricting suffrage was spelled out already by Montesquieu, who started from the principle that "All inequality under democracy should be derived from the nature of democracy and from the very principle of democracy."[50] His example was that people who must continually work to live are not prepared for public office or would have to neglect their functions. As barristers of Paris put it on the eve of the Revolution, "Whatever respect one might wish to show for the rights of humanity in general, there is no denying

the existence of a class of men who, by virtue of their education and the type of work to which their poverty had condemned them, is . . . incapable at the moment of participating fully in public affairs."[51] "In such cases," Montesquieu went on, "equality among citizens can be lifted in a democracy for the good of democracy. But it is only apparent equality which is lifted. . . ." The generic argument, to be found in slightly different versions, was that: (1) Representation is acting in the best interest of all. (2) To determine the best interest of all one needs reason.[52] (3) Reason has sociological determinants: not having to work for a living ("disinterest"), or not being employed or otherwise dependent on others ("independence"). As a Chilean statesman put it in 1865, to exercise political rights it is necessary "to have the intelligence to recognize the truth and the good, the will to want it, and the freedom to execute it."[53] In turn, the claim that only apparent equality is being violated was built in three steps: (1) Acting in the best common interest considers everyone equally, so that everyone is equally represented. (2) The only quality that is being distinguished is the capacity to recognize the common good. (3) No one is barred from acquiring this quality, so that suffrage is potentially open to all.[54]

The self-serving nature of these convoluted arguments for restricting suffrage was apparent. A French conservative polemicist, J. Mallet du Pan, was perhaps first to insist in 1796 that legal equality must lead to equality of wealth: "Do you wish a republic of equals amid the inequalities which the public services, inheritances, marriage, industry and commerce have introduced into society? You will have to overthrow property."[55] Madison, who in Federalist #10 maintained that representative government would protect property,[56] was less sanguine some decades later: "the danger to the holders of property can not be disguised, if they are undefended against a majority without property. Bodies of men are not less swayed by interest than individuals. . . . Hence, the liability of the rights of property. . . ."[57] The Scottish philosopher James Mackintosh predicted in 1818 that "if the laborious classes gain franchise, a permanent animosity between opinion and property must be the consequence."[58] David Ricardo was prepared to extend suffrage only to "that part of them which cannot be supposed to have an interest in overturning the right to property."[59] Thomas Macaulay in the 1842 speech on the Chartists vividly summarized the danger presented by universal suffrage:[60]

> The essence of the Charter is universal suffrage. If you withhold that, it matters not very much what else you grant. If you grant that, it matters not at all what else you withhold. If you grant that, the country is lost. . . . My firm conviction is that, in our country, universal suffrage is incompatible, not only with this or that form of government, and with everything for the sake of which government exists; that it is incompatible with property and that it is consequently incompatible with civilization.

Systems of representative government were born under a mortal fear that participation by the broad masses of the population, a large part of whom were poor and illiterate, would threaten property. Suffrage was a dangerous weapon. Yet the poor did not think that their best interests were being represented by the propertied, and they would struggle for suffrage. The elites resisted as long as they could and yielded when they could not. Political rights were conquered by the poorer classes. As Georges Sorel put it on the very eve of the World War I, "the bourgeoisie was so troubled by the fear of revolution that it accepted out of resignation the claims of a democracy whose inevitable triumph had been predicted by so many ideologies."[61]

Partisan Politics and Women's Suffrage

Extensions to women present, however, several puzzles. The first one is "Why so late?" Indeed, if the elites had wanted, as Lizzeri and Persico thinks they did, to dilute the value of transfers relative to public goods, they should have extended suffrage to women while preserving class restrictions: the number of voters would have increased, thus diminishing the value of transfers, while the demand for redistribution would not be enhanced by enfranchising poorer people. Yet, while J. S. Mill moved an amendment to give votes to women in 1867, this amendment was defeated, and the first women could vote in the United Kingdom only in 1918. With the notable exception of New Zealand, women were barred from participating in national politics throughout the nineteenth century, and in many European and Latin American countries they gained the right to vote only after the Second World War.

The assumption that women are not capable of exercising political rights was so self-evident to founders of representative institutions that Kant referred to it as "natural."[62] While early proponents of female suffrage observed that reason is not distributed along gender lines—after all, some rulers had been queens[63]—the main argument against giving the right to vote to women was that, like children, they were not independent, had no will of their own. To enfranchise them would be only to double the votes of their husbands.[64] Women were already represented by the males in their households and their interests were to be represented through a tutelary, rather than an electoral, connection. The "fact" that women are not capable of acting independently in the political sphere was so obvious to the male founders of representative institutions that often they did not even bother to explicitly restrict suffrage to men. According to Johnson, the 1776 Constitution of New Jersey, "through an error in wording," admitted as voters "all inhabitants" who held a certain amount of property. Many women did vote until 1807 when "male" was explicitly added as a qualification.[65] A similar situation ensued in Chile, where the electoral law of 1874 failed to mention sex as a qualification for citizenship. Only when some women took this opportunity to register to vote, did the Congress pass in 1884 a law explicitly excluding females. This was clearly an omission: as one senator admitted: "it did not occur to anyone to concede such rights" (*a nadie se le ha ocurrido concederle tales derechos*).[66] Again the same occurred in France, where Mme Barbarousse claimed the right to vote pointing out that *tout français* had this right according to the constitution and it took a court ruling in 1885 to decide that *français* did not include *française* women.[67]

In turn, after World War II female suffrage became almost inevitable. The evidence in favor of the importance of international norms is overwhelming. The introduction of universal suffrage in New Zealand in 1893, Australia in 1901, and in Finland in 1906 broke the dam for other countries. Beginning with Poland in 1919, six out of fourteen countries that emerged between the two world wars immediately adopted universal, male and female, suffrage. With the proclamation by the United Nations in 1948 of the Universal Declarations of Human Rights, which banned all kinds of discrimination and asserted quality of rights between men and women, all but three Moslem countries—Bahrain, Kuwait, and Maldives—that became independent after this date extended suffrage to all men and women.

Giving women the vote was inconceivable before 1860 and inevitable after 1948. But why were women fully enfranchised in New Zealand in 1893 and in Belgium in 1949? Although the literature on women's suffrage is enormous—the lion's share of writings about suffrage is dedicated to women—it tends to be hagiographic rather than analytical, implicitly assuming that suffrage was conquered as a result of heroic protagonism of eminent suffragettes. But while in some countries the struggle for women's suffrage did indeed entail militancy and sacrifice, and while the statistical results indicate that extensions by gender followed outbursts of mobilization, actions of militant women are not sufficient to explain the timing of these extensions.

If one thinks in the long run, sociological determinants seem predominant, the very issue of female suffrage appeared on the political agenda only when a significant part of middle-class and upper-class women could find work outside the household (Trevor 1971). Note that poor women were always forced to work in factories and fields, as domestic servants, and often on the streets. But they were poor and illiterate, and would have been excluded by these criteria alone. Jobs for educated women became available only toward the end of the nineteenth century. Hence, the sociological hypothesis is that women's suffrage became possible only when a sufficient number of educated women entered the public sphere by finding employment outside the household.

The effect of the two world wars is not obvious. They did accelerate the entrance of women to the labor market.[68] But the issue of women's suffrage was on the political agenda in many countries well before 1914 and in four countries women were enfranchised before the First World War. Hence, the question is whether suffrage would not have been extended to women, perhaps just a few years later, had the war not occurred. Indeed, Lloyd suggests that women would have been enfranchised in the United Kingdom before 1918 had the war not suppressed controversial domestic issues, while Collier makes the same argument with regard to the Netherlands and Belgium.[69] What does seem apparent is that the success of revolution in Russia, which introduced universal suffrage in 1918, and its role in World War II sparked revolutionary crises in several countries.

While participation of educated women in the labor force and the international norms concerning women's rights created a climate of opinion in which conflicts about female enfranchisement would proceed in particular countries, they provide only background conditions but do not explain the outcomes. The protagonists in these conflicts were organized groups that included political parties, women's movements, including some that were opposed to suffrage, in some countries the Catholic Church and in some temperance movements and their opponents, liquor lobbies. Did these groups behave strategically?

One would think that if a party expects that women would vote disproportionately in its favor, it would enfranchise them simply in its search for votes. Here is a sketch of an explanation of the timing of female suffrage. If parties seek to maximize their vote shares, any party wants to enfranchise women if it expects that the share of the vote it would receive from them would be larger than its current share in the male electorate. Assume that left and right-wing male voters have different preferences: this is why they vote for left or right parties. Now suppose that it is known that, while preferences of women are in some aspects different from those of men,[70] in some countries women were seen as more likely and in others as less likely to vote left (right) than men. Then different parties should have enfranchised women in different countries.

A clue to the partisan preferences is that none of the six countries which first enfranchised women were predominantly Catholic. The first Catholic countries that established universal suffrage were the newly independent Austria in 1918, Poland in 1919, and Ireland in 1923, followed by republican Spain in 1931. Five Latin American countries extended suffrage to women in the 1930s, but the rest of them, as well as the Catholic countries in Western Europe, waited until the end of World War II. But this delay was not due to the position of the Catholic Church. While the Church had long opposed female suffrage, arguing that the place of the woman is at home, by 1919 Pope Benedict XV abruptly changed this stance,[71] supporting the cause of vote for women, perhaps expecting that they would vote for conservative parties.

In turn, the timing of women's suffrage makes sense if the preferences of non-Catholic women were seen as closer to those of male left-wing voters, while the preferences of Catholic women as nearer to those of right-wing males. Some evidence that this is what the protagonists had thought is available. The French Radical Party thought that Catholic women would be influenced by the Church to vote for the Right and did nothing to advance their suffrage rights when it was in office in the 1920s.[72] In Belgium, Socialists adopted women's suffrage as a part of their platform but had to give it up in 1906 as a price for entering a coalition with Liberals, who had a larger vote share and were opposed to votes for women. Still in 1923, a Socialist feared: "If you give the vote to women, . . . Belgium will become one large house of Capuchins (*capucinière*)."[73] In Spain in 1931 even some women Socialists, notably Victoria Kent, feared that women would vote for conservative parties under the influence of the Church, but in the end their principles prevailed and women won franchise.

The earliest data concerning the actual voting patterns of women date to several years after they obtained suffrage. Tingsten used the fact that in (some) German districts and in Austria votes were tabulated separately for the two sexes. His calculations show that in Germany, where the proportions of Catholics and Protestants were more balanced, women were almost as likely as men to vote for the SPD in the Reichstag elections of 1924, 1938, and 1930, while the gap was much larger in the 1927 and 1930 elections in predominantly Catholic Austria.[74] Earliest survey results are available only for the 1950s: they show that women were in fact somewhat more likely than men to vote for the Social Democrats in Protestant Finland,[75] slightly more likely to vote for the Christian Democrats in West Germany,[76] and much less likely to vote for the Left in Catholic Italy.[77] Obviously, these are just bits and pieces, but they show that party leaders may not have been wrong.

Assume, then, that Catholic women are less likely to vote for the Left than Protestant ones. Left-wing parties would want to extend suffrage to women in Catholic countries when their share of vote among males is lower than the proportion of women who would vote for them if they were enfranchised. Since this proportion is low, left-wing parties want to do so only if their current vote share is very low, and when it is very low they cannot do it. Hence, no extensions occur when the share of the Left is low. In turn, conservative parties of any stripe would want to enfranchise women if the share of the Left among males exceeds the proportion of women who would vote Left. Hence, in Catholic countries women are enfranchised by the Right when it fears that Left might win a sizeable share of the vote among the voting males. In Protestant countries, however, the Left wants to enfranchise women even when it wins a large share of the male vote and does so when this share is sufficiently large to elect a Left party or coalition. The Right, in turn, wants to give women the vote only if the share of the Left among males is very large but this means that the share of the Right is small and it is unable to do it. Moreover, if the Left had a chance to do it, women would have been already enfranchised.

Hence, woman enfranchisement is likely to occur in Catholic countries only if the right-wing parties are in office but fear they would lose it because the proportion of males voting against them is increasing, which clearly was the rationale of Social Christians in Belgium in 1919, when suffrage was extended to some women, and again in 1949 when it became universal. Note that in the two countries with a sizeable but minority proportion of Catholics, Conservatives enfranchised women in Canada in 1921 even though Liberals had a chance to do it when they were in office between 1896 and 1911, while Catholics extended suffrage to women in the Netherlands in 1922 even though Liberals controlled governments between 1913 and 1918. In predominantly Catholic countries, France and Belgium, even Socialists did not use their tenure in government to enfranchise women. In France neither the Cartel des Gauches nor Front Populaire did it when they were in power during the inter-war period, but Christian Democrats did in 1945. In Belgium, Socialists were in office immediately before and after World War II, but women were enfranchised only when Christian Democrats came into office in 1949.

In non-Catholic countries, in turn, left-wing parties can enjoy a large vote share among males and still support female suffrage. Right-wing parties, however, should never enfranchise women. Indeed, among countries with a low proportion of Catholics, franchise was extended to women by Liberal governments in New Zealand and Norway,[78] a Protection-ist Party in Australia, and by the first Liberal-Social Democratic coalitions in Denmark and Sweden. The odd case is the United Kingdom, where women were enfranchised by a conservative government and, along with the United States, this may be a case where women's protagonism truly mattered.

Obviously, the model oversimplifies, as models do. At least in New Zealand, where as of 1880 Catholics constituted 15 percent of the popula-tion,[79] the electoral effect of enfranchising women was far from apparent to the protagonists: "Some believed women were a radical force; others that they were conservative upholders of traditional values. . . . The suffrage issue cut across conven-tional lines of political allegiance."[80] Hence, while Liberal backbenchers supported female suffrage, the leadership was divided. In Sweden, Conserva-tives opposed the 1918 Reform Bill even though "The extension of the franchise to women seemed harmless enough, since it could be assumed that their vote would be distributed roughly in the same proportion as men's."[81] Yet this argument goes a long way in predicting the timing of extensions to women. In most Protestant countries women were enfranchised by left-wing parties, pretty much as soon as they had a chance, while in Catholic coun-tries left-wing parties continued to procrastinate. At least for the handful of countries for which data are available, the relation between the propor-tion of population that is Catholic and the date at which women were enfranchised on the same basis as men is quite tight.

This argument is applicable only to countries where religions are a reliable predictor of potential voting patterns. But at least for these countries it suggests that, in contrast to extensions to poorer classes, enfranchisement of women was only in rare cases, notably those of the United Kingdom and the United States, a consequence of a threat women's movements presented to the incumbent elite. As Sulkunen observed, "Countries with the most militant suffragettism had to wait for years, even decades, before they could enjoy the fruits of their struggle, while many small, peripheral countries gave women full parliamentary representation at an early date without much ado."[82] These extensions seem to have resulted from the electoral calculus of political parties. Many women were active and some important protagonists in these parties before they had voting rights, but the calculus was electoral. Hence, in terms of the dichotomy posed here, women's rights were granted, not conquered.

Figure 8.8 includes three Latin American countries for which Lindert provides data on religious distribution: Brazil, Argentina, and Mexico. *Mutatis mutandis* these cases support the conclusion reached above: in Brazil literate women were enfranchised under the populist regime of Getulio Vargas in 1934 after a series of military insurrections; in Argentina women gained suffrage after the 1946 election that brought into office the populist regime of Juan Domingo Peron; and in Mexico suffrage was extended to women under the authoritarian reign of *Partido Revolucionario Institucional* in 1953. In fact, the first Latin American country to extend suffrage to all literate women was the arch-Catholic Ecuador in 1929, while the first one to make suffrage universal was Uruguay in 1932.

They were followed by Cuba in 1935, El Salvador in 1939, and the Dominican Republic in 1942. In all these countries suffrage was granted (*otorgado*) to women by ruling or prospective dictators who sought political support, mostly for changing constitutions in their favor.

Conclusion

For almost a century after representative institutions were first established, conflicts over suffrage were organized along class lines. Until well into the second half of the nineteenth century, whatever issues that may have divided the propertied men were not sufficient for partisan considerations to prevail over the fear of the distributional consequences that would ensue from incorporating the poor into representative institutions. But the poorer classes fought their way into the representative institutions. Once admitted, they were organized by different political parties. In pursuit of their economic and social goals, these parties sought to enhance their electoral positions, treating the issue of female suffrage as an instrument of electoral competition.

Figure 8.8 Year of equal female suffrage by proportion Catholic

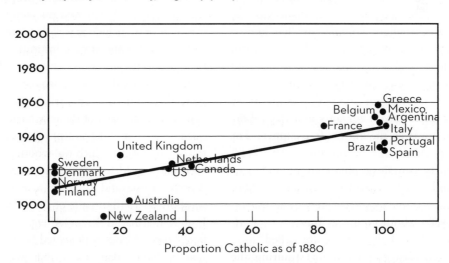

Note: Source for Catholic: Peter H. Lindert, *Growing Public*, Vol. 1 (Cambridge: Cambridge University Press, 2004), Table 5.5.

Appendix: Data

The data cover independent countries that existed at any time after 1919 and colonies that would become independent countries before 2001. The period begins from the origins of any kind of unit-level (country or territory) elective institutions and ends in 2000.

Suffrage Data

Information about suffrage rules is available for 187 political units, including periods before independence, for the total of 14,604 country-years.[83] The sources include regional volumes by Nohlen and his collaborators, Caramani for Western Europe, and histories of particular countries.[84] Only those franchise qualifications that were implemented at least once are considered, which also means that we date changes of suffrage rules by the time of the first election under the new rules, not by the time a law was passed.

Note that some franchise qualifications, in particular 4, 6, and 7, are often difficult to distinguish. The category 6, "independent males," is particularly amorphous, for reasons spelled out in the body of the text. The general coding rule was that if suffrage rules mention any specific thresholds (of income or tax), franchise was coded as 4; if they contained only vague phrases, such as "earns an honest living" or "has known sources of income," they were coded as 6. In turn, "independent" males are distinguished from all males, coded as 7, by the requirement of having a "regular," "known," or "honest" income or by an explicit exclusion of servants and day laborers. Again, however, the line is often slippery. For example, the Mexican Constitution of 1917, still in force today, contains a phrase about "independence," while the Swedish Constitution of 1866, in force until 1975, required voters to appear on tax rolls, yet in both countries franchise was *de facto* universal, and these cases are coded as 7. Similarly, the Ottoman provision requiring the payment of taxes was enforced in 1877 but not

when elections resumed in 1908: we code 1877 as 6 and the post 1908 period as 7.

Identifying suffrage extensions is surprisingly complex, both conceptually and practically. First, one must be careful about the units themselves. If one were to code all the information at the level of units that were not independent countries, one would introduce some observations that were clearly not independent. For example, in 1947 the French colonial authority reformed suffrage in seventeen of its African possessions. We treat this event as one, rather than seventeen independent observations. In general, whenever political decisions were taken at the level of some "supra" unit and were uniform for the component territories, suffrage qualifications are coded only at this level. In turn, countries that broke away from these "supra" units are considered to have inherited their suffrage rules, unless their suffrage qualifications were already distinct. Thus, for example, the French colonial authorities introduced suffrage restricted by income qualification for men and women (code = 42) in French Africa, of which one part was Dahomey. These restrictions were relaxed in 1947 and in 1951 and universal suffrage was introduced in 1956, still under colonial rule. The newly independent country of Benin inherited this qualification. One purely conceptual issue is whether to consider as "extensions" only those cases in which some people already had the right to vote before new categories were granted this right or to include as well the instances in which suffrage qualifications were institutionalized for the first time in the history of a country. The definition of extensions used in the analysis does include them. Note that some new countries may have had suffrage at least in parts of the new territory before the country became independent. This is, for example, the case of Poland, which was reborn in 1918 having been partitioned for more than a century between Austria, Prussia, and Russia. In turn, Czechoslovakia was born in 1918 of parts of the Austro-Hungarian Empire that had different suffrage rules. Still a different type of cases is presented by India and Pakistan (including Bangladesh) that were born out of British India, which had heterogeneous suffrage rules that did not correspond to the new boundaries. Finally, pre-1901 Australia consisted of provinces each of which regulated suffrage independently. In general, one can be almost certain that whenever the first recorded suffrage qualification falls short of universal for both sexes, this was indeed the first rule instituted. In some cases, however, in which the first recorded rule is universal suffrage, some or all parts of the new country may have had suffrage earlier.

The second conceptual issue is how to treat periods in which elections are abolished or suspended. A country holds elections under some suffrage rules, a dictator takes over, during some period no elections take place, and then electoral competition is reestablished. Suffrage rules are irrelevant during some period. The practical aspect of this issue is that while some dictators change the constitution, formally abolishing elections and thus the attendant rules, most of them do not bother to declare formally that suffrage rules are no longer valid; they simply do not hold elections. The coding rule adopted here maintains the extant suffrage rules as long as they are not formally altered. Hence, if some suffrage qualification is in place before elections cease to take place, this qualification is recorded until and unless a new one is instituted.

Another practical issue is presented by instances in which there are gaps in the data and the first suffrage rule observed after the information is again available differs from the last observed previously. For example, we know that male owners of property and some females on a narrower basis (code = 21) had the right to vote in Ghana as of 1945 and that as of 1950 qualified to vote were individuals of both genders if they earned some minimum income (code = 42). We cannot determine, however, when between 1946 and 1959 the reform occurred. There are eight such cases and in seven of them there was some other information which led us to believe that the reform took place at the latest date possible. Hence, the missing years are coded as having previously existing rules. The only exception is Colombia between 1863 and 1885, when suffrage qualifications were determined at the provincial level. These years were left as having missing data.

Given these decisions, current rules differ from those in force during the previous year in 389 instances. [In] forty-seven countries first qualifications provided for universal suffrage and in none of these countries was suffrage subsequently restricted. In addition, five countries maintained other suffrage rules during the entire period of observation. Hence, we observe at least one change of qualifications in 135 political units either before or after independence.

Now, in forty instances suffrage was contracted, meaning that qualifications became more restrictive. In addition, one case (Iran in 1963) ambiguous, since suffrage was extended to women while it was restricted by class. This leaves 348 suffrage extensions.

Table 8.4 Samples for which Different Variables are Available

	Independent only	Including colonies
Post-1918 only	*unrest*	
Entire period	*milper, urban, wars, farms*	*infmor, gdpcap*

Other Data

To follow the statistical analyses, it is important to keep track of the fact that different variables and consequently their combinations are available for different periods and different samples. Table 8.4 summarizes this coverage.

The variables are constructed as follows:

unrest: Sum of demonstrations, riots, and strikes from Banks,[85] lagged one year. The unlagged values are available for the period between 1919 and 1995 and only for independent countries, yielding 7,023 observations. Values are missing for the years of World War II. Hence, lagged values were not available for the year of independence as well as for 1919 and 1946. In the variable used in the text these missing lagged values were replaced by the current values for the years of independence but not for the years following wars. All the analyses were replicated with the unmodified lagged values, and in all cases these results were even stronger than those reported. Hence, the results reported in the text are conservative.

milper: Military personnel as a proportion of the population. Covers independent countries between 1815 and 1981, with 6,194 observations. Constructed by taking absolute numbers from Banks' (variable S08f6) and dividing by population, rather than from Banks' original per 10,000 numbers (S08f7). The absolute numbers are available from the Correlates of War Project for years preceding wars, or 445 observations. The correlation between the two sources is 0.87.

urban: Population in cities of 25,000 and above per hundred, from Banks (1996). Covers independent countries between 1815 to 1980, with 7,239 observations.

infmor: Mortality of infants during the first year of life, per hundred, from Mitchell.[86] Covers independent countries as well as colonies between 1809 and 1998, for the total of 4,886 observations.

gdpcap: Income per capita, from Maddison.[87] Covers independent countries as well as colonies between 1820 and 2000, yielding 8,814 observations.

before_war, war, after_war: The original data are from the Correlates of War Project. All these variables concern international wars, that is, wars between states as distinct from wars against non-state actors or civil wars. The dummy variable for *war* was created using the dates for the beginning and end of wars, but the ending date was modified for some countries during World War II, by extending it to the year when last hostilities occurred on a particular territory. (The original data seem to include only the initial hostilities, so that, for example, the World War II in Poland begins and ends in 1939.) The variable *before_war* dummies five years before an international war in which a country participated and *after_war* codes five years after the war ended. Note that the coverage begins in 1815, so that Napoleonic wars are not recorded. Also note that wars are not coded for colonies, even if they took an active part in them.

family farms: Proportion of land holdings owned and operated by families, from Vanhanen.[88] Linearly interpolated between dates for which observations were available, yielding 5,850 observations. Covers independent countries between 1850 and 1971.

NOTES

1. Bernard Manin, *A Theory of Representative Government* (New York: Cambridge University Press, 1997); John Dunn, *Democracy: A History* (New York: Atlantic Monthly Press, 2005).

2. Reinhard Bendix and Stein Rokkan, "The Extension of National Citizenship to the Lower Classes: A Comparative Perspective" (paper presented at the Fifth World Congress of Sociology, Washington, D.C., 1962), p. 30.

3. Adam Przeworski and Fernando Cortés, "Sistemas partidistas, movilización electoral y la estabilidad de sociedades capitalistas," *Revista Latinoamericana de Ciencia Política*, 2 (1971), 220–41.

4. John R. Freeman and Duncan Snidal, "Diffusion, Development, and Democratisation: Enfranchisement in Western Europe," *Canadian Journal of Political Science*, 55 (1982), 299–329.

5. John P. Conley and Akram Temini, "Endogenous Enfranchisement when Group Preferences Conflict," *Journal of Political Economy*, 109 (2001), 79–102.

6. Daron Acemoglu and James Robinson, "Why Did the West Extend the Franchise? Democracy, Inequality, and Growth in Historical Perspective," *Quarterly Journal of Economics*, 115 (2000), 1167–99. A more general treatment is by William Jack and Roger Lagunoff, "Dynamic Enfranchisement" (unpublished, Department of Economics, Georgetown University, 2003).

7. Alessandro Lizzeri and Nicola Persico, "Why Did the Elites Extend the Suffrage? Democracy and the Scope of the Government, with an Application to Britain's 'Age of Reform,'" *Quarterly Journal of Economics*, 118 (2004), 707–65.

8. Davide Ticchi and Andrea Vindigni, "On Wars and Political Development: The Role of International Conflicts in the Democratization of the West" (unpublished, Department of Politics, Princeton University, 2006).

9. Nicolò Machiavelli, *The Discourses*, edited by Bernard Crick (London: Penguin Books, 1970), Book 1, Discourse 32.

10. Ruth Berins Collier, *Paths Toward Democracy: The Working Class and Elites in Western Europe and South America* (Cambridge: Cambridge University Press, 1999).

11. Humberto Llavador and Robert Oxoby, "Partisan Competition, Growth and the Franchise," *Quarterly Journal of Economics*, 119 (2005), 1155–89.

12. Acemoglu and Robinson, "Why Did the West Extend the Franchise?," p. 1168, explicitly note that their model is not intended to apply to enfranchisement of women: "Since extending voting rights to women does not have major consequences for redistribution from the rich to the poor, social values rather than redistributive motives should be more important."

13. Moreover, this type of evidence seems to be based on the assumption that whatever happened later was a consequence of whatever occurred earlier. Since the lags between suffrage extensions and fis-

cal transformations vary according to the availability of data on the distribution of income, tax rates and expenditures on public goods, the causal effect of extensions cannot be identified.

14. While interpreting the variable that makes the threat of revolution credible in the Acemoglu–Robinson model is slippery, they observe: "The fact that μ fluctuates captures the notion that some periods may be more conducive to social unrest than others" (Acemoglu and Robinson, "Why Did the West Extend the Franchise?," p. 1170).

15. Arthur S. Banks, "Cross-National Time-Series Data Archive," 1996 version. See <http://www.databanks.sitchosting.net>.

16. B. R. Mitchell, *International Historical Statistics: The Americas, 1750–2000*, 5th edn (London: Palgrave Macmillan, 2003); B. R. Mitchell, *International Historical Statistics: Europe, 1750–2000*, 5th edn (London: Palgrave Macmillan, 2003); B. R. Mitchell, *International Historical Statistics: Africa, Asia and Oceania, 1750–2000*, 4th edn (London: Palgrave Macmillan, 2003).

17. One of the pieces of evidence Lizzeri and Persico cite in favour of their model is that suffrage reforms increased spending on public health (see Lizzeri and Persico, "Why Did the Elites Extend the Suffrage?" Section V.F).

18. Adam Przeworski and Fernando Limongi, "Modernization Theories and Facts," *World Politics*, 39 (1997), 155–83.

19. Angus Maddison, *The World Economy: Historical Statistics* (Paris: OECD Development Centre, 2003).

20. B. Peter Rosendorf, "Choosing Democracy," *Economics and Politics*, 13 (2001), 1–31.

21. Göran Therborn, "The Rule of Capital and the Rise of Democracy," *New Left Review* 103 (1977), 3–41.

22. Stanley L. Engerman and Kenneth L. Sokoloff, "Factor Endowments, Institutions, and Differential Paths of Growth Among New World Economies: A View from Economic Historians of the United States," in Stephen Haber, ed., *How Latin America Fell Behind: Essays on the Economic*

Histories of Brazil and Mexico, 1800–1914 (Palo Alto, Calif.: Stanford University Press, 1997), pp. 260–306; Stanley L. Engerman and Kenneth L. Sokoloff, "Inequality, Institutions, and Differential Paths of Growth Among New World Economies" (paper presented at the meeting of the MacArthur Research Network on Inequality and Economic Performance, Boston, 2001).

23. Tatu Vanhanen, *The Polyarchy Dataset* (Norwegian University of Science and Technology, see <http://www.svt.ntnu.no/iss/data/vanhanen>, 1996).

24. Multinomial logit estimates, conditioned on lagged franchise being less than universal, generate very similar results.

25. Since according to Ticchi and Vindigni, "On Wars and Political Development," extensions should precede military mobilizations, I also replicated all the analyses using the rate of growth of military personnel during the next year. This variable behaves in the same way as the current size of the military, that is, it never matters.

26. I replicated all the analyses using gross death rates rather than infant mortality. The results are always the same.

27. Ticchi and Vindigni, "On Wars and Political Development," p. 3; italics added.

28. Aberdam *et al.*, *Voter, élire pendant la Révolution française* 1789–1799, p. 265.

29. Gabriela Soriano, "Introducción," to *Simón Bolívar, Escritos políticos* (Madrid: Alianza Editorial, 1996), pp. 11–41.

30. Cited by Therborn, "The Rule of Capital and the Rise of Democracy," p. 14.

31. War periods are never distinct from periods that are neither before nor after wars.

32. Extensions that consist of lowering the age of eligibility are also less likely before wars, much more likely during post-war periods, and much more likely when more countries have universal suffrage. Of the other variables, only per capita income matters, with a highly significant positive sign. There were 158 such extensions, thirty coinciding with extensions by other criteria, but most of them, ninety-eight, occurred when franchise was already universal.

33. Note that Lott and Kenny, as well as Abrams and Settle, find that welfare expenditures increased, respectively in the United States and in Switzerland, when women gained the right to vote. But this is not evidence that the men who supported votes for women were motivated by a desire to expand these expenditures. Moreover, neither study considers selection bias (see John R. Lott and Lawrence W. Kenny, "Did Women's Suffrage Change the Size and the Scope of Government?" *Journal of Political Economy*, 107 (1999), 1163–98; Burton A. Abrams and Russell F. Settle, "Women's Suffrage and the Growth of the Welfare State," *Public Choice*, 100 (1999), 289–300.

34. Przeworski and Limongi, "Modernization."

35. Peter H. Lindert, *Growing Public*, Vol. 1 (Cambridge: Cambridge University Press, 2004), pp. 171–4.

36. Wilhelmine Germany is a complicated case. Acemoglu and Robinson, "Why Did the West Extend the Franchise?" use it in support of their claim that suffrage came later in countries with strong working-class movements, but in fact a broad male suffrage was introduced in Germany at the time of unification and they have to revert to *ad hoc* arguments that it was ineffective. Moreover, Lindert (*Growing Public*, p. 173) points out that Bismarck's insurance programmes had a minuscule redistributive component.

37. Adam Przeworski, *Capitalism and Social Democracy* (New York: Cambridge University Press, 1986).

38. Cited by Ralph Miliband, *Parliamentary Socialism: A Study in the Politics of Labour*, 2nd edn (London: Merlin Press, 1975), p. 69.

39. Douglas Verney, *Parliamentary Reform in Sweden, 1866–1921* (London: Oxford University Press, 1967), p. 208.

40. William Alexander Jencks, *The Austrian Electoral Reform of 1907* (New York: Columbia University Press, 1950), pp. 41–5.

41. Adrien de Mecus, *History of the Belgians* (New York: Frederick A. Praeger, 1962), p. 332.

42. Therborn, "The Rule of Capital and the Rise of Democracy," p. 8.

43. Törnudd, *The Electoral System of Finland*, p. 28.

44. Cited in Susan Dunn, *Jefferson's Second Revolution: The Election Crisis of 1800 and the Triumph of Republicanism* (Boston, Mass: Houghton Mifflin), p. 23.

45. Cited in Crook. *Elections in the French Revolution*, p. 46.

46. Francisco Gutiérrez Sanin, "La literatura plebeya y el debate alrededor de la propriedad (Nueva Granada, 1849–1854)," in Hilda Sabato, ed., *Ciudadania politica y formacion de las naciones. Perspectivas históricas de América Latina* (Mexico: El Colegio de Mexico, 2003), pp. 181–201, at p. 185.

47. Natalia Sobrevilla, "The Infuence of the European 1848 Revolutions in Peru," in Guy Thomson, ed., *The European Revolutions of 1848 and the Americas* (London: Institute of Latin American Studies, 2002), pp. 191–216, at p. 196.

48. Roberto Gargarella, *Los fundamentos legales de la desigualidad: El constitucionalismo en América (1776–1860)* (Madrid: Siglo XXI, 2005), p. 120.

49. Walter Bagehot, *The English Constitution* (Ithaca, N.Y.: Cornell University Press, 1963), p. 277.

50. Montesquieu, *De l'ésprit des lois* (Paris: Gallimard), p. 155.

51. Cited in Crook, *Elections in the French Revolution*, p. 13.

52. Restrictions of political rights based on religion were also couched in a universalistic language, but the appeal was not to reason but to common values. From Rousseau and Kant to J. S. Mill, everyone believed that a polity could function only if it is based on common interests, norms or values. Following on the Spanish Constitution of 1812, the cement holding societies together was to be Catholicism: of the 103 Latin American constitutions studied by Loveman, eighty-three proclaimed Catholicism as the official religion and fifty-five prohibited worship of other religions. While many arguments for restricting political rights to Catholics were openly directed against the principle of popular sovereignty—"it is not for people to change what God willed"—quite a few were pragmatic. For example, the Mexican thinker Lucas Alamán maintained in 1853 that Catholic religion deserves support by the state, "even if we do not consider it as divine" because it constitutes the only common tie that connects all Mexicans, when all others are broken (cited after Gargarella, who provides other examples). See Brian Loveman, *The Constitution of Tyranny: Regimes of Exception in Spanish America* (Pittsburgh: Pittsburgh University Press, 1993); Gargarella, *Los fundamentas legales de la desigualidad*, p. 93.

53. A speech by Senator Abdón Cifuentes, cited in Erika Maza Valenzuela, "Catolicismo, Anticlericalismo y la Extensión del Sufragio a la Mujer en Chile," *Estudios Politicos*, 58 (1995), 137–97, p. 153.

54. This is not to say that all restrctions of franchise were justified in a universalistic manner. For example, the Polish Constitution of 2 May 1791 asserted in Paragraph VI that "deputies to the local parliaments . . . should be considered as *representatives of the entire nation*" (italics in the original). Yet to become a deputy to the local parliaments (*sejniki*, which, in turn elect deputies to the national legislature, the *sejm*) one had to be a member of a legally defined group, the gentry (*szlachta*). In turn, only members of the hereditary gentry could own land entitling them to political rights. In fact, the Polish justification for privileging gentry was not reason but "Respect for the memory of our forefathers as founders of free government" (Article II) (Jerzy Kowecki, *Konstytucja 3 Maja 1791* (Warsaw: Państwowe Wydawnictwo Naukowe, 1991). Simón Bolívar used the same principle in 1819 when he offered positions of hereditary senators to the "liberators of Venezuela, . . . to whom the Republic owns its existence" (Bolívar, *Escritos politicos*, p. 109).

55. Cited in R. R. Palmer, *The Age of the Democratic Revolution: Vol. II. The Struggle* (Princeton, N.J.: Princeton University Press, 1964), p. 230. Hamilton formulated something like this syllogism

in his Plan for the National Government, delivered at the Convention on 18 June: "In every community where industry is encouraged, there will be a division of it into the few and the many. Hence separate interests will arise. There will be debtors and creditors, etc. Give all power to the many, they will oppress the few." Yet he thought, like Madison, that this effect could be prevented. Hamilton's speech is in Ralph Ketcham, ed., *The Anti-Federalist Papers and the Constitutional Convention Debates* (New York: Mentor Books, 1986), p. 75.

56. James Madison, *The Federalist Papers by Alexander Hamilton, James Madison and Jolm Jay*, edited by Gary Wills (New York: Bantam Books, 1982).

57. A note written at sometime between 1821 and 1829, in Ketcham, ed., *The Anti-Federalist Papers*, p. 152.

58. Stefan Collini, Donald Winch and John Burrow, *That Noble Science of Politics* (Cambridge: Cambridge University Press, 1983), p. 98.

59. Collini, Winch and Burrow, *That Noble Science of Politics*, p. 107.

60. Thomas B. Macaulay, *Complete Writings*, Vol. 17 (Boston and New York: Houghton-Mifflin, 1900), p. 263.

61. Cited by Charles Maier, *Recasting Bourgeois Europe* (Princeton. N.J.: Princeton University Press, 1975), p. 23.

62. Immanuel Kant. "The Principles of Political Right" [1793], in *Kant's Principles of Politics*, edited and translated by W. Hardie, B.D. (Edinburgh: T. & T. Clark, 1891), p. 38.

63. An observation made by Sieyes, according to Pasquale Pasquino, *Sieyes et L'Invention de la Constitution en France* (Paris: Editions Odile Jacob, 1998), p. 71. Note, however, that perhaps the most powerful of them all, Queen Victoria, adamantly opposed female suffrage.

64. Why were women not independent in the same way as some men were? If women could not own property, they were legally barred from qualifying for suffrage just by this criterion. But where they could and did own property in their own name, why would property ownership not be a sufficient indicator of reason? Condorcet, who defended property qualifications, thought it should be: "The reason for which it is believed that they [women] should be excluded from public function, reasons that albeit are easy to destroy, cannot be a motive for depriving them of a right which would be so simple to exercise [voting], and which men have not because of their sex, but because of their quality of being reasonable and sensible, which they have in common with women." Condorcet [1785], "Essai sur l'application de l'analyse a la probabilite des décisions rendues a la pluralité des voix" in *Sur les élections et autres texts*, textes choisis et revus par Olivier de Bernon (Paris: Fayard, 1986), pp. 9–176, at p. 293. And Chilean suffragettes claimed. "Wives and mothers, widows and daughters, we all have time and money to devote to the happiness of Chile." (An article in *El Eco*, 3 August 1865, cited in Maza Valenzuela, "Catolicismo," p. 156.) Yet these were isolated voices.

65. Helen Kendrick Johnson, *Woman and the Republic* (1913), http://www.womenhistory.about.com. Klinghofer and Elkis, "The Petticoat Electors," dispute that including women was simply an error, but I find their evidence unpersuasive.

66. Maza Valenzuela, "Catolicismo."

67. Trevor Lloyd, *Suffragettes International* (London: American Heritage Press, 1971), p. 14.

68. Indeed, in the four countries for which this information is available, only 1.6 percent of adult women were employed in non-manual occupations in Germany as late as of 1907, only 2.4 percent in Denmark in 1901, 2.8 percent in France in 1901, and 1.5 percent in Sweden in 1900. Only after World War I did this proportion surpass 5 percent in all these countries.

69. Lloyd, *Suffragettes International*; Collier, *Paths Toward Democracy*, p. 78.

70. For the argument that women are more risk-averse than men, see Lott and Kenny, "Did Women's Suffrage . . . ?"

71. According to Lloyd, *Suffragettes International*, p. 101.

72. Therborn, "The Rule of Capital and the Rise of Democracy"; Lloyd, *Suffragettes International*, p. 101.

73. Jean Stengers, "Histoire de la législation électorale en Belgique," in Serge Noiret, ed., *Political Strategies and Electoral Reforms: Origins of the Voting Systems in Europe in the 19th and 20th Centuries* (Baden-Baden: Nomos, 1990), pp. 76–107, at p. 87.

74. Herbert Tingsten, *Political Behavior: Studies in Election Statistics* (Totowa, N.J.: Becminster Press, 1973).

75. Erik Allardt and Pertti Pesonen, "Cleavages in Finnish Politics," in Seymour M. Lipset and Stein Rokkan, eds. *Party Systems and Voter Alignments* (New York: The Free Press, 1967), pp. 325–66.

76. Juan J. Linz, "Cleavage and Consensus in West German Politics: The Early Fifties," in Lipset and Rokkan, eds., *Party Systems and Voter Alignments*, pp. 283–322, at p. 191.

77. Mattei Dogan, "Political Cleavage and Social Stratification in France and Italy," in Lipset and Rokkan, eds., *Party Systems and Voter Alignments*, pp. 129–96, at p. 161.

78. The timing in Norway is perhaps explained by the defeat of the Liberal party by the Right in 1909.

79. Lindert, *Growing Public*, Table 5.5.

80. See (www.nzhistory.net.nz).

81. Verney, *Parliamentary Reform in Sweden*, p. 205.

82. Irma Sulkunen, "The Women's Movement," in Max Engman and David Kirby, eds., *Finland: People, Nation, State* (Bloomington: Indiana University Press, 1989), pp. 178–92.

83. Bhuttan, which had family-based representation is not included below. Saudi Arabia had no franchise rules before 2001.

84. Dieter Nohlen, *Enciclopedia Electoral Latinoamericana y del Caribe* (San Jose: Instituto Americano de Derechos Humanos, Costa Rica, 1993); Dieter Nohlen, ed., *Elections in the Americas: A Data Handbook, Volume 1: North America, Central America, and the Caribbean* (New York: Oxford University Press, 2005); Dieter Nohlen, Michael Krennerich and Bernhard Thibaut, eds, *Elections in Africa: A Data Handbook* (New York: Oxford University Press, 1999); Dieter Nohlen, Florian Grotz and Christof Hartmann, eds., *Elections in Asia and the Pacific: A Data Handbook* (New York: Oxford University Press, 2001); Dieter Nohlen, ed., *Elections in the Americas. A Data Handbook, Volume 1: North America, Central America, and the Caribbean* (New York: Oxford University Press, 2005); Danièle Caramani, *Elections in Western Europe since 1815: Electoral Results by Constituencies* (London: Macmillan, 2000).

85. See Banks, "Cross-National Time-Series Data Archive."

86. See Mitchell, *International Historical Statistics*, volumes cited in fn. 16.

87. See Maddison, *The World Economy*.

88. See Vanhanen, *The Polyarchy Dataset*.

Maurice Duverger
THE NUMBER OF PARTIES

Only individual investigation of the circumstances in each country can determine the real origins of the two-party system. The influence of such national factors is certainly very considerable; but we must not in their *favour* underestimate the importance of one general factor of a technical kind, the electoral system. Its effect can be expressed in the following formula: *the simple-majority single-ballot system favours the two-party system.* Of all the hypotheses that have been defined in this book, this approaches the most nearly perhaps to a true sociological law. An almost complete correlation is observable between the simple-majority single-ballot system and the two-party system: dualist countries use the simple-majority vote and simple-majority vote countries are dualist. The exceptions are very rare and can generally be explained as the result of special conditions.

We must give a few details about this coexistence of the simple-majority and the two-party systems. First let us cite the example of Great Britain and the Dominions: the simple-majority system with a single ballot is in operation in all; the two-party system operates in all, with a Conservative-Labour antagonism tending to replace the Conservative-Liberal antagonism. It will be seen later that Canada, which appears to present an exception, in fact conforms to the general rule.[1] Although it is more recent and more restricted in time the case of Turkey is perhaps more impressive. In this country, which had been subjected for twenty years to the rule of a single party, divergent tendencies were manifest as early as 1946; the secession of the Nationalist party,

which broke away from the opposition Democratic party in 1948, might have been expected to give rise to a multi-party system. On the contrary, at the 1950 elections the simple-majority single-ballot system, based on the British pattern (and intensified by list-voting), gave birth to a two-party system: of 487 deputies in the Great National Assembly only ten (i.e., 2.07%) did not belong to one or other of the two major parties, Democrats and Popular Republicans. Nine were Independents and one belonged to the Nationalist party. In the United States the traditional two-party system also coexists with the simple-majority single-ballot system. The American electoral system is, of course, very special, and the present-day development of primaries introduces into it a kind of double poll, but the attempt sometimes made to identify this technique with the "second ballot" is quite mistaken. The nomination of candidates by an internal vote inside each party is quite a different thing from the real election. The fact that the nomination is open makes no difference: the primaries are a feature of party organization and not of the electoral system.

The American procedure corresponds to the usual machinery of the simple-majority single-ballot system. The absence of a second ballot and of further polls, particularly in the presidential election, constitutes in fact one of the historical reasons for the emergence and the maintenance of the two-party system. In the few local elections in which proportional representation has from time to time been tried it shattered the two-party system: for example in New York between 1936 and 1947, where there were represented on the City Council 5 parties in 1937 (13 Democrats, 3 Republicans, 5 American Labor, 3 City Fusionists, 2 dissident Democrats), 6 parties in 1941 (by the addition of 1 Communist), and 7 parties in 1947 (as a result of an internal split

From *Political Parties: Their Organization and Activity in the Modern State* (New York: Wiley, 1954), pp. 217–28.

in the American Labor party supported by the Garment Trade Unions).

■   ■   ■

Elimination [of third parties] is itself the result of two factors working together: a mechanical and a psychological factor. The mechanical factor consists in the "under-representation" of the third, i.e. the weakest party, its percentage of seats being inferior to its percentage of the poll. Of course in a simple-majority system with two parties the vanquished is always under-represented by comparison with the victor, as we shall see below, but in cases where there is a third party it is under-represented to an even greater extent than the less favoured of the other two. The example of Britain is very striking: before 1922, the Labour party was under-represented by comparison with the Liberal party; thereafter the converse regularly occurred (with the one exception of 1931, which can be explained by the serious internal crisis in the Labour party and the crushing victory of the Conservatives); in this way the third party finds the electoral system mechanically unfair to it (Fig. 8.9). So long as a new party which aims at competing with the two old parties still remains weak the system works against it, raising a barrier against its progress. If, however, it succeeds in outstripping one of its forerunners, then the latter takes its place as third party and the process of elimination is transferred.

The psychological factor is ambiguous in the same way. In cases where there are three parties operating under the simple-majority single-ballot system the electors soon realize that their votes are wasted if they continue to give them to the third party: whence their natural tendency to transfer their vote to the less evil of its two adversaries in order to prevent the success of the greater evil. This "polarization" effect works to the detriment of a new party so long as it is the weakest party but is turned against the less favoured of its older rivals as soon as the new party outstrips it. It operates in fact in the same way as "under-representation." The reversal of

the two effects does not always occur at the same moment, under-representation generally being the earlier, for a certain lapse of time is required before the electors become aware of the decline of a party and transfer their votes to another. The natural consequence is a fairly long period of confusion during which the hesitation of the electors combines with the transposition of the "under-representation" effect to give an entirely false picture of the balance of power amongst the parties: England experienced such drawbacks between 1923 and 1935. The impulse of the electoral system towards the creation of bipartism is therefore only a long-term effect.

The simple-majority single-ballot system appears then to be capable of maintaining an established dualism in spite of schisms in old parties and the birth of new parties. For a new party to succeed in establishing itself firmly it must have at its disposal strong backing locally or great and powerful organization nationally. In the first case, moreover, it will remain circumscribed within the geographical area of its origin and will only emerge from it slowly and painfully, as the example of Canada demonstrates. Only in the second case can it hope for a speedy development which will raise it to the position of second party, in which it will be favoured by the polarization and under-representation effects. Here perhaps we touch upon one of the deep-seated reasons which have led all Anglo-Saxon Socialist parties to organize themselves on a Trade Union basis; it alone could put at their disposal sufficient strength for the "take-off," small parties being eliminated or driven back into the field of local campaigns. The simple-majority system seems equally capable of re-establishing dualism when it has been destroyed by the appearance of a third party. The comparison between Great Britain and Belgium offers a striking contrast: in both countries a traditional two-party system was broken up at the beginning of the century by the emergence of Socialism. Fifty years later the majority system restored bipartism in Great Britain by the elimination of the Liberals (Fig. 8.10), whereas in Belgium proportional representation saved the Liberal party and later made possible the

Figure 8.9 Disparity between percentage of votes and percentage of seats in Great Britain

I Gross disparity

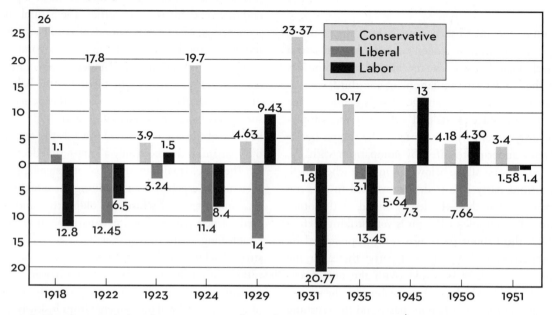

II Net disparity (related to percentage of votes).

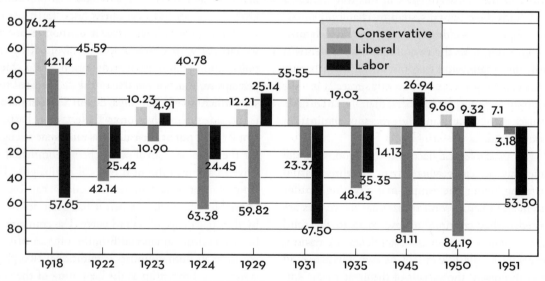

Figure 8.10 Elimination of Liberal Party in Great Britain

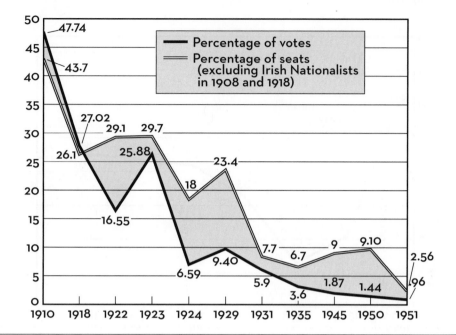

birth of the Communist party, without counting a few other parties between the wars (Fig. 8.11).

Can we go further and say that the simple-majority system is capable of producing bipartism in countries where it has never existed? If they already show a fairly clear tendency towards two parties, the answer would unquestionably be in the affirmative. The establishment of the simple-majority single-ballot system in Western Germany would undoubtedly have the effect of gradually destroying the small and medium-sized parties, leaving the Socialists and Christian Democrats face to face; there is undoubtedly no country in which the technical conditions more nearly approach those required for the establishment of a parliamentary system after the British pattern. In Italy an electoral reform of the same kind would have the same results—with the sole difference that the Communists would be one of the two parties, which would greatly imperil the future of the democratic system. However, the brutal application of the single-ballot system in a country in which multipartism has taken deep root, as in

France, would not produce the same results, except after a very long delay. The electoral system works in the direction of bipartism; it does not necessarily and absolutely lead to it in spite of all obstacles. The basic tendency combines with many others which attenuate it, check it, or arrest it. With these reserves we can nevertheless consider that dualism of parties is the "brazen law" (as Marx would have said) of the simple-majority single-ballot electoral system.

NOTE

1. Australia too offers an exception since the development of the *Country party*. But the system of preferential voting in operation there profoundly modifies the machinery of the simple-majority poll and makes it more like a two-ballot system by allowing a regrouping of the scattered votes. It is moreover a striking fact that the appearance of the Country party coincided with the introduction of the preferential vote.

Figure 8.11 "Rescue" of Belgian Liberal Party by P.R. (No. of seats in Chamber of Deputies.)

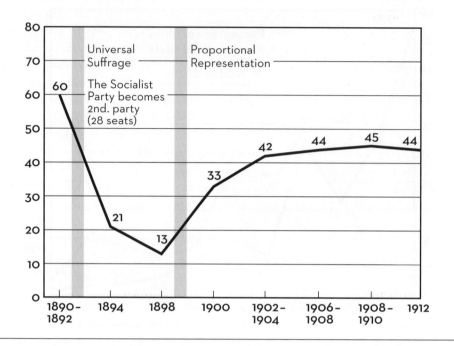

Torben Iversen and David Soskice

ELECTORAL INSTITUTIONS AND THE POLITICS OF COALITIONS: WHY SOME DEMOCRACIES REDISTRIBUTE MORE THAN OTHERS

Why do some countries redistribute more than others? Most work on the politics of redistribution starts from the premise that democratic institutions empower those who stand to benefit from redistribution. The basic logic is succinctly captured in the Meltzer–Richard (1981) model, where the voter with the median income is also the decisive voter. With a typical right-skewed distribution of income, the median voter will push for redistributive spending up to the point where the benefit of such spending to the median voter is outweighed by the efficiency costs of distortionary taxation.

This argument implies that redistribution is much greater in democracies than in nondemocracies (at least of the right-authoritarian variety), and

From *American Political Science Review* 100, no. 2 (May 2006), pp. 165–181.

that, among the latter, inegalitarian societies redistribute more than egalitarian ones. There is some evidence to support the first implication, although it is disputed (see Ross 2005), but most of the variance in redistribution is probably within the same regime type. According to data from the Luxembourg Income Study, for example, the reduction in the poverty rate in United States as a result of taxation and transfers was 13% in 1994, whereas the comparable figure for Sweden was 82% (the poverty rate is the percentage of households below 50% of the median income). To explain this variance, we have to look at political and economic differences among democracies, but the second implication — that inegalitarian societies redistribute more — turns out to be of little help. In fact the empirical relationship between inequality and redistribution is the opposite of the predicted one (see Bénabou 1996; Moene and Wallerstein 2001; Perotti 1996). Sweden not only redistributes more than the United States, but also is a much more egalitarian society. So the explanation for why some democracies redistribute more than others would seem to lie more or less wholly outside the standard framework in political economy to explain democratic redistribution.

One possibility is that the power of the working class and left political parties varies across countries (see, e.g., Korpi 1983, 1989; Hicks and Swank 1992; Huber and Stephens 2001). Because it is plausible that redistribution is a function of government policies, and such policies reflect the preferences of those who govern, looking for differences in government partisanship is a promising avenue. Furthermore, if left governments not only redistribute more but also reduce inequality of earnings by, say, investing heavily in public education, partisanship may also explain why equality and redistribution tend to co-vary. Indeed, there is much evidence to the effect that government partisanship helps explain cross-national differences in redistribution (Boix 1998; Bradley et al. 2003; Kwon and Pontusson 2003), and our findings corroborate this evidence. But it raises another puzzle: why are some democracies dominated by left governments, whereas others are dominated by right governments?

Although government partisanship is often assumed to reflect the level of working-class mobilization, we argue that it is in fact mainly determined by differences in coalitional dynamics associated with particular electoral systems. Table 8.5 shows the strong empirical relationship using a new dataset on

Table 8.5 Electoral System and the Number of Years With Left and Right Governments (1945–98)

		GOVERNMENT PARTISANSHIP		Proportion of Right Governments
		Left	Right	
Electoral system	Proportional	342	120	0. 26
		(8)	(1)	
	Majoritarian	86	256	0. 75
		(0)	(8)	

Note: Excludes centrist governments (see text for details).

parties and legislatures (see Cusack and Engelhardt 2002; Cusack and Fuchs 2002). The figures are the total number of years with right and left governments in 17 advanced democracies between 1945 and 1998, organized by type of electoral system. Mirroring a similar finding by Powell (2002), about three fourths of governments in majoritarian systems were center-*right*, whereas three fourths of governments under PR were center-*left* (excluding here "pure" center governments). The numbers in parentheses convey a sense of the evidence at the level of countries, classifying countries according to whether they have an overweight (more than 50%) of center-left or center-right governments during the 1945–98 period. We discuss the data (and the one outlier) in detail next.

Our explanation for the association of Table 8.5 builds on an emerging literature on the effects of electoral formulae on economic policies and outcomes (see, e.g., Persson and Tabellini 1999, 2000, 2003; Rogowski and Kayser 2002; Austen-Smith 2000). In particular, we argue that the electoral formula affects coalition behavior and leads to systematic differences in the partisan composition of governments—hence, to different distributive outcomes. The model we propose assumes that parties represent classes, or coalition of classes, and that it is difficult for parties to commit credibly to electoral platforms that deviate from the preferences of their constituents. We also make a critical departure from standard models based on Meltzer–Richard (1981) by allowing taxes and transfers to vary across classes, thereby transforming redistributive politics into a multidimensional game. In particular, we move away from a simple rich-poor model to one in which the middle class will fear taxation by the poor, even as it faces an incentive to ally with the poor to take from the rich. The only constraint is that the rich cannot "soak" the middle class and poor under democracy—a condition that can be justified on empirical, normative, and institutional grounds.

Based on these very general assumptions we show that in a two-party majoritarian system the center-right party is more likely to win government power, and redistribute less, than in a multi-party PR system where the center party is more likely to ally with parties to its left. The intuition is that in a majoritarian system where parties cannot fully commit, the median voter faces low taxes if a center-right party deviates to the right if elected, but faces high taxes and redistribution to low-income groups if a center-left party in government deviates to the left. With PR, on the other hand, the middle-class party has an incentive to form a coalition with the left party because they can together "exploit" the rich. No such exploitation of the poor is feasible under realistic assumptions. Remarkably, therefore, the same set of assumptions about redistributive policies leads to opposite predictions about government partisanship depending on the electoral system. We test the model on postwar data for redistribution and government partisanship for advanced democracies since the Second World War.

The Evidence

We test our argument in two parts. In the first part, we use partisanship and electoral system as explanatory variables to account for differences in the level of redistribution. In the second part, we use partisanship as the dependent variable, testing the proposition that the electoral system shapes coalition behavior and therefore the composition of governments.

Data

We base our analysis of redistribution on the Luxembourg Income Study (LIS), which has been compiling a large database on pre- and post-tax and transfer income inequality during the past three decades. The LIS data used for this study cover 14 countries from the late 1960s (the first observation is 1967) to the late 1990s (the last observation is 1997). All 14 countries have been democracies since the Second World War. There are a total of 61 observations, with the number of observations for each country ranging from 2 to 7. About one fifth of the observations are from the 1970s and late 1960s, about 40% from the 1980s, and the remainder from the 1990s. The data are based on separate national surveys, but considerable effort has gone into harmonizing (or "Lissifying") them to ensure comparability across countries and time. The LIS data are widely considered to be of high quality and the best available for the purposes of studying distribution and redistribution (see Brady 2003; OECD 1995).

As noted previously, we use the data specifically to explore the determinants of redistribution as measured by the percentage reduction in the Gini coefficient from before to after taxes and transfers. The Gini coefficient is perhaps the best summary measure of inequality, and varies from 0 (when there is a perfectly even distribution of income) to 1 (when all income goes to the top decile). Using an adjusted version of the LIS data—constructed by Huber, Stephens, and their associates (Bradley et al. 2003)[1]—we include only working age families, primarily because generous public pension systems (especially in Scandinavia) discourage private savings and therefore exaggerate the degree of redistribution among older people. Furthermore, because data are only available at the household level, income is adjusted for household size using a standard square root divisor (see OECD 1995).

On the independent side, the key variables for explaining redistribution are government partisanship and electoral system. The first is an index of the partisan left-right "center of gravity" of the cabinet based on (1) the average of three expert classifications of government parties' placement on a left-right scale, weighted by (2) their decimal share of cabinet portfolios. The index goes from left to right and is standardized to vary between 0 and 1. The measure was conceived by Gross and Sigelman (1984) and has been applied to OECD countries by Cusack in a new comprehensive data set on parties and partisanship (see Cusack and Fuchs 2002 and Cusack and Engelhardt 2002 for details). The expert codings are from Castles and

Mair (1984), Laver and Hunt (1992), and Huber and Inglehart (1995).

One issue raised by this measure is how we can be sure that partisan effects are due to differences in "who governs" as opposed to differences in voter preferences. Our argument is that the electoral system affects the party composition of governments, and hence government policies—*not* that electorates in different countries want different governments and policies (although that might of course also be the case). One way of making sure is to use the difference between the ideological center of gravity of the government and the ideological position of the median voter. Because the position of each party represented in the legislature is known, we can use the position of the party with the median legislator as a proxy for the median voter preference. Hence, we also test our model using this relative center of gravity measure. In cases with single-party majority governments (such as the current British Labour government)—where the government party controls the median legislator by definition—we use the *mean* position of the legislative parties weighted by the parties' seat shares (so that the Labour government would be recorded as being left of center).[2]

Turning to measurement of electoral system, the theoretical distinction between majoritarian two-party systems and proportional multiparty systems is roughly matched by differences in actual electoral systems (see Table 8.6). With the partial exception of Austria (because of the strong position of the two main parties), all PR systems tend to have multiple parties and coalition governments, whereas the non-PR systems have few parties and frequent single-party majority governments (although Australia and Ireland *have* experienced several instances of coalition governments).[3] This is indicated in the third column of Table 8.6 using Laasko and Taagepera's (1979) measure of the effective number of parties in parliament.[4] France is somewhat of an outlier among the majoritarian cases, but the second round of voting in the French runoff system usually involves candidates from only two parties.

Table 8.6 Key Indicators of Party and Electoral Systems

	Electoral System	Effective Number of Legislative Parties	Proportionality of Electoral System
Majoritarian			
Australia	Majority[a]	2.5	0.19
Canada	SMP	2.2	0.13
France	Runoff[b]	3.8	0.16
Ireland	STV[c]	2.8	0.70
Japan	SNTV[d]	2.7	0.61
New Zealand	SMP	2.0	0.00
UK	SMP	2.1	0.16
USA	SMP	1.9	0.39
Average		2.5	0.30
Proportional			
Austria	PR	2.4	0.89
Belgium	PR	5.2	0.86
Denmark	PR	4.4	0.96
Finland	PR	5.1	0.87
Germany	PR	2.6	0.91
Italy	PR	4.0	0.91
Netherlands	PR	4.6	1.00
Norway	PR	3.3	0.76
Sweden	PR	3.3	0.90
Average		3.9	0.90

a. The use of the single transferable vote in single-member constituencies makes the Australian electoral system a majority rather than plurality system.
b. The two-round runoff system has been in place for most of the postwar period with short interruptions of PR (1945 until early 1950s and 1986–88).
c. The Irish single transferable vote system (STV) is unique. Although sometimes classified as a PR system, the low constituency size (five or less) and the strong centripetal incentives for parties in the system makes it similar to a median-voter-dominated SMP system.
d. The single nontransferable voting (SNTV) in Japan (until 1994) deviates from SMP in that more than one candidate is elected from each district, but small district size and nontransferability make it clearly distinct from PR list systems.

The division of countries into two electoral systems is bolstered by the quantitative proportionality measure in the last column. This is a composite index based on Lijphart's measure of the effective threshold of representation and Gallagher's measure of the disproportionality between votes and seats (data are from Lijphart 1994). Note that the index is consistent with the division into a majoritarian and a proportional group: there are no cases that should be "switched" based on their value on the index. All our results go through if we use this index instead of the PR-majoritarian dichotomy.

We also controlled for variables that are commonly assumed to affect redistribution and/or partisanship. These variables, with definitions, sources, as well as a short discussion of causal logic, are listed next.

PRETAX AND TRANSFER INEQUALITY

This variable is included to capture the Meltzer–Richard logic that more inequality leads to more redistribution. It is measured as the earnings of a worker in the 90th percentile of the earnings distribution as a share of the earnings of the worker with a median income. We are using earnings data, despite their limitations, because the Meltzer–Richard model applies to individuals, not households. The data is from OECD's wage dispersion data set (unpublished electronic data).

CONSTITUTIONAL VETO POINTS

Composite measure of federalism, presidentialism, bicameralism, and the frequency of referenda, based on Huber, Ragin, and Stephens (1993). The more independent decision nodes, the more veto points. The left in countries with many veto points may have found it harder to overcome opposition to redistributive spending.

UNIONIZATION

According to power resource theory, high union density should lead to more political pressure for redistribution and a stronger left, whereas simultaneously reducing primary income inequality. The data are from Visser (1989, 1996).

VOTER TURNOUT

Lijphart (1997) argues that there is much evidence to the effect that voter nonturnout is concentrated among the poor. Higher turnout may therefore be associated with less redistribution. The turnout data are from annual records in Mackie and Rose (1991) and in International Institute for Democracy and Electoral Assistance (1997).

UNEMPLOYMENT

Because the unemployed receive no wage income, they are typically poor in the absence of transfers. Because all countries have public unemployment insurance, higher unemployment will therefore "automatically" be linked to more redistribution. We use standardized rates from OECD, *Labour Force Statistics* (Paris: OECD, various years).

REAL PER CAPITA INCOME

This is a standard control to capture "Wagner's Law," which says that demand for social insurance is income elastic. The data are expressed in constant 1985 dollars and are from the World Bank's Global Development Network Growth Database (http://www.worldbank.org/research/growth/GDNdata.htm)—itself based on Penn World Table 5.6, Global Development Finance and World Development Indicators.

FEMALE LABOR FORCE PARTICIPATION

Women's participation in the labor market is likely to affect redistributive spending because it entitles some women to benefits (unemployment insurance, health insurance, etc.) for which they would otherwise be ineligible. Because women tend to be lower paid it may also increase support for the left and for redistributive policies. The measure is female labor force participation as a percentage of the working age population and is taken from OECD, *Labour Force Statistics*, Paris: OECD, various years.

■ ■ ■

Findings

REDISTRIBUTION

We begin our presentation with the results from estimating a simple baseline model with economic variables only (column 1 in Table 8.6). As expected, female labor force participation and unemployment are associated with more redistribution. Contrary to Wagner's Law, higher per capita income slightly reduces redistribution, although the result is not statistically significant across model specifications.

As in other studies, we also find that inequality of pretax and transfer earnings has a *negative* effect on redistribution, contrary to the Meltzer-Richard model expectation. This negative effect is statistically significant at a .01 level, and the substantive impact is strong: a 1 SD increase in inequality is associated with a .3 standard deviation reduction in redistribution.

Yet the effect of inequality *reverses* (though the positive effect is not significant) when we include controls for the political-institutional variables (columns 2–4). One likely reason for this change is that left governments, as well as strong unions and PR, not only cause an increase in redistribution but also reduce inequality. Ansell (2005), for example, has found strong evidence that left governments spend more on primary education, which is likely to increase the equality of the wage structure. If so, excluding partisanship produces an omitted variable bias on the coefficient for inequality.

The most important result in Table 8.7 is that right partisanship has a strong and statistically significant negative effect on redistribution, regardless of whether we use the absolute (column 2) or the relative (column 3) measure of partisanship. A 1 SD

shift to the right reduces redistribution by about 1/3 SD. This confirms previous research, especially that of Bradley et al. (2003), and it adds the finding that partisanship matters *even* when measured relative to the ideological center of the legislature. This is important to our story because it implies that political parties, and the coalitions they form, matter for redistribution—not just differences in the preferences of electorates.

The results also suggest that multiple veto points, as expected, reduce redistribution, and that PR has a direct (positive) effect on redistribution. The latter effect holds regardless of which measure of electoral system in Table 8.6 that we use. Our model suggests one possible reason for this because if the probability of left deviation from a median voter platform is not too high, center-left governments will always redistribute more to the poor under PR than under majoritarian rules. To test this, we ran the same model using the percentage reduction in the poverty rate instead of reduction in the gini coefficient as the dependent variable. Consistent with this proposition it turns out that whereas the effect of partisanship is about the same, the direct effect of PR is notably stronger.[5]

There may also be effects of electoral systems that we have not modeled. Persson and Tabellini (2003), for example, have argued that single member plurality systems incentivize politicians to target spending on geographically concentrated constituencies, whereas PR, with ideally only one electoral district, encourages politicians to spend more on universalistic benefit programs. Because universalistic programs are likely to be more redistributive than geographically targeted programs, this would mean that PR has a direct effect on redistribution. But our focus is on the effect of electoral system on partisanship, to which we now turn.

PARTISANSHIP

Whereas both government partisanship and electoral system are important in explaining redistribution, partisanship itself is shaped by the distinct

Table 8.7 Regression Results for Reduction in Inequality (Standard Errors in Parentheses)

	(1)	(2)	(3)
Inequality	−16.75***	13.17	12.48
	(5.68)	(9.36)	(8.96)
Political–institutional variables			
Government partisanship (right)	–	−2.38***	–
		(0.73)	
Government partisanship relative to median legislator	–	–	−2.93***
			(0.75)
Voter turnout	–	0.01	−0.06
		(0.10)	(0.10)
Unionization	–	0.16*	0.15*
		(0.09)	(0.09)
Number of veto points	–	−1.57**	−1.79***
		(0.62)	(0.59)
Electoral system (PR)	–	5.00**	4.44**
Controls		(2.15)	(2.06)
Per capita income	−0.001***	−0.001	−0.001
	(0.00)	(0.00)	(0.000)
Female labor force participation	0.73***	0.36	0.45***
	(0.11)	(0.20)	(0.20)
Unemployment	0.81***	0.99***	1.08***
	(0.27)	(0.27)	(0.26)
ρ	.4	.7	.7
R-squared	0.648	0.746	0.765
N	47	47	47

Note: *Significance levels*: ***<. 01; **<. 05; *<. 10 (two-tailed tests). All independent variables are measures of the cumulative effect of these variables between observations on the dependent variable. See regression equation and text for details.

coalitional politics associated with different electoral systems. A key implication of our argument is that center-left governments tend to dominate over long periods of time under PR, whereas center-right governments tend to dominate under majoritarian institutions. Although the electoral system has a direct effect on redistribution, we argue that partisanship is one of the key mechanisms through which it exerts an effect on redistribution. * * *

Conclusion

The details of actual tax-and-spend policies for the purpose of redistribution are complex, but the explanation for redistribution in advanced democracies is arguably fairly simple. We propose here that to a very considerable extent, redistribution is the result of electoral systems and the class coalitions they engender. The contribution of this paper is to provide a very general model that explains the electoral system effect, and to empirically test this model.

To explain redistributive policies under democracy, it is essential to understand that policies are multidimensional and that groups have to form partisan coalitions to govern. Both features of redistributive politics are assumed away in standard political economy models that follow the setup in Meltzer and Richard (1981). In our model, by contrast, there is nothing that prevents the poor from taking from the middle class, or the middle class taking from the rich. This means that the middle class, which tends to decide who governs, has an incentive to ally with the poor to exploit the rich, but also an incentive to support the rich to avoid being exploited by the poor. In a majoritarian two-party system, the latter motive dominates because the middle-class cannot be sure that the poor will not set policies in a center-left leadership party. In a PR system with three representative parties, on the other hand, the first motive dominates because the middle-class party *can* make sure that a coalition with the left party will not deviate from pursuing their common interest in tax-ing and redistributing from the rich. The center-right governments therefore tend to dominate in majoritarian systems, whereas the center-left governments tend to dominate in PR systems.

NOTES

1. We are grateful to the authors for letting us use their data.
2. We did the same in a small number of cases where the government position is equivalent to the median legislator, but where it is not a single-party majority government.
3. Ireland is perhaps the most ambiguous case, but it is not part of the redistribution regression, and the results for partisanship are not sensitive to the particular electoral system measure we use or whether Ireland is included or excluded.
4. The effective number of parties is defined as one divided by the sum of the square root of the shares of seats held by different parties (or one divided by the Hilferding index).
5. The effect of going from a majoritarian system to a PR system is to increase redistribution to the poor by .7 SD whereas the effect on the gini coefficient is .5 SD.

REFERENCES

Ansell, Ben. 2005. "From the Ballot to the Blackboard? Partisan and Institutional Effects on Human Capital Policy in the OECD. Department of Government." Harvard University. Typescript.

Austen-Smith, David. 2000. "Redistributing Income Under Proportional Representation." *Journal of Political Economy* 108 (6): 1235–69.

Bénabou, Roland. 1996. "Inequality and Growth." In *National Bureau of Economic Research Macro Annual*, ed. Ben S. Bernanke and Julio J. Rotemberg, Cambridge: MIT Press, Vol. 11, pp. 11–74.

Boix, Carles. 1998. *Political Parties, Growth and Equality.* New York: Cambridge University Press.

Bradley David, Evelyne Huber, Stephanie Moller, François Nielsen, and John Stephens. 2003. "Distribution and Redistribution in Postindustrial Democracies." *World Politics* 55 (2): 193–228.

Brady, David. 2003. "Rethinking the Sociological Measure of Poverty." *Social Forces* 81 (3): 715–52.

Castles, Francis, and Peter Mair. 1984. "Left-Right Political Scales: Some Expert Judgments." *European Journal of Political Research* 12: 73–88.

Cusack, Thomas R., and Lutz Engelhardt. 2002. "The PGL File Collection: File Structures and Procedures." Wissenschaftszentrum Berlin für Sozialforschung.

Cusack, Thomas R., and Susanne Fuchs. 2002. "Documentation Notes for Parties, Governments, and Legislatures Data Set." Wissenschaftszentrum Berlin für Sozialforschung.

Gross, Donald A., and Lee Sigelman. 1984. "Comparing Party Systems: A Multidimensional Approach." *Comparative Politics* 16: 463–79.

Hicks, Alexander, and Duane Swank. 1992. "Politics, Institutions, and Welfare Spending in Industrialized Democracies, 1960–82." *American Political Science Review* 86 (3): 649–74.

Huber, Evelyne, Charles Ragin, and John Stephens. 1993. "Social Democracy, Christian Democracy, Constitutional Structure and the Welfare State." *American Journal of Sociology* 99 (3): 711–49.

Huber, Evelyne, and John D. Stephens. 2001. *Development and Crisis of the Welfare State: Parties and Policies in Global Markets.* Chicago: University of Chicago Press.

Huber, John D., and Ronald Inglehart. 1995. "Expert Interpretations of Party Space and Party Locations in 42 Societies." *Party Politics* 1: 73–111.

International Institute for Democracy and Electoral Assistance. 1997. *Voter Turnout from 1945 to 1997: A Global Report on Political Participation.* Stockholm: IDEA Information Services.

Korpi, Walter. 1983. *The Democratic Class Struggle.* London: Routledge & Kegan Paul.

Korpi, Walter. 1989. "Power, Politics and State Autonomy in the Development of Social Citizenship — Social Rights During Sickness in 18 OECD Countries Since 1930." *American Sociological Review* 54 (3): 309–28.

Kwon, Hyeok Yong, and Jonas Pontusson. 2003. "The Zone of Partisanship, Parties, Unions and Welfare Spending on OECD Countries, 1962–99." Unpublished Manuscript, Department of Political Science, Cornell University.

Laasko, Markku, and Rein Taagepera. 1979. "Effective Number of Parties: A Measure with Applications to Western Europe." *Comparative Political Studies* 12 (3): 3–27.

Laver, Michael, and W. Ben Hunt. 1992. *Policy and Party Competition.* New York: Routledge.

Lijphart, Arend. 1994. *Electoral Systems and Party Systems: A Study of Twenty-Seven Democracies, 1945–90.* New York: Oxford University Press.

Lijphart, Arend. 1997. "Unequal Participation: Democracy's Unresolved Dilemma." *American Political Science Review* 91: 1–14.

Mackie, Thomas T., and Richard Rose. 1991. *The International Almanac of Electoral History*, 3rd edition. London: Macmillan.

Meltzer, Allan H., and Scott F. Richard. 1981. "A Rational Theory of the Size of Government." *Journal of Political Economy* 89: 914–27.

Moene, Karl Ove, and Michael Wallerstein. 2001. "Inequality, Social Insurance and Redistribution." *American Political Science Review* 95 (4): 859–74.

OECD. 1995. "Income Distribution in OECD Countries: Evidence from the Luxembourg Income Study." *Social Policy Studies* No. 18.

Perotti, Roberto. 1996. "Growth, Income Distribution and Democracy: What the Data Say." *Journal of Economic Growth* 1 (2): 149–87.

Persson, Torsten, and Guido Tabellini. 1999. "The Size and Scope of Government: Comparative Politics with Rational Politicians." *European Economic Review* 43: 699–735.

Persson, Torsten, and Guido Tabellini. 2000. *Political Economics: Explaining Economic Policy.* Cambridge: MIT Press.

Persson, Torsten, and Guido Tabellini. 2003. *The Economic Effects of Constitutions.* MIT Press.

Powell, Bingham. 2002. "PR, the Median Voter, and Economic Policy: An Exploration." Paper presented at the 2002 Meetings of the American Political Science Association, Boston.

Rogowski, Ronald, and Mark Andreas Kayser. 2002. "Majoritarian Electoral Systems and Consumer Power: Price-level Evidence from the OECD Countries." *American Journal of Political Science* 46 (3): 526–39.

Ross, Michael. 2005. "Does Democracy Reduce Infant Mortality?" Paper presented in Workshop on Democratic Institutions and Economic Performance. Duke University. April 1–2, 2005.

Visser, Jelle. 1989. *European Trade Unions in Figures.* Deventer/Netherlands: Kluwer Law and Taxation Publishers.

Visser, Jelle. 1996. "Unionization Trends Revisited." Mimeo. University of Amsterdam.

Margarita Estévez-Abe, Torben Iversen, and David Soskice
SOCIAL PROTECTION AND THE FORMATION OF SKILLS: A REINTERPRETATION OF THE WELFARE STATE

Introduction

Social protection rescues the market from itself by preventing market failures. More specifically, * * * social protection * * * [helps] economic actors overcome market failures in skill formation. We show, in this chapter, that different types of social protection are complementary to different skill equilibria. * * *

Young people are less likely to invest in specific skills if the risk of loss of employment opportunities that require those specific skills is high. Employers who rely on specific skills to compete effectively in international markets therefore need to institutionalize some sort of guarantee to insure workers against potential risks. Without implicit agreements for long-term employment and real wage stability, their specific skills will be under-supplied. Employ-

From Peter A. Hall and David Soskice, eds., *Varieties of Capitalism: The Institutional Foundations of Comparative Advantage* (New York: Oxford University Press, 2001), pp. 145–183.

ers' promises are not, however, sufficiently credible by themselves. This is why social protection as governmental policy becomes critical. * * *

Institutional differences that safeguard returns on specific skills explain why workers and employers invest more in specific skills. The absence of such institutions, in countries such as the USA and UK, gives workers a strong incentive to invest in transferable skills. In such an environment, it then also makes more economic sense for firms to pursue product market strategies that use these transferable skills intensely. * * *

The model of micro-level links between skills and social protection we develop in this chapter has important policy implications. First, our model predicts what types of political alliance are likely to emerge in support of a particular type of social protection. For example, in economies where companies engage in product market strategies that require a combination of firm- and industry-specific skills, and where a large number of workers invest in such skills, a strong alliance between skilled workers and their employers in favor of social protection advantageous to them is likely to emerge—even if this means reducing job opportunities for low-skilled workers. By contrast, where business has no common interest in the promotion of specific skills, it will have no interest in defending * * * social protection. Second, we show that different systems of social protection have deeper ramifications for inequality than commonly assumed. Some skill equilibria—sustained by different systems of social protection—produce more inequalities based on the academic background of workers, while others produce more inequalities based on gender.

■   ■   ■

Product Market Strategies, Skill Types, and The Welfare State

■   ■   ■

Skills and Product Market Strategies

[We distinguish] three types of skills associated with different product market strategies: (i) firm-specific skills; (ii) industry-specific skills; and (iii) general skills.[1] These skills differ significantly in terms of their asset specificity (i.e., portability). Firm-specific skills are acquired through on-the-job training, and are least portable. They are valuable to the employer who carried out the training but not to other employers. Industry-specific skills are acquired through apprenticeship and vocational schools. These skills, especially when authoritatively certified, are recognized by any employer within a specific trade. General skills, recognized by all employers, carry a value that is independent of the type of firm or industry. Of course, any actual production system will involve all three types of skills to some degree.

Nonetheless, we can characterize distinctive product market strategies based upon the "skill profile" they require.

* * * [M]ass production of standardized goods does not require a highly trained workforce. Production work is broken into a narrow range of standardized tasks that only require semi-skilled workers. Traditional US manufacturing industries such as automobile and other consumer durables fall into this category. There is, however, a variant of mass production called diversified mass production (DMP). The DMP strategy, in contrast, aims at producing a varied range of products in large volumes. Japanese auto-makers and domestic electronic appliances industry are good examples. This production strategy depends on workers capable of performing a wide range of tasks to enable frequent product changes in the line (Koike 1981). Workers are also expected to solve problems that emerge in the production line themselves to minimize downtime (Shibata 1999). The tasks these workers perform involve high levels of knowledge about their company products and machineries in use, and hence are highly firm-specific.

There are product market strategies that do not mass produce. One strategy is a high-quality product niche market strategy. It requires a highly trained workforce with industry-specific craft skills. The prototype of this production strategy does not involve any scale merit, and the process tends to involve highly craft-intensive workshops. Custom-made clothing, jewelry, and fine porcelain may be examples of such production. Another strategy is a hybrid. It pursues high-quality product lines, but takes the production out of small-scale craft shops in order to increase the volume of production. Streeck (1992b) calls this diversified quality production. This production strategy requires firm-specific skills in addition to high levels of craft skills. Germany is a prototype of this type of production.

All the above strategies require firm-specific and industry-specific skills to varying degrees. It is important, however, to note that relative abundance of high levels of general skills (i.e., university and postgraduate qualifications) brings comparative advantages in radical product innovation. Let us take the example of the USA to illustrate this point. For example, start-up software companies in the USA take advantage of a highly flexible labor market with university-educated people combining excellent general skills with valuable knowledge about the industry acquired from switching from one job to another. Another example would be American financial institutions, which have taken advantage of an abundant supply of math Ph.D.s to develop new products such as derivatives. Complex systems development (for e-commerce, for example), biotechnology, segments of the telecommunications industry, and advanced consulting services are other examples that fall into this class of industries.

The Welfare-Skill Formation Nexus

We make the three following assumptions about workers' economic behavior:

(i) *People calculate overall return to their educational/training investment before deciding to commit themselves. (The investment cost of further training and education can be conceptualized in terms of wages forgone during the period of training and education, in addition to any tuition or training fees incurred.)*

(ii) *People choose to invest in those skills that generate higher expected returns, provided that the riskiness of the investments is identical.*

(iii) Ceteris paribus, *people refrain from investing in skills that have more uncertain future returns (i.e., people are risk averse).*

From these assumptions, it follows that a rational worker must consider three factors in making skill investment decisions: (i) the initial cost of acquiring the skills as, for instance, when a worker receives a reduced wage during the period of training; (ii) the

future wage premium of specific skills; and (iii) the risks of losing the current job and the associated wage premium.

The core skills required by an industry are critical for this analysis because they vary in the degree to which they expose workers to the risk of future income losses. Highly portable skills are less risky than highly specific skills because in the former case the market value of the skill is not tied to a particular firm or industry. Faced with future job insecurity, a rational worker will not invest his or her time and money in skills that have no remunerative value outside the firm or industry. In other words, in the absence of institutional interventions into workers' payoff structure, general rather than asset-specific skill acquisition represents the utility-maximizing strategy.

Let us now examine what types of institutions are necessary in order to protect investments in asset-specific skills. We can distinguish three different types of protection, which might be called *employment protection, unemployment protection*, and *wage protection. Employment protection* refers to institutionalized employment security. The higher the employment protection, the less likely that a worker will be laid off even during economic downturns. *Unemployment protection* means protection from income reduction due to unemployment, and can thus reduce the uncertainty over the wage level throughout one's career. *Wage protection*, finally, is an institutional mechanism that protects wage levels from market fluctuations. In this section, we first contrast the significance of *employment protection* and *unemployment protection* for firm-specific and industry-specific skills. We will discuss wage protection in a separate section, because it is generally not considered to be part of the welfare system.

Firm-specific skills are, *ex hypothesi*, worthless outside that specific firm, and they therefore require a high level of *employment protection* in order to convince workers to invest in such skills (Aoki 1988). Since workers will only be paid the value of their non-firm-specific skills in the external market, the greater their investment in specific skills the greater the discrepancy between current wages and the wages they could fetch in the external market. In order to invest heavily in firm-specific skills, workers therefore need assurances that they can remain in the company for a long enough period to reap the returns on such investments (see Lazear and Freeman 1996; Osterman 1987; Schettkat 1993). If not, the expenditures of training must be commensurably lower, and/or the premium on future wages higher. In either case, the cost of training for the firm goes up, and it will offer less training.

Because rational workers weigh higher expected income later in their career against the risks of losing their current job, the only way to encourage workers to carry a substantial part of the costs of firm-specific training is to increase job security and/or reduce the insecurity of job loss. Hence we can interpret institutionalized lifetime employment, or subsidies to keep redundant workers within the firm, as safeguarding mechanisms for firm-specific skill investment.

■ ■ ■

For firms pursuing product market strategies which depend heavily on firm- and industry-specific skills, promise of employment and unemployment security can thus provide a cost-effective path to improving the firms' competitive position in international markets (cf. Ohashi and Tachibanaki 1998; Koike 1994). Contrary to conventional neoclassical theory, which sees efforts to increase protection against job loss as an interference with the efficient operation of labor markets, measures to reduce future uncertainty over employment status—hence uncertainty over future wage premiums—can significantly improve firms' cost effectiveness (Schettkat 1993). And the more successful these firms are, the greater their demand for specific skills. We are in a specific skills equilibrium.

If there is little protection built into either the employment or the unemployment system, the best insurance against labor market risks for the worker is to invest in general, or portable, skills that are highly valued in the external labor market. If general skills are what firms need for pursuing their product market strategies successfully, low employment protection can thus give these firms a competitive edge. Indeed, if most firms are pursuing general skills strategies, then higher protection will undermine workers' incentives to invest in these skills, *without* significantly increasing their appropriation of specific skills (because there is little demand for such skills). In this general skills equilibrium the neoclassical efficiency argument for little protection is more valid.[2]

The predictions of the argument are summarized in Fig. 8.12, which identifies the four main welfare production regimes and gives an empirical example of each (discussed below).

Figure 8.12 Social Protection and Predicted Skill Profiles

Unemployment protection		Employment protection: Low	Employment protection: High
	High	Industry-specific skills Example: Denmark	Industry-specific, firm-specific skill mix Example: Germany
	Low	General skills Example: United States	Firm-specific skills Example: Japan

■ ■ ■

Self-Reinforcing Inequalities and Political Preferences

So far the discussion has focused on the efficiency aspects of social protection. In this section we extend the core argument to unravel two sets of previously neglected logics by which welfare production regimes perpetuate inequalities. First, we point out that general skill systems are more likely to create a "poverty trap." Second, we cast light upon the gender inequality consequences of different product market strategies. Finally, we discuss how these distributive implications of different welfare state regimes are reproduced and perpetuated through distinct patterns of political support for social protection.

Distribution, Poverty Traps, and Product Market Strategies

Our argument has far-reaching implications for equality and labor market stratification, some of which are poorly understood in the existing welfare state literature. Product market strategies that rely on high levels of industry-specific and firm-specific skills are likely to create more egalitarian societies than product market strategies based on general skills. They therefore help us understand large and persistent cross-national differences in the distribution of wages and incomes. The existing literature can only account for these differences in so far as they are caused by redistributive state policies. This is far too narrow an approach. We contend that most inequalities result from particular welfare production regimes (i.e., combinations of product market strategies, skill profiles, and the political-institutional framework that supports them).

The basic logic of our argument is straightforward. We argue that different skill systems and accompanying training systems have important economic implications for those who are academically weak and strong respectively. For the bottom one third, or so, of the academic ability distribution, a highly developed vocational training system offers the best opportunities for students to acquire skills that are valued by employers. When entry into vocational training is competitive, these students have an incentive to be as good as they can academically in order to get into the best training programs with the most promising career prospects (Soskice 1994). Therefore, countries with well-developed (and competitive) vocational training systems provide a stable economic future even to those students who are not academically strong. General education systems, in contrast, offer these students relatively few opportunities for improving their labor market value outside of the school system. As a result, there are fewer incentives for them to work hard inside the school system.

In firm-specific skill-training systems, employers develop strong stakes in overseeing the quality of potential employees (i.e., trainees) and developing clear job entry patterns.[3] Since employers are committed to make significant initial human capital investment in new job entrants, they will be interested in monitoring the quality of the pool of the new school leavers. As a result, they are likely to establish a working relationship with various schools for systematic hiring of new school leavers. Since employers in a firm-specific skill system carry out initial job training, new school graduates have a chance of building careers as skilled workers. This gives young schoolgoers a strong incentive to work hard in school. The "from-school-to-work" transition is likely to be more institutionalized (Dore and Sako 1989). Similarly, in the case of industry-specific skills where employers are involved, employers take an interest in ensuring the quality of vocational training and the certification of skills (Finegold and Soskice 1988). In these systems, education-work transition is also relatively institutionalized (Ni Cheallaigh 1995; Blossfeld and Mayer 1988).

In general skill regimes, in contrast, the "from-school-to-work" transition is less institutionalized (see Allmendinger 1989). Hiring is more flexible. Employers hire new job entrants with different educational backgrounds. Promotion and opportunities for further skill training are themselves contingent upon the job performance of the worker. There is not so much initial human capital investment by employers as there is in firm-specific skill systems. Because of the absence of a clear vocational track, systems based on general skills therefore tend to disadvantage those who are not academically inclined. Regardless of the presence or absence of vocational schools and apprenticeship programs, for employers who emphasize general skills a certificate from a vocational school does not add much value to the worker. Potential workers therefore have to demonstrate their competence in terms of general scholarly achievement, and getting a tertiary degree becomes an essential component. Because there is a hierarchy of post-secondary schools, if the student thinks there is a possibility of making it into the tertiary educational system, he or she has a strong incentive to work hard. For those who are not academically inclined, by contrast, the system produces the unintended consequence of undermining the incentive to work hard in school. In the absence of a specialized vocational track, unless a student believes that he or she can make the cut into college, there is not much gained by being a good student.

In short, in general skill systems, since the completion of elementary and secondary school does not qualify them for a vocational certificate that leads to secure jobs, academically weak students face lower returns from their educational investment. Since the opportunity for vocational training—both on the job and off the job—for these students will remain low, it creates an impoverished labor pool. In contrast, at the top end of the ability distribution, a general education system offers the largest returns to those with advanced graduate and postgraduate degrees. These returns tend to be more modest in specific skills systems because a large number of companies depend more on industry-specific and firm-specific skills than professional degrees or broad academic qualifications. General skill systems, therefore, reward those students who are academically talented in terms of labor market entry. Distribution of academic aptitude thus translates into distribution of skills, and consequently into a very skewed distribution of earnings. As a consequence, academically weak students in general skill regimes are worse off than their counterparts elsewhere: they are more likely to be trapped in low-paid unskilled jobs.

Gender Equality and Skill Types

Compared to men, women face an additional set of issues when making skill investment choices (see Estévez-Abe 1999). In addition to the probability of layoff, women have to take into consideration the likelihood of career interruption due to their role as mothers (see Daly 1994; Rubery et al. 1996). For a woman to invest in specific skills, she has to be assured that potential career interruptions will not (i) lead to dismissal; or (ii) reduce her wage level in the long run. A high probability of dismissal reduces the incentives to acquire firm-specific skills. A high probability of reduction in wages after becoming a mother—because of time off due to childbirth and-rearing—reduces the incentives to invest in either firm-specific or industry-specific skills.

For women, therefore, employment protection necessarily involves two factors in addition to the employment and unemployment protection discussed earlier. These two factors are (i) protection against dismissal, such as maternity, parental, and family leave policies; and (ii) income maintenance during leaves and guarantees of reinstatement to the same job at the same wage level upon return to work.

As for industry-specific skill investments, leave programs and generous income maintenance during the leave function in the same way as unemployment protection for male skilled workers. A higher wage replacement ratio thus encourages specific skill investment. Firm-specific and industry-specific skills again require slightly different institutional guarantees. While income maintenance during leave is sufficient for industry-specific skills, firm-specific skill investment by women faces another issue. In firm-specific skill regimes, reinstatement to the original job after the leave means that women fall behind their male cohort in skill formation and promotion. This means that despite generous income replacement during the leave, time off due to childbirth and -rearing reduces women's overall earnings. The very fact that the child-rearing years for women coincide with the critical early years of employment compounds the problem. Therefore, for women to invest in firm-specific skills, affordable childcare is more important than a family leave policy. In short, compared to men, it takes more institutional support to encourage women to make specific skill investments. This means that employers' incentives differ significantly from the earlier descriptions of employment and unemployment protection. From the employers' perspective, it costs more to provide incentives for women to invest in specific skills than it does for men (Spencer 1973). Not only do additional income maintenance and childcare create a greater financial burden, but they come with the organizational cost of hiring replacement workers during regular workers' maternal and childcare leaves. And not only is it expensive to hire highly skilled workers as replacement workers, but it is also very difficult to seek those skills in the external labor market—especially in the case of firm-specific skills.

Given these additional financial and organizational costs, employers are unlikely to support family leave or childcare programs except under two circumstances: (i) when someone other than the employer covers the program expenses; or (ii) when there is an acute shortage of men willing to invest in the skills they need.

From a woman's perspective, this means that it does not pay to invest in skills for which there is an abundant supply of males. Even if a woman invests to acquire a specific skill, as far as there is an abundant supply of male skilled workers, her skill investment will not be protected to the same degree as men's. Given this situation, women are more likely than men to invest in general skills. Furthermore, even women who are willing to invest in skill training will rationally choose trades and professions where there are few men. Hence a vicious cycle of occupational segregation of women arises. In countries where there is an established vocational training system, women's enrollment choices will reflect women's tendency to avoid "male jobs."

In short, product market strategies that rely on firm-specific and industry-specific skills are more gender segregating than product market strategies based on general skills. As we argued, general skills provide more flexibility without penalizing career interruptions, precisely because they do not require any external guarantee and reinforcement. We can thus predict that economies with a large presence of companies with specific skill strategies demonstrate high occupational gender segregation, while general skill systems are more gender neutral.

■   ■   ■

Comparative Patterns

Our argument implies a tight coupling between employment protection, unemployment protection, and skill formation. The dominant mode of firm structure, as well as circumstances in the historical development of different welfare production regimes, have led some countries to emphasize *employment protection* over *unemployment protection*, or vice versa. As we noted in the theoretical discussion, political opposition to strong *employment protection* legislation will be greater in countries with a high proportion of small firms.

The predictions of our model are summarized in Fig. 8.12.

When *neither* employment *nor* unemployment protection is high, workers have a strong incentive to protect themselves against labor market insecurities by investing heavily in highly portable skills. Since workers are reluctant to take on specific skills in this scenario—or at least unlikely to share much of the cost of training such skills—firms have an incentive to use technologies that rely least on specific skills. This, in turn, increases demand for general skills, and availability of general skill jobs makes general education more attractive for workers, thus creating a self-reinforcing dynamic. In this case we expect skill profiles to be heavily tilted toward general and broad occupational skills, with a weak or absent vocational training system.

When employment and unemployment protection are both high, on the other hand, workers will find it more attractive to invest in firm- and industry-specific skills. In turn, this makes it more cost-efficient for firms to engage in production that require large inputs of labor with specific skills. As firms specialize in this type of production, the job market for general skills shrinks. Note here that a standard trade argument supports the idea of self-reinforcing dynamics in both types of systems: institutional comparative advantage makes an intensive use of relatively more abundant skills an efficient production strategy. Yet, not all countries necessarily conform to these two ideal types. Where companies can offer very high levels of job protection and a large and attractive internal labor market, firm-specific skill formation can flourish in the absence of strong unemployment protection (represented by the south-east corner of Fig. 8.12). If career opportunities are extensive within the firm, and if the firm makes credible commitments to job security, the external labor market will be small and workers will have an incentive to take advantage of internal career opportunities by investing in company-specific skills. This, essentially, is the Japanese situation (see Aoki 1988; Koike 1981). In most other cases, firms neither have the size nor the resources and institutional capacity to commit credibly to lifetime employment. It is for this reason that we would *ordinarily* expect the development of firm-specific skills to be coupled with generous protection against unemployment.

On the flip side of the Japanese system, we find welfare production regimes with extensive unemployment protection, but low or only modest employment protection. Especially in economies dominated by small firms, with small internal labor markets and little organizational capacity to adapt to business cycles, employment protection is a costly and unattractive option for employers. Denmark is an archetypal example of an economy with a small-firm industrial structure. Yet, generous unemployment protection for skilled workers is still a requisite for workers to invest in industry-specific skills in these cases, much the same way as employment protection is a requisite for investment in firm-specific skills. In effect, unemployment protection increases employment security *within the industry* as opposed to security within a particular firm. At a high level of abstraction, therefore, the *industry* in a country with high unemployment and low employment protec-

tion becomes functionally equivalent to the *firm* in a country with low unemployment and high employment protection.

◼   ◼   ◼

Putting the Pieces Together

Fig. 8.13 plots the eighteen OECD countries on the employment and unemployment protection indexes [that we have adopted]. Countries are distributed along a primary axis, corresponding to the south-west–north-east diagonal in Fig. 8.12, with some countries further divided along a secondary axis, corresponding to the north-west–south-east diagonal in Fig. 8.12. The main axis separates countries into two distinct welfare production regimes: one combining weak employment and unemployment protection with a general skills profile, represented by the Anglo-Saxon countries and Ireland; and one combining high protection on at least one of the two social protection dimensions with firm- and/or industry-specific skills, represented by the continental European countries and Japan. The secondary axis divides the latter group into one with greater emphasis on employment protection and the creation of firm-specific skills, exemplified primarily by Japan and Italy,[4] and one with greater emphasis on unemployment protection and the production of industry-specific skills, exemplified by Denmark, the Netherlands, and Switzerland.

The data on skills * * * have been summarized in the form of averages for each cluster of countries (only tenure rates are relevant for the division along the secondary axis). The high protection countries are also those with the most developed vocational training systems, and tenure rates decline with employment protection. Clearly, the empirical patterns we observe correspond rather closely to our main theoretical thesis, namely that skill formation is closely linked to social protection.

The coupling of social protection and skill systems helps us understand the product market strategies of companies and the creation of comparative

Figure 8.13 Social Protection and Skill Profiles

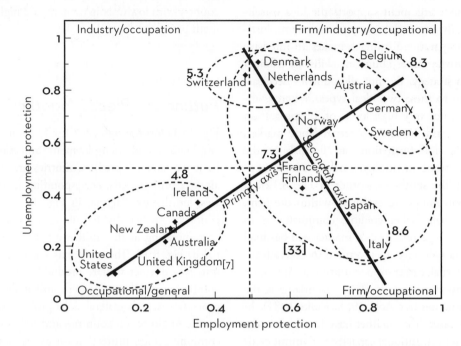

Source: OECD, *Database on Unemployment Benefit Entitlements and Replacement Rates* (undated); Huber, Ragin, Stephens (1997); OECD Economic Outlook (Paris: OECD, various years); OECD, *Labour Force Statistics* (Paris: OECD, various years); European Commission, *Unemployment in Europe* (various years); and national sources; Income Data Services, *Industrial Relations and Collective Bargaining*. London, Institute of Personnel and Development, 1996.

advantages in the global economy. Thus, where there is a large pool of workers with advanced and highly portable skills, and where social protection is low, companies enjoy considerable flexibility in attracting new workers, laying off old ones, or starting new production lines. This flexibility allows for high responsiveness to new business opportunities, and facilitates the use of rapid product innovation strategies. In economies with a combination of firm- and industry-specific skills, such strategies are hampered by the difficulty of quickly adapting skills to new types of production, and by restrictions in the ability of firms to hire and fire workers. On the other hand, these welfare-production regimes advantage companies that seek to develop deep competencies within established technologies, and to continuously upgrade and diversify existing product lines ("diversified quality production" in the terminology of Streeck 1991).

There is considerable case-oriented research to support these propositions (see especially Soskice 1999 and Hollingsworth and Boyer 1997), and they can be bolstered by quantitative evidence constructed by Thomas Cusack from U.S. Patent Office data. Broken into thirty technology classes, Cusack counted the number of references to scientific articles for patents in each technology class and country, and then divided this number by the world number of scientific citations per technology class.[5] The idea is that the number of scientific citations, as opposed to citations to previous patents and non-scientific sources, is a good proxy for the extent to which national firms are engaged in radical innovation strategies. The results are shown in the first column of Table 8.8, with countries ranked by the average ratio of scientific citations for patents secured by national firms. As it turns out, the Anglo-Saxon countries and Ireland all have ratios that are significantly higher than in the specific skills countries of continental Europe and Japan. Precisely as we would expect.

At the low-tech end of product markets, we have to rely on a different type of data to detect cross-national differences. In column (2) of Table 8.8 we used the proportion of the working-age population employed in private social and personal services as a proxy. As argued by Esping-Andersen (1990: ch. 8) and Iversen and Wren (1998), firms that rely heavily on low-skilled and low-paid labor for profitability tend to be concentrated in these industries. Although we only have data for a subset of countries, the numbers display a rather clear cross-national pattern. Producers of standardized and low-productivity services thrive in general skills countries such as Australia and the United States because they can hire from a large pool of unskilled workers who are afforded much job protection and whose wages are held down by low unemployment protection. By contrast, firms trying to compete in this space in specific skills countries such as Germany and Sweden are inhibited by higher labor costs and lower flexibility in hiring and firing. These differences have magnified during the 1980s and 1990s, and Britain is now closer to the mean for the general skills countries.

In an open international trading system, differences in product market strategies will tend to be perpetuated, which in turn feed back into organized support for existing social protection regimes. Contrary to the popular notion of a "race to the bottom" in social policies, differences across countries persist and are even attenuated through open trade. Correspondingly, from the 1970s to the 1980s and 1990s, unemployment benefits remained stable or rose in most continental European countries, but they were cut in Ireland and all the Anglo-Saxo countries with the exception of Australia.[6] Moreover, whereas labor markets have become even more deregulated in the latter countries, employment protection has remained high in the former. Although some countries have seen a notable relaxation in the protection of temporary employment, there is no reduction

Table 8.8 Scientific Citation Rates and Low-Wage Service Employment in Eighteen OECD Countries

	(1) Scientific citation ratio[a]	(2) Private service employment[b]
Ireland	1.514	—
United States	1.310	23
New Zealand	1.267	—
Canada	1.032	20
United Kingdom	0.837	16
Australia	0.804	26
Sweden	0.757	14
The Netherlands	0.754	14
Norway	0.690	17
Switzerland	0.639	—
France	0.601	11
Belgium	0.598	13
Germany	0.592	14
Japan	0.586	—
Austria	0.575	—
Finland	0.552	11
Denmark	0.536	11
Italy	0.491	9

a. The average number of scientific citations per patent by national firms in each of 30 technology classes as a proportion of the average number of citations in each class for the entire world.
b. The number of people employed in wholesale, retail trade, restaurants and hotels, and in community, social and personal services, 1982–91 as a percentage of the working-age population.
Source: Col. 1: United States Patent Office Data. Col. 2: OECD (1996).

in the level of protection for regular employment (*OECD Employment Outlook* 1999). This evidence, and the theoretical explanation we provide for it, seriously challenge the notion, popular in much of the economic literature, that social protection is simply inefficient forms of labor market "rigidities." Social protection can provide important competitive advantages. By the same token we question the prevalent approach in the sociological and political science literature, which understands social protection solely in terms of its redistributive effects.

Implications for Labor Market Stratification

That said, we are not implying that welfare production regimes are irrelevant for distributive outcomes. To the contrary, our argument has important implications for equality and labor market stratification, and

it helps account for the political divisions over the welfare state. Partly these effects are direct consequences of particular product market strategies and their associated skill profiles; partly they reflect the effects of the collective wage-bargaining system that is itself an important component of the wage protection system.

With respect to wage protection, the most important issue is what we have previously referred to as wage protection for the unemployed. Such protection implies that workers with similar skills are paid the same amount across firms and industries, and in practice this is accomplished through collective wage-bargaining at the industry level or at higher levels. It is striking, though not surprising, that all countries with a strong emphasis on industry-specific skills have developed effective wage coordination at the industry level. Conversely, general skills countries, and countries with a strong emphasis on firm-specific skills (Japan in particular), lack such coordination.

Figure 8.14 Vocational Training and Wage Inequality

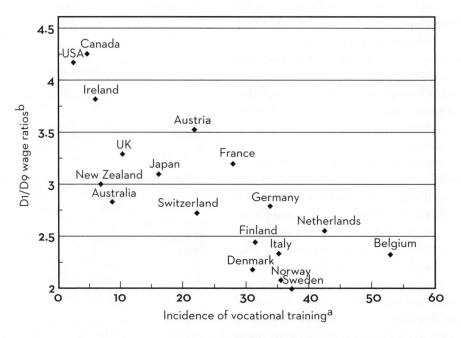

a. The share of an age cohort in either secondary or post-secondary (ISCED5) vocational training. *Source*: UNESCO (1999).
b. The earnings of worker in the top decile of the earnings distribution relative to a worker in the bottom decile of the earnings distribution.
Sources: D1/D9 wage ratios: UNESCO (1999). Incidence of vocational training: OECD, *Electronic Data Based on Wage Dispersion* (undated).

Very extensive evidence has now been accumulated that demonstrates the importance of the structure of the wage-bargaining system for the wage structure (see especially Rowthorn 1992; Wallerstein 1999; and Rueda and Pontusson 2000), but we believe the skill system is equally important. Fig. 8.14, which uses the incidence of vocational training as the indicator for skill system, clearly shows the empirical association between skills and earnings equality, and there is a good reason. Because specific skills systems generate high demand for workers with good vocational training, young people who are not academically inclined have career opportunities that are largely missing in general skills systems. Whereas a large proportion of early school leavers in the former acquire valuable skills through the vocational training system, in the latter most early school leavers end up as low-paid unskilled workers for most or all of their working lives.

In combination, the wage-bargaining system—i.e., whether it is industry coordinated or not—and the skill system—i.e., whether it is specific skills or general skills biased—provides a powerful explanation of earnings inequality as we have illustrated in Fig. 8.15. The figure shows earnings and income inequality for each combination of bargaining and skill system. The big drop in earnings equality occurs as we move from specific skills systems with industry-coordinated bargaining to general skills systems where industry-coordinated wage-bargaining is lacking. By themselves this pair of dichotomous variables account for nearly 70 percent of the cross-national variance in income inequality.[7] Yet, despite their importance for explaining inequality, neither variable is accorded much attention in the established welfare state literature, notwithstanding the focus on distribution in this literature. In our theoretical framework, on the other hand, they are integral parts of the story, even though we have focused on micro mechanisms that emphasize the importance of efficiency.

The hypothesized relationship between product market strategies, skill composition, and equality points to another, and quite different, source of evidence: academic test scores. Because specific skills systems create strong incentives among young schoolgoers to do as well as they can in school in order to get the best vocational training spots, whereas those at the bottom of the academic ability distribution in general skills systems have few such incentives, we should expect the number of early school leavers who fail internationally standardized tests to be higher in general skills countries than in specific skills countries.

Although the data are limited in coverage, this is in fact what we observe (see Fig. 8.16). Whereas the percentage failing the test varies between 15 and 22 per cent in the Anglo-Saxon countries, it is only between 8 and 14 in the countries emphasizing more specific skills for which we have data. Although these differences could be due to the overall quality of the educational system, it is not

Figure 8.15 Skills, the Bargaining System, and Equality[a]

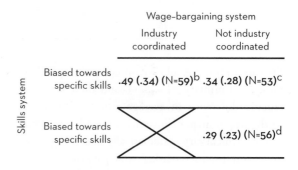

a. Numbers are D9/D1 earnings ratios based on gross earnings (including all employer contributions for pensions, social security, etc.) of a worker at the bottom decile of the earnings distribution relative to the worker at the top decile. Figures are averages for the period 1977–1993. Numbers in parentheses are D9/D1 income ratios based on disposable income of a person at the bottom decile of the earnings distribution relative to a person at the top decile. Most figures are from the early 1990s, with a few from the 1980s.
b. Austria, Belgium, Denmark, Finland, Germany, Netherlands, Norway, Sweden, Switzerland
c. France, Italy, Japan
d. Australia, Canada, Ireland, New Zealand, UK, US
Sources: Skills: see Table 8.8. Bargaining system: see Iversen (1999a: ch. 3. Inequality measures: see OECD Employment Outlook (1991, 1996); Gottschalk and Smeeding (2000: fig. 2).

Figure 8.16 The Failure of Early School Leavers to Pass Standardized Tests in Eleven OECD Countries

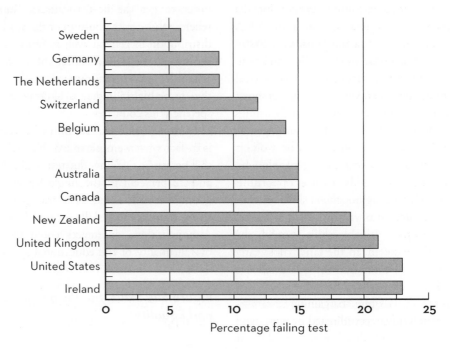

Source: OECD (2000).

the case that the Anglo-Saxon countries spend less money on primary education, and there is no systematic difference in average scorers. This points to the importance of incentives outside the school system, which vary systematically according to the dominant product market strategies of firms and their associated demand for particular skills.

But general skills systems are not necessarily bad for all types of inequality. They perform better in terms of gender equality at work (Estévez-Abe 1999). When we compare degrees of occupational segregation, specific skills systems fare worse than general skills systems. Specific skills systems segregate women into "female occupations" such as low-rank clerical and service jobs. Table 8.9 shows the occupational breakdown of women employed expressed in terms of a percentage of women over total workforce within the same category. While the data are not conclusive, it nonetheless shows that countries (see Germany and

Sweden in Table 8.9) that adopt high-quality product market strategies—thus dependent on high industry-specific skills—employ women for production jobs to a lesser degree. The USA, the archetypal general skills system, shows significantly higher ratios of women in technical and managerial positions when compared to specific skills systems. Our findings support Esping-Andersen's argument about the US employment system being more gender equal than that found in Germany and Sweden (Esping-Andersen 1999). Our explanation, however, differs from his.

Conclusion

Protection of employment and income is widely seen in the welfare state literature as reducing workers' dependence on the market and employers ("decommodification" in Esping-Andersen's terminology). In turn, this is argued to reflect a particular balance of power between labor and capital. We reject both theses. Although strong unions and left governments undoubtedly affect distributive outcomes, we have argued that employment and income protection can be seen as efforts to *increase* workers' dependence on particular employers, as well as their exposure to labor market risks. Moreover, social protection often stems from the strength rather than the weakness of employers.

The key to our argument is the link between social protection and the level and composition of skills. In a modern economy, skills are essential for firms to compete in international markets, and depending on the particular product market strategy of firms, they rely on a workforce with a certain combination of firm-specific, industry-specific, and general skills. To be cost-effective firms need workers who are willing to make personal investments in these skills. And if firms want to be competitive in product markets that require an abundance of specific skills, workers must be willing to acquire these skills at the cost of increasing their dependence on a particular employer or group of employers. Because investment in specific skills increases workers' exposure to risks, only by insuring against such risks can firms satisfy their need for specific skills.

The particular combination of employment protection and unemployment protection determines the profile of skills that is likely to emerge in an economy. Thus employment protection increases the propensity of workers to invest in firm-specific skills, whereas unemployment protection facilitates investment in industry-specific skills. The absence of both gives people strong incentives to invest in general skills. These predictors are borne out by the comparative data, which show that most countries combine either low protection with general skills, or high protection with specific skills.

Two factors contribute to the distinctiveness and resilience of particular welfare production regimes. The first is that such regimes tend to be reinforced by institutions—collective wage-bargaining systems,

Table 8.9 Share of Women by Occupation (%)[a]

	(1) Professional, technical, and related workers	(2) Administrative and managerial workers	(3) Clerical and related workers	(4) Sales workers	(5) Service workers	(6) Production and related workers
USA (1989)	22	26	70	33	30	30
Japan (1988)	10	7	58	11	40	39[b]
Germany (1986)	15	11	59	52	67	21
The Netherlands (1993)	14	0	55	32	45	12
Sweden (1989)	15		57	25	72	24
Australia (1987)	8	18	20	43	76	31

a. Percentages represent the ratio of women over the total of men and women employed within each occupational category.
b. The female ratio for occupational category (6) in Japan is exceptionally high due to a demographically shrinking pool of young male workers (Estévez-Abe 1999).
Source: ILO (1989–90).

business organizations, employee representation, and financial systems—that facilitate the credible commitment of actors to particular strategies, such as wage restraint and long-term employment, that are necessary to sustain cooperation in the provision of specific skills. The second is that those workers and employers who are being most advantaged by these institutional complementaries also tend to be in strong political positions, in terms of both economic clout and sheer numbers. For example, the more a welfare production system emphasizes the creation of specific skills, the more likely it is that the median voter will be someone with considerable investments in specific skills, and the more likely it is that employers' interest organizations will be dominated by firms pursuing specific skills strategies. Both will contribute to perpetuating institutions and policies that advantage firms and workers with heavy investments in specific skills.

Our argument has broader implications for our understanding of the welfare state that reach well beyond the immediate effects of employment and income protection. In particular, earnings dispersion, by far the most important determinant of the overall distribution of income, is closely related to particular skill systems as well as the wage-bargaining institutions that tend to go with these systems. Similarly, the combination of particular product market strategies and skills has distinct effects on the career opportunities of particular groups, especially women. Thus, our theory implies that gender-based segmentation of the labor market varies systematically across welfare production systems.

■   ■   ■

NOTES

1. Our framework builds upon Gary Becker's distinction between general and specific skills (1964: ch. 3). In Becker's definition, firm-specific training increases productivity only in the firm where training takes place. General training, in contrast, raises produc-

tivity equally in all firms. In an analogous manner, industry-specific training can be defined as training that raises productivity in all firms in the industry, but not in other industries. Firm-, industry-, and general skills are skills acquired through firm-specific, industry-specific, and general training.

2. Since the general skills are portable, there is no risk associated with separation from current employer. See Gary Becker (1964). This does not mean that high turnover in countries with more general skills does not produce negative welfare consequences from the economy-wide efficiency perspective. For an interesting elaboration on this issue, see Chang and Wang (1995).

3. It is worth noting that monitoring the quality of the general education system becomes important where a lot of human capital investment takes place beyond the general education system, because poor general education increases the cost of training workers in industry-specific and firm-specific skills.

4. Although the position of Italy is probably exaggerated by the failure to account for semipublic unemployment insurance arrangements, as noted above.

5. The data are coded into references to previous patents and others, where many of the latter are references to scientific articles. To get a good estimate for the number of scientific articles in the "other" category, the proportion of scientific references to other references was calculated for a random sample (6,000) for each country and technology class. These factors were then used to correct the overall dataset so as to get a better measure of scientific citations.

6. Based on gross unemployment replacement rates published in OECD's *Database on Unemployment Benefit Entitlements and Replacement Rates* (undated).

7. The estimated regression equation is:
   Income equality = 0.23 + 0.048 × Specific skills + 0.055 × Industry coordination, where R^2 = 0.69

REFERENCES

Allmendinger, Jutta. 1989. "Educational Systems and Labor Market Outcomes." *European Sociological Review* 5 (3): 231–50.

Aoki, Masahiko. 1988. *Information, Incentives and Bargaining in the Japanese Economy.* Cambridge: Cambridge University Press.

Becker, Gary. 1964. *Human Capital: A Theoretical and Empirical Analysis, with Special Reference to Education.* New York: Columbia University Press.

Blossfeld, Hans-Peter, and Karl Ulrich Mayer. 1988. "Labor Market Segmentation in the Federal Republic of Germany: An Empirical Study of Segmentation Theories from a Life Course Perspective." *European Sociologic Review* 4 (2): 123–40.

Daly, Mary. 1994. "A Matter of Dependency? The Gender Dimension of British Income-Maintenance Provision." *Sociology* 28 (3): 779–97.

Dore, Ronald. and Mari Sako. 1989. *How the Japanese Learn to Work.* London: Routledge.

Esping-Andersen, Gøsta. 1990. *Three Worlds of Welfare Capitalism.* Princeton: Princeton University Press.

———. 1999. *Social Foundations of Postindustrial Economies.* Oxford: Oxford University Press.

Estévez-Abe, Margarita. 1999. "Comparative Political Economy of Female Labor Force Participation." Paper presented at the meeting of the American Political Science Association, Atlanta, 2–5 September.

Finegold, David, and David Soskice. 1988. "The Failure of Training in Britain: Analysis and Prescription." *Oxford Review of Economic Policy* 4 (3): 21–53.

Gottschalk, Peter, and T. M. Smeeding. 2000. "Empirical Evidence on Income Inequality in Industrialized Countries." In *The Handbook of Income Distribution*, ed. A. B. Atkinson and F. Bourguignon. London: North Holland Press.

Hollingsworth, J. Rogers and Robert Boyers, eds. 1997. *Contemporary Capitalism: The Embeddedness of Institutions.* Cambridge: Cambridge University Press.

Huber, Evelyne, John D. Stephens, Charles Ragin, and John Stephens. 1993. "Social Democracy, Christian Democracy, Constitutional Structure and the Welfare State." *American Journal of Sociology* 99 (3): 711–49.

ILO. 1989–90. *Yearbook of Labour Statistics.* Geneva: ILO.

Income Data Services. 1996. *Industrial Relations and Collective Bargaining.* London: Institute of Personnel and Development.

Iversen, Torben. 1999. *Contested Economic Institutions: The Politics of Macroeconomics and Wage Bargaining in Advanced Democracies.* New York: Cambridge University Press.

———. and Anne Wren. 1998. 'Equality, Employment, and Budgetary Restraint: The Trilemma of the Service Economy.' *World Politics* 50 (July): 507–46.

Koike, Kazuo. 1981. *Nihon no Jukuren: Sugureta Jinzai Keisei Shisutemu* [Skills in Japan: An Effective Human Capital Formation System]. Tokyo: Yuhikaku.

———. 1994. "Learning and Incentive Systems in Japanese Industry." In *The Japanese Firm*, ed. Masahiko Aoki and Ronald Dore. Oxford: Clarendon Press: 41–65.

Lazear, Edward, and Richard Freeman. 1996. "Relational Investing: The Workers' Perspective." NBER Working Paper 5346.

Ni Cheallaigh, Martina. 1995. *Apprenticeship in the EU Member States: A Comparison.* Berlin: European Center for the Development of Vocational Training.

OECD. 1991. "Unemployment Benefit Rules and Labour Market Policy." *OECD Employment Outlook.* Paris: OECD: 199–236.

———. 1996. *OECD International Sectoral Data Base.* Paris: OECD.

———. 1999. *OECD Education Database.* Paris: OECD.

———. *OECD Employment Outlook.* Paris: OECD (various years).

———. *Labour Force Statistics.* Paris: OECD (various years).

Ohashi, Isao, and Toshiaki Tachibanaki, eds. 1998. *Internal Labor Markets, Incentives and Employment.* New York: St Martin's Press.

Osterman, Peter. 1987. "Choice of Employment Systems in Internal Labour Markets." *Industrial Relations* 26 (1): 46–67.

Rowthorn, Robert. 1992. "Corporatism and Labour Market Performance." In *Social Corporatism:*

A Superior Economic System?, ed. Jukka Pekkarinen, Matti Pohjola, and Bob Rowthorn. Oxford: Clarendon Press: 44–81.

Rubery, Jill, Colette Fagan, and Friederike Maier. 1996. "Occupational Segregation, Discrimination and Equal Opportunity." In *International Handbook of Labour Market Policy and Evaluation*, ed. Gunther Schmid, Jacqueline O'Reilly, and Klaus Schomann. Cheltenham: Edward Elgar: 431–61.

Rueda, David, and Jonas Pontusson. 2000. "Wage Inequality and Varieties of Capitalism." *World Politics* 52 (April): 350–83.

Schettkat, Ronald. 1993. "Compensating Differentials? Wage Differentials and Employment Stability in the U.S. and German Economies." *Journal of Economic Issues* 27 (1): 153–70.

Shibata, Hiromichi. 1999. "Comparison of American and Japanese Work Practices: Skill Formation, Communications and Conflict Resolution." *Industrial Relations* 38 (2): 192–214.

Soskice, David. 1994. "Reconciling Markets and Institutions: The German Apprenticeship System." In *Training and the Private Sector: International Comparisons*, ed. Lisa M. Lynch. Chicago: Chicago University Press: 25–60.

———. 1999. "Divergent Production Regimes: Coordinated and Uncoordinated Market Economies in the 1980s and 1990s." In *Continuity and Change in Contemporary Capitalism*, ed. Herbert Kitschelt et al. Cambridge: Cambridge University Press: 101–34.

Spencer, Michael. 1973. "Job Market Signaling." *Quarterly Journal of Economics* 87 (3): 355–74.

Streeck, Wolfgang. 1991. "On the Institutional Conditions of Diversified Quality Production." In *Beyond Keynesianism: The Socioeconomics of Production and Full Employment*, ed. Egon Matzner and Wolfgang Streeck. Aldershot: Elgar: 21–61.

———. 1992. *Social Institutions and Economic Performance: Studies on Industrial Relations in Advanced European Capitalist Countries.* London: Sage.

UNESCO. 1999. *UNESCO Statistical Yearbook.* New York: UNESCO.

Wallerstein, Michael. 1999. "Wage-Setting Institutions and Pay Inequality in Advanced Industrial Societies." *American Journal of Political Science* 43 (3): 649–80.

9 COMMUNISM AND POSTCOMMUNISM

This section traces the concept of communism: its limitations, collapse, and future prospects. We begin with the most commonly read work of Karl Marx and Friedrich Engels, *Manifesto of the Communist Party* (1848), in which they lay out their understanding of human history and its dynamics, and the inevitability of the communist revolution to come. For Marx and Engels, economic relations are the driving force of all human relations, and it is these changes in economic relations that drive history. History is a succession of revolutions by those who are exploited against those who exploit them. At the midpoint of the nineteenth century, with the Industrial Revolution well under way, the authors predicted that capitalism's own limitations would soon bring about its overthrow and replacement by a system in which resources and wealth would be shared equally. Marx and Engels thus combined research with activism. Their ideas would go on to spark communist movements across the globe and revolutions in such places as Russia in 1917 and China in 1949.

But communism in practice was more challenging than Marx or Engels anticipated. Implementing the idea of eliminating private property and market forces led to an economy administered by the state and backed by authoritarian rule. In addition to denying democratic freedoms, communism also grew increasingly unable to provide for material needs and economic growth. By the 1980s, attempts to reform this ossified structure in the Soviet Union and Eastern Europe quickly led to its undoing.

The dynamics of communism's collapse, like all revolutions, are difficult to understand and generalize. In Chapter 7 we considered theories of revolution in some detail, including those revolutions that brought communism into power as well as swept it away. In particular, one selection in that chapter, Timur Kuran's "Now Out of Never" (1991) emphasizes the role of private preferences for political changes which may be unseen in an authoritarian order. Using the case of Eastern Europe, he argues that widespread opposition to communism emerged only when shifts in the international environment (reforms in the Soviet Union) signaled to the public that political change was possible and public opposition was no longer as risky a venture. This, he argues, is one of the main reasons why dramatic political change, such as that in Eastern Europe and the Soviet Union, was such a surprise—small shifts in the environment can lead people to reassess their power, leading to a cascade of protest that can bring down a regime.

But understanding the surprising nature of communism's collapse does not necessarily tell us anything about what will come next. What are the dynamics of building new post-communist institutions, specifically democratic regimes? Krastev's "Paradoxes of the New Authoritarianism" (2011) tackles the issue of those postcommunist countries whose transition to democracy did not occur, notably Russia and a number of other former Soviet republics. Krastev notes the observations of Levitsky and Way and Diamond (see Chapter 6), and in some ways turns their arguments upside down. Whereas it is often assumed that international linkages—whether in the form of pressure from other states or greater globalization—can powerfully undermine postcommunist regimes, Krastev argues that these regimes' very openness is the source of their strength. The absence of any meaningful ideology and the relative openness of borders makes postcommunist authoritarian regimes a difficult target for opposition forces. It is hard to articulate alternative values when those in power lack a clear ideology, or to mobilize the public when there are easy alternatives for "opting out," whether online or through immigration. To return to Kuran, postcommunist authoritarianism is well able to blur individual preferences, both public and private.

Bunce and Wolchik are less skeptical than Krastev. In their 2011 book *Defeating Authoritarianism*, they assert that active and strategic efforts on the part of political opponents can bring down postcommunist dictatorships. Although they acknowledge the assets that competitive, authoritarian regimes bring to bear, they emphasize that opposition forces can bring these regimes down, especially when backed by international actors that can provide training and other logistical resources in order to contest elections. In this view, the kind of openness that Krastev sees as an asset of postcommunist dictatorships allows for the space in which civil society and international actors can cooperate.

These debates lead us to the final puzzle regarding communism—the future of China. Scholars and observers of China are deeply divided as to the prospects for democracy there in the near future. For some, the path of political change will be the same as that of Eastern Europe or Russia: modernization will inevitably lead to a more public activism, and growing opposition will eventually bring down the regime. Others contend that a combination of political culture, economic development, and political repression mean that the Chinese Communist Party will be able to maintain power indefinitely. He and Warren's "Authoritarian Deliberation" (2011) describes a situation that combines both paths, in which civil society and public opposition are carefully channeled into the party-state in order to forestall demands for greater change. In such a system, the end of communism may come about incrementally and only over a very long period of time.

In the meantime, authoritarian Russia and China will represent a significant political force. Azar Gat (2007) argues that the rise of Russia and China has brought a new era of international relations akin to the 1930s. Russia and China will be a major challenge to liberal democracy in the coming decades, as Germany and Japan were in the interwar period—an alternative to the assumption that capitalism and liberal democracy must go hand in hand.

Karl Marx and Friedrich Engels
MANIFESTO OF THE COMMUNIST PARTY

A spectre is haunting Europe—the spectre of communism. All the powers of old Europe have entered into a holy alliance to exorcise this spectre: Pope and Tsar, Metternich and Guizot, French Radicals and German police-spies.

Where is the party in opposition that has not been decried as communistic by its opponents in power? Where is the opposition that has not hurled back the branding reproach of communism, against the more advanced opposition parties, as well as against its reactionary adversaries?

Two things result from this fact:

I. Communism is already acknowledged by all European powers to be itself a power.
II. It is high time that Communists should openly, in the face of the whole world, publish their views, their aims, their tendencies, and meet this nursery tale of the spectre of communism with a manifesto of the party itself.

To this end, Communists of various nationalities have assembled in London and sketched the following manifesto, to be published in the English, French, German, Italian, Flemish and Danish languages.

I—Bourgeois and Proletarians

The history of all hitherto existing society is the history of class struggles.

Freeman and slave, patrician and plebian, lord and serf, guild-master and journeyman, in a word, oppressor and oppressed, stood in constant opposition to one another, carried on an uninterrupted, now hidden, now open fight, a fight that each time ended, either in a revolutionary reconstitution of society at large, or in the common ruin of the contending classes.

In the earlier epochs of history, we find almost everywhere a complicated arrangement of society into various orders, a manifold gradation of social rank. In ancient Rome we have patricians, knights, plebians, slaves; in the Middle Ages, feudal lords, vassals, guild-masters, journeymen, apprentices, serfs; in almost all of these classes, again, subordinate gradations.

The modern bourgeois society that has sprouted from the ruins of feudal society has not done away with class antagonisms. It has but established new classes, new conditions of oppression, new forms of struggle in place of the old ones.

Our epoch, the epoch of the bourgeoisie, possesses, however, this distinct feature: it has simplified class antagonisms. Society as a whole is more and more splitting up into two great hostile camps, into two great classes directly facing each other—bourgeoisie and proletariat.

From the serfs of the Middle Ages sprang the chartered burghers of the earliest towns. From these burgesses the first elements of the bourgeoisie were developed.

The discovery of America, the rounding of the Cape, opened up fresh ground for the rising bourgeoisie. The East-Indian and Chinese markets, the colonisation of America, trade with the colonies, the increase in the means of exchange and in commodities generally, gave to commerce, to navigation, to industry, an impulse never before known, and thereby, to the revolutionary element in the tottering feudal society, a rapid development.

From *Selected Works in Three Volumes*, Vol. 1 (Moscow, USSR: Progress Publishers, 1969), pp. 98–137.

The feudal system of industry, in which industrial production was monopolized by closed guilds, now no longer suffices for the growing wants of the new markets. The manufacturing system took its place. The guild-masters were pushed aside by the manufacturing middle class; division of labor between the different corporate guilds vanished in the face of division of labor in each single workshop.

Meantime, the markets kept ever growing, the demand ever rising. Even manufacturers no longer sufficed. Thereupon, steam and machinery revolutionized industrial production. The place of manufacture was taken by the giant, MODERN INDUSTRY; the place of the industrial middle class by industrial millionaires, the leaders of the whole industrial armies, the modern bourgeois.

Modern industry has established the world market, for which the discovery of America paved the way. This market has given an immense development to commerce, to navigation, to communication by land. This development has, in turn, reacted on the extension of industry; and in proportion as industry, commerce, navigation, railways extended, in the same proportion the bourgeoisie developed, increased its capital, and pushed into the background every class handed down from the Middle Ages.

We see, therefore, how the modern bourgeoisie is itself the product of a long course of development, of a series of revolutions in the modes of production and of exchange.

Each step in the development of the bourgeoisie was accompanied by a corresponding political advance in that class. An oppressed class under the sway of the feudal nobility, an armed and self-governing association of medieval commune: here independent urban republic (as in Italy and Germany); there taxable "third estate" of the monarchy (as in France); afterward, in the period of manufacturing proper, serving either the semi-feudal or the absolute monarchy as a counterpoise against the nobility, and, in fact, cornerstone of the great monarchies in general—the bourgeoisie has at last, since the establishment of Modern Industry and of the world market, conquered for itself, in the modern represen-

tative state, exclusive political sway. The executive of the modern state is but a committee for managing the common affairs of the whole bourgeoisie.

The bourgeoisie, historically, has played a most revolutionary part.

The bourgeoisie, wherever it has got the upper hand, has put an end to all feudal, patriarchal, idyllic relations. It has pitilessly torn asunder the motley feudal ties that bound man to his "natural superiors," and has left no other nexus between people than naked self-interest, than callous "cash payment." It has drowned out the most heavenly ecstacies of religious fervor, of chivalrous enthusiasm, of philistine sentimentalism, in the icy water of egotistical calculation. It has resolved personal worth into exchange value, and in place of the numberless indefeasible chartered freedoms, has set up that single, unconscionable freedom—Free Trade. In one word, for exploitation, veiled by religious and political illusions, it has substituted naked, shameless, direct, brutal exploitation.

The bourgeoisie has stripped of its halo every occupation hitherto honored and looked up to with reverent awe. It has converted the physician, the lawyer, the priest, the poet, the man of science, into its paid wage laborers.

The bourgeoisie has torn away from the family its sentimental veil, and has reduced the family relation into a mere money relation.

The bourgeoisie has disclosed how it came to pass that the brutal display of vigor in the Middle Ages, which reactionaries so much admire, found its fitting complement in the most slothful indolence. It has been the first to show what man's activity can bring about. It has accomplished wonders far surpassing Egyptian pyramids, Roman aqueducts, and Gothic cathedrals; it has conducted expeditions that put in the shade all former exoduses of nations and crusades.

The bourgeoisie cannot exist without constantly revolutionizing the instruments of production, and thereby the relations of production, and with them the whole relations of society. Conservation of the old modes of production in unaltered form, was, on the contrary, the first condition of existence for all earlier industrial classes. Constant revolutionizing of production, uninterrupted disturbance of all social conditions, everlasting uncertainty and agitation distinguish the bourgeois epoch from all earlier ones. All fixed, fast frozen relations, with their train of ancient and venerable prejudices and opinions, are swept away, all new-formed ones become antiquated before they can ossify. All that is solid melts into air, all that is holy is profaned, and man is at last compelled to face with sober senses his real condition of life and his relations with his kind.

The need of a constantly expanding market for its products chases the bourgeoisie over the entire surface of the globe. It must nestle everywhere, settle everywhere, establish connections everywhere.

The bourgeoisie has, through its exploitation of the world market, given a cosmopolitan character to production and consumption in every country. To the great chagrin of reactionaries, it has drawn from under the feet of industry the national ground on which it stood. All old-established national industries have been destroyed or are daily being destroyed. They are dislodged by new industries, whose introduction becomes a life and death question for all civilized nations, by industries that no longer work up indigenous raw material, but raw material drawn from the remotest zones; industries whose products are consumed, not only at home, but in every quarter of the globe. In place of the old wants, satisfied by the production of the country, we find new wants, requiring for their satisfaction the products of distant lands and climes. In place of the old local and national seclusion and self-sufficiency, we have intercourse in every direction, universal interdependence of nations. And as in material, so also in intellectual production. The intellectual creations of individual nations become common property. National one-sidedness and narrow-mindedness become more and more impossible, and from the numerous national and local literatures, there arises a world literature.

The bourgeoisie, by the rapid improvement of all instruments of production, by the immensely facilitated means of communication, draws all, even the most barbarian, nations into civilization. The cheap prices of commodities are the heavy artillery with which it forces the barbarians' intensely obstinate hatred of foreigners to capitulate. It compels all nations, on pain of extinction, to adopt the bourgeois mode of production; it compels them to introduce what it calls civilization into their midst, i.e., to become bourgeois themselves. In one word, it creates a world after its own image.

The bourgeoisie has subjected the country to the rule of the towns. It has created enormous cities, has greatly increased the urban population as compared with the rural, and has thus rescued a considerable part of the population from the idiocy of rural life. Just as it has made the country dependent on the towns, so it has made barbarian and semi-barbarian countries dependent on the civilized ones, nations of peasants on nations of bourgeois, the East on the West.

The bourgeoisie keeps more and more doing away with the scattered state of the population, of the means of production, and of property. It has agglomerated population, centralized the means of production, and has concentrated property in a few hands. The necessary consequence of this was political centralization. Independent, or but loosely connected provinces, with separate interests, laws, governments, and systems of taxation, became lumped together into one nation, with one government, one code of laws, one national class interest, one frontier, and one customs tariff.

The bourgeoisie, during its rule of scarce one hundred years, has created more massive and more colossal productive forces than have all preceding generations together. Subjection of nature's forces to man, machinery, application of chemistry to industry and agriculture, steam navigation, railways, electric telegraphs, clearing of whole continents for cultivation, canalization or rivers, whole populations conjured out of the ground—what earlier century had even a presentiment that such productive forces slumbered in the lap of social labor?

We see then: the means of production and of exchange, on whose foundation the bourgeoisie built itself up, were generated in feudal society. At a certain stage in the development of these means of production and of exchange, the conditions under which feudal society produced and exchanged, the feudal organization of agriculture and manufacturing industry, in one word, the feudal relations of property became no longer compatible with the already developed productive forces; they became so many fetters. They had to be burst asunder; they were burst asunder.

Into their place stepped free competition, accompanied by a social and political constitution adapted in it, and the economic and political sway of the bourgeois class.

A similar movement is going on before our own eyes. Modern bourgeois society, with its relations of production, of exchange and of property, a society that has conjured up such gigantic means of production and of exchange, is like the sorcerer who is no longer able to control the powers of the nether world whom he has called up by his spells. For many a decade past, the history of industry and commerce is but the history of the revolt of modern productive forces against modern conditions of production, against the property relations that are the conditions for the existence of the bourgeois and of its rule. It is enough to mention the commercial crises that, by their periodical return, put the existence of the entire bourgeois society on its trial, each time more threateningly. In these crises, a great part not only of the existing products, but also of the previously created productive forces, are periodically destroyed. In these crises, there breaks out an epidemic that, in all earlier epochs, would have seemed an absurdity—the epidemic of over-production. Society suddenly finds itself put back into a state of momentary barbarism; it appears as if a famine, a universal war of devastation, had cut off the supply of every means of subsistence; industry and commerce seem to be destroyed. And why? Because there is too much civilization, too much means of subsistence, too much industry, too much commerce. The productive forces at the disposal of society no longer tend to further the development of the conditions of bourgeois property; on the contrary, they have become too powerful for these conditions, by which they are fettered, and so soon as they overcome these fetters, they bring dis-

order into the whole of bourgeois society, endanger the existence of bourgeois property. The conditions of bourgeois society are too narrow to comprise the wealth created by them. And how does the bourgeoisie get over these crises? On the one hand, by enforced destruction of a mass of productive forces; on the other, by the conquest of new markets, and by the more thorough exploitation of the old ones. That is to say, by paving the way for more extensive and more destructive crises, and by diminishing the means whereby crises are prevented.

The weapons with which the bourgeoisie felled feudalism to the ground are now turned against the bourgeoisie itself.

But not only has the bourgeoisie forged the weapons that bring death to itself; it has also called into existence the men who are to wield those weapons—the modern working class—the proletarians.

In proportion as the bourgeoisie, i.e., capital, is developed, in the same proportion is the proletariat, the modern working class, developed—a class of laborers, who live only so long as they find work, and who find work only so long as their labor increases capital. These laborers, who must sell themselves piecemeal, are a commodity, like every other article of commerce, and are consequently exposed to all the vicissitudes of competition, to all the fluctuations of the market.

Owing to the extensive use of machinery, and to the division of labor, the work of the proletarians has lost all individual character, and, consequently, all charm for the workman. He becomes an appendage of the machine, and it is only the most simple, most monotonous, and most easily acquired knack, that is required of him. Hence, the cost of production of a workman is restricted, almost entirely, to the means of subsistence that he requires for maintenance, and for the propagation of his race. But the price of a commodity, and therefore also of labor, is equal to its cost of production. In proportion, therefore, as the repulsiveness of the work increases, the wage decreases. What is more, in proportion as the use of machinery and division of labor increases, in the same proportion the burden of toil also increases, whether by prolongation of the working hours, by the increase of the work exacted in a given time, or by increased speed of machinery, etc.

Modern Industry has converted the little workshop of the patriarchal master into the great factory of the industrial capitalist. Masses of laborers, crowded into the factory, are organized like soldiers. As privates of the industrial army, they are placed under the command of a perfect hierarchy of officers and sergeants. Not only are they slaves of the bourgeois class, and of the bourgeois state; they are daily and hourly enslaved by the machine, by the overlooker, and, above all, in the individual bourgeois manufacturer himself. The more openly this despotism proclaims gain to be its end and aim, the more petty, the more hateful and the more embittering it is.

The less the skill and exertion of strength implied in manual labor, in other words, the more modern industry becomes developed, the more is the labor of men superseded by that of women. Differences of age and sex have no longer any distinctive social validity for the working class. All are instruments of labor, more or less expensive to use, according to their age and sex.

No sooner is the exploitation of the laborer by the manufacturer, so far at an end, that he receives his wages in cash, than he is set upon by the other portion of the bourgeoisie, the landlord, the shopkeeper, the pawnbroker, etc.

The lower strata of the middle class—the small tradespeople, shopkeepers, and retired tradesmen generally, the handicraftsmen and peasants—all these sink gradually into the proletariat, partly because their diminutive capital does not suffice for the scale on which Modern Industry is carried on, and is swamped in the competition with the large capitalists, partly because their specialized skill is rendered worthless by new methods of production. Thus, the proletariat is recruited from all classes of the population.

The proletariat goes through various stages of development. With its birth begins its struggle with the bourgeoisie. At first, the contest is carried on by individual laborers, then by the work of people of a factory, then by the operative of one trade, in one locality, against the individual bourgeois who directly exploits them. They direct their attacks not against the bourgeois condition of production, but against the instruments of production themselves; they destroy imported wares that compete with their labor, they smash to pieces machinery, they set factories ablaze, they seek to restore by force the vanished status of the workman of the Middle Ages.

At this stage, the laborers still form an incoherent mass scattered over the whole country, and broken up by their mutual competition. If anywhere they unite to form more compact bodies, this is not yet the consequence of their own active union, but of the union of the bourgeoisie, which class, in order to attain its own political ends, is compelled to set the whole proletariat in motion, and is moreover yet, for a time, able to do so. At this stage, therefore, the proletarians do not fight their enemies, but the enemies of their enemies, the remnants of absolute monarchy, the landowners, the non-industrial bourgeois, the petty bourgeois. Thus, the whole historical movement is concentrated in the hands of the bourgeoisie; every victory so obtained is a victory for the bourgeoisie.

But with the development of industry, the proletariat not only increases in number; it becomes concentrated in greater masses, its strength grows, and it feels that strength more. The various interests and conditions of life within the ranks of the proletariat are more and more equalized, in proportion as machinery obliterates all distinctions of labor, and nearly everywhere reduces wages to the same low level. The growing competition among the bourgeois, and the resulting commercial crises, make the wages of the workers ever more fluctuating. The increasing improvement of machinery, ever more rapidly developing, makes their livelihood more and more precarious; the collisions between individual workmen and individual bourgeois take more and more the character of collisions between two classes. Thereupon, the workers begin to form combinations (trade unions) against the bourgeois; they club together in order to keep up the rate of wages; they found permanent associations in order to make provision beforehand for these occasional revolts. Here and there, the contest breaks out into riots.

Now and then the workers are victorious, but only for a time. The real fruit of their battles lie not in the immediate result, but in the ever expanding union of the workers. This union is helped on by the improved means of communication that are created by Modern Industry, and that place the workers of different localities in contact with one another. It was just this contact that was needed to centralize the numerous local struggles, all of the same character, into one national struggle between classes. But every class struggle is a political struggle. And that union, to attain which the burghers of the Middle Ages, with their miserable highways, required centuries, the modern proletarian, thanks to railways, achieve in a few years.

This organization of the proletarians into a class, and, consequently, into a political party, is continually being upset again by the competition between the workers themselves. But it ever rises up again, stronger, firmer, mightier. It compels legislative recognition of particular interests of the workers, by taking advantage of the divisions among the bourgeoisie itself. Thus, the Ten-Hours Bill in England was carried.

Altogether, collisions between the classes of the old society further in many ways the course of development of the proletariat. The bourgeoisie finds itself involved in a constant battle. At first with the aristocracy; later on, with those portions of the bourgeoisie itself, whose interests have become antagonistic to the progress of industry; at all time with the bourgeoisie of foreign countries. In all these battles, it sees itself compelled to appeal to the proletariat, to ask for help, and thus to drag it into the political arena. The bourgeoisie itself, therefore, supplies the proletariat with its own elements of political and general education, in other words, it furnishes the proletariat with weapons for fighting the bourgeoisie.

Further, as we have already seen, entire sections of the ruling class are, by the advance of industry, precipitated into the proletariat, or are at least threatened in their conditions of existence. These also supply the proletariat with fresh elements of enlightenment and progress.

Finally, in times when the class struggle nears the decisive hour, the progress of dissolution going on within the ruling class, in fact within the whole range of old society, assumes such a violent, glaring character, that a small section of the ruling class cuts itself adrift, and joins the revolutionary class, the class that holds the future in its hands. Just as, therefore, at an earlier period, a section of the nobility went over to the bourgeoisie, so now a portion of the bourgeoisie goes over to the proletariat, and in particular, a portion of the bourgeois ideologists, who have raised themselves to the level of comprehending theoretically the historical movement as a whole.

Of all the classes that stand face to face with the bourgeoisie today, the proletariat alone is a genuinely revolutionary class. The other classes decay and finally disappear in the face of Modern Industry; the proletariat is its special and essential product.

The lower middle class, the small manufacturer, the shopkeeper, the artisan, the peasant, all these fight against the bourgeoisie, to save from extinction their existence as fractions of the middle class. They are therefore not revolutionary, but conservative. Nay, more, they are reactionary, for they try to roll back the wheel of history. If, by chance, they are revolutionary, they are only so in view of their impending transfer into the proletariat; they thus defend not their present, but their future interests; they desert their own standpoint to place themselves at that of the proletariat.

The "dangerous class," the social scum, that passively rotting mass thrown off by the lowest layers of the old society, may, here and there, be swept into the movement by a proletarian revolution; its conditions of life, however, prepare it far more for the part of a bribed tool of reactionary intrigue.

In the condition of the proletariat, those of old society at large are already virtually swamped. The proletarian is without property; his relation to his wife and children has no longer anything in common with the bourgeois family relations; modern industry labor, modern subjection to capital, the same in England as in France, in America as in Germany, has stripped him of every trace of national character. Law, morality, religion, are to him so many bourgeois prejudices, behind which lurk in ambush just as many bourgeois interests.

All the preceding classes that got the upper hand sought to fortify their already acquired status by subjecting society at large to their conditions of appropriation. The proletarians cannot become masters of the productive forces of society, except by abolishing their own previous mode of appropriation, and thereby also every other previous mode of appropriation. They have nothing of their own to secure and to fortify; their mission is to destroy all previous securities for, and insurances of, individual property.

All previous historical movements were movements of minorities, or in the interest of minorities. The proletarian movement is the self-conscious, independent movement of the immense majority, in the interest of the immense majority. The proletariat, the lowest stratum of our present society, cannot stir, cannot raise itself up, without the whole superincumbent strata of official society being sprung into the air.

Though not in substance, yet in form, the struggle of the proletariat with the bourgeoisie is at first a national struggle. The proletariat of each country must, of course, first of all settle matters with its own bourgeoisie.

In depicting the most general phases of the development of the proletariat, we traced the more or less veiled civil war, raging within existing society, up to the point where that war breaks out into open revolution, and where the violent overthrow of the bourgeoisie lays the foundation for the sway of the proletariat.

Hitherto, every form of society has been based, as we have already seen, on the antagonism of oppressing and oppressed classes. But in order to oppress a class, certain conditions must be assured to it under which it can, at least, continue its slavish existence. The serf, in the period of serfdom, raised himself to membership in the commune, just as the petty bourgeois, under the yoke of the feudal absolutism, managed to develop into a bourgeois. The modern laborer, on the contrary, instead of rising with the process of industry, sinks deeper and deeper below the conditions of existence of his own class. He becomes a pauper, and pauperism develops more rapidly than population and wealth. And here it becomes evident that the bourgeoisie is unfit any longer to be the ruling class in society, and to impose its conditions of existence upon society as an overriding law. It is unfit to rule because it is incompetent to assure an existence to its slave within his slavery, because it cannot help letting him sink into such a state, that it has to feed him, instead of being fed by him. Society can no longer live under this bourgeoisie, in other words, its existence is no longer compatible with society.

The essential conditions for the existence and for the sway of the bourgeois class is the formation and augmentation of capital; the condition for capital is wage labor. Wage labor rests exclusively on competition between the laborers. The advance of industry, whose involuntary promoter is the bourgeoisie, replaces the isolation of the laborers, due to competition, by the revolutionary combination, due to association. The development of Modern Industry, therefore, cuts from under its feet the very foundation on which the bourgeoisie produces and appropriates products. What the bourgeoisie therefore produces, above all, are its own grave-diggers. Its fall and the victory of the proletariat are equally inevitable.

II—Proletarians and Communists

In what relation do the Communists stand to the proletarians as a whole? The Communists do not form a separate party opposed to the other working-class parties.

They have no interests separate and apart from those of the proletariat as a whole.

They do not set up any sectarian principles of their own, by which to shape and mold the proletarian movement.

The Communists are distinguished from the other working-class parties by this only:

1. In the national struggles of the proletarians of the different countries, they point out and bring to the front the common interests of the entire proletariat, independently of all nationality.
2. In the various stages of development which the struggle of the working class against the bourgeoisie has to pass through, they always and everywhere represent the interests of the movement as a whole.

The Communists, therefore, are on the one hand practically, the most advanced and resolute section of the working-class parties of every country, that section which pushes forward all others; on the other hand, theoretically, they have over the great mass of the proletariat the advantage of clearly understanding the lines of march, the conditions, and the ultimate general results of the proletarian movement.

The immediate aim of the Communists is the same as that of all other proletarian parties: Formation of the proletariat into a class, overthrow of the bourgeois supremacy, conquest of political power by the proletariat.

The theoretical conclusions of the Communists are in no way based on ideas or principles that have been invented, or discovered, by this or that would-be universal reformer.

They merely express, in general terms, actual relations springing from an existing class struggle, from a historical movement going on under our very eyes. The abolition of existing property relations is not at all a distinctive feature of communism.

All property relations in the past have continually been subject to historical change consequent upon the change in historical conditions.

The French Revolution, for example, abolished feudal property in favor of bourgeois property.

The distinguishing feature of communism is not the abolition of property generally, but the abolition of bourgeois property. But modern bourgeois private property is the final and most complete expression of the system of producing and appropriating products that is based on class antagonisms, on the exploitation of the many by the few.

In this sense, the theory of the Communists may be summed up in the single sentence: Abolition of private property.

We Communists have been reproached with the desire of abolishing the right of personally acquiring property as the fruit of a man's own labor, which property is alleged to be the groundwork of all personal freedom, activity and independence.

Hard-won, self-acquired, self-earned property! Do you mean the property of petty artisan and of the small peasant, a form of property that preceded the bourgeois form? There is no need to abolish that; the development of industry has to a great extent already destroyed it, and is still destroying it daily.

Or do you mean the modern bourgeois private property?

But does wage labor create any property for the laborer? Not a bit. It creates capital, i.e., that kind of property which exploits wage labor, and which cannot increase except upon conditions of begetting a new supply of wage labor for fresh exploitation. Property, in its present form, is based on the antagonism of capital and wage labor. Let us examine both sides of this antagonism.

To be a capitalist, is to have not only a purely personal, but a social STATUS in production. Capital is a collective product, and only by the united action of many members, nay, in the last resort, only by the united action of all members of society, can it be set in motion.

Capital is therefore not only personal; it is a social power.

When, therefore, capital is converted into common property, into the property of all members of society, personal property is not thereby transformed into social property. It is only the social character of the property that is changed. It loses its class character.

Let us now take wage labor.

The average price of wage labor is the minimum wage, i.e., that quantum of the means of subsistence which is absolutely requisite to keep the laborer in bare existence as a laborer. What, therefore, the wage laborer appropriates by means of his labor merely suffices to prolong and reproduce a bare existence. We by no means intend to abolish this personal appropriation of the products of labor, an appropriation that is made for the maintenance and reproduction of human life, and that leaves no surplus wherewith to command the labor of others. All that we want to do away with is the miserable character of this appropriation, under which the laborer lives merely to increase capital, and is allowed to live only in so far as the interest of the ruling class requires it.

In bourgeois society, living labor is but a means to increase accumulated labor. In communist society, accumulated labor is but a means to widen, to enrich, to promote the existence of the laborer.

In bourgeois society, therefore, the past dominates the present; in communist society, the present dominates the past. In bourgeois society, capital is independent and has individuality, while the living person is dependent and has no individuality.

And the abolition of this state of things is called by the bourgeois, abolition of individuality and freedom! And rightly so. The abolition of bourgeois individuality, bourgeois independence, and bourgeois freedom is undoubtedly aimed at.

By freedom is meant, under the present bourgeois conditions of production, free trade, free selling and buying.

But if selling and buying disappears, free selling and buying disappears also. This talk about free selling and buying, and all the other "brave words" of our bourgeois about freedom in general, have a meaning, if any, only in contrast with restricted selling and buying, with the fettered traders of the Middle Ages, but have no meaning when opposed to the communist abolition of buying and selling, or the bourgeois conditions of production, and of the bourgeoisie itself.

You are horrified at our intending to do away with private property. But in your existing society, private property is already done away with for nine-tenths of the population; its existence for the few is solely due to its non-existence in the hands of those nine-tenths. You reproach us, therefore, with intending to do away with a form of property, the necessary condition for whose existence is the non-existence of any property for the immense majority of society.

In one word, you reproach us with intending to do away with your property. Precisely so; that is just what we intend.

From the moment when labor can no longer be converted into capital, money, or rent, into a social power capable of being monopolized, i.e., from the moment when individual property can no longer be transformed into bourgeois property, into capital, from that moment, you say, individuality vanishes.

You must, therefore, confess that by "individual" you mean no other person than the bourgeois, than the middle-class owner of property. This person must, indeed, be swept out of the way, and made impossible.

Communism deprives no man of the power to appropriate the products of society; all that it does is to deprive him of the power to subjugate the labor of others by means of such appropriations.

It has been objected that upon the abolition of private property, all work will cease, and universal laziness will overtake us.

According to this, bourgeois society ought long ago to have gone to the dogs through sheer idleness; for those who acquire anything, do not work. The whole of this objection is but another expression of the tautology: There can no longer be any wage labor when there is no longer any capital.

All objections urged against the communistic mode of producing and appropriating material products, have, in the same way, been urged against the communistic mode of producing and appropriating intellectual products. Just as to the bourgeois, the disappearance of class property is the disappearance of production itself, so the disappearance of class culture is to him identical with the disappearance of all culture.

That culture, the loss of which he laments, is, for the enormous majority, a mere training to act as a machine.

But don't wrangle with us so long as you apply, to our intended abolition of bourgeois property, the standard of your bourgeois notions of freedom, culture, law, etc. Your very ideas are but the outgrowth of the conditions of your bourgeois production and bourgeois property, just as your jurisprudence is but the will of your class made into a law for all, a will whose essential character and direction are determined by the economical conditions of existence of your class.

The selfish misconception that induces you to transform into eternal laws of nature and of reason the social forms stringing from your present mode of production and form of property—historical relations that rise and disappear in the progress of production—this misconception you share with every ruling class that has preceded you. What you see clearly in the case of ancient property, what you admit in the case of feudal property, you are of course forbidden to admit in the case of your own bourgeois form of property.

Abolition of the family! Even the most radical flare up at this infamous proposal of the Communists.

On what foundation is the present family, the bourgeois family, based? On capital, on private gain. In its completely developed form, this family exists only among the bourgeoisie. But this state of things finds its complement in the practical absence of the family among proletarians, and in public prostitution.

The bourgeois family will vanish as a matter of course when its complement vanishes, and both will vanish with the vanishing of capital.

Do you charge us with wanting to stop the exploitation of children by their parents? To this crime we plead guilty.

But, you say, we destroy the most hallowed of relations, when we replace home education by social.

And your education! Is not that also social, and determined by the social conditions under which you educate, by the intervention direct or indirect, of society, by means of schools, etc.? The Communists have not intended the intervention of society in education; they do but seek to alter the character of that intervention, and to rescue education from the influence of the ruling class.

The bourgeois claptrap about the family and education, about the hallowed correlation of par-

ents and child, becomes all the more disgusting, the more, by the action of Modern Industry, all the family ties among the proletarians are torn asunder, and their children transformed into simple articles of commerce and instruments of labor.

But you Communists would introduce community of women, screams the bourgeoisie in chorus.

The bourgeois sees his wife a mere instrument of production. He hears that the instruments of production are to be exploited in common, and, naturally, can come to no other conclusion that the lot of being common to all will likewise fall to the women.

He has not even a suspicion that the real point aimed at is to do away with the status of women as mere instruments of production.

For the rest, nothing is more ridiculous than the virtuous indignation of our bourgeois at the community of women which, they pretend, is to be openly and officially established by the Communists. The Communists have no need to introduce free love; it has existed almost from time immemorial.

Our bourgeois, not content with having wives and daughters of their proletarians at their disposal, not to speak of common prostitutes, take the greatest pleasure in seducing each other's wives. (Ah, those were the days!)

Bourgeois marriage is, in reality, a system of wives in common and thus, at the most, what the Communists might possibly be reproached with is that they desire to introduce, in substitution for a hypocritically concealed, an openly legalized system of free love. For the rest, it is self-evident that the abolition of the present system of production must bring with it the abolition of free love springing from that system, i.e., of prostitution both public and private.

The Communists are further reproached with desiring to abolish countries and nationality.

The workers have no country. We cannot take from them what they have not got. Since the proletariat must first of all acquire political supremacy, must rise to be the leading class of the nation, must constitute itself *the* nation, it is, so far, itself national, though not in the bourgeois sense of the word.

National differences and antagonism between peoples are daily more and more vanishing, owing to the development of the bourgeoisie, to freedom of commerce, to the world market, to uniformity in the mode of production and in the conditions of life corresponding thereto.

The supremacy of the proletariat will cause them to vanish still faster. United action of the leading civilized countries at least is one of the first conditions for the emancipation of the proletariat.

In proportion as the exploitation of one individual by another will also be put an end to, the exploitation of one nation by another will also be put an end to. In proportion as the antagonism between classes within the nation vanishes, the hostility of one nation to another will come to an end.

The charges against communism made from a religious, a philosophical and, generally, from an ideological standpoint, are not deserving of serious examination.

Does it require deep intuition to comprehend that man's ideas, views, and conception, in one word, man's consciousness, changes with every change in the conditions of his material existence, in his social relations and in his social life?

What else does the history of ideas prove, than that intellectual production changes its character in proportion as material production is changed? The ruling ideas of each age have ever been the ideas of its ruling class.

When people speak of the ideas that revolutionize society, they do but express that fact that within the old society the elements of a new one have been created, and that the dissolution of the old ideas keeps even pace with the dissolution of the old conditions of existence.

When the ancient world was in its last throes, the ancient religions were overcome by Christianity. When Christian ideas succumbed in the eighteenth century to rationalist ideas, feudal society fought its death battle with the then revolutionary bourgeoisie. The ideas of religious liberty and freedom of conscience merely gave expression to the sway of free competition within the domain of knowledge.

"Undoubtedly," it will be said, "religious, moral, philosophical, and juridicial ideas have been modified in the course of historical development. But religion, morality, philosophy, political science, and law, constantly survived this change."

"There are, besides, eternal truths, such as Freedom, Justice, etc., that are common to all states of society. But communism abolishes eternal truths, it abolishes all religion, and all morality, instead of constituting them on a new basis; it therefore acts in contradiction to all past historical experience."

What does this accusation reduce itself to? The history of all past society has consisted in the development of class antagonisms, antagonisms that assumed different forms at different epochs.

But whatever form they may have taken, one fact is common to all past ages, viz., the exploitation of one part of society by the other. No wonder, then, that the social consciousness of past ages, despite all the multiplicity and variety it displays, moves within certain common forms, or general ideas, which cannot completely vanish except with the total disappearance of class antagonisms.

The communist revolution is the most radical rupture with traditional relations; no wonder that its development involved the most radical rupture with traditional ideas.

But let us have done with the bourgeois objections to communism.

We have seen above that the first step in the revolution by the working class is to raise the proletariat to the position of ruling class to win the battle of democracy.

The proletariat will use its political supremacy to wrest, by degree, all capital from the bourgeoisie, to centralize all instruments of production in the hands of the state, i.e., of the proletariat organized as the ruling class; and to increase the total productive forces as rapidly as possible.

Of course, in the beginning, this cannot be effected except by means of despotic inroads on the rights of property, and on the conditions of bourgeois production; by means of measures, therefore, which appear economically insufficient and untenable, but which, in the course of the movement, outstrip themselves, necessitate further inroads upon the old social order, and are unavoidable as a means of entirely revolutionizing the mode of production.

These measures will, of course, be different in different countries.

Nevertheless, in most advanced countries, the following will be pretty generally applicable.

1. Abolition of property in land and application of all rents of land to public purposes.
2. A heavy progressive or graduated income tax.
3. Abolition of all rights of inheritance.
4. Confiscation of the property of all emigrants and rebels.
5. Centralization of credit in the banks of the state, by means of a national bank with state capital and an exclusive monopoly.
6. Centralization of the means of communication and transport in the hands of the state.
7. Extension of factories and instruments of production owned by the state; the bringing into cultivation of waste lands, and the improvement of the soil generally in accordance with a common plan.
8. Equal obligation of all to work. Establishment of industrial armies, especially for agriculture.
9. Combination of agriculture with manufacturing industries; gradual abolition of all the distinction between town and country by a more equable distribution of the populace over the country.
10. Free education for all children in public schools. Abolition of children's factory labor in its present form. Combination of education with industrial production, etc.

When, in the course of development, class distinctions have disappeared, and all production has been concentrated in the hands of a vast association of the whole nation, the public power will lose its political character. Political power, properly so called, is merely the organized power of one class for oppressing another. If the proletariat during its contest with the bourgeoisie is compelled, by the force of circumstances, to organize itself as a class; if, by means of a revolution, it makes itself the ruling class, and, as such, sweeps away by force the old conditions of production, then it will, along with these conditions, have swept away the conditions for the existence of class antagonisms and of classes generally, and will thereby have abolished its own supremacy as a class.

In place of the old bourgeois society, with its classes and class antagonisms, we shall have an association in which the free development of each is the condition for the free development of all.

■ ■ ■

IV—Position of the Communists in Relation to the Various Existing Opposition Parties

Section II has made clear the relations of the Communists to the existing working-class parties, such as the Chartists in England and the Agrarian Reformers in America.

The Communists fight for the attainment of the immediate aims, for the enforcement of the momentary interests of the working class; but in the movement of the present, they also represent and take care of the future of that movement. In France, the Communists ally with the Social Democrats against the conservative and radical bourgeoisie, reserving, however, the right to take up a critical position in regard to phases and illusions traditionally handed down from the Great Revolution.

In Switzerland, they support the Radicals, without losing sight of the fact that this party consists of antagonistic elements, partly of Democratic Socialists, in the French sense, partly of radical bourgeois.

In Poland, they support the party that insists on an agrarian revolution as the prime condition for national emancipation, that party which fomented the insurrection of Krakow in 1846.

In Germany, they fight with the bourgeoisie whenever it acts in a revolutionary way, against the absolute monarchy, the feudal squirearchy, and the petty-bourgeoisie.

But they never cease, for a single instant, to instill into the working class the clearest possible recognition of the hostile antagonism between bourgeoisie and proletariat, in order that the German workers may straightway use, as so many weapons against the bourgeoisie, the social and political conditions that the bourgeoisie must necessarily introduce along with its supremacy, and in order that, after the fall of the reactionary classes in Germany, the fight against the bourgeoisie itself may immediately begin.

The Communists turn their attention chiefly to Germany, because that country is on the eve of a bourgeois revolution that is bound to be carried out under more advanced conditions of European civilization and with a much more developed proletariat than that of England was in the seventeenth, and France in the eighteenth century, and because the bourgeois revolu-tion in Germany will be but the prelude to an immediately following proletarian revolution.

In short, the Communists everywhere support every revolutionary movement against the existing social and political order of things.

In all these movements, they bring to the front, as the leading question in each, the property question, no matter what its degree of development at the time.

Finally, they labor everywhere for the union and agreement of the democratic parties of all countries.

The Communists disdain to conceal their views and aims. They openly declare that their ends can be attained only by the forcible overthrow of all existing social conditions. Let the ruling classes tremble at a communist revolution. The proletarians have nothing to lose but their chains. They have a world to win.

Proletarians of all countries, unite!

Valerie Bunce and Sharon Wolchik
Conclusions: Democratizing Elections, International Diffusion, and U.S. Democracy Assistance

Democracy is not the voting, it's the counting.

TOM STOPPARD[1]

It is a good thing that U.S. democracy assistance is so chaotic. Otherwise, people might see it as a plot.

NINO KOBAKHIDZE[2]

Why do authoritarian leaders lose elections? This question is important for three reasons. First, regimes that combine authoritarian politics

From *Defeating Authoritarian Leaders in Postcommunist Countries* (New York: Cambridge University Press, 2011), pp. 327–52.

with electoral competition have proliferated over the course of the global wave of democratization. For example, these hybrid political systems have been estimated to comprise between one-fourth and one-fifth of all regimes that currently exist in the world.[3] Second, elections have a habit of fore-shadowing important changes in politics. The rise, consolidation, and termination of both democracy and dictatorship, for instance, seem to be very sensitive to the electoral calendar.[4] Finally, because incumbents have more resources than their opponents in mixed regimes, electoral turnovers in such political settings are rare events.[5] The norm of continuity in leadership has led some analysts to characterize elections in these political contexts not as a constraint on what authoritarian leaders can do, but rather "as a means by which dictators hold on to power."[6]

The purpose of this book has been to address the puzzle of electoral turnover in mixed regimes by comparing two sets of elections that took place in postcommunist Europe and Eurasia from 1998 to 2008. In the first set, we placed six elections that had the similar and surprising outcome of producing a victory for the opposition over the authoritarian incumbent or his designated successor. The cases here included Slovakia (1998), Croatia and Serbia (2000), Georgia (2003), Ukraine (2004), and Kyrgyzstan (2005).[7] The second set, by contrast, consisted of five elections that produced continuity in authoritarian rule, that is, in Armenia (2003 and 2008), Azerbaijan (2003 and 2005), and Belarus (2006). What made this comparison so illuminating for our purposes, aside from the contrast in election results, were the many similarities between our two groups of regimes and elections. For example, all of these regimes are located in new states that were formed in the early 1990s as a consequence of the collapse of Communist Party hegemony and the accompanying dissolution of the Soviet, Yugoslav, and Czechoslovak states. Just as important is the fact that all of the elections featured a united opposition, and most of them were rigged and prompted large-scale postelection popular protests. These are characteristics that, according to some recent studies, should have made the opposition a more formidable political opponent.[8]

In the course of testing a number of hypotheses in order to explain why electoral results diverged, we addressed some other issues of considerable interest to specialists in comparative and international politics. One was whether these elections were related to one another through a process of international diffusion. This possibility was suggested by recent findings regarding the spread of democracy as a diffusion dynamic and by the fact that our electoral breakthroughs followed a pattern consistent with a role for cross-national diffusion—for example, the clustering of these electoral turnovers across time and space.[9] A related question that we examined was the impact of outside actors on these electoral confrontations between authoritarian incumbents and opposition groups. Here, we were particularly interested in the role of the U.S. democracy assistance community, although we also examined the influence of the European Union and European governments and foundations.[10] Finally, we analyzed variations in the longer-term consequences of these elections. Why was democratic progress greater in some countries that experienced electoral turnover than in others, and what political difference did it make that oppositions won or lost elections?

Difficult questions such as these demand detailed data and diverse approaches. With respect to the first issue: we gathered a wide range of information, including over two hundred interviews conducted with local and international participants in our eleven elections. We then assembled this information in several different ways in order to shed light on the key factors shaping electoral outcomes.

Negative Findings: Structural and Institutional Factors

What did we discover? We can begin our summary by noting briefly some of the hypotheses that we were able to reject. Perhaps the most surprising negative finding in this study was that familiar indicators of the strength of the regime versus that of the opposition on the eve of the election—in particular, the political character of the regime itself and long-term trends in economic and political performance—failed to account in a consistent way for variations in electoral outcomes. For example, while it is true (as one would expect) that all of the failures to dislodge authoritarian leaders took place in relatively authoritarian regimes, it is also the case that many opposition victories were registered in regimes that were just as authoritarian. At the same time, there was significant overlap between our two sets of elections with respect to trends in such areas as economic performance and the frequency of governmental turnovers and anti-regime protests.[11] These findings do not, of course, challenge the fact that some political settings are more supportive of opposition victories than others, or that extreme degrees of political repression foreclose the possibility of an opposition electoral victory. However, what we would argue is that the structural and institutional parameters on political change are surprisingly elastic in mixed regimes.

Two other negative findings were also unexpected. One was that liberalization of politics in the years leading up to the pivotal elections had *no* relationship to the success of electoral challenges mounted by the opposition. Indeed, virtually all of the elections, whether producing continuity in or a break with authoritarian rule, were preceded by a period of growing authoritarianism.[12] We also failed to find, even when expanding our study to include earlier electoral confrontations between the regime and the opposition in our nine countries, the expected role for unity of the opposition, electoral fraud, or popular protests following the election. None of these developments correlated very well with opposition victories.[13]

The Electoral Model

By contrast, explanatory factors of a more short-term character that focused on the dynamics of the elections emerged as being more influential. In particular, what proved to be decisive in distinguishing between opposition victory and defeat was whether oppositions and their allies ran sophisticated and energetic political campaigns. When they did, they succeeded in taking office—either immediately after the election or, where incumbents or their chosen successors attempted to steal the election, following popular protests.

What did this ensemble of innovative electoral strategies—which we have termed the electoral model—mean in practice? Included in this tool kit was, first, the formation of a united front among major opposition parties. In addition, for the opposition the electoral model included such activities as mounting large-scale voter registration and turnout drives; carrying out creative and ambitious nationwide campaigns; and collaborating closely with civil society groups, including youth organizations, women's organizations, and organizations devoted to organizing and analyzing the elections and the electorate. The electoral model also made extensive use of cultural events such as rock concerts, marches, and even bicycle tours to increase public interest in the election, and of the media, public opinion polls, exit polls, and external and internal vote monitoring and parallel vote tabulation. When combined, these wide-ranging and interrelated activities put in place all the pieces that were required for an opposition victory. To put the issue succinctly: these strategies highlighted the costs of continuing the regime in office and demonstrated the credibility of the opposition. As a result, citizens became more optimistic about the possibilities for political change; they were more willing to vote; and they were more ready to throw their support to the opposition. In more authoritarian regimes, moreover, these critical shifts in the perceptions, preferences, and behaviors of ordinary citizens, when joined with the contrast between the official vote tally and the real results of the election, provided the necessary conditions for large-scale public protests that succeeded in forcing a transfer of power to the victorious opposition.

Thus, the electoral model solved long-standing coordination and collective action problems.[14] In this sense, the most important impact of the electoral model was to level the political playing field in mixed regimes by empowering the opposition and its supporters. However, this conclusion introduces an obvious question. What explains the failure of authoritarian incumbents or their anointed successors to adopt the electoral model as well? After all, they had a lot to lose by allowing the opposition to run a more sophisticated campaign. Our response to this question is twofold. First, authoritarian incumbents or their chosen successors were prisoners of their previous successes. Why go to the trouble of doing something different, especially since elections could always be stolen at the last minute? Second, authoritarian incumbents paid a steep price for their isolation—from information about the real distribution of their political support within the population (votes, for instance, were a poor guide, since opponents of the regime tended not to vote); from the international democracy assistance community, which provided detailed information about how campaigns could be run and elections won; and, more generally, from the cross-national diffusion dynamic described earlier that brought the electoral model to oppositions in these countries, but not to authoritarian incumbents. The fact is that the electoral model was a foreign import, and there was a good reason for this. Elections were too new to these countries to have spawned such an elaborate and sophisticated ensemble of electoral strategies. Thus, while commanding impressive resources in most respects, authoritarian leaders were in fact disadvantaged in one area vital to their tenure. They did not understand what they needed to do to fend off strong electoral challenges to their power. Indeed, they mistakenly assumed that, as in the past, the opposition would be divided, weak, and unpopular.

International Diffusion

It was far from accidental that the electoral model was adopted by opposition groups in so many countries in postcommunist Europe and Eurasia within such a brief span of time. The wave of electoral breakthroughs reflected, in particular, a two-stage diffusion dynamic that we have traced through the more than 200 interviews we conducted with participants in this process. The first stage involved a cross-regional transfer of innovative electoral strategies from the Philippines and Chile, where oppositions had mounted successful challenges to authoritarian rule in the second half of the 1980s, to Bulgaria in 1990, where competitive elections were being held for the first time since World War II. A number of factors facilitated the transfer of electoral strategies from Latin America and Southeast Asia to the postcommunist region. One was that members of the International Republican Institute and especially the National Democratic Institute had become convinced that democratic change was well served by bringing opposition groups (including political parties and civil society associations) that had successfully challenged authoritarian rule to meet with similar groups in other countries that wanted to accomplish the same objective. These "learning delegations," as Larry Garber characterized them, were efficient mechanisms for passing on useful political strategies, and they also flattened the hierarchical relationship between the international democracy assistance community and local democratic activists.[15]

Second, Bulgaria was chosen as the focus of such activities in 1990 because the new regime in power was relatively open, yet widely perceived by local and international democracy activists as likely to move in a decidedly more authoritarian direction if the Bulgarian Socialist Party won the election.[16] Finally, democratic change both in Latin America and in Central and Eastern Europe had been a high priority for the National Endowment for Democracy, the International Republican Institute (as it came to be called), the National Democratic Institute, the Free Trade Union Institute, and Freedom House since their founding in 1983. This is why, for example, we see so much personnel overlap between activists who had been involved in Latin America in the 1980s and the activists who played key roles in the postcommunist transitions in the 1990s.

The second stage of the diffusion process concentrated on regimes within the postcommunist region. Here, the Slovak case looms large. It was in that country's 1998 election where we find the first full application in the postcommunist region of the electoral model as described earlier in this chapter, and the first case as well of this model succeeding in its mission to replace authoritarians with democrats. The Slovak approach to defeating authoritarian leaders was then transferred in quite deliberate fashion to oppositions and their allies in Croatia, Serbia, Georgia, Ukraine, and, to a lesser extent, Kyrgyzstan from 2000 to 2005. Three mechanisms were responsible for the cross-national transfer of the electoral model within postcommunist Europe and Eurasia. One was the portability of the model and its widespread appeal because of its success and its ability to provide efficient solutions to many problems that had long prevented oppositions from winning power. A second driver of diffusion was the existence of an assumption shared by both exporters and importers of the model that it was widely applicable (with some tinkering) to many other regimes in the postcommunist region. Finally, the model was transferred to new sites because of the hard work of transnational networks that defined, shared, amended, and implemented the model. Members of this transnational network included groups funded by USAID and private foundations, U.S. ambassadors and their staffs, and European-based public and private democracy assistance organizations. In addition, local oppositions and civil society groups played a key role, as did another less widely recognized set of players: political activists from neighboring countries in the postcommunist region who had been successful in mounting electoral challenges to authoritarian rule.

The spread of the electoral model was also typical of diffusion dynamics in several other respects. One was that the cycle of adoption moved from using elements of the model and then putting together a well-rounded tool kit for domestic use and international export to modifying this ensemble of strategies in response to new environments that were much less hospitable to electoral change. That is why, for example, we see the addition of postelection popular protests in the final four cases of electoral turnover. Another pattern that we found in our cases and that is typical of the way diffusion works, particularly when the innovation of interest

is (as ours was) very threatening to the prevailing distribution of money and power, is a thinning of transnational networks as they spread out from their original site of operation to more far-flung locales over the course of the wave. This development, plus the growing awareness among authoritarian leaders that they needed to take strong actions to defend themselves from electoral challenges and the tendency of oppositions, witnessing the wave in their neighborhood, to underestimate what they needed to do to make it happen in their own countries, explains the geographical and temporal limits of the spread of the diffusion dynamic.

International Democracy Assistance

Our analysis of electoral stability and change also generated insights about how international democracy assistance works and its role in electoral stability and change in postcommunist Europe and Eurasia. Here, three conclusions stand out. One is that international democracy assistance is, in practice, a relatively chaotic process.[17] The field itself is very crowded because of the involvement of so many governments and private foundations, along with the vast array of civil society groups they support. In addition, priorities on the ground and in the home organizations shift rapidly; there is no consensus about the kinds of activities that contribute to democratic progress; and there is limited capacity to evaluate the impact of interventions. Moreover, especially in the case of the United States, the process is very decentralized, and turnover rates of members of the U.S. democracy assistance community are extremely high.[18] As a consequence, despite what happened with respect to the elections analyzed in this book, lack of coordination among the Western foundations and governments involved in democracy assistance is the norm.

Second, contrary to the assumptions underlying the very use of the term "exporting democracy," the relationship between donors and recipients—at least in the cases of interest in this study—is neither as hierarchical nor as unidirectional as many critical accounts assume. Thus, just as donors do not always dictate what recipients can and should do, so donors often learn from recipients.[19] Transnational networks that bring together local, regional, and Western activists in a common cause serve as the key players in international democracy assistance.

Finally, in the particular case of the elections of interest in this study, while a number of international actors played important roles, it was the United States that in fact dominated the field, though always in collaboration, we must emphasize, with other actors, local and international. Here, we refer, for example, to U.S.-based foundations, such as the Open Society, the Charles Stuart Mott foundation, Rockefeller Brothers, and the German Marshall Fund of the United States, as well as to U.S. government–funded actors, such as the United States Institute of Peace and especially the National Endowment for Democracy, the International Republican Institute, the National Democratic Institute, and Freedom House. The role of the United States in these electoral struggles grew in part out of U.S. foreign policy priorities. The United States became involved in democracy assistance in the postcommunist world before other international players, and USAID outlays on democracy and governance favored the postcommunist region in the 1990s in particular.[20]

While money matters, however, so does the fact that the United States took a distinctive approach to democracy assistance that was particularly critical in influencing electoral outcomes. Thus, as we discovered through our interviews and analysis of relevant documents, the United States specialized in five areas of assistance: 1) extending financial and technical support for free and fair elections, including putting pressure on regimes to improve their electoral procedures and providing support for exit polls and parallel vote tabulation, along with civil society organizations that were involved in voter registration and turnout drives; 2) supporting greater engagement in politics and policy by such under-represented and demobilized groups as women, minorities, and citizens located in smaller towns and rural areas; 3) working with the opposition parties to encourage them to collaborate with each other and to reach out to civil society groups; 4) assisting in the development, transfer, and implementation of the electoral model; and 5) providing sizeable long-term support for civil society.[21]

At the same time, as local participants in these elections emphasized repeatedly in interviews with us, the United States was far more "nimble" than the Europeans, who were less concerned with the politics of the moment and far more committed to longer-term capacity building. U.S. assistance also was more likely to involve civil society groups directly, while European assistance, particularly through the EU, focused more on aid to government organizations or, as in the case of aid to civil society, had to be channeled through the government. Part of the reason for this difference was the strong interest of the United States in elections—what Kenneth Wollack characterized as "the heart of the country's political process."[22] But part of it was also the decentralized character of U.S. democracy assistance, and part, too, the differences in the professional backgrounds of individuals involved in democracy assistance. While the Europeans were largely bureaucrats by training and experience, the Americans had prior histories in U.S. politics—in Washington and in the states. Finally, the United States was important for the simple reason that it is the most powerful country in the international system. As a result, it mattered to the political calculations of local players when the United States signaled strong interest in the conduct of elections, when it withdrew support from authoritarian incumbents, and when it engaged in all the other activities highlighted earlier.

Postelection Trajectories

This observation leads to our final set of conclusions: patterns of democratic progress after successful and failed attempts to defeat authoritarian rulers. While all of the successful breakthroughs produced a democratic opening, if only because they removed authoritarian leaders from office and led to a more competitive politics, they varied nonetheless in whether these opportunities translated into significant or limited democratic development after the opposition took power. Thus, while Croatia and Serbia made virtual leaps from dictatorship to democracy, democracy returned to Slovakia, and Ukraine made significant steps in becoming more democratic, the outcomes in Georgia and especially in Kyrgyzstan were far more mixed.

This contrast reflected three factors in particular: long-term trends in the development of civil society; variations in whether the elections had led to a constitutional transition in leadership or one that forced sitting presidents, even though they were not up for reelection, to vacate office; and electoral mandates. Thus, it is striking that, of the successful cases of electoral turnover, it is only in Georgia and Kyrgyzstan that we find extra-legal removals of authoritarians from office by the opposition and a draining of what had already been a small and fragile civil society as a result (especially in Georgia) of activists joining the new government. These two cases also stand out because of the one-sided electoral victories in the presidential elections that followed the parliamentary elections that had served as pretexts for leadership change. Landslide victories gave the new leaders of Georgia and Kyrgyzstan the luxury—unlike their counterparts of Serbia, Georgia, Ukraine, Croatia, Bulgaria, and Slovakia—of ruling without much opposition.

In this sense, the continuing political struggles between authoritarian and democratic forces in Serbia and Ukraine—which have led many analysts to question how much the pivotal elections contributed to democratic change—have been a blessing insofar as democratic change is concerned.[23] While both Viktor Yushchenko, who lost the presidency in the 2010 election, and Boris Tadić, who was elected and then reelected president of Serbia in 2004 and 2008, respectively, were very constrained in their actions by oppositions on the left and on the right, they were at the same time blocked, unlike their counterparts in Georgia and Kyrgyzstan, from becoming increasingly autocratic over time or recycling the patronage networks left behind by their predecessors. Moreover, competitive politics in Ukraine and Serbia, as in Croatia and Slovakia after their electoral breakthroughs, is rooted in policy differences among relatively well-defined political parties. As a result, although they are still fluid in many respects, and although new parties enter and old parties exit the political scene between elections, the party systems in these countries are far more institutionalized and more supportive of democracy than the party systems—or, more accurately, the loose-knit patronage-based networks arrayed around specific leaders—that we find in Georgia and Kyrgyzstan.

While the political trajectories of the breakthrough cases varied, however, the postelection experiences of the failed attempts to remove authoritarians from office were remarkably similar. Fraudulent elections, followed by popular protests, led to growing authoritarianism in Armenia, Azerbaijan, and Belarus. What we have seen, therefore, is a deepening of earlier political trends favoring authoritarian politics—in sharp contrast, in most of our successful cases, to a sharp break with similar pre-election trends. Thus, regimes that were similar at the time of the pivotal elections—politics in Serbia, Georgia, Ukraine, and Kyrgyzstan was as repressive, we must remember, as politics in Armenia and Azerbaijan in particular—began to diverge from one another following the elections of concern in this book.

This contrast, especially when combined with similarities between regime trends in Armenia, Azerbaijan, and Belarus, on the one hand, and in Russia and Kazakhstan, on the other, which also began the transition as mixed systems but did not feature the syndrome of opposition cohesion and postelection protests after manipulated elections, led us to draw another conclusion. In the absence of electoral breakthroughs, there seems to be little to stop mixed regimes in this part of the world from tilting in an increasingly authoritarian direction over time. In fact, the growing pessimism among many analysts over the past few years about the future of democracy is based in large measure on one regional trend: growing authoritarianism in postcommunist Eurasia.[24]

Thus, electoral turnovers in mixed regimes matter for two reasons. More than any other factor, they are likely to improve democratic performance, and—again, more than any other factor—they play a key role in reversing an ongoing slide into increasingly repressive politics. However, there is another implication that we can draw from our analysis of postelection political trends. There are extremely high stakes attached to launching popular protests in response to fraudulent elections. If the demonstrations succeed, democratic progress is likely to follow. However, if they fail, the regime invariably becomes more repressive.

In the remainder of this chapter, we return to the theoretical debates and draw some implications from our findings. We begin with the issue of mixed regimes and their potential for democratic change.

Mixed Regimes

Are authoritarian leaders in mixed regimes weak or strong? Our analysis supports both points of view. On the one hand, authoritarian leaders emerge in this study as relatively powerful. Even when they are vulnerable according to a variety of measures, they can withstand the challenge of even united oppositions and popular protests. Moreover, our finding about the electoral model suggests that unseating authoritarian leaders requires enormous effort.

On the other hand, while we discovered significant constraints on the ability of oppositions to win elections, we also found evidence suggesting that in some respects analysts have overestimated the freedom to maneuver of authoritarian leaders in regimes featuring competition for political power. Here, we would question the recent trend in the study of authoritarianism that emphasizes how powerful authoritarian leaders are as a result, for example, of political repression and the economic tools they have at their disposal and the role of even seemingly democratic institutions in enhancing their ability to monopolize politics.[25] In response, we would draw attention, on the basis of the behavior of authoritarian incumbents or their anointed successors in Serbia, Georgia, Kyrgyzstan, and Ukraine, to several important facts on the ground. One is the cost for their own political survival of resorting to more authoritarian practices over time, and the other is the cost of unchallenged rule. In the first instance, in the cases of Serbia, Ukraine, and Georgia in particular, despotism was widely interpreted by democratic activists and ordinary citizens as a sign of desperation. Thus, the leader was seen as more, not less, vulnerable.

We can also point to some of the costs attached to what appears to be political invincibility. These costs are particularly high when the duration of authoritarian rule has been built upon repeated successes by the leader in defeating challenges to his power—from oppositions and from actions taken by the international community. Thus, long-serving leaders, such as Milošević, Kuchma, Shevardnadze, and Akaev (at least before protesters appeared in Bishkek), assumed that the behavior of the opposition, civil society groups, ordinary citizens, Western governments, and the international democracy assistance community would not change. In this sense, leaders can be punished for relying too much on past precedents.

Thus, while we are sympathetic to the arguments that students of democratization have been biased as a result of their selective attention to indicators of democratic development and their pronounced tendency to ignore alternative interpretations, we think that the decision to counter these problems by focusing on the many ways authoritarian leaders are strong, creative, resilient, and the like suffers from serious biases as well.[26] If nothing else, these assumptions about the power of authoritarians are problematic in view of our limited knowledge about politics within the palace, the tendency to project onto the present and into the future the resilience of authoritarian rule in the past, and, finally, the puzzling belief, contrary to the way politics often works, that politicians can control what happens after they introduce changes, including seemingly democratic reforms, that they see as serving their interests. We argue this, not just because of the data presented in this book, but also because of our professional resumes. Before we analyzed transitions to democracy and mixed regimes in the postcommunist region, we were students of communism.

Moreover, if transitology suffered in its early development from a research design that often involved looking only at cases of successful transitions from authoritarian rule, then students of authoritarianism sometimes suffer from looking only at long-standing authoritarian polities, such as those in the Middle East or in China (a communist regime, we must note, that is still less long-lived than its Soviet counterpart). The tendency to predict durable authoritarianism is also a reaction to studies of the Middle East and China in the 1990s that wrestled repeatedly, because of the events of 1989 and the global wave of democratization, with the possibility of democratic change.

The role of different area studies in supporting very different expectations about the power of autocrats and the potential for democratic change leads to another insight about mixed regimes. Whether autocrats in mixed regimes are presumed by scholars to be vulnerable or powerful, careless or calculating, may depend on how the mixed regimes came into existence. While in the Middle East, for example, regimes that feature authoritarian leaders but competitive politics arose as part of a continuing state and authoritarian political project, the formation of mixed regimes in the post-communist region followed dramatic political and economic ruptures. As a consequence, while mixed regimes in many regions of the world grew out of decisions by autocrats to implement certain types of political reforms, mixed regimes in the postcommunist region in particular grew out of a rough balance of power between two sets of players. One was discredited authoritarian incumbents, who were intent on maintaining power in the new domestic and international circumstances they confronted, and the other was the opposition, which was often divided and inexperienced but

empowered, at least potentially, by the same new circumstances. Balancing and bargaining between authoritarians and democrats in a time of regime and state transition, therefore, produced a very different type of mixed regime—and one where authoritarians were likely more constrained—than a dynamic involving a sprinkling of the polity by well-ensconced leaders with some carefully selected democratic decorations.

Whether such democratic decorations actually contribute to democratic development, however, may very well depend not so much on the institutional and structural vulnerability of the regime as on the willingness and capacity of oppositions and their allies to exploit openings provided by the combination of authoritarian rule and electoral competition for office. Thus, we would also question the tendency in more structural accounts of political change in mixed systems to argue that the key issue insofar as regime change is concerned is whether the regime is in decline as a result of structural considerations.[27] Weak regimes can survive for a very long time, especially if there are few alternatives on the horizon and if they are supported by outside actors. In addition, many of the structural weaknesses of the regimes analyzed in this book were evident in many of the elections that preceded those that led to opposition victories. Finally, it is telling that, despite all the hard work of oppositions and their allies in the successful cases, victories were usually razor-thin. If the regime was ready to fall and everyone knew it, why were the votes so close?

Finally, this study counsels us to rethink how we conceptualize regimes that combine authoritarian and democratic elements. In particular, we are skeptical about the value and validity of placing too much emphasis on the "regime-ness" of these political formations. This is a practice that is implied, for example, in the preoccupation with giving various names to these regimes, drawing increasingly fine-grained distinctions among them, and treating them as political outcomes equal to those polities that are fully democratic or authoritarian and therefore amenable to comparison to them in the quest to identify the causes behind divergent regime pathways.[28] The very act of calling them "regimes" and freezing them in time suggests a certain jelling of their characteristics and the parameters on how they will evolve in the future. However, both implications are countered not just by the trends toward and away from democracy and authoritarianism that we have analyzed in this book, but also by the finding in the literature that such regimes are, quite simply, unusually resistant to "staying put."

Elections and Democratization

As we noted in the introductory chapters of this book, while some scholars see elections as sites that merely register long-term political and economic developments, other scholars give elections causal import in their own right and argue, as a result, that elections can be considered a mode of regime transition.[29] This study provides strong support for the second characterization, while recognizing, like Andreas Schedler, that elections have contingent effects.[30] For example, it is striking that the elections of interest in this book had very different outcomes, despite similarities in regime points of departure. Also notable are the facts that the contrast in these electoral outcomes reflected differences in electoral efforts on the part of the opposition and their allies, and that political developments after the pivotal elections widened the regime gap between the countries where oppositions won power and those where they did not.

As with other, more commonly discussed modes of transition from authoritarianism to democracy, such as mass protests unrelated to elections and elite pacting, then, democratizing elections do not necessarily lead to the consolidation of democracy. Like protests and pacting, electoral breakthroughs can be followed not just by democratic progress, but also by democratic backsliding or even breakdowns. But these possibilities do not negate the importance of the fact that elections in semi-authoritarian regimes often play the role of creating an opening for a transition to democracy. It is precisely for these reasons that we have used the term "democratizing elections" throughout this book.

But these conclusions lead to an obvious question: what is it about elections that expands the potential for democratic change? Most obviously, elections can remove key obstacles to democratic progress in mixed regimes by removing authoritarian leaders from office and thereby, albeit to varying degrees, disassembling patronage networks and the security forces that backed them, redefining international alliances, and bringing new voters and groups into politics and bringing their interests into the policy calculus of governments.[31] However, whether they set in motion this train of important developments depends, as we have seen, on how oppositions and their allies campaign for power and the impact of their efforts on electoral outcomes.

It is here that we need to recognize the contributions of the electoral model to democratic development. At the most general level, the electoral model exploits the fact that elections are regular and well-defined events in terms of their beginnings and endings, and that they combine high stakes, expectations of popular participation, and widely visible political outcomes. Elections, therefore, are uniquely energizing events.[32] More specifically, the electoral model creates a new type of election by helping solve the collective action and coordination problems that not only prevent ordinary citizens, opposition parties, and civil society groups from embracing the same cause and taking concerted action to further their common agenda, but also inhibit international democracy promoters, who suffer as well from difficulties in defining a common mission and working together to achieve shared goals. The deployment of the electoral model can surmount these problems because elections can serve as focal points for action. The model, moreover, specifies what needs to be done while communicating a distinctive message—that change is possible, especially when everyone works together to make it happen.

But do these arguments about electoral efforts, in conjunction with the limited impact of structural and institutional factors, mean that our explanation of variations in electoral outcomes can be reduced to the powerful effects of agency? On the one hand, this is precisely what we are arguing in the sense that the election-related activities of individuals made all the difference in who won and who lost. However, we would nonetheless caution strongly against reducing agency in this case—as the term has been used in so many other studies—to the ad hoc and last-minute actions of a handful of individuals. What is striking about these electoral efforts is that they were planned, widely and deeply collaborative, and quite task-oriented. They were also based upon a sophisticated and tested model that was invented outside the postcommunist region and then transferred, applied, and adapted to local conditions within that region by a large cast of players. While one could argue that the key in these elections was a short-term dynamic involving the actions of individuals, therefore, this did not mean that there was anything idiosyncratic, accidental, or individualistic about why, how, or where authoritarian rulers were defeated.

International Diffusion of Democracy

This study also contributes to an area of growing interest in the study of democratization, that is, the impact of international influences on democratic change in general and, more specifically, the role of cross-national diffusion in the spread of democracy.[33] It is obvious from what we have argued in this book that we agree with the more recent position that the introduction and development of democracy, especially during the Third Wave, cannot be understood without reference to the influence of international actors, institutions, and norms. That recognized, however, it is also important to note that, while international actors were important in the electoral breakthroughs that took place in the postcommunist region from 1998 to 2005, they worked in conjunction with local actors who, in the final analysis, were the ones who carried out the tasks

that led to the defeat of authoritarian rulers and the empowerment of the democratic opposition. In this sense, while international influences figured prominently in our study, so did domestic politics. Indeed, it was the electoral model that joined these two key arenas of democratic struggle.

What also emerged in this study is the value of looking at democratization through the lens of international diffusion. Here, we would offer some suggestions. First, analysts of diffusion processes need to assume more of a burden of proof than they have in the past when claiming that similar developments in a group of cases in a relatively short span of time testify necessarily to the impact of international diffusion. * * * [W]hat is often missing from studies of the diffusion of democracy in particular is clear specification of the innovation (and one not to be confused with similar outcomes) and mechanisms of cross-national transfer. For example, it is unhelpful to argue on behalf of the spread of democracy without specifying what exactly is being diffused—for example, democratic institutions, the idea of democracy, or specific modes of transition that can counter effectively the power of authoritarians and/or empower democrats. At the same time, without the specification of the mechanisms involved in the transfer of innovation among sites, the case for diffusion is necessarily weak.

This discussion of mechanisms leads in turn to another requirement in making a compelling case for diffusion: assessing alternative hypotheses to explain the clustered pattern of similar changes across time and space. For example, such patterns could reflect similar local conditions prompting similar responses or the role of powerful outside actors dictating similar changes in a group of weak countries. In either case, the cross-national similarities of interest would not reflect the work of diffusion dynamics.

Gaps in diffusion must be explained as well. It is striking how often analysts overlook the obvious fact that innovative precedents in the neighborhood do not just resonate with supporters of such changes in other sites, but also elicit fears on the part of actors in those other sites who find such changes threatening to their values and interests. Rather than being a nearly automatic and indeed bloodless process, which is the way it is often depicted, the cross-national spread of innovation usually involves fierce local struggles. This is particularly the case when a wave of adoptions has already taken place, and opponents of the innovation in neighboring sites have been amply forewarned and therefore forearmed. As a result, it is a mistake to restrict one's analytical focus to cases in which innovations have been adopted. Such an approach is particularly suspect on methodological grounds. As in comparative politics we cannot be secure in identifying causes in the absence of examining cases that vary in their outcomes, so we cannot nail down the drivers of diffusion, and thus the very fact that it has taken place, without confronting the issue of uneven adoption rates.

In this sense, there are in fact clear similarities between the more familiar methods used in comparative politics—that is, examining variable outcomes by selecting cases that are otherwise similar—and methods that should be used to analyze international diffusion. In fact, as we have argued in this book, the two approaches to political change can be seen as complimentary rather than conflicting. They feature a similar logic with respect to the optimal approach to identifying causality, and they can be partnered with one another to specify how, why, and where similar political changes take place. Just as our comparison of similarities and differences among our countries and elections helped us understand the importance of the electoral model, so the analysis of diffusion helped us explain the origins, modifications, and uneven spread of that model.

While the analysis we have presented in this book meets these standards for establishing the role of cross-national diffusion of innovation, it also reminds us of how rare diffusion must be in view of its formidable requirements. This insight, in turn, carries one final lesson for students of diffusion. It is very important to draw a distinction between innovations that amend the status quo and those that have the explicit purpose of subverting it. For the latter type of innovation, it is fair to argue that purposive and planned transmission plays an unusually important role, that the mechanisms driving diffusion are usually multiple in nature, and that the establishment of diffusion rests, even more than usual, on analyzing the process as it played out on the ground.[34]

Two Cheers for Democracy Assistance?

We can now conclude this book by addressing a final issue: the implications of this study for our understanding of the role of U.S. democracy assistance and for those involved in a practical way in that effort. We can begin by observing that U.S. democracy promotion is a very controversial enterprise. For example, in a recent survey carried out by the German Marshall Fund of the United States, less than half of all Americans said that they supported international democracy assistance programs. Sixty-four percent of Americans who identified with the Republican Party did so, but only thirty-five percent of Democratic Party identifiers took a similar position.[35] It is not surprising that people disagree about the value of U.S. support for democratic development abroad. Most obviously, the controversial wars in Iraq and Afghanistan have linked U.S. democracy assistance to military interventions and the escalation of violence in the countries where the U.S. has intervened. Second, even for the cases of interest in this book, the struggle for democratic change remains a largely domestic political project. Thus, international democracy assistance necessarily takes place at the margins, and it can only build upon, rather than substitute for, a domestic arena ripe for democratic development.[36]

Finally, the United States has no special claim to knowing how to promote democracy in other countries, as members of the U.S. democracy assistance community readily admitted in the interviews we conducted with them. While there is strong evidence that democracy is good in itself and has the additional advantages of promoting peaceful relations among states and enhancing the quality of human life, there is mixed evidence in support of the corollary argument that the United States, as a result, can and should promote democracy abroad. The problem with drawing such a conclusion is that U.S. commitment to democratic change has been inconsistent, even since the end of the Cold War. Equally telling is the fact that the evidence demonstrating the positive effects of U.S. democracy and governance assistance is uneven, as is the quality of such assessments.[37]

All of these concerns about the value and validity of U.S. democracy promotion have merit. However, many critiques of U.S. democracy assistance are very removed from what actually happens on the ground, and they rely in many instances on only a few cases or on only one (often rare and far from representative) form of assistance, such as military intervention in Iraq.[38] At the same time, many critics wrongly assume that U.S. democracy assistance is engineered by Washington, and that it is an enterprise that involves clearly specified goals, a list of fixed activities, and considerable coordination among the actors involved. As Richard Miles, a former U.S. ambassador to Azerbaijan and Georgia and chief of mission in Yugoslavia, argued in the interview we conducted with him: "It is very unusual for the State Department to dictate specific development or democracy assistance programs to U.S. embassies. Instead, most decisions are made on the ground. Moreover, the flow of information between Washington and the field is primarily from the field to Washington rather than vice-versa."[39]

Many analysts also seem to assume that international democracy promoters work in isolation from local actors, are ignorant of local circumstances, and are in a position to dictate what happens. However, if, as in this study, we look at democracy assistance from the ground up (in the postcommunist region and in Washington), take into account the perspectives and actions of both donors and recipients, look at a variety of programs and players, and examine a range of cases where democracy assistance has been

in play, we necessarily operate from a broader and deeper data base and on the basis of some very different assumptions.

All of these considerations lead us to draw more nuanced conclusions regarding such questions as the costs and benefits of, along with the limits on and possibilities for, U.S. support of democratic change abroad. Based on the electoral breakthroughs analyzed in this book, we would conclude that the United States can be, and in most of our successful cases was, an important and effective contributor to democratic change.

However, having made this broad claim, we must quickly amend it by recognizing that, as in the case of international diffusion, the devil is very much in the details. First, and most obviously, democracy assistance is only one, and often not the most important, aspect of U.S. foreign policy and actions in particular countries. As the lack of U.S. interest in assisting actors seeking to oust autocrats in Azerbaijan and Armenia illustrates, security and energy concerns (as in the first case) and U.S. domestic political considerations (as in the second) frequently trump the U.S. commitment to supporting movement toward democracy abroad. While the United States did not "engineer" any of the successful breakthroughs we analyzed, and U.S. commitment to regime change was not the determining factor, U.S. interest in an opposition victory clearly varied in the elections we examined.

Second, the standard used to assess U.S. influence on democratic development matters a great deal. If we argue that the United States can contribute to democratic change, we are not by any means asserting that the United States can, let alone should, "export" democracy, "create" a democracy, "guarantee" democratic progress in the future, or "construct" a full-scale democratic polity overnight. Instead, we are suggesting that the United States can take actions that expand *opportunities* for democratic development in other countries.[40] Whether these opportunities are seized, however, seems to depend largely on local political dynamics. U.S. democracy assistance, in short, contributes at the margins, and it is within these parameters that one should judge the impact of U.S. democracy assistance on democratic change and whether its effects are positive or negative.

In addition, as we have repeatedly emphasized throughout this book, the United States hardly acted alone in our electoral breakthroughs. Other international actors, including the EU, European governments, European and U.S. foundations, the Organization for Security and Cooperation in Europe, and regional graduates of these electoral breakthroughs, along with domestic actors—including opposition parties, civil society organizations, youth movements, and ordinary citizens—played a critical and, just as importantly, a deeply collaborative role in the defeat of authoritarian leaders. The effort, in short, was both cross-national and transnational. * * * The implication here is that if the United States acts alone, it will certainly fail, if not make matters worse.

We also need to unpack the United States as an international actor involved in these elections. Here, we refer, for example, to the role not just of specific U.S. administrations and the State Department, along with USAID and the groups it has funded—such as Freedom House, the United States Institute of Peace, the National Endowment for Democracy and its International Republican Institute and National Democratic Institute for Foreign Affairs, and the Free Trade Union Institute—but also of private foundations based in the United States, such as the Open Society Institute, Rockefeller Brothers, the Mott Foundation, and the German Marshall Fund of the United States. While often engaging in parallel play, these varied organizations and players nonetheless were able to come together in order to provide important assistance to local oppositions and their allies. But such assistance, as James O'Brien, the special envoy to the Balkans during the Clinton administration and the Washington-based director of the campaign to defeat Milošević, noted, merely "built on the plumbing of the past."[41] While elections provided an opportunity for creative and collaborative work among interna-

tional democracy promoters in general and those in the United States in particular, therefore, local struggle and a ripening of local capacities for change were essential.

Finally, U.S. "success" in the specific way we have understood it was also based upon several other considerations that are often overlooked in debates about the value of international democracy assistance. One is that the focus of assistance in our cases was on countries that were situated between democracy and dictatorship. While not always halfway houses on the road to democracy, mixed regimes provide the raw material in general—and regular political and especially electoral opportunities in particular—for improved democratic performance. At the same time, the very nature of elections can enhance the prospects for oppositions, civil society groups, ordinary citizens, and international democracy promoters to work in concert, rather than separately, and to mobilize in support of democratic change, rather than remain in their usual roles as atomized political bystanders or political actors at war with one another. While many aspects of the U.S. experience may be of little help or relevance to other countries—for instance, the unusual character of the U.S. party system, federalism, and a presidential form of government that, for some reason, has not encouraged democratic breakdown in the United States as it has in other parts of the world—the U.S. experience with how elections can be won is very different. It is a model that travels relatively well, and it is a form of assistance that U.S. democracy promoters know well. The politics of getting out the vote, therefore, is less specific to individual countries than questions involving, say, the optimal design of political institutions and public policy.

The results of our research also have a great deal to say regarding the debate, which took place a few years ago and which is being repeated, although in somewhat different terms, today, concerning which strategy is likely to have the bigger payoff: long-term efforts to assist the development of civil society and the rule of law in semi-authoritarian regimes or an infusion of funding and training for the opposition and NGO communities "just in time," as it were—that is, in the context of an upcoming election. Clearly, as we have argued, the latter has had important payoffs in the short term. Thus, the electoral model can be very effective in getting citizens to vote and support the opposition and in creating, as a result, a democratic opening. And, as we have emphasized, such an opening is a necessary, though not sufficient, condition for further democratic progress. However, as the differing results after our breakthrough elections illustrate, long-term support for the development of civil society and the rule of law is also important, if success in removing authoritarian leaders is to translate into longer-term progress toward creating consolidated democratic systems. Thus, there is little to be gained from forcing a choice between short-term and longer-term approaches to democracy assistance. The two approaches play critical and complementary roles.

What we are arguing, therefore, is that the United States has contributed in important ways to democratic development abroad. However, this has been the case only under the very special—indeed, stringent—conditions discussed here. Thus, we can conclude this study of democratizing elections, borrowing from Irving Kristol's characterization of capitalism and E. M. Forster's earlier characterization of democracy, by offering "two cheers" in support of U.S. democracy assistance.[42]

NOTES

1. Quoted in Thomas Friedman, "Bullets and Barrels," *New York Times*, June 21, 2009, 8.
2. Interview with Nino Kobakhidze, Tbilisi, October 19, 2005.
3. Larry Diamond, "Thinking about Hybrid Regimes," *Journal of Democracy* 13:2 (April 2002), 21–35; Andreas Schedler, "The Nested Game of Democratization by Elections," *International Political Science Review/Revue Internationale De Science Politique* 23:1 (January 2002), 103–122; Philip G. Roessler, and Marc Morjé Howard, "Post-Cold-War Political Regimes: When Do Elections Matter?," in *Democratization by Elections: A New Mode of Transition*, ed. Staffan Lindberg (Baltimore: Johns Hopkins University Press, 2009), 101–127.
4. Jan Teorell and Axel Hadenius, "Elections as Levers of Democracy: A Global Inquiry," in *Democratization by Elections: A New Mode of Transition*, ed. Staffan Lindberg (Baltimore: Johns Hopkins University Press, 2009), 77–100; Staffan I. Lindberg, *Democracy and Elections in Africa* (Baltimore: Johns Hopkins University Press, 2006); Valerie Bunce, "Sequencing Political and Economic Reforms," in *East-Central European Economies in Transition*, ed. John Hardt and Richard Kaufman (Washington, DC: Joint Economic Committee, 1994), 46–63; M. Steven Fish, "Democratization's Prerequisites," *Post-Soviet Affairs* 14:3 (July–September 1998), 212–247; Nancy Bermeo, *Ordinary People in Extraordinary Times: The Citizenry and the Breakdown of Democracy* (Princeton, NJ: Princeton University Press, 2003).
5. Marc Morjé Howard and Philip G. Roessler, "Liberalizing Electoral Outcomes in Competitive Authoritarian Regimes," *American Journal of Political Science* 50:2 (April 2006), 362–368; Roessler and Howard, "Post-Cold-War Political Regimes"; Grigore Pop-Eleches and Graeme Robertson, "Elections, Information and Liberalization in the Post–Cold War Era," unpublished manuscript, Princeton University and the University of North Carolina, 2009; Andreas Schedler, "Sources of Competition under Electoral Authoritarianism," in *Democratization by Elections: A New Mode of Transitions?*, ed. Staffan Lindberg (Baltimore: Johns Hopkins University Press, 2009), 179–201; Andreas Schedler, *Electoral Authoritarianism: The Dynamics of Unfree Competition* (Boulder, CO: Lynne Rienner Publishers, 2006); and see Kristin McKie, "The Politics of Adopting Term Limits in Sub-Saharan Africa," paper presented at the annual meeting of the American Political Science Association, Boston, MA, August 29, 2008, on the impact of term limits.
6. Jennifer Gandhi and Ellen Lust Okar, "Elections under Authoritarianism," *Annual Review of Political Science* 12 (June 2009), 404.

7. This wave of electoral change was followed by a wave of studies of the "color revolutions." See, for example, Michael McFaul, "Transitions from Postcommunism," *Journal of Democracy* 16:3 (July 2005), 5–19; Joerg Forbrig and Pavol Demeš, eds., *Reclaiming Democracy: Civil Society and Electoral Change in Central and Eastern Europe* (Bratislava: German Marshall Fund of the United States, 2007); Taras Kuzio, ed., "Democratic Revolutions in Post-Communist States," special issue of *Communist and Postcommunist Studies* 39:3 (September 2006); Menno Fenger, "The Diffusion of Revolutions: Comparing Recent Regime Turnovers in Five Post-Communist Countries," *Demokratizatsiya* 15:1 (Winter 2007), 5–28; Mark Beissinger, "Structure and Example in Modular Political Phenomena: The Diffusion of Bulldozer/Rose/Orange/Tulip Revolutions," *Perspectives on Politics* 5:2 (June 2007), 259–276; Joshua Tucker, "Enough! Electoral Fraud Collective Action Problems and Post-Communist Colored Revolutions," *Perspectives on Politics* 5:3 (September 2007), 537–553.

8. Nicolas Van de Walle, "Meet the New Boss: Same as the Old Boss: The Evolution of Political Clientelism in Africa," in *Patrons, Clients and Policies: Patterns of Democratic Accountability and Political Competition*, ed. Herbert Kitschelt and Steven I. Wilkinson (Cambridge: Cambridge University Press, 2007), 50–67; Nicolas Van de Walle, *Why Do Oppositions Coalesce in Electoral Autocracies?*, Einaudi Center for International Studies Working Paper Series, No. 01–05, Cornell University, August 2005; Nicolas Van de Walle, "Tipping Games: When Do Opposition Parties Coalesce?," in *Electoral Authoritarianism: The Dynamics of Unfree Competition*, ed. Andreas Schedler (Boulder, CO: Lynne Rienner Publishers, 2006), 77–94; Howard and Roessler, "Liberalizing Electoral Outcomes in Competitive Authoritarian Regimes"; Mark R. Thompson and Philipp Kuntz, "Stolen Elections: The Case of the Serbian October," *Journal of Democracy* 15:4 (October 2004): 159–172; Tucker, "Enough!"

9. Pam Oliver and Dan Myers, "Network Diffusion and Cycles of Collective Action," in *Social Movements and Networks: Relational Approaches to Collective Action*, ed. Mario Diani and Doug McAdam (Oxford: Oxford University Press, 2003), 173–203; Doug McAdam and Dieter Rucht, "The Cross-National Diffusion of Movement Ideas," *The Annals of the American Academy of Political and Social Science* 528:1 (July 2003), 56–74; David Strang and Sarah A. Soule, "Diffusion in Organizations and Social Movements: From Hybrid Corn to Poison Pills," *Annual Review of Sociology* 24:1 (August 1998), 265–290; Mark Beissinger, *Nationalist Mobilization and the Collapse of the Soviet State* (Cambridge: Cambridge University Press, 2002); Wade Jacoby, "Inspiration, Coalition and Substitution: External Influences on Postcommunist Transformations," *World Politics* 58:4 (July 2006), 623–651; Everett Rogers, *Diffusion of Innovations* (New York: Free Press, 1996); Beth Simmons and Zachary Elkins, "The Globalization of Liberalization: Policy Diffusion in the International Political Economy," *American Political Science Review* 98:1 (February 2004), 171–189; Zachary Elkins and Beth Simmons, "On Waves, Clusters, and Diffusion: A Conceptual Framework," *The Annals of the American Academy of Political and Social Science* 598 (March 2005), 33–51; Beth Simmons, Frank Dobbin, and Geoffrey Garrett, *The Global Diffusion of Markets and Democracy* (Cambridge: Cambridge University Press, 2008); Daniel Brinks and Michael Coppedge, "Diffusion Is No Illusion: Neighbor Emulation in the Third Wave of Democracy," *Comparative Political Studies* 39:4 (May 1, 2006), 463–489; Kristian Skrede Gleditsch and Michael D. Ward, "Diffusion and the International Context of Democratization," *International Organization* 60:4 (October 2006), 911–933; Kurt Weyland, "The Diffusion of Revolution: '1848' in Europe and Latin America," *International Organization* 63:3 (Summer 2009), 391–423; Kurt Weyland, "Diffusion Dynamics in European and Latin American Democratization," paper presented at the 105th annual meeting of the American Political Science Association,

Toronto, September 3–6, 2009; and Scott Mainwaring and Aníbal Pérez-Liñán, "International Factors and Regime Change in Latin America, 1945–2005," paper presented at the 105th annual meeting of the American Political Science Association, Toronto, September 3–6, 2009.

10. See, for example, Gordon Crawford, *Foreign Aid and Political Reform: A Comparative Analysis of Democracy Assistance and Conditionality* (Basingstoke, UK: Palgrave, 2001); Eric C. Bjornlund, *Beyond Free and Fair: Monitoring Elections and Building Democracy* (Washington, DC: Woodrow Wilson Center Press, 2004); Jon C. Pevehouse, *Democracy from Above: Regional Organizations and Democratization* (Cambridge: Cambridge University Press, 2005); Thomas Carothers, "The End of the Transition Paradigm," *Journal of Democracy* 13:1 (January 2002), 5–21; Thomas Carothers, *Critical Missions: Essays on Democracy Promotion* (Washington, DC: Carnegie Endowment for International Peace, 2004); Thomas Carothers, *Aiding Democracy Abroad: The Learning Curve* (Washington, DC: Carnegie Endowment for International Peace, 1999); Michael Cox, G. John Ikenberry, and Takashi Inoguchi, *American Democracy Promotion: Impulses, Strategies, and Impacts* (Oxford: Oxford University Press, 2000); Richard Youngs, *International. Democracy and the West: The Roles of Governments, Civil Society, and Multinational Business* (Oxford: Oxford University Press, 2004); Gideon Rose, "Democracy Promotion and American Foreign Policy: A Review Essay," *International Security* 25:3 (Winter 2000), 186–203; Scott Mainwaring and Aníbal Pérez-Liñán, *Why Regions of the World Are Important: Regional Specificities and Region-Wide Diffusion of Democracy,* Kellogg Institute, University of Notre Dame, Working Paper 322 (October 2005); Ronald Haly Linden, *Norms and Nannies: The Impact of International Organizations on the Central and East European States* (Lanham, MD: Rowman & Littlefield Publishers, 2002); Stephen Knack, "Does Foreign Aid Promote Democracy?," *International Studies Quarterly* 48:1 (March 2004), 251–266; Wade Jacoby, *The Enlargement of the European Union and NATO: Ordering from the Menu in Central Europe* (Cambridge: Cambridge University Press, 2004); Anna Milada Vachudová, *Europe Undivided: Democracy, Leverage, and Integration after Communism* (Oxford: Oxford University Press, 2005); Steven F. Finkel, Aníbal Pérez-Liñán, Mitchell A. Seligson, and Dinorah Azpuru, *Effects of U.S. Foreign Assistance on Democracy Building: Results of a Cross-National Quantitative Study, Final Report, USAID* (January 12, 2006), http://www.usaid.gov/ourwork/democracyandgovernance/publications/pdfs/impactof-democracyassistance.pdf; Ralph Morris Goldman and William A. Douglas, *Promoting Democracy: Opportunities and Issues: Democracy in the World* (New York: Praeger, 1988); Peter J. Schraeder, *Exporting Democracy: Rhetoric vs. Reality* (Boulder, CO: Lynne Rienner Publishers, 2002); and Michael Mandelbaum, "Foreign Policy as Social Work," *Foreign Affairs* 75:1 (January–February 1996). See also detailed case studies of democracy promotion in one country: Walt Bogdanich and Jenny Nordberg, "Democracy Undone: Back Channels versus Policy; Mixed U.S. Signals Helped Tilt Haiti toward Chaos," *New York Times*, January 29, 2006, http://www.nytimes.com/2006/01/29/international/americas/29haiti.html; David Backer and David Carroll, "NGOs and Constructive Engagement: Promoting Civil Society, Good Governance and Rule of Law in Liberia," *International Politics* 38:1 (March 2001), 1–26; Andrew Ng, "Accompanying the King: Building a Democratic Governance State in Morocco" (honors thesis, Department of Government, Cornell University, April 16, 2007). But see Laurence Whitehead, *The International Dimensions of Democratization: Europe and the Americas* (Oxford: Oxford University Press, 1996) for a longer-term perspective. Also see Strobe Talbott, "Democracy and the National Interest," *Foreign Affairs* 75:6 (November–December 1996), 47–63; Jaba Devdariani, *The Impact of International Assistance on Georgia*, International Institute for Democracy and Electoral Assistance

(IDEA) Building Democracy in Georgia Discussion Paper no. 11 (May 2003), http://www.idea.int/publications/georgia/upload/Book-11_scr.pdf; Jonathan Monten, "The Roots of the Bush Doctrine," *International Security* 29:4 (Spring 2005), 112–156; and Eric Hershberg, "Democracy Promotion in Latin America," *Democracy and Society* 4:2 (Spring 2007), 3–5. On the role of international influences on democratic change, see, for instance, Guillermo A. O'Donnell, Philippe C. Schmitter, and Laurence Whitehead, *Transitions from Authoritarian Rule: Comparative Perspectives* (Baltimore: Johns Hopkins University Press, 1988); Laurence Whitehead, "Three International Dimensions of Democratization," in *The International Dimensions of Democratization: Europe and the Americas*, ed. Laurence Whitehead (Oxford: Oxford University Press, 2001), 3–25; Youngs, *International Democracy and the West*; and Jan Zielonka, *Democratic Consolidation in Eastern Europe* (Oxford: Oxford University Press, 2001).

11. Lucan Way, "The Real Causes of the Color Revolutions," *Journal of Democracy* 19:3 (July 2008), 55–69; Valerie Bunce and Sharon L. Wolchik, "Debating the Color Revolutions: Getting Real about 'Real Causes,'" *Journal of Democracy* 20:1 (January 2009), 69–73; Steven Levitsky and Lucan A. Way, "Competitive Authoritarian Regimes: The Evolution of Post-Soviet Competitive Authoritarianism 1992–2005," paper presented at the conference Why Communism Didn't Collapse: Understanding Regime Resilience in China, Vietnam, Laos, North Korea and Cuba, Dartmouth College, Hannover, NY, May 25–26, 2007; Jason Brownlee, *Authoritarianism in an Age of Democratization* (Cambridge: Cambridge University Press, 2007); Steven Levitsky and Lucan Way, *Competitive Authoritarianism: Hybrid Regimes after the Cold War* (Cambridge: Cambridge University Press, 2010).

12. Wayne Francisco, "After the Massacre: Mobilization in the Wake of Harsh Repression," *Mobilization: An International Journal* 9:2 (January 2004), 107–126. Also see Sidney Tarrow, *Power in Movement: Social Movements and Contentious Politics* (Cambridge:

Cambridge University Press, 1998). However, it is important to recognize at the same time that growing authoritarianism did correlate with propensity to protest—as we saw not just in Serbia, Georgia, Ukraine, and Kyrgyzstan, but also in Armenia, Azerbaijan, and Belarus.

13. Tucker, "Enough!"; Van de Walle, "Meet the New Boss: Same as the Old Boss"; Van de Walle, "Why Do Oppositions Coalesce in Electoral Autocracies?"; Van de Walle, "Tipping Games: When Do Opposition Parties Coalesce?"; Howard and Roessler, "Liberalizing Electoral Outcomes in Competitive Authoritarian Regimes"; Mark R. Thompson and Philipp Kuntz, "Stolen Elections."

14. Our thanks to David Patel for drawing the important distinction between coordination and collective action.

15. Interview with Larry Garber, Washington, DC, April 9, 2010.

16. Interviews with Patrick Merloe, Washington, DC, April 30, 2009; Larry Garber, Washington, DC, April 9, 2010; Kenneth Wollack, Washington, DC, May 12, 2010; and Thomas Melia, Washington, DC, April 12, 2010.

17. See, especially, National Research Councils of the National Academies, Committee on Evaluation of USAID Democracy Assistance Programs, *Improving Democracy Assistance: Building Knowledge through Evaluations and Research* (Washington, DC: National Academies Press, 2008).

18. Finkel et al., "Effects of US Foreign Assistance on Democracy Building"; Lincoln Abraham Mitchell, *Uncertain Democracy: U.S. Foreign Policy and Georgia's Rose Revolution* (Philadelphia: University of Pennsylvania Press, 2009); National Research Councils of the National Academies, Committee on Evaluation of USAID Democracy Assistance Programs, *Improving Democracy Assistance*; Erzsebet Fazekas, "Exporting Ideas for Institution-Building: U.S. Foundation Grant-Making for Civil Society Development in Postcommunist Hungary, 1989–2004," paper presented at the annual meeting of the American Association for the Advancement of Slavic Stud-

ies, November 14–18, 2007; Andrew Green, "Democracy and Donor Funding: Patterns and Trends," *Eastern European Studies Newsletter*, Woodrow Wilson Center for International Scholars (September–October, 2007), 5–11; Devdariani, *The Impact of International Assistance on Georgia*; Carothers, "The End of the Transition Paradigm"; Carothers, *Critical Missions*; Carothers, *Aiding Democracy Abroad*; Thomas Carothers, "Misunderstanding Gradualism," *Journal of Democracy* 18:3 (July 2007), 18–22; Thomas Carothers, "The 'Sequencing' Fallacy," *Journal of Democracy* 18:1 (January 2007), 12–27. Moreover, as Florian Bieber has suggested in a personal exchange, European democracy promoters tend to be professional bureaucrats who are committed primarily to capacity building and who have a well-defined and relatively apolitical portfolio of tasks that they apply wherever they serve. This is in sharp contrast to many of their American counterparts, who have greater room to maneuver in the field and who more often come from backgrounds in the political world.

19. See Diamond, "Thinking about Hybrid Regimes"; but see Beate Sissenich, *Building States without Society: European Union Enlargement and the Transfer of EU Social Policy to Poland and Hungary* (Lanham, MD: Lexington Books, 2007), especially on the asymmetries built into certain aspects of EU expansion.

20. As calculated from Finkel et al., "Effects of U.S. Foreign Assistance on Democracy Building," 28, 32. Also see Valerie Bunce and Sharon L. Wolchik, "Favorable Conditions and Electoral Revolutions," *Journal of Democracy* 17:4 (October 2006): 5–18.

21. We especially thank Barbara Haig, Carl Gershman, and Kenneth Wollack for defining these activities.

22. Interview with Kenneth Wollack, Washington, DC, May 12, 2010.

23. Theodor Tudoroiu, "Rose, Orange and Tulip: The Failed Post-Soviet Revolutions," *Communist and Postcommunist Studies* 40:3 (September 2007), 315–342; but see Lucia Kureková, "Electoral Revolutions and their Socio-Economic Impact: Bulgaria and Slovakia in Comparative Perspective" (master's thesis, Department of International Relations and European Studies, Central European University, Budapest, 2006), for a more nuanced assessment.

24. See, especially, Thomas Carothers, *Stepping Back from Democratic Pessimism*, Carnegie Endowment for International Peace, Democracy and Rule of Law Program, Paper no. 99 (February 2009).

25. Ellen Lust Okar, "Divided They Rule: The Management and Manipulation of Political Opposition," *Comparative Politics* 36:2 (January 2004), 159–179; Gandhi and Lust Okar, "Elections under Authoritarianism"; Lisa Blaydes, "Authoritarian Elections and Elite Management: Theory and Evidence from Egypt," unpublished manuscript, April 2008; Jennifer Gandhi and Adam Przeworski, "Cooperation, Cooptation, and Rebellion under Dictatorships," *Economics & Politics* 18:1 (March 2006), 1–26; Brownlee, *Authoritarianism in an Age of Democratization*.

26. Lisa Anderson, "Searching Where the Light Shines: Studying Democratization in the Middle East," *Annual Review of Political Science* 9 (June 2006), 189–214; Eva Bellin, "The Robustness of Authoritarianism in the Middle East," *Comparative Politics* 36:2 (January 2004), 139–157; Jason Brownlee, "Low Tide after the Third Wave: Exploring Politics under Authoritarianism," *Comparative Politics* 34:4 (July 2002), 477–498. Also see David Shambaugh, *China's Communist Party: Atrophy and Adaptation* (Berkeley: University of California Press, 2008).

27. See, for example, Lucan Way, "Authoritarian State-Building and the Sources of Regime Competitiveness in the Fourth Wave: The Cases of Belarus, Moldova, Russia and Ukraine," *World Politics* 57:2 (January 2005), 231–61; Way, "The Real Causes of the Color Revolutions"; Levitsky and Way, *Competitive Authoritarianism*; and Brownlee, *Authoritarianism in an Age of Democracy*. In some other work, however, both Brownlee and Way seemed to give more explanatory power to agency and processes, such as elections. See, for example, Lucan Way, "Deer in Headlights: Authoritarian Skill and Regime Trajectories after the Cold War," paper presented at the Conference on Central Asia and Sub-Saharan Africa, Cornell University, September

26–28, 2008; and Jason Brownlee, "Harbingers of
Change: Competitive Elections before the End of
Authoritarianism," in *Democratization by Elections:
A New Mode of Transition?*, ed. Staffan Lindberg
(Baltimore: Johns Hopkins University Press, 2009),
128–147.

28. Valerie Bunce, *Subversive Institutions: The
Design and the Destruction of Socialism and the
State* (Cambridge: Cambridge University Press,
1999); Michael McFaul, "The Fourth Wave of
Democracy and Dictatorship: Noncooperative
Transitions in the Postcommunist World," *World
Politics* 54:2 (January 2002), 212–244; Marina
Ottaway, *Democracy Challenged: The Rise of
Semi-Authoritarianism* (Washington, DC: Carnegie
Endowment for International Peace, 2003);
Diamond, "Thinking about Hybrid Regimes";
Levitsky and Way, *Competitive Authoritarianism*.

29. Compare, for example, Brownlee, *Authoritarianism
in an Age of Democratization*, to Staffan I. Lindberg,
"The Surprising Significance of African Elections," *Journal of Democracy*, 17:1 (January 2006),
139–151; Staffan Lindberg, ed., *Democratization
by Elections: A New Mode of Transition?* (Baltimore:
Johns Hopkins University Press, 2009); Teorell and
Hadenius, "Elections as Levers"; Tucker, "Enough!";
and Valerie Bunce, "Reflections on Elections,"
*Newsletter of the Comparative Politics Section of the
American Political Science Association* 19 (Fall 2008),
1–5. For a distinction between electoral processes
and leadership turnover as influences on policy
innovation, see Valerie Bunce, *Do New Leaders Make
a Difference? Executive Succession and Public Policy
under Capitalism and Socialism* (Princeton, NJ:
Princeton University Press, 1981).

30. Andreas Schedler, "The Contingent Power of
Authoritarian Elections," in Staffan Lindberg, ed.,
*Democratization by Elections: A New Mode of Transi-
tion?* (Baltimore: Johns Hopkins University Press,
2009), 291–313.

31. Interview with Larry Garber, Washington, DC,
April 9, 2010.

32. Doug McAdam and Sidney Tarrow, "Ballots
and Barricades: On the Reciprocal Relationship
between Elections and Social Movements," paper
presented at the conference Hot Models and Hard
Conflicts: The Agenda of Comparative Political Science in the 21st Century, a symposium
in honor of Hanspeter Kriesi, Center for Comparative and International Studies (CIS), Zurich,
Switzerland, June 26, 2009; Guillermo Trejo,
"The Political Foundations of Ethnic Mobilization and Territorial Conflict in Mexico,
1975–2000," in *Federalism and Territorial Cleavages*, ed. Ugo Amoretti and Nancy Bermeo
(Baltimore: Johns Hopkins University Press, 2004),
355–386.

33. Barbara Wejnert, "Diffusion, Development, and
Democracy, 1800–1999," *American Sociological
Review* 70:1 (February 2005), 53–81; Mainwaring
and Pérez-Liñán, "Why Regions of the World
Are Important"; Brinks and Coppedge, "Diffusion
Is No Illusion"; Gleditsch and Ward, "Diffusion
and the International Context of Democratization";
Harvey Starr and Christina Lindborg, "Democratic
Dominoes Revisited: The Hazards of Governmental
Transitions, 1974–1996," *Journal of Conflict
Resolution* 47:4 (August 2003), 490–519; John
Markoff, *Waves of Democracy: Social Movements and
Political Change* (Thousand Oaks, CA: Pine Forge
Press, 1996); Pevehouse, *Democracy from Above*;
Youngs, *International Democracy and the West*;
Finkel et al., "Effects of U.S. Foreign Assistance on
Democracy Building."

34. Jacoby, "Inspiration, Coalition and Substitution."

35. "German Marshall Fund Survey: Transatlantic
Trends," German Marshall Fund of the United
States, 2006, www.transatlantictrends.org.

36. Carothers, "The End of the Transition Paradigm";
Carothers, *Critical Missions*; Carothers, *Aiding
Democracy Abroad*; Carothers, "Misunderstanding
Gradualism"; Carothers, "The 'Sequencing' Fal-
lacy"; Mitchell, *Uncertain Democracy*.

37. The National Councils of the National Academies,
Committee on Evaluation of USAID Democ-
racy Assistance Programs, *Improving Democracy
Assistance*; Finkel et al., "Effects of U.S. Foreign
Assistance on Democracy Building"; Martha

Finnemore, *The Purpose of Intervention: Changing Beliefs about the Use of Force* (Ithaca, NY: Cornell University Press, 2003); Devdariani, *The Impact of International Assistance on Georgia*; Paul Drake, "From Good Men to Good Neighbors, 1912–1932," in *Exporting Democracy: The U.S. and Latin America*, ed. Abraham Lowenthal (Baltimore: Johns Hopkins University Press, 1991), 3–40; Lise Rakner and Lars Svåsand, "The Politics of the Elections (or How Incumbents Remain in Office): The Cases of Malawi and Uganda," paper presented at the workshop Democratization by Elections?, University of Florida, Gainesville, November 30–December 2, 2007; Alexander Cooley, "Base Politics," *Foreign Affairs* 84:6 (November–December 2005), 79–92; Alexander Cooley, "U.S. Bases and Democratization in Central Asia," *Orbis* 52:1 (January 2008), 65–90; Alexander Cooley and James Ron, "The NGO Scramble: Organizational Insecurity and the Political Economy of Transnational Action," *International Security* 27:1 (Summer 2002), 5–39; Jeff Erlich, "Uzbekistan after the Backlash: How Can the U.S. Promote Democracy Where It Is Not Welcome?" (MA thesis, Global Master of Arts Program, Tufts University, Fletcher School, March 12, 2006); Sarah Elizabeth Mendelson and John K. Glenn, *The Power and Limits of NGOs: A Critical Look at Building Democracy in Eastern Europe and Eurasia* (New York: Columbia University Press, 2002); Lisa McIntosh Sundstrom, "Foreign Assistance, International Norms, and NGO Development: Lessons from the Russian Campaign," *International Organization* 59:2 (Spring 2005), 419–449; Sarah Mendelson and Theodore P. Gerber, "Local Activist Culture and Transnational Diffusion: An Experiment in Social Marketing among Human Rights Groups in Russia," unpublished manuscript, April 2005; Laurence Jarvik, "NGOs: A New Class in International Relations," *Orbis* 51:2 (Spring 2007), 217–238; Frederic Charles Schaffer, *The Hidden Costs of Clean Election Reforms* (Ithaca, NY: Cornell University Press, 2008); Frederick Charles Schaffer, *Democracy in Translation: Understanding Politics in an Unfamiliar Culture* (Ithaca, NY: Cornell University Press, 1998); Carothers, "Misunderstanding Gradualism"; Carothers, "The 'Sequencing' Fallacy"; Crawford, *Foreign Aid and Political Reform*; Kristina Kaush and Richard Youngs, *Algeria: Democratic Transition Case Study*, CDDRL Working Paper No. 84, Center for Democracy, Development and the Rule of Law, Freeman Spogli Institute for International Studies, Stanford University (August 2008); Bogdanich and Norberg, "Democracy Undone"; Sarah L. Henderson, "Selling Civil Society: Western Aid and the Nongovernmental Organization Sector in Russia," *Comparative Political Studies* 35:2 (March 2002), 139–167; Sarah L. Henderson, *Building Democracy in Contemporary Russia: Western Support for Grassroots Organizations* (Ithaca, NY: Cornell University Press, 2006); Janine R. Wedel, *Collision and Collusion: The Strange Case of Western Aid to Eastern Europe, 1989–1998* (New York: St. Martin's Press, 1998).

38. Steve Watts, "Military Interventions and the Construction of Political Order," paper presented at the annual meeting of the American Political Science Association, Washington, DC, September 1–4, 2005; Mark Peceny, "Democracy Promotion and American Foreign Policy: Afghanistan, Iraq, and the Future," in *American Foreign Policy in a Globalized World*, ed. David Forsythe, Patrice McMahon, and Andrew Wedeman (New York: Routledge, 2006), 324–360; Mark Peceny, *Democracy at the Point of Bayonets* (University Park: Pennsylvania State University Press, 1999); Margaret G. Hermann and Charles Kegley, "The U.S. Use of Military Intervention to Promote Democracy: Evaluating the Record," *International Interactions* 24:2 (June 1998), 91–114.

39. Interview with Richard Miles, Washington, DC, September 25, 2009.

40. Interviews with Barbara Haig, Washington, DC, May 14, 2010; Carl Gershman, Washington, DC, May 14, 2010; and Kenneth Wollack, Washington, DC, May 12, 2010.

41. Interview with James C. O'Brien, Washington, DC, November 16, 2006.

42. Irving Kristol, *Two Cheers for Capitalism* (New York: New American Library, 1979). Kristol, in turn, borrowed his title from E. M. Forster, *Two Cheers for Democracy* (New York: Harcourt Brace Jovanovich, 1966). Our thanks to Marc Plattner for pointing this out.

Ivan Krastev

PARADOXES OF THE NEW AUTHORITARIANISM

In early 1991, as a young Bulgarian scholar still fired by the revolutionary passions of 1989, I sat in the library room of St. Antony's College at Oxford reading Seymour Martin Lipset's classic, *Political Man*. This was an unforgettable time when reading daily newspapers was much more exciting than reading political science, so perhaps it is unsurprising that Lipset's analysis seemed to me to be, if sound, also a bit dull. Now I realize that this is the fate of any classic book in the social sciences. You feel that you have "read" it long before opening the first page, and the more revolutionary were its conclusions when they were first published, the more banal and obvious they seem decades later. So in my first encounter with Lipset's work, I was neither particularly impressed by the book nor intrigued by its author.

Now, rereading Lipset twenty years on, I have discovered not only the originality of his mind but—what is even more striking—the amazing power of his personality. Lipset is the embodiment of the type of intellectual presence that we so badly miss today. He fascinates by both his curiosity and his seriousness. In his scholarly life, he succeeded in researching and publishing about any problem that concerned him. He crossed disciplinary boundaries with the ease of a Balkan smuggler. He was consistent without being dogmatic and political without being partisan, and he succeeded in influencing both his academic colleagues and the general public. In short, he was among the best representatives of the great generation of American public intellectuals who devoted themselves to "arguing the world."[1]

In his autobiographical essay "Steady Work," Lipset wrote:

> As a Trotskyist or socialist from high school through graduate school, I became interested in three questions. The biggest one was—why had the Bolshevik revolution in the Soviet Union led to an oppressive, exploitive society? . . . The second question that concerned me was: Why had the democratic socialist movement . . . failed to adhere to policies that would further socialism? . . . The third political question that interested me greatly was why the United States had never had a major socialist party. . . . Attempting to answer these questions was to inform much of my academic career.[2]

Asking the right questions and struggling with them all his life was Lipset's way of engaging with the world. It is probably a good model for the rest of us to follow, even when we are doubtful about the answers that we find. Thus I would like to use the

From *Journal of Democracy* 22, no. 2 April 2011), pp. 5–16.

opportunity given to me by this Lipset Memorial Lecture to try to address three questions that have been haunting me recently: *1) Why are authoritarian regimes surviving in the age of democratization? 2) Why did political science fail to anticipate the resilience of these regimes? and 3) Why it is so difficult to resist contemporary authoritarianism?*

Most of my observations will be based primarily on Russia's postcommunist experience. This focus on Russia in a lecture that tries to reflect on the challenges of the new authoritarianism may come as a surprise to many, for it is fair to say that Russia's moment in history has passed. Political scientist Stephen Holmes has argued that "the ideological polarity between democracy and authoritarianism, inherited from the Cold War, obscures more than it reveals when applied to Russian political reality."[3] This suggests that the dichotomy between democracy and authoritarianism will not help us much in understanding the nature of the current regime in Moscow—a weak state weakly connected to a weak society. Russia is also not a good example to explain the attractiveness of the new authoritarianism, as it is not the trendsetter when it comes to authoritarianism's return to fashion. Russia's authoritarianism looks dull and tawdry compared with China's capitalism with a communist face. While the Chinese experiment and innovate, the Russians are stagnant. Russia has lost not only its status as a great power, but also its aura of mystery.

User-Friendly Authoritarianism

Why, then, since Russia is neither a trendsetter nor an intellectual mystery, should we focus on Russia in order to understand the paradoxes of modern authoritarianism? There are three good reasons to do so.

First, as Robert Kagan has observed, Russia was the place where history ended and also where it has returned.[4] In this sense, Russia's political experience over the last two decades has been critically important for our understanding of both democracy and autocracy. It was Russia's development in the 1990s that shaped our expectations about the global advance of democracy, and it was Russia's failed democratization in the 2000s that led many to change their views about the prospects for a global democratic revolution. So making sense of the confusing nature of Putin's authoritarianism may be more important for understanding where the world is going than is explaining the sources of popularity of China's authoritarian success.

Second, Russia is an interesting case because it highlights the key features of the new competitive authoritarianism. Russia's regime is only moderately repressive. Putin's authoritarianism is a "vegetarian" one. While political repression exists and human-rights organizations have documented the persecution of journalists and other opponents of the regime, it is fair to say that most Russians today are freer than in any other period of their history. They can travel, they can freely surf the Web—unlike in China or Iran, the government is not trying to control the Internet—and they can do business if they pay their "corruption tax." Unlike the Soviet Union, which was a self-contained society with closed borders, Russia is an open economy with open borders. Almost ten-million Russians travel abroad annually.

Putin's regime is also a nonideological one. The fate of the concept of "sovereign democracy," the Kremlin's most ambitious attempt to date to come up with an ideology, is the best demonstration of this. Like any political regime, Putin's Kremlin is doing its best to construct some collective identities and to exploit nationalist sentiments or Soviet nostalgia, but the insistence that you do not want to be lectured by the United States is not an ideology. The ease with which Russian elites recently shifted their slogan from "sovereign democracy" to "modernization" exemplifies the postideological character of the current regime. It presents itself as a variant of, and not as an alternative to, Western democracy, and it has managed to adapt some key democratic institutions—most notably elections—for its own purposes.

Third, unlike the Chinese regime, which survives because both the elites and the people perceive it as successful, Putin's regime survives even though elites and ordinary people alike view it as dysfunctional and uninspiring. The latest survey by Russia's Levada Center shows that a majority sees the current situation as one of stagnation. The paradox of Russian authoritarianism today is that its backers no less than its foes consider it a flop, yet it slogs on, oblivious and unmoved. Why are people ready to accept such "zombie authoritarianism" rather than opt for democratic change? This is the real question that Putin's Russia poses to the world.

It is the contradictory nature of Russia's authoritarianism—stable and dysfunctional, open and nonideological—that can best help us to understand why authoritarianism is surviving in the age of democratization, and why it is so difficult to resist contemporary authoritarian regimes.

An Unexpected Resilience

First, however, let us address the question of why democratic theorists were blind to the resilience of authoritarianism.

Among Seymour Martin Lipset's many books and articles, there is one that remains mostly unknown. It is a tiny booklet that he wrote in 1994 together with the Hungarian philosopher and former dissident Gyorgy Bence.[5] This essay was meant to contribute not to theory, but to the self-knowledge of theorists. The question it addressed was why political science had failed to anticipate the collapse of communism.

Lipset pointed to two major reasons for this dismal failure of political science. First, during the Cold War an ideological consensus prevailed in the West that presumed the stability of the Soviet system. The political right believed that the Soviet system was stable because of effective repression, and always tended to portray Soviet institutions such as the KGB or the army as ruthless, smart, and efficient. This was the delusion of the right. The political left, accepting the view that the Soviet Union was an egalitarian society providing free education and health care, tended to overestimate the social legitimacy of the Soviet system. This was the delusion of the left. So even though the left and the right in the days of the Cold War were in disagreement about almost everything when it came to communism, both agreed that the Soviet Union was there to stay.

Lipset and Bence's second reason was the institutional bias of those who studied the Soviet world for a living. Political scientists were experts on how the Soviet system worked, but were blind to the possibility that it could collapse. Cold War political science simply took the continued existence of the Soviet Union for granted. It was those outside the academy—journalists, dissidents, political activists—who foresaw the coming crash.

As history showed, the Soviet Union was not as stable as the Sovietologists had assumed it to be. It seemed destined to last forever until it suddenly began to crumble. The divine surprise of 1989 revealed to scholars that the USSR's seemingly rock-solid "stability" had always been a fragile thing. What was thought to be made of steel turned out to be made of paper.

Like mirror images of the Sovietologists who once assumed communist regimes to be inherently stable, many theorists of democratization have since the end of the Cold War come to see today's authoritarian regimes as inherently fragile. Thus any serious rethinking of the nature of new authoritarian regimes such as Russia's or China's should start with a critical examination of the assumptions that make us rate authoritarianism as bound for the ash heap of history.

Samuel P. Huntington best captured the prevailing mood about the transitory nature of these regimes when he observed in 1991 that "liberalized authoritarianism is not a stable equilibrium; the halfway house does not stand."[6] If authoritarian regimes "do not perform, they lose legitimacy since performance is their only justification for holding power. But . . . if they do perform socioeconomically, they tend to refocus popular aspirations around political goals for voice and participation that they cannot satisfy without terminating their existence."[7]

Why should we believe that today's authoritarian regimes are so unstable? The first argument comes from the core of modernization theory and might be termed the "Lipset hypothesis." Modernization theorists tend to view democracy as a necessary element of the modernity package, in the same way as urbanization, industrialization, or secularization. In his major work, Lipset asserts that high incomes and economic development enhance the chances for democracy to be sustained. He also insists on the elective affinity between democracy and capitalism. So, the global spread of capitalism and the unprecedented rise in incomes in developing countries strengthen the expectation that authoritarian regimes are a transitory phenomenon. The latest research supports the notion that as societies grow wealthier, values begin to change in democracy-friendly ways.

The second argument about the obsolescence of authoritarian regimes can be described as "the effect of openness." Ian Bremmer spoke for many when, in his widely read book *The J Curve*, he argued that under conditions of free trade, free travel, and the free flow of information, only democracies can be stable.[8] If autocratic regimes want to achieve stability, they must either close their "borders" (meaning not only their geographical frontiers but also their multifarious forms of exposure to the wider world) or open their political systems.

The third argument that made us deem authoritarianism doomed to obsolescence is the "imitation argument." As we have already shown in the case of Russia, over the last two decades authoritarian rulers have tried to imitate democratic institutions and to adopt democratic language. Holding elections, the rulers calculated, would gain them acceptability and less international pressure for real change. Advocates of the imitation argument insist that by adopting democratic institutions in some form and to some degree, such rulers unavoidably put their electoral authoritarian regimes at risk. "If in the first act you have hung a pistol on the wall," Anton Chekhov once reportedly advised his fellow playwrights, "then in the following one it should be fired." Political scientists contend that if authoritarians adopt elections and other democratic institutions—even in a limited, manipulative way—at some point these institutions will "fire." The presence of democratic institutions, even if perverted ones, will eventually bite authoritarian regimes where it hurts.

The change in the international environment—that is, the effect of "geopolitical warming"—offered still another argument for expecting that authoritarian regimes would not survive the age of democratization, just as dinosaurs had been unable to survive the Ice Age. The demise of the Soviet Union and the end of the Cold War deprived autocrats of their foreign protectors.

For all these reasons, political scientists at the end of the twentieth century tended to believe that autocratic regimes were doomed to fail. But while the end of authoritarianism has long been forecast, it has yet to occur. Why authoritarian regimes can survive and even flourish in an age of democratization is a question that should be asked anew.

The Search for Explanations

In recent years, scholars such as Jason Brownlee, Steven Levitsky, and Lucan Way have made significant contributions toward determining what factors contribute to the survival of twenty-first-century authoritarianism. Brownlee has demonstrated that "the shift to authoritarianism with multiparty elections . . . does not represent an unwitting step toward full democratization, but neither do manipulated elections automatically protect rulers by reducing international pressure and corralling the opposition."[9] In short, faking democracy can both strengthen and weaken authoritarian regimes.

Levitsky and Way have concluded, based on a study of numerous cases of competitive authoritarianism, that authoritarian regimes have the best chance of surviving in countries where Western leverage is limited and where linkages with the West are low. The existence of a functional state with a capacity for repression and the presence of an efficient ruling party are other critical factors that boost the survival chances of authoritarian regimes. Such regimes are harder to dislodge in big, nuclear-armed countries that have never been Western colonies, that are governed by a consolidated ruling party, and that are ready to shoot when students come to protest on the main square. Authoritarians are less likely to stay in power in states that are small and weak, that are located near the European Union or United States, that need IMF loans, that are economically and culturally connected with the West, that lack a strong ruling party, and that cannot or will not shoot protesters.

While enhancing our understanding of the survival capacity and strategies of twenty-first-century authoritarians, Levitsky and Way are not particularly interested in the question of why resisting these regimes is so difficult. Why do even unpopular nondemocratic regimes in most cases not face mass political protests? Thinking exclusively in terms of the opposition between democracy and authoritarianism threatens to trap democratic theorists within the two assumptions that this opposition implicitly contains: first, that when an authoritarian system collapses, democracy will naturally arise by default; and second, that if democracy fails to develop, authoritarian forces must be to blame.

Paradoxically, in order to understand the survival capacity of contemporary authoritarianism, we should be very careful in using the dichotomy of authoritarianism versus democracy. The truth is that today authoritarianism survives best in the no-man's land *between* democracy and authoritarianism.

What I want to argue is that the weakness of the resistance to contemporary authoritarian regimes is less a fruit of effective repression—the fear factor—than it is of the very openness of these regimes. Contrary to the usual assumption of democratic theory, the opening of borders can actually stabilize rather than destabilize the new authoritarian regimes. In a similar fashion, I will try to demonstrate that the nonideological nature of the new authoritar-

ian regimes can also strengthen them rather than increase their vulnerability.

The Perversity of Ideology

In her famous November 1979 article in *Commentary*, "Dictatorships and Double Standards," Jeane Kirkpatrick argued that totalitarian regimes grounded in revolutionary ideology are not only more repressive than traditional authoritarian regimes but are also much harder to liberalize or democratize. In her view, ideology is a source of transcendental legitimacy for these regimes, giving them some of the qualities of theocracies.

Ideology also served as a means of securing the ruling elite's coherence. The notion of "the correct party line," as Ken Jowitt has argued, did for Leninist regimes what democratic procedures did in the West. The existence of a ruling party rooted in an ideology was vital to solving the problem of succession, the most dangerous source of instability in autocratic regimes. The ruling ideology also served as a tool for political mobilization. As the history of the Soviet Union shows, it was sometimes easier to die for the regime than to live under it. The heroism of the Soviet people during World War II provided the ultimate demonstration of the power of the ideological authoritarians.

The notion of ideology as a source of strength for autocratic regimes is so much a part of the Cold War's legacy in the West that one is surprised to encounter the post-Soviet elite's view of communist ideology as one of the old regime's weaknesses. The USSR's collapse showed that ideology corrodes autocratic regimes in two ways: It feeds the reformist delusions of the elites, and it gives the regime's opponents a language and a platform by holding up an ideal against which the regime can be measured and found wanting.

During the last twenty years, thousands of books have been published on the nature of Mikhail Gorbachev's revolution. But for my argument, the key point is that Gorbachev started his reforms not because he had lost faith in communism, but because he remained a true believer who was firmly convinced that the genuine socialism he hoped to install would prove itself decisively superior to the democratic capitalism of the West. Reforms from above often are generated by rulers' misperceptions, not their accurate grasp of reality.

Ideology not only breeds reformist delusions on the part of elites, it also gives the opposition a discourse that it can use to press the regime, from below. As a rule, dissidents in the Soviet bloc were former believers; before opposing Marxist regimes, root and branch, they had often criticized these regimes in the language of Marxism itself. One cannot fully understand the power of the Prague Spring or of Solidarity's "self-limiting revolution" without understanding the self-consciously "dialectical" nature of these movements. The revolutions of 1989 were the *joint* product of communist elites who contributed to the demise of their own regimes by genuinely trying to reform them *and* of oppositionists who fueled the regimes' demise by pretending to want reform when in reality they had come to desire complete uprooting.

Resisting Putin's regime is so difficult precisely because of its lack of any ideology beyond a meaningless mélange of Kremlin-produced sound bites. Public-relations experts are not fit for the role of ideologues because an ideology, unlike an ad campaign, is something in which its authors must believe. The new authoritarian regimes' lack of any real ideology explains their tendency to view themselves as corporations. In order to stay in power, they try to eradicate the very idea of the public interest. In this context, the glorification of the market does not undermine the new authoritarian capitalism; it can even strengthen it. If the public interest is nothing more than the unintended outcome of millions of individuals pursuing their private interests, then any sacrifice in the name of the public interest is a waste.

The new authoritarian regimes' lack of any ideology also partly explains why the democratic world is reluctant to confront them. They do not seek to export their political models, and hence they are not threatening. The new authoritarian regimes do not want to transform the world or to impose their system on other countries. So the axis of conflict today is no longer the free world versus the world of authoritarianism—it is more the free world versus the world of free riding.

The Perversity of Open Borders

Also lurking behind the belief that authoritarianism is doomed to the slow death of reform or the sudden death of collapse is the assumption that the opening of borders must be fatal to autocracy. In the middle of the nineteenth century, the Marquis de Custine, the French aristocrat who went to Russia in 1839 looking for arguments to support his conservatism and came back as an advocate of constitutionalism, had already claimed that "the political system of Russia could not withstand twenty years of free communication with Western Europe."[10] His proposition is a common belief today—open borders allow people to see a different way of life and to struggle to achieve it, thus encouraging demands for change. Open borders also make it easier for people to organize with help from abroad.

But do open borders really destabilize authoritarian regimes? Joseph Stalin, of course, very much believed so. He sent to the gulag millions of Soviet soldiers whose only crime was that they had seen Western or even Central Europe. But Putin is not Stalin. He does not try to govern Russia by preventing people from traveling; he governs it by allowing them to travel. While open borders place some limits on a government's ability to manipulate and persecute, they also afford opportunities to promote the survival of the regime.

Almost forty years ago, economist Albert O. Hirschman, in his brilliant little book *Exit, Voice, and Loyalty*, explained why railways in Nigeria had performed so poorly in the face of competition from trucks and buses:

> The presence of a ready alternative to rail transport makes it less, rather than more, likely that the weaknesses of the railways will be fought rather

than indulged. With truck and bus transportation available, a deterioration in the rail service is not so serious a matter as if the railways held a monopoly for long distance transport—it can be lived with for a long time without arousing strong public pressures for the . . . reforms in administration and management that would be required. This may be the reason public enterprise . . . has strangely been at its weakest in sectors such as transportation and education where it is subjected to competition: instead of stimulating improved or top performance, the presence of a ready and satisfactory substitute for the services public enterprise offers merely deprives it of a precious feedback mechanism that operates at its best when the customers are securely locked in. For the management of public enterprise, always fairly confident that it will not be let down by the national treasury, may be less sensitive to the loss of revenue due to the switch of customers to a competing mode than to the protests of an aroused public that has a vital stake in the service, has no alternative, and will therefore "raise hell."[11]

In Hirschman's view, consumers or members of organizations can offer two opposing responses to the deterioration of the goods they buy or the services they receive. The first is *exit*—simply the act of leaving, such as buying another shampoo, resigning from the party, or departing from the country. *Voice*, by contrast, is an act of complaining or protesting. As Hirschman points out, however, the easy availability of exit tends to diminish the use of voice, because exit requires less time and commitment.

Exit is particularly attractive for middle-class Russians who have managed to become consumers and at the same time are discouraged about the potential for collective action. Russia's demographic situation—its aging and shrinking populace—and Russia's weak national identity have made exit a very natural option for those who are disappointed with the regime. The emergence of an exit-minded middle class in Russia is at the heart of the regime's sur-

vival capacity. Russian economist Leonid Grigoriev recently suggested that more than "two million Russian democrats have left the country in the last decade." Voting with one's feet to leave Russia because it is undemocratic is not the same as voting to make Russia democratic.

In fact, Hirschman's explanation of why the Nigerian railways performed so poorly in the face of competition from trucks and buses may be the key to understanding why it is so difficult to resist Putin's authoritarianism. It explains the failure of reforms and the resulting loss of the reformist spirit in Russia. Paradoxically, the opening of the borders and the opportunity to live and work abroad have led to the decline of political reformism. The people who are the most likely to be upset by the poor quality of governance in Russia are the very same people who are the most ready and able to exit Russia. For them, leaving the country in which they live is easier than reforming it. Why try to turn Russia into Germany, when there is no guarantee that a lifetime is long enough for that mission, and when Germany is but a short trip away? The opinion polls demonstrate that Russia's middle class prefers to work abroad and to come home to Russia during the holidays to see their friends and relatives.

Comparing the outburst of reformist energy in the 1980s with the lack of such energy today makes me believe that, while the sealing of the borders destroyed Soviet communism, the opening of the borders helps the new Russian authoritarianism to survive. The Soviet system locked its citizens in. Changing the system was the only way to change your life. Today's Russia, on the other hand, very much resembles the Nigerian railways—it will remain inefficient as long as there is enough oil money to compensate for its inefficiency. The major reason why Russians are reluctant to protest is not fear; it is because the people who care most have already left the country or have resolved to do so in the near future—or they may simply have moved to the virtual reality of the Internet (Russians on average spend twice as much time using online social networks as do their Western counterparts).

The consequence is that there is no critical mass of people demanding change.

Where will all this lead? It is not easy to predict. But I would say that the future of dysfunctional authoritarian regimes like the one we see in Russia today is less likely to eventuate in democracy than in decay. It is not "after Putin, the deluge," but "after Putin, the dry rot."

NOTES

1. This phrase is from the title of the 1997 documentary *Arguing the World*, directed by Joseph Dorman for Riverside Film Productions.
2. Seymour Martin Lipset, "Steady Work: An Academic Memoir," *Annual Review of Sociology* 22 (1996): 2–3.
3. Stephen Holmes, "Imitating Democracy, Imitating Authoritarianism," Dju Memorial Lecture, Sofia, Bulgaria, November 2010.
4. Robert Kagan, *The Return of History and the End of Dreams* (New York: Vintage, 2009).
5. Seymour Martin Lipset and Gyorgy Bence, "Anticipations of the Failure of Communism," *Theory and Society* 23 (April 1994): 169–210.
6. Samuel P. Huntington, *The Third Wave: Democratization in the Late Twentieth Century* (Norman: University of Oklahoma Press, 1991), 137.
7. Larry Diamond, "Introduction: Persistence, Erosion, Breakdown, and Renewal," in Larry Diamond, Juan J. Linz, and Seymour Martin Lipset, *Democracy in Developing Countries: Asia* (Boulder, Colo.: Lynne Rienner, 1989), 39.
8. Ian Bremmer, *The J Curve: A New Way to Understand Why Nations Rise and Fall* (New York: Simon and Schuster, 2006).
9. Jason Brownlee, *Authoritarianism in an Age of Democratization* (Cambridge: Cambridge University Press, 2007), 9.
10. Astolphe de Custine, *Journey for Our Time* (New York: Pellegrini and Cudahy, 1951), 98.
11. Albert O. Hirschman, *Exit, Voice, and Loyalty: Responses to Decline in Firms, Organizations, and States* (Cambridge: Harvard University Press, 1970), 44–45.

Baogang He and Mark E. Warren

AUTHORITARIAN DELIBERATION: THE DELIBERATIVE TURN IN CHINESE POLITICAL DEVELOPMENT

Over the last two decades, authoritarian regimes in Asia have increasingly experimented with controlled forms of political participation and deliberation, producing a variety of "hybrid" regimes. These regimes mix authoritarian rule with political devices including elections, consultative forums, political parties, and legislatures that we would normally associate with democracy.[1] China is a particularly important case; though it remains an authoritarian country led by the Chinese Communist Party (CCP), its government is

From *Perspectives on Politics* 9 (2011), pp. 269–89.

now permeated with a wide variety of participatory and deliberative practices.[2] Two decades ago, leaders introduced village-level elections. Other innovations have followed, including approval and recall voting at the local level, public hearings, deliberative polls, citizen rights to sue the state, initiatives to make government information public, an increasing use of Peoples' Congresses to discuss policy, and acceptance of some kinds of autonomous civil society organizations. While very uneven in scope and effectiveness, many of these innovations appear to have genuinely deliberative elements, from which political leaders take guidance, and upon which they rely for the legitimacy of their decisions.[3] Typically, however, deliberation is limited in scope and focused on particular problems of governance. Curiously these practices are appearing within an authoritarian regime led by a party with no apparent interest in regime-level democratization. We refer to this paradoxical phenomenon as *authoritarian deliberation*, and its associated ideal-type regime as *deliberative authoritarianism*. In the Chinese case, we argue, authoritarian deliberation is conceptually possible, empirically existent, and functionally motivated. Authoritarian deliberation is normatively significant—but, as the concept implies, it is also normatively ambiguous.

Although we focus on the Chinese case, our analysis "should be understood as a contribution to comparative political theory, an emerging style of political theory that elaborates normatively-significant concepts in ways that are both attentive to contexts, particularly non-Western contexts, while enabling comparisons across contexts.[4] Our primary aim is not to provide new empirical knowledge of China, but rather to develop the concept of authoritarian deliberation from within democratic theory by combining two familiar concepts into an unfamiliar concept, and then to argue that this concept helps to both explain and illuminate a distinctive set of normative potentials and risks for democracy within Chinese political development.

Our first claim is oriented by democratic theory. We argue that authoritarian deliberation is theoretically possible. Democracy, as we conceive it, involves the empowered inclusion of individuals in matters that affect them by means of votes, voice, and related rights. Deliberation is mode of communication in which participants in a political process offer and respond to the substance of claims, reasons, and perspectives in ways that generate persuasion-based influence.[5] There are important structural and institutional relations between democratic empowerment and deliberative influence: democratic empowerments ensure that actors are able to resolve conflicts by means of arguments and votes. However, it is possible for deliberative influence to affect political decision-making in the absence of democratic empowerments, assuming that (authoritarian) elites have other kinds of incentives, such as functional needs for cooperation and legitimacy. That is, the linkages between democracy and deliberation are contingent rather than necessary, leaving open the theoretical possibility of authoritarian deliberation as a form of rule.

Following this logic, we then develop the ideal type of deliberative authoritarianism—a regime style that makes frequent use of authoritarian deliberation. In developing this ideal type, we depart from much of the literature on hybrid regimes. The literature has focused extensively on incomplete democratic transitions, especially those involving regime change from authoritarian to electoral democracy, while retaining many of the elements of authoritarian rule, including weak rights and uncertain freedoms, weak rule of law, on-going patronage relationships, weak civilian control of the military, and corruption.[6] Viewed in these terms, the Chinese case is distinctive: to date, there has been no regime-level democratization. Lacking this kind of regime trajectory, China is not an "incomplete," "pseudo," or "illiberal" democracy, terms often applied to dynamic cases.[7] Nor do the terms "competitive" or "electoral" authoritarianism describe its distinctive one-party rule. The regime exhibits, rather, a resilient form of authoritarianism that, as Nathan argues, draws its strength from reforms that increase "the adaptability, complexity, autonomy, and coherence of state organization." The regime is achieving these capacities through an increasingly norm-bound succession process, an increasing use of merit-based considerations in top leadership selection, an increasing functional differentiation and specialization of state organizations, and new participatory institutions that enhance the CCP's legitimacy.[8] We agree with Nathan. In ideal-typing features of the Chinese case as deliberative authoritarianism, however, we are focusing our analysis on mechanisms of conflict management and decision-making rather than regime nature and classification as such. Thus we intend the concept of deliberative authoritarianism to compare to those concepts of "hybrid" authoritarian regimes that identify supplements to command and control decision-making. These supplements include limited elections and institutional consultations, some citizens rights and protections, some local and autonomy, and segmentation by level policy and level of government. They result in regime identifiers such as "competitive authoritarianism,"[9] "consultative Leninism,"[10] and "conditional autonomy within authority structures."[11] These kinds of classifications are distinct from those based on leadership types, such as personalist, military, and single-party hegemonic authoritarianisms,[12] as well as from concepts that describe consequences, such as "resilient" authoritarianism,[13] although China is most certainly a single-party hegemonic system that is proving to be extraordinarily resilient. By developing the concept deliberative authoritarianism, we are ideal-typing an apparently paradoxical supplement to authoritarian decision-making—deliberation—that appears to be assuming an increasing important role in Chinese political development.

As we develop the concepts of authoritarian deliberation and deliberative authoritarianism as they apply to the Chinese case, we also extend the ideal-typical analysis to identify the complex ways in which deliberative features of political development mix with other kinds of institutions and practices, including protests, some rights, and elections. The analysis we offer here ideal-types a

regime strategy of channeling political conflict away from regime-level participation, such as multi-party competition, and into "governance-level" participation, segmented into policy-focused, often administratively- or juridically-organized venues. We then survey some of the emerging deliberative features of these governance-level venues in order to indicate that authoritarian deliberation is empirically existent and (we believe) an important feature of recent Chinese political development. We next discuss a key methodological problem: under authoritarian conditions, it is not always easy to distinguish forms of participation common under authoritarianisms that mobilize people for shows of support as in the former Soviet Union, Cuba, and Maoist China, from those that generate deliberative influence. We argue, however, that the theoretical categories developed here show us where to look for empirical indicators that would distinguish deliberative influence from, say, coerced participation.

We then return to theory to ask why would an authoritarian regime resort to deliberative politics. Our initial take is functional: problems of governance in complex, multi-actor, high-information, high-resistance environments may provide elites with incentives to rely on deliberation in the absence of democratic empowerments, thus producing a systemic (though contingent) relationship between authoritarianism and deliberation. These functionally-driven deliberative developments are not unique to China: governments in the developed democracies have been innovating with new forms of governance over the last few decades in response to many of the same kinds of pressures. Winning elections is often insufficient to provide legitimacy for particular policies, leaving administrative agencies with the problem of manufacturing legitimacy through stakeholder meetings, consensus conferences, hearing and comment periods, partnerships with non-governmental organizations, and other kinds of "governance" devices.[14] What distinguishes China is that governance-level participation is developing in the absence of regime-level democratization, combined with a high degree of experimentalism with consultation, deliberation, and limited forms of democracy.[15]

Finally, we speculate that authoritarian deliberation is contingently dynamic. We illustrate the claim by stylizing two possible (but not exhaustive) trajectories of political development. One possibility is that deliberative mechanisms will transform authoritarianism supportively in ways that are compatible with complex, de-centered, multi-actor market societies, thus forestalling regime democratization. Although the challenges are significantly greater in China due to geographic size and vast population, we believe this scenario to be the most likely in the short term. A second possibility, however, is that the CCP's increasing reliance on deliberative influence for its legitimacy effectively locks it into incremental advances in democratic empowerments, just because they provide a means of broadening and regularizing deliberative influence. Under this scenario, democracy would be driven by functional problems of governance and led by deliberation, in contrast to regime change following the more familiar "liberal" model, in which autonomous social forces propel regime-level democratization—the pattern most evident in the democratic transitions of the last three decades. We conclude by identifying several possible mechanisms of such a transition.

The Concept of Authoritarian Deliberation

Since deliberation is often seen as an element of democracy, authoritarian deliberation is not part of our arsenal of concepts within democratic theory. The concept is, however, theoretically possible and—as we suggest below—identifies an empirically existent phenomenon. The theoretical possibility follows from a distinction between democracy and deliberation. Democracy, as we conceive it, involves the inclusion of individuals in matters that potentially affect them, realized through distributions of empowerments such as votes, voice, and related rights. Deliberation is mode of communication in which participants in a political process offer and respond to the substance of claims, reasons, and perspectives in ways that generate persuasion-based influence.

Under most circumstances democracy and deliberation are structurally related. On the one hand, deliberation needs protection from coercion, economic dependency, and traditional authority if it is to function as a means of resolving conflict and making decisions. Democratic institutions provide these protections by limiting and distributing power in ways that provide the inducements and spaces for persuasion, argument, opinion, and demonstration. These spaces allow for the formation of preferences and opinions, enable legitimate bargains and, sometimes, consensus. On the other hand, though highly imperfect, established democracies have a high density of institutions that underwrite deliberative approaches to politics, such as politically-oriented media, courts, legislatures, advocacy groups, ad hoc committees and panels, and universities. Relative to other kinds of regimes, democracies are more likely to have institutions that enable deliberative influence in politics. Whatever their other differences, all theories of deliberative democracy presuppose this close and symbiotic relationship between democratic institutions and deliberation.[16]

It is because of this theoretically and empirically robust connection between democracy and deliberation that democratic theorists have typically not focused on the more difficult problem of identifying and theorizing deliberative influence under authoritarian circumstances—with the exception that increasing attention is being paid to deliberation within (nominally authoritarian) bureaucracies in the established democracies.[17] For good reason, authoritarian systems such as China have seemed unpromising terrain for political deliberation.[18] Countries with authoritarian regimes are, on average, unfriendly to deliberative approaches to conflict, evidenced not only by the (typically) closed nature of decision-making itself, but also in limits on spaces of public discourse and its agents—the press, publishing houses, the internet, advocacy groups, and universities. The ideal means of authoritarian rule is command, not deliberation. The ideal outcome is—to use Max Weber's terms—legitimate domination, in which the conduct of the ruled "occurs as if the ruled had made the content of the command the maxim of their conduct for its very own sake."[19] When authoritarian rule is legitimate, the ruled accept commands because they originate in an authoritative source such as traditions, leaders, or because the ruled accept the reasons provided by rulers.

Yet democratic empowerments are contingently rather than necessarily linked to deliberative politics. Theoretically, deliberation can occur under authoritarian conditions when rulers decide to use it as a means to form preferences and policies, but do so without institutionalized distributions of democratic powers to those affected. To identify the theoretical possibility of deliberative politics under authoritarian conditions, then, deliberation should identify persuasive influence about matters of common concern under a wide variety of non-ideal settings. In contrast, democracy should identify empowerments such as votes and rights that function to include those affected by decisions in making those decisions.

When successful, deliberation generates what Parsons calls *influence*, which he conceives as a

> generalized symbolic medium of interchange in the same general class as money and power. It consists in the capacity to bring about desired decisions on the part of the other social units without directly offering them a valued quid pro quo as an inducement or threatening them with deleterious consequences. Influence must operate through persuasion, however, in that its object must be convinced that to decide as the influencer suggests is to act in the interest of a collective system with which both are solidary.[20]

Following Parsons, we understand deliberation broadly, as any act of communication that motivates others through persuasion "without a quid pro quo"—that is, in ways that are not reducible to threats, economic incentives, or sanctions based on tradition or religion. As we use the term, "deliberative influence" is generated by the offering and receiving of claims and arguments, where the inducements follow from the acceptability of the claims and arguments themselves. Deliberation does *not* encompass all communication, and in particular it excludes communications which simply convey incentives or threats that are not, in themselves, cognitively persuasive. Persuasive influence in this sense *can* include bargains and negotiations, but only if they depend upon the commitments of parties to fair procedures and their outcomes—that is, to rules that can themselves be justified by reference to claims to fairness or other normative validity claims.[21] We also understand styles of deliberation broadly, as any kind of communication—demonstrations, rhetoric, or storytelling—that is intended to persuade without resort to coercion or quid pro quos.[22]

Importantly, deliberation excludes two other kinds of communication, a distinction that will become important later. Deliberation excludes communications that are purely *instrumental*, and intended to convey information about, say, the content of a command and the incentives for obedience. In this kind of case, the communication motivates *only* because it references incentives that are external to the content of the communication. An ideal-typical example of an instrumental communication would be a coercively-enforced command. Deliberation also excludes communications that are purely *strategic*, in the sense that the party offering the claim does so to induce a response to the content of the claim that furthers goals external to the cognitive content of the claim. An ideal-typical example would be a promise made by a candidate solely for the sake of gaining a vote.

In contrast, democracy refers not to communication, but a distribution of powers of decision to those potentially affected by collective decisions. Democratic means of empowerment include the rights and opportunities to vote for political representatives in competitive elections, and sometimes to vote directly for policies, as in referendums and town meetings. In addition, democratic means of empowerment include representative oversight and accountability bodies; the rights to speak, to write, and to be heard;

rights to information relevant to public matters; rights to associate for the purposes of representation, petition, and protest; as well as due process rights against the state and other powerful bodies.[23]

Considered genetically then, democracies disperse these kinds of empowerments in ways that those affected by decisions have some influence over them. The conceptual opposite of democracy is "authoritarianism." Authoritarian systems concentrate the power of decision, typically in the hands of a ruler who dictates, a military structure, or at the apex of a single organization structure, such as a hegemonic political party.

In making the distinction between kinds of communication and distributions of decision-making powers, then, we follow Habermas and Goodin[24] rather than Thompson and Cohen, both of whom view democratic deliberation as a kind of deliberation oriented toward the making of binding decisions.[25] While there are very good reasons for this kind of stipulation—to distinguish political deliberation from other kinds of deliberation for example—our purposes are different. Because we want to identify the conceptual possibility of authoritarian deliberation, we need to sort out kinds of communication from locations of decision-making power. Within democratic settings, the distinction is straightforward: deliberation often leads to a decision. But the decision itself is (typically) a consequence of voting or consensus—procedures that assign each member of the decision-making unit a piece of binding decision-making power, or authorize representatives to make decisions—whether or not members have successfully persuaded others of the merits of the decision. However important deliberation may be to the legitimacy of a vote-based decision, deliberation, as Goodin argues, is about discovery and persuasion, and is not in itself a decision-making procedure: "First talk, then vote."[26] In democracies, decisions are typically the consequence of voting or vote-based authorization of representatives, not deliberation. Even in cases of consensus, voting still stands as an implicit part of the process—the moment in which the work of deliberation is trans-

formed, unanimously, into a collectively binding decision.

Once we distinguish between deliberative influence and decision-making, we can then conceptually describe contexts within which deliberation is followed *not* by democratic decisions, but rather by the decisions of (unelected) political authorities—party officials or bureaucrats, for example. Thus, for example, participants in a process might deliberate an issue, influencing one another through persuasion and generating a common position which all find acceptable. An authority might then make a decision that reflects and accepts the substance of the deliberation, or defers to the weight of opinion developed within a deliberative process. The authority retains the power of decision, but the decision borrows, as it were, its legitimacy from deliberation.

If deliberation and democracy are distinct in theory—the one a kind of communication, the other a distribution of powers to decide—they have often been distinct in practice as well. Historically, deliberation has appeared in numerous nondemocratic contexts, as in the many instances in which palace courts and religious institutions sought to legitimize their political rule through consultative and deliberative means, just as early legislative institutions with narrow representative bases engaged in deliberation.[27] Indeed, deliberation within representative institutions has often been thought to trade off against democracy: the more accountable representatives are to constituents, the less room they have for deliberative judgments, a trade-off evident in majoritarian, strong-party legislatures.[28] Likewise, today's democracies have many spaces of deliberative decision-making that are not democratic in a robust sense because they exclude those affected or their representatives. Closed jury sessions and hearings, Supreme Court decisions, expert panels, and many deliberative public forums all fit into this category.[29] These non-democratic deliberations may be entirely justified by other reasons—just not by their origins in democratic empowerments, at least as we use the term here. And democracy, famously, can be non-deliberative, as it is with any inclusive decision-making mechanism that simply aggregates preferences such as voting-based majoritarianism.

Deliberative Authoritarianism as an Ideal Type

These observations can be ideal typed. If deliberation is a phenomenon different in kind from democracy, then (in theory) it might combine with non-democratic (authoritarian) distributions of power. We illustrate the ideal types in Table 9.1, where the terms "authoritarian" and "democratic" refer to the relative dispersion of means of empowerment (dispersion, by implication, provides more opportunities for the affected to exercise power), while communication can vary from "instrumental" to "strategic" and "deliberative." The combinations produce five familiar types, and one unfamiliar type, deliberative authoritarianism.

Working across the table, the term *instrumental communication* refers to the use of communication to express preferences, without regard to the preferences of others. *Aggregative democracy* describes situations in which decisions reflect preferences that are aggregated (typically) by voting, and communication is primarily about expressing preferences. Instrumental communication combined with concentrated

powers of decision produces *command authoritarianism*, in which power holders use communication solely to indicate the content of commands.

Strategic communication refers to the use of communication to express preferences, with the aim of maximizing an agent's preferences while taking into account the preferences of others. *Bargaining-based democracy* describes a form of rule in which participants use communication to express their preferences and to negotiate, and in which they are able to use powers such as votes and rights induce others to take their preferences into account. But when strategic communication combines with concentrated powers of decision, we might refer to *consultative authoritarianism*, a form of rule in which power holders use communication to collect the preferences of those their decisions will affect and take those preferences into account as information relevant to their decision-making.

Deliberative communication, as suggested above, refers to the use of communication to influence the preferences, positions, arguments, reasons, and justifications of others. *Deliberative democracy* refers to the form of rule in which powers of decision are widely dispersed in the form of votes and rights, but the legitimacy of the decision is based on the persuasive influence generated by communication, or the acceptability of the process. Following this logic,

Table 9.1. Deliberative Authoritarianism

Distribution of powers of decision	MODE OF COMMUNICATION		
	More instrumental	More strategic	More deliberative
More democratic (dispersed, egalitarian)	Aggregative democracy	Bargaining-based democracy	Deliberative democracy
More authoritarian (concentrated, inegalitarian)	Command authoritarianism	Consultative authoritarianism	**Deliberative authoritarianism**

deliberative authoritarianism describes a form of rule in which powers of decision are concentrated, but power holders enable communicative contexts that generate influence (responsiveness to claims and reasons) among the participants. Power holders are influenced in their decisions by the reasons generated by communication among participants and/or by the legitimacy of the process of reason-giving. Although both democratic and authoritarian deliberation make use of persuasive influence, the ideal type implies that authoritarian control of decision-making involves not just concentrated control over decisions that may have been widely deliberated, but also—and importantly—control over the agenda. In an ideal democracy, citizens have the powers necessary to introduce deliberative claims into any issue area, and any level of government. In an authoritarian regime, elites control the domain and scope of deliberation, and limit citizens' capacities to put issues onto the political agenda. Authoritarianism thus implies that elites control not just what policies or issues are deliberated, but also the forums, levels of organization, timing, and duration.

In short, these combinations produce three familiar types of democracy: aggregative democracy, bargaining-based democracy, and deliberative democracy, as well as two familiar types of authoritarianism: traditional (command) authoritarianism, and consultative authoritarianism—a type increasingly recognized in the literature, and evidenced by political tactics in Singapore, Malaysia, and Vietnam,[30] certain features of the old Soviet Union,[31] as well as in contemporary China.[32] The unfamiliar possibility, deliberative authoritarianism—rule via authoritarian deliberation—is an ideal type of regime that combines concentrated power—that is, power not distributed to those affected by collective decisions—with deliberative communication.

For authoritarian deliberation to exist, deliberative influence must also exist, in the sense that it could be shown (in principle) that elite decisions respond to persuasive influence, generated either among participants, or in the form of arguments made by participants to decision-makers. This point underwrites the distinction between authoritarian deliberation and consultation—a distinction that is subtle but important for our argument. Consultation, in which decision-makers take into account the preferences of those their decisions will affect, is pervasive in most kinds of regimes—including authoritarian regimes. In China, "consultative" processes often shade into "deliberative" processes. As ideal types, however, the processes are distinct. Whereas "consultation" implies that decision-makers ask for, and receive information from those their decisions will affect, "deliberation" implies that decision-makers will do more than solicit input; they will enable (or permit) space for people to discuss issues, and to engage in the give and take of reasons, to which decisions are then responsive. While many instances of public deliberation in China today are continuations of Maoist consultation, they also have distinctive features. Maoist consultations lacked deliberative elements as well as any procedural elements that might ensure fair and equal discussion. They served primarily as tools for ideological political study imposed from above. In contrast, many public deliberations in China today focus on conflicts surrounding concrete governance issues. There are often norms and procedures that promote deliberative virtue and ensure equality and fairness. Some deliberative forums like deliberative polling have direct impact on decision-making. Finally, as we will argue below, these new deliberative processes may have the potential to set in motion dynamics that are potentially democratic even under authoritarianism, owing to the fact that its norms and procedures that are more reciprocal and egalitarian than those in which decision-makers merely consult, as well as to the fact that persuasive influence requires more deliberate protection.

Ideal Types and the Chinese Case

Ideal types do not, of course, describe empirical cases. But they do help to identify features of cases of normative interest. The Chinese case exhibits a mix of types; command and consultative authoritarianism are clearly evident, as are some forms of democracy. Indeed, as we shall argue, it is in part *because* elites do not possess all the resources necessary to command or even consultative authoritarianism, so that the third form of authoritarianism—deliberative authoritarianism—has been emerging. Its development should be understood within the context of a political and administrative system within which the powers of decision are too dispersed to support command authoritarianism alone. The dispersions are consequences of numerous factors, including a political culture with Confucian and Maoist roots that holds leaders to moral standards; patterns of economic development that multiply veto players; insufficient administrative capacity to rule a huge, complex country; and—last but not least—political institutions that decentralize huge numbers of decisions. In addition, there are some voting powers, as in village elections and an increasing number of intra-party elections.[33] Citizens have more and more rights, though the extent to which they are actionable varies widely owing to the relatively new and uneven development of supporting judicial structures. There are some kinds of accountability mechanisms, as with the right to vote on the performance of village-level officials, as well as some kinds of legal standing enabling citizens to sue officials, although such standing is highly uneven. And there are powers of obstruction and de facto petition; Chinese citizens are often insistently ingenious in organizing protests or engaging in public discussions in ways that work around official controls, while leveraging official rules and promises.[34]

Thus, as a first rough take on the Chinese case, we should note that the most obviously applicable ideal type, command authoritarianism, is not descriptive of the regime capacities, largely owing to these broad dispersions of powers. But it does not follow that the CCP response to these dispersions maps onto the democratic ideal types. What we do see, rather, is a strategy of channeling political demand that makes selective use of consultation, deliberation, voting, and other forms of controlled

participation that, for the time being, appear to be compatible with, and perhaps expand the capacities of, authoritarian rule—a point to which we return later.[35] Table 9.2 maps this story. Here we are assuming that political demand is, in large part, a function of dispersed powers, which we can class into types of participatory resources—obstruction, protest, voice, rights, accountability mechanisms, voting for policies, and voting for representatives in competitive elections—identified in the left-hand column of the table. The top row identifies the domains over which these mechanisms are operative. Thus, we can find many political devices in China that are familiar in the developed democracies. The difference is that, in contrast to the developed democracies, the CCP seeks to channel political participation into the domains of administrative decision-making, the economy, the judiciary, and—to a very limited extent—a nascent civil society. Let us call this domain "governance level" political participation, reflecting its problem-focused, issue and domain segmented nature.[36] At the same time, we find little or no development of political participation at what might be called the "regime level"; powers of decision have not dispersed to the extent that they produce autonomous public spheres, independent political organizations, independent oversight bodies or oversight through separations of powers. Nor have they produced open-agenda public meetings, citizen initiatives, or—most obviously—multiparty elections. These limited governance-focused empowerments do not add up to regime democratization. But they do contribute to the overall pattern of authoritarian deliberation by empowering domain and scope-limited forms of voice, and there exist functioning pockets of democracy constrained by geographical scope, policy, and level of government. The conjunction of these resources with domain constraints maps the spaces of authoritarian deliberation now emerging in China.

Table 9.2 also ideal types a regime strategy to channel the baseline political resources—obstruction and protest—into functionally-specified, controlled arenas of participation, typically within the

Table 9.2. Regime Strategies by Domain and Individual-Level Resources

DOMAINS OF PARTICIPATION

Individual political resources	Regime-level participation (Legislative and executive)	Governance-level participation	
		Administrative and judicial	Civil society and economy
Obstruction, protest			Protests, mass mobilization, consumer actions, labor actions
Voice	Autonomous public sphere	Surveys, admin and legislative hearings, deliberative forum	Bounded petitions, media, internet
Rights	Independent political organizations	Some judicial rights	Property rights, some associative rights
Accountability	Independent oversight bodies, elections, separation of powers	Citizen evaluation forums, village elections, local approval voting	Party approved NGO and media watchdogs
Voting for policies	Initiatives, open-agenda town meetings	Empowered deliberative forums, councils, and committees	
Voting for representatives in competitive elections	Multiparty elections		

administrative and judicial domains of government, as well as issue-specified discourse in civil society (the shaded cells), while seeking to avoid regime-level democratization. In short, Table 9.2 specifies modes of participation that have deliberative—and sometimes democratic—dimensions, but which occur in the absence of independent political organizations, autonomous public spheres, independent oversight and separations of powers, open-agenda meetings, and multiparty elections.

These distinctions help to identify apparently contradictory developments in the Chinese case.

On the one hand, we agree with Pei's observation that regime-level democratic change has stalled in China.[37] Nor should we identify these developments as political liberalization. The Freedom House index for political and civic liberties shows that China's record has remained almost unchanged over the last decade. On the other hand, when we look outside of regime-level institutions, we find significant changes in governance, producing a regime that combines authoritarian control of domains and agendas with just "enough" democratization — "orderly participation" in Chinese official terminology — to enable controlled deliberation.[38] Indeed, what distinguishes China from the established democracies is not the emergence of governance-level participation in itself: as noted above, governance-level participation is evolving rapidly in the established democracies as well.[39] What distinguishes China is that these modes of participation, among them deliberative forms of politics, are evolving in the *absence* of regime-level democratization. Indeed, they are sometimes justified as an alternative to "western" adversarial, multi-party democracy.[40]

The Development of Deliberative Politics in China

The distinctive features of deliberation — responsiveness to reasons, discussion, and attentiveness to what others are saying — have deep roots within Chinese political culture.[41] Some are traditional, building on Confucian practices of consultation and common discussion.[42] Centuries ago Confucian scholars established public forums in which they deliberated national affairs.[43] Though elitist, the Confucian tradition took seriously elite duties to deliberate conflicts, as well as certain duties to procedures of discussion.[44] These traditions are alive today, expressed in the high value intellectuals and many leaders place on policy-making through combinations of reasoned deliberation, scientific evidence, and experimentation-based policy cycles.[45] In modern China, the *Ziyiju* (Bureau of Consulta-tion and Deliberation) played a significant role in deliberating and advocating constitutional reform before the 1911 Revolution in China. During Mao's time, elites were indoctrinated into the "mass line" — a method of leadership that emphasized learning from the people through direct engagement with their conditions and struggles. That said, as suggested above, while today's public deliberation is a continuation of Maoist consultation and contains elements of consultation, it has distinctive features. Maoist consultation lacked infrastructures of procedures and rights, and for the most part failed to achieve deliberation of high quality. For the most part, they were elite-directed exercises in ideological political study. In contrast, public deliberation in China today tends to be focused on concrete issues of governance, often in direct response to conflict. And, as we will note later, unlike Maoist consultation, contemporary forums are increasingly regulated by procedural guarantees to promote equal voice and fairness, as well as norms inculcating deliberative virtues. Moreover, as we will also note, in direct contrast to Maoist consultation, some processes are directly empowered. But there are also continuities. The Maoist mass line emphasized inclusiveness, equality, and reciprocal influence between the people and political elites. Indeed, like the Maoist mass line, the current system remains justified by the Confucian notion of *minben* (people-centric) rule. According to this ideal, elites express the voice of and serve the people. No doubt these inheritances help to explain why "deliberative democracy" is now a common topic in academic and policy circles within China, indeed, so much so that the CCP has developed a system of rewards for party officials who develop new deliberative processes.

The contemporary wave of deliberative practices dates to the late 1980s, concurrent with the introduction of village elections and other participatory practices[46] and administrative reforms.[47] Indicative evidence includes changes in official terminology. In Maoist China, for example, participatory activities were called "political study," and they were ideologically oriented and politically compulsory.

Deliberative forums are now often called *kentan* (heart-to-heart talks), or other names with deliberative connotations. In 1987 General Party Secretary Zhao Ziyang outlined a "social consultative dialogue system" as one major initiative in political reform in the Thirteenth Party Congress, followed by a comprehensive scheme of popular consultation to be implemented in a number of areas across China. These experiments were derailed by the events of Tiananmen Square in 1989, which resulted in a period of authoritarian repression and retrenchment. Nevertheless, they survived as ideational precursors of institutionalized deliberative practices, not least because CCP elites were keenly aware of the damage wrought by Tiananmen, and quite consciously sought ways of channeling dissent even as they engaged in repression.

In 1991 President Jiang Zemin stressed that China needs to develop both electoral and "consultative democracy," identifying the National People's Congress as the proper location of former, and Chinese People's Political Consultative Conference (CPPCC: a body which engages in often lengthy deliberations, but lacks either the power of decision or veto) as the site of the latter.[48] In 2005 Li Junru, Vice President of the Central Party School, openly advocated deliberative democracy—as did the Central Party School's official journal *Study Times*, which published an editorial endorsing a deliberative polling experiment in Zeguo, Wenling.[49] In 2006, "deliberative democracy" was endorsed in the *People's Daily*, the official document of the Central Party Committee, as a way of reforming the CPPCC.[50] And in 2007, the official document of the 2007 Seventeenth Party Congress specified that all major national policies must be deliberated in the CPPCC. More generally, deliberative venues have become widespread, though they are widely variable in level, scale, design, and frequency. They exhibit a variety of forms such as elite debates in different levels of Peoples' Congress, lay citizen discussions via the Internet, formal discussions in the public sphere, and informal debate in non-governmental domains. The more formal events can be, and often are, held monthly, bimonthly, or even quarterly in streets, villages, townships and cities.

In rural areas, deliberative politics have emerged alongside empowerments such as village elections, village representative assemblies, independent deputy elections for local Peoples' Congresses, and similar institutions. Beginning in the 1990s, many villages developed meetings in which officials deliberate village affairs with citizens, an innovation probably encouraged by imperatives of election, re-election, and approval voting.[51] Indeed, the meaning of township elections was not that elections would produce majority rule—as we might assume in the West—but rather that they would serve as a mechanism of consultation—though in practice they can induce deliberation, particularly when issues are contentious.[52] Electoral empowerments are often buttressed by protests, obstruction, and "rightful resistance" movements that have generated pressures for elites to consult with the people,[53] but which can, in practice, shade into deliberation.

There are some indications that these trends are widespread, though by no means universal. In 2004, the total number of meetings with deliberative elements at village level was estimated to be 453,000, a number considerably higher than the government's estimated number of protests (74,000) for the same year.[54] The 2005 National Survey provided some indications as to the (uneven) penetration of village level democratic institutions that we might expect to generate deliberation.[55] Ten percent of respondents (298) reported that decisions on schools and roads in their town or city over the last three years were decided by an all-villagers' meeting attended by each household. By contrast, 616 (20.7 percent) said these decisions had been made by village representative meetings, and 744 (25 percent) by villager leaders. The largest fraction—1,318 (44.3 percent)—were not sure. The same survey also found that the 547 (18.8 percent) of respondents reported that decisions on village land contracts were made by an all-villagers' meeting; 524 (18 percent) by village representatives 650 (22.3 percent) by village leaders; while 1,192

(40.9 percent) were not sure. The survey also found that 28.3 percent reported that their villages held two village representative meetings in 2004 (while 59.3 percent were unsure).[56] Such findings indicate that penetration of deliberative devices such as the all-villagers' meeting is at least broad enough for demonstration effects, and probably broad enough to begin to alter the incentives of the 3.2 million village officials in the 734,700 villages in China.[57]

While broad data about the uses of deliberative venues are not available, some cases in rural areas exhibit an impressive density. From 1996 to 2000 within Wenling City, a municipality with almost a million residents, more than 1,190 of these deliberative and consultative meetings were held at the village level, 190 at the township level, and 150 in governmental organizations, schools, and business sectors. Wenling has by increments developed a form of democracy that combines popular representation with deliberation.[58] A case in point is Zeguo township in Wenling, where in 2005 officials introduced deliberative polling, using the device to set priorities for the township's budget. Deliberative polling uses random sampling in order to constitute small (typically a few hundred) bodies of ordinary citizens that are descriptively representative of the population. These bodies engage in facilitated processes of learning and deliberation about an issue, typically over a period of one or two days, and can produce results that represent considered public opinion.[59] Officials in Wenling altered the device by elevating the outcomes of the deliberative poll from its typical advisory function to an empowered status, committing in advance of the process to abide by the outcomes.[60] In 2006, ten out of twelve projects chosen through deliberative polling were implemented. The device has also evolved: in the most recent uses (February–March 2008, 2009, 2010, and 2011), the government opened every detail of the city's budget to participants.

Whereas deliberative venues in rural locales are often related to village elections, in urban locales deliberative and participatory institutions are more likely to emerge as consequences of administra-tive rationalization and accountability.[61] Some of these accountability measures generate deliberative approaches to conflict. Local leaders are increasingly using devices such as consultative meetings and public hearings designed to elicit people's support for local projects. Observations from Hangzhou, Fujian, Shanghai, Beijing, and other urban areas suggest that such deliberative practices are becoming more widespread, with more than a hundred public hearings per year being held in each district.[62]

The practice of holding public hearings—a consultative institution that may sometimes produce deliberation—has also developed within the area of law. In 1996, the first national law on administrative punishment introduced an article stipulating that a public hearing must be held before any punishment is given. More than 359 public hearings on administrative punishment were held in Shanghai alone between 1996 and 2000.[63] Another example is the well-known Article 23 of the Law on Price passed by China's National People's Congress in December 1997, which specified that the price of public goods must be discussed in public hearings. At least eleven provinces developed regulations to implement this provision with ten referring specifically to the idea of transparency and openness, and nine to the idea of democracy.[64] More than 1,000 public hearings on prices were held across China between 1998 and 2001.[65] The Legislation Law, passed in 2000 by the National People's Congress, requires public hearings to be an integral part of decision-making process for new legislation.[66] More than 39 public hearings on new legislation were held at the provincial level between 1999 and 2004,[67] including, for example, a national public hearing on income taxes. In Hangzhou, the government has developed a web-based public hearing process for comment on the various drafts of laws or regulations.[68]

Finally, there are some emerging practices that include elements of democracy or deliberation, but which are quite limited in scope. They are nonetheless worth mentioning because they help to fill out the broader picture of a polity permeated by a diversity of highly uneven deliberative practices. In one state-owned factory, allocations of apartments were decided after an intense deliberation among ordinary workers and managers.[69] Intra-party elections with secret ballots were held in Ya'An in 2002. There has also been a trend toward publicly-visible deliberation in the National Legislature, as was evident in the deliberations over the Draft New Labor Contract Law in 2006–07. In addition, there have been experiments with participatory budgeting with varying degrees of participation as well as consultation—ranging from a highly constrained process in Wuxi to more inclusive and consultative processes in Xinhe and Huinan from 2004 to 2008 (He 2011). There are also instances of deliberation among government bodies, as in the case in which a committee of Municipal Peoples' Congress now examines the budget submitted by Shenzhen City. Instances of rights-based representation are beginning to induce deliberation as well. In 1999, for example, the official trade union in Yiwu City began to actively represent workers, producing effective rights, which in turn led to broader forums on workers' rights. And in 2006, the government funded the Poverty Reduction Foundation, which invites international non-governmental organizations (NGOs) to not only invest, but to engage recipients' ideas for poverty reduction.

We can make some sense of this high diversity of participatory, consultative, and deliberative practices by mapping them according to the characteristics relevant to identifying authoritarian deliberation. Table 9.3 distinguishes practices by level (local versus national), the extent of participation, the likelihood that deliberation exists, and (in bold) the extent of democratic empowerment. Most practices combine a high degree of government control of the agenda with either consultation or deliberation (indicated by the shaded cells). Participation is likely to be encouraged in the more local venues rather than in higher-level venues, though deliberation is increasingly a characteristic of higher-level bodies such as National Peoples' Congress. Some of the local practices combine with limited empowerments—rights to vote, rights

to initiate meeting and organize agendas, rights to equal concern, and rights to express one's voice—to produce highly robust instances of deliberative influence.[70] The overall pattern suggests *authoritarian deliberation*: that is, a high density of venues in which deliberation seems to exert influence, but within the context of government-defined agendas and formal government control of outcomes.

A Methodological Issue

Although we can point to instances of deliberative politics in China, our analysis has been primarily theoretical, driven by our interests in democratic theory, and related to the Chinese case primarily by means of theoretically-derived ideal types. The evidence is primarily indicative, and not sufficient to generalize about the occurrence of authoritarian deliberation relative to other forms of rule.

Identifying authoritarian deliberation faces another significant problem of evidence as well. Because the concept identifies situations in which persuasive influence (the effects of deliberation) combine with authoritarian decision-making, it will often be unclear as to whether any particular decision reflects the influence generated by deliberation or the (authoritarian) power of decision-making.

Identifying the "authoritarian" part of the concept is not difficult, as the evidence is well known and self evident. The Chinese state still maintains a Leninist political structure.[71] Most power remains in the hands of unelected elites, operating within the structures of one-party domination, and without the kinds of empowerments and protections necessary for democratic inclusion.[72] Party officials still decide whether or not to introduce deliberative meetings; they determine the agenda as well as the extent to which the people's opinion will be taken into account. They seek to avoid spillover onto non-approved topics, holding deliberations to specific topics. Democracy, Premier Wen Jiabao has said, is "one hundred years away"—possible only when China becomes a "'mature socialist system."[73]

Table 9.3. *Kinds and Locations Deliberative Politics in China*

DEGREE OF DELIBERATION

Extent of participation	Domain	Limited	Consultation	Reasoning
More concentrated, inegalitarian	More local	Intra-party elections Elite-driven participatory budgeting	Participant-limited public hearings Consultations on wages Trade union representation of workers	Local Peoples' Congress deliberations on and oversight of municipal budgets
	More national	Standard (closed) law and policy making	Public hearing on individual tax income held by National People's Congress	High-level deliberation on the New Labor Contract Law
More dispersed, egalitarian	More local	Village elections Independent deputy elections in local People's Congresses	Participatory budgeting NGO-led participatory poverty reduction Township and county elections with consultative features Rights-driven public consultation	Issue-limited debate in press and internet Electorally-driven deliberative village meetings Empowered deliberative polling
	More national	No cases	No cases	Issue-limited debate in the press and internet

But precisely because of the authoritarian context it will often be difficult to know whether talk counts as deliberation. Does the context produce subtle forms of intimidation? Do participants self-censor, anticipating the powers of authorities? Under authoritarian circumstances, it is also difficult to know whether authorities are merely consulting with citizens, or whether they are influenced by their deliberations.

The other ideal types we develop here suffer from fewer ambiguities. In the cases of the democratic ideal types, the relative influence of communication and powers of decision can be inferred from outcomes; the modes of empowerment align with the influence of communication, such that, for example, dissent can be inferred from minority votes, while winning arguments are reflected in majority votes. Likewise, the outcomes of command authoritarianism can be inferred from the powers of decision. In the case of authoritarian deliberation—and, to a lesser extent, consultative authoritarianism—researchers must look for evidence of communicative influence on decisions.

This methodological problem reflects a problem of normative significance: authoritarian and totalitarian regimes have, historically, mobilized participation to provide legitimacy for command-based decisions. There are numerous examples, from Franco's corporatist authoritarianism to Cuba today. The most obvious comparison, however, is with the former Soviet Union prior to *glasnost*, which can be broadly characterized as a form of dictatorship with a high level of institutionalized participation, as well as the involvement of officially recognized groups in the initial stages of decision-making.[74] Stalin, like many dictators, used professional groups as information "transmission belts," primarily to convey information about decisions. More substantive consultation with groups existed under Khrushchev, particularly with key technocratic elites,[75] while under Brezhnev, numerous councils were created to draw the citizens into public life.[76] But as Hough notes, even when Lenin, Stalin, and Khrushchev used consultative procedures, they "were ruthless in overriding society's preferences on important matters."[77]

In the authoritarian and post-authoritarian regimes in Southeast Asia, particularly Singapore, consultation is now a regularized feature of rule.[78] These regimes seek to generate legitimacy for policies through public consultations; they understand the economic benefits of transparent, competent, and clean public administration, and they show an increasing openness to various forms of NGO participation within state-sponsored institutions—processes Rodan and Jayasuriya appropriately term "administrative incorporation."[79] It is likely that consultation is fully consistent with, and probably functional for, consolidated authoritarianism.

But at the level of broad comparisons, Chinese authoritarianism differs from cases of mobilized participation: most Chinese people now have opportunities to exit participatory pressures, effectively blunting this political strategy. China's Maoist past also favors decentralizing judgment to the people to a degree not found in the Soviet and Southeast Asian cases. We also find widespread inducements for deliberation such as village elections; there are increasing numbers of relatively large-scale deliberative experiments, such as deliberative polling in Wenling City. Deliberation as an ethos is now widely pursued within representative and governmental bodies.

And yet, as suggested, identifying instances in which deliberation rather than mere consultation exits suffers from the difficulties of inferring sources of influence under authoritarian conditions. But it is not impossible. Although the burden of evidence for generalization across China is higher than we can meet here, in principle it can be met in the following ways. First, cases sometimes generate counterfactuals from which causality can be inferred. In the case of the Wenling City deliberative poll, for example, city officials changed their previously held infrastructure priorities in response to the deliberations, suggesting an influence that could only be accounted for by the outcomes of the deliberative process.[80] Second, researchers are developing indicators of the quality of deliberation,[81] some of which have been applied to the Wenling case.[82] Finally, in-depth case studies, including participant observation, ethnographic techniques, and interviews can document the generation of deliberative influence—all techniques used to document deliberation in the Wenling case.[83] Such techniques are resource intensive. But to *fail* to frame the evidence through the concept of authoritarian deliberation owing to these methodological challenges risks missing what may be a normatively important dynamic in Chinese political development.

Why Would an Authoritarian Regime Use Deliberative Mechanisms?

Problems of evidence aside, let us now turn to another question implied in the concept of authoritarian deliberation: Why would elites in an authoritarian regime ever resort to devising and encouraging deliberative practices and institutions? We should not rule out normative motivations, of course: the post-Maoist, neo-Confucian culture of China imposes moral responsibilities on leaders to rule in accordance with the common good, to demonstrate virtue and to attend to the well-being of the communities they oversee.[84] Contemporary Confucians sometimes argue that democracy is a second-best route to wise rule, given the failures of guardianship.[85] And a lasting effect of the Maoist "mass line" is the norm that elites should listen to the people.

But even where such motivations exist, they would also need to align with the strategic interests of powerful elites and with established institutions for such practices to evolve. From a strategic perspective, Table 9.2 identifies the CCP's gamble, that opening the participatory venues at the governance level will channel political demand into deliberative and some highly constrained democratic venues, while containing popular obstruction as well as demand for regime-level democratization. Behind this gamble is a functionalist story, one that, in its broad outlines, is common to developing contexts. In using the term "functionalist," we are not proposing causal explanations—that is not what functionalist frames do. Rather, they identify broad classes of problems by calling attention to the social environments to which a political regime must adapt on pain of losing capacity, legitimacy, and power.

In the Chinese case the environments conducive to deliberative experimentation are largely the result of rapid market-oriented economic development, which has increased the size of the middle class, pluralized sources of tax revenue, created new demands for development-related administrative systems, generated extreme inequalities and environmental problems, produced internal migrations, and reduced the overall capacities of the state to engage in command and control government.[86]

While there is no necessary relationship between the legitimacy and capacity needs of authoritarian elites and deliberation (as the history of authoritarian regimes amply illustrates), there may be contingent relationships under conditions that limit the effectiveness of command authoritarianism. For example, the relationship between legitimacy and deliberation is sometimes evident in international diplomacy and, increasingly, within global civil society. In global relations, for example, power is not distributed democratically. But there is often a plurality of powers that limit the capacities of powerful states and other actors to impose their wills without incurring high costs. In many cases, the perceptions of costs are sufficient to motivate deliberation, despite the absence of democratic mechanisms of inclusion.[87] By analogy, under authoritarian circumstances at the domestic level, states are rarely powerful enough to control all means of opposition. When they do (as in North Korea), they pay a high economic penalty, which subsequently limits a regime's power simply through resource constraint. In contrast, owing to its rapid economic development, sources (and resources) of power in China are rapidly pluralizing. Under these conditions, rule through command and control is likely to be dysfunctional because it is insensitive to information and learning, and will fail to generate legitimate agreements that motivate participants. Deliberation may simply function more effectively to maintain order, generate information, and produce legitimate decisions.

Under these circumstances, some of the incentives for deliberative politics will be negative, following from the dispersion of veto players that accompanies development, as well as from controlled distribution of political powers, such as village elections. Where there are many veto players, development-oriented elites will have incentives to deliberate: to gather information, to bring conflicting public and private parties to the table, and to forge coalitions sufficient to governance.

Other kinds of incentives are more positive. Deliberation should be functional for governance, enabling bargaining, negotiation, and learning, and it should enable the legitimate forms of cooperation that underwrite collective actions in politically complex situations. Development-oriented elites such as China's CCP need not merely compliance, but the *willing* compliance of multiple actors. Thus if deliberation generates legitimacy, even in the absence of democratically dispersed empowerments, then elites will have incentives to pursue deliberation. If these conditions exist, then we might expect to see the emergence of what might be called "governance-striven deliberation"—that is, the use and encouragement of deliberative mechanisms by elites for the purposes of expanding the governance capacities of the state.

That there are functional reasons why an authoritarian regime pursuing a development agenda might use deliberative mechanisms does not mean, of course, that it will do so. But in China's case, these functional pressures are real and immediate. In order to maintain its legitimacy based on development, the CCP must provide basic living standards and social services for a population of over 1.3 billion, which requires, according to the CCP's own calculations, a minimum annual economic growth of around seven or eight percent. Internally, it manages

74 million party members, a number which—if it were a country—would be the seventeenth largest in the world. It faces myriad political, social, and economic problems, ranging from daily peasant and labor actions to collecting taxes from the newly wealthy, environmental issues, security problems, and corruption. These functional demands do not immediately explain authoritarian deliberative responses. But they do suggest a series of more specific hypotheses as to why Chinese political elites might adopt deliberative mechanisms.

First, and perhaps most importantly, deliberative mechanisms can co-opt dissent and maintain social order. Following Hirschman's typology of exit, voice, and loyalty, the CCP faces functional limits in two of the three means of controlling dissent. Currently, the CCP controls high profile political dissent with an exit strategy, allowing dissidents to immigrate to the U.S. and other countries to minimize their domestic impact. Internally, the CCP buys the loyalty of party members with senior positions, privileges, and grants. But simply owing to their numbers, neither strategy can be applied to the hundreds of millions of ordinary Chinese, who are quite capable of collective forms of dissent.[88] Suppression is always possible and often used selectively against internal dissidents. But like all overtly coercive tactics, overuse produces diminishing returns.[89] In the case of China, suppression risks undermining the increasing openness that supports its development agenda, as well as generating international attention that may also have economic consequences. Thus *voice* is the remaining option for controlling dissent and maintaining order. The CCP has for some time pursued a policy of channeling dissent onto a developing court system,[90] as well as into low level elections.[91] But CCP officials are discovering, often through trial and error, that regular and frequent deliberative meetings can reduce dissent, social conflict and complaints, while saving money, personnel, and time.[92] As Hirschman has noted, relative to multiparty systems, one-party systems may even increase voice incentives, since limited options for exit options are more likely to increase internal pressures for voice. There are "*a great many* ways in which customers, voters, and party members can impress their unhappiness on a firm or a party and make their managers highly uncomfortable; only a few of these ways, and not necessarily the most important ones, will result in a loss of sales or votes, rather than in, say, a loss of sleep by the managers."[93] Indeed, just because the CCP cannot claim legitimacy based on electoral victories, it must be attentive to other ways of generating legitimacy.[94]

Second, deliberative mechanisms can generate information about society and policy, and thus help to avoid mistakes in governing. As noted, authoritarian regimes face a dilemma with regard to information. Under conditions of rapid development, authoritarian techniques are often at odds with the information resources necessary to govern — information about operational and administrative matters, as well as the preferences of citizens and other actors. Command-based techniques, however, limit communication and expression, while increasing the incentives for subordinates to husband and leverage information. Controlled deliberation is one response to this dilemma. And as we have been suggesting in China we in fact see an increasing number of policies subjected to deliberation within controlled settings such as in the National and local Peoples' Congresses, within university centers, and within the Party Schools. The CCP also commonly uses the mass media and internet to test policy ideas or new policy by encouraging debate and discussion on specific topics.[95]

Third, deliberation can function to provide forums for and exchanges with business in a marketizing economy. In China, market-style economic development is dramatically increasing the number and independence of business stakeholders with veto powers not only over new investments, but also over tax payments, which can make up the bulk of revenues for many locales.[96] Pressures for deliberation can and do come from an increasingly strong business sector. Consultations among public and private interests are increasingly institutionalized[97] — a process reminiscent, perhaps, of the early history of parliaments in England and Europe in which the middle classes bargained with monarchs for liberty and political voice in exchange for their tax revenues.[98]

Fourth, open deliberative processes can protect officials from charges of corruption by increasing credible transparency. In a context in which local government revenues increasingly depend upon business, almost all officials are regarded as corrupt, not only in public opinion but also often by superiors. Officials may learn to use transparent and inclusive deliberative decision-making to avoid or reduce accusations that their decisions have been bought by developers and other business elites.[99]

Fifth, in cases where decisions are difficult and inflict losses, deliberative processes enable leaders to deflect responsibility onto processes and thus avoid blame. In China, elites are recognizing that "I decide" implies "I take responsibility." But "we decide" implies that citizens are also responsible, thus providing (legitimate) political cover for officials who have to make tough decisions. In Wenling City, to take one example, it is now common for local officials to begin a decision-making process by asking a governmental organization to establish a deliberative meeting or forum.[100] The government then passes the results of the meeting to local legislative institutions, which then replicate the results in legislation.

Finally, to summarize the preceding points, deliberative processes can generate *legitimacy* within a context in which ideological sources are fading for the CCP, while development-oriented policies create winners and losers. Legitimacy is a political resource that even authoritarian regimes must accumulate to reduce the costs of conflict.[101] While we do not have broad-based evidence to support the claim that deliberation is an important source of legitimacy in China, there is some indicative evidence: the results of annual deliberative polling suggest that deliberative polling has enhanced citizens' trust in the local government in Zeguo.[102]

The Developmental Logic of Authoritarian Deliberation I: Deliberative Authoritarianism

Our argument is that the apparently puzzling combination of authoritarian rule and deliberative influence—authoritarian deliberation—is conceptually possible, empirically existent, and functionally motivated in the Chinese case. But the concept also highlights two important structural instabilities: deliberative influence tends to undermine the power of authoritarian command, and deliberation is more effective as a legitimacy-generating resource for elites when it flows from democratic empowerments. These instabilities are currently bridged in China through internal differentiations among the scope, domain, and levels of government authority, some limited democracy, deliberative venues within authoritarian institutions, and the authoritarian leadership of the CCP. The standard expectation is that the CCP has developed a form of rule that is relatively stable and highly resilient.[103] The instabilities identified by the concept of authoritarian deliberation are important, however, because they frame two possibilities of normative interest from the perspective of deliberative democratic theory that are consistent with Chinese political development, though not exhaustive of other possibilities. It is certainly possible, for example, for China to evolve into a clientist- or crony-style capitalist state based on the successive co-optation of stakeholders into the governing structures of the CCP—a scenario that would follow from the continuing transference of state assets into private hands, combined with the CCP's encouragement of wealthy stakeholders to join the party.[104] It is also possible for the CCP to use more coercive powers to maintain its rule in spite of costs performance and legitimacy: the habits and resources for command authoritarianism are deeply entrenched in China. The government does not hesitate to use these resources if it sees the stakes as high enough—as evidenced by the centralization surveillance in the period leading up to the 2008 Beijing Olympics, as well as more recent attempts to suppress dissent by Uighur minorities.

Here, however, we style two possibilities, which we call simply, deliberative authoritarianism and deliberation-led democratization. These two possibilities focus on strategies of political conflict management and decision-making rather than patterns of economic ownership and influence or coercive state power. In the short term we expect deliberative authoritarianism to prevail, though we believe deliberation-led democratization is a longer-term possibility.

The first possibility, deliberative authoritarianism, implies that deliberative influence can stabilize authoritarian rule, which in turn is increasingly bounded in such a way that it is compatible with processes that generate deliberative influence.[105] Under this scenario, authoritarian political resources are used to mobilize deliberative mechanisms. Deliberative influence is limited in scope and agenda, and detached from political movements and independent political organizations. Deliberative experiments are localized and well-managed so as to prevent them from expanding beyond particular policy areas, levels of government, or regions. Following this logic, if deliberation is successful at demobilizing and co-opting opposition while generating administrative capacity, then it will enable the CCP to avoid regime-level democratization. Under this scenario, authoritarian rule will continue to transform in ways that channel and manage the political demands generated by economic development in such a way that authoritarian rule is maintained and strengthened. More specifically, we might expect the following, all of which can be observed in China today.

Coercion is targeted and limited. While state power is still ubiquitous, the way in which the power is exercised is modified in ways that both enable and require deliberative approaches to political contestation. Under deliberative authoritarianism, the use of coercion continues to be tamed and regulated. Coercive force is carefully and selectively used to eliminate organized political dissidents,[106] while governance-related forms of conflict are channeled into deliberative problem-solving venues.

Power is regularized through rights and deliberation. The CCP continues to incrementally grant rights to citizens including rights to own property, to consent to transfers, and to consent to public projects with individual impacts; rights to elect local committees and officials, and to manage local funds; and certain welfare rights. Limited rights of private association are institutionalized. Importantly, China is likely to continue to incrementally but systematically establish a judicial system that institutionalizes the rule of law, enabling these rights to have autonomous effects.[107]

The CCP gives up some power as a political investment its future. The CCP calculates that giving over some powers to local and administrative processes will generate specific policy- or problem-related solutions to problems, thus forming a piecemeal but resilient basis for its continued legitimacy—a process Pierre Rosanvallon has called "destructive legitimation" that can be more generally observed in the governance strategies of complex societies.[108] These local and segmented sites of legitimacy shore up the global legitimacy of the party in the face of weaknesses of the official ideology, which in turn increases its political capacities.

Under this scenario, then, the functional effectiveness of authoritarian deliberation substitutes for regime-level democratization. The current nascent form of deliberative authoritarianism in China would evolve into a more consistent and developed type of rule, under which cruder exercises of power are replaced with more limited, subtle, and effective forms. Political legitimacy would be generated by deliberative means, locale by locale, and policy by policy. The CCP continues to encourage local officials to develop participatory and deliberative institutions to curb rampant corruption, reduce coercion, and promote reason-based persuasion. It invites ordinary citizens, experts, and think tanks to participate in decision-making processes. But ultimate control over agendas as well as outcomes remains with the Party and beyond the reach of democratic processes. Of course, this kind of softening, regularizing, and civilizing of power remains contingent on the wisdom of the CCP elites and local leaders, who must be sufficiently enlightened as to be motivated by the legitimating effects of deliberation. Where these conditions hold, however, it is theoretically possible for deliberative political processes to become an important ingredient in the reproduction and resilience of authoritarian rule—a possibility that remains under-explored in the literatures on regime transitions as well as the literature of deliberative democracy.

The Developmental Logic of Authoritarian Deliberation II: Deliberation-led Democratization

Democratic transitions from England in the eighteenth and nineteenth centuries to Spain in the 1970s have mostly been society-led, often conjoined with market-driven development. These transitions were "liberal" in the sense that autonomous social forces propelled democratization. The democratic transitions of the late 1970s and 1980s tended to be driven by regime-level changes from authoritarian to multi-party electoral rule, and accompanied by constitutional changes that institutionalized legislative power and judicial independence, as well as the rights that secured social freedom and autonomy. The Polish Solidarity model of democratic transition, for instance, involved a strong opposition from civil society that forced government to the negotiating table.

Most students of China focus on democratization through regime change from one-party rule to multiparty electoral democracy. Reforms below the regime level—at the local level, in administrative and policy processes, and in the judiciary—are unlikely to lead to broader democratization of the political system.[109] Yet an increasing number of Chinese intellectuals see the development of deliberative processes within authoritarian institutions as a pathway to democracy. Some hold that democratization could develop from within one-party rule, if the kinds, level, and density of reforms alter its character in ways that produce the functional effects of democracy.[110] If this trajectory were to materialize, it would be unique: we know of no examples of regime democratization as a consequence of progressively institutionalized deliberation. Nor, indeed, is such a possibility conceptualized in the transitions literature.

But we can theorize the possibility. If authoritarian elites increasingly depend upon deliberation as a source of legitimacy for their decisions, then it is also possible for the democratic empowerments to grow incrementally, driven in part by the fact that deliberation provides legitimacy only if it has the space and inclusiveness to generate influence.[111] This kind of development would have the effect of layering new institutions over old ones for the purpose of enhancing their effectiveness, while also transforming their character in democratic directions.[112] Deliberation might then serve as a leading edge of democratization, possibly through the following mechanisms.

Deliberative legitimacy tends toward inclusion of all affected. When other sources of legitimacy fail—ideology, traditional deference, or economic benefits—deliberation provides a means of generating legitimacy. However, deliberation generates legitimacy that is "usable" by the state primarily when those whose cooperation the state requires have been

included in the deliberations, either directly or through credible representation mechanisms, and participants believe they have had influence or accept the legitimacy of the process. Because the tactics of obstruction (both rights-based and protest-based) and exit are widely available in China, elites have incentives to expand institutions to include those affected by policies. For example, local officials in Wenling required each household to send one family member to attend public hearings about land appropriation or house demolition. When this tactic failed to include all they believed to be affected, they resorted to random selection methods to ensure wide representation.[113]

Experiences of consultative and deliberative engagement change citizen expectations. Closely related, democratic institutions are easier for regimes to initiate than to retract.[114] Once voice and rights are granted by the state, they become part of the culture of expectations, transforming supplicants into citizens, and making it difficult for regimes to dial back democratic reforms.[115] The party secretary of Wenling City, for example, reported that he regularly receives complaints from peasants when local officials make decisions without first holding deliberative meetings. Officials in Zeguo, a township in Wenling, continue to repeat deliberative polling in part because they worry that *not* to do so would violate expectations created by earlier experiments. The anecdotal evidence is backed by poll results which suggest that citizens of Zeguo expect their government to conduct annual deliberative polls on the budget, and trust them to do so. The mean response to the question "Will the government take deliberative polling seriously," on a 0 to 10 scale, where one is "unlikely" and 10 is "the most likely" was 7.55 in the 2005 survey, but increased to 8.43 in the 2006 survey. With regard to the question "Do you think the government will use the results of the Deliberative Democracy meeting," the mean score increased from 7.33 in 2005 to 8.16 in 2006.[116] Zegui officials are now working on a regularized annual procedure for budgeting through deliberative polls.

Deliberation tends towards institutionalized decision-making procedures. When deliberation is regularized, it tends toward institutionalization. Institutionalization can be driven by citizen expectations. But it can also be driven by elite desires to retain control of political demand by channeling into scope- and domain-specific venues. This kind of tendency is visible in the government's concern with creating a non-arbitrary, constitutionally-regulated judicial system, the existence of which is a condition of democratization.[117] China seems to be changing, gradually, from an instrumental "rule by law" to a normative "rule of law" which binds not only citizens but also government officials.[118] The institutionalization of decision-making procedures is also visible more directly; in 2004, for example, the government of Fujian Province issued requirements that each village hold at least four public meetings a year and detailed procedures for selecting participants and conducting the meetings, the role of chairperson, note-taking, and linking meetings with village decision-making processes.[119] As early as 2002, Wenling City ruled that townships must hold four democratic roundtables each year. In 2004, the city further specified the procedures of these meetings, with the apparent aim of deepening their democratic credentials.[120] In July 2008 the State Council issued a national regulation requiring all county and city level governments to hold open public hearings when making major social policies. Importantly, the regulation specified procedures, apparently intending to secure legal, "scientific," and democratic legitimacy for the hearings. In 2010 the State Council drafted three National Guidelines

regulating public participation. One provision requires parties to present the supporting argument first, followed by all opposing arguments. Another procedure focuses on encouraging and managing open debates in public hearings. Interestingly, such provisions reflect and institutionalize the principles of deliberative democracy, emphasizing equality, fairness, and openness to public participation.[121]

The logic of deliberative inclusion leads to voting. Political elites in China often emphasize the relationship between deliberation and consensual decision-making, consistent with authoritarian deliberation. However, when interests conflict even after deliberation, elites may find that if they nonetheless claim, counterfactually, that their preferred decisions are the result of "consensus," they erode the legitimacy of their decisions. It is increasingly common for officials to respond to contentious deliberation by holding votes in public meetings, by submitting decisions to the community through referendums, or by deferring to voting by the deputies of local people's congresses. More generally, the notion that deliberation and voting should function together within political processes is now more common in China; of the 27 projects awarded national prizes for local political innovations with deliberative elements between 2000 and 2005, ten involved various kinds of elections.[122]

While all of these processes can be described as CCP strategies to co-opt opposition and expand state capacities, each can also result in lasting democratic transformations in the form of rule. As Tilly notes, "trajectories of regimes within a two-dimensional space defined by degree of governmental capacity and extent of protected consultation significantly affect both their prospects for democracy and the character of their democracy if it arrives."[123]

Conclusion

Our argument should not be taken as a prediction that should China democratize, it will be governance-driven and deliberation-led. Instead, our argument is both more modest and speculative. By conceptualizing authoritarian deliberation and exemplifying its existence in China, we are identifying a trajectory of democratization that is conceptually possible and normatively significant. While our theoretical speculations do align with observed developments in China, our aims are primarily theoretical. The key distinction—between democratic empowerments and deliberative influence—allows us to frame democratizing tendencies as the legitimacy-producing capacities of deliberation. In so doing, we are pushing the democratic imagination beyond familiar democratic institutions and toward the transformative practices out of which democratic innovations arise. It is in non-ideal cases such as China that democratization is likely to give the biggest payoff in human well-being—which is why normative democratic theory must be able to meet them halfway. Last but not least, we hope to expand the domain of comparative political theory by setting western concepts into conversation with non-western concepts and contexts.[124]

NOTES

1. Rodan and Jayasuriya 2007, Diamond 2002, Ghandi 2008.
2. He 2006a; Mohanty et al. 2007; Nathan 2003; Ogden 2002.
3. Leib and He 2006; Lin 2003; He 2006a, 2006b; Ogden 2002.
4. Dallmayr 2004.
5. Habermas 1987, 1996.
6. Karl 1995, 72–86; Diamond 2002, 21–35; Collier and Levitsky 1997, 441, Levitsky and Way 2002.
7. Zakaria 2003.
8. Nathan 2003, 6–7.
9. Levitsky and Way 2002, Diamond 2002; see also Ghandi 2008.
10. Tsang 2009.
11. Cai 2008.
12. Geddes 1999.
13. Nathan 2003.
14. Rodan and Jayasuriya 2007; Cain, Dalton, and Scarrow 2003; Fung 2006; Warren 2009.
15. See also Frug 1990; Bellone and Goerl 1992.
16. Bohman 1998; Chambers 2003; Cohen 1996; Elster 1998; Gutmann and Thompson 1996; Habermas 1996; Sunstein 2002; Warren 2002, 2006; Young 2000.
17. Dryzek 2009; Richardson 2003: Warren 2009.
18. Cf. Leib and He 2006.
19. Weber 1978, 946.
20. Parsons 1971, 14.
21. Habermas 1996; see also Habermas 1987, Rawls 1993.
22. Young 2000, Dryzek 2010.
23. Dahl 1998.
24. Habermas 1996, Goodin 2008.
25. Thompson 2008, 502–5, and Cohen 1996.
26. Goodin 2008, 108.
27. Urbinati 2006.
28. Schmitt, 1988; Manin 2002; Elster 1998; Steiner et al. 2004.
29. See Dryzek et al. 2003.
30. Rodan and Jayasuriya 2007.
31. Harding 1987; Hough 1997, 142–43; Unger 1981, 117.
32. Tsang 2009, Nathan 2003.
33. He 2010c.
34. O'Brien and Li 2006.
35. See also Rodan and Jayasuriya 2007.
36. Cai 2008.
37. Pei 2006.
38. Nathan 2003; Ogden 2002; He 2007, ch. 13.
39. Fung 2006; Warren 2009.
40. Lin. 2003.
41. Rosenberg 2006.
42. Bell and Chaibong 2003, He 2010a.

43. Chen 2006.

44. Ogden 2002, ch. 2; Chan 2007.

45. Heilmann 2008, 10.

46. Shi 1997, He 2007.

47. Yang 2004.

48. Zhou 2007.

49. *Study Times* 2005.

50. *People's Daily* 2006.

51. Tan 2006.

52. He and Thøgersen 2010.

53. O'Brien and Li 2006.

54. He 2007.

55. Cf. Tsai 2007, ch. 7.

56. He 2007, 96–7.

57. Ibid.; Diamond and Myers 2004; Mohanty et al. 2007.

58. Mo and Chen 2005; Wenling Department of Propaganda 2003, 98.

59. Fishkin 1995.

60. Fishkin et al., 2006, 2010.

61. Yang 2004; Ogden 2002, 220–28.

62. He, personal observations in Hangzhou and Shanghai in 2003 and 2005.

63. Zhu 2004, 2.

64. Peng, Xue, and Kan 2004, 49.

65. Hangzhou Municipal Office of Legislative Affairs 2007a.

66. Wang 2003.

67. Chen and He 2006, 445.

68. Hangzhou Municipal Office of Legislative Affairs 2007b.

69. Unger and Chan 2004.

70. He 2006a.

71. Tsang 2009.

72. Nathan 2003.

73. McDonald 2007; cf. Gilley 2004.

74. Hough 1997, 142–43.

75. Skilling and Griffiths 1971.

76. Hough 1976, 6–7.

77. Hough 1997, 143.

78. Rodan and Jayasuriya 2007.

79. Ibid.

80. Fishkin et at., 2010.

81. Nanz and Steffek 2005; Steiner et al., 2004.

82. He 2008, 2010b; Fishkin et al., 2010.

83. Fishkin et al., 2010.

84. Ogden 2002, ch. 2; Bell and Chaibong 2003.

85. Chan 2007.

86. Cai 2008; Nathan 2003; Gilley 2004; Ogden 2002; Tsai 2007, chap. 8.

87. Dryzek 2006; Buchanan and Keohane, 2006; Linklater, 1998.

88. O'Brien and Li 2006.

89. Cai 2008.

90. Cai 2008, 431.

91. Ogden 2002, chap. 6, Tsai 2007.

92. Zhejiang Province 2005.

93. Hirschman 1970, 73–4.

94. Cai 2008, 412–13.

95. Heilmann 2008.

96. Dickson 2003; Gilley 2004.

97. Nathan 2003.

98. Bates 1991.

99. He 2006a.

100. Leib and He, 2006.

101. Hess 2009.

102. He 2008, ch. 13.

103. Nathan 2003; Cai 2008; Tsang 2009.

104. Oi 1991; Ogden 2002, ch. 8.

105. See Tucher 2008.

106. Cai 2008.

107. Peerenboom 2002; Zhao 2003; Pan 2003; Cai 2008.

108. Rosanvallon 2008, 264.

109. For such a debate see He 2006b.

110. He 2008.

111. Dryzek 2009.

112. See Ogden 2002, 257; Thelen 2003.

113. He and Thøgersen 2010.

114. Przeworski et al, 2000, ch. 4.

115. Kelly 2006; see also O'Donnell, Schmitter, and Whitehead 1986.

116. He 2008, 157.

117. Ogden 2002, ch. 6.

118. Peerenboom 2002; Liu 1998; O'Brien and Li 2006; Potter 1994.

119. Sanduao.com 2006.
120. He, interview in 2005.
121. He was invited to comment on these three draft documents in Feb 2010 in Beijing.
122. China Innovation 2006.
123. Tilly 2004, 7.
124. Dallmayr 2004; Rosenberg 2006; He 2006b.

REFERENCES

Angle, Steven C. 2005. "Decent Democratic Centralism." *Political Theory* 33(4): 518–546.

Bates, Robert H. 1991. "The Economics of Transitions to Democracy." *PS: Political Science and Politics* 24(1): 24–27.

Bell, Daniel, and Hahm Chaibong, eds. 2003. *Confucianism for the Modern World.* Cambridge: Cambridge University Press.

Bellone, Carl J., and George Frederick Goerl. 1992. "Reconciling Public Entrepreneurship and Democracy." *Public Administration Review* 52(2): 130–34.

Bohman, James. 1998. "The Coming of Age of Deliberative Democracy." *Journal of Political Philosophy* 6(4): 400–25.

———. 2000. *Public Deliberation: Pluralism, Complexity, and Democracy.* Cambridge, Mssachusetts: MIT Press.

Buchanan, Allen, and Robert O. Keohane. 2006. "The Legitimacy of Global Governance Institutions." *Ethics and International Affairs* 20: 405–37.

Cai, Yongshun. 2008. "Power Structure and Regime Resilience: Contentious Politics in China." *British Journal of Political Science* 38(3): 411–32.

Cain, Bruce, Russell Dalton, and Susan Scarrow. 2003. "Democratic Publics and Democratic Institutions." In *Democracy Transformed? Expanding Political Opportunities in Advanced Industrial Democracies*, ed. Bruce Cain, Russell Dalton, and Susan Scarrow. Oxford: Oxford University Press.

"The Central Party's Ideas on Strengthening the Chinese Peoples Political Consultative Conference." 2006. *People's Daily* March 2.

Chambers, Simone. 2003. "Deliberative Democracy Theory." *Annual Review of Political Science* 6: 307–26.

Chan, Joseph. 2007. "Democracy and Meritocracy: Toward a Confucian Perspective." *Journal of Chinese Philosophy* 34(2): 179–93.

Chen, Shengyong. 2006. "The Native Resources of Deliberative Politics in China." In *The Search for Deliberative Democracy in China*, ed. Ethan Leib and Baogang He. New York: Palgrave.

Chen, Shengyong, and Baogang He, eds. 2006. *Development of Deliberative Democracy.* Beijing: China Social Sciences Press.

China Innovation. 2006. "Results of Local Government Innovation." http://www.chinainnovations.org/default.html, accessed February 5, 2008.

Cohen, Joshua. 1996. "Procedure and Substance in Deliberative Democracy." In *Democracy and Difference*, ed. Seyla Benhabib. Princeton: Princeton University Press.

Collier, David, and Steven Levitsky. 1997. "Democracy with Adjectives." *World Politics* 49(3): 430–51.

Croissant, Aurel. 2004. "From Transition to Defective Democracy: Mapping Asian Democratization." *Democratization* 11(5): 156–78.

Dahl, Robert. 1998. *On Democracy.* New Haven: Yale University Press.

Dallmayr, Fred. 2004. "Beyond Monologue: For a Comparative Political Theory." *Perspectives on Politics* 2(2): 249–57.

Diamond, Larry. 2002. "Elections without Democracy: Thinking about Hybrid Regimes." *Journal of Democracy* 13(2): 21–35.

Diamond, Larry, and Ramon H. Myers, eds. 2004. *Elections and Democracy in Greater China.* Oxford: Oxford University Press.

Dickson, Bruce J. 2003. *Red Capitalists in China: The Party, Private Entrepreneurs, and the Prospects for Political Change.* Cambridge: Cambridge University Press.

Difranceisco, Wayne, and Zvi Gitelman. 1984. "Soviet Political Culture and 'Covert Participation' in Policy Implementation." *American Political Science Review* 78(3): 603–21.

Dryzek, John S. 2006. *Deliberative Global Politics: Discourse and Democracy in a Divided World.* Cambridge: Polity Press.

———. 2009. "Democratization as Deliberative Capacity Building." *Comparative Political Studies* 42(11): 1379–402.

———. 2010. "Rhetoric in Democracy: A Systemic Appreciation." *Political Theory* 38(3): 319–39.

Dryzek, John S., David Downes, Christian Hunold, David Schlosberg, Hans-Kristian Hemes. 2003. *Green States and Social Movements: Environmentalism in the United States, United Kingdom, Germany, and Norway.* New York: Oxford University Press.

Elster, Jon, ed. 1998. *Deliberative Democracy.* Cambridge: Cambridge University Press.

Estlund, David. 1997. "Beyond Fairness and Deliberation: The Epistemic Dimension of Democratic Authority." In *Deliberative Democracy*, ed. James Bohman and William Rehg. Cambridge, MA: MIT Press.

Fishkin, James S. 1995. *The Voice of the People: Public Opinion and Democracy.* New Haven: Yale University Press.

Fishkin, James, Baogang He, Robert C. Luskin, and Alice Siu. 2010. "Deliberative Democracy in an Unlikely Place: Deliberative Polling in China." *British Journal of Political Science* 40(2): 435–48.

Fishkin, James S., and Peter Laslett, eds. 2003. *Debating Deliberative Democracy.* Oxford: Blackwell.

Fishkin, James S., Baogang He, and Alice Siu. 2006. "Public Consultation through Deliberation in China: The First Chinese Deliberative Poll." In *Governance Reform under Real-world Conditions: Citizens, Stakeholders, and Voice*, ed. Sina Odugbemi and Thomas Jacobson. Washington: The World Bank.

Frug, Jerry. 1990. "Administrative Democracy." *University of Toronto Law Journal* 40(3): 559–86.

"A Fruitful Experiment in Developing Grass-root Democracy." 2005. *Study Times*, December 12, 2005. Beijing: Central Party School.

Fung, Archon. 2006. "Varieties of Participation in Complex Governance." *Public Administration Review* 66: 66–75.

Geddes, Barbara. 1999. "What Do We Know about Democratization after Twenty Years?" *Annual Review of Political Science* 2: 115–44.

Ghandi, Jennifer. 2008. *Political Institutions under Dictatorship.* New York: Cambridge University Press.

Gibson, Edward L. 2005. "Boundary Control: Subnational Authoritarianism in Democratic Countries." *World Politics* 58(1): 101–32.

Gilley, Bruce. 2004. *China's Democratic Future: How It Will Happen and Where It Will Lead.* New York: Columbia University Press.

Goodin, Robert. 2008. *Innovating Democracy: Democratic Theory and Practice after the Deliberative Turn.* Oxford: Oxford University Press.

Gutmann, Amy, and Dennis Thompson. 1996. *Democracy and Disagreement.* Cambridge, MA: Harvard University Press.

Habermas, Jürgen. 1987. *The Theory of Communicative Action.* Vol. 2. Trans. Thomas McCarthy. Boston: Beacon Press.

———. 1996. *Between Facts and Norms: Contributions to a Discourse Theory of Law and Democracy.* Trans. William Rehg. Cambridge, MA: MIT Press.

Hangzhou Municipal Office of Legislative Affairs. 2007a. "The Current Situation and Problems of China's Administrative Public Hearings." http://www.hangzhoufz.gov.cn/fzb/xsyd/llyd0l4.htm, accessed July 26, 2007.

Hangzhou Municipal Office of Legislative Affairs. 2007b. "Online Deliberation on Various Drafts of Legislation." http://www.hangzhoufz.gov.cn/fzb/, accessed July 26, 2007.

Harding, Harry, 1987. *China's Second Revolution: Reform after Mao.* Washington: The Brookings Institution.

He. Baogang. 2003. "The Theory and Practice of Chinese Grassroots Governance: Five Models." *Japanese Journal of Political Science* 4(2): 293–314.

———. 2006a. "Participatory and Deliberative Institutions in China." In *The Search for Deliberative Democracy in China*, ed. Ethan Leib and Baogang He. New York: Palgrave.

———. 2006b. "Western Theories of Deliberative Democracy and the Chinese Practice of Complex Deliberative Governance." In *The Search for Deliberative Democracy in China*, ed. Ethan Leib and Baogang He. New York: Palgrave.

———. 2007. *Rural Democracy in China.* New York: Palgrave/Macmillan.

———. 2008. *Deliberative Democracy: Theory, Method and Practice.* Beijing: China's Social Science Publishers.

———. 2010a. "Four Models of the Relationship between Confucianism and Democracy." *The Journal of Chinese Philosophy* 37(1): 18–33.

———. 2010b. "The Deliberative Approach to the Tibet Autonomy Issue." *Asian Survey* 50(4): 709–34.

———. 2010c. "Intra-Party Democracy in China." In *Political Parties and Democracy: Volume III: Post-Soviet and Asian Political Parties*, eds. Kay Lawson, Anatoly Kulik, and Baogang He. [city]: Praeger Publishers.

———. 2011. "Civic Engagement through Participatory Budgeting in China." *Public Administration and Development* 31(2): 122–133.

He, Baogang, and Stig Thøgersen. 2010. "Giving the People a Voice? Experiments with Consultative Authoritarian Institutions in China." *Journal of Contemporary China* 19(66): 675–92.

Heilmann, Sebastian. 2008. "Policy Experimentation in China's Economic Rise." *Studies in Comparative International Development* 41: 1–26.

Held, David. 1996. *Models of Democracy.* Stanford: Stanford University Press.

Hess, Steve. 2009. "Deliberative Institutions as Mechanisms for Managing Social Unrest: The Case of the 2008 Chongqing Taxi Strike." *China: An International Journal* 7(2): 336–52.

Hirschman, Albert O. 1970. *Exit, Voice, and Loyalty: Response to Decline in Firms, Organizations, and States.* Cambridge, MA: Harvard University Press.

Hough, Jerry F. 1976. "Political Participation in the Soviet Union." *Soviet Studies* 28(1): 3–20.

———. 1997. Democratization and revolution in the USSR, 1985–1991. Washington, DC: The Brookings Institution.

Karl, Terry Lynn. 1995. "The Hybrid Regimes of Central America." *Journal of Democracy* 6: 72–86.

Kelly, David. 2006. "Citizen Movements and China's Public Intellectuals in the Hu-Wen Era." *Pacific Affairs* 79(2): 183–204.

Leib, Ethan, and Baogang He, eds. 2006. *The Search for Deliberative Democracy in China.* New York: Palgrave.

Levirsky, Steven, and Lucan A. Way. 2002. "The Rise of Competitive Authoritarianism." *Journal of Democracy* 13(2): 51–65.

Li, Junru. 2005. "What Kind of Democracy Should China Establish?" *Beijing Daily*, September 26.

Lin, Shangli. 2003. "Deliberative Politics: A Reflection on the Democratic Development of China." *Academic Monthly* 4: 19–25.

Linklater, Andrew. 1998. *The Transformation of Political Community: Ethical Foundations of the Post-Westphalian Era.* Cambridge: Polity Press.

Linz, Juan. 1964. "An Authoritarian Regime: Spain." In *Mass Politics*, ed. E. Allardt and S. Rokkan, New York: Free Press.

Liu, Junning. 1998. "From Rechtsstaat to rule of law." In *Political China*, ed. Dong Yuyu and Shi Binhai. Bejing: Jinri Zhongguo Chubanshe.

Luwan District 2003. *Collected Materials on Public Hearings in Luwan.* Shanghai. Luwan District.

Macedo, Stephen, ed. 1999. *Deliberative Politics: Essays on Democracy and Disagreement.* New York: Oxford University Press.

Manin, Bernard. 2002. *Principles of Representative Government Representative Democracy.* Cambridge: Cambridge University Press.

McDonald, Scott. 2007. "Wen: China Democracy 100 Years Off." *Time Magazine*, March 1. http://www. time.com/time/world/article/0,8599, 1594010,00. html, accessed March 28, 2007.

Mo, Yifei, and Chen Yiming. 2005. *Democratic Deliberation: The Innovation from Wenling.* Beijing: Central Compliance and Translation Press.

Mohanty, Manoranjan, George Mathew, Richard Baum, and Rong Ma, eds. 2007. *Grassroots Democracy in India and China.* Thousand Oaks, CA: Sage Publications.

Nanz, Patrizia, and Jens Steffek. 2005. "Assessing the Democratic Quality of Deliberation in International Governance: Criteria and Research Strategies." *Acta Politica* 40: 368–83.

Nathan, Andrew. 2003. "Authoritarian Resilience." *Journal of Democracy* 14: 6–17.

O'Brien, Kevin J., and Li Lianjiang. 2006. *Rightful Resistance in Rural China*. Cambridge: Cambridge University Press.

O'Donnell, Guillermo. 1994. "Delegative Democracy." *Journal of Democracy* 5: 55–69.

O'Donnell, Guillermo, Philippe Schmitter, and Laurence Whitehead. 1986. *Transitions from Authoritarian Rule*. Baltimore: Johns Hopkins University Press.

Ogden, Suzanne. 2002. *Inklings of Democracy in China*. Cambridge: Harvard University Press.

Oi, Jean. 1991. *State and Peasant in Contemporary China*. Berkeley: University of California Press.

Ottaway, Marina. 2003. *Democracy Challenged: The Rise of Semi-Authoritarianism*. Washington: Carnegie Endowment for International Peace.

Pan, Wei. 2003. "Toward a Consultative Rule of Law Regime in China." *Journal of Contemporary China* 12(34): 3–43.

Parsons, Talcott. 1971. *The System of Modern Societies*. Englewood Cliffs: Prentice-Hall.

Peerenboom, Randall 2002. *China's Long March toward Rule of Law*. Cambridge: Cambridge University Press.

Pei, Minxin. 2006. *China's Trapped Transition: The Limits of Developmental Autocracy*. Cambridge: Harvard University Press.

Peng, Zhongzhao, Xue Lan, and Kan Ke. 2004. *The Public Hearing System in China*. Beijing: Qinghua University Press.

Potter, Pitman. 1994. "Riding the Tiger: Legitimacy and Legal Culture in Post-Mao China." *China Quarterly* 138: 325–58.

Przeworski, Adam, Michael E. Alvarez, Jose Antonio Cheibub, and Fernando Limongi. 2000. *Democracy and Development: Political Institutions and Well-Being in the World: 1950–1990*. Cambridge: Cambridge University Press.

Rawls, John. 1993. *Political Liberalism*. New York: Columbia University Press.

Richardson, Henry. 2003. *Democratic Autonomy: Public Reasoning about the Ends of Policy*. Oxford: Oxford University Press.

Rodan, Garry, and Kanishka Jayasuriya. 2007. "Beyond Hybrid Regimes: More Participation, Less Contestation in Southeast Asia." *Democratization* 14(5): 773–94.

Rosanvallon, Pierre. 2008. *Counter-Democracy: Politics in the Age of Distrust*. Cambridge: Cambridge University Press.

Rosenberg, Shawn. 2006. "Human Nature, Communication and Culture: Rethinking Democratic Deliberation in China and the West." In *The Search for Deliberative Democracy in China*, ed. Ethan Leib and Baogang He. New York: Palgrave.

Sanduao.com. 2006. "On Village Public Hearings in Fujian." http://www.sanduao.com/danjian/JCDJ/nc/files/20.htm, accessed February 23, [year].

Schmitt, Carl. 1988. *The Crisis of Parliamentary Democracy*. Translated by Ellen Kennedy. Cambridge, MA: MIT Press.

Shen, Fei, Ning Wang, Zhongshi Guo and Liang Guo. 2009. "Online Network Size, Efficacy, and Opinion Expression: Assessing the Impacts of Internet Use in China." *International Journal of Public Opinion Research* 21(4): 451–76.

Shen, Ronghua, ed. 1988. *Social Consultative Dialogue*. Beijing: Spring and Autumn Press.

Shi, Tianjian. 1997. *Political Participation in Beijing*. Cambridge, MA: Harvard University Press.

Skilling, H. D., and F. Griffiths. 1971. *Interest Groups in Soviet Politics*, N.J.: Princeton University.

Steiner, Jürg, André Bachtiger, Markus Sporndli, and Marco R. Steenbergen. 2004. *Deliberative Politics in Action: Analysing Parliamentary Discourse*. Cambridge: Cambridge University Press.

Sunstein, Cass. 2002. *Designing Democracy: What Constitutions Do*. Oxford: Oxford University Press.

Tan, Qingshan. 2006. "Deliberative Democracy and Village Self-government in China." In *The Search for Deliberative Democracy in China*, ed. Ethan Leib and Baogang He. New York: Palgrave.

Thelen, Kathleen. 2003. "How Institutions Evolve: Insights from Comparative Historical Analysis." In *Comparative Historical Analysis in the Social Sciences*, ed. James Mahoney and Dietrich

Rueschemeyer. Cambridge: Cambridge University Press.

Thompson, Dennis F. 2008. "Deliberative Democratic Theory and Empirical Political Science." *Annual Review of Political Science* 11: 497–520.

Tilly, Charles. 2004. *Contention and Democracy in Europe, 1650–2000.* Cambridge: Cambridge University Press.

Tsai, Lilly. 2007. *Accountability without Democracy: Solidarity Groups and Public Goods Provision in Rural China.* New York: Cambridge University Press.

Tsang, Steve. 2009. "Consultative Leninism: China's New Political Framework." *Journal of Contemporary China* 18(62): 865–80.

Tucher, Aviezer. 2008. "Pre-Emptive Democracy: Oligarchic Tendencies in Deliberative Democracy." *Political Studies* 56: 127–47.

Unger, Aryeh. 1981. "Political Participation in the USSR: YCL and CPSU." *Soviet Studies* 34(1): 107–24.

Unger, Jonathan, and Anita Chan. 2004. "The Internal Politics of an Urban Chinese Work Community: A Case Study of Employee Influence on Decisionmaking at a State-Owned Factory." *China Journal* 52: 1–24.

Urbinati, Nadia. 2006. *Representative Democracy: Principles and Genealogy.* Chicago: University of Chicago Press.

Wang, Quansheng. 2003. *A Study of Legislative Hearing,* Beijing: Beijing University Press.

Warren, Mark E. 2002. "Deliberative Democracy." In *Democratic Theory Today,* ed. April Carter and Geoffrey Stokes. Cambridge: Polity Press.

Warren, Mark E. 2006. "Democracy and the State." In *The Oxford Handbook of Political Theory,* ed. John Dryzek, Bonnie Honig, and Anne Phillips. Oxford: Oxford University Press.

Warren, Mark. 2009. "Governance-Driven Democratization." *Critical Policy Analysis* 3(1): 3–13.

Weber, Max. 1978. *Economy and Society: An Outline of Interpretive Sociology.* Vol. 2. ed. Guenther Roth and Claus Wittich. Berkeley: University of California Press.

Wenling Department of Propaganda. 2003. *Democratic Sincerely Talk: The Innovation from Wenling.* Wenling: Wenling Department of Propaganda.

Yang, Dali. 2004. *Remaking the Chinese Leviathan.* Stanford: Stanford University Press.

Young, Iris Marion. 2000. *Inclusion and Democracy.* Oxford: Oxford University Press.

Zakaria, Fareed. 2003. *The Future of Freedom: Illiberal Democracy at Home and Abroad.* New York: W. W. Norton.

Zhao, Suisheng. 2003. "Political Liberalization without Democratization: Pan Wei's Proposal for Political Reform." *Journal of Contemporary China* 12: 333–55.

Zhejiang Province. 2005. *Zhejiang Social Security Governance* 21, June 28.

Zhou, Tianrong. 2007. "Deliberative Democracy and the Chinese People's Political Consultative Conference." *Zhongguo Renmin Zhengxie Lilun Yanjiuhui Huikan* 1: 18–21.

Zhu, Mang. 2004. *Multiple Dimensions of Administrative Law.* Beijing: Beijing University Press.

Azar Gat

THE RETURN OF AUTHORITARIAN GREAT POWERS

The End of the End of History

Today's global liberal democratic order faces two challenges. The first is radical Islam—and it is the lesser of the two challenges. Although the proponents of radical Islam find liberal democracy repugnant, and the movement is often described as the new fascist threat, the societies from which it arises are generally poor and stagnant. They represent no viable alternative to modernity and pose no significant military threat to the developed world. It is mainly the potential use of weapons of mass destruction—particularly by nonstate actors—that makes militant Islam a menace.

The second, and more significant, challenge emanates from the rise of nondemocratic great powers: the West's old Cold War rivals China and Russia, now operating under authoritarian capitalist, rather than communist, regimes. Authoritarian capitalist great powers played a leading role in the international system up until 1945. They have been absent since then. But today, they seem poised for a comeback.

Capitalism's ascendancy appears to be deeply entrenched, but the current predominance of democracy could be far less secure. Capitalism has expanded relentlessly since early modernity, its lower-priced goods and superior economic power eroding and transforming all other socioeconomic regimes, a process most memorably described by Karl Marx in *The Communist Manifesto*. Contrary to Marx's expectations, capitalism had the

same effect on communism, eventually "burying" it without the proverbial shot being fired. The triumph of the market, precipitating and reinforced by the industrial-technological revolution, led to the rise of the middle class, intensive urbanization, the spread of education, the emergence of mass society, and ever greater affluence. In the post–Cold War era (just as in the nineteenth century and the 1950s and 1960s), it is widely believed that liberal democracy naturally emerged from these developments, a view famously espoused by Francis Fukuyama. Today, more than half of the world's states have elected governments, and close to half have sufficiently entrenched liberal rights to be considered fully free.

But the reasons for the triumph of democracy, especially over its nondemocratic capitalist rivals of the two world wars, Germany and Japan, were more contingent than is usually assumed. Authoritarian capitalist states, today exemplified by China and Russia, may represent a viable alternative path to modernity, which in turn suggests that there is nothing inevitable about liberal democracy's ultimate victory—or future dominance.

Chronicle of a Defeat Not Foretold

The liberal democratic camp defeated its authoritarian, fascist, and communist rivals alike in all of the three major great-power struggles of the twentieth century—the two world wars and the Cold War. In trying to determine exactly what accounted for this decisive outcome, it is tempting to trace it to the special traits and intrinsic advantages of liberal democracy.

From *Foreign Affairs* 86, no. 4 (July/August 2007), pp. 59–69.

One possible advantage is democracies' international conduct. Perhaps they more than compensate for carrying a lighter stick abroad with a greater ability to elicit international cooperation through the bonds and discipline of the global market system. This explanation is probably correct for the Cold War, when a greatly expanded global economy was dominated by the democratic powers, but it does not apply to the two world wars. Nor is it true that liberal democracies succeed because they always cling together. Again, this was true, at least as a contributing factor, during the Cold War, when the democratic capitalist camp kept its unity, whereas growing antagonism between the Soviet Union and China pulled the communist bloc apart. During World War I, however, the ideological divide between the two sides was much less clear. The Anglo-French alliance was far from preordained; it was above all a function of balance-of-power calculations rather than liberal cooperation. At the close of the nineteenth century, power politics had brought the United Kingdom and France, bitterly antagonistic countries, to the brink of war and prompted the United Kingdom to actively seek an alliance with Germany. Liberal Italy's break from the Triple Alliance and joining of the Entente, despite its rivalry with France, was a function of the Anglo-French alliance, as Italy's peninsular location made it hazardous for the country to be on a side opposed to the leading maritime power of the time, the United Kingdom. Similarly, during World War II, France was quickly defeated and taken out of the Allies' side (which was to include nondemocratic Soviet Russia), whereas the right-wing totalitarian powers fought on the same side. Studies of democracies' alliance behavior suggest that democratic regimes show no greater tendency to stick together than other types of regimes.

Nor did the totalitarian capitalist regimes lose World War II because their democratic opponents held a moral high ground that inspired greater exertion from their people, as the historian Richard Overy and others have claimed. During the 1930s and early 1940s, fascism and Nazism were exciting new ideologies that generated massive popular enthusiasm, whereas democracy stood on the ideological defensive, appearing old and dispirited. If anything, the fascist regimes proved more inspiring in wartime than their democratic adversaries, and the battlefield performance of their militaries is widely judged to have been superior.

Liberal democracy's supposedly inherent economic advantage is also far less clear than is often assumed. All of the belligerents in the twentieth century's great struggles proved highly effective in producing for war. During World War I, semiautocratic Germany committed its resources as effectively as its democratic rivals did. After early victories in World War II, Nazi Germany's economic mobilization and military production proved lax during the critical years 1940–42. Well positioned at the time to fundamentally alter the global balance of power by destroying the Soviet Union and straddling all of continental Europe, Germany failed because its armed forces were meagerly supplied for the task. The reasons for this deficiency remain a matter of historical debate, but one of the problems was the existence of competing centers of authority in the Nazi system, in which Hitler's "divide and rule" tactics and party functionaries' jealous guarding of their assigned domains had a chaotic effect. Furthermore, from the fall of France in June 1940 to the German setback before Moscow in December 1941, there was a widespread feeling in Germany that the war had practically been won. All the same, from 1942 onward (by which time [it] was too late), Germany greatly intensified its economic mobilization and caught up with and even surpassed the liberal democracies in terms of the share of GDP devoted to the war (although its production volume remained much lower than that of the massive U.S. economy). Likewise, levels of economic mobilization in imperial Japan and the Soviet Union exceeded those of the United States and the United Kingdom thanks to ruthless efforts.

Only during the Cold War did the Soviet command economy exhibit deepening structural weaknesses—weaknesses that were directly responsible for the Soviet Union's downfall. The Soviet system had successfully generated the early and intermediate stages of industrialization (albeit at a frightful human cost) and excelled at the regimentalized techniques of mass production during World War II. It also kept abreast militarily during the Cold War. But because of the system's rigidity and lack of incentives, it proved ill equipped to cope with the advanced stages of development and the demands of the information age and globalization.

There is no reason, however, to suppose that the totalitarian capitalist regimes of Nazi Germany and imperial Japan would have proved inferior economically to the democracies had they survived. The inefficiencies that favoritism and unaccountability typically create in such regimes might have been offset by higher levels of social discipline. Because of their more efficient capitalist economies, the rightwing totalitarian powers could have constituted a more viable challenge to the liberal democracies than the Soviet Union did; Nazi Germany was judged to be such a challenge by the Allied powers before and during World War II. The liberal democracies did not possess an inherent advantage over Germany in terms of economic and technological development, as they did in relation to their other great-power rivals.

So why did the democracies win the great struggles of the twentieth century? The reasons are different for each type of adversary. They defeated their nondemocratic capitalist adversaries, Germany and Japan, in war because Germany and Japan were medium-sized countries with limited resource bases and they came up against the far superior—but hardly preordained—economic and military coalition of the democratic powers and Russia or the Soviet Union. The defeat of communism, however, had much more to do with structural factors. The capitalist camp—which after 1945 expanded to include most of the developed world—possessed much greater economic power than the communist bloc, and the inherent inefficiency of the communist economies prevented them from fully exploiting their vast resources and catching up to the West. Together, the Soviet Union and China were larger

and thus had the potential to be more powerful than the democratic capitalist camp. Ultimately, they failed because their economic systems limited them, whereas the nondemocratic capitalist powers, Germany and Japan, were defeated because they were too small. Contingency played a decisive role in tipping the balance against the nondemocratic capitalist powers and in favor of the democracies.

American Exception

The most decisive element of contingency was the United States. After all, it was little more than a chance of history that the scion of Anglo-Saxon liberalism would sprout on the other side of the Atlantic, institutionalize its heritage with independence, expand across one of the most habitable and thinly populated territories in the world, feed off of massive immigration from Europe, and so create on a continental scale what was—and still is—by far the world's largest concentration of economic and military might. A liberal regime and other structural traits had to do with the United States' economic success, and even with its size, because of its attractiveness to immigrants. But the United States would scarcely have achieved such greatness had it not been located in a particularly advantageous and vast ecological-geographic niche, as the counterexamples of Canada, Australia, and New Zealand demonstrate. And location, of course, although crucial, was but one necessary condition among many for bringing about the giant and, indeed, United States as the paramount political fact of the twentieth century. Contingency was at least as responsible as liberalism for the United States' emergence in the New World and, hence, for its later ability to rescue the Old World.

Throughout the twentieth century, the United States' power consistently surpassed that of the next two strongest states combined, and this decisively tilted the global balance of power in favor of whichever side Washington was on. If any factor gave the liberal democracies their edge, it was above all the existence of the United States rather than any inherent advantage. In fact, had it not been for the United States, liberal democracy may well have lost the great struggles of the twentieth century. This is a sobering thought that is often overlooked in studies of the spread of democracy in the twentieth century, and it makes the world today appear much more contingent and tenuous than linear theories of development suggest. If it were not for the U.S. factor, the judgment of later generations on liberal democracy would probably have echoed the negative verdict on democracy's performance, issued by the fourth-century-BC Greeks, in the wake of Athens' defeat in the Peloponnesian War.

The New Second World

But the audit of war is, of course, not the only one that societies—democratic and nondemocratic—undergo. One must ask how the totalitarian capitalist powers would have developed had they not been defeated by war. Would they, with time and further development, have shed their former identity and embraced liberal democracy, as the former communist regimes of eastern Europe eventually did? Was the capitalist industrial state of imperial Germany before World War I ultimately moving toward increasing parliamentary control and democratization? Or would it have developed into an authoritarian oligarchic regime, dominated by an alliance between the officialdom, the armed forces, and industry, as imperial Japan did (in spite of the latter's liberal interlude in the 1920s)? Liberalization seems even more doubtful in the case of Nazi Germany had it survived, let alone triumphed. Because all these major historical experiments were cut short by war, the answers to these questions remain a matter of speculation. But perhaps the peacetime record of other authoritarian capitalist regimes since 1945 can offer a clue.

Studies that cover this period show that democracies generally outdo other systems economically. Authoritarian capitalist regimes are at least as successful—if not more so—in the early stages of development, but they tend to democratize after crossing a certain threshold of economic and social development. This seems to have been a recurring pattern in East Asia, southern Europe, and Latin America. The attempt to draw conclusions about development patterns from these findings, however, may be misleading, because the sample set itself may be polluted. Since 1945, the enormous gravitational pull exerted by the United States and the liberal hegemony has bent patterns of development worldwide.

Because the totalitarian capitalist great powers, Germany and Japan, were crushed in war, and these countries were subsequently threatened by Soviet power, they lent themselves to a sweeping restructuring and democratization. Consequently, smaller countries that chose capitalism over communism had no rival political and economic model to emulate and no powerful international players to turn to other than the liberal democratic camp. These small- and medium-sized countries' eventual democratization probably had as much to do with the overwhelming influence of the Western liberal hegemony as with internal processes. Presently, Singapore is the only example of a country with a truly developed economy that still maintains a semiauthoritarian regime, and even it is likely to change under the influence of the liberal order within which it operates. But are Singapore-like great powers that prove resistant to the influence of this order possible?

The question is made relevant by the recent emergence of nondemocratic giants, above all formerly communist and booming authoritarian capitalist China. Russia, too, is retreating from its postcommunist liberalism and assuming an increasingly authoritarian character as its economic clout grows. Some believe that these countries could ultimately become liberal democracies through a combination of internal development, increasing affluence, and outside influence. Alternatively, they may have enough weight to create a new nondemocratic but economically advanced Second World. They could establish a powerful authoritarian capitalist order that allies political elites, industrialists, and the military; that is nationalist in orientation; and that participates in the global economy on its own terms, as imperial Germany and imperial Japan did.

It is widely contended that economic and social development creates pressures for democratization that an authoritarian state structure cannot contain. There is also the view that "closed societies" may be able to excel in mass manufacturing but not in the advanced stages of the information economy. The jury on these issues is still out, because the data set is incomplete. Imperial and Nazi Germany stood at the forefront of the advanced scientific and manufacturing economies of their times, but some would argue that their success no longer applies because the information economy is much more diversified. Nondemocratic Singapore has a highly successful information economy, but Singapore is a city-state, not a big country. It will take a long time before China reaches the stage when the possibility of an authoritarian state with an advanced capitalist economy can be tested. All that can be said at the moment is that there is nothing in the historical record to suggest that a transition to democracy by today's authoritarian capitalist powers is inevitable, whereas there is a great deal to suggest that such powers have far greater economic and military potential than their communist predecessors did.

China and Russia represent a return of economically successful authoritarian capitalist powers, which have been absent since the defeat of Germany and Japan in 1945, but they are much larger than the latter two countries ever were. Although Germany was only a medium-sized country uncomfortably squeezed at the center of Europe, it twice nearly broke out of its confines to become a true world power on account of its economic and military might. In 1941, Japan was still behind the leading great powers in terms of economic development, but its growth rate since 1913 had been the highest in the world. Ultimately, however, both Germany and Japan were too small—in terms of population, resources, and potential—to take on the United States. Present-day China, on the other hand, is the largest player in the international system in terms

of population and is experiencing spectacular economic growth. By shifting from communism to capitalism, China has switched to a far more efficient brand of authoritarianism. As China rapidly narrows the economic gap with the developed world, the possibility looms that it will become a true authoritarian superpower.

Even in its current bastions in the West, the liberal political and economic consensus is vulnerable to unforeseen developments, such as a crushing economic crisis that could disrupt the global trading system or a resurgence of ethnic strife in a Europe increasingly troubled by immigration and ethnic minorities. Were the West to be hit by such upheavals, support for liberal democracy in Asia, Latin America, and Africa—where adherence to that model is more recent, incomplete, and insecure—could be shaken. A successful nondemocratic Second World could then be regarded by many as an attractive alternative to liberal democracy.

Making the World Safe for Democracy

Although the rise of authoritarian capitalist great powers would not necessarily lead to a nondemocratic hegemony or a war, it might imply that the near-total dominance of liberal democracy since the Soviet Union's collapse will be short-lived and that a universal "democratic peace" is still far off. The new authoritarian capitalist powers could become as deeply integrated into the world economy as imperial Germany and imperial Japan were and not choose to pursue autarky, as Nazi Germany and the communist bloc did. A great-power China may also be less revisionist than the territorially confined Germany and Japan were (although Russia, which is still reeling from having lost an empire, is more likely to tend toward revisionism). Still, Beijing, Moscow, and their future followers might well be on antagonistic terms with the democratic countries, with all the potential for suspension, insecurity, and conflict that this entails—while holding considerably more power than any of the democratics' past rivals ever did.

So does the greater power potential of authoritarian capitalism mean that the transformation of the former communist great powers may ultimately prove to have been a negative development for global democracy? It is too early to tell. Economically, the liberalization of the former communist countries has given the global economy a tremendous boost, and there may be more in store. But the possibility of a move toward protectionism by them in the future also needs to be taken into account—and assiduously avoided. It was, after all, the prospect of growing protectionism in the world economy at the turn of the twentieth century and the protectionist bent of the 1930s that helped radicalize the nondemocratic capitalist powers of the time and precipitate both world wars.

On the positive side for the democracies, the collapse of the Soviet Union and its empire stripped Moscow of about half the resources it commanded during the Cold War, with eastern Europe absorbed by a greatly expanded democratic Europe. This is perhaps the most significant change in the global balance of power since the forced postwar democratic reorientation of Germany and Japan under U.S. tutelage. Moreover, China may still eventually democratize, and Russia could reverse its drift away from democracy. If China and Russia do not become democratic, it will be critical that India remain so, both because of its vital role in balancing China and because of the model that it represents for other developing countries.

But the most important factor remains the United States. For all the criticism leveled against it,

the United States—and its alliance with Europe—stands as the single most important hope for the future of liberal democracy. Despite its problems and weaknesses, the United States still commands a global position of strength and is likely to retain it even as the authoritarian capitalist powers grow. Not only are its GDP and productivity growth rate the highest in the developed world, but as an immigrant country with about one-fourth the population density of both the European Union and China and one-tenth of that of Japan and India, the United States still has considerable potential to grow—both economically and in terms of population—whereas those others are all experiencing aging and, ultimately, shrinking populations. China's economic growth rate is among the highest in the world, and given the country's huge population and still low levels of development, such growth harbors the most radical potential for change in global power relations. But even if China's superior growth rate persists and its GDP surpasses that of the United States by the 2020s, as is often forecast, China will still have just over one-third of the United States' wealth per capita and, hence, considerably less economic and military power. Closing that far more challenging gap with the developed world would take several more decades. Furthermore, GDP alone is known to be a poor measure of a country's power, and evoking it to celebrate China's ascendancy is highly misleading. As it was during the twentieth century, the U.S. factor remains the greatest guarantee that liberal democracy will not be thrown on the defensive and relegated to a vulnerable position on the periphery of the international system.

10 LESS-DEVELOPED AND NEWLY INDUSTRIALIZING COUNTRIES

Few people in any developed country can imagine the grinding burden of poverty, and the horrible moral dilemmas it brings, that people experience in the typical "less-developed" country. Do famine-stricken parents, themselves the only support of several children, feed themselves or their children first? Do they sell or abandon some children to keep the others alive? We recoil at even contemplating such choices. William Easterly, a World Development Bank economist, confronts us directly with such images in the opening chapter of his important book *The Elusive Quest for Growth* (2001).

The intellectual puzzle of developing world poverty is that according to all our standard economic models, it should not persist. Investment in poor countries should earn much higher returns than in rich ones—a phenomenon known technically as "declining marginal productivity of capital." Hence, investment rates and economic growth should also be much higher. This standard result of economic theory is usually called the theory of *convergence*. It holds that initially, poor countries should grow so much faster than rich ones that their growth rates (and, allowing for random variation, their levels of wealth) should very quickly "converge" on those of rich countries. In short, all poor countries should be duplicating the experience of the Asian "tigers." Korea, Taiwan, and China should be the rule, not the exception. More shocking, perhaps, rapid growth and rapid convergence should occur especially where poorer countries are open to foreign investment (because foreign investors will want those higher returns) and even more under imperialism (because it opens countries to foreign investment and guarantees foreign investors' property rights).

It seems at first self-evident that nothing like this has happened in the real world. Lant Pritchett, a development economist at the World Bank, argues forcefully in his influential article "Divergence, Big-Time" (1997) that virtually all of the predictions of convergence theory have been wrong over the last century and more: countries have diverged, not converged, in their rates of growth and levels of wealth. But this turns out to be true only if we weight all countries, big and small, equally. As Branko Milanovic, the lead economist in the World Bank's research department, showed in his 2005 book *Worlds Apart*, population-weighted, between-nation inequality has been trending almost uniformly downward since the 1960s. This is due chiefly to the very rapid economic growth of China, and, to a lesser extent, that of India, both with huge populations. Thus, convergence has been happening, in one important sense, at the world level; but this does not resolve the mystery of why so many smaller nations have remained impoverished.

The region that has failed most signally to grow is sub-Saharan Africa. Indeed, a significant number of African countries are poorer today than they were at independence. Thus, Paul Collier (another World Bank economist) and Jan Willem Gunning (an Oxford University economist who specializes in Africa) ask simply, "Why Has Africa Grown Slowly?" and weigh the major competing explanations: "policy" versus "destiny," and external versus internal factors (1999). They conclude that policy—rather than the longer-term factors emphasized by such scholars as Daron Acemoglu (see Chapter 4)—is mostly to blame. In the past, this largely meant external policies, that is, the intrusive policies of richer and more powerful countries. More recently, internal policies have played a larger role.

It is also possible that the rapid growth of the Asian "tigers" has been in part illusory. So argued the Nobel laureate Paul Krugman in his influential 1994 piece, "The Myth of Asia's Miracle." Krugman distinguished between growth in per capita production due simply to an increase in capital per worker, and the more important growth in total factor productivity (TFP, or technical or process improvements that yield more product from the same inputs). Asia, Krugman contended, had seen much of the former, but very little of the latter, whereas historically (for example, in the United States) the great majority of growth had come from improvements in TFP. Krugman argued that hence, Asia's growth resembled that of the early USSR: seemingly rapid, but in the long run likely to peter out. Although more recent evidence suggests a strong growth in Asian TFP, Krugman's perspective continues to influence policy and analysis and to focus scholars' attention (rightly) on TFP growth.

The most recent "Asian miracle" has been happening in Vietnam, whose growth is of interest both for its causes and for its ability to prosper against Chinese competition. Both issues are addressed in the influential Wayne Arnold article included here.

Our inherited view of developing world poverty includes the ideas of rampant disease, low life expectancy, and (in part as a result of high death rates) a propensity to have many children and to invest little in the education of any one of them. As Acemoglu and Johnson note at the outset of "Disease and Development" (2007), this picture is woefully outdated. Amazing improvements in public health (better sanitation, almost universal immunization) have led to much lower death rates (particularly among infants and children) and much higher life expectancies. As demographers would expect, those improvements have in turn lowered fertility rates (the number of children born to each woman) and increased incentives to educate each child. Whereas as recently as the 1960s the average couple in a poor country gave birth to six children, in the 1990s the rate was only three children per couple. Those worries about the "population explosion" are exaggerated. Indeed, both in the advanced economies and in some of the rapidly growing ones (such as China), the bigger problem will be an aging and declining population—too few young people, with the average couple giving birth to fewer than two children, thus failing to replace themselves fully in the next generation. And although we might assume that higher life expectancy would lead to higher per capita production, Acemoglu and Robinson show that this seems not to be the case. A lower death rate does not, by itself, translate into more rapid economic growth—although, over the long run, the greater propensity to invest in human capital (education) should have that effect.

To summarize bluntly: the quest for growth indeed remains elusive. Although the great success stories, particularly that of China, hold out hope, and although improvements in public health have greatly increased quality of life in even the poorest countries, comparativists remain baffled about why so many nations remain mired in poverty, and especially about why growth in TFP seems so hard to achieve. The issue has more than moral implications, for the growing gap between rich and poor countries raises incentives to migrate: if I am doomed to poverty in Chad or Bolivia or North Korea, I will be willing to risk and spend a lot to get to higher wages in Europe, North America, or (in the case of North Korea) China. Thus, the richer or more rapidly growing countries have a strong self-interest in solving the riddle of self-perpetuating poverty.

William Easterly
TO HELP THE POOR

When I see another child eating, I watch him, and if he doesn't give me something I think I'm going to die of hunger.

—A TEN-YEAR-OLD CHILD IN GABON, 1997

I am in Lahore, a city of 6 million people in Pakistan, on a World Bank trip as I write this chapter. Last weekend I went with a guide to the village of Gulvera, not far outside Lahore. We entered the village on an impossibly narrow paved road, which the driver drove at top speed except on the frequent occasions that cattle were crossing the road.

We continued as the road turned into a dirt track, where there was barely enough space between the village houses for the car. Then the road seemed to dead-end. But although I could not detect any road, the guide pointed out to the driver how he could make a sharp right across an open field, then regain a sort of a road—flat dirt anyway. I hated to think what would happen to these dirt roads in rainy season.

The "road" brought us to the community center for the village, where a number of young and old men

From *The Elusive Quest for Growth: Economists' Adventures and Misadventures in the Tropics* (Cambridge, Mass.: MIT Press, 2001), pp. 5–19. Author's notes have been omitted.

were hanging out (no women, on which more in a moment). The village smelled of manure. The men were expecting us and were extremely hospitable, welcoming us in to the brick-and-mortar community center, everyone grasping each of our right hands with their two hands and seating us on some rattan benches. They provided pillows for us to lean on or with which to otherwise make ourselves comfortable. They served us a drink of lassi, a sort of yogurt-milk mixture. The lassi pitcher was thickly covered with flies, but I drank my lassi anyway.

The men said that during the week, they worked all day in the fields, then came to the community center in the evenings to play cards and talk. The women couldn't come, they said, because they still had work to do in the evenings. Flocks of flies hummed everywhere, and some of the men had open sores on their legs. There was one youngish but dignified man nicknamed Deenu to whom everyone seemed to defer. Most of the men were barefoot, wearing long dusty robes. A crowd of children hung around the entrance watching us—only boys, no girls.

I asked Deenu what the main problems of Gulvera village were. Deenu said they were glad to have gotten electricity just six months before. Imagine getting electricity after generations spent in darkness. They were glad to have a boys' elementary school. However, they still lacked many things: a girls' elementary school, a doctor, drainage or sewerage (everything was dumped into a pool of rancid water outside the community center), telephone connections, paved roads. The poor sanitary conditions and lack of access to medical care in villages like Gulvera may help explain why a hundred out of every thousand babies die before their first birthday in Pakistan.

I asked Deenu if we could see a house. He walked with us over to his brother's house. It was an adobe-walled dirt-floor compound, which had two small rooms where they lived, stalls for the cattle, an outside dung-fired oven built into a wall, piles of cattle dung stacked up to dry, and a hand pump hooked up to a well. Children were everywhere, including a

few girls finally, staring curiously at us. Deenu said his brother had seven children. Deenu himself had six brothers and seven sisters. The brothers all lived in the village; the sisters had married into other villages. The women in the household hung back near the two small rooms. We were not introduced to them.

Women's rights have not yet come to rural Pakistan, a fact reflected in some grim statistics: there are 108 men for every 100 women in Pakistan. In rich countries, women slightly outnumber men because of their greater longevity. In Pakistan, there are what Nobel Prize winner Amartya Sen called "missing women," reflecting some combination of discrimination against girls in nutrition, medical care, or even female infanticide. Oppression of women sometimes takes an even more violent turn. There was a story in the Lahore newspaper of a brother who had killed his sister to preserve the family honor; he had suspected her of an illicit affair.

Violence in the countryside is widespread in Pakistan, despite the peaceful appearance of Gulvera. Another story in the Lahore paper described a village feud in which one family killed seven members of another family. Bandits and kidnappers prey on travelers in parts of the countryside in Pakistan.

We walked back to the community center, passing a group of boys playing a game, where they threw four walnuts on the ground and then tried to hit one of the walnuts with another one. Deenu asked us if we would like to stay for lunch, but we politely declined (I didn't want to take any of their scarce food), said our good-byes, and drove away. One of the villagers rode away with us, just to have an adventure. He told us that they had arranged for two cooks to prepare our lunch. I felt bad about having declined the lunch invitation.

We drove across the fields to where four brothers had grouped their compounds into a sort of a village and went through the same routine: the men greeting us warmly with two hands and seating us on rattan benches outside. No women were to be seen. The children were even more numerous and uninhibited than in Gulvera; they were mostly boys but this time also a few girls. They crowded around us watching everything we did, frequently breaking into laughter at some unknown faux pas by one of us. The men served us some very good milky sweet tea. I saw a woman peeking out from inside the house, but when I looked in her direction, she pulled back out of sight.

We walked into one of the brothers' compounds. Many women stood at the doors into their rooms, hanging back but watching us. The men showed us a churn that they used to make butter and yogurt. One of the men tried to show us how to use it, but he himself didn't know; this was woman's work. The children nearly passed out from laughing. The men brought us some butter to taste. They said they melted the butter to make ghee—clarified butter—which was an important ingredient in their cooking. They said if you ate a lot of ghee, it made you stronger. Then they gave us some ghee to taste. Most of their food seemed to consist of dairy products.

I asked what problems they faced. They had gotten electricity just one month before. They otherwise had the same unfulfilled needs as Gulvera: no telephone, no running water, no doctor, no sewerage, no roads. This was only a kilometer off the main road just outside Lahore, so we weren't in the middle of nowhere. They were poor, but these were relatively well-off villagers compared to more remote villages in Pakistan. The road leading to their minivillage was a half-lane track constructed of bricks that they had made themselves.

The majority of people in Pakistan are poor: 85 percent live on less than two dollars a day and 31 percent live in extreme poverty at less than one dollar a day. The majority of the world's people live in poor nations like Pakistan, where people live in isolated poverty even close to a major city. The majority of the world's people live in poor nations where women are oppressed, far too many babies die, and far too many people don't have enough to eat. We care about economic growth for the poor nations because it makes the lives of poor people like those in Gulvera better. Economic growth frees the poor from hunger and disease. Economy-wide GDP growth per capita translates into rising incomes for the poorest of the poor, lifting them out of poverty.

The Deaths of the Innocents

The typical rate of infant mortality in the richest fifth of countries is 4 out of every 1,000 births; in the poorest fifth of countries, it is 200 out of every 1,000 births. Parents in the poorest countries are fifty times more likely than in the richest countries to know grief rather than joy from the birth of a child. Researchers have found that a 10 percent decrease in income is associated with about a 6 percent higher infant mortality rate.

The higher rates of babies dying in the poorest countries reflect in part the higher rates of communicable and often easily preventable diseases such as tuberculosis, syphillis, diarrhea, polio, measles, tetanus, meningitis, hepatitis, sleeping sickness, schistosomiasis, river blindness, leprosy, trachoma, intestinal worms, and lower respiratory infections. At low incomes, disease is more dangerous because of lower medical knowledge, lower nutrition, and lower access to medical care.

Two million children die every year of dehydration from diarrhea. Another 2 million children die annually from pertussis, polio, diphtheria, tetanus, and measles.

Three million children die annually from bacterial pneumonia. Overcrowding of housing and indoor wood or cigarette smoke make pneumonia among children more likely. Malnourished children are also more likely to develop pneumonia than well-fed children. Bacterial pneumonia can be cured by a five-day course of antibiotics, like cotrimoxazole, that costs about twenty-five cents.

Between 170 million and 400 million children annually are infected with intestinal parasites like hookworm and roundworm, which impair cognition and cause anemia and failure to thrive.

Deficiency of iodine causes goiters—swelling of the thyroid gland at the throat—and lowered mental capacity. About 120,000 children born each year suffer from mental retardation and physical paralysis caused by iodine deficiency. About 10 percent of the world's population, adults and children both, suffer from goiter.

Vitamin A deficiency causes blindness in about half a million children and contributes to the deaths of about 8 million children each year. It is not independent of the other diseases discussed here; it makes death more likely from diarrhea, measles, and pneumonia.

Medicines that would alleviate these diseases are sometimes surprisingly inexpensive, a fact that UNICEF often uses to dramatize the depths of poverty of these suffering people. Oral rehydration therapy, at a cost of less than ten cents for each dose, can alleviate dehydration. Vaccination against pertussis, polio, diphtheria, measles, and tetanus costs about fifteen dollars per child. Vitamin A can be added to diets through processing of salt or sugar or administered directly through vitamin A capsules every six months. Vitamin A capsules cost about two cents each. Iodizing salt supplies, which costs about five cents per affected person per year, alleviates iodine deficiency. Intestinal parasites can be cured with inexpensive drugs like albendazole and praziquantel.

Wealthier and Healthier

Lant Pritchett, from Harvard's Kennedy School of Government, and Larry Summers, the former U.S. secretary of the treasury, found a strong association between economic growth and changes in infant mortality. They pointed out that a third factor that was unchanging over time for each country, like "culture" or "institutions," could not be explaining the simultaneous change in income and change in infant mortality. Going further, they argued that the rise in income was causing the fall in mortality rather than the other way around. They used a statistical argument that we will see more of later in this book. They observed some income increases that were probably unrelated to mortality, like income increases due to rises in a country's export prices. They traced through the effect of such an income increase, finding that it still did result in a fall in infant mortality. If an income increase that has nothing to do with mortality changes is still associated with a fall in mortality, this suggests that income increases are causing reduced mortality.

Pritchett and Summers's findings, if we can take them literally, imply huge effects of income growth on the death of children. The deaths of about half a million children in 1990 would have been averted if Africa's growth in the 1980s had been 1.5 percentage points higher.

The Poorest of the Poor

The statistics presented so far are national averages. Behind the averages of even the poorest nation, there is still regional variation. Mali is one of the poorest nations on earth. The countryside along the Niger River around the city of Tombouctou (Timbuktu) is one of the poorest regions in Mali and thus one of the poorest places on earth. At the time of a survey in 1987, over a third of the children under age five had had diarrhea in the preceding two weeks. Very few of them were on simple and cheap oral rehydration therapy. None had been vaccinated for diphtheria, pertussis, or typhoid. Forty-one percent of children born do not live to the age of five, three times the mortality rate in the capital of Bamako and one of the highest child mortality rates ever recorded.

As in Tomboctou, there are some regions or peoples at the very bottom of the economic pyramid, despised even by other poor. "In Egypt they were *madfoun*—the buried or buried alive; in Ghana, *ohiabrubro*—the miserably poor, with no work, sick with no one to care for them; in Indonesia, *endek arak tadah*; in Brazil, *miseraveis*—the deprived; in Russia, *bomzhi*—the homeless; in Bangladesh *ghrino gorib*—the despised/hated poor." In Zambia the *balandana sana* or *bapina* were described in these terms: "Lack food, eat once or twice; poor hygiene, flies fall over them, cannot afford school and health costs, lead miserable lives, poor dirty clothing, poor sanitation, access to water, look like made people, live on vegetables and sweet potatoes." In Malawi, the bottom poor were *osaukitsitsa*, "mainly households headed by the aged, the sick, disabled, orphans and widows." Some were described as *onyentchera*, "the stunted poor, with thin bodies, short stature and thin hairs, bodies that did not shine even after bathing, and who experience frequent illnesses and a severe lack of food."

Eating

High mortality in the poorest countries also reflects the continuing problem of hunger. Daily calorie intake is one-third lower in the poorest fifth of countries than in the richest fifth.

A quarter of the poorest countries had famines in the past three decades; none of the richest countries faced a famine. In the poorest nations like Burundi, Madagascar, and Uganda, nearly half of all children under the age of three are abnormally short because of nutritional deficiency.

An Indian family housed in a thatched hut seldom "could have two square meals a day. The lunch would be finished munching some sugarcane. Once in a while they would taste 'sattu' (made of flour), pulses [dried beans], potatoes etc. but for occasions only."

In Malawi, the poorest families "stay without food for 2–3 days or even the whole week . . . and may simply cook vegetables for a meal . . . some households literally eat bitter maize bran (*gaga/deya owawa*) and *gmelina* sawdust mixed with a little maize flour especially during the hunger months of January and February."

Oppression of the Poor

Poor societies sometimes have some form of debt bondage. To take one example, observers of India report "a vicious cycle of indebtedness in which a debtor may work in a moneylender's house as a servant, on his farm as a laborer. . . . The debt may accumulate substantially due to high interest rates, absence due to illness, and expenses incurred for food or accommodations."

Ethnic minorities are particularly prone to oppression. In Pakistan in 1993, the Bengali community of Rehmanabad in Karachi "had been subject to evictions and bulldozing, and on returning to the settlement and constructing temporary housing of reeds and sacks, have faced on-going harassment by land speculators, the police and political movements."

Poor children are particularly vulnerable to oppression. Forty-two percent of children aged ten to fourteen are workers in the poorest countries. Less than 2 percent of children aged ten to fourteen are workers in the richest countries. Although most countries have laws forbidding child labor, the U.S. Department classifies many countries as not enforcing these laws. Eighty-eight percent of the poorest countries are in this no-enforcement category; none of the richest countries is. For example, we have this story of Pachawak in western Orissa state in India: "Pachawak dropped out of class 3 when one day his teacher caned him severely. Since then he has been working as child labor with a number of rich households. Pachawak's father owns 1.5 acres of land and works as a laborer. His younger brother of 11-years-old also became a bonded laborer when the family had to take a loan for the marriage of the eldest son. The system is closely linked to credit, as many families take loans from landlords, who in lieu of that obligation keep the children as 'kuthia.' Pachawak worked as a cattle grazer from 6 A.M. to 6 P.M. and got paid two to four sacks of paddy a year, two meals a day, and one lungi [wrap-around clothing]."

One particularly unsavory kind of child labor is prostitution. In Benin, for example, "the girls have no choice but to prostitute themselves, starting at 14, even at 12. They do it for 50 francs, or just for dinner."

Another occupation in which children work in poor countries is particularly dangerous: war. As many as 200,000 child soldiers from the ages of six to sixteen fought wars in poor countries like Myanmar, Angola, Somalia, Liberia, Uganda, and Mozambique.

Women are also vulnerable to oppression in poor countries. Over four-fifths of the richest fifth of countries have social and economic equality for women most of the time, according to the *World Human Rights* Guide by Charles Humana. None of the poorest fifth of countries has social and economic equality for women. In Cameroon, "Women in some regions require a husband's, father's, or brother's permission to go out. In addition, a woman's husband or brother has access to her bank accounts, but not vice versa." A 1997 survey in Jamaica found that "in all communities, wife-beating was perceived as a common experience in daily life." In Georgia in the Caucasus, "women confessed that frequent household arguments resulted in being beaten." In Uganda in 1998, when women were asked, "What kind of work do men in your area do?" they laughed and said, "Eat and sleep then wake up and go drinking again."

Growth and Poverty

My World Bank colleagues Martin Ravallion and Shaohua Chen collected data on spells of economic growth and changes in poverty covering the years 1981 to 1999. They get their data from national surveys of household income or expenditure. They require that the methodology of the survey be unchanged over the period that they are examining so as to exclude spurious changes due to changing definitions. They found 154 periods of change in 65 developing countries with data that met this requirement.

Ravallion and Chen defined poverty as an absolute concept within each country: the poor were defined as the part of the population that had incomes below $1 a day at the beginning of each period they were examining. Ravallion and Chen keep this poverty line fixed within each country during the period they analyze. So the question was, How did aggregate economic growth change the share of people below this poverty line?

The answer was quite clear: fast growth went with fast poverty reduction, and overall economic contraction went with increased poverty. Here I summarize Ravallion and Chen's data by dividing the number of episodes into four equally sized groups from the fastest growing to the fastest declining. I compare the change in poverty in countries with the fastest growth to the poverty change in countries with the fastest decline [see table below].

The increases in poverty were extremely acute in the economies with severe economic declines — most of them in Eastern Europe and Central Asia. These were economies that declined with the death of the old communist system and kept declining while awaiting the birth of a new system. Several of these poverty-increasing declines also occurred in Africa. Poverty shot up during severe recessions in Zambia, Mali, and Côte d'Ivoire, for example.

Countries with positive income growth had a decline in the proportion of people below the

	Percentage change in average incomes per year	Percent change in poverty rate per year
Strong contraction	−9.8	23.9
Moderate contraction	−1.9	1.5
Moderate expansion	1.6	−0.6
Strong expansion	8.2	−6.1

poverty line. The fastest average growth was associated with the fastest poverty reductions. Growth was reaching the poor in Indonesia, for example, which had average income growth of 76 percent from 1984 to 1996. The proportion of Indonesians beneath the poverty line in 1993 was one-quarter of what it was in 1984. (A bad reversal came with Indonesia's crisis over 1997–1999, with average income falling by 12 percent and the poverty rate shooting up 65 percent, again confirming that income and poverty move together.)

All of this in retrospect seems unsurprising. For poverty to get worse with economic growth, the distribution of income would have to get much more unequal as incomes increased. There is no evidence for such disastrous deteriorations in income inequality as income rises. In Ravallion and Chen's data set, for example, measures of inequality show no tendency to get either better or worse with economic growth. If the degree of inequality stays about the same, then income of the poor and the rich must be rising together or falling together.

This is indeed what my World Bank colleagues David Dollar and Aart Kraay have found. A 1 percent increase in average income of the society translates one for one into a 1 percent increase in the incomes of the poorest 20 percent of the population. Again using statistical techniques to isolate direction of causation, they found that an additional one percentage point per capita growth *causes* a 1 percent rise in the poor's incomes.

There are two ways the poor could become better off: income could be redistributed from the rich to the poor, and the income of both the poor and the rich could rise with overall economic growth. Ravallion and Chen's and Dollar and Kraay's findings suggest that on average, growth has been much more of a lifesaver to the poor than redistribution.

To Begin the Quest

The improvement in hunger, mortality, and poverty as GDP per capita rises over time motivates us on our quest for growth. Poverty is not just low GDP; it is dying babies, starving children, and oppression of women and the downtrodden. The well-being of the next generation in poor countries depends on whether our quest to make poor countries rich is successful. I think again back to the woman I saw peering out at me from a house in a village in Pakistan. To that unknown woman I dedicate the elusive quest for growth as we economists, from rich countries and from poor countries, trek the tropics trying to make poor countries rich.

■   ■   ■

Paul Collier and Jan Willem Gunning
WHY HAS AFRICA GROWN SLOWLY?

In the 1960s, Africa's future looked bright. On the basis of Maddison's (1995) estimates of per capita GDP for a sample of countries, during the first half of the century Africa had grown considerably more rapidly than Asia; by 1950, the African sample had overtaken the Asian sample. In the 1950s there were uncertainties of political transition, but after 1960 Africa was increasingly free of colonialism, with the potential for governments that would be more responsive to

From *Journal of Economic Perspectives* 13, No. 3 (Summer 1999) pp. 3–22.

domestic needs. During the period 1960–73, growth in Africa was more rapid than in the first half of the century. Indeed, for this period, African growth and its composition were indistinguishable from the geographically very different circumstances of south Asia (Collins and Bosworth, 1996). Political self-determination in Africa and economic growth seemed to be proceeding hand-in-hand.

However, during the 1970s both political and economic matters in Africa deteriorated. The leadership of many African nations hardened into autocracy and dictatorship. Africa's economies first faltered and then started to decline. While Africa experienced a growth collapse, nations of south Asia modestly improved their economic performance. A good example of this divergence is the comparison of Nigeria and Indonesia. Until around 1970, the economic performance of Nigeria was broadly superior to that of Indonesia, but over the next quarter-century outcomes diverged markedly, despite the common

Map 10.1 The Political Geography of Africa

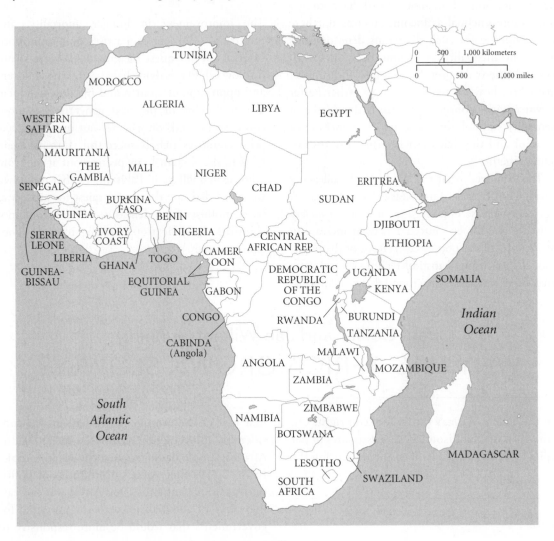

Table 10.1 The Economies of Sub-Saharan Africa

Country	Population (Millions) 1997	GDP US$m at 1990 Prices 1997	GNP per Capita (PPP $) 1997	GNP Average Annual % Growth per Capita 1965–97	Life Expectancy at Birth (years) 1995	% of Population below $1 a Day (early 1990s)	Trade as % of GDP (in PPP) 1997
Angola	11.6	9,886	728	. . .	48	. . .	77
Benin	5.7	2,540	1,240		48	. . .	17
Botswana	1.5	4,458	7,440	7.7	66	33	. . .
Burkina Faso	11.1	3,643	936	0.9	47	. . .	7
Burundi	6.4	939	661	1.1	51	. . .	5
Cameroon	13.9	11,254	1,739	1.4	57	. . .	13
Cape Verde	0.4	393	. . .	. . .	66	. . .	. . .
Central African Republic	3.4	1,420	1,254	–1.2	50	. . .	10
Chad	6.7	1,492	978	0.1	49	. . .	4
Comoros	0.7	251	. . .	. . .	57	. . .	. . .
Congo	2.7	2,433	1,275	1.7	53	. . .	80
Congo, Dem. Rep.	48.0	6,094	698	–3.7	. . .	. . .	7
Côte d'Ivoire	14.3	13,320	1,676	–0.9	50	18	30
Djibouti	0.4	384	. . .	. . .	49	. . .	. . .
Equatorial Guinea	0.4	541	. . .	. . .	49	. . .	. . .
Eritrea	3.4	1,010	990	. . .	52	. . .	. . .
Ethiopia	60.1	11,327	493	–0.5	49	46	7
Gabon	1.1	7,280	6,480	0.4	55	. . .	58
Gambia	1.0	332	1,372	0.5	46	. . .	30
Ghana	18.3	7,892	1,492	–0.9	57	. . .	19
Guinea	7.6	3,699	1,763	. . .	46	26	14
Guinea-Bissau	1.1	306	1,041	0.1	45	88	13

(Continued)

Table 10.1 The Economies of Sub-Saharan Africa (Continued)

Country	Population (Millions) 1997	GDP US$m at 1990 Prices 1997	GNP per Capita (PPP $) 1997	GNP Average Annual % Growth per Capita 1965–97	Life Expectancy at Birth (years) 1995	% of Population below $1 a Day (early 1990s)	Trade as % of GDP (in PPP) 1997
Kenya	28.4	9,879	1,150	1.3	55	50	16
Lesotho	2.1	998	2,422	3.2	62	49	. . .
Liberia	2.5	. . .	. . .	. . .	57	. . .	. . .
Madagascar	15.8	3,187	892	–1.9	58	72	11
Malawi	10.1	2,480	688	0.5	45	. . .	21
Mali	11.5	3,132	715	0.5	47	. . .	19
Mauritania	2.4	1,346	1,654	–0.2	53	31	28
Mauritius	1.1	3,755	9,147	3.8	71	. . .	37
Mozambique	18.3	2,144	541	–0.1	47	. . .	15
Namibia	1.6	3,141	4,999	0.7	60	. . .	. . .
Niger	9.8	2,776	824	–2.5	48	62	9
Nigeria	118.4	34,418	854	0.0	51	31	23
Rwanda	5.9	1,979	643	0.1	47	46	9
São Tomé & Principe	0.1	56	. . .	. . .	. . .	. . .	. . .
Senegal	8.8	6,708	1,670	–0.5	50	54	11
Seychelles	0.1	435	. . .	. . .	. . .	. . .	. . .
Sierra Leone	4.4	. . .	401	–1.4	40	. . .	24
Somalia	10.4	. . .	. . .	. . .	48	. . .	. . .
South Africa	43.3	117,089	7,152	0.1	64	24	23
Sudan	27.9	13,119	. . .	–0.2	54	. . .	. . .
Swaziland	0.9	1,031	. . .	. . .	59	. . .	. . .
Tanzania	31.5	4,956	608	. . .	52	11	14
Togo	4.3	1,726	1,408	–0.6	56	. . .	24
Uganda	20.8	6,822	1,131	. . .	44	69	6
Zambia	8.5	3,564	900	–2.0	48	85	26
Zimbabwe	11.7	7,904	2,207	0.5	52	41	21

Sources: African Development Report (1998); and World Development Indicators (1999).

Table 10.2 Africa Compared With Other Developing Regions

(*figures are unweighted country averages*)	Sub-Saharan Africa	Other LDCs
Domestic-Destiny		
Life expectancy in 1970 (years)	45.2	57.3
Income in 1960 (1985 $ PPP-adjusted)	835.5	1855.2
Ethnic Fractionalization	67.6	32.7
Domestic-Policy		
Political Rights, 1973–90	6.0	4.0
Bureaucracy	1.38	1.72
External-Destiny		
Population <100 km from the sea or river (%)	21.0	52.0
Terms of trade volatility	16.4	12.8
External-Policy		
Parallel market exchange rate premium	40.0	26.0
Average tariffs 1996–98 (%)	21.0	13.0
Quantitative Restrictions, 1988–90 (%)	46.0	21.0
Endogenous		
Growth of GDP per capita, 1965–90	0.5	1.7
Investment rate in 1997 (%)	18.0	25.0
Population growth rate, 1980–97 (%)	2.8	1.8
Capital flight/private wealth, 1990 (%)	39.0	14.0

Sources: Life expectancy, World Development Indicators, 1998. Income and growth: Penn World Tables 5.6. The index of ethno- linguistic diversity is on the scale 0–100 with 0 being homogenous (Mauro, 1995). The Gastil index of political rights is on the range 1–7 with 1 being fully democratic.

The index of bureaucracy is on the scale 0–6 with high score indicating better quality (Knack and Keefer, 1995). Population living less than 100 km from the sea or a navigable river, from Bloom and Sachs (1999), Table 2, (other LDCs is the weighted average for Asia and Latin America). Terms of trade volatility is the standard deviation of annual log changes 1965–92, (Collins and Bosworth, 1996). Parallel exchange rate premium (%), (Easterly and Levine, 1997).

Average tariff: simple average, computed by IMF, we would like to thank Robert Sharer for these numbers. QRs: weighted average incidence of non-tariff measures over product lines; other LDCs is simple average of Latin America and East Asia; from Rodrik (1999, Table 12).

Investment rate and population growth rate, World Development Indicators, 1999 Capital flight/private wealth as of 1990 (Collier and Pattillo, 1999).

experience for both countries of an oil boom in a predominantly agricultural economy. Since 1980, aggregate per capita GDP in sub-Saharan Africa has declined at almost 1 percent per annum. The decline has been widespread: 32 countries are poorer now than in 1980. Today, sub-Saharan Africa is the lowest-income region in the world. Map 10.1 and Table 10.5, taken together, offer a snapshot of Africa today. Map 10.1 is a map of the continent. Table 10.5 gives some basic information on population, GDP, standard of living, and growth rates for countries of sub-Saharan Africa. We focus on the sub-Saharan countries, setting aside the north African countries of Algeria, Egypt, Libya, Morocco and Tunisia. This is conventional for the studies of this area, since the north African countries are part of a different regional economy — the Middle East — with its own distinctive set of economic issues. It is clear that Africa has suffered a chronic failure of economic growth. The problem for analysis is to determine its causes.

The debate on the causes of slow African growth has offered many different explanations. These can be usefully grouped into a two-by-two matrix, distinguishing on the one hand between policy and exogenous "destiny" and, on the other, between domestic and external factors. Table 10.6 compares Africa to other developing regions, using this grouping. Until recently it has largely been accepted that the main causes of Africa's slow growth were external, with the debate focusing upon whether external problems were policy-induced or exogenous. Especially during the 1980s, the World Bank, the International Monetary Fund and bilateral donors came to identify exchange rate and trade policies as the primary causes of slow growth in Africa. Table 10.6 offers some evidence that official exchange rates in sub-Saharan Africa have been more overvalued relative to (often illegal) market rates than is common for other less developed economies of Asia and Latin America. Tariffs and quantitative trade restrictions have also been higher in Africa than elsewhere. The rival thesis, often favored by African governments,

was that the crisis was due to deteriorating and volatile terms of trade, and as Table 10.6 shows, terms of trade have indeed been more volatile for Africa than for other less developed economies. Jeffrey Sachs and his co-authors have emphasized a further adverse external "destiny" factor: Africa's population is atypically landlocked. As shown in Table 10.6, a high proportion of the population is remote from the coast or navigable waters.

Recently, attention has shifted to possible domestic causes of slow growth within African nations, but the debate as to the relative importance of policy-induced and exogenous problems has continued. Sachs and his co-authors have attributed slow growth to "the curse of the tropics." Africa's adverse climate causes poor health, and so reduces life expectancy below that in other regions, which puts it at a disadvantage in development. The adverse climate also leads to leached soils and unreliable rainfall, which constrains African agriculture. African nations also appear to have more ethnic diversity than other poor nations of the world, which may make it harder to develop an interconnected economy. In contrast to the domestic destiny argument, Collier and Gunning (1999) have emphasized domestic policy factors such as poor public service delivery. African governments have typically been less democratic and more bureaucratic than their Asian and Latin American counterparts.

Of course, once the conditions for slow growth are established by any combination of these reasons, they can become self-reinforcing in an endogenous process. Weak economic growth helps explain a lower saving rate and a higher proportion of flight capital for Africa compared to the less developed nations of Asia and Africa. Richer countries tend to see their population growth rates drop off, so the poverty of Africa has helped to keep its birth rates high, even as compared to the world's other less developed economies. Similarly, poverty may have increased the incidence of Africa's numerous civil wars, as well as being a consequence of them.

In the discussion that follows, we assess the policy/destiny and domestic/external distinctions in various combinations. During the mid-1990s, African performance started to improve, with a few countries growing quite rapidly. We conclude by assessing these different explanations as guides to whether this improvement is likely to be transient or persistent.

Four Types of Explanation

Domestic-Destiny

Africa has several geographic and demographic characteristics which may predispose it to slow growth. First, much of the continent is tropical and this may handicap the economy, partly due to diseases such as malaria and partly due to hostile conditions for livestock and agriculture. Life expectancy has historically been low, with the population in a high-fertility, high infant-mortality equilibrium. With the advent of basic public health measures, population growth became very high. In particular, Africa has not been through the demographic transition whereby fertility rates decline which occurred in Asia and Latin America over the past 40 years. On one estimate, Africa's low life expectancy and high population growth account for almost all of Africa's slow growth (Bloom and Sachs, 1998). The argument is not clear-cut, however. Low life expectancy and high fertility are consequences of low income as well as causes, so the estimates are likely to be biased upwards. The household-level evidence suggests that the effects of poor health on income are small, although these in turn will be biased downwards by the omission of large-scale changes in economic activity which cannot be detected at the household level.

Whether or not Africa's past demographic characteristics have contributed to its slow growth, some African countries seem certain to go through a distinctive and disastrous demographic transition during the next two decades. As a result of AIDS, adult mortality rates will rise dramatically. In Africa, AIDS is a heterosexual disease. During the 1980s in parts of Africa it spread rapidly across the population before the risks became apparent, with up to 20–25 percent of adults now HIV-positive in some countries (World Bank, 1997). This human tragedy will have substantial economic effects during the next decade, especially since infection rates appear to be higher among the more educated, but it does not account for historically slow growth.

A second key characteristic of Africa which may predispose it to slow growth is that soil quality is poor and much of the continent is semi-arid, with rainfall subject to long cycles and unpredictable failure. Soils derive disproportionately from a very old type of rock ("Basement Complex"), which is low in micronutrients and varies considerably between localities. The application of additional macronutrients, which is the fertilizer package associated with the Green Revolution, is generally ineffective with low levels of micronutrients. Africa probably has scope for its own agricultural revolution, but it will depend upon locality-specific packages of micronutrients (Voortman et al., 1999). Since the 1960s, the semi-arid areas of Africa have been in a phase of declining rainfall (Grove, 1991). While there are no estimates of the output consequences of this decline, it may be significant, since agriculture is typically about one-quarter of GDP in this region. Given the lack of irrigation, the unpredictability of rainfall implies high risks in agriculture. With incomplete insurance and a high rate of time preference, households have to use assets for purposes of consumption-smoothing rather than investment. Households can thus become trapped in low-income, high-liquidity equilibria (Dercon, 1997).

A third relevant characteristic of Africa's economies, which can be seen as a result of these semi-arid conditions, is that the continent has very low population density. One by-product is high costs of transport which in turn have added to risk: poor market integration has hampered the use of trade for risk sharing. Another consequence of low population density is that Africa has relatively high natural resource endowments per capita (Wood and Mayer, 1998). High levels of natural resources can cause several problems. High levels of exported natural resources may lead to an appreciation of the exchange rate, which in turn makes manufacturing less competitive. Yet manufacturing may offer larger growth externalities, such as learning, than natural resource extraction. Natural resources may also increase "loot-seeking" activities. Collier and Hoeffler (1998) find that a dependence on natural resources strongly increases the risk of civil war, which has been a widespread phenomenon in Africa.

A further consequence of low population density is that African countries have much higher ethno-linguistic diversity than other regions; when groups come together less, there is less mingling and merging. Easterly and Levine (1997) find that this high level of diversity is the most important single cause of Africa's slow growth. There are various interpretations of this result. A common perception is that Africa's high ethnic diversity accounts for its high incidence of civil war. This turns out to be false: high levels of ethnic and religious diversity actually make societies significantly safer (Collier and Hoeffler, 1999). The effects of ethnic diversity on growth turn out to be contingent upon the political system; diversity has deleterious effects only when it occurs in the context of governments which are undemocratic. Collier (1999) finds that in democratic societies, ethnic diversity has no effect on either growth or the quality of public projects, but that in dictatorships, high levels of diversity reduce growth rates by 3 percentage points and double the rate of project failure relative to homogeneity. Dictatorships tend not to transcend the ethnic group of the dictator, so that the more ethnically fragmented the society, the more narrowly based a dictatorship will be, whereas democratic governments in such societies must be ethnically cross-cutting. In turn, the more narrowly based the government, the greater the payoff to predation relative to the inducement of generalized growth. Africa's problem was thus not its ethnic diversity but its lack of democracy in the context of diversity.

A fourth characteristic of Africa that may hinder its growth prospects is that because of its colonial heritage, Africa has much smaller countries in terms of population than other regions. Sub-Saharan Africa has a population about half that of India, divided into 48 states. These many states, combined with low levels of income, make Africa's national economies radically smaller than those of other regions. Very small states might be economically disadvantaged for several reasons. If government has some fixed costs, either in its administrative role or as a provider of services, then it may be hard for a small state to perform at minimum cost. Moreover, the society may forfeit much more extensive scale economies if it combines small scale with isolation. Some domestic markets will be too small even for the minimum efficient scale of production of a single producer; all domestic markets taken alone will be less competitive than in larger economies. Small economies are also perceived by investors as significantly more risky (Collier and Dollar, 1999b). Finally, they may have a slower rate of technological innovation; Kremer (1993) argues the incidence of discoveries may be broadly proportional to the population, so that if discoveries cannot readily spread between societies, low-population societies will have less innovation. However, in aggregate these effects cannot be large, because growth regressions generally find that state size does not affect a nation's rate of economic growth.

Domestic-Policy

For much of the post-colonial period, most African governments have been undemocratic. The median African government during the 1970s and 1980s was close to autocracy, and far less democratic than the median non-African developing country (as measured by the Gastil scale of political rights shown in Table 10.6). A typical pattern was that governments were captured by the educated, urban-resident population, with few agricultural or commercial interests. They expanded the public sector while imposing wide-ranging controls on private activity. These choices have been economically costly.

Public employment was expanded, often as an end in itself. For example, in Ghana by the late

1970s the public sector accounted for three-quarters of formal wage employment (Ghana Central Bureau of Statistics, 1988), and even in a more market-oriented economy like Kenya, the figure was 50 percent as of 1990 (Kenya Central Bureau of Statistics, 1996). Indeed, economic decline may have increased pressure for public sector employment. The large number of public sector employees was reconciled with limited tax revenue by reducing wage rates and non-wage expenditures. The ratio of wage to non-wage expenditures in African governments is double that in Asia, and this has lowered the quality of public services; for example, in education, teaching materials are often lacking. The large, ill-paid public sector became the arena in which ethnic groups struggled for resources. For example, in the Ghanaian public sector, the locally dominant ethnic group received a wage premium of 25 percent over other groups after controlling for worker characteristics, and cognitive skills were completely unrewarded (Collier and Garg, 1999). The combination of low wage levels and payment structures, which rewarded social connections rather than skill, made it difficult for managers to motivate staff, and the difficulties of service delivery were compounded by the low ratio of non-wage to wage expenditures.

Since public sector employment was the main priority, managers were not under severe pressure for actual delivery of services from their political masters. Because of the lack of democracy, neither were they accountable to the broader public. As a result, Africa experienced a paradox of poor public services despite relatively high public expenditure (Pradhan, 1996). Poor service delivery handicapped firms through unreliable transport and power, inadequate telecommunications networks, and unreliable courts. For example, manufacturing firms in Zimbabwe need to hold high levels of inventories, despite high interest rates, due to unreliable delivery of inputs tied to poor transportation infrastructure (Fafchamps et al., 1998). A survey of Ugandan firms found that shortage of electricity was identified as the single most important constraint upon firm growth; indeed, the provision of electricity by firms for their own use was almost as large as the public supply of electricity (Reinikka and Svensson, 1998). A study in Nigeria found that their own generators accounted for three-quarters of the capital equipment of small manufacturers (Lee and Anas, 1991). The poor state of African telecommunications was estimated to reduce African growth rates by 1 percentage point, according to Easterly and Levine (1997). (However, since telecommunications was the main infrastructure variable which they could quantify, and since lack of different kinds of infrastructure is probably highly correlated, their estimate is probably a proxy for a wider range of infrastructural deficiencies.) African commercial courts are more corrupt than those in other regions (Widner, 1999). As a result, firms face greater problems of contract enforcement. Some firms can overcome these by relying upon their social networks to screen potential clients, but it is common to restrict business to long-standing clients (Bigsten et al., 1999). Ethnic minorities, such as Asians in East Africa and Lebanese in West Africa, tend to have more specialized social networks and so are better able than African firms to screen new clients (Biggs et al., 1996). The problem of contract enforcement thus makes markets less competitive and reduces the potential gains from trade, while tending to perpetuate the dominant position of minorities in business.

Poor public service delivery also handicapped households through inefficient education, health and extension services. A survey of primary education expenditures in Uganda found that, of the non-wage money released by the Ministry of Finance, on average, less than 30 percent actually reached the schools (Ablo and Reinikka, 1998). The expansion of the public sector has reduced private initiative. Since major areas of economic activity were reserved for the public sector—often including transport, marketing and banking—and African elites looked to the public sector rather than the private sector for advancement, Africa was slow to develop indigenous entrepreneurs.

African governments built various economic control regimes. A few nations, such as Ethiopia, Angola and Tanzania, had wide-ranging price controls under which private agents had an incentive to reduce production—at least officially marketed production. These governments often attempted to counterbalance these incentives with coercive production targets, but the net effect was usually dramatic declines in economic activity. More commonly, firms were subject to considerable regulation. For example, for many years manufacturing firms wishing to set up in Kenya had to acquire letters of no objection from existing producers, which resulted in a predictably low level of competition. In Uganda, when the government removed the requirement that coffee could only be transported by rail, the market for road haulage expanded sufficiently to induce new entry, which in turn broke an existing cartel, nearly halving haulage rates. Similarly, in Tanzania during the long period when agricultural marketing was heavily regulated, marketing margins for grain were double what they were both before regulation and after deregulation (Bevan et al., 1993). In this period, food prices became much more volatile: between 1964 and 1980 the coefficient of variation (that is, the ratio of the standard deviation to the mean) of maize prices at regional centers doubled, falling again sharply when markets were liberalized.

Government interventions undermined the functioning of product markets in many countries. Private trading, which was often associated with ethnic minorities such as the Indians in East Africa and the Lebanese in West Africa, was sometimes banned. A particularly damaging intervention, practiced even in relatively market-friendly economies such as Kenya, was to ban private inter-district trade in food. Where government marketing monopolies were focused on ensuring the food supply to urban areas, this provision discouraged farmers from specializing in non-food export crops, since they could not rely on being able to buy food locally.

Since the political base of governments was urban, agriculture was heavily taxed and the public agronomic research needed to promote an African green revolution, based on locally specific packages of micronutrients, was neglected. The main source of agricultural growth has been the gradual adoption of cash crops by smallholders, a process slowed down by government pricing policies (Bevan et al., 1993). While governments favored manufacturing, the basis for industrial growth in this area was also undermined, since trade and exchange rate policies induced industrial firms to produce under uncompetitive conditions and only for small and captive domestic markets.

The same urban bias initially led governments to favor the urban wage labor force. In the immediate post-colonial period, minimum wages rose and unions acquired influence, so that wages increased substantially. However, post-independence inflation has usually eroded minimum wages, so that in most of Africa, wage rigidities in the labor market are not currently a significant impediment to the growth process. The exceptions are South Africa, where the labor market may just be going through such a real wage adjustment now, and the low inflation environments of Ethiopia and the countries in the "franc zone," the 13 former colonies of France in west and central Africa which had currencies pegged to the French franc. While high wage levels are not normally a hindrance to African economies, the job matching process appears to be inefficient, so that job mobility offers unusually high returns (Mengistae, 1998). This is an instance of the high costs of market information; for example, newspapers are expensive and have low circulation.

Financial markets were heavily regulated, with bank lending directed to the government, public enterprises or "strategic" sectors, very limited financial intermediation and virtually no competition between financial institutions. A common proxy for the extent of financial intermediation, known as "financial depth," is the broad money supply, M2, relative to GDP. But although Africa has even less financial depth than other developing areas, currently available evidence suggests that this may have had only a modest impact on its growth. For example, Easterly and Levine (1997) estimate that lack of financial depth reduced the annual growth rate by only 0.3 percentage points. Similarly, micro-economic survey evidence on manufacturing firms indicates that the lack of external finance is not currently the binding constraint on industrial investment (Bigsten et al., 1999).

External-Destiny

Africa is better located than Asia for most developed economy markets. However, most Africans live much further from the coast or navigable rivers than in other regions and so face intrinsically higher transport costs for exports (as shown in Table 10.6). Further, much of the population lives in countries which are land-locked, so that problems of distance are compounded by political barriers. Even a relatively open border like the one between Canada and the United States appears to be a substantial impediment to trade, in the sense that trade across Canadian provinces or across Uinted states is far greater than trade of equal distance between Canada and the United States (McCallum, 1995). Landlocked countries face national borders on all sides, which may constitute an irreducible barrier to trade even if they have good relations with their neighbors. Typically, growth regressions find that being landlocked reduces a nation's annual growth rate by around half of 1 percent.

A further aspect of external destiny is that Africa's exports are concentrated in a narrow range of commodities, with volatile prices that have declined since the 1960s. The deterioration in the terms of trade for such commodities has undoubtedly contributed to Africa's growth slowdown. However, there is controversy over whether its atypical exposure to terms of trade volatility has been damaging. Deaton and Miller (1996) find little evidence of detrimental effects in the short run. However, case study evidence suggests that shocks have often had longer-run deleterious effects. Investment has been concertinaed into short periods, during which construction booms have raised the unit cost of capital, and government budgets have been destabilized, with spending rising during booms but being

difficult to reduce subsequently (Schuknecht, 1999; Collier and Gunning, 1999b).

Africa has attracted much more aid per capita than other regions. Donor allocation rules have typically favored countries which have small populations and low incomes, and were recent colonies — and African countries met all three criteria. There has been a long debate as to whether aid has been detrimental or beneficial for the growth process (for recent overviews, see Gwin and Nelson, 1997; World Bank, 1998). Early critics claimed that aid reduced the incentive for good governance (for example, Bauer, 1982). Since the 1980s, the World Bank and the International Monetary Fund have attempted to make policy improvement a condition for the receipt of aid. Econometric work does not find that aid has had a significant effect on policy: to the extent that aid encourages or discourages policy changes, the two effects apparently offset each other. However, the effect of aid on growth has been shown to be policy-dependent. Where policies are good, aid substantially raises growth rates, where they are poor, diminishing returns rapidly set in so that aid cannot significantly contribute to growth. This result holds whether the measure of policy is objective indicators of the fiscal and exchange rate stance (Burnside and Dollar, 1997), or subjective but standardized ratings of a broader range of policies done by the World Bank (Collier and Dollar, 1999a). Until recently, many African policy environments were not good enough for aid to raise growth substantially. Hence, the evidence does not support Bauer's (1982) claim that Africa's large aid receipts were a cause of its slow growth, but does suggest that Africa largely missed the opportunity for enhanced growth which aid provided.

Excluding South Africa and the oil exporters (whose terms of trade have improved), the net aid inflows since 1970 have been around 50 percent greater than the income losses from terms of trade deterioration. The combination was thus somewhat analogous to an increase in export taxation: the terms of trade losses taking money from exporters, while the aid provided money to governments.

External-Policy

In recent decades, African governments adopted exchange rate and trade policies which were atypically anti-export and accumulated large foreign debts. On a range of indicators, Africa has had much higher trade barriers and more misaligned exchange rates than other regions (Dollar, 1992; Sachs and Warner, 1997). Exchange rates were commonly highly overvalued, reflecting the interest of the political elite in cheap imports. Tariffs and export taxes were higher in Africa than in other regions of the world, partly because of the lack of other sources of tax revenue to finance the expansion of the public sector. Exports were sharply reduced as a result of export crop taxation. For example, Dercon (1993) shows that Tanzanian cotton exports would have been 50 percent higher in the absence of taxation. Quantitative restrictions on imports were also used much more extensively, despite yielding no revenue. They often arose because of the difficulties of fine-tuning import demand in a situation where government was attempting to keep exchange rates fixed with few reserves. They probably persisted because they generated large opportunities for corruption, since someone could often be bribed to circumvent the quantitative limits.

The international growth literature has reached a consensus that exchange rate overvaluation and tight trade restrictions are damaging, but controversy continues over the effects of more moderate trade restrictions (Rodrik, 1999). However, there are reasons why Africa's poor export performance may have been particularly damaging. Since 1980, African export revenue per capita has sharply declined, which in turn has induced severe import compression of both capital goods and intermediate inputs. Moreover, because African economies are so much smaller than other economies, external barriers of a given height have been significantly more damaging (Collier and Gunning, 1999).

By the 1990s, several African economies had accumulated unsustainable international debts, largely from public agencies. Clearly, this is one way in which poor decisions of the past become embedded in the present. There is a good theoretical argument that high indebtedness discourages private investment due to the fear of the future tax liability. There is some supporting evidence for this claim, although since poor policies lower GDP, using high debt/GDP as an explanatory variable may simply be a proxy for poor policies more broadly (Elbadawi et al., 1997).

Policy or Destiny?

The dichotomy between policy and destiny is of course an oversimplification: some apparently exogenous features of Africa have often been induced by policy, and conversely, African policies may reflect exogenous factors.

Consider, first, some of the "exogenous" factors that we have discussed under destiny. For example, the claim by Sachs and Warner (1997) that geography and demography almost fully account for Africa's slow growth rests largely upon the lack of a demographic transition to lower fertility rates in Africa, as has happened in most of Latin America and Asia. However, it is more plausible to regard these continuing high fertility rates as a consequence of slow growth than a cause. The lack of employment opportunities for young women has prevented the opportunity cost of children from rising, and the low returns to education in an environment where many of the "good" jobs are allocated by political criteria have reduced the incentive for parents to educate their children.

Similarly, the argument that the concentration of Africa's population in the interior is an external force holding down growth can also be seen as an endogenous outcome; specifically, the population has remained in the interior because of the failure of Africa's coastal cities to grow. In turn, this is partly because the failure to industrialize has slowed urbanization, and partly because policy has often been biased against coastal cities; for example, in both Nigeria and Tanzania the capital was relocated from the coast to the interior. Where policy was less biased, as in the Côte d'Ivoire during the 1970s, the coastal population grew so rapidly that it supported massive emigration from the landlocked economy of Burkina Faso: at its peak, around 40 percent of the Ivorien population were immigrants.

Further, being landlocked need not be an economic disadvantage. Developed landlocked economies, such as Switzerland, have atypically low international transport costs because they have oriented their trade towards their neighbors. By contrast, Africa's landlocked economies trade with Europe, so that neighboring countries are an obstacle rather than a market. These patterns of trade are partly a legacy of the colonial economy, but they also reflect the high trade barriers within Africa erected by postindependence governments, and the slow rate of growth. Ultimately, landlocked economies were faced with neighboring markets that were both inaccessible and unattractive, which did not make it desirable to reorient the economy to trade with them. Finally, Africa's continued export concentration in a narrow range of primary commodities, which we discussed earlier as reflecting the destiny of resource endowments, probably also reflects a number of public policy decisions. Other export activities have been handicapped either directly through overvalued exchange rates, or indirectly, through high transactions costs. Poor policy has given Africa a comparative disadvantage in "transaction-intensive" activities such as manufacturing.

Now consider the reverse situation; that is, how some of the dysfunctional policies that we have discussed can also be considered the outcome of exogenous forces. The anti-export policies which we argue hindered growth can be viewed as a consequence of the fact that most of the population lives far from the coast (Gallup and Sachs, 1999). In such societies, it might be argued that the elasticity of growth with respect to openness is lower and so the incentive for openness is reduced. However, at present Africa offers little evidence for this hypothesis. According to the World Bank's standardized ratings of policy (currently confidential), all five of the worst-rated countries on the continent are coastal whereas many of the best-rated countries are landlocked. As another example, it is possible that restrictive import policies are adopted, at least initially, in response to trade shocks like those created by an external dependence on commodity exports (Collier and Gunning, 1999b). The prevalence of natural resources may bring forth a variety of other policy errors, as well. For example, it may worsen policy by turning politics into a contest for rents or, through crowding out manufactured exports, prevent the emergence of potentially the most potent lobby for openness.

Along with being endogenous to fixed effects like geography, policies are also affected by experience. Societies which have experienced high levels of economic risk may place a higher priority on income-sharing arrangements such as expanded opportunities of public employment, rather than focusing on income generation. Societies also learn from past failure. The African nations which have recently implemented the strongest economic reforms, such as Ghana and Uganda, tended to be those which had earlier experienced the worst economic crises. However, African countries facing the challenge of reversing economic failure have lacked significant role models within the continent. In east Asia, Hong Kong, Singapore, Taiwan and Korea provided early role models, as did Chile since the late 1970s in Latin America. Within-continent models may be important because the information is both closer to hand and more evidently pertinent. Once Africa develops examples of success, the scope for societal learning across the continent will make it unlikely that Africa is "destined" to poor policies by its geography: although its geographic characteristics may have given it some weak tendencies towards poor policies in the initial post-independence period.

Sorting out the policy effects from the destiny effects is a difficult econometric problem. In the ordinary least squares regressions common in the analysis of African growth, the dependent variable is typically the average growth rate over a long period, and a variety of policy and destiny variables enter as the explanatory variables. Depending upon the specification, either policy or destiny can appear important.

An alternative approach is to consider the extent to which African slow growth has been persistent, to take advantage of the insight that policies have varied, whereas destiny-like geographic disadvantages remain constant over time. Along these lines, Diamond (1998) provides a convincing explanation from a historical perspective of why geographic reasons, such as the north-south axis of the continent, caused African agriculture to develop only slowly prior to European colonization, due to a combination of technological isolation and small scale. However, since colonization gradually relaxed some of these constraints (while introducing others), pre-20th century experience is of limited pertinence for explaining patterns of growth in the last few decades.

More recent experience tends to argue that destiny plays less of a role than policy. After all, the economies of Africa did grow relatively quickly through the first half of the 20th century, and up until the early 1970s, which tends to argue that they were not obviously destined for lower growth. The arrival of slow economic growth in the 1970s coincides with a phase in which African economic policy became both statist and biased against exports. Moreover, the main exception to African economic collapse, Botswana, experienced the most rapid growth in the world despite the seeming exogenous disadvantages of being landlocked and having very low population density.

The most sophisticated econometric test of whether something about Africa seems intrinsically connected to slow growth is the study by Hoeffler (1999). She searches for a continental fixed effect using panel regressions of five-year periods over 1965–90. She first estimates a simple growth model in which the explanatory variables are initial income, investment, population growth, and schooling. She then uses the coefficients on these variables to compute the residuals, and regresses the residuals on regional dummies. The Africa dummy is small and insignificant, that is, there is no continental fixed effect to explain. However, she does find that both being landlocked and being tropical significantly reduce growth, and these are indeed locational characteristics of much of Africa. Between them they would reduce the African growth rate by around 0.4 percentage points relative to that of other developing regions.

Whereas in the distant past the economies of Africa may well have been intrinsically disadvantaged by factors like less easy access to water transportation or the geography of the continent, the thesis that this has persisted into recent decades is less plausible. Remember that by 1950 Africa had a higher per capita income than south Asia and its subsequent performance was indistinguishable from that region until the mid-1970s. Coastal Africa is not intrinsically markedly worse-endowed in any geographical sense than much of coastal Asia or Brazil, although its soil types pose distinct challenges for agronomic research.

By contrast, it is easy to point to policies which until very recently have been dysfunctional. Even as of 1998, Africa had the worst policy environment in the world according to the World Bank ratings. Microeconomic evidence shows how these policies damaged the growth of firms. Poor infrastructure, poor contract enforcement and volatile policies all make the supply of inputs unreliable. Firms have responded to this risky environment partly by reducing risks: they hold large inventories, invest in electricity generators, and restrict their business relations to known enterprises. They have also responded by reducing investment. A striking implication is the conjunction of a high marginal return on capital and a very low rate of investment, even for firms that are not liquidity constrained. In Africa, the elasticity of investment with respect to profits may be as low as 0.07 (Bigsten et al., 1999). Some of the effects of poor policy are highly persistent. Most notably, the colonial governments of Africa provided little education, especially at the secondary level. Although independent governments rapidly changed these priorities, for the past 30 years Africa has had a markedly lower stock of human capital than other continents. The rapid growth in education has, however, gradually narrowed the gap with other regions.

Even if one disagrees with this view that policy is more important in explaining Africa's slow rate of growth and finds the "destiny" explanations more persuasive, this by no means condemns Africa to growing more slowly than other regions. Some of the economic disadvantages of being tropical may be overcome, for example, by the discovery of vaccines or new strains of crops. Moreover, Africa has two potential growth advantages over other regions which should offset against any locational disadvantage. It has lower per capita income and so could benefit from a convergence effect with richer countries, and it has higher aid inflows and so could benefit from aid-induced growth. If public policies were as good as in other regions, aid and convergence should enable even those countries which are land-locked and tropical to grow more rapidly than other developing regions for several decades. Although the growth regressions would imply that in the long term such countries would converge on a lower steady-state income than more favorably located countries, even this is doubtful. If the coastal African nations grew, then being landlocked would cease to be disadvantageous, since the gains from trading with close neighbors would expand.

Domestic or External?

Until recently, there was broad agreement that Africa's problems were predominantly associated with its external relations, although some analysts emphasized the policy-induced lack of openness and markets, while others attributed poor performance to over-dependence on a few commodities, the prices of which were declining and volatile. In our view, the argument that Africa's poor performance originates in its overdependence on commodities has looked weaker in recent years: Africa has lost global market share in its major exports, often spectacularly. The focus of the discussion has consequently shifted to underlying reasons for poor domestic performance, and in turn to domestic factors. The domestic factors, as we have argued, can be divided into those that smack of destiny, like the fact that much of Africa has a tropical climate, and those that are related to policy. Indeed, we believe that domestic policies largely unrelated to trade may now be the main obstacles to growth in much of Africa.

To illustrate our argument, we focus on Africa's failure to industrialize. It might appear that Africa is intrinsically uncompetitive in manufactures because of its high natural resource endowments give it a comparative advantage in that area (Wood and Mayer, 1998). But while Africa may have a comparative advantage in natural resources in the long run, at present African wages are often so low that were African manufacturing to have similar levels of productivity to other regions, it would be competitive. Hence, it is low productivity which needs to be explained.

African manufacturing has been in a low-productivity trap. Because African firms are oriented to small domestic markets, they are not able to exploit economies of scale, nor are they exposed to significant competition, and their technology gap with the rest of the world is unusually wide—yielding large opportunities for learning. This suggests that African manufacturing might have atypically large potential to raise productivity through exporting. However, most African firms fail to step onto this productivity escalator. This is because they face high costs for other reasons. As discussed already, transactions costs are unusually high. With transport unreliable, firms typically need to carry very large stocks of inputs to maintain continuity of production, despite higher interest rates than elsewhere. Telecommunications are much worse than other regions. Malfunctioning of the courts makes contract enforcement unreliable, so that firms are reluctant to enter into deals with new partners, in turn making markets less competitive.

These high transactions costs have a relatively large impact on manufacturing. Compared with natural resource extraction, manufacturing tends to have a high share of intermediate inputs and a low share of value-added to final price. Consequently, transactions costs tend to be much larger relative to value-added. Africa's intrinsic comparative advantage in natural resource exports may thus have been reinforced by public policies which have made manufacturing uncompetitive relative to resource extraction. African policies may have given the region a comparative disadvantage in transactions-intensive activities.

Conclusion: Will Africa Grow?

During the mid-1990s, average African growth accelerated and performance became more dispersed. A few countries such as Uganda, Côte d'Ivoire, Ethiopia and Mozambique started to grow very fast, whereas others such as the Democratic Republic of the Congo and Sierra Leone descended into social disorder. "Africa" became less meaningful as a category. Both the improvement in the average performance and the greater dispersion among countries were consistent with what had happened to policy. During the 1990s many of the most egregious exchange rate, fiscal and trade policies were improved. By 1998, although Africa still ranked as the region with the worst policies on the World Bank ratings, it was also the region with by far the greatest policy dispersion.

However, the faster growth coincided not only with better policies but with improvements in the terms of trade. Further, investment in Africa as a share of GDP is currently only 18 percent. This is much lower than other regions: for example, 23 percent in South Asia and 29 percent on average in lower middle-income countries. Even these figures may understate Africa's true investment shortfall. Capital goods are more expensive in Africa than the international average, so that once the investment share is recalculated at international relative prices it approximately halves. Although it is not possible to disaggregate investment into its public and private components with complete accuracy, estimates suggest that the shortfall in African investment is due to low private investment. Thus, growth may be unsustainable unless there is a substantial increase in private investment.

On an optimistic interpretation of the evidence, Africa's slow growth from the early 1970s into the 1990s has been due to policies which reduced its openness to foreign trade. Since these policies have largely been reversed during the last decade, if this is correct then Africa should be well-placed for continued growth.

The pessimistic interpretation is that Africa's problems are intrinsic, often rooted in geography. This view implies that economic progress in Africa will be dependent upon international efforts to make its environment more favorable, such as research to eradicate tropical diseases, and finance to create transport arteries from the coast to the interior. The thesis that Africa's economic problems are caused by ethno-linguistic fractionalization has similarly intractable implications.

Our own interpretation lies between these extremes. We suggest that while the binding constraint upon Africa's growth may have been externally-oriented policies in the past, those policies have now been softened. Today, the chief problem is those policies which are ostensibly domestically-oriented, notably poor delivery of public services. These problems are much more difficult to correct than exchange rate and trade policies, and so the policy reform effort needs to be intensified. However, even widespread policy reforms in this area might not be sufficient to induce a recovery in private investment, since recent economic reforms are never fully credible. Investment rating services list Africa as the riskiest region in the world. Indeed, there is some evidence that Africa suffers from being perceived by investors as a "bad neighborhood." Analysis of the global risk ratings shows that while they are largely explicable in terms of economic fundamentals, Africa as a whole is rated as significantly more risky than is warranted by these fundamentals (Haque et al., 1999). Similarly, private investment appears to be significantly lower in Africa than is explicable in terms of economic fundamentals (Jaspersen et al., 1999). "Africa" thus seems to be treated as a meaningful category by investors.

The perception of high risk for investing in Africa may partly be corrected by the passage of time, but reforming African governments can also take certain steps to commit themselves to defend economic reforms. Internationally, governments may increasingly make use of rules within the World Trade Organization, and shift their economic relations with the European Union from unreciprocated trade preferences to a wider range of reciprocated commitments. Domestically, there is a trend to freedom of the press, and the creation of independent centers of authority in central banks and revenue authorities, all of which should generally help to reinforce a climate of openness and democracy, which is likely to be supportive of economic reform.

REFERENCES

Ablo, Emanuel and Ritva Reinikka. 1998. "Do Budgets Really Matter? Evidence from Public Spending on Education and Health in Uganda." Policy Research Working Paper No. 1926, World Bank.

African Development Bank. 1998. *African Development Report*. Oxford: Oxford University Press.

Bates, Robert, H. 1983. *Essays in the Political Economy of Rural Africa*. Cambridge: Cambridge University Press.

Bauer, Peter T. 1982. "The Effects of Aid." *Encounter*. November.

Bevan, David L., Paul Collier and Jan Willem Gunning. 1993. *Agriculture and the policy environment: Tanzania and Kenya*. Paris: OECD.

Biggs, T., M. Raturi and P. Srivastava. 1996. "Enforcement of Contracts in an African Credit Market: Working Capital Financing in Kenyan Manufacturing." RPED Discussion Paper, Africa Region, World Bank.

Bigsten, Arne, P. Collier, S. Dercon, B. Gauthier, J. W. Gunning, A. Isaksson, A. Oduro, R. Oostendorp, C. Pattillo, M. Soderbom, M. Sylvain, F. Teal and A. Zeufack. 1999, forthcoming. "Investment by Manufacturing Firms in Africa: a Four-Country Panel Data Analysis." *Oxford Bulletin of Economics and Statistics*.

Bloom, John and Jeffrey Sachs. 1998. "Geography, Demography and Economic Growth in Africa." *Brookings Papers in Economic Activity*. 2, 207–95.

Burnside, Craig and David Dollar. 1997. "Aid, Policies and Growth." Policy Research Working Paper No. 1777, World Bank.

Collier, Paul. 1999. "The Political Economy of Ethnicity," in *Proceedings of the Annual Bank Conference on Development Economics*. Pleskovic, Boris and Joseph E. Stiglitz, eds. World Bank, Washington, D.C.

Collier, Paul and David Dollar. 1999a. "Aid Allocation and Poverty Reduction." Policy Research Working Paper 2041, World Bank, Washington, DC.

Collier, Paul and David Dollar. 1999b. "Aid, Risk and the Special Concerns of Small States." Mimeo, Policy Research Department, World Bank, Washington, DC.

Collier, Paul and Ashish Garg. 1999, forthcoming. "On Kin Groups and Wages in the Ghanaian Labour Market." *Oxford Bulletin of Economics and Statistics*, 61:2, pp. 131–51.

Collier, P. and J. W. Gunning. 1999. "Explaining African Economic Performance." *Journal of Economic Literature*. March, 37:1, 64–111.

Collier, P. and J.W. Gunning. 1999a, forthcoming. "The IMF's Role in Structural Adjustment." *Economic Journal*. World Bank, Washington, DC.

Collier, P. and J. W. Gunning with associates. 1999b. *Trade Shocks in Developing Countries: Theory and Evidence*. Oxford: Oxford University Press (Clarendon).

Collier, Paul and Anke Hoeffler. 1998. "On the Economic Causes of Civil War." *Oxford Economic Papers*. 50, pp. 563–73.

Collier, Paul and Anke Hoeffler. 1999. "Loot-Seeking and Justice-Seeking in Civil War." Mimeo, Development Research Department, World Bank, Washington, DC.

Collier, Paul and Catherine Pattillo, eds. 1999. *Investment and Risk in Africa*. Macmillan: London.

Collins, S. and B. P. Bosworth. 1996. "Economic Growth in East Asia: Accumulation versus Assimilation." *Brookings Papers in Economic Activity*, 2, pp. 135–203.

Deaton, A. and R. Miller. 1996. "International Commodity Prices, Macroeconomic Performance and Politics in Sub-Saharan Africa." *Journal of African Economies*. 5 (Supp.), pp. 99–191.

Dercon, Stefan. 1993. "Peasant supply response and macroeconomic policies: cotton in Tanzania." *Journal of African Economies*. 2, pp. 157–94.

Dercon, Stefan. 1997. "Wealth, Risk and Activity Choice: Cattle in Western Tanzania." *Journal of Development Economics*. 55:1, pp. 1–42.

Diamond, Jared. 1998. *Guns, Germs, and Steel: The Fates of Human Societies*. New York: W. W. Norton & Co.

Dollar, David. 1992. "Outward-Oriented Developing Economies Really do Grow More Rapidly: Evidence from 95 LDCs 1976–85." *Economic Development and Cultural Change*. 40, pp. 523–44.

Easterly, William and Ross Levine. 1997. "Africa's Growth Tragedy: Policies and Ethnic Divisions." *Quarterly Journal of Economics*. CXII, pp. 1203–1250.

Elbadawi, Ibrahim A., Benno J. Ndulu, and Njuguna Ndung'u. 1997. "Debt Overhang and Economic Growth in Sub-Saharan Africa," in *External Finance for Low-Income Countries*. Iqbal, Zubair and Ravi Kanbur, eds. IMF Institute, Washington, DC.

Fafchamps, Marcel, Jan Willem Gunning and Remco Oostendorp. 1998. "Inventories, Liquidity and Contractual Risk in African Manufacturing." Department of Economics, Stanford University, mimeo.

Gallup, John L. and Jeffrey D. Sachs. 1999. "Geography and Economic Growth," in *Proceedings of the Annual World Bank Conference on Development Economics*. Pleskovic, Boris and Joseph E. Stiglitz, eds. World Bank, Washington, DC.

Ghana Central Bureau of Statistics. 1988. *Quarterly Digest of Statistics*. Accra.

Grove, A. T. 1991. "The African Environment," in *Africa 30 Years On*. Rimmer, Douglas, ed. London: James Currey.

Gwin, Catherine and Joan Nelson. 1997. *Perspectives on Aid and Development*. Johns Hopkins for Overseas Development Council, Washington, DC.

Haque, Nadeem U., Nelson Mark and Donald J. Mathieson. 1999. "Risk in Africa: its Causes and its Effects on Investment," in *Investment and Risk in Africa*. Collier, Paul and Catherine Pattillo, eds. London: Macmillan.

Hoeffler, Anke A. 1999. "Econometric Studies of Growth, Convergence and Conflicts." D. Phil. Thesis, Oxford University.

Jaspersen, Frederick, Anthony H. Aylward and A. David Cox. 1999. "Risk and Private Investment: Africa Compared with Other Developing Areas," in *Investment and Risk in Africa*. Collier, Paul and Catherine Pattillo, eds. London: Macmillan.

Knack, Stephen and Phillip Keefer. 1995. Institutions and Economic Performance: Cross-Country Tests Using Alternative Institutional Measures." *Economics and Politics*. 7:3, pp. 207–28.

Kenya Central Bureau of Statistics. 1996. *Statistical Abstract*. Nairobi.

Kremer, Michael. 1993. "Population Growth and Technological Change: One Million B.C. to 1990." *Quarterly Journal of Economics*. 108:3, pp. 681–716.

Lee, K. S. and A. Anas. 1991. "Manufacturers' Responses to Infrastructure Deficiencies in Nigeria: Private Alternatives and Policy Options," in *Economic Reform in Africa*. Chibber, A. and S. Fischer, eds. World Bank, Washington, DC.

Maddison, Angus. 1995. *Monitoring the World Economy*. Paris: OECD.

Mauro, P. 1995. "Corruption and Growth." *Quarterly Journal of Economics*. 110, pp. 681–712.

McCallum, J. 1995. "National Borders Matter: Canada-U.S. Regional Trade Patterns." *American Economic Review*. 85, pp. 615–23.

Mengistae, Taye. 1998. "Ethiopia's Urban Economy: Empirical Essays on Enterprise Development and the Labour Market." D.Phil. Thesis, University of Oxford.

Pradhan, Sanjay. 1996. "Evaluating Public Spending." World Bank Discussion Paper 323, Washington, DC.

Reinikka, Ritva and Jakob Svensson. 1998. "Investment Response to Structural Reforms and Remaining Constraints: Firm Survey Evidence from Uganda." Mimeo, Africa Region, World Bank.

Rodrik, Dani. 1999. *Making Openness Work: The New Global Economy and the Developing Countries.* Overseas Development Council, Washington, DC.

Sachs, J. D. and Mark Warner. 1997. "Sources of Slow Growth in African Economies." *Journal of African Economies.* 6, pp. 335–76.

Schuknecht, Ludger. 1999. "Tying Governments' Hands in Commodity Taxation." *Journal of African Economies.* 8:2, 152–81.

Voortman, R. L., B.G.J.S. Sonneveld and M. A. Keyzer. 1999. "African Land Ecology: Opportunities and Constraints for Agricultural Development." Mimeo, Centre for World Food Studies, Free University, Amsterdam.

Widner, Jennifer, A. 1999. "The Courts as Restraints," in *Investment and Risk in Africa.* Collier, Paul and Catherine Pattillo, eds. London: Macmillan.

Wood, Adrian and J. Mayer. 1998. "Africa's Export Structure in Comparative Perspective," Study No. 4 of the UNCTAD series *Economic Development and Regional Dynamics in Africa: Lessons from the East Asian Experience.*

World Bank. 1997. *Confronting Aids*, Policy Research Report. Oxford University Press.

World Bank. 1998. *Assessing Aid: What Works, What Doesn't, and Why*, Policy Research Report. Oxford University Press.

World Bank. 1999. *World Development Indicators.* Development Data Center, Washington, D.C.

Paul Krugman

THE MYTH OF ASIA'S MIRACLE

A Cautionary Fable

Once upon a time, Western opinion leaders found themselves both impressed and frightened by the extraordinary growth rates achieved by a set of Eastern economies. Although those economies were still substantially poorer and smaller than those of the West, the speed with which they had transformed themselves from peasant societies into industrial powerhouses, their continuing ability to achieve growth rates several times higher than the advanced nations, and their increasing ability to challenge or even surpass American and European technology in certain areas seemed to call into question the dominance not only of Western power but of Western ideology. The leaders of those nations did not share our faith in free markets or unlimited civil liberties. They asserted with increasing self-confidence that their system was superior: societies that accepted strong, even authoritarian governments and were willing to limit individual liberties in the interest of the common good, take charge of their economies, and sacrifice short-run consumer interests for the sake of long-run growth would eventually outperform the increasingly chaotic societies of the West. And a growing minority of Western intellectuals agreed.

The gap between Western and Eastern economic performance eventually became a political issue. The Democrats recaptured the White House under the leadership of a young, energetic new president who pledged to "get the country moving again"— a pledge that, to him and his closest advisers, meant accelerating America's economic growth to meet the Eastern challenge.

The time, of course, was the early 1960s. The dynamic young president was John F. Kennedy. The technological feats that so alarmed the West were the launch of Sputnik and the early Soviet lead in space. And the rapidly growing Eastern economies were those of the Soviet Union and its satellite nations.

While the growth of communist economies was the subject of innumerable alarmist books and

From *Foreign Affairs* 73, no. 6 (November/December 1994), pp. 62–78.

polemical articles in the 1950s, some economists who looked seriously at the roots of that growth were putting together a picture that differed substantially from most popular assumptions. Communist growth rates were certainly impressive, but not magical. The rapid growth in output could be fully explained by rapid growth in inputs: expansion of employment, increases in education levels, and, above all, massive investment in physical capital. Once those inputs were taken into account, the growth in output was unsurprising—or, to put it differently, the big surprise about Soviet growth was that when closely examined it posed no mystery.

This economic analysis had two crucial implications. First, most of the speculation about the superiority of the communist system—including the popular view that Western economies could painlessly accelerate their own growth by borrowing some aspects of that system—was off base. Rapid Soviet economic growth was based entirely on one attribute: the willingness to save, to sacrifice current consumption for the sake of future production. The communist example offered no hint of a free lunch.

Second, the economic analysis of communist countries' growth implied some future limits to their industrial expansion—in other words, implied that a naive projection of their past growth rates into the future was likely to greatly overstate their real prospects. Economic growth that is based on expansion of inputs, rather than on growth in output per unit of input, is inevitably subject to diminishing returns. It was simply not possible for the Soviet economies to sustain the rates of growth of labor force participation, average education levels, and above all the physical capital stock that had prevailed in previous years. Communist growth would predictably slow down, perhaps drastically.

Can there really be any parallel between the growth of Warsaw Pact nations in the 1950s and the spectacular Asian growth that now preoccupies policy intellectuals? At some levels, of course, the parallel is far-fetched: Singapore in the 1990s does not look much like the Soviet Union in the 1950s, and

Singapore's Lee Kuan Yew bears little resemblance to the U.S.S.R.'s Nikita Khrushchev and less to Joseph Stalin. Yet the results of recent economic research into the sources of Pacific Rim growth give the few people who recall the great debate over Soviet growth a strong sense of déjà vu. Now, as then, the contrast between popular hype and realistic prospects, between conventional wisdom and hard numbers, remains so great that sensible economic analysis is not only widely ignored, but when it does get aired, it is usually dismissed as grossly implausible.

Popular enthusiasm about Asia's boom deserves to have some cold water thrown on it. Rapid Asian growth is less of a model for the West than many writers claim, and the future prospects for that growth are more limited than almost anyone now imagines. Any such assault on almost universally held beliefs must, of course, overcome a barrier of incredulity. This article began with a disguised account of the Soviet growth debate of 30 years ago to try to gain a hearing for the proposition that we may be revisiting an old error. We have been here before. The problem with this literary device, however, is that so few people now remember how impressive and terrifying the Soviet empire's economic performance once seemed. Before turning to Asian growth, then, it may be useful to review an important but largely forgotten piece of economic history.

"We Will Bury You"

Living in a world strewn with the wreckage of the Soviet empire, it is hard for most people to realize that there was a time when the Soviet economy, far from being a byword for the failure of socialism, was one of the wonders of the world—that when Khrushchev pounded his shoe on the U.N. podium and declared, "We will bury you," it was an economic rather than a military boast. It is therefore a shock to browse through, say, issues of *Foreign Affairs* from the mid-1950s through the early 1960s and discover that at least one article a year dealt with the implications of growing Soviet industrial might.

Illustrative of the tone of discussion was a 1957 article by Calvin B. Hoover.[1] Like many Western economists, Hoover criticized official Soviet statistics, arguing that they exaggerated the true growth rate. Nonetheless, he concluded that Soviet claims of astonishing achievement were fully justified: their economy was achieving a rate of growth "twice as high as that attained by any important capitalistic country over any considerable number of years [and] three times as high as the average annual rate of increase in the United States." He concluded that it was probable that "a collectivist, authoritarian state" was inherently better at achieving economic growth than free-market democracies and projected that the Soviet economy might outstrip that of the United States by the early 1970s.

These views were not considered outlandish at the time. On the contrary, the general image of Soviet central planning was that it might be brutal, and might not do a very good job of providing consumer goods, but that it was very effective at promoting industrial growth. In 1960 Wassily Leontief described the Soviet economy as being "directed with determined ruthless skill"—and did so without supporting argument, confident he was expressing a view shared by his readers.

Yet many economists studying Soviet growth were gradually coming to a very different conclusion. Although they did not dispute the fact of past Soviet growth, they offered a new interpretation of the nature of that growth, one that implied a reconsideration of future Soviet prospects. To understand this reinterpretation, it is necessary to make a brief detour into economic theory to discuss a seemingly abstruse, but in fact intensely practical, concept: growth accounting.

Accounting for the Soviet Slowdown

It is a tautology that economic expansion represents the sum of two sources of growth. On one side are increases in "inputs": growth in employment, in the education level of workers, and in the stock of physical capital (machines, buildings, roads, and so on). On the other side are increases in the output per unit of input; such increases may result from better management or better economic policy, but in the long run are primarily due to increases in knowledge.

The basic idea of growth accounting is to give life to this formula by calculating explicit measures of both. The accounting can then tell us how much of growth is due to each input—say, capital as opposed to labor—and how much is due to increased efficiency.

We all do a primitive form of growth accounting every time we talk about labor productivity; in so doing we are implicitly distinguishing between the part of overall national growth due to the growth in the supply of labor and the part due to an increase in the value of goods produced by the average worker. Increases in labor productivity, however, are not always caused by the increased efficiency of workers. Labor is only one of a number of inputs; workers may produce more, not because they are better managed or have more technological knowledge, but simply because they have better machinery. A man with a bulldozer can dig a ditch faster than one with only a shovel, but he is not more efficient; he just has more capital to work with. The aim of growth accounting is to produce an index that combines all measurable inputs and to measure the rate of growth of national income relative to that index—to estimate what is known as "total factor productivity."[2]

So far this may seem like a purely academic exercise. As soon as one starts to think in terms of growth accounting, however, one arrives at a crucial insight about the process of economic growth: sustained growth in a nation's per capita income can only occur if there is a rise in output *per unit of input*.[3]

Mere increases in inputs, without an increase in the efficiency with which those inputs are used—investing in more machinery and infrastructure—must run into diminishing returns; input-driven growth is inevitably limited.

How, then, have today's advanced nations been able to achieve sustained growth in per capita income over the past 150 years? The answer is that technological advances have led to a continual increase in total factor productivity—a continual rise in national income for each unit of input. In a famous estimate, MIT Professor Robert Solow concluded that technological progress has accounted for 80 percent of the long-term rise in U.S. per capita income, with increased investment in capital explaining only the remaining 20 percent.

When economists began to study the growth of the Soviet economy, they did so using the tools of growth accounting. Of course, Soviet data posed some problems. Not only was it hard to piece together usable estimates of output and input (Raymond Powell, a Yale professor, wrote that the job "in many ways resembled an archaeological dig"), but there were philosophical difficulties as well. In a socialist economy one could hardly measure capital input using market returns, so researchers were forced to impute returns based on those in market economies at similar levels of development. Still, when the efforts began, researchers were pretty sure about what they would find. Just as capitalist growth had been based on growth in both inputs and efficiency, with efficiency the main source of rising per capita income, they expected to find that rapid Soviet growth reflected both rapid input growth and rapid growth in efficiency.

But what they actually found was that Soviet growth was based on rapid growth in inputs—end of story. The rate of efficiency growth was not only unspectacular, it was well below the rates achieved in Western economies. Indeed, by some estimates, it was virtually nonexistent.[4]

The immense Soviet efforts to mobilize economic resources were hardly news. Stalinist planners had moved millions of workers from farms to cities, pushed millions of women into the labor force and millions of men into longer hours, pursued massive programs of education, and above all plowed an ever-growing proportion of the country's industrial output back into the construction of new factories. Still, the big surprise was that once one had taken the effects of these more or less measurable inputs

into account, there was nothing left to explain. The most shocking thing about Soviet growth was its comprehensibility.

This comprehensibility implied two crucial conclusions. First, claims about the superiority of planned over market economies turned out to be based on a misapprehension. If the Soviet economy had a special strength, it was its ability to mobilize resources, not its ability to use them efficiently. It was obvious to everyone that the Soviet Union in 1960 was much less efficient than the United States. The surprise was that it showed no signs of closing the gap.

Second, because input-driven growth is an inherently limited process, Soviet growth was virtually certain to slow down. Long before the slowing of Soviet growth became obvious, it was predicted on the basis of growth accounting. (Economists did not predict the implosion of the Soviet economy a generation later, but that is a whole different problem.)

It's an interesting story and a useful cautionary tale about the dangers of naive extrapolation of past trends. But is it relevant to the modern world?

Paper Tigers

At first, it is hard to see anything in common between the Asian success stories of recent years and the Soviet Union of three decades ago. Indeed, it is safe to say that the typical business traveler to, say, Singapore, ensconced in one of that city's gleaming hotels, never even thinks of any parallel to its roach-infested counterparts in Moscow. How can the slick exuberance of the Asian boom be compared with the Soviet Union's grim drive to industrialize?

And yet there are surprising similarities. The newly industrializing countries of Asia, like the Soviet Union of the 1950s, have achieved rapid growth in large part through an astonishing mobilization of resources. Once one accounts for the role of rapidly growing inputs in these countries' growth, one finds little left to explain. Asian growth, like that of the Soviet Union in its high-growth era, seems to be driven by extraordinary growth in inputs like labor and capital rather than by gains in efficiency.[5]

Consider, in particular, the case of Singapore. Between 1966 and 1990, the Singaporean economy grew a remarkable 8.5 percent per annum, three times as fast as the United States; per capita income grew at a 6.6 percent rate, roughly doubling every decade. This achievement seems to be a kind of economic miracle. But the miracle turns out to have been based on perspiration rather than inspiration: Singapore grew through a mobilization of resources that would have done Stalin proud. The employed share of the population surged from 27 to 51 percent. The educational standards of that work force were dramatically upgraded: while in 1966 more than half the workers had no formal education at all, by 1990 two-thirds had completed secondary education. Above all, the country had made an awesome investment in physical capital: investment as a share of output rose from 11 to more than 40 percent.[6]

Even without going through the formal exercise of growth accounting, these numbers should make it obvious that Singapore's growth has been based largely on one-time changes in behavior that cannot be repeated. Over the past generation the percentage of people employed has almost doubled; it cannot double again. A half-educated work force has been replaced by one in which the bulk of workers has high school diplomas; it is unlikely that a generation from now most Singaporeans will have Ph.D.s. And an investment share of 40 percent is amazingly high by any standard; a share of 70 percent would be ridiculous. So one can immediately conclude that Singapore is unlikely to achieve future growth rates comparable to those of the past.

But it is only when one actually does the quantitative accounting that the astonishing result emerges: all of Singapore's growth can be explained by increases in measured inputs. There is no sign at all of increased efficiency. In this sense, the growth of Lee Kuan Yew's Singapore is an economic twin of the growth of Stalin's Soviet Union—growth achieved purely through mobilization of resources.

Of course, Singapore today is far more prosperous than the U.S.S.R. ever was—even at its peak in the Brezhnev years—because Singapore is closer to, though still below, the efficiency of Western economies. The point, however, is that Singapore's economy has always been relatively efficient; it just used to be starved of capital and educated workers.

Singapore's case is admittedly the most extreme. Other rapidly growing East Asian economies have not increased their labor force participation as much, made such dramatic improvements in educational levels, or raised investment rates quite as far. Nonetheless, the basic conclusion is the same: there is startlingly little evidence of improvements in efficiency. Kim and Lau conclude of the four Asian "tigers" that "the hypothesis that there has been no technical progress during the postwar period cannot be rejected for the four East Asian newly industrialized countries." Young, more poetically, notes that once one allows for their rapid growth of inputs, the productivity performance of the "tigers" falls "from the heights of Olympus to the plains of Thessaly."

This conclusion runs so counter to conventional wisdom that it is extremely difficult for the economists who have reached it to get a hearing. As early as 1982 a Harvard graduate student, Yuan Tsao, found little evidence of efficiency growth in her dissertation on Singapore, but her work was, as Young puts it, "ignored or dismissed as unbelievable." When Kim and Lau presented their work at a 1992 conference in Taipei, it received a more respectful hearing, but had little immediate impact. But when Young tried to make the case for input-driven Asian growth at the 1993 meetings of the European Economic Association, he was met with a stone wall of disbelief.

In Young's most recent paper there is an evident tone of exasperation with this insistence on clinging to the conventional wisdom in the teeth of the evidence. He titles the paper "The Tyranny of Numbers"—by which he means that you may not want to believe this, buster, but there's just no way around the data. He begins with an ironic introduction, written in a deadpan, Sergeant Friday, "Just the facts, ma'am" style: "This is a fairly boring and tedious paper, and is intentionally so. This paper provides no new interpretations of the East Asian experience to interest the historian, derives no new theoretical implications of the forces behind the East Asian growth process to motivate the theorist, and draws no new policy implications from the subtleties of East Asian government intervention to excite the policy activist. Instead, this paper concentrates its energies on providing a careful analysis of the historical patterns of output growth, factor accumulation, and productivity growth in the newly industrializing countries of East Asia."

Of course, he is being disingenuous. His conclusion undermines most of the conventional wisdom about the future role of Asian nations in the world economy and, as a consequence, in international politics. But readers will have noticed that the statistical analysis that puts such a different interpretation on Asian growth focuses on the "tigers," the relatively small countries to whom the name "newly industrializing countries" was first applied. But what about the large countries? What about Japan and China?

The Great Japanese Growth Slowdown

Many people who are committed to the view that the destiny of the world economy lies with the Pacific Rim are likely to counter skepticism about East Asian growth prospects with the example of Japan. Here, after all, is a country that started out poor and has now become the second-largest industrial power. Why doubt that other Asian nations can do the same?

There are two answers to that question. First, while many authors have written of an "Asian system"—a common denominator that underlies all of the Asian success stories—the statistical evidence tells a different story. Japan's growth in the 1950s and 1960s does not resemble Singapore's growth in the 1970s and 1980s. Japan, unlike the East Asian "tigers," seems to have grown both through high rates

of input growth and through high rates of efficiency growth. Today's fast-growth economies are nowhere near converging on U.S. efficiency levels, but Japan is staging an unmistakable technological catch-up.

Second, while Japan's historical performance has indeed been remarkable, the era of miraculous Japanese growth now lies well in the past. Most years Japan still manages to grow faster than the other advanced nations, but that gap in growth rates is now far smaller than it used to be, and is shrinking.

The story of the great Japanese growth slowdown has been oddly absent from the vast polemical literature on Japan and its role in the world economy. Much of that literature seems stuck in a time warp, with authors writing as if Japan were still the miracle growth economy of the 1960s and early 1970s. Granted, the severe recession that has gripped Japan since 1991 will end soon if it has not done so already, and the Japanese economy will probably stage a vigorous short-term recovery. The point, however, is that even a full recovery will only reach a level that is far below what many sensible observers predicted 20 years ago.

It may be useful to compare Japan's growth prospects as they appeared 20 years ago and as they appear now. In 1973 Japan was still a substantially smaller and poorer economy than the United States. Its per capita GDP was only 55 percent of America's, while its overall GDP was only 27 percent as large. But the rapid growth of the Japanese economy clearly portended a dramatic change. Over the previous decade Japan's real GDP had grown at a torrid 8.9 percent annually, with per capita output growing at a 7.7 percent rate. Although American growth had been high by its own historical standards, at 3.9 percent (2.7 percent per capita) it was not in the same league. Clearly, the Japanese were rapidly gaining on us.

In fact, a straightforward projection of these trends implied that a major reversal of positions lay not far in the future. At the growth rate of 1963–73, Japan would overtake the United States in real per capita income by 1985, and total Japanese output would exceed that of the United States by 1998! At the time, people took such trend projections very seriously indeed. One need only look at the titles of such influential books as Herman Kahn's *The Emerging Japanese Superstate* or Ezra Vogel's *Japan as Number One* to remember that Japan appeared, to many observers, to be well on its way to global economic dominance.

Well, it has not happened, at least not so far. Japan has indeed continued to rise in the economic rankings, but at a far more modest pace than those projections suggested. In 1992 Japan's per capita income was still only 83 percent of the United States', and its overall output was only 42 percent of the American level. The reason was that growth from 1973 to 1992 was far slower than in the high-growth years: GDP grew only 3.7 percent annually, and GDP per capita grew only 3 percent per year. The United States also experienced a growth slowdown after 1973, but it was not nearly as drastic.

If one projects those post-1973 growth rates into the future, one still sees a relative Japanese rise, but a far less dramatic one. Following 1973–92 trends, Japan's per capita income will outstrip that of the United States in 2002; its overall output does not exceed America's until the year 2047. Even this probably overestimates Japanese prospects. Japanese economists generally believe that their country's rate of growth of potential output, the rate that it will be able to sustain once it has taken up the slack left by the recession, is now no more than 3 percent. And that rate is achieved only through a very high rate of investment, nearly twice as high a share of GDP as in the United States. When one takes into account the growing evidence for at least a modest acceleration of U.S. productivity growth in the last few years, one ends up with the probable conclusion that Japanese efficiency is gaining on that of the United States at a snail's pace, if at all, and there is the distinct possibility that per capita income in Japan may never overtake that in America. In other words, Japan is not quite as overwhelming an example of economic prowess as is sometimes thought, and in any case Japan's experience has much less in common with that of other Asian nations than is generally imagined.

The China Syndrome

For the skeptic, the case of China poses much greater difficulties about Asian destiny than that of Japan. Although China is still a very poor country, its population is so huge that it will become a major economic power if it achieves even a fraction of Western productivity levels. And China, unlike Japan, has in recent years posted truly impressive rates of economic growth. What about its future prospects?

Accounting for China's boom is difficult for both practical and philosophical reasons. The practical problem is that while we know that China is growing very rapidly, the quality of the numbers is extremely poor. It was recently revealed that official Chinese statistics on foreign investment have been overstated by as much as a factor of six. The reason was that the government offers tax and regulatory incentives to foreign investors, providing an incentive for domestic entrepreneurs to invent fictitious foreign partners or to work through foreign fronts. This episode hardly inspires confidence in any other statistic that emanates from that dynamic but awesomely corrupt society.

The philosophical problem is that it is unclear what year to use as a baseline. If one measures Chinese growth from the point at which it made a decisive turn toward the market, say 1978, there is little question that there has been dramatic improvement in efficiency as well as rapid growth in inputs. But it is hardly surprising that a major recovery in economic efficiency occurred as the country emerged from the chaos of Mao Zedong's later years. If one instead measures growth from before the Cultural Revolution, say 1964, the picture looks more like the East Asian "tigers": only modest growth in efficiency, with most growth driven by inputs. This calculation, however, also seems unfair: one is weighing down the buoyant performance of Chinese capitalism with the leaden performance of Chinese socialism. Perhaps we should simply split the difference: guess that some, but not all, of the efficiency gains since the turn toward the market represent a one-time recovery, while the rest represent a sustainable trend.

Even a modest slowing in China's growth will change the geopolitical outlook substantially. The World Bank estimates that the Chinese economy is currently about 40 percent as large as that of the United States. Suppose that the U.S. economy continues to grow at 2.5 percent each year. If China can continue to grow at 10 percent annually, by the year 2010 its economy will be a third larger than ours. But if Chinese growth is only a more realistic 7 percent, its GDP will be only 82 percent of that of the United States. There will still be a substantial shift of the world's economic center of gravity, but it will be far less drastic than many people now imagine.

The Mystery That Wasn't

The extraordinary record of economic growth in the newly industrializing countries of East Asia has powerfully influenced the conventional wisdom about both economic policy and geopolitics. Many, perhaps most, writers on the global economy now take it for granted that the success of these economies demonstrates three propositions. First, there is a major diffusion of world technology in progress, and Western nations are losing their traditional advantage. Second, the world's economic center of gravity will inevitably shift to the Asian nations of the western Pacific. Third, in what is perhaps a minority view, Asian successes demonstrate the superiority of economies with fewer civil liberties and more planning than we in the West have been willing to accept.

All three conclusions are called into question by the simple observation that the remarkable record of East Asian growth has been matched by input growth so rapid that Asian economic growth, incredibly, ceases to be a mystery.

Consider first the assertion that the advanced countries are losing their technological advantage. A heavy majority of recent tracts on the world economy have taken it as self-evident that technology now increasingly flows across borders, and that newly industrializing nations are increasingly able to match the productivity of more established economies. Many writers warn that this diffusion of technology will place huge strains on Western society as capital flows to the Third World and imports from those nations undermine the West's industrial base.

There are severe conceptual problems with this scenario even if its initial premise is right.[7] But in any case, while technology may have diffused within particular industries, the available evidence provides absolutely no justification for the view that overall world technological gaps are vanishing. On the contrary, Kim and Lau find "no apparent convergence between the technologies" of the newly industrialized nations and the established industrial powers; Young finds that the rates in the growth of efficiency in the East Asian "tigers" are no higher than those in many advanced nations.

The absence of any dramatic convergence in technology helps explain what would otherwise be a puzzle: in spite of a great deal of rhetoric about North-South capital movement, actual capital flows to developing countries in the 1990s have so far been very small—and they have primarily gone to Latin America, not East Asia. Indeed, several of the East Asian "tigers" have recently become significant exporters of capital. This behavior would be extremely odd if these economies, which still pay wages well below advanced-country levels, were rapidly achieving advanced-country productivity. It is, however, perfectly reasonable if growth in East Asia has been primarily input-driven, and if the capital piling up there is beginning to yield diminishing returns.

If growth in East Asia is indeed running into diminishing returns, however, the conventional wisdom about an Asian-centered world economy needs some rethinking. It would be a mistake to overstate this case: barring a catastrophic political upheaval, it is likely that growth in East Asia will continue to outpace growth in the West for the next decade and beyond. But it will not do so at the pace of recent years. From the perspective of the year 2010, current projections of Asian supremacy extrapolated from recent trends may well look almost as silly as 1960's-vintage forecasts of Soviet industrial supremacy did from the perspective of the Brezhnev years.

Finally, the realities of East Asian growth suggest that we may have to unlearn some popular lessons. It has become common to assert that East Asian economic success demonstrates the fallacy of our traditional laissez-faire approach to economic policy and that the growth of these economies shows the effectiveness of sophisticated industrial policies and selective protectionism. Authors such as James Fallows have asserted that the nations of that region have evolved a common "Asian system," whose lessons we ignore at our peril. The extremely diverse institutions and policies of the various newly industrialized Asian countries, let alone Japan, cannot really be called a common system. But in any case, if Asian success reflects the benefits of strategic trade and industrial policies, those benefits should surely be manifested in an unusual and impressive rate of growth in the efficiency of the economy. And there is no sign of such exceptional efficiency growth.

The newly industrializing countries of the Pacific Rim have received a reward for their extraordinary mobilization of resources that is no more than what the most boringly conventional economic theory would lead us to expect. If there is a secret to Asian growth, it is simply deferred gratification, the willingness to sacrifice current satisfaction for future gain.

That's a hard answer to accept, especially for those American policy intellectuals who recoil from the dreary task of reducing deficits and raising the national savings rate. But economics is not a dismal science because the economists like it that way; it is because in the end we must submit to the tyranny not just of the numbers, but of the logic they express.

NOTES

1. Hoover's tone—critical of Soviet data but nonetheless accepting the fact of extraordinary achievement—was typical of much of the commentary of the time (see, for example, a series of articles in *The Atlantic Monthly* by Edward Crankshaw, beginning with "Soviet Industry" in the November 1955 issue). Anxiety about the political implications of Soviet growth reached its high-water mark in 1959, the year Khrushchev visited America. *Newsweek* took Khrushchev's boasts seriously enough to warn that the Soviet Union might well be "on the high road to economic domination of the world." And in hearings held by the Joint Economic Committee late that year, CIA Director Allen Dulles warned, "If the Soviet industrial growth rate persists at eight or nine percent per annum over the next decade, as is forecast, the gap between our two economies . . . will be dangerously narrowed."

2. At first, creating an index of all inputs may seem like comparing apples and oranges, that is, trying to add together noncomparable items like the hours a worker puts in and the cost of the new machine he uses. How does one determine the weights for the different components? The economists' answer is to use market returns. If the average worker earns $15 an hour, give each person-hour in the index a weight of $15; if a machine that costs $100,000 on average earns $10,000 in profits each year (a 10 percent rate of return), then give each such machine a weight of $10,000; and so on.

3. To see why, let's consider a hypothetical example. To keep matters simple, let's assume that the country has a stationary population and labor force, so that all increases in the investment in machinery, etc., raise the amount of capital per worker in the country. Let us finally make up some arbitrary numbers. Specifically, let us assume that initially each worker is equipped with $10,000 worth of equipment; that each worker produces goods and services worth $10,000; and that capital initially earns a 40 percent rate of return, that is, each $10,000 of machinery earns annual profits of $4,000. Suppose, now, that this country consistently invests 20 percent of its output, that is, uses 20 percent of its income to add to its capital stock. How rapidly will the economy grow?

Initially, very fast indeed. In the first year, the capital stock per worker will rise by 20 percent of $10,000, that is, by $2,000. At a 40 percent rate of return, that will increase output by $800: an 8 percent rate of growth.

But this high rate of growth will not be sustainable. Consider the situation of the economy by the time that capital per worker has doubled to $20,000. First, output per worker will not have increased in the same proportion, because capital stock is only one input. Even with the additions to capital stock up to that point achieving a 40 percent rate of return, output per worker will have increased only to $14,000. And the rate of return is also certain to decline—say to 30 or even 25 percent. (One bulldozer added to a construction project can make a huge difference to productivity. By the time a dozen are on-site, one more may not make that much difference.) The combination of those factors means that if the investment share of output is the same, the growth rate will sharply decline. Taking 20 percent of $14,000 gives us $2,800; at a 30 percent rate of return, this will raise output by only $840, that is, generate a growth rate of only 6 percent; at a 25 percent rate of return it will generate a growth rate of only 5 percent. As capital continues to accumulate, the rate of return and hence the rate of growth will continue to decline.

4. This work was summarized by Raymond Powell, "Economic Growth in the U.S.S.R.," *Scientific American*, December 1968.

5. There have been a number of recent efforts to quantify the sources of rapid growth in the Pacific Rim. Key readings include two papers by Professor Lawrence Lau of Stanford University and his associate Jong-Il Kim, "The Sources of Growth of the East Asian Newly Industrialized Countries," *Journal of the Japanese and International Economies*, 1994, and "The Role of Human Capital in the Economic Growth of the East Asian Newly Industrialized Countries," mimeo, Stanford University, 1993; and three papers by Professor Alwyn Young, a rising star in growth economics, "A Tale of Two Cities: Factor Accumulation and Technical Change in Hong Kong and Singapore," *NBER Macroeconomics Annual 1992*, MIT Press; "Lessons from the East Asian NICS: A Contrarian View," *European Economic Review Papers and Proceedings*, May 1994; and "The Tyranny of Numbers: Confronting the Statistical Realities of the East Asian Growth Experience," NBER Working Paper No. 4680, March 1994.

6. These figures are taken from Young, *ibid.* Although foreign corporations have played an important role in Singapore's economy, the great bulk of investment in Singapore, as in all of the newly industrialized East Asian economies, has been financed out of domestic savings.

7. See Paul Krugman, "Does Third World Growth Hurt First World Prosperity?" *Harvard Business Review*, July 1994.

Wayne Arnold

VIETNAM HOLDS ITS OWN WITHIN CHINA'S VAST ECONOMIC SHADOW

One of the biggest beneficiaries of China's rapid economic ascent is not China at all, but rather its historic rival, occasional enemy and fellow socialist neighbor to the south, Vietnam.

From *The New York Times* (January 1, 2011).

Less than a decade ago, many economists and executives believed that China's allure was creating a "giant sucking sound" of investment that could be heard in distant Hanoi and Ho Chi Minh City.

Vietnam has instead managed to tag along, however, thanks to its own program of economic overhauls, a fast-growing population of 87 million people, cheap labor and a free-trade agreement that has enabled Vietnam to become part of the vast global supply chain that feeds China's manufacturing machine.

After following China down the path toward communism after World War II, therefore, Vietnam finds itself back in China's ideological slipstream. This time, Hanoi is driving toward what it calls a "socialist-oriented market economy," largely to keep from being run over by China's economic juggernaut.

"If China had not been there," said Jonathan Anderson, an economist at UBS in Hong Kong, "Vietnam may not have opened up." Vietnam officially reopened its doors to foreign investors in 1986. But it did not really become part of the Asian economic boom until it won back its former enemy, the United States, which lifted a trade embargo in 1994 and normalized trade with Vietnam in 2000.

The U.S. trade agreement provided special incentives to textile and garment makers, since it immediately cut U.S. tariffs on Vietnamese made brassieres and panties from roughly 60 percent to zero. Textile and garment makers from South Korea and Taiwan flocked to Vietnam to open new factories.

Other light manufacturing soon followed, like home appliances and motorbike assemblers, and another industry hitherto dominated by China—furniture. "That whole industry just gradually moved into Vietnam," said Frederick Burke, a lawyer at Baker & McKenzie in Ho Chi Minh City who has been working in Vietnam and advising its government for more than a decade.

When China joined the World Trade Organization in 2002, however, many feared that Vietnam and indeed much of Southeast Asia's days as a favored destination for foreign manufacturing investment were over. Some economists even warned that the region would have to surrender manufactured export-led development and instead focus on feeding China's voracious demand for raw materials.

China signed a free-trade agreement with Vietnam and the nine other members of the Association of Southeast Asian Nations in 2002 that seemed to reinforce such fears. While the agreement gave poorer nations like Vietnam until 2015 to open up to Chinese goods, China eliminated tariffs on their agricultural products in 2003.

The agreement was a boon for Vietnam, which aside from being a leading exporter of rice, pepper and coffee, is a net oil exporter. But as other nations like Singapore, Malaysia and Thailand scrambled to climb the value-added ladder with niche products or more technologically advanced products that enabled them at the least to stay in the race with China, Vietnam seemed destined to become a pantry for a rapidly developing China.

Then China stumbled. Rampant technological piracy, nationalist demonstrations and shortages of skilled labor prompted many foreign companies, particularly Japanese, to move some production back to Southeast Asia. Worse, wages in China were rising fast. "In the late 1990s and early 2000s, you could hire as much labor as you wanted in China. People now talk about rising labor costs," said Mr. Anderson.

Waiting with its own well-educated, disciplined but much cheaper work force was Vietnam. The minimum wage in Vietnam's two largest cities is still about $75 a month, as little as half what it costs to hire a worker in China's factory province of Guangdong, according to Dinh Tuan Viet, senior economist at the World Bank in Hanoi.

This year, Intel opened a new, $1 billion semiconductor factory near Ho Chi Minh City to replace facilities in Malaysia, the Philippines and China. Canon's printer factory near Hanoi, with more than 18,000 employees, is the company's largest.

Vietnam has now managed to establish itself firmly in China's supply chain. Many of the parts for Canon's factory come from China, for example, a fact that underscores the downside to Vietnamese efforts to follow in China's manufacturing footsteps—imports of machinery and equipment from China contribute to a roughly $11.5 billion trade deficit with China as Vietnam races to build up its infrastructure and manufacturing capacity.

Now, with China trying to take its next major leap forward into cleaner, more consumer-focused industries, the question is whether Vietnam has gotten far enough to advance in step with China, Mr. Viet said. "Is Vietnam ready and capable of absorbing a new wave of foreign investment resulting from 'structural change' in China?" he asked. "It seems to me there are still a lot of constraints for Vietnam to take this chance: poor infrastructure and an underdeveloped logistics industry, an abundant but unskilled labor force, etc."

For all of China's many obstacles, Vietnam still ranks below it in the World Bank's survey on the ease of doing business.

That survey ranks Vietnam above China in starting a business and employing workers, but below China in protecting investors and enforcing contracts. Vietnam also ranks low on Transparency International's Corruption Perceptions Index — 116th, compared with 78th for China.

Still, Vietnam seems to have won favor as an alternative to China for foreign investors. Foreign direct investment into Vietnam rose almost fourfold between 2005 and 2008, according to the World Bank, to $9.58 billion, and slipped 20 percent during the crisis in 2009 to $7.6 billion. In China it almost halved.

Daron Acemoglu and Simon Johnson

DISEASE AND DEVELOPMENT: THE EFFECT OF LIFE EXPECTANCY ON ECONOMIC GROWTH

I. Introduction

Improving health around the world today is an important social objective, which has obvious direct payoffs in terms of longer and better lives for millions. There is also a growing consensus that improving health can have equally large indirect payoffs through accelerating economic growth (see, e.g., Bloom and Sachs 1998; Gallup and Sachs 2001; WHO 2001; Alleyne and Cohen 2002; Bloom and Canning 2005; Lorentzen, McMillan, and Wacziarg 2005). For example, Gallup and Sachs (2001, 91) argue that wiping out malaria in sub-Saharan Africa could increase that continent's per capita growth rate by as much as 2.6 percent a year, and a recent report

by the World Health Organization states that "in today's world, poor health has particularly pernicious effects on economic development in sub-Saharan Africa, South Asia, and pockets of high disease and intense poverty elsewhere" (WHO 2001, 24) and "extending the coverage of crucial health services . . . to the world's poor could save millions of lives each year, reduce poverty, spur economic development and promote global security" (i).

The evidence supporting this recent consensus is not yet conclusive, however. Although cross-country regression studies show a strong correlation between measures of health (e.g., life expectancy) and both the level of economic development and recent economic growth, these studies have not established a causal effect of health and disease on economic growth. Since countries suffering from short life expectancy and ill health are also disadvantaged in

From *Journal of Democracy* 11, no. 6 (2007), pp. 925–930, 975–976.

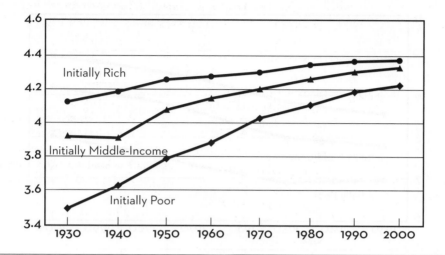

other ways (and often this is the reason for their poor health outcomes), such macro studies may be capturing the negative effects of these other, often omitted, disadvantages. While a range of micro studies demonstrate the importance of health for individual productivity,[1] these studies do not resolve the question of whether health differences are at the root of the large income differences we observe because they do not incorporate general equilibrium effects. The most important general equilibrium effect arises because of diminishing returns to effective units of labor, for example, because land and/or physical capital are supplied inelastically. In the presence of such diminishing returns, micro estimates may exaggerate the aggregate productivity benefits from improved health, particularly when health improvements are accompanied by population increases.

This article investigates the effect of general health conditions, proxied by life expectancy at birth, on economic growth. We exploit the large improvements in life expectancy driven by international health interventions, more effective public health measures, and the introduction of new chemicals and drugs starting in the 1940s. This episode, which we refer to as the *international epidemiological transition*, led to an unprecedented improvement in life expectancy in a large number of countries.[2] Figure 10.1 shows this by plotting life expectancy in countries that were initially (circa 1940) poor, middle-income, and rich. It illustrates that while in the 1930s life expectancy was low in many poor and middle-income contries, this transition brought their levels of life expectancy close to those prevailing in richer parts of the world.[3] As a consequence, health conditions in many poor countries today, though still in dire need of improvement, are significantly better than the corresponding health conditions were in the West at the same stage of development.[4]

The international epidemiological transition provides us with an empirical strategy to isolate potentially exogenous changes in health conditions. The effects of the international epidemiological transition on a country's life expectancy were related to the extent to which its population was initially (circa 1940) affected by various specific diseases, for example, tuberculosis, malaria, and pneumonia, and to the timing of the various health interventions.

The early data on mortality by disease are available from standard international sources, though they have not been widely used in the * * *

Fig 10.2 Log GDP per capita for initially rich, middle-income, and poor countries in the base sample

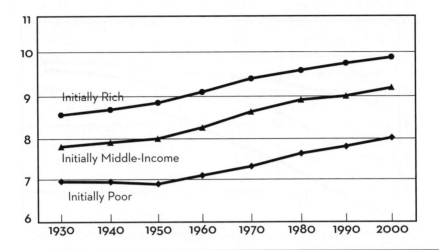

literature. These data allow us to create an instrument for changes in life expectancy based on the preintervention distribution of mortality from various diseases around the world and the dates of global intervention (e.g., discovery and mass production of penicillin and streptomycin, or the discovery and widespread use of DDT against mosquito vectors). * * * We document that there were large declines in disease-specific mortality following these global interventions. More important, we show that the predicted mortality instrument has a large and robust effect on changes in life expectancy starting in 1940, but has no effect on changes in life expectancy prior to this date (i.e., before the key interventions).

The instrumented changes in life expectancy have a fairly large effect on population: a 1 percent increase in life expectancy is related to an approximately 1.7–2 percent increase in population over a 40–60–year horizon. The magnitude of this estimate indicates that the decline in fertility rates was insufficient to compensate for increased life expectancy, a result that we directly confirm by looking at the relationship between life expectancy and total births.

However, we find no statistically significant effect on total GDP * * *. More important, GDP per capita and GDP per working age population show relative declines in countries experiencing large increases in life expectancy. In fact, our estimates exclude any positive effects of life expectancy on GDP per capita within 40- or 60-year horizons. This is consistent with the overall pattern in Figure 10.2, which, in contrast to Figure 10.5, shows no convergence in income per capita between initially poor, middle-income, and rich countries. We document that these results are robust to a range of specification checks and to the inclusion of various controls. We also document that our results are not driven by life expectancy at very early ages. The predicted mortality instrument has a large, statistically significant and robust effect on life expectancy at 20 (and at other ages), and using life expectancy at 20 instead of life expectancy at birth as our measure of general health conditions leads to very similar results.

The most natural interpretation of our results comes from neoclassical growth theory. Increased life expectancy raises population, which initially reduces capital-to-labor and land-to-labor ratios, thus depressing income per capita. This initial decline is later compensated by higher output as more people enter the labor force and as more capital is accumulated. This compensation can be complete and may even exceed the initial level of income per capita if there are significant productivity benefits from longer life expectancy. Yet, the compensation may also be incomplete if the benefits from higher life expectancy are limited and if some factors of production, for example, land, are supplied inelastically.

Our findings do not imply that improved health has not been a great benefit to less developed nations during the postwar era. The accounting approach of Becker, Philipson, and Soares (2005), which incorporates information on longevity and health as well as standards of living, would suggest that these interventions have considerably improved "overall welfare" in these countries. What these interventions have not done, and in fact were not intended to do, is to increase output per capita in these countries.

Our article is most closely related to two recent contributions: Weil (2007) and Young (2005). Weil calibrates the effects of health using a range of micro estimates and finds that these effects could be quite important in the aggregate.[5]*** Young evaluates the effect of the recent HIV/AIDS epidemic in Africa. Using micro estimates and calibration of the neoclassical growth model, he shows that the decline in population resulting from HIV/AIDS may increase income per capita despite significant disruptions and human suffering caused by the disease.[6]

■　　■　　■

VIII. Concluding Remarks

A recent consensus in academic and policy circles holds that differences in disease environments and health conditions lie at the root of large income differences across countries today and argues that improving health not only will improve lives but will by itself spur rapid economic growth.

■　　■　　■

Our results indicate that the increase in life expectancy led to a significant increase in population; birth rates did not decline sufficiently to compensate for the increase in life expectancy. We find a small positive effect of life expectancy on total GDP over the first 40 years, and this effect grows somewhat over the next 20 years, but not enough to compensate for the increase in population. Overall, the increases in life expectancy (and the associated increases in population) appear to have reduced income per capita. There is no evidence that the increase in life expectancy led to faster growth of income per capita or output per worker. This evidence casts doubt on the view that health has a first-order impact on economic growth.

Considerable caution is necessary in interpreting our results for at least two reasons. The most important limitation is that because our approach exploits the international epidemiological transition around the 1940s, the results may not be directly applicable to today's world; the international epidemiological transition was a unique event, and perhaps similar changes in life expectancy today would not lead to an increase in population and the impact on GDP per capita may be more positive. Second, the diseases that take many lives in the poorer parts of the world today are not the same ones as those 60 years ago; most notably HIV/AIDS is a major killer today but was not so in 1940. Many of the diseases we focus on had serious impacts on children (with the notable exception of tuberculosis), whereas HIV/AIDS affects individuals at the peak of their labor productivity and could have a larger negative impact on growth. Further study of the effects of the HIV/AIDS epidemic on economic outcomes as well as more detailed analysis of different measures of health on human capital investments and economic outcomes are major areas for future research.

NOTES

1. See Strauss and Thomas (1998) for an excellent survey of the research through the late 1990s. For some of the more recent research, see Schultz (2002),

Bleakley (2003, 2007), Behrman and Rosenzweig (2004), and Miguel and Kremer (2004).

2. The term "epidemiological transition" was coined by demographers and refers to the process of falling mortality rates after about 1850, associated with the switch from infectious to degenerative disease as the major cause of death (Omran 1971). Some authors prefer the term "health transition," since this includes the changing nature of ill health more generally (e.g., Riley 2001). We focus on the rapid decline in mortality (and improvement in health) in poorer countries after 1940, most of which was driven by the fast spread of new technologies and practices around the world (hence the adjective "international"). The seminal works on this episode include Stolnitz (1955), Omran (1971), and Preston (1975).

3. In this figure and throughout the article, rich countries are those with income per capita in 1940 above the level of Argentina (the richest Latin American country at that time, according to Maddison's [2003] data, in our base sample).

4. For example, life expectancy at birth in India in 1999 was 60 compared to 40 in Britain in 1820, when income per capita was approximately the same level as in India today (Maddison 2001, 30). According to Maddison (264), income per capita in Britain in 1820 was $1,707, whereas it stood at $1,746 in India in 1998 (all figures in 1990 international dollars).

5. Weil's baseline estimate uses the return to the age of menarche from Knaul's (2000) work on Mexico as a general indicator of "overall return to health." Using Behrman and Rosenzweig's (2004) estimates from returns to birth weight differences in monozygotic twins, he finds smaller effects.

6. For more pessimistic views on the economic consequences of HIV/AIDS, see Arndt and Lewis (2000), Bell, Devarajan, and Gersbach (2003), Forston (2006), and Kalemli-Ozcan (2006).

REFERENCES

Alleyne, George A. O., and Daniel Cohen. 2002. "The Report of Working Group I of the Commission on Macroeconomics and Health." WHO Comm. on Macroeconomics and Health, Geneva.

Arndt, Channing, and Jeffrey D. Lewis. 2000. "The Macro Implications of HIV/AIDS in South Africa: A Preliminary Assessment." *South African J. Econ.* 68 (December): 380–92.

Becker, Gary S., Tomas J. Philipson, and Rodrigo R. Soares. 2005. "The Quantity and Quality of Life and the Evolution of World Inequality." *A.E.R.* 95 (March): 277–91.

Behrman, Jere R., and Mark R. Rosenzweig. 2004. "Returns to Birthweight." *Rev. Econ. and Statis.* 86 (May): 586–601.

Bell, Clive, Shantanyanan Devarajan, and Hans Gersbach. 2003. "The Long-Run Economic Costs of AIDS: Theory and an Application to South Africa." Policy Research Paper no. 3152 (October), World Bank, Washington, DC.

Bleakley, Hoyt. 2003. "Disease and Development: Evidence from the American South." *J. European Econ. Assoc.* 1 (April–May): 376–86.

———. 2007. "Disease and Development: Evidence from Hookworm Eradication in the American South." *Q.J.E.* 122 (February): 73–117.

Bloom, David E., and David Canning. 2005. "Health and Economic Growth: Reconciling the Micro and Macro Evidence." Working Paper no. 42 (February), Center Democracy, Development, and Rule of Law, Stanford Inst. Internat. Studies, Stanford, CA. http://cddrl.stanford.edu.

Bloom, David E., and Jeffrey D. Sachs. 1998. "Geography, Demography, and Economic Growth in Africa." *Brookings Papers Econ. Activity*, no. 2: 207–73.

Forston, Jane. 2006. "Mortality Risks in Human Capital Investment: The Impact of HIV AIDS in Sub-Saharan Africa." Manuscript, Princeton Univ.

Gallup, John Luke, and Jeffrey D. Sachs. 2001. "The Economic Burden of Malaria." *American J. Tropical Medicine and Hygiene* 64, suppl. 1 (January): 85–96.

Kalemli-Ozcan, Sebnem. 2006. "AIDS, Reversal of the Demographic Transition and Economic Development: Evidence from Africa." Manuscript, Univ. Houston.

Knaul, Felicia Marie. 2000. "Health, Nutrition and Wages: Age at Menarche and Earnings in Mexico." In *Wealth from Health: Linking Social Investments to Earnings in Latin America*, edited by William D. Savedoff and T. Paul Schultz, Washington, DC: Inter-American Development Bank.

Lorentzen, Peter, John McMillan, and Romain Wacziarg. 2005. "Death and Development." Working paper no. 11620 (September), NBER, Cambridge, MA.

Maddison, Angus. 2001. *The World Economy: A Millennial Perspective*. Paris: OECD, Development Centre.

———. 2003. *The World Economy: Historical Statistics*. Paris: OECD, Development Centre.

Miguel, Edward, and Michael Kremer. 2004. "Worms: Identifying Impacts on Education and Health in the Presence of Treatment Externalities." *Econometrica* 72 (January): 159–217.

Omran, Abdel R. 1971. "The Epidemiologic Transition: A Theory of the Epidemiology of Population Change." *Milbank Memorial Fund Q.* 49, no. 4, pt. 1 (October): 509–38.

Preston, Samuel H. 1975. "The Changing Relation between Mortality and Level of Economic Development." *Population Studies* 29 (July): 231–48.

Riley, James C. 2001. *Rising Life Expectancy: A Global History*. Cambridge: Cambridge Univ. Press.

Schultz, T. Paul. 2002. "Wage Gains Associated with Height as a Form of Health Human Capital." *A.E.R. Papers and Proc.* 92 (May): 349–53.

Stolnitz, George J. 1955. "A Century of International Mortality Trends: I." *Population Studies* 0 (July): 24–55.

Strauss, John, and Duncan Thomas. 1998. "Health, Nutrition, and Economic Development." *J. Econ. Literature* 36 (June): 766–817.

Weil, David N. 2007. "Accounting for the Effect of Health on Economic Growth." *Q.J.E.* 122 (August): 1265–1306.

WHO (World Health Organization). 2001. *Macroeconomics and Health: Investing in Health for Economic Development*. http://www3.who.int/whosis/cmh.

Young, Alwyn. 2005. "The Gift of the Dying: The Tragedy of AIDS and the Welfare of Future African Generations." *Q.J.E.* 120 (May): 423–66.

11 GLOBALIZATION

We conclude this reader with selections that relate to globalization. Evocative and rather vague, this term can be incorporated into just about any kind of politics that has some "global" aspect to it. However, here we refer specifically to the extensive and intensive connections between political, societal, and economic institutions among countries. To political scientists, *globalization* describes the modern intersection between comparative politics (the study of domestic politics across countries) and international relations (the study of foreign relations between countries). As a result, scholars of both international relations and comparative politics have been drawn to this contentious topic. Just as globalization blurs the lines between the domestic and the international, it also blurs the lines between comparative politics and international relations.

These increased interconnections have many possible implications. One of the most common arguments, coined by Thomas Friedman, is that globalization has made the world "flat," removing many of the traditional barriers and obstacles that separate states and markets from each other. This has not only increased competition (think of outsourcing, for example) but has also forced states into what Friedman calls a "golden straitjacket," where they are compelled to give up a great deal of autonomy in both domestic and international politics in order to reap the benefits of globalized trade. Implicit in these arguments is that anyone can share in the benefits of the flat world. Not all scholars agree. One critic of Friedman is Richard Florida, whose 2006 piece "The World Is Spiky" argues that globalization has helped cluster intellectual capital and technological innovation around the world, creating "spiky" areas that are increasingly interlinked across the globe while the peoples physically around them are left out and left behind.

Florida's piece questions the idea that globalization will benefit all comers, as the "flat earth" view of globalization suggests, but it accepts as a given the power of globalization as an unstoppable, if problematic, force. The recent economic recession, however, has helped bring attention to scholars who are more broadly critical of globalization, among them the economist Dani Rodrik. In his 2011 book *The Globalization Paradox*, he returns to his frequent argument that globalization, sovereignty, and democracy are essentially incompatible. In the selection included here, he asks whether the problems caused by globalization (such as those Florida suggests) can be managed by institutions of global governance that would transcend the nation-state. Rodrik is skeptical, looking at the European

Union as an example of the limits of such institutions. Beyond his discussion of the technical difficulties in creating global governance, Rodrik points out that the very desire for globalization can be found precisely among those elites that Florida speaks of—well educated and highly mobile citizens. For the majority of people in the world, however, globalization entails more risk than reward, as economic security and political authority move beyond their representative control. For this majority, the nation-state remains an important institution of sovereignty, and Rodrik suggests that states and societies must remain active in managing and limiting globalization.

Florida's and Rodrik's contributions are important reminders that globalization does not necessarily mean a more level playing field or a more just vision of world politics. Nor, in fact, does it even necessarily mean a fundamental change in politics. The short article from the *Economist*, "Leviathan Stirs Again" (2010), argues that the past few years have in fact seen precisely what Rodrik suggests—the reemergence of the state as a major force in economics and other areas, belying the idea of a flat earth or golden straightjacket. As Rodrik noted, states have played a central role in intervening in markets in order to stave off global recession. The U.S. wars since 2001 have also led to a massive increase in government spending and increased security measures. Aging populations across the advanced democracies have increased their demands for greater social expenditures. In developing and post-communist countries, too, states retain a powerful role in their economies in such areas as planning and national ownership of industry. The authors conclude that what is currently emerging in many of these cases is a new economic hybrid that they call *state capitalism*. Such systems focus on the pursuit of sovereign power and are more than willing to check and roll back globalization when necessary. The state, in short, is back, if ever it were gone—just as Fukuyama suggested in our first reading in this volume.

The power of the state over globalization extends beyond the market. Jiang's "Authoritarian Informationalism" (2010) looks at the role of the Internet in China and considers clashing notions of "Internet sovereignty." Many observers of globalization consider it indistinguishable from the Internet. The Internet is the ultimate expression of globalization, it would appear, in how it collapses time and space in a way that renders traditional barriers, such as national borders, obsolete. In this view, the Internet is sovereign over states. But as Jiang points out, countries such as China view Internet sovereignty as the desire and ability of states to assert sovereignty over the Internet, not vice versa. This takes the form not only of censorship but also of using the Internet as a space where the regime can promote its own values and ideology, boosting its legitimacy in the process. The Internet can amplify state power as well as undermine it. States not only have failed to disappear in the face of globalization but also are finding ways to assert their sovereignty over new territories and realms, just as they have done for centuries.

Richard Florida

THE WORLD IS SPIKY: GLOBALIZATION HAS CHANGED THE ECONOMIC PLAYING FIELD, BUT HASN'T LEVELED IT

The world, according to the title of the *New York Times* columnist Thomas Friedman's book, is flat. Thanks to advances in technology, the global playing field has been leveled, the prizes are there for the taking, and everyone's a player—no matter where on the surface of the earth he or she may reside. "In a flat world," Friedman writes, "you can innovate without having to emigrate."

Friedman is not alone in this belief: for the better part of the past century economists have been writing about the leveling effects of technology. From the invention of the telephone, the automobile, and the airplane to the rise of the personal computer and the Internet, technological progress has steadily eroded the economic importance of geographic place—or so the argument goes.

But in partnership with colleagues at George Mason University and the geographer Tim Culden, of the Center for International and Security Studies, at the University of Maryland, I've begun to chart a very different economic topography. By almost any measure the international economic landscape is not at all flat. On the contrary, our world is amazingly "spiky." In terms of both sheer economic horsepower and cuttingedge innovation, surprisingly few regions truly matter in today's global economy. What's more, the tallest peaks—the cities and regions that drive the world economy—are growing ever higher, while the valleys mostly languish.

The most obvious challenge to the flat-world hypothesis is the explosive growth of cities worldwide. More

and more people are clustering in urban areas—the world's demographic mountain ranges, so to speak. The share of the world's population living in urban areas, just three percent in 1800, was nearly 30 percent by 1950. Today it stands at about 50 percent; in advanced countries three out of four people live in urban areas. Map 11.1 shows the uneven distribution of the world's population. Five megacities currently have more than 20 million inhabitants

PEAKS, HILLS, AND VALLEYS

When looked at through the lens of economic production, many cities with large populations are diminished and some nearly vanish. Three sorts of places make up the modern economic landscape. First are the cities that generate innovations. These are the tallest peaks; they have the capacity to attract global talent and create new products and industries. They are few in number, and difficult to topple. Second are the economic "hills"—places that manufacture the world's established goods, take its calls, and support its innovation engines. These hills can rise and fall quickly; they are prosperous but insecure. Some, like Dublin and Seoul, are growing into innovative, wealthy peaks; others are declining, eroded by high labor costs and a lack of enduring competitive advantage. Finally there are the vast valleys—places with little connection to the global economy and few immediate prospects.

From *The Atlantic Monthly* (October 2005), pp. 48–51.

each. Twenty-four cities have more than 10 million inhabitants, sixty more than 5 million, and 150 more than 2.5 million. Population density is of course a crude indicator of human and economic activity. But in does suggest that at least some of the tectonic forces of economics are concentrating people and resources, and pushing up some places more than others.

Still, differences in population density vastly understate the spikiness of the global economy; the continuing dominance of the world's most productive urban areas is astounding. When it comes to actual economic output, the ten largest U.S. metropolitan areas combined are behind only the United States as a whole and Japan. New York's economy alone is about the size of Russia's or Brazil's, and Chicago's is on a par with Sweden's. Together New York, Los Angeles, Chicago, and Boston have a bigger economy than all of China. If U.S. metropolitan areas were countries, they'd make up forty-seven of the biggest 100 economies in the world.

Unfortunately, no single, comprehensive information source exists for the economic production of all the world's cities. A rough proxy is available, though. Map 11.2 shows a variation on the widely circulated view of the world at night, with higher concentrations of light—indicating higher energy use and, pre-sumably, stronger economic production—appearing in greater relief. U.S. regions appear almost Himalayan on this map. From their summits one might look out on a smaller mountain range stretching across Europe, some isolated peaks in Asia, and a few scattered hills throughout the rest of the world.

Population and economic activity are both spiky, but it's innovation—the engine of economic growth—that is most concentrated. The World Intellectual Property Organization recorded about 300,000 patents from resident inventors in more than a hundred nations in 2002 (the most recent year for which statistics are available). Nearly two thirds of them went to American and Japanese inventors. Eighty-five percent went to the residents of just five countries (Japan, the United States, South Korea, Germany, and Russia).

Worldwide patent statistics can be somewhat misleading, since different countries follow different standards for granting patents. But patents granted in the United States—which receives patent applications for nearly all major innovations worldwide, and holds them to the same strict standards—tell a similar story. Nearly 90,000 of the 170,000 patents granted in the United States in 2002 went to Americans. Some 35,000 went to Japanese inventors, and 11,000 to Germans. The next ten most innovative

Map 11.1 A Population

Urban areas house half of all the world's people, and continue to grow in both rich and poor countries.[1]

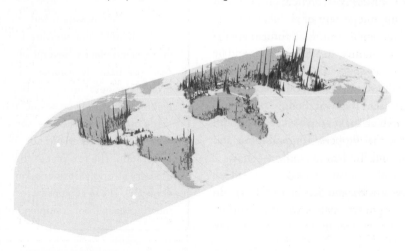

Map 11.2 Light Emissions

Economic activity—roughly estimated here using light-emissions data—is remarkably concentrated. Many cities, despite their large population barely register.[2]

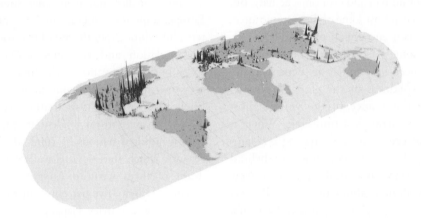

countries—including the usual suspects in Europe plus Taiwan, South Korea, Israel, and Canada—produced roughly 25,000 more. The rest of the broad, flat world accounted for just five percent of all innovations patented in the United States. In 2003 India generated 341 U.S. patents and China 297. The University of California alone generated more than either country. IBM accounted for five times as many as the two combined.

This is not to say that Indians and Chinese are not innovative. On the contrary, AnnaLee Saxenian, of the University of California at Berkeley, has shown that Indian and Chinese entrepreneurs founded or co-founded roughly 30 percent of all Silicon Valley startups in the late 1990s. But these fundamentally creative people had to travel to Silicon Valley and be absorbed into its innovative ecosystem before their ideas became economically viable. Such ecosystems matter, and there aren't many of them.

Map 11.3—which makes use of data from both the World Intellectual Property Organizations and the U.S. Patent and Trademark Office—shows a world composed of innovation peaks and valleys. Tokyo, Seoul, New York, and San Francisco remain the front-runners in the patenting competition. Boston, Seattle, Austin, Toronto, Vancouver, Berlin,

Stockholm, Helsinki, London, Osaka, Taipei, and Sydney also stand out.

Map 11.4 shows the residence of the 1,200 most heavily cited scientists in leading fields. Scientific advance is even more concentrated than patent production. Most occurs not just in a handful of countries but in a handful of cities—primarily in the United States and Europe. Chinese and Indian cities

THE GEOGRAPHY OF INNOVATION

Commercial innovation and scientific advance are both highly concentrated—but not always in the same places. Several cities in East Asia—particularly in Japan—are home to prolific business innovation but still depend disproportionately on scientific breakthroughs made elsewhere. Likewise, some cities excel in scientific research but not in commercial adaptation. The few places that do both well are very strongly positioned in the global economy. These regions have little to fear, and much to gain, from continuing globalization.

Map 11.3 Patents

Just a few places produce most of the world's innovations. Innovation remains difficult without a critical mass of financiers, entrepreneurs, and scientists, often nourished by world-class universities and flexible corporations.[3]

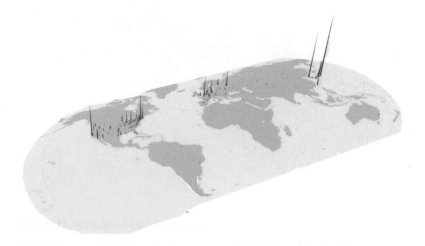

do not even register. As far as global innovation is concerned, perhaps a few dozen places worldwide really compete at the cutting edge.

Concentrations of creative and talented people are particularly important for innovation, according to the Nobel Prize–winning economist Robert Lucas. Ideas flow more freely, are honed more sharply, and can be put into practice more quickly when large numbers of innovators, implementers, and financial backers are in constant contact with one another, both in and out of the office. Creative people cluster not simply because they like to be around one another or they prefer cosmopolitan centers with lots of amenities, though both those things count. They and their companies also cluster because of the powerful productivity advantages, economies of scale, and knowledge spillovers such density brings.

So although one might not *have* to emigrate to innovate, it certainly appears that innovation, economic growth, and prosperity occur in those places that attract a critical mass of top creative talent. Because globalization has increased the returns to innovation, by allowing innovative products and services to quickly reach consumers worldwide, it

has strengthened the lure that innovation centers hold for our planet's best and brightest, reinforcing the spikiness of wealth and economic production.

The main difference between now and even a couple of decades ago is not that the world has become flatter but that the world's peaks have become slightly more dispersed—and that the world's hills, the industrial and service centers that produce mature products and support innovation centers, have proliferated and shifted. For the better part of the twentieth century the United States claimed the lion's share of the global economy's innovation peaks, leaving a few outposts in Europe and Japan. But America has since lost some of those peaks, as such industrial-age powerhouses as Pittsburgh, St. Louis, and Cleveland have eroded. At the same time, a number of regions in Europe, Scandinavia, Canada, and the Pacific Rim have moved up.

The world today looks flat to some because the economic and social distances between peaks worldwide have gotten smaller. Connection between peaks has been strengthened by the easy mobility of the global creative class—about 150 million people worldwide. They participate in a global technology system and a global labor market that allow them

Map 11.4 Scientific Citations

The world's most prolific and influential scientific researchers overwhelmingly reside in U.S. and European cities.[4]

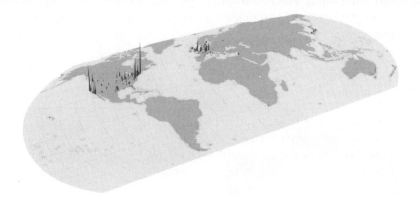

to migrate freely among the world's leading cities. In a Brookings Institution study the demographer Robert Lang and the world-cities expert Peter Taylor identify a relatively small group of leading city-regions—London, New York, Paris, Tokyo, Hong Kong, Singapore, Chicago, Los Angeles, and San Francisco among them—that are strongly connected to one another.

But Lang and Taylor also identify a much larger group of city-regions that are far more locally oriented. People in spiky places are often more connected to one another, even from half a world away, than they are to people and places in their veritable backyards.

The flat-world theory is not completely misguided. It is a welcome supplement to the widely accepted view (illustrated by the Live 8 concerts and Bono's forays into Africa, by the writings of Jeffrey Sachs and the UN Millennium project) that the growing divide between rich and poor countries is the fundamental feature of the world economy. Friedman's theory more accurately depicts a developing world with capabilities that translate into economic development. In his view, for example, the emerging economies of India and China combine cost advantages, high-tech skills, and entrepreneurial energy, enabling those countries to compete effectively for industries and jobs. The

tensions set in motion as the playing field is leveled affect mainly the advanced countries, which see not only manufacturing work but also higher-end jobs, in fields such as software development and financial services, increasingly threatened by offshoring.

But the flat-world theory blinds us to far more insidious tensions among the world's growing peaks, sinking valleys, and shifting hills. The innovative, talent-attracting "have" regions seem increasingly remote from the talent-exporting "have-not" regions. Second-tier cities, from Detroit and Wolfsburg to Nagoya and Mexico City, are entering an escalating and potentially devastating competition for jobs, talent, and investment. And inequality is growing across the world and within countries.

This is far more harrowing than the flat world Friedman describes, and a good deal more treacherous than the old rich-poor divide. We see its effects in the political backlash against globalization in the advanced world. The recent rejection of the EU constitution by the French, for example, resulted in large part from high rates of "no" votes in suburban and rural quarters, which understandably fear globalization and integration.

But spiky globalization also wreaks havoc on poorer places. China is seeing enormous concentrations of talent and innovation in centers such as Shanghai, Shenzhen, and Beijing, all of which are a world apart from its vast, impoverished rural areas. According to detailed polling by Richard Burkholder, of Callup, average household incomes in urban China are now triple those in rural regions, and they've grown more than three times as fast since 1999; perhaps as a result, urban and rural Chinese now have very different, often conflicting political and lifestyle values. India is growing even more divided, as Bangalore, Hyderabad, and parts of New Delhi and Bombay pull away from the rest of that enormous country, creating destabilizing political tensions. Economic and demographic forces are sorting people around the world into geographically clustered "tribes" so different (and often mutually antagonistic) as to create a somewhat Hobbesian vision.

We are thus confronted with a difficult predicament. Economic progress requires that the peaks grow stronger and taller. But such growth will exacerbate economic and social disparities, fomenting

political reactions that could threaten further innovation and economic progress. Managing the disparities between peaks and valleys worldwide—raising the valleys without shearing off the peaks—will be among the top political challenges of the coming decades.

NOTES

1. Map data source: Center for International Earth Science Information Network, Columbia University, and Centro Internacional de Agricultura Tropical.
2. Map data source: U.S. Defense Meteorological Satellite Program.
3. Map data source: World Intellectual Property Organization; U.S. Patent and Trademark Office.
4. Map data source: Michael Batty, Centre for Advanced Spatial Analysis, University College London (www.casa.ucl.ac.uk).

Dani Rodrik

IS GLOBAL GOVERNANCE FEASIBLE? IS IT DESIRABLE?

The nation state is passé. Borders have disappeared. Distance is dead. The earth is flat. Our identities are no longer bound by our places of birth. Domestic politics is being superseded by newer, more fluid forms of representation that transcend national boundaries. Authority is moving from domestic rule-makers to transnational networks of regulators. Political power is shifting to a new wave of activists organized around international non-governmental organizations. The decisions that shape our economic lives are made by

large multinational companies and faceless international bureaucrats.

How many times have we heard these or similar statements, heralding or decrying the dawn of a new era of global governance?

And yet look at the way events have unfolded in the recent crisis of 2007–08. Who bailed out the global banks to prevent the financial crisis from becoming even more cataclysmic? Who pumped in the liquidity needed to soothe international credit markets? Who stimulated the global economy through fiscal expansion? Who provided unemployment compensation and other safety nets for the workers who lost their jobs? Who is setting the new rules on compensation, capital adequacy, and

From *The Globalization Paradox: Democracy and the Future of the World Economy* (New York: W. W. Norton, 2011), pp. 207–32.

liquidity for large banks? Who gets the lion's share of the blame for everything that went wrong before, during, and after?

The answer to each one of these questions is the same: *national governments*. We may think we live in a world whose governance has been radically transformed by globalization, but the buck still stops with domestic policy makers. The hype that surrounds the decline of the nation state is just that: hype. Our world economy may be populated by a veritable alphabet soup of international agencies—everything from ADB to WTO[1]—but democratic decision making remains firmly lodged within nation states. "Global governance" has a nice ring to it, but don't go looking for it anytime soon. Our complex and variegated world allows only a very thin veneer of global governance—and for very good reasons, too.

Overcoming the Tyranny of Nation States

It's no longer just cranks and wide-eyed utopians who entertain the idea of global government. Many economists, sociologists, political scientists, legal scholars, and philosophers have joined the search for new forms of governance that leave the nation state behind. Of course, few of these analysts advocate a truly global version of the nation state; a global legislature or council of ministers is too much of a fantasy. The solutions they propose rely instead on new conceptions of political community, representation, and accountability. The hope is that these innovations can replicate many of constitutional democracy's essential functions at the global level.

The crudest form of such global governance envisages straightforward delegation of national powers to international technocrats. It involves autonomous regulatory agencies charged with solving what are essentially regarded as "technical" problems arising from uncoordinated decision making in the global economy. For obvious reasons, economists are particularly enamored of such arrange-

ments. For example, when the European economics network VoxEU.org solicited advice from leading economists on how to address the frailties of the global financial system in the wake of the 2008 crisis, the proposed solutions often took the form of tighter international rules administered by some kind of technocracy: an international bankruptcy court, a world financial organization, an international bank charter, an international lender of last resort, and so on.[2] Jeffrey Garten, undersecretary of commerce for international trade in the Clinton administration, has long called for the establishment of a global central bank.[3] Economists Carmen Reinhart and Ken Rogoff have proposed an international financial regulator.

These proposals may seem like the naive ruminations of economists who don't understand politics, but in fact they are often based on an explicit political motive. When Reinhart and Rogoff argue for an international financial regulator, their goal is as much to fix a political failure as it is to address economic spillovers across nations; perhaps the political motive even takes precedence over the economic one. They hope to end political meddling at the national level that they perceive has emasculated domestic regulations. They write: "a well-endowed, professionally staffed international financial regulator—operating without layers of political hacks—would offer a badly needed counterweight to the powerful domestic financial service sector."[4] The political theory that underpins this approach holds that delegating regulatory powers to an insulated and autonomous global technocracy leads to better governance, both global and national.

In the real world, delegation requires legislators to give up their prerogative to make the rules and reduces their ability to respond to their constituents. As such, it typically takes place under a narrow set of conditions. In the United States, for example, Congress delegates rulemaking powers to executive agencies only when its political preferences are quite similar to the president's and when the issues under consideration are highly technical.[5] Even then, delegation remains partial and comes with elaborate accountability mechanisms. Delegation is a *political* act. Hence, many preconditions have to be satisfied before delegation to supranational bodies can become widespread and sustainable. We would need to create a "global body politic" of some sort, with common norms, a transnational political community, and new mechanisms of accountability suited to the global arena.

Economists don't pay much attention to these prerequisites, but other scholars do. Many among them see evidence that new models of global governance are indeed emerging. Anne-Marie Slaughter, a scholar of international relations at Princeton, has focused on transnational networks populated by regulators, judges, and even legislators. These networks can perform governance functions even when they are not constituted as intergovernmental organizations or formally institutionalized. Such networks, Slaughter argues, extend the reach of formal governance mechanisms, allow persuasion and information sharing across national borders, contribute to the formation of global norms, and can generate the capacity to implement international norms and agreements in nations where the domestic capacity to do so is weak.[6]

The governance of financial markets is in fact the arena where such networks have advanced the furthest and which provides Slaughter's most telling illustrations. The International Organization of Securities Commissions (IOSCO) brings together the world's securities regulators and issues global principles. The Basel Committee on Banking Supervision performs the same role for banking regulators. These networks have small secretariats (if any at all) and no enforcement power. Yet they certainly exert influence through their standard-setting powers and legitimacy—at least in the eyes of regulators. Their deliberations often become a reference point in domestic discussions. They may not entirely substitute for nation states, but they end up creating internationally intertwined networks of policy makers.

To achieve legitimacy, global governance must transcend exclusive clubs of regulators and techno-crats. Can these networks go beyond narrowly technical areas and encompass broader social purposes? Yes, says John Ruggie, the Harvard scholar who coined the term "embedded liberalism" to describe the Bretton Woods regime. Ruggie agrees that transnational networks have undermined the traditional model of governance based on nation states. To right this imbalance, he argues, we need greater emphasis on corporate social responsibility at the global level. An updated version of embedded liberalism would move beyond a state-centered multilateralism to "a multilateralism that actively embraces the potential contributions to global social organization by civil society and corporate actors." These actors can advance new global norms—on human rights, labor practices, health, anti-corruption, and environmental stewardship—and then enshrine them in the operations of large international corporations and policies of national governments. Multinational corporations' funding of HIV/AIDS treatment programs in poor nations represents one prominent example.

The United Nation's Global Compact, which Ruggie had a big hand in shaping, embodies this agenda. The Compact aims to transform international corporations into vehicles for the advancement of social and economic goals. Such a transformation would benefit the communities in which these corporations and their affiliates operate. But, as Ruggie explains, there would be additional advantages. Improving large corporations' social and environmental performance would spur emulation by other, smaller firms. It would alleviate the widespread concern that international competition creates a race to the bottom in labor and environmental standards at the expense of social inclusion at home. And it would allow the private sector to shoulder some of the functions that states are finding increasingly difficult to finance and carry out, as in public health and environmental protection, narrowing the governance gap between international markets and national governments.[7]

Arguments on behalf of new forms of global governance—whether of the delegation, network, or corporate social responsibility type—raise troubling questions. To whom are these mechanisms supposed to be accountable? From where do these global clubs of regulators, international non-governmental organizations, or large firms get their mandates? Who empowers and polices them? What ensures that the voice and interests of those who are less globally networked are also heard? The Achilles' heel of global governance is lack of clear accountability relationships. In a nation state, the electorate is the ultimate source of political mandates and elections the ultimate vehicle for accountability. If you do not respond to your constituencies' expectations and aspirations, you are voted out. Global electoral accountability of this sort is too far-fetched a notion. We would need different mechanisms.[8]

Probably the best argument for an alternative *global* conception of accountability comes from two distinguished political scientists, Joshua Cohen and Charles Sabel. These scholars begin by arguing that the problems global governance aims to solve don't lend themselves to traditional notions of accountability. In the traditional model, a constituency with well-defined interests empowers its representative to act on behalf on those interests. Global regulation presents challenges that are new, often highly technical, and subject to rapidly evolving circumstances. The global "public" typically has only a hazy notion of what problems need solving and how to solve them.

In this setting, accountability hinges on the international regulator's ability to provide "a good explanation" for what she chooses to do. "Questions are decided by argument about the best way to address problems," write Cohen and Sabel, "not [by] simply exertions of power, expressions of interest, or bargaining from power positions on the basis of interest."[9] There is no presumption here that the solutions will be "technocratic" ones. Even when values and interests diverge and disagreement prevails, the hope is that the process of transnational deliberation will generate the explanations that all or most can acknowledge as legitimate. Global rule-making becomes accountable to the extent that the reasoning behind the rules is found to be compelling by those to whom the rules would apply.

Cohen and Sabel's scheme provides room, at least in principle, for variation in institutional practices across nation states within an overall framework of global cooperation and coordination. A country and its policy makers are free to experiment and implement different solutions as long as they can explain to their peers—policy makers in the other countries—why they have arrived at those solutions. They must justify their choices publicly and place them in the context of comparable choices made by others. A skeptic may wonder, however, if such mechanisms will not lead instead to widespread hypocrisy as policy makers continue with business-as-usual while rationalizing their actions in loftier terms.

Ultimately, Cohen and Sabel hope that these deliberative processes would feed into the development of a global political community, in which "dispersed peoples might come to share a new identity as common members of an organized global populace."[10] It is difficult to see how their conception of global governance would work in the absence of such a transformation in political identities. At the end of the day, global governance requires individuals who feel that they are global citizens.

Maybe we are not too far from that state of affairs. The Princeton ethicist Peter Singer has written powerfully about the development of a new global ethic that follows from globalization. "If . . . the revolution in communications has created a global audience," he writes, "then we might need to justify our behavior to the whole world."[11] The economist and philosopher Amartya Sen has argued that it is quite misleading to think of ourselves as bound by a single, unchanging identity—ethnic, religious, or national—with which we are born. Each one of us has multiple identities, based on our profession, gender, occupation, class, political leanings, hobbies and interests, sports teams we support, and so on.[12] These identities do not come at the expense of each other, and we freely choose how much weight we put on them. Many identities cross national boundaries, allowing us to form transnational associations and define our "interests" across a broad geography. This flexibility and multiplicity creates room, in principle, for the establishment of a truly global political community.

There is much that is attractive in these ideas about the potential for global governance. As Sen puts it, "there is something of a tyranny of ideas in seeing the political divisions of states (primarily, national states) as being, in some way, fundamental, and in seeing them not only as practical constraints to be addressed, but as divisions of basic significance in ethics and political philosophy."[13] Furthermore, political identity and community have been continuously redefined over time in ever more expansive terms. Human associations have moved from the tribal and local to city states and then on to nation states. Shouldn't a global community be next?

The proof of the pudding is in the eating. How far can these emergent forms of global governance go and how much globalization can they support? A good place to start is the European Union, which has traveled further along the road of transnational governance than any other collection of nation states.

European Union: The Exception That Tests the Rule

When Cohen and Sabel were developing their ideas on global governance through deliberation, they had one concrete example in mind: the European Union. The European experiment shows both the potential and the limitations of these ideas.

European nations have achieved an extraordinary amount of economic integration among themselves. Nowhere is there a better approximation of deep integration or hyperglobalization, albeit at the regional level. Underneath Europe's single market lies an enormous institutional artifice devoted to removing transaction costs and harmonizing regulations. EU members have renounced barriers on the movement of goods, capital, and labor. But beyond

that they have signed on to 100,000-plus pages of EU-wide regulations—on everything from science policy to consumer protections—that lay out common standards and expectations. They have set up a European Court of Justice that assiduously enforces these regulations. They have empowered an administrative arm in the form of the European Commission to propose new laws and implement common policies in external trade, agriculture, competition, regional assistance, and many other areas. They have established a number of programs to provide financial assistance to lagging regions of the Union and foster economic convergence. Sixteen of the members have adopted a common currency (the euro) and succumbed to a common monetary policy administered by the European Central Bank. In addition to all this, the EU has many specialized agencies that are too numerous to list here.

The EU's democratic institutions are less well developed. The directly elected European Parliament operates mostly as a talking shop rather than as a source of legislative initiative or oversight. Real power lies with the Council of Ministers, which is a collection of ministers from national governments. How to establish and maintain democratic legitimacy and accountability for Europe's extensive supranational setup has long been a thorny question. Critics from the right blame EU institutions for overreaching while critics from the left complain about a "democratic deficit."

European leaders have made significant efforts in recent years to boost the *political* infrastructure of the European Union, but it has been a bumpy and arduous road. An ambitious effort to ratify a European Constitution failed after voters in France and The Netherlands rejected it in 2005. In the wake of this failure came the Lisbon Treaty, which entered into force in December 2009—but only after the United Kingdom, Poland, Ireland, and the Czech Republic secured exclusions from some of the requirements of the treaty. The treaty reforms the voting rules in the Council of Ministers, gives more power to the European Parliament, renders the European Union's human rights charter legally binding, and establishes a new executive position in the form of the president of the European Council.

As the opt-outs received by Britain and others suggest, there remain significant differences among member states on the desirability of turning Europe into a true political federation. Britain zealously guards its distinctive constitution and legal system from the encroachment of EU rules or institutions. In many areas such as financial regulation and monetary policy, it has little interest in bringing its practices in line with those of the others. Britain's interest in Europe remains primarily economic. Its minimalist approach to European institution building contrasts sharply with France's and Germany's occasionally more ambitious federalist goals.

As important as these broad debates over the European Union's constitutional architecture may be, much of the organization's real work gets done under an informal, evolving set of practices that Charles Sabel calls "experimentalist governance." The member states and the higher-level EU institutions decide on the goals to be accomplished. These could be as ambitious and ill-defined as "social inclusion" or as narrow as "a unified energy grid." National regulatory agencies are given freedom to advance these goals in the ways they see fit, but the quid pro quo is that they must report their actions and results in what are variably called forums, networked agencies, councils of regulators, or open methods of coordination. Peer review allows national regulators to compare their approaches to those of others and revise them as necessary. Over time, the goals themselves are updated and altered in light of the learning that takes place in these deliberations.[14]

Experimentalist governance helps create Europe-wide norms and contributes to building transnational consensus around common approaches. They need not necessarily result in complete homogenization. Where differences continue to exist, they do so in the context of mutual understanding and accountability, so that they are much less likely to turn into sources of friction. The requirement that national practices be justified renders national differences easier to accommodate.

The members of the European Union may seem like a diverse bunch, but compared to the nations that make up the world economy they are a model of concord. These twenty-seven nations are bound together by a common geography, culture, religion, and history. Excluding Luxembourg, where measured income per head is very high, the richest among them (Ireland, in 2008) is only 3.3 times wealthier than the poorest (Bulgaria), compared to a multiple of almost 190 across the world. EU members are driven by a strong sense of strategic purpose that extends considerably beyond economic integration. European unity in fact looms larger as a political goal than it does as an economic one.

Despite all these comparative advantages, the European Union's institutional evolution has progressed slowly and large differences remain among the member states. Most telling is the well recognized tension between deepening the Union and expanding it to incorporate new members. Consider the long-simmering debate over Turkey. French and German opposition to Turkey's entrance into the European Union derives in part from cultural and religious reasons. But the fear that Turkey's divergent political traditions and institutions would greatly hamper European political integration also plays a large role. Britain, on the other hand, welcomes anything that would temper French and German ambitions for a *political* Europe, and for that reason supports eventual membership for Turkey. Everyone understands that the deepening of Europe's political integration becomes more problematic as the number of members increases and the European Union's composition becomes more diverse.

Europe's own dilemma is no different from that faced by the world economy as a whole. As we saw in previous chapters, deep economic integration requires erecting an extensive transnational governance structure to support it. Ultimately, the European Union will either bite the political bullet or resign itself to a more limited economic union. Those who push for a political Europe stand a greater chance of achieving a truly single European market than those who want to limit the conversation to the economic level. But political advocates have yet to win the argument. They face great opposition both from their national electorates and from other political leaders with differing visions.

Thus Europe has become a halfway house—economically more integrated than any other region of the world, but with a governance structure that remains a work in progress. It has the potential to turn itself into a true economic union, but it is not there yet. When European economies come under stress, the responses are overwhelmingly national.

The governance gaps became particularly obvious during the crisis of 2008 and its aftermath. Europe's banks are supervised by national regulators. When they started going bust, there was practically no coordination among EU governments. Bailouts of banks and other firms were carried out separately by individual governments, often in ways that harmed other EU members. There was also no coordination in the design of recovery plans and fiscal stimulus programs, even though there are clear spillovers (German firms benefit from a French fiscal stimulus almost as much as French firms do, given how intertwined the two economies are). When European leaders finally approved a "common" framework for financial oversight in December 2009, Britain's finance minister underscored the limited nature of the agreement by emphasizing that "responsibility lies with national regulators."[15]

The poorer and worse-hit members of the European Union could count on only grudging support from Brussels. Latvia, Hungary, and Greece were forced to turn to the IMF for financial assistance as a condition for getting loans from richer EU governments.[16] (Imagine what it would look like if Washington were to require California to submit to IMF monitoring in order to benefit from Federal Recovery Funds.) Others dealing with crushing economic problems were left to fend for themselves (Spain and Portugal). In effect, these countries had the worst of both worlds: economic union prevented their resort to currency devaluation for a quick boost to their competitiveness, while the lack of political

union precluded their receiving much support from the rest of Europe.

In light of all this it would be easy to write off the European Union, but that would be too harsh a judgment. Membership in the Union did make a difference to the willingness of smaller countries to live by hyperglobalization rules. Consider Latvia, the small Baltic country, which found itself experiencing economic difficulties similar to those Argentina had lived through a decade earlier. Latvia had grown rapidly since joining the European Union in 2004 on the back of large amounts of borrowing from European banks and a domestic property bubble. It had run up huge current account deficits and foreign debts (20 percent and 125 percent of GDP, respectively, by 2007). Predictably, the global economic crisis and the reversal in capital flows in 2008 left the Latvian economy in dire straits. As lending and property prices collapsed, unemployment rose to 20 percent and GDP declined by 18 percent in 2009. In January 2009, the country had its worst riots since the collapse of the Soviet Union.

Latvia had a fixed exchange rate and free capital flows, just like Argentina. Its currency had been pegged to the euro since 2005. Unlike Argentina, however, the country's politicians managed to tough it out without devaluing the currency and introducing capital controls (the latter would have explicitly broken EU rules). By early 2010, it looked as if the Latvian economy had begun to stabilize.[17] The difference with Argentina was that Latvia's membership in a larger political community changed the balance of costs and benefits of going it alone. The right to free circulation of labor within the European Union allowed many Latvian workers to emigrate, serving as a safety valve for an economy under duress. Brussels prevailed on European banks to support their subsidiaries in Latvia. Most important, the prospect of adopting the euro as the domestic currency and joining the Eurozone compelled Latvian policy makers to foreclose any options—such as devaluation—that would endanger that objective, despite the very high short-term economic costs.

For all its teething problems, Europe should be viewed as a great success considering its progress down the path of institution building. For the rest of the world, however, it remains a cautionary tale. The European Union demonstrates the difficulties of achieving a political union robust enough to underpin deep economic integration even among a comparatively small number of like-minded countries. At best, it is the exception that tests the rule. The European Union proves that transnational democratic governance is workable, but its experience also lays bare the demanding requirements of such governance. Anyone who thinks global governance is a plausible path for the world economy at large would do well to consider Europe's experience.

Would Global Governance Solve Our Problems?

Let's give global governance enthusiasts the benefit of the doubt and ask how the mechanisms they propose would resolve the tensions that hyperglobalization generates.

Consider how we should deal with the following three challenges:

1. Chinese exports of toys to the United States are found to contain unsafe levels of lead.
2. The subprime mortgage crisis in the United States spreads to the rest of the world as many of the securities issued by U.S. banks and marketed in foreign countries turn out to be "toxic."
3. Some of the goods exported from Indonesia to the United States and Europe are manufactured using child labor.

In all three cases, a country exports a good, service, or asset that causes problems for the importing country. Chinese exports of lead-tainted toys endanger the health of American children; U.S. exports of mispriced mortgage-based assets endanger financial stability in the rest of the world, and

Indonesian exports of child-labor services threaten labor standards and values in the United States and Western Europe. Prevailing international rules do not provide clear-cut solutions for these challenges, so we need to think our way through them. Can we address them through markets alone? Do we need specific rules, and if so, should they be national or global? Might the answers differ across these three areas?

Consider the similarities between these problems, even though they are drawn from quite different domains of the world economy. At the core of each is a dispute about standards, with respect to lead content, rating of financial securities, and child labor. In all three cases there are differences in the standards applied (or desired) by the exporting and importing countries. Exporters may have lower standards and therefore possess a competitive advantage in the markets of the importing countries. However, purchasers in the importing country cannot directly observe the standard under which the exported good or service has been produced. A consumer cannot tell easily whether the toy contains lead paint or has been manufactured using child labor under exploitative conditions; nor can a lender fully identify the risk characteristics of the bundled assets it holds. Everything else held constant, importers are less likely to buy the good or the service in question if it contains lead paint, has been made by children, or is likely to cause financial havoc.

At the same time, consumers' preferences vary. Each one of us probably places somewhat different weights on upholding the standard versus obtaining other benefits, such as a low price. You may be willing to pay an extra $2 for a T-shirt certified as child-labor-free, but I may want to pay no more than $1. You may be willing to trade off some extra risk for additional yield on a security, while I am more conservative in my investment philosophy. Some may be willing to purchase lead-tainted toys if it makes a big enough difference to the price, while others would consider it abhorrent. For this reason, any standard creates gainers and losers when applied uniformly.

How do we respond to these three challenges? The default option is to neglect them until they loom too large to ignore. We may choose this option for several reasons. First, we may trust the standard applied in the exporting country. The credit rating agencies in the United States are supposedly the best in the world, so why would any country worry about buying triple-A-rated U.S. mortgage securities? Chinese lead regulations are, on paper, more stringent than those in the United States, so why get concerned about the health hazards of Chinese toys? Second, we may think standards and regulations in foreign countries are none of our business. Buyers simply beware. Third, we may actually think that differences in regulatory standards are a source of comparative advantage—and hence of gains from trade—just like differences in productivity or skills across nations. If lax labor standards enable Indonesia to sell us cheaper goods, this is just another manifestation of the benefits of globalization.

These shortsighted arguments undercut the efficiency of the global economy and ultimately undermine its legitimacy. The challenges presented raise legitimate concerns and deserve serious responses. Consider therefore some of the possibilities.

Global standards. We may be tempted to seek global standards by which all countries would have to abide. We might require compliance with core labor standards of all producers, a common set of banking regulations, and uniform product safety codes. This is the global governance solution par excellence. In many areas we are gravitating toward this kind of approach, as we have seen, but obvious limitations remain. Nations are unlikely to agree on the appropriate standards and often for very good reasons.

Labor standards offer the easiest example. The argument that rich countries' restrictions on child labor may be a poor fit for developing countries has long prevented a global consensus from emerging. Child labor of the type that activists in rich nations object to is often an unavoidable consequence of poverty. Preventing young children from working in factories may end up doing more harm than good if the most likely alternative for the children is not going to school but employment in domestic trades that are even more odious (prostitution is an oft-mentioned illustration). This argument against homogenization applies to other labor regulations too, such as maximum hours of work or minimum wages. More broadly, as long as basic human rights such as non-discrimination and freedom of association are not violated, nations ought to be free to choose the labor standards that best fit their own circumstances and social preferences. Common standards are costly, even if they may facilitate acceptance of certain kinds of imports in the rich countries.

This is also true in the area of financial regulation. What is "safe" for the United States may not be "safe enough" for France or Germany. The United States may accept happily a bit more risk than the other two countries as the price of financial innovation. On the other hand, the U.S. may want its banks to have higher capital requirements as a cushion against risk taking than French or German policy makers think necessary. In each case, neither position is necessarily right and the other wrong. Nations have different views because they have different preferences and circumstances.

Product safety rules seem the easiest to organize around a common standard, but even here there are important constraints. Note first that Chinese lead paint standards are in fact quite stringent. The problem arises not from differences in standards as written, but from differences in standards as practiced. As in most developing countries, the Chinese government has trouble enforcing and monitoring product standards. These difficulties often arise not from lack of willingness, but from lack of ability stemming from administrative, human resource, and financial constraints. No global standard can change this underlying reality. Perhaps, as Slaughter suggests, participation in global networks can help Chinese regulators improve by enabling information sharing and transfer of "best practices." Don't hold your breath. Improving domestic institutions is a long, drawn-out process over which foreigners typically have a very limited influence.

Even if nations were to agree on global standards, they may end up converging on the wrong set of regulations. Global finance provides an apt illustration. The Basel Committee on Banking Supervision, the global club of bank regulators, has been widely hailed as the apogee of international financial cooperation, but has produced largely inadequate agreements.[18] The first set of recommendations (Basel I) encouraged risky short-term borrowing and may have played a role in precipitating the Asian financial crisis. The second (Basel II) relied on credit rating agencies and banks' own models to generate risk weights for capital requirements, and is now widely viewed as inappropriate in light of the recent financial crisis. By neglecting the fact that the risks created by an individual bank's actions depend on the liquidity of the system as a whole, the Basel Committee's standards have, if anything, magnified systemic risks. In light of the great uncertainty about the merits of different regulatory approaches, it may be better to let a variety of regulatory models flourish side by side.

Market-based solutions. There is a more market-friendly alternative. Instead of mandating adherence to global standards, it entails mandating provision of *information*. If we enhance the information available to importers about the standards under which goods and services have been produced, every buyer can then make the decision that best fits his or her circumstances.

Consider child labor. We can imagine a system of certification and labeling that lets consumers in the advanced nations distinguish between imported goods that have been produced by children and those that have not. There are already many such labeling schemes in operation. RugMark, for example, is an international non-governmental organization that certifies that no child labor has been used in carpets from India and Nepal. Presumably, child-labor-free products cost more to produce and are more expensive. Consumers can express their preferences through the products they want to buy. Those who oppose the use of child labor can pay extra and buy the appropriately labeled goods while others remain free to consume the cheaper product. An attractive feature of labeling is that it doesn't impose a common standard on everyone in the importing country. I don't have to pay for your high standard if a lower one is good enough for me.

This would seem like a good solution, especially since it makes limited demands on global governance. And there may be certain areas where it makes a lot of sense. But as a generic solution, it falls far short.

Until the recent financial crisis we would have pointed to credit rating agencies as a successful instance of labeling. These agencies functioned, in principle, in the way that labeling is supposed to work. If you were risk-averse, you could restrict yourself to triple-A-rated, low-yield securities. If you wanted more yield, at the expense of higher risk, you could invest in lower-rated securities instead. These ratings allowed investors, again in principle, to decide where they wanted to be on the risk spectrum. The government did not need to micromanage portfolio decisions.

We have learned since that the information conveyed by credit ratings was not nearly as meaningful as it appeared at the time. For a variety of reasons, not least that the credit rating agencies were paid by the very firms whose securities they were evaluating, toxic assets received top ratings. Too many investors got burned because they took the ratings seriously. The market for information worked quite poorly.

The costs of faulty ratings were borne not just by the investors in those securities but by society at large. This is the problem of systemic risk: when large, highly leveraged institutions go bust, they threaten to take the entire financial system with them. The failure of credit rating agencies had consequences well beyond those who purchased the toxic securities.

Every system of labeling in fact raises a higher-order governance question: To whom are the certifiers accountable, or who certifies the certifiers?

Credit rating worked poorly in financial markets because credit rating agencies maximized their income and neglected their fiduciary duties to society. A complicated governance problem was "solved" by handing it over to private profit-seeking entities whose incentives weren't properly aligned with society's.

The problem with labeling is no less serious in the case of labor or environmental standards, where diverse coalitions of non-governmental organizations and private corporations have taken the lead in the face of governmental deadlock. All of the participants have their own agenda, with the result that the meaning the labels convey can become quite ambiguous. For example, "fair trade" labels denote products such as coffee, chocolates, or bananas that are grown in an environmentally sustainable manner and which pay the farmers a certain minimum price. This seems like a win-win. Consumers can sip their coffee knowing that they are contributing to alleviating poverty and safeguarding the environment. But does the consumer really know or understand what the "fair trade" label on her coffee means?

We have very little reliable information on how labeling efforts such as "fair trade" work out in practice. One of the few academic studies on the subject looked at coffee in Guatemala and Costa Rica and found very little interest on the part of growers in fair trade certification. This is quite surprising in light of the apparent advantages, most notably in terms of better prices. In reality, the price premium the growers received seems to have been low compared to what they could get from growing specialty coffees. Often, the price was not high enough to cover the investments necessary to fit the requirements for certification. Moreover, the benefits did not necessarily flow to the poorest farmers, who are the landless indigenous growers.[19] Other reports suggest that only a tiny share of the price premium for fair trade coffee finds its way to the growers.[20]

Fair trade or other labeling programs like Rug-Mark may be doing some good on the whole, but we should be skeptical about how informative these labels are and the likely magnitude of their effects.

And what is true of NGO-led efforts is all the more true of corporate social responsibility. Corporations, after all, are motivated by the bottom line. They may be willing to invest in social and environmental projects if doing so buys them customers' goodwill. Yet we shouldn't assume their motives align closely with those of society at large, nor exaggerate their willingness to advance societal agendas.

The most fundamental objection to labeling and other market-based approaches is that they overlook the *social* dimension of standard-setting. For example, the conventional approach to dealing with health and safety hazards calls for standards, not labeling. If labeling works so well, why don't we deal with these issues in the same way, by letting individuals decide how much risk they want to take? As far as I know, not even libertarian economists have proposed that the best way to deal with the problem of lead-tainted Chinese toys is to *label* Chinese-made toys as having uncertain or high lead content and let consumers choose according to their own preferences and health-hazard/price trade-offs. Instead, our natural instinct is to push for more regulation and better enforcement of existing standards. Even the U.S. toy industry has asked the federal government to impose mandatory safety-testing standards for all toys sold in the United States.[21]

We prefer uniform, government-mandated standards in these cases for several reasons. We may be skeptical that consumers will have enough information to make the right choices or the capacity to process the information they have. We may believe in the importance of social goals and norms in addition to individual preferences. Even though a few people in our midst may be willing to sign on as indentured servants for a price, we are unlikely as a society to allow them to do so. Finally, individuals acting in their own best interest may create problems for the rest of society and as a consequence their freedom to choose may need to be restricted. Think again of the mess that the banks that invested in toxic assets created for the rest of us or how sweatshops can undermine employment conditions for others in the economy.

These reasons apply as much to social and economic issues as they do to health and safety risks. They suggest that labeling and certification will play only a limited role in addressing the governance challenges of the global economy.

The limits of global governance. Global governance offers little help in solving these challenges we have considered. We are dealing with problems rooted in deep divisions among different societies in terms of preferences, circumstances, and capabilities. Technical fixes don't help. Neither do networks of regulators, market-based solutions, corporate social responsibility, or transnational deliberation. At best, these new forms of governance provide a kind of global governance-light. They simply cannot carry the weight of a hyperglobalized world economy. The world is too diverse to be shoehorned into a single political community.

In the case of lead-tainted toys, most people would agree that the obvious and correct solution is to let the domestic standard prevail. The United States should determine its own health and safety standards, and allow only toys that satisfy those standards to be imported. If other countries want to have different standards, or are unable to match U.S. standards for practical reasons, they would be similarly entitled to their own variants. But they cannot expect to export their products freely to the United States unless they meet the U.S. standards. This approach enables countries to uphold their own regulations, even if it comes at the cost of barriers at the border.

Can we not apply the same principle to financial regulation labor standards, or other areas of conflict arising from differences in national standards? We can, and we should.

Globalization and Identity Redux

In Nick Hornby's comic novel *Juliet, Naked* (2009), one of the main characters, Duncan, obsesses over an obscure and reclusive American rock musician named Tucker Crowe. Duncan's life revolves around Crowe: he lectures on him, organizes meetings and conventions, and has written an unpublished book on the great man. Initially, Duncan has few people nearby with whom he can share his passion. The nearest Tucker Crowe fan lives sixty miles away and Duncan can meet up with him only once or twice a year. Then the Internet comes along. Duncan sets up a Web site and makes contact with hundreds of equally passionate Tucker Crowe aficionados scattered around the world. As Hornby writes, "now the nearest fans lived in Duncan's laptop," and he could talk to them all the time.[22]

New information and communication technologies are bringing ordinary people like Duncan together around shared interests in ways that scholars including Peter Singer and Amartya Sen hope will shrink the world. Thanks to these global links, local attachments are becoming less important as transnational moral and political communities loom ever larger. Or are they?

Even though Duncan's story sounds familiar—we've all had similar transformations in our own lives thanks to the Internet—it doesn't tell us the full story. Do our global interactions really erode our local and national identities? Evidence from the real world presents a very different and quite surprising picture. Consider the case of Netville.

In the mid-1990s, a new housing development in one of the suburbs of Toronto engaged in an interesting experiment. The houses in this Canadian residential community were built from the ground up with the latest broadband telecommunications infrastructure and came with a host of new Internet technologies. Residents of Netville (a pseudonym) had access to high-speed Internet, a videophone, an online jukebox, online health services, discussion forums, and a suite of entertainment and educational applications.[23]

These new technologies made the town an ideal setting for nurturing global citizens. The people of Netville were freed from the tyranny of distance. They could communicate with anyone in the world as easily as they could with a neighbor, forge their own global links, and join virtual communities in cyberspace. They would begin, observers expected, to define their identities and interests increasingly in global, rather than local, terms.

What actually transpired was quite different. Glitches experienced by the telecom provider left some homes without a link to the broadband network. This allowed researchers to compare across wired and non-wired households and reach some conclusions about the consequences of being wired. Far from letting local links erode, wired people actually strengthened their existing local social ties. Compared to non-wired residents, they recognized more of their neighbors, talked to them more often, visited them more frequently, made many more local phone calls. They were more likely to organize local events and mobilize the community around common problems. They used their computer network to facilitate a range of social activities—from organizing barbecues to helping local children with their homework. Netville exhibited, as one resident put it, "a closeness that you don't see in many communities." What was supposed to have unleashed global engagement and networks had instead strengthened local social ties.

As powerful as information and communication technologies are, we should not assume that they will lead us down the path of global consciousness or transnational political communities. Distance matters. Our local attachments largely still define us and our interests.

The World Values Survey periodically polls random samples of individuals around the world on their attitudes and attachments. A recent round of surveys asked people in fifty-five countries about the strength of their local, national, and global identities. The results were similar across the world—and quite instructive. They reveal that attachment to the nation state overwhelms all other forms of identity. People see themselves primarily as citizens of their nation, next as members of their local community, and only last as "global citizens." The sole exceptions, where people identified more with the world than with their nation, were violence-ridden Colombia and tiny Andorra.[24]

These surveys uncover an important divide between elites and the rest of society. A strong sense of global citizenship tends to be confined, where it exists, to wealthy individuals and those with the highest levels of educational attainment. Conversely, attachment to the nation state is generally much stronger (and global identities correspondingly weaker) among individuals from lower social classes. This cleavage is perhaps not that surprising. Skilled professionals and investors can benefit from global opportunities wherever they may arise. The nation state and what it does matters a lot less to these people than it does to less mobile workers and others with fewer skills who have to make do with what's nearby. This opportunity gap reveals a certain dark side to the clamor for global governance. The construction of transnational political communities is a project of globalized elites attuned largely to their needs.

If Not Global Governance, Then What?

The new forms of global governance are intriguing and deserve further development, but ultimately they run up against some fundamental limits: political identities and attachments still revolve around nation states; political communities are organized domestically rather than globally; truly global norms have emerged only in a narrow range of issues; and there remain substantial differences across the world on desirable institutional arrangements. These new transnational mechanisms can take the edge off some contentious issues, but they are no substitute for real governance. They are insufficient to underpin extensive economic globalization.

We need to accept the reality of a divided world polity and make some tough choices. We have to be explicit about where one nation's rights and responsibilities end and another nation's begin. We cannot fudge the role of nation states and proceed on the assumption that we are witnessing the birth of a global political community. We must acknowledge and accept the restraints on globalization that a divided global polity entails. *The scope of workable global regulation limits the scope of desirable globalization.* Hyper-globalization cannot be achieved, and we should not pretend that it can.

Ultimately, this reality check can lead us to a healthier, more sustainable world order.

NOTES

1. African Development Bank and World Tourism (not Trade) Organization, respectively.

2. See http://voxeu.org/index.php?q=node/2544.

3. See Jeffrey Garten, "The Case for a Global Central Bank," Yale School of Management, posted online, September 21, 2009, at http://ba.yale.edu/news_events/CMS/Articles/6958.shtml.

4. Carmen Reinhart and Kenneth Rogoff, "Regulation Should Be International," *Financial Times*, November 18, 2008 (http://www.ft.com/cms/s/0/983724fc-b589-11dd-ab71-0000779fd18c.html?nclick_check=1).

5. David Epstein and Sharyn O'Halloran, *Delegating Powers: A Transaction Cost Politics Approach to Policy Making Under Separate Powers* (Cambridge and New York: Cambridge University Press, 1999).

6. Anne-Marie Slaughter. *A New World Order* (Princeton and Oxford: Princeton University Press, 2004).

7. John G. Ruggie, "Reconstituting the Global Public Domain—Issues, Actors, and Practices," *European Journal of International Relations*, 10 (2004), pp. 499–531.

8. There is a parallel debate in international law on whether it is possible to institute effective legal norms and practices at the global level in the absence of global government. See, e.g., Jeffrey L. Dunoff and Joel P. Trachtman, eds., *Ruling the World?: Constitutionalism, International Law, and Global Governance* (Cambridge and New York: Cambridge University Press, 2009), and Eric Posner, *The Perils of Global Legalism* (Chicago: University of Chicago Press, 2009), in addition to the work of Anne-Marie Slaughter already cited. The case against "global legalism" is stated succinctly by Posner, who argues that without legal institutions—legislators, enforcers, and courts—law cannot control behavior.

9. Joshua Cohen and Charles F. Sabel, "Global Democracy?" *International Law and Politics*, 37 (2005), p. 779.

10. Ibid., p. 796.

11. Peter Singer, *One World: The Ethics of Globalization* (New Haven: Yale University Press, 2002), p. 12.

12. Amartya Sen, *Identity and Violence: The Illusion of Destiny* (New York: W. W. Norton, 2006).

13. Amartya Sen, *The Idea of Justice* (Cambridge, MA: Harvard University Press, 2009), p. 143.

14. See Cohen and Sabel, "Global Democracy," and Charles F. Sabel and Jonathan Zeitlin, "Learning from Difference: The New Architecture of Experimentalist Governance in the EU," *European Law Journal*, vol. 14, no. 3 (May 2008), pp. 271–327.

15. Stephen Castle, "Compromise with Britain Paves Way to Finance Rules in Europe," *New York Times*, December 2, 2009 (http://www.nytimes.com/2009/12/03/business/global/03eubank.html?_r=1& sudsredirect=true).

16. The decision to send Greece to the IMF caused a certain amount of controversy within the European Union since, unlike the other two countries, Greece is a member of not only the European Union but also of the Eurozone. Ultimately, insistence on this score by German chancellor Angela Merkel overcame opposition from French president Nicolas Sarkozy and the European Central Bank president Jean-Claude Trichet.

17. See "After Severe Recession, Stabilization in Latvia," IMF Survey online, February 18, 2010, http://www.imf.org/external/pubs/ft/survey/so/2010/CAR021810A.htm.

18. The national regulators that negotiate these international agreements have their own interests, of course, and they enter into agreements in part as a counterweight to domestic political pressures. See David Andrew Singer, *Regulating Capital: Setting Standards for the International Financial System* (Ithaca, NY: Cornell University Press, 2007).

19. Colleen E. H. Berndt, "Is Fair Trade in Coffee Production Fair and Useful? Evidence from Costa Rica and Guatemala and Implications for Policy," Mercatus Policy Series, Policy Comment No. 11, George Mason University, June 2007.

20. Andrew Chambers, "Not So Fair Trade," *The Guardian*, December 12, 2009. (http://www.guardian .co.uk/commentisfree/cif-green/2009/ dec/12/ fair-trade-fairtrade-kitkat-farmers).

21. See "Toy Makers Seek Standards for U.S. Safety," *New York Times*, September 7, 2007 (http://www .nytimes.com/2007/09/07/business/07toys .html?_r=2).

22. Nick Hornby, *Juliet, Naked* (New York: Penguin, 2009).

23. This account is based on Keith Hampton, "Netville: Community On and Offline in a Wired Suburb," in Stephen Graham, ed., *The Cybercities Reader* (London: Routledge, 2004), pp. 256–62. I owe the reference to this study to Nicholas A. Christakis and James H. Fowler, *Connected: The Surprising Power of Our Social Networks and How They Shape Our Lives* (New York: Little, Brown, 2009).

24. The data that I summarize here come from the World Values Survey databank at http://www .worldvaluessurvey.org/services/index.html.

LEVIATHAN STIRS AGAIN

Fifteen years ago it seemed that the great debate about the proper size and role of the state had been resolved. In Britain and America alike, Tony Blair and Bill Clinton pronounced the last rites of "the era of big government." Privatising state-run companies was all the rage. The Washington consensus reigned supreme: persuade governments to put on "the golden straitjacket," in Tom Friedman's phrase, and prosperity would follow.

Today big government is back with a vengeance: not just as a brute fact, but as a vigorous ideology. Britain's public spending is set to exceed 50% of GDP. America's financial capital has shifted from New York to Washington, DC, and the government has been trying to extend its control over the health-care industry. Huge state-run companies such as Gazprom and PetroChina are on the march. Nicolas Sarkozy, having run for office as a French Margaret Thatcher, now argues that the main feature of the credit crisis is "the return of the state, the end of the ideology of public powerlessness."

"The return of the state" is stirring up fiery opposition as well as praise. In America the Republican Party's anti-government base is more agitated than it has been at any time since the days of the Gingrich revolution in 1994. "Tea-party" protesters have been marching across the country with an amusing assortment of banners and buttons: "Born free, taxed to death" and "God only requires 10%." On January 19th Scott Brown, a Republican, captured the Massachusetts Senate seat long held by the late Ted Kennedy, America's most prominent supporter of big-government liberalism.

Many European countries have devoted a high proportion of their GDP to public spending for years. And many governments cannot wait to get out of their new-found business of running banks and car companies. But the past decade has clearly produced changes which, taken cumulatively, have put the question of the state back at the centre of political debate.

The obvious reason for the change is the financial crisis. As global markets collapsed, governments intervened on an unprecedented scale, injecting liquidity into their economies and taking over, or otherwise rescuing, banks and other companies that were judged "too big to fail." A few months after Lehman Brothers had collapsed, the American government was in charge of General Motors

From *The Economist* (January 21, 2010).

and Chrysler, the British government was running high street banks and, across the OECD, governments had pledged an amount equivalent to 2.5% of GDP.

The crisis upended conventional wisdom about the relative merits of governments and markets. Where government, in Ronald Reagan's aphorism, was once the problem, today the default villain is the market. Free-marketeers such as Alan Greenspan, the former head of the Federal Reserve, have apologised for their ideological zeal. A line from Rudyard Kipling sums it up best: "The gods of the market tumbled, and their smooth-tongued wizards withdrew."

Yet even before Lehman Brothers collapsed the state was on the march—even in Britain and America, which had supposedly done most to end the era of big government. Gordon Brown, Britain's chancellor and later its prime minister, began his ministerial career as "Mr. Prudent." During Labour's first three years in office public spending fell from 40.6% of GDP to 36.6%. But then he embarked on an Old Labour spending binge. He increased spending on the National Health Service by 6% a year in real terms and boosted spending on education. During Labour's 13 years in power two-thirds of all the new jobs created were driven by the public sector, and pay has grown faster there than in the private sector.

In America, George Bush did not even go through a prudent phase. He ran for office believing that "when somebody hurts, government has got to move." And he responded to the terrorist attacks of September 11th, 2001 with a broad-ranging "war on terror." The result of his guns-and-butter strategy was the biggest expansion in the American state since Lyndon Johnson's in the mid-1960s. He added a huge new drug entitlement to Medicare. He created the biggest new bureaucracy since the second world war, the Department of Homeland Security. He expanded the federal government's control over education and over the states. The gap between American public spending and Canada's has tumbled from 15 percentage points in 1992 to just two percentage points today.

The Public's Demands

The expansion of the state in both Britain and America met with widespread approval. The opposition Conservative Party applauded Mr. Brown's increase in NHS spending. Mr. Bush met no significant opposition from his fellow Republicans to his spending binge. It was clear that, when it came to their own benefits, suburban Americans wanted government on their side. A banner at one of those tea-parties sums up the confused attitude of many of the so-called anti-government protesters: "Keep the government's hands off my Medicare."

The demand for public services will soar in the coming decades, thanks to the ageing of the population. The United Nations points out that the proportion of the world's population that is over 60 will rise from 11% today to 22% in 2050. The situation is especially dire in the developed world: in 2050 one in three people in the rich world will be pensioners, and one in ten will be over 80. In America more than 10,000 baby-boomers will become eligible for Social Security and Medicare every day for the next two decades. The Congressional Budget Office (CBO) calculates that entitlement spending will grow from 9% of GDP today to 20% in 2025. If America keeps its distaste for taxes, it will face fiscal Armageddon.

The level of public spending is only one indication of the state's power. America's federal government employs a quarter of a million bureaucrats whose job it is to write and apply federal regulations. They have cousins in national and supranational capitals all around the world. These regulators act as force multipliers: a regulation promulgated by a few can change the behaviour of entire industries. Periodic attempts to build "bonfires of regulations" have gotten nowhere. Under Mr. Bush the number of pages of federal regulations increased by 7,000, and eight of Britain's ten biggest regulatory bodies were set up under the current government.

The power of these regulators is growing all the time. Policymakers are drawing up new rules on everything from the amount of capital that banks have to set aside to what to do about them when they fail. Britain is imposing additional taxes on bankers' bonuses, America is imposing extra taxes on banks' liabilities, and central bankers are pondering ingenious ways to intervene in overheated markets. Worries about climate change have already led to a swathe of new regulations, for example on carbon emissions from factories and power plants and on the energy efficiency of cars and light bulbs. But, since emissions are continuing to grow, such regulations are likely to proliferate and, at the same time, get tighter. The Kerry-Boxer bill on carbon emissions, which is now in the Senate, runs to 821 pages.

Fear of terrorism and worries about rising crime have also inflated the state. Governments have expanded their ability to police and supervise their populations. Britain has more than 4m CCTV cameras, one for every 14 people. In Liverpool the police have taken to using unmanned aerial drones, similar to those used in Afghanistan, to supervise the population. The Bush administration engaged in a massive programme of telephone tapping before the Supreme Court slapped it down.

Another form of the advancing state is more insidious. Annual lists of the world's biggest companies have begun to feature new kinds of corporate entities: companies that are either directly owned or substantially controlled by the state. Four state-controlled companies have made it into the top 25 of the 2009 Forbes Global 2000 list, and the number is likely to grow. Chinese state-controlled companies have been buying up private companies during the financial crisis. Russia's state-controlled companies have a long record of snapping up private companies on the cheap. Sovereign wealth funds are increasingly important in the world's markets.

This is partly a product of the oil boom. Three-quarters of the world's crude-oil reserves are owned by national oil companies. (By contrast, conventional multinationals control just 3% of the world's reserves and produce 10% of its oil and gas.)

But it is also the result of something more fundamental: the shift in the balance of economic power to countries with a very different view of the state from the one celebrated in the Washington consensus. The world is seeing the rise of a new economic hybrid—what might be termed "state capitalism."

Under state capitalism, governments do not so much reject the market as use it as an instrument of state power. They encourage companies to take advantage of global capital markets and venture abroad in search of opportunities. Malaysia's Petronas and China's National Petroleum Corporation run businesses in some 30 countries. But they also use them to control the economy at home—to direct resources to favoured industries or reward political clients. Politicians in China and elsewhere not only make decisions about the production of cars and mobile phones; they are also the hidden hands behind companies that are scouring the world for the raw materials that go into them.

The revival of the state is creating a series of fierce debates that will shape policymaking over the coming decades. Governments are beginning to cut public spending in an attempt to deal with surging deficits. But the inevitable quarrels over cuts will be paltry compared with those about the growth of entitlements. America's deficit, boosted by recession, is already hovering at a post-war high of 12% of GDP, and the American economy depends on the willingness of other countries (particularly China) to fund its debt. The CBO calculates that the deficit could rise to 23% of GDP in the next 40 years if it fails to tackle the yawning imbalance between revenue and expenditure.

Crises can be the midwives of serious thinking. The stagflation of the 1970s prepared the way for the Reagan and Thatcher revolutions. More recently, several countries have dealt with out-of-control spending by introducing dramatic cuts: New Zealand, Canada and the Netherlands all reduced public spending by as much as 10% from 1992 onwards.

In the early 1990s Sweden faced a home-grown economic crisis that foreshadowed many of the features of the global crisis. The property bubble burst and the government stepped in to save the banks and pump up demand. Public debt doubled, unemployment tripled and the budget deficit increased tenfold. The Social Democrats were elected in 1994 and re-elected twice thereafter on a programme of raising taxes and slashing spending.

This points to an irony: a crisis which promotes state growth in the short term may lead to pruning in the longer term. In Britain power is almost certain to shift from Labour to the Conservatives, who are much keener on cutting public spending. In America the Republicans will make big gains in the mid-term elections and Mr. Obama, already sobered by his loss in Massachusetts, will have to move to the centre.

But pruning will still be more difficult than it has ever been before. Getting the public sector to do "more with less" is harder after two decades of public-sector reforms. Across the OECD more than 40% of public goods are provided by the private sector (thanks to privatisation and contracting out) and 75% of public officials are on some sort of pay-for-performance scheme. The ageing of the population makes earlier reforms look easy. Governments will have to ask fundamental questions—such as whether it makes sense to let people retire at 65 when they are likely to live for another 20 years.

The rise of state capitalism is fraught with problems. It may be hard to argue with China's 30 years of hefty economic growth and $2.3 trillion in foreign-currency reserves. But subordinating economic decisions to political ones can come with a price-tag in the long term: politicians are reluctant to let "strategic" companies fail, and companies become adjuncts of the state patronage machine. Giving the imprimatur of the state to global companies is also fraught with risks. America's Congress prevented Dubai from taking over American ports on grounds of national security.

Anatomising Failure

The most interesting arguments over the next few years will weigh government failure against market failure. The market-failure school had been gaining strength even before the credit crunch struck. The rise of cowboy capitalism in Russia under Boris Yeltsin persuaded many people—not least the Chinese—of the importance of strong government. And the threat of global warming is an obvious example of how government intervention is needed to deter people from overheating the world. Advocates of market failure have also been advancing a broad range of arguments for using the government to "nudge" people's behaviour in the right direction.

But the fact that markets are prone to sometimes spectacular failure does not mean that governments are immune to it. Government departments are good at expanding their empires. Thus a welfare state that was designed to help people deal with unavoidable risks, such as sickness and old age, is increasingly in the business of trying to eliminate risk in general through a proliferating health-and-safety bureaucracy. Government workers are also good at protecting their own interests. In America, where 30% of people in the public sector are unionised compared with just 7% in the private sector, public-sector workers enjoy better pension rights than private-sector workers, as well as higher average pay.

The public sector is subjected to all sorts of perverse incentives. Politicians use public money to "buy" votes. America is littered with white elephants such as the John Murtha Airport in Jonestown, Pennsylvania, which cost hundreds of millions of dollars but serves only a handful of passengers, including Mr. Murtha, who happens to be chairman of a powerful congressional committee. Interest groups spend hugely to try to affect political decisions: there are 1,800 registered lobbyists in the European Union, 5,000 in Canada and no fewer than 15,000 in America. Mr. Bush's energy bill was so influenced by lobbyists that John McCain dubbed it the "No Lobbyist Left Behind" act.

These perverse incentives mean that governments can frequently spend lots of money without producing any improvement in public services. Britain's government doubled spending on education between fiscal 1999 and fiscal 2007, but the spending splurge coincided with a dramatic decline in

Britain's position in the OECD's ranking of educational performance. Bill Watkins of the University of California, Santa Barbara, calculates that, once you adjust for inflation and population growth, his state's government spent 26% more in 2007–08 than in 1997–98. No one can argue that California's public services are now 26% better.

"The question that we ask today," said Barack Obama in his inaugural address, "is not whether our government is too big or too small, but whether it works." This is clearly naive: with deficits soaring, nobody can afford to ignore the size of government. Mr. Obama's appeal for pragmatism has some value: conservative attempts to roll back government regulations have led to disaster in the finance industry. But left-wing attempts to defend entitlements and public-sector privileges willy-nilly will condemn the state to collapse under its own weight. Policymakers will not be able to give a serious answer to Mr. Obama's question of whether "government works" without first asking themselves some more fundamental questions about what the state should be doing and what it should be leaving well alone.

Min Jiang

AUTHORITARIAN INFORMATIONALISM: CHINA'S APPROACH TO INTERNET SOVEREIGNTY

In a speech given at the Paul H. Nitze School of Advanced International Studies at Johns Hopkins University, President Bill Clinton made light of Beijing's effort to regulate the Internet. "Good luck! That's sort of like trying to nail Jell-O to the wall." He was confident that the United States would benefit economically from greater access to Chinese markets and that the Internet would spread liberty in China.[1]

In retrospect, Clinton was right about the growing economic ties between the two countries and, to his credit, there is a greater degree of economic, cultural, and political freedoms in China than before, aided by active Internet use. But he seriously underestimated Beijing's determination and capabilities to regulate the Chinese Internet to its liking. Following Google's high profile spat with Beijing over censorship, alleged cyber attacks, and the Internet giant's license renewal saga to operate in China, issues of Internet freedom and cybersecurity were elevated to new heights. Speaking at the Newseum in Washington, D.C. on 2010, January 21 Secretary of State Hillary Clinton conceded that "technologies are not an unmitigated blessing" and that the U.S. government stands to promote the freedom of expression, and notably, the freedom to connect.[2]

Six months later, the Chinese State Council Information Office responded with *The Internet in China*, a white paper on Chinese Internet policy. As the first document of its kind, the paper outlines Beijing's basic principles of Internet regulation in a country of 420 million Internet users: "active use, scientific development, law-based administration and ensured security." The paper proclaims that:

> Within Chinese territory the Internet is under the jurisdiction of Chinese sovereignty. The Internet sovereignty of China should be respected and protected. Citizens of the People's Republic of China and foreign citizens, legal persons and other

From *SAIS Review* 30, no. 2 (Summer–Fall 2010), pp. 71–89.

organizations within Chinese territory have the right and freedom to use the Internet; at the same time, they must obey the laws and regulations of China and conscientiously protect Internet security.[3]

Looming large here is a clash between two different visions for the future of the Web: a single, connected Internet endorsed by Secretary Clinton and a bordered Internet based on national sovereignty supported by Beijing. This article outlines the clashing views on Internet sovereignty and analyzes, in particular, China's Internet policies from the standpoint of state legitimacy. Grounded in its fundamental interest in maintaining regime legitimacy by delivering economic growth and domestic stability, Beijing's cyber approach and practices are inseparable from its promotion of legitimacy in five major areas: the economy, nationalism, ideology, culture, and governance. State efforts, orchestrated both online and offline, have been arguably successful in gaining popular compliance, thus cementing Beijing's political authority despite some grassroots challenges to its rule. In the foreseeable future, China's Internet policies will continue to reflect what I call authoritarian informationalism, an Internet development and regulatory model that combines elements of capitalism, authoritarianism, and Confucianism. Engagement with the regime's cyber policies and its Internet users needs to recognize not only an audible outcry to tear down the Great Firewall, but also the larger Chinese populace's aspiration for economic growth, social stability as well as greater transparency, accountability, and freedom. Meaningful social change comes not only from outside, but also from within.

Whose Sovereignty? Clashing Views on Internet Sovereignty

The Chinese white paper catapulted the term "Internet sovereignty" to prominence. Though the Chinese government is not claiming sovereignty over the entire Internet, it is asserting its right to regulate the Internet within its borders. It also signals the maturity of an authoritarian Internet regulatory model from an increasingly confident China.

Overall, Washington and Beijing's approaches toward Internet governance and Internet sovereignty are at odds. The U.S. State Department advocates a single connected Internet that is, to a degree, sovereign in its own right while China's State Council Information Office is pushing for a bordered Internet based on territorial sovereignty. The U.S. approach, is individual-based, rights-centered, and market-driven. The Chinese approach, on the other hand, is state-centered. It emphasizes individual responsibilities over individual rights, maximum economic benefits, and minimal political risk for the one-party state.

Secretary Clinton's speech on Internet freedom evokes a libertarian aura, depicting an Internet that celebrates free information, unlimited computer access, and individualism.[4] Clinton's call to build "a single Internet where all of humanity has equal access to knowledge and ideas" certainly appeals to freedom seekers around the world. Beijing's view of the Internet, on the other hand, is fundamentally a utilitarian one, viewing it as "useful and conducive to economic and social development." Rather than placing emphasis on the Internet as an extension of individual freedom and a marketplace of ideas, Beijing stresses its importance in driving China's economy and raising people's living standards.

Individuals who inhabit cyberspace are also ascribed somewhat different characteristics. Clinton's speech, in essence, is an affirmation of the American First Amendment in cyberspace. Under the umbrella of Internet freedom, she argues that netizens should have the rights to freedom of expression and freedom to connect. Here, not only does the State Department frame these individual rights on the Internet as universal, it also underscores the potential of the Internet in promoting a form of global citizenship that transcends national boundaries. Rhetorically, Beijing also guarantees its citizens and those residing in China online speech freedom. The public, according to the Chinese Internet white paper, has the "right to know, to participate, to be heard, and to oversee in accordance with the law."

The same paper also asserts that Chinese netizens' active use of online commentary and discussion services and their oversight of government activities online are "a manifestation of China's socialist democracy and progress."

Notwithstanding the improvement made in certain areas of civil rights in China, individuals' speech rights, especially political speech rights are limited. In its characteristically sweeping language, the Chinese Internet white paper states the Chinese government forbids Internet content:

> against the cardinal principles set forth in the Constitution; endangering state security, divulging state secrets, subverting state power and jeopardizing national unification; damaging state honor and interests; instigating ethnic hatred or discrimination and jeopardizing ethnic unity; jeopardizing state religious policy, propagating heretical or superstitious ideas; spreading rumors, disrupting social order and stability; disseminating obscenity, pornography, gambling, violence, brutality and terror or abetting crime; humiliating or slandering others, trespassing on the lawful rights and interests of others; and other contents forbidden by laws and administrative regulations.[5]

Given the wide spectrum of Internet content prohibited by Chinese laws as well as the arbitrary interpretation and enforcement of law, critical online expressions of dissent are often silenced to preserve often-social stability even though doing so impinges on the rights of individual Internet users.

Although the U.S. State Department was able to claim the moral high ground of liberty and freedom over the dispute between Google and Beijing, one cannot help but realize that the U.S. is constrained by the same standard it needs to live up to as well as the international norm of cyber governance based largely on the nation-state. Under the expansive umbrella of Internet freedom, the apparition of Internet censorship is no less palpable than that of online privacy breaches. While both Beijing and Google try to gain control over data and informa-

tion in China, the former motivated by political concerns and the latter by advertising dollars, it is not unreasonable for the Chinese netizen to be wary that both may fail the "Don't be evil" test at some point although government censorship is pervasive and prominent at the moment.

Moreover, although the Internet has been popularly viewed and used as border-crossing infrastructure, its governance is far from borderless. Realists have long argued that territorial sovereignty in the form of a state, with its political and legal institutions such as an elected government and the rule of law, is the proper organization to regulate the Internet and such regulation would be no more problematic than that of the real world.[6] This framework tends to refrain from judging the legitimacy of specific state actions, leave Internet regulation to individual states, and adjudicate conflicts based on a limited set of existing international laws. This reality allows countries, including authoritarian countries like China, to deflect criticism and reject international interference, citing territorial supremacy.

The rising specter of government-backed online censorship and the commercial rush to hoard user information and data points to the increasing tension between state sovereignty and a growing public demand to protect netizen rights in the face of both governmental and market obtrusion. It is indeed ironic that the nation-state and national economy have never seemed so relevant even as we speak of their alleged passing and increasing global connectivity. As China grows more integrated with the rest of the world economically, there is a discernible tendency within the Communist Party to rein in political reforms and reaffirm Chinese values. Beijing's recent roll-back in its Internet policies and its bold assertion of Internet sovereignty are symptoms of this trend. However, one would be remiss not to notice the tangible signs of public demands for economic equality, social justice, and political freedoms as they surface on the Chinese Internet. Unfortunately, all too often the debate on the Internet's potential in authoritarian regimes winds up as a dead-end between techno-utopians and pessimists. I argue, however, modest goals of engagement with the Chinese populace is possible if one understands the essence of the Chinese government's Internet approach as well as the interest, needs, and aspirations of its people.

Chinese Internet: Beyond Techno-Utopians and Pessimists

As early as 1982, three years after the Party adopted the reform and open door policy, the State Council set up a committee to study and plan for the development of computing and information technology.[7] In 1994, China first connected to the World Wide Web and in 1998 had a million Internet users. Today that number stands at a dizzying 420 million (larger than the U.S. population). Among them, 200 million have blogs. Additionally, 277 million of China's 740 million phone users can access the Web via their cell devices.[8]

Beijing's adoption and promotion of the Web, however, has gone hand in hand with its physical manipulation of Internet architecture and control of Internet use. For the Party, the Web is not something inherently emancipating but an intermediary that can be configured and regulated in an *ad hoc* manner. Wu Jichuan, the then-Minister of Posts and Telecommunications was quoted in 1995 saying:

> By linking with the Internet, we don't mean absolute freedom of information. I think there is a general understanding about this. If you go through customs, you have to show your passport. It's the same with management of information. There is no contradiction at all between the development of telecommunications infrastructure and the exercise of state sovereignty.[9]

Beyond the well-known "Great Firewall of China," a technological filtering system blocking "harmful" foreign content at China's international gateway to the World Wide Web, the state also adopts a multi-layered censorship approach, from blunt suppression of dissidents, Internet policing, content removal, and discipline of cyber cafes, to more subtle forms: regulation of Internet service providers, promotion of self-censorship among users, and employment of cyber commentators to shape public opinion.[10]

Such extensive control does not go unchallenged. Beyond the high-profile cyber dissidents and activists who frequently make headlines in Western media, there is considerable online public discussion and debate on various economic, social, and political issues, forming a unique phenomenon of authoritarian deliberation.[11] Although such debates, not always critical of the government, take place largely within the expanding boundaries consented to by the Chinese state, they contribute to an impressive degree of cyber activism that pressures the government to be more accountable and have, in some cases, been able to change government policies.[12] Walking a fine line between self-expression and self-censorship, many Chinese Internet users have become more keenly aware of their rights as netizens and grown more adept at using euphemism, parody, and humor to criticize local and national government policies.[13]

Taken altogether, there is an unmistakable parallel in the growth of both state Internet control and online activism in China. Techno-utopians often cite instances of empowered individuals who express opinions, expose wrongdoing, scrutinize officials, mobilize protests, and hold the government accountable, all of which contribute to an expanding public sphere and an emergent civil society. Pessimists, on the other hand, point out that the authoritarian prowess of surveillance, censorship, and control has also been strengthened by the same tools and may well survive the age of digital activism relatively unscathed by diffusing the opposition of a small number of cyber dissidents while keeping the populace at large insulated or apolitical.[14]

So far, the Chinese state continues to embrace the "architectures of liberty" without succumbing to an irreversible loss of control over either the architecture or the empowered populace. More peculiarly, most Chinese approve of state Internet regulation. In a 2007 survey conducted by Pew Internet & American Life

Project on Chinese Internet use, almost 85 percent of Chinese respondents say they think the government should be responsible for managing and controlling the Internet.[15] Why the overwhelming consent to state control? This paradox may be explained partially by an unquestioned faith in the Web as a tool against tyranny in the West, in part by Beijing's ability to adapt, and more fundamentally by a broad public acceptance of the state as a provider of social goods, guarantor of social order, and preserver of public values.

A blind faith in technology as liberating ignores political, social, and economic factors that determine the Internet's effect on governance and civil society. To move beyond the debate between optimists and pessimists over the political future of China and the role the Internet could play in its democratization, one has to see past the binary view of authoritarian politics as a perpetual struggle between the state and its antistate, prodemocracy population and try to understand China's peculiars in its own terms.

Unfortunately, Western democracies have long dismissed stable nondemocratic states as illegitimate and resorted to an "elite-driven, top-down, outside-in, technocratic and overly formulaic experiment in social engineering that lacked local legitimacy."[16] This is not to say the values "liberal peacebuilding" tries to promote such as rule of law, human rights protection, democracy, and good governance do not have merit, but the manner in which peacebuilding has been pursued often seems hypocritical and imperialistic to the target countries and consequently has met resistance and produced counterproductive results. Engagement with China's Internet policies and its netizens may benefit from a better grasp of the Chinese government's popular sources of legitimacy and the needs and interests of the diverse Chinese population.

The Promotion of Harmony: Boost Authoritarian Legitimacy

Without competitive elections, functioning rule of law, or adequate human rights protection, China would have failed to pass as a legitimate state by liberal democratic standards. On the other hand, however, China has enjoyed relative stability despite serious challenges to Communist rule in 1989 and experienced high-speed economic growth in the past three decades. Most measurements on state legitimacy agree that the post-1989 Communist Party has successfully rebuilt its popular legitimacy. Bruce Gilley's study found in 2006 that China was a "high legitimacy" state among seventy-two countries considered, higher than Japan and second only to Taiwan in Asia.[17] Internationally, China is increasingly viewed more favorably as well, largely due to its economic achievements, according to Pew Research.[18] To understand and effectively engage such countries, there seems to be a need to evaluate state legitimacy empirically, not based solely on a realist's focus on stability or an idealist's emphasis on democratic consent, but grounded in a sense of common good and justice historically and locally defined.[19]

Beijing's relationship with the Internet is ambivalent. For any authoritarian regime, controlling information and public discourse has always been a cornerstone of authoritarian rule.[20] It is because legitimacy, understood as the right to rule, or the public's belief that the existing political institutions are the most appropriate for the society, requires subjects to obey not only out of self-interest, but also consent to the state's moral authority.[21] This acceptance implies knowledge and judgment about the state on the part of the ruled. A broad base of legitimacy can thus enable an authoritarian government like China's to regulate the Internet more to its liking, which in turn, reinforces its authority online. Following Holbig and Gilley's scheme,[22] I discuss next Beijing's popular legitimacy in five areas: economy, nationalism, ideology, culture, and governance and democracy. With their online presence, these various sources of legitimacy serve to solidify the party-state's claim to Internet sovereignty.

Economy

Economic growth is undoubtedly the Party's top priority and a main source of legitimacy. It is particularly the case as China emerged out of the recent global financial crisis triumphantly, with the government announcing a four trillion yuan (US$560 billion) stimulus package. Pew's 2010 survey shows in a widespread gloom, only China has an overwhelming portion of the population (87 percent) expressing satisfaction with the national conditions.[23] The Party's economic performance, framed as Party-led societal progress, scored points with many Chinese who now enjoy a higher standard of living compared to abject poverty levels twenty or thirty years ago.

Unlike the focus on individual rights in Anglo-American political thought, there is an enduring emphasis on collective socioeconomic justice in China, dating back to Mencius, a Confucian philosopher who stressed the links between economic welfare and legitimate rule.[24] This idea continues to find resonance in current Chinese politics as the 2004 Chinese White Paper on human rights states: "The Chinese government continues to put the safeguarding and promotion of the people's rights to subsistence and development on the top of its agenda."[25]

Knowing all too well that economic growth and rising standards of living are its fundamental raison d'être, Beijing relentlessly promoted IT development. Shortly after China introduced economic reform and the open door policy in 1979, the leadership under Deng Xiaoping quickly realized its Western counterparts were transitioning from an industrial society to an informational one and felt the urgency to catch up. Deng himself approved the National 863 Projects in 1986, investing 10 billion yuan (roughly $1.4 billion) in high tech industries between 1986 and 2000, two-thirds of which went to IT.[26] Today, IT contributes about 10 percent towards China's GDP. With the government's backing, many Chinese IT companies emerged as global competitors, including ZTE Communications, Huawei (networking and telecom), Tencent (instant messaging, online gaming and virtual currency, the world's third largest Internet company by market capitalization), and Baidu (search engine, the fourth most-visited website in ̣10).[27] The rise of such firms continues to fuel the ̣e economy and Beijing's claim to legitimacy.

Economy-based legitimacy, however, has its limits. It not only creates unprecedented inequalities and environmental deterioration in China, but also feeds rising expectations and alternative social values and political cultures.[28] So far, Beijing has managed to rally dominant social forces around economic growth. An elite class of business and political leaders has accepted authoritarian rule in exchange for cash. The growing middle class, intent on guarding their wealth from instability, is far from challenging state legitimacy as previously expected.[29]

Nationalism

Besides economy, nationalism is often seen as the other pillar of authoritarian legitimacy. Both state-sponsored and grassroots-driven nationalism serve as a bedrock for personal and social identities at a time of uncertainty induced by marketization and social pluralism. An official cultivation of "patriotism" becomes an "ersatz ideology"[30] to fill the vacuum left by an erosion of communist ideology. State media, through news and entertainment, regularly remind citizens of the nation's sufferings in its not so distant past: Western imperialism in the nineteenth century, cruelties inflicted by the Japanese "devils" during the Sino-Japanese War, and more recently the virulent Western "China threat" rhetoric fixed on preventing China from its inevitable rise.[31] Similar endless chains of "national humiliations" are repeated in textbooks to perpetuate a mode of "victimhood" expected to be internalized by youths born in the 1980s or 1990s.

Grassroots pent-up frustration of perceived foreign disrespect towards China is invariably channeled through the catharsis of nationalism. Western leaders' meetings with the Dalai Lama are framed as a gesture of open provocation. Popular protests against foreign powers such as the anti-Carrefour rally against French disruptions of [the] Beijing Olympics torch relay in 2008 are often delicately sanctioned by the state.[32] Books like *China Can Say No* published in 1996 and *Unhappy China* of 2009 became instant bestsellers, transmitting popular anger toward perceived unfair Western, particularly U.S., criticism and containment of China.

In the age of new media, nationalistic sentiments find new platforms of expression and coordination. *People's Net*, the official party mouthpiece, for instance, maintains a highly popular online forum, Strengthening the Nation Forum. Many netizens consider it a freer space and credit the government for listening to the people.[33] The growth of the Anti-CNN movement also bears out the state's sophisticated guiding of popular patriotism. Started out as a project of a 23-year-old student in response to "the lies and distortions of facts in Western media" in covering the 2008 Tibetan unrest, the online group sets out to "collect, classify, and distribute biased Western media reports against China"[34] but shuns criticizing the failures of Chinese official media.

While popular nationalism often comes from an authentic place, state nationalism has a tendency to manipulate public sentiments, extol state achievements, and obscure inequalities. By erasing the differences between "nation" and "state," the government continues to promote the logic that a Chinese citizen's love for the country inevitably translates into support for the Party.[35] Conversely, a challenge to the state and praise for Western values such as freedom and democracy are seen as unpatriotic and a denial of one's Chinese identity.

Ideology

The Internet has not put an end to ideology. The Communist Party cannot disown the revolution that brought it into power or the 75 million party members, one in every twelve Chinese adults, who are part of its ranks. The world's largest party is a sprawling governing edifice with branches throughout government, the military, schools, state-owned enterprises and even private firms.[36]

Over the years, the Party has adapted. Unlike Mao, who threw himself behind "thought work" to induce popular obedience, his successors, from Deng Xiaoping, Jiang Zemin to Hu Jingtao, have been more pragmatic. All of them de-emphasized class struggles that defined the Mao era and put economic development on the top of the Party's priority list. Deng's famous "cat-ism"—"I don't care if it's a white cat or black cat. It's a good cat so long as it catches mice"—perhaps best captures this pragmatism in ensuring public support for the Party's leadership.

After 1989, the Party under Jiang paid more attention to thought work. Jiang summarized his approach as "seize with both hands, both hands must be strong," meaning Party legitimacy relies on both economic growth and a renewed emphasis on political thought work.[37] Jiang's 2002 legacy of the "three represents" broadened party membership to include "the most advanced social productive forces," i.e., the newly affluent segments of the society. Hu, on the other hand, made "harmony" his political centerpiece to reduce confrontations in China's tumultuous economic and social transition.[38] The idea openly acknowledges China's societal tensions but prescribes a socially acceptable and politically legitimate goal for the Party. Chinese citizens are no longer assessing their political leaders based on party principles but rather on performance, such as capacity and efficiency in solving social problems.[39]

It certainly can be said that contrary to bringing harmony to Chinese society, the Party had in effect consolidated "crony capitalism" and created a corrupt class largely above the law.[40] But attracting the best and brightest also lends legitimacy to the Party's claim to reduce arbitrary decision-making and improve governance. Top Party leaders have repeatedly vowed to address popular discontent over issues of land grabs, political corruption, and wealth gaps, and moved in 2006 to abolish the agricultural tax to appeal to China's 800 million plus farmers. Premier Wen Jiabao, for instance, famously said during his online chat with netizens in 2010: "He who knows the leakage of a house lives under the roof. He who knows the mishandling of a state is among the populace."[41] The central government subtly manages to maintain public confidence in the top leadership by assigning blame to unprincipled and corrupt local officials.

Culture

Similar to ideological renewal, Chinese culture is also undergoing reconstruction. But rather than directly referencing national sovereignty or socialist ideology, the Party has increasingly aligned itself to represent the legacy of Chinese cultural traditions and a revival of China's cultural identities.[42] At the forefront of this movement is the renaissance of Confucianism. Traces of Confucianism in contemporary Chinese society can be found in both public and private life, through architecture, fashion, education, lifestyle, and over 300 Confucius Institutes worldwide. Its rejuvenation is all the more remarkable given Mao's open condemnation of this quasi-religious philosophy four decades ago.[43]

The rediscovery of Confucianism in the 1980s was both populist and intellectual. Besides initiatives from local authorities, Confucianism was seen in the academy as an inherently humanistic bridge between Eastern and Western values. Tu Weiming, for instance, argues that Confucian core values are not only compatible with human rights but can enhance the universal appeal of human rights: persons are at the center of relationships rather than in isolation; society is a community of trust rather than a mere system of adversarial relationships.[44]

The Party has promoted the revival of Confucianism by appropriating it as an alternative strategy to legitimize party rule. There is some resemblance of Confucian thoughts in the official ideology of "harmonious society." Perhaps most appealing to the ruling party are such Confucian ideas as the love of social order and stability, cultivation of personal virtues and social responsibility, obedience, acceptance of hierarchy, and devotion to the family and the state. These values, from the Party perspective, ᵉ not only intuitively compatible with Chinese ⁱᵒⁿs, but more importantly can help promote ʳ and stability. By claiming a moral high ground, the state is able to intervene and regulate aspects of Internet use such as pornography and gaming from the standpoint of benevolence and protection.

Governance and Democracy

If resorting to nationalism, ideology, and culture to bolster the Party's political legitimacy seems elusive at times, the government has been delivering more concrete, if consistent, results in the governance realm. Striving to build a Chinese version of "socialist democracy," the party-state has improved its governance in a few key areas: bureaucratic efficiency, empowerment of the people's congress, the rule of law, and inner-party democracy.[45] Such changes are important in that they developed more autonomous, capacity-rich public institutions not easily manipulated by single individuals.

In addition, authorities have also tried to adopt various input institutions that allow citizens to apprise the state of their concerns. Such institutions include: the Administrative Litigation Act of 1989 that allows citizens to sue government agencies for alleged violations of government policies; Letters-and-Visits department (*Xinfangju*) for citizen complaints; village elections; people's congresses; people's consultative conferences (where citizen grievances are addressed); and use of mass media as the people's tribunes.[46] These institutions, even if not well implemented, are legitimacy-enhancing. They provide, at the very minimum, a symbolic gesture from the state toward protecting human rights and restoring social justice.

The advent of the Internet has extended and in some ways transformed such practices by adding an online dimension to many rights- and justice-seeking activities. It is estimated that the states has committed to investing trillion-yuans (US$121 billion) in government IT projects since the early 1990s. As a result, provincial, city, and county governments now feature online government portals at rates of 100 percent, 93 percent, and 69 percent respectively.[47] Aside from making more information available online, government networks have also created spaces for public discourse including e-consultation functions such as Q&A sessions with government officials; e-petitions; e-discussion features such as real-time "gov. chat" between citizens and policy makers; and policy discussion forums. Local citizens have more access to government information, services, and means to articulate their rights and seek social justice. As a result, citizens are gaining access to local politics, and with it, political knowledge. By granting limited public spaces, these government networks help deflate social tension and re-establish state legitimacy.[48]

All these initiatives indicate that the state is promoting good governance and defining democracy in its own terms, although not in the liberal democratic sense. There are still many profound contradictions in its governance structure that place the party's leadership above the law, social harmony above dissent and social "instabilities," and individual responsibilities to society above personal rights and freedoms.

Authoritarian Informationalism

Given the government's active and largely successful promotion of legitimacy in various quarters including economy, nationalism, ideology, culture, and governance, it is perhaps not too astonishing to come across reports such as the 2007 Pew survey on Chinese Internet use which found an overwhelming amount of netizen trust in the government regulation of the Internet. Three-quarters of respondents said that they trusted information on government websites more than any other kind of online information, compared with 46 percent for established media, 28 percent for search engine results, 11 percent for content on bulletin boards and in advertisements, 4 percent for information from individuals' web pages, and 3 percent for postings in chat rooms.[49]

Indeed, the state's grip on power has been strengthened, not weakened. Although the regime still has many legitimacy deficits, largely in corruption, rule of law, public safety, and social inequality, the government is still viewed legitimate by most Chinese citizens. With no viable political alternative to the status quo, the government is able to regulate the Internet more to its liking, which in turn, reinforces its authority online.

In the foreseeable future, China's Internet policies will continue to reflect what I call authoritarian informationalism, an Internet development and regulatory model that combines elements of capitalism, authoritarianism, and Confucianism. From the government's perspective, although the Internet poses some fundamental challenge to the regime, it is possible to mitigate such challenges and ensure its own survival by producing economic growth, social stability, and national identity. In this respect, the Chinese government actually expects to use the Internet not only to extend its control in society but also to enhance its legitimacy.

Beijing will continue down the path of capitalism with a vision to turn China into a technologically advanced economic powerhouse. The past three decades of market-driven development have made China the second largest economy by being the world's factory, producing low-end manufacturing products. In order to consistently deliver high-rate economic growth, the government is clearly committed to the next stage of development by ramping up domestic consumption and creating cutting edge technological innovations. Sustained Internet growth, in both user base, goods and service delivery, fits into the bigger picture. China already has the world's largest number of Internet users, a market that draws both domestic and foreign companies. Ongoing urbanization will add more consumers who can afford Internet products and services in the near future. With the government's backing, many Chinese Internet and telecommunications companies, state-owned and private ones, have been expanding overseas, particularly in Asia, Africa, South America and the Middle East, places that prefer inexpensive Chinese technological products or have an interest in China's surveillance technologies.

Such an economic development strategy, however, is unlikely to deter the Chinese government from tweaking the Internet infrastructure or manipulating public opinion. By securing a broad base of political legitimacy, the state legitimizes and legalizes restriction of online expressions or dissent on the basis of security, law and order, arguing that doing so will be in the interest of the majority of its citizens and for the greater good of the Chinese society. Without strong legal protection for individual rights, the state's claim to national sovereignty invariably puts netizens at a disadvantage, while also deflecting international criticism and interference. But it would be inaccurate to conclude that Chinese netizens are not free. There remains a lot of give and take between the government and citizens compared to the pre-Internet era. Netizens have a greater deal of freedom than before, enjoy a lot more benefits and conveniences the Internet affords, and sometimes can even influence policy-making. But the boundaries of political discourse and actions are largely prescribed by the state and enforced behind the scene with cooperation from Internet companies. With an expanded toolbox of sophisticated censoring techniques and technologies, modern authoritarianism differs from its classic counterparts in that it grants a much bigger degree of freedom to its citizens, including political ones, to diffuse radical opposition and enhance its rule.

The revival of Confucianism boosts the state's image as the ultimate caretaker of the Chinese society and embodiment of Chinese cultural legacy. From the government's perspective, Confucianism has both internal and external appeal. Its emphasis on social order and stability, obedience and devotion to family and state reinforces the government's official ideology on social harmony. Politically, Confucianism can be used as an excuse to diffuse individual and group challenges to state authority and arbitrariness. Such challenges are often dismissed for causing "social instabilities" and disrupting social order although neither the constitution nor other provisions clearly define "social instabilities" concrete terms. Externally, the benevolent and humanistic essence of Confucianism helps promote Chinese cultural heritage and values overseas.

Engage Authoritarian Informationalism

The options for engaging Chinese netizens are few given the Chinese government's firm stance. Major Internet services like Twitter, Facebook, YouTube, and Blogger are still blocked. Google, after weeks of deliberation with the Chinese government, renewed its license in July 2010 to continue its operation in China. Now Google.cn provides a landing page and sends users directly to its uncensored Hong Kong site, although for mainland users, specific searches containing sensitive words are still blocked by the Great Firewall.[50] Other major Internet companies like Microsoft and Yahoo! continue to comply with Chinese regulations and offer censored search engines.

Such blockage and restriction place limits on speech as well as business. The U.S. State Department voiced concerns and vowed to promote Internet freedom. Various proposals have been put forth to increase freedom of speech on the Internet, particularly in response to Chinese Internet censorship.[51] They fall largely into four categories: (1) technical: developing tools for censorship circumvention, anonymity and security measures such as secure login, storage and redistribution of deleted content, and mirror sites to replicate at-risk materials; (2) legislative: enacting legislations such as the Global Online Freedom Act to prevent U.S. Internet companies from engaging in Internet censorship; (3) trade: pursuing actions through international trade organizations such WTO that treat censorship as an unfair barrier to trade, controlling the export of U.S. and European censorship technologies; (4) research, education and community of practice: funding research and innovation against Internet censorship such as building block resistance platforms, sharing "opposition research" to identify problems and solutions in an international anticensorship community, educating users on privacy and rights issues, supporting international exchange to increase the influence of indigenous experts, implementing corporate responsibility mechanisms, promoting international acceptance of Internet freedom and respect for the rights of Internet users for instance through the U.N.

These and many more ideas highlight a multilayered thinking behind Internet freedom that attempt to address the various interests involved, such as users, businesses, civil society groups, and governments. As far as China is concerned, many of these recommendations may have some limited effects on the Chinese government, and perhaps a more profound impact on U.S. Internet companies operating in China more than Chinese Internet users. This is because these are largely technical, external solutions to an inherently human, political and internal problem.

Anti-censorship technologies, in no way easy and inexpensive, may help a small number of users break through the Great Firewall of China or other filtering systems to reach restricted content overseas (which most web savvy Chinese users are already doing), but they will have a limited effect on far more complicated domestic censorship issues: human censors, closure of domestic websites, arrest of cyberdissidents, discipline of Chinese Internet companies, and self-censorship. Although Google has kept its promise not to censor by directing mainland search traffic to its uncensored server located in Hong Kong, sensitive searches are still blocked. So search results are unlikely to have been changed for Chinese mainland users although the burden and cost of censoring seem to have shifted more to the Chinese government.

Moreover, the proposed technologies, if created and deployed online, can potentially be blocked online as well. They cannot protect the creation and sharing of politically sensitive materials on domestic websites (though domestic platforms are far more effective to gain influence over the target audience within the country). Nor can these technologies necessarily change Chinese citizens' views on western norms of freedom and democracy and turn them into "global citizens." Circumvention tools have existed since 1990s but technologies and information do not automatically lead people to start a revolution. Political and human problems demand more than mere technological answers.

In the eyes of the Chinese government, most of the discussion on the topic seems more or less a plot to overthrow its rule. American Internet giants Google, Facebook, and Twitter somehow seem like extensions of the U.S. State Department.[52] U.S. funding to a Falun Gong Internet freedom group preceded Beijing's announcement of its Internet White Paper to restate its national sovereignty over the issue. Somewhere in the context of the spat between the government and Google as well as the high-profile involvement of the U.S. State Department, Internet freedom had been much more narrowly defined than its original intent, which is to create and maintain a single connected Internet for ideas, knowledge, and expressions. The sheer political focus of the conversation may not address the broader American foreign policy goals in authoritarian societies as much as intended. Given the current level of legitimacy the Chinese state enjoys and the democracy deficit the U.S. government has overseas, radical political change is not only unlikely but also undesirable. However, incremental, progressive changes are possible to achieve on the issue of Internet freedom if the issue itself is more broadly defined beyond the attempt to tear down the Great Firewall.

At the government level, economy and trade are more likely to change the Chinese state's behavior given Beijing's priority in economic development and international trade. Framing censorship as a trade barrier may rally the larger foreign business community, not just a few U.S. Internet companies. As much as the government wants to censor political content with its borders, it also desires to retain foreign investment and trade relations. In addition, Beijing prizes technological and business innovation, which it sees as the primary driving force for the next wave of economic growth. Although it wishes Google would comply with its censorship rules, the Chinese government also views companies like Google as a useful leverage to spur technological innovation at home.

At the Internet-user level, the question of Internet freedom is not so much about turning Chinese netizens into cyberdissidents, but rather about engaging the majority Internet users on issues they care about, increasing their living standards and helping them to be more conscious of their rights and hold local governments to account. This is not foreign policy of the "social engineering," "regime changing" kind, but the kind that can effectively raise awareness and build long-term engagement. It implies local problems need local solutions. The "App <4> Africa" contest, a contest funded by the State Department, for instance, is engaging local people to develop mobile phone applications most useful to citizens and civil society organizations in Africa as mobile phones have become central to African everyday living. Projects as such do not presuppose or impose solutions but instead invests in the ingenuity of the local population.[53]

China is a big country with its own unique set of problems. Engaging Chinese netizens via the Internet and social media requires a unique understanding of these issues, China's media landscape, regulations, as well as the interests and preferences of Chinese Internet users.[54] Guided by a broadly conceived framework of Internet freedom, it is possible to connect with diverse Chinese Internet population segments, including youths, women, and migrant workers on issues of common interest, including public health, environment, education, and intellectual property. Citizens can be engaged in these issues through a variety of platforms like music, gaming, and mobile phones. Research, education, and community of practice can aid in this endeavor. Virtual connection with Chinese Internet users can be achieved through key players such as U.S. Internet firms operating in China, Chinese Internet companies, as well as bilingual online communities to raise awareness among Internet users and educate users ⌐ issues of security and privacy.

Just as there is no single silver bullet to tackle ⌐ of censorship, there is also no single way to engage the numerous Chinese Internet users who share common needs, interests, and aspirations with their Western counterparts despite the controls and parameters set by a popular authoritarian regime. Internet sovereignty is ultimately about restoring users' rights and giving users the necessary tools and experience to govern themselves.

NOTES

1. Bill Clinton, "America's Stake in China," *The Democratic Leadership Council's Blueprint Magazine*, 1 June 2000, http://www.dlc.org/ndol_ci.cfm?kaid=108&subid=128&contentid=963 (accessed April 20, 2008), Goldsmith and Wu (2006) noted that around the same time President Clinton made the remark, an effective government crackdown on Chinese cyber-dissidents was taking place.

2. Hillary Clinton, "Internet Freedom," *Foreign Policy*, 21 January 2010, http://www.foreignpolicy.com/articles/2010/01/21/internet_freedom?page=full (accessed January 25, 2010).

3. State Council Information Office of People's Republic of China (SCIO), "The Internet in China," *China Daily*, 8 June 2010, http://www.chinadaily.com.cn/china/2010-06/08/content_9950198.htm (accessed June 10, 2010). China Internet Network Information Center (CNNIC), *26th Statistical Survey Report on the Internet Development in China*, 15 July, 2010, http://www.cnnic.net.cn/uploadfiles/pdf/2010/7/15/100708.pdf (accessed on July 15, 2010).

4. Steven Levy, *Hackers: The Heroes of the Computer Revolution*, New York: Anchor, 1984.

5. State Council Information, Office of People's Republic of China (SCIO).

6. Viktor Mayer-Schonberger, "The Shape of Governance: Analyzing the World of Internet Regulation," *Virginia Journal of International Law 43*, (2003): 605–673. Jack Goldsmith & Tim Wu, *Who Controls the Internet? Illusions of a Borderless World* (New York, NY: Oxford University Press, 2006). Jack Goldsmith, "The Internet and the Abiding Significance

of Territorial Sovereignty," *Indiana Journal of Global Legal Studies* 5, (1998): 475.

7. Ministry of Industry and Information Technology of the People's Republic of China (MIIT), "Telecommunication Industry's 60 Years: Now a Strategic Industry Pillar of National Economy," *Ministry of Industry and Information Technology*, August 28, 2009, http://zwgk.miit.gov.cn/n11293472/n11293877/n12511031/n12511136/12544641.html (accessed January 10, 2010).

8. State Council Information Office (SCIO). China Internet Network Information Center (CNNIC).

9. Quoted in Jack Goldsmith & Tim Wu, *Who Controls the Internet? Illusions of a Borderless World* (New York, NY: Oxford University Press, 2006), 467.

10. Ronald Deibert et al., *Access Controlled* (Cambridge, MA: MIT Press, 2010), 449–487.

11. Jiang, "Spaces of Authoritarian Deliberation: Online Public Deliberation in China."

12. Guobin Yang, *The Power of the Internet in China* (New York, NY: Columbia University Press, 2009).

13. Ashley Esarey and Qiang Xiao, "Below the Radar: Political Expression in the Chinese Blogosphere," *Asian Survey 48*, no. 5: 752–772.

14. Evgeny Morozov, "How Dictators Watch Us on the Web," *Prospect*, no. 165, November 18, 2009, http://www.prospectmagazine.co.uk/2009/11/how-dictators-watch-us-on-the-web/ Clay Shirky, "The Net Advantage," *Prospect*, no. 165, December 11, 2009, http://www.prospectmagazine.co.uk/2009/12/the-net-advantage

15. Deborah Fallows, "Few in China Complain about Internet Controls," *Pew Internet & American Life Project*. March 27, 2008. http://pewresearch.org/pubs/776/china-internet (accessed August 28, 2008).

16. Mark Hoffman, "What Is Left of the 'Liberal Peace,'" *LSE Connect*, no. 21(2009): 10–11.

17. Bruce Gilley, "The Determinants of State Legitimacy: Results for 72 Countries," *International Political Science Review 27*, no. 1 (2006): 47–71.

18. Pew Internet Research Center, "Obama More Popular Abroad Than at Home, Global Image of U.S. Continues to Benefit," *Pew Research Center: Pew Global Attitudes Project,* June 17, 2010. http://pewresearch.org/pubs/1630/obama-more-popular-abroad-global-american-image-benefit-22-nation-global-survey (accessed June 22, 2010).

19. John Kane and Haig Patapan, "Recovering Justice: Political Legitimacy Reconsidered," *Politics & Policy 38*, no. 3 (2010), 589–610.

20. Shanthi Kalathil, "Dot.Com for Dictators," *Foreign Policy 135*, (March–April 2003), 42–49. Min Jiang, "Spaces of Authoritarian Deliberation: Online Public Deliberation in China," in *In Search for Deliberative Democracy in China* (2nd ed.), edited by Ethan Leib and Baogang He, (New York, NY: Palgrave, 2010), 261–287.

21. Kane and Patapan, "Recovering Justice: Political Legitimacy Reconsidered," 590.

22. Heike Holbig and Bruce Gilley, "Reclaiming Legitimacy in China," *Politics & Policy 38*, no. 3: 395–422.

23. Pew Internet Research Center, "Obama More Popular Abroad Than at Home, Global Image of U.S. Continues to Benefit."

24. Elizabeth Perry, "Chinese Conceptions of 'Rights': From Mencius to Mao—and Now," *Perspectives on Politics 6*, no. 1 (2008): 37–50.

25. State Council Information Office of the People's Republic of China, "China's Progress in Human Rights in 2004," Beijing, 2004.

26. Ministry of Industry and Information Technology of the People's Republic of China (MIIT), "Telecommunication Industry's 60 Years: Now a Strategic Industry Pillar of National Economy."

27. Stuart Corner, "China's Tencent Outranks Google but Microsoft Leads in Australia," *iTWire*, July 12, 2010, http://www.itwire.com/it-industry-news/market/40336-chinas-tencent-outranks-google-but-microsoft-leads-in-australia (accessed July 15, 2010). *The Economist*, "The Emerging Online Giants," *The Economist*, July 8, 2010, http://www.economist.com/node/16539424 (accessed July 18, 2010).

28. Perry Link and Joshua Kurlantzick, "China's Modern Authoritarianism," *Wall Street Journal*, May 25, 2010, http://online.wsj.com/article/ NA_WSJ_PUB:SB124319304482150525.html

29. Holbig and Gilley, "Reclaiming Legitimacy in China," 400. Perry Link and Joshua Kurlantzick, "China's Modern Authoritarianism," *Wall Street Journal*, May 25, 2010, http://online.wsj.com/article/NA_WSJ_PUB:SB124319304482150525.html

30. Holbig and Gilley, "Reclaiming Legitimacy in China," 402.

31. Yinan He, "History, Chinese Nationalism, and the Emerging Sino-Japanese Conflict," *Journal of Contemporary China 16*, no. 50 (2007): 1–24.

32. William Callahan, "History, Identity, and Security: Producing and Consuming Nationalism in China," *Critical Asian Studies 38*, no. 2 (2006): 179–298.

33. Guobin Yang, "The Internet and Civil Society in China: A Preliminary Assessment," *Journal of Contemporary China 12*, no. 36 (2003): 453–75.

34. Anti-CNN, http://anti-cnn.com

35. Youyu Xu, "What Kind of Nationalism Do We Need?" *China Elections & Governance*, March 25, 2010, http://www.chinaelections.org/newsinfo.asp?newsid=172417

36. Richard McGregor, *The Party: The Secret World of China's Communist Rulers*, New York: Harpers, 2010.

37. Anne-Marie Brady, "Guiding Hand: The Role of the CCP Central Propaganda Department in the Current Era," *Westminster Papers in Communication and Culture 3*, no. 1 (2006): 58–77.

38. People's Daily Online, "Construct a Harmonious Socialist Society," *People's Daily Online*, http://politics.people.com.cn/GB/8198/70195/index.html (accessed April 24, 2010).

39. Holbig and Gilley, "Reclaiming Legitimacy in China," 407.

40. McGregor, *The Party: The Secret World of China's Communist Rulers*.

41. XinhuaNet, "Premier Wen Jiaobao Chats with Netizens Online," *Xinhua News Agency Online*, February 27, 2010, http://www.xinhuanet.com/zlft2010_index.htm

42. Holbig and Gilley, "Reclaiming Legitimacy in China," 408.

43. Daniel Bell, *China's New Confucianism: Politics and Everyday Life in a Changing Society*, Princeton, NJ: Princeton University Press, 2008.

44. William de Bary and Tu Weiming, *Confucianism and Human Rights*, New York: Columbia University Press, 1998.

45. Holbig and Gilley, "Reclaiming Legitimacy in China," 411.

46. Andrew Nathan, "Authoritarian Resilience," *Journal of Democracy 14*, 1 (2003): 6–17.

47. James Yong, "Enter the Dragon: Informatization in China," in *E-Government in Asia: Enabling Public Service Innovation in the 21st Century*, edited by James Yong (Hong Kong: Times Media, 2003), 65–96. CCID Consulting, *2005 Chinese Government Websites Performance Evaluation*, 2006, http://www.ccidconsulting.com/2005govtop/default.shtml (accessed June 24, 2009).

48. Min Jiang and Heng Xu, "Exploring Online Structures on Chinese Government Portals: Citizen Political Participation and Government Legitimation." *Social Science Computer Review 27*, no. 2 (2009), 174–195.

49. Deborah Fallows, "Few in China Complain about Internet Controls."

50. Rebecca MacKinnon, "On Google's License Renewal and Principled Engagement," *RConversation*, July 9, 2010, http://rconversation.blogs.com/rconversation/2010/07/on-googles-license-renewal-and-principled-engagement.html

51. Rebecca MacKinnon, "China, the Internet and Google: Congressional Testimony," *RConversation*, March 23, 2010, http://rconversation.blogs.com/rconversation/2010/03/china-the-internet-and-google.html Ethan Zuckerman, "Internet Freedom: Protect, then Project," *My Heart's in Accra*, March 22, 2010 http://ww.ethanzuckerman.com/blog/2010/03/22/internet-freedom-protect-then-project/ Daniel Calingaert, "Authoritarianism vs. the Internet: The Race between Freedom and Oppression," *Policy Review 160*, April & May (2010), http://www.hoover.org/publications/policy-review/article/5269

52. Jiangwei Zhang, "China Doesn't Need a Politicized Google," *China Daily*, 20 March 2010, http://

www.chinadaily.com.cn/china/2010-03/20/content_9618252.htm (accessed March 24, 2010).

53. Sam Dupont, "Digital diplomacy," *Foreign Policy*, August 3, 2010, http://www.foreignpolicy.com/articles/2010/08/03/digital_diplomacy?sms_ss=twitter

54. Guo Liang, "Surveying Internet Usage and Impact in Five Chinese Cities," *Chinese Academy of Social Sciences (CASS) and Markle Foundation*, November 2005, http://www.markle.org/downloadable_assets/china_final_11_2005.pdf (accessed May 2, 2007).

CREDITS

Chapter 1: What Is Comparative Politics?

p. 3: Mark Irving Lichbach and Alan S. Zuckerman: "Research Traditions and Theory in Comparative Politics: An Introduction," *Comparative Politics: Rationality, Culture, and Structure*, pp. 3–10. © Mark Irving Lichbach and Alan S. Zuckerman 1997. Reprinted with the permission of Cambridge University Press.

p. 7: Gary King, Robert O. Keohane, and Sidney Verba: "The Science in Social Science," *Designing Social Inquiry: Scientific Inference in Qualitative Research*, pp. 4–12. © 1994 Princeton University Press. Reprinted by permission of Princeton University Press.

p. 13: Larry M. Bartles: "Some Unfulfilled Promises of Quantitative Imperialism," *Rethinking Social Inquiry*, 2nd Edition, Brady and Collier, eds. Reprinted by permission of Rowman & Littlefield Publishing Group.

p. 17: Ronald Rogowski: "How Inference in the Social (but not Physical) Sciences Neglects Theoretical Anomaly," *Rethinking Social Inquiry: Diverse Tools, Shared Standards*, August 19, 2004. Reprinted by permission of Rowman & Littlefield Publishing Group.

Chapter 2: The State

p. 26: Francis Fukuyama: "Chapter 1: The Necessity of Politics," from *The Origins of Political Order* by Francis Fukuyama. Copyright © 2011 by Francis Fukuyama. Reprinted by permission of Farrar, Straus and Giroux, LLC.

p. 45: Jeffrey Herbst: "War and the ‚State in Africa," *International Security*, 14:4 (Spring, 1990), pp. 117–139. © 1990 by the President and Fellows of Harvard College and the Massachusetts Institute of Technology. Reprinted by permission of MIT Press.

p. 60: Robert Rotberg: "The New Nature of Nation-State Failure," *The Washington Quarterly*, 25:3, Summer 2002, pp. 85–96. Copyright © 2002 by The Center for Strategic and International Studies and the Massachusetts Institute of Technology. Reprinted by permission of the publisher (Taylor & Francis Ltd, http://www.informaworld.com).

p. 68: Stephen D. Krasner: "Sovereignty," *Foreign Policy*, January-February 2001, pp. 20–29. www.foreignpolicy.com. Copyright 2001 by Foreign Policy. Reproduced with permission of Foreign Policy in the format Textbook via Copyright Clearance Center.

Chapter 3: Nations and Society

p. 77: Eric Hobsbawm: From *The Age of Revolution*, pp. 163–177. © 1996 by Eric Hobsbawm. Reprinted by permission of George Weidenfeld and Nicolson, Ltd., an imprint of The Orion Publishing Group, London.

p. 86: James D. Fearon and David D. Laitin: "Ethnicity, Insurgency, and Civil War," *American Political Science Review*, Vol. 97, No. 1, 2003, pp. 75–76, 77–78, 82–83, 88–89. Copyright © 2003 by the American Political Science Association. Reprinted with the permission of Cambridge University Press.

p. 96: Alberto Alesina and Eliana La Ferrara: "Ethnic Diversity and Economic Performance," *Journal of Economic Literature*, VOL XLII, September 2005. Reprinted with permission.

p. 114: Kate Baldwin and John Huber: "Economic vs. Cultural Differences: Forms of Ethnic Diversity and Public Goods Provision," *American Political Science Review*, Vol. 104, No. 4, November 2010. Copyright © 2010 by the American Political Science Association. Reprinted with the permission of Cambridge University Press.

Chapter 4: Political Economy

p. 143: Douglass C. North: "Institutions," *Journal of Economic Perspectives*, Vol. 5, No. 1, Winter 1991, pp. 97–112. Copyright © 1991 by the American Economic Association. Reprinted by permission of the American Economic Association.

p. 155: Daron Acemoglu: "Root Causes," *Finance and Development*, Vol. 40, No. 2, June 2003, pp. 27–30. Copyright © 2003 by the International Monetary Fund. Reprinted by permission of the International Monetary Fund. "Income and Democracy," *American Economic Review*, Vol. 98, 2008, pp. 808–842. Reprinted with permission.

p. 160: Abhijit Banerjee and Lakshmi Iyer: "History, Institutions and Economic Performance: The Legacy of Colonial Land Tenure Systems in India," *The American Economic Review*, Vol. 95, No. 4. Reprinted with permission.

p. 184: N. Gregory Mankiw: "The Trilemma of International Finance," From *The New York Times*, July 10, 2010. Copyright © 2010 The New York Times. All

Chapter 5: Democratic Regimes

p. 188: Fareed Zakaria: "A Brief History of Human Liberty" from *The Future of Freedom Illiberal Democracy at Home and Abroad* by Fareed Zakaria. Copyright © 2003 by Fareed Zakaria. Used by permission of W.W. Norton & Company, Inc.

p. 203: Phillippe C. Schmitter and Terry Lynn Karl: "What Democracy Is... And Is Not," *Journal of Democracy* 2:3 (1991), 75–88. © National Endowment for Democracy and The Johns Hopkins University Press. Reprinted with permission of The Johns Hopkins University Press.

p. 213: Arend Lijphart: "Constitutional Choices for New Democracies," *Journal of Democracy* 2:1 (1991), 72–84. © National Endowment for Democracy and The Johns Hopkins University Press. Reprinted with permission of The Johns Hopkins University Press.

p. 222: Robert Putnam: "Tuning In, Tuning Out: The Strange Disappearance of Social Capital in America," *PS: Political Science & Politics*, Dec. 1995, pp. 664-683. Reprinted by permission of the author.

p. 250: Alfred Stephan, Jaun J. Linz, and Yogendra Yadav: The Rise of "State-Nations," *Journal of Democracy*, Vol. 21, No. 3, July 2010. © National Endowment for Democracy and The Johns Hopkins University Press. Reprinted with permission of The Johns Hopkins University Press.

Chapter 6: Nondemocratic Regimes

p. 267: Juan J. Linz and Alfred Stepan: "Modern Non-Democratic Regimes," *Problems of Democratic Transition and Consolidation: Southern Europe, South America, and Post-Communist Europe*, pp. 38–54. © 1996 The Johns Hopkins University Press. Reprinted with permission of The Johns Hopkins University Press.

p. 279: Erika Weinthal and Pauline Jones Luong: "Combating the Resource Curse: An Alternative Solution to Managing Mineral Wealth," *Perspectives on Politics*, Vol. 4, No. 1, March 2006, pp. 35–38, 43–53. Copyright © 2006 American Political Science Association. Reprinted with the permission of Cambridge University Press.

p. 294: Larry Diamond: "The Rule of Law vs. the Big Man," *Journal of Democracy* Vol.19, No. 2, April

2008. © 2008 The Johns Hopkins University Press. Reprinted with permission of The Johns Hopkins University Press.

p. 303: Steve Levitsky and Lucan A. Way: "The Rise of Competitive Authoritarianism," Journal of Democracy, Vol. 13, No. 2, April 2002. © 2002 The National Endowment for Democracy and The Johns Hopkins University Press. Reprinted with permission of The Johns Hopkins University Press.

Chapter 7: Political Violence

p. 316: Theda Skocpol: "France, Russia, and China: A Structural Analysis of Social Revolutions," *States and Social Revolutions: A Comparative Analysis of France, Russia, & China*, pp. 175–210. © Cambridge University Press 1979. Reprinted with the permission of Cambridge University Press.

p. 333: Martha Crenshaw: "The Causes of Terrorism," *Comparative Politics*, 13 (July 1981). Reprinted by permission of *Comparative Politics*.

p. 349: Timur Kuran: "Now out of Never: The Element of Surprise in the East European Revolution of 1989," *World Politics*, 44, October 1991. © World Politics 1991. Reprinted with the permission of Cambridge University Press.

p. 366: Jack Goldstone: "Understanding the Revolutions of 2011," *Foreign Affairs*, May/June 2011, Vol. 90, Issue 3. Copyright © 2011 Council on Foreign Relations, Publisher of *Foreign Affairs*. All rights reserved. Distributed by Tribune Media Services.

p. 372: Max Abrahms: "What Terrorists Really Want: Terrorist Motives and Counter Terrorism Strategies," *International Security*, Vol. 32, No. 4, Spring 2008. © 2008 Massachusetts Institute of Technology. Reprinted by permission of the MIT Press.

Chapter 8: Advanced Democracies

p. 411: Adam Przeworski: "Conquered or Granted? A History of Suffrage Extensions," *British Journal of Political Science*, 39, November 10, 2008. © Cambridge University Press 2008. Reprinted with the permission of Cambridge University Press.

p. 436: Maurice Duverger: "The Number of Parties," from *Les Partis Politiques* (Paris: Armand Colin, 1976), *Political Parties: Their Organization and Activity in the Modern State*, translated by Barbara and Robert North (New York: Wiley, 1954). Reprinted by permission of Armand Colin.

p. 440: Torben Iversen and David Soskice: "Electoral Institution and the Politics of Coalitions: Why

Some Democracies Redistribute More Than Others," *American Political Science Review*, Vol. 100, No. 2, May 2006, pp. 165–166, 171–175, 178–179. Copyright © 2006 by the American Political Science Association. Reprinted with the permission of Cambridge University Press.

p. 450: Margarita Estevez-Abe, Torben Iversen, and David Soskice: "Social Protection and the Formation of Skills: A Reinterpretation of the Welfare State." Reproduced from *Varieties of Capitalism: The Institutional Foundations of Comparative Advantage*, eds. Peter A. Hall and David Soskice, © 2001, by permission of Oxford University Press.

Chapter 9: Communism and Postcommunism

p. 469: Karl Marx and Freidrich Engels: "Manifesto of the Communist Party," *The Marx-Engels Reader*, Second Edition, 1978. pp. 473–477. Courtesy of W.W. Norton & Company.

p. 481: Valerie J. Bunce and Sharon Wolchik: "Democratizing Elections, International Diffusion and U.S. Democracy Assistance," *Defeating Authoritarian Leaders in Postcommunist Countries*, June 3, 2011. © Cambridge University 2011. Reprinted by permission of Cambridge University Press.

p. 502: Ivan Krastev: "Paradoxes of the New Authoritarianism," *Journal of Democracy*, Vol. 22, No. 2, April 2011. © 2011 The National Endowment for Democracy and The Johns Hopkins University Press. Reprinted with permission of The Johns Hopkins University Press.

p. 509: Baogang He and Mark E. Warren: "Authoritarian Deliberation: The Deliberative Turn in Chinese Political Development," *Perspectives on Politics*, Vol. 9, No. 2, June 2011. © 2011. Reprinted with the permission of Cambridge University Press.

p. 539: Azar Gat: "The Return of Authoritarian Great Powers." Reprinted by permission of *Foreign Affairs*, Vol. 86, No. 4, July/August 2007. Copyright 2007 by the Council on Foreign Relations, Inc. www.ForeignAffairs.org.

Chapter 10: Less-Developed and Newly Industrializing Countries

p. 547: William Easterly: "Chapter 2: To Help the Poor," from *The Elusive Quest for Growth: Economists' Adventures and Misadventures in the Tropics*. © 2001

Massachusetts Institute of Technology. Reprinted by permission of the MIT Press.

p. 553: Paul Collier and Jan Willem Gunning: "Why Has Africa Grown Slowly?," *Journal of Economic Perspectives*, Vol. 13, No. 3, Summer 1999, pp. 3–22. Copyright © 1999 by the American Economic Association. Reprinted by permission of the American Economic Association.

p. 571: Paul Krugman: "The Myth of Asia's Miracle," *Foreign Affairs* Vol. 73, No. 6, Nov/Dec 1995. Reprinted by permission of Foreign Affairs. Copyright © 1995 by the Council on Foreign Relations, Inc. www.ForeignAffairs.com.

p. 580: Wayne Arnold: "Vietnam Holds Its Own Within China's Vast Economic Shadow," from the *New York Times*, January 1, 2011. Copyright © 2010 The New York Times. All rights reserved. Used by permission and protected by the Copyright Laws of the United States. The printing, copying, redistribution, or retransmission of this Content without express written permission is prohibited.

p. 582: Daron Acemoglu and Simon Johnson: "Disease and Development: The Effect of Life Expectancy on Economic Growth," *Journal of Political Economy*, Vol. 115, No. 6, 2007. Reprinted by permission of the University of Chicago Press.

Chapter 11: Globalization

p. 590: Richard Florida: "The World is Spiky: Globalization has Changed the Economic Playing Field," *The Atlantic Monthly*, October 2005. Reprinted by permission of the author.

p. 595: Dani Rodrik: "Is Global Governance Feasible? Is it Desirable?" from *The Globalization Paradox: Democracy and the Future of World Economy*. Copyright © 2011 by Dani Rodrik. Used by permission of W.W. Norton & Company, Inc.

p. 609: The Economist: "Leviathan Stirs Again" *The Economist*, January 21, 2010. © 2010 The Economist Newspaper Ltd. All rights reserved. Further reproduction prohibited, www.economist.com.

p. 613: Min Jiang: "Authoritarian Informationalism: China's Approach to Internet Sovereignty," *SAIS Review*, Vol. 30, No. 2, Summer-Fall 2010. © 2010 The Johns Hopkins University Press. Reprinted with permission of The Johns Hopkins University Press.